Writing is a political instrument.

James Baldwin

I write to find out what I'm thinking. I write to find out who I am. I write to understand things.

Julia Alvarez

If I had to say what writing is, we would define it essentially as an act of courage.

Cynthia Ozick

Writing is the act of saying *I*, of imposing yourself upon other people, of saying *listen to me, see it my way, change your mind.*

Joan Didion

The beautiful part of writing is that you don't have to get it right the first time — unlike, say, brain surgery.

Robert Cormier

Writing and rewriting are a constant search for what one is saying.

John Updike

Eighth Edition

The St. Martin's Guide to Writing

Rise B. Axelrod

University of California, Riverside

Charles R. Cooper

University of California, San Diego

Bedford/St. Martin's

Boston ◆ New York

For Bedford/St. Martin's

Senior Developmental Editor: John Elliott
Production Editor: Bernard Onken
Senior Production Supervisor: Dennis J. Conroy
Senior Marketing Manager: Karita dos Santos
Art Director: Lucy Krikorian
Text Design: Claire Seng-Niemoeller
Copy Editor: Diana P. George
Indexer: Riofrancos & Co. Indexes
Photo Research: Naomi Kornhauser
Cover Design: Donna L. Dennison
Composition: Monotype LLC
Printing and Binding: R.R. Donnelley & Sons Company

President: Joan E. Feinberg
Editorial Director: Denise B. Wydra
Editor in Chief: Karen S. Henry
Director of Development: Erica T. Appel
Director of Marketing: Karen Melton Soeltz
Director of Editing, Design, and Production: Marcia Cohen
Managing Editor: Shuli Traub

Library of Congress Control Numbers: 2009929970 (with Handbook; 2009 MLA update)
2006925053 (without Handbook)

Manufactured in the United States of America.

4 3 2 1 0 9
f e d c b

For information, write: Bedford/St. Martin's, 75 Arlington Street,
Boston, MA 02116   (617-399-4000)

ISBN-10: 0-312-60354-1   ISBN-13: 978-0-312-60354-0 (with Handbook; 2009 MLA update)
ISBN-10: 0-312-44633-0   ISBN-13: 978-0-312-44633-8 (without Handbook)

Acknowledgments

Acknowledgments and copyrights appear at the back of the book on pages A1–A2, which constitute an extension of the copyright page.

Advisory Board

We owe an enormous debt to all the rhetoricians and composition specialists whose theory, research, and pedagogy have informed *The St. Martin's Guide to Writing*. We would be adding many pages if we were to name everyone to whom we are indebted.

The members of the Advisory Board for the eighth edition, a group of dedicated composition instructors from across the country, have provided us with extensive insights and suggestions for the chapters in Part One and have given us the benefit of their advice on new features, in many cases testing them in their own classrooms. *The St. Martin's Guide to Writing* has been greatly enhanced by their contributions.

Lawrence Barkley
Mt. San Jacinto College–Menifee

Sandie McGill Barnhouse
Rowan-Cabarrus Community College

Melissa Batai
Triton College

Susan Callender
Sinclair Community College

Jack Halligan
Johnson County Community College

Maurice Hunt
Baylor University

Scott Payne
The University of Findlay

Sharran S. Slinkard
Des Moines Area Community College

Rachelle Smith
Emporia State University

Kim Stallings
University of North Carolina–Charlotte

Rosemary Winslow
Catholic University of America

Preface for Instructors

When we first wrote *The St. Martin's Guide to Writing*, we took what we had learned from classical rhetoric as well as from contemporary composition theory and research and did our best to make it accessible to students. We aimed to demystify writing and authorize students as writers. We wanted to help students learn to commit themselves to writing projects, communicate effectively with chosen readers, and question their own certainties. We also wanted them to understand that knowledge of writing comes both from analyzing published and student writing and from working seriously on their own writing and giving and getting advice on work in progress.

The response from instructors and students has been overwhelmingly positive ever since the first publication of *The Guide* in 1985. That first edition immediately became the most widely adopted text of its kind in the nation, and the book has maintained that position through seven editions. Although *The Guide* has changed in many ways since we wrote the first draft in 1983, our basic goals for this eighth edition remain the same: to take the best of current composition research and practice and turn it into forms that are as useful as possible for both instructors and students. In this edition, as explained below, we have focused our efforts on better preparing students for writing in today's academy, including enhanced coverage of working with sources, working online, and considering document design and other visual aspects of writing.

■ An Overview of the Book

As a rhetoric and reader, *The St. Martin's Guide to Writing* can serve as a comprehensive introduction to nine genres of writing. It comprises several parts:

Part One, Writing Activities, presents nine different essay assignments, all reflecting actual writing situations that students may encounter both in and out of college, genres of writing that they should learn to read insightfully and to write compellingly. Among the types of essays included are narrating a remembered event, explaining a concept, arguing a position, proposing a solution to a problem, and interpreting a short story.

You may choose among these chapters and teach them in any sequence you wish, though they are sequenced here from writing based on personal experience and reflection, to writing based on first-hand observation and library or Internet research on established information, and then to writing about ongoing debates over controversial issues and problems.

Each chapter follows the same organizational plan:

Chapter Organization for Part One

- Three brief illustrated **scenarios** based on the genre covered in the chapter and suggesting the range of occasions when such writing is done — in college courses, in the community, and in the workplace

- A brief **introduction** to the genre suggesting why it is a valuable kind of writing for students to study

- A **collaborative activity** that gets students working with the genre

- A set of four **readings** accompanied by a **critical apparatus** designed to help students explore connections to their culture and experience and to analyze writing strategies used in the genre

- A summary of the **purpose and audience** and the **basic features** of the genre

- A flexible **guide to writing,** tailored to the particular genre, that scaffolds students as they research and compose their essays and includes a critical reading guide for peer review of drafts

- **Editing and proofreading guidelines,** based on our nationwide study of error in first-year college students' writing in nine genres, to help students check for one or two sentence-level problems likely to occur in a genre

- A look at one **writer at work,** focusing on some aspect of the process of writing a student essay featured in the chapter

- A box exploring how writers think about **document design,** expanding on one of the scenarios presented at the beginning of the chapter

- A trio of **critical thinking activities** designed to help students reflect on and consolidate what they learned about writing and reading and consider the social dimensions of the genre taught in the chapter

Part Two, Critical Thinking Strategies, collects in two separate chapters practical heuristics for invention and reading. The catalog of invention strategies includes clustering, looping, dramatizing, and questioning, while the catalog of reading strategies includes annotating, summarizing, exploring the significance of figurative language, and evaluating the logic of an argument.

Part Three, Writing Strategies, looks at a wide range of writers' strategies: paragraphing and coherence; logic and reasoning; and the familiar methods of presenting information, such as narrating, defining, and classifying. Examples and exercises have been drawn from a wide range of contemporary publications as well as reading selections appearing in Part One. Because of the extensive cross-referencing between Parts One and Three, instructors will find it easier to teach writing strategies as students work on full essays.

Part Four, Research Strategies, discusses field as well as library and Internet research and includes thorough, up-to-date guidelines for using and documenting sources, with detailed examples of the Modern Language Association (MLA) and American Psychological Association (APA) documentation styles. An annotated sample student research paper models ways students can integrate citations into their own work in accordance with the MLA documentation style.

Part Five, Writing for Assessment, covers essay examinations, showing students how to analyze different kinds of exam questions and offering strategies for writing answers. It also addresses portfolios, helping students select, assemble, and present a representative sample of their writing.

Part Six, Writing and Speaking to Wider Audiences, helps students design written and online documents and prepare oral presentations. This part of *The Guide* also includes chapters on collaborative learning and service learning, designed to help students work together on individual and joint writing projects and to write in and for their communities.

The Handbook offers a complete reference guide to grammar, word choice, punctuation, mechanics, common ESL problems, sentence structure, and usage. We have designed the Handbook so that students will find the answers they need quickly, and we have provided student examples from our nationwide study so that students will see errors similar to the ones in their own essays. In addition to the section on ESL problems, boxes throughout the rest of the Handbook offer specific support for ESL students.

Proven Features

Since the first edition, two central features have made *The Guide* such an effective textbook: the practical guides to writing different genres and the systematic integration of reading and writing.

Practical Guides to Writing. We do not merely talk about composing; rather, we offer practical, flexible guides that help students with different parts of writing, such as invention or revision, as they write. Commonsensical and easy to follow, these writing guides teach students to assess a rhetorical situation, identify the kinds of information they will need, ask probing questions and find answers, and organize writing to achieve a particular purpose for chosen readers.

Systematic Integration of Reading and Writing. Because we see a close relationship between the ability to read critically and the ability to write thoughtfully, *The Guide* combines reading instruction with writing instruction. Each chapter in Part One introduces one genre, which students are led to consider both as readers and as writers. Each reading is accompanied by carefully focused apparatus to guide purposeful, productive rereading. First is a response activity, Making Connections to Personal and Social Issues, that relates a central theme of the reading to students' own lives and cultural knowledge. The two sections following, Analyzing Writing Strategies and a brief Commentary, examine how each writer makes telling use of some of the basic features and strategies typical of the genre. Taken together, these activities and commentaries provide students with a comprehensive rhetorical introduction that prepares them to write an essay of their own in a genre. Finally, in Considering Topics for Your Own Essay, students approach the most important decision they have to make with a genre-centered assignment: choosing a workable topic that inspires their commitment to weeks of thinking and writing.

Continuing Attention to Changes in Composition

With each new edition, we have tried to respond to new thinking and new issues in the field of composition and to continue our tradition of turning current theory and research into practical classroom activities — with a minimum of jargon. As a result, from the first to the seventh editions *The Guide* incorporated a number of added features that have contributed to its continued effectiveness, including activities that promote group discussion and inquiry and encourage students to reflect on what they have learned as well as material on document design, oral presentations, and writing in the community.

Collaborative Activities.   *The Guide* offers multiple opportunities for group work throughout each chapter in Part One. At the start of each chapter is a collaborative activity that invites students to try out some of the thinking and planning they will be engaged in as they complete the chapter's assignment. The Making Connections to Personal and Social Issues section that follows each reading is designed to provoke thoughtful small-group discussions about the social and cultural dimensions of the reading. The Guide to Writing offers a collaborative activity that invites students to discuss their work in progress with two or three other students. A Critical Reading Guide focuses a student's comments on another student's essay draft. At the end of each chapter, a discussion activity invites students to explore the social dimensions of the genre they have been learning to write. Each activity includes questions and prompts to guide students to work productively together. In addition to these activities in Part One, the book includes a variety of small-group activities in the chapters in Part Three and an entire chapter in Part Six (Chapter 27) on working with others on individual and joint writing projects.

Critical Thinking Activities.   Each chapter in Part One concludes with three metacognitive activities to help students become aware of what they have learned about the process of writing, about the influences of reading on writing, and about the social and political dimensions of the genres in which they have written. These activities are based on research showing that reflecting on what they have learned deepens students' understanding and improves their recall.

Attention to Document Design, Oral Presentations, and Writing in the Community.   We offer full chapters in Part Six on each of these current issues in composition, as well as material in the rest of the book related to document design and service learning.

Attention to the Computerization of Writing and Research. In the previous (seventh) edition, *The Guide* was thoroughly revised to reflect the many diverse ways that both students and instructors now rely on computers, ranging from the keyword-searching, editing-tracking, and cutting-and-pasting capabilities of word processors to the use of chat rooms, online collaboration and peer review, and other aspects of the increasingly electronic classroom. Sidebars in the assignment chapters in Part One provide concise information and advice about technological topics such as grammar- and spell-checkers and software-based commenting tools, and the Invention section in each Guide to Writing includes an activity that suggests ways students can use the Web selectively and productively for that genre.

Changes in the Eighth Edition

In this edition, in response to instructors' concerns about the need to better prepare students for the kinds of writing specific to academic discourse, we introduce a new writing assignment chapter — the first such change since the second edition of *The Guide* — on the genre of explaining opposing positions on an issue. In addition to this new chapter, which is based on close analysis and citation of two pieces of published writing, in every assignment chapter we have added specific advice to support students' work with sources. We also seek to address another area of growing concern in composition — visual issues — in a number of ways. These range from the book's new design, featuring a brighter color palette and fresh, contemporary look, to the extensive use of color-coded annotations in place of discursive text and the updating and expansion of the parts of the book dealing with visuals and document design. As always, we have inserted many new readings on engaging topics. In addition, *The Guide's* companion Web site has been significantly expanded and enhanced in ways that allow students and instructors to use much of the book in an online format.

A New Assignment Chapter. Along with focusing students' attention on the conventions of academic writing and the skills of objective analysis that they will need to use in many of their college courses, the new "Explaining Opposing Positions" chapter serves as a bridge between the more personal, expository genres in the earlier chapters of the book and the more argument-based genres that follow it. (To make room for it, we dropped the chapter on Remembering People.) More specifically, as Chapter 5, it creates a new related sequence of chapters:

Chapter 4: Explaining a Concept

Chapter 5: Explaining Opposing Positions

Chapter 6: Arguing a Position

The writing strategies that students use in explaining concepts can then be used to explain opposing positions. By learning how to analyze opposing positions in order to compare and contrast them, students become better prepared to argue a position of their own. In all these chapters, students must work closely with published sources.

Like the chapter on Interpreting Stories, the new chapter teaches students to closely analyze given texts, in this case two essays taking opposing positions on a controversial issue. As in all of the chapters in Part One, students first read examples of the genre, and then a special Guide to Writing supports their work through a challenging assignment. The new chapter closes with two debates for students to choose to analyze and explain, with several additional debates provided on *The Guide's* companion Web site.

New Advice on Working with Sources.   The Revision section of every Guide to Writing now includes a boxed feature that gives special attention to an issue related to using sources for the chapter's assignment, with examples drawn from the chapter's readings. Issues include using speaker tags to introduce information from sources, citing a variety of sources rather than just one or two, and citing statistics to establish a problem's existence and seriousness.

A New Overall Design with Marginal Annotations of Essays and Examples. Perhaps the most noticeable feature of the new design is that the first reading in each chapter in Part One is now a student essay with color-screened marginal annotations instead of the apparatus that accompanies the other readings. Each annotation refers to a specific strategy or feature of the essay that is also screened in the same color. These color-coded links model the kind of close reading students must do in order to learn to recognize and use a genre's characteristic features and strategies. Similar annotations have been added to many of the brief examples in Part Three to replace discursive explanations.

Updated and Expanded Coverage of Visuals and Document Design.   The sections in each chapter in Part One dealing with visual aspects of writing — both the advice to the student writer in the Guide to Writing and the discussion of another writer's use of visual elements in the retitled Thinking About Document Design (formerly Designing Your Work) section — have been revised, updated, and in many cases expanded. In addition, Chapter 25, "Designing Documents," has been thoroughly revised, with many new examples and more discussion of such issues as the use of color.

New Readings.   Half of the readings (17 out of 34) are new to this edition, including 4 of the 12 student essays. Selected from a wide variety of contemporary sources, the new readings will engage students with topics such as the ethics of downloading music from the Web, the causes of increasing violence among sports fans and players, the usefulness of online professor-evaluation sites, and the desirability of same-sex schooling.

An Expanded Web Site Available in an Enhanced Version.   A new, enhanced version of *The Guide's* companion Web site, accessible with a code that is available free with the purchase of a new copy of the book, includes an e-book that lets students integrate reading and writing in a new way and makes *The Guide* an even more effective teaching tool. Another major feature of the enhanced site is *Marriage 101 and Other Student Essays*, a new collection of 32 essays inspired by *The Guide* and organized according to the chapter structure of Part One. *Marriage 101* also highlights the revision process with three annotated draft-and-revision pairs. Also featured on this version of the site are a peer-review lesson module and online role-playing game and more pairs of opposing-position essays for use with the new Chapter 5.

Like the enhanced site, an expanded open version of the site also continues to offer many other resources for both instructors and students, including a PDF version of the Instructor's Resource Manual, prompts for journaling and discussion, electronic versions of the Critical Reading Guides and collaborative activities, tutorials for the sentence strategies in the Part One chapters, a variety of resources for research and documentation, and the Exercise Central database of grammar, punctuation, and word choice exercises (which includes customized feedback for students and a reporting feature that lets instructors monitor student progress).

Additional Resources

In addition to the companion Web site, numerous other resources, both print and electronic, accompany *The St. Martin's Guide to Writing*.

The Instructor's Resource Manual, by Rise B. Axelrod, Charles R. Cooper, and Lawrence Barkley of Mt. San Jacinto College–Menifee Valley, includes a catalog of helpful advice for new instructors (by Alison M. Warriner of California State University, East Bay), guidelines on common teaching practices such as assigning journals and setting up group activities, guidelines on responding to and evaluating student writing, course plans, detailed chapter plans, an annotated bibliography in composition and rhetoric, and a selection of background readings. This edition includes coverage of technology and an expanded background readings section with annotated articles on theory, pedagogy, and plagiarism.

Sticks and Stones and Other Student Essays, Sixth Edition, edited by Rise B. Axelrod, Charles R. Cooper, and Ruthe Thompson of Southwest Minnesota State University, is a collection of essays written by students across the nation using *The Guide.* The chapters in the book correspond to those in Part One of *The Guide.* In addition to the 14 most popular essays from the fifth edition, we have chosen 23 new and engaging pieces — more new essays than ever before. Each essay is now accompanied by a headnote that spotlights some of the ways the writer uses the genre successfully, invites students to notice other achievements, and supplies context where necessary.

Who Are We? Readings in Identity and Community and Work and Career, prepared by Rise B. Axelrod and Charles R. Cooper, contains selections that expand on themes foregrounded in *The Guide.* Full of ideas for classroom discussion and writing, the readings offer students additional perspectives and thought-provoking analysis.

Additional Resources for Teaching with The St. Martin's Guide to Writing supports classroom instruction with over fifty transparency masters, including lists of important features for each genre, critical reading guides, collaborative activities, and checklists, all adapted from the text. It also provides more than fifty exercises designed to accompany the Handbook section of *The Guide.* All the pages are perforated for easy removal and copying.

The Elements of Teaching Writing (A Resource for Instructors in All Disciplines), by Katherine Gottschalk and Keith Hjortshoj, provides time-saving strategies and practical guidance in a brief reference form. Drawing on their extensive experience training instructors in all disciplines to incorporate writing into their courses, Gottschalk and Hjortshoj offer reliable advice, accommodating a wide range of teaching styles and class sizes, about how to design effective writing assignments and how to respond to and evaluate student writing in any course.

Our content cartridge for course management systems like WebCT, Blackboard, and Angel makes it simple for instructors using this online learning architecture to build a course around *The Guide.* The content is drawn from the Web site and includes activities, models, reference materials, and the new Exercise Central 3.0 gradebook.

Comment, a powerful and easy-to-use Web-based tool, allows instructors and students to comment on writing quickly and easily, making the drafting and peer-review processes more visible and shareable. Comment with *The St. Martin's Guide* offers *The Guide's* complete e-book online, so reviewers can include direct links to specific parts of the text.

CompClass for The St. Martin's Guide provides the best writing support available in the best online course environment. With e-books, tutorials, model documents, and other premium media from Bedford/St. Martin's, CompClass helps you snap together the pieces you want for your online course. You can connect your syllabus to your e-book, a blog project, or a portfolio assignment and immediately comment, discuss, and respond to the reading and writing that's at the core of your course.

◼ Acknowledgments

We owe an enormous debt to all the rhetoricians and composition specialists whose theory, research, and pedagogy have informed *The St. Martin's Guide to Writing.* We would be adding many pages to an already long book if we were to name everyone to whom we are indebted; suffice it to say that we have been eclectic in our borrowing.

We must also acknowledge immeasurable lessons learned from all the writers, professional and student alike, whose work we analyzed and whose writing we used in this and earlier editions.

So many instructors and students have contributed ideas and criticism over the years. Charles acknowledges the valuable contributions of many instructors in the first-year writing and core-course programs that he directed at Marshall College (formerly Third College) of the University of California, San Diego. We are still benefiting from the astute insights of M. A. Syverson, Sheryl Fontaine, Kate Gardner, Kristin Hawkinson, Michael Pemberton, Irv Peckham, Keith Grant-Davie, Evelyn Torres, Gesa Kirsch, and James Degan. Charles also acknowledges the support of members of the English Department at Sacramento City College, where he has tutored their students, and of Steven Tchudi, Susan Tchudi, and Katherine Boardman of the English Department, University of Nevada, Reno, who have invited him to teach summer-session writing courses for first-year students. Rise similarly acknowledges the many instructors and students both at the University of California, Riverside, where she currently teaches and directs the composition program, and at California State University, San Bernardino, where she previously taught. We want especially to thank the instructors and students who tested early versions of the new chapter on "Explaining Opposing Positions"; the instructors were Melissa Batai at Triton College; Monica Jobes at Catholic University of America; and Sandra Baringer, Paul Beehler, and Stephanie Kay at University of California, Riverside.

The members of the advisory board for the eighth edition, a group of dedicated composition instructors from across the country, have provided us with extensive insights and suggestions for the chapters in Part One and have given us the benefit of their advice on new readings and other new features. For all of their many contributions, we would like to thank Lawrence Barkley, Mt. San Jacinto College–Menifee Valley; Sandie McGill Barnhouse, Rowan-Cabarrus Community College; Melissa Batai, Triton College; Susan Callender, Sinclair Community College; Jack Halligan, Johnson County Community College; Maurice Hunt, Baylor University; Scott Payne, University of Findlay; Sharran S. Slinkard, Des Moines Area Community College; Rachelle Smith, Emporia State University; Kim Stallings, University of North Carolina–Charlotte; and Rosemary Winslow, Catholic University of America.

Many other instructors have also helped us improve the book. For responding to detailed questionnaires about the seventh edition, we thank Teresa Trvathan, South Plains College; Emily Anderson, University of California, Riverside; Lenny Cavallaro, Northern Essex Community College; Nancy V. Daniels, William Rainey Harper College; Tiffany Gilmartin, Copper Mountain College; Sarah Waddle, Des Moines Area Community College–West Campus; Paul Beehler, University of California, Riverside; Marlys Cervantes, Cowley College; Hank Galmish, Green River Community College; Kimberly Harrison, Florida International University; Lesa Hildebrand, Triton College; Ellen Monroe, Copper Mountain College; Ruthe Thompson, Southwest Minnesota State University; James Yates, Northwestern Oklahoma State University; Nolan Belk, Wilkes Community College; Joette Whims, Barstow Community College; Kristin C. Brunnemer, University of California, Riverside and Mt. San Jacinto College–Menifee Valley; Maureen Fonts, Florida International University; James Dervin, Winston-Salem State University; Diane C. Reed, Lincoln Trail College; Tad Wakefield, Riverside Community College, Moreno Valley Campus; R. W. Chapman, Des Moines Area Community College; Philip Mayfield, Fullerton College; Anna M. Lang, University of Indianapolis; Connie R. Miller, Minnesota State University; Rachel Chaffee, Roberts Wesleyan College; Thomas C. Reber, Canisius College; Susan Achziger, Community College of Aurora; Irene Anders, IPFW; Robert E. Gibbons, Our Lady of the Lake University; Patricia R. Granstra, Des Moines Area Community College; Dawn Hubbell-Staeble, Bowling Green State University; Michael O. Kent, San Bernardino Valley College; Damon

Kraft, University of Missouri; Shirley Myers, DeAnza College; Matthew W. Schmeer, Johnson County Community College; Charles Sieracki, Portland Community College; Noel J. Sloboda, Penn State York; Rick Van Noy, Radford University; Delinda Wunder, Community College of Aurora; Cheyenne M. Bonnell, Copper Mountain College; John J. Halligan, Johnson County Community College; Rachelle M. Smith, Emporia State University; Mary Bishop, Holmes Community College; Rhonda Dean Kyncl, University of Oklahoma; Rosemary Winslow, Catholic University of America; Carrie Krantz Fischer, Washtenaw Community College; Susan Kimberleigh Stallings, UNC Charlotte; Sharran S. Slinkard, Des Moines Area Community College; Scott Payne, University of Findlay; Melissa Batai, Triton College; Sandie McGill Barnhouse, Rowan-Cabarrus Community College; Maurice Hunt, Baylor University; Susan Callender, Sinclair Community College; Laura Hope, Chaffey College; and Lawrence Barkley, Mt. San Jacinto College–Menifee Valley.

For this new edition of *The Guide*, we also gratefully acknowledge the special contributions of six people. Debora A. Person, a librarian at the University of Wyoming, reviewed Chapter 21, "Library and Internet Research," and suggested updates and other revisions. Mark Gallaher, who has made many creative contributions to *The Guide* from the beginning, both as a St. Martin's editor and as a teacher of an early draft of a *Guide* chapter, edited and updated a number of chapters in Part One and also researched the additional paired essays for the new "Explaining Opposing Positions" chapter that appear on the companion Web site. Danielle Nicole DeVoss of Michigan State University extensively updated and revised much of the material in the book related to document design and the use of visuals, including the advice in the Guides to Writing and the Thinking About Document Design sections of the Part One chapters as well as all of Chapter 25. Grateful thanks are likewise due to Ruthe Thompson of Southwest Minnesota State University and Larry Barkley of Mt. San Jacinto College–Menifee Valley, our co-editors for *Sticks and Stones* and for the Instructor's Resource Manual, respectively, and to Graham Scott, a University of California, Riverside, graduate student who composed the new technology chapter and the Tech Tips for the manual. Finally, we are especially grateful to the student authors for allowing us to use their work in *Sticks and Stones, Marriage 101,* and *The Guide.*

We want to thank many people at Bedford/St. Martin's, especially John Elliott, who ushered us through the editorial process with unwavering grace, skill, and caring. Thank you, John, for your patience and professionalism as well as your superb writing and editing. We are also grateful to Beth Ammerman, whose patient and intelligent editorial guidance helped launch this new edition, and to our production team of Bernie Onken, Shuli Traub, and Dennis Conroy. Bernie, thanks especially for your skillful juggling during the final stages of the process. Diana Puglisi George, who had served as our editor on an earlier edition, made many additional valuable contributions to this revision with her careful copyediting and especially her suggestions for the new chapter. Laura King managed, contributed to, and edited all of the most important ancillaries to the book: the Instructor's Resource Manual, *Sticks and Stones, Marriage 101,* and the rest of the *Guide* Web site as well as the preview versions of it. Laura always writes and edits precisely and gracefully, never showing off or inflicting jargon or abstractions on her readers when accessible language is available. Consequently her edits and revisions were unerringly helpful. Without the expertise and leadership of Laura, Kim White, and Cate Kashem, the new electronic supplements to *The Guide* would not have been possible. Nathan Odell made important contributions to the Instructor's Resource Manual and to *Sticks and Stones* as well. He helped us correspond with many instructors around the country to invite them to encourage their students to contribute essays; the result was the best-ever pool of essays from which to select, making possible the addition of twenty-one new essays in *Sticks and Stones*.

Thanks also to the immensely talented design team — book designers Wanda Kossak and Claire Seng-Niemoeller as well as Bedford/St. Martin's art directors Anna Palchik and Lucy Krikorian — for making the eighth edition so attractive and usable. Our gratitude also goes to Sandy Schechter and Fred Courtright for their hard work clearing permissions, Katie Paarlberg and Ester Bloom for their invaluable assistance throughout the project, and Naomi Kornhauser for her imaginative photo research.

We wish finally to express our heartfelt appreciation to Nancy Perry for helping us to launch *The Guide* successfully so many years ago and continuing to stand by us. Over the years, Nancy has generously and wisely advised us on everything from planning new editions to copyediting manuscript, and now she is helping us develop the new customized publication of *The Guide*. We also want to thank Erica Appel, who has long helped with the redesign and production of *The Guide* and now lends her considerable experience as our new director of development. Thanks as well to Joan Feinberg and Denise Wydra for their adroit leadership of Bedford/St. Martins, and to marketing managers Karen Melton Soeltz and Karita Dos Santos — along with the extraordinarily talented and hardworking sales staff — for their tireless efforts on behalf of *The Guide*.

Charles dedicates this edition to his three children: Vince, the guitarist and composer; Laura, the artist and garden designer; and Susanna, the writer and political consultant. Rise wishes to thank her husband, Steven, and their son, Jeremiah, for their abiding love, patience, and support. Rise dedicates this edition to the person who has been her guiding light, her beloved mother, Edna Borenstein.

Preface for Students: How to Use *The St. Martin's Guide*

As the authors of *The St. Martin's Guide to Writing*, we have written the book with you, the student reading and using it, always in the forefront of our minds. Although it is a big book that covers many different topics, at its heart is a simple message. The best way to become a good writer is to study examples of good writing, then to apply what you have learned from those examples to your own work, and finally to learn even more by reflecting on the challenges that the particular writing task posed for you. We have set out to provide those examples for specific kinds of writing you are likely to do both in and out of college. Then we provide as much detailed support as possible to show you how to use the strategies familiar to you from those examples to write your own essays. Here we explain how the various parts of the book work together to achieve this goal.

The Organization of the Book

Following Chapter 1 — an introduction to writing that gives general advice about how to approach different parts of a writing assignment — *The St. Martin's Guide to Writing* is divided into six major parts:

Part One: Writing Activities (Chapters 2–10)

Part Two: Critical Thinking Strategies (Chapters 11 and 12)

Part Three: Writing Strategies (Chapters 13–19)

Part Four: Research Strategies (Chapters 20–22)

Part Five: Writing for Assessment (Chapters 23 and 24)

Part Six: Writing and Speaking to Wider Audiences (Chapters 25–28)

This hardcover version of the book also includes a Handbook that you can refer to for help with grammar, punctuation, word choice, common ESL problems, and similar issues.

The Part One Chapters

For now, to understand how to use the book effectively to improve your writing, you first need to know that the most important part — the part that all of the rest depends on — is Part One, Chapters 2 through 10. Each of these chapters is organized to teach you about one important specific *genre*, or type of writing:

- autobiography
- profile
- explanation of concepts
- explanation of opposing positions
- position paper
- proposal
- evaluation
- causal analysis
- literary interpretation

Each Part One chapter except Chapter 10 follows the same structure, beginning with three scenarios that provide examples of how that kind of writing could be used in a college course, in a workplace, and in a community setting such as a volunteer program or civic organization. Then, after a brief introduction, there are four readings, essays that will help you become familiar with the basic features of the genre and the particular challenges it poses. The first reading in each chapter is always one written by a first-year college student who was using *The St. Martin's Guide*, and it includes color-coded marginal annotations that refer to particular parts of the essay screened in the same color. These annotations point out ways the student writer incorporated the basic features of the genre into his or her essay and

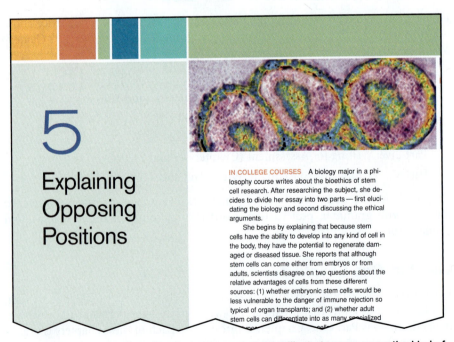

5
Explaining Opposing Positions

IN COLLEGE COURSES   A biology major in a philosophy course writes about the bioethics of stem cell research. After researching the subject, she decides to divide her essay into two parts — first elucidating the biology and second discussing the ethical arguments.

She begins by explaining that because stem cells have the ability to develop into any kind of cell in the body, they have the potential to regenerate damaged or diseased tissue. She reports that although stem cells can come either from embryos or from adults, scientists disagree on two questions about the relative advantages of cells from these different sources: (1) whether embryonic stem cells would be less vulnerable to the danger of immune rejection so typical of organ transplants; and (2) whether adult stem cells can differentiate into as many specialized

Scenarios at the beginning of each assignment chapter illustrate some ways the kind of writing taught in the chapter could be used in college and elsewhere.

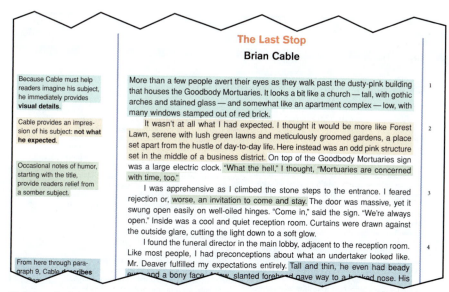

The Last Stop

Brian Cable

Because Cable must help readers imagine his subject, he immediately provides **visual details.**

More than a few people avert their eyes as they walk past the dusty-pink building that houses the Goodbody Mortuaries. It looks a bit like a church — tall, with gothic arches and stained glass — and somewhat like an apartment complex — low, with many windows stamped out of red brick. 1

Cable provides an impression of his subject: **not what he expected.**

It wasn't at all what I had expected. I thought it would be more like Forest Lawn, serene with lush green lawns and meticulously groomed gardens, a place set apart from the hustle of day-to-day life. Here instead was an odd pink structure set in the middle of a business district. On top of the Goodbody Mortuaries sign was a large electric clock. "What the hell," I thought, "Mortuaries are concerned with time, too." 2

Occasional notes of humor, starting with the title, provide readers relief from a somber subject.

I was apprehensive as I climbed the stone steps to the entrance. I feared rejection or, worse, an invitation to come and stay. The door was massive, yet it swung open easily on well-oiled hinges. "Come in," said the sign. "We're always open." Inside was a cool and quiet reception room. Curtains were drawn against the outside glare, cutting the light down to a soft glow. 3

I found the funeral director in the main lobby, adjacent to the reception room. Like most people, I had preconceptions about what an undertaker looked like. Mr. Deaver fulfilled my expectations entirely. Tall and thin, he even had beady eyes and a bony face. A low, slanted forehead gave way to a hooked nose. His 4

From here through paragraph 9, Cable describes

Color-coded annotations of the first reading in each assignment chapter point out basic features of that kind of writing and particular strategies used by the student writer.

also call attention to particular writing strategies — such as quoting, using humor, providing definitions, and comparing and contrasting — that the writer used.

Usually, the other three readings in the chapter are by professional writers. Each of these additional essays is accompanied by the following groups of questions, activities, and commentary to help you learn how essays in that genre work:

Making Connections to Personal and Social Issues invites you to explore with other students an issue raised by the reading that is related to your own experience and often to broader social or cultural issues.

Analyzing Writing Strategies helps you examine closely some specific strategies the writer used.

Commentary points out and discusses the ways one or more of the basic features are represented in the essay.

Considering Topics for Your Own Essay suggests subjects related to the reading that you might write about in your own essay.

Following the readings, each assignment chapter (except Chapter 10) also includes the following six parts:

- a discussion of possible purposes and audiences for the genre.
- a summary of the genre's basic features, with examples from the chapter's readings (see next page).
- a Guide to Writing that will help you write an effective essay in the genre for your particular audience and purpose. The Guides to Writing, the most important parts of the entire book, will be explained fully in the next section.

Basic Features: Arguing Positions

A Focused Presentation of the Issue

Writers use a variety of strategies to present the issue and prepare readers for their argument. For current, hotly debated issues, the title may be enough to identify the issue. Estrada's allusion to the familiar children's chant in his title "Sticks and Stones and Sports Team Names" is enough to identify the issue for many readers. Statsky gives a brief history of the debate about competitive sports for children. Many writers provide concrete examples early on to make sure that readers can understand the issue. Statsky mentions Peewee Football and Little League Baseball as examples of the kind of organized sports she opposes.

How writers present the issue depends on what they assume readers already know and what they want readers to think about the issue. Therefore, they try to define the issue in a way that promotes their position. Estrada defines the issue of naming sports

qualified, and clearly arguable. For example, to avoid ambiguity, Estrada uses common words like *wrong*. But because readers may differ on what they consider to be wrong, Estrada demonstrates exactly what he thinks is wrong about naming teams for ethnic groups. To show readers he shares their legitimate concerns about hypersensitivity, Estrada qualifies his thesis to apply only to genuine cases of political insensitivity. Finally, to show that his position is not based solely on personal feelings, Estrada appeals to readers' common sense of right and wrong.

Plausible Reasons and Convincing Support

To argue for a position, writers must give reasons. Even in relatively brief essays, writers sometimes give more than one reason and state their reasons explicitly. Estrada, for instance, gives two reasons for his

The basic features of the genre in each assignment chapter are summarized on two facing pages tinted grayish green.

A Writer at Work

■ The Interview Notes and Write-Up

Most profile writers take notes when interviewing people. Later, they may summarize their notes in a short write-up. In this section, you will see some of the interview notes and a write-up that Brian Cable prepares for his mortuary profile, "The Last Stop," printed on pp. 76–78.

Cable arranged to tour the mortuary and conduct interviews with the funeral director and mortician. Before each interview, he wrote out a few questions at the top of a sheet of paper and then divided it into two columns; he used the left-hand column for descriptive details and personal impressions and the right-hand column for the information he got directly from the person he interviewed. Following are Cable's notes and write-up for his interview with the funeral director, Howard Deaver.

Cable used three questions to guide his interview with Howard and then took brief notes during the interview. He did not concern himself too much with note-taking because he planned to spend a half-hour directly afterward to complete his notes. He focused his attention on Howard, trying to keep the interview comfortable and conversational and jotting down just enough to jog his memory and catch especially meaningful quotations. A typescript of Cable's interview notes follows.

The Interview Notes

QUESTIONS

1. How do families of the deceased view the mortuary business?
2. How is the concept of death approached?
3. How did you get into this business?

A Writer at Work section shows part of a student's work on one of the essays in the chapter.

Thinking About Document Design

Effective document design is an important factor for the marketing manager who volunteers to teach fifth graders about the concept of surveys (see the community writing project described on p. 135). Because the marketer is teaching students about surveys by having them take a survey, she knows that the design of the survey will be crucial to the students' understanding.

She recognizes that students need to be interested in the questionnaire and able to fill it out quickly; she also knows that it is important that they not feel intimidated by its appearance — by page after page and question after question. After first drafting the questionnaire, she realizes that although the questions all fit on one page (cutting down on paper and photocopying costs), the page is very cluttered and difficult to read.

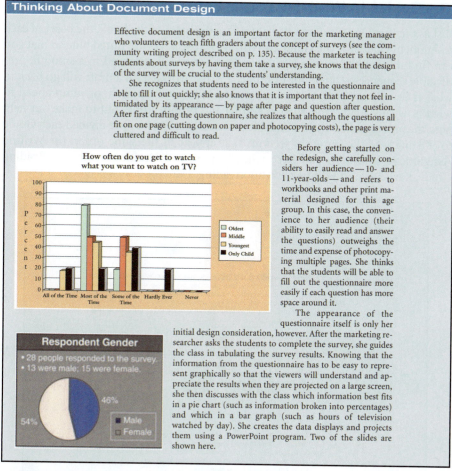

Before getting started on the redesign, she carefully considers her audience — 10- and 11-year-olds — and refers to workbooks and other print material designed for this age group. In this case, the convenience to her audience (their ability to easily read and answer the questions) outweighs the time and expense of photocopying multiple pages. She thinks that the students will be able to fill out the questionnaire more easily if each question has more space around it.

The appearance of the questionnaire itself is only her initial design consideration, however. After the marketing researcher asks the students to complete the survey, she guides the class in tabulating the survey results. Knowing that the information from the questionnaire has to be easy to represent graphically so that the viewers will understand and appreciate the results when they are projected on a large screen, she then discusses with the class which information best fits in a pie chart (such as information broken into percentages) and which in a bar graph (such as hours of television watched by day). She creates the data displays and projects them using a PowerPoint program. Two of the slides are shown here.

A Thinking About Document Design section, on blue pages, shows possible ways to use visual illustrations in the genre.

- a Writer at Work narrative showing a student's work on one of the readings in the chapter.

- a Thinking About Document Design section, illustrating possible ways to use visuals in the genre and based on one of the scenarios at the beginning of the chapter. This section is tinted blue.

- a concluding section titled Thinking Critically About What You Have Learned, which invites you to reflect on your experience with the genre and to consider some of its wider social and cultural implications.

The Guides to Writing

Just as the Part One assignment chapters are the heart of the book, the heart of each assignment chapter is the Guide to Writing, whose pages are tinted blue so that you can find them easily. Writing an essay does not usually proceed in a smooth, predictable sequence — often, for example, a writer working on a draft will go back to what is usually an earlier step, such as invention and research, or jump ahead to what is usually a later one, such as editing and proofreading. But to make our help with the process more understandable and manageable, we have divided each Guide to Writing into the same six sections that appear in the same order: the Writing Assignment, Invention and Research, Planning and Drafting, a Critical Reading Guide, Revising, and Editing and Proofreading.

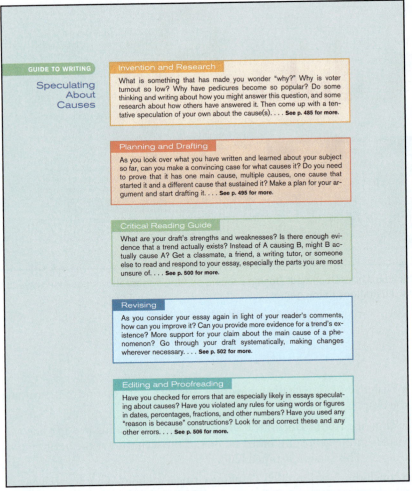

The color-coded "menu" at the beginning of each Guide to Writing shows you at a glance the six sections of the Guide and some of the things you will need to think about and do in each section.

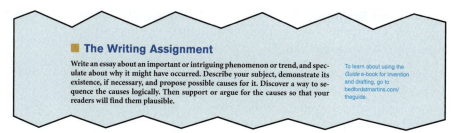

The Writing Assignment

Write an essay about an important or intriguing phenomenon or trend, and speculate about why it might have occurred. Describe your subject, demonstrate its existence, if necessary, and propose possible causes for it. Discover a way to sequence the causes logically. Then support or argue for the causes so that your readers will find them plausible.

To learn about using the *Guide* e-book for invention and drafting, go to bedfordstmartins.com/theguide.

Each Guide to Writing begins with a clearly defined assignment.

To understand how the Guide to Writing works, look closely at the types of activities included in each section:

The Writing Assignment.   Each Guide to Writing begins with an assignment that defines the general purpose and basic features of the genre you have been studying in the chapter. The assignment does not tell you what subject to write about or who your readers will be. You will have to make these decisions, guided by the invention and research activities in the next section.

Invention and Research.   Every Guide to Writing includes invention activities designed to help you

- find a topic
- discover what you already know about the topic
- consider your purpose and audience
- research the topic further — in the library, on the Internet, through observation and interviews, or some combination of these methods — to see what others have written about it
- explore and develop your ideas, and
- compose a tentative thesis statement to guide your planning and drafting.

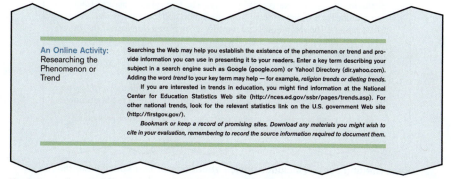

An Online Activity: Researching the Phenomenon or Trend

Searching the Web may help you establish the existence of the phenomenon or trend and provide information you can use in presenting it to your readers. Enter a key term describing your subject in a search engine such as Google (google.com) or Yahoo! Directory (dir.yahoo.com). Adding the word *trend* to your key term may help — for example, *religion trends or dieting trends*.

If you are interested in trends in education, you might find information at the National Center for Education Statistics Web site (http://nces.ed.gov/ssbr/pages/trends.asp). For other national trends, look for the relevant statistics link on the U.S. government Web site (http://firstgov.gov/).

Bookmark or keep a record of promising sites. Download any materials you might wish to cite in your evaluation, remembering to record the source information required to document them.

Each Invention and Research section includes a box with suggestions for researching your topic on the Web.

Planning and Drafting. To get you started writing a draft of your essay, each Guide to Writing includes suggestions for planning — setting goals that you try to implement as you write a draft. The section is divided into four parts:

- *Seeing What You Have* involves reviewing what you have discovered about your subject, purpose, and audience.
- *Setting Goals* helps you think about your overall purpose as well as your goals for the various parts of your essay.
- *Outlining* suggests some of the ways you might organize your essay.
- *Drafting* launches you on the writing of your draft, providing both general advice and suggestions about one or two specific sentence strategies that you might find useful for the particular genre.

Critical Reading Guide. Once you have finished a draft, you will want to make an effort to have someone else read the draft and comment on how to improve it. Each Guide to Writing includes a Critical Reading Guide, tinted in beige for easy reference, that will help you get a good assessment of your draft as well as help you assess others' drafts.

A Sentence Strategy: Rhetorical Questions. As you draft an essay proposing a solution to a problem, you will want to connect with your readers. You will also want readers to become concerned with the seriousness of the problem and thoughtful about the challenge of solving it. Sentences that take the form of **rhetorical questions** can help you achieve these goals.

A rhetorical question is conventionally defined as a sentence posing a question to which the writer expects no answer from the reader. In proposals, however, rhetorical questions do important rhetorical work — that is, they assist a writer in realizing a particular purpose and they influence readers in certain ways. Here are three examples from Matt Miller's proposal:

- How should we address this crisis? (paragraph 5)
- How to do this? (paragraph 6)
- How much would this plan cost? (paragraph 11)

These questions, each placed at the beginning of a paragraph, function like headings. They announce the main parts of the proposal. The first question makes a transition from defining the problem to describing the solution, and the word *we* reaches out to include readers. The second question introduces the plan to implement the writer's proposed solution: the word *this* refers back to the sentence that immediately precedes the question and states the thesis of the essay. Similarly, the last question lets readers know that the focus is shifting to Miller's argument about the feasibility of his proposed solution.

Following is another pair of rhetorical questions from Miller's essay, but note that these are placed at the end of a brief paragraph instead of at the beginning:

In determining pay rates, who will decide which teachers are better performers? And what standards will be used to assess teachers? (paragraph 20)

Each Drafting section includes advice about one or two specific sentence strategies that writers often find useful in that genre.

Now is the time to get a good critical reading of your draft. Your instructor may arrange such a reading as part of your coursework — in class or online. If not, you can ask a classmate, friend, or family member to read your draft using this guide. If your campus has a writing center, you might ask a tutor there to read and comment on your draft. (If you are unable to have someone else review your draft, turn ahead to the Revision section for help reading your own draft with a critical eye.)

Critical Reading Guide

▶ **If You Are the Writer.**   To provide focused, helpful comments, your reader must know your essay's intended audience, your purpose, and a problem in the draft that you need help solving. Briefly write out this information at the top of your draft.

- *Readers:* To whom are you directing your concept explanation? What do you assume they know about the concept? How do you plan to engage and hold their interest?
- *Purpose:* What do you hope to achieve with your readers?
- *Problem:* Ask your reader to help you solve the most important problem you see in the draft. Describe this problem briefly.

▶ **If You Are the Reader.**   Use the following guidelines to help you give constructive, helpful comments to others on essays explaining concepts.

1. *Read for a First Impression.*   Read first to get a sense of the concept. Then briefly write out your impressions. What in the draft do you think will especially interest the intended readers? Where might they have difficulty in following the explanation? Next, consider the problem the writer identified, and respond briefly to that concern now. (If you find that the problem is covered by one of the other guidelines listed below, respond to it in more detail there if necessary.)

Making Comments Electronically
Most word processing software offers features that allow you to insert comments directly into the text of someone else's document. Many readers prefer to make their comments in this way because it tends to be faster than writing on a hard copy and space is virtually unlimited; from the writer's point of view, it also eliminates the problem of deciphering handwritten comments. Even where such special comment features are not available, simply typing comments directly into a document in a contrasting color can provide the same advantages.

Each Critical Reading Guide provides specific, detailed questions to help you or someone else assess a draft.

Ask whether your critical reader would prefer an electronic version of your draft or a hard copy. Even a reader who is going to comment on the draft electronically may prefer to read a hard copy.

Revising.   Each Guide to Writing includes a Revising section to help you get an overview of your draft, consider readers' comments, chart a plan for revision, and carry out the revisions. The Revising section also includes a boxed feature called Working with Sources, which offers advice (using examples from one or more of the readings) on a particular issue related to incorporating materials from research sources into your essay. An example is shown on the next page.

Editing and Proofreading.   Each Guide to Writing ends with a section intended to help you recognize and fix specific kinds of errors in grammar, punctuation, sentence structure, and so on that are common in essays in that genre of writing. An example appears on the next page. In some chapters, the errors include ones particular to students whose first language is not English.

Working with Sources

Integrating quotations from your interviews

In addition to describing people, your profile will also quote them. These quotations can be especially revealing because they let readers hear different people speaking for themselves, rather than being presented through your eyes. Nevertheless, it is the writer who decides which quotations to use and how. Therefore, one major task you face in drafting and revising your essay is to choose quotations from your notes, present them in a timely way to reveal the style and character of people you interviewed, and integrate these quotations smoothly into your sentences.

For more help integrating quotations, go to bedfordstmartins.com/theguide and click on Bedford Research Room.

When you directly quote (rather than paraphrase or summarize) what someone has said, you will usually need to identify the speaker. The principal way to do so is to create what is called a **speaker tag**. You may rely on a *general* or all-purpose speaker tag, using the forms of *say* and *tell*:

"I don't see a policeman," Lewis *says* to him. (John McPhee, paragraph 15)

"Three pounds for a dollar," I *tell* her. (John McPhee, paragraph 1)

Other speaker tags are more *specific* or precise:

"It was a large service," *remarked* Howard. (Brian Cable, paragraph 16)

"Something deep within us demands a confrontation with death," Tim *explained*. (Brian Cable, paragraph 22)

"Take me out to the" — and Toby *yells out*, "Banana store!" (Amanda Coyne, paragraph 21)

As you draft your profile, consider using specific speaker tags. They give readers more help with imagining speakers' attitudes and personal styles. Nevertheless, keep in mind that experienced writers rely on general speaker tags using forms of *say* and *tell* for most of their sentences with quotations.

In addition, you may add a word or phrase to any speaker tag to identify or describe the speaker or to reveal more about *how, where, when,* or *why* the speaker speaks:

A Working with Sources box in each Revising section helps you with a specific issue related to using source material.

■ Editing and Proofreading

A Note on Grammar and Spelling Checkers
These tools are good at catching certain types of errors, but currently there is no replacement for a good human proofreader. Grammar checkers in particular are extremely limited in what they can usually find, and often they only give you summary information that isn't helpful if you do not already understand the rule in question. They are also prone to give faulty advice for fixing problems and to flag correct items as wrong. Spelling checkers cause fewer problems but cannot catch misspellings that are themselves words, such as *to* for *too*.

For practice, go to bedfordstmartins.com/theguide/exercisecentral and click on Comparisons.

Now is the time to check your revised draft for errors in grammar, punctuation, and mechanics and to consider matters of style. Our research has identified several errors that are especially likely to occur in evaluative writing. The following guidelines will help you proofread and edit your revised draft for these common errors.

Checking Comparisons.   Whenever you evaluate something, you are likely to engage in comparison. You might want to show that a new recording is inferior to an earlier one, that one film is stronger than another, that this café is better than that one. Make a point of checking to see that all comparisons in your writing are complete, logical, and clear.

Editing to Make Comparisons Complete

▶ *Jazz* is as good, if not better than, Morrison's other novels. *as*

▶ I liked the Lispector story because it's so different. *from anything else I've ever read*

Editing to Make Comparisons Logical

▶ Will Smith's Muhammad Ali is more serious than any role he's played. *other*

▶ Ohio State's offense played much better than Michigan. *Michigan's did.*

Check also to see that you say *different from* instead of *different than*.

▶ Carrying herself with a confident and brisk stride, Katherine Parker seems different than the other women in the office. *from*

The Editing and Proofreading section shows examples of errors common in the genre, with corrections in blue type.

The Other Parts of the Book

Parts Two through Five provide more help and practice with specific kinds of strategies for reading critically as well as for different aspects of writing and research. Also included are up-to-date guidelines for choosing, using, and documenting different kinds of sources (library sources, the Internet, and your own field research); taking essay exams; and assembling a portfolio of your writing. See the next two pages for illustrations of Chapter 22, "Using and Acknowledging Sources."

Part Six presents four brief chapters that will help you in writing and speaking for audiences beyond your first-year composition classroom, covering the diverse topics of writing in the community (sometimes referred to as service learning), collaborative learning (consulting and writing with others), print and electronic document design, and oral presentations. (See p. xxx for an illustration from Chapter 25, "Designing Documents.")

Finding and Navigating between Different Parts of the Book

In a book as large and complex as this one, it can sometimes be hard to tell where you are or to find the information you need on a particular topic in the book. To help you find your way around, besides the color-coded sections that have already been mentioned, you can use the running heads at the tops of the pages and, in the Part One chapters, the color-coded tabs used to mark the four main sections of those chapters. (See the illustrations on p. xxx.) To locate information or additional material on particular topics, besides using the table of contents in the front of the book and the index in the back, you can benefit from the cross-references that appear in the margins throughout the book. (See the illustration on p. xxxi.) As you may have noticed in the illustrations on the previous pages, other marginal notes refer you to the companion Web site, where related material or electronic versions of material in the book are available. Still other notes provide useful information and advice about computer-related topics such as editing-tracking, collaborating and reviewing others' work online, and software-based commenting tools.

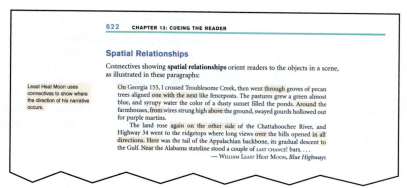

In Part Three, Chapters 13–19, color-coded annotations of examples point out the use of particular strategies.

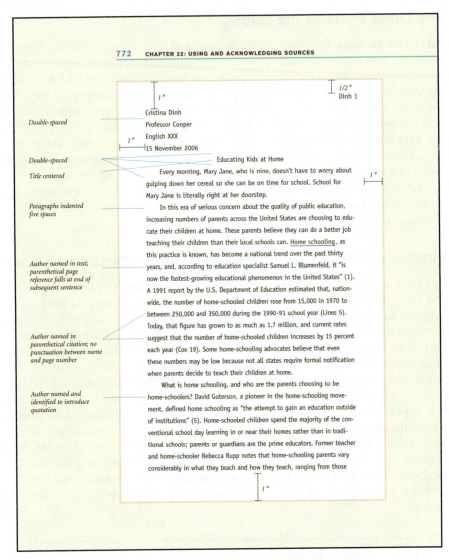

1/2 "
Dinh 1

1 "

Cristina Dinh

Double-spaced   Professor Cooper

1 "   English XXX

15 November 2006

Double-spaced   Educating Kids at Home

Title centered   Every morning, Mary Jane, who is nine, doesn't have to worry about

gulping down her cereal so she can be on time for school. School for   1 "

Mary Jane is literally right at her doorstep.

Paragraphs indented   In this era of serious concern about the quality of public education,

five spaces   increasing numbers of parents across the United States are choosing to edu-

cate their children at home. These parents believe they can do a better job

teaching their children than their local schools can. Home schooling, as

this practice is known, has become a national trend over the past thirty

Author named in text;   years, and, according to education specialist Samuel L. Blumenfeld, it "is

parenthetical page   now the fastest-growing educational phenomenon in the United States" (1).

reference falls at end of   A 1991 report by the U.S. Department of Education estimated that, nation-

subsequent sentence   wide, the number of home-schooled children rose from 15,000 in 1970 to

between 250,000 and 350,000 during the 1990-91 school year (Lines 5).

Today, that figure has grown to as much as 1.7 million, and current rates

Author named in   suggest that the number of home-schooled children increases by 15 percent

parenthetical citation; no   each year (Cox 19). Some home-schooling advocates believe that even

punctuation between name   these numbers may be low because not all states require formal notification

and page number   when parents decide to teach their children at home.

What is home schooling, and who are the parents choosing to be

Author named and   home-schoolers? David Guterson, a pioneer in the home-schooling move-

identified to introduce   ment, defined home schooling as "the attempt to gain an education outside

quotation   of institutions" (5). Home-schooled children spend the majority of the con-

ventional school day learning in or near their homes rather than in tradi-

tional schools; parents or guardians are the prime educators. Former teacher

and home-schooler Rebecca Rupp notes that home-schooling parents vary

considerably in what they teach and how they teach, ranging from those

1 "

Several parts of Chapter 22, "Using and Acknowledging Sources," are color-coded for easy reference. The pages tinted beige contain a sample research paper using MLA (Modern Language Association) format and documentation style, the format and style you are most likely to use in this class. The pages containing guidelines for and examples of how to cite various kinds of sources in MLA style have a dark blue stripe down the side. And a dark orange stripe indicates the pages containing guidelines and examples for APA (American Psychological Association) style, which you may also need to use in this or other college courses.

The MLA System of Documentation

Citations in Text

The MLA author-page system generally requires that in-text citations include the author's last name and the page number of the passage being cited. There is no punctuation between author and page. The parenthetical citation should follow the quoted, paraphrased, or summarized material as closely as possible without disrupting the flow of the sentence.

> Dr. James is described as a "not-too-skeletal Ichabod Crane" (Simon 68).

Note that the parenthetical citation comes before the final period. With block quotations, however, the citation comes after the final period, preceded by a space (see p. 742 for an example).

If you mention the author's name in your text, supply just the page reference in parentheses.

> Simon describes Dr. James as a "not-too-skeletal Ichabod Crane" (68).

A WORK WITH MORE THAN ONE AUTHOR

To cite a source by two or three authors, include all the authors' last names; for works with more than three authors, use all the authors' names or just the first author's name followed by *et al.*, meaning "and others," in regular type (not italicized or underlined).

> Dyal, Corning, and Willows identify several types of students, including the "Authority-Rebel" (4).

> The Authority-Rebel "tends to see himself as superior to other students in the class" (Dyal, Corning, and Willows 4).

> The drug AZT has been shown to reduce the risk of transmission from HIV-positive mothers to their infants by as much as two-thirds (Van de Perre et al. 4-5).

TWO OR MORE WORKS BY THE SAME AUTHOR

Include the author's last name, a comma, a shortened version of the title, and the page number(s).

> When old paint becomes transparent, it sometimes shows the artist's original plans: "a tree will show through a woman's dress" (Hellman, *Pentimento* 1).

A WORK WITH AN UNKNOWN AUTHOR

Use a shortened version of the title, beginning with the word by which the title is alphabetized in the works-cited list. ("Awash in Garbage" was the title in the following example.)

Electronic Sources

For more information on using the Internet for research, see Chapter 21, pp. 730–31.

For answers to frequently asked questions on citing Internet sources in the APA style, go to http://www.apastyle.org/elecref/html.

While the APA guidelines for citing online resources are still something of a work in progress, a rule of thumb is that citation information must allow readers to access and retrieve the information cited. The following guidelines are derived from the *Publication Manual of the American Psychological Association*, Fifth Edition (2001), and the APA Web site.

For most sources accessed on the Internet, you should provide the following information:

- Name of author (if available)
- Date of publication or most recent update (in parentheses; if unavailable, use the abbreviation *n.d.*)
- Title of document
- Publication information, including volume and issue numbers for periodicals
- Retrieval information, including date of access and URL or path followed to locate the site

A WEB SITE

When you cite an entire Web site, the APA does not require an entry in the list of references. You may instead give the name of the site in your text and its Web address in parentheses. To cite a document that you have accessed through a Web site, follow these formats:

> American Cancer Society. (2003). How to fight teen smoking. Retrieved April 10, 2006, from http://www.cancer.org/docroot/ped/content/ped_10_14_how_to_fight_teen_smoking.asp

> Heims, M. (2003, January 24). The strange case of Sarah Jones. *The Free Expression Policy Project.* Retrieved January 12, 2006, from http://www.fepproject.org/commentaries/sarahjones.html

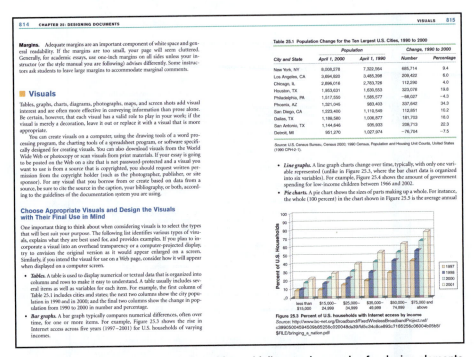

Chapter 25, "Designing Documents," provides guidelines and examples for design elements and visual illustrations for many kinds of documents, both print and electronic, such as photographs, charts, and tables.

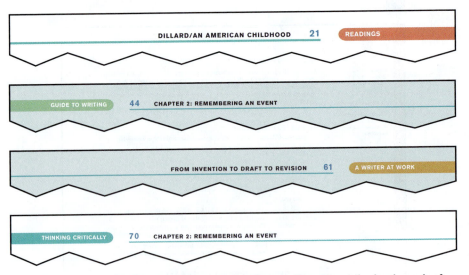

In addition to the running heads at the top of each page throughout the book, each of the four main sections of the Part One assignment chapters is marked with a color-coded tab to help you identify where you are in the chapter.

The Handbook

The Handbook, on the beige pages in the back of the book, offers a complete reference guide to grammar, word choice, punctuation, capitalization, use of numbers and abbreviations, spelling, ESL troublespots, sentence structure, and words that are frequently misused. We have designed the Handbook so that you can find the answers you need quickly, and we have provided examples from a nationwide study we did of college students' writing. The examples appear in regular black type, with the corrections in blue in a different font. The grammatical and other specialized terms that are used in the Handbook are all highlighted in white boxes in the text and defined in white boxes in the margins, so that you never have to look elsewhere in the book to understand the explanation. In addition to a section on ESL problems, blue boxes throughout the rest of the Handbook offer specific support for ESL students.

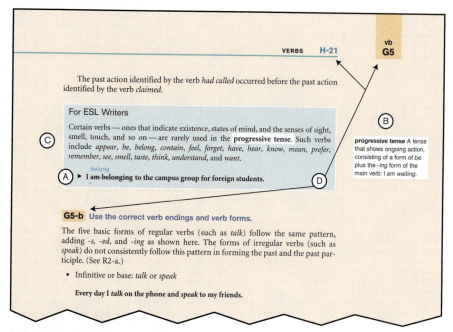

A Corrections appear in blue type.
B White boxes highlight terms defined in the margins.
C Blue boxes offer ESL support.
D Codes for different sections of the Handbook, along with symbols and abbreviations for specific issues, make it easier to find the exact information that you need or that your instructor needs to refer you to.

A Brief Contents

Contents

PART TWO CRITICAL THINKING STRATEGIES

PART THREE   WRITING STRATEGIES

PART FIVE WRITING FOR ASSESSMENT

HANDBOOK

Introduction

"Why should learning to write well be important to me? What is the connection between writing and thinking? How will reading help me learn to write better? How can I learn to write more inventively, effectively, efficiently?" These are some of the questions you may be asking as you begin this writing course. Read on — for *The St. Martin's Guide to Writing* offers some answers to these and other questions you may have.

◼ Why Writing Is Important

Writing influences and changes the way you think and learn, enhances your chances of success, contributes to your personal development, and strengthens your relationships with other people.

Writing Influences the Way You Think

The very act of writing encourages you to be creative as well as organized and logical in your thinking. When you write sentences, paragraphs, and whole essays, you generate ideas and connect these ideas in systematic ways. For example, by combining words into phrases and sentences with conjunctions such as *and, but,* and *because,* you create complex new ideas. By grouping related ideas into paragraphs, you develop their similarities and differences and anchor your general ideas in specific facts and concrete examples.

By writing essays for different purposes, you develop your thinking in different ways. For example, writing about a remembered event stimulates you to reflect on your personal memories and their meaning for you; arguing for your position on a controversial issue encourages logical reasoning; explaining opposing positions deepens your ability to notice similarities and differences; and making evaluations helps you to understand why you value certain things more than others.

> The mere process of writing is one of the most powerful tools we have for clarifying our own thinking. I am never as clear about any matter as when I have just finished writing about it.
> — JAMES VAN ALLEN

Writing Contributes to Learning

Writing helps you learn by making you a more attentive critical reader and thinker. When you take notes in class, for example, writing helps you identify and remember what is important. Writing in the margins as you read encourages you to question the reading's ideas and information in light of your experience and other reading. Writing consolidates your understanding of and response to what you are learning.

Writing essays of various kinds helps you to organize and present what you have learned and, in the process, clarify and extend your own ideas. Different kinds of writing contribute to learning in different ways. When you explain opposing positions on a controversial issue, you learn the points on which people agree and disagree. Arguing your own position teaches you not only to support your reasons but also to refute likely objections to your argument. Researching a profile, you learn to make precise observations and arrange them to create a particular impression. Composing an evaluation requires you to learn about your subject and the values or standards typically used to judge it.

> I've always thought best when I wrote.   — TONI MORRISON

> Writing has been for a long time my major tool for self-instruction and self-development.   — TONI CADE BAMBARA

Writing Fosters Personal Development

In addition to influencing the ways you think and learn, writing can help you grow as an individual. Writing leads you to reflect deeply on your personal experience, for example, when you write to understand the significance of a particular event in your life. Writing about a controversial issue can make you examine some of your most basic beliefs. Writing an evaluation requires that you think about what you value and how your values compare to those of others. Perhaps most important, becoming an author confers authority on you; it gives you confidence to assert your own ideas and feelings.

> In a very real sense, the writer writes in order to teach himself, to understand himself, to satisfy himself. . . .   — ALFRED KAZIN

> Some of the things that happen to us in life seem to have no meaning, but when you write them down, you find the meanings for them. . . .   — MAXINE HONG KINGSTON

Writing Connects You to Others

It is easier now than ever before to connect with others via e-mail and the Internet. You may use writing to keep in touch with friends and family, take part in academic discussions, and participate actively in civic debate and decision making. By writing about your experiences, ideas, and observations, you reach out to readers, offering them your own point of view and inviting them to share theirs in return. Writing your own argument, for example, you not only assert your position on the issue but also try to anticipate and respond to readers' likely objections and questions. Moreover, when you respond constructively to other people's arguments, you clarify your different perspectives, reexamine your own reasoning, and may ultimately influence other people's opinions as they influence yours. Similarly, writing a proposal invites you to work collaboratively with others to invent new, creative ways of solving complex problems.

> Writing is the act of saying I, of imposing oneself upon other people, of saying listen to me, see it my way, change your mind.   — JOAN DIDION

> It's the sense of being in contact with people who are part of a particular audience that really makes a difference to me in writing.
> — SHERLEY ANNE WILLIAMS

Writing Promotes Success in College and at Work

As a student, you are probably most aware of the many ways writing can contribute to your success in school. Students who learn to write for different readers and purposes do well in courses throughout the curriculum. No doubt you have been able to use writing to demonstrate your knowledge as well as to add to it. Eventually, you will need to use writing to advance your career by writing persuasive application letters for jobs or graduate school admission. At work, you will be expected to write effective e-mail messages, formal letters, and reports that present clear explanations, well-reasoned arguments, convincing evaluations, or constructive proposals.

> People think it's sort of funny that I went to graduate school as a biologist and then became a writer. . . . What I learned [in science] is how to formulate or identify a new question that hasn't been asked before and then to set about solving it, to do original research to find the way to an answer. And that's what I do when I write a book.   — BARBARA KINGSOLVER

EXERCISE 1.1

Think of an occasion when writing helped you accomplish something important. For example, you may recall a time when writing helped you better understand a difficult subject you were studying, when you used writing to influence someone else, when you expressed your feelings or worked through a problem by writing, or when you used writing for some other worthwhile purpose.

Write a page or two describing what happened on this particular occasion. Describe how you came to write and what you wrote about. Then explain how you used writing on this occasion and what you wanted your writing to accomplish. For example, did you use it to help you learn something, express yourself, or connect to others?

■ How Writing Is Learned

Writing is important. But can it be learned? There are many myths about writing and writers. For example, some people believe that writers are born, not made. They assume that people who are good at writing do not have to spend a lot of time learning to write — that they just naturally know how. Another myth is that "real" writers write perfectly the first time, every time, dashing off an essay with minimal effort. Writers' testimonies, however, together with extensive research on how people write and learn to write, show that writing can — indeed, must — be learned. All writers, especially gifted writers, work at their writing. Some writers may be more successful and influential than others. Some may find writing easier and more satisfying. But no one is born knowing how to write.

> However great a [person's] natural talent may be, the art of writing cannot be learned all at once.
> — JEAN JACQUES ROUSSEAU

> Learning to write well takes time and much effort, but it can be done.
> — MARGARET MEAD

The St. Martin's Guide to Writing, now in its eighth edition, has helped many students become more thoughtful, effective, confident writers. From reading and analyzing an array of different kinds of essays, you will learn how other writers make their texts work for their particular readers. From writing the kinds of essays you are reading, you will learn to compose texts that readers want to read. To help you take full advantage of what you are learning, *The Guide* will also help you reflect on your learning so that you will be able to remember, apply, and build on what you have learned.

Reading

Most professional writers are avid readers who read not only for enjoyment and information but also to learn how other writers write. As a college student, you will do a great deal of reading, much of which will help you learn about the types of writing you aspire to do for personal, academic, and career reasons. This section shows how *The St. Martin's Guide* supports your learning about writing from reading.

How Written Texts Work.   The expectations of readers are aroused when they recognize a text as a particular *genre* or type of writing. For example, a story about a past event in the writer's life is immediately recognizable as a form of autobiography, which leads readers to expect an engaging story about an event that seems significant, a story that changes, challenges, or complicates the writer's sense of self or connection with others. If the event seems trivial or the story lacks interest, then readers' expectations will be disappointed and the text will not succeed. Similarly, if the text takes a position on a controversial issue, readers will recognize it as an opinion piece and expect it to not only assert and support that position, but also refute possible objections. If the argument lacks credible support or ignores objections that thoughtful readers may have raised, readers are likely to decide that the essay is not convincing and is therefore ineffective.

Although individual texts within the same genre vary a great deal because of the different contents and emphases (no two proposals, even those arguing for the same solution, will be identical), they nonetheless follow a general pattern that provides a certain amount of predictability without which communication would be difficult, if not impossible. But these language patterns, also called *conventions*, should not be thought of as rigid formulas that must be followed mechanically. Not only does language allow for variation and innovation, but it evolves as society changes — for example, developing new genres for new media, such as text messaging and blogs. Genre conventions are broad frameworks within which writers are free to be creative. Most writers, in fact, find that working within a framework allows them to be more creative, not less so.

> You would learn very little in this world if you were not allowed to imitate. And to repeat your imitations until some solid grounding . . . was achieved and the slight but wonderful difference — that made you and no one else — could assert itself.
> — MARY OLIVER

How *The Guide* Helps You Write Texts That Work.   To learn the conventions of a particular genre, you need to read examples of that genre so that you begin to recognize its predictable patterns as well as the possibilities for innovation. At the same time, you should also practice writing in the genre.

> Read, read, read. . . . Just like a carpenter who works as an apprentice and studies the master. Read!
> — WILLIAM FAULKNER

The St. Martin's Guide to Writing provides an array of sample essays in the genres you are learning to write and helps you analyze patterns in these essays. It also helps you practice using these patterns in your own writing to achieve your own purposes. Studying how others write in the genre you are learning is practical education, not slavish imitation. Seeing, for example, how writers define key terms and integrate quotations from their sources in an essay explaining a concept or how they anticipate objections to their proposal to solve a problem gives you an array of strategies you may use when you write in these genres.

> I practiced writing in every possible way that I could. I wrote a pastiche of other people. Just as a pianist runs his scales for ten years before he gives his concert: because when he gives that concert, he can't be thinking of his fingering or of his hands, he has to be thinking of his interpretation. He's thinking of what he's trying to communicate.
> — KATHERINE ANNE PORTER

How *The Guide* Helps You Design Texts That Work.   Writers have long recognized that no matter how well organized, well reasoned, or compelling a piece of writing may be, the way it looks on the page influences to some extent how well it works for readers. Today, writers have many more options for designing their documents than ever before. Recent advances in computer technology, digital photography and scanning, and integrated word processing and graphics programs make it relatively easy for writers to heighten the visual impact of the page. For example, they can change type fonts and add colors, charts, diagrams, and photographs to written documents. To construct multimedia Web pages or DVDs, writers can add sound, moving images, and hyperlinks.

These multiple possibilities, however, do not guarantee a more effective document. Writers need to learn to design effective texts by studying texts in their everyday lives that capture readers' attention and enhance understanding. As someone who has grown up watching television shows and videos, playing computer games, and looking at the photos, advertisements, cartoons, tables, and graphs in magazines, newspapers, and other sources, you are already a sophisticated visual consumer who has unconsciously learned many of the conventions of document design for different genres and writing situations. This book will help you become aware of what you already know and help you make new discoveries about document design that you may be able to use in your own writing.

> Design is a funny word. Some people think design means how it looks. But of course, if you dig deeper, it's really how it works. — STEVE JOBS

EXERCISE 1.2

Make two lists — one of the genres you have *read* recently, such as explanations of how to do something, stories, news reports, opinion pieces, and movie reviews, and the other of the genres you have *written* recently, both for courses and for other purposes. Then write a few sentences speculating about how your reading influences your writing and the design of your texts.

Writing

This section shows how your writing can become more thoughtful and productive. It also suggests how *The St. Martin's Guide to Writing* helps you develop a richer and more flexible repertoire of writing strategies to meet the demands of different writing situations.

How Writing Helps You Think.   Writing does not get done without commitment and effort. We all know what it is like to stare at a blank computer screen or stark white page of paper waiting for inspiration. "Invention," as the great inventor Thomas Alva Edison famously said, "is one percent inspiration and ninety-nine percent perspiration." This quotation (which incidentally has also been attributed to Albert Einstein, Pablo Picasso, and even Yogi Berra) simply states what is common knowledge to anyone who has tried to write: Writing is work.

Inspiration usually comes during work, rather than before it.

— MADELEINE L'ENGLE

Sitting around waiting for inspiration is for amateurs.   — TOM ROBBINS

Writing is work, but the work of writing can also be a joy as the writing leads to new and surprising discoveries. The challenge most writers face is how to make writing inventive yet also efficient. In other words, how can you take advantage of the naturally creative but messy and unpredictable act of writing and still get your paper done by the due date?

Waiting for inspiration is not a very promising composing strategy, as all writers who are members of Procrastinators Anonymous can testify. Like people who write for a living, students need to develop a repertoire of reliable strategies they can use in different writing situations, strategies they can use not only to get writing done but also to make writing a way of learning. *The St. Martin's Guide to Writing* offers many strategies to help you learn to write productively in a range of genres about different topics. The composing strategies and suggestions that follow come from research examining the experience of writers as well as from writers' reflections. Try many of the strategies in this book to discover which ones work especially well for you. Of particular importance are the invention activities in each Part 1 chapter's Guide to Writing.

Invention or discovery is not a part of writing you can skip. It is the basic, ongoing preoccupation of all writing that goes on before, during, and after composing a draft. Invention is what makes writing new. As writers, you cannot choose *whether* to invent; you can only decide *how*.

Few writers begin writing with a complete understanding of a subject. Most use writing as a way to learn about the subject — trying out ideas and information they have collected, exploring connections and implications, reviewing what they have written in order to expand and develop their ideas — letting the writing lead them to greater understanding.

When I start a project, the first thing I do is write down, in longhand, everything I know about the subject, every thought I've ever had on it. This may be twelve or fourteen pages. Then I read it through, for quite a few days . . . then I try to find out what are the salient points that I must make. And then it begins to take shape.

— MAYA ANGELOU

Using writing for discovery in this way means that you do not think and then write, but that the writing helps you think. Most writers come to rely on the very act of writing to help them learn the questions to ask, work out problems, and forge new connections. Writers often reflect on this so-called generative aspect of writing, echoing E. M. Forster's much repeated adage: "How do I know what I think until I see what I say?" Here are some other versions of the same insight:

Every book that I have written has been an education, a process of discovery.

— AMITAV GHOSH

> I don't see writing as a communication of something already discovered, as "truths" already known. Rather, I see writing as a job of experiment. It's like any discovery job; you don't know what's going to happen until you try it.
> — WILLIAM STAFFORD

Writers obviously do not give birth to a text as a whole, but must work cumulatively, focusing first on one aspect, then on another. Writing therefore may seem to progress in a linear, step-by-step fashion. But in fact it almost always proceeds *recursively*, which means that writers return periodically to earlier stages of their work to reconsider and build upon what they are discovering. In this way, the experience of writing is less like marching in a straight line from first sentence to last and more like climbing a steep trail with frequent switchbacks. It may appear that you are retracing old ground, but you are really rising to new levels.

> It's a matter of piling a little piece here and a little piece there, fitting them together, going on to the next part, then going back and gradually shaping the whole piece into something.
> — DAVE BARRY

Discovery does not stop when you finish a draft. Most writers plan and revise their plans, draft and revise their drafts, write and read what they have written, and then write some more. The continual shifting of attention — from discovering new ideas to choosing words, from setting goals to planning, from rereading to reorganizing, from anticipating questions to adding details — characterizes writing as a dynamic, recursive process.

How to Make Your Writing Inventive, Yet Efficient. Writers, then, need strategies that make writing more systematic but do not stifle inventiveness. Using writing to explore ideas and collect information can make drafting relatively easy. The main task becomes one of weaving the parts and pieces together seamlessly rather than figuring out how to get started and what to say. Most writers begin drafting with some type of plan — a list, a scratch outline, or a detailed storyboard like that used by filmmakers. Outlines can be very helpful, but they should not be written in stone; they must be tentative and flexible if writers are to benefit from writing's natural recursiveness.

> I began [*Invisible Man*] with a chart of the three-part division. It was a conceptual frame with most of the ideas and some of the incidents indicated.
> — RALPH ELLISON

> You are always going back and forth between the outline and the writing, bringing them closer together, or just throwing out the outline and making a new one.
> — ANNIE DILLARD

While composing a draft, writers can benefit from frequent pauses to reread what they have written. Rereading often leads to further discovery — adding an example, choosing different words that unpack or separate ideas, filling in a gap in the logic of an argument. In addition, rereading frequently leads to substantial rethinking and revising: cutting, reorganizing, rewriting whole sections to make the writing more effective. Consequently, drafting always involves both invention and revision.

> You have to work problems out for yourself on paper. Put the stuff down and read it — to see if it works.
> — Joyce Cary

> As a writer, I would find out most clearly what I thought, and what I only thought I thought, when I saw it written down.
> — Anna Quindlen

As you write your first draft, keep in mind the following practical suggestions:

Make Revision Easy. If possible, compose your draft on a computer so that you can easily move, add, and cut sections. Be sure to save your work and also back it up on a flash drive or other removable digital media in case of hard disk crash. Save anything you cut in a separate file so that you can go back to it if needed. If you choose to or have to draft on paper, leave plenty of space in the margins for notes and revisions.

Do the Easy Parts First. Divide your task into manageable portions and start with the parts you understand best or feel most confident about. Then just aim to complete one small part of the essay — a section or paragraph — at a time. Try not to agonize over problem areas, such as the first paragraph or places where you know the wording isn't quite right, because you can revisit them later.

Lower Your Expectations — for the Time Being. Be satisfied with less than perfect writing in a first draft, and do not be overly critical of what you are getting down on paper. For now, try things out. Follow digressions. Let your ideas flow. Later you can go back and cut parts that do not fit or find ways to suture them together, do more research to develop or clarify a section, and finally check your spelling and grammar.

With a more or less complete draft, writers shift their focus to discovering ways to improve it. Rereading your own writing in order to improve it can be difficult, though, because it is hard to see what the draft actually says, as opposed to what you were trying to say. For this reason, most writers also give their drafts to others to read. Students generally seek advice from their teachers and other students in the class because they understand the assignment. Published writers also share their work in progress with others. Poets, novelists, historians, scientists, newspaper reporters, magazine essayists, and even textbook writers actively seek constructive critical comments by joining writers' workshops or getting help from editors.

> I was lucky because I was always going to groups where the writers were at the same level or a little better than me. That really helped.
> — Manil Suri

> [Ezra Pound] was a marvelous critic because he didn't try to turn you into an imitation of himself. He tried to see what you were trying to do.
>
> — T. S. Eliot

Writers have a responsibility to listen to advice from others, but they rarely act on all of it. "Then why go to all the trouble?" you might ask. There are at least two good reasons. First, when you read someone else's draft, you learn more about writing — about the decisions writers make, about how a thoughtful reader reads, about the constraints of particular kinds of writing. Second, as a critical reader you embody for the writer the abstraction called "audience." By sharing your reactions with the writer, you complete the circuit of communication.

Writers who take advantage of the recursiveness of writing often say writing is revising. As they write, they also reread what they have just written and use rewriting to clarify, extend, and connect their ideas by rephrasing, moving, deleting, and adding material.

> Don't tear up the page and start over again when you write a bad line — try to write your way out of it. Make mistakes and plunge on. . . . Writing is a means of discovery, always.
>
> — Garrison Keillor

As writers write, reread, and revise their drafts recursively, they also tend to do minor editing — correcting spelling and fixing garbled sentences. But all writers — from people who only write a little bit on the job to people who write professionally — know that they eventually need to proofread carefully and edit to ensure correct spelling and grammar. Errors can be distracting and lessen writers' credibility with readers. Students have a special need to edit carefully because their readers are teachers grading their writing.

Fortunately, word processing programs make checking spelling easy. Checking for grammar and word choice takes more time and is harder, but here is some advice that can make your proofreading and editing more effective.

Keep a List of Your Common Errors. From teachers' comments on your writing over the years, you probably already know whether you tend to write sentence fragments, occasionally use commas incorrectly to splice together complete sentences, have trouble with verb tenses, are inclined to wordiness, or typically make another kind of error. It is a good idea to keep a list of your typical problems and to check for them as you edit your work.

Get Help with Common Errors. If you persistently make the same errors, study the Handbook to make sure you understand the rules, consult a tutor in the Writing Center at your school, or go online to do practice exercises with a service like Exercise Central.

Begin Proofreading with the Last Word. To focus your attention on spelling and typing errors, it may help to read backward word for word, beginning with the last word of your essay. When you read backward, it is harder to pay attention to content and thus easier to recognize typos.

How *The Guide* Helps You Learn To Write.   As you have seen, students learning to write need to be flexible and yet systematic. The Guides to Writing in Part One of this book are designed to meet precisely this need. The first few times you write in a new genre, you can rely on these guides. They provide scaffolding to support your work until you become more familiar with the demands and possibilities of each genre. The Guides will help you develop a repertoire of strategies for creatively solving problems in your writing, such as deciding how to interest readers, how to refute opposing arguments, what to quote from a source, and how to integrate quotations into your writing.

When engaging in any new and complex activity — driving, playing an instrument, skiing, or writing — people have to learn how to break down the activity into a series of manageable tasks. In learning to play tennis, for example, you can isolate lobbing from volleying or work on your backhand or serve. Similarly, in writing an argument on a controversial issue, you can separate tasks such as defining the issue, developing your reasons, and anticipating readers' objections. What is important is focusing on one aspect at a time. Dividing your writing in this way enables you to take advantage of writing's natural recursiveness and tackle a complex subject without oversimplifying it.

Here is a writer's quotation that has been especially helpful for us as we have written and revised *The St. Martin's Guide to Writing* over eight editions:

> You know when you think about writing a book, you think it is overwhelming. But, actually, you break it down into tiny little tasks any moron could do.
> — ANNIE DILLARD

EXERCISE 1.3

Write a page or two describing how you went about writing the last time you wrote an essay (or something else) that took time and effort. Use the following questions to help you recall what you did, but feel free to write about any other aspects of your writing that you remember.

- What initially led you to write? Who were you writing for, and what was the purpose of your writing?

- What kinds of thinking and planning did you do, if any, before you began writing the first draft?

- If you discussed your ideas and plans with someone, how did discussing them help you? If you had someone read your draft, how did getting a response help?

- If you rewrote, moved, added, or cut anything in your first draft, describe what you changed.

Creating the Best Conditions for Reading and Writing

As you probably already know, people sometimes read and write under the most surprising or arduous conditions. As you probably also know, however, both reading and writing are most productive if you can find a time and place ideally suited for sustained and thoughtful work. Many professional writers have a place where they can concentrate for a few hours without repeated interruptions. Try to find such a place for yourself.

Consider, too, the sound — or the silence — that surrounds you in this place. In a wired world with all its distractions and stimulations and pleasures, most people experience little silence and therefore grow less accustomed to it, maybe even uncomfortable with it. Disconnecting is certainly hard to do, but eliminating or at least greatly reducing distraction for sustained periods of time — even an hour here, an hour there — is likely to help you concentrate on intellectually demanding college reading and writing. If at all possible, turn off your cell phone. If you are used to listening to music while reading or writing, you might experiment with turning it off, too, just to see if your attention is better focused with or without it. Or if you find complete silence stressful — or a certain amount of background noise impossible to escape — music might help. Whatever the conditions that prove best for you, make a real effort to create them.

As a college student you desire lasting knowledge, knowledge you can savor and put to use throughout your entire lifetime. You want the opportunity not only to accumulate large amounts of knowledge but also to gain insights into how it is interrelated. You also hope to prepare yourself for different kinds of writing situations and to develop confidence as a writer. These are grand, demanding ambitions, and the time you spend reading and writing is your time to fulfill them. Find the quiet places where you can do so.

Thinking Critically

This section explains how thinking critically about your learning can help you write more effectively and how *The St. Martin's Guide* helps you think critically about your reading, your writing, and the genres you are using.

How to Think Critically about Your Learning.   Thinking critically means becoming aware or conscious of your own thinking and learning processes.

When writing, you will find that many of your decisions do not require conscious effort. You can rely on familiar strategies that usually produce effective writing for you in the genre. But there will nearly always be occasions as you write when you become aware of problems that require your full attention. Some problems may be fairly easy to remedy, such as an inappropriate word choice or a confusing sequence of events. Other problems may require considerable rethinking and rewriting — for example, if you discover that your readers' likely objections seriously undermine your argument.

> That's what a writer is: someone who sees problems a little more clearly than others.
> — Eugene Ionesco

After you have completed a final draft, reflecting on how you identified and tried to solve such problems can be a powerful aid to learning. Understanding a problem may enable you to anticipate and avoid similar problems in the future. It may also give you a firmer grip on the standards you need to apply when rereading your drafts. Most important, reflecting on a problem you solved should enhance your confidence as a writer, helping you realize that problems are not signs of bad writing but that problem-solving signifies good writing.

To think critically about your learning, it also helps to reflect on what you have learned from reading texts in the genre you are writing. Much of human language and genre-learning comes from modeling. As young children, for example, we learn from hearing our parents, teachers, and peers tell stories and from watching stories portrayed on television and in film. We learn ways of beginning and ending, strategies for building suspense, techniques for making time sequences clear, how to use dialogue to develop character, and so on. As adults, we can reinforce and increase our repertoire of storytelling patterns by analyzing how stories that we admire work and by consciously trying out in our own writing the strategies we have seen work in those stories.

> I went back to the good nature books that I had read. And I analyzed them. I wrote outlines of whole books — outlines of chapters — so that I could see their structure. And I copied down their transitional sentences or their main sentences or their closing sentences or their lead sentences.
>
> — ANNIE DILLARD

Finally, thinking critically about what you have learned about writing different genres can help you understand what could be called the social dimensions of genres and the power that they exert as models: how they promote certain kinds of thinking and action while discouraging others. Concept explanations, for example, enable the efficient exchange of established knowledge, but they also discourage questioning about how certain kinds of knowledge, and not other kinds, get established as authoritative and by whom. Similarly, proposals are essential responses to problems in public life, but they raise questions about who has the power to define something as a problem.

> The obligation of a writer . . . is to state, to elucidate, how we are all part of something larger, something grander.
>
> — TOM SANCHEZ

How *The Guide* Helps You Think Critically.   Thinking critically about your reading and writing experiences is not difficult. It simply requires that you shift focus from *what* you are reading and writing to *how* you are reading and writing.

The St. Martin's Guide to Writing helps you talk and write about the hows of reading and writing different genres by providing a shared vocabulary of words and phrases that you can easily learn and add to others which you already know. Words like *significance, narrating,* and *thesis,* for example, will help you identify the features and strategies of essays you are reading in different genres. Words and phrases like *invention, setting goals,* and *revising* will help you describe what you are doing as you write your own essays in these genres. Phrases like *established knowledge* and *essential self* will help you examine and question the social dimensions of the genres you are reading and writing.

Each writing assignment chapter in Part One of *The Guide* includes many opportunities for you to think critically about your understanding of the genre you are writing and to reflect on your learning. A section entitled Thinking Critically about What You Have Learned concludes each chapter, giving you an opportunity to look back and reflect on these three aspects of your learning:

- how writing worked for you as creative problem-solving
- how your reading of other essays in the genre helped you write your own essay
- how you understand the social dimensions of writing in the genre.

EXERCISE 1.4

Read the following quotes to see how writers use similes ("Writing is like") and metaphors ("Writing is") to describe the processes and products of writing.

Writing is like exploring . . . as an explorer makes maps of the country he has explored, so a writer's works are maps of the country he has explored.
— Lawrence Osgood

The writer must soak up the subject completely, as a plant soaks up water, until the ideas are ready to sprout.
— Marguerite Yourcenar

Writing is manual labor of the mind: a job, like laying pipe.
— John Gregory Dunne

If we had to say what writing is, we would define it essentially as an act of courage.
— Cynthia Ozick

Write two or three similes or metaphors of your own that express aspects of your experience as a writer. Then write a page or so explaining and expanding on the ideas and feelings expressed in your similes and metaphors.

Part One

Writing
Activities

2

Remembering an Event

IN COLLEGE COURSES   For a linguistics course, a student is required to select a subject, report research on that subject, and connect findings or conclusions by the researchers to a specific instance of language use in her own experience. Drawn to the differences between men's and women's conversational styles, the student goes to the library to search for information. After several hours of skimming and reading reports on men's and women's conversational styles, she lists a dozen promising reports, including one by a very readable researcher, Deborah Tannen. The student decides to focus on the finding that in problem-solving discussions women expect to spend a lot of time talking about the problem itself, especially their feelings about it. Men, in contrast, typically want to cut short the analysis of the problem and the talk about feelings; they would rather discuss solutions.

Applying Tannen's findings to her own experience, the student recalls a recent conversation with her brother, who is one year older, about a family problem: their father's drinking, which seems to be increasing. When she talks, she turns to look at him. When he talks, he mostly looks straight ahead. Her inflection is even, his sometimes urgent. She reconstructs as much of the conversation as she can remember, setting it up as dialogue with "he said/she said" signals and with quotation marks around the sentences and phrases that make up the conversation itself. In her paper, she strives to sequence the conversation much as it occurred. Next she explains which parts constitute feelings talk and which indicate problem-solving talk. She concludes that her conversation with her brother well illustrates Tannen's findings.

IN THE COMMUNITY   As part of a local history project in a small western ranching community, a college student volunteers to help an elderly rancher write about some of his early experiences. They meet and talk about life on the ranch. One experience seems especially dramatic and significant — a time in the winter of 1938 when a six-foot snowstorm isolated the rancher's family for nearly a month. The student tape-records the rancher talking about how he and his wife made preparations to survive and ensure the health of their infant sons and how he snowshoed eight miles to a logging train track, stopped the train, and gave the engineer a message to deliver to relatives in the nearest town 18 miles away explaining that they were going to be okay. On a second visit, the student and the rancher listen to the tape recording and afterward talk about further details that might make the event more complete and dramatic for readers. They focus on the rancher's efforts to bring large amounts of firewood into the house. Then they focus on the rancher's wait in the intense cold on a still, bright morning by the railroad tracks, not knowing whether the train would even come by.

The rancher then writes drafts of these two remembered events, and the student later helps him revise and edit them. The essay and some of the rancher's photographs are published in a special supplement to the newspaper. (For more information on how the student and rancher chose visuals and selected quotations from the story to accompany the visuals, turn to Thinking About Document Design, p. 67).

IN THE WORKPLACE   The highway department offices of a large midwestern state have recently been the site of violence and threats of violence. One worker has killed another, and several managers have been threatened. To keynote a statewide meeting of highway department regional managers seeking solutions to this problem, a respected manager writes a speech to address the problem.

He begins his talk in a very personal way, by describing an incident when he was confronted in his office by an unhappy employee. Coming into the manager's office without knocking, the employee refused to sit down when invited to do so. He complained loudly about an overtime assignment, to work through the weekend to prepare for a predicted large snowstorm, and he threatened to harm the manager and his family if the manager did not give him the weekend off. When asked to leave, he initially refused and remained, cursing, for several minutes. The manager reflects on his fear and on his frustration about not knowing what to do when the employee finally left, since the department's published procedures seemed not to apply to this case. He acknowledges his reluctance to report the incident to the state office because he did not want to appear to be ineffective and indecisive.

Then he connects each element of this frightening confrontation — its unpredictability, the employee's cursing, threats, and refusal to leave the office, and his own reluctance to report it — to sound advice he later got from the resources he recommends in the handout. He wins loud, extended applause for his talk.

When you write about remembered events in your life, you rely on a genre of writing known as autobiography. It is a popular genre because reading as well as writing it leads people to reflect deeply on their own lives. Reflecting on the meaning of your experience, you examine the forces within yourself and within society that have shaped you into the person you have become.

When you write about a remembered event, your purpose is to present yourself to readers by telling a story that discloses something significant about you. Autobiographical writers do not just pour out their memories and feelings, however. Instead, they shape those memories into a compelling story that conveys the meaning and importance of an experience.

A Collaborative Activity:
Practice Remembering an Event

The preceding scenarios suggest some occasions for writing about events in one's life. Think of an event in your life that you would feel comfortable describing to others in your class. The only requirements are that you remember the event well enough to tell the story and that the story lets your classmates learn something about you. Your instructor may schedule this collaborative activity as a face-to-face in-class discussion or ask you to conduct an online real-time discussion in a chatroom. Whatever the medium, here are some guidelines to follow:

Part 1. Consider several events, and choose one you feel comfortable telling in this situation. Then, for two or three minutes, make notes about how you will tell your story.

Now, get together with two or three other students, and take turns telling your stories. Be brief: Each story should take only a few minutes.

Part 2. Take ten minutes to discuss what happened when you told about a remembered event:

- Tell each other how you chose your particular story. What did you think about when you were choosing an event? How did your purpose and audience — what you wanted your classmates to know and think about you — influence your choice?
- Review what each of you decided to include in your story. Did you plunge right into telling what happened, or did you first provide some background information? Did you describe any of the people, including yourself, or mention any specific dialogue? Did you tell your listeners how you felt at the time the event occurred, or did you say how you feel now looking back on it?
- What was the easiest part of telling a story about a remembered event in your life? What was the most difficult part?

JEAN BRANDT wrote this essay as a first-year college student. In it, she tells about a memorable event that occurred when she was thirteen. Reflecting on how she felt at the time, Brandt writes, "I was afraid, embarrassed, worried, mad." As you read, look for places where these tumultuous and contradictory remembered feelings are expressed.

Calling Home

Jean Brandt

1   As we all piled into the car, I knew it was going to be a fabulous day. My grandmother was visiting for the holidays; and she and I, along with my older brother and sister, Louis and Susan, were setting off for a day of last-minute Christmas shopping. On the way to the mall, we sang Christmas carols, chattered, and laughed. With Christmas only two days away, we were caught up with holiday spirit. I felt light-headed and full of joy. I loved shopping — especially at Christmas.

2   The shopping center was swarming with frantic last-minute shoppers like ourselves. We went first to the General Store, my favorite. It carried mostly knick-knacks and other useless items which nobody needs but buys anyway. I was thirteen years old at the time, and things like buttons and calendars and posters would catch my fancy. This day was no different. The object of my desire was a 75-cent Snoopy button. Snoopy was the latest. If you owned anything with the Peanuts on it, you were "in." But since I was supposed to be shopping for gifts for other people and not myself, I couldn't decide what to do. I went in search of my sister for her opinion. I pushed my way through throngs of people to the back of the store where I found Susan. I asked her if she thought I should buy the button. She said it was cute and if I wanted it to go ahead and buy it.

3   When I got back to the Snoopy section, I took one look at the lines at the cashiers and knew I didn't want to wait thirty minutes to buy an item worth less than one dollar. I walked back to the basket where I found the button and was about to drop it when suddenly, instead, I took a quick glance around, assured myself no one could see, and slipped the button into the pocket of my sweatshirt. I hesitated for a moment, but once the item was in my pocket, there was no turning back. I had never before stolen anything; but what was done was done. A few seconds later, my sister appeared and asked, "So, did you decide to buy the button?"

4   "No, I guess not." I hoped my voice didn't quaver. As we headed for the entrance, my heart began to race. I just had to get out of that store. Only a few more yards to go and I'd be safe. As we crossed the threshold, I heaved a sigh of relief. I was home free. I thought about how sly I had been and I felt proud of my accomplishment.

5   An unexpected tap on my shoulder startled me. I whirled around to find a middle-aged man, dressed in street clothes, flashing some type of badge and

The action in this remembered event begins with the first sentence. Verbs move the action along.

Actors other than the narrator are introduced and two of them are named.

A remembered conversation is summarized.

Specific narrative action slows the narrative and focuses readers on a fateful moment.

A remembered conversation is reconstructed as dialogue.

Remembered feelings help to create suspense.

This startling, dramatic moment is simply narrated

without any dialogue, perhaps leaving readers feeling disappointed. The restraint at this point in the narrative, however, heightens the effect of the even more dramatic interactions later in the essay.

Beginning here, the story of the narrator's arrest is narrated mostly through remembered conversations.

More remembered feelings heighten the suspense.

Through a simile, the narrator compares her situation to that of the main character in Nathaniel Hawthorne's novel *The Scarlet Letter*.

Remembered feelings of detachment and even pleasure provide a surprise for readers.

The climax and resolution of the narrative begins here, revealed through a combination of reconstructed conversation and expression of remembered feelings.

politely asking me to empty my pockets. Where did this man come from? How did he know? I was so sure that no one had seen me! On the verge of panicking, I told myself that all I had to do was give this man his button back, say I was sorry, and go on my way. After all, it was only a 75-cent item.

Next thing I knew, he was talking about calling the police and having me arrested and thrown in jail, as if he had just nabbed a professional thief instead of a terrified kid. I couldn't believe what he was saying. 6

"Jean, what's going on?" 7

The sound of my sister's voice eased the pressure a bit. She always managed to get me out of trouble. She would come through this time too. 8

"Excuse me. Are you a relative of this young girl?" 9

"Yes, I'm her sister. What's the problem?" 10

"Well, I just caught her shoplifting and I'm afraid I'll have to call the police." 11

"What did she take?" 12

"This button." 13

"A button? You are having a thirteen-year-old arrested for stealing a button?" 14

"I'm sorry, but she broke the law." 15

The man led us through the store and into an office, where we waited for the police officers to arrive. Susan had found my grandmother and brother, who, still shocked, didn't say a word. The thought of going to jail terrified me, not because of jail itself, but because of the encounter with my parents afterward. Not more than ten minutes later, two officers arrived and placed me under arrest. They said that I was to be taken to the station alone. Then, they handcuffed me and led me out of the store. I felt alone and scared. I had counted on my sister being with me, but now I had to muster up the courage to face this ordeal all by myself. 16

As the officers led me through the mall, I sensed a hundred pairs of eyes staring at me. My face flushed and I broke out in a sweat. Now everyone knew I was a criminal. In their eyes I was a juvenile delinquent, and thank God the cops were getting me off the streets. The worst part was thinking my grandmother might be having the same thoughts. The humiliation at that moment was overwhelming. I felt like Hester Prynne being put on public display for everyone to ridicule. 17

That short walk through the mall seemed to take hours. But once we reached the squad car, time raced by. I was read my rights and questioned. We were at the police station within minutes. Everything happened so fast I didn't have a chance to feel remorse for my crime. Instead, I viewed what was happening to me as if it were a movie. Being searched, although embarrassing, somehow seemed to be exciting. All the movies and television programs I had seen were actually coming to life. This is what it was really like. But why were criminals always portrayed as frightened and regretful? I was having fun. I thought I had nothing to fear — until I was allowed my one phone call. I was trembling as I dialed home. I didn't know what I was going to say to my parents, especially my mother. 18

"Hi, Dad, this is Jean." 19

"We've been waiting for you to call." 20

"Did Susie tell you what happened?" 21

"Yeah, but we haven't told your mother. I think you should tell her what you did and where you are." 22

"You mean she doesn't even know where I am?" 23

"No, I want you to explain it to her." 24

There was a pause as he called my mother to the phone. For the first time that 25
night, I was close to tears. I wished I had never stolen that stupid pin. I wanted to
give the phone to one of the officers because I was too ashamed to tell my mother
the truth, but I had no choice.

"Jean, where are you?" 26

"I'm, umm, in jail." 27

"Why? What for?" 28

"Shoplifting." 29

"Oh no, Jean. Why? Why did you do it?" 30

"I don't know. No reason. I just did it." 31

"I don't understand. What did you take? Why did you do it? You had plenty of 32
money with you."

"I know but I just did it. I can't explain why. Mom, I'm sorry." 33

"I'm afraid sorry isn't enough. I'm horribly disappointed in you." 34

Long after we got off the phone, while I sat in an empty jail cell, waiting for my 35
parents to pick me up, I could still distinctly hear the disappointment and hurt in
my mother's voice. I cried. The tears weren't for me but for her and the pain I had
put her through. I felt like a terrible human being. I would rather have stayed in jail
than confront my mom right then. I dreaded each passing minute that brought our
encounter closer. When the officer came to release me, I hesitated, actually not
wanting to leave. We went to the front desk, where I had to sign a form to retrieve
my belongings. I saw my parents a few yards away and my heart raced. A large
knot formed in my stomach. I fought back the tears.

Not a word was spoken as we walked to the car. Slowly, I sank into the back 36
seat anticipating the scolding. Expecting harsh tones, I was relieved to hear almost
the opposite from my father.

"I'm not going to punish you and I'll tell you why. Although I think what you did 37
was wrong, I think what the police did was more wrong. There's no excuse for lock-
ing a thirteen-year-old behind bars. That doesn't mean I condone what you did, but
I think you've been punished enough already."

As I looked from my father's eyes to my mother's, I knew this ordeal was over. 38
Although it would never be forgotten, the incident was not mentioned again.

ANNIE DILLARD won the Pulitzer Prize for nonfiction writing with her first book,
Pilgrim at Tinker Creek (1974). Since then, she has written 10 other books in a variety of
genres, including the essay collections *Teaching a Stone to Talk* (1988) and *For the Time
Being* (1999); a novel, *The Living* (1993); poetry, *Mornings Like This* (1996); literary theory, *Living by Fiction* (1988); and an account of her work as a writer, *The Writing Life*
(1990). Dillard also wrote an autobiography of her early years, *An American Childhood*
(1987), from which the following reading comes.

Dillard is a professor of English and writer in residence at Wesleyan College and a Fellow of the American Academy of Arts and Letters. In *The Writing Life*, she describes her writing as a process of discovery: "When you write, you lay out a line of words. The line of words is a miner's pick, a woodcarver's gouge, a surgeon's probe. You wield it, and it digs a path you follow. Soon you find yourself in new territory." Through this process, she explains, the writing "changes from an expression of your notions to an epistemological tool." In other words, the very act of writing helps her learn more about herself and others.

The reading that follows relates an event that occurred one winter morning when the seven-year-old Dillard and a friend were chased relentlessly by an adult stranger at whom they had been throwing snowballs. Dillard admits that she was terrified at the time, and yet she asserts that she has "seldom been happier since." As you read, think about how this paradox helps you grasp the autobiographical significance of this experience for Dillard.

An American Childhood
Annie Dillard

1 Some boys taught me to play football. This was fine sport. You thought up a new strategy for every play and whispered it to the others. You went out for a pass, fooling everyone. Best, you got to throw yourself mightily at someone's running legs. Either you brought him down or you hit the ground flat out on your chin, with your arms empty before you. It was all or nothing. If you hesitated in fear, you would miss and get hurt: you would take a hard fall while the kid got away, or you would get kicked in the face while the kid got away. But if you flung yourself wholeheartedly at the back of his knees — if you gathered and joined body and soul and pointed them diving fearlessly — then you likely wouldn't get hurt, and you'd stop the ball. Your fate, and your team's score, depended on your concentration and courage. Nothing girls did could compare with it.

2 Boys welcomed me at baseball, too, for I had, through enthusiastic practice, what was weirdly known as a boy's arm. In winter, in the snow, there was neither baseball nor football, so the boys and I threw snowballs at passing cars. I got in trouble throwing snowballs, and have seldom been happier since.

3 On one weekday morning after Christmas, six inches of new snow had just fallen. We were standing up to our boot tops in snow on a front yard on trafficked Reynolds Street, waiting for cars. The cars traveled Reynolds Street slowly and evenly; they were targets all but wrapped in red ribbons, cream puffs. We couldn't miss.

4 I was seven; the boys were eight, nine, and ten. The oldest two Fahey boys were there — Mikey and Peter — polite blond boys who lived near me on Lloyd Street, and who already had four brothers and sisters. My parents approved Mikey and Peter Fahey. Chickie McBride was there, a tough kid, and Billy Paul and Mackie Kean too, from across Reynolds, where the boys grew up dark and furious,

grew up skinny, knowing, and skilled. We had all drifted from our houses that morning looking for action, and had found it here on Reynolds Street.

It was cloudy but cold. The cars' tires laid behind them on the snowy street a complex trail of beige chunks like crenellated castle walls. I had stepped on some earlier; they squeaked. We could not have wished for more traffic. When a car came, we all popped it one. In the intervals between cars we reverted to the natural solitude of children.   5

I started making an iceball — a perfect iceball, from perfectly white snow, perfectly spherical, and squeezed perfectly translucent so no snow remained all the way through. (The Fahey boys and I considered it unfair actually to throw an iceball at somebody, but it had been known to happen.)   6

I had just embarked on the iceball project when we heard tire chains come clanking from afar. A black Buick was moving toward us down the street. We all spread out, banged together some regular snowballs, took aim, and, when the Buick drew nigh, fired.   7

A soft snowball hit the driver's windshield right before the driver's face. It made a smashed star with a hump in the middle.   8

Often, of course, we hit our target, but this time, the only time in all of life, the car pulled over and stopped. Its wide black door opened; a man got out of it, running. He didn't even close the car door.   9

He ran after us, and we ran away from him, up the snowy Reynolds sidewalk. At the corner, I looked back; incredibly, he was still after us. He was in city clothes: a suit and tie, street shoes. Any normal adult would have quit, having sprung us into flight and made his point. This man was gaining on us. He was a thin man, all action. All of a sudden, we were running for our lives.   10

Wordless, we split up. We were on our turf; we could lose ourselves in the neighborhood backyards, everyone for himself. I paused and considered. Everyone had vanished except Mikey Fahey, who was just rounding the corner of a yellow brick house. Poor Mikey, I trailed him. The driver of the Buick sensibly picked the two of us to follow. The man apparently had all day.   11

He chased Mikey and me around the yellow house and up a backyard path we knew by heart: under a low tree, up a bank, through a hedge, down some snowy steps, and across the grocery store's delivery driveway. We smashed through a gap in another hedge, entered a scruffy backyard and ran around its back porch and tight between houses to Edgerton Avenue; we ran across Edgerton to an alley and up our own sliding woodpile to the Halls' front yard; he kept coming. We ran up Lloyd Street and wound through mazy backyards toward the steep hilltop at Willard and Lang.   12

He chased us silently, block after block. He chased us silently over picket fences, through thorny hedges, between houses, around garbage cans, and across streets. Every time I glanced back, choking for breath, I expected he would have quit. He must have been as breathless as we were. His jacket strained over his body. It was an immense discovery, pounding into my hot head with every sliding, joyous step, that this ordinary adult evidently knew what I thought only children who trained at football knew: that you have to fling yourself at what you're doing, you have to point yourself, forget yourself, aim, dive.   13

Mikey and I had nowhere to go, in our own neighborhood or out of it, but away from this man who was chasing us. He impelled us forward; we compelled him to follow our route. The air was cold; every breath tore my throat. We kept running, block after block; we kept improvising, backyard after backyard, running a frantic course and choosing it simultaneously, failing always to find small places or hard places to slow him down, and discovering always, exhilarated, dismayed, that only bare speed could save us — for he would never give up, this man — and we were losing speed.

14

He chased us through the backyard labyrinths of ten blocks before he caught us by our jackets. He caught us and we all stopped.

15

We three stood staggering, half blinded, coughing, in an obscure hilltop back-yard: a man in his twenties, a boy, a girl. He had released our jackets, our pursuer, our captor, our hero: he knew we weren't going anywhere. We all played by the rules. Mikey and I unzipped our jackets. I pulled off my sopping mittens. Our tracks multiplied in the backyard's new snow. We had been breaking new snow all morn-ing. We didn't look at each other. I was cherishing my excitement. The man's lower pants legs were wet; his cuffs were full of snow, and there was a prow of snow be-neath them on his shoes and socks. Some trees bordered the little flat backyard, some messy winter trees. There was no one around: a clearing in a grove, and we the only players.

16

It was a long time before he could speak. I had some difficulty at first recall-ing why we were there. My lips felt swollen; I couldn't see out of the sides of my eyes; I kept coughing.

17

"You stupid kids," he began perfunctorily.

18

We listened perfunctorily indeed, if we listened at all, for the chewing out was redundant, a mere formality, and beside the point. The point was that he had chased us passionately without giving up, and so he had caught us. Now he came down to earth. I wanted the glory to last forever.

19

But how could the glory have lasted forever? We could have run through every backyard in North America until we got to Panama. But when he trapped us at the lip of the Panama Canal, what precisely could he have done to pro-long the drama of the chase and cap its glory? I brooded about this for the next few years. He could only have fried Mikey Fahey and me in boiling oil, say, or dismembered us piecemeal, or staked us to anthills. None of which I really wanted, and none of which any adult was likely to do, even in the spirit of fun. He could only chew us out there in the Panamanian jungle, after months or years of exalting pursuit. He could only begin, "You stupid kids," and continue in his ordinary Pittsburgh accent with his normal righteous anger and the usual common sense.

20

If in that snowy backyard the driver of the black Buick had cut off our heads, Mikey's and mine, I would have died happy, for nothing has required so much of me since as being chased all over Pittsburgh in the middle of winter — running ter-rified, exhausted — by this sainted, skinny, furious redheaded man who wished to have a word with us. I don't know how he found his way back to his car.

21

Making Connections to Personal and Social Issues: Behaving Fearlessly

"The point," Dillard tells us near the end, "was that he had chased us passionately without giving up" (paragraph 19). What seems to fascinate her is not that the man chased the kids to bawl them out, but that an adult could still do what she thought only children knew how to do: "you have to fling yourself at what you're doing, you have to point yourself, forget yourself, aim, dive" (paragraph 13). In fact, she explains at the beginning of the essay that in teaching her to play football, the neighborhood boys taught her something that she says few girls learned about: the joy of flinging yourself wholeheartedly, fearlessly, into play or, indeed, into anything you do in life.

With other students in your class, discuss what you have learned about being fearless from team sports or any goal-directed activity in small groups. Begin by telling one another about a particular team or group you belonged to for at least a few months where you had to coordinate your activities to achieve a common goal, activities that posed some risk or challenge or required special effort. It could have been a baseball, badminton, soccer, or swimming team. Or maybe it was a theater or dance group, a debating team, a newspaper staff with deadlines, a science project or writing contest, a group effort to provide help following a natural disaster or to alleviate the effects of poverty.

Then, together, discuss what you learned about being challenged, taking risks, or exerting yourself in unexpected ways in this group. Into what other activities, if any, were you able to carry forward this "[flinging] yourself wholeheartedly" and "fearlessly"? If it has not happened again, what special conditions in the activity made it possible that one time? How might the expectations of your family, friends, and community have encouraged or thwarted your accepting challenge, behaving fearlessly?

Analyzing Writing Strategies

1. Early in the essay, once we are oriented to the scene and actors, the black Buick appears. The essay ends with a reference to the Buick. **Framing**, a narrative device, echoes something from the beginning in the ending. The writer assumes that you will think of the beginning as you are reading the ending. Speculate about why writers of remembered event essays might want to use framing. (It is sometimes used in other types of essays.) What effect does it have on you as a reader? At the end of the story, what further ideas does the frame suggest to you about the man, what he might represent, and the significance to Dillard of her confrontation with him? Consider that in the late 2000s, when you are reading the essay, a black Mercedes sedan would be the equivalent of the black Buick sedan of the 1950s. Why at this point is Dillard not afraid of the man or angry at him? Should she be, do you think?

2. **Visual description** — naming objects and detailing their colors, shapes, sizes, textures, and other qualities — is an important writing strategy in remembered-event essays. To see how writers use **naming** and **detailing** to create vivid word

For more on the describing strategies of naming and detailing, see Chapter 15.

pictures or images, let us look closely at Dillard's description of an iceball: "I started making an iceball — a perfect iceball, from perfectly white snow, perfectly spherical, and squeezed perfectly translucent so no snow remained all the way through" (paragraph 6). Notice that she names two things: *iceball* and *snow*. She adds to these names descriptive details — *white* (color), *spherical* (shape), and *translucent* (appearance) — that help readers imagine more precisely what an iceball looks like. She also repeats the words *perfect* and *perfectly* to emphasize the color, shape, and appearance of this particular iceball.

To analyze Dillard's use of naming and detailing to present scenes and people, reread paragraphs 10–13, where she describes the man and the neighborhood through which he chases her and Mikey. As you read these paragraphs, underline the names of objects and people (nearly always nouns), and put brackets around all of the words and phrases that modify the nouns they name. Here are two examples from paragraph 10 to get you started: "[snowy] Reynolds sidewalk" and "[city] clothes."

Notice first how frequently naming and detailing occur in these paragraphs. Notice also how many different kinds of objects and people are named. Then consider these questions: Does naming sometimes occur without any accompanying detailing? How do you think the naming helps you as a reader visualize the scene and people? What do you think the detailing contributes?

Commentary: Organizing a Well-Told Story

An American Childhood is a **well-told story**. It provides a dramatic structure that arouses readers' curiosity, builds suspense, and concludes the action in a rather surprising way.

Writers of remembered-event essays usually begin at the beginning or even before the beginning. That is how Annie Dillard organizes *An American Childhood* — opening with two introductory paragraphs that give readers a context for the event and prepare them to appreciate its significance. Readers can see at a glance, by the space that separates the second paragraph from the rest of the essay, that the first two paragraphs are meant to stand apart as an introduction. They also are general, broad statements that do not refer to any particular incident.

In contrast, paragraph 3 begins by grounding readers in specifics. It is not any "weekday morning" but "one" in particular, one morning "after Christmas" and after a substantial snowfall. Dillard goes on to locate herself in a particular place "on a front yard on trafficked Reynolds Street," engaged in a particular set of actions with a particular group of individuals. She has not yet begun to tell what happened but is giving us the cast of characters (the "polite blond" Fahey boys, "tough" Chickie McBride) and setting the scene ("cloudy but cold"). The narrative, up to this point, has been moving slowly, like the cars making their way down Reynolds Street. But in paragraph 9, when the driver of the Buick "got out of it, running," Dillard's narrative itself suddenly springs into action, moving at breakneck speed for the next six paragraphs until the man catches up with the kids in paragraph 15.

We can see this simple narrative organization in the following paragraph-by-paragraph scratch outline:

1. explains what she learned from playing football
2. identifies other sports she learned from boys in the neighborhood
3. sets the scene by describing the time and place of the event
4. describes the boys who were playing with her
5. describes what typically happened: a car would come down the street, they would throw snowballs, and then they would wait for another car
6. describes the iceball-making project she had begun while waiting
7. describes the Buick's approach and how they followed the routine
8. describes the impact of the snowball on the Buick's windshield
9. describes the man's surprising reaction: getting out of the car and running after them
10. narrates the chase and describes the man
11. explains how the kids split up and the man followed her and Mikey
12. narrates the chase and describes how the neighborhood looked as they ran through it
13. continues the narration, describing the way the man threw himself into the chase
14. continues the narration, commenting on her thoughts and feelings
15. narrates the ending or climax of the chase, when the man caught the kids
16. describes the runners trying to catch their breath
17. describes her own physical state
18. relates the man's words
19. explains her reactions to his words and actions
20. explains her later thoughts and feelings
21. explains her present perspective on this remembered event

From this simple scratch outline, we can see that Dillard's essay focuses on the chase. This focus on a single incident that occurred in a relatively short span of time is the hallmark of the remembered-event essay. A chase is by nature dramatic because it is suspenseful: Readers want to know whether the man will catch the kids and, if he does, what will happen.

For more on scratch outlining, see Chapter 12.

Dillard heightens the drama in a couple of ways. One strategy she uses is identification: She lets us into her point of view, helping us to see what she saw and feel what she felt. In addition, she uses surprise. In fact, Dillard surprises us from beginning to end. The first surprise is that the man gets out of the car. But the fact that he chases the kids and that he continues to chase them beyond the point that any reasonable person would do so ratchets up the suspense. We simply cannot know what such a man is capable of doing. Finally, the story reaches its climax when the man catches Mikey and Dillard. Even then, Dillard surprises readers by what the man says and doesn't say or do. He does not shove them or hit them. Instead, he gives them only a "chewing out," a harsh lecture about their reckless, dangerous behavior. Moreover, Dillard tells us, he says it "perfunctorily," as if it is something he is supposed to say as an adult "in his ordinary Pittsburgh accent with his normal righteous anger and the usual common sense" (paragraph 20). Dillard's language here is ironic because it is obvious that she feels that the man's behavior was anything but *ordinary, normal,* or *usual*—which is, of course, precisely what Dillard wants us to appreciate.

Considering Topics for Your Own Essay

Like Dillard, you could write about a time when an adult did something entirely unexpected during your childhood, perhaps by the time you were eleven or twelve years old, before you had come to understand adults' motives. It could have been an action that seemed dangerous or threatening to you, or it could have been something humorous, kind, or generous. You still remember it and have thought about it several times over the years. There is a story about it you could tell. List two or three of these occasions when some adult behaved unpredictably and unforgettably. Consider unpredictable actions of adults in your immediate or extended family, adults you had come to know outside your family, and strangers.

TOBIAS WOLFF is probably best known for his short-story collections *Back in the World* (1985), *In the Garden of the North American Martyrs* (1981), and *The Night in Question* (1996) and for his novel *The Barracks Thief* (1984), which won the PEN/Faulkner Award in 1985. Wolff has also written two autobiographies. The first, *A Boy's Life* (1989), won the *Los Angeles Times* Book Award for biography and was made into a movie (1993) in which Wolff was played by Leonardo DiCaprio. The second autobiography, *In Pharaoh's Army: Memories of the Lost War* (1994), about his experience serving as a Green Beret in the Vietnam War, was a finalist for a National Book Award and a *Los Angeles Times* Award for biography. In addition to his fiction and autobiography, Wolff has also edited several short-story collections, including *The Best American Short Stories.* Wolff has taught creative writing at Syracuse University and is currently a professor at Stanford University, where he also has directed the creative writing program.

In this selection from *A Boy's Life,* Wolff tells the story of an experience he had when he was ten years old. He and his mother had just moved west from Florida to Salt Lake City, followed by Roy, his divorced mother's boyfriend. "Roy was handsome," Wolff writes, "in the conventional way that appeals to boys. He had a tattoo. He'd been to war and kept a silence about it that was full of heroic implication." As you read, notice how the young Wolff is motivated, at least in part, by a desire to be the kind of self-sufficient man he associates with soldiers and cowboys.

On Being a Real Westerner
Tobias Wolff

Just after Easter Roy gave me the Winchester .22 rifle I'd learned to shoot with. It was a light, pump-action, beautifully balanced piece with a walnut stock black from all its oilings. Roy had carried it when he was a boy and it was still as good as new. Better than new. The action was silky from long use, and the wood of a quality no longer to be found. 1

The gift did not come as a surprise. Roy was stingy, and slow to take a hint, but I'd put him under siege. I had my heart set on that rifle. A weapon was the first condition of self-sufficiency, and of being a real Westerner, and of all acceptable employment — trapping, riding herd, soldiering, law enforcement, and outlawry. I needed that rifle, for itself and for the way it completed me when I held it. 2

My mother said I couldn't have it. Absolutely not. Roy took the rifle back but promised me he'd bring her around. He could not imagine anyone refusing him anything and treated the refusals he did encounter as perverse and insincere. Normally mute, he became at these times a relentless whiner. He would follow my mother from room to room, emitting one ceaseless note of complaint that was pitched perfectly to jelly her nerves and bring her to a state where she would agree to anything to make it stop. 3

After a few days of this my mother caved in. She said I could have the rifle if, and only if, I promised never to take it out or even touch it except when she and Roy were with me. Okay, I said. Sure. Naturally. But even then she wasn't satisfied. She plain didn't like the fact of me owning a rifle. Roy said he had owned several rifles by the time he was my age, but this did not reassure her. She didn't think I could be trusted with it. Roy said now was the time to find out. 4

For a week or so I kept my promises. But now that the weather had turned warm Roy was usually off somewhere and eventually, in the dead hours after school when I found myself alone in the apartment, I decided that there couldn't be any harm in taking the rifle out to clean it. Only to clean it, nothing more. I was sure it would be enough just to break it down, oil it, rub linseed into the stock, polish the octagonal barrel and then hold it up to the light to confirm the perfection of the bore. But it wasn't enough. From cleaning the rifle I went to marching around the apartment with it, and then to striking brave poses in front of the mirror. Roy had saved one of his army uniforms and I sometimes dressed up in this, together with martial-looking articles of hunting gear: fur trooper's hat, camouflage coat, boots that reached nearly to my knees. 5

The camouflage coat made me feel like a sniper, and before long I began to act like one. I set up a nest on the couch by the front window. I drew the shades to darken the apartment, and took up my position. Nudging the shade aside with the rifle barrel, I followed people in my sights as they walked or drove along the street. At first I made shooting sounds — kyoo! kyoo! Then I started cocking the hammer and letting it snap down. 6

Roy stored his ammunition in a metal box he kept hidden in the closet. As with everything else hidden in the apartment, I knew exactly where to find it. There was a layer of loose .22 rounds on the bottom of the box under shells of bigger caliber, dropped there by the handful the way men drop pennies on their dressers at night. I took some and put them in a hiding place of my own. With these I started loading up the rifle. Hammer cocked, a round in the chamber, finger resting lightly on the trigger, I drew a bead on whoever walked by — women pushing strollers, children, garbage collectors laughing and calling to each other, anyone — and as they passed under my window I sometimes had to bite my lip to keep from laughing in the ecstasy of my power over them, and at their absurd and innocent belief that they were safe.

7

But over time the innocence I laughed at began to irritate me. It was a peculiar kind of irritation. I saw it years later in men I served with, and felt it myself, when unarmed Vietnamese civilians talked back to us while we were herding them around. Power can be enjoyed only when it is recognized and feared. Fearlessness in those without power is maddening to those who have it.

8

One afternoon I pulled the trigger. I had been aiming at two old people, a man and a woman, who walked so slowly that by the time they turned the corner at the bottom of the hill my little store of self-control was exhausted. I had to shoot. I looked up and down the street. It was empty. Nothing moved but a pair of squirrels chasing each other back and forth on the telephone wires. I followed one in my sight. Finally it stopped for a moment and I fired. The squirrel dropped straight into the road. I pulled back into the shadows and waited for something to happen, sure that someone must have heard the shot or seen the squirrel fall. But the sound that was so loud to me probably seemed to our neighbors no more than the bang of a cupboard slammed shut. After a while I sneaked a glance into the street. The squirrel hadn't moved. It looked like a scarf someone had dropped.

9

When my mother got home from work I told her there was a dead squirrel in the street. Like me, she was an animal lover. She took a cellophane bag off a loaf of bread and we went outside and looked at the squirrel. "Poor little thing," she said. She stuck her hand in the wrapper and picked up the squirrel, then pulled the bag inside out away from her hand. We buried it behind our building under a cross made of popsicle sticks, and I blubbered the whole time.

10

I blubbered again in bed that night. At last I got out of bed and knelt down and did an imitation of somebody praying, and then I did an imitation of somebody receiving divine reassurance and inspiration. I stopped crying. I smiled to myself and forced a feeling of warmth into my chest. Then I climbed back in bed and looked up at the ceiling with a blissful expression until I went to sleep.

11

For several days I stayed away from the apartment at times when I knew I'd be alone there.

12

Though I avoided the apartment, I could not shake the idea that sooner or later I would get the rifle out again. All my images of myself as I wished to be were images of myself armed. Because I did not know who I was, any image of myself, no matter how grotesque, had power over me. This much I understand now. But the man can give no help to the boy, not in this matter nor in those that follow. The boy moves always out of reach.

13

Making Connections to Personal and Social Issues: Role Playing

Wolff shows us that he took great delight in playing the role of a soldier — looking at himself in the mirror dressed in camouflage and "striking brave poses" (paragraph 5). The word *brave* suggests that the young Wolff wanted to see himself as possessing certain traits, like bravery, that we often associate with soldiers. Another part of the attraction of playing soldier, he admits, is the sense of power he experienced holding a rifle.

    With other students in your class, discuss the roles you played as children. What personal and cultural factors influenced the roles that you and your classmates imagined for yourselves? You might begin by comparing your own childhood imaginings with Wolff's desire to play soldier. In addition to having firsthand experience with Roy, a soldier who impressed him with his masculine authority and power, Wolff grew up during World War II, when children were bombarded by media images of brave soldiers fighting heroic wars and lone cowboys bringing justice to the Wild West. What media images — from television, film, the Internet, and computer games — do you think influenced the kinds of role play that you engaged in as a child or young adult?

Analyzing Writing Strategies

1. Writers convey the **significance** of autobiographical events by telling how they felt at the time the event occurred and by telling how they feel now as they look back on the event. Skim paragraphs 7, 8, and 13, noting where Wolff expresses his feelings and thoughts about the event. Try to distinguish between what he remembers thinking and feeling at the time and what he thinks and feels as he looks back on the event. What impression do you get of the young Wolff? What does the adult Wolff seem to think about his younger self?

2. Good stories show people in action — what we call **specific narrative action** — people moving or gesturing. Analyze paragraphs 7 and 9 by underlining the narrative actions and then putting brackets around the verb or verbal in each narrative action that specifically names the action. (A verbal is the *-ing* or *to* form of a verb: *laughing, to laugh.*) For example, here are the narrative actions (underlined) with their action verbs or verbals (in brackets) in paragraph 6:

   [set up] a nest, [drew] the shades, [took up] my position, [nudging] the shade aside, [followed] people, [walked] or [drove], [made] shooting sounds — kyoo! kyoo!, [started cocking] the hammer, [letting] it [snap] down.

      Now that you have completed your analysis of paragraphs 7 and 9, how do you think specific narrative action contributes to autobiographical stories?

3. Like other autobiographers, Wolff sometimes uses relatively short sentences. To understand why he might do so, compare the short and long sentences in the most dramatic and revealing action in the event. Begin by underlining every sentence of nine words or fewer (in paragraph 9). Then put brackets around the

For more on the role of short sentences in remembered-event essays, turn to A Sentence Strategy, p. 53.

relatively long sentence at the end of paragraph 7 and the three relatively long sentences beginning "I had been aiming," "I pulled back," and "But the sound" in paragraph 9. Compare what the long and short sentences contribute to the action. How do their contents differ? What effect do the short sentences have on you as a reader?

Commentary: Narrative Cueing in a Well-Told Story

This is a gripping story. The subject makes it inherently dramatic: Putting a rifle in a child's hands immediately alerts readers to the possibility that something dreadful could happen. Thus the potential for suspense is great. Contributing to the drama is Wolff's use of narrative strategies that move the action through time and help readers keep track of what happened.

If we look closely at Wolff's narration, we can see how two **narrating strategies** — **verb tenses** and **temporal transitions** — create the impression of time passing. These strategies serve as cueing devices because, like road signs, they enable readers to follow the action.

Verb Tenses.   Verb tenses signal when the action occurred — in the past, present, or future. Because remembered-event essays tell about past events, most of the verbs are in the past tense. Looking at the verbs in Wolff's essay, we can find several different kinds of past tense. In the first sentence of the essay, for example, Wolff shows an action that occurred at one point in the past (underlined) together with an action that was already completed (in brackets): "Just after Easter Roy gave me the Winchester .22 rifle [I'd learned to shoot with]." ("I'd learned" is a shortened form of "I had learned.") A second example shows an earlier action that was still going on (in brackets) when the more recent action occurred (underlined): "One afternoon I pulled the trigger. I [had been aiming] at two old people . . ." (paragraph 9).

Our final example is a little more complicated: "Roy took the rifle back but promised me [he'd bring] her around" (paragraph 3). This example presents three past actions. Whereas the first two actions (underlined) occurred at roughly the same time, the third (in brackets) predicts a future action that occurred after the first two actions were completed. (Here "he'd" is a short form of "he would.")

You probably do not know the technical names for these tenses, nor do you need to know them. However, you do need to know what the different verb tenses mean and how to use them. In your remembered-event essay, you will want to be sure that the verb tenses you use accurately indicate the time relations among various actions in your story.

Temporal Transitions.   In addition to using verb tense to show time, writers use transitions to move the narrative action forward in time and thereby keep readers oriented. Wolff uses many transitional words and phrases to locate an action at a particular point in time or to relate an action at one point in time to an action at another time. He uses four in the first paragraph alone: *just after, when, still,* and *no longer.* Time markers may appear at the beginning of a sentence or within a sentence.

Notice how many paragraphs in Wolff's story include such a transition in the opening sentence: "Just after" (paragraph 1), "After a few days" (4), "For a week or so" (5), "before long" (6), "One afternoon" (9), "When" (10), "again" (11), and "For several days" (12). This extensive use of temporal transitions is not unusual in remembered-event essays. You will want to use them liberally in your essay to make it easy for your readers to follow the action.

Considering Topics for Your Own Essay

In this selection, Wolff describes experiencing what he calls the "ecstasy of my power" to inflict harm on others (paragraph 7). Try to recall two or three incidents when you were in a position to exercise power over another person or when you were subject to someone else's power. Select only those relationships that can be well illustrated by one key incident that occurred within a day or two. Pick one such incident. Think about how you would narrate what happened and declare its significance for you personally.

RICK BRAGG was twenty when he began working as a journalist for his hometown newspaper, the *Anniston* (Alabama) *Star*. After honing his writing skills at several small southern newspapers, he joined the staff of the *St. Petersburg Times*, where he became Miami bureau chief, and eventually the *Los Angeles Times* and the *New York Times*. Bragg has won the Pulitzer Prize for feature writing in 1996, the American Society of Newspaper Editors' Distinguished Writing Award twice, and more than fifty other awards. His journalism has been collected in a book titled *Somebody Told Me: The Newspaper Stories of Rick Bragg* (2000). In addition, he has written two autobiographical books: *All Over but the Shoutin'* (1997), about his small-town Alabama childhood, and *Ava's Man* (2001), about the grandfather he never met. Bragg, who has taught writing at the University of South Florida, Boston University, and Harvard, says he learned storytelling "at the knees of some of the best storytellers — back-porch talkers."

The following selection from *All Over but the Shoutin'* tells what happened the summer before Bragg was a senior in high school. As you read about this remembered event, pay attention to Bragg's vivid descriptions. For example, notice how he helps readers imagine the car and appreciate his feelings for it right down to its orange houndstooth-pattern upholstery and the eight-track *Eagles' Greatest Hits* tape.

100 Miles per Hour, Upside Down and Sideways
Rick Bragg

Since I was a boy I have searched for ways to slingshot myself into the distance, faster and faster. When you turn the key on a car built for speed, when you hear that car rumble like an approaching storm and feel the steering wheel tremble in your hands from all that power barely under control, you feel like you can run away from anything, like you can turn your whole life into an insignificant speck in the rearview mirror.

In the summer of 1976, the summer before my senior year at Jacksonville High School, I had the mother of all slingshots. She was a 1969 General Motors convertible muscle car with a 350 V-8 and a Holley four-barreled carburetor as long as my arm. She got about six miles to the gallon, downhill, and when you started her up she sounded like Judgment Day. She was long and low and vicious, a mad dog cyclone with orange houndstooth interior and an eight-track tape player, and looked fast just sitting in the yard under a pine tree. I owned just one tape, that I remember, *The Eagles' Greatest Hits*.

I worked two summers in the hell and heat at minimum wage to earn enough money to buy her and still had to borrow money from my uncle Ed, who got her for just nineteen hundred dollars mainly because he paid in hundred-dollar bills. "You better be careful, boy," he told me. "That'un will kill you." I assured him that, Yes, Sir, I would creep around in it like an old woman.

I tell myself I loved that car because she was so pretty and so fast and because I loved to rumble between the rows of pines with the blond hair of some girl who had yet to discover she was better than me whipping in the breeze. But the truth is I loved her because she was my equalizer. She raised me up, at least in my own eyes, closer to where I wanted and needed to be. In high school, I was neither extremely popular nor one of the great number of want-to-bes. I was invited to parties with the popular kids, I had dates with pretty girls. But there was always a distance there, of my own making, usually.

That car, in a purely superficial way, closed it. People crowded around her at the Hardee's. I let only one person drive her, Patrice Curry, the prettiest girl in school, for exactly one mile.

That first weekend, I raced her across the long, wide parking lot of the TG&Y, an insane thing to do, seeing as how a police car could have cruised by at any minute. It was a test of nerves as well as speed, because you actually had to be slowing down, not speeding up, as you neared the finish line, because you just ran out of parking lot. I beat Lyn Johnson's Plymouth and had to slam on my brakes and swing her hard around, to keep from jumping the curb, the road and plowing into the parking lot of the Sonic Drive-In.

It would have lasted longer, this upraised standing, if I had pampered her. I guess I should have spent more time looking at her than racing her, but I had too much of the Bragg side of the family in me for that. I would roll her out on some lonely country road late at night, the top down, and blister down the blacktop until I knew the tires were about to lift off the ground. But they never did. She held the road, somehow, until I ran out of road or just lost my nerve. It was as if there was no limit to her, at how fast we could go, together.

It lasted two weeks from the day I bought her.

On Saturday night, late, I pulled up to the last red light in town on my way home. Kyle Smith pulled up beside me in a loud-running Chevrolet, and raced his engine. I did not squall out when the light changed — she was not that kind of car — but let her rpm's build, build and build, like winding up a top.

I was passing a hundred miles per hour as I neared a long sweeping turn on Highway 21 when I saw, coming toward me, the blue lights of the town's police. I cannot really remember what happened next. I just remember mashing the gas pedal down hard, halfway through that sweeping turn, and the sickening feeling as the car just seemed to lift and twist in the air, until I was doing a hundred miles per hour still, but upside down and sideways.

She landed across a ditch, on her top. If she had not hit the ditch in just the right way, the police later said, it would have cut my head off. I did not have on my seat belt. We never did, then. Instead of flinging me out, though, the centrifugal force — I had taken science in ninth grade — somehow held me in.

Instead of lying broken and bleeding on the ground beside my car, or headless, I just sat there, upside down. I always pulled the adjustable steering wheel down low, an inch or less above my thighs, and that held me in place, my head covered with mud and broken glass. The radio was still blaring — it was the Eagles' "The Long Run," I believe — and I tried to find the knob in the dark to turn it off. Funny. There I was in an upside-down car, smelling the gas as it ran out of the tank, listening to the tick, tick, tick of the hot engine, thinking: "I sure do hope that gas don't get nowhere near that hot manifold," but all I did about it was try to turn down the radio.

I knew the police had arrived because I could hear them talking. Finally, I felt a hand on my collar. A state trooper dragged me out and dragged me up the side of the ditch and into the collective glare of the most headlights I had ever seen. There were police cars and ambulances and traffic backed up, it seemed, all the way to Piedmont.

"The Lord was riding with you, son," the trooper said. "You should be dead."

My momma stood off to one side, stunned. Finally the police let her through to look me over, up and down. But except for the glass in my hair and a sore neck, I was fine. Thankfully, I was too old for her to go cut a hickory and stripe my legs with it, but I am sure it crossed her mind.

The trooper and the Jacksonville police had a private talk off to one side, trying to decide whether or not to put me in prison for the rest of my life. Finally, they informed my momma that I had suffered enough, to take me home. As we drove away, I looked back over my shoulder as the wrecker dragged my car out of the ditch and, with the help of several strong men, flipped it back over, right-side up. It looked like a white sheet of paper someone had crumpled up and tossed in the ditch from a passing car.

"The Lord was riding with that boy," Carliss Slaughts, the wrecker operator, told my uncle Ed. With so many people saying that, I thought the front page of the *Anniston Star* the next day would read: LORD RIDES WITH BOY, WRECKS ANYWAY.

I was famous for a while. No one, no one, flips a convertible at a hundred miles per hour, without a seat belt on, and walks away, undamaged. People said I

10

11

12

13

14

15

16

17

18

had a charmed life. My momma, like the trooper and Mr. Slaughts, just figured God was my copilot.

The craftsmen at Slaughts' Body Shop put her back together, over four months. My uncle Ed loaned me the money to fix her, and took it out of my check. The body and fender man made her pretty again, but she was never the same. She was fast but not real fast, as if some little part of her was still broken deep inside. Finally, someone backed into her in the parking lot of the Piggly Wiggly, and I was so disgusted I sold her for fourteen hundred dollars to a preacher's son, who drove the speed limit.

19

Making Connections to Personal and Social Issues: Social Status

Bragg worked hard and saved his money for two years when he was a teenager in high school to buy the convertible. Probably he had several motives for doing so; but after he started driving the car, he came to think of it as "my equalizer," which "closed" the distance between the most popular students and himself and gave him immediate "upraised standing" (paragraphs 4, 5, 7).

With other students, discuss this concern with standing or status in high school. Was it a concern of yours personally? If not, speculate about the reasons. If so, what did you try to do, if anything, to raise (or maintain) your status? Why do you think you made this effort?

Analyzing Writing Strategies

For more on comparing strategies, including similes and metaphors, see Chapter 15, pp. 642–43. For more on creating a dominant impression, see Chapter 15, pp. 648–49.

1. One important strategy used for describing people, places, and objects in autobiographical writing is **comparing** — using similes and metaphors to help readers imagine what happened. Similes use *like* or *as* to make explicit comparisons: "you hear that car rumble like an approaching storm" (paragraph 1). Metaphors are implied comparisons: "Since I was a boy I have searched for ways to slingshot myself into the distance, faster and faster" (paragraph 1). Here Bragg implies a comparison between himself and a stone launched from a hand-held slingshot; the stone speeds into space as Bragg hopes to speed into the future, to get to any place other than the place where he was at the time of this event. Comparisons are not a requirement of successful remembered-event essays, but they can contribute to readers' understanding of the significance of the event to the writer if they are not merely decorative.

   There are several comparisons in paragraph 1 and one each in paragraphs 3, 7, 9, 13, and 16. Locate and underline the comparisons in these paragraphs. Choose one comparison that you think works especially well, and explain briefly why you think so. Then consider the comparisons as a group. What impression do these comparisons give you of the young Bragg and the event he is writing about?

2. In the central incident (paragraphs 9–16), the defining element of a remembered-event essay, Bragg **narrates** a compelling story. To understand more fully how Bragg organizes the incident, make a paragraph scratch outline of it. Does the order of events make sense? Are there further details you need to know to follow easily what happens? What does Bragg do to arouse your curiosity and build **suspense**?

For an example of a paragraph scratch outline, turn to the Commentary following Annie Dillard's essay on p. 22. For more information on scratch outlining, see Chapter 12, p. 593.

Commentary: Autobiographical Significance

Bragg's essay illustrates the two main ways writers convey the **autobiographical significance** of a remembered event: showing and telling. Bragg shows the event's significance through details and action. For example, he shows us how the car raised his status by describing its power and imposing appearance and the girls he took for rides in it. He shows the importance of the car by recounting how terribly hard he worked to buy it and then to have it repaired after the wreck. He reveals perhaps his resigned acceptance that the car would not change his life by selling it after it was dented in a parking lot. The least Bragg must do to succeed is to show consistently through details and action what the remembered event meant to him. Bragg also tells readers what he believes the autobiographical significance might be, and he does so in two ways: by telling his remembered thoughts and feelings from the time of the event as well as by giving his present perspective on the event.

Bragg's **remembered thoughts and feelings** frame his essay. In the first paragraph, he remembers thinking that owning a powerful car makes "you feel like you can run away from anything, like you can turn your whole life into an insignificant speck in the rearview mirror." In the final paragraphs, he remembers his temporary fame for surviving the accident and his disgust when someone damaged his car in a parking lot. These remembered thoughts and feelings reveal perhaps a change of values, from materialism to some yet-to-be-defined values, from Bragg's relying on a car for status to his parting with it readily for far less money than he had invested in it.

Bragg's **present perspectives** on this remembered event occur in paragraphs 4–7, between the time he bought the car and had the accident. From his perspective in his midthirties, as he was writing *All Over but the Shoutin'*, Bragg writes, "I tell myself I loved that car because she was so pretty and so fast. . . . But the truth is I loved her because she was my equalizer" (paragraph 4). He acknowledges that as a high school student he wanted the car because it made him popular, "upraised" his social "standing" (paragraph 7). But he also admits that he loved the feeling the car gave him that he could "run away from anything" (paragraph 1). By inserting these present-perspective comments, Bragg reflects on desires that are contradictory but all too familiar: the wish to be accepted socially and, at the same time, the need to feel free and powerful. From his adult perspective, he knows that racing was "an insane thing to do" (paragraph 6). But instead of moralizing about the recklessness of his wild ride, he tries to give readers a sense of the joy he felt when he would "slingshot" himself "into the distance, faster and faster" (paragraph 1), as well as the amazement he felt later that he had lived to tell the tale.

Considering Topics for Your Own Essay

Bragg has focused on a particular incident that tells us something about himself both as an adolescent and as the man he would become by his midthirties. Think of incidents early in your life (before you were eleven or twelve years old) that are particularly revealing about you, both as a child and as a person of your present age. You might try to think of incidents that tested or challenged you or incidents in which you behaved either typically or atypically in relation to the way you remember yourself to have been or think of yourself now. Perhaps you experienced a dreadful disappointment or an unexpected delight. Perhaps you were in danger, or you accomplished something you now think you were unprepared for.

▮ Purpose and Audience

Writing autobiography, writers relive moments of pleasure and pain, and they also gain insight, learning who they are now by examining who they used to be and the forces that shaped them. Because autobiographers write to be read, though, they are as much concerned with self-presentation as with self-discovery. Writers present themselves to readers in the way they want to be perceived. The rest they keep hidden, though readers may read between the lines.

We read about others' experiences for much the same reason that we write about our own — to learn how to live our lives. Reading autobiography can validate our sense of ourselves, particularly when we see our own experience reflected in another's life. Reading about others' lives can also challenge our complacency and help us appreciate other points of view.

Basic Features: Remembering Events

A Well-Told Story

An essay about a remembered event should tell an interesting story. Whatever else the writer may attempt to do, he or she must shape the experience into a story that is entertaining and memorable. This is done primarily by building suspense, leading readers to wonder, for example, whether the driver of the Buick will catch Annie Dillard, Tobias Wolff will shoot the rifle, or Jean Brandt will get caught for shoplifting. The principal technique for propelling the narrative and heightening suspense is specific narrative action with its action verbs and verbals. Suspense increases, for instance, when Wolff gives a detailed close-up of his play with the rifle. In addition, writers use temporal transitions to cue readers and move the narrative through time, as when Rick Bragg begins paragraphs with "In the summer of 1976," "That first weekend," and "On Saturday night." Finally, writers often use dialogue to convey immediacy and drama, as Brandt does to dramatize her confrontation with her mother on the phone.

A Vivid Presentation of Places and People

Instead of giving a generalized impression, skillful writers attempt to re-create the place where the event occurred and let us hear what people said. Vivid language and specific details make the writing memorable. By moving in close, a writer can name specific objects at a place, such as when Brandt catalogs the store's knickknacks, calendars, and buttons. A writer may also provide details about some of the objects, as when Brandt describes the coveted "75-cent Snoopy button." Finally, writers use similes and metaphors to draw comparisons and thereby help readers understand the point. For example, when Brandt says she "felt like Hester Prynne being put on public display" (paragraph 17), readers familiar with *The Scarlet Letter* can imagine how embarrassed Brandt must have felt.

To present people who played an important role in a remembered event, autobiographers often provide some descriptive details and a snatch of dialogue. They may detail the person's appearance, as Annie Dillard does by describing the man who chased her "in city clothes: a suit and tie, street shoes" as "a thin man, all action" (paragraph 10). Dialogue can be an especially effective way of giving readers a vivid impression of someone. Wolff, for example, describes his mother by combining specific narrative actions with her empathetic words: "She took a cellophane bag off a loaf of bread and we went outside and looked at the squirrel. 'Poor little thing,' she said. She stuck her hand in the wrapper and picked up the squirrel, then pulled the bag inside out away from her hand" (paragraph 10).

An Indication of the Event's Significance

There are two ways a writer can communicate an event's autobiographical significance: by showing us that the event was important or by telling us directly what it meant. Most writers do both. Showing is necessary because the event must be dramatized for readers to appreciate its importance and understand the writer's feelings about it. Seeing the important scenes and people from the writer's point of view naturally leads readers to identify with the writer. We can well imagine what that "unexpected tap on [the] shoulder" (paragraph 5) must have felt like for Brandt, how Dillard felt when the man chased her and Mikey "silently over picket fences, through thorny hedges, between houses, around garbage cans, and across streets" (paragraph 13), and what Bragg was thinking as he hung upside down in his overturned car.

Telling also contributes to a reader's understanding, so most writers comment on the event's meaning and importance. Readers expect to understand the significance of the event, but they do not expect the essay to begin with the kind of thesis statement typical of argumentative writing. Instead, as the story moves along, writers tell us how they felt at the time or how they feel now as they look back on the experience. Often writers do both. Wolff, for example, tells us some of his remembered feelings when he recalls feeling "like a sniper" and delighting in the "ecstasy" of power. He also tells us what he thinks looking back on the experience: "Because I did not know who I was, any image of myself, no matter how grotesque, had power over me. This much I understand now" (paragraph 13). Telling is the main way that writers interpret the event for readers, but skillful writers are careful not to append these reflections artificially, like a moral tagged on to a fable.

Remembering Events

Invention and Research

What are some events that have been important in your life, ones whose details you remember and would not mind sharing with your class? Think about several possible events, choose one of them, and do some more thinking and some writing about it. Then consider how you would express what it meant — and means — to you. . . . **See p. 43 for more.**

Planning and Drafting

As you look over what you have written so far, can you present the event vividly to readers and make them understand its importance to you? How can you engage their attention? What details and dialogue will bring the story to life? Make a plan for your narrative, and start drafting it. . . . **See p. 50 for more.**

Critical Reading Guide

What are your draft's strengths and weaknesses? Is the sequence of actions confusing? Is it unclear why the event was important to you? Ask a classmate, a friend, a writing tutor, or someone else to read and respond to your essay, especially the parts you are most unsure of. . . . **See p. 53 for more.**

Revising

As you consider your essay again in light of your reader's comments, how can you improve it? Did the beginning fail to engage the reader? Do you need more dialogue? Are you giving the wrong impression of how you felt at the time? Go through your draft systematically, making changes wherever necessary. . . . **See p. 55 for more.**

Editing and Proofreading

Have you checked for errors that are especially likely in essays about remembered events? Have you left out commas after introductory time references in sentences? Have you forgotten to use the past perfect tense to indicate a past action that was completed at the time of another one? Look for and correct these and any other errors. . . . **See p. 59 for more.**

■ The Writing Assignment

Write an essay about an event in your life that will engage readers and that will, at the same time, help them understand the significance of the event. Tell your story dramatically and vividly.

To learn about using the *Guide* e-book for invention and drafting, go to bedfordstmartins.com/theguide.

■ Invention and Research

The following invention activities will help you choose an appropriate event, recall specific details, sketch out the story, test your choice, and explore the event's auto-biographical significance.

Each invention activity is easy to complete and takes only a few minutes. If you can spread out the activities over several days, it will be easier for you to recall details of the event and to reflect deeply on the event's meaning in your life. Keep a written record of your invention work to use when you draft the essay and later when you revise it. Also, by never being without a small notebook and pencil or your laptop computer, you can write down some of the relevant details and ideas that will inevitably arise in your inner speech.

Finding an Event to Write About

To find the best possible event to write about, consider several possibilities rather than automatically choosing the first event that comes to mind.

Listing Remembered Events. *Make a list of significant events from your past. Include only those events about which you can recall details about what happened, where and when it happened, and the people involved.* For this assignment, an event is something that happened on *one day or just a part of a day*. Begin your list now, and add to it over the next few days. Aim for at least four or five events you might write about. Include possibilities suggested by the Considering Topics for Your Own Essay activities following the readings by Annie Dillard, Tobias Wolff, and Rick Bragg in this chapter. The following categories may give you some more ideas:

- An incident that you find yourself thinking about occasionally or one you know you will never forget
- A difficult situation, such as when you had to make a tough choice, when someone you admired let you down (or you let someone else down), or when you struggled to learn or understand something hard

- An occasion when things did not turn out as expected, such as when you expected to be praised but were criticized or ignored or when you were convinced you would fail but succeeded
- An incident charged with strong emotion, such as love, fear, anger, embarrassment, guilt, frustration, hurt, pride, happiness, or joy
- An occasion when you realized you had a special skill, ambition, or problem
- A time when you became aware of injustice, selflessness, heroism, sexism, or racism

■ *Listing Events Related to Identity and Community.*   Whenever you write about events in your life, you are likely to reveal important aspects of your sense of identity and your relationships with others. The suggestions that follow, however, will help you recall events that are particularly revealing of your efforts to know yourself and to discover your place in the communities to which you belong.

- An event that shaped you in a particular way or revealed an aspect of your personality you had not seen before, such as your independence, insecurity, ambitiousness, or jealousy
- An incident that made you reexamine one of your basic values or beliefs, such as when you were expected to do something that went against your better judgment or when your values conflicted with someone else's values
- An occasion when others' actions led you to consider seriously a new idea or point of view
- An incident that made you feel the need to identify yourself with a particular community, such as an ethnic group, a political or religious group, or a group of coworkers
- An event that made you realize that you were playing a role you were uncomfortable with, such as a friend or partner, a parent or sibling, a worker or boss, a believer in a particular religious faith, or a member of a particular community
- An incident in which a single encounter with another person changed the way you view yourself or changed your ideas about how you fit into a particular community

■ *Listing Events Related to Work and Career.*   The following suggestions will help you think of events involving your work experiences as well as your career aspirations.

- An event that made you aware of your capacity for or interest in a particular kind of work or career or an event that convinced you that you were not cut out for a particular kind of work or career
- An incident of great achievement, breakthrough, or insight at work
- An incident of harassment or mistreatment at work

- An event that revealed to you other people's assumptions, attitudes, or prejudices about you as a worker, your likelihood of succeeding at a particular job, your fitness for a particular job, or your career goals
- An incident of conflict or serious misunderstanding with a customer, a fellow employee, a supervisor, or someone you supervised

An Online Activity: Finding an Event to Write About

Exploring Web sites that collect personal narratives of U.S. citizens from different historical periods, ethnic groups, and social classes will give you a broad view of the importance of autobiography in American life. Not all of the narratives at the sites we recommend here focus on a single remembered event, as your essay will, but any one of them might nevertheless suggest to you an event from your own life you might want to write about. You can certainly gain insights into the kinds of life experiences people remember as significant. You could read several narratives from one site or one or two narratives from each site.

American Life Histories. Manuscripts from the Federal Writers' Project, 1936–1940. You can focus on stories from your own state. (rs6.loc.gov/wpaintro/wpahome.html)

First-Person Narratives of the American South. Written between 1860–1920. A project of the University of North Carolina at Chapel Hill. (docsouth.unc.edu/fpn)

Sixties Personal Narrative Project. This site collects personal narratives by men and women who came of age during the decade of the Vietnam war. A project of the University of Virginia. (www3.iath.Virginia.edu/sixties/HTML_docs/Narrative.html)

Add to your list of possibilities any events suggested by your online research. Do not be disappointed if other people's stories do not help you think of events in your own life that you could write about.

Choosing an Event.   *Look over your list of possibilities, and choose one event that you think will make an interesting story.* Your event should be limited to one day or part of a day. You should be eager to explore its significance and comfortable about sharing it with your instructors and classmates, who will be your first readers. You may find the choice easy to make, or you may have several equally promising possibilities from which to choose.

It may help you in choosing an event if you tentatively identify your ultimate readers, the people with whom you most want to share the story. They could include, for example, your personal friends, members of your family, people you work with, members of a group with which you identify or of an organization to which you belong, your classmates, or even the public at large.

Make the best choice you can now. If this event does not work out, you can try a different one later.

Describing the Place

The following activities will help you decide which places are important to your story and what you remember about them. Take the time now to explore your memory and imagination. This exploration will yield descriptive language you can use in your essay.

Listing Key Places.   *Make a list of all the places where the event occurred, skipping some space after each entry on your list.* Your event may have occurred in one or more places. For now, list all the places you remember without worrying about whether they should be included in your story.

Describing Key Places.   *In the space after each entry on your list, make some notes describing each place.* As you remember each place, what do you see (excluding people for the moment)? What objects stand out? Are they large or small, green or brown, square or oblong? What sounds do you hear? Do you detect any smells? Does any taste come to mind? Do you recall anything soft or hard, smooth or rough?

Recalling Key People

These activities will help you remember the people who played a role in the event — what they looked like, did, and said.

Listing Key People.   *List the people who played more than a casual role in the event.* You may have only one person to list, or you may have several.

Describing a Key Person.   *Write a brief description of a person other than yourself who played a major role in the event.* For this person, name and detail a few distinctive physical features or items of dress. Briefly describe in a few phrases this person's way of moving and gesturing.

Re-Creating a Conversation.   *Reconstruct one important conversation you had during the event.* It could have lasted only a moment or several minutes. Try to recall any especially memorable comments, any unusual choice of words, or any telling remarks that you made or were made to you. You will not remember exactly what was said during an entire conversation, but try to partially re-create it so that readers will be able to imagine what was going on and how your language and the other person's language reveal who you were and your relationship.

Sketching the Story

Write for a few minutes, telling what happened. You may find it easier to outline what happened rather than writing complete sentences. Any way you can put the main activities or actions into words is fine.

Filling Out Your Invention Notes

Over the next few days, add newly remembered details to your notes in each invention category.

Testing Your Choice

Now you need to decide whether you recall enough of the event and care enough about it to write a good story. If at any point you lose confidence in your choice, return to the list of possible events you made, and choose another event.

Do You Know Enough?   *Reread your invention notes to see whether your initial memories seem promising.* To make this decision, *try to answer the following questions:*

- Do I recall enough of what happened during the event to narrate a complete and coherent story?
- Do I well remember feelings associated with the event?
- Have I been able to reconstruct conversations partially and to recall details of my appearance, dress, movements, and gestures to help readers imagine me as I was then?

Do You Care Enough?   In writing about the event you have chosen, you are accepting an obligation both to yourself and to your readers to work hard and imaginatively to tell a story they will want to read. To decide whether you can make this commitment, *try to answer the following questions:*

- *Do you look forward to uncovering more details about the event?* The event can come alive in readers' minds only if you provide enough details of the place, people, and interactions to stimulate readers' imaginations.
- *Do you feel drawn toward understanding what this event meant to you then and means to you now?* Readers will enjoy your story, but they want more from you: what it meant to you then and what meaning or significance you find in it now. You need not yet know the significance or feel entirely confident about your remembered feelings and present perspective, but you have to feel compelled to discover them — and not fearful of what you may discover. (Keep in mind that you decide what you want to disclose.)
- *Do you anticipate the pleasure your completed essay will give your readers?* You are not writing a diary entry. Rather, you are writing a public document to be shared with classmates and your instructor and perhaps with others, ranging from current friends to your grandchildren. You are giving them a great gift. This certainty can inspire and motivate you.

At this point, you will find it useful to get together with two or three other students to try out your story. Your classmates' reactions to your remembered event will help you determine whether you have chosen an event you can present in an interesting way.

A Collaborative Activity:
Testing Your Choice

Storytellers: Take turns telling your story briefly. As you tell your story, describe the place and key people. Try to pique your listeners' curiosity and build suspense.

Listeners: Briefly tell each storyteller what you found most intriguing about the story. For example, were you eager to know how the story would turn out? Were you curious about any of the people? Were you able to identify with the storyteller? Could you imagine the place? Could you understand why the event might be memorable and significant for the storyteller?

Exploring Memorabilia

Memorabilia are visual images, sounds, and objects that can help you remember details and understand the significance of an event. Examples include photographs, newspaper or magazine clippings, recordings of popular music, and items like restaurant menus and movie, theater, or concert stubs and programs. Memorabilia are not a requirement for success with this assignment, but they may prove helpful in stimulating your memory. *If you can obtain access to memorabilia relevant to the remembered event you will write about, take time to do so now. Add to your invention notes any details about the period, places, or people the memorabilia suggest.*

You might also consider including memorabilia in your essay. You can simply append photographs or other items to your printed-out essay, or you can scan them into your electronic document. If you include visual memorabilia in your essay, you should label and number them as Figure 1, Figure 2, and so on, and include captions identifying them. For more information about including visuals in your essay, see Chapter 25.

Reflecting on the Event's Significance

You should now feel fairly confident that you can tell an interesting story about the event you have chosen. The following activities will help you to understand the meaning that the event holds in your life and to develop ways to convey this significance to your readers.

Recalling Your Remembered Feelings and Thoughts. *Write for a few minutes about your feelings and thoughts during and immediately after the event.* The following questions may help stimulate your memory:

- What were my expectations before the event?
- What was my first reaction to the event as it was happening and right after it ended?
- How did I show my feelings? What did I say?
- What did I want the people involved to think of me? Why did I care what they thought of me?
- What did I think of myself at the time?
- How long did these initial feelings last?
- What were the immediate consequences of the event for me personally?

Pause now to reread what you have written. *Then write another sentence or two about the event's significance to you at the time it occurred.*

Exploring Your Present Perspective. *Write for a few minutes about your current feelings and thoughts as you look back on the event.* These questions may help you get started:

- Looking back, how do I feel about this event? If I understand it differently now than I did then, what is the difference?

- What do my actions at the time of the event say about the kind of person I was then? How would I respond to the same event if it occurred today?

- Can looking at the event historically or culturally help explain what happened? For example, did I upset gender expectations? Did I feel torn between two cultures or ethnic identities? Did I feel out of place?

- Do I now see that there was a conflict underlying the event? For example, did I struggle with contradictory desires within myself? Did I feel pressured by others? Were my desires and rights in conflict with someone else's? Was the event about power or responsibility?

Pause now to reflect on what you have written about your present perspective. *Then write another sentence or two, commenting on the event's significance as you look back on it.*

Defining Your Purpose for Your Readers

Write a few sentences, defining your purpose in writing about this particular event for your readers. Use these questions to focus your thoughts:

- Who are my readers? (Remember that in choosing an event, you considered several possible readers: your personal friends, members of your family, people you work with, members of a group with which you identify or of an organization to which you belong, your classmates, even the public at large.)

- What do my readers know about me?

- What do my readers expect when they read autobiography?

- How do I expect my readers to understand or react to the event?

- How do I want my readers to feel about what happened? What is the dominant impression or mood I want my story to create?

- What specifically do I want my readers to think of me? What do I expect or fear they might think?

It is unlikely, but you may decide at this point that you feel uncomfortable disclosing this event. If so, choose another event to write about.

Formulating a Tentative Thesis Statement

Review what you wrote for Reflecting on the Event's Significance, and add another two or three sentences, not necessarily summarizing what you already have written but extending your insights into the significance of the event, what it meant to you at the time, and what it means now. These sentences must necessarily be speculative and tentative because you may not fully understand the event's significance in your life.

Keep in mind that readers do not expect you to begin your essay with the kind of explicit thesis statement typical of argumentative or explanatory writing. If you do decide to tell readers explicitly why the event was meaningful or significant, you will most likely do so as you tell the story, by commenting on or evaluating what happened, instead of announcing the significance at the beginning. Keep in mind that you are not obliged to tell readers the significance, but you must show it through the way you tell the story.

■ Planning and Drafting

This section will help you review your invention writing and get started on your first draft.

Seeing What You Have

You have now done a lot of thinking and writing about the basic elements of a remembered-event essay: what happened, where it happened, who was involved, what was said, and how you felt. You have also begun to develop your understanding of why the event is so important to you. If you have done your invention writing on the computer, you may have sentences or whole paragraphs that can be copied and pasted into your draft. Reread what you have written so far to see what you have. Watch for specific narrative actions, vivid descriptive details, and choice bits of dialogue. Note also any language that resonates with feeling or that seems especially insightful. Highlight any writing you think could be used in your draft.

Then ask yourself the following questions:

- Do I remember enough specific details about the event to describe it vividly?
- Do I understand how the event was significant to me?
- Does my invention material provide what I need to convey that significance to my readers?
- Does my present perspective on this event seem clear to me?
- Does the dominant impression I want to create in my essay seem relevant?

If you find little that seems promising, you are not likely to be able to write a good draft. Consider starting over with another event.

If, however, your invention writing offers some promising material, the following activities may help you develop more:

- To remember more of what actually happened, discuss the event with someone who was there or who remembers having heard about it at the time.
- To recall additional details about a person who played an important role in the event, look at any available photographs or letters, talk with the person, or talk

with someone who remembers the person. If that is impossible, you might imagine having a conversation with the person today about the event: What would you say? How do you think the person would respond?

- To remember how you felt at the time of the event, try to recall what else was happening in your life during that period. What music, television shows, movies, sports, books, and magazines did you like? What concerns did you have at home, school, work, play?

- To develop your present perspective on the event, try viewing your experience as a historical event. If you were writing a news story or documentary about the event, what would you want people to know?

- To decide on the dominant impression you want your story to have on readers, imagine that you are making a film based on this event. What would your film look like? What mood or atmosphere would you try to create? Alternatively, imagine writing a song or poem about the event. Think of an appropriate image or refrain. What kind of song would you write — blues, hip-hop, country, ranchera, rock?

Setting Goals

Before starting to draft, set goals that will help you make decisions and solve problems as you draft and revise. Here are some questions that will help you set your goals:

Your Purpose and Readers

- What do I want my readers to think of me and my experience? Should I tell them how I felt and what I thought at the time of the event, as Dillard does? Should I tell them how my perspective has changed, as Bragg does?

- If my readers are likely to have had a similar experience, how can I convey the uniqueness of my experience or its special importance in my life? Should I tell them more about my background or the particular context of the event, as Bragg does? Should I give them a glimpse, as Dillard does, of its impact years later?

- If my readers are not likely to have had a similar experience, how can I help them understand what happened and appreciate its importance? Should I reveal the cultural influences acting on me, as Wolff and Bragg do?

The Beginning

- What can I do in the opening sentences to arouse readers' curiosity? Should I begin with a surprising announcement, as Wolff does, or should I establish the setting and situation, as Dillard and Brandt do?

- How can I get my readers to identify with me? Should I tell them a few things about myself, as Bragg does?

- Should I do something unusual, such as begin in the middle of the action or with a funny bit of dialogue?

The Story

- What should be the climax of my story — the point that readers anticipate with trepidation or eagerness?
- What specific narrative actions or dialogue would intensify the drama of the story?
- Should I follow strict chronological order? Or would flashback (referring to an event that occurred earlier) or flashforward (referring to an event that will occur later) make the narrative more interesting?
- How can I use vivid descriptive detail to dramatize the story?

The Ending

- If I conclude with some reflections on the meaning of the experience, how can I avoid tagging on a moral or being too sentimental?
- If I want readers to think well of me, should I conclude with a philosophical statement, as Wolff does? Should I end with a paradoxical statement, like Dillard? Should I be satirical? Should I be self-critical to avoid seeming smug?
- If I want to underscore the event's continuing significance in my life, can I show that the conflict was never fully resolved, as Brandt does? Could I contrast my remembered and current feelings and thoughts?
- Should I frame the essay by echoing something from the beginning to give ⸢readers at least a superficial sense of closure, as Brandt does by setting the last scene, like the first, in a car?

Outlining

For an example of a paragraph scratch outline, turn to the Commentary following Annie Dillard's essay on p. 26. For more information on scratch outlining, see Chapter 12, p. 593.

The goals you have set should help you draft your essay, but first you might want to make a quick scratch outline to refocus on the basic story line. You could use the outlining function of your word processing program. In your outline, list the main actions in order, noting where you plan to describe the place, introduce particular people, present dialogue, and insert remembered or current feelings and thoughts. Use this outline to guide your drafting, but do not feel tied to it. As you draft, you may find a better way to sequence the action and integrate these features.

Drafting

General Advice. Start drafting your essay, keeping in mind the goals you have set for yourself, especially the goal of telling the story dramatically. Turn off your grammar checker and spelling checker at this stage if you find them distracting. Don't be afraid to skip around in your story. Jump back and fill in a spontaneous idea, or leap ahead and write a later section first if you find that easier. Refer to your outline to help you sequence the action. If you get stuck while drafting, either make a note of what you need to fill in later or see if you can use something from your invention writing.

As you read over your first draft, you may see places where you can add new material to make the story dramatic. Or you may even decide that after this first draft you can finally see the story you want to write and set out to do so in a second draft.

A Sentence Strategy: Short Sentences.   As you draft a remembered-event essay, you will be trying to help readers feel the suspense of your story and recognize its significance. In thinking about how to achieve this goal, you can often benefit by paying attention to how long your sentences are.

   Use short sentences to heighten the drama or suspense, point out autobiographical significance, and summarize action. Experienced writers of autobiography usually use both short and long sentences, as a glance at any reading in this chapter demonstrates. They write short sentences not to relieve the monotony or effort of writing long sentences but to achieve certain purposes they cannot achieve as easily with long sentences.

   To dramatize actions or heighten suspense:

   Finally, I felt a hand on my collar. (Rick Bragg, paragraph 13)

   He caught us and we all stopped. (Annie Dillard, paragraph 15)

   To emphasize the significance of the event to the writer:

   I wanted the glory to last forever. (Annie Dillard, paragraph 19)

   The humiliation at that moment was overwhelming. (Jean Brandt, paragraph 17)

   To summarize actions:

   One afternoon, I pulled the trigger. (Tobias Wolff, paragraph 9)

Short sentences are not the only way to achieve these purposes, but they do so notably well. Note, though, that most of these writers use short sentences infrequently. Because short sentences are infrequent, they attract the reader's attention: They seem to say, "Pay close attention here." But short sentences achieve this effect only in relation to long sentences, in context with them. (Some of the sentence strategies presented in other chapters of this book illustrate ways that writers construct and purposefully deploy relatively long, complex sentences.) See how Dillard uses a series of longer sentences to build suspense that she brings to a peak with a short one:

For more on using short sentences, go to bedfordstmartins.com/theguide and click on Sentence Strategies.

   On one weekday morning after Christmas, six inches of new snow had just fallen. We were standing up to our boot tops in snow on a front yard on trafficked Reynolds Street, waiting for cars. The cars traveled Reynolds Street slowly and evenly; they were targets all but wrapped in red ribbons, cream puffs. We couldn't miss. (paragraph 3)

Now is the time to get a good critical reading of your draft. Your instructor may schedule readings of drafts as part of your coursework — in class or online. If not, ask a classmate, friend, or family member to read your draft. You could also seek comments from a tutor at your campus writing center. The guidelines in this section can be used by anyone reviewing an essay about a remembered event. (If

Critical Reading Guide

Making Comments Electronically

Most word processing software offers features that allow you to insert comments directly into the text of someone else's document. Many readers prefer to make their comments in this way because it tends to be faster than writing on a hard copy and space is virtually unlimited; from the writer's point of view, it also eliminates the problem of deciphering handwritten comments. Even where such special comment features are not available, simply typing comments directly into a document in a contrasting color can provide the same advantages.

For a printable version of this critical reading guide, go to bedfordstmartins.com/theguide.

you are unable to have someone read your draft, turn ahead to the Revising section, where you will find guidelines for reading your own draft critically.)

▶ **If You Are the Writer.**   To provide focused, helpful comments, your reader must know your essay's intended audience, your purpose, and a problem in the draft that you need help solving. Briefly write out this information at the top of your draft.

- *Readers:* Identify the intended readers of your essay.
- *Purpose:* What do you hope to achieve in writing this remembered-event essay? What features of your story do you hope will most interest readers? What do you want to disclose about yourself?
- *Problem:* Ask your reader to help you solve the single most important problem with your draft. Describe this problem briefly.

▶ **If You Are the Reader.**   Use the following guidelines to help you give critical comments to others on remembered-event essays.

1. *Read for a First Impression.*   Begin by reading the draft quickly, to enjoy the story and to get a sense of its significance. Then, in just a few sentences, describe your first impression. If you have any insights about the meaning or importance of the event, share your thoughts.

    Next, consider the problem the writer identified, and respond briefly to that concern now. (If you find that the problem is covered by one of the other guidelines listed below, respond to it in more detail there if necessary.)

2. *Analyze the Effectiveness of the Storytelling.*   Review the story, looking at the way the suspense builds and resolves itself. Point to any places where the drama loses intensity — perhaps where the suspense slackens, where specific narrative action is sparse or action verbs are needed, where narrative transitions would help readers, or where dialogue could be added to dramatize people's interactions.

3. *Consider How Vividly the Places and People Are Described.*   Point to any descriptive details, similes, or metaphors that are especially effective. Note any places or people that need more specific description. Also indicate any descriptive details that seem unnecessary. Identify any quoted dialogue that might be summarized instead or any dialogue that does not seem relevant.

4. *Assess Whether the Autobiographical Significance Is Clear.*   Explain briefly what you think makes this event significant for the writer. Point out any places in the draft where the significance seems so overstated as to be sentimental or so understated as to be vague or unclear. If the event seems to lack significance, speculate about what you think the significance could be. Then point to one place in the draft where you think the significance could

be made clearer by telling the story more fully or dramatically or by stating the significance.

5. ***Assess the Use of Memorabilia.*** If the writer makes use of memorabilia, evaluate how successfully each item is used. How is it relevant? Does it seem integrated into the narrative or merely appended? Is it placed in the most appropriate location? Does it make a meaningful contribution to the essay?

6. ***Analyze the Effectiveness of the Organization.*** Consider the overall plan, perhaps by making a scratch outline. Pay special attention to temporal transitions and verb tenses so that you can identify any places where the order of the action is unclear. Also indicate any places where you think the description or background information interrupts the action. If you can, suggest other locations for this material.

   - Look at the beginning. If it does not arouse curiosity, point to language elsewhere in the essay that might serve as a better opening — for example, a bit of dialogue, a striking image, or a remembered feeling.

   - Look at the ending. Indicate whether the conflict in the story is too neatly resolved at the end, whether the writer has tagged on a moral, or whether the essay abruptly stops without really coming to a conclusion. If there is a problem with the ending, try to suggest an alternative ending, such as framing the story with a reference to something from the beginning or projecting into the future.

7. ***Give the Writer Your Final Thoughts.*** What is the draft's strongest part? What part is most in need of further work?

Revising

Now you have the opportunity to revise your essay. Your instructor or other students may have given you advice. You may have begun to realize that your draft requires not so much revising as rethinking. For example, you may recognize that the story you told is not the story you meant to tell. Or maybe you realize only now why the incident is important to you. Consequently, you may need to reshape your story radically or draft a new version of it, instead of working to improve the various parts of your first draft. Many students — and professional writers — find themselves in this situation. Often a writer produces a draft or two and gets advice on them from others and only then begins to see what might be achieved.

However, if instead you feel satisfied that your draft mostly achieves what you set out to do, you can focus on refining the various parts of it. Very likely you have thought of ways to improve your draft, and you may even have begun revising it. This section will help you get an overview of your draft and revise it accordingly.

Getting an Overview

Consider the draft as a whole, following these two steps:

1. *Reread.* If at all possible, put the draft aside for a day or two. When you do reread it, start by reconsidering your purpose. Then read the draft straight through, trying to see it as your intended readers will.

2. *Outline.* Make a quick scratch outline on paper, or use the headings and outline or summary functions of your word processor.

Planning for Revision. Resist the temptation to dive in and start changing your text until you have a comprehensive view of what needs to be done. Using your outline as a guide, move through the document, using the change-highlighting or commenting tools of your word processor to note comments received from others and problems you want to solve (or mark on a hard copy if you prefer).

Turn to pp. 40–41 to review the basic features.

Analyzing the Basic Features of Your Own Draft. Turn to the Critical Reading Guide on the preceding pages (pp. 53–55). Using this guide, reread the draft to identify problems you need to solve. Note the problems on your draft.

Studying Readers' Comments. Review all of the comments you have received from other readers and add to your notes any that you intend to act on. For each comment, refer to the draft to see what might have led the reader to make that particular point. Try to be objective about any criticism. Ideally, these comments will help you to see your draft as others see it (rather than as you hoped it would be) and to identify specific problems.

Working with Sources

Using references to time to keep readers oriented to the stages of the event

In the essays you will write in later chapters of this book, you will rely on interviews and observation and print or visual sources to support your explanations or arguments. In writing about a remembered event, however, you will rely almost entirely on your memory. From your memory, if you complete the invention work, will come several pages of notes; and these notes will stimulate your memory further and lead to further notes. As you draft and revise, still more memories may flood in and be incorporated in your essay.

Among these rich, varied mental and written sources are ones related to the setting and unfolding of an event in time. Some action that occurs at a particular time starts the event, and other actions follow in a sequence that you determine and that your readers will accept as representing what really happened. Consequently, readers expect you to keep them oriented to the story you tell by giving them frequent, explicit cues about time. Without these cues, readers may not know in which decade, year, or season the event occurred; whether it unfolded slowly or quickly; or in what sequence the various actions took place.

When experienced writers of autobiography use these cues, they nearly always place them at the beginnings of sentences (or main clauses), as Annie Dillard does in this sentence from *An American Childhood*:

> *On one weekday morning after Christmas,* six inches of new snow had just fallen. (paragraph 3)

Placing these two important times cues — day of the week and time of the year — at the beginning of a sentence may not seem noteworthy, but in fact time cues can usually be placed nearly anywhere in a sentence. Dillard might have written

> Six inches of new snow had just fallen *on one weekday morning after Christmas.*

> Or she could have written

> *After Christmas,* six inches of new snow had just fallen one weekday morning.

Why might Dillard decide to locate these time cues at the beginning of the sentence, as she does with nearly all the time cues in her essay? Why not begin the sentence with the subject or main idea, in this case *six inches of snow*? The answer is that experienced writers of autobiography give highest priority to keeping readers oriented to time, including the overall time frame of the remembered event as well as the order and the speed of each action in the sequence of actions that make it up. To do so, they can rely on words, phrases, or clauses:

> Slowly, . . . (Jean Brandt, paragraph 36)

> For a week or so . . . (Tobias Wolff, paragraph 5)

> A few seconds later, . . . (Jean Brandt, paragraph 3)

> As we drove away, . . . (Rick Bragg, paragraph 16)

As you draft and revise, look to locating your time cues at the beginnings of your sentences. It is easy to do, and your readers will be grateful.

Carrying Out Revisions

Having identified problems in your draft, you now need to figure out solutions and — most important — to carry them out. Basically, there are three ways to find solutions:

1. Review your invention and planning notes for material you can add to your draft.
2. Do additional invention writing to provide material you or your readers think is needed.
3. Look back at the readings in this chapter to see how other writers have solved similar problems.

The following suggestions, which are organized according to the basic features of remembered-event essays, will get you started solving some writing problems that are common in them.

A Well-Told Story

- *Is the climax difficult to identify?* Check to be sure your story has a climax. Perhaps it is the point when you get what you were striving for (Dillard), when you do what you were afraid you might do (Wolff), when something frightening happens (Bragg), or when you get caught (Brandt). If you cannot find a climax in your story or reconstruct your story so that it has one, then you may have a major problem. If this is the case, you should discuss with your instructor the possibility of starting over with another event.

- *Does the suspense slacken instead of building to the climax?* Try showing people moving or gesturing, adding narrative transitions to propel the action, or substituting quoted dialogue for summarized dialogue. Remember that writers of autobiography often use short sentences to summarize action and heighten suspense, as when Dillard writes "We couldn't miss" and "He didn't even close the car door."

A Vivid Presentation of Places and People

- *Do any places or people need more specific description?* Try naming objects and adding sensory details to help readers imagine what the objects look, feel, smell, taste, or sound like. For people, describe a physical feature or mannerism that shows the role the person plays in your story.

- *Does any dialogue seem irrelevant or poorly written?* Eliminate any unnecessary dialogue, or summarize quoted dialogue that has no distinctive language or dramatic purpose. Liven up quoted dialogue with faster repartee to make it more dramatic. Instead of introducing each comment with the dialogue cue "he said," describe the speaker's attitude or personality with phrases like "she gasped" or "he joked."

- *Do any descriptions weaken the dominant impression?* Omit extraneous details or reconsider the impression you want to make. Add similes and metaphors that strengthen the dominant impression you want your story to have.

- *Do readers question any visuals you used?* Might you move a visual to a more appropriate place or replace an ineffective visual with a more appropriate one? Could you make clear the relevance of a visual by mentioning it in your text?

An Indication of the Event's Significance

- *Are readers getting a different image of you from the one you want to create?* Look closely at the language you use to express your feelings and thoughts. If you project an aspect of yourself you did not intend to, reconsider what the story reveals about you. Ask yourself again why the event stands out in your memory. What do you want readers to know about you from reading this essay?

- *Are your remembered or current feelings and thoughts about the event coming across clearly and eloquently?* If not, look in your invention writing for more expressive language. If your writing seems too sentimental, try to express your feelings more directly and simply, or let yourself show ambivalence or uncertainty.

- *Do readers appreciate the event's uniqueness or special importance in your life?* If not, consider giving them more insight into your background or cultural heritage. Also consider whether they need to know what has happened since the event took place to appreciate why it is so memorable for you.

The Organization

- *Is the overall plan ineffective or the story hard to follow?* Look carefully at the way the action unfolds. Fill in any gaps. Eliminate unnecessary digressions. Add or clarify temporal transitions. Fix confusing verb tenses. Remember that writers of autobiography tend to place references to time at the beginnings of sentences — "*When a car came*, we all popped it one" — to keep readers on track as the story unfolds.

- *Does description or other information disrupt the flow of the narrative?* Try integrating this material by adding smoother transitions. Or consider removing the disruptive parts or placing them elsewhere.

- *Is the beginning weak?* See whether there is a better way to start. Review the draft and your notes for an image, a bit of dialogue, or a remembered feeling that might catch readers' attention or spark their curiosity.

- *Does the ending work?* If not, think about a better way to end — with a memorable image, perhaps, or a provocative assertion. Consider whether you can frame the essay by referring back to something in the beginning.

For a revision checklist, go to bedfordstmartins.com/theguide.

■ Editing and Proofreading

Now is the time to check your revised draft for errors in grammar, punctuation, and mechanics and to consider matters of style. Our research has identified several errors that occur often in essays about remembered events: missing commas after introductory elements, fused sentences, and misused past-perfect verbs. The following guidelines will help you check your essay for these common errors. This book's Web site also provides interactive online exercises to help you learn to identify and correct each of these errors; to access the exercises for a particular error, go to the URL listed in the margin next to that section of the guidelines.

Checking for Missing Commas after Introductory Elements.   Introductory elements in a sentence can be words, phrases, or clauses. A comma tells readers that the introductory information is ending and the main part of the sentence is about to begin. If there is no danger of misreading, you can omit the comma after single words or short phrases or clauses, but you will never be wrong to include the comma. Remembered-event essays require introductory elements, especially those showing time passing. The following sentences, taken from drafts written by college

A Note on Grammar and Spelling Checkers
These tools are good at catching certain types of errors, but currently there is no replacement for a good human proofreader. Grammar checkers in particular are extremely limited in what they can usually find, and often they only give you summary information that is not helpful if you do not already understand the rule in question. They are also prone to give faulty advice for fixing problems and to flag correct items as wrong. Spelling checkers cause fewer problems but cannot catch misspellings that are themselves words, such as *to* for *too*.

For practice, go to bedfordstmartins.com/theguide/exercisecentral and click on Commas after Introductory Elements.

students using this book, show several kinds of introductory sentence elements that should have a comma after them.

▶ Through the nine-day run of the play↑the acting just kept getting better and better.

▶ Knowing that the struggle was over↑I felt through my jacket to find tea bags and cookies the robber had taken from the kitchen.

▶ As I stepped out of the car↑I knew something was wrong.

Checking for Fused Sentences.   Fused sentences occur when two independent clauses are joined with no punctuation or connecting word between them. When you write about a remembered event, you try to re-create a scene. In so doing, you might write a fused sentence like this one:

Sleet glazed the windshield the wipers were frozen stuck.

There are several ways to edit fused sentences:

- Make the clauses separate sentences.

▶ Sleet glazed the windshield. ~~the~~ *The* wipers were frozen stuck.

- Join the two clauses with a comma and *and, but, or, nor, for, so,* or *yet.*

▶ Sleet glazed the windshield ↑*and* the wipers were frozen stuck.

- Join the two clauses with a semicolon.

▶ Sleet glazed the windshield↑the wipers were frozen stuck.

For practice, go to bedfordstmartins.com/theguide/exercisecentral and click on Fused Sentences.

- Rewrite the sentence, subordinating one clause.

▶ *As sleet* ~~Sleet~~ glazed the windshield↑the wipers *became* ~~were~~ frozen stuck.

Checking Your Use of the Past Perfect.   Verb tenses indicate the time an action takes place. As a writer, you will generally use the present tense for actions occurring at the time you are writing (we *see*), the past tense for actions completed in the past (we *saw*), and the future tense for actions that will occur in the future (we *will see*). When you write about a remembered event, you will often need to use various forms of the past tense: the past perfect to indicate an action that was completed at the time of another past action (she *had finished* her work when we saw her) and the past progressive to indicate a continuing action in the past (she *was finishing* her

For practice, go to bedfordstmartins.com/theguide/exercisecentral and click on The Past Perfect.

work). One common problem in writing about a remembered event is the failure to use the past perfect when it is needed. For example:

▶ I had three people in the car, something my father *had* told me not to do on several occasions.

In the following sentence, the meaning is not clear without the past perfect:

▶ Coach Kernow told me I ~~ran~~ *had run* faster than ever before.

A Common ESL Problem.   It is important to remember that the past perfect is formed with *had* followed by a past participle. Past participles usually end in *-ed*, *-d*, *-en*, *-n*, or *-t*: *worked, hoped, eaten, taken, bent.*

▶ Before Tania went to Moscow last year, she had not really ~~speak~~ *spoken* Russian.

For practice, go to bedfordstmartins.com/theguide/exercisecentral and click on A Common ESL Problem: Forming the Past Perfect.

A Writer at Work

■ From Invention to Draft to Revision

In this section, we look at the writing process that Jean Brandt follows in composing her essay, "Calling Home." You will see some of her invention writing and her complete first draft, which you can then compare to the final draft printed on pp. 19–21.

Invention

Brandt's invention work produced about nine pages, but it took her only two hours, spread out over four days, to complete. Here is a selection of her invention writings. She begins by choosing an event and then recalling specific sensory details of the scene and the other people involved. She writes two dialogues, one with her sister Sue and the other with her father. Following is the dialogue between her and her sister:

Re-Creating Conversations

SUE: Jean, why did you do it?

ME: I don't know. I guess I didn't want to wait in that long line. Sue, what am I going to tell Mom and Dad?

SUE: Don't worry about that yet, the detective might not really call the police.

ME: I can't believe I was stupid enough to take it.

SUE: I know. I've been there before. Now when he comes back, try crying and acting like you're really upset. Tell him how sorry you are and that it was the first time you ever stole something, but make sure you cry. It got me off the hook once.

ME: I don't think I can force myself to cry. I'm not really that upset. I don't think the shock's worn off. I'm more worried about Mom.

SUE: Who knows? Maybe she won't have to find out.

ME: God, I hope not. Hey, where's Louie and Grandma? Grandma doesn't know about this, does she?

SUE: No, I sort of told Lou what was going on so he's just taking Grandma around shopping.

ME: Isn't she wondering where we are?

SUE: I told him to tell her we would meet them in an hour.

ME: How am I ever going to face her? Mom and Dad might possibly understand or at least get over it, but Grandma? This is gonna kill her.

SUE: Don't worry about that right now. Here comes the detective. Now try to look like you're sorry. Try to cry.

This dialogue helps Brandt to recall an important conversation with her sister. Dialogues are an especially useful form of invention, for they enable writers to remember their feelings and thoughts.

Brandt writes this dialogue quickly, trying to capture the language of excited talk, keeping the exchanges brief. She includes a version of this dialogue in her first revision but excludes it from the final essay printed earlier in this chapter (pp. 19–21). The dialogue with her father does not appear in any of her drafts. Even though she eventually decides to feature other, completely different conversations, these invention dialogues enable her to evaluate how various conversations would work in her essay.

Next, Brandt makes her first attempt to bring the autobiographical significance of the event into focus. She explores her remembered as well as her current feelings and thoughts about the experience:

> Being arrested for shoplifting was significant because it changed some of my basic attitudes. Since that night I've never again considered stealing anything. This event would reveal how my attitude toward the law and other people has changed from disrespectful to very respectful.

Brandt begins by stating tentatively that the importance of the event was the lesson it taught her. Reading this statement might lead us to expect a moralistic story of how someone learned something the hard way. As we look at the subsequent invention activities and watch the draft develop, however, we will see how her focus shifts to her relations with other people.

Recalling Remembered Feelings and Thoughts

I was scared, humiliated, and confused. I was terrified when I realized what was happening. I can still see the manager and his badge and remember what I felt when I knew who he was. I just couldn't believe it. I didn't want to run. I felt there wasn't anything I could do--I was afraid, embarrassed, worried, mad that it happened. I didn't show my feelings at all. I tried to look very calm on the outside, but inside I was extremely nervous. The nervousness might have come through in my voice a little. I wanted the people around me to think I was tough and that I could handle the situation. I was really disappointed with myself. Getting arrested made me realize how wrong my actions were. I felt very ashamed. Afterward I had to talk to my father about it. I didn't say much of anything except that I was wrong and I was sorry. The immediate consequence was being taken to jail and then later having to call my parents and tell them what happened. I hated to call my parents. That was the hardest part. I remember how much I dreaded that. My mom was really hurt.

Brandt's exploration of her first reaction is quite successful. Naming specific feelings, she focuses on the difference between what she felt and how she acted. She remembers her humiliation at being arrested as well as the terrible moment when she had to tell her parents. As we will see, this concern with her parents' reaction, more than her own humiliation, becomes the focus of her remembered feelings and thoughts.

In exploring her first response to the event, Brandt writes quickly, jotting down memories as they come to mind. Next, she rereads this first exploration and attempts to state briefly what the incident really reveals about her:

I think it reveals that I was not a hard-core criminal. I was trying to live up to Robin Files's (supposedly my best girlfriend) expectations, even though I actually knew that what I was doing was wrong.

Stopping to focus her thoughts like this helps Brandt see the point of what she has just written in her longer pieces of exploratory writing. Specifically, it helps her connect diverse invention writings to her main concern: discovering the autobiographical significance of the event. She reflects on what her remembered feelings of the event reveal about the kind of person she was at the time: not a hard-core criminal. She identifies a friend, who will disappear from the writing after one brief mention. Next, she looks at her present perspective on the event.

Exploring Present Perspectives

At first I was ashamed to tell anyone that I had been arrested. It was as if I couldn't admit it myself. Now I'm glad it happened, because who knows where I'd be now if I hadn't been caught. I still don't tell many people about it. Never before have I written about it. I think my response was appropriate. If I'd broken down and cried, it wouldn't have helped me any, so it's better that I reacted calmly. My actions and responses show that I was trying to be tough. I thought that that was the way to gain respectability. If I were to get arrested now (of course it wouldn't be for shoplifting), I think I'd react the same way because it doesn't do any good to get emotional. My current feelings are ones of appreciation. I feel lucky because I was set straight early. Now I can look back on it and laugh, but at the same time know how serious it was. I am emotionally distant now because I can view the event objectively rather than subjectively. My feelings are settled now. I don't get upset thinking about it. I don't feel angry at the manager or the police. I think I was more upset about my parents than about what was happening to me. After the first part of it was over I mainly worried about what my parents would think.

By writing about her present perspective, Brandt reassures herself that she feels comfortable enough to write for class about this event. Having achieved a degree of emotional distance, she no longer feels humiliated, embarrassed, or angry. Reassessing her reaction at the time, she is obviously pleased to recall that she did not lose control and show her true feelings. Staying calm, not getting emotional, looking tough — these are the personal qualities Brandt wants others to see in her. Exploring her present perspective seems to have led to a new, respectable self-image she can proudly display to her readers:

> My present perspective shows that I'm a reasonable person. I can admit when I'm wrong and accept the punishment that was due me. I find that I can be concerned about others even when I'm in trouble.

Next, Brandt reflects on what she has written to express the meaning of the event for her.

Defining the Event's Autobiographical Significance

> The event was important because it entirely changed one aspect of my character. I will be disclosing that I was once a thief, and I think many of my readers will be able to identify with my story, even though they won't admit it.

After the first set of invention work, completed in about forty-five minutes on two separate days, Brandt is confident she has chosen an event with personal significance. She knows what she will be disclosing about herself and feels comfortable doing it. In her brief focusing statements, she begins by moralizing ("my attitude . . . changed") and blaming others ("Robin Files") but concludes by acknowledging what she did. She is now prepared to disclose it to readers ("I was once a thief"). Also, she thinks readers will like her story because she suspects many of them will recall doing something illegal and feeling guilty about it, even if they never got caught.

The First Draft

The day after completing the invention writing, Brandt reviews her invention and composes her first draft on a word processor. It takes her about an hour to write the draft, and she writes steadily without doing a lot of rearranging or correcting of obvious typos and grammatical errors. She knows this will not be her only draft.

Before you read Brandt's first draft, reread the final draft, "Calling Home," in the Readings section of this chapter (p. 19). Then, as you read the first draft, consider what part it plays in the total writing process.

1 It was two days before Christmas and my older sister and brother, my grandmother, and I were rushing around doing last-minute shopping. After going to a few stores we decided to go to Lakewood Center shopping mall. It was packed with other frantic shoppers like ourselves from one end to the other. The first store we went to (the first and last for me) was the General Store. The General Store is your typical gift shop. They mainly have the cutesy knick-knacks, posters, frames and that sort. The store is decorated to resemble an old-time western general store but the appearance doesn't quite come off.

2 We were all browsing around and I saw a basket of buttons so I went to see what the different ones were. One of the first ones I noticed was a Snoopy button. I'm not sure what it said on it, something funny I'm sure and besides I was in love with anything Snoopy when I was 13. I took it out of the basket and showed it to my sister and she said "Why don't you buy it?" I thought about it but the lines at the cashiers were outrageous and I didn't think it was worth it for a 75 cent item. Instead I figured just take it and I did. I thought I was so sly about it. I casually slipped it into my pocket and assumed I was home free since no one pounced on me. Everyone was ready to leave this shop so we made our way through the crowds to the entrance.

3 My grandmother and sister were ahead of my brother and I. They were almost to the entrance of May Co. and we were about 5 to 10 yards behind when I felt this tap on my shoulder. I turned around already terror struck, and this man was flashing some kind of badge in my face. It happened so fast I didn't know what was going on. Louie finally noticed I wasn't with him and came back for me. Jack explained I was being arrested for shoplifting and if my parents were here then Louie should go find them. Louie ran to get Susie and told her about it but kept it from Grandma. By the time Sue got back to the General Store I was in the back office and Jack was calling the police. I was a little scared but not really. It was sort of exciting. My sister was telling me to try and cry but I couldn't. About 20 minutes later two cops came and handcuffed me, led me through the mall outside to the police car. I was kind of embarrassed when they took me through the mall in front of all those people.

4 When they got me in the car they began questioning me, while driving me to the police station. Questions just to fill out the report--age, sex, address, color of eyes, etc.

Then when they were finished they began talking about Jack and what a nui- ⁵
sance he was. I gathered that Jack had every single person who shoplifted, no matter what their age, arrested. The police were getting really fed up with it because it
was a nuisance for them to have to come way out to the mall for something as petty
as that. To hear the police talk about my "crime" that way felt good because it was
like what I did wasn't really so bad. It made me feel a bit relieved. When we walked
into the station I remember the desk sergeant joking with the arresting officers
about "well we got another one of Jack's hardened criminals." Again, I felt my crime
lacked any seriousness at all. Next they handcuffed me to a table and questioned me
further and then I had to phone my mom. That was the worst. I never was so humiliated in my life. Hearing the disappointment in her voice was worse punishment
than the cops could ever give me.

Brandt's first draft establishes the main sequence of actions. About a third of it
is devoted to the store manager, an emphasis that disappears by the final draft. What
ends up having prominence in the final draft — Brandt's feelings about telling her
parents and her conversations with them — appears here only in a few lines at the
very end. But mentioning the interaction suggests its eventual importance, and we
are reminded of its prominence in Brandt's invention writing.

Brandt revises this first draft for another student to read critically. In this revised draft, she includes dialogues with her sister and with the police officers. She
also provides more information about her actions as she considered buying the
Snoopy button and then decided to steal it instead. She includes visual details of the
manager's office. This draft is not much different in emphasis from the first draft,
however, and still ends with a long section about the police officers and the station.
The parents are mentioned briefly only at the very end.

The reader tells Brandt how much he likes her story and admires her frankness.
However, he does not encourage her to develop the dramatic possibilities in calling
her parents and meeting them afterward. In fact, he encourages her to keep the dialogue with the police officers about the manager and to include what the manager
said to the police.

Brandt's final revision shows that she does not take her reader's advice. She reduces the role of the police officers, eliminating any dialogue with them. She greatly
expands the role of her parents: The last third of the essay is now focused on her remembered feelings about calling them and seeing them afterward. In terms of dramatic importance, the phone call home now equals the arrest. When we recall
Brandt's earliest invention writings, we can see that she was headed toward this conclusion all along, but she needed invention, a first draft with many changes and re-
finement, a critical reading, and about two weeks to get there.

As the student and rancher were working on the text of the local history project described earlier in this chapter (see p. 17), they considered visual and textual elements appropriate to writing about remembered events — including, for instance, photographs of the area — and quotations from the rancher's tape-recorded story.

Selecting Visuals

To begin, the student and rancher discussed what visuals might accompany the final written piece and how photographs could enhance the telling of the rancher's story. The student found old snow-day photographs from the local newspaper's archives, and the rancher selected a compelling photo of his wife standing on the roof of the family home after the storm. The student and the rancher also considered including a painting of an isolated homestead and an early snapshot that the rancher had taken of his house in 1941, but decided that the painting was too abstract for a newspaper story, and the snapshot did not capture the snowstorm itself, which was the focus of the newspaper's special supplement. For their final product, they narrowed their selections to pictures that gave readers the strongest basis for engaging with the rancher's story. They knew that their story would run in a newspaper printed in black and white, and thus they assessed whether the color photos they had would still be as compelling printed in black and white. They narrowed their selection to two black-and-white photos — the photo of his wife standing on the house, representing the adversity the family faced, and the family photo taken in the spring, to include on the second page of the story — both of which emphasized the key points they wanted readers to pull from the story — the importance of family in the face of adversity.

The Rocky Valley Times

Special Supplement, Volume XCII, Number 2   January 14, 2006

This Sunday marks the 68th anniversary of the legendary "Storm of the Century" that blitzed the Rocky Valley area with up to 8 feet of snow in just a few hours.

In this era of cell phones and fax machines, it's all too easy to forget the danger and difficulties the regions' widely scattered settlers faced at that time.

In this special 6-page supplement, we salute the resourceful individuals who "made it through" and helped to establish our community as we know it today. —The Editor

INSIDE
The General Store, 2
An Engineer's Tale, 2
Women Saved Lives, 2
Born During Storm, 3
Animals in Snowstorm, 4
Forecast Went Wrong, 5
Logger's Perspective, 5
Happen Today? 6

RANCHER REMEMBERS THE STORM OF THE CENTURY
By George Valentino

"It was only a few days, but it seemed like a lifetime."

Jim and Anne Austin were new to Rocky Valley, and when it became clear that a major blizzard was imminent, relatives urged the couple and their two young children to stay in town lest supplies become scarce. But Austin and Anne had lived off the land for years, and had weathered storms before.

Anne Austin standing on the roof of the Austin home after the 1938 snowstorm.

They felt safest returning to their ranch to tend their livestock. They were confident they had enough food, water, and candles at the ranch to carry them through any storm. Nothing in their past experience had prepared the couple, however, for the onslaught of what quickly came to be known as "the storm of the century." In a recent interview for the *Times*, Austin unfolded an inspiring tale of resourcefulness and courage in a desperate situation.

The date was January 1938. Young Jim Jr. was only two, and Mark was just a few months old. Austin remembered that, despite the frigid temperature, the children were happy and excited on the ride home from town as the first few flakes of snow started to fall—innocently enough, it seemed at first.

While Anne put the children to bed, Austin went about his usual evening chores. "Within the span of a few hours, the wind started to blow quite a bit harder," he recalls, "but the animals were calm and comfortable in their quarters. Anne and I retired for the night without suspicion about what was to come."

Anne checked on Mark "at about 2:45 in the morning," Austin recalls wryly," and when she came back down the hall, I knew something was wrong just from the look on her face. She said—and this is what I'll never forget—that Mark was crying because there were snowdrifts up to the windowsills." The snow was blocking the scant light from the moon, leaving the room in total darkness. SEE STORM, 4

Pulling Revealing Quotations

After reviewing the draft of their newspaper story and the two photographs they selected, the student and the rancher chose two quotes from the story to highlight. As they prepared their story, they reviewed other newspaper stories recollecting historical events, and noticed that newspapers often used compelling quotations in text boxes or as subheadings to grab readers' attention. They thus suggested to the editor of the newspaper special supplement two short passages that they thought would capture readers' attention and convey some of the story's drama: "It was only a few days, but it seemed like a lifetime" and "I knew I had to make a decision — to continue on through the storm, or to head back to the house. Either way, I was unsure of my fate." The idea was not to summarize the rancher's story in these quotations, but to emphasize to readers the significance of the event as well as to leave readers with a good understanding of the event as they finished reading the piece. The newspaper selected the first quotation as the story lead.

Thinking Critically About What You Have Learned

Now that you have worked extensively in autobiography — reading it, talking about it, writing it — take some time to reflect on what you have learned: What problems did you have while you were writing, and how did you solve them? How did reading about events in other people's lives help you write about a remembered event in your own life? Finally, you might stop to reflect on autobiography as a genre of writing: How does it influence the way you think about yourself and other people?

Reflecting on Your Writing

Write a page or so telling your instructor about a problem you encountered in writing your essay and how you solved it. Before you begin, gather all of your writing — invention and planning notes, outlines, drafts, critical comments, revision plans, and final revision. Review these materials as you complete this writing task.

1. ***Identify one problem you needed to solve as you wrote about a remembered event.*** Do not be concerned with grammar and punctuation; concentrate on problems unique to writing a story about your experience. For example: Did you puzzle over how to present a particular place or person? Was it difficult to structure the narrative so it held readers' interest? Did you find it hard (or uncomfortable) to convey the event's autobiographical significance?

2. ***Determine how you came to recognize the problem.*** When did you first discover it? What called it to your attention? Did you notice it yourself, or did another reader point it out? Can you now see hints of it in your invention writing, your planning notes, or an earlier draft? If so, where specifically?

3. ***Reflect on how you went about solving the problem.*** Did you work on a particular passage, cut or add details, or reorganize the essay? Did you reread one of the essays in the chapter to see how another writer handled similar material? Did you look back at the invention guidelines? Did you discuss the problem with another student, a tutor, or your instructor? If so, how did talking about it help, and how useful was the advice you got?

4. ***Write a brief explanation of the problem and your solution.*** Be as specific as possible in reconstructing your efforts. Quote from your invention notes or early drafts, from readers' comments, from your revision plan, and from your final revision to show the various changes your writing underwent as you worked to solve the problem. Taking the time now to think about how you recognized and solved a real writing problem will help you become more aware of what works and does not work, making you a more confident writer.

Reviewing What You Learned from Reading

Write a page or so explaining to your instructor how the readings in this chapter influenced your final draft. Your own essay about a remembered event has no doubt been influenced by the essays you have read in this chapter. These readings may have helped you decide which of your own experiences would seem significant to your readers, or they may have given you ideas about how to evoke a vivid sense of place or how to convey your feelings about the event.

Before you start writing, take some time to reflect on what you have learned from the four reading selections.

1. ***Reread the final revision of your essay; then review the selections you read before completing your own essay, looking for specific influences.*** If you were impressed, for example, with the way one of the readings described a place, used dialogue, dramatized the action, or conveyed autobiographical significance, look to see where you might have been striving for similar effects in your own essay. Look also for ideas you got from your reading: writing strategies you were inspired to try, specific details you were led to include, effects you sought to achieve.

2. ***Write a page or so explaining these influences.*** Did a single reading selection influence you, or were you influenced by several selections? Quote from the selections and your final revision to show how your essay was influenced by the other essays. If, in reviewing the selections, you have found another way to improve your own essay, indicate briefly what you would change and which of the selections inspired the change.

Considering the Social Dimensions of Essays about Remembered Events

Writing about events that have special significance for you can lead you to recognize personal strengths and weaknesses and to clarify your beliefs and values. At the same time, reading others' autobiographical writing can help forge connections between you and other people. Another person's life often reflects our own experience, enabling us to identify and empathize. Just as often, however, another person's life does not resemble ours, and we learn that people can have radically different experiences, even within the same society. Although reading about other people's lives may not completely bridge these differences, it can help us better understand one another and the circumstances affecting all of us. (Wolff's experience, for example, gives us insight into how the American myth of the cowboy has defined manliness partly in terms of guns and power.) Likewise, striving as writers to forge connections with other people is important, but so is respecting and acknowledging the differences.

These ideas about autobiographical writing lead to some basic questions about how we understand ourselves and our relationships with others.

Autobiography and Self-Discovery.

If autobiography leads to self-discovery, what do we mean by the "self"? Should we think of the self as our "true" essence or as the different roles we play in different situations?

If we accept the idea of an essential self, autobiographical writing helps us in the search to discover who we truly are. Given this idea of the self, we might see Tobias Wolff, for example, as searching to understand whether he is the kind of person who shoots squirrels or the kind of person who cries over dead animals. If, on the other hand, we accept the idea that the various roles we play are what create the self, then autobiographical writing allows us to reveal the many sides of our personalities. This view of the self assumes that we present different self-images to different people in different situations. Given this idea, we might see Wolff as presenting his sympathetic side to his mother but keeping his aggressive, "manly" side hidden from her.

1. *Consider how your remembered-event essay might be considered an exercise in self-discovery.* Planning and writing your essay, did you see yourself as discovering your true self or examining how you reacted in a particular situation? Do you think your essay reveals your single, essential, true self, or does it show only one aspect of the person you understand yourself to be?

2. *Write a page or so explaining your ideas about self-discovery and truth in remembered-event essays.* Connect your ideas to your own essay and to the readings in this chapter.

Ways of Interpreting Our Experience.

How might we interpret autobiography? Should we view it psychologically, in terms of personal feelings, relationships, conflicts, and desires, or more publicly, in terms of the social, political, and cultural conditions of our lives? You can understand these different perspectives by applying them to the selections in this chapter. Wolff's essay, for example, could be seen in psychological terms as the story of an adolescent boy trying to assert his manhood. Or it could be seen in political terms as a critique of power and war. Brandt's essay could be interpreted psychologically, either in terms of her childish desire to have what she wants when she wants it, or socially in terms of her relationship with her mother.

1. *Consider how you have generally interpreted other people's essays about remembered events.* Have you understood the essays primarily in personal, psychological terms? Or in social or possibly political terms? Or in some of both? When you read Annie Dillard's essay, for example, you may have wondered why she thought of the man who chased her as "sainted"? If you interpreted Dillard's essay in psychological terms, you may have thought that the man represented a father figure, or even a Christ figure, someone who would make great sacrifices to teach her an important lesson. If, on the other hand, you tended to interpret the essay in social terms, perhaps you noted that the young Dillard preferred to play with boys rather than with girls. Or you may have noticed a socioeconomic or ethnic bias in Dillard's distinction between the "polite blond" Fahey brothers who lived on her street and the boys who lived "across Reynolds," who she describes as *dark, furious, skinny,* and *knowing.* She makes the point that her parents "approved" of the polite boys, but she lets us imagine what they thought of the others.

2. *Reflect on whether you adopted a primarily psychological or primarily social perspective when you were writing about your own life.* How did you think about your experience? Did you see

yourself as being motivated more by personal needs or fears, or by external forces?

3. ***Write a page or two about whether you find yourself interpreting autobiography more psychologically or more socially.*** Neither is preferred over the other; they are simply quite different perspectives. Try to connect your ideas to readings in the chapter and to your experience writing your essay. What do you think we gain or lose by looking at experience in these different ways?

3

Writing Profiles

IN COLLEGE COURSES To fulfill an important requirement for an upper-division education course, a student who plans to teach sixth grade decides to study collaborative learning (CL), which is learning achieved by a group of three to five students who work together toward a common goal. The student's course reading includes theory and research about CL, and she wants to write about CL in action among students like the ones she hopes to teach. The student arranges to visit an elementary school class that is beginning an Internet project about immigration. On three separate visits, she observes a group of three students working together on the project and interviews them individually and as a group.

The student organizes her profile narratively, combining her observations over the course of three visits into the story of one typically erratic but ultimately productive group meeting. She begins by describing the classroom. Then she briefly describes each child and details the activities they engaged in together. She provides information about the project itself from what she has learned talking to the teacher and the students and quoting statements the students made to one another. She reports as a detached observer, standing back from the students' work and weaving her insights about collaborative learning into a narrative of a typical half-hour meeting. From her profile emerges the central idea that sixth graders' collaborative work is unlikely to succeed unless the students, along with their teacher, frequently reflect on what they are learning and how they can work together more productively.

IN THE COMMUNITY A reporter on the arts and culture staff of a city's newspaper profiles a local artist recently commissioned to paint a mural on a section of a high wall sheltering a section of the city's central park.

Having scheduled an appointment, he visits the artist's studio and talks with him about mural painting. The artist invites the reporter to spend the following day with a team of local art students and neighborhood volunteers working on the mural under his direction. Before he leaves, the reporter takes several digital images of the artist and the studio.

The next day when the reporter arrives at the mural site, the artist hands him a brush and a small can of pale blue paint and puts him to work alongside two volunteers who are already filling in a large section of sky in a high corner of the mural. This firsthand experience helps the reporter describe the process of mural painting from a participant-observer's point of view. He takes more digital images.

Later, writing about the mural and its creation for the Sunday arts section of the paper, the reporter organizes the profile around the main stages of this collaborative mural project, from conception to completion. As he describes each stage, he weaves in details about the artist, his helpers, and the mural itself, seeking to capture the civic spirit that pervades the entire project.

IN THE WORKPLACE For a company newsletter circulated monthly to all employees at the various offices of a large banking and investment corporation, a public-relations officer profiles a day in the life of the corporation's new chief operating officer (COO). He follows the COO from meeting to meeting at corporate headquarters, taking photographs and observing her interactions with others. Between meetings, he interviews her about her management philosophy and her plans for handling the challenges facing the corporation. With her permission, he records these brief interviews. Immediately after the interviews he listens and re-listens to the recordings, making notes about key ideas and themes and writing down questions to ask in a follow-up interview.

A day later, to his surprise, the COO invites the writer to visit her at home and meet her family. He stays for dinner, helps clear the table, and then watches the COO help her daughter with homework. He converses with her husband to get his perspective on the family and to learn about his new job at a nearby medical research center. He also takes more photographs.

The writer illustrates the completed profile with two images, one showing the COO engaged in an intense business meeting and the other showing her helping her daughter with homework. As he reports on some of the immediate operational and competitive challenges she anticipates for the corporation, he tries to convey the ease and confidence she shows throughout a typical day of her life.

Profiles tell about people, places, and activities. Some profile writers try to reveal the not-so-obvious workings of places or activities we consider familiar. Others introduce us to exotic places or people — peculiar hobbies, unusual places of business, bizarre personalities. In general, a profile describes a person, place, or activity the writer has observed closely. The profile writers in the scenarios that open this chapter describe young students involved in a complex learning activity, an artist and his helpers creating a public mural, and a high-ranking business executive expressing her views and going about her daily activities.

Whatever their subject, profile writers strive most of all to enable readers to imagine the person, place, or activity that is the focus of the profile. Writers succeed only through specific and vivid details: how the person dresses, gestures, and talks; what the place looks, sounds, and smells like; what the activity requires of those who participate in it. Not only must the details be vivid, but they also must help to convey a writer's perspective — some insight, idea, or interpretation — on the subject.

Because profiles share many features with essays about remembered events — such as description, narration, and dialogue — you may use many of the strategies learned in Chapter 2: Remembering Events when you write your profile. Yet the differences are significant. To write about a remembered event, you look inside for personal memories in order to write about yourself and your intimate experiences with other people. To write a profile, you look outside for fresh observations of an unfamiliar subject in order to understand it better. Yet both remembered event and profile require you to strive for understanding, to recognize significance or uniqueness, to gain a new perspective.

The scope of your profile may be large or small, depending on your subject. You could attend a single event such as a parade, dress rehearsal for a play, or city council meeting and write your observations of the place, people, and activities. Or you might conduct an interview with a person who has an unusual occupation and write a profile based on your interview notes. If you have the time to do more extensive research, you might write a more complete profile based on several visits to a place and interviews with various people there.

More immediately, reading profiles and writing your own will make you a more insightful consumer of profiles, a popular feature in many media: for example, think about how often you watch interviews on television or the Internet or read them in newspapers and magazines. Observing and interviewing and then writing your own profile will also give you confidence in observing, ordering, and reporting your own world. You will practice asking probing questions that produce revealing answers and discover that strangers will talk to you at length about their work and interests. You will learn how to get under the surface or go behind facades to better understand other people and your world. You may even learn some of the ways that businesses, institutions, and people are often not what they appear to be.

Imagine that you have been assigned to write a profile of a person, a place, or an activity on your campus, in your community, or at your workplace. Think of subjects that you would like to know more about. Your instructor may schedule this collaborative activity as a classroom discussion or ask you to conduct an online discussion in a chat room.

A Collaborative Activity: Practice Choosing a Profile Subject

Part 1. List three to five subjects you are curious about. Choose subjects you can imagine yourself visiting and learning more about. If possible, name a specific subject — a particular musician, day-care center, or local brewery. Consider interesting people (for example, store owners, distinguished teachers, accomplished campus or community musicians or sports figures, newspaper columnists, public defenders, CEOs, radio talk show hosts), places (for example, a college health center or student newspaper office, day-care center, botanical garden, community police department, zoo, senior citizen center, farmer's market, artist's studio, museum or sculpture garden, historic building, public transportation center, or garage), and businesses or activities (for example, a comic-book store, wrecking company, motorcycle dealer, commercial fishing boat, local brewery or winery, homeless shelter, building contractor, dance studio, private tutoring service, or dog kennel).

Now get together with two or three other students, and take turns reading your lists of subjects to one another. The other group members will tell you which item on your list they personally find most interesting and why they chose that item, and ask you any questions they have about it.

Part 2. After you have all read your lists and received responses, discuss these questions as a group:

- What surprised you most about group members' choices of interesting subjects from your list?
- If you were now choosing a subject from your list to write about, how would group members' comments and questions influence your choice?
- How might their comments and questions influence your approach to learning more about this subject?

Readings

BRIAN CABLE wrote the following selection when he was a first-year college student. Cable's profile of a mortuary combines both seriousness and humor. He lets readers know his feelings as he presents information about the mortuary and the people working there. As you read, notice how Cable manages to inform you about the business of a mortuary while taking you on a guided tour of the premises. Notice also how he expresses his lack of seriousness about a serious place, a place of death and grief.

The Last Stop

Brian Cable

Because Cable must help readers imagine his subject, he immediately provides **visual details**.

More than a few people avert their eyes as they walk past the dusty-pink building that houses the Goodbody Mortuaries. It looks a bit like a church — tall, with gothic arches and stained glass — and somewhat like an apartment complex — low, with many windows stamped out of red brick. 1

Cable provides an impression of his subject: **not what he expected**.

It wasn't at all what I had expected. I thought it would be more like Forest Lawn, serene with lush green lawns and meticulously groomed gardens, a place set apart from the hustle of day-to-day life. Here instead was an odd pink structure set in the middle of a business district. On top of the Goodbody Mortuaries sign was a large electric clock. "What the hell," I thought, "Mortuaries are concerned with time, too." 2

Occasional notes of humor, starting with the title, provide readers relief from a somber subject.

I was apprehensive as I climbed the stone steps to the entrance. I feared rejection or, worse, an invitation to come and stay. The door was massive, yet it swung open easily on well-oiled hinges. "Come in," said the sign. "We're always open." Inside was a cool and quiet reception room. Curtains were drawn against the outside glare, cutting the light down to a soft glow. 3

From here through paragraph 9, Cable **describes** Mr. Deaver: his stature, skin, hair, dress, personality, way of speaking, work space, and nervous tics.

I found the funeral director in the main lobby, adjacent to the reception room. Like most people, I had preconceptions about what an undertaker looked like. Mr. Deaver fulfilled my expectations entirely. Tall and thin, he even had beady eyes and a bony face. A low, slanted forehead gave way to a beaked nose. His skin, scrubbed of all color, contrasted sharply with his jet black hair. He was wearing a starched white shirt, gray pants, and black shoes. Indeed, he looked like death on two legs. 4

To fill out his presentation of Mr. Deaver, Cable **quotes** him extensively.

He proved an amiable sort, however, and was easy to talk to. As funeral director, Mr. Deaver ("Call me Howard") was responsible for a wide range of services. Goodbody Mortuaries, upon notification of someone's death, will remove the remains from the hospital or home. They then prepare the body for viewing, whereupon features distorted by illness or accident are restored to their natural condition. The body is embalmed and then placed in a casket selected by the family of the deceased. Services are held in one of three chapels at the mortuary, and afterward the casket is placed in a "visitation room," where family and friends can pay their last respects. Goodbody also makes arrangements for the purchase of a burial site and transports the body there for burial. 5

Cable begins providing **information about the mortuary business** from notes he made during this meeting with Mr. Deaver.

All this information Howard related in a well-practiced, professional manner. It was obvious he was used to explaining the specifics of his profession. We sat alone in the lobby. His desk was bone clean, no pencils or paper, nothing — just a telephone. He did all his paperwork at home; as it turned out, he and his wife lived right upstairs. The phone rang. As he listened, he bit his lips and squeezed his Adam's apple somewhat nervously. 6

"I think we'll be able to get him in by Friday. No, no, the family wants him cremated." 7

8   His tone was that of a broker conferring on the Dow Jones. Directly behind him was a sign announcing "Visa and Master Charge Welcome Here." It was tacked to the wall, right next to a crucifix.

9   "Some people have the idea that we are bereavement specialists, that we can handle the emotional problems which follow a death: Only a trained therapist can do that. We provide services for the dead, not counseling for the living."

10   Physical comfort was the one thing they did provide for the living. The lobby was modestly but comfortably furnished. There were several couches, in colors ranging from earth brown to pastel blue, and a coffee table in front of each one. On one table lay some magazines and a vase of flowers. Another supported an aquarium. Paintings of pastoral scenes hung on every wall. The lobby looked more or less like that of an old hotel. Nothing seemed to match, but it had a homey, lived-in look.

11   "The last time the Goodbodys decorated was in '59, I believe. It still makes people feel welcome."

12   And so "Goodbody" was not a name made up to attract customers but the owner's family name. The Goodbody family started the business way back in 1915. Today, they do over five hundred services a year.

13   "We're in *Ripley's Believe It or Not*, along with another funeral home whose owners' names are Baggit and Sackit," Howard told me, without cracking a smile.

14   I followed him through an arched doorway into a chapel that smelled musty and old. The only illumination came from sunlight filtered through a stained glass ceiling. Ahead of us lay a casket. I could see that it contained a man dressed in a black suit. Wooden benches ran on either side of an aisle that led to the body. I got no closer. From the red roses across the dead man's chest, it was apparent that services had already been held.

15   "It was a large service," remarked Howard. "Look at that casket — a beautiful work of craftsmanship."

16   I guess it was. Death may be the great leveler, but one's coffin quickly reestablishes one's status.

17   We passed into a bright, fluorescent-lit "display room." Inside were thirty coffins, lids open, patiently awaiting inspection. Like new cars on the showroom floor, they gleamed with high-gloss finishes.

18   "We have models for every price range."

19   Indeed, there was a wide variety. They came in all colors and various materials. Some were little more than cloth-covered cardboard boxes, others were made of wood, and a few were made of steel, copper, or bronze. Prices started at $400 and averaged about $1,800. Howard motioned toward the center of the room: "The top of the line."

20   This was a solid bronze casket, its seams electronically welded to resist corrosion. Moisture-proof and air-tight, it could be hermetically sealed off from all outside elements. Its handles were plated with 14-karat gold. The price: a cool $5,000.

Cable conveys a **perspective** on Goodbody Mortuaries: though it provides a highly personal service to grieving family members, it operates like a business.

Cable has been piling up **visual details** like these since the first paragraph — and will continue to do so.

Readers may infer by this point that Cable's plan for his profile is **narrative**: he tells the story of one visit from beginning to end.

With attention to caskets from here through paragraph 20, Cable reminds readers that a mortuary is a business.

The facts in this paragraph come from Cable's **Internet research**.

A proper funeral remains a measure of respect for the deceased. But it is expensive. In the United States the amount spent annually on funerals is about $2 billion. Among ceremonial expenditures, funerals are second only to weddings. As a result, practices are changing. Howard has been in this business for forty years. He remembers a time when everyone was buried. Nowadays, with burials costing $2,000 a shot, people often opt instead for cremation — as Howard put it, "a cheap, quick, and easy means of disposal." In some areas of the country, the cremation rate is now over 60 percent. Observing this trend, one might wonder whether burials are becoming obsolete. Do burials serve an important role in society? [21]

For Tim, Goodbody's licensed mortician, the answer is very definitely yes. Burials will remain in common practice, according to the slender embalmer with the disarming smile, because they allow family and friends to view the deceased. Painful as it may be, such an experience brings home the finality of death. "Something deep within us demands a confrontation with death," Tim explained. "A last look assures us that the person we loved is, indeed, gone forever." [22]

Cable provides **further details** about caskets.

Apparently, we also need to be assured that the body will be laid to rest in comfort and peace. The average casket, with its inner-spring mattress and pleated satin lining, is surprisingly roomy and luxurious. Perhaps such an air of comfort makes it easier for the family to give up their loved one. In addition, the burial site fixes the deceased in the survivors' memory, like a new address. Cremation provides none of these comforts. [23]

Cable **defines key terms** of the mortuary business: mortuary science and embalming fluid.

Tim started out as a clerk in a funeral home but then studied to become a mortician. "It was a profession I could live with," he told me with a sly grin. Mortuary science might be described as a cross between pre-med and cosmetology, with courses in anatomy and embalming as well as in restorative art. [24]

Tim let me see the preparation, or embalming, room, a white-walled chamber about the size of an operating room. Against the wall was a large sink with elbow taps and a draining board. In the center of the room stood a table with equipment for preparing the arterial embalming fluid, which consists primarily of formaldehyde, a preservative, and phenol, a disinfectant. This mixture sanitizes and also gives better color to the skin. Facial features can then be "set" to achieve a restful expression. Missing eyes, ears, and even noses can be replaced. [25]

I asked Tim if his job ever depressed him. He bridled at the question: "No, it doesn't depress me at all. I do what I can for people and take satisfaction in enabling relatives to see their loved ones as they were in life." He said that he felt people were becoming more aware of the public service his profession provides. Grade-school classes now visit funeral homes as often as they do police stations and museums. The mortician is no longer regarded as a minister of death. [26]

Cable approaches one other person before he leaves, reinforcing his **participant role** in the profile.

Before leaving, I wanted to see a body up close. I thought I could be indifferent after all I had seen and heard, but I wasn't sure. Cautiously, I reached out and touched the skin. It felt cold and firm, not unlike clay. As I walked out, I felt glad to have satisfied my curiosity about dead bodies, but all too happy to let someone else handle them. [27]

JOHN T. EDGE directs the Southern Foodways Symposium, which is part of the Center for the Study of Southern Culture at the University of Mississippi. He coordinates an annual conference on southern food. Food writer for the national magazine *Oxford American*, he has also written for *Cooking Light, Food & Wine, Gourmet*, and *Saveur* magazines. He has published several books, including *A Gracious Plenty: Recipes and Recollections from the American South* (1999); and *Southern Belly* (2000), a portrait of southern food told through profiles of people and places. Edge has also written a series of books on more specific food topics: *Fried Chicken* and *Apple Pie* (2000) were followed by *Hamburgers and Fries* (2005), and *Donuts* is promised.

This reading, including the photograph shown on p. 80, first appeared in a 1999 issue of *Oxford American* and was reprinted in 2000 in *Utne Reader*. Edge profiles an unusual manufacturing business, Farm Fresh Food Supplier, in a small Mississippi town. He introduces readers to its pickled meat products, which include pickled pig lips. Like many other profile writers, Edge participates in his subject, in his case not by joining in the activities undertaken at Farm Fresh but by attempting to eat a pig lip at Jesse's Place, a nearby "juke" bar. You will see that the reading begins and ends with this personal experience.

As you read, enjoy Edge's struggle to eat a pig lip, but notice also how much you are learning about this bar snack food as Edge details his discomfort in trying to eat it. Be equally attentive to the information he offers about the history and manufacturing of pig lips at Farm Fresh.

I'm Not Leaving Until I Eat This Thing

John T. Edge

It's just past 4:00 on a Thursday afternoon in June at Jesse's Place, a country juke 17 miles south of the Mississippi line and three miles west of Amite, Louisiana. The air conditioner hacks and spits forth torrents of Arctic air, but the heat of summer can't be kept at bay. It seeps around the splintered doorjambs and settles in, transforming the squat particleboard-plastered roadhouse into a sauna. Slowly, the dank barroom fills with grease-smeared mechanics from the truck stop up the road and farmers straight from the fields, the soles of their brogans thick with dirt clods. A few weary souls make their way over from the nearby sawmill. I sit alone at the bar, one empty bottle of Bud in front of me, a second in my hand. I drain the beer, order a third, and stare down at the pink juice spreading outward from a crumpled foil pouch and onto the bar.

I'm not leaving until I eat this thing, I tell myself.

Half a mile down the road, behind a fence coiled with razor wire, Lionel Dufour, proprietor of Farm Fresh Food Supplier, is loading up the last truck of the day, wheeling case after case of pickled pork offal out of his cinder-block processing plant and into a semitrailer bound for Hattiesburg, Mississippi.

His crew packed lips today. Yesterday, it was pickled sausage; the day before that, pig feet. Tomorrow, it's pickled pig lips again. Lionel has been on the job since

2:45 in the morning, when he came in to light the boilers. Damon Landry, chief cook and maintenance man, came in at 4:30. By 7:30, the production line was at full tilt: six women in white smocks and blue bouffant caps, slicing ragged white fat from the lips, tossing the good parts in glass jars, the bad parts in barrels bound for the rendering plant. Across the aisle, filled jars clatter by on a conveyor belt as a worker tops them off with a Kool-Aid-red slurry of hot sauce, vinegar, salt, and food coloring. Around the corner, the jars are capped, affixed with a label, and stored in pasteboard boxes to await shipping.

Unlike most offal — euphemistically called "variety meats" — lips belie their provenance. Brains, milky white and globular, look like brains. Feet, the ghosts of their cloven hoofs protruding, look like feet. Testicles look like, well, testicles. But lips are different. Loosed from the snout, trimmed of their fat, and dyed a preternatural pink, they look more like candy than like carrion.

At Farm Fresh, no swine root in an adjacent feedlot. No viscera-strewn killing floor lurks just out of sight, down a darkened hallway. These pigs died long ago at some Midwestern abattoir. By the time the lips arrive in Amite, they are, in essence, pig Popsicles, 50-pound blocks of offal and ice.

"Lips are all meat," Lionel told me earlier in the day. "No gristle, no bone, no nothing. They're bar food, hot and vinegary, great with a beer. Used to be the lips ended up in sausages, headcheese, those sorts of things. A lot of them still do."

Lionel, a 50-year-old father of three with quick, intelligent eyes set deep in a face the color of cordovan, is a veteran of nearly 40 years in the pickled pig lips business. "I started out with my daddy when I wasn't much more than 10," Lionel

5

6

7

8

told me, his shy smile framed by a coarse black mustache flecked with whispers of gray. "The meatpacking business he owned had gone broke back when I was 6, and he was peddling out of the back of his car, selling dried shrimp, napkins, straws, tubes of plastic cups, pig feet, pig lips, whatever the bar owners needed. He sold to black bars, white bars, sweet shops, snowball stands, you name it. We made the rounds together after I got out of school, sometimes staying out till two or three in the morning. I remember bringing my toy cars to this one joint and racing them around the floor with the bar owner's son while my daddy and his father did business."

For years after the demise of that first meatpacking company, the Dufour family sold someone else's product. "We used to buy lips from Dennis Di Salvo's company down in Belle Chasse," recalled Lionel. "As far as I can tell, his mother was the one who came up with the idea to pickle and pack lips back in the '50s, back when she was working for a company called Three Little Pigs over in Houma. But pretty soon, we were selling so many lips that we had to almost beg Di Salvo's for product. That's when we started cooking up our own," he told me, gesturing toward the cast-iron kettle that hangs from the rafters by the front door of the plant. "My daddy started cooking lips in that very pot."   9

Lionel now cooks lips in 11 retrofitted milk tanks, dull stainless-steel cauldrons shaped like oversized cradles. But little else has changed. Though Lionel's father has passed away, Farm Fresh remains a family-focused company. His wife, Kathy, keeps the books. His daughter, Dana, a button-cute college student who has won numerous beauty titles, takes to the road in the summer, selling lips to convenience stores and wholesalers. Soon, after he graduates from business school, Lionel's younger son, Matt, will take over operations at the plant. And his older son, a veterinarian, lent his name to one of Farm Fresh's top sellers, Jason's Pickled Pig Lips.   10

"We do our best to corner the market on lips," Lionel told me, his voice tinged with bravado. "Sometimes they're hard to get from the packing houses. You gotta kill a lot of pigs to get enough lips to keep us going. I've got new customers calling every day; it's all I can do to keep up with demand, but I bust my ass to keep up. I do what I can for my family — and for my customers.   11

"When my customers tell me something," he continued, "just like when my daddy told me something, I listen. If my customers wanted me to dye the lips green, I'd ask, 'What shade?' As it is, every few years we'll do some red and some blue for the Fourth of July. This year we did jars full of Mardi Gras lips — half purple, half gold," Lionel recalled with a chuckle. "I guess we'd had a few beers when we came up with that one."   12

Meanwhile, back at Jesse's Place, I finish my third Bud, order my fourth. *Now*, I tell myself, my courage bolstered by booze, *I'm ready to eat a lip*.   13

They may have looked like candy in the plant, but in the barroom they're carrion once again. I poke and prod the six-inch arc of pink flesh, peering up from my reverie just in time to catch the barkeep's wife, Audrey, staring straight at me. She fixes me with a look just this side of pity and asks, "You gonna eat that thing or make love to it?"   14

Her nephew, Jerry, sidles up to a bar stool on my left. "A lot of people like 'em with chips," he says with a nod toward the pink juice pooling on the bar in front of me. I offer to buy him a lip, and Audrey fishes one from a jar behind the counter, wraps it in tinfoil, and places the whole affair on a paper towel in front of him. 15

I take stock of my own cowardice, and, following Jerry's lead, reach for a bag of potato chips, tear open the top with my teeth, and toss the quivering hunk of hog flesh into the shiny interior of the bag, slick with grease and dusted with salt. Vinegar vapors tickle my nostrils. I stifle a gag that rolls from the back of my throat, swallow hard, and pray that the urge to vomit passes. 16

With a smash of my hand, the potato chips are reduced to a pulp, and I feel the cold lump of the lip beneath my fist. I clasp the bag shut and shake it hard in an effort to ensure chip coverage in all the nooks and crannies of the lip. The technique that Jerry uses — and I mimic — is not unlike that employed by home cooks mixing up a mess of Shake 'n Bake chicken. 17

I pull from the bag a coral crescent of meat now crusted with blond bits of potato chips. When I chomp down, the soft flesh dissolves between my teeth. It tastes like a flaccid cracklin', unmistakably porcine, and not altogether bad. The chips help, providing texture where there was none. Slowly, my brow unfurrows, my stomach ceases its fluttering. 18

Sensing my relief, Jerry leans over and peers into my bag. "Kind of look like Frosted Flakes, don't they?" he says, by way of describing the chips rapidly turning to mush in the pickling juice. I offer the bag to Jerry, order yet another beer, and turn to eye the pig feet floating in a murky jar by the cash register, their blunt tips bobbing up through a pasty white film. 19

Making Connections to Personal and Social Issues: Gaining Firsthand Experience

Undoubtedly, Edge believed that he should visit a place where Farm Fresh Food Supplier's most popular product is consumed. He went further, however: He decided to experience the product firsthand by handling, smelling, and tasting it. Except for his own squeamishness, nothing prevented him from gaining the firsthand experience he sought. Aside from experiences in family and personal relationships, think about times when you have sought to gain firsthand experience and either succeeded or failed. Perhaps you yearned to sing but never took lessons, challenged yourself to go beyond watching basketball or soccer on television and won a spot on a school team, dreamed of an internship at a certain workplace but never could find the time to arrange it, imagined visiting a natural or historic site you had only read about and found a way to do so, or thought about joining others to protest a social injustice but never took action.

Identify one longed-for personal experience you missed out on and one you achieved, and think about why you failed in one case and succeeded in the other. At the time, how ready and able were you to gain access to the experience? What part did your personal decisiveness and effort play? Did you feel timid or bold about seeking what you wanted? Did you try to be accommodating, or did you have to be challenging or even disruptive? What roles did other people play? Who supported you, and who attempted to silence or exclude you? With whom did you have to negotiate? How did your gender or age affect the outcome? How important was money or other resources?

With two or three other students, discuss your attempts to gain longed-for personal experience. Begin by telling each other about one experience, explaining briefly what drew you to it, what happened, how you felt about the outcome, and why you think you succeeded or failed. Then, as a group, discuss what your stories reveal about what motivates and helps young Americans and what frustrates them as they try to gain longed-for experiences that may open new opportunities to them.

Analyzing Writing Strategies

1. Edge focuses on one of Farm Fresh's products, pickled pig lips. He probably assumes that most of his readers have never seen a pickled pig lip, much less eaten one. Therefore, he **describes** this product carefully. To see how he does so, underline or highlight in paragraphs 4, 5, 7, 14, and 18 every detail of a pickled pig lip's appearance, size, texture or consistency, smell, and taste. If you have never seen a pickled pig lip, what more do you need to know to imagine what it looks like? Which details make a lip seem appealing to you? Which ones make it seem unappealing?

2. The scene in the bar begins in the first two paragraphs, then picks up again in paragraph 13 and continues to the end of the profile. In these paragraphs Edge **narrates** the story of his attempt to eat a pig lip. Three strategies dominate: reconstructed conversation or dialogue, narrative action, and suspense. Begin by putting brackets around the dialogue so that you can see it more clearly at a glance. Then underline the action, instances of people physically moving or gesturing. Finally, at the end of the essay write a few brief notes in the margin explaining how Edge creates suspense to keep you reading to learn whether he ever eats the pig lip.

3. To present their subjects, profile writers occasionally make use of a strategy that relies on a sentence structure known as an **absolute phrase**. To discover what absolute phrases contribute, underline these absolutes in Edge's profile: in paragraph 1, sentence 4, from "the soles" to the end of the sentence, and sentence 6, from "one empty bottle" to the end; in paragraph 8, sentence 2, from "his shy smile" to the end; and in paragraph 19, sentence 3, from "their blunt tips" to the end. Make notes in the margin about how the absolute phrase seems to be related to what comes before it in the sentence. Given that Edge's goal is to help readers imagine what he observes, what does each absolute contribute toward that goal? How are these four absolutes alike and different in what they add to their sentences?

Commentary: A Topical Plan

A profile may be presented **narratively**, as a sequence of events observed by the writer during an encounter with the place, person, or activity; or it may be presented **topically**, as a series of topics of information gathered by the writer about the person, place, or activity. Though Edge **frames** (begins and ends) his profile with the narrative or story about attempting to eat a pig lip, he presents the basic information about Farm Fresh Food Supplier topically.

The following scratch outline of Edge's profile shows at a glance the topics he chose and how they are sequenced:

> loading meat products on a truck (paragraph 3)
>
> an overview of the production process, with a focus on that day's pig lips (4)
>
> pig lips' peculiarity in not looking like where they come from on the pig (5)
>
> the origin of Farm Fresh's materials — shipped frozen from the Midwest (6)
>
> some characteristics of a pig lip (7)
>
> Lionel's introduction to marketing food products and services (8)
>
> Lionel's resurrection of the family meatpacking business (9)
>
> family involvement in the business (10)
>
> Lionel's marketing strategy (11)
>
> Lionel's relations with customers (12)

Reviewing his interview and observation notes taken while he was at Farm Fresh, Edge apparently decided to organize them not as a narrative in the order in which he took them but as topics sequenced to be most informative for readers. He begins with the finished product, with Lionel loading the truck for shipment. Then he outlines the production process and mentions the various products. From there, he identifies the source of the products and briefly describes a pig lip, his main interest. Then he offers a history of Farm Fresh and concludes with Lionel's approach to his business. When you plan your profile essay, you will have to decide whether to organize your first draft topically or chronologically.

Considering Topics for Your Own Essay

Consider writing about a place that serves, produces, or sells something unusual, perhaps something that, like Edge, you could try yourself for the purpose of further informing and engaging your readers. If such places do not come to mind, you could browse the Yellow Pages of your local phone directory. There are many possibilities: producer or packager of a special ethnic or regional food or a local café that serves it, licensed acupuncture clinic, caterer, novelty and toy balloon store, microbrewery, chain saw dealer, boat builder, talent agency, manufacturer of ornamental iron, bead store, nail salon, pet fish and aquarium supplier, detailing shop, tattoo parlor, scrap metal recycler, fly fishing shop, handwriting analyst, dog or cat sitting service, photo restorer, burglar alarm installer, Christmas tree farm, wedding specialist, reweaving specialist, wig salon. You need not evaluate the quality of the work provided at a place as part of your observational essay. Instead, keep the focus on informing readers about the service or product the place offers. Relating a personal experience with the service or product is a good idea but not a requirement for a successful essay.

JOHN McPHEE (b. 1931) lives in Princeton, New Jersey, where he occasionally teaches a writing workshop in the "literature of fact" at Princeton University. He is highly regarded as a writer of profiles, in which he integrates information from shrewd observations, masterful interviews, and thorough research into engaging, readable prose. Readers marvel at how clearly he explains such complex subjects as experimental aircraft or modern physics and how he reveals the complexities of such ordinary subjects as bears or oranges. Among his books are *Oranges* (1967); *The Control of Nature* (1989); *Assembling California* (1993); *Annals of the Former World* (1998), a four-volume explanation of the geology of North America, for which he was awarded the Pulitzer Prize; *The Founding Fish* (2002); and *Uncommon Carriers*. In a recent interview, McPhee spoke frankly about his struggles with writing: "When I start work on a piece, I start at a zero level of confidence. . . . I have a very mild form of writer's block that I have to break through each day. . . . [O]ver time I've learned to be alone and to work alone and to enjoy it."

As you read, notice how McPhee introduces pickpockets and their crimes, mentioning some and describing others at length. A sociologist would offer statistics on petty crimes in Brooklyn, New York. McPhee instead offers strikingly different individual criminals, describing different kinds of pickpocketing and other kinds of theft, all in a colorful outdoor farmers' market that attracts a wide range of Brooklyn residents. Notice from what single perspective he views all of this activity.

The New York Pickpocket Academy
John McPhee

Brooklyn, and the pickpocket in the burgundy jacket appears just before noon. Melissa Mousseau recognizes him much as if he were an old customer and points him out to Bob Lewis, who follows him from truck to truck. Aware of Lewis, he leaves the market. By two, he will have made another run. A woman with deep-auburn hair and pale, nervous hands clumsily attracts the attention of a customer whose large white purse she is rifling. Until a moment ago, the customer was occupied with the choosing of apples and peppers, but now she shouts out, "Hey, what are you doing? Your hand is in my purse. What are you doing?" The auburn-haired woman not only has her hand in the purse but most of her arm as well. She withdraws it, and with intense absorption begins to finger the peppers. "How much are the peppers? Mister, give me some of these!" she says, looking up at me with a gypsy's dark, starburst eyes. "Three pounds for a dollar," I tell her, with a swift glance around for Lewis or a cop. When I look back, the pickpocket is gone. Other

1

faces have filled in — people unconcernedly examining the fruit. The woman with the white purse has returned her attention to the apples. She merely seems annoyed. Lewis once sent word around from truck to truck that we should regularly announce in loud voices that pickpockets were present in the market, but none of the farmers complied. Hodgson shrugged and said, "Why distract the customers?" Possibly Fifty-ninth Street is the New York Pickpocket Academy. Half a dozen scores have been made there in a day. I once looked up and saw a well-dressed gentleman under a gray fedora being kicked and kicked again by a man in a green polo shirt. He kicked him in the calves. He kicked him in the thighs. He kicked him in the gluteal bulge. He kicked him from the middle of the market out to the edge, and he kicked him into the street. "Get your ass out of here!" shouted the booter, redundantly. Turning back toward the market, he addressed the curious. "Pickpocket," he explained. The dip did not press charges.

People switch shopping carts from time to time. They make off with a loaded one and leave an empty cart behind. Crime on such levels is a part of the background here, something in the urban air, so many parts per million. The condition is accepted with a resignation that approaches nonchalance. [2]

Most thievery is petty and is on the other side of the tables. As Rich describes it, "Brooklyn, Fifty-ninth Street, people rip off stuff everywhere. You just expect it. An old man comes along and puts a dozen eggs in a bag. Women choosing peaches steal one for every one they buy — a peach for me, a peach for you. What can you do? You stand there and watch. When they take too many, you complain. I watched a guy one day taking nectarines. He would put one in a plastic bag, then one in a pocket, then one in a pile on the ground. After he did that half a dozen times, he had me weigh the bag." [3]

"This isn't England," Barry Benepe informed us once, "and a lot of people are pretty dishonest." [4]

Now, in Brooklyn, a heavyset woman well past the middle of life is sobbing pitifully, flailing her arms in despair. She is sitting on a bench in the middle of the market. She is wearing a print dress, a wide-brimmed straw hat. Between sobs, she presents in a heavy Russian accent the reason for her distress. She was buying green beans from Don Keller, and when she was about to pay him she discovered that someone had opened her handbag — even while it was on her arm, she said — and had removed several books of food stamps, a telephone bill, and eighty dollars in cash. Lewis, in his daypack, stands over her and tells her he is sorry. He said, "This sort of thing will happen wherever there's a crowd." [5]

Another customer breaks in to scold Lewis, saying, "This is the biggest rip-off place in Brooklyn. Two of my friends were pick-pocketed here last week and I had to give them carfare home." [6]

Lewis puts a hand on his forehead and, after a pensive moment, says, "That was very kind of you." [7]

The Russian woman is shrieking now. Lewis attends her like a working dentist. "It's all right. It will be O.K. It may not be as bad as you think." He remarks that he would call the police if he thought there was something they could do. [8]

Jeffrey Mack, eight years old, has been listening to all this, and he now says, "I see a cop." 9

Jeffrey has an eye for cops that no one else seems to share. (A squad car came here for him one morning and took him off to face a truant officer. Seeing his fright, a Pacific Street prostitute got into the car and rode with him.) 10

"Where, Jeffrey?" 11

"There," Jeffrey lifts an arm and points. 12

"Where?" 13

"There." He points again — at trucks, farmers, a falafel man. 14

"I don't see a policeman," Lewis says to him. "If you see one, Jeffrey, go and get him." 15

Jeffrey goes, and comes back with an off-duty 78th Precinct cop who is wearing a white apron and has been selling fruits and vegetables in the market. The officer speaks sternly to the crying woman. "Your name?" 16

"Catherine Barta." 17

"Address?" 18

"Eighty-five Eastern Parkway." 19

Every Wednesday, she walks a mile or so to the Greenmarket. She has lived in Brooklyn close to half her life, the rest of it in the Ukraine. Heading back to his vegetables, the officer observes that there is nothing he can do. 20

Out from behind her tables comes Joan Benack, the baker, of Rocky Acres Farm, Milan, New York — a small woman with a high, thin voice. Leaving her tropical carrot bread, her zucchini bread, her anadama bread, her beer bread, she goes around with a borrowed hat collecting money from the farmers for Catherine Barta. Bills stuff that hat, size 7 — the money of Alvina Frey and John Labanowski and Cleather Slade and Rich Hodgson and Bob Engle, who has seen it come and go. He was a broker for Merrill Lynch before the stock market imploded, and now he is a blond-bearded farmer in a basketball shirt selling apples that he grows in Clintondale, New York. Don Keller offers a dozen eggs, and one by one the farmers come out from their trucks to fill Mrs. Barta's shopping cart with beans and zucchini, apples, eggplants, tomatoes, peppers, and corn. As a result, her wails and sobs grow louder. 21

A man who gave Rich Hodgson a ten-dollar bill for a ninety-five-cent box of brown eggs asks Rich to give the ten back after Rich has handed him nine dollars and five cents, explaining that he has smaller bills that he wants to exchange for a twenty. Rich hands him the ten. Into Rich's palm he counts out five ones, a five, and the ten for a twenty and goes away satisfied, as he has every reason to be, having conned Rich out of nine dollars, five cents, and a box of brown eggs. Rich smiles at his foolishness, shrugs, and sells some cheese. If cash were equanimity, he would never lose a cent. One day, a gang of kids began taking Don Keller's vegetables and throwing them at the Hodgson truck. Anders Thueson threw an apple at the kids, who then picked up rocks. Thueson reached into the back of the truck and came up with a machete. While Hodgson told him to put it away, pant legs went up, switchblades came into view. Part of the gang bombarded the truck with debris from a nearby roof. Any indication of panic might have been disastrous. Hodgson packed deliberately, and drove away. 22

Todd Jameson, who comes in with his brother Dan from Farmingdale, New Jersey, weighed some squash one day, and put it in a brown bag. He set the package down while he weighed something else. Then, reaching for the squash, he picked up an identical bag that happened to contain fifty dollars in rolled coins. He handed it to the customer who had asked for the squash. Too late, Todd discovered the mistake. A couple of hours later, though, the customer — "I'll never forget him as long as I live, the white hair, the glasses, the ruddy face" — came back. He said, "Hey, this isn't squash. I didn't ask for money, I asked for squash." Whenever that man comes to market, the Jamesons give him a bag full of food. "You see, where I come from, that would never, never happen," Todd explains. "If I made a mistake like that in Farmingdale, no one — no one — would come back with fifty dollars' worth of change." 23

Dusk comes down without further crime in Brooklyn, and the farmers are packing to go. John Labanowski — short, compact, with a beer in his hand — is expounding on his day. "The white people are educating the colored on the use of beet greens," he reports. "A colored woman was telling me today, 'Cut the tops off,' and a white woman spoke up and said, 'Hold it,' and told the colored woman, 'You're throwing the best part away.' They go on talking, and pretty soon the colored woman is saying, 'I'm seventy-three on Monday,' and the white says, 'I don't believe a word you say.' You want to know why I come in here? I come in here for fun. For profit, of course, but for relaxation, too. I like being here with these people. They say the city is a rat race, but they've got it backwards. The farm is what gets to be a rat race. You should come out and see what I —." He is interrupted by the reappearance in the market of Catherine Barta, who went home long ago and has now returned, her eyes hidden by her wide-brimmed hat, her shopping cart full beside her. On the kitchen table, at 85 Eastern Parkway, she found her telephone bill, her stamps, and her cash. She has come back to the farmers with their food and money. 24

Making Connections to Personal and Social Issues: Petty Crime

Petty crime occurs in every town, rural area, and city in the United States, just as it does at the Brooklyn Greenmarket. This category of crime takes its name from a word meaning small, trivial, or unimportant. It is rarely violent or immediately threatening to anyone; yet it can contribute to a sense of social or public insecurity. Petty crimes include pickpocketing, purse or handbag snatching, house or car break-ins, tire slashing or puncturing, shoplifting, vandalism, graffiti and other forms of defacing property, bumping or shoving, and verbal, sexual or racial harassment. Larceny, any theft of property without use of force, is legally considered a petty theft. Petty crimes may occur in any public space, including schools and college campuses. Most of them are never reported to the police.

Think of a time when you were a victim of a petty crime, observed one, or heard about one from a victim you knew or from the news. With two or three other students, take turns describing your experiences. If you were the victim, explain where you were, why you were there, who you were with, and what happened. Report your reaction and feelings at the time. If you observed a petty crime or heard about one, describe it. Then, together, discuss these questions about the social implications of petty crime. How has petty crime influenced your feelings about your community? Has it placed any constraints on your public activities? If so, what are they? Has it influenced your attitudes toward law enforcement? Some cities have tried to take a "zero tolerance" approach to petty crime in order to reduce citizens' feelings of insecurity in public. This strategy requires high-visibility police foot patrols. Do you think this strategy — or a car-based version of it — could work in your community? Would you be willing to pay the taxes to support a much more visible police presence in your community, perhaps doubling the number of police officers? Would you support a higher arrest rate for petty crimes even if prison and court costs would rise sharply?

Analyzing Writing Strategies

1. McPhee intends to entertain readers, but he also wishes to inform them. His information is primarily about one type of urban crime, petty theft. The activity at the market is so entertaining and diverting readers may overlook or underestimate on first reading the sheer quantity of **information** the essay offers them. For example, McPhee classifies the petty thefts he observed over the course of a day at the market, creating distinct categories of this kind of crime. With your pencil or highlighter in hand, reread paragraphs 1–3 and 22 and underline a phrase or sentence that best defines each separate kind of crime. Then list, name, and describe each crime in a phrase or two. Finally, write two or three sentences explaining what surprised you most in this information about these kinds of petty crimes.

2. In spite of the threat from pickpockets, the market seems a peaceful, even quiet place. In this context, a writer might report noise to dramatize key scenes, and that is what McPhee does. He mentions shouting (paragraph 1, twice), sobbing (paragraphs 5 and 21), shrieking (paragraph 8), and wailing (paragraph 21). Find and highlight or underline these words. Then write two or three sentences about how your imagining of these abrupt, loud noises within a relatively quiet scene influences your response to what is going on.

Commentary: A Narrative Plan

John McPhee profiles his subject primarily through telling stories about it, through narrative. His profile of petty crime at the Brooklyn market opens with three brief narratives relating attempts at thievery by the man in the burgundy jacket, the woman with the starburst eyes, and the man wearing the gray fedora. The longest narrative tells the story of the woman, Catherine Barta, who thought someone had stolen her food stamps and money but later discovered that she had left them at home. The resourceful eight-year-old Jeffrey Mack plays a role in this story. Reread this part of the Barta narrative, paragraphs 8–20. Notice the importance of dialogue. Only a brief amount of time passes, yet several characters are involved. People move and gesture. We get bits of background information about Barta and Mack. This brief narrative illustrates the complex interactions of quite different people at the market, none of them pickpockets.

Both John Edge and John McPhee begin and end their profiles with narratives, a common strategy in a genre where writers aim to entertain as much as inform. A profile writer, like a novelist or filmmaker, attempts to create a scene with action, showing individuals moving, talking, gesturing — with information about the subject woven into and around this activity.

Considering Topics for Your Own Essay

Public scenes crowded with people and action offer good material for profiles. Crowds also present problems for profile writers, however, mainly because of their size and scope: So many people are present and so much is happening at once that the observer may not be able to decide where to focus. Notice how McPhee solves this problem by remaining in one location, the stall where he is selling vegetables. The action takes place in one small area of a large outdoor market, focusing on only a few people and events.

You could likewise find such a focus for a profile in some large, crowded public place. Here are a few examples to start you thinking: a lifeguard station at the beach, one stall at a flea market, one car dealer at an auto show, a musician playing for donations in a subway station, one librarian at work in your college library, a coach supervising a team at a sporting event. In each of these situations, you would not limit your observations and information-gathering to one or two individuals but would also survey the larger scene and observe the individual's interactions with the various other people there.

Throughout his profile McPhee assumes the role of **detached observer**. He positions himself at the site where he makes his observations, and he is keenly aware of everything that is going on. He participates in that he helps the farmers sell vegetables from the stand where he is observing the market, but he never shifts the focus to himself, except briefly in the first paragraph when the pickpocket with the starburst eyes asks him the price of the peppers and he answers, "Three pounds for a dollar." When you visit a place to profile, you can often choose to remain detached or to participate. Or the kind of place you profile may determine whether it is at all possible for you to participate in the activity there. It may be too dangerous, for example.

AMANDA COYNE (b. 1966), an award-winning staff writer for the *Anchorage Press*, earned an MFA in nonfiction writing from the University of Iowa. She wrote "The Long Goodbye," her first piece of published writing, for a 1997 issue of *Harper's*, a monthly general-interest magazine covering politics, culture, and the arts. She is now writing a memoir and has read her essays on National Public Radio's popular program *All Things Considered.*

As Coyne explains in this essay, her observations are based on a visit to a minimum-security women's prison where her sister is incarcerated and where Coyne has visited her before. The sister had been imprisoned without the possibility of parole (opportunity for early release) for aiding a drug dealer.

As you read, pay particular attention to Coyne's focus on two inmates, Jennifer (her sister) and Stephanie, and their relationships with their young sons, whom they now see only on rare prison visits like the one described in this profile.

The Long Good-Bye: Mother's Day in Federal Prison
Amanda Coyne

You can spot the convict-moms here in the visiting room by the way they hold and touch their children and by the single flower that is perched in front of them — a rose, a tulip, a daffodil. Many of these mothers have untied the bow that attaches the flower to its silver-and-red cellophane wrapper and are using one of the many empty soda cans at hand as a vase. They sit proudly before their flower-in-a-Coke-can, amid Hershey bar wrappers, half-eaten Ding Dongs, and empty paper coffee cups. Occasionally, a mother will pick up her present and bring it to her nose when one of the bearers of the single flower — her child — asks if she likes it. And the mother will respond the way that mothers always have and always will respond when presented with a gift on this day. "Oh, I just love it. It's perfect. I'll put it in the middle of my Bible." Or, "I'll put it on my desk, right next to your school picture." And always: "It's the best one here." 1

But most of what is being smelled today is the children themselves. While the other adults are plunking coins into the vending machines, the mothers take deep whiffs from the backs of their children's necks, or kiss and smell the backs of their knees, or take off their shoes and tickle their feet and then pull them close to their noses. They hold them tight and take in their own second scent — the scent assuring them that these are still their children and that they still belong to them. 2

The visitors are allowed to bring in pockets full of coins, and today that Mother's Day flower, and I know from previous visits to my older sister here at the Federal Prison Camp for women in Pekin, Illinois, that there is always an aberrant urge to gather immediately around the vending machines. The sandwiches are stale, the coffee weak, the candy bars the ones we always pass up in a convenience store. But after we hand the children over to their mothers, we gravitate toward those machines. Like milling in the kitchen at a party. We all do it, and nobody knows why. Polite conversation ensues around the microwave while the popcorn is popping and the processed-chicken sandwiches are being heated. We ask one another where we are from, how long a drive we had. An occasional whistle through the teeth, a shake of the head. "My, my, long way from home, huh?" "Staying at the Super 8 right up the road. Not a bad place." "Stayed at the Econo 3

Lodge last time. Wasn't a good place at all." Never asking the questions we really want to ask: "What's she in for?" "How much time's she got left?" You never ask in the waiting room of a doctor's office either. Eventually, all of us — fathers, mothers, sisters, brothers, a few boyfriends, and very few husbands — return to the queen of the day, sitting at a fold-out table loaded with snacks, prepared for five or so hours of attempted normal conversation.

Most of the inmates are elaborately dressed, many in prison-crafted dresses and sweaters in bright blues and pinks. They wear meticulously applied makeup in corresponding hues, and their hair is replete with loops and curls — hair that only women with the time have the time for. Some of the better seamstresses have crocheted vests and purses to match their outfits. Although the world outside would never accuse these women of making haute-couture fashion statements, the fathers and the sons and the boyfriends and the very few husbands think they look beautiful, and they tell them so repeatedly. And I can imagine the hours spent preparing for this visit — hours of needles and hooks clicking over brightly colored yards of yarn. The hours of discussing, dissecting, and bragging about these visitors — especially the men. Hours spent in the other world behind the door where we're not allowed, sharing lipsticks and mascaras, and unraveling the occasional hair-tangled hot roller, and the brushing out and lifting and teasing . . . and the giggles that abruptly change into tears without warning — things that define any female-only world. Even, or especially, if that world is a female federal prison camp. 4

While my sister Jennifer is with her son in the playroom, an inmate's mother comes over to introduce herself to my younger sister, Charity, my brother, John, and me. She tells us about visiting her daughter in a higher-security prison before she was transferred here. The woman looks old and tired, and her shoulders sag under the weight of her recently acquired bitterness. 5

"Pit of fire," she says, shaking her head. "Like a pit of fire straight from hell. Never seen anything like it. Like something out of an old movie about prisons." Her voice is getting louder and she looks at each of us with pleading eyes. "My *daughter* was there. Don't even get me started on that place. Women die there." 6

John and Charity and I silently exchange glances. 7

"My daughter would come to the visiting room with a black eye and I'd think, 'All she did was sit in the car while her boyfriend ran into the house.' She didn't even touch the stuff. Never even handled it." 8

She continues to stare at us, each in turn. "Ten years. That boyfriend talked and he got three years. She didn't know anything. Had nothing to tell them. They gave her ten years. They called it conspiracy. Conspiracy? Aren't there real criminals out there?" She asks this with hands outstretched, waiting for an answer that none of us can give her. 9

The woman's daughter, the conspirator, is chasing her son through the maze of chairs and tables and through the other children. She's a twenty-four-year-old blonde, whom I'll call Stephanie, with Dorothy Hamill hair and matching dimples. 10

She looks like any girl you might see in any shopping mall in middle America. She catches her chocolate-brown son and tickles him, and they laugh and trip and fall together onto the floor and laugh harder.

Had it not been for that wait in the car, this scene would be taking place at home, in a duplex Stephanie would rent while trying to finish her two-year degree in dental hygiene or respiratory therapy at the local community college. The duplex would be spotless, with a blown-up picture of her and her son over the couch and ceramic unicorns and horses occupying the shelves of the entertainment center. She would make sure that her son went to school every day with stylishly floppy pants, scrubbed teeth, and a good breakfast in his belly. Because of their difference in skin color, there would be occasional tension — caused by the strange looks from strangers, teachers, other mothers, and the bullies on the playground, who would chant after they knocked him down, "Your Momma's white, your Momma's white." But if she were home, their weekends and evenings would be spent together transcending those looks and healing those bruises. Now, however, their time is spent eating visiting-room junk food and his school days are spent fighting the boys in the playground who chant, "Your Momma's in prison, your Momma's in prison."

He will be ten when his mother is released, the same age my nephew will be when his mother is let out. But Jennifer, my sister, was able to spend the first five years of Toby's life with him. Stephanie had Ellie after she was incarcerated. They let her hold him for eighteen hours, then sent her back to prison. She has done the "tour," and her son is a well-traveled six-year-old. He has spent weekends visiting his mother in prisons in Kentucky, Texas, Connecticut (the Pit of Fire), and now at last here, the camp — minimum security, Pekin, Illinois.

Ellie looks older than his age. But his shoulders do not droop like his grandmother's. On the contrary, his bitterness lifts them and his chin higher than a child's should be, and the childlike, wide-eyed curiosity has been replaced by defiance. You can see his emerging hostility as he and his mother play together. She tells him to pick up the toy that he threw, say, or to put the deck of cards away. His face turns sullen, but she persists. She takes him by the shoulders and looks him in the eye, and he uses one of his hands to swat at her. She grabs the hand and he swats with the other. Eventually, she pulls him toward her and smells the top of his head, and she picks up the cards or the toy herself. After all, it is Mother's Day and she sees him so rarely. But her acquiescence makes him angrier, and he stalks out of the playroom with his shoulders thrown back.

Toby, my brother and sister and I assure one another, will not have these resentments. He is better taken care of than most. He is living with relatives in Wisconsin. Good, solid, middle-class, churchgoing relatives. And when he visits us, his aunts and his uncle, we take him out for adventures where we walk down the alley of a city and pretend that we are being chased by the "bad guys." We buy him fast food, and his uncle, John, keeps him up well past his bedtime enthralling him with stories of the monkeys he met in India. A perfect mix, we try to convince one another. Until we take him to see his mother and on the drive back he asks the question that most confuses him, and no doubt all the other children who spend much of their lives in prison visiting rooms: "Is my Mommy a bad guy?" It is the question that most seriously disorders his five-year-old need to clearly separate right from wrong. And because our own need is perhaps just as great, it is the question that haunts us as well.

Now, however, the answer is relatively simple. In a few years, it won't be. In a few years we will have to explain mandatory minimums, and the war on drugs, and the murky conspiracy laws, and the enormous amount of money and time that federal agents pump into imprisoning low-level drug dealers and those who happen to be their friends and their lovers. In a few years he might have the reasoning skills to ask why so many armed robbers and rapists and child-molesters and, indeed, murderers are punished less severely than his mother. When he is older, we will somehow have to explain to him the difference between federal crimes, which don't allow for parole, and state crimes, which do. We will have to explain that his mother was taken from him for five years not because she was a drug dealer but because she made four phone calls for someone she loved.

But we also know it is vitally important that we explain all this without betraying our bitterness. We understand the danger of abstract anger, of being disillusioned with your country, and, most of all, we do not want him to inherit that legacy. We would still like him to be raised as we were, with the idea that we live in the best country in the world with the best legal system in the world — a legal system carefully designed to be immune to political mood swings and public hysteria; a system that promises to fit the punishment to the crime. We want him to be a good citizen. We want him to have absolute faith that he lives in a fair country, a country that watches over and protects its most vulnerable citizens: its women and children.

So for now we simply say, "Toby, your mother isn't bad, she just did a bad thing. Like when you put rocks in the lawn mower's gas tank. You weren't bad then, you just did a bad thing."

Once, after being given this weak explanation, he said, "I wish I could have done something really bad, like my Mommy. So I could go to prison too and be with her."

It's now 3:00. Visiting ends at 3:30. The kids are getting cranky, and the adults are both exhausted and wired from too many hours of conversation, too much coffee and candy. The fathers, mothers, sisters, brothers, and the few boyfriends, and the very few husbands are beginning to show signs of gathering the trash. The mothers of the infants are giving their heads one last whiff before tucking them and their paraphernalia into their respective carrying cases. The visitors meander toward the door, leaving the older children with their mothers for one last word. But the mothers never say what they want to say to their children. They say things like, "Do well in school," "Be nice to your sister," "Be good for Aunt Berry, or Grandma." They don't say, "I'm sorry I'm sorry I'm sorry. I love you more than anything else in the world and I think about you every minute and I worry about you with a pain that shoots straight to my heart, a pain so great I think I will just burst when I think of you alone, without me. I'm sorry."

We are standing in front of the double glass doors that lead to the outside world. My older sister holds her son, rocking him gently. They are both crying. We give her a look and she puts him down. Charity and I grasp each of his small hands, and the four of us walk through the doors. As we're walking out, my brother sings one of his banana songs to Toby. [20]

"Take me out to the — " and Toby yells out, "Banana store!" [21]

"Buy me some —" [22]

"Bananas!!" [23]

"I don't care if I ever come back. For it's root, root, root for the —" [24]

"Monkey team!" [25]

I turn back and see a line of women standing behind the glass wall. Some of them are crying, but many simply stare with dazed eyes. Stephanie is holding both of her son's hands in hers and speaking urgently to him. He is struggling, and his head is twisting violently back and forth. He frees one of his hands from her grasp, balls up his fist, and punches her in the face. Then he walks with purpose through the glass doors and out the exit. I look back at her. She is still in a crouched position. She stares, unblinking, through those doors. Her hands have left her face and are hanging on either side of her. I look away, but before I do, I see drops of blood drip from her nose, down her chin, and onto the shiny marble floor. [26]

Making Connections to Personal and Social Issues: Unfair Punishment

Recall a time when you believed you were unfairly punished for breaking some rule or guideline or neglecting to fulfill some obligation. (For this discussion, exclude the formal laws that local, state, and national courts adjudicate.) You understood that you had violated some rule or expectation, and you did not feel that you could challenge or question the reasonableness of that rule or expectation. Nevertheless, you were convinced that your punishment was too severe. Perhaps you broke a school regulation, violated a rule at work or on a sports team, or failed to meet a reasonable expectation of your parents or a friend. Perhaps you failed someone who trusted you and whose trust you valued. You did not question that you had done something wrong. You were even willing to admit it. Yet you deeply resented the punishment, even felt angry or bitter about it.

With two or three other students, take turns telling about your incidents of perceived unfair punishment. Be specific about what rule or expectation you violated and the punishment that followed. Then try to explain why you believed at the time that the punishment was unfair. With these incidents in mind, discuss where rules governing your behavior and other people's expectations of you come from. How are they sometimes negotiated or changed, especially if many people begin to see them as restrictive, limiting, or confining? What if they seem to you to serve other people's interests and not your own? How do punishments get attached to them, and how are these punishments reevaluated? (If you like, you can anchor your discussion of these broader social questions to the specific incident of unfair punishment you described.)

Analyzing Writing Strategies

1. Coyne conveys a lot of **information** about the **effects** of separation on both the mothers and the children. The most dramatic effects are revealed in Coyne's descriptions of interactions between Stephanie and her son Ellie on this one visit. In paragraphs 13 and 26, underline once the words that Coyne uses to present Ellie's hostile actions, and underline twice the words that present his mother's actions. Then write two or three sentences that summarize the effects on each of them of their seeing each other so rarely.

2. Coyne's plan for her profile is **narrative**; that is, she starts at the beginning of the day, relating interactions among the people visiting the prison and between the incarcerated mothers and their children, and stops at the end of the day when visiting time ends. Underline two or three phrases in paragraph 3 that indicate the visit is getting underway and underline some phrases in paragraphs 19 and 20 which signal that the visit is ending. Write a sentence or two about the appropriateness of this plan. (Keep in mind that Coyne could have informed readers about these visits by organizing topically, that is by presenting a series of insights and impressions from the many visits she reveals she has made.)

Commentary: Conveying a Perspective

Coyne makes a judgment about the fairness of the laws that sent these women to prison, but she does not state it explicitly like a thesis in an essay taking a position on a controversial issue. Instead, she implies it or **conveys a perspective** indirectly through the scenes, stories, interactions, and details of her profile. Rather than telling readers what to think about this issue, she shows them mothers and sons caught in a cycle of regret, bitterness, anxiety, blame, and self-blame. In paragraphs 5–10, Coyne cleverly uses the story Stephanie's mother tells to introduce the perspective she wishes to convey of her own sister's imprisonment without parole: The inmate's mother says, "I'd think, 'All she did was sit in the car while her boyfriend ran into the house'. . . . Ten years. That boyfriend talked and he got three years. . . . They called it conspiracy. Conspiracy? Aren't there real criminals out there?" In paragraph 11, Coyne imagines Stephanie and Ellie leading an ordinary life unlike that of their nightmarish separation. In paragraph 15, Coyne speculates about all that will have to be explained to Toby, her nephew, when he is older and how hard it will be for him to understand his mother's long, harsh punishment. Through these three episodes, Coyne clearly conveys her perspective that the punishment these women received for participating in selling or delivering drugs is too severe.

Considering Topics for Your Own Essay

In researching her profile, Coyne spends the day in the visitor's room of a prison where she can observe and talk to prisoners and visitors, both adults and children. She has the unusual advantage of having made many previous visits to this same prison's visitor's room, yet nearly all of the information presented in her profile comes from this one visit. You can gain the same advantages by profiling an activity occurring in a relatively small space and involving only a few people. You should visit the place three or four times, observing and talking to people on every visit, making notes in the process, and perhaps capturing a few digital images (though that is not a requirement, as the profiles in this chapter confirm.) You should probably plan to be a detached observer, but you may find an opportunity to participate in some way in order to learn more about the activity. Between visits you can review your notes and decide what else your readers would likely want you to learn about the place, the activities pursued, and the people there. Here are some manageable possibilities:

The waiting room of the student health service's clinic on your campus.

The desk or computer station of a campus librarian.

The equipment room used by participants in a large-team college sport (football, soccer, or track, for example) or music ensemble (band, orchestra) — a place where equipment may be stored, checked in and out, and repaired.

The practice sessions of a small-team college sport (fencing, tennis, wrestling, boxing, swimming).

The broadcast room of a campus radio station.

A production studio where film students are viewing, cutting, and assembling a film.

A research lab where a small group of students is collaborating on the same project.

Rehearsals of a small music ensemble on campus — jazz band, clarinet quartet, string quartet, brass choir, singing duet or trio.

Or you could profile the activities of a relatively small group of people who come together in another space in your community, such as a day-care center, the waiting area of a hospital emergency room, or a fishing pier.

Because you need to view the activity naïvely in order to understand what your readers who have never experienced it will want to know, you must not be a member of the group you profile. You want to portray the people, their tools and surroundings, their interactions, and their activities as an outsider, on the basis of what you can learn from your visits and perhaps a little background research. After your final visit, you will still have many unanswered questions; but that is the experience of all profile writers.

■ Purpose and Audience

A profile writer's primary purpose is to inform readers about the subject of the profile. Readers expect a profile to present information in an engaging way, however. Readers of profiles expect to be surprised by unusual subjects. If they read about a familiar subject, they expect it to be presented from an unusual perspective. When writing a profile, you will have an immediate advantage if your subject is a place, an activity, or a person that is likely to surprise and intrigue your readers. For example, John Edge, the writer of "I'm Not Leaving Until I Eat This Thing" (pp. 79–82) has the triple advantage of being able to describe an unusual snack food, a little-known production process, and a colorful bar in which he can try out the unusual snack. Even when your subject is familiar, however, you can still engage your readers by presenting it in a way they have never before considered. For example, in "The Last Stop" (pp. 76–78) Brian Cable describes a mortuary owner as an ordinary, efficient businessman and not a "bereavement specialist."

A profile writer has one further concern: to be sensitive to readers' knowledge of a subject. Since readers must imagine the subject profiled and understand the new information offered about it, the writer must carefully assess what readers are likely to know already. For a profile of a pig-products processor, the decisions of a writer whose readers have likely never seen a pickled pig lip or foot will be quite different from those of a writer whose readers occasionally hang out in jukes and other bars where pickled pig products are visible floating in a bottle of garish-colored vinegar. Given Edge's attention to detail, he is clearly writing for a general audience that has never before seen a pickled pig lip or foot, much less considered eating one.

Basic Features: Profiles

Description of People and Places

Successful profile writers master the strategies of description. The profiles in this chapter, for example, evoke all the senses: **sight** ("the pink juice pooling on the bar in front of me," Edge, paragraph 15; "switchblades came into view," McPhee, 22); **touch** ("slick with grease," Edge, paragraph 16; "the skin . . . felt cold and firm, not unlike clay," Cable, 27; "grasp each of his small hands," Coyne, 20); **smell** ("take in their own second scent," Coyne, paragraph 2); **taste** ("hot and vinegary," Edge, paragraph 7; "the sandwiches are stale, the coffee weak," Coyne, 3); **hearing** ("woman is shrieking now," McPhee, paragraph 8); and **physical sensation** ("a gag that rolls from the back of my throat," Edge, paragraph 16; "my stomach ceases its fluttering," Edge, 18; "the adults are both exhausted and wired" Coyne, 19). **Similes** ("Lewis attends her like a working dentist," McPhee, paragraph 8), and **metaphors** ("the air conditioner hacks and spits forth torrents of Arctic air," Edge, paragraph 1) appear occasionally.

Profile writers often describe people in graphic detail ("his shy smile framed by a coarse black mustache," Edge, paragraph 8; "beady eyes and a bony face," Cable, 4; "deep-auburn hair and pale, nervous hands" McPhee, paragraph 1). They show people moving and gesturing ("he bit his lips and squeezed his Adam's apple," Cable, 6; "I poke and prod the six-inch arc of pink flesh," Edge, 14). These writers also rely on dialogue to reveal character ("Look at that casket — a beautiful work of craftsmanship," Cable, 15; "You gonna eat that thing or make love to it?" Edge, 14; "Is my mommy a bad guy?" Coyne, 14).

Information about the Subject

Profile writers give much thought to how and where to introduce information to their readers. After all, readers expect to be informed — to learn something surprising or useful. To meet this expectation, profile writers' basic strategy is to interweave information with descriptions of the subject (as Cable does profiling a mortuary) and with narratives of events (as Edge does when he struggles to eat a pig lip). Throughout their profiles, writers make good use of several strategies relied on by all writers of explanation: classification, example or illustration, comparison and contrast, definition, process narration, and cause and effect.

Edge **classifies** information about Farm Fresh when, in one part of his profile, he divides information about the business into four categories: rebirth of the family business, family involvement, marketing strategies, and customer relations. McPhee gives many **examples** of pickpocketing. Coyne **contrasts** the desirability of candy bars from vending machines in the prison's visiting area and in convenience stores. Cable **defines** the terms "mortuary science" and "embalming fluid." Edge **narrates** the process of preparing and bottling pig lips and, after receiving instruction, of eating one. Edge presents the **causes** of Farm Fresh's failure as a business and of its rebirth, and he discloses frankly the effects of his attempts to eat a pig lip. Coyne emphasizes the **effects** of separation on incarcerated mothers and their children.

A Topical or Narrative Plan

Profile writers rely on two basic plans for reporting their observations: **topical**, with the information grouped into topics; and **narrative**, with the information interwoven with elements of a story. The profiles by Cable, McPhee, and Coyne are all organized narratively. In all three, the narrative is a story of a single visit to a place. For Cable, the visit is one of indeterminate length, probably two or three hours, to Goodbody Mortuaries. McPhee's and Coyne's visits last all or most of a day. (Some profile writers present the information they gathered from several visits as though it was learned in a single visit, as Coyne does in part.)

In the central segment of his profile of a southern pig-products producer, Edge organizes the information topically: He creates topics out of the many bits of information he gathers on the tour of Farm Fresh led by the owner, Lionel Dufour, and then sequences them in the profile in a way that he thinks will be most informative to readers. Yet Edge frames the information about Farm Fresh with a narrative of his attempts to eat one of its products, illustrating that a profile can be organized topically in some parts and narratively in others. Usually, however, one plan or the other predominates. Which plan you adopt will depend on your subject, the kinds of information you collect, and your assessment of what might be most engaging and informative for your readers.

A Role for the Writer

Profile writers must adopt a role or stance for themselves when they present their subjects. There are two basic options: **detached observer** and **participant observer**. McPhee is a detached observer of pickpockets and the swirl of activity at the outdoor market. In the central part of his profile, where he presents what he learned on his visit to Farm Fresh Food Supplier, Edge, too, is a detached observer. We can easily infer that he asked questions and made comments, but he decides not to report any of them; instead, he focuses unwaveringly on the equipment, canning process, workers, and Dufour family members. By contrast, Cable adopts a participant-observer role. Even before he enters the mortuary, he inserts himself personally into the profile, reflecting on death, expressing his disappointment in the appearance of the place, admitting his apprehension about entering, revealing his sense of humor. Readers know where he is at all times as his tour of the building

proceeds, and he seems as much a participant in the narrative of his visit as Deaver and Tim are. Before he leaves the mortuary, he touches a corpse to satisfy his curiosity. Both Edge and Coyne participate briefly — Edge when he tries to eat a pig's lip in the juke, Coyne when she takes her young nephew by the hand and tries to reassure him.

A Perspective on the Subject

Profile writers do not simply present their observations of a subject; they also offer insights into the person, place, or activity being profiled. They may convey a perspective on their subjects by stating it explicitly, by implying it through the descriptive details and other information they include, or both. Cable shares his realization that Americans seem to capitalize on death as a way of coping with it. McPhee seems resigned to the petty crime that he observes. Coyne is explicit in her judgment of the unreasonable hardships that federal sentencing rules create for prisoners' families. Edge's perspective on pig products is less explicit, but perhaps, as a specialist in southern cooking, he hopes to convey the impression that regional foods remain important to many of the people who live in a region. In small southern towns, bar patrons are not satisfied by peanuts, pretzels, and packaged cheese and crackers. They want a soft, pink, vinegary pig lip shaken in a bag of crushed potato chips.

Writing Profiles

Invention and Research

What is a person, place, or activity you are curious about and could interview or observe? A campus personality? A local hangout? An online community? Set up your interview or observation, take good notes, and do some thinking and writing about your subject. Then come up with a possible approach for presenting it to readers. . . . **See p. 103 for more.**

Planning and Drafting

As you look over what you have written about your subject so far, how can you describe it in an interesting, informative way? Should you present your profile as a narrative? Should you mention yourself? What perspective on the subject have you developed? Make a plan for your profile, and start drafting it. . . . **See p. 112 for more.**

Critical Reading Guide

What are your draft's strengths and weaknesses? Are there key aspects of your subject that seem vague? Does the profile seem to ramble, with no shape or point? Get a classmate, a friend, a writing tutor, or someone else to read and respond in detail to your essay, especially the parts you are most unsure of. . . . **See p. 117 for more.**

Revising

As you consider your essay again in light of your reader's comments, how can you improve it? Do you provide too little information about the subject? Too much? Is your own presence in the profile too prominent? Does the ending seem weak? Go through your draft systematically, making changes wherever necessary. . . . **See p. 119 for more.**

Editing and Proofreading

Have you checked for errors that are especially likely in profiles? For example, have you forgotten to include quotation marks around someone's exact words? Have you put commas and periods outside rather than inside closing quotation marks? Look for and correct these and any other errors. . . . **See p. 123 for more.**

■ The Writing Assignment

Write an essay about an intriguing person, place, or activity in your community. Observe your subject closely, and then present what you have learned in a way that both informs and engages readers.

To learn about using the *Guide* e-book for invention and drafting, go to bedfordstmartins.com/theguide.

■ Invention and Research

Preparing to write a profile involves several activities, such as finding a subject, exploring your preconceptions about it, planning your project, and posing some preliminary questions. Each step takes no more than a few minutes, yet together these activities will enable you to anticipate problems likely to arise in a complex project like a profile, to arrange and schedule your interviews wisely, and to take notes and gather materials in a productive way. There is much to learn about observing, interviewing, and writing about what you have learned, and these activities will support your learning.

Finding a Subject to Write About

When you choose a subject, you consider various possibilities, select a promising one, and check that particular subject's accessibility.

Listing Subjects.   *Make a list of subjects you want to consider for your profile.* Even if you already have a subject in mind, take a few minutes to consider some other possibilities. The more possibilities you consider, the more confident you can be about your choice. Do not overlook the subjects suggested by the Considering Topics for Your Own Essay activities following readings in this chapter. (Turn to pp. 84, 90, and 97.)

Before you list possible subjects, consider realistically the time you have available and the amount of observing and interviewing you will be able to accomplish. Whether you have a week to plan and write up one observational visit or interview or a month to develop a full profile will determine what kinds of subjects will be appropriate for you. Consult with your instructor if you need help defining the scope of your profile project.

Here we present some ideas you might use as *starting points* for a list of subjects. Try to extend your list to ten or twelve possibilities. You may decide to profile one of the subjects listed here. More likely, however, these lists of subjects will suggest to you a subject not listed here. Consider every subject you can think of, even unlikely ones. People like to read about the unusual.

People

- Anyone with an unusual or intriguing job or hobby — a private detective, bee-keeper, classic-car owner, or dog trainer
- A prominent local personality — a parent of the year, labor organizer, politician, consumer advocate, television or radio personality, or community activist
- A campus personality — a coach, distinguished teacher, or ombudsman
- Someone recently recognized for outstanding service or achievement — a volunteer, mentor, or therapist

Places

- A weight-reduction clinic, martial arts studio, body-building gym, or health spa
- A small-claims court, juvenile court, or consumer fraud office
- A used-car lot, old movie house, used-book store, antique shop, historic site, auction hall, flower or gun show, or farmers' or flea market
- A hospital emergency room, hospice, birthing center, or psychiatric unit
- A local diner; the oldest, biggest, or quickest restaurant in town; or a coffeehouse
- A campus radio station, computer center, agricultural research facility, student center, faculty club, museum, newspaper office, or health center
- A book, newspaper, or Internet publisher; florist shop, nursery, or greenhouse; pawnshop; boatyard; or automobile restorer or wrecking yard
- A recycling center; fire station; airport control tower; theater, opera, or symphony office; refugee center; orphanage; or convent or monastery

Activities

- A citizens' volunteer program — a voter registration service, public television auction, meals-on-wheels project, tutoring program, or election campaign
- A sports event — a marathon, a Frisbee tournament, chess match, or wrestling or boxing meet
- The activities of a particular group of hobbyists — folk dancers, roller bladers, rock climbers, poetry readers, comic book collectors, investors, or car customizers

Listing Subjects Related to Identity and Community.   Writing a profile about a person or a place in your community can help you learn more about particular individuals in your community and about institutions and activities fundamental to community life. By *community* we mean both geographic communities, such as towns and neighborhoods, and institutional and temporary communities, such as religious congregations, college students majoring in the same subject, volunteer organizations, and sports teams. The following suggestions will enable you to list several possible subjects.

People

- Someone who has made or is currently making an important contribution to a community
- Someone who is a prominent member of one of the communities you belong to and can help you define and understand that community
- Someone in a community who is generally tolerated but is not liked or respected, such as a homeless person, a gruff store owner, an unorthodox church member, or someone who has been or is in danger of being shunned or exiled from a community
- Someone who has built a successful business, overcome a disability or setback, supported a worthy cause, served as a role model, or won respect from coworkers or neighbors

Places

- A facility that provides a needed service in a community, such as a legal advice bureau, child-care center, medical clinic, or shelter offering free meals
- A place where people of different ages, genders, ethnic groups, or some other attribute have formed a kind of ongoing community, such as a chess table in the park, political or social action headquarters, computer class, local coffeehouse, or barber or beauty shop
- A place where people come together because they are of the same age, gender, or ethnic group, such as a seniors-only housing complex, a boathouse for a men's crew team, a campus women's center, or an African American or Asian American student center

Activities

- A team practicing a sport or other activity (one you can observe as an outsider, not as a participant)
- A community improvement project, such as graffiti cleaning, tree planting, house repairing, church painting, or highway litter pickup
- A group of researchers working collaboratively on a project and meeting regularly so that you could meet with them more than one time before drafting your profile

Listing Subjects Related to Work and Career.   The following categories will help you consider work- and career-related subjects. Writing a profile on one of these possibilities can help you learn more about your attitudes toward your own work and career goals by examining how others do their work and pursue their careers.

People

- A college senior or graduate student in a major you are considering
- Someone working in the career you are thinking of pursuing
- Someone who trains people to do the kind of work you would like to do

Places

- A place on campus where students work part-time at some well-defined job — the library, computer center, cafeteria, bookstore, office, or tutoring or learning center
- A place where you could learn more about the kind of career you would like to pursue — a law office, medical center, veterinary hospital, research institute, television station, newspaper, school, software manufacturer, or engineering firm
- A place where people do a kind of work you would like to know more about — a clothing factory, coal mine, dairy farm, racetrack, restaurant, bakery, commercial fishing boat, gardening nursery, nursing home, or delicatessen
- A place where people are trained for a certain kind of work or career — a police academy, cosmetology program, video repair course, or truck drivers' school

Activities

- The actual activities performed by someone doing a kind of work represented on television, such as that of a police detective, judge, attorney, newspaper reporter, taxi driver, novelist, or emergency room doctor
- The activities involved in preparing for a particular kind of work, such as a boxer preparing for a fight, an attorney preparing for a trial, a teacher or professional preparing a course, an actor rehearsing a role, or a musician practicing a new piece for the first time

Choosing a Subject.   *Look over your list of possibilities, and choose a subject that you find you want to know more about and that your readers will find interesting.* Note, too, that most profile writers report the greatest satisfaction and the best results when they profile an *unfamiliar* person, place, or activity. If you choose a subject with which you are somewhat familiar, try to study it in an unfamiliar setting. For example, if you are a rock climber and decide to write a profile on rock climbing, do not rely exclusively on your own knowledge of and authority on the subject. Seek out other rock-climbing enthusiasts, even interview some critics of the sport to get another perspective, or visit a rock-climbing event or training class where you can observe without participating. By adopting an *outsider's perspective* on a familiar subject, you can make writing your profile a process of discovery for yourself as well as for your readers.

Stop now to focus your thoughts. *In a sentence or two, identify the subject you have chosen, and explain why you think it is a good choice for you and your readers.*

Checking on Accessibility. *Take steps to ensure that your subject will be accessible to you.* Having chosen a subject, you need to be certain you will be able to make observations and conduct interviews to learn more about it. Find out who might be able to give you information by making some preliminary phone calls. (Keep in mind your own deadline for completing the first draft of your profile.) Explain that you need information for a school research project. You will be surprised how helpful people can be when they have the time. If you are unable to contact knowledgeable people or get access to the place you need to observe, you may not be able to write on this subject. Therefore, try to make these initial contacts early.

Exploring Your Preconceptions

Explore your initial thoughts and feelings about your subject in writing before you begin observing or interviewing. Write for a few minutes about your thoughts, using the following questions as a guide:

What I already know about this subject

- How can I define or describe it?
- What are its chief qualities or parts?
- Do I associate anyone or anything with it?
- What is its purpose or function?
- How does it compare with other, similar subjects?

My attitude toward this subject

- Why do I consider it intriguing?
- What about it most interests me?
- Do I like it? Respect it?

My own and my classmates' expectations

(For now, consider your classmates your readers.)

- How do my preconceptions of this subject compare with my classmates'?
- What might be unique about my preconceptions?
- What attitudes about this subject do I share with my classmates?
- How is this subject represented in the media?
- What values and ideas are associated with subjects of this kind?

Testing Your Choice

Decide whether you should proceed with this particular subject. Giving up on a profile subject after the work you have completed already is bound to be frustrating, but if the subject does not seem a strong possibility for you to research and write about, starting over may be the wisest course of action. (The questions that follow and the collaborative activity following them may also help you decide whether to go on with this subject or begin looking for an alternative.)

Are you confident enough about your choice of subject? To make this decision, try to answer the following questions:

- After reviewing the possible subjects listed under the earlier section Finding a Subject to Write About, does any subject you overlooked before now grab your attention?

- Does reviewing the list confirm for you that you have likely made the best possible choice?

- If you have learned about the subjects other students in your class have chosen, do any of their choices suggest to you one you might like to change to?

Do you care enough about your choice of subject? You have already assessed what you may know now about your subject and how you feel about approaching it and learning about it. There have been no constraints on your choice, except those of time and access to the location of your profile subject. As a writer this gives you a huge advantage — choice and control — that can be very motivating. Even after your first visit to the place, you can change to a new subject if there seem to be too many constraints or uncertainties. Given these advantages, reflect on these questions:

- Do you feel curious about the subject?

- Are you eager to apply to this project what you have learned about the genre so far, taking inspiration from the published and student writers, and looking forward to presenting your subject to readers?

- Do you believe that you can fulfill your profile subjects' expectations that you will be serious and responsible, thorough and fair?

A Collaborative Activity:
Testing Your Choice

At this point, you will find it useful to get together with two or three other students and describe the subject you have chosen to profile. This collaborative activity will help you decide whether you have chosen a good subject to write about, one that will allow you to proceed confidently as you develop your profile.

Presenters: Take turns identifying your subjects. Explain your interest in the subject, and speculate about why you think it will interest readers.

Listeners: Briefly tell each presenter what you already know about his or her subject, if anything, and what might make it interesting to you.

Planning Your Project

Set up a tentative schedule for your observational and interview visits. Whatever the scope of your project — a single observation, an interview with one follow-up exchange, or multiple observations and interviews — you will want to get the most out of your time with your subject. Chapter 20 offers guidance in observing and interviewing and will give you an idea of how much time you will need to plan, carry out, and write up an observation or interview.

Take time now to consult Chapter 20. Figure out the amount of time you have to complete your essay, and then decide what visits you will need to make, whom you will need to interview, and what library or Internet research you might want to do, if any. Estimate the time necessary for each. You might use a chart like the following one:

Date	Time Needed	Purpose	Preparation
10/23	1 hour	Observe	Bring map, directions, paper
10/25	2 hours	Library research	Bring references, change or copy-card for copy machine
10/26	45 minutes	Interview	Read brochure and prepare questions
10/30	3 hours	Observe and interview	Confirm appointment; bring questions and extra pen

You will probably have to modify your plan once you actually begin work, but it is a good idea to keep some sort of schedule in writing.

If you are developing a full profile, your first goal is to get your bearings. Some writers begin by observing; others start with an interview. Many read up on the subject before doing anything else to get a sense of its main elements. You may also want to read about other subjects similar to the one you have chosen. Save your notes.

An Online Activity: Researching Your Profile Subject

One way to get a quick initial overview of the information available on the subject of your profile is to search for the subject online. Use Google (http://google.com) or Yahoo! Directory (http://dir.yahoo.com) to discover possible sources of information about the subject:

- For example, if you are profiling a beekeeper, you could get some useful background information to guide you in planning your interview by entering "bee keeping."

- If you are profiling a person, enter the full name to discover whether he or she has a personal Web site. If you are profiling a business or institution, the chances are even better that it offers a site. Either kind of site would orient and inform you prior to your interview or first visit.

Bookmark or keep a record of promising sites. After your interview with or visit to the subject, download any materials, including visuals, you might consider including in your own essay. If you find little or no information about your subject online, do not lose confidence in your choice. All of the information you need to develop your profile can come from your observations and interviews when you visit your subject.

Posing Some Preliminary Questions

Write questions to prepare for your first visit. Before beginning your observations and interviews, try writing some questions for which you would like to find answers. These questions will orient you and allow you to focus your visits. As you work, you will find answers to many of these questions. Add to this list as new questions occur to you, and delete any that come to seem irrelevant.

Each subject invites its own special questions, and every writer has particular concerns. Consider, for example, how one student prepares interview questions for her profile of a local office of the Women's Health Initiative, a nationwide fifteen-year study of women's health established by the National Institutes of Health in 1991. (Follow-up studies are planned through 2010.) After reading about the long-term studies in her local newspaper, the student calls the local WHI office to get further information. The administrator faxes her a fact sheet on the studies and her office's special part in them. The student knows that she will need to mention studies and findings in her profile of the local office and the people who work there. She also hopes to interview women who volunteered to participate in the research. Consequently, she devises the following questions to launch her research:

- Why has so little research been done until recently on women's health?
- How did the studies come about, and what is the role of the National Institutes of Health?
- Why do the studies focus only on women between the ages of fifty and eighty?
- Are women from all income levels involved?
- Why did it take fifteen years to complete the first studies?
- When was this office established, and what role does it play in the national studies?
- Does the office simply coordinate the studies, or does it also provide health and medical advice to women participating in the study?
- Who works at the office, and what are their qualifications to work there?
- Will I be able to interview women who volunteer to participate in the research?
- Will I be permitted to take photographs in the office?
- Would it be appropriate to take photographs of the researchers and participants, if they give their consent?

Discovering a Perspective

After you have completed your observations and interviews, write for a few minutes, reflecting on what you now think is interesting and meaningful about the person, place, or activity you have chosen for your profile. Consider how you would answer these questions about your subject:

- What visual or other sensory impression is most memorable?
- What does this impression tell me about the person, place, or activity?

- What mood do I associate with my subject?
- What about my subject is most striking and likely to surprise or interest my readers?
- What is the most important thing I have learned about my subject? Why is it important?
- If I could find out the answer to one more question about my subject, what would that question be? Why is this question important?
- What about my subject says something larger about our culture and times?
- Which of my ideas, interpretations, or judgments do I most want to share with readers?

Considering Your Own Role

Decide tentatively whether you will adopt a detached-observer or participant-observer role to present your profile. As a detached observer, you would focus solely on the place, people, and activities, keeping yourself invisible to readers. As a participant observer, you would insert yourself personally into the profile by reporting what you said or thought during interviews and commenting on the activities you observed.

Defining Your Purpose for Your Readers

Write a few sentences, defining your purpose in writing about this particular person, place, or activity for your readers. Use these questions to focus your thoughts:

- Who are my readers? Who would be interested in reading an essay about this particular subject? If I were to try to publish my essay, what kind of magazine, newspaper, newsletter, or Web site might want a profile on this particular subject?
- What do I want my readers to learn about the person, place, or activity from reading my essay?
- What insight can I offer my readers about the person, place, or activity?

Formulating a Tentative Thesis Statement

Review what you wrote for Discovering a Perspective (p. 110), and add another two or three sentences that will help you tell readers what you understand about the person, place, or activity on which you are focusing. Try to write sentences that extend your insights and interpretations and that do not simply summarize what you have already written.

Keep in mind that readers do not expect you to begin a profile essay with the kind of explicit thesis statement typical of argumentative essays. If you decide to spell out your perspective on the person, place, or activity, you can do so. You may, however, decide to convey your perspective through the ways you describe people and places, present dialogue, and narrate what you observed.

Designing Your Document

Think about whether visual or audio elements — photographs, postcards, menus, or snippets from films, television programs, or songs — would strengthen your profile. These are not at all a requirement of an effective profile, but they sometimes are helpful. Consider also whether your readers might benefit from design features such as headings, bulleted or numbered lists, or other typographic elements that can make an essay easier to follow.

For more information about including visuals in your work, see Chapter 25.

Think of the types of profiles you have seen — perhaps in a magazine or on a Web page or as a biography on a television show. Did the profile show, not just tell, you about the person, place, or activity? What visual or audio elements, if any, were used to create a strong sense of the person, place, or activity being profiled? Photographs? Postcards? Menus? Signs? Song lyrics?

As you review the questions on the next few pages, especially those in the "Setting Goals" section on pages 113–14, think about the ways in which you might show as well as tell readers about your object of study. Remember that you should cite the source of any visual or audio element you do not create yourself, and you should also request permission from the source if your essay is going to be posted on a Web site that is not password-protected.

■ Planning and Drafting

This section will help you review your invention writing and research notes and get started on your first draft.

Seeing What You Have

Read over your invention materials to see what you have. You probably have a great deal of material — notes from observational and interview visits or from library research, some idea of your preconceptions, a list of questions, and perhaps even some answers. You should also have a tentative perspective on the subject, some idea about it or insight into it. Your goals at this point are to digest all of the information you have gathered; to pick out the promising facts, details, anecdotes, and quotations; and to see how it all might come together to present your subject and your perspective on it to readers.

If you have done your invention writing on the computer, you may have sentences or whole paragraphs that can be copied and pasted into your draft. Whether your material is on screen or on paper, highlight key words, phrases, and sentences, and either make annotations in the margins or use your computer's annotating function.

As you sort through your material, try asking yourself the following questions to help clarify your focus and interpretation:

- How do my preconceptions of the subject contrast with my findings about it?
- Can I compare or contrast what different people say about my subject? Do I see any discrepancies between people's words and their behavior?

- How do my reactions compare with those of the people directly involved?
- How could I consider the place's appearance in light of the activity that occurs there?
- If I examine my subject as an anthropologist or archaeologist would, what evidence could explain its role in society at large?
- Could I use a visual or other graphic to complement the text?

Setting Goals

The following questions will help you establish goals for your first draft. Consider each question briefly now, and then return to them as necessary as you draft and revise.

Your Purpose and Readers

- Are my readers likely to be familiar with my subject? If not, what details do I need to provide to help them understand and visualize it?
- If my readers are familiar with my subject, how can I present it to them in a new and engaging way? What information do I have that is likely to be unfamiliar or entertaining to them?
- What design elements might make my writing more interesting or easier for readers to understand?

The Beginning

The opening is especially important in a profile. Because readers are unlikely to have any particular reason to read a profile, the writer must arouse their curiosity and interest. The best beginnings are surprising and specific; the worst are abstract. Here are some strategies you might consider:

- Should I open with a brief anecdote, as Edge does, action, as McPhee does, or on the street outside the place, as Cable does?
- Can I start with an amazing fact, anecdote, or question that would catch readers' attention?

Description of People and Places

- How might I give readers a strong visual image of people and places?
- Can I think of a simile or metaphor that would help me present an evocative image?
- Which bits of dialogue would convey information about my subject as well as a vivid impression of the speaker?
- What specific narrative actions can I include to show people moving and gesturing?

For more about specific narrative action, see Chapter 14.

Information about the Subject

- How can I fully satisfy readers' needs for information about my subject?
- How can I manage the flow of information so that readers do not lose interest?
- What special terms will I need to define for my readers?
- What comparisons or contrasts might make the information clearer and more memorable?

A Narrative or Topical Plan

Profile writers use two basic methods of organizing information, arranging it narratively like a story or topically by grouping related materials.

If You Use a Narrative Plan

- How can I make the narrative interesting, perhaps even dramatic?
- What information should I present through dialogue, and what information should I interrupt the narrative to present?
- How much space should I devote to describing people and places and to telling what happened during a visit?
- If I have the option of including images or other design elements, how might I use them effectively — to clarify the sequence of events, highlight a dramatic part of the narrative, or illustrate how the people and places in the profile changed over time?

If You Use a Topical Plan

- Which topics will best reflect the information I have gathered, inform my readers, and hold their interest?
- How can I sequence the topics to bring out significant comparisons or contrasts in the information I have?
- What transitions will help readers make connections between topics?
- If I have the option of including design elements, are there ways I can use them effectively to illustrate topics and reinforce the topical organization?

A Perspective on the Subject

- How can I convey a perspective on the subject that seems original or at least fresh?
- Should I state my perspective or leave readers to infer it from the details of my presentation?

The Ending

- Should I try to frame the essay by repeating an image or phrase from the beginning or by completing an action begun earlier in the profile?

- Would it be effective to end by stating or restating my perspective?
- Should I end with a telling image, anecdote, or bit of dialogue or with a provocative question or connection?

Outlining

If you plan to arrange your material *narratively*, plot the key events on a timeline. If you plan to arrange your material *topically*, you might use clustering or topic outlining to help you divide and group related information.

The following outline suggests one possible way to organize a *narrative profile* of a place:

Begin by describing the place from the outside.

Present background information.

Describe what you see as you enter.

Introduce the people and activities.

Tour the place, describing what you see as you move from one part to the next.

Fill in information wherever you can, and comment about the place or the people.

Conclude with reflections on what you have learned about the place.

Here is a suggested outline for a topical profile about a person:

Begin with a vivid image of the person in action.

Use dialogue to present the first topic. (A topic could be a characteristic of the person or one aspect of his or her work.)

Narrate an anecdote or a procedure to illustrate the first topic.

Present the second topic.

Describe something related to it.

Evaluate or interpret what you have observed.

Present the third topic, etc.

Conclude with a bit of action or dialogue.

All of the material for these hypothetical essays would come from observations, interviews, and background reading. The plan you choose should reflect the possibilities in your material as well as your purpose and readers. At this point, your decisions must be tentative. As you begin drafting, you will almost certainly discover new ways of organizing your material. Once you have written a first draft, you and others may see better ways to organize the material for your particular audience.

Drafting

General Advice.   Start drafting your essay, keeping in mind the goals you set while you were planning. As you write, try to describe your subject in a way that conveys your perspective on it. Turn off your grammar checker and spelling checker at this stage if you find them distracting. Don't be afraid to skip around in your draft. Jump back and fill in a spontaneous idea, or leap ahead and write a later section first if you find that easier. If you get stuck while drafting, explore the problem by using some of the writing activities in the Invention and Research section of this chapter (pp. 103–112).

As you read over your first draft, you may see places where you can add new material to reveal more about the person, place, or activity. You may even decide that after this first draft, you can finally understand the complexity of your subject and set out to convey it more fully in a second draft.

A Sentence Strategy: Absolute Phrases.   As you draft a profile, you will need to help your readers imagine the actions, people, and objects you have encountered. A grammatical structure called an **absolute phrase** is useful for this purpose. This structure adds meaning to a sentence but does not modify any particular word in the rest of the sentence. (You need not remember its name or the grammatical explanation for it to use the absolute phrase effectively in your writing.) Here is an example, with the absolute phrase in italics:

> I offer the bag to Jerry, order yet another beer, and turn to eye the pig feet floating in a murky jar by the cash register, *their blunt tips bobbing up through a pasty white film.* (John Edge, paragraph 19)

For more on using absolute phrases, go to bedfordstmartins.com/theguide and click on Sentence Strategies.

Edge could have presented his observation of the pickled pig feet in a separate sentence, but the sentence he wrote brings together his turning and looking and what he actually saw, emphasizing the at-a-glance instant of another possible stomach flutter. Absolute phrases nearly always are attached to the end of a main clause, adding various kinds of details to it to create a more complex, informative sentence. They are usually introduced by a noun or a possessive pronoun like *his* or *their*. Here are three further examples of absolute phrases from this chapter's readings:

> This was a solid bronze casket, *its seams electronically welded to resist corrosion.* (Brian Cable, paragraph 20)

> Inside were thirty coffins, *lids open,* patiently awaiting inspection. (Cable, paragraph 17)

> He is interrupted by the reappearance in the market of Catherine Barta, who went home long ago and has now returned, *her eyes hidden by her wide-brimmed hat, her shopping cart full beside her.* (John McPhee, paragraph 24)

Absolute phrases are certainly not required for a successful profile — experienced writers use them only occasionally — yet they do offer writers an effective sentence option. Try them out in your own writing.

In addition to using absolute phrases, you can strengthen your profile with other kinds of sentences as well, and you may want to review the discussions of short sentences (p. 53) and sentences that place references to time at the beginning (pp. 56–57).

Now is the time to get a close reading of your draft. Writers usually find it help-ful to have someone else read and comment on their drafts, and all writers know how much they learn about writing when they read other writers' drafts. Your in-structor may schedule readings of drafts as part of your coursework — in class or online. If not, you can ask a classmate, friend, or family member to read your draft. You could also seek comments from a tutor at your campus writing center. The guidelines in this section can be used by anyone reviewing a profile. (If you are unable to have someone else read your draft, turn ahead to the Revising sec-tion on p. 121, where you will find guidelines for analyzing and evaluating your own draft.)

Critical Reading Guide

▶ **If You Are the Writer.** To provide comments that are focused and helpful, your reader must know your essay's intended audience, your purpose, and a problem in the draft that you need help solving. Briefly write out this information at the top of your draft.

- *Readers:* Identify the intended readers of your essay.
- *Purpose:* What do you hope your readers will see and learn about your subject?
- *Problem:* Ask your draft reader to help you solve the most important prob-lem you see with your draft. Describe this problem briefly.

▶ **If You Are the Draft Reader.** The following guidelines can be useful for approach-ing a draft with a well-focused, questioning eye.

1. *Read for a First Impression.* Begin by reading the draft straight through to get a general impression. Read for enjoyment, ignoring spelling, punctuation, and other kinds of errors for now. Try to imagine the subject and to understand the perspective that the profile offers on its subject.

   When you have finished this first quick reading, write a few sentences about your overall impression. State the profile's perspective on its subject or main insight into it, as you best understand it. Next, consider the problem the writer identified, and respond briefly to that concern now. (If you find that the problem is covered by one of the other guidelines listed below, re-spond to it in more detail there if necessary.)

2. *Analyze the Effectiveness of the Organization.* Consider the overall plan, perhaps by making a scratch outline. Keep in mind that the plan may be nar-rative or topical or a combination of the two. If the plan narrates a visit (or visits) to a place, point out passages where the narrative slows unnecessarily or shows gaps. Point out where time markers and transitions would help. Let the writer know whether the narrative arouses and holds your curiosity. Where does dialogue fall flat, and where does it convey immediacy and valu-able information? If the plan is organized topically, note whether the writer

Making Comments Electronically
Most word processing software offers features that allow you to insert com-ments directly into the text of someone else's document. Many readers prefer to make their comments in this way because it tends to be faster than writing on a hard copy and space is virtually unlimited; from the writer's point of view, it also elimi-nates the problem of deci-phering handwritten comments. Even where such special comment fea-tures are not available, sim-ply typing comments directly into a document in a con-trasting color can provide the same advantages.

For a printable version of this critical reading guide, go to bedfordstmartins.com/ theguide.

presents too much or too little information for a topic and whether topics might be sequenced differently or connected more clearly. Finally, decide whether the writer might strengthen the profile by reordering any of the parts or the details.

- *Look again at the beginning* of the essay to see whether it captures your attention. If not, is there a quotation, a fact, or an anecdote elsewhere in the draft that might make a better opening?

- *Look again at the ending* to see whether it leaves you hanging, seems too abrupt, or oversimplifies the subject. If it does, suggest another way of ending, possibly by moving a part or a quotation from elsewhere in the essay.

- *Look again at any visuals.* Tell the writer how well the visuals — headings, lists, tables, photographs, drawings, video — are integrated into the profile. Advise the writer about any visuals that seem misplaced or unnecessary.

3. *Evaluate the Writer's Role.*   Decide whether the writer has adopted the participant-observer or detached-observer role or a combination of the two roles to present the profile subject. The writer has likely chosen one role or the other, but if both roles are visibly present, evaluate whether the writer really needs both roles or whether the alternation between the two is too frequent or confusing in any way. If the writer remains throughout in a participant-observer role, look for places where the writer is perhaps too prominent, dominating rather than featuring the subject. Point out where the writer-participant is most appealing and informative and also, perhaps, most distracting and tiresome. If the writer remains throughout in the detached-observer role, notice whether the writer consistently directs you where and how to look at the subject, keeping you confidently moving through the profile.

4. *Analyze the Description of People and Places.*   Begin by pointing out two or three places in the profile where the description of people, places, and activities or processes is most vivid for you, where your attention is held and you can readily imagine who or what is being described. Identify places where you would like more descriptive details. Also indicate where you need to see people in action — moving, talking, gesturing — to understand what is going on.

5. *Assess the Quality and Presentation of the Information about the Subject.* Show the writer where you learned something truly interesting, surprising, or useful. Point out where the information is too complex, coming at you too quickly, or incomplete. Ask for definitions of words you do not understand or clarification of definitions that do not seem immediately clear. Ask for a fuller description of any activity or process you cannot readily

understand. Assess the clarity and informativeness of all visuals and design features. If there are parts of the information about the subject that you think could be better presented or complemented by visuals, let the writer know. Show the writer where the interweaving of description and information seems out of balance — too much of one or the other for too long.

6. ***Question the Writer's Perspective on the Subject.*** Begin by trying to state briefly what you believe to be the writer's perspective on the subject — some idea or insight the writer wants to convey. (This perspective statement may differ from the one you wrote at the beginning of your critical reading of this draft.) Then look for and underline one or two places where the writer explicitly states or implies a perspective. If the perspective is stated, tell the writer whether you fully understand or would welcome some elaboration. If the perspective is only implied, let the writer know whether you are content with the implication or whether you would prefer to have the perspective explicitly stated. With the writer's perspective in mind, skim the draft one last time looking for unneeded or extraneous description and information.

7. ***Give the Writer Your Final Thoughts.*** What is the draft's strongest part? What part is most memorable? What part is weakest or most in need of further work?

■ Revising

This section will help you get an overview of your draft and revise it accordingly.

Getting an Overview

Consider your draft as a whole, following these two steps:

1. ***Reread.*** If at all possible, put the draft aside for a day or two. When you do reread it, start by reconsidering your purpose. Then read the draft straight through, trying to see it as your intended readers will.

2. ***Outline.*** Make a quick scratch outline on paper, or use the headings and outline/summary functions of your word processor.

Planning for Revision. Resist the temptation to dive in and start changing your text until after you have a comprehensive view of what needs to be done. Using your outline as a guide, move through the document, using the change-highlighting or commenting tools of your word processor to note comments received from others and problems you want to solve (or mark on a hard copy if you prefer).

Analyzing the Basic Features of Your Own Draft.   Turn to the Critical Reading Guide on pp. 117–19. Using this guide, reread the draft to identify problems you need to solve. Note the problems on your draft.

Studying Readers' Comments.   Review all of the comments you have received from other readers. For each comment, look at the draft to determine what might have led the reader to make that particular point. Try to be open-minded about any criticism. Ideally, these comments will help you see your draft as others see it (rather than as you hoped it would be) and identify specific problems. Add to your notes any problems readers have identified.

Working with Sources

Integrating quotations from your interviews

In addition to describing people, your profile will also quote them. These quotations can be especially revealing because they let readers hear different people speaking for themselves, rather than being presented through your eyes. Nevertheless, it is the writer who decides which quotations to use and how. Therefore, one major task you face in drafting and revising your essay is to choose quotations from your notes, present them in a timely way to reveal the style and character of people you interviewed, and integrate these quotations smoothly into your sentences.

When you directly quote (rather than paraphrase or summarize) what someone has said, you will usually need to identify the speaker. The principal way to do so is to create what is called a **speaker tag**. You may rely on a *general* or all-purpose speaker tag, using the forms of *say* and *tell*:

For more help integrating quotations, go to bedfordstmartins.com/theguide and click on Bedford Research Room.

"I don't see a policeman," Lewis *says* to him. (John McPhee, paragraph 15)

"Three pounds for a dollar," I *tell* her. (John McPhee, paragraph 1)

Other speaker tags are more *specific* or precise:

"It was a large service," *remarked* Howard. (Brian Cable, paragraph 16)

"Something deep within us demands a confrontation with death," Tim *explained*. (Brian Cable, paragraph 22)

"Take me out to the" — and Toby *yells out*, "Banana store!" (Amanda Coyne, paragraph 21)

As you draft your profile, consider using specific speaker tags. They give readers more help with imagining speakers' attitudes and personal styles. Nevertheless, keep in mind that experienced writers rely on general speaker tags using forms of *say* and *tell* for most of their sentences with quotations.

In addition, you may add a word or phrase to any speaker tag to identify or describe the speaker or to reveal more about *how, where, when,* or *why* the speaker speaks:

"It was a profession I could live with," he told me *with a sly grin*. (Brian Cable, paragraph 24)

"We do our best to corner the market on lips," Lionel told me, *his voice tinged with bravado*. (John Edge, paragraph 11)

"A lot of people like 'em with chips," he says *with a nod toward the pink juice pooling on the bar in front of me*. (John Edge, paragraph 15)

"Kind of look like Frosted Flakes, don't they?" he says, *by way of describing the chips rapidly turning to mush in the pickling juice*. (John Edge, paragraph 19)

"How much are the peppers? Mister, give me some of these!" she says, *looking up at me with a gypsy's dark starburst eyes*. (John McPhee, paragraph 1)

In addition to being carefully introduced, quotations must be precisely punctuated, and fortunately there are only two general rules:

1. Enclose all quotations in quotation marks. These always come in pairs, one at the beginning, one at the end of the quotation. Be especially careful not to forget to include the one at the end.

2. Separate the quotation from its speaker tag with appropriate punctuation, usually a comma.

You can readily see how these rules apply by glancing over each of the examples in this section. In special situations other rules apply. For details, see the Editing and Proofreading section of this chapter on pp. 123–25 and the sections on quotations in Chapter 22, pp. 739–44.

Carrying Out Revisions

Having identified problems in your draft, you now need to figure out solutions and carry them out. Basically, you have three options for finding solutions:

1. Review your observation or interview notes for other information and ideas.

2. Do additional observations or interviews to answer questions that you or other readers raised.

3. Look back at the readings in this chapter to see how other writers have solved similar problems.

The following suggestions, which are organized according to the basic features of profiles, will get you started solving some problems common to this kind of writing.

A Description of People and Places

- **Can the description of the person who is the focus of the profile be improved?** Add details to help readers see the person. Think, for example, of McPhee's description of a distraught woman: "She is wearing a print dress, a wide-brimmed straw hat" (paragraph 5). Recall, for example, how Edge describes Lionel Dufour: "his shy smile framed by a coarse black mustache flecked with whispers of gray" (paragraph 8).

- *Should other people be described briefly?* Consider naming and detailing a few physical features of each person. Recall, for example, McPhee's description of a pickpocket: "A woman with deep-auburn hair and pale, nervous hands" (paragraph 1). Consider adding comparisons, as Cable does when he says Howard Deaver "looked like death on two legs" (paragraph 4). Also consider adding specific narrative action. Think of Deaver again, on the phone: "As he listened, he bit his lips and squeezed his Adam's apple" (paragraph 6).

- *Can you enliven the description of the place?* Add other senses to visual description. Recall, for example, these sensory descriptions from the readings: sound (the clattering of a conveyer belt, a door creaking open), texture (a splintered door jamb, the soft flesh of a pig lip, a cold and firm cadaver), smell (children being their mothers' "second scent," vinegar vapors), and taste (a pig lip that tastes porcine, stale sandwiches).

- *Do readers have difficulty seeing people in action or imagining what is involved in the activity?* Add specific narrative actions to show people moving, gesturing, or talking. For example, recall from Edge's profile how he smashes the bag of potato chips, from Cable's how he reaches out to touch the cadaver's skin, from McPhee's how and where the man in the green polo shirt kicks the well-dressed pickpocket.

Information about the Subject

- *Do readers feel bogged down by information?* Look for ways to reduce information or to break up long blocks of informational text with description of scenes or people, narration of events, lists, or other design elements. Consider presenting information through dialogue, as Edge and Cable do.

A Topical or Narrative Plan

- *Does your narratively arranged essay seem to drag or ramble?* Try adding drama through dialogue or specific narrative action, as Edge does in the bar.

- *Does your topically arranged essay seem disorganized or out of balance?* Try rearranging topics to see whether another order makes more sense. Add clearer, more explicit transitions or topic sentences. Move or condense information to restore balance.

- *Does the opening fail to engage readers' attention?* Consider alternatives. Think of questions you could open with, or look for an engaging image or dialogue later in the essay to move to the beginning. Go back to your observational or interview notes for other ideas. Recall how the writers in this chapter open their profile essays: Cable stands on the street in front of the mortuary, Edge sits at a juke bar staring at a pig lip, McPhee immediately shows you a pickpocket at work, Coyne points out the single flower-in-a-Coke-can in front of every convict mom.

- *Are transitions between stages in the narrative or between topics confusing or abrupt?* Add appropriate words or phrases, or revise sentences to make transitions clearer or smoother.

- *Does the ending seem weak?* Consider ending at an earlier point or moving something striking to the end. Review your invention and research notes to see if you overlooked something that would make for a strong ending. Cable touches the cold, firm flesh of a cadaver. Edge stares at floating pig feet. McPhee returns to the Barta story introduced earlier. Coyne sees a boy hit his mother and blood dripping down her face.

- *Are the visual features effective?* Use an image, as Edge does. Consider adding textual references to any images in your essay or positioning images more effectively. Think of other possible design features — drawings, lists, tables, graphs, cartoons, headings — you might incorporate to enhance your profile to make the place and people easier to imagine or the information more understandable.

A Role for the Writer

- *Do readers want to see more of you in the profile?* Consider revealing yourself participating in some part of the activity. Add yourself to one of the conversations you participated in, re-creating dialogue for yourself.

- *Do readers find your participation so dominant that you seem to eclipse other participants?* Bring other people forward into more prominent view by adding material about them, reducing the material about yourself, or both.

For a revision checklist, go to bedfordstmartins.com/theguide.

A Perspective on the Subject

- *Are readers unsure what your perspective is?* Try stating it more directly. Be sure that the descriptive and narrative details reinforce the perspective you want to convey.

- *Are your readers' ideas about the person, place, or activity being profiled different from yours?* Consider whether you can incorporate any of their ideas into your essay or use them to develop your own ideas.

- *Do readers point to any details that seem especially meaningful?* Consider what these details suggest about your own perspective on the person, place, or activity.

A Note on Grammar and Spelling Checkers
These tools are good at catching certain types of errors, but currently there is no replacement for a good human proofreader. Grammar checkers in particular are extremely limited in what they can usually find, and often they only give you summary information that is not helpful if you do not already understand the rule in question. They are also prone to give faulty advice for fixing problems and to flag correct items as wrong. Spelling checkers cause fewer problems but cannot catch misspellings that are themselves words, such as *to* for *too*.

■ Editing and Proofreading

Now is the time to check your revised draft for errors in grammar, punctuation, and mechanics. Our research has identified several errors that occur often in profiles, including problems with the punctuation of quotations and the order of adjectives. The following guidelines will help you check your essay for these common errors. This book's Web site also provides interactive online exercises to help you learn to identify and correct each of these errors; to access the exercises for a particular error, go to the URL listed in the margin next to that section of the guidelines.

Checking the Punctuation of Quotations.   Because most profiles are based in part on interviews, you probably have quoted one or more people in your essay. When you quote someone's exact words, you must enclose those words in quotation marks and observe strict conventions for punctuating quotations. Check your revised draft for your use of the following specific punctuation marks.

All quotations should have quotation marks at the beginning and the end.

▶ "What exactly is civil litigation?" I asked.

Commas and periods go *inside* quotation marks.

▶ "I'm here to see Anna Post," I replied nervously.

▶ Tony explained, "Fraternity boys just wouldn't feel comfortable at the Chez Moi Café."

Question marks and exclamation points go *inside* closing quotation marks if they are part of the quotation, *outside* if they are not.

▶ After a pause, the patient asked, "Where do I sign?"

▶ Willie insisted, "You can *too* learn to play Super Mario!"

▶ When was the last time someone you just ticketed said to you, "Thank you, Officer, for doing a great job?"

Use commas with speaker tags (*he said, she asked,* etc.) that accompany direct quotations.

▶ "This sound system costs only four thousand dollars," Jorge said.

▶ I asked, "So where were these clothes from originally?"

A Common ESL Problem: Adjective Order.   In trying to present the subject of your profile vividly and in detail, you probably have included many descriptive adjectives. When you include more than one adjective in front of a noun, you may have difficulty sequencing them. For example, do you write *a large old ceramic pot* or *an old large ceramic pot?* The following list shows the order in which adjectives are ordinarily arranged in front of a noun.

For practice, go to bedfordstmartins.com/theguide/exercisecentral and click on Punctuation of Quotations.

1. *Amount:* a/an, the, a few, six
2. *Evaluation:* good, beautiful, ugly, serious
3. *Size:* large, small, tremendous
4. *Shape, length:* round, long, short
5. *Age:* young, new, old
6. *Color:* red, black, green
7. *Origin:* Asian, Brazilian, German
8. *Material:* wood, cotton, gold
9. *Noun used as an adjective:* computer (as in *computer program*), cake (as in *cake pan*)
10. *The noun modified*

For practice, go to bedfordstmartins.com/theguide/exercisecentral and click on A Common ESL Problem: Adjective Order.

A Writer at Work

▉ The Interview Notes and Write-Up

Most profile writers take notes when interviewing people. Later, they may summarize their notes in a short write-up. In this section, you will see some of the interview notes and a write-up that Brian Cable prepares for his mortuary profile, "The Last Stop," printed on pp. 76–78.

Cable arranged to tour the mortuary and conduct interviews with the funeral director and mortician. Before each interview, he wrote out a few questions at the top of a sheet of paper and then divided it into two columns; he used the left-hand column for descriptive details and personal impressions and the right-hand column for the information he got directly from the person he interviewed. Following are Cable's notes and write-up for his interview with the funeral director, Howard Deaver.

Cable used three questions to guide his interview with Howard and then took brief notes during the interview. He did not concern himself too much with note-taking because he planned to spend a half-hour directly afterward to complete his notes. He focused his attention on Howard, trying to keep the interview comfortable and conversational and jotting down just enough to jog his memory and catch especially meaningful quotations. A typescript of Cable's interview notes follows.

The Interview Notes

QUESTIONS

1. How do families of the deceased view the mortuary business?
2. How is the concept of death approached?
3. How did you get into this business?

DESCRIPTIVE DETAILS & PERSONAL IMPRESSIONS	INFORMATION
weird-looking tall long fingers big ears low, sloping forehead Like stereotype--skin colorless	Howard Deaver, funeral director, Goodbody Mortuaries "Call me Howard" How things work: Notification, pick up body at home or hospital, prepare for viewing, restore distorted features-- accident or illness, embalm, casket-- family selects, chapel services (3 in bldg.), visitation room--pay respects, family & friends.
	Can't answer questions about death-- "Not bereavement specialists. Don't handle emotional problems. Only a trained therapist can do that." "We provide services for dead, not counseling for the living." (great quote) Concept of death has changed in last 40 yrs (how long he's been in the business) Funeral cost: $500 – $600, now $2,000

plays with lips
blinks
plays with Adam's apple
desk empty--phone, no
   paper or pen
 	
angry
disdainful of the
   Neptune Society
	Phone call (interruption)
	"I think we'll be able to get him in
	on Friday. No, no, the family wants
	him cremated."
	Ask about Neptune Society--cremation
	Cremation "Cheap, quick, easy means of
	disposal."
	Recent phenomenon. Neptune Society--erroneous
	claim to be only one.

	"We've offered them since the beginning. It's only now it's come into vogue." Trend now back toward burial. Cremation still popular in sophisticated areas 60% in Marin Co. and Florida Ask about paperwork--does it upstairs, lives there with wife, Nancy.
musty, old stained glass sunlight filtered	Tour around (happy to show me around) Chapel--large service just done, Italian.

man in black suit	"Not a religious institution--a
roses	business."
wooden benches	casket--"beautiful craftsmanship"--
	admires, expensive
contrast brightness	Display room--caskets, about 30 of them
fluorescent lights	Loves to talk about caskets "models in every price
Plexiglas stands	range" glossy (like cars in a showroom) cardboard
	box, steel, copper, bronze $400 up to $1,800.
	Top of line: bronze, electronically welded, no
	corrosion--$5,000

Cable's interview notes include many descriptive details of Howard as well as of various rooms in the mortuary. Though most entries are short and sketchy, much of the language found its way into the final essay. In describing Howard, for example, Cable noted that he fits the stereotype of the cadaverous undertaker, a fact that Cable emphasized in his essay.

He put quotation marks around Howard's actual words, some of them written in complete sentences, others in fragments. We will see how Cable filled these quotes in when he wrote up the interview. In only a few instances did he take down more than he could use. Even though profile writers want good quotes, they should not use quotes to present information that can be more effectively expressed in their own words. In profiles, writers use direct quotation both to provide information and to capture the mood or character of the person speaking.

As you can see, Howard was not able to answer Cable's questions about the families of the deceased and their attitudes toward death or mortuaries. The gap between these questions and Howard's responses led Cable to recognize one of his own misperceptions about mortuaries — that they serve the living by helping people adjust to the death of loved ones. This misperception would become an important theme of his essay.

Immediately after the interview, Cable filled in his notes with details while they were still fresh in his mind. Next, he took some time to reflect on what he had learned from his interview with Howard. Here are some of his thoughts:

I was surprised by how much Howard looked like the undertakers in scary movies. Even though he couldn't answer some of my questions, he was friendly enough. It's obviously a business for him (he loves to talk about caskets and to point out all their features, like a car dealer kicking a tire). Best quote: "We offer services to the dead, not counseling to the living." I have to bring up these issues in my interview with the mortician.

The Interview Write-Up

Writing up an account of the interview a short time afterward helped Cable fill in more details and reflect further on what he had learned. His write-up shows him already beginning to organize the information he had gained from his interview with the funeral director.

I. His physical appearance.

Tall, skinny, with beady blue eyes embedded in his bony face. I was shocked to see that he looks just like the undertakers in scary movies. His skin is white and colorless, from lack of sunshine. He has a long nose and a low, sloping forehead. He was wearing a clean white shirt. A most unusual man--have you ever seen those Ames Home Loan commercials? But he was friendly, and happy to talk with me. "Would I answer some questions? Sure."

II. What people want from a mortuary.

A. Well first of all, he couldn't answer my second question, about how families cope with the loss of a loved one. "You'd have to talk to a psychologist about that," he said. He did tell me how the concept of death has changed over the last ten or so years.

B. He has been in the business for forty years(!). One look at him and you'd be convinced he'd been there at least that long. He told me that in the old times, everyone was buried. Embalmed, put in a casket, and paid final homage before being shipped underground forever. Nowadays, many people choose to be cremated instead. Hence comes the success of the Neptune Society and others specializing in cremation. You can have your ashes dumped anywhere. "Not that we don't offer cremation services. We've offered them since the beginning," he added with a look of disdain. It's just that they've become so popular recently because they offer a "quick, easy, and efficient means of disposal." Cheap too--I think it is a reflection of a "no nonsense" society. The Neptune Society has become so successful because it claims to be the only one to offer cremations as an alternative to expensive burial. "We've offered it all along. It's just only now come into vogue."

Sophisticated areas (I felt "progressive" would be more accurate) like Marin County have a cremation rate of over 60 percent. The phone rang. "Excuse me," he said. As he talked on the phone, I noticed how he played with his lips, pursing and squeezing them. He was blinking a lot, too. I meant to ask him how he got into this business, but I forgot. I did find out his name and title: Mr. Howard Deaver, funeral director of Goodbody Mortuaries (no kidding, that's the real name). He lives on the premises, upstairs with his wife. I doubt if he ever leaves the place.

III. It's a business!

Some people have the idea that mortuaries offer counseling and peace of mind--a place where everyone is sympathetic and ready to offer advice. "In some mortuaries, this is true. But by and large, this is a business. We offer services to the dead, not counseling to the living." I too had expected to feel an awestruck respect for the dead upon entering the building. I had also expected green lawns, ponds with ducks, fountains, flowers, peacefulness--you know, a "Forest Lawn" type deal. But it was only a tall, Catholic-looking building. "Mortuaries do not sell plots for burial," he was saying. "Cemeteries do that, after we embalm the body and select a casket. We're not a religious institution." He seemed hung up on caskets--though maybe he was just trying to impress upon me the differences between caskets. "Oh, they're very important. A good casket is a sign of respect. Sometimes if the family doesn't have enough money, we rent them a nice one. People pay for what they get just like any other business." I wondered when you had to return the casket you rented.

I wanted to take a look around. He was happy to give me a tour. We visited several chapels and visiting rooms--places where the deceased "lie in state" to be "visited" by family and friends. I saw an old lady in a "fairly decent casket," as Mr. Deaver called it. Again I was impressed by the simple businesslike nature of it all. Oh yes, the rooms were elaborately decorated, with lots of shrines and stained glass, but these things were for the customers' benefit. "Sometimes we have up to eight or nine corpses here at one time, sometimes none. We have to have enough rooms to accommodate." Simple enough, yet I never realized how much (trouble?) people were after they died. So much money, time, and effort go into their funerals.

As I prepared to leave, he gave me his card. He'd be happy to see me again, or maybe I could talk to someone else. I said I was going to interview the mortician on another day. I shook his hand. His fingers were long and his skin was warm.

Writing up the interview helped Cable probe his subject more deeply. It also helped him express a humorous attitude toward his subject. Cable's interview notes and write-up were quite informal; later, he integrated this material more formally into his full profile of the mortuary.

Thinking About Document Design

The education student working on a paper about collaborative learning principles (see p. 72) published her essay as a Web site so that classmates and other interested people could read her work. For this student, whose paper reported on her field research in a sixth-grade classroom, Web-based publishing allowed her to not only include photographs and materials from her research, but also to show her final product to the sixth graders and the teacher she had profiled.

Web documents can be more visually complex and interactive than most essays written for print. In her Web-based essay, the education student incorporated photographs, links, and color highlights to make the material both more interesting and helpful to her readers. As the screen shot on this page shows, she also took advantage of the navigational tools Web publishing provides, and embedded links on the left side of the page so readers can easily move through her essay. She also used a graphic

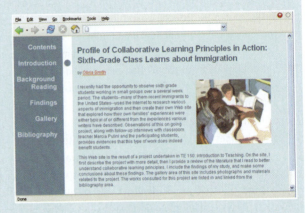

(the dark blue circle) to mark where readers are on the site. Web readers tend to skim, surf, and bounce around, so the student organized the information in a way that enabled her to provide several different points of entry into and through her site.

As for links, the student carefully broke her essay into logical chunks: a table of contents ("Contents"); an introduction that included information about the assignment and some context for the site ("Introduction"); a page that summarized the work she researched, read, and reviewed for the project ("Background Reading"); a section that reported on her research ("Findings"); and a page that included photos taken during the project ("Gallery"). She also included a page with her works cited ("Bibliography") — the list of scholarly essays about collaborative learning that served as background reading and links to the online material she cited in her essay. In addition, within several of the pages on the site, the student writer included links to the sixth-grade class's Web site, which contained the final projects that resulted from the Internet research she had watched the children engage in. She encouraged readers to view the variety and quality of these projects as evidence of collaborative learning as a classroom tool.

Because the student was working with children who were minors, she would have needed parent and teacher (and perhaps even school board) permission to take and include their photographs. Instead, she decided to include photos that let readers see the space in which the children worked — photos of the classroom and of the computers. Because her topic was collaboration, she knew she needed a photograph showing children working together. She used her graphic software to alter a picture of four children working so that the meaning was still clear, although the children's faces were not identifiable. At key points in her essay, the student writer also included quotes from the sixth graders themselves. She used these quotes as subtitles for individual sections of her essay, and to draw more attention to the quotes, she used a font larger than the body of the essay — a technique borrowed from print publishing.

Thinking Critically About What You Have Learned

Now that you have spent several days discussing profiles and writing one of your own, take some time to think critically about what you have learned about this genre. You can use this knowledge — your new expertise — to analyze and reflect on what you have learned. What problems did you encounter while you were writing your profile, and how did you solve them? How did what you learned as a reader of profiles help you write your own profile? Finally, in what ways might profiles influence your thinking about yourself and the society we live in?

Reflecting on Your Writing

Write a one-page explanation, telling your instructor about a problem you encountered in writing your profile and how you solved it. Before you begin, gather all of your written invention material, planning and interview notes, drafts, advice on improving your draft, revision notes and plans, and final revision. Review these materials as you complete this writing task.

1. *Identify one writing problem you needed to solve as you worked on your profile.* Do not be concerned with grammar or punctuation; concentrate instead on problems unique to developing a profile. For example: Did you puzzle over how to organize your diverse observations into a coherent essay? Was it difficult to convey your own perspective? Did you have any concerns about presenting your subject vividly or controlling the flow of information?

2. *Determine how you came to recognize the problem.* When did you first discover it? What called it to your attention? If someone else pointed out the problem to you, can you now see hints of it in your invention writings? If so, where specifically? When you first recognized the problem, how did you respond?

3. *Reflect on how you went about solving the problem.* Did you work on the wording of a passage, cut or add details about your subject, or move paragraphs or sentences around? Did you reread one of the essays in this chapter to see how another writer handled a similar problem, or did you look back at the invention suggestions? If you talked about the problem with another student, your instructor, or someone else, what specific help did you receive?

4. *Write a brief explanation of the problem and your solution.* Reconstruct your efforts as specifically as possible. Quote from your invention notes or draft essay, others' advice, your revision plan, or your revised essay to show the various changes your writing underwent as you tried to solve the problem. When you have finished, consider how explaining what you have learned about solving this writing problem can help you solve future writing problems.

Reviewing What You Learned from Reading

Write a page or so explaining to your instructor how the reading selections in this chapter influenced your final essay. Before you write, take time to reflect on what you have learned from the readings in this chapter and how your reading has influenced your writing.

1. *Reread the final revision of your profile essay; then look back at the selections you read before completing it.* Do you see any specific influences? For example, if you were impressed with the way one of the readings presented a place through concrete details, made an ordinary activity seem interesting, focused all of the materials around a compelling and unexpected interpretation, or reconstructed dialogue from interview notes, look

to see where you might have been striving to use the same writing strategies, include comparable details, or achieve similar effects in your own writing.

2. *Write an explanation of these influences.* Did one selection in particular influence you, or were you influenced by several readings in different ways? Quote from the readings and from your final revision to show how your profile essay was influenced by the selections in this chapter. Finally, now that you have reviewed the other readings again, point out any ways in which you might further improve your profile.

Considering the Social Dimensions of Profiles

Profiles offer some of the same pleasures as autobiographies, novels, and films: good stories, memorable characters, exotic places or familiar places viewed freshly, vivid images of people at work and play. They divert and entertain. They may even shock or fascinate. In addition, they offer information that may surprise and should interest readers. This special combination of entertainment and information makes profiles unique among all the kinds of reading and writing available to us.

Like travel writing and natural history, profiles nearly always take us to a particular place, usually a place we have never been. For example, Cable provides many visual details of Goodbody Mortuaries, with its gothic arches and stained glass, its hotel-like lobby with couches and coffee tables, aquarium, and pastoral paintings.

But the larger appeal of profiles is that they present real people that most readers will never have a chance to meet. Often, profiles present people the writer admires and assumes that readers will admire for their achievements, endurance, dedication, skill, or unselfishness. For example, Edge clearly admires Lionel Dufour for his persistence and success. McPhee implies that if farmer Rich Hodgson were not so unflappable, there might have been a riot at the farmers' market, the day people started throwing fruit and

rocks. Profiles also present less admirable people; these people may occasionally be shown as cruel, greedy, or selfish, but more often they are people, such as the forgetful Catherine Barta at the Brooklyn farmers' market, with whom we can empathize. The strongest profiles present us not with saints, monsters, or helpless victims but with people of mixed motives, human failings, and some resources even in dire situations.

Entertain Readers, or Show the Whole Picture?

Profiles broaden our view of the world by entertaining and informing us with portraits of unusual people in particular places. It is important to recognize, however, that profiles sometimes offer a more limited view of their subjects than they seem to. For example, the impulse to entertain readers may lead a profile writer to focus exclusively on the dramatic, bizarre, colorful, or humorous aspects of a person, place, or activity, ignoring the equally important humdrum, routine, or even disturbing aspects. Imagine a profile that focuses on the free trips that a travel agent enjoys as part of the job but ignores the everyday demands of dealing with clients and the energy-draining precision required by computerized airline reservation systems. Such a profile would provide a limited and distorted picture of a travel agent's work.

In addition, by focusing on the dramatic or glamorous aspects of a subject, profile writers tend to ignore economic or social consequences and to slight supporting players. Profiling the highly praised chef in a trendy new restaurant, a writer might not ask whether the chef participates in the city's leftover-food-collection program for the homeless or find out who the kitchen workers and wait staff are, how the chef treats them, or how much they are paid. Profiling the campus bookstore, a writer might become so caught up in the details of ordering books for hundreds of courses and selling them efficiently to hordes of students during the first week of a semester that he or she could forget to ask about textbook costs, pricing policies, profit margins, and payback on used textbooks.

1. *Consider whether any of the profiles you have read glamorize or sensationalize their subjects.* Do they ignore less colorful but centrally impor-

tant everyday activities? Is this a problem with your own profile?

2. ***Single out a profile you read that seems to overlook potential social or economic consequences.*** What is overlooked? Why do you think the writer omits these aspects?

3. ***Write a page or so explaining what the omissions signify.*** What do they suggest about the readers' desires to be entertained and the profile writer's reluctance to present the subject as boring or disturbing in some way?

Be Aware of the Writer's Viewpoint. Though profiles may seem impartial and objective, they inevitably reflect the views of their writers. The choice of subject, the details observed, the questions asked, the ultimate focus and presentation — all are influenced by the writer's interests and values, gender and ethnicity, and beliefs about social and political issues. For example, we would expect a vegetarian to write a

very different profile of a cattle ranch than a beef lover would. Consequently, profiles are likely to reflect a writer's unstated values.

1. ***Consider the attitudes, values, and views expressed in your favorite profile in this chapter.*** Identify two or three attitudes and values. Are they obvious or hidden? How can you tell?

2. ***Consider your own profile essay in the same terms.*** Are your attitudes obvious or hidden? If obvious, how did you make them so, and did you feel as though you were taking a risk? If hidden, why did you think it best to keep your personal views out of sight?

3. ***Write a page or so about how your viewpoint influenced your writing.*** How have your own assumptions, values, gender, ethnicity, or other characteristics influenced your choice of a subject to profile, your approach to learning about it, and your attitudes toward it?

4

Explaining a Concept

IN COLLEGE COURSES For a linguistics course, a student writes a term paper tracing children's gradual development of control of sentences — or *syntax*, as linguists say — from about eighteen months to five or six years of age. To get started, she goes to the library and does some preliminary research in sources listed in her linguistics textbook. She then goes to her professor's office hours, describes her paper idea, and asks for other articles or books she should consult. These sources become the basis of the first section of her paper, which explains how researchers go about studying children's syntax and cites several well-known examples.

From lectures and one of the books her professor recommends, she learns about a widely accepted classification of stages that children go through as they gain control of syntax, beginning with the one-word or holophrastic stage (such as *mommy*) and progressing through the two-word or duose stage, when children put words together in subject + verb (*baby sleep*) or verb + object (*want toy*) constructions, and the multi-word or telegraphic stage, when children leave out words not required for meaning (*no sit there*). She decides to organize her essay around these stages. From the many excerpts of children's monologues and conversations in the published research studies, she chooses examples to illustrate each stage. Even though she writes for her professor, who is an expert in child language development, she carefully defines key terms to show that she understands what she is writing about.

IN THE WORKPLACE Returning from a small invitational seminar on the national security implications of satellite photography, the CEO of a space-imaging company prepares a report to his employees on the international debate about *symmetrical transparency*. This concept involves using satellite photography to make everything on the planet visible to everyone on the planet at one-meter resolution — enough detail to reveal individual cars in parking lots, small airplanes on runways, backyard swimming pools, and individual shrubs and trees planted in parks. Aware of the financial implications for his company of the outcome of the debate, the executive carefully organizes his information. He prepares a written text to read aloud to his employees, a one-page handout that lists key issues in the debate, and a transparency to project on a large screen during his presentation.

He begins by reminding employees that the company's cameras already provide high-resolution images to government and corporate purchasers. Addressing the question of whether symmetrical transparency and the multinational monitoring that it makes possible compromise national security — or promise greater worldwide security and peace — the CEO gives a brief overview of key issues in the debate. These issues include how closed societies (like that of North Korea) will be affected differently from more open ones, whether global terrorism will be reduced or become more prevalent or more effective, and whether the chance of a nuclear stand-off will be lessened. The CEO concludes by pointing out that the big question for the U.S. government to answer soon is whether to attempt to control space or insist that it be open to everyone.

IN THE COMMUNITY As part of her firm's plan to encourage community volunteering, a manager at a marketing research firm has been tutoring fifth-grade students in math for a few hours each month. Learning about the manager's market research expertise, the teacher encourages her to plan a presentation to the class about *surveying*, an important research method in the social sciences. The manager agrees to do so and spends the weeked before her presentation planning an impromptu in-class survey to engage fifth-graders.

She begins the lesson by having students fill out a brief questionnaire on their television-watching habits. When they are done, she discusses with them how such data could be used for different purposes such as deciding where to place commercials and developing a schedule of programs. Then she gets the students to help decide how to categorize the information from the questionnaire. With the students' help, she tabulates the results on a computer, separating the results into three categories: the viewer's gender, the time of the program, and the type of television show. Using a PowerPoint program, she projects the data onto a large screen so that everyone can see how the tables represent the survey results.

She concludes by putting on the screen examples of questions from other surveys and explaining who does such surveys, what they hope to learn, and how they report and use the results. She explains that the state tests that the students take every year are a form of survey. Finally, she passes out a short-answer quiz so that she and each student can find out how much has been learned about surveys.

Concept explanations inform readers about processes, phenomena, theories, principles, or ideas. The scenarios that open this chapter illustrate a variety of kinds of concepts and situations in which they may be explained. For example, the concept of *surveying* refers to a process by which data is collected and analyzed. *Symmetrical transparency* is a term for the use of satellite photography. *Syntax* refers to the grammatical patterning of sentences.

Every student entering a new academic field is introduced to a sometimes bewildering array of new concepts like these. Introductory courses and their textbooks teach a whole new vocabulary of technical terms and specialized jargon. The opening chapter of this textbook, for example, introduced many concepts important to the study of writing, such as *genre, critical thinking, recursiveness,* and *invention.* As a high-school student studying literature, you may have encountered the concepts of *figurative language, irony, realism,* and *sonnet form.* In your college literature courses, you will learn many additional concepts such as *intertextuality, modernism,* and *postcolonialism.* Every field of study has concepts which students starting out, as well as those in more advanced courses, must learn and be able to explain and apply. Physics has *entropy, mass,* and *quantum mechanics;* music has *harmonics, counterpoint,* and *sonata form;* mathematics has *probability, proportionality,* and *geometric progression;* psychology has *subconscious, transference, attachment disorder,* and so on. Just think of the courses you are taking this term and all the new concepts you are learning.

In this chapter, you will read essays explaining the concepts of *cannibalism* (an anthropological concept), *romantic love* (a cultural concept), *hyperthymia* (a psychological concept focusing on the happy-go-lucky temperament), and *contemporary evolution* (a biological concept dealing with the kinds of changes in species that happen quickly, often as a result of environmental change). Two of these essays were written by experts on the subject—the explanation of hyperthymia by research psychologist Richard A. Friedman and the explanation of contemporary evolution by evolutionary biologist Bob Holmes. The other essays were written by student Linh Kieu Ngo and science reporter Anastasia Toufexis, both of whom explain concepts they have learned about from researching what experts have discovered.

Your instructor may encourage you to explain a concept related to a subject on which you are an expert. For example, if you are knowledgeable about music, you might choose to explain a phenomenon like *hip hop* or a theory like *counterpoint.* If you are an avid video game player, you could explain *game mechanics, mods,* or *real time strategy* games. If you are a sports enthusiast, you could write about the *curve ball* in baseball or the *Wing-T offense* in football. Or your instructor may ask you to write about an academic concept you have learned or are just now learning in your English or other courses.

Learning to explain a concept is especially important for you as a college student. It will help you read critically a staple of academic discourse; it will prepare you to write a common type of exam and paper assignment; it will acquaint you with the basic strategies common to all types of explanatory writing — definition, classification, comparison and contrast, cause and effect, and process narration; and it will sharpen your skill in researching and using sources, abilities essential for success in college, whatever your major.

Think of concepts you are currently studying or have recently studied or concepts connected to a job, sport, or hobby you know a lot about. Here are some possibilities: *krumping, squeeze play, critical thinking, honor, interval training, freedom of speech, photosynthesis, manifest destiny, open source, nanotechnology.* Here are some guidelines to follow:

Part 1. Choose one concept to explain to two or three other students. When you have chosen your concept, think about what others in the group are likely to know about it and how you can inform them about it in two or three minutes. Consider how you will define the concept and what other strategies you might use – description, comparison, and so on – to explain it in an interesting, memorable way.

Get together with two or three other students, and explain your concepts to one another. You might begin by indicating where you learned the concept and in what area of study or work or leisure it is usually used.

Part 2. When all group members have explained their concepts, discuss what you learned from the experience of explaining a concept. Begin by asking one another a question or two that elicits further information that you need to understand each concept more fully. Then consider these questions:

- How did you decide what to include in your explanation and what to leave out?
- What surprised you in the questions that readers asked about your presentation?
- If you were to repeat your explanation to a similar group of listeners, what would you add, subtract, or change?

A Collaborative Activity:
Practice Explaining a Concept

Readings

LINH KIEU NGO wrote this essay as a first-year college student. In it, he defines a concept that is of importance in anthropology and of wide general interest — cannibalism, the eating of human flesh by other humans. Most Americans know about survival cannibalism — eating human flesh to avoid starvation — but Ngo also explains the historical importance of dietary and ritual cannibalism in his essay. As you read, notice how he relies on examples to illustrate the three types of cannibalism.

Cannibalism: It Still Exists

Linh Kieu Ngo

1   Fifty-five Vietnamese refugees fled to Malaysia on a small fishing boat to escape communist rule in their country following the Vietnam War. During their escape attempt, the captain was shot by the coast guard. The boat and its passengers

By beginning with a dramatic anecdote, Ngo tries to interest readers and make the concept seem less abstract and distant. As you read, notice how much you are learning about the concept even before he gives it a name.

managed to outrun the coast guard to the open sea, but they had lost the only person who knew the way to Malaysia, the captain.

The men onboard tried to navigate the boat, but after a week fuel ran out, and they drifted farther out to sea. Their supply of food and water was gone; people were starving, and some of the elderly were near death. The men managed to produce a small amount of drinking water by boiling salt water, using dispensable wood from the boat to create a small fire near the stern. They also tried to fish but had little success.

A month went by, and the old and weak died. At first, the crew threw the dead overboard, but later, out of desperation, they turned to human flesh as a source of food. Some people vomited as they attempted to eat it, while others refused to resort to cannibalism and see the bodies of their loved ones sacrificed for food. Those who did not eat died of starvation, and their bodies in turn became food for others. Human flesh was cut out, washed in salt water, and hung to dry for preservation. The liquids inside the cranium were drunk to quench thirst. The livers, kidneys, hearts, stomachs, and intestines were boiled and eaten.

Five months passed before a whaling vessel discovered the drifting boat, looking like a graveyard of bones. There was only one survivor.

Cannibalism, the act of human beings eating human flesh (Sagan 2), has a long history and continues to hold interest and create controversy. Many books and research reports offer examples of cannibalism, but a few scholars have questioned whether it actually was ever practiced anywhere, except in cases of ensuring survival in times of famine or isolation (Askenasy 43-54). Recently, some scholars have tried to understand why people in the West have been so eager to attribute cannibalism to non-Westerners (Barker, Hulme, and Iversen). Cannibalism has long been a part of American popular culture. For example, Mark Twain's "Cannibalism in the Cars" tells a humorous story about cannibalism by well-to-do travelers on a train stranded in a snowstorm, and cannibalism is still a popular subject for jokes ("Cannibal Jokes").

If we assume there is some reality to the reports about cannibalism, how can we best understand this concept? Cannibalism can be broken down into two main categories: exocannibalism, the eating of outsiders or foreigners, and endocannibalism, the eating of members of one's own social group (Shipman 70). Within these categories are several functional types of cannibalism, three of the most common being survival cannibalism, dietary cannibalism, and religious and ritual cannibalism.

Survival cannibalism occurs when people trapped without food have to decide "whether to starve or to eat fellow humans" (Shipman 70). In the case of the Vietnamese refugees, the crew and passengers on the boat ate human flesh to stay alive. They did not kill people to get human flesh for nourishment but instead waited until the people had died. Even after human carcasses were sacrificed as food, the boat people ate only enough to survive. Another case of survival cannibalism occurred in 1945, when General Douglas MacArthur's forces cut supply lines to Japanese troops stationed in the Pacific Islands. In one incident, Japanese troops were reported to have sacrificed the Arapesh people of northeastern New Guinea for food in order to avoid death by starvation (Tuzin 63). The most famous example of survival cannibalism in American history comes from the diaries, letters, and interviews of survivors of the California-bound Donner Party, who in the win-

Margin notes:

Ngo works to make the anecdote dramatic, but not melodramatic. His narrative does not manipulate readers' emotions, but simply details what he learned from his reading.

Here Ngo shifts from narrating to explaining what experts have written about cannibalism. The parenthetical citations are keyed to the Works Cited list at the end of the essay. Ngo cites a range of sources, showing readers that the information he presents is well established.

Ngo poses a rhetorical question that anticipates what his readers may be thinking.

Ngo's thesis statement names the three types of cannibalism he will discuss, forecasting his essay's plan.

Ngo uses topic sentences to announce what he is about to discuss because readers expect essays explaining a concept to be clear and easy to follow.

Ngo refers to the opening anecdote and then presents additional examples to illustrate survival cannibalism.

ter of 1846 were snowbound in the Sierra Nevada Mountains for five months. Thirty-five of eighty-seven adults and children died, and some of them were eaten (Hart 116-117; Johnson).

8   Unlike survival cannibalism, in which human flesh is eaten as a last resort after a person has died, in dietary cannibalism humans are purchased or trapped for food and then eaten as a part of a culture's traditions. In addition, survival cannibalism often involves people eating other people of the same origins, whereas dietary cannibalism usually involves people eating foreigners.

Another topic sentence cues readers that Ngo is making a transition to the second category of cannibalism.

9   In the Miyanmin society of the west Sepik interior of Papua, New Guinea, villagers do not value human life over that of pigs or marsupials because human flesh is part of their normal diet (Poole 7). The Miyanmin people observe no differences in "gender, kinship, ritual status, and bodily substance"; they eat anyone, even their own dead. In this respect, then, they practice both endocannibalism and exocannibalism; and to ensure a constant supply of human flesh for food, they raid neighboring tribes and drag their victims back to their village to be eaten (Poole 11). Perhaps, in the history of this society, there was at one time a shortage of wild game to be hunted for food, and because people were more plentiful than fish, deer, rabbits, pigs, or cows, survival cannibalism was adopted as a last resort. Then, as their culture developed, the Miyanmin may have retained the practice of dietary cannibalism, which has endured as a part of their culture.

Ngo presents examples to illustrate dietary cannibalism.

Ngo cites Poole twice in this paragraph but quotes only one phrase. To gain insight into what he decided to quote and what to paraphrase, see A Writer at Work on p. 187.

10   Similar to the Miyanmin, the people of the Leopard and Alligator societies in South America eat human flesh as part of their cultural tradition. Practicing dietary exocannibalism, the Leopard people hunt in groups, with one member wearing the skin of a leopard to conceal the face. They ambush their victims in the forest and carry their victims back to their village to be eaten. The Alligator people also hunt in groups, but they hide themselves under a canoelike submarine that resembles an alligator, then swim close to a fisherman's or trader's canoe to overturn it and catch their victims (MacCormack 54).

11   Religious or ritual cannibalism is different from survival and dietary cannibalism in that it has a ceremonial purpose rather than one of nourishment. Sometimes only a single victim is sacrificed in a ritual, while at other times many are sacrificed. For example, the Bangala tribe of the Congo River in central Africa honors a deceased chief or leader by purchasing, sacrificing, and feasting on slaves (Sagan 53). The number of slaves sacrificed is determined by how highly the tribe members revered the deceased leader.

Another topic sentence cues readers that Ngo is making a transition to the third category of cannibalism.

12   Ritual cannibalism among South American Indians often serves as revenge for the dead. Like the Bangalas, some South American tribes kill their victims to be served as part of funeral rituals, with human sacrifices denoting that the deceased was held in high honor. Also like the Bangalas, these tribes use outsiders as victims. Unlike the Bangalas, however, the Indians sacrifice only one victim instead of many in a single ritual. For example, when a warrior of a tribe is killed in battle, the family of the warrior forces a victim to take the identity of the warrior. The family adorns the victim with the deceased warrior's belongings and may even force him to marry the deceased warrior's wives. But once the family believes the victim has assumed the spiritual identity of the deceased warrior, the family kills

Ngo presents examples to illustrate religious or ritual cannibalism.

him. The children in the tribe soak their hands in the victim's blood to symbolize their revenge of the warrior's death. Elderly women from the tribe drink the victim's blood and then cut up his body for roasting and eating (Sagan 53-54). The people of the tribe believe that by sacrificing a victim, they have avenged the death of the warrior and the soul of the deceased can rest in peace.

In the villages of certain African tribes, only a small part of a dead body is used in ritual cannibalism. In these tribes, where the childbearing capacity of women is highly valued, women are obligated to eat small, raw fragments of genital parts during fertility rites. Elders of the tribe supervise this ritual to ensure that the women will be fertile. In the Bimin-Kuskusmin tribe, for instance, a widow eats a small, raw fragment of flesh from the penis of her deceased husband in order to enhance her future fertility and reproductive capacity. Similarly, a widower may eat a raw fragment of flesh from his deceased wife's vagina along with a piece of her bone marrow; by eating her flesh, he hopes to strengthen the fertility of his daughters borne by his dead wife, and by eating her bone marrow, he honors her reproductive capacity. Also, when an elder woman of the village who has shown great reproductive capacity dies, her uterus and the interior parts of her vagina are eaten by other women who hope to benefit from her reproductive power (Poole 16-17).

13

Members of developed societies in general practice none of these forms of cannibalism, with the occasional exception of survival cannibalism when the only alternative is starvation. It is possible, however, that our distant-past ancestors were cannibals who through the eons turned away from the practice. We are, after all, descended from the same ancestors as the Miyanmin, the Alligator, and the Leopard people, and survival cannibalism shows that people are capable of eating human flesh when they have no other choice.

14

Ngo's conclusion anticipates another likely question readers may have: Why should I be interested in this concept?

Works Cited

Askenasy, Hans. *Cannibalism: From Sacrifice to Survival.* Amherst, NY: Prometheus, 1994. Print.

Barker, Francis, Peter Hulme, and Margaret Iversen, eds. *Cannibalism and the New World.* Cambridge: Cambridge UP, 1998. Print.

Brown, Paula, and Donald Tuzin, eds. *The Ethnography of Cannibalism.* Washington: Society of Psychological Anthropology, 1983. Print.

"Cannibal Jokes." *Bored.com.* N.p., n.d. Web. 2 Sept. 2008.

Hart, James D. *A Companion to California.* Berkeley: U of California P, 1987. Print.

Johnson, Kristin. "New Light on the Donner Party." Kristin Johnson, 5 Nov. 2006. Web. 28 Sept. 2008.

MacCormack, Carol. "Human Leopard and Crocodile." Brown and Tuzin 54-55.

Poole, Fitz John Porter. "Cannibals, Tricksters, and Witches." Brown and Tuzin 16-17.

Sagan, Eli. *Cannibalism.* New York: Harper, 1976. Print.

Shipman, Pat. "The Myths and Perturbing Realities of Cannibalism." *Discover* Mar. 1987: 70+. Print.

Tuzin, Donald. "Cannibalism and Arapesh Cosmology." Brown and Tuzin 61-63.

Twain, Mark. "Cannibalism in the Cars." *The Complete Short Stories of Mark Twain.* Ed. Charles Neider. New York: Doubleday, 1957. 9-16. Print.

Ngo uses MLA documentation style with the title centered, the entries in alphabetical order, and subsequent lines of the same entry indented one-half inch.

ANASTASIA TOUFEXIS has been an associate editor of *Time*, senior editor of *Discover*, and editor in chief of *Psychology Today*. She has written major reports, including some best-selling cover stories, on subjects as diverse as medicine, health and fitness, law, environment, education, science, and national and world news. Toufexis received a bachelor's degree from Smith College in 1967 and spent several years reporting for medical and pharmaceutical magazines. She has won a number of awards for her writing, including a Knight-Wallace Fellowship at the University of Michigan and an Ocean Science Journalism Fellowship at Woods Hole Oceanographic Institution. She has also lectured on science writing at Columbia University, the University of North Carolina, and the School of Visual Arts in New York.

The following essay was originally published in 1993 in *Time* magazine. As you read, notice how Toufexis brings together a variety of sources of information to present a neuro-chemical perspective on love.

Love: The Right Chemistry
Anastasia Toufexis

> Love is a romantic designation for a most ordinary biological — or, shall we say, chemical? — process. A lot of nonsense is talked and written about it.
> — GRETA GARBO to Melvyn Douglas in *Ninotchka*

1 O.K., let's cut out all this nonsense about romantic love. Let's bring some scientific precision to the party. Let's put love under a microscope.

2 When rigorous people with Ph.D.s after their names do that, what they see is not some silly, senseless thing. No, their probe reveals that love rests firmly on the foundations of evolution, biology and chemistry. What seems on the surface to be irrational, intoxicated behavior is in fact part of nature's master strategy — a vital force that has helped humans survive, thrive and multiply through thousands of years. Says Michael Mills, a psychology professor at Loyola Marymount University in Los Angeles: "Love is our ancestors whispering in our ears."

3 It was on the plains of Africa about 4 million years ago, in the early days of the human species, that the notion of romantic love probably first began to blossom or at least that the first cascades of neurochemicals began flowing from the brain to the bloodstream to produce goofy grins and sweaty palms as men and women gazed deeply into each other's eyes. When mankind graduated from scuttling around on all fours to walking on two legs, this change made the whole person visible to fellow human beings for the first time. Sexual organs were in full display, as were other characteristics, from the color of eyes to the span of shoulders. As never before, each individual had a unique allure.

4 When the sparks flew, new ways of making love enabled sex to become a romantic encounter, not just a reproductive act. Although mounting mates from the rear was, and still is, the method favored among most animals, humans began to enjoy face-to-face couplings; both looks and personal attraction became a much greater part of the equation.

Romance served the evolutionary purpose of pulling males and females into long-term partnership, which was essential to child rearing. On open grasslands, one parent would have a hard — and dangerous — time handling a child while foraging for food. "If a woman was carrying the equivalent of a 20-lb. bowling ball in one arm and a pile of sticks in the other, it was ecologically critical to pair up with a mate to rear the young," explains anthropologist Helen Fisher, author of *Anatomy of Love*.

While Western culture holds fast to the idea that true love flames forever (the movie *Bram Stoker's Dracula* has the Count carrying the torch beyond the grave), nature apparently meant passions to sputter out in something like four years. Primitive pairs stayed together just "long enough to rear one child through infancy," says Fisher. Then each would find a new partner and start all over again.

What Fisher calls the "four-year itch" shows up unmistakably in today's divorce statistics. In most of the 62 cultures she has studied, divorce rates peak around the fourth year of marriage. Additional youngsters help keep pairs together longer. If, say, a couple have another child three years after the first, as often occurs, then their union can be expected to last about four more years. That makes them ripe for the more familiar phenomenon portrayed in the Marilyn Monroe classic *The Seven-Year Itch*.

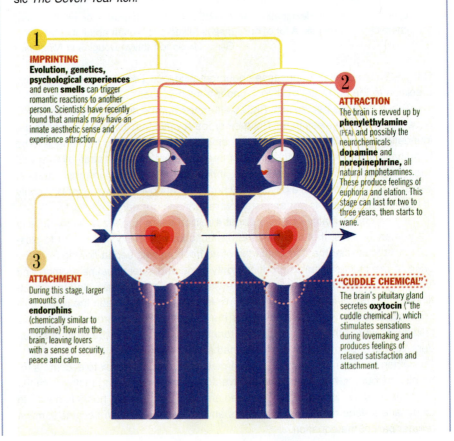

1

IMPRINTING
Evolution, genetics, psychological experiences and even **smells** can trigger romantic reactions to another person. Scientists have recently found that animals may have an innate aesthetic sense and experience attraction.

2

ATTRACTION
The brain is revved up by **phenylethylamine** (PEA) and possibly the neurochemicals **dopamine** and **norepinephrine,** all natural amphetamines. These produce feelings of euphoria and elation. This stage can last for two to three years, then starts to wane.

3

ATTACHMENT
During this stage, larger amounts of **endorphins** (chemically similar to morphine) flow into the brain, leaving lovers with a sense of security, peace and calm.

"CUDDLE CHEMICAL"
The brain's pituitary gland secretes **oxytocin** ("the cuddle chemical"), which stimulates sensations during lovemaking and produces feelings of relaxed satisfaction and attachment.

If, in nature's design, romantic love is not eternal, neither is it exclusive. Less than 5% of mammals form rigorously faithful pairs. From the earliest days, contends Fisher, the human pattern has been "monogamy with clandestine adultery." Occasional flings upped the chances that new combinations of genes would be passed on to the next generation. Men who sought new partners had more children. Contrary to common assumptions, women were just as likely to stray. "As long as prehistoric females were secretive about their extramarital affairs," argues Fisher, "they could garner extra resources, life insurance, better genes and more varied DNA for their biological futures. . . ."   8

Lovers often claim that they feel as if they are being swept away. They're not mistaken; they are literally flooded by chemicals, research suggests. A meeting of eyes, a touch of hands or a whiff of scent sets off a flood that starts in the brain and races along the nerves and through the blood. The results are familiar: flushed skin, sweaty palms, heavy breathing. If love looks suspiciously like stress, the reason is simple: the chemical pathways are identical.   9

Above all, there is the sheer euphoria of falling in love — a not-so-surprising reaction, considering that many of the substances swamping the newly smitten are chemical cousins of amphetamines. They include dopamine, norepinephrine and especially phenylethylamine (PEA). Cole Porter knew what he was talking about when he wrote, "I get a kick out of you." "Love is a natural high," observes Anthony Walsh, author of *The Science of Love: Understanding Love and Its Effects on Mind and Body*. "PEA gives you that silly smile that you flash at strangers. When we meet someone who is attractive to us, the whistle blows at the PEA factory."   10

But phenylethylamine highs don't last forever, a fact that lends support to arguments that passionate romantic love is short-lived. As with any amphetamine, the body builds up a tolerance to PEA; thus it takes more and more of the substance to produce love's special kick. After two to three years, the body simply can't crank up the needed amount of PEA. And chewing on chocolate doesn't help, despite popular belief. The candy is high in PEA, but it fails to boost the body's supply.   11

Fizzling chemicals spell the end of delirious passion; for many people that marks the end of the liaison as well. It is particularly true for those whom Dr. Michael Liebowitz of the New York State Psychiatric Institute terms "attraction junkies." They crave the intoxication of falling in love so much that they move frantically from affair to affair just as soon as the first rush of infatuation fades.   12

Still, many romances clearly endure beyond the first years. What accounts for that? Another set of chemicals, of course. The continued presence of a partner gradually steps up production in the brain of endorphins. Unlike the fizzy amphetamines, these are soothing substances. Natural pain-killers, they give lovers a sense of security, peace and calm. "That is one reason why it feels so horrible when we're abandoned or a lover dies," notes Fisher. "We don't have our daily hit of narcotics."   13

Researchers see a contrast between the heated infatuation induced by PEA, along with other amphetamine-like chemicals, and the more intimate attachment   14 fostered and prolonged by endorphins. "Early love is when you love the way the other person makes you feel," explains psychiatrist Mark Goulston of the University of California, Los Angeles. "Mature love is when you love the person as he or she is." It is the difference between passionate and compassionate love, observes Walsh, a psychobiologist at Boise State University in Idaho. "It's Bon Jovi vs. Beethoven."

Oxytocin is another chemical that has recently been implicated in love. Produced by the brain, it sensitizes nerves and stimulates muscle contraction. In women it helps uterine contractions during childbirth as well as production of breast milk, and seems to inspire mothers to nuzzle their infants. Scientists speculate that oxytocin might encourage similar cuddling between adult women and men. The versatile chemical may also enhance orgasms. In one study of men, oxytocin increased to three to five times its normal level during climax, and it may soar even higher in women. . . . 15

Chemicals may help explain (at least to scientists) the feelings of passion and compassion, but why do people tend to fall in love with one partner rather than a myriad of others? Once again, it's partly a function of evolution and biology. "Men are looking for maximal fertility in a mate," says Loyola Marymount's Mills. "That is in large part why females in the prime childbearing ages of 17 to 28 are so desirable." Men can size up youth and vitality in a glance, and studies indeed show that men fall in love quite rapidly. Women tumble more slowly, to a large degree because their requirements are more complex; they need more time to check the guy out. "Age is not vital," notes Mills, "but the ability to provide security, father children, share resources and hold a high status in society are all key factors." 16

Still, that does not explain why the way Mary walks and laughs makes Bill dizzy with desire while Marcia's gait and giggle leave him cold. "Nature has wired us for one special person," suggests Walsh, romantically. He rejects the idea that a woman or a man can be in love with two people at the same time. Each person carries in his or her mind a unique subliminal guide to the ideal partner, a "love map," to borrow a term coined by sexologist John Money of Johns Hopkins University. 17

Drawn from the people and experiences of childhood, the map is a record of whatever we found enticing and exciting — or disturbing and disgusting. Small feet, curly hair. The way our mothers patted our head or how our fathers told a joke. A fireman's uniform, a doctor's stethoscope. All the information gathered while growing up is imprinted in the brain's circuitry by adolescence. Partners never meet each and every requirement, but a sufficient number of matches can light up the wires and signal, "It's love." Not every partner will be like the last one, since lovers may have different combinations of the characteristics favored by the map. 18

O.K., that's the scientific point of view. Satisfied? Probably not. To most people — with or without Ph.D.s — love will always be more than the sum of its natural parts. It's a commingling of body and soul, reality and imagination, poetry and phenylethylamine. In our deepest hearts, most of us harbor the hope that love will never fully yield up its secrets, that it will always elude our grasp. 19

Making Connections to Personal and Social Issues: Love Maps

The chemistry of love is easily summarized: Amphetamines fuel romance; endorphins and oxytocin sustain lasting heterosexual relationships. As Toufexis makes clear, however, these chemical reactions do not explain why specific people are initially attracted to each other. Toufexis observes that an initial attraction occurs because each of us carries a "unique subliminal guide" or "love map" (paragraph 17) that leads us unerringly to a partner. Moreover, she explains that men look for maximal fertility, whereas women look for security, resources, status, and a willingness to father children.

With two or three other students, discuss these explanations for attraction between the sexes. Consider where your love map comes from and how much it may be influenced by your family traditions, your friends and community, or images in the media and advertising. Consider also whether it is possible for an individual's love map to change over time — and whether your own has changed. What might contribute to such changes?

Analyzing Writing Strategies

1. Put yourself in the position of a *Time* magazine reader turning pages and encountering Toufexis's essay. Would you stop and read it? What does Toufexis do to **catch readers' attention**? Look, for example, at the title — "Love: The Right Chemistry" — and the epigraph quoting Greta Garbo's line from the film *Ninotchka*. What appeal might these features have for readers?

   Reread the opening paragraph, paying special attention to its tone. Note the conversational "O.K." with which it begins and the use of a contraction (*let's*) instead of the more formal (*let us*). What other characteristics of Toufexis's language in this opening paragraph seem designed to entice readers to read on?

2. Toufexis's essay includes a **visual** that combines words with drawings. Consider what it contributes to your understanding of her concept explanation. Begin by examining how you read it. Do you start with the words, the images, or some combination of the two? Do you read from left to right and top to bottom, as you would a written text in English, or do you follow some other path? How do the numbers together with the colored and dotted lines guide your eye?

   There is no title or caption to explain the role the visual plays in the essay. What seems to you to be its role? Does it illustrate something already discussed in the essay, add new information, do both, or do something else altogether?

Commentary: A Focused Concept, Logical Plan, and Careful Use of Sources

Toufexis's published concept explanation resembles the opening essay by student Linh Kieu Ngo in that both authors obviously thought a lot about their readers when planning their essays. Neither Ngo nor Toufexis tries to present everything there is to know about the concept; instead, each focuses the explanation on aspects that are likely to be new and interesting to readers. Assuming that the information she is presenting will be unfamiliar to most readers, Toufexis, like Ngo, carefully plans the essay and provides cues that make it easy to follow. Moreover, to reassure readers that the information they are being given is trustworthy, both Ngo and Toufexis cite authoritative sources.

Unless they are writing encyclopedic books, writers of essays explaining concepts must limit the scope of their explanation. In her relatively brief magazine article, Toufexis writes about a narrowly **focused concept**. She focuses on certain scientific aspects of romantic love, specifically the evolutionary biology and neurochemistry of love between adult human heterosexual mates. Because she is explaining the evolutionary pressures that promote reproduction of the species, she excludes other love relationships such as romantic love between members of the same gender as well as platonic or nonsexual love between friends, siblings, or parents and children. Because she focuses on science, Toufexis chooses not to discuss views on love held by various cultures and religions, the history of romance as reflected in literature, courtship rituals through time, and dozens of other possible subjects related to love. Toufexis keeps her focus scientific throughout the essay, except for a brief but relevant digression about "love maps" toward the end. When readers finish the essay, they are well informed about the evolutionary biology and chemistry of love. By keeping to this focus, Toufexis is able to present information that is likely to be unfamiliar to most readers and therefore is more likely to hold their attention.

The unfamiliarity of the information in concept explanations makes it imperative that writers develop a **logical plan** that lays out the information in a way that is clear and easy for readers to follow. Toufexis gives readers cues to help them anticipate how the essay will unfold: a *thesis statement* that identifies the focused concept that is the subject of the essay and a *forecast* of the topics that will be addressed in the essay. In paragraph 1, Toufexis announces that she is writing about "romantic love," a concept she will address with "scientific precision." In paragraph 2, she states the essay's thesis ("What seems on the surface to be irrational, intoxicated behavior is in fact part of nature's master strategy — a vital force that has helped humans survive, thrive and multiply through thousands of years"). She also forecasts the topics she will discuss in the essay ("love rests firmly on the foundations of evolution, biology and chemistry"). Here's a simple scratch outline of the topics she goes on to develop, showing that she delivers on the promise of this forecast:

introduction (epigraph and paragraphs 1–2)

evolutionary biology (3–8)

neurochemistry (9–15)

love maps (16–18)

conclusion (19)

By constructing visible transitions, Toufexis also lets readers know when she is leaving one topic and beginning the next. For example, at the beginning of paragraph 9, where she moves from discussing evolutionary biology to neurochemistry, Toufexis writes: "Lovers often claim that they feel as if they are being swept away. They're not mistaken; they are literally flooded by chemicals, research suggests." Similarly, when the topic shifts to love maps, Toufexis uses the whole paragraph (17) to make the transition. She also uses transitions within her discussion of each topic. Look, for example, at the way she introduces each neurochemical involved in romantic feelings:

> Above all, there is the sheer euphoria of falling in love — a not-so-surprising reaction, considering that many of the substances swamping the newly smitten are chemical cousins of amphetamines. They include dopamine, norepinephrine and especially phenylethylamine (PEA). (paragraph 10)

> Still, many romances clearly endure beyond the first years. What accounts for that? Another set of chemicals, of course. (13)

> Oxytocin is another chemical that has recently been implicated in love. (15)

You can feature these types of cues — thesis, forecasting, and transitions — in your essay explaining a concept. Whereas forecasting is optional, a thesis and transitions are essential; without them, your readers will have to struggle to follow your explanation and may become confused and irritated.

To learn more about cueing readers, see Chapter 13.

In addition to giving readers a focused concept and a logical plan, writers have to convince readers that the information they've used to explain the concept is reliable. They do this by acknowledging their expert **sources**. Like most journalists, Toufexis relies primarily on interviews, although it appears that she also read at least parts of the two books she names in paragraphs 5 and 10. Perhaps she also read other sources, which may have led her to some of the professors she interviewed. She apparently arranged telephone or in-person interviews (or possibly e-mail exchanges) with six different professors specializing in diverse academic disciplines: psychology, anthropology, psychiatry, and sexology. Identifying her sources by their specialization, academic institution, and books or articles on the subject helps to establish that they are indeed credible authorities.

What is most notable about Toufexis's use of sources is that she does not indicate precisely where she obtained all the information she includes. For example, she does not cite the source of the anthropological information in paragraphs 3–5, although a reader might guess that she summarized it from *Anatomy of Love*, cited at the end of paragraph 5. We cannot be certain whether the quote at the end of paragraph 5 comes from the book or from an interview with its author. Because she is writing for a respected publication, *Time* magazine, Toufexis can probably assume that her readers will not fault her for failing to provide exact bibliographical citations as long as she gives general indications of where her information comes from. These liberties in citing sources are expected by experienced readers of magazines and newspapers, including the leading ones that educated readers count on to keep them up to date regarding developments in various fields. Readers would be surprised to find footnotes or works cited lists in popular publications.

In most college writing, however, sources must be cited. Moreover, college writers — whether students or professors — are expected to follow certain styles for source citations, such as MLA style in English and APA style in psychology.

Academic writers cite sources because credit must be given to the authors of any publication that contributes to a new piece of writing. The only essay in this chapter that includes a bibliography and follows an academic style (MLA) of citing sources was written for a college composition course by student Linh Kieu Ngo. Your instructor will expect you to cite your sources in a conventional academic way.

Considering Topics for Your Own Essay

Like Toufexis, you could write an essay about love or romance, but you could choose a different focus: its history (how and when did romantic love develop as an idea in the West?), its cultural characteristics (how is love regarded currently among different American ethnic groups or world cultures?), its excesses or extremes, or the phases of falling in and out of love. Also consider writing about other concepts involving personal relationships, such as jealousy, codependency, idealization, stereotyping, or homophobia.

RICHARD A. FRIEDMAN is the director of Psychopharmacology at the New York Weill Cornell Medical Center and a Professor of Clinical Psychiatry. Specializing in clinical depression, anxiety, and mood disorders, he has published his research in distinguished academic journals such as the *American Journal of Psychiatry*, the *Journal of Affective Disorders*, and the *Journal of Clinical Psychopharmacology*. He also writes a regular column in *The New York Times* on health issues, which is where this article originally appeared. As you read, notice how Friedman makes the concept of hyperthymia accessible to readers who may not be knowledgeable about science.

Born to Be Happy, Through a Twist of Human Hard Wire
Richard A. Friedman

In the course of the last year, the woman lost her husband to cancer and then her job. But she did not come to my office as a patient; she sought advice about her teenage son who was having trouble dealing with his father's death. Despite crushing loss and stress, she was not at all depressed — sad, yes, but still upbeat. I found myself stunned by her resilience. What accounted for her ability to weather such sorrow with buoyant optimism? So I asked her directly. "All my life," she recalled recently, "I've been happy for no good reason. It's just my nature, I guess." But it was more than that. She was a happy extrovert, full of energy and enthusiasm who was indefatigably sociable. And she could get by with five or six hours of sleep each night. 1

Like this woman, a journalist I know realized when she was a teenager that she was different from others. "It's actually kind of embarrassing to be so cheerful and happy all the time," she said. "When I was in high school I read the Robert Browning poem 'My Last Duchess.' In it, the narrator said he killed his wife, the 2 duchess, because 'she had a heart — how shall I say — too soon made glad?' And I thought, uh-oh, that's me."

These two women were lucky to be born with a joyous temperament, which in its most extreme form is called hyperthymia. Cheerful despite life's misfortunes, energetic and productive, they are often the envy of all who know them because they don't even have to work at it. In a sense, they are the psychiatric mirror image of people who suffer from a chronic, often lifelong, mild depression called dysthymia, which affects about 3 percent of American adults. Always down, dysthymics experience little pleasure and battle through life with a dreary pessimism. Despite whatever fortune comes their way, they remain glum. But hyperthymia certainly doesn't look like an illness; there appears to be no disadvantage to being a euphoric extrovert, except, perhaps, for inspiring an occasional homicidal impulse from jealous friends or peers. But little is actually known about people with hyperthymia for the simple reason that they don't see psychiatrists complaining that they are happy.

If dysthymia is hyperthymia's dark twin, then hyperthymia may not always be so rosy. That is because about 90 percent of dysthymic people experience episodes of more severe depression in their lifetimes. Are hyperthymics at risk of some mood disorders, too?

If hyperthymics bear a kinship with any psychiatric illness, it may be bipolar disorder. Bipolar patients live on a roller coaster of depressive troughs and manic peaks. But unlike hyperthymia, mania is an inherently unstable state of euphoria, irritability and often psychosis that causes profound morbidity and impaired functioning. Some researchers believe hyperthymics may be at increased risk of depression or hypomania, a mild variant of mania. And they may have high rates of affective disorders in their closest relatives. Hyperthymic and bipolar people may also share a tendency to be highly creative, given the strong association between bipolar disorder and creativity. For example, a 1987 study of creative writers at the University of Iowa Writers' Workshop by Dr. Nancy Andreasen showed that writers had bipolar illness at a rate four times as high as control group members who were not writers.

Of course, the notion of a hyperthymic temperament is hardly new. Some 2,400 years ago, Hippocrates proposed that a mixture of four basic humors — blood, phlegm, yellow bile and black bile — determined human temperament; depending on which humor predominates, one's nature is happy, phlegmatic, irritable or sad. Modern science has renamed the humors neurotransmitters, like serotonin and dopamine, and tried to link them to abnormal mental states. For example, depression was thought to result from a functional deficit of serotonin or norepinephrine in the brain. But one problem with this theory is that antidepressants increase the levels of these neurotransmitters within days, yet their clinical effects take several weeks. If the theory were correct, then depression should clear up within days of taking an antidepressant, not weeks. Still, many dysthymic people respond to antidepressants and watch their unhappiness melt away in a matter of weeks. If a lifelong depressive state like dysthymia can be erased in some cases with medication, is it possible then to make a person better than well, let's say hyperthymic?

Of course, humans have experimented with various recreational drugs for this purpose since recorded history without much success. Cocaine, to name one, produces an instant and intense euphoria by flooding the brain with dopamine. But the pleasure of cocaine is fleeting because the neurons that are activated by dopamine become rapidly desensitized to it, leading to a state of apathy and depression. Ecstasy can induce tranquil euphoria, largely by enhancing brain serotonin activity, but it is short-lived. And it can permanently damage serotonin-containing neurons in animals, hardly good news for humans. In fact, the pleasure brought on by all recreational drugs will fade sooner or later because of the brain's own homeostatic mechanisms.

7

What about psychotropic medications? A study by Dr. Brian Knutson at the University of California at San Francisco looked at the effects of the serotonin-enhancing antidepressant Paxil among normal volunteers, randomly assigned to either Paxil or a placebo. Neither the volunteers nor the researchers knew who was taking Paxil and who was taking the placebo. Compared with the placebo, Paxil reduced hostile feelings and slightly increased social affiliation. But Paxil did not make the normal people any happier.

8

In short, no drug — recreational or prescribed — comes close to creating the stable euphoria of hyperthymic people. Of course, antidepressants, unlike recreational drugs, are nonaddicting and retain their benefits over time. So if some people are just born happy and stay happy for no good reason, does this mean that happiness is nothing more than a lucky combination of neurotransmitters? For most people, no. Circumstance and experience count for a lot, and being happy takes work. But hyperthymic people have it easy: they have won the temperamental sweepstakes and may be hard-wired for happiness.

9

Making Connections to Personal and Social Issues: Temperament

Everyone has good and bad moods and everyone suffers setbacks that have emotional consequences, but Friedman explains that some people also tend to be either dysthymic or hyperthymic. That is, their temperaments and possibly their genes incline them either to be depressed or to be happy no matter what the circumstances. If you think of these categories as extremes on a continuum, with dysthymia on one extreme and hyperthymia on the other, where would you place yourself at this or some other period in your life? Or if you would prefer not to focus on yourself, consider where on the continuum you would place someone you know.

With two or three other students, discuss Friedman's categories as they apply to you or someone you know. Take turns giving examples that would illustrate each person's temperament. Then, consider how social and cultural influences — family and community as well as the media — affect not only how we express our feelings but possibly also what we think we should feel at certain moments in our lives.

Analyzing Writing Strategies

1. Effective concept explanations present **clear definitions**. In a sense, Friedman's entire essay, like most concept explanations, can be seen as an extended definition. But Friedman also uses brief definitions to explain new terms to his nonspecialist readers. For example, look at the first sentence of paragraph 3 where he defines *hyperthymia* and the third sentence where he defines *dysthymia*. Both of these sentence definitions take the same form, using the word "called" to signal to readers that a key term is being defined.

   Definitions, however, do not need to announce themselves so explicitly. Reread paragraph 5 and underline the definitions you find. Compare your findings with those of other students in the class. What do you learn from this analysis about some of the different sentence patterns you can use to define important words?

For more on sentence patterns for defining, turn to Chapter 16.

2. A common way of explaining something is to compare it to something else, perhaps something that readers already know. In paragraph 3, right after naming the concept he is explaining (*hyperthymia*), Friedman also mentions a second concept (*dysthymia*), which he calls hyperthymia's "psychiatric mirror image." He **compares and contrasts** these two concepts in paragraphs 3, 4, and 6. Reread these paragraphs, noting the comparisons and contrasts he draws between them. Why do you think Friedman decided to spend so much space in this brief essay to this comparison? As a reader, how does the comparison with dysthymia help you understand the concept of hyperthymia?

   Friedman also compares and contrasts hyperthymia to the mania typical of bipolar disorder (paragraph 5) and the euphoria produced by drugs like cocaine and ecstasy (paragraph 7). Reread these paragraphs and consider what these comparisons add to your understanding.

Commentary: Engaging Readers' Interest with Anecdotes and Rhetorical Questions

As a psychiatrist and experienced newspaper writer, Friedman knows that one of the challenges of effectively explaining scientific concepts to the general reader is **capturing readers' interest** before getting into technical details. He therefore opens his essay with **anecdotes**, stories about real people that serve primarily as examples to illustrate the concept being explained.

To be effective, anecdotes need to strike readers as realistic. The first anecdote tells about a woman who sought Friedman's professional advice and the second tells about a friend. His narrative about how he met the first woman is concise but detailed enough to enable readers to picture their first conversation. In fact, Friedman not only gives us an impression of the woman by reporting her own words, but he also describes his initial "stunned" reaction. As readers, we can readily sympathize with the woman's situation; and like Friedman, most of us will be surprised that although the woman is evidently "sad," she also seems "upbeat." The anecdote is designed to make us curious, wanting to learn more about why this woman reacted as she did. But instead of telling us more about this particular woman, the next paragraph presents an anecdote about another person. The word "like" at the beginning of the paragraph lets us know that we are about to learn about someone else who behaves similarly.

The similarities between these two women — the fact that they are naturally happy and resilient (not doing anything to raise their spirits) and have been that way their whole lives — gives us important information about the concept. Beginning an essay with anecdotes in this way enables readers to begin to understand essential elements of the concept even before they know it is being explained to them. This strategy is especially useful when explaining new or abstract concepts with technical terminology like "hyperthymia" and "dysthymia" that tends to make some readers anxious. The anecdotes lead readers to compare themselves and other people they know to these two women and to wonder either what's wrong with them or what's wrong with us. This question prepares readers for the more technical explanation of the "twin" psychological concepts of hyperthymia and dysthymia.

In beginning his explanatory essay with anecdotes, Friedman is following a common newspaper writing convention of opening with a "hook," so called because it is supposed to catch and hold readers' attention. This strategy is especially useful in a newspaper or on the Internet where readers usually skim headlines, graphics, and opening paragraphs looking for items of interest. For college essays, it might not seem to be necessary — after all, you know ahead of time that your instructor is going to read your essay whether it captures his or her attention or not. But if the opening also vividly illustrates the concept, your instructor is likely to give you credit for explaining it well and may think your essay stands out from the less intriguing concept explanations of your classmates.

Whereas opening with anecdotes can capture readers' attention, **rhetorical questions** can keep readers reading. Rhetorical questions are questions writers pose but do not expect readers to answer. Instead, writers usually go on to answer the questions themselves, as is the case with all of Friedman's rhetorical questions.

- What accounted for her ability to weather such sorrow with buoyant optimism? (paragraph 1)
- Are hyperthymics at risk of some mood disorders, too? (paragraph 4)
- If a lifelong depressive state like dysthymia can be erased in some cases with medication, is it possible then to make a person better than well, let's say hyperthymic? (paragraph 6)
- What about psychotropic medications? (paragraph 8)
- So if some people are just born happy and stay happy for no good reason, does this mean that happiness is nothing more than a lucky combination of neurotransmitters? (paragraph 9)

Rhetorical questions engage readers by anticipating questions they may have as they read. For example, the first rhetorical question in the opening paragraph comes right after Friedman describes the woman's unusually cheery frame of mind in spite of the "crushing loss and stress" she has suffered. As we suggested above, readers may share Friedman's "stunned" reaction. Like him, we might ask ourselves at that very point in the essay, "What accounted for her ability to weather such sorrow with buoyant optimism?" By giving voice to our thoughts, Friedman strengthens our identification with him and encourages us to trust what he tells us.

Depending on where it is placed, the rhetorical question can also serve as a kind of topic sentence or as a transition to introduce a new topic. The question that concludes paragraph 4 — "Are hyperthymics at risk of some mood disorders, too?" — works this way. It prepares us for the next paragraph's discussion of the kinds of mood disorders associated with hyperthymia. The rhetorical question ending paragraph 6 and the one opening paragraph 8 work in similar ways, making a transition to the following paragraph or introducing the topic of the paragraph, respectively. Rhetorical questions certainly are not a requirement of explanatory writing, but they are a useful strategy. Nevertheless, like anything else, they can be overused. As you look back at the way Friedman uses rhetorical questions in his essay, ask yourself whether he relies too much on this one device and consider what other writing strategies he could use to engage his readers and keep them reading.

Considering Topics for Your Own Essay

Friedman mentions several concepts you might think about exploring further for your own essay, such as pessimism, extroversion (or introversion), apathy, addiction, psychosis, and the placebo effect. Other psychological concepts you might consider writing about include agoraphobia, obsessive-compulsive disorder, seasonal affective disorder, malingering, kleptomania, dyslexia, or attention deficit disorder (ADD). You could focus instead on the history of psychology and write about Freudian concepts such as psychoanalysis, ego, id, superego, repression, libido; Jungian concepts such as anima, archetype, collective unconscious; behavioral psychology concepts such as conditioning, positive and negative reinforcement; or social psychology concepts such as socialization, conformity, "the looking-glass self," altruism, narcissism, empathy, or codependency.

BOB HOLMES has a B.S. in zoology from the University of Alberta in Canada and a Ph.D. in ecology and evolutionary biology from the University of Arizona. After obtaining a certificate in science writing from the University of California, Santa Cruz, Holmes taught in UCSC's writing program for several years. He has been a science writer for over a decade and has written about 600 magazine articles, mostly for *New Scientist,* for which he is a correspondent. *New Scientist* is a popular science magazine "for everyone, both young & old, amateur & professional." It is published in England and has a worldwide readership. Holmes writes on a wide range of topics in a variety of genres, including profiles and interviews with noted researchers, book reviews, and concept explanations. "In the Blink of an Eye" originally appeared in the *New Scientist* in July 2005.

In the Blink of an Eye

Bob Holmes

Every weekend angler knows to throw back the tiddlers. Likewise, commercial fish-ermen use large-meshed nets to spare smaller fish. Both are working on the prin-ciple that by reducing their haul this way, they can keep fish populations vigorous and healthy. But they could be making a terrible mistake. It is becoming increas-ingly clear that such well-meaning strategies may actually have the opposite effect to what the fishermen intend.

What they and most of the rest of us have overlooked is evolution — not the familiar glacier-slow process found in textbooks, which takes millennia to work its wonders, but a burbling freshet of evolutionary change that can occur in a matter of years or decades. By leaving the smaller fish, fishermen may be shifting the evolutionary goalposts, reshaping fish species as they go. In fact, biologists are starting to suspect that this phenomenon, which they have dubbed contemporary evolution, is happening all around us. Besides emptying fishing nets, rapid evolu-tionary change cripples the efforts of doctors and farmers, thwarts trophy hunters in search of the big prize, and frustrates conservation biologists trying to rescue endangered species.

What's more, in the decades to come, the pace of evolution may quicken still further, as human activities transform the Earth, forcing species to adapt or die. That makes our need to understand the forces at work even more compelling. If

By taking only the biggest cod, fishermen favour fish that grow slowly and stay small.

we know what's going on, we may be able to find ways to control evolution, and even shape it for our benefit and that of the world around us.

Evolutionary biologists have long known that the process can happen rapidly — Charles Darwin himself pointed out the observable changes wrought by pigeon fanciers and dog breeders. A century later biologists showed that peppered moths in England's industrial heartland had evolved darker colours to camouflage themselves against soot-blackened trees. And by the end of the 20th century everyone knew that bacteria, insects and weeds were able to evolve resistance to antibiotics and pesticides within a few years. But few thought such speedy evolution was more than just a special case.

"When I was a graduate student in the 1970s, the prevailing idea was that evolution was this gradual, slow process," says David Reznick of the University of California, Riverside. "We already knew there were instances of evolution that people had witnessed, but it was considered to be exceptional, not the usual pattern."

The experts had good reason to be sceptical that evolution could happen quickly. After all, evolution is driven by a mismatch between an organism's needs and its abilities to meet them. The prevailing wisdom was that most organisms were already well adapted to their circumstances. Although there would be genetic variation between individuals within a population, no combination of genes would be particularly better adapted than any other, so there would be little pressure for natural selection to favour the survival and reproduction of some individuals over others. In other words, selection would generally be low and evolution slow — except where humans used antibiotics or pesticides to wipe out all but the one-in-a-million resistant individuals, or allowed only the gaudiest pigeons to breed.

All Change

But in the 1980s biologists began to realise that adaptation might be a more dynamic process than they had thought. For example, on one of the Galapagos Islands, Peter and Rosemary Grant of Princeton University discovered that among one species of finch, individuals with small beaks do best in wet years, when small-seeded plants thrive, while their larger-beaked nestmates have the edge in drier years, when larger-seeded plants predominate. As a result, beak size seesaws back and forth rapidly.

More recently, a team led by Barry Sinervo of the University of California, Santa Cruz, has found the same kind of rapid change in the side-blotched lizard in the south-western U.S. Male lizards pursue one of three different genetically determined mating strategies, each corresponding with a different throat colour. Orange-throated males are big and aggressive, and easily bully the more timid blue-throated males into ceding their females. Yellow-throated males, which sneak in disguised as females, can steal mating opportunities from the orange males while they are busy blustering, but fail to fool the blue males as these pay close attention to their precious mates. The result is a game of evolutionary rock-paper-scissors, with each strategy becoming dominant every four to five years.

No one knows how common this sort of contemporary evolution is, because it is hard to spot in the wild. The change happens so fast that biologists are likely to miss it unless they keep very detailed records of exactly the right characters — a complete reversal of the old view that evolution is too slow to see in real time. "There's no reason this couldn't be going on all the time in organisms all over the place," says Reznick.

Adaptation is a dynamic process for Galapagos finches and side-blotched lizards.

Nor is rapid evolution confined to the cycling of different versions of the same trait. Sometimes evolution drives steadily in one direction. This may be crucial to our understanding of the biology of invasive species. Biologists have often noted that introduced species, such as zebra mussels or garlic mustard in the U.S., can lurk inconspicuously in their new home for decades or even centuries before suddenly exploding into problem pests. One possible, though not yet well tested, explanation is that the invaders are at first poorly adapted to their new setting, and cannot take off until they evolve a better match. And once that happens, the result can be dramatic. "Many of these invasions may reflect a genetic shift in the invading population," says Donald Waller from the University of Wisconsin–Madison. "A lot of [organisms] are just a couple of percentage points above or below break-even, so it only takes a little change to make a big difference."   10

Human activity is changing some ecosystems faster, and more dramatically, than ever before, and strong directional selection may be especially common in these cases. "It's possible these human-induced changes are not just greater, but more consistent and more permanent. They may be resulting in evolutionary changes that are rapid, but may also be persistent as well," says Andrew McAdam from Michigan State University in East Lansing. For example, ivory hunting has favoured the evolution of tuskless elephants in parts of Africa and Asia.   11

One of the best places to see evolution in action is high in the Rocky Mountains of Alberta, Canada, home of the largest bighorn sheep in North America. Hunters can pay six-figure sums for the right to shoot a big ram, the massive, curling horns of which make it the continent's most highly prized hunting trophy. On one peak, aptly named Ram Mountain, hunting has been so intense that rams can expect to live only a year or two after their horns reach the almost-360-degree curl that makes them a legal target for hunters. Not surprisingly, this has led to intense selection in favour of males whose horns never grow to reach trophy status.   12

Sure enough, a study led by Dave Coltman, now at the University of Alberta in Edmonton, found that average horn size has declined by about 25 per cent over the past 30 years (Nature, vol 426, p 655). And the genetic erosion doesn't end there because larger-horned rams tend to have better genes in general. "You start taking out the prime-quality rams and the next generation will be missing those genes, because their fathers will be lower quality," says Coltman. In other words, every time they pull the trigger, hunters are working against their own long-term interests. "It's a form of artificial selection where instead of getting more of what you want you're actually going to end up with less," he says.   13

The same thing happens at sea, where fishermen are typically only allowed to keep fish larger than a particular size. Three years ago, David Conover from Stony Brook University in New York showed just how counterproductive this might be. Conover and his colleague Stephan Munch simulated intense size-selective fishing on lab populations of a small commercial fish called the Atlantic silverside. After just four generations, fish from the "fished" populations — in which the largest 90 per cent of fish were removed before breeding — averaged barely half the size of fish in the "anti-fished" populations, in which the smallest 90 per cent were removed. As a result of the size difference, the total weight of fish removed   14

Hunting has reduced horn size by a quarter among Canada's bighorn sheep.

(analogous to the fishery harvest) in the fifth generation of the fished population was barely half that of the anti-fished one (Science, vol 297, p 94).

Since then other researchers have shown that cod off the coast of Newfoundland, Canada, have also evolved toward maturing at smaller sizes — presumably as a result of the capture of the largest fish. As well as contributing to the crash of the area's fishery, this shift may also hinder the cod's ability to recover, since small fish produce many fewer eggs than large fish. This could help explain why cod populations have failed to bounce back on the Grand Banks, off southeast Newfoundland, despite closure of the fishery there for the past 13 years. 15

If contemporary evolution really is a dominant force in heavily fished populations, then fisheries managers may unwittingly be doing just the opposite of what they should to maintain healthy stocks. Instead of catching the biggest fish and letting the rest go, we need to treasure the big fish as bearers of the best genes. One solution, says Conover, would be to let fishers take only medium-sized fish. If we did that, he says, a fish's best strategy would then be to grow through that window as fast as possible. Such a scheme would select for fast growth rates — a big improvement over the present system, which selects for scrawny fish that never reach the minimum catch size. 16

Turning evolution back from the "dark side" in fisheries can be done, but it won't be easy. "If you had a maximum size limit, under present trawl technology there wouldn't be a way to let the large ones go except by picking them out on your 17

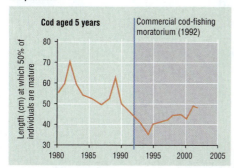

The adult body size of cod off the Atlantic coast of Labrador, Canada, shrank progressively over the time commercial fishing was permitted

Cod aged 5 years

Commercial cod-fishing moratorium (1992)

Length (cm) at which 50% of individuals are mature

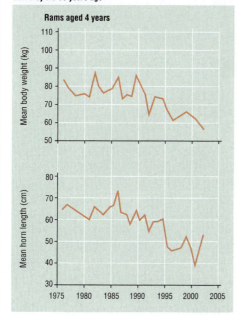

Mature bighorn rams weigh less and have much smaller horns than they did 30 years ago

Rams aged 4 years

Mean body weight (kg)

Mean horn length (cm)

deck and throwing them back, and a lot of them wouldn't survive," says Conover. But, he notes, modern trawls often use large-mesh metal grates to shunt sea turtles away from the net mouth while allowing fish through, and these might be adapted to exclude large fish as well.

18 But there is another, more drastic way to put the brakes on evolution: introduce no-fishing zones before stocks become too depleted. Such protected areas provide a refuge where larger fish can survive and continue to produce disproportionate numbers of eggs, so diluting the selection that would otherwise drive fish toward smaller sizes. No-hunting zones for bighorn sheep — or regulations that allow hunters to take a small number of sheep, but of any size — would similarly blunt selection for smaller horns.

19 Contemporary evolution is not always a bad thing, though. It is already being used to fit microbes for useful work. . . . And with man-made climate change looming, plants and animals will need the ability to adapt quickly. Biologists have noticed that several species have already responded to the warmer temperatures, and hence earlier springs, of the past few years by migrating or breeding earlier. For example, Stan Boutin and his colleagues at the University of Alberta found that red squirrels in Canada's Yukon territory now give birth about 18 days earlier than they did just a decade ago. Using tissue samples to determine each squirrel's parentage, the researchers could see how much of the variation in birth date ran in families. From this they calculated that at least 13 percent of the change — representing a shift of almost a full day per generation — was due to evolution and not behavioural flexibility.

Red squirrels are among several species adapting to global warming.

Fast Forward

Whether evolution can move fast enough to cope with the unprecedented rates of climate change expected over the next century remains to be seen. Clearly though, a species cannot evolve a new adaptation unless it has the right genes — and larger populations are more likely to possess this genetic capital than small ones. This means the losers in the climate-change shuffle are likely to be the species that are already rare. Conservationists might even need to consider abandoning some marginal populations and concentrating on those with the genetic resources to evolve successfully, says Boutin. "That means we maybe don't save every caribou herd in Alberta, but we focus on the ones with the highest probability of success."   20

And if rapid contemporary evolution really is as widespread as some researchers are beginning to suspect, it has one more unsettling implication: we may have to modify our notion of "preserving" rare species because every effort to rescue a species through captive breeding, founding new wild populations, or modifying existing habitats may cause it to evolve away from its starting point.   21

"This brings up an interesting philosophical question," says McAdam. "What is it that we're hoping to conserve? Is it particular species, or is it something about those species? Would we be happy if we were able to maintain all the species we have today, but human-induced evolutionary changes were so great that they essentially became functionally domesticated? Would we be satisfied with that? I would say no, that's not satisfying — at least to me."   22

Making Connections to Personal and Social Issues: Implications of Scientific Research

If it is true, as Holmes explains in paragraph 3, that "human activities transform the Earth, forcing species to adapt or die," then what are our moral responsibilities as individuals and as nations? What can people do to prevent or reverse the climate change that apparently is causing rapid contemporary evolution? For example, should the United States change its position and join the 140 nations that signed the 2005 Kyoto treaty agreeing to reduce carbon dioxide and other gases that contribute to global warming?

With two or three other students, discuss your views on these issues. Try to think of how you as individuals can make a difference. If you drive a gas-guzzling SUV or sporty car, would you trade it in for a hybrid car? Would you take public transportation to school or to work? What do you think your family and friends would be willing to do? Then, think about the role that governments and business leaders should take to reduce greenhouse emissions. Should government provide incentives and/or fines to encourage industry and individuals?

Analyzing Writing Strategies

1. We have said that essays explaining concepts present a **focused concept**. That is, writers do not try to explain everything that is known about the concept, but focus on certain aspects of it that they think will interest readers. For example, we have seen that Toufexis explains the concept of romantic love by detailing its evolutionary biology and neurochemistry. What is the concept Holmes explains and how does he focus his explanation? Reread the opening paragraphs to find where he first names the concept. How does he present his focus and interest readers in it?

2. Reread paragraphs 14–18 where Holmes discusses the effects of efforts to protect fish by restricting fishing. In paragraph 15, he presents the **problem** of Newfoundland cod. What exactly is the problem with the cod population?

   In paragraphs 16–18, Holmes discusses various **solutions** that have been proposed. Why do you think he devotes so much space in this relatively brief essay to discussing possible solutions to this problem?

   Notice also that Holmes first introduced the problem in paragraph 1. How does introducing it at the beginning of the essay and returning to it at the end help readers?

Commentary: Explaining Concepts through Illustration

Concepts typically are abstract. They name ideas, not things; therefore, they are often hard to grasp. Among the strategies writers use to bring concepts down to earth and make them more tangible for readers is to provide illustrations, as Bob Holmes does in this essay on the concept of rapid contemporary evolution. Holmes uses two kinds of illustration: examples and visuals.

Examples provide specific, often vivid illustrations that help readers understand and remember abstract concepts. Writers explaining concepts may give several brief examples or they may focus on an extended example; often, like Holmes, they do both. Paragraph 4 shows how a writer might sprinkle an explanation with multiple, brief examples. In this short paragraph, Holmes refers to examples of rapid evolutionary changes in pigeons, dogs, peppered moths, bacteria, insects, and weeds. Holmes also develops several paragraph-long examples such as his discussion in paragraph 7 of how Galapagos finches adapt and in paragraph 10 of how invasive species like zebra mussels and garlic mustard can suddenly become "problem pests." Finally, Holmes uses two multiparagraph extended examples: showing how hunting bighorn sheep for their "trophy" horns has led to a reduction in the size of the horns (paragraphs 12–13) and how catching big Newfoundland cod has endangered the health of the species (paragraphs 15–18). All of these examples help to establish the fact that rapid contemporary evolution exists and that it represents a potential problem for conservationists.

Examples like these apply the general concept to specific species, helping readers form a mental image of the effects of rapid evolutionary change. Holmes also illustrates the concept with two kinds of **visuals**: photographs and graphs. The article includes photographs of some of the species used as examples: cod, Galapagos finches, side-blotched lizards, bighorn sheep, and red squirrels. These photographs give readers memorable visual images. But the photographs are static and do not portray the process of rapid evolution. To represent the process, Holmes adds captions (listed below with the paragraphs in which each example is discussed). Notice that the captions are carefully composed to state directly and concisely the information presented in the written text about how these species are affected by the evolutionary process:

- Adaptation is a dynamic process for Galapagos finches (paragraph 7) and side-blotched lizards. (paragraph 8).
- By taking only the biggest cod, fishermen favour fish that grow slowly and stay small. (14–18)
- Hunting has reduced horn size by a quarter among Canada's bighorn sheep. (12–13)
- Red squirrels are among several species adapting to global warming. (19)

Although the photographs together with captions help illustrate the concept, Holmes adds a second type of visual — graphs — to emphasize and make plain to readers the rapidity of the process of contemporary evolution. Under the heading "Evolving Fast," three graphs are presented with captions. The first graph shows the effect of fishing on the size of Atlantic cod over the last twenty-five years. The caption tells the story that the graph illustrates visually. The next two graphs go together. They show how over a thirty-year period hunting has affected both the bighorn rams' weight and the size of their horns. These graphs show at a glance the fact that a significant change has occurred over a relatively short time, demonstrating with clarity and force the concept of rapid contemporary evolution.

When you are planning your essay, you will undoubtedly want to include examples — every essay in this chapter relies on examples. But you should also consider whether visuals might be added to illustrate and clarify your concept.

Considering Topics for Your Own Essay

Holmes refers to several concepts you might consider explaining, such as conservation, endangered species, natural and artificial selection, ecosystems, and global warming. You may also be interested in exploring related concepts like ecology, mutation, biodiversity, eugenics, genetic drift, adaptation, creationism, and intelligent design. Concepts related to global warming include the greenhouse effect, fossil fuels, deforestation, ozone depletion, renewable energy, fuel cells, and hybrid technology.

Purpose and Audience

Though it seeks to engage readers' interests, explanatory writing gives prominence to facts about a subject. It aims to engage readers' intellects rather than their imaginations, to instruct rather than entertain or argue.

Setting out to teach readers about a concept is no small undertaking. To succeed, you must know the concept so well that you can explain it simply, with a minimum of potential jargon or other confusing language. You must be authoritative without showing off or talking down. You must also estimate what your readers already know about the concept to decide which information will be truly new to them. You need to define unfamiliar words and pace the information carefully so that your readers are neither bored nor overwhelmed.

This assignment requires a willingness to cast yourself in the role of expert. Like Toufexis, Friedman, and Holmes, you could assume a general audience of informed adults, people who regularly read a newspaper, magazines, or Internet sites. Even though some readers may be highly educated, you can readily and confidently assume the role of expert after a few hours of research into your concept. If your readers are unfamiliar with the concept, you will be introducing it to them. If they know something about the concept, the particular focus you have chosen may broaden their knowledge and give them a new way of understanding the concept. If you choose a concept in a course you are currently taking, explaining it may help you understand it better and may make it more interesting and comprehensible to other students as well. Even if you are told to consider your instructor your sole reader, you can assume that your instructor will be eager to be informed about nearly any concept you choose.

Basic Features: Explaining a Concept

A Focused Concept

The primary purpose for explaining a concept is to inform readers, but writers of explanatory essays do not hope to communicate everything that is known about a concept. Instead, they make choices about what to include, what to emphasize, and what to omit. Most writers focus their explanations by discussing a particular aspect of the concept. Linh Kieu Ngo focuses on three specific types of cannibalism. Anastasia Toufexis centers her explanation of love on the evolutionary biology and neurochemistry of this phenomenon. In explaining the particular personality trait of hyperthymia, Richard A. Friedman concentrates on its relationship — or lack of one — to psychological disorders and the effects of recreational drugs. Bob Holmes's explanation of rapid contemporary evolution zeroes in on the role humans play in it and whether that role should change.

An Appeal to Readers' Interests

Most people read explanations of concepts for work or study. Consequently, they expect the writing to be simply informative and not necessarily entertaining. Yet readers appreciate explanations that both identify the concept's importance and engage them with lively writing and vivid detail. The essays in this chapter show some of the ways in which writers may appeal to readers. For example, Toufexis uses everyday language and humor, opening her essay with this direct address to readers: "O.K., let's cut out all this nonsense about romantic love." Calling romantic love "nonsense" arrests readers' attention as they thumb through the magazine in which the essay originally appeared. Ngo and Friedman each open their essays with a dramatic or surprising anecdote, Ngo's about a horrendous situation in which a group of refugees found themselves and Friedman's about a person whose behavior "stunned" him. Holmes also tries to surprise readers by telling them that what leisure and professional fishermen typically do to "keep fish populations vigorous and healthy" actually may endanger these populations. Opening strategies like these can do much to interest readers in the concept.

A Logical Plan

Since concept explanations present information that is new to readers and can therefore be hard to understand, writers need to develop a plan that presents new material step by step in a logical order. The most effective explanations are carefully organized and give readers all the obvious cues they need, such as forecasting statements, topic sentences, transitions, and summaries. In addition, the writer may try to frame the essay for readers by relating the ending to the beginning. We see these features repeatedly in the readings in this chapter. For example, Toufexis frames her essay with references to Ph.D.s, forecasts the three sciences from which she has gleaned her information about the neurochemistry of love, and begins nearly all of her paragraphs with a transition sentence. Following the opening anecdote, Ngo organizes his essay around the three kinds of cannibalism he introduces in paragraph 6. After discussing the first type, survival cannibalism (paragraph 7), his topic sentences make a transition from one type to another: "Unlike survival cannibalism, in which . . ., in dietary cannibalism humans are . . ." (paragraph 8); and "Religious or ritual cannibalism is different from survival and dietary cannibalism in that it . . ." (paragraph 11).

Good writers never forget that their readers need clear signals. Because writers already know the information and are aware of how their essays are organized, they can find it difficult to see the essay the way someone reading it for the first time would. That is precisely how it should be seen, however, to be sure that the essay includes all the necessary cues.

Clear Definitions

Essays explaining concepts depend on clear definitions. To relate information clearly, a writer must be sensitive to readers' knowledge; any key terms that are likely to be unfamiliar or misunderstood must be explicitly defined, as Toufexis defines *attraction junkies* (paragraph 12) and *endorphins* (paragraph 13) and as Ngo defines the categories of cannibalism (paragraph 6) and types of cannibalism (at the beginnings of paragraphs where he illustrates them). Friedman defines the concepts of *hyperthymia* and its opposite, *dysthymia* (3). He also defines the related concepts of *bipolar disorder, mania,* and *hypomania.* Holmes defines *rapid contemporary evolution* as well as the more familiar gradual form of evolutionary change. In a sense, all the readings in this chapter are extended definitions of concepts, and all the authors offer relatively concise, clear definitions of their concepts at some point in their essays.

Careful Use of Sources

To explain concepts, writers usually draw on information from many different sources. Although they often draw on their own experiences and observations, they almost always do additional research into what others have to say about their subject. Referring to expert sources always lends authority to an explanation.

How writers treat sources depends on the writing situation. Certain formal situations, such as college assignments or scholarly papers, have rules for citing and documenting sources. Students and scholars are expected to cite their sources formally because readers judge their work in part by what the writers have read and how they have used their reading. Ngo's essay illustrates this academic form of citing sources. For more informal writing — magazine articles, for example — readers do not expect or want page references or publication information, but they do expect sources to be identified. This identification often appears within the text of the article, for example when Friedman refers to "a 1987 study of creative writers at the University of Iowa Writers' Workshop by Dr. Nancy Andreasen" (paragraph 5). Holmes quotes several authorities and summarizes the findings of their research, being careful to identify each source by name and university affiliation. In two instances (paragraphs 13 and 14), he also gives a parenthetical citation with the journal name, volume number, and page number in case readers want to look up the research themselves.

Explaining a Concept

Invention and Research

What is an idea that you enjoy explaining to other people — or would like to learn more about? How much do you already know about it? Do some library or online research if necessary, and do some thinking and writing about the concept. Then consider how you'd interest readers in it and explain it clearly to them. . . . **See p. 167 for more.**

Planning and Drafting

As you look over what you have written so far, how can you present the concept clearly to readers and engage their interest? How much do they already know about it? What terms do you need to define? What organization would be easiest to follow? Make a plan for your explanation, and start drafting it. . . . **See p. 175 for more.**

Critical Reading Guide

What are your draft's strengths and weaknesses? For example, does your focus seem too broad? Would visuals or better transitions make your explanation clearer? Get a classmate, a friend, a writing tutor, or someone else to read and respond in detail to your essay, focusing especially on the parts you are most unsure of. . . . **See p. 179 for more.**

Revising

As you consider your essay again in light of your reader's comments, how can you improve it? If the beginning failed to engage the reader's interest, how else could you begin? How could you integrate quotations more smoothly into your own text? Go through your draft systematically, making changes wherever necessary. . . . **See p. 181 for more.**

Editing and Proofreading

Have you checked for errors that are especially likely in explanations of concepts? Have you forgotten to include commas around adjective clauses that are not essential to the meaning or around phrases that interrupt the flow of a sentence? Look for and correct these and any other errors. . . . **See p. 185 for more.**

The Writing Assignment

Write an essay about a concept that interests you and that you want to study further. When you have a good understanding of the concept, explain it to your readers, considering carefully what they already know about it and how your essay might add to what they know.

To learn about using the *Guide* e-book for invention and drafting, go to bedfordstmartins.com/theguide.

Invention and Research

The following guidelines will help you find a concept, understand it fully, select a focus that is appropriate for your readers, test your choice, and devise strategies for presenting your discoveries in a way that will be truly informative for your particular readers. Each activity is easy to do and takes only a few minutes. If you can spread out the activities over several days, you will have adequate time to understand the concept and decide how to present it. Keep a written record of your invention work to use when you draft the essay and later when you revise it. If you write on the computer, you may be able to copy and paste into your draft material from your invention and research notes.

Finding a Concept to Write About

Even if you already have a concept in mind, completing the following activities will help you to be certain of your choice.

Listing Concepts. *Make a list of concepts you could write about.* The longer your list, the more likely you are to find just the right concept for you. And should your first choice not work out, you will have a ready list of alternatives. Include concepts you already know something about as well as some you know only slightly and would like to research further. Also include concepts suggested by the Considering Topics for Your Own Essay activities following each reading in this chapter.

Your courses provide many concepts you will want to consider. Here are some typical concepts from a number of academic and other subjects. Your class notes or textbooks will suggest many others.

- *Literature:* irony, metaphysical conceit, semiotics, hero, dystopian novel, humanism, picaresque, the absurd, canon, representation, figurative language, modernism, identity politics, queering
- *Philosophy:* existentialism, nihilism, logical positivism, determinism, metaphysics, ethics, natural law, Zeno's paradox, epistemology, ideology
- *Business management:* autonomous work group, quality circle, cybernetic control system, management by objectives, zero-based budgeting, liquidity gap

- *Psychology:* metacognition, Hawthorne effect, assimilation/accommodation, social cognition, moratorium, intelligence, divergent/convergent thinking, operant conditioning, short-term memory, the Stroop effect, sleep paralysis
- *Government:* majority rule, minority rights, federalism, popular consent, exclusionary rule, political party, political machine, interest group, hegemony
- *Biology:* photosynthesis, mitosis, karyotype analysis, morphogenesis, electron transport, plasmolysis, phagocytosis, homozygosity, diffusion
- *Art:* cubism, Dadaism, surrealism, expressionism, perspective, collage
- *Math:* polynomials, boundedness, null space, permutations and combinations, factoring, Rolle's theorem, continuity, derivative, indefinite integral
- *Physical sciences:* matter, mass, weight, energy, gravity, atomic theory, law of definite proportions, osmotic pressure, first law of thermodynamics, entropy
- *Public health:* alcoholism, seasonal affective disorder, contraception, lead poisoning, prenatal care, toxicology, glycemic index
- *Environmental studies:* acid rain, recycling, ozone depletion, toxic waste, endangered species, sustainability
- *Sports:* squeeze play, hit and run (baseball); power play (hockey); nickel defense, wishbone offense (football); serve and volley offense (tennis); setup (volleyball); pick and roll, inside game (basketball)
- *Personal finance:* reverse mortgage, budget, insurance, deduction, revolving credit, interest rates, dividend, bankruptcy, socially conscious investing
- *Law:* tort, contract, garnishment, double indemnity, reasonable doubt, class-action suits, product liability, lemon law
- *Sociology:* norm, deviance, role conflict, ethnocentrism, class, social stratification, conflict theory, action theory, acculturation, Whorf-Sapir hypothesis, machismo

■ *Listing Concepts Related to Identity and Community.*   Many concepts are important in understanding identity and community. As you consider the following concepts, try to think of others in this category: self-esteem, character, personality, autonomy, individuation, narcissism, multiculturalism, ethnicity, race, racism, social contract, communitarianism, community policing, social Darwinism, identity politics, special-interest groups, diaspora, colonialism, public space, the other, agency, difference, yuppie, generation Y.

■ *Listing Concepts Related to Work and Career.*   Concepts like the following enable you to gain a deeper understanding of your work experiences and career aspirations: free enterprise, minimum wage, affirmative action, stock option, sweatshop, glass ceiling, downsizing, collective bargaining, service sector, market, entrepreneur, bourgeoisie, underclass, working class, middle class, division of labor, monopoly, automation, robotics, management style, deregulation, multinational corporation.

Choosing a Concept.   *Look over your list of possibilities and select one concept to explore.* Pick a concept that interests you, one you feel eager to learn more about.

Consider also whether it might interest others. You may know very little about the concept now, but the guidelines that follow will help you research it and understand it fully.

Surveying Information about the Concept

Your research efforts for a concept essay must be divided into two stages. First, you want to achieve quickly a far-reaching survey or overview of information about the concept you have chosen. Your goal in this first stage is to learn as much as you can from diverse sources so that you may decide whether you want to write about this topic and whether you can identify an aspect of it to focus on.

In the second stage, when you know what your focus will be, you begin in-depth research for information that will educate you about this focus. When Linh Kieu Ngo arrived at this stage, he would have been digging for information on ways to classify the different types of cannibalism.

The activities that follow will guide you through this two-stage research process.

Discovering What You Already Know.   *Before doing any research on your concept or even looking at any handy references, take a few minutes to write about what you already know about the concept.* Also say why you have chosen the concept and why you find it interesting and worth knowing about. Write quickly, without planning or organizing. Write phrases or lists as well as sentences. You could even add drawings or quick sketches or write down questions about the concept, questions that express your curiosity or uncertainty. If you find that you know very little about the concept, you still might want to write about it — out of personal motivation, which is not a bad reason to commit yourself to the study of an unfamiliar concept.

Sorting Through Your Personal Resources.   *Check any materials you already have at hand that explain your concept.* If you are considering a concept from one of your academic courses, you will find explanatory material in your textbook or perhaps your lecture notes.

To acquire a comprehensive, up-to-date understanding of your concept, however, you will need to know how experts other than your textbook writer and instructor define and illustrate it. To find this information, you might locate relevant articles and books in the library, search for resources or make inquiries on the Internet, or consult experts on campus or in the community.

Going to the Library.   To learn about your concept and explore aspects that you could focus on, you may want to do some research in the library. Ask the librarian for help finding relevant encyclopedias, disciplinary guides, databases, or online resources available through the library. While at the library, look for your concept name in the subject headings of the Library of Congress Subject Headings and search the book catalog, using the keyword search option. Chapter 21, Library and Internet Research, has general information that will help you use your college library productively. Be sure to take notes of any potentially useful information or make a photocopy and write down the exact source information for your Works Cited list.

Going Online.   An Internet search could turn up interesting information about your concept and help you find a focus for your essay. Bookmark Web sites you find that invite more than a quick glance, and copy into a word processing document any potentially useful information — making sure to include the URL, the title of the site, the date the information was posted (if available), and the date you accessed the site. Also keep a list of possible aspects of the concept you might focus on. Your goal at this stage is to educate yourself quickly about the concept and look for a possible focus for your essay. It is too early to begin printing or downloading a lot of material.

An Online Activity:
Researching
Concepts

One way to get a quick initial overview of the information available on a concept is to search for the concept online. You can do this in several ways:

- Enter the name of your concept in a search tool such as Google (http://google.com) or Yahoo! Directory (http://dir.yahoo.com) to discover possible sources of information about the concept.

- Check an online encyclopedia in the field to which the concept belongs. Here are a few specialized encyclopedias that may be helpful:

  - *Encyclopedia of Psychology* http://www.psychology.org/
  - *The Internet Encyclopedia of Philosophy* http://www.utm.edu/research/iep/
  - *Webopedia* http://www.webopedia.com

Bookmark or keep a record of promising sites. When you proceed to a narrower search for information about your topic focus, you could then download any materials, including visuals, that you might consider including in your own essay.

Focusing the Concept

Once you have an overview of your concept, you must choose a focus for your essay. More is known about most concepts than you can include in an essay, and concepts can be approached from many perspectives (for example, history, definition, significance), so you must limit your explanation. Doing this will help you avoid the common problem of trying to explain too much. Because the focus must reflect both your special interest in the concept and your readers' likely knowledge and interest, you will want to explore both.

Exploring Your Own Interests.   *Make a list of two or three aspects of the concept that could become a focus for your essay, and evaluate what you know about each focus.* Leave some space after each item in the list. Under each possible focus in your list, make notes about why it interests you and why it seems just the right size (not so small that it is trivial and not so large that it is overwhelming). Indicate whether you know enough to begin writing about that aspect of the concept, what additional questions you would need to answer, and what is important or interesting to you about that particular aspect.

Analyzing Your Readers.   *Take a few minutes to analyze your readers in writing.* To decide what aspect of the concept to focus on, you also need to think about who your prospective readers are likely to be and to speculate about their knowledge of and interest in the concept. Even if you are writing only for your instructor, you should give some thought to what he or she knows and thinks about the concept.

The following questions are designed to help you with your analysis:

- Who are my readers, and what are they likely to know about this concept?
- What, if anything, might they know about the field of study to which this concept applies?
- What could I point out that would be useful for them to know about this concept, perhaps something that could relate to their life or work?
- What connections could I make between this concept and others that my readers are likely to be familiar with?

Choosing a Focus.   *With your interests and those of your readers in mind, choose an aspect of your concept on which to focus, and write a sentence justifying its appropriateness.*

Testing Your Choice

Decide whether you should proceed with this particular concept and focus. As painful as it may be to consider, starting fresh with a new concept is better than continuing with an unworkable or unfocused one. The questions and the collaborative activity that follow will help you test your choice.

Do You Know Enough?   *Review your invention notes to see whether you understand the concept well enough to continue working with it.* To make this decision, *try to answer the following questions*:

- Do I now know enough or can I learn what I need to know in the time I have available to write a concept explanation with this focus?
- Do I understand the concept well enough to make it clear to my readers?

Do You Care Enough?   Unless your instructor has chosen the concept for you, pick a concept you are truly interested in, because you will be devoting a lot of time and energy to researching and writing about it. In choosing a concept, you are making a commitment both to yourself and to your readers. You are obligating yourself to do the work that is necessary to learn what you need to know about the concept in order to explain it effectively. At the same time, you are making a commitment to your readers to make your explanation understandable, informative, and interesting. To decide whether you can make this commitment, try to answer the following questions:

- *Do you feel a personal interest in the concept and the particular focus you have chosen?* If so, what in your experience or learning might be the basis for this interest? Have you chosen a concept related to a hobby, sport, or other area of special interest to you? Have you known something about this concept for a long time or are you just now beginning to learn about it? Is the concept so interesting to you that you are willing to arrange your time over the next two or three weeks to work on your essay explaining the concept?

- *Do you think you can make the concept and the focus you have chosen interesting to readers?* If so, what can you do to engage readers' attention? Can you relate the concept to something readers already know or give them a reason to want to learn about the particular aspect of the concept you are focusing on? Can you think of any anecdotes or examples that will make the concept less abstract and more meaningful to your particular readers?

A Collaborative Activity: Testing Your Choice

Get together with two or three other students to find out what your readers are likely to know about your subject and what might interest them about it. Your instructor may ask you to complete this activity in class or online in a chat room.

Presenters: Take turns briefly explaining your concept, describing your intended readers, and identifying the aspect of the concept that you will focus on.

Listeners: Briefly tell the presenter whether the focus sounds appropriate and interesting for the intended readers. Share what you think readers are likely to know about the concept and what information might be especially interesting and memorable for them.

Researching Your Topic Focus

Now begins stage two of your research process. With a likely focus in mind, you are ready to mine both the Internet and the library for valuable nuggets of information. Your research becomes selective and deliberate, and you will now want to keep careful records of all sources you believe will contribute in any way to your essay. If possible, make photocopies of print sources, and print out sources you download from CD-ROMs or the Internet. If you must rely on notes, be sure to copy any quotations exactly and enclose them in quotation marks so that later you can quote sources accurately.

Since you do not know which sources you will ultimately use, keep a careful record of the author, title, publication information, page numbers, and other required information for each source you gather. Check with your instructor about whether you should follow the Modern Language Association (MLA) or American Psychological Association (APA) style of acknowledging sources. In this chapter, the Ngo essay follows the MLA style.

Going Online. *Return to online searching, with your focus in mind.* Download and print out essential material if possible, or take careful notes. Record all of the details you will need to acknowledge sources in your essay, should you decide to use them.

Going to the Library.   *Return to the library to search for materials relevant to your focus.* Photocopy, print out, or take notes on promising print and electronic materials. Keep careful records so that you can acknowledge your sources.

Considering Explanatory Strategies

Before you move on to plan and draft your essay, consider some possible ways of presenting the concept. Try to answer each of the following questions in a sentence or two. Questions that you can answer readily may identify strategies that can help you explain your concept.

- What term is used to name the concept, and what does it mean? (definition)
- How is this concept like or unlike related concepts? (comparison and contrast)
- How can an explanation of this concept be divided into parts? (classification)
- How does this concept happen, or how does one go about doing it? (process narration)
- What are this concept's known causes or effects? (cause and effect)
- What examples can make the concept less abstract and more memorable? (example)

Designing Your Document

Think about whether visual elements — tables, graphs, drawings, photographs — would make your explanation clearer. These are not a requirement of an essay explaining a concept, but they could be helpful. Consider also whether your readers might benefit from design features such as headings, bulleted or numbered lists, or other elements that would present information efficiently or make your explanation easier to follow. You could construct your own graphic elements (using your word processing software to create bar graphs or pie charts, for example), download materials from the Internet, copy images from television or DVDs, or scan into your document visuals from books and magazines. Remember that you should cite the source of any visual you do not create yourself, and you should also request permission from the source of the visual if your paper is going to be posted on a Web site that is not password-protected.

For more information about including visuals in your work, see Chapter 25.

Defining Your Purpose for Your Readers

Write a few sentences that define your purpose in writing about this particular concept for your readers. Remember that you have already identified and analyzed your readers and that you have begun to research and develop your explanation with these readers in mind. Given these readers, try now to define your purpose in explaining the concept to them. Use these questions to focus your thoughts:

- Are my readers familiar with the concept? If not, how can I overcome their resistance or puzzlement? Or, if so, will my chosen focus allow my readers to see the familiar concept in a new light?

- If I suspect that my readers have misconceptions about the concept, how can I correct the misconceptions without offending readers?
- Do I want to arouse readers' interest in information that may seem at first to be less than engaging?
- Do I want readers to see that the information I have to report is relevant to their lives, families, communities, work, or studies?

Formulating a Tentative Thesis Statement

Write one or more sentences that could serve as a thesis statement. State your concept and focus. You might also want to forecast the topics you will use to explain the concept.

Anastasia Toufexis begins her essay with this thesis statement:

> O.K., let's cut out all this nonsense about romantic love. Let's bring some scientific precision to the party. Let's put love under a microscope.
>
> When rigorous people with Ph.D.s after their names do that, what they see is not some silly, senseless thing. No, their probe reveals that love rests firmly on the foundations of evolution, biology and chemistry.

Toufexis's concept is love, and her focus is the scientific explanation of love — specifically the evolution, biology, and chemistry of love. In announcing her focus, she forecasts the order in which she will present information from the three most relevant academic disciplines — anthropology (which includes the study of human evolution), biology, and chemistry. These discipline names become her topics.

In his essay on cannibalism, Linh Kieu Ngo offers his thesis statement in paragraph 6:

> Cannibalism can be broken down into two main categories: exocannibalism, the eating of outsiders or foreigners, and endocannibalism, the eating of members of one's own social group (Shipman 70). Within these categories are several functional types of cannibalism, three of the most common being survival cannibalism, dietary cannibalism, and religious and ritual cannibalism.

Ngo's concept is cannibalism, and his focus is on three common types of cannibalism. He carefully forecasts how he will divide the information to create topics and the order in which he will explain each of the topics, the common types of cannibalism.

As you draft your own tentative thesis statement, take care to make the language clear and unambiguous. Although you may want to revise your thesis statement as you draft your essay, trying to state it now will give your planning and drafting more focus and direction. Keep in mind that the thesis in an explanatory essay merely announces the subject; it never asserts a position that requires an argument to defend it.

■ Planning and Drafting

The following guidelines will help you get the most out of your invention notes, determine specific goals for your essay, and write a first draft.

Seeing What You Have

Reread everything you have written so far. This is a critically important time for reflection and evaluation. Before beginning the actual draft, you must decide whether your subject is worthwhile and whether you have sufficient information for a successful essay.

It may help, as you read, to annotate your invention writings. Look for details that will help you explain the concept in a way that your readers can grasp. Highlight key words, phrases, or sentences; make marginal notes or electronic annotations of any material you think could be useful. If you have done your invention writing on the computer, you may have sentences or whole paragraphs that can be copied and pasted into your draft.

Be realistic. If at this point your notes do not look promising, you may want to choose a different focus for your concept or select a different concept to write about. If your notes seem thin but promising, do further research to find more information before continuing.

Setting Goals

Successful writers are always looking beyond the next sentence to larger goals. Indeed, the next sentence is easier to write if you keep larger goals in mind. The following questions can help you set these goals. Consider each one now, and then return to them as necessary while you write.

Your Purpose and Readers

- How can I build on my readers' knowledge?
- What new information can I present to them?
- How can I organize my essay so that my readers can follow it easily?
- What tone would be most appropriate? Would an informal tone like Toufexis's or a formal one like Ngo's be more appropriate to my purpose?

The Beginning

- Can I begin in a way that will interest readers? Should I open with a provocative quotation, as Toufexis does? With an anecdote illustrating the concept, as Ngo and Friedman do? With a startling example, as Holmes does?
- How can I orient readers? Should I forecast the topics I will address, as Toufexis and Ngo do?

Presentation of the Information

- Should I name and define my concept early in the essay, as Ngo, Toufexis, Friedman, and Holmes all do?
- Could I develop my explanation by dividing my concept into different categories, as Ngo does? By giving a series of examples, like Holmes? By comparing my concept to related concepts, like Friedman?
- How can I establish the authority of my sources? Should I give their names and credentials, as Toufexis, Friedman, and Holmes do? Refer to specific publications or research, as Ngo, Toufexis, and Holmes do? Will my instructor require me to use the MLA, APA, or some other documentation style, as Ngo's instructor did?
- How can I make it easy for readers to follow my explanation? Should I simply use clear and explicit transitions when I move from one topic to another, as Ngo does, or also include rhetorical questions, like Friedman? Should I use headings and visuals, like Holmes?

The Ending

- Should I frame the essay by relating the ending to the beginning, as Toufexis and Holmes do?
- Should I end by suggesting what is special about the concept, as Friedman does?
- Should I end with a speculation, as Ngo does?
- Should I end by formulating a question suggested by the concept, as Holmes does?

Outlining

The goals that you have set should help you draft your essay, but first you might want to make a quick scratch outline to refocus on the basic story line. You could use the outlining function of your word processing program. In your outline, list the main topics into which you have divided the information about your concept. Use this outline to guide your drafting, but do not feel tied to it. As you draft, you may find a better way to sequence the action and integrate these features.

An essay explaining a concept is made up of four basic parts:

- An attempt to engage readers' interest
- The thesis statement, announcing the concept, its focus, and its topics
- An orientation to the concept, which may include a description or definition of the concept
- Information about the concept

Here is a possible outline for an essay explaining a concept:

An attempt to gain readers' interest in the concept

Thesis statement

Definition of the concept

Topic 1 with illustration

Topic 2 with illustration

(etc.)

Conclusion

An attempt to gain readers' interest could take as little space as two or three sentences or as much as four or five paragraphs. The thesis statement and definition are usually quite brief — sometimes only a few sentences. A topic illustration may occupy one or several paragraphs, and there can be few or many topics, depending on how the information has been divided up. A conclusion might summarize the information presented, give advice about how to use or apply the information, or speculate about the future of the concept.

Consider any outlining that you do before you begin drafting to be tentative. As you draft, be ready to revise your outline, shift parts around, or drop or add parts. If you use the outlining function of your word processing program, changing your outline will be simple, and you may be able to write the essay simply by expanding the outline.

Drafting

General Advice.   Start drafting your essay, keeping in mind the goals you set while you were planning. Remember also the needs and expectations of your readers; organize, define, and explain with them in mind. Work to increase readers' understanding of your concept. Turn off your grammar checker and spelling checker at this stage if you find them distracting. Do not be afraid to skip around in your document. Jump back and fill in a spontaneous idea, or leap ahead and write a later section first if you find that easier. If you get stuck while drafting, try using some of the writing activities in the Invention and Research section of this chapter.

A Sentence Strategy: Appositives.   As you draft an essay explaining a concept, you have a lot of information to present, such as definitions of terms and credentials of experts. **Appositives** provide an efficient, clear way to integrate these kinds of information into your sentences. An appositive can be defined as a noun or pronoun, that, along with modifiers, gives more information about another noun or pronoun. Here is an example from Linh Kieu Ngo's concept essay (the appositive is in italics and the noun it refers to is underlined):

> Cannibalism, *the act of human beings eating human flesh* (Sagan 2), has a long history and continues to hold interest and create controversy. (paragraph 5)

By placing the definition in an appositive phrase right after the word it defines, this sentence locates the definition exactly where readers need it.

For more on using appositives, go to bedfordstmartins.com/theguide and click on Sentence Strategies.

Not only are they a precise way to present information, but appositives are efficient. By using an appositive, Ngo merges two potential sentences into one or shrinks a potential clause to a phrase:

Cannibalism can be defined as the act of human beings eating human flesh. It has a long history and continues to hold interest and create controversy.

Cannibalism, which can be defined as the act of human beings eating human flesh, has a long history and continues to hold interest and create controversy.

Writers explaining concepts rely on appositives because they serve many different purposes needed in concept essays, as the following examples demonstrate. (Again, the appositive is in italics and the noun it refers to is underlined.)

Defining a New Term

Some researchers believe hyperthymics may be at increased risk of depression or hypomania, *a mild variant of mania* (Richard Friedman, paragraph 5)

Cannibalism can be broken down into two main categories: exocannibalism, *the eating of outsiders or foreigners*, and endocannibalism, *the eating of members of one's own social group* (Shipman 70). (Linh Kieu Ngo, paragraph 6)

Introducing a New Term

Each person carries in his or her mind a unique subliminal guide to the ideal partner, *a "love map."* (Anastasia Toufexis, paragraph 17)

Giving Credentials of Experts

"Love is a natural high," observes Anthony Walsh, *author of The Science of Love: Understanding Love and Its Effects on Mind and Body.* (Anastasia Toufexis, paragraph 10)

Identifying People and Things

When I was in high school I read the Robert Browning poem 'My Last Duchess.' In it, the narrator said he killed his wife, *the duchess*, because . . . (Richard Friedman, paragraph 2)

One of the best places to see evolution in action is high in the Rocky Mountains of Alberta, Canada, *home of the largest bighorn sheep in North America.* (Bob Holmes, paragraph 12)

Giving Examples or Specifics

Some 2,400 years ago, Hippocrates proposed that a mixture of four basic humors — *blood, phlegm, yellow bile and black bile* — determined human temperament . . . (Richard Friedman, paragraph 6)

Notice that this last example uses dashes instead of commas to set off the appositive from the rest of the sentence. Although commas are more common, either punctuation will do the job. Dashes are often used if the writer wants to give the appositive more emphasis or if the appositive itself contains commas, as in this example.

In addition to using appositives, you can strengthen your concept explanation with other kinds of sentences as well, and you may want to review the information about sentences that express comparison and contrast (pp. 435–37). If you frequently quote from sources, you may want to review some examples of integrating quoted material into your sentences (pp. 741–42).

Critical Reading Guide

Now is the time to get a good critical reading of your draft. Your instructor may arrange such a reading as part of your coursework — in class or online. If not, you can ask a classmate, friend, or family member to read your draft using this guide. If your campus has a writing center, you might ask a tutor there to read and comment on your draft. (If you are unable to have someone else review your draft, turn ahead to the Revising section for help reading your own draft with a critical eye.)

▶ **If You Are the Writer.**   To provide focused, helpful comments, your reader must know your essay's intended audience, your purpose, and a problem in the draft that you need help solving. Briefly write out this information at the top of your draft.

- *Readers:* To whom are you directing your concept explanation? What do you assume they know about the concept? How do you plan to engage and hold their interest?

- *Purpose:* What do you hope to achieve with your readers?

- *Problem:* Ask your reader to help you solve the most important problem you see in the draft. Describe this problem briefly.

▶ **If You Are the Reader.**   Use the following guidelines to help you give constructive, helpful comments to others on essays explaining concepts.

1. *Read for a First Impression.*   Read first to get a sense of the concept. Then briefly write out your impressions. What in the draft do you think will especially interest the intended readers? Where might they have difficulty in following the explanation? Next, consider the problem the writer identified, and respond briefly to that concern now. (If you find that the problem is covered by one of the other guidelines listed below, respond to it in more detail there if necessary.)

Making Comments Electronically
Most word processing software offers features that allow you to insert comments directly into the text of someone else's document. Many readers prefer to make their comments in this way because it tends to be faster than writing on a hard copy and space is virtually unlimited; from the writer's point of view, it also eliminates the problem of deciphering handwritten comments. Even where such special comment features are not available, simply typing comments directly into a document in a contrasting color can provide the same advantages.

2. ***Assess Whether the Concept Is Clearly Explained and Focused.***   Restate, in one sentence, what you understand the concept to mean. Indicate any confusion or uncertainty you have about its meaning. Given the concept, does the focus seem appropriate, too broad, or too narrow for the intended readers? Can you think of a more interesting aspect of the concept on which to focus the explanation?

3. ***Consider Whether the Content Is Appropriate for the Intended Readers.*** Does it tell them all that they are likely to want to know about the concept? Can you suggest additional information that should be included? What unanswered questions might readers have about the concept? Point out any information that seems either superfluous or too predictable.

For a printable version of this critical reading guide, go to bedfordstmartins.com/theguide.

4. ***Evaluate the Organization.***   Look at the way the essay is organized by making a scratch outline. Does the information seem to be logically divided? If not, suggest a better way to divide it. Also consider the order or sequence of information. Can you suggest a better way of sequencing it?

   - Look at the *beginning*. Does it pull readers into the essay and make them want to continue? Does it adequately forecast the direction of the essay? If possible, suggest a better way to begin.

   - Look for obvious *transitions* in the draft. Tell the writer how they are helpful or unhelpful. Try to improve one or two of them. Look for additional places where transitions would be helpful.

   - Look at the *ending*. Explain what makes it particularly effective or less effective than it might be, in your opinion. If you can, suggest a better way to end.

5. ***Assess the Clarity of Definitions.***   Point out any definitions that may be unclear or confusing to the intended readers. Identify any other terms that may need to be defined.

6. ***Evaluate the Use of Sources.***   If the writer has used sources, review the list of sources cited. Given the purpose, readers, and focus of the essay, does the list seem balanced, and are the selections appropriate? Try to suggest concerns or questions about sources that readers knowledgeable about the concept might raise. Then consider the use of sources within the text of the essay. Are there places where summary or paraphrase would be preferable to quoted material or vice versa? Note any places where the writer has placed quotations awkwardly into the text, and recommend ways to smooth them out.

7. ***Evaluate the Effectiveness of Visuals.***   If charts, graphs, tables, or other visuals are included, let the writer know whether they help you understand the concept. Suggest ideas you have for changing, adding, moving, or deleting visuals.

8. ***Give the Writer Your Final Thoughts.***   Which part needs the most work? What do you think the intended readers will find most informative or memorable? What do you like best about the draft essay?

■ Revising

Now you are ready to revise your essay. Your instructor or other students may have given you advice on improving your draft. Nevertheless, you may have begun to realize that your draft requires not so much revision as rethinking. For example, you may recognize that the focus you chose is too broad to be explained adequately in a few pages, that you need to make the information more engaging or interesting for your intended readers, or that you need substantially more information to present the concept adequately. Consequently, instead of working to improve parts of the draft, you may need to write a new draft that radically reenvisions your explanation. It is not unusual for students — and professional writers — to find themselves in this situation. Seek your instructor's advice if you must plan a radical revision.

On the other hand, you may feel quite satisfied that your draft achieves most, if not all, of your goals. In that case, you can focus on refining specific parts of your draft. Very likely you have thought of ways to improve your draft, and you may even have begun improving it. This section will help you get an overview of your draft and revise it accordingly.

Getting an Overview

Consider your draft as a whole. It may help to do so in two steps:

1. *Reread.* If at all possible, put the draft aside for a day or two before rereading it. When you return to it, start by reconsidering your readers and purpose. Then read the draft straight through, trying to see it as your intended readers will.

2. *Outline.* Make a scratch outline to get an overview of the essay's development. Consider using the headings and outline/summary functions of your word processor.

Planning for Revision.   Resist the temptation to dive in and start changing your text until after you have a clear view of the big picture. Using your outline as a guide, move through the document, using the highlighting or commenting tools of your word processor to note comments received from others and problems you want to solve (or mark on a hard copy if you prefer).

Analyzing the Basic Features of Your Own Draft.   Using the Critical Reading Guide on the preceding pages, reread the draft to identify problems you need to solve. Note the problems on your draft.

Studying Readers' Comments.   Review all of the comments you have received from other readers, and add to your notes any that you intend to act on. Try not to react defensively. For each comment, look at the draft to determine what might have led the reader to make the comment. By letting you see how others respond to your draft, these comments provide valuable information about how you might improve it.

Working with Sources

Using descriptive verbs to introduce information from sources

When explaining concepts, writers usually need to present information from different sources. There are many verbs writers can choose to introduce the information they quote or summarize. Here are a few examples from the concept essays in this chapter (the verbs are in italics):

> "When I was a graduate student in the 1970s, the prevailing idea was that evolution was this gradual, slow process," *says* David Reznick of the University of California, Riverside. (Bob Holmes, paragraph 5)

> "That is one reason why it feels so horrible when we're abandoned or a lover dies," *notes* Fisher. (Anastasia Toufexis, paragraph 13)

> In one incident, Japanese troops *were reported* to have sacrificed the Arapesh people of northeastern New Guinea for food in order to avoid death by starvation (Tuzin 63). (Linh Kieu Ngo, paragraph 7)

For help working with sources, go to bedfordstmartins.com/theguide.

By using the verb *says*, Holmes takes a neutral stance toward the information he got from Reznick. Similarly, Toufexis's *notes* and Ngo's *were reported* indicate that they are not characterizing or judging their sources, but simply reporting them.

Often, however, writers are more descriptive — even evaluative — when they introduce information from sources, as these examples demonstrate:

> For example, on one of the Galapagos Islands, Peter and Rosemary Grant of Princeton University *discovered* that among one species of finch, individuals with small beaks do best in wet years, when small-seeded plants thrive, while their larger-beaked nestmates have the edge in drier years, when larger-seeded plants predominate. (Bob Holmes, paragraph 7)

> "As long as prehistoric females were secretive about their extramarital affairs," *argues* Fisher, "they could garner extra resources, life insurance, better genes and more varied DNA for their biological futures. . . ." (Anastasia Toufexis, paragraph 8)

> Lovers . . . are literally flooded by chemicals, research *suggests*. (Anastasia Toufexis, paragraph 9)

> Some researchers *believe* hyperthymics may be at increased risk of depression or hypomania, a mild variant of mania. And they may have high rates of affective disorders in their closest relatives. (Richard A. Friedman, paragraph 5)

The verbs in these examples — *discovered, argues, suggests,* and *believe* — do not neutrally report the source material but describe the particular role played by the source in explaining the concept. Verbs like *found, showed,* and *discovered* are used to introduce information resulting from scientific research. When Holmes explains what Peter and Rosemary Grant *discovered* about finches, he is demonstrating that the concept of rapid contemporary evolution has been supported by research and is not an abstract theory but one based on observable facts. In contrast, verbs like *contends* and *argues* emphasize that what is being reported is an interpretation that others may disagree with. *Suggests* indicates that in this case Toufexis is referring to broad implications of research rather than to specific findings. Friedman chooses *believe* to designate a conclusion or speculation made by researchers.

As you refer to sources in your concept explanation, you will want to choose carefully among a wide variety of precise verbs. Every writer in this chapter uses many different verbs for this purpose — sometimes for the sake of variety, no doubt, but usually in an effort to help readers better understand how he or she is using each source. You may find these additional verbs helpful in selecting precisely the right verbs to introduce your sources when you are explaining a concept: *reveals, recalls, looks at, questions, brings into focus, pulls together, tries to understand, documents, finds, notices, observes, emphasizes.* When you are introducing sources in an argumentative essay, you also will want to draw from another set of verbs that claim, disagree, or agree, such as *argues, contends, asserts, claims, supports, refutes, repudiates, advocates, contradicts, rejects, corroborates, acknowledges.* You can find more information about integrating sources into your sentences and constructing signal phrases in Chapter 22, Using and Acknowledging Sources.

Notice that except for the one example quote on p. 182, Ngo does not introduce his sources in the body of his essay. Instead, he simply integrates the information from them into his sentences, and readers can see where he got it from the parenthetical citation and the Works Cited list. Here is an example from paragraph 9 in which Ngo includes a quotation together with information he paraphrases from his source:

> The Miyanmin people observe no differences in "gender, kinship, ritual status, and bodily substance"; they eat anyone, even their own dead. In this respect, then, they practice both endocannibalism and exocannibalism; and to ensure a constant supply of human flesh for food, they raid neighboring tribes and drag their victims back to their village to be eaten (Poole 11).

This strategy of integrating but not introducing source material allows Ngo to report the information and show how it helps explain the concept. It is useful when you want to emphasize the information and play down the source. (To learn more about Ngo's use of quoting and paraphrasing, see A Writer at Work on page 187.)

Carrying Out Revisions

Having identified problems in your draft, you now need to come up with solutions and — most important — to carry them out. Basically, there are three ways to find solutions:

1. Review your invention and planning notes and your sources for information and ideas to add to the draft.

2. Do further invention or research to answer questions your readers raised.

3. Look back at the readings in this chapter to see how other writers have solved similar problems.

The following suggestions, which are organized according to the basic features of explanatory essays, will get you started solving some writing problems common to them.

A Focused Concept

- *Is the focus too broad?* Consider limiting it further so that you can explain one part of the concept in more depth. If readers were uninterested in the aspect you focused on, consider focusing on some other aspect.

- *Is the focus too narrow?* You may have isolated too minor an aspect. Go back to your invention and research notes, and look for larger or more significant aspects.

An Appeal to Readers' Interests

- *Do you fail to connect to readers' interests and engage their attention throughout the essay?* Help readers see the significance of the information to them personally. Eliminate superfluous or too-predictable content. Open with an unusual piece of information that catches readers' interest.

- *Do you think readers will have unanswered questions?* Review your invention writing and sources for further information to answer them.

A Logical Plan

- *Does the beginning successfully orient readers to your purpose and plan?* Try making your focus obvious immediately. Forecast the plan of your essay.

- *Is the explanation difficult to follow?* Look for a way to reorder the parts so that the essay is easier to follow. Try constructing an alternative outline. Add transitions or summaries to help keep readers on track. Or consider ways you might classify and divide the information to make it easier to understand or provide a more interesting perspective.

- *Is the ending inconclusive?* Consider moving important information there. Try summarizing highlights of the essay or framing it by referring to something in the beginning. Or you might speculate about the future of the concept or assert its usefulness.

Clear Definitions

- *Do readers need a clearer or fuller definition of the concept?* Add a concise definition early in your essay, or consider adding a brief summary that defines the concept later in the essay (in the middle or at the end). Remove any information that may blur readers' understanding of the concept.

- *Are other key terms inadequately defined?* Supply clear definitions, searching your sources or checking a dictionary if necessary.

Careful Use of Sources

- *Do readers find your sources inadequate?* Return to the library or the Internet to find additional ones. Consider dropping weak or less reliable sources. Make sure that your sources provide coverage in a comprehensive, balanced way.

- ***Do you rely too much on quoting, summarizing, or paraphrasing?*** Change some of your quotations to summaries or paraphrases, or vice versa.

- ***Does quoted material need to be more smoothly integrated into your own text?*** Revise to make it so. Remember to use precise verbs to introduce sources and authors.

- ***Are there discrepancies between your in-text citations and the entries in your list of sources?*** Compare each citation and entry against the examples given in Chapter 22 for the documentation style you are using. Be sure that all of the citations and entries follow the style exactly. Check to see that your list of sources has an entry for each source that you cite in the text.

For a revision checklist, go to bedfordstmartins.com/theguide.

Editing and Proofreading

Now is the time to check your revised draft carefully for errors in usage, punctuation, and mechanics and to consider matters of style. Our research on students' writing has identified several errors that are especially common in writing that explains concepts. The following guidelines will help you check and edit your essay for these errors. This book's Web site also provides interactive online exercises to help you learn to identify and correct each of these errors; to access the exercises for a particular error, go to the URL listed in the margin next to that section of the guidelines.

A Note on Grammar and Spelling Checkers
These tools are good at catching certain types of errors, but currently there is no replacement for a good human proofreader. Grammar checkers in particular are extremely limited in what they can usually find, and often they only give you summary information that is not helpful if you do not already understand the rule in question. They are also prone to give faulty advice for fixing problems and to flag correct items as wrong. Spelling checkers cause fewer problems but cannot catch misspellings that are themselves words, such as *to* for *too.*

Checking the Punctuation of Adjective Clauses.   Adjective clauses include both a subject and a verb. They give information about a noun or a pronoun. They often begin with *who, which,* or *that.* Here is an example from a student essay explaining the concept of schizophrenia, a type of mental illness:

> **It is common for schizophrenics to have delusions** *that they are being persecuted.*

Because adjective clauses add information about the nouns they follow — defining, illustrating, or explaining — they can be useful in writing that explains a concept. Adjective clauses may or may not need to be set off with a comma or commas. To decide, first you have to determine whether the clause is essential to the meaning of the sentence. Clauses that are essential to the meaning of a sentence should not be set off with a comma; clauses that are not essential to the meaning must be set off with a comma. Here are two examples from the student essay about schizophrenia:

ESSENTIAL   **It is common for schizophrenics to have delusions** *that they are being persecuted.*

The adjective clause defines and limits the word *delusions.* If the clause were removed, the basic meaning of the sentence would change, saying that schizophrenics commonly have delusions of all sorts.

NONESSENTIAL   **Related to delusions are hallucinations,** *which are very common in schizophrenics.*

The adjective clause gives information that is not essential to understanding the main clause (*Related to delusions are hallucinations*). Taking away the adjective clause (*which are very common in schizophrenics*) in no way changes the basic meaning of the main clause.

To decide whether an adjective clause is essential or nonessential, mentally delete the clause. If taking out the clause changes the basic meaning of the sentence or makes it unclear, the clause is probably essential and should not be set off with commas. If the meaning of the main part of the sentence or the main clause does not change enormously, the clause is probably nonessential and should be set off with commas.

For practice, go to bedfordstmartins.com/theguide/exercisecentral and click on Adjective Clauses.

▶ Postpartum neurosis͵which can last for two weeks or longer͵can adversely affect a mother's ability to care for her infant.

▶ The early stage starts with memory loss͵which usually causes the patient to forget recent life events.

▶ Seasonal affective disorders are mood disturbances͵ that occur with a change of season.

▶ The coaches͵ who do the recruiting should be disciplined.

Adjective clauses following proper nouns always require commas.

▶ Nanotechnologists defer to K. Eric Drexler͵who speculates imaginatively about the uses of nonmachines.

Checking for Commas around Interrupting Phrases.   When writers are explaining a concept, they need to supply a great deal of information. They add much of this information in phrases that interrupt the flow of a sentence. Words that interrupt are usually set off with commas, one at the beginning of the phrase and one at the end:

For practice, go to bedfordstmartins.com/theguide/exercisecentral and click on Commas around Interrupting Phrases.

▶ People on the West Coast, especially in Los Angeles͵have always been receptive to new ideas.

▶ Alzheimer's disease͵named after the German neuropathologist Alois Alzheimer, is a chronic degenerative illness.

▶ These examples͵though simple, present equations in terms of tangible objects.

A Writer at Work

Selecting and Integrating Information from Sources

This section describes how student writer Linh Kieu Ngo selected information from a source and integrated it into one part of his essay on cannibalism.

One paragraph from Ngo's essay illustrates a sound strategy for integrating sources into your essay, relying on them fully — as you nearly always must do in explanatory writing — and yet making them your own. Here is paragraph 9 from Ngo's essay (the five sentences are numbered for ease of reference):

(1) In the Miyanmin society of the west Sepik interior of Papua, New Guinea, villagers do not value human life over that of pigs or marsupials because human flesh is part of their normal diet (Poole 7). (2) The Miyanmin people observe no differences in "gender, kinship, ritual status, and bodily substance"; they eat anyone, even their own dead. (3) In this respect, then, they practice both endocannibalism and exocannibalism; and to ensure a constant supply of human flesh for food, they raid neighboring tribes and drag their victims back to their village to be eaten (Poole 11). (4) Perhaps, in the history of this society, there was at one time a shortage of wild game to be hunted for food, and because people were more plentiful than fish, deer, rabbits, pigs, or cows, survival cannibalism was adopted as a last resort. (5) Then, as their culture developed, the Miyanmin may have retained the practice of dietary cannibalism, which has endured as a part of their culture.

Most of the information in this paragraph comes from a twenty-six-page research report by an anthropologist, Fitz John Porter Poole. Given Ngo's purpose in this paragraph — to illustrate some forms of dietary cannibalism — he selects only a limited amount of information from small sections of text on two different pages of the Poole report. Notice first that Ngo quotes only once (sentence 2, a phrase that emphasizes what indiscriminate dietary cannibals the Miyanmin people are). Otherwise, Ngo paraphrases information from Poole. (When you **paraphrase**, you construct your own sentences and phrases but rely necessarily on the key words in your source.) For example, in his sentence 1, Ngo paraphrases this sentence: "For Miyanmin, they claim, humans do indeed become food in an ordinary sense and are seen as comparable to pigs and marsupials." Toward the end of sentence 3, Ngo again paraphrases Poole. By contrast, Ngo's sentences 4 and 5 seem to be his own speculations about the possible origins of Miyanmin cannibalism because this information does not appear in Poole.

The paragraph illustrates a careful balance between a writer's ideas and information gleaned from sources. Ngo is careful not to let the sources take over the explanation. The paragraph also illustrates judicious use of quotations and paraphrases. Ngo avoids stringing quotes together to illustrate an explanation.

Effective document design is an important factor for the marketing manager who volunteers to teach fifth graders about the concept of surveys (see the community writing project described on p. 135). Because the marketer is teaching students about surveys by having them take a survey, she knows that the design of the survey will be crucial to the students' understanding.

She recognizes that students need to be interested in the questionnaire and able to fill it out quickly; she also knows that it is important that they not feel intimidated by its appearance — by page after page and question after question. After first drafting the questionnaire, she realizes that although the questions all fit on one page (cutting down on paper and photocopying costs), the page is very cluttered and difficult to read.

Before getting started on the redesign, she carefully considers her audience — 10- and 11-year-olds — and refers to workbooks and other print material designed for this age group. In this case, the convenience to her audience (their ability to easily read and answer the questions) outweighs the time and expense of photocopying multiple pages. She thinks that the students will be able to fill out the questionnaire more easily if each question has more space around it.

The appearance of the questionnaire itself is only her initial design consideration, however. After the marketing researcher asks the students to complete the survey, she guides the class in tabulating the survey results. Knowing that the information from the questionnaire has to be easy to represent graphically so that the viewers will understand and appreciate the results when they are projected on a large screen, she then discusses with the class which information best fits in a pie chart (such as information broken into percentages) and which in a bar graph (such as hours of television watched by day). She creates the data displays and projects them using a PowerPoint program. Two of the slides are shown here.

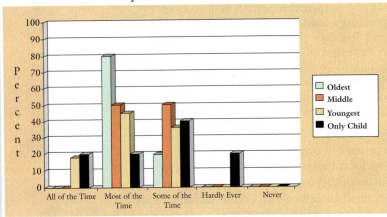

How often do you get to watch what you want to watch on TV?

Respondent Gender

- 28 people responded to the survey.
- 13 were male; 15 were female.

46% Male
54% Female

Thinking Critically About What You Have Learned

Now that you have read and discussed several essays that explain concepts and written one of your own, take some time to reflect on the act of reading and writing concept essays and to think critically about how explanations of concepts influence the way we think about ourselves and our culture.

Reflecting on Your Writing

Write a one-page explanation, telling your instructor about a problem you encountered in writing your essay and how you solved it. Before you begin, gather all of your writing — invention and planning notes, drafts, critical comments, revision notes and plans, and final revision. Review these materials, and refer to them as you complete this writing task.

1. ***Identify one writing problem you had to solve as you worked to explain the concept in your essay.*** Do not be concerned with grammar and punctuation; concentrate instead on problems unique to developing a concept explanation. For example: Did you puzzle over how to focus your explanation? Did you worry about how to appeal to your readers' interests or how to identify and define the terms that your readers would need explained? Did you have trouble integrating sources smoothly?

2. ***Determine how you came to recognize the problem.*** When did you first discover it? What called it to your attention? If you did not become aware of the problem until someone else pointed it out, can you now see hints of it in your invention writings? If so, where specifically? How did you respond when you first recognized the problem?

3. ***Reflect on how you went about solving the problem.*** Did you work on the wording of a particular passage, cut or add information, move paragraphs or sentences around, add transitions

or forecasting statements, experiment with different writing strategies? Did you reread one of the essays in this chapter to see how another writer handled the problem, or did you look back at the invention suggestions? If you talked about the writing problem with another student, a tutor, or your instructor, did talking about it help? How useful was the advice you received?

4. ***Write a brief explanation of how you identified the problem and how you solved it.*** Be as specific as possible in reconstructing your efforts. Quote from your invention notes and draft essay, others' critical comments, your revision plan, or your revised essay to show the various changes your writing underwent as you tried to solve the problem. If you are still uncertain about your solution, say so. Thinking in detail about how you identified a particular problem, how you went about solving it, and what you learned from this experience can help you solve future writing problems more easily.

Reviewing What You Learned from Reading

Write a page or two explaining to your instructor how the readings in this chapter influenced your final draft. To some extent, your own essay has been influenced by the concept explanations that you have read in this chapter and by classmates' essays that you have read. Your reading may have helped you choose a topic, suggested that you needed to do research, or shown you how to structure your essay or how to use examples or comparisons. Before you write, take time to reflect on what you have learned about concept explanations from the readings in this chapter and how the readings have influenced your own writing.

1. *Reread the final revision of your essay; then look back at the selections you read before completing your essay.* Name any specific influences. For example, if you were impressed by the way one of the readings described the origins or originators of the concept, organized the information, or connected to the reader's knowledge through analogy or comparison, look in your revised essay to see where you might have been striving for similar effects in your own writing. Also look for ideas you got from your reading: writing strategies you were inspired to try, specific details you were led to include, effects you sought to achieve.

2. *Write an explanation of these influences.* Did one reading have an especially strong influence on your essay, or were several readings influential in different ways? Quote from the readings and from your final revision to show how your essay explaining a concept was influenced by the readings in this chapter. Finally, based on this review of the chapter's readings, briefly explain any further improvements you would now make in your essay.

Considering the Social Dimensions of Concept Explanations

Concepts are the building blocks of knowledge, essential to its creation and acquisition. We use concepts to name and organize ideas and information in areas as diverse as snowboarding and psychiatry. Academic disciplines and most professions are heavily concept-based, enabling newcomers to be introduced efficiently, if abstractly, to the basic knowledge they need to begin learning.

The Nature of Knowledge. As you have learned from your reading, research, and writing for this chapter, writers explaining concepts present knowledge as established and uncontested. They presume to be unbiased and objective, and they assume that

readers will not doubt or challenge the truth or the value of the knowledge they present. This stance encourages readers to feel confident about the validity of the explanation.

However, explanatory writing should not always be accepted at face value. Textbooks and reference materials, in particular, sometimes present a limited view of knowledge in an academic discipline. Because introductory textbooks must be highly selective, they necessarily leave out certain sources of information and types of knowledge.

1. *Consider the claim that concept explanations attempt to present their information as uncontested truths.* Identify a reading in this chapter that particularly seems to support this claim, and then think about how it does so. Do the same for a chapter or section in a textbook you are reading for another course.

2. *Reflect on how concept explanations present established knowledge.* How do you think knowledge gets established in academic disciplines such as biology, psychology, and history? How might the prominent researchers and professors in a discipline go about deciding what is to be considered established knowledge for now? How might they decide when that established knowledge needs to be revised? If possible, ask these questions of a professor in a subject you are studying.

3. *Write a page or two explaining your initial assumptions about the knowledge or information you presented about a concept in your essay.* When you were doing research on the concept, did you discover that some of the information was being challenged by experts? Or did the body of knowledge seem settled and established? Did you at any point think that your readers might question any of the information you were presenting? How did you decide what information might seem new or even surprising to readers? Did you feel comfortable in your roles as the selector and giver of knowledge?

5

Explaining Opposing Positions

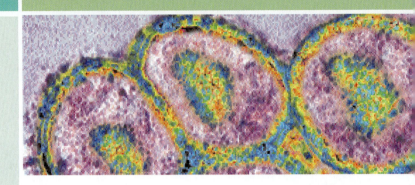

IN COLLEGE COURSES A biology major in a philosophy course writes about the bioethics of stem cell research. After researching the subject, she decides to divide her essay into two parts — first elucidating the biology and second discussing the ethical arguments.

She begins by explaining that because stem cells have the ability to develop into any kind of cell in the body, they have the potential to regenerate damaged or diseased tissue. She reports that although stem cells can come either from embryos or from adults, scientists disagree on two questions about the relative advantages of cells from these different sources: (1) whether embryonic stem cells would be less vulnerable to the danger of immune rejection so typical of organ transplants; and (2) whether adult stem cells can differentiate into as many specialized cell types as embryonic stem cells can.

The second part of the student's essay presents the ethical debate over whether surplus embryos from in vitro fertilization clinics should be used to harvest stem cells for research. She explains that this debate hinges on the fundamental question of when life begins, a question that she points out has been addressed in several ways. Bioethicists have debated whether consciousness or the ability to develop independent of the mother's body should be the criterion for determining life. The debate has also been influenced by religious teachings: Whereas some religions believe that life begins at conception and consequently object to the use of embryonic stem cells for research, others believe life begins at a later stage of gestation or at birth and therefore support such research. Throughout the essay, the writer tries to present the opposing positions in a fair and balanced way, keeping her own opinion to herself.

IN THE COMMUNITY   A reporter and photographer from a local newspaper rush out early one morning to report on students leaving their classrooms to protest Congressional efforts to control immigration from Mexico and elsewhere in Latin America. Meanwhile, at the newspaper office, a college intern researches the national debate on immigration, gathers facts and statistics, and reviews the television and Internet coverage of similar protests around the country. Late in the afternoon, working with the front-page editor, the team plans a report to appear the next morning. They begin by selecting photographs, one showing a student close up, her mouth open wide in a shout, her braces showing, part of a Mexican flag just behind her head, in the distance a corner of the state capitol building. The editor and reporter choose a tentative headline, "Students Denounce Border Proposals."

The reporter writes the news article, which includes vivid details describing the protest march and interviews with students, educators, and local politicians. Meanwhile, the intern writes a background explanatory "sidebar" article to accompany the news story. His explanation is organized around the various aspects of the debate over illegal immigration and the feasibility of proposals to secure the border, as well as whether to crack down on employers who illegally hire undocumented immigrants, to create a guest worker program, or to grant amnesty to illegal immigrants who have lived in the United States and paid taxes for many years and whose children are American citizens.

IN THE WORKPLACE   A science writer attends a conference at which sixty scientists from eleven countries discuss a proposed new way of classifying biological organisms called PhyloCode. He learns that there is a lively debate among scientists about whether PhyloCode should replace the current classification system, which was originated by the eighteenth-century Swedish botanist Carolus Linnaeus. The journalist reports that conference goers were greeted by people wearing T-shirts that read "Join the Rebellion!" and "PhyloCode, May the Force Be With Us!" Although the writer does not say that supporters of the Linnaean system wore opposing T-shirts, he does suggest a slogan that Linneaus himself invented: "God created, Linneaus arranged."

Later the writer searches the Internet for additional information on the two classification systems and phones one of the scientists he met at the conference to make sure he got a quote right. His article begins by identifying the issue and introducing a few of the scientists who have taken opposing positions. Then he explains the main practical and philosophical differences between the two systems. His article discusses some of the topics raised in the debate, such as what each side thinks would be gained and lost if the PhyloCode taxonomy were to replace the Linnaean one and the agenda of some PhyloCode proponents who want to use the new classification system to advance the goal of saving endangered species. To help readers see at a glance the difference between the two systems, he designs a graphic that shows not only how the basic structures of the two systems compare but also how each system handles the discovery of new species or the reclassification of an existing one.

Essays explaining opposing positions aim to help readers understand a disagreement over some issue. They inform and educate readers. In doing so, they satisfy readers' desires to understand the sometimes confusing or even bewildering public arguments, misunderstandings, and antagonisms that continuously swirl through a democracy, in groups of all kinds, small and large, from a city council to a university research institute to the U.S. Senate. Sometimes the disagreement is local and relatively trivial — whether traffic should flow two ways or one way on a busy city street. Sometimes it has broader and longer-term implications — whether to build a new campus for a state university system. Sometimes it is fateful on a global scale — whether Congress should give the president its support for going to war. Citizens are listening in, curious, maybe even anxious, hoping to learn what is going on. Sometimes they may want to read or hear the debaters arguing with each other. At other times, however, they may want an overview of the debate, a sorting out of the main points of disagreement, a comparison and contrast of the different positions debaters are taking — the kind of writing you will be reading and eventually writing as you work through this chapter.

Learning to write a clear and unbiased explanation of the opposing positions on a controversial issue can be helpful in college courses where you are likely to encounter opposing views among scholars. For example, anthropologists are currently debating when humans who were physically like us began thinking creatively or symbolically. The issue, launched by recent discoveries in South Africa of polished weapons and decorated stones, is whether such thinking began around 40,000 years ago in Europe or much earlier, around 80,000 years ago in Africa. Similarly, medical researchers are debating three possible causes of SAD or seasonal affective disorder, also known as the winter blues. Every winter, health magazines inform readers of this disorder and explain the debate, taking care not to favor one of the proposed causes. Reports of disputes about public policy issues as well as scientific research often appear in newsmagazines and on the Internet. They are also featured in college textbooks, and you can expect to be asked to write about conflicting views on issues you are studying in your college courses.

In this chapter, you will read essays explaining opposing positions on a wide range of issues. Student Alexander Cheung starts us off by comparing and contrasting two essays that argue opposing positions on whether exchanging music online should be considered theft. Science writer Amos Esty next explains the opposing theories researchers have developed about what caused the mass extinction of large animals during the Pleistocene era. Law Professor Noah Feldman then examines two schools of thought about the proper relationship between church and state in America today. Finally, student Athena Alexander reports on the debate over the No Child Left Behind Act. Reading these essays will help you prepare to write an essay of your own explaining opposing positions on an issue that interests you.

Think of a controversial issue about which there has been considerable debate. You may know something about the issue from the news, from blogs, from a class you are taking, or from friends or coworkers. Here are some possibilities:

- Should government surveillance of American citizens without court approval be allowed?
- Should torture of people suspected of involvement with terrorist organizations be permitted?
- Should legal marriage rights be granted to gays and lesbians?
- Should intelligent design be taught in science classes as an alternative theory to evolution?
- Should athletes who use steroids be forced out of their sport in disgrace?
- Should college athletes be paid like professionals?
- Should students be required to pass a standardized test to receive a high school diploma? A college diploma?
- Should colleges lower admission standards for athletes?
- Should embryonic stem cell research be funded by the government?
- Should oil drilling in the Arctic National Wildlife Refuge be allowed?

Your instructor may schedule this collaborative activity as a face-to-face in-class discussion or ask you to conduct an online real-time discussion in a chat room. Whatever the medium, here are some guidelines to follow:

Part 1. Individually, choose one issue, make notes on what you know about the opposing positions people have taken on this issue, and consider what you think your fellow students should know about the debate.

Get together with two or three other students, and take two to three minutes each explaining your debates to one another. You might begin by indicating what positions people tend to take on the issue and explaining what seems to concern them most.

After explaining your debate, allow a minute or two for your listeners to ask questions, but do not answer them at this point. The purpose of the questions is to help you understand what readers need in an explanation of opposing positions.

Part 2. When all group members have explained their debates, discuss what you learned from the experience of explaining opposing positions. Begin by discussing the kinds of questions whose answers your listeners felt would help them understand each debate more fully. Then consider these questions:

- How did you decide what was essential to explain and what you could leave out?
- What surprised you in the questions that your group asked about your explanation? What confused them?

Readings

ALEXANDER CHEUNG was a first-year student majoring in bioengineering when he wrote this essay explaining opposing positions on the controversial issue of downloading music from the Internet. In a composition class where he used a draft version of this chapter, Cheung read the essays arguing a position on which his explanation is based. (You can access these essays online at bedfordstmartins.com/theguide.) However, he told us he has been following the debate "since the hype first began with the closure of Napster in 2001." Reading online message boards had led him to a cyberjournalist's history of the MP3 revolution and the debate over intellectual property on the Internet that he was able to use for background information in his essay. As someone who used to, but no longer, downloads copyrighted content, Cheung's interest in the issue continues to be intense because "the future of music," he believes, "is being decided right now through this very debate."

Consider, as you read the essay, how well Cheung succeeds in explaining the two opposing positions without arguing a position of his own. Indicate where in the essay, if anywhere, you see evidence of Cheung's own position.

The Perfect Crime?

Alexander Cheung

Cheung wants his introduction to engage the reader, so he uses words and phrases that stick in readers' minds. He also puns for insiders who know about the BitTorrent file-sharing program.

1 In June 1999, a man named Shawn Fanning opened a modern day Pandora's Box. In the ensuing months, a torrent of music fans all over the world discovered a revolutionary means by which they could obtain their favorite music tracks without having to shell out a Jackson to purchase an entire album. As the number of people who flocked to cash in on free music continued to grow exponentially without any sign of cessation, the music industry resolved to strike back. To them, the face of evil was a cat. And it wore headphones. Its name: Napster.

Cheung cites Alderman's book as the source of his background knowledge. He uses MLA-style parenthetical citations throughout the essay, keyed to a Works Cited list at the end.

2 With the instinctive reaction of a jazzed mongoose, the music industry (i.e., large record companies) immediately realized the severity of the situation that they were now in. They realized that the decentralization of music would cut them, the middlemen, out of the music distribution equation. And so they took action. In a series of highly publicized court cases that pitted Fanning, creator of Napster, and his supporters against the giant labels that dominate the recording industry, the music industry succeeded in shutting down the peer-to-peer file sharing giant (Alderman 172). But it didn't succeed in destroying the notion of peer-to-peer music sharing.

Assuming some readers do not know how peer-to-peer file sharing works, Cheung briefly explains the process.

3 Peer-to-peer (P2P) file sharing software, such as Napster, enables people all over the world to trade files. By downloading and installing a simple application, Web surfers can use these P2P programs as a cheap (often free) and convenient search engine to find their favorite songs and other media files and save them to their computer.

4 In his essay "In Defense of Music Downloading: Why Internet File-Sharing Is Necessary for the Survival of Music," Matthew Scrivner provides support for one side

of this debate. Scrivner is a volunteer staff writer for *2 Walls Webzine*, where the essay was published in February 2004, as well as an assistant editor for a literary magazine. The essay "Thou Shalt Not Pirate Thy Neighbor's Songs," cowritten by Graham Spanier and Cary H. Sherman, offers an opposing perspective to that of Scrivner. This essay was originally published in *The Chronicle of Higher Education* in December 2005. Spanier and Sherman are co-chairs of the Committee on Higher Education and the Entertainment Industry, a national organization of college administrators and music and film executives. Spanier, the president of Pennsylvania State University, testified before Congress in 2002 on the issue of file sharing. Sherman is president of the Recording Industry Association of America (RIAA), and is described on RIAA's Web site as "one of the top copyright attorneys in the country" ("About Us"). Not only do these two essays take opposing sides on the legality of file sharing, they disagree about definitions of key terms and even about basic facts.

5   Scrivner makes the bold claim that "Music is a form of information. . . . It cannot, no matter what they [the music industry] would have you believe, be wrapped in cellophane and sold back to you for $18.99" (par. 2). He maintains that music is not a tangible object, but rather that it is an "experience" that cannot be owned by anyone save for the individual listener. "What you are really paying for" when you buy a CD, according to Scrivner, "is the medium . . . the means by which the experience is transmitted to you" (par. 3).

6   In contrast, Spanier and Sherman contend that music, particularly copyrighted music, is "intellectual property" (par. 6). If it is property, music can be owned, bought, and sold — and therefore also stolen. Defining music as intellectual property protected by copyright is essential to Spanier and Sherman's agenda, which is to convince college administrators to crack down on students' music downloading using their campuses' high-speed Internet connections. Spanier and Sherman argue by analogy that downloading deserves the same treatment as plagiarism: "Higher-education institutions all across the country view plagiarism as an issue on which they must intercede. Copyright infringement should be no different." Copyright infringement, they assert, "is unacceptable in any instance but should be particularly disturbing at colleges and universities where creators and inventors thrive" (par. 8).

7   It is clear that how you define music determines whether you think music downloading is legal or illegal. Spanier and Sherman conclude that downloading music files that one did not pay for constitutes theft and that if educational institutions do nothing to discourage downloading, they may "be liable for infringement themselves." For support, they refer to the authority of the Supreme Court ruling in the Grokster case, carefully explaining that the "ramifications for colleges and universities are yet to be determined," but insisting that "the underlying message is straightforward: Stealing intellectual property is wrong" (par. 2). On the other hand, Scrivner maintains that "the term *theft* is misleading" (par. 6). He asks the following rhetorical questions:

> A hundred years ago, if I heard a song at church, and rode my horse home and found myself humming it, I was stealing? And fifty years ago, if I heard a song on the radio, and it was so catchy that I found myself singing it out loud later on

---

Here Cheung identifies the writers whose positions he will compare, describing their professional affiliations so that readers can judge their knowledge about and stake in the debate.

Cheung's thesis statement forecasts the main points of disagreement he will discuss.

Cheung begins with the major question of differing definitions.

Cheung uses transitions to signal differences and similarities in the opposing positions.

Cheung points out the analogy Spanier and Sherman use.

Cheung explains that the disagreement over definition is central to the debate about legality.

Following MLA style, Cheung indents this long quotation, which he included because he thought it helped explain Scrivner's argument that music cannot be owned.

while I cooked dinner, I committed theft? And ten years ago, when I waited hours for the top 40 countdown to play that one song just so I could tape it to cassette for my girlfriend. I was taking something that wasn't mine? It's never ever worked that way before, despite what they would have us believe. No one has ever been sued for singing their favorite song around the campfire. No one has ever been sued for making mix tapes for their best friends. Why is it that the presence of the Internet has made this so much more the case? (par. 7)

In essence, Scrivner is attesting that what Spanier and Sherman call theft is something that has always been committed throughout history by musicians as well as music lovers.

Although the question of the legality of downloading copyrighted music is just about the span of Spanier and Sherman's argument, Scrivner takes the debate a step further by asking why this is becoming an issue now and whose interests would actually be served by outlawing music downloading. From a historical perspective, he claims, it can be seen that music traditionally has been built on theft: "There are pieces of Buddy Guy and B.B. King in the Beatles and Jimi Hendrix. There are pieces of the Beatles in probably every rock and roll band that has ever come since" (par. 8). Because this is the case, as he sees it, Scrivner wonders why the music industry is putting its foot down with fiery passion *now*, and not ever before. His answer is simply that the big record labels are starting to realize financial losses that they attribute to the rise of music downloading. Scrivner questions this causal analysis, suggesting that the real cause may be the "downward trend in the rest of the economy" (par. 11). Scrivner also asserts that when music industry spokesmen claim as fact "that artists will not get paid for their work if the free (i.e., uncontrolled) exchange of music continues" (par. 11), they are misleading the public because "there has been no concrete proof offered so far that music downloading has caused financial loss for musicians" (par. 12). Finally, Scrivner points out the "Fact" that "Musicians and artists do not receive the majority of their income from royalties on record sales" anyway — the record companies do (par. 13). Although Scrivner raises these questions of fact, neither essay gives supporting evidence to settle the matter.

These authors obviously stand on opposite ends of the spectrum in their perspectives on this issue. Whereas Spanier and Sherman rest their argument on the legal definition of music as intellectual property, Scrivner contends that artists benefit from the free "exchange of ideas" and that their interests are not the same as those of the music industry (par. 9). This debate is still being fought both in the courts and at the computer, and it doesn't seem as if a resolution will come about any time soon.

8

9

Here, Cheung shifts the discussion from whether downloading is legal to who benefits from it.

Cheung brings up the question of what should be taken as "fact."

Cheung concludes by summarizing the main points of disagreement and speculating about the future.

Works Cited

"About Us." *RIAA*. Recording Industry Association of America, 2003. Web. 10 Jan. 2006.
Alderman, John. *Sonic Boom: Napster, MP3, and The New Pioneers of Music.* Cambridge: Perseus, 2001. Print.

Scrivner, Matthew. "In Defense of Music Downloading: Why Internet File-Sharing Is Necessary for the Survival of Music." *2 Walls Webzine.* N.p., 15 Feb. 2004. Web. 10 Jan 2006.

Spanier, Graham, and Cary H. Sherman. "Thou Shalt Not Pirate Thy Neighbor's Songs." *Chronicle of Higher Education.* Chronicle of Higher Education, 2 Dec. 2005. Web. 10 Jan. 2006.

AMOS ESTY is assistant book review editor for *American Scientist* magazine, which is published by an international science organization, Sigma Xi, founded in 1886. In addition to writing book reviews, Esty also conducts interviews with distinguished authors and writes essays for the *American Scientist* and other publications such as the e-zine *Freezerbox*. In 2005, the Society of National Association of Publications honored Esty with the Gold Excel award for his *American Scientist* feature article "The Evolution of Jealousy." Esty's explanation of the debate about the causes of the mass extinction of large animals in the Pleistocene era, "Investigating a Mega-Mystery," appeared in August 2005.

As you read the essay, underline any technical terms with which you may be unfamiliar, such as "megafauna," "Pleistocene," and "proboscideans." Because Esty assumes most of his readers will not know these words, he defines them. Notice how efficiently he defines terms likely to be unfamiliar to readers.

Investigating a Mega-Mystery
Amos Esty

When, at least 12,000 years ago, human beings first crossed into North America from Siberia, the continent teemed with large animals. Today, of course, our only encounters with giant short-faced bears, enormous sloths and dozens of other such extinct species come in museums. On this much, archaeologists and paleontologists agree. The causes of this mass extinction, however, remain clouded by conflicting findings and holes in the archaeological record. [1]

The mystery extends far beyond North America. Between about 50,000 and 10,000 years ago, near the end of the Pleistocene, much of the world's megafauna (usually defined as animals weighing at least 100 pounds) disappeared. At the same time, *Homo sapiens* was expanding from Africa into Eurasia, Australia and the Americas. The late Pleistocene also witnessed dramatic climate change, especially during the period of warming and deglaciation that followed the Last Glacial Maximum some 20,000 years ago. [2]

This convergence of events makes for exciting — and sometimes contentious — science. High-impact human hunting, referred to by archaeologists as "overkill," and climate change are the two most cited possible causes of the extinctions, but the role of each remains contested. [3]

The debate began to heat up in the late 1960s after Paul S. Martin, a professor of geosciences at the University of Arizona, first proposed a "blitzkrieg" model of human overkill for North America — basically, overkill on fast forward. In this scenario, humans moved rapidly through the continent, slaughtering mammoths, mastodons and other large prey as they went. Within about 1,000 years, most North American endemic megafauna were gone.

The blitzkrieg hypothesis has since been applied elsewhere, but it remains controversial. Criticism has focused on the lack of archaeological evidence, a charge Martin has responded to by arguing that, if the extinctions occurred quickly, there would be little trace of the massacre in the fossil record. Archaeologists Donald Grayson of the University of Washington and David Meltzer of Southern Methodist University have been particularly critical of Martin's response, calling it "faith-based" science.

Two recent papers, both published in *Proceedings of the National Academy of Sciences of the U.S.A.*, try to help settle the question. Todd Surovell and Nicole Waguespack of the University of Wyoming and P. Jeffrey Brantingham of the University of California, Los Angeles, studied the timing and location of Pleistocene encounters between humans and proboscideans (the order that includes mammoths, mastodons and elephants) and found evidence supporting the overkill hypothesis. Meanwhile, Clive N. G. Trueman of the University of Portsmouth and Judith H. Field of the University of Sydney were part of a multinational team that confirmed the age of megafauna fossils at a site in eastern Australia, concluding that their work weakens claims for overkill in the land Down Under.

Surovell, Waguespack and Brantingham outlined two possible extinction scenarios, one based on human overkill and the other on climate change. They then plugged into their models data from 41 archaeological sites in Africa, Europe, Asia and the Americas that contain remains of proboscideans hunted or scavenged by humans. If people hunted these animals to extinction, the authors argue, the kill sites should appear along the border between proboscidean and human ranges. So, as humans expanded south across North America, for example, the sites would also be located farther and farther south. If climate was the culprit, then people and proboscideans should have shared some of the same territory, at least until climate change shrunk proboscidean habitat. Thus, kill sites would be found both along and behind the frontier of human expansion.

The authors concluded that the location and age of the sites correlate closely with an overkill model. As humans moved north into Eurasia from Africa and, later, south from Alaska across the Americas, proboscidean range contracted correspondingly. Climate change, then, cannot account for proboscidean extinction "unless one were to invoke serial climatic change that perfectly tracks human global colonization." The odds, they're saying, aren't good.

Although the authors do not claim to have proved that humans drove other species to extinction, Surovell is skeptical of arguments for climate change. "I would like to see somebody explain how climate change could cause mass extinction on such a large geographical scale," he says. "Climate is constantly changing."

In Australia, much of the evidence for overkill relies on proving that many large animals became extinct within several millennia of the first appearance of humans, usually estimated at about 50,000 years ago. Unlike other parts of the world, nothing in Australia's fossil record proves that humans hunted megafauna. As Trueman and Field note in their paper, there aren't even any sites with evidence that early inhabitants had the tools to kill large animals.

Trueman and Field discuss the dates of a controversial archaeological site, Cuddie Springs, that might prove that at least some Australian megafauna survived much longer than previously thought, dealing a blow to arguments for overkill. The site includes remains of several extinct animals, including *Diprotodon*, a two-ton marsupial, and *Genyornis*, a large, flightless bird. Previous efforts, made using radiocarbon dating and other methods, have concluded that some megafauna remains found there are 36,000 to 30,000 years old, but the findings have been disputed. Trueman and Field used a newer technique in their recent work, an analysis of rare earth elements (REEs) in bone fragments, and confirmed these dates. As they're buried, bones adsorb REEs, leaving a "fingerprint" that links the bones to their original layer of deposition.

Proving that people coexisted with large animals for 10,000 years or more would not necessarily remove humans from the extinction equation, but it would make it more likely that other factors, such as climate, also played a key part. Field, for one, is convinced that the findings at Cuddie Springs disprove the possibility of blitzkrieg in Australia and cast doubt on the overkill hypothesis. It's about time, she says, "to start entertaining other ideas about the extinction process."

Not everyone is convinced. In a 2001 paper published in *Science*, Richard G. Roberts of the University of Wollongong and a team of investigators found evidence of widespread Australian megafauna extinctions by about 46,000 years ago, concluding that humans must have played an important role. Roberts says that he still has "some strong reservations" about the recent paper. He notes that REEs are usually used to date much older bones, for which an error of thousands of years one way or the other would be insignificant. Although he himself is not entirely persuaded by blitzkrieg, he does think that it remains a possibility.

If Pleistocene humans hunted some large animals to extinction but blitzkrieg is ruled out as a possibility in Australia, as the recent findings suggest, the search for an overarching theory may be futile. In a review of recent research on the extinctions, published in the October 1, 2004, issue of *Science*, coauthors Anthony D. Barnosky, Paul L. Koch, Robert S. Feranec, Scott L. Wing and Alan B. Shabel argued that it will be more productive to look for localized, species-by-species explanations than a single cause. Some combination of climate change and human activity, they think, probably determined the fate of much of the world's megafauna.

Implicating multiple factors might not be as satisfying as convicting a single perpetrator, but it may better explain the evidence at hand. And as the *Science* authors point out, the combination of climate change and human action can have a much greater effect on the world's animal species than either factor alone. There's no debate that both are today affecting the viability of the remaining megafauna.

Making Connections to Personal and Social Issues: Coexisting with Other Animals

Esty refers to the hypothesis that during the Pleistocene era "humans moved rapidly through the [North American] continent, slaughtering mammoths, mastodons and other large prey as they went," ultimately wiping out most megafauna (paragraph 4). In the past, humans killed large animals primarily for food; however, in recent times, such killings seem to result primarily not from hunting for food or even for trophies, but from conflicts with humans. Human encounters with large wild animals occur frequently in many parts of the world. You may have seen news reports about bears foraging for food in people's backyards or even kitchens and mountain lions attacking hikers.

One of the debates in this chapter that you will have the opportunity to write about addresses the issue of whether suburban sprawl in the United States has hurt or helped wildlife survival. Whatever the reasons, many megafauna populations have declined and are facing the threat of extinction. In Africa, twenty years ago there were 100,000 to 200,000 lions; today, only 16,000 to 30,000 exist. Similarly, an estimated 1,500 to 2,000 wild elephants roamed Vietnam in 1975; today, only 76 survive. During the last one hundred years, grizzly bears have been eliminated from 98 percent of their original range in the western United States. Despite conservation efforts, the Yellowstone National Park grizzly population has dropped from 588 in 2004 to approximately 350 bears in 2006.

With two or three other students in your class, consider the question of how — or whether — humans can coexist with wild animals, especially large, dangerous ones. You might begin by telling each other about any encounters with wild animals you have had personally or have heard about. For example, have you seen deer or moose when driving on the highway, black bear in mountain areas, coyotes in suburban neighborhoods? Then discuss whether you think something *should* be done to protect megafauna, and if so, what *could* be done.

Analyzing Writing Strategies

1. For readers to understand the opposing positions, they first have to know what is being argued about. Therefore, writers typically introduce **the issue** or main point of disagreement early in the essay. Reread paragraphs 1–5 to see how Esty presents the issue, noticing the words he uses to cue readers. For example, at the end of paragraph 1, he uses the word "agree" to establish what scientists accept as fact and the expression "conflicting findings" to identify the issue. Look for and underline the other words Esty uses in paragraphs 2–5 to keep readers focused on the issue. How do the words you underlined help readers understand what is at issue?

2. In addition to informing readers about the issue, the writer also has to introduce **the opposing positions**. Opposing positions may be identified by key words or by the names of their proponents; Esty uses both to label the opposing positions in this essay. To see how Esty labels the two "possible causes of the extinctions,"

reread paragraphs 3–5 and put brackets around the key words used to identify the two different causes.

Esty also uses scientists' names to help readers follow the explanation of these two different causal theories. Reread paragraphs 4–12 and underline the scientists' names. Notice that in paragraph 4, he identifies one hypothesis proposed by Paul S. Martin. Then in paragraph 5, he names two scientists who have criticized Martin's hypothesis and in paragraph 6 names the authors of two recent publications that "try to help settle the question." Their work is explained in subsequent paragraphs: research that supports Martin's hypothesis is explained in paragraphs 7–9 and research that calls it into question is discussed in paragraphs 10–12. How well does this strategy of using key words and names help you keep track of the opposing positions in the debate?

Commentary: A Logical Plan and a Fair and Unbiased Presentation

Writers explaining opposing positions want their explanations to be clear and engaging for readers who do not know very much about the subject. Therefore, they lay out the information in a systematic and unbiased way.

Readers can best understand a debate if a writer explains it to them **topic by topic** — considering each aspect of the debate in turn and comparing and contrasting the debaters' treatment of it — rather than explaining one argument entirely and then the opposing argument entirely. Like the other authors in this chapter, Esty has closely analyzed the debate he is explaining. To help readers understand the disagreement among scientists about the causes of the sudden disappearance of large animals in the Pleistocene era, Esty has organized his explanation around these three topics:

- facts pertaining to the location and age of fossil sites (paragraphs 6–10)
- research methods for dating these sites (paragraphs 11–13)
- a possible resolution of the debate involving multiple causes of mass extinction (paragraphs 14–15)

Like all writers explaining opposing positions, Esty had to identify the significant topics in the debate he wished to write about, and then come up with a **logical plan** for his essay — an order, from first to last, for presenting the topics. In deciding on a plan, he considered the kind of information he would put under each topic, readers' likely familiarity with the information, and readers' need to know certain information related to one topic so that they would more readily comprehend the information in subsequent topics. Esty therefore begins by presenting readers with the debate about the fundamental questions guiding the research on this issue:

- what are the locations of mass extinction of megafauna on the planet?
- how does the age of these sites correlate with evidence of human population movements?

Next comes a topic that reveals the dispute among researchers about methods of dating these sites — specifically the use of REEs instead of the older method of radiocarbon dating. The final topic Esty presents refers to the possibility that human hunting of large animals may not be the sole cause of mass extinctions. An alternative solution to the research problem might be that there is no single "overarching theory" that will explain extinctions throughout the world, but that it would be "more productive to look for localized, species-by-species explanations" (paragraph 14). When you plan your own explanation of a debate, you will first need to create a logical plan or sequence for the topics you have discovered.

In addition to organizing the essay in a way that is logical and easy to follow, writers of essays explaining opposing positions have to be careful to present others' views in a **fair and unbiased** way. Notice that Esty does not voice his own opinion on whether overkill or climate change best explains the Pleistocene mass extinction, at least until the last paragraph where he writes that multiple causes "may better explain the evidence at hand" (paragraph 15). It could be said that even here Esty is not advocating his own view, but reporting the view of others such as the authors of the *Science* article who argue for a different way to resolve the dispute by looking for "localized" explanations rather than one overarching cause (paragraph 14). Another way Esty tries to make his presentation of opposing positions balanced is by giving each position a roughly equivalent amount of space in his essay — three paragraphs each: paragraphs 7–9 to Surovell, Waguespack and Brantingham, and paragraphs 10–12 to Trueman and Field.

While maintaining his own stance of impartiality, Esty quotes the criticism researchers have made about one another's findings. For example, Esty quotes Surovell's criticism of the argument for climate change (paragraph 9), explains how Trueman and Field's findings "cast doubt on the overkill hypothesis" (paragraph 12), and reports Roberts' "reservations" about the use of REEs (paragraph 13). Consequently, his essay informs readers about the debate and also makes them aware of the important questions they should be asking.

NOAH FELDMAN is a professor at the New York University School of Law, where he teaches courses in constitutional law, the history of legal theory, and law and religion. Feldman has a Ph.D. from Oxford University in Islamic political thought and a J.D. from Yale Law School. He has combined his interests in the Islamic world and constitutional law in his books *After Jihad: America and the Struggle for Islamic Democracy* (2003) and *What We Owe Iraq: War and the Ethics of Nation Building* (2004). His expertise in these areas also led to his appointment in 2003 as senior advisor for constitutional law to the Iraq Coalition Provisional Authority. Feldman also serves as an adjunct Senior Fellow of the Council on Foreign Relations, a fellow at the New America Foundation, and a contributing writer for the *New York Times Magazine*.

"America's Church-State Problem" comes from a much longer essay that was published in the *Times Magazine* and excerpted from Feldman's book *Divided by God: America's Church-State Problem — and What We Should Do About It* (2005). Both the book and the original article (entitled "A Church-State Solution") not only present Feldman's analysis of the church-state problem but also include an argument for his proposed solution. The excerpt here presents only Feldman's explanation of the problem. Essays or books arguing a solution to a problem or a position on a controversial issue frequently begin by explaining opposing positions.

As you read Feldman's essay, notice that he creates labels for the opposing positions: "values evangelicals" and "legal secularists." He uses the term "values evangelicals" to describe people who are not necessarily evangelical Christians but who think the government should evangelize or promote certain values. Similarly, "legal secularists" are not necessarily secular in the sense that they are not personally religious, but rather in that they think the "government should be secular" (paragraph 6).

America's Church-State Problem
Noah Feldman

For roughly 1,400 years, from the time the Roman Empire became Christian to the American Revolution, the question of church and state in the West always began with a simple assumption: the official religion of the state was the religion of its ruler. Sometimes the king fought the church for control of religious institutions; other times, the church claimed power over the state by asserting religious authority over the sovereign himself. But the central idea, formally enshrined at Westphalia in 1648 by the treaty that ended the wars of religion in Europe, was that each region would have its own religion, namely that of the sovereign. The rulers, meanwhile, manipulated religion to serve their own ends. . . .

All this changed with the radical idea, introduced during the American Revolution, that the people were sovereign. This arrangement profoundly disturbed the old model of church and state. To begin with, America was religiously diverse: how could the state establish the religion of the sovereign when the sovereign people in America belonged to many faiths — Congregationalist, Anglican, Presbyterian, Baptist, Quaker? Furthermore, the sovereign people would actively believe in religion instead of cynically manipulating it. . . . Religion would be a genuinely popular, even thriving, political force.

This model called for a new understanding of church and state, and the framers of the American Constitution rose to the occasion. They designed a national government that, for the first time in Western history, had no established religion at all. The Articles of Confederation, which were drawn up during the Revolutionary War, had been silent on religion — itself something of an innovation. But the Constitution went further by prohibiting any religious test for holding office. And the first words of the First Amendment stated that "Congress shall make no law respecting an establishment of religion, or prohibiting the free exercise thereof." If the people were to be sovereign, and belonged to different religions, the state religion would be no religion at all. Otherwise, the reasoning went, too many religious denominations would be in competition to make theirs the official choice, and none could prevail without coercing dissenters to support a church other than their own — a violation of the liberty of conscience that Americans had come to believe was a God-given right. Establishment of religion at the national level was prohibited. Religious diversity had ensured it. The experiment had begun.

During the two and a quarter centuries since America's founding, the experi- 4 ment has progressed fitfully. The non-establishment of religion, with a simultane- ous guarantee of its free exercise, was an elegant solution but not a complete one. Generation after generation, fresh infusions of religious diversity into American life have brought with them original ideas about church and state — new answers to the challenge of preserving the unity of the sovereign people in the face of their flourishing spiritual variety and often conflicting religious needs. . . .

In our own era, two camps dominate the church-state debate in American life, 5 corresponding to what are now the two most prominent approaches to the proper relation of religion and government. One school of thought contends that the right answers to questions of government policy must come from the wisdom of reli- gious tradition. You might call those who insist on the direct relevance of religious values to political life "values evangelicals." Not every values evangelical is, tech- nically speaking, an evangelical or a born-again Christian, although many are. Values evangelicals include Jews, Catholics, Muslims and even people who do not focus on a particular religious tradition but care primarily about identifying tradi- tional moral values that can in theory be shared by everyone.

What all values evangelicals have in common is the goal of evangelizing for 6 values: promoting a strong set of ideas about the best way to live your life and urg- ing the government to adopt those values and encourage them wherever possible. To them, the best way to hold the United States together as a nation, not just a country, is for us to know what values we really hold and to stand up for them. As Ralph Reed recently told an audience at Harvard, "While we are sometimes di- vided on issues, there remains a broad national consensus on core values and principles."

On the other side of the debate are those who see religion as a matter of 7 personal belief and choice largely irrelevant to government and who are con- cerned that values derived from religion will divide us, not unite us. You might call those who hold this view "legal secularists," not because they are necessarily strongly secular in their personal worldviews — though many are — but because they argue that government should be secular and that the laws should make it so. To the legal secularists, full citizenship means fully sharing in the legal and political commitments of the nation. If the nation defines itself in terms of values drawn from religion, they worry, then it will inevitably tend to adopt the religious values of the majority, excluding religious minorities and nonreligious people from full citizenship.

Despite the differences, each approach, values evangelicalism and legal 8 secularism, is trying to come to terms with the same fundamental tension in American life. The United States has always been home to striking religious diversity — diversity that has by fits and starts expanded over the last 230 years. At the same time, we strive to be a nation with a common identity and a common project. Religious division threatens that unity, as we can see today more clearly than at any time in a century in the disputes over stem-cell research, same-sex marriage and end-of-life issues. Yet almost all Americans want to make sure that we do not let our religious diversity pull us apart. Values evangelicals say that the solution lies in finding and embracing traditional values we can all share and without which we will never hold together. Legal secularists counter that we can maintain our national unity only if we treat religion as a personal, private matter, separate from concerns of citizenship. The goal of reconciling national unity and religious diversity is the same, but the methods for doing it are deeply opposed.

Yet neither legal secularism nor values evangelicalism has lived up to its own aspirations. Each promises inclusion, but neither has delivered. To make matters worse, the conflict between these two approaches is becoming a political and constitutional crisis all its own. Talk of secession of blue states from red in the aftermath of the 2004 election was not meant seriously; but this kind of dark musing, with its implicit reference to the Civil War, is also not coincidental. It bespeaks a division deeper than any other in our public life, a division that cannot be healed by the victory of either side. . . .

Even a joint commitment to "the culture of life" turns out to be very thin. Catholics and conservative Protestants may agree broadly on abortion and euthanasia; but what about capital punishment, which Pope John Paul II condemned as an immoral usurpation of God's authority to determine life and death but which many evangelical Christians support as biblically mandated? To reach consensus, the values evangelicals have to water down the "values" they say they accept to the point where they would mean nothing at all. They are left either acknowledging disagreement about values or else falling into a kind of relativism (I'm O.K., you're O.K.) that is inconsistent with the very goal of standing for something rather than nothing.

Meanwhile, the legal secularists have a different problem. They claim that separating religion from government is necessary to ensure full inclusion of all citizens. The problem is that many citizens — values evangelicals among them — feel excluded by precisely this principle of keeping religion private. Keeping nondenominational prayer out of the public schools may protect religious minorities who might feel excluded; but it also sends a message of exclusion to those who believe such prayer would signal commitment to shared values. Increasingly, the symbolism of removing religion from the public sphere is experienced by values evangelicals as excluding them, no matter how much the legal secularists tell them that is not the intent. . . .

Legal secularists may fear that when facing arguments with religious premises, they have the deck stacked against them. If values evangelicals begin by asserting that God has defined marriage as the union of one man and one woman, then, say the secularists, the conversation about same-sex marriage is over. But in fact, secularists can make arguments of their own, which may be convincing: if

9

10

11

12

the state is going to regulate marriages, shouldn't they be subject to the same equality requirement as every other law? Some might even go further and ask the evangelicals how they can be so sure that they have correctly identified God's will on the question. They may discover that few evangelicals treat faith as a conversation stopper, and most consider it just the opposite.

In any event, when the debate is over, the people will vote, and they will decide the matter. Legal secularists cannot realistically expect that they will win more democratic fights by banning the evangelicals' arguments, which can usually be recast, however disingenuously, as secular. Once in a while they may, if the composition of the Supreme Court is just right, thwart the values evangelicals' numerical superiority with a judicial override; but in the long run, all they will accomplish is to alienate the values evangelicals in a way that undercuts the meaningfulness of participatory democracy. . . .

If we could be more tolerant of sincere religious people drawing on their beliefs and practices to inform their choices in the public realm, and at the same time be more vigilant about preserving our legacy of institutional separation between government and organized religion, the shift would redirect us to the uniqueness of the American experiment with church and state. Until the rise of legal secularism, Americans tended to be accepting of public, symbolic manifestations of faith. Until values evangelicalism came on the scene, Americans were on the whole insistent about maintaining institutional separation. These two modern movements respectively reversed both those trends.

Making Connections to Personal and Social Issues: Shared Values

In paragraph 5, Feldman describes "values evangelicals" as including not only evangelical Protestants but also "Jews, Catholics, Muslims and even people who do not focus on a particular religious tradition but care primarily about identifying traditional moral values that can in theory be shared by everyone." In the next paragraph, he quotes Ralph Reed's assertion that "there remains a broad national consensus on core values and principles."

To examine this idea, discuss with two or three other students in your class the "core values and principles" that underlie your individual positions on a highly controversial issue. First, choose the issue that you will discuss. One possible issue is whether government should support research on embryonic stem cells. If you are unfamiliar with this issue, you can learn something about it from the opening scenario in this chapter. Here are several alternative issues you might prefer to discuss: whether the minimum wage should be raised, whether doctors should be permitted to help dying patients end their lives, whether the government should be allowed to torture people suspected of terrorism, whether capital punishment should continue to be legal.

After choosing an issue, take turns briefly stating your position on the issue and one or two values or principles upon which you base your position. Think of these values or principles as reasons why you take the position you do. If you have not made up your mind on the issue, explain which values you think are relevant to the issue. Do not get into an argument. The objective of this activity simply is to see whether you share the same values or prioritize your values in the same way. On the issue of embryonic stem cell research, for example, opponents and supporters may base their opposing positions on the same value for human life. But whereas supporters think the lives of sick or injured people (which might be saved by such research) are the most important consideration, opponents believe that the lives of the unborn (which are destroyed by the research) are more important. Explore the similarities and differences in the values and principles that you think are relevant to the issue you have chosen.

Analyzing Writing Strategies

1. Feldman **introduces the issue** in paragraphs 1–4 by presenting a brief history so that contemporary Americans can better understand the implications of the current debate and appreciate why it is important. Even though the separation of church and state is an issue that affects all Americans whatever their religious beliefs, the dispute may still seem rather abstract to many readers. Therefore, Feldman later refers to a variety of examples to make the issue more specific and relevant for readers. For instance, in paragraph 8, he writes: "Religious division threatens that unity, as we can see today more clearly than at any time in a century in the disputes over stem-cell research, same-sex marriage and end-of-life issues." Other examples of disputes appear in paragraphs 10, 11, and 12.

   Notice that Feldman does not explain how these examples illustrate the church-state debate; he simply asserts that they do because he assumes many of his readers will be familiar with them. With which of these examples are you familiar? How well do the examples with which you are familiar work to help you understand the church-state debate? What additional information, if any, would be helpful to you?

2. Writers explaining two opposing positions try to be **fair and unbiased**. In paragraph 9, for example, Feldman makes the point that values evangelicals and legal secularists both fail to achieve their goal: "Each promises inclusion, but neither has delivered." The fact that Feldman discusses the failure of both camps suggests he is being evenhanded. Reread paragraphs 10–12 to see whether he treats the two camps equivalently.

   From your analysis of these paragraphs, how well do you think Feldman succeeds in impartially pointing out the failure of both camps? Consider, for example, whether the failure of values evangelicals to agree among themselves on "core values" is as serious a shortcoming as the failure of legal secularists to convince values evangelicals that keeping religion private is not a way of excluding them.

Commentary: Comparing and Contrasting Topics Raised in the Debate

To explain opposing positions, writers use the common writing strategy of **comparing and contrasting**. They identify the topics that are important in the debate and organize their essays around these topics, pointing out similarities and differences in how each topic is treated by the debaters. Comparing and contrasting opposing positions can be confusing for readers if writers do not make very clear which position is being referred to at each point in the essay. Feldman relies on three strategies to help readers follow the comparison/contrast: He labels the opposing positions in a way that readers will remember; he uses transitions that clearly mark the differences and similarities he is pointing out; and he employs juxtaposition with parallel sentence structure to place alongside each other the contrasting views of the two camps.

Let us begin by looking at the way Feldman uses labels in paragraph 5:

> (1) In our own era, two camps dominate the church-state debate in American life, corresponding to what are now the two most prominent approaches to the proper relation of religion and government. (2) One school of thought contends that the right answers to questions of government policy must come from the wisdom of religious tradition. (3) You might call those who insist on the direct relevance of religious values to political life "values evangelicals." (4) Not every values evangelical is, technically speaking, an evangelical or a born-again Christian, although many are. (5) Values evangelicals include Jews, Catholics, Muslims and even people who do not focus on a particular religious tradition but care primarily about identifying traditional moral values that can in theory be shared by everyone.

This paragraph opens by introducing what Feldman calls the "two camps" that "dominate the church-state debate." The second sentence identifies one of the camps with the phrase "One school of thought." Sentence three labels this camp "values evangelicals" and is followed by two more sentences (4 and 5) in which the same label appears prominently so that readers know the same camp is being described. Feldman marks the switch to describing the second camp with a new paragraph — paragraph 7 — and the transitional phrase "On the other side of the debate." He then labels this "other side" "legal secularists."

We can also see the strategy of labeling the two camps carried out in the opening sentence of paragraph 8, where the words "each approach" are followed immediately by an appositive phrase identifying the two approaches with the familiar labels "values evangelicalism and legal secularism." Here is the complete sentence: "Despite the differences, each approach, values evangelicalism and legal secularism, is trying to come to terms with the same fundamental tension in American life."

This sentence plays a crucial role as a shift from pointing out differences between the two camps to discussing an important similarity between them. To help readers follow this turn his explanation is taking, Feldman uses transitional words and phrases that readers recognize immediately as signaling comparison or contrast. He begins the sentence with the phrase "Despite the differences." *Despite* is a preposition used to signal a contrast. It also serves to refer back to what was said previously. The preceding three paragraphs point out differences between the two camps on the issue of church and state. So this sentence begins by reminding readers of the differences they just read about, but then goes on to talk about something the two camps agree on, indicated by the word *same* — namely, the need to solve the problem of religious tension in America and find common ground for unity.

To see how Feldman uses juxtaposition with parallel sentence structure, look at one last example from paragraph 8. The second and third sentences from the end show how he juxtaposes the two camps' positions by placing them in adjacent sentences. Beginning each sentence with the same subject-verb-*that* structure ("Values evangelicals say that" and "Legal secularists counter that") makes the juxtaposition hard to miss. The verb *counter* signals clearly that the relation between these two sentences is one of contrast or difference, not similarity.

Feldman's use of these comparison/contrast strategies for cueing the reader — consistent labeling, transitions, and juxtaposition with parallelism — helps readers follow the explanation without getting confused. When you write your own essay explaining opposing positions, be sure to use these strategies. You can find an extensive list of connectives that signal a comparison (such as *like* and *in the same way*) or a contrast (such as *despite* and *although*) in Chapter 13: Cueing the Reader.

ATHENA ALEXANDER is a sociology major who hopes to become a doctor. In a composition class that used a draft version of this chapter, she wrote this essay to explain the debate over the No Child Left Behind Act. The two position essays by Rod Paige and Reg Weaver that she uses as the basis of her explanation are reproduced in the Writer at Work section of this chapter on pp. 241–53.

Reflecting on the challenges posed by the assignment, Alexander wrote that when she began work on this essay she did not know anything about the No Child Left Behind Act. Following the suggestions in the Guide to Writing, she did some background research, beginning with the Web site of the U.S. Department of Education. From there, she discovered that to find out what happens to schools that do not show improvement under the requirements of the act, she would have to search the sites of individual state departments of education, which is how she happened to find and quote from the Georgia state Web site. As you read the opening paragraphs of Alexander's essay, notice how she uses the information she learned from these two sources.

No Child Left Behind: "Historic Initiative" or "Just an Empty Promise"?

Athena Alexander

In 2001, an overwhelming bipartisan majority in Congress approved President George W. Bush's No Child Left Behind Act (NCLB), designed to improve the quality of education in American schools. Under this law, every state must test public school students in grades 3–8 annually to assess their progress in

1

reading and math. The NCLB also sets "adequate yearly progress" (AYP) goals for schools to meet. According to the U.S. Department of Education Web site, "schools that fail to make adequate yearly progress toward statewide proficiency goals will, over time, be subject to improvement, corrective action, and restructuring measures aimed at getting them back on course to meet State standards" ("Overview").

Each state determines how its own failing schools will be handled. For example, according to the Georgia State Department of Education's Web site, low-performing Georgia schools must meet AYP goals within five years. After a school has fallen below the AYP target for two years, school administrators are "required to seek outside expert assistance." This is also the point at which parents are permitted to transfer their children to a higher-performing school; if they choose a private school, they are given vouchers to pay the tuition. If the problem persists after three years, additional actions may be taken. For example, students may be given additional tutoring. After four or five years, more severe measures may go into effect, such as replacing teachers, administrators, or both; putting the failing school under "private management"; or even permanently closing it ("Consequences").

As the effects of the law began to be felt at the state and local level, the debate about it intensified. One particular pair of opposing essays appeared in *Insight on the News* (2004), a magazine published by *The Washington Times*. In "Testing Has Raised Students' Expectations, and Progress in Learning Is Evident Nationwide," Rod Paige, the secretary of education under President George W. Bush from 2001 to 2005, defends NCLB, claiming that major improvements in schools have resulted in the short time the law has been in effect. Reg Weaver, president of the National Education Association, a union representing teachers, argues the opposite position in his essay, "NCLB's Excessive Reliance on Testing Is Unrealistic, Arbitrary and Frequently Unfair." Weaver calls for changes in the law, arguing that in its present form, NCLB will destroy the public education system in America (par. 4). Paige and Weaver differ on the role standardized testing should play in assessing students' progress and the NCLB's effectiveness. Ultimately, however, their disagreement is political — with Paige accusing NCLB critics of being cynical and Weaver accusing its supporters of having a hidden agenda.

Whether testing should be the only, or even the most important, diagnostic tool for assessing the rate of learning is a central topic of debate between Paige and Weaver. Paige defends the NCLB's reliance on standardized testing, claiming that testing is an integral "part of life" (par. 1). He compares testing of students to tests that certify drivers, pilots, doctors, and teachers (par. 2). Furthermore, he argues that testing is essential because it indicates "whether the system is performing as it should" (par. 3).

Weaver, however, disagrees with Paige on the role standardized testing should play in assessment. He argues that the NCLB should not rely on "only one type of assessment" because "good teachers" know that "judgments about what has been learned" should be based on "a variety of assessments" (par. 3).

He also points out that teachers complain about the reliance on standardized testing because it makes preparing students for the test the focus of coursework, "push[ing] more and more of the important things that prepare us for life . . . off the curriculum plate" (par. 1). He reports that the majority of teachers believe that "teaching to the test 'inevitably stifles real teaching and learning'" (par. 2). In addition, Weaver questions the "one-size-fits-all approach" standardized testing imposes on special needs students, who he says require more "complex and multifaceted assessment" procedures (par. 3). Therefore, unlike Paige, who defends standardized tests as "scientifically based research techniques" (Paige par. 12), Weaver calls for a change in the NCLB's method of assessing adequate yearly progress.

Although Weaver and Paige both agree that, as Weaver puts it, the "focus should be on helping the individual student," they appear to have different information about whether NCLB, in fact, is being used for this purpose (Weaver, par. 19). Weaver apparently believes the tests are used only to compare schools and not to diagnose individual students' problems. He asserts: "Measuring this year's fourth-graders against next year's fourth-graders tells us little that we need to know about the improvement of individual students" (par. 17). Paige, on the other hand, confidently affirms that the tests identify "problems" individual students have "so that they can be fixed" (par. 3). To support his claim that the law is helping individual students, Paige points to the example of Cheltenham, Pennsylvania, "where the district provides schools with specific information about each student's abilities and weaknesses in specific academic areas" that teachers use to develop their lesson plans for the coming school year (par. 15). Another example Paige cites shows that school administrators are using grant money to invest in computerized assessment programs like "Yearly Progress Pro" to track individual student progress (par. 13). Whether such grants are funded by NCLB or in some other way is not clear from Paige's essay. But what is clear from both Paige and Weaver's essays is that they both agree the goal of any assessment should be to help individual students receive the teaching they need to improve.

Indeed, the need to improve America's educational system is unquestioned by both writers. But whereas Paige argues passionately that the NCLB is not only necessary but effective, Weaver contends that it fails to deliver on its promise. Paige makes a strong economic argument for the need to improve high school education so that students are prepared for the "fastest-growing occupations in the United States" and can compete in the new "global economy" (pars. 8, 9). To support his argument, Paige cites statistics from the National Assessment of Educational Progress and quotes from authorities like Federal Reserve Chairman Alan Greenspan. He also refers to a research study that claims the "vast majority of employers sadly expect that a high-school graduate will not write clearly or have even fair math skills" (par. 8). Perhaps most important, Paige argues that "the status quo result of a decades-old education system before the NCLB" results in a disparity in student performance along race and ethnic lines: "only one in six African Americans and one in five Hispanics are proficient in reading by the time they are high-school seniors" (par. 7). These are impressive and depressing statistics. But, according to studies Paige cites, the NCLB is making progress in reversing this trend. For example, he explains that the "Beating the Odds IV report showed that since NCLB has been implemented, public-school students across the country" — and especially those in large metropolitan school systems — "have shown a marked improvement in reading" (par. 14).

Weaver also cites authorities, studies, and statistics, but his purpose is to question the NCLB's effectiveness in solving the problem. He focuses his criticism on the concept of "adequate yearly progress" that is used by the NCLB to measure progress. Weaver claims that the AYP sets an unrealistic standard for schools. He bases this argument on economic scenarios or projections, together with preliminary results after two years under the NCLB Act. As he says, "the prediction became reality last summer when nearly 25 percent of schools in Connecticut were identified as having failed to make AYP" (par. 9). Projections also estimate that at the end of twelve years, 93 percent (744 of 802) of Connecticut's elementary and middle schools will have failed to reach AYP targets (par. 10). Weaver's point is that if Connecticut, "a state that is regarded nationally as a high performer[,] is not adequate to meet the statistical demands of this law," there must be something wrong with the AYP standard (par. 11).

The problem, according to Weaver, is that the "current formula for AYP fails to consider the difference between where you start and how quickly you must reach the goal." He therefore calls the formula "irresponsible" (par. 13). He criticizes the NCLB's grouping of English-language learners and special-education students with the general student population, and its requirement that all students progress at the same rate. Moreover, he asserts that using standardized tests to determine progress is "totally inappropriate and emotionally injurious" for some of these groups of students (par. 13).

Paige refutes Weaver's argument by labeling critics of the NCLB "cynics" and claiming that they exercise what President Bush has called the "soft bigotry of low expectations." He argues that "pessimism" sets up a self-fulfilling prophecy, in which the expectation a teacher has of a student affects the performance of that student. Paige adamantly insists that such "excuses must stop" and that every child should be treated equally (par. 11). He reminds readers of NCLB's theme: "if you challenge students, they will rise to the occasion" (par. 16). Paige is making a political argument here, implying that if you oppose the law, you do not cherish the American ideal of equal opportunity for all, or you are prejudiced in your assumptions about the abilities of students.

Weaver, in turn, counters Paige's political argument with a political argument of his own. He suggests that the NCLB Act has a hidden agenda to privatize education in America by replacing public schools with private schools funded by government vouchers (par. 15). He presents this argument gingerly through rhetorical questions: "Is this all the law of unintended consequences? Or is there, as many believe, an insidious intent to discredit public education, paving the way for a breakup of the current system — an opening of the door to a boutique system with increased privatization and government vouchers?" (par. 15). Weaver contends that if the goal is really to improve "student achievement," then before encouraging parents to abandon a school that is failing according to NCLB measures, "shouldn't we offer tutoring to struggling students first?" (par. 19). But vouchers are offered, in Georgia at least, only after two years of failing to meet AYP targets, and tutoring is not offered until the third year. Weaver seems to think that by making AYP goals so hard to reach, the NCLB will frighten parents into taking their children out of public schools and with the help of vouchers put them into private schools that are likely to have higher scores because they have more selective enrollments and are not required to take in English-language learners, disabled students, and others who bring down the school average. Private schools, in any case, are not held to NCLB requirements.

If you look up school vouchers on the Internet, you see that the debate over them has been going on for years. Many of the arguments that were made about vouchers in the past are echoed in the arguments about the No Child Left Behind Act. Wikipedia, for example, points out that whereas supporters of vouchers, like Paige, argue they "promote competition among schools of all types," opponents, like Weaver, contend that the funding for vouchers would compete with the funding for public education. Similarly, although proponents of vouchers argue that the poor would benefit by being able to "attend private schools that were previously inaccessible," opponents fear that "vouchers are tantamount to providing taxpayer-subsidized white flight from urban public schools, whose student bodies are predominantly non-white in most large cities" ("Education voucher"). Readers who are aware of the history of this debate over school vouchers cannot fail to see how these same arguments support the opposing positions Weaver and Paige take on No Child Left Behind. 12

Even though Paige and Weaver are part of a long history of debate on how to improve American education, they do agree with the sentiment behind the slogan "no child left behind." Both support "high standards and accountability" (Weaver par. 21). But they disagree on the means to achieve these goals. For Weaver, adequate yearly progress as measured by standardized tests — the backbone of the law — is a stumbling block rather than a building block to quality education for all. He recommends significant changes in the law that he believes would make it more effective and fairer. Paige, on the other hand, characterizes Weaver's recommendations as "complaints of the unwilling," arguing that instead of changing the NCLB Act, we should give it time and "work to make the law successful" (pars. 18, 19). Time will tell whether No Child Left Behind is viewed as an "historic initiative," as Paige predicts (par. 4), or as "just an empty promise," as Weaver warns (par. 21). 13

Works Cited

"Consequences for Schools and Districts Not Making Adequate Yearly Progress AYP." *Georgia Department of Education.* 2002. 5 April 2006 <http://www.doe.k12.ga.us/support/plan/nclb.asp/ayp_consequences>.
"Education Voucher." *Wikipedia.* 27 April 2006. 29 April 2006 <http://en.wikipedia.org/wiki/Education_voucher>.

"Overview: Executive Summary." *U.S. Department of Education*. 10 Feb. 2004. 5 April 2006 <http://www.ed.gov/nclb/overview/intro/execsumm.html>.

Paige, Rod. "Testing Has Raised Students' Expectations, and Progress in Learning Is Evident Nationwide." *Insight on the News*. 11 May 2004. 17 April 2006 <http://findarticles.com/p/articles/mi_m1571/is_2004_May_11/ai_n6143345>.

Weaver, Reg. "NCLB's Excessive Reliance on Testing Is Unrealistic, Arbitrary and Frequently Unfair." *Insight on the News*. 11 May 2004. 17 April 2006 <http://findarticles.com/p/articles/mi_m1571/is_2004_May_11/ai_n9778520>.

Making Connections to Personal and Social Issues: Improving Schools

Everyone appears to agree that schools in the United States need improvement. Whether you attended public or private schools or both — and even if you were schooled at home or in another country — you have had extensive experience in schooling and could be considered an expert on it. Get together with two or three classmates and share with them your insights about what was wrong — and right — about your own schooling. Take turns telling each other what in your experience is the most pressing problem with schools and also what you value most about your school experience. Focus on any part of your experience from kindergarten through high school.

Then discuss what you think should be done to make schools better. Athena Alexander reports that the debate over the No Child Left Behind Act has focused on using standardized tests to determine whether students are progressing at the prescribed rate in reading and math. In addition to making changes in the curriculum or in the faculty, what other, perhaps more fundamental changes in people's attitudes do you think would improve schooling in America?

Analyzing Writing Strategies

1. To help readers understand a debate about a controversial issue, writers usually organize their explanation around a series of points of comparison and contrast based on topics, or specific aspects of the argument, presented in a sequence that follows a **logical plan**. To see how Alexander's plan works, begin by rereading the last two sentences of paragraph 3. Underline the topics introduced in these forecasting sentences. Then, reread the rest of the essay, identifying in the margin where each of these topics is brought up again and developed.

   Finally, consider whether placing the topics in this order seems logical to you. In other words, how does each topic prepare you for the next one? Do any of the topics seem out of order? If so, why do you think so?

2. Writers explaining opposing positions focus readers' attention on the points of agreement and disagreement among those debating a controversial issue. Alexander relies on two strategies for presenting her **comparison and contrast**: she labels the opposing positions in a way that readers will remember and she uses transitions that clearly mark the similarities and differences she is pointing out.

   Reread paragraphs 5 and 6 to find examples of these two strategies. What labels does she use to identify the opposing positions and avoid confusing readers? Note any places where you think additional labels could be helpful or where labels that she includes are not needed. Then, put brackets around or highlight the transitions Alexander uses. (Transitional words and phrases perform different functions: pointing to differences [such as *but* and *in contrast*], similarities [*like* and *similarly*], additional items [*as well as* and *in addition to*], conclusions [*in conclusion* and *thus*], etc.) Group the transitions in paragraphs 5 and 6 according to their purpose. Finally, assess the effectiveness of Alexander's use of labels and transitions to present her comparison and contrast.

3. Read the **Writer at Work** section on pages 241–53 to see how Alexander based her essay on the topics in the Guide to Writing. The list of Topics to Look For on pages 226–27 identifies topics that may be addressed in essays arguing a position. As she analyzed the essays by Paige and Weaver, Alexander looked for these topics and filled in the Topics Chart on page 228. Reread paragraphs 7 and 8 of her essay to see which topics from this chart she discusses.

Commentary: Introducing the Issue and the Opposing Positions

Writers explaining opposing positions typically explain the issue and identify the opposing positions early in the essay. Because she is writing about a complex issue that few readers are likely to know about or fully understand, Athena Alexander devotes the first three paragraphs (almost a fourth of the paragraphs in the entire essay) to **introducing the issue and the opposing positions**. She explains the purpose of the No Child Left Behind Act ("designed to improve the quality of education in American schools," paragraph 1), when and how it was passed by Congress ("in 2001" by an "overwhelming bipartisan majority," paragraph 1) and what the new law requires ("test public school students in grades 3–8 annually to assess their progress in reading and math," paragraph 1). Finally, to explain what happens when schools "fail to make adequate yearly progress," she gives the example of Georgia (paragraph 2). This example is helpful because the No Child Left Behind Act only legislated a mechanism for assessing progress; states establish their own targets ("statewide proficiency goals") and are responsible for figuring out how to use the assessments to actually improve education.

This information gives readers a basic understanding of the law. Paragraph 3 clarifies what is at issue in the debate about this law. In identifying the two essays arguing opposing positions that her own essay will explain, she helps readers understand what the disagreement is about. She lays out each essay's position: Rod "Paige . . . defends NCLB" and Reg "Weaver calls for changes in the law." Notice that Alexander makes clear from the outset that Weaver does not want to eliminate the No Child Left Behind Act, but to modify it. Of course, Paige and other supporters of the NCLB might regard Weaver's proposed changes in the law as having the effect of destroying it. But Alexander does not evaluate or even characterize these two positions; she simply tries to report them as accurately and clearly as she can. She also very briefly summarizes each essay's main argument: whereas for Paige, the NCLB has already been effective ("major improvements in schools have resulted"), for Weaver, it threatens to have a different and disastrous effect ("NCLB will destroy the public education system in America").

Alexander specifies in the last two sentences of paragraph 3 the points of disagreement between Paige and Weaver that her explanation will cover. These sentences offer readers a further clarification of the issue and also provide a road map to help readers follow the intricacies of the explanation. Her characterization of the disagreement as ultimately "political" is interesting in light of the fact that Alexander noted in the opening paragraph that the No Child Left Behind Act initially passed by "an overwhelming bipartisan majority." As she explains at the end of her essay, given the history of the debate about school vouchers and the funding of public and private education in America, it should not be surprising that the debate over the NCLB has become political. She does not explicitly identify Paige and Weaver as politicians, but she does indicate that they represent different groups. Paige, as she explains, wrote his essay defending the No Child Left Behind Act when he was the secretary of education, the person responsible for developing the law as well as getting it passed and implemented. In criticizing the way the law has been implemented, Weaver as union president speaks for teachers who work primarily in the public school system. As spokesmen for these different constituencies, Paige and Weaver represent two important points of view on this highly controversial issue that affects students and teachers nationwide.

As you introduce the issue and the opposing positions in your essay, think about what background information would help your readers understand the debate and the debaters. Think about how you can inform yourself and your readers about the historical and political as well as the economic and social implications of the issue.

■ Purpose and Audience

The primary purpose for writing an essay explaining opposing positions is to give readers an understanding of the debate. The information you present will help readers grasp why the issue is important and what is at stake. Most writers of debate explanations also try to interest their readers, perhaps even to entice them to care about the issue and possibly to join in the debate.

People who read essays explaining opposing positions are unlikely to know very much about the debate. For many, reading an explanation is likely to be only the first step. For these readers, think of your essay as an introduction designed to alert them to some of the important points of disagreement and agreement on the issue. You will want to help them understand the topics that have been raised in the debate and where the different debaters position themselves in relation to these topics.

Basic Features:
Explaining Opposing Positions

An Introduction to the Issue and the Opposing Positions

Writers need to introduce the issue as well as the opposing positions on it. All of the writers in this chapter assume their readers will not know or remember very much about the issue; consequently, they spend the opening section of their essays introducing it. Alexander Cheung, Noah Feldman, and Athena Alexander all devote the first three paragraphs of their essays to informing readers about the issue, and Amos Esty uses the first five paragraphs. Writers use various strategies to describe the issue and interest readers. They may indicate why the issue is timely or urgent, offer a brief history of the debate, or give examples or anecdotes. For example, Cheung recounts more recent history relating to the court case that led to the demise of Napster. Esty begins his essay by describing the "mystery" of the megafauna extinction and then tells what made the debate about its cause (or causes) "heat up" (paragraph 4). Alexander describes the No Child Left Behind Act and gives an example to show how it is being implemented.

Writers also introduce the debaters, nearly always giving their names and some further information that establishes their authority to speak on the issue and also suggests what their interest in it may be. For example, Cheung gives the title and publication source for the two essays on which he bases his explanation. He names the authors and briefly describes their professions and other credentials. Readers can decide the relevance of such facts as that Matthew Scrivner, who argues for free exchange of information on the Internet, writes for an online literary magazine and that one of the writers who takes the opposing position is president of the Recording Industry Association of America and a copyright attorney. Feldman is the exception: he describes and labels the "two camps" but does not mention individual people who advocate either position.

A Comparison and Contrast of Topics Raised in the Debate

The most informative essays explaining a debate present the debate topic by topic, comparing and contrasting the debaters' presentation of each topic. In addition to explaining the issue itself and the opposing debaters' basic positions on it, writers focus on more specific topics — such as argumentative strategies used or kinds of evidence provided — that are important to readers' understanding of the debate. Cheung, for example, focuses on the contrasting positions on legal matters of Scrivner on the one hand and Spanier and Sherman on the other, their concern with defining whether music should be considered "information," which is free, or "intellectual property," which can be owned and therefore stolen. He also points out that Scrivner raises questions about whose interests are served by outlawing music downloading and that Spanier and Sherman do not address this topic.

Writers draw from an array of strategies for comparing and contrasting. For example, they may label the opposing positions and use those labels consistently so that readers are never confused about which side is being discussed. Cheung, Esty, and Alexander use the essayists' names as labels, and Feldman creates memorable labels of his own: "values evangelicals" and "legal secularists." Another valuable strategy that makes it easy for readers to follow points of agreement and disagreement is to use transitional words and phrases. Cheung, Feldman, and Alexander use transitions liberally to signal similarity ("Despite the differences, each approach . . . is trying to come to terms with the same") as well as difference ("In contrast" and "On the other hand").

A Logical Plan

Writers sequence the topics they compare or contrast in various ways: according to which topics are likely to be most and least familiar to readers, which topics are most and least complex to present, which topic contrast is likely to be most helpful in orienting readers to the debate or in concluding the debate. Here is the order in which Cheung takes up topics: the writers' overall positions, their definitions of music, their concern with legal matters, questions about who would benefit from outlawing music downloading, and questions of fact. This plan seems likely to be helpful to readers. Cheung begins by ensuring that readers understand that the debaters hold sharply different positions and follows with their different ways of defining music, which are central to the legal dispute. He concludes by presenting questions raised by one of the writers that invite further inquiry by readers interested in learning more about the issue.

A Fair and Unbiased Presentation of the Opposing Positions

Writers strive to be fair and unbiased in explaining a debate. They know that they will only hold readers' confidence if they accurately report the similarities and differences between the opposing positions and do not give preferential treatment to one position over the other. All of the writers in this chapter try to make their explanation of opposing positions balanced by giving each position a roughly equivalent amount of space in the essay. Esty, for example, gives three paragraphs to each side: paragraphs 7–9 to Surovell, Waguespack and Brantingham, and paragraphs 10–12 to Trueman and Field. Writers also try to present both the strengths and the weaknesses of each position rather than emphasizing the strengths of one and the weaknesses of the other. Feldman, for example, discusses how neither legal secularism nor values evangelicalism has fulfilled the promise of inclusion. Esty maintains his impartiality by quoting various writers' criticisms rather than presenting his own.

Although both Cheung and Alexander told us that they felt strongly about the issue they were writing about, they keep their views to themselves. Esty and Feldman, on the other hand, each let readers know where they stand, but only at the end of the essay. Esty indicates his preference for the multiple-causes solution, suggesting that it "may better explain the evidence" (paragraph 15). Similarly, Feldman concludes with a compromise: ". . . we could be more tolerant of sincere religious people drawing on their beliefs and practices to inform their choices in the public realm, and at the same time be more vigilant about preserving our legacy of institutional separation between government and organized religion . . ." (paragraph 14). If you do feel the need to enter the debate, consider doing so only as part of your conclusion, as Esty and Feldman do.

Explaining Opposing Positions

Invention and Research

Which of the debates at the end of this chapter (or on the Web site) would you like to learn more about and explain to other people? Go on-line if necessary to get some background on the issue, and do some thinking and writing about the opposing essays. Then consider how to explain the debate clearly to readers. . . . **See p. 223 for more.**

Planning and Drafting

As you look over what you have written and learned so far, how can you present the debate clearly to readers and engage their interest in it? How much do they already know about it? What are the most important differences between the two essays? Make a plan for your explanation, and start drafting it. . . . **See p. 230 for more.**

Critical Reading Guide

What are your draft's strengths and weaknesses? For example, is it clear exactly what the opposing positions are? Have you failed to stay impartial in your explanation? Get a classmate, a friend, a writing tutor, or someone else to read and respond in detail to your essay, especially the parts you're most unsure of. . . . **See p. 235 for more.**

Revising

As you consider your essay again in light of your reader's comments, how can you improve it? Have you misrepresented either of the writers? Is there too much or too little detail about any of the topics? Is the sequence of topics hard to follow? Go through your draft systematically, making changes wherever necessary. . . . **See p. 237 for more.**

Editing and Proofreading

Have you checked for errors that are especially likely in explanations of opposing positions? For example, have you used pronouns like *this*, *that*, *it*, or *which* to refer only to a vague idea rather than to a specific noun in your sentence? Look for and correct these and any other errors. . . . **See p. 240 for more.**

The Writing Assignment

Write an essay about opposing positions on an issue that interests you and that you want to learn more about. When you have reached a good understanding of the debate on the issue, explain it to your readers. Consider carefully what they already know about the debate and try to interest them in it. Your goal is to explain the debate in an unbiased way — to report on it — while taking care not to express your own position on the issue of the debate, should you have one.

To learn about using the *Guide* e-book for invention and drafting, go to bedfordstmartins.com/theguide.

Invention and Research

The following guidelines and activities provide comprehensive support for your work on this assignment. They guide you from choosing a debate to write about to formulating a tentative thesis statement for your essay. You will learn to understand a debate by identifying and charting its important topics, the different ways in which the debaters present their ideas and make their points. This method will enable you to collect and organize the information in two essays taking opposing positions on the issue, so that you can compare and contrast them for your readers.

Choosing a Debate to Write About

If your instructor has not assigned one of the debates in the Appendix to this chapter or on the companion Web site for this book at bedfordstmartins.com/theguide, choose one now to read closely and write about. Choose a debate that you feel drawn to learn more about. It may or may not be the one you already know the most about or the one that connects most immediately to your personal experience or interests. It could be the debate that touches on your planned college academic major or your hoped-for career. It could be the one that you assume would most stretch and challenge you. You will discover that the close reading required, the topic-charting challenge, and the planning and drafting of the comparisons and contrasts between the opposing positions will pose about the same challenge, whichever debate you choose. You need not agonize over the choice.

Take time now to skim and read a bit of all of the debates. Then make a choice and dive into the work.

Getting an Overview of the Debate You Have Chosen

Read the debate just as though you had come across it in a magazine or newspaper. If you have neither read nor viewed recent reports and discussions about the debate you have chosen to write about, you can expect that your understanding will grow only gradually as you read and reread. You need not understand every detail, but you need a good general understanding before you proceed with the invention work that follows.

Researching the Issue

Gather some information about the background of the issue. Your essay explaining opposing positions on an issue will have two distinctly different parts, each requiring of you quite different kinds of reading, thinking, and writing. One part is the comparison and contrast of topics based on your close reading of the two essays. For this part, all of the information you need is in the two essays themselves.

The other part is informing your readers about the issue itself before you begin to explain the opposing positions on it. This part will form the introduction to your essay. Some of this information can come from the position essays if one or both of the writers describe the history or context of the debate (most likely as part of the introduction to the essay). You will need to know more, however, in order to be well informed about the issue yourself and to orient your readers to it. Therefore, you will need to research the background or history of the issue and its present status. Start in your college library, where a librarian can give you advice about the online catalog of all the library's resources and also direct you to the Library of Congress Subject Headings, where you can find a useful search term for the issue you want to learn more about. Also consult Chapter 21, Library and Internet Research, for help with using the library productively. This research into the issue underlying the debate will necessarily be limited in time and scope. To introduce your explanation of the debate, you will need to write only a paragraph or two of information about the issue. Most of the space in your essay will be devoted to your explanation of the two opposing positions in the debate you have chosen.

An Online Activity:
Researching the Issue of Your Chosen Debate

One way to get a quick overview of the issue in the debate you have chosen is to go online. For the issues in the two debates printed in the Appendix at the end of this chapter, the following online sites offer comprehensive information:

Urban Sprawl and Wildlife

- Sprawl City, which offers information based on the U.S. Bureau of Census Data on Urbanized Areas (www.sprawlcity.org)
- Sierra Club (www.sierraclub.org/sprawl)
- Urban Sprawl: the Big Picture, which offers visual images of urban areas from the National Aeronautics and Space Administration (science.nasa.gov//headlines/y2002/11Oct_sprawl.htm)

Torture

- *Frontline: The Torture Question*, a comprehensive television report on the War on Terror prisoner interrogations by the U.S. military. You can view the 90-minute program online (www.pbs.org./wgbh/pages/frontline/torture/etc/faqs.html).

- *The New Yorker* magazine, which published a report by Seymour Hersh that first attracted national attention to the treatment of prisoners at Abu Ghraib Prison in Iraq (www.newyorker.com/fact/content/?040510fa_fact).
- Photos (www.antiwar.com/news/?articleid=2444). At this site you can view photos taken inside Abu Ghraib Prison.

You can get information online about other issues by entering keywords about the issue into a search tool such as Google (google.com) or Yahoo! Directory (http://dir.yahoo.com). *Bookmark or keep a record of promising sites. Download any material that you think might help you explain the issue to your readers. Keep in mind that you need only enough information to orient your readers to the issue before you explain the two-essay debate you have been studying, and remember that you will need to cite your sources of background information.*

Testing Your Choice

If you have the option of choosing a debate to explain, pause now to decide whether you want to stay with the debate you originally chose or consider choosing a different one. Now that you are familiar with your first choice and with the issue it engages, take some time to review the material you have collected about the issue. Skim or reread the two debate essays. Then consider these questions.

Does the issue seem timely and important to you?

Does the debate itself engage your interest?

Do you feel drawn to studying the two opposing positions carefully, so that you can learn precisely how they are alike and different?

Identifying Topics in Your Debate

A **topic** is an aspect of the argument the writer is making, such as the basic position asserted, a specific kind of information used for support, or a specific strategy used to persuade. The following activities will help you identify topics in the debate by annotating where they appear in the essays and by filling in a chart showing the paragraphs where the topics appear. This chart will be the focus for the planning, organizing, and drafting of your explanation of the debate. This challenging and rewarding activity involves several rereadings of all or parts of the two essays. It is a good idea to spread your study of the debate over two or three days so that you can gradually gain confidence at identifying the topics.

Annotating the Essays to Identify Topics.   *Either on paper or electronically, annotate both essays in the debate you have chosen, writing or typing the names of topics from the list on pages 226–27 wherever the topics appear in the essays. In addition, highlight in some way the text to which each annotation refers.*

Search every paragraph for these topics. Some of them are easy to identify. Others will become apparent only after you have become more familiar with the

Topics to Look For

These first two topics are basic elements that you can expect to find in any essay arguing a position. (The writer mentioned in the description of each topic is the writer of the essay you are reading.)

ISSUE.   The writer defines and describes the issue that is the focus of the debate. Usually you will find the issue presented in the first paragraph or the first two or three paragraphs of the essay.

These subtopics may contribute to the presentation of the issue:

KEY WORDS The writer uses these words to identify just this issue and not some other.

EXAMPLE or **ANALOGY** or **SCENARIO** or **OBSERVATION** The writer explains the issue using one of these strategies. (An analogy compares two similar things and a scenario briefly narrates a hypothetical or possible event)

OTHER DEFINITION The writer mentions another author's definition of the issue.

HISTORY The writer locates the issue historically or narrates some of its history.

IMPORTANCE The writer states the importance or seriousness of the issue.

POSITION.   The writer asserts a position on the issue. (Look for a concise assertion of one to three sentences. It may appear anywhere in the definition or description of the issue.)

The following topics are specific ways of arguing to support a position that may appear in either, both, or neither of the essays you are annotating. Some topics may appear more than once in the same essay.

OPPOSING The writer mentions or discusses an opposing position by identifying the position, naming those who argue for it, or giving the titles of their publications.

RESOLVE The writer attempts to resolve a difference with an opposing position or to find common ground on the issue.

REFUTE The writer attempts to refute (question, discredit, undermine, attack) another position on the issue.

SOLUTION OR **ACTION** The writer proposes a solution to a problem raised by the issue or advocates actions to be taken.

CAUSE OR **CONSEQUENCE** The writer speculates about how the issue arose, what the basis or origins of opponents' views are, or why people involved behaved as they did. Or the writer predicts future consequences of the issue.

STATISTIC OR **FACT** The writer uses a statistic or established fact.

RESEARCH The writer refers to a specific research study.

EXAMPLE The writer gives an example or illustration.

OBSERVATION The writer introduces a recent personal observation of people or places.

ANECDOTE OR **SCENARIO** The writer narrates an anecdote (a one-time personally experienced event) or a scenario (a hypothetical or possible event).

U.S. IDEALS The writer reveals concern for traditional U.S. ideals of freedom, equality, democracy, opportunity, fair elections, and so on.

MORAL OR **ETHICAL** The writer refers to moral or ethical values or to particular religious beliefs.

LEGAL The writer focuses on legal issues or questions, such as court cases, laws, or the U.S. Constitution.

WHAT GAINED OR **WHAT LOST** The writer focuses on what may be gained or lost by taking one position or another.

WHO GAINS OR **WHO LOSES** The writer identifies individuals or groups who have an interest in, or may benefit or suffer from, how the issue is resolved.

PUBLIC GOOD The writer expresses a concern for the public good, for policies or conditions that benefit society in general, such as clean air and water, safe neighborhoods, and ethical behavior among corporate executives.

AGENDA The writer states or implies a broader cultural or political agenda, that is, a personal preference for the way things ought to be that extends beyond this issue to other issues.

ATTITUDE The writer reveals an attitude toward possible readers or other writers who are participating in the debate.

If you find any other topic that you consider important but that is not on the list above, name it and include it in your annotations.

---

essay. Some topics may be expressed in a word, a phrase, or a sentence, others in several sentences or a paragraph.

Guided by the Topics to Look For list, first look for statements of the *issue* being debated and of the *position* taken in each of the essays. Then search for the other topics. You will find yourself reading and rereading and rereading still more in order to find and name the topics that appear in the debate. Your goal is to use the topics list to help you identify all the topics that you can recognize. The more topics you identify, the more likely you are to have the information you need to explain the debate comprehensively to your readers.

In the Writer at Work section on pp. 241–53, you will find an example of Athena Alexander's topic annotations of three paragraphs from an essay in the debate she explains, along with a discussion of her approach to this assignment.

Charting the Topics. Either fill in the chart on the next page or set up a chart of your own on paper or in a computer file. Put in the names or abbreviations of those topics you have identified in the essays you are analyzing. Another student's chart of topics may not resemble yours in every detail. Below the blank chart is a part of Alexander's filled-in topics chart.

Your Topics Chart

Instructions:

1. At the top of the second and third columns, put the names of each debater.
2. In the column labeled Topic, put the name of every topic you identify in either or both essays.
3. In the column under the debater's name, put the paragraph numbers where the topics you have listed in the left column are brought up in the essay.
4. Begin by charting topics in the paragraphs where the issue and position are presented in each essay. Then, chart every other topic you identify in either essay.

Topic		

Part of Athena Alexander's Topics Chart

Topic	Paige	Weaver
issue	4, 7–9	1–3, 20
position	5, 9–10	4–5, 8, 13
key words		6
refute	11	19
attitude	11	16
solution	12	17–19
consequences	8–9	1, 10–11
ideals	6, 16, 18	13, 16, 21
scenarios/examples	13–15	2, 9–11, 17–19
observations	17	1

Identifying and Understanding Your Readers

Take a few minutes to write about your readers. Now that you have a good understanding of the debate you will be explaining, think about who your prospective readers are likely to be and to speculate about their knowledge of and interest in the issue. The following questions will help you identify your readers and develop a better understanding of them. To collect your thoughts, make notes about your answers to the questions.

- What specific category or group of readers do I want to write for? What are they likely to know about this issue, and how interested in it are they?
- What connections could I make between this issue and other related issues that these readers are likely to be familiar with?
- How can I interest them in this particular debate on the issue? From my research on the issue, what have I learned that might interest them?
- Are there specialized terms used in the debate, terms my readers may not be familiar with? (List them.) Do the readings give me enough information to define these important terms, or will I have to search out further information?
- What opinions are my readers likely to hold on the issue, and how could this influence the way I present the debate?

Selecting Topics to Explain the Debate

Select and list the topics you will present in your debate. You may not want to use all the topics in your chart. Review your list of topics and your Topic Chart with these questions in mind:

- What topics in the debate should I focus on for my readers? Which ones will give my readers a good understanding of the debate without exhausting or irritating them with too much detail?
- What topic should I begin with? End with?
- How should I sequence the topics most logically, given the content of the debate and my readers' likely prior knowledge of the debate?

Trying Out a Topic Comparison or Contrast

Choose a topic you are almost certain to include in your essay, and write about a page comparing and contrasting the ways the two essays in the debate treat the topic. Before writing, go back into both essays looking at the paragraphs where the topic appears. Review how each writer treats the topic and identify the most relevant information. You may not need all of it. Make notes about an orderly way to present the comparison and contrast. Consider which parts you should quote, paraphrase, or summarize. (To review these options for using sources, turn to Chapter 22: Using and Acknowledging Sources, p. 738.) Then write your comparison or contrast. You will be comparing what the two opposing essays say on the topic if they seem to agree, contrasting what they say if they seem to disagree.

This writing activity will likely give you a paragraph you can insert into the full draft of your essay. Even more important for now, however, is that it will enable you to try out and refine two writing strategies essential to your success with this assignment: setting up orderly comparisons or contrasts between both debate essays and smoothly integrating topic information from the essays into your explanation of the debate.

Formulating a Tentative Thesis Statement

Write one or more sentences that could serve as a thesis statement for your essay. These sentences from the end of paragraph 3 in Athena Alexander's essay assert her thesis:

> Paige and Weaver differ on the role standardized testing should play in assessing students' progress and the NCLB's effectiveness. Ultimately, however, their disagreement is political — with Paige accusing NCLB critics of being cynical and Weaver accusing its supporters of having a hidden agenda.

As you write your own tentative thesis statement now, think about how you could help readers see immediately both what the issue is and what positions the debaters take. Although you may want to revise your thesis statement as you draft your essay, trying to state it now will give you more focus and direction.

■ Planning and Drafting

The following guidelines will help you get the most out of your invention work, determine specific goals for your essay, and write a promising first draft.

Seeing What You Have

Now comes a very important time for reflection and evaluation. Before beginning work on the first complete draft of your explanation of the opposing positions, you must decide whether your chart captures all the significant topics in the debate, whether you have made an astute selection of these topics (since you would not want to say everything that could possibly be said about the two essays), and whether the page or so that you wrote for the invention activity Trying Out a Topic Comparison or Contrast gives you confidence that you can meaningfully compare and contrast the opposing positions of the two essays you have been learning so much about.

It may help to reread the debate, confirming the accuracy of your marginal annotations and perhaps adding new annotations about topics you notice for the first time. Look for details that will help you explain the different positions in a way that your readers can understand. Mark key words, phrases, or sentences; make marginal notes or electronic annotations of any material you think could be useful.

If you feel you need a fuller understanding of the history and significance of the debate, consider going online to learn more about the issue and the debaters who wrote the two position essays you have analyzed. This further reading might increase your interest in the issue and widen your knowledge of the nature of current debate. It might increase your confidence that you can entice readers to read your explanation and give them a context for following what you have to say. Keep in mind, however, that your presentation of the debate itself should be limited to the topics discussed in the two opposing position essays you have studied.

It may be that your work thus far has convinced you that you would prefer to write about one of the other debates. If you are permitted that choice, you should probably take it. If you cannot decide, consult your instructor to determine whether you should make a change or whether you just need to think about your project in new ways. (Your instructor will be very familiar with all of the debates.)

Setting Goals

Successful writers are always looking beyond the next sentence to their larger goals for the whole essay. Indeed, that next sentence is easier to write if you keep larger goals in mind. The following questions can help you set these goals. Consider each one now, and then return to them as necessary while you write.

Your Purpose and Readers

- How can I present the debate in an impartial way that will not alienate readers who have strong views about the issue? For example, after he introduces the issue of file sharing, Cheung limits himself to explaining what Spanier and Sherman say on the one hand and what Scrivner says on the other. Esty and Feldman also keep the focus on the debaters and do not even suggest a possible outcome of the debate until the end of their essays. Alexander concerns herself with the opposing positions of Paige and Weaver.

- How can I interest readers who are unfamiliar with the issue? Esty, for example, suggests that the issue of large animal extinctions promises both mystery and contentiousness. Cheung tries to engage readers with lively language as he tells the story of the shutdown of Napster.

- What information about the history of the issue or its current relevance would interest my particular readers? Recall that Esty devotes his first three paragraphs to establishing the prehistorical timeline and locations on the planet for his promised debate over the "mega-mystery." Feldman tries to interest readers by giving the historical context for the church-state debate.

- Which topics from my analysis chart should I choose to focus on for my particular readers? In addition to discussing the issue and positions, Cheung centers his explanation of the debate on topics of key words, legality, interests of stakeholders, history, cause, and consequence. Alexander's explanation focuses on a wide range of topics besides history, issue, and positions: solution, authority, facts, public good, statistics, consequence, ethics, attitude, and what may be lost.

The Beginning

- How shall I begin? Should I open by explaining the current relevance of the issue, as Cheung does? Should I begin with the issue's history, as Esty and Feldman do?

- How can I help readers follow my explanation? How early in my essay should I introduce the two opposing essays on which I am basing my explanation? Should I offer a forecast indicating the plan of my essay, as Cheung does?

Writing Strategies

- How can I clearly mark the different positions being compared and contrasted so that readers can follow my explanation? Cheung, Esty, and Feldman all carefully label each position and use the labels consistently. They also make extensive use of transitions or connectives such as *similarly, although,* and *whereas* to signal similarities and differences as well as juxtaposition as they move from one position to another.

- What concepts or terms do I need to define? Can I rely on brief sentence definitions, or will I need to write extended definitions? Esty and Feldman both insert a definition in parentheses: "megafauna (usually defined as animals weighing at least 100 pounds)" (Esty, paragraph 2) and "a kind of relativism (I'm O.K., you're O.K.)" (Feldman, paragraph 9). Feldman and Cheung also present extended definitions. For example, Feldman defines "values evangelicalism" (paragraphs 4–5). Cheung presents Scrivner's definition of music as "information" (paragraph 5) as well as Spanier and Sherman's definition of music as "intellectual property" (paragraph 6).

- What examples can I use to make the issue or the different positions more concrete? Recall that Esty refers to specific examples of large animals of the Pleistocene: "giant short-faced bears, enormous sloths" (paragraph 1). Feldman gives examples of current church-state issues such as abortion, euthanasia, and capital punishment (paragraph 9).

- Do I need to explain any known causes or effects? Cheung reports the disagreement about what caused the downturn in CD sales (paragraph 9). The debate over the cause of megafauna extinction is at the center of Esty's essay.

The Ending

- Should I conclude by speculating about how the debate could be resolved, as both Esty and Feldman do?

- Should I end by summarizing the major differences, as Cheung and Alexander do?

- Could I frame the essay by relating the ending to the beginning, as all the authors do?

Outlining

The goals that you have set should help you draft your essay, but first you might want to make a quick scratch outline based on a logical ordering of topics from Your Topic Chart. You could use the outlining function of your word processing program. In your outline, list the main topics in the order you think will help your readers best understand the likeness and differences between the opposing opinions. Use this outline to guide your drafting, but do not feel tied to it.

Here is an outline of the topics as they appear in the essay by Athena Alexander:

The issue

History

Issue

Positions and debaters

The opposing positions

Solution

Authority

Facts

Public good

Statistics

Consequences

Ethics

Public good

Attitude

Consequences

What lost

The introduction to the issue and to the positions and debaters could take from one to four paragraphs, but it should never dominate your explanation. The thesis statement is usually quite brief — sometimes only a sentence or two — and may appear in your introduction of the issue or a bit later. A topic comparison and contrast may occupy one or several paragraphs, and there can be few or many topics, depending on what you have discovered about the content of the two essays debating opposing positions. You may take up one topic and then return to it later after intervening topics, as Alexander does with her topics of consequences and public good. A conclusion might summarize the main differences in the debate, discuss the possibility of a resolution, or speculate about the future of the debate.

Consider any outlining that you do before you begin drafting to be tentative. As you draft, be ready to revise your outline, shift parts around, or drop or add parts. You will find that you are continually returning to the two position essays to focus on topics and select the material you require to compare and contrast the positions.

You will almost certainly notice a topic or two that escaped your first search. Add them to your chart. Remember that your readers are counting on you to represent the opposing positions accurately and impartially.

Drafting

General Advice.   With every sentence you plan and draft, with every pause to reread what you have written in order to draft the next sentence or two or three, keep in mind your purpose and readers. Your purpose is to enable your readers to understand a complex debate. You will first need to introduce them to the issue and to interest them in it by pointing out how it is relevant to them personally. If you can explain to them its social, economic, or political significance, all the better. And they will need an introduction to the debaters themselves. You might find it easier to draft your introduction after you have explained the opposing positions to your readers topic by topic. There really is no need to draft the introduction first.

For more on introducing a quotation with a colon, go to bedfordstmartins.com/theguide and click on Sentence Strategies.

A Sentence Strategy: Introducing a Quotation with a Colon.   As you draft an essay explaining a debate, you will need to quote frequently from the two opposing positions. Quoting does more than prove your fidelity to the words of the writers. If you allow readers to see some of the writers' actual language, you help them understand the two debaters as writers and thinkers. There are several strategies available to you for inserting writers' language directly into the sentences of your debate explanation. You may use speaker tags alone — "Johnson *says*" or "Lopez *claims*" — or you may rely on the word *that*, as in "Kynard counters *that* 'Graff greatly exaggerates the amount of damage this hurricane will cause.'" And there is another way, not necessarily better but a very useful alternative: setting up or preparing for a quotation from the beginning of a sentence that leads the reader towards a colon, with the quotation immediately following the colon. Here is an example:

> He [Paige] reminds readers of NCLB's theme: "if you challenge students, they will rise to the occasion." (Athena Alexander, paragraph 10)

Alexander might have written a different sentence: "NCLB's theme is something he wants to remind you of when he says, 'if you challenge students, they will rise to the occasion.'" The advantage to the sentence she did write is that it is more precise, and it puts the mention of a theme right next to the quotation that illustrates or defines it.

Here are three more examples:

> He [Weaver] presents this argument gingerly through rhetorical questions: "Is this all the law of unintended consequences? . . ." (Athena Alexander, paragraph 11)

> Spanier and Sherman argue by analogy that downloading deserves the same treatment as plagiarism: "Higher-education institutions all across the country view plagiarism as an issue on which they must intercede. Copyright infringement should be no different." (Alexander Cheung, paragraph 6)

> From a historical perspective, he claims, it can be seen that music traditionally has been built on theft: "There are pieces of Buddy Guy and B.B. King in the Beatles and Jimi Hendrix." (Alexander Cheung, paragraph 8)

Now is the time to get advice on improving your draft. Your instructor may arrange a guided reading of your draft as part of your coursework — in class or online. If not, you can ask a classmate, friend, or family member to read your draft using this guide. If your campus has a writing center, you might ask a tutor there to read and comment on your draft. If you do, however, be sure to ask the tutor to follow this guide. (If you are unable to have someone else review your draft, turn ahead to the Revising section for help with evaluating and revising your own draft.)

▶ **If You Are the Writer.**   To provide focused, helpful comments, your reader must know your essay's intended audience, your purpose, and, as a starting point for commenting, a problem in the draft that you need help solving. Briefly write out this information at the top of your draft or on a separate page.

- *Readers:* To whom are you directing your explanation? What do you assume they already know about the debate? How do you plan to engage and hold their interest?

- *Purpose:* What do you hope your readers will learn from reading your explanation?

- *Problem:* Ask your reader to help you solve the most important problem you see in the draft. Describe this problem briefly.

▶ **If You Are the Reader.**   Use the following guidelines to help you give constructive, helpful comments to others on essays explaining debates.

1. *Read for a First Impression.* Read all the way through to get a sense of the debate being explained. Then briefly write out your impressions. What one aspect of the draft do you think will especially interest the intended readers? Point to one place where they might have difficulty in following the explanation.

    Next, consider the problem the writer identified, and respond briefly to that concern now. (If you find that the problem is covered by one of the other guidelines listed below, respond to it in more detail there if necessary.)

2. *Evaluate the Way the Issue Is Presented.* Look at the way the issue is presented. If you are familiar with the essays on which the draft is based, let the writer know if any aspect of the issue or context has been left out or represented incorrectly. Consider also the information the writer provides — historical background, information about the current relevance or importance of the issue, the credentials of the essays' authors — and tell the writer about any part that needs to be added, expanded, reduced, or eliminated. If you have any additional unanswered questions about the presentation of the issue, share them with the writer.

Critical Reading Guide

For a printable version of this critical reading guide, go to bedfordstmartins.com/theguide.

3. ***Assess Whether the Opposing Positions Are Clearly and Impartially Explained.*** Write a sentence or two summarizing the opposing positions presented in the essay. Let the writer know whether either of the positions taken in the debate needs further clarification for readers. Try to pose specific questions for the writer. Point to language in the draft that you find confusing or difficult to understand, including any quotations from the essays themselves that would benefit from the writer's commentary. If you are familiar with the essays on which the draft is based, let the writer know whether the opposing positions have been represented fairly and completely. Point to any word choices that suggest a lack of balance or impartiality. If you think the debate is being oversimplified or limited in some way, explain how.

4. ***Identify Each Comparison and Contrast of a Topic in the Debate and Evaluate How Well Each One Is Developed.*** Identify each separate topic the writer has chosen from the debate. Indicate specific places in the draft where the comparison or contrast could be clarified or better balanced. Point to places, if any, where examples, definitions, or additional commentary are needed. If you are familiar with the opposing position which this draft seeks to explain, note whether anything important has been left out in the discussion of each topic. Also explain whether the writer has left out any important topics that appear in those essays.

5. ***Review the Organization and Suggest How It Could Be Improved.*** Look at the way the essay is organized by making a scratch outline showing the paragraph-by-paragraph sequence of topics compared or contrasted. Can you suggest a better, more logical way to sequence the topics?

   - Look at the *beginning*. Does it engage readers and make them want to continue reading? Does it adequately forecast the direction of the essay? If possible, suggest a better way to begin.

   - Look for *transitions* in the draft from one topic to the next or from the writer's explanation of a topic in one essay to its explanation in the other essay. Point to one transition that seems especially helpful and one that seems less than helpful. Try to improve one or two of them. Look for additional places where transitions would be helpful.

   - Look at the *ending*. Explain what makes it particularly effective or less effective than it might be, in your opinion. If you can, suggest a different way to end.

6. ***Give the Writer Your Final Thoughts.*** Which part needs the most work? What do you think the intended readers will find most informative or memorable? What do you like best about the draft?

■ Revising

Now you are ready to revise your essay. Your instructor or other students may have given you advice on improving your draft. Nevertheless, you may have begun to realize that your draft requires not so much revision as rethinking. For example, you may recognize that you discuss too many topics and cannot develop them adequately in just a few pages, that you need to help readers appreciate why the debate is important, or that the contrasts (or similarities) between the different positions on some of the topics are not clear enough. Consequently, instead of working to improve parts of the draft, you may need to write a new draft that radically reenvisions your explanation. It is not unusual for students — and professional writers — to find themselves in this situation. Seek your instructor's advice if you must plan a radical revision.

On the other hand, you may feel quite satisfied that your draft achieves most, if not all, of your goals. In that case, you can focus on refining specific parts of your draft. Very likely you have thought of ways to improve your draft, and you may even have begun improving it. This section will help you get an overview of your draft and revise it accordingly.

Getting an Overview

Consider your draft as a whole, following these two steps:

1. *Reread.* If at all possible, put the draft aside for a day or two before rereading it. When you return to it, start by reconsidering your purpose. Then read the draft straight through, trying to see it as your intended readers will.

2. *Outline.* Make a scratch outline, indicating the basic features as they appear in the draft. Consider using the headings and outline/summary functions of your word processor.

Planning for Revision.   Resist the temptation to dive in and start changing your text until you have a solid grasp of the big picture. Using your outline as a guide, move through the document, using the highlighting or commenting tools of your word processor to note useful comments received from others and problems you want to solve (or mark on a hard copy if you prefer).

Analyzing the Basic Features of Your Own Draft.   Use the Critical Reading Guide on the preceding pages to guide your analysis of your own draft to identify problems you need to solve.

Studying Readers' Comments.   Review all of the comments you have received from other readers, and add to your revision plan any that you intend to act on. For each comment, look at the draft to determine what might have led the reader to make that particular point. Try to keep an open mind about any criticism. By letting you see how other readers respond to your draft, these comments provide valuable information about how you might improve it.

Carrying Out Revisions

Having identified problems in your draft, you now need to come up with solutions and — most important — to carry them out. Basically, there are four ways to find solutions:

1. Look for answers in your invention and planning notes, especially in Your Topics Chart.

Working with Sources

Weaving quoted materials into your own sentences

Your essay explaining opposing positions is based sentence after sentence on sources: your background research on the issue and the two debate essays you have studied. In nearly every sentence, you will be quoting, summarizing, or paraphrasing these sources. When you quote from them, you have many options for integrating a quotation smoothly into your explanation.

One familiar, common strategy is to create a noun clause beginning with *that*, as in this example:

> On the other hand, Scrivner maintains that "the term theft is misleading." (Alexander Cheung, paragraph 7)

Another common strategy is to lead into the quotation with a verb like *say*, or alternatives to it like *assert, claim, ask, argue, explain*:

> As he *says*, "the prediction became reality last summer when nearly 25 percent of schools in Connecticut were identified as having failed to make AYP." (Athena Alexander, paragraph 8)

Beyond relying on *that* or a verb alone, you can weave the quotations right into your own sentence structures. This option is especially useful when the material you want to quote is a phrase rather than a clause or a complete sentence.

> Scrivner questions this causal analysis, suggesting that the cause may be the "downward trend in the rest of the economy." (Alexander Cheung, paragraph 8)

This approach allows you to easily accommodate two or more quotations in one of your own sentences:

> Paige makes a strong economic argument for the need to improve high school education so that students are prepared for the "fastest-growing occupations in the United States" and can compete in the new "global economy." (Athena Alexander, paragraph 7)

> Paige, on the other hand, characterizes Weaver's recommendations as "complaints of the unwilling," arguing that instead of changing the NCLB Act, we should give it time and "work to make the law successful." (Athena Alexander, paragraph 13)

For more help on using sources in your writing, turn to Chapter 22: Using and Acknowledging Sources, p. 738.

For more help weaving quoted materials into your own sentences, go to bedfordstmartins.com/theguide and click on Bedford Research Room.

2. Do further invention writing to answer questions your readers raised.

3. Look back at the readings in this chapter to see how other writers have solved similar problems.

4. Reread the debate you are trying to explain.

The following suggestions, which are organized according to the basic features of essays explaining a debate, will get you started solving some writing problems common to the genre.

An Introduction to the Issue and the Opposing Positions

- **Is the issue unclear?** Consider dividing the issue into one or two questions about which people disagree, providing more background information, or explaining the principles or values at stake.

- **Do readers fail to appreciate the debate's significance?** Consider providing examples to show how the issue affects people's lives or an anecdote or scenario that would help readers understand why people have strong feelings about the issue.

- **Do readers have difficulty identifying the opposing positions?** You may need to announce the positions more explicitly or provide readers with a concise statement of how they differ from each other. Or you may need to explain the positions in more depth, perhaps providing examples to make them more concrete. Also reconsider your word choice or try defining key terms and concepts.

A Comparison and Contrast of Topics Raised in the Debate

- **Do readers think any topics need further elaboration?** Extend your discussion of the topic, spelling out the comparison or contrast. Also consider where you might need to add examples or define unfamiliar terms.

- **Do readers have a problem understanding any of the comparisons and contrasts?** Revise so that the comparison or contrast is brought into clearer focus for the reader. Consider adding more details or examples or defining unfamiliar terms.

- **Do readers think there is too much information or detail?** Consider how you can emphasize the most important topics or eliminate some of the less important ones.

- **Have any important topics been left out?** You may need to review your analysis chart or the essays themselves to reconsider whether what you have left out now seems important enough to include.

A Logical Plan

- **Do the opening paragraphs successfully orient readers to your purpose and plan?** Try forecasting the plan of your essay.

- **Is the explanation difficult to follow?** Look for a way to reorder the topics so that the explanation is easier to follow. Try constructing an alternative outline. Add transitions or summaries to help keep readers on track.

- ***Is the ending inconclusive?*** Consider moving important information there. Try summarizing highlights of the essay or framing it by referring to something in the beginning. Or you might speculate about the future of the debate or assert its social or political significance.

A Fair and Unbiased Presentation of the Opposing Positions

- ***Do readers notice any places where there seems to be a lack of balance or impartiality in your presentation of the different positions?*** Reconsider your word choice to make sure you do not unfairly characterize or misrepresent either position. Add brief quotations from the essays in places where readers think you may have not been accurate. Make sure you do not oversimplify the position either writer has taken.

- ***Do readers point to any places where the position essays have been represented incorrectly or incompletely?*** You may need to reread the position essays to make sure you have not misrepresented them. Consider quoting more words and phrases to help you present them more impartially.

For a revision checklist, go to bedfordstmartins.com/theguide.

■ Editing and Proofreading

Now is the time to check your revised draft for problems in grammar, punctuation, and mechanics and to consider matters of style. It may help you to recognize problems if you study your draft in separate passes — first for paragraphs, then for sentences, and finally for words. Our research has identified two problems that occur often in essays explaining opposing positions: missing commas around interrupting phrases and vague pronoun reference. The following guidelines will help you check your draft for these common problems.

For practice, go to bedfordstmartins.com/theguide/exercisecentral and click on Commas around Interrupting Phrases.

Checking for Commas around Interrupting Phrases.   When a phrase within a sentence interrupts the flow of the sentence, it must be marked visibly so that readers do not stumble through it to come out the other side quite confused. Such a phrase must be set off with two commas, one at the beginning and one at the end:

▶ Live Nation, without hesitating, paid $350 million to buy HOB Entertainment, which owns the popular House of Blues clubs.

▶ Virtual football, to hold onto its fans and gain more, soon has to move beyond solitary players to teams of players on the Internet, each player taking a different position.

For practice, go to bedfordstmartins.com/theguide/exercisecentral and click on Vague Pronoun Reference.

Correcting Vague Pronoun Reference.   Pronouns replace and refer to nouns, making writing more efficient and cohesive. Unless the reference is clear and precise, this advantage is lost. A common problem is vague use of *this, that, it,* or *which.*

▶ TV evangelists seem to be perpetually raising money, ~~which~~ makes some viewers question their motives.

This habit

▶ By the late 1960s, plate tectonics was a new science. It was based on the notion of

the earth's crust as a collection of plates or land masses above and below sea

startling new geological theory

level, constantly in motion. This took a while for most people to accept ~~because~~

~~of its unexpected novelty~~.

▶ Inside the Summit Tunnel the Chinese laborers were using as much as

500 kegs a day of costly black powder to blast their way through the solid rock.

The unexpected expense

~~It~~ was straining the Central Pacific's budget.

A Writer at Work

Making and Using a Topic Analysis

In this section, you can learn how one writer, Athena Alexander, the author of "No Child Left Behind: 'Historic Initiative' or 'Just an Empty Promise'?" in the Readings section of this chapter (see pages 211–16), prepared to write her essay. Alexander first read and annotated two essays taking opposing positions on the No Child Left Behind Act. Then she charted the results of her analysis and relied on the chart to guide her drafting and revision of the essay. You can rely on this same productive pattern of work to write your own essay explaining a debate.

To learn from this Writer-at-Work demonstration and to prepare yourself for your own work, first read the two essays in the next section just as though you had come across them in a magazine or on the Internet. The first essay argues in favor of the No Child Left Behind Act. The second argues against it. Read the essays to understand this important debate and to prepare yourself to follow Alexander through her work analyzing the two readings, planning her essay, and drafting a portion of it.

Understanding the Debate: Can the No Child Left Behind Act Improve Learning in U.S. Schools?

If you are unfamiliar with the No Child Left Behind Act and the debate it has generated, you can expect that your understanding will grow as you read the essays by Paige and Weaver. You may find that you want to reread parts of one or both of the essays. You need not understand every detail of both essays, but you need a good general understanding of them to appreciate Alexander's explanation of these opposing positions.

The No Child Left Behind Act (NCLB) became law in 2001 under President George W. Bush. A nationwide initiative to improve America's schools, the NCLB requires every state to test students yearly to assess progress in reading and math in grades 3–8 and to develop appropriate remedies for schools that perform poorly on the standardized tests. Although the law was passed with a bipartisan majority of 381–41, it has always had critics as well as defenders.

Rod Paige, who served as the secretary of education from 2001–2005, has been the NCLB's most vocal defender. Paige was a teacher, coach, and school board member before becoming the superintendent of the Houston public school system and subsequently joining President Bush's cabinet. His essay is titled "Testing Has Raised Students' Expectations, and Progress in Learning Is Evident Nationwide." The second essay, "NCLB's Excessive Reliance on Testing Is Unrealistic, Arbitrary, and Frequently Unfair," was written by Reg Weaver, president of the National Education Association (NEA), the union that represents teachers and educational support personnel. A science teacher for thirty years, Weaver is also a member of the executive boards of the National Council for the Accreditation of Teacher Education and the National Board for Professional Teaching Standards. Both essays were initially published in the online publication *Insight on the News* in 2004, as part of a symposium titled "Are the Tests Required by No Child Left Behind Making Schools More Accountable?" *Insight* is published by the conservative newspaper *The Washington Times*.

Testing Has Raised Students' Expectations, and Progress in Learning Is Evident Nationwide
Rod Paige

Testing is a part of life. In fact, testing starts at the beginning stages of life: The moment we are born, neonatologists measure our reflexes and responses and give us what is called an Apgar score on a scale of one to ten. As we grow up, our teachers test us in school and we take other standardized tests that compare us with the rest of the nation's students. We are tested if we want to practice a trade — whether it be to get a cosmetology license, a driver's permit, or pilot training. And often we are retested and retested again to show that our skills remain at peak level.   1

In short, tests exist for a reason. In the case of a doctor, they certify that he or she is capable of practicing medicine. In the case of a teacher, they show that he or she has the knowledge to help children learn a given subject. And in the case of a student, they demonstrate whether a child has indeed learned and understood the lesson or the subject.   2

At their core, tests are simply tools — they subjectively measure things. In education, they are particularly important because they pinpoint where students are   3 doing well and where they need help. In fact, testing has been a part of education since the first child sat behind the first desk. Assessments are an important component of educational accountability; in other words, they tell us whether the system is performing as it should. They diagnose, for the teacher, the parent and the student, any problems so that they can be fixed.

Educational accountability is the cornerstone of the No Child Left Behind Act (NCLB), President George W. Bush's historic initiative that is designed to raise student performance across America. The law embraces a number of commonsense ways to reach that goal: accountability for results, empowering parents with information about school performance and giving them options, more local control, and flexibility to tailor the law to local circumstances. 4

No Child Left Behind is a revolutionary change, challenging the current educational system and helping it to improve. It aims to challenge the status quo by pushing the educational system into the twenty-first century so that American students leave school better prepared for higher education or the workforce. 5

Educational accountability is not a new concept — several states have been instituting accountability reforms for years. No Child Left Behind builds on the good work of some of these states that were at the forefront of the reform movement. The truth is that this law has one goal: to get all children reading and doing math at grade level. It's that simple. The law itself is a federal law, but it is nothing more than a framework. Elementary and secondary education are the traditional province of state and local governments, which is why the specific standards, tests and most of the other major tenets of the law are designed and implemented by the state departments of education, because they are in the best position to assess local expectations and parental demands. . . . 6

Let's examine what we do know. According to the nation's report card (the National Assessment of Educational Progress, or NAEP), only one in six African Americans and one in five Hispanics are proficient in reading by the time they are high-school seniors. NAEP math scores are even worse: Only 3 percent of blacks and 4 percent of Hispanics are testing at the proficient level. This is the status quo result of a decades-old education system before the NCLB. 7

Of the ten fastest-growing occupations in the United States, the top five are computer-related, which are jobs that require high-level skills. High-school dropouts need not apply. We are all concerned about outsourcing jobs overseas, and we should note that the unemployment rate for high-school dropouts is almost twice that of those with high-school diplomas (7.3 percent compared with 4.2 percent) and nearly four times that of college graduates (7.3 percent vs. 2.3 percent). For young black men the unemployment rate is a staggering 26 percent. Even a high-school diploma isn't the cure: A vast majority of employers sadly expect that a high-school graduate will not write clearly or have even fair math skills. No wonder a recent study claimed a high-school diploma has become nothing more than a "certificate of attendance." For millions of children, they were given a seat in the school but not an education of the mind. 8

It is clear that our system as a whole is not preparing the next generation of workers for the global economy ahead of them. As Federal Reserve Chairman 9

Alan Greenspan noted recently, "We need to be forward looking in order to adapt our educational system to the evolving needs of the economy and the realities of our changing society. . . . It is an effort that should not be postponed." That's why I am so passionate about making these historic reforms and drawing attention to the issue.

The old system — the status quo — is one that we must fight to change. That's why the president and both parties in Congress understood the urgency of the situation and put NCLB into law. They also ensured that the money would be there to get the job done, providing the means to states fully to implement the law; indeed, there's been 41 percent more federal support for education since President Bush took office. 10

But some defenders of the status quo have aired complaints about the law, saying its requirements are unreasonable and the tests are arbitrary. The bottom line is, these cynics do not believe in the worth of all children — they have written some of them off. You can guess which ones fall into that category. This pessimism relegates these children to failure. The president aptly refers to this phenomenon as the "soft bigotry of low expectations." But NCLB says the excuses must stop — all children must be given a chance. 11

NCLB helps us zero in on student needs. With little information about individual students' abilities with different skills, most teachers must rely on a "buckshot" approach to teaching their classes, aiming for the middle and hoping to produce a decent average. With an emphasis on scientifically based research techniques and effective use of information, NCLB helps fund programs that teachers can use to identify specific areas of weakness among their students. 12

For example, the Granite School District in Utah used Title I funds (support for economically disadvantaged students) to procure the "Yearly Progress Pro" computer program. Now a fourth-grade class at Stansbury Elementary School visits the computer lab for a quick 15-minute test each week; the teacher walks out with a printout identifying changes in performance in specific skill areas over the week. 13

Child by child, the improvements add up. For example, a study by the Council of Great City Schools examined the recent gains in large metropolitan school systems. The Beating the Odds IV report showed that since NCLB has been implemented, public-school students across the country have shown a marked improvement in reading. The report found that the achievement gap in reading and math between African Americans and whites, and Hispanics and whites in large cities, is narrowing for fourth- and eighth-grade students. And it appears, according to the report, that our big-city schools are closing the gap at a faster rate than the statewide rate. Not only are the achievement gaps closing, the report states, but also math and reading achievement are improving. 14

For a concrete example of how the law is working, look at the Cheltenham School District in Pennsylvania, where leaders are disaggregating data to find the cracks they must fill. Drawing on test results, the district provides schools with specific information about each student's abilities and weaknesses in specific academic areas. Schools receive this data in easily accessible electronic formats in July, before the students arrive, giving them time to plan for the year. Now teachers 15 can account for the effectiveness of their strategies and, if they are not working for some students, adapt to alternatives.

These findings are especially significant because research shows that it is often the students in the large-city schools who need the most help and face the greatest odds. Clearly, this report demonstrates that if you challenge students, they will rise to the occasion. This concept is at the fundamental core of NCLB because we can no longer mask our challenges in the aggregate of our successes. We must make sure that all children, regardless of their skin color and zip codes, have the opportunity to receive a high-quality education.

16

While the press focuses on the complaints of the unwilling, whole communities are taking on the challenge of accountability and achieving great results. Perhaps my favorite example is in the Peck School in rural Michigan, where I visited in late March and found that the school culture had embraced the accountability treatment. A huge poster hangs in the hallway of the school emblazoned with No Child Left Behind! Showing creativity and commitment, the school launched a tutoring program, began intervening sooner with low-performing students, and even created a peer-counseling program to address the conflicts that often spill into the classroom and distract from learning. Everyone in the Peck School is taking responsibility for the students' education, truly fostering the character of good citizenship.

17

It is time to think of the children and to give them what they need. It is time to work to make the law successful. We need to create an American public educational system that matches the vision of this law, where we strive for excellence without exclusion, where our children achieve greatness rather than greatly underachieving, and where 10 or 20 years from now a new generation of adults realize that we gave them a better life because we had courage and conviction now.

18

NCLB's Excessive Reliance on Testing Is Unrealistic, Arbitrary, and Frequently Unfair

Reg Weaver

As I travel around the country visiting schools and talking with National Education Association (NEA) members, I sense a growing concern among teachers and parents about the overwhelming emphasis given to standardized testing in America's schools. This concern is heightened when high stakes are attached to the outcomes of such tests. Teachers and parents worry that more and more of the important things that prepare us for life will be pushed off the curriculum plate to make room for test preparation.

1

According to a recent poll by Public Agenda, 88 percent of teachers say the amount of attention their school pays to standardized test results has increased

2

during the last several years. And 61 percent agreed that teaching to the test "inevitably stifles real teaching and learning."

As any good teacher knows, there is no one-size-fits-all approach to either teaching or learning. In fact, we now have a solid body of research about cognition and learning styles that provides ample confirmation of this. Any good teacher also knows that proper assessment of learning is both complex and multifaceted. Tests — particularly paper and pencil tests that are standardized — are only one type of assessment. Good teachers make judgments about what has been learned on the basis of a variety of assessments. Finally, we know that what constitutes spectacular achievement for a child who suffers serious challenges may not equal the progress of his or her peers, but we honor this progress nonetheless.

The NEA has a proud history of supporting and nurturing our system of public education. When we are critical of the so-called No Child Left Behind (NCLB) Act, our interest is to fix those elements of the law that we see as destructive to public education and, ultimately, to the children we serve.

A consensus is emerging from coast to coast and across the political spectrum that this is a law in need of repair. And the present definition of adequate yearly progress is at the heart of what is wrong with the law.

The concept of adequate yearly progress is relatively simple: Set a lofty goal, establish a time frame for accomplishing the goal, establish incremental targets or steps toward achieving the goal, and hold schools accountable for meeting the targets and, ultimately, the goal. The goal is 100 percent proficiency in reading and math, and all schools must meet it by 2014.

Wouldn't life, and particularly parenting and teaching, be simple if progress in learning were linear and time-sensitive? Parents, teachers and cognitive psychologists alike know that learning is anything but linear. And yet we now have a federal law that not only violates what we know to be true about human learning but says that unless schools achieve linear progress, the federal government will punish you.

Do we have a problem with this? You bet we do. Can it be fixed? We think so.

One of our state affiliates, the Connecticut Education Association (CEA), is a leader in recognizing and studying the problems with the federal definition of "adequate yearly progress" (AYP). Shortly after the law was adopted, the CEA had an independent economist develop a scenario based on existing test data in Connecticut in an attempt to visualize the impact of AYP in one of the highest achieving states in the nation. The initial results were shocking; however, because the law had yet to be implemented, the results were still hypothetical. Nonetheless, the prediction became reality last summer when nearly 25 percent of schools in Connecticut were identified as having failed to make AYP. An astonishing 155 elementary and middle schools and 88 high schools were identified as "in need of improvement" under the federal law.

More recently, armed with two years of test data, the CEA asked its economist, Ed Moscovitch of Massachusetts, to update the scenarios. This time the CEA asked what failure rates might look like over the full 12 years of implementation.

The new scenario, based on a model that allows for the rate of growth that students actually achieved in the last two years of testing, is very revealing. At the end of 12 years, 744 of 802 elementary and middle schools in Connecticut will have failed to make adequate yearly progress — that's 93 percent of its elementary and middle schools.

In the first year none of the schools identified had the white non-Hispanic subgroup failing to make AYP. In the final year 585 of the 744 schools will have the white subgroup failing to do so. Even the powerful combination of social capital and great schools in a state that is regarded nationally as a high performer is not adequate to meet the statistical demands of this law.   11

Only in Lake Wobegon, perhaps, where all the students are above average, is there a chance of meeting the requirements set forth in the so-called No Child Left Behind law.   12

The current formula for AYP fails to consider the difference between where you start and how quickly you must reach the goal. That is, in my opinion, irresponsible. It is particularly irresponsible as it applies to English-language learners and special-education subgroups. While the Department of Education (DOE) finally has acknowledged that students whose first language is not English may not perform well when given a test in English, it does not go far enough to correct the problem. With respect to special-education students, the DOE has granted some leeway for the small percentage of severely cognitively disabled students, but there are thousands of other students in this subgroup for whom the test is totally inappropriate and emotionally injurious.   13

What's more, while the department has acknowledged the unfairness of how English-language learners and students with disabilities were tested, it has refused to go back and reconsider schools labeled "in need of improvement" under the old procedures.   14

Is this all the law of unintended consequences? Or is there, as many believe, an insidious intent to discredit public education, paving the way for a breakup of the current system — an opening of the door to a boutique system with increased privatization and government vouchers?   15

We believe that for every ideologue who wants to subject public education to market forces, there are scores of policymakers and political officials who supported this law based solely on its stated, laudable intent. Many of them still do not understand the full import of what they supported. So what do we believe needs to be done?   16

First, we need to ask whether the measurement of AYP is an accurate barometer of a student's progress or a school's effectiveness. We have urged the adoption of multiple indicators. Measuring this year's fourth-graders against next year's fourth-graders tells us little that we need to know about the improvement of individual students. Wouldn't it make more sense to follow the progress of individual children? We have called for this kind of cohort analysis, and recently 14 state superintendents asked for the same change in a meeting with President George W. Bush.   17

Second, is it fair to have the same starting point for all groups? We need to find a more rational way to acknowledge the dramatic gaps in performance among   18 subgroups. As an example, high-achieving students in Connecticut wait for years for targeted low-achieving subgroups to catch up with their performance, while other groups are asked to fill an unachievable gap in one year just to get to the starting gate. Yet the race begins at the same time and at the same pace for all. For certain subgroups, even dramatic increases in performance relative to their prior performance will only lead to failure. We need to acknowledge and honor progress.

Third, if we really have a goal of improving student achievement, shouldn't we offer tutoring to struggling students first? Right now NCLB adopts an "abandon ship" philosophy of allowing parents to change schools. The focus should be on helping the individual student in the subgroup in need of attention. And by the way, why is it less important to have a highly qualified tutor, or supplemental service provider, than it is to have a highly qualified teacher? Academic tutors should be certified, as well. Current law prohibits states from requiring that tutors be certified. [19]

So in answer to the question "Does AYP increase school accountability?" our answer is no. But it could with serious and thoughtful revision. [20]

The NEA and its state affiliates have always supported high standards and accountability. And we believe that no child should be left behind. We believe that every child in a public school should be taught by a highly qualified teacher in an atmosphere that is safe and conducive to learning, and all students should have access to a rich and deep curriculum. We also believe that each child is unique and brings to the classroom a variety of gifts and challenges. We have built a system in the United States that has struggled to honor this notion of gifts and challenges — our doors are open to all — and we have huge systemic challenges in meeting this philosophical ideal. There's much more that the federal government must do to guarantee that No Child Left Behind is more than just an empty promise. [21]

How Alexander Analyzed the Debate between Paige and Weaver

After reading the same two essays you just read, Alexander reread them looking for the topics listed in the section Identifying Topics in Your Debate from the Guide to Writing. Using the list of Topics to Look For (see pages 226–27) ensured that Alexander would be able to identify important, relevant parts of both essays.

Alexander searched every paragraph for the topics in the chart. Some were easy to identify. Others became apparent only after she had charted other topics and become more familiar with each essay. She first looked for statements of the issue and each author's position on the issue. Then she searched for other topics, not expecting to find all of them and assuming that a topic could be addressed in a sentence or two or a whole paragraph.

As she identified a topic, Alexander wrote its name in the margin of the essay where the topic appeared and underlined or bracketed the relevant language in the text. She used pencil so that she could easily change these annotations if she later decided the text material should be categorized under a different topic. Then she completed the topic chart, which recorded the results of her topic identification paragraph by paragraph. An example of her annotations of the Paige essay and her completed chart of topics she identified in both essays are shown below.

Let's examine what we do know. According to the nation's report card (the National Assessment of Educational Progress, or NAEP), only one in six African Americans and one in five Hispanics are proficient in reading by the time they are high-school seniors. NAEP math scores are even worse: Only 3 percent of blacks and 4 percent of Hispanics are testing at the proficient level. This is the status quo result of a decades-old education system before the NCLB. — 7

statistics

importance

Of the ten fastest-growing occupations in the United States, the top five are computer-related, which are jobs that require high-level skills. High-school dropouts need not apply. We are all concerned about outsourcing jobs overseas, and we should note that the unemployment rate for high-school dropouts is almost twice that of those with high-school diplomas (7.3 percent compared with 4.2 percent) and nearly four times that of college graduates (7.3 percent vs. 2.3 percent). For young black men the unemployment rate is a staggering 26 percent. Even a high-school diploma isn't the cure: A vast majority of employers sadly expect that a high-school graduate will not write clearly or have even fair math skills. No wonder a recent study claimed a high-school diploma has become nothing more than a "certificate of attendance." For millions of children, they were given a seat in the school but not an education of the mind. — 8

consequences

statistics

consequences

research

consequences　　　It is clear that <u>our system as a whole is not preparing the next</u>　9

<u>generation of workers for the global economy ahead of them.</u> As

Federal Reserve Chairman Alan Greenspan noted recently, "We

need to be forward looking in order to adapt our educational sys-

tem to the <u>evolving needs of the economy and the realities of our</u>

public good　　<u>changing society</u>.... It is an effort that should not be postponed."

That's why I am so passionate about making these historic re-

forms and drawing attention to the issue.

Athena Alexander's Topics Chart		
Topic	**Paige**	**Weaver**
issue	4, 7–9	1–3, 20
position	5, 9–10	4–5, 8, 13
key words		6
refute	11	19
attitude	11	16
solution	12	17–19
consequences	8–9	1, 10–11
ideals	6, 16, 18	13, 16, 21
scenarios/examples	13–15	2, 9–11, 17–19
observations	17	1
statistics/facts	7–10	2, 3, 7, 9–11
agenda		15
public good	9, 16, 18	13, 21
importance	8–9	1, 13
research	8	

How Alexander Used the Chart to Plan and Draft Her Essay

Alexander relied on the chart as a guide to planning her essay (see pages 211–16). She chose to open with the topics *issue* and *position*. In the first two paragraphs, she presents her background research on the No Child Left Behind Act, using the example of Georgia to show how one state chose to implement the law. Like Alexander, you may turn up relevant details in your background research about the issue — facts, history, current news — that you can use to present it to readers.

In paragraph 3, Alexander introduces the two opposing position essays, identifying the writers. To represent their positions, she consulted her chart and then looked at her highlighted and annotated essays to identify the language she would paraphrase. Now her essay was well launched. Her patience in charting the topics ensured that she would not overlook any important material that would help her compare and contrast these writers' essays.

Alexander also made good use of her topic chart in paragraphs 7 and 8 where she deals with the topics *statistics* and *scenarios*. The chart helped her locate Paige's statistics, and she explains how he uses them to argue for the need to improve the U.S. educational system. In contrast, she shows that Weaver uses statistics combined with economists' scenarios to support his argument about the inappropriateness of the "adequate yearly progress" goals. You can see from the chart that she made use of information from several paragraphs in both readings.

Most important, she does not cover every topic in her chart but selected those that enabled her to fairly represent what she considered the most interesting and important points of agreement and disagreement between the two writers.

Thinking About Document Design

In the science writer's article explaining the two competing biological classification systems (see the workplace writing project described on page 193), document design played an important role in helping readers visualize the alternatives. The greatest challenge for the writer was to design a graphic that would make the contrast between the two systems apparent at a glance.

His first impulse was to juxtapose side by side two schematic trees — one showing an example of the current Linnaean system and the other showing the same example of the proposed PhyloCode. But he soon realized that two trees would not be sufficient to show what happens when an organism is reclassified into a different evolutionary group, or clade. A clade includes the ancestral species and all its descendants, and is graphically represented as an evolutionary "tree" with branching limbs. So, he decided to develop a visual with four trees — before and after images of what happens when an organism is reclassified, in both the Linnaean system and the PhyloCode system.

The graphic the writer developed has four sections of equal size, with the PhyloCode system in the top section and the Linnaean system in the bottom. To distinguish the two systems, he put labels at the bottom of each section in bold print and used two different background colors. To show what happens when an organism needs to be reclassified, he placed the "before" versions

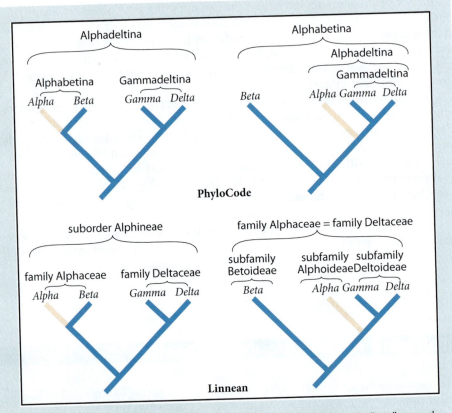

In a hypothetical example of how Linnaean naming works (bottom), Alpha is the "type" genus, the representative genus used to determine the name for a family, Alphaceae, in the suborder Alphineae (left). Delta belongs to the family Deltaceae. If new molecular data suggest that the existing taxonomy is wrong and that Alpha is more closely related to Gamma and Delta than to Beta, the ranking changes. Linnaean rules require that several groups be renamed (right) with changes in suffixes. With Deltaceae's demotion to subfamily status, a name change to Deltoideae is required. Under PhyloCode rules (top), names do not change when the new data are incorporated. Alphabetina becomes the name of the clade containing all four genera (right) since Alphabetina is defined as the smallest clade containing both Alpha and Beta.

on the left and the "after" versions on the right. Reading from left to right, readers first see the way the classification looks before it has to be changed and then how it looks after the change. Interestingly, the writer chose not to label the before and after sides. Instead, he wrote a detailed caption to explain the relationship between the trees on the left and the right.

He also decided to use a different color (orange) to focus readers' attention on the limb of the tree that is moved when the organism is reclassified. As you can see from the graphic, the trees are changed in exactly the same way when an organism is reclassified. What is different is the naming system. The key difference that becomes apparent is that the Linnaean system involves a greater number of name changes.

The writer could have used real biological names, but he wanted the visual to be abstract so that he could direct readers' attention to the name changes required in each system. Linnaean rules require that family names end in *aceae* and subfamily names end in *ideae*. Therefore, if a group once considered a family is changed to a subfamily, it has to be renamed. As the caption explains: "With Deltaceae's demotion to subfamily status, a name change to Deltoideae is required." The only significant name change proposed for the PhyloCode system is the change from Alpha*del*tina to Alpha*bet*ina. The renaming emphasizes and clarifies the new understanding of the evolutionary relationship among the branches of this particular tree, their clade name.

Thinking Critically About What You Have Learned

Now that you have read and discussed several explanations of debates and written one of your own, take some time to think critically and write about what you have learned. To think critically means to use all of your new genre knowledge — acquired from the information in this chapter, your own writing, the writing of other students, and discussions with them and your instructor — to reflect deeply on your work for this assignment. It also requires that you consider the social implications of your new knowledge. Critical thinking is sustained by analysis, a thoughtful, patient survey of all of the materials you have read and produced during your work in this chapter. The benefit is proven and important: you will remember longer what you have learned, ensuring that you will be able to put it to good use well beyond this writing course.

Reflecting on Your Writing

Write a one-page explanation, telling your instructor about a problem you encountered in writing your essay and how you solved it. Before you begin, gather all of your writing — topics chart, invention and planning notes, drafts, analyses and evaluations by others of your draft, revision notes and plans, and final revision. Review these materials as you complete this writing task.

1. ***Identify one writing problem you needed to solve as you worked on the essay.*** Do not be concerned with grammar and punctuation problems; concentrate instead on problems unique to developing an essay explaining a debate. For example: Did you have trouble identifying the topics covered in each debate or organizing the topics in your essay? Was it difficult to give an impartial account of each author's position? Did you encounter difficulty in drafting and organizing comparisons and contrasts? Or any other problem you encountered.

2. ***Determine how you came to recognize the problem.*** When did you first discover it? What called it to your attention? If you did not become aware of the problem until someone else pointed it out to you, can you now see hints of it

in your invention writings? If so, where specifically? When you first recognized the problem, how did you respond?

3. ***Reflect on how you went about solving the problem.*** Did you work on the wording of a passage, cut or add information, add transitions or forecasting statements, or move paragraphs or sentences around? Did you reread one of the debate explanations in this chapter to see how another writer handled a similar problem? Did you look back at your topic chart or find that you had overlooked important topics in the debate? If you talked about the problem with another student, a tutor, or your instructor, what advice did you receive and how was it helpful?

4. ***Write a brief explanation of the problem and your solution.*** Be as specific as possible in reconstructing your efforts. Quote from your invention notes or draft essay, others' comments or advice on your draft, your revision plan, or your revised essay to show the various changes that your writing — and thinking — underwent as you tried to solve the problem. If you are still uncertain about your solution, say so. Taking time to explain how you identified a particular problem, how you went about trying to solve it, and what you learned from this experience will help you solve future writing problems more easily.

Reviewing What You Learned from Reading

Write a page or two explaining to your instructor how the readings in this chapter influenced your final draft. Your own essay may have been influenced to some extent by one or more of the essays in this chapter as well as by classmates' essays that you have read. These other essays may have helped you decide that you needed to do further searching for debate topics before you could give a complete and accurate account of the debate or that you could more effectively quote or paraphrase the debate essays as part of your explanation. These essays may also have shown you the best way to develop a topic comparison or contrast or to structure your essay. Before you write, take some

time to reflect on what you have learned from these selections about explaining a debate.

1. ***Reread the final revision of your essay; then look back at the four selections that you read and analyzed at the beginning of this chapter.*** Look for specific influences on your own essay. For example, did any reading influence how you decided to present each position, maintain impartiality, appeal to readers' interest, or organize your information? Also in these readings look for writing strategies you were inspired to try, types of sentences you relied on, or goals you sought to emulate.

2. ***Write an explanation of these influences.*** Did one reading have a particularly strong influence on your essay, or were several readings influential in different ways? Quote from the readings and from your final revision to show how your essay was influenced by other essays you read. Finally, based on your review of this chapter's readings, point out any further improvements you would now make in your essay.

Considering the Social Dimensions of Explanations of Opposing Positions

Published explanations of opposing positions on issues are unquestionably helpful. As they are intended to do, they can help readers understand a complicated debate of great social or political importance, such as the debate in the U.S. Congress over whether to grant amnesty and eventual citizenship to millions of illegal immigrants. Explanations of opposing positions can also have immediate personal significance: for example, an explanation of the debate over whether high school graduates should be immediately registered for the military draft or the debate between liberal and conservative Christians (or other groups) over gay marriage.

The Pose of Impartiality. As you have learned from your reading and writing in this chapter, readers must rely on explainers of opposing positions to be impartial. Unlike writers who take positions on issues, seeking to convince you to consider their position carefully if not to adopt it, writers explaining opposing positions must never take sides. If readers suspect they are doing so, the pact of restraint and impartiality, the implicit trust between reader and writer, is broken. Such disappointment can lead to suspicion and mistrust, undermining social ties, civic life, and political participation.

1. *Consider how difficult it is to remain completely impartial,* never showing even a hint of favoritism toward one side in the debate. It seems almost too much to ask of ordinary human beings. Yet citizens often have to rely on presumed experts to report impartially the debates on issues of the day they care about.

2. *Consider the possibility that you are likely to be deceived when you seek information or advice about important issues of the day.* It is certainly possible for people to pose as reliable, impartial explainers when they are really trying to deceive other people for personal gain, or out of a desire to support one side of the debate. Can you think of any social factors that might disguise a writer's intentions?

3. *Write a page or so about your own experience of attempting to be an impartial explainer. Also speculate about the inevitable risks you accept as a citizen when relying on people to explain important issues of the day to you.* If you believe you succeeded in explaining your debate's opposing positions impartially, reflect on what guidelines if any in the chapter contributed to your success. Did your confidence come all at once or gradually, and what influenced you? Then identify one significant issue you face right now as a student and one as a citizen. Describe in a few sentences the issue and the debate you are having with yourself about what to do. Then write about what information you believe you need to make a decision, how you might find it, and how you would decide whether it was impartially presented, reliable information that you could trust to guide you toward a decision.

Appendix: Two Debates

Following are two pairs of essays taking opposing positions on an issue. Your instructor may assign you to write about one of these pairs, or you may be given a choice. These essays are available electronically on the companion Web site for this book, bedfordstmartins.com/theguide, which also includes several other debates for you or your instructor to choose from.

Debate: Urban Sprawl and Wildlife

As more and more Americans move into previously rural areas and suburbs penetrate deeply into undeveloped natural habitats, controversy over the impact of suburban sprawl on the environment has grown. You may have seen news stories in various parts of the country about bears and moose wandering into backyards, deer becoming a pest for gardeners and an increasing menace for drivers, and people occasionally becoming victims of mountain lion attacks. The central question addressed in the following debate is whether the spread of suburbs presents a threat to the environment, especially to wildlife such as bears, moose, deer, and mountain lions.

The first essay, "Unwelcome (Human) Neighbors: The Impacts of Sprawl on Wildlife," is by Jutka Terris, an urban planner who serves as a policy analyst for the Natural Resources Defense Council (NRDC) in Washington, D.C., a group that describes itself on its Web site as "the nation's most effective environmental action organization" (http://www.nrdc.org). The article was originally published in 1999 by NRDC. Before joining the NRDC, Terris was national field director for 20/20 Vision, a grassroots environmental and peace advocacy organization, and also a member of the AmeriCorps/Neighborhood Green Corps. Terris has co-authored a book called *Solving Sprawl: Models of Smart Growth in Communities across America* (2001).

The second essay, "Nature in the Suburbs," is by Jane S. Shaw, a Senior Fellow at the Property and Environment Research Center (PERC) in Bozeman, Montana, an organization that according to its Web site is "dedicated to original research that brings market principles to resolving environmental problems" (http://www.perc.org). The article was adapted from a chapter in *A Guide to Smart Growth* and was published in 2004 by The Heritage Foundation, a conservative research institute. Before joining PERC, Shaw was a journalist and editor at *Business Week* magazine. She directs PERC's editorial outreach program and has written numerous articles about environmental and economic issues in publications such as the *Wall Street Journal*, the *Washington Times*, and the *Cato Journal*. Shaw also has co-authored several books, including *Facts, Not Fear: A Parents' Guide to Teaching Children about the Environment* (1999) and *A Guide to Smart Growth: Shattering Myths, Providing Solutions* (2000).

Unwelcome Human Neighbors: The Impact of Sprawl on Wildlife

Jutka Terris

"Bears know their landscape like we know our houses. I have data on one female bear who, I am convinced, has used the same babysitter tree for all the litters of cubs she's had for the last twelve years. Imagine if she woke up after hibernation with her new cubs to find a road and a sprawling suburban neighborhood in place of that tree. What would she do?"

— SUSAN MORSE, forester, carnivore expert and founder of Keeping Track

Roads and sprawling neighborhoods are replacing pristine wildlife habitats at an alarming pace, putting the survival and reproduction of plants and animals at risk. In just the last few decades, rapidly growing human settlements have consumed large amounts of land in our country, while wildlife habitats have shrunk, fragmented, or disappeared altogether. If the current land use pattern — expansion of built areas at rates much faster than population growth — continues, sprawl could become the problem for U.S. wildlife in the 21st century. [1]

At-Risk Species

First there were tents, then huts, then farmhouses and fields, then towns and cities. Ever since humans set foot on this continent, permanent human settlements [2]

have been built and expanded on landscapes that were previously home to wildlife. While loss of habitat to human settlement is not new, the last few decades have seen a dramatic increase in its pace. Nearly one-sixth of the total base of land developed in our country's long history was claimed for development in just 10 years, from 1982 to 1992. But this expansion was not due to an unprecedented population boom in the 80s. Instead, urban sprawl was rapidly outpacing population growth. From 1960 to 1990, the amount of developed land in all U.S. metropolitan areas more than doubled — while population grew by less than 50 percent. Today, this rapid growth continues. Moreover, some of the fastest growth is occurring far beyond our urban areas, in still-rural communities 60 to 70 miles from metropolitan beltways. Such exurbs already account for 60 million people and one-quarter of the recent population growth of the lower 48 states. In the exurbs, developments are often far away from each other, connected only by a system of highways and roads. Such "leapfrog developments" exacerbate the fragmentation of wildlife habitats.

3   There is wildlife in all these fast-growing areas, metropolitan and rural, and species do not fare well when the natural landscapes are paved over and built on. What kind of wildlife is most at risk? Since sprawl is claiming open lands nationwide across a varied landscape, the species affected by it are also varied.

4   One victim of sprawl, the Florida panther, is among the most endangered large mammals in the world. It is now reduced to a single population of an estimated 30 to 50 adults. This is especially tragic, considering that the panther — also known as cougar, mountain lion, puma and catamount — was once the most widely distributed mammal (other than humans) in North and South America. In the eastern United States, only the Florida subspecies survives. But for how long? Its southern Florida habitat of hardwood hammocks, pine flatwoods and wetlands is still rapidly giving way to residential developments and agricultural fields. Habitat loss has already driven the Florida panther into a small area, where the few remaining animals are highly inbred, causing such genetic flaws as heart defects and sterility.

5   In the Southwest, where especially rapid growth is taking place, plant and animal species of the fragile desert ecosystem are at risk. For example, the silent victims of Tucson's rapid expansion into the Sonoran Desert in Arizona include the ancient ironwood, the creosote bush and the graceful saguaro cactus. Growing painfully slowly in the arid lands, these beautiful plants survive for hundreds of years (indeed, some may date back thousands of years). But they take only a few seconds to bulldoze. Disappearing with them are animal species such as the endangered pygmy owl, a beautiful, hand-sized, brown-and-white flecked raptor, and the sonoran pronghorn, a graceful creature that looks like an antelope but is, in fact, the sole survivor of a distinct ancient family dating back 20 million years.

6   In Southern California, another booming area, the coastal sage ecosystem is unraveling. Sprawling development has wiped out over 90 percent of this landscape, identified by the U.S. Fish and Wildlife Service as "one of the most depleted habitat types in the United States." What is left is badly fragmented and, as a result, the region has experienced a dramatic loss of native species of birds and

small mammals. A rare bird with an unfortunately unheroic name, the coastal California gnatcatcher is one that has suffered most. The gnatcatcher has lost some three-fourths of its natural habitat, and its remaining population, now dwindled to perhaps 2,500 pairs, is hanging on in shrinking, isolated patches where it is more exposed to predators. It has recently been classified as a threatened species. The coastal sage ecosystem is also home to such endangered species as the kangaroo rat and the quino checkerspot, a large butterfly with a life cycle that makes it especially vulnerable to habitat loss.

Other species in trouble include the redleg frog and the Pacific pond turtle in Sonoma Valley, California; the piping plover, a tiny bird living and nesting on the Atlantic coast; the dusky salamander in New York state's streams; the hawksbill sea turtle in the Gulf of Mexico; the desert tortoise in the Mojave and Colorado deserts and the nocturnal lynx, with its trademark bobbed tail, in parts of the Northwest and New York state.   7

Habitats Are Being Destroyed

Before we can talk about change, it is important to understand the many ways that our current patterns of growth hurt wildlife. Habitat loss is one of the most familiar. This concept is perhaps easiest to grasp when a complete transformation of the natural landscape occurs. Almost no on-site wildlife can survive the transition from a meadow to a large new factory, or to an office complex or "big-box" retail outlet surrounded by a vast concrete parking lot. But can wildlife survive when the new use is a residential suburb with some grass and trees? Or an office campus, where buildings are surrounded by green landscaping?   8

While a few species can adapt to such human-shaped environments, many cannot. And since our suburbs and office campuses are remarkably similar all around the country (and are thus often completely oblivious to their natural surroundings), we are essentially cultivating the few species that do well with irrigated lawns and Norway maples and have learned to eat from our garbage cans and bird feeders. All this is at the expense of the many species that depend on more fragile local habitats.   9

This trend is called generalization of habitat, and results in the survival of hardy species such as pigeons, squirrels and raccoons. While the overall biomass may not decline — the generalists take over where more sensitive species are disappearing — the total number of species plummets. Standing in a suburban backyard, one may still hear birds singing, but the choir is not nearly as diverse as it was before the subdivisions came and the mature trees were chopped down.   10

Another serious problem is habitat fragmentation. When roads, houses and malls break up ecosystems, large populations that once were genetically diverse are broken up into small groups. With amphibians, for example, even a single road across their habitat may be enough to create genetically divergent groups. A result may be a lack of enough genetic variety within each subgroup, resulting in degenerative inbreeding. This has been a significant factor in the decline of the   11

Florida panther, as fragmentation of wetland and forest habitats has resulted in new generations suffering serious, sometimes fatal, genetic flaws.

Fragmentation of habitat may also separate a species from its feeding or breeding grounds. In some cases, not even the first generation survives. Or, a species may survive only until the first environmental stress, such as a drought, occurs, when it is trapped in a small and isolated area. Prior to habitat fragmentation, the thirsty wildlife could find relief at a nearby river during droughts. After development, that river may now be on the other side of a five-lane highway or a strip mall, impossible to reach. The more fragmented, the more vulnerable to any stress an ecosystem is.

Further Effects of Sprawl

Habitat loss, generalization and fragmentation are sprawl's three most damaging impacts on wildlife. But sprawl does more: it also pollutes our rivers, lakes and air, further threatening species. It is easy to see why Michael Klemens of the Wildlife Conservation Society described sprawl as an "extremely severe problem for wildlife," and why ecologist Joseph McAuliffe calls sprawl "an environmental abomination."

Twenty-seven ecosystem types have already declined by as much as 98 percent or more since Europeans settled North America. As of mid-1997, the U.S. Fish and Wildlife Service reported that 1,082 species of plants and animals were listed as threatened and endangered, with another 119 proposed for listing. In a comprehensive assessment of some 20,000 species of plants and animals native to the United States, The Nature Conservancy reports that fully a third are "of conservation concern," believed to be extinct, imperiled or vulnerable. According to the Conservancy, "current extinction rates are conservatively estimated to be at least 10,000 times greater than background levels."

However, not all is lost — yet. The United States still has an abundance of natural areas where wildlife thrives. The question is what we can do now to save them from the rising tide of development.

Conservation Measures

When feasible, buying land that is threatened by development and setting it aside as a nature preserve is a dramatic and secure way to protect some wildlife. But we cannot save our natural areas by land purchases alone: there is simply not enough money to go around. Developers have just as deep, if not deeper, pockets than conservation groups do, and there is too much land around the country that needs to be protected. Buying conservation easements (paying landowners to restrict development on their property) is a more economical approach, but still insufficient.

If money alone won't fix the problem, what about national laws that protect wildlife? The most widely influential of these has been the Endangered Species Act, which has succeeded in rehabilitating some endangered species that are now recovering, among them the bald eagle, the gray wolf, the peregrine falcon, the

12

13

14

15

16

17

whooping crane and the mountain lion. Indirectly, the law has also benefited additional species in the protected areas. However, by its nature, the law's scope is limited to the last remaining habitat of the last remaining individuals of a particular species. Surely, we should start protecting our unique ecosystems and dependent species long before the edge of disaster.

Ultimately, purely defensive strategies — setting aside wildlife reserves, attempting to prevent the diminution of endangered species — are insufficient. We need to change the way we plan and manage our growth. 18

Citizens concerned about sprawl should advocate at least three approaches. First, ecological considerations should play a larger role in our local land use planning decisions. Activities such as mapping wildlife habitats and evaluating a proposed project's impact on those habitats should be routinely incorporated in the planning process. Planners should receive some training in ecology, and interdepartmental cooperation between planners and environmental and wildlife specialists should be encouraged. 19

Second, ecological thinking does not stop at a local jurisdiction's border; regional cooperation is essential. Ideally, regions should correspond to biological units, such as watersheds, in order to provide maximum benefit for wildlife. This approach has been coined bioregional planning, and has already yielded some promising results. Some states, for example, have designated "areas of critical state concern" based on these areas' unique natural resources. Development in these areas is to be carefully managed, so as to minimize environmental damage, by regional bodies or state agencies. Ecosystems as diverse as New Jersey's pine barrens, Virginia's tidewater region and Florida's wetlands are already enjoying some degree of regional protection. 20

Third, and perhaps most critically, the ultimate answer to reversing the tide of sprawling development should be to grow differently, to accommodate our housing and commercial needs in a more thoughtful way. The alternative to sprawl, smart growth, is not one simple formula, but rather a set of guiding principles. These should be flexible enough to be adapted to diverse and ever-changing local conditions, and to be achieved by a variety of creative policies and market mechanisms. 21

Guiding Principles

Among the guiding principles are the following: 22

- strong central cities and more efficient use of already developed areas;
- compact, walkable developments with several transportation choices;
- a range of housing opportunities and choices; mixed land uses;
- growth management and protection of open spaces.

Maybe the most important lesson for those of us who care deeply about the well-being of our nation's wildlife is that intimate connections exist between the 23 health of our cities (and inner suburbs) and the health of wildlife at the far edges of the metropolitan areas these cities anchor. Protecting open space and wildlife is essential, but not enough, if we want to reverse the damage that urban sprawl inflicts on our wildlife. A more comprehensive approach that aims both to strengthen the urban core and to tame growth at the edge — smart growth — is called for.

Nature in the Suburbs

Jane S. Shaw

A decade ago, who would have thought that New Jersey would host a black bear hunt — the first in 33 years? Or that Virginia, whose population of bald eagles was once down to 32 breeding pairs, would have 329 known active bald eagle nests? Who would have expected *Metropolitan Home* magazine to be advising its readers about ornamental grasses to keep away white-tailed deer, now found in the millions around the country? [1]

Such incidents illustrate a transformed America. This nation, often condemned for being crowded, paved over, and studded with nature-strangling shopping malls, is proving to be a haven for wild animals. [2]

An Upsurge of Wild Animals

It is difficult to ignore this upsurge of wildlife, because stories about bears raiding trashcans and mountain lions sighted in subdivisions frequently turn up in the press or on television. Featured in these stories are animals as large as moose, as well as once-threatened birds such as eagles and falcons and smaller animals like wolverines and coyotes. [3]

One interpretation of these events is that people are moving closer to wilderness and invading the territory of wild animals. But this is only a small part of the story. As this essay will show, wild animals increasingly find suburban life in the United States to be attractive. [4]

The stories, while fascinating, are not all upbeat. Americans are grappling with new problems — the growing hazard of automobile collisions with deer, debates over the role of hunting, the disappearance of fragile wild plants gobbled up by hungry ruminants, and even occasional human deaths caused by these animals. [5]

At the same time, the proliferation of wildlife should assure Americans that the claim that urban sprawl is wiping out wildlife is simply poppycock. Human settlement in the early 21st century may be sprawling and suburban — about half the people in this country live in suburbs — but it is more compatible with wildlife than most people think. There may be reasons to decry urban sprawl or the suburbanization of America, but the loss of wildlife is not one of them. [6]

Two phenomena are fueling this increase in wild animals. One is natural refor- 7
estation, especially in the eastern United States. This is largely a result of the
steady decline in farming, including cotton farming, a decline that allows forests to
retake territory they lost centuries ago. The other is suburbanization, the expansion
of low-density development outside cities, which provides a variety of landscapes
and vegetation that attract animals. Both trends undermine the claim that wild open
spaces are being strangled and that habitat for wild animals is shrinking.

The trend toward regrowth of forest has been well-documented. The percent 8
of forested land in New Hampshire increased from 50 percent in the 1880s to 86
percent 100 years later.

Forested land in Connecticut, Massachusetts, and Rhode Island increased 9
from 35 percent to 59 percent over that same period. "The same story has been
repeated in other places in the East, the South, and the Lake States," writes
forestry expert Roger Sedjo.

Environmentalist Bill McKibben exulted in this "unintentional and mostly un- 10
noticed renewal of the rural and mountainous East" in a 1995 article in the *Atlantic
Monthly*. Calling the change "the great environmental story of the United States,
and in some ways of the whole world," he added, "Here, where 'suburb' and 'mega-
lopolis' were added to the world's vocabulary, an explosion of green is under way."
Along with the reforestation come the animals; McKibben cites a moose "ten miles
from Boston," as well as an eastern United States full of black bears, deer, alligators, and perhaps even mountain lions.

This re-greening of the eastern United States explains why some large wild 11
animals are thriving, but much of the wildlife Americans are seeing today is a
direct result of the suburbs. Clearly, suburban habitat is not sterile.

The Return of Deer

When people move onto what once was rural land, they modify the landscape. Yes, 12
they build more streets, more parking lots, and more buildings. Wetlands may be
drained, hayfields may disappear, trees may be cut down, and pets may prolifer-
ate. At the same time, however, the new residents will create habitat for wildlife.
They will create ponds, establish gardens, plant trees, and set up bird nesting-
boxes. Ornamental nurseries and truck farms may replace cropland, and parks
may replace hedgerows.

This new ecology is different, but it is often friendly to animals, especially 13
those that University of Florida biologist Larry Harris calls "meso-mammals," or
mammals of medium size. They do not need broad territory for roaming to find
food, as moose and grizzly bears do. They can find places in the suburbs to feed,
nest, and thrive, especially where gardens flourish.

One example of the positive impact of growth is the rebound of the endan- 14
gered Key deer, a small white-tailed deer found only in Florida and named for the
Florida Keys. According to *Audubon* magazine, the Key deer is experiencing a "remarkable recovery." The news report continues: "Paradoxically, part of the reason
for the deer's comeback may lie in the increasing development of the area."

Paraphrasing the remarks of a university researcher, the reporter says that human development "tends to open up overgrown forested areas and provide vegetation at deer level — the same factors fueling deer population booms in suburbs all over the country."

Indeed, white-tailed deer of normal size are the most prominent species proliferating in the suburbs. In the *New York Times*, reporter Andrew C. Revkin has commented that "suburbanization created a browser's paradise: a vast patchwork of well-watered, fertilizer-fattened plantings to feed on and vest-pocket forests to hide in, with hunters banished to more distant woods." 15

The increase in the number of deer in the United States is so great that many people, especially wildlife professionals, are trying to figure out what to do about them. In 1997, the Wildlife Society, a professional association of wildlife biologists, devoted a special 600-page issue of its *Bulletin* to "deer overabundance." The lead article noted, "We hear more each year about the high costs of crop and tree-seedling damage, deer-vehicle collisions, and nuisance deer in suburban locales." Insurance companies are worried about the increase in damage from automobile collisions with deer and similar-sized animals. And there are fears that the increase in deer in populated areas means that the deer tick could be causing the increased number of reported cases of Lyme disease. 16

Yes, the proliferation of deer poses problems, as do geese, whose flocks can foul ponds and lawns and are notorious nuisances on golf courses, and beaver, which can cut down groves of trees. Yet the proliferation of deer is also a wildlife success story. At least that is the view of Robert J. Warren, editor of the *Bulletin*, who calls the resurgence of deer "one of the premier examples of successful wildlife management." Today's deer population in the United States may be as high as 25 million, says Richard Nelson, writing in *Sports Afield*. 17

People have mixed feelings about deer. In the *Wildlife Society Bulletin*, Dale R. McCullough and his colleagues reported on a survey of households in El Cerrito and Kensington, two communities near Berkeley, California. Twenty-eight percent of those who responded reported severe damage to vegetation by the deer, and 25 percent reported moderate damage. Forty-two percent liked having the deer around, while 35 percent disliked them and 24 percent were indifferent. The authors summarized the findings by saying: "As expected, some residents loved deer, whereas others considered them 'hoofed rats.'" 18

James Dunn, a geologist who has studied wildlife in New York State, believes that suburban habitat fosters deer more than forests do. Dunn cites statistics on the harvest of buck deer reported by the New York State government. Since 1970 the deer population has multiplied 7.1 times in suburban areas (an increase of 610 percent), but only 3.4 times (an increase of 240 percent) in the state overall. 19

Other Suburban Species

Dunn explains that the forests have been allowed to regrow without logging or burning, so they lack the "edge" that allows sunlight in and encourages vegetation suitable for deer. In his view, that explains why counties with big cities (and 20 therefore with suburbs) have seen a greater increase in deer populations than have the isolated, forested rural counties. Supporting this point, Andrew Revkin quotes a wildlife biologist at the National Zoo in Washington, D.C.: "Deer are an edge species," he says, "and the world is one big edge now."

Deer are not the only wild animals that turn up on lawns and doorsteps, however. James Dunn lists species in the Albany, New York, suburbs in addition to deer: birds such as robins, woodpeckers, chickadees, grouse, finches, hawks, crows, and nuthatches, as well as squirrels, chipmunks, opossums, raccoons, foxes, and rabbits. Deer attract coyotes too. According to a 1999 article in *Audubon*, biologists estimate that the coyote population (observed in all states except Hawaii) is about double what it was in 1850.

Joel Garreau, author of *Edge City*, includes black bears, red-tailed hawks, peregrine falcons, and beaver on his list of animals that find suburban niches. Garreau still considers these distant "edge city" towns a "far less diverse ecology than what was there before." However, he writes, "if you measure it by the standard of city, it is a far more diverse ecology than anything humans have built in centuries, if not millennia."

For one reason or another, some environmental activists tend to dismiss the resurgence of deer and other wildlife. In an article criticizing suburban sprawl, Carl Pope, executive director of the Sierra Club, says that the suburbs are "very good for the most adaptable and common creatures — raccoons, deer, sparrows, starlings, and sea gulls" but "devastating for wildlife that is more dependent upon privacy, seclusion, and protection from such predators as dogs and cats."

Yet the suburbs attract animals larger than meso-mammals, and the suburban habitat may be richer than what they replace. In many regions, suburban growth comes at the expense of agricultural land that was cultivated for decades, even centuries. Cropland doesn't necessarily provide abundant habitat. Environmental essayist Donald Worster, for example, has little favorable to say about land cultivated for crops or used for livestock grazing. In Worster's view, there was a time when agriculture was diversified, with small patches of different crops and a variety of animals affecting the landscape. Not now. "The trend over the past two hundred years or so," he writes, "has been toward the establishment of monocultures on every continent." In contrast, suburbs are not monocultures.

Even large animals can be found at the edges of metropolitan areas. Early in 2004, a mountain lion attacked a woman riding a bicycle in the Whiting Ranch Wilderness Park in the foothills above populous Orange County, and the same animal may have killed a man who was found dead nearby. According to the *Los Angeles Times*, if the man's death is confirmed as caused by the mountain lion, it would be the first death by a mountain lion in Orange County. The *Times* added, however, that "mountain lions are no strangers in Orange County's canyons and wilderness parks." Indeed, in 1994, mountain lions killed two women in state parks near San Diego and Sacramento. Deer may be attracting the cats, suggests Paul Beier, a professor at the University of California at Berkeley. . . .

21

22

23

24

25

Learning to Live with Animals

The fact that wildlife finds a home in suburban settings does not mean that all wildlife will do so. The greening of the suburbs is no substitute for big stretches of land — both public and private — that allow large mammals such as grizzly bears, elk, antelope, and caribou to roam. The point of this essay is that the suburbs offer an environment that is appealing to many wild animal species.

26

If the United States continues to prosper, the 21st century is likely to be an environmental century. Affluent people will seek to maintain or, in some cases, restore an environment that is attractive to wildlife, and more parks will likely be nestled within suburban developments, along with gardens, arboreta, and environmentally compatible golf courses. As wildlife proliferates, Americans will learn to live harmoniously with more birds and meso-mammals. New organizations and entrepreneurs will help integrate nature into the human landscape. There is no reason to be pessimistic about the ability of wildlife to survive and thrive in the suburbs.

27

Debate: Torture

Torture is the intentional infliction of pain to kill, punish, intimidate, or gather information. It has ancient origins, and it continues today. The earliest civilizations in the West, the Greeks and Romans, practiced torture to gather information about crimes, although the Romans tortured not to persuade a suspect to confess but to gather evidence from witnesses. Because they believed that so long as witnesses could think and reason they would make up lies, the Romans concluded that witnesses would tell the truth only under extreme pain.

Throughout the Middle Ages, the Catholic Church tortured nonbelievers and heretics, and later, especially in Scotland, Protestants also tortured those they considered religious subversives, some of them presumed witches. In the early American colonies, accused witches, some of them harmless midwives, were tortured and killed. Not until the eighteenth-century Enlightenment, a time of aggressively secular thinking, did the widespread use of torture begin to be seriously challenged. For the first time, states from Sweden to Tuscany began abolishing the official use of torture, though it continued during wars.

Current United States and international laws forbid torture. After reviewing relevant U.S. Supreme Court cases over the last 40 years, Jerome Skolnick, an expert on legal aspects of torture, recently wrote, "I feel confident in maintaining that there is no longer any torture by American police detectives who are seeking evidence to be introduced at a trial." Internationally, the United States has ratified the United Nations Convention against Torture (1987), which asserts that "[n]o exceptional circumstances whatsoever, whether a state of war or a threat of war, internal political instability or any other public emergency may be invoked as a justification for torture." Since the terrorist attacks of September 11, 2001, and the subsequent revelations of abuse of prisoners by the U.S. military and others at the Abu Ghraib and

Guantanamo Bay prisons and elsewhere, however, torture has again become a subject of debate in the United States.

Because torture has a long history and is such a complex subject, a great many debatable issues arise from it. For example, writers have debated whether torture is effective in obtaining the truth, affects the torturers, threatens the international standing of the United States, or undermines justice. Other contested issues include what qualifies as torture, whether the United States must observe international laws forbidding torture, or whether the United States should set an example by not torturing. Fundamental to the torture issue, however, are moral or ethical considerations; and that is the question the following two essays debate: Can torture be moral?

The first essay, "A Case for Torture," is by Mirko Bagaric, professor of law and coordinator of the Graduate Law Program at the Deakin Law School in Melbourne, Australia. His recent books include *Criminal Laws of Australia*, with Ken Arenson (2004); *How to Live: Being Happy and Living with Moral Dilemmas* (2006); and *Torture: When the Unthinkable Is Morally Permissible*, with Julie Clark (2006). His essay, a summary of an article that he and Clark wrote for the *University of San Francisco Law Review*, was published in 2005 in *The Age*, a Melbourne, Australia, newspaper.

The second essay, "Inhuman Behavior," was written by Major General Kermit D. Johnson, a retired chaplain in the U.S. Army. Johnson is a graduate of the U.S. Military Academy, the Princeton Theological Seminary, the U.S. Command and General Staff College, and the U.S. Army War College. As an infantry officer, he commanded a heavy mortar company in the Korean War. As a chaplain, he served in the United States, Germany, and Vietnam, completing his service as Chief of Chaplains from 1979 to 1982. His essay was published in 2006 in *The Christian Century*, a national magazine concerned with "faithful living, critical thinking."

A Case for Torture

Mirko Bagaric

Recent events stemming from the "war on terrorism" have highlighted the prevalence of torture. This is despite the fact that torture is almost universally deplored. The formal prohibition against torture is absolute — there are no exceptions to it. [1]

The belief that torture is always wrong is, however, misguided and symptomatic of the alarmist and reflexive responses typically emanating from social commentators. It is this type of absolutist and short-sighted rhetoric that lies at the core of many distorted moral judgements that we as a community continue to make, resulting in an enormous amount of injustice and suffering in our society and far beyond our borders. [2]

Torture is permissible where the evidence suggests that this is the only means, due to the immediacy of the situation, to save the life of an innocent per- [3]

son. The reason that torture in such a case is defensible and necessary is because the justification manifests from the closest thing we have to an inviolable right: the right to self-defence, which of course extends to the defence of another. Given the choice between inflicting a relatively small level of harm on a wrongdoer and saving an innocent person, it is verging on moral indecency to prefer the interests of the wrongdoer.

The analogy with self-defence is sharpened by considering the hostage-taking scenario, where a wrongdoer takes a hostage and points a gun to the hostage's head, threatening to kill the hostage unless a certain (unreasonable) demand is met. In such a case it is not only permissible, but desirable for police to shoot (and kill) the wrongdoer if they get a "clear shot". This is especially true if it's known that the wrongdoer has a history of serious violence, and hence is more likely to carry out the threat. [4]

There is no logical or moral difference between this scenario and one where there is overwhelming evidence that a wrongdoer has kidnapped an innocent person and informs police that the victim will be killed by a co-offender if certain demands are not met. [5]

In the hostage scenario, it is universally accepted that it is permissible to violate the right to life of the aggressor to save an innocent person. How can it be wrong to violate an even less important right (the right to physical integrity) by torturing the aggressor in order to save a life in the second scenario? [6]

There are three main [objections] to even the above limited approval of torture. The first is the slippery slope argument: if you start allowing torture in a limited context, the situations in which it will be used will increase. [7]

This argument is not sound in the context of torture. First, the floodgates are already open — torture is used widely, despite the absolute legal prohibition against it. Amnesty International has recently reported that it had received, during 2003, reports of torture and ill-treatment from 132 countries, including the United States, Japan and France. It is, in fact, arguable that it is the existence of an unrealistic absolute ban that has driven torture beneath the radar of accountability, and that legalisation in very rare circumstances would in fact reduce instances of it. [8]

The second main argument is that torture will dehumanise society. This is no more true in relation to torture than it is with self-defence, and in fact the contrary is true. A society that elects to favour the interests of wrongdoers over those of the innocent, when a choice must be made between the two, is in need of serious ethical rewiring. [9]

A third [objection] is that we can never be totally sure that torturing a person will in fact result in us saving an innocent life. This, however, is the same situation as in all cases of self-defence. To revisit the hostage example, the hostage-taker's gun might in fact be empty, yet it is still permissible to shoot. As with any decision, we must decide on the best evidence at the time. [10]

Torture in order to save an innocent person is the only situation where it is clearly justifiable. This means that the recent high-profile incidents of torture, apparently undertaken as punitive measures or in a bid to acquire information where [11] there was no evidence of an immediate risk to the life of an innocent person, were reprehensible.

Will a real-life situation actually occur where the only option is between torturing a wrongdoer or saving an innocent person? Perhaps not. However, a minor alteration to the Douglas Wood situation illustrates that the issue is far from moot. If Western forces in Iraq arrested one of Mr. Wood's captors, it would be a perverse ethic that required us to respect the physical integrity of the captor, and not torture him to ascertain Mr. Wood's whereabouts, in preference to taking all possible steps to save Mr. Wood.

Even if a real-life situation where torture is justifiable does not eventuate, the above argument in favour of torture in limited circumstances needs to be made because it will encourage the community to think more carefully about moral judgements we collectively hold that are the cause of an enormous amount of suffering in the world.

First, no right or interest is absolute. Secondly, rights must always yield to consequences, which are the ultimate criteria upon which the soundness of a decision is gauged. Lost lives hurt a lot more than bent principles.

Thirdly, we must take responsibility not only for the things that we do, but also for the things that we can — but fail to — prevent. The retort that we are not responsible for the lives lost through a decision not to torture a wrongdoer because we did not create the situation is code for moral indifference.

Equally vacuous is the claim that we in the affluent West have no responsibility for more than 13,000 people dying daily due to starvation. Hopefully, the debate on torture will prompt us to correct some of these fundamental failings.

Inhuman Behavior: A Chaplain's View of Torture
Kermit D. Johnson

The historian Arnold Toynbee called war "an act of religious worship." Appropriately, when most people enter the cathedral of violence, their voices become hushed. This silence, this reluctance to speak, is based in part on not wishing to trivialize or jeopardize the lives of those who have been put in harm's way. We want to support the men and women in our armed forces, whether we are crusaders, just warriors or pacifists.

Furthermore, those who interrupt this service of worship become a source of public embarrassment, if not shame. The undercurrent seems to be that dissent or critique in the midst of war is inherently unpatriotic because it violates a sacred wartime precept: support our troops.

From the standpoint of Christian faith, how do we respond? I would say that if war causes us to suppress our deepest religious, ethical and moral convictions, then we have indeed caved in to a "higher religion" called war.

Since this obeisance to war is packaged in the guise of patriotism, it is well to admit to the beauty of patriotism, the beauty of unselfishness and love of country, land, community, family, friends and, yes, our system of government. But this fabulous beauty makes us appreciate all the more what Reinhold Niebuhr called the "ethical paradox in patriotism." The paradox is that patriotism can transmute individual unselfishness into national egoism. When this happens, when the critical attitude of the individual is squelched, this permits the nation, as Niebuhr observed, to use "power without moral constraint."

I believe this has been the case, particularly since 9/11, in the treatment of prisoners under U.S. custody.

We must react when our nation breaks the moral constraints and historic values contained in treaties, laws and our Constitution, as well as violating the consciences of individuals who engage in so-called "authorized" inhuman treatment. Out of an unsentimental patriotism we must say no to torture and all inhuman forms of interrogation and incarceration. It is precisely by speaking out that we can support our troops and at the same time affirm the universal values which emanate from religious faith.

A clear-cut repudiation of torture or abuse is also essential to the safety of the troops. If the life and rule of Jesus and his incarnation is to be normative in the church, then we must stand for real people, not abstractions: for soldiers, their families, congregations to which they belong, and the chaplains and pastors who minister to their needs from near and far. By "real people" we also mean that tiny percentage of the armed forces who are guards and interrogators and the commanders responsible for what individuals and units do or fail to do in treating prisoners.

Too often the topic of torture is reduced to a Hollywood drama, a theoretical scenario about a ticking time bomb and the supposed need to torture someone so the bomb can be discovered and defused in the nick of time. Real torture is what takes place in the daily interchange between guards, interrogators and prisoners, and in the everyday, unglamorous, intricate job of collecting intelligence.

U.S. troops in Iraq are fighting an insurgency. It is a battle for the "hearts and minds" of the people. Mao Zedong referred to guerrillas or insurgents as the fish and the supporting population as the water. This is an asymmetrical battle. As a weaker force, the insurgents cannot operate without the support of the people. So the classic formula for combating an insurgency is to drain the swamp — cut the insurgents off from their life support. Both sides are trying to win the "hearts and the minds" of the people.

Imagine, then, the consequences when people learn that U.S. forces have tortured and abused captives. A strengthened and sustained insurgency means danger and death for U.S. forces. Never mind that the other side routinely tortures. It is we who lay claim to a higher morality.

Nor should we take comfort that we do not chop off heads or field suicide bombers. What we must face squarely is this: whenever we torture or mistreat prisoners, we are capitulating morally to the enemy — in fact, adopting the terrorist ethic that the end justifies the means. And let us not deceive ourselves: torture is a form of terrorism. Never mind the never-ending debate about the distinctions between "cruel, inhuman and degrading treatment" and "torture." The object of all such physical and mental torment is singularly clear: to terrify prisoners so they will yield information. Whenever this happens to prisoners in U.S. control, we are handing terrorists and insurgents a priceless ideological gift, known in wartime as aid and comfort to the enemy.

As for individual guards or interrogators, whenever they are encouraged or ordered to use torture, two war crimes are committed: one against the torturer and the other against the prisoner. The torturer and the tortured are both victims, unless the torturer is a sadist or a loose cannon who needs to be court-martialed. This violation of conscience is sure to breed self-hatred, shame and mental torment for a lifetime to come.

12

Finally, the most obvious reason for repudiating torture and inhuman treatment is that our nation needs to claim the full protection of the Geneva Conventions on behalf of our troops when they are captured, in this or any war.

13

The congressional votes for and the presidential capitulation to the amendment offered by Senator John McCain prohibiting torture and inhuman treatment have to be seen as positive (despite the president's statement in signing it, in which he claimed an exception to the rule when acting as commander in chief). But reasons for concern remain.

14

- The most passionate defenders of the Geneva Conventions, the judge advocate generals, the military lawyers, were completely cut off from providing input on the torture issue.

- The government has denigrated international treaties that the U.S. has signed and that constitute U.S. law regarding torture and inhuman treatment.

- The definition of torture has been reinterpreted by the Justice Department as follows: "Physical pain amounting to torture must be equivalent in intensity to the pain accompanying serious physical injury, such as organ failure, impairment of bodily function, or even death."

- There is no indication that the outsourcing or "rendition" of brutal treatment will cease. Is it not odd that some of the countries the U.S. State Department faults for torture are the very countries we utilize in outsourcing interrogations? What credence can we put in their assurances that they will not torture?

- In Senate testimony, Senator Jack Reed (D., R.I.) asked the military this question: "If you were shown a video of a United States Marine or an American citizen [under the] control of a foreign power, in a cell block, naked with a bag over their head, squatting with their arms uplifted for 45 minutes, would you describe that as a good interrogation technique or a violation of the Geneva Convention?" The chairman of the Joint Chiefs of Staff, Marine General Peter Pace, answered: "I would describe it as a violation." The next question might be: Why have these and other violations of the Geneva Conventions been certified as legal when employed by the U.S.?

- The public has been dragged through a labyrinth of denials, retractions, redefinitions and tortured arguments, all designed to justify and rationalize lowered moral standards in the treatment of prisoners, not to strengthen and defend high ethical standards.

In a letter to Senator McCain, Captain Ian Fishback, a West Point graduate in the 82nd Airborne Division, said, "Some argue that since our actions are not as horrifying as al-Qaeda's we should not be concerned. When did al-Qaeda become any type of standard by which we measure the morality of the United States? I strongly urge you to do justice to your men and women in uniform. Give them clear standards of conduct that reflect the ideals they risk their lives for." Torture is not one of those ideals. . . .

15

6

Arguing
a Position

IN COLLEGE COURSES For a business course, a student writes an essay arguing that a "glass ceiling" still prevents women in the United States from advancing up the corporate ladder or being elected to national office. After a brief conference with her professor, she decides she needs to define the phenomenon carefully and to collect statistics to support her position. With the help of a college librarian, the student readily finds a great deal of information.

She begins her essay by explaining that the term "glass ceiling" was first used by a writer at the *Wall Street Journal* in 1986 and refers to barriers that are largely invisible but nonetheless quite real. The student takes the position that since 1986 women's opportunities have not measurably improved. She cites statistics that in 2006 only 11 percent of corporate officers were women and that in 2004 only 15 percent of the members of the U.S. Congress were women, whereas in Sweden 45 percent of the members of Parliament were women. Among chief executives of corporations, she finds, women make up only 0.7 percent of the total in the United States; they are 5 percent in France. The student quotes one authority who concludes that the U.S. figure is not only very low but "not getting any higher." She argues that few male CEOs make the development of women's potential a high priority. While conceding that some ambitious women decide to give their families priority, she insists that more women would claim top jobs and national office if the climb up were not such a struggle.

Ambitious herself, the student is pleased to receive an "A" for her research effort and writing.

IN THE COMMUNITY   In a letter to the school board, a group of parents protest a new Peacekeepers program that is being implemented at the local middle school. Meeting in a home to discuss their opposition, the group at the end of the meeting talk two of the parents into working together to draft a strong, assertive, but diplomatic argument to support their position.

The writers acknowledge that the aim of the program — to teach students to avoid conflict — is worthwhile. But they argue that its methods unduly restrict students' freedom and may teach children to become passive and submissive rather than thinking adults who can make their way in the world and speak up for what is right. They express the concern that Peacekeepers will not prepare students for the give and take of public and professional life, depriving them of the opportunity to begin developing assertiveness, frankness, and self-confidence. To support their argument, they list some of the rules that have been instituted at the middle school: Students must wear uniforms, must keep their hands clasped behind their backs when walking down the halls, may not raise their voices in anger or use obscenities, and cannot play aggressive games like dodge ball or contact sports like basketball and football. Although the parents plan to propose that the school board drop Peacekeepers and institute a different program they believe to be more practical and realistic, they focus this first letter on weakening the board's belief in the worth of Peacekeepers in order to understand how resolved the board is to keep it and why.

IN THE WORKPLACE   For a business magazine, an executive writes an article arguing that protecting the environment is not only good citizenship, but also good business. Protecting the environment was given high priority at his company just because it was a deeply held value for him personally. Initially, he acknowledges, there were some costs and inconveniences. Gradually, however, with outside advice and several years' experience, his management team began to save the company money by buying the most modern technology to reduce heating and cooling costs along with carbon dioxide emissions at the headquarters and nearby factory buildings. Recently they had added rooftop solar cells to generate electricity. He supports his argument with a table showing that after the first five years, the costs and maintenance of the needed equipment steadily declined in relation to profits.

For readers of the magazine, the writer knew it would take more than his own fervor and experience to convince them to spend large amounts of money to make their business practices environmentally friendly. Consequently, he supports his position with examples of two other companies in his city that reduced manufacturing, packaging, and shipping costs by developing innovative methods of reducing hazardous wastes. He also points out that the eight deciding factors in *Fortune* magazine's annual ranking of America's Most Admired Corporations include community and environmental responsibility.

To his surprise, the magazine article produces several e-mails of comment, questions, and thanks as well as a dozen requests to visit his company to see its environmental efforts firsthand.

You may associate arguing with quarreling or with the in-your-face debating we hear so often on radio and television talk shows. These ways of arguing may let us vent strong feelings, but they seldom lead us to consider seriously other points of view or to reflect on our own thinking.

This chapter presents a more deliberative way of arguing that we call **reasoned argument** because it depends on giving reasons rather than raising voices. It demands that positions be supported rather than merely asserted. It also commands respect for the right of others to disagree with you as you may disagree with them. Reasoned argument requires more thought than quarreling but no less passion or commitment, as you will see when you read the essays in this chapter arguing about controversial issues.

Controversial issues are, by definition, issues about which people may have strong feelings. The issue may involve a practice that has been accepted for some time, like allowing college athletes to register for their courses before all other students to accommodate the athletes' practice and travel schedules. Or it may concern a newly proposed or recently instituted policy, like the U.S. military's use of torture to get information from prisoners. People may agree about goals but disagree about the best way to achieve them, as in the perennial debate over how to make a public-college education affordable to all qualified students. Or they may disagree about fundamental values and beliefs, as in the debate over gay marriage or granting citizenship to immigrants who have entered the United States illegally.

As you can see from these examples, controversial issues have no obvious right answer, no truth that everyone accepts, no single authority on which everyone relies. Writers cannot offer absolute proof in debates about controversial issues because such issues are matters of opinion and judgment. Simply gathering information — finding the facts or learning from experts — will not settle disputes like these, although the more that is known about an issue, the more informed the positions will be.

Although it is not possible to prove that a position on a controversial issue is right or wrong, it is possible through reasoned argument to convince others to accept or reject a particular position. To be convincing, not only must an argument present convincing reasons and plausible support for its position, but it also should anticipate readers' likely objections and opposing arguments, conceding those that are reasonable and refuting those that are not. Vigorous debate that sets forth arguments and counterarguments on all sides of an issue can advance everyone's thinking.

Learning to make reasoned arguments on controversial issues and to evaluate our own as well as others' arguments is not a luxury; it is a necessity if our form of government is to survive and flourish. As citizens in a democracy, we have a special duty to inform ourselves about pressing issues and to participate constructively in the public debate. Improving our research and argument strategies also has practical advantages in school, where we often are judged by our ability to write convincingly, and in the workplace, where we may want to take a stand on issues concerning working conditions, observing environment regulations, or pay and promotional policies.

To construct an effective argument, you must assert a position and offer reasons and support for it. You must also anticipate readers' likely objections to your reasons. This activity gives you a chance to practice constructing an argument and to discover how much you already know about doing so.

Part 1. Get together with two or three other students and choose an issue from the following list. None of you needs to be an expert on the issue you choose. Each of you can participate fully in the discussion, no matter what issue you have chosen.

- Should community service be a requirement for graduation from high school or college?
- Should the U.S. government ignore its own and international laws that forbid torture for any reason?
- Should the primary purpose of a college education be job training?
- Should the racial, ethnic, or gender makeup of a local police force parallel the community it serves?
- Should U.S. state governments continue to sponsor lotteries?

Then complete the following activities:

- Choose someone in your group to make notes about each of the following parts of your discussion.
- In your group, quickly exchange your opinions about the issue you have chosen. Then agree together to argue to support the same position on the issue, whether you personally agree with the position or not. As you will see, you can contribute just as much to the discussion whether or not you support it.
- Define the key term in your position statement, for example, *community service* or *torture*.
- Decide whom you would want to read your argument. Imagine that you plan to send it to a group or agency that could take action, and identify that audience (your state governor's office, a committee of the U.S. Senate, or your local city council, for example).
- List three reasons why you support the position and briefly discuss how you would support each reason in order to ensure that your readers will consider it seriously. Also list three likely objections your readers would make to your argument as you have developed it so far.

Part 2. Discuss your efforts at constructing an argument. What part of the task was easiest, and what part hardest? What most surprised you about the kind of argument that takes a position on an issue?

JESSICA STATSKY wrote the following essay about children's competitive sports for her college composition course. Before reading, recall your own experiences as an elementary student playing competitive sports, either in or out of school. If you were not actively involved yourself, did you know anyone who was? Looking back, do you think that winning was unduly emphasized? What value was placed on having a good time? On learning to get along with others? On developing athletic skills and confidence?

Children Need to Play, Not Compete

Jessica Statsky

Over the past three decades, organized sports for children have increased dramatically in the United States. And though many adults regard Little League Baseball and Peewee Football as a basic part of childhood, the games are not always joyous ones. When overzealous parents and coaches impose adult standards on children's sports, the result can be activities that are neither satisfying nor beneficial to children.

I am concerned about all organized sports activities for children between the ages of six and twelve. The damage I see results from noncontact as well as contact sports, from sports organized locally as well as those organized nationally. Highly organized competitive sports such as Peewee Football and Little League Baseball are too often played to adult standards, which are developmentally inappropriate for children and can be both physically and psychologically harmful. Furthermore, because they eliminate many children from organized sports before they are ready to compete, they are actually counterproductive for developing either future players or fans. Finally, because they emphasize competition and winning, they unfortunately provide occasions for some parents and coaches to place their own fantasies and needs ahead of children's welfare.

One readily understandable danger of overly competitive sports is that they entice children into physical actions that are bad for growing bodies. Although the official Little League Web site acknowledges that children do risk injury playing baseball, it insists that "severe injuries . . . are infrequent," the risk "far less than the risk of riding a skateboard, a bicycle, or even the school bus" ("What about My Child?"). Nevertheless, Leonard Koppett in *Sports Illusion, Sports Reality* claims that a twelve-year-old trying to throw a curve ball, for example, may put abnormal strain on developing arm and shoulder muscles, sometimes resulting in lifelong injuries (294). Contact sports like football can be even more hazardous. Thomas Tutko, a psychology professor at San Jose State University and coauthor of the book *Winning Is Everything and Other American Myths*, writes:

I am strongly opposed to young kids playing tackle football. It is not the right stage of development for them to be taught to crash into other kids. Kids under

1

2

3

the age of fourteen are not by nature physical. Their main concern is self-preservation. They don't want to meet head on and slam into each other. But tackle football absolutely requires that they try to hit each other as hard as they can. And it is too traumatic for young kids. (qtd. in Tosches A1)

4   As Tutko indicates, even when children are not injured, fear of being hurt detracts from their enjoyment of the sport. The Little League Web site ranks fear of injury as the seventh of seven reasons children quit ("What about My Child?"). One mother of an eight-year-old Peewee Football player explained, "The kids get so scared. They get hit once and they don't want anything to do with football anymore. They'll sit on the bench and pretend their leg hurts . . ." (qtd. in Tosches A1). Some children are driven to even more desperate measures. For example, in one Peewee Football game, a reporter watched the following scene as a player took himself out of the game:

> "Coach, my tummy hurts. I can't play," he said. The coach told the player to get back onto the field. "There's nothing wrong with your stomach," he said. When the coach turned his head the seven-year-old stuck a finger down his throat and made himself vomit. When the coach turned back, the boy pointed to the ground and told him, "Yes there is, coach. See?" (Tosches A33)

5   Besides physical hazards and anxieties, competitive sports pose psychological dangers for children. Martin Rablovsky, a former sports editor for the *New York Times*, says that in all his years of watching young children play organized sports, he has noticed very few of them smiling. "I've seen children enjoying a spontaneous pre-practice scrimmage become somber and serious when the coach's whistle blows," Rablovsky says. "The spirit of play suddenly disappears, and sport becomes joblike" (qtd. in Coakley 94). The primary goal of a professional athlete — winning — is not appropriate for children. Their goals should be having fun, learning, and being with friends. Although winning does add to the fun, too many adults lose sight of what matters and make winning the most important goal. Several studies have shown that when children are asked whether they would rather be warming the bench on a winning team or playing regularly on a losing team, about 90 percent choose the latter (Smith, Smith, and Smoll 11).

6   Winning and losing may be an inevitable part of adult life, but they should not be part of childhood. Too much competition too early in life can affect a child's development. Children are easily influenced, and when they sense that their competence and worth are based on their ability to live up to their parents' and coaches' high expectations — and on their ability to win — they can become discouraged and depressed. Little League advises parents to "keep winning in perspective" ("Your Role"), noting that the most common reasons children give for quitting, aside from change in interest, are lack of playing time, failure and fear of failure, disapproval by significant others, and psychological stress ("What about My Child?"). According to Dr. Glyn C. Roberts, a professor of kinesiology at the Institute of Child Behavior and Development at the University of Illinois, 80 to 90 percent of children who play competitive sports at a young age drop out by sixteen (Kutner).

To support her second reason — **psychological damage** — Statsky cites authoritative sources, quoting, summarizing, and commenting on them.

Statsky makes a smooth transition to her third reason.

This first sentence in this paragraph, which introduces Statsky's fourth reason, may be the most challenging assertion in the essay for many readers. Statsky risks losing some of her readers by offending them, but she tries to keep them aboard by promising specific horror stories as support.

The argument takes a new direction as, in paragraphs 9 and 11, Statsky describes two practical, tested alternatives to overly competitive children's sports teams. She may well have become concerned that readers would tire of her criticisms and that she needed to mention more positive possibilities.

In response to her awareness that some readers will resist, if not dismiss, her argument, Statsky acknowledges the value many parents place on training their children for a life of competition and struggle. After conceding some wisdom in this value, however, she suggests that it is one-sided and short-sighted for children in this age range.

This statistic illustrates another reason I oppose competitive sports for children: because they are so highly selective, very few children get to participate. Far too soon, a few children are singled out for their athletic promise, while many others, who may be on the verge of developing the necessary strength and ability, are screened out and discouraged from trying out again. Like adults, children fear failure, and so even those with good physical skills may stay away because they lack self-confidence. Consequently, teams lose many promising players who with some encouragement and experience might have become stars. The problem is that many parent-sponsored, out-of-school programs give more importance to having a winning team than to developing children's physical skills and self-esteem. 7

Indeed, it is no secret that too often scorekeeping, league standings, and the drive to win bring out the worst in adults who are more absorbed in living out their own fantasies than in enhancing the quality of the experience for children (Smith, Smith, and Smoll 9). Recent newspaper articles on children's sports contain plenty of horror stories. *Los Angeles Times* reporter Rich Tosches, for example, tells the story of a brawl among seventy-five parents following a Peewee Football game (A33). As a result of the brawl, which began when a parent from one team confronted a player from the other team, the teams are now thinking of hiring security guards for future games. Another example is provided by an *L.A. Times* editorial about a Little League manager who intimidated the opposing team by setting fire to one of their team's jerseys on the pitching mound before the game began. As the editorial writer commented, the manager showed his young team that "intimidation could substitute for playing well" ("The Bad News"). 8

Although not all parents or coaches behave so inappropriately, the seriousness of the problem is illustrated by the fact that Adelphi University in Garden City, New York, offers a sports psychology workshop for Little League coaches, designed to balance their "animal instincts" with "educational theory" in hopes of reducing the "screaming and hollering," in the words of Harold Weisman, manager of sixteen Little Leagues in New York City (Schmitt). In a three-and-one-half-hour Sunday morning workshop, coaches learn how to make practices more fun, treat injuries, deal with irate parents, and be "more sensitive to their young players' fears, emotional frailties, and need for recognition." Little League is to be credited with recognizing the need for such workshops. 9

Some parents would no doubt argue that children cannot start too soon preparing to live in a competitive free-market economy. After all, secondary schools and colleges require students to compete for grades, and college admission is extremely competitive. And it is perfectly obvious how important competitive skills are in finding a job. Yet the ability to cooperate is also important for success in life. Before children are psychologically ready for competition, maybe we should emphasize cooperation and individual performance in team sports rather than winning. 10

Many people are ready for such an emphasis. In 1988, one New York Little League official who had attended the Adelphi workshop tried to ban scoring from six- to eight-year-olds' games — but parents wouldn't support him (Schmitt). An innovative children's sports program in New York City, City Sports for Kids, emphasizes fitness, self-esteem, and sportsmanship. In this program's basketball games, 11 every member on a team plays at least two of six eight-minute periods. The basket is seven feet from the floor, rather than ten feet, and a player can score a point just by hitting the rim (Bloch). I believe this kind of local program should replace overly competitive programs like Peewee Football and Little League Baseball. As one coach explains, significant improvements can result from a few simple rule changes, such as including every player in the batting order and giving every player, regardless of age or ability, the opportunity to play at least four innings a game (Frank).

12   Authorities have clearly documented the excesses and dangers of many competitive sports programs for children. It would seem that few children benefit from these programs and that those who do would benefit even more from programs emphasizing fitness, cooperation, sportsmanship, and individual performance. Thirteen- and fourteen-year-olds may be eager for competition, but few younger children are. These younger children deserve sports programs designed specifically for their needs and abilities.

In her conclusion, Statsky firmly reasserts her position and reasons for it, while again limiting its scope to younger children and conceding that it may not apply to older ones.

Works Cited

Bloch, Gordon B. "Thrill of Victory Is Secondary to Fun." *New York Times* 2 Apr. 1990, late ed.: C12. *LexisNexis*. Web. 16 May 1999.

"The Bad News Pyromaniacs?" Editorial. *Los Angeles Times* 16 June 1990: B6. *LexisNexis*. Web. 16 May 1999.

Coakley, Jay J. *Sport in Society: Issues and Controversies.* St. Louis: Mosby, 1982. Print.

Frank, L. "Contributions from Parents and Coaches." *CYB Message Board.* AOL, 8 July 1997. Web. 14 May 1999.

Koppett, Leonard. *Sports Illusion, Sports Reality.* Boston: Houghton, 1981. Print.

Kutner, Lawrence. "Athletics, through a Child's Eyes." *New York Times* 23 Mar. 1989, late ed.: C8. *LexisNexis*. Web. 15 May 1999.

Schmitt, Eric. "Psychologists Take Seat on Little League Bench." *New York Times* 14 Mar. 1988, late ed.: B2. *LexisNexis*. Web. 15 May 1999.

Smith, Nathan, Ronald Smith, and Frank Smoll. *Kidsports: A Survival Guide for Parents.* Reading: Addison, 1983. Print.

Tosches, Rich. "Peewee Football: Is It Time to Blow the Whistle?" *Los Angeles Times* 3 Dec. 1988: A1+. *LexisNexis*. Web. 22 May 1999.

"What about My Child?" *Little League Online.* Little League Baseball, Incorporated, 1999. Web. 30 May 1999.

"Your Role as a Little League Parent." *Little League Online.* Little League Baseball, Incorporated, 1999. Web. 30 May 1999.

Statsky lists eleven sources, all of which are cited in her essay — that is, identified and referenced to this alphabetical list of sources. The sources not only provide material for her argument, but also contribute to her authority because readers can look over the list and get an impression about whether the sources as a group seem reputable and trustworthy.

RICHARD ESTRADA was the associate editor of the *Dallas Morning News* editorial page and a syndicated columnist whose essays appeared regularly in the *Washington Post*, the *Los Angeles Times*, and other major newspapers. He was best known as a thoughtful, independent-minded commentator on immigration and social issues. Before joining the *Dallas Morning News* in 1988, Estrada worked as a congressional staff member and as a researcher at the Center for Immigration Studies in Washington, D.C. In the 1990s, he was appointed to the U.S. Commission on Immigration Reform. Following his death at the age of forty-nine in 1999, the Richard Estrada Fellowship in Immigration Studies was established in his honor.

Estrada wrote this essay during the 1995 baseball World Series in which the Atlanta Braves played the Cleveland Indians. The series drew the public's attention to the practice of dressing team mascots like Native Americans on the warpath and encouraging fans to rally their team with gestures like the "tomahawk chop" and pep yells like the "Indian chant." The controversy over these practices revitalized a longstanding debate over naming sports teams with words associated with Native Americans. Several high schools and at least one university, Stanford, have changed the names of their sports teams because of this ongoing controversy. A coworker remarked that in his newspaper columns, Estrada "firmly opposed separating the American people into competing ethnic and linguistic groups." As you read this essay, think about his purpose in writing this position essay and how it seeks to bring different groups together.

Sticks and Stones and Sports Team Names
Richard Estrada

When I was a kid living in Baltimore in the late 1950s, there was only one professional sports team worth following. Anyone who ever saw the movie *Diner* knows which one it was. Back when we liked Ike, the Colts were the gods of the gridiron and Memorial Stadium was their Mount Olympus. 1

Ah, yes: The Colts. The Lions. Da Bears. Back when defensive tackle Big Daddy Lipscomb was letting running backs know exactly what time it was, a young fan could easily forget that in a game where men were men, the teams they played on were not invariably named after animals. Among others, the Packers, the Steelers and the distant 49ers were cases in point. But in the roll call of pro teams, one name in particular always discomfited me: the Washington Redskins. Still, however willing I may have been to go along with the name as a kid, as an adult I have concluded that using an ethnic group essentially as a sports mascot is wrong. 2

The Redskins and the Kansas City Chiefs, along with baseball teams like the Atlanta Braves and the Cleveland Indians, should find other names that avoid highlighting ethnicity. 3

By no means were such names originally meant to disparage Native Americans. The noble symbols of the Redskins or college football's Florida State Seminoles or the Illinois Illini are meant to be strong and proud. Yet, ultimately, the practice of using a people as mascots is dehumanizing. It sets them apart from the rest of society. It promotes the politics of racial aggrievement at a moment when our storehouse is running over with it. 4

The World Series between the Cleveland Indians and the Atlanta Braves reignited the debate. In the chill night air of October, tomahawk chops and war chants suddenly became far more familiar to millions of fans, along with the ridiculous and offensive cartoon logo of Cleveland's "Chief Wahoo." 5

The defenders of team names that use variations on the Indian theme argue that tradition should not be sacrificed at the altar of political correctness. In truth, 6 the nation's No. 1 P.C. [politically correct] school, Stanford University, helped matters some when it changed its team nickname from "the Indians" to "the Cardinals." To be sure, Stanford did the right thing, but the school's status as P.C. without peer tainted the decision for those who still need to do the right thing.

Another argument is that ethnic group leaders are too inclined to cry wolf in alleging racial insensitivity. Often, this is the case. But no one should overlook genuine cases of political insensitivity in an attempt to avoid accusations of hypersensitivity and political correctness.   7

The real world is different from the world of sports entertainment. I recently heard a father who happened to be a Native American complain on the radio that his child was being pressured into participating in celebrations of Braves baseball. At his kid's school, certain days are set aside on which all children are told to dress in Indian garb and celebrate with tomahawk chops and the like.   8

That father should be forgiven for not wanting his family to serve as somebody's mascot. The desire to avoid ridicule is legitimate and understandable. Nobody likes to be trivialized or deprived of their dignity. This has nothing to do with political correctness and the provocations of militant leaders.   9

Against this backdrop, the decision by newspapers in Minneapolis, Seattle and Portland to ban references to Native American nicknames is more reasonable than some might think.   10

What makes naming teams after ethnic groups, particularly minorities, reprehensible is that politically impotent groups continue to be targeted, while politically powerful ones who bite back are left alone. How long does anyone think the name "Washington Blackskins" would last? Or how about "the New York Jews"?   11

With no fewer than 10 Latino ballplayers on the Cleveland Indians' roster, the team could change its name to "the Banditos." The trouble is, they would be missing the point: Latinos would correctly object to that stereotype, just as they rightly protested against Frito-Lay's use of the "Frito Bandito" character years ago.   12

It seems to me that what Native Americans are saying is that what would be intolerable for Jews, blacks, Latinos and others is no less offensive to them. Theirs is a request not only for dignified treatment, but for fair treatment as well. For America to ignore the complaints of a numerically small segment of the population because it is small is neither dignified nor fair.   13

Making Connections to Personal and Social Issues: Name-Calling

As children, we may say, "Sticks and stones will break my bones, but words will never hurt me." Most children, however, recognize the power of words, especially words that make them feel different or inferior.

Make a list of words that are used to refer to groups with which you identify. Try to think of words associated with your ethnicity, religion, gender, interests, geographic region, or any other factor. (Are you perhaps a redneck Okie good ole boy religious fanatic?) Which of the words on your list, if any, do you consider insulting? Why? Would you consider someone who called you these names insensitive?

With two or three other students, discuss your name-calling lists, giving examples from your list. Tell when, where, and by whom you or others in your group have been called these names. Then discuss how these names belittle, condescend, hurt, and insult. Consider what other effects you have felt from name-calling. Some people have speculated that this kind of behavior is motivated by the desire to isolate and establish power over other people or groups. With this power comes more influence and opportunity, purposefully creating inequality. In other words, the name-caller's gain is your loss. Speculate about this view of name-calling in light of your own experience.

Analyzing Writing Strategies

1. Like most writers taking a position, Estrada **states the position** early. To identify it and keep it in view as you learn more about his argument, underline the final sentence in paragraph 2 and the first sentence of paragraph 3. In those sentences, circle Estrada's key terms: *ethnic, mascot,* and *ethnicity.* Then search paragraphs 1, 2, and 3 to determine whether Estrada gives you enough information to let you know unmistakably what the key terms mean. To find out, write your own brief definition of these terms.

2. Reread paragraphs 11 and 12, where Estrada offers hypothetical **examples** of three team names for ethnic groups. Underline each example. Then decide how these examples support Estrada's position. Given his readers, subscribers to the *Dallas Morning News,* how convincing do you think the examples are likely to be? What reactions would you expect from his readers? Write a few sentences about your insights.

Commentary: Presenting the Issue and Plausible Reasons

Although the title of his essay implies its subject, Estrada does not identify the **issue** explicitly until the end of the second paragraph. He begins the essay by remembering his childhood experience as a football fan and explaining that, even as a child, he was made uncomfortable by the practice of naming sports teams for Native Americans. In paragraphs 2–4, he lists team names (Washington Redskins, Kansas City Chiefs, Atlanta Braves, Cleveland Indians, Florida State Seminoles, Illinois Illini) to remind readers how common the practice is. Then, in paragraph 8, he relates an anecdote about a father who not only feels uncomfortable but also feels personally ridiculed as a Native American when his son's school celebrates Braves' victories with Indian costumes and tomahawk chops. Estrada uses this anecdote to demonstrate that the issue is important and worth taking seriously.

Estrada presents the issue in this way to appeal to the readers of his column in the politically conservative *Dallas Morning News.* He apparently assumes that unless he can convince his readers that the issue of sports teams' names is significant, many readers would dismiss it as unimportant or as advancing a liberal agenda. Therefore, Estrada tries to make his readers empathize with what he calls a real-world issue, one that actually hurts kids (paragraph 8). When you present the issue of your own essay, you also may need to help readers understand why it is important and for whom.

Presenting the issue is just a beginning. To convince readers, Estrada has to give the **reasons** that he believes naming sports teams for ethnic groups is detrimental. He gives two: because it treats people like team mascots and it singles out a politically weak group. Moreover, to be convincing, the reasons have to seem plausible to readers; and if readers are convinced by the support Estrada provides to show the effects of treating people like mascots, then they will be inclined to agree with Estrada that the practice is wrong. Similarly, if readers are convinced also that naming sports teams for Native Americans unfairly singles out a politically weak group, then they would be even more likely to agree with Estrada's conclusion.

Considering Topics for Your Own Essay

List some issues that involve what you believe to be unfair treatment of any group. For example, should a law be passed to make English the official language in this country, requiring that election ballots and drivers' tests be printed only in English? Should teenagers be required to get their parents' permission to obtain birth-control information and contraception? What is affirmative action, and should it be used in college admissions for underrepresented groups? Should colleges publish guidelines for discussions in classes to protect any group from either blatant or inadvertent discrimination? Should telling jokes about any group be banned from workplaces?

AMITAI ETZIONI (b. 1929) has written numerous articles and books reflecting his commitment to a communitarian agenda, including, most recently, *My Brother's Keeper: A Memoir and a Message* (2003) and *From Empire to Community: A New Approach to International Relations* (2004). Professor of sociology at George Washington University for many years, he is also Director of the Institute for Communitarian Policy Studies there.

The following essay was originally published in 1986 in the *Miami Herald*, a major newspaper that circulates in South Florida. The original headnote identifies Etzioni as the father of five sons, including three teenagers, and points out that his son Dari helped Etzioni write this essay — although it does not say what Dari contributed.

Before you read, think about the part-time jobs you held during high school — not just summer jobs but those you worked during the months when school was in session. Recall the pleasures and disappointments of these jobs. In particular, think about what you learned that might have made you a better student and prepared you for college. Perhaps you worked at a fast-food restaurant. If not, you have probably been in many such places and have observed students working there.

Working at McDonald's

Amitai Etzioni

McDonald's is bad for your kids. I do not mean the flat patties and the white-flour buns; I refer to the jobs teen-agers undertake, mass-producing these choice items.   1

As many as two-thirds of America's high school juniors and seniors now hold down part-time paying jobs, according to studies. Many of these are in fast-food chains, of which McDonald's is the pioneer, trend-setter and symbol.

At first, such jobs may seem right out of the Founding Fathers' educational manual for how to bring up self-reliant, work-ethic-driven, productive youngsters. But in fact, these jobs undermine school attendance and involvement, impart few skills that will be useful in later life, and simultaneously skew the values of teen-agers — especially their ideas about the worth of a dollar.

It has been a longstanding American tradition that youngsters ought to get paying jobs. In folklore, few pursuits are more deeply revered than the newspaper route and the sidewalk lemonade stand. Here the youngsters are to learn how sweet are the fruits of labor and self-discipline (papers are delivered early in the morning, rain or shine), and the ways of trade (if you price your lemonade too high or too low . . .).

Roy Rogers, Baskin Robbins, Kentucky Fried Chicken, *et al.* may at first seem nothing but a vast extension of the lemonade stand. They provide very large numbers of teen jobs, provide regular employment, pay quite well compared to many other teen jobs and, in the modern equivalent of toiling over a hot stove, test one's stamina.

Closer examination, however, finds the McDonald's kind of job highly uneducational in several ways. Far from providing opportunities for entrepreneurship (the lemonade stand) or self-discipline, self-supervision and self-scheduling (the paper route), most teen jobs these days are highly structured — what social scientists call "highly routinized."

True, you still have to have the gumption to get yourself over to the hamburger stand, but once you don the prescribed uniform, your task is spelled out in minute detail. The franchise prescribes the shape of the coffee cups; the weight, size, shape and color of the patties; and the texture of the napkins (if any). Fresh coffee is to be made every eight minutes. And so on. There is no room for initiative, creativity, or even elementary rearrangements. These are breeding grounds for robots working for yesterday's assembly lines, not tomorrow's high-tech posts.

There are very few studies on the matter. One of the few is a 1984 study by Ivan Charper and Bryan Shore Fraser. The study relies mainly on what teen-agers write in response to questionnaires rather than actual observations of fast-food jobs. The authors argue that the employees develop many skills such as how to operate a food-preparation machine and a cash register. However, little attention is paid to how long it takes to acquire such a skill, or what its significance is.

What does it matter if you spend 20 minutes to learn to use a cash register, and then — "operate" it? What "skill" have you acquired? It is a long way from learning to work with a lathe or carpenter tools in the olden days or to program computers in the modern age.

A 1980 study by A. V. Harrell and P. W. Wirtz found that, among those students who worked at least 25 hours per week while in school, their unemployment rate four years later was half of that of seniors who did not work. This is an impressive statistic. It must be seen, though, together with the finding that many who begin as part-time employees in fast-food chains drop out of high school and are gobbled up in the world of low-skill jobs.

Some say that while these jobs are rather unsuited for college-bound, white, middle-class youngsters, they are "ideal" for lower-class, "non-academic," minority youngsters. Indeed, minorities are "over-represented" in these jobs (21 percent of fast-food employees). While it is true that these places provide income, work and even some training to such youngsters, they also tend to perpetuate their disadvantaged status. They provide no career ladders, few marketable skills, and undermine school attendance and involvement.

11

The hours are often long. Among those 14 to 17, a third of fast-food employees (including some school dropouts) labor more than 30 hours per week, according to the Charper-Fraser study. Only 20 percent work 15 hours or less. The rest: between 15 and 30 hours.

12

Often the stores close late, and after closing one must clean up and tally up. In affluent Montgomery County, Md., where child labor would not seem to be a widespread economic necessity, 24 percent of the seniors at one high school in 1985 worked as much as five to seven days a week; 27 percent, three to five. There is just no way such amounts of work will not interfere with school work, especially homework. In an informal survey published in the most recent yearbook of the high school, 58 percent of seniors acknowledged that their jobs interfere with their school work.

13

The Charper-Fraser study sees merit in learning teamwork and working under supervision. The authors have a point here. However, it must be noted that such learning is not automatically educational or wholesome. For example, much of the supervision in fast-food places leans toward teaching one the wrong kinds of compliance: blind obedience, or shared alienation with the "boss."

14

Supervision is often both tight and woefully inappropriate. Today, fast-food chains and other such places of work (record shops, bowling alleys) keep costs down by having teens supervise teens with often no adult on the premises.

15

There is no father or mother figure with which to identify, to emulate, to provide a role model and guidance. The work-culture varies from one place to another: Sometimes it is a tightly run shop (must keep the cash registers ringing); sometimes a rather loose pot party interrupted by customers. However, only rarely is there a master to learn from, or much worth learning. Indeed, far from being places where solid adult work values are being transmitted, these are places where all too often delinquent teen values dominate. Typically, when my son Oren was dishing out ice cream for Baskin Robbins in upper Manhattan, his fellow teen-workers considered him a sucker for not helping himself to the till. Most youngsters felt they were entitled to $50 severance "pay" on their last day on the job.

16

The pay, oddly, is the part of the teen work-world that is most difficult to evaluate. The lemonade stand or paper route money was for your allowance. In the old days, apprentices learning a trade from a master contributed most, if not all, of their income to their parents' household. Today, the teen pay may be low by adult standards, but it is often, especially in the middle class, spent largely or wholly by the teens. That is, the youngsters live free at home ("after all, they are high school kids") and are left with very substantial sums of money.

17

Where this money goes is not quite clear. Some use it to support themselves, especially among the poor. More middle-class kids set some money aside to help pay for college, or save it for a major purchase — often a car. But large amounts

18

seem to flow to pay for an early introduction into the most trite aspects of American consumerism: flimsy punk clothes, trinkets and whatever else is the last fast-moving teen craze.

One may say that this is only fair and square; they are being good American consumers and spend their money on what turns them on. At least, a cynic might add, these funds do not go into illicit drugs and booze. On the other hand, an educator might bemoan that these young, yet unformed individuals, so early in life driven to buy objects of no intrinsic educational, cultural or social merit, learn so quickly the dubious merit of keeping up with the Joneses in ever-changing fads, promoted by mass merchandising.   19

Many teens find the instant reward of money, and the youth status symbols it buys, much more alluring than credits in calculus courses, European history or foreign languages. No wonder quite a few would rather skip school — and certainly homework — and instead work longer at a Burger King. Thus, most teen work these days is not providing early lessons in the work ethic; it fosters escape from school and responsibilities, quick gratification and a short cut to the consumeristic aspects of adult life.   20

Thus, parents should look at teen employment not as automatically educational. It is an activity — like sports — that can be turned into an educational opportunity. But it can also easily be abused. Youngsters must learn to balance the quest for income with the needs to keep growing and pursue other endeavors that do not pay off instantly — above all education.   21

Go back to school.   22

Making Connections to Personal and Social Issues: Job Skills

Etzioni argues that working at McDonald's (or any other fast-food place) does not teach the kinds of skills and habits required for success in jobs requiring personal initiative and self-monitoring. He points out that at McDonald's workers never get to practice "entrepreneurship [initiative, risk-taking, speculation, self-promotion] . . . or self-discipline, self-supervision and self-scheduling" (paragraph 6). He asserts that there is "no room for initiative, creativity, or even elementary rearrangements" (paragraph 7).

With two or three other students, describe in turn the most McDonald's-like job you have held. Then, in turn again, describe a job (if you've had one) that gave you practice in even one of the work virtues Etzioni mentions and explain how it did so. (If you have never held a job, talk about why you have focused your priorities elsewhere.) Finally, describe for each other the ideal job or career you envision for yourself and how you think your work or other out-of-school experience has — or has not — helped prepare you for it. (You may have noticed that your work on the writing assignments in this course enables you to practice many of the virtues in Etzioni's list.)

Analyzing Writing Strategies

1. To see how Etzioni makes use of statistics (numbers) to **support** his argument, underline the statistics in paragraphs 2, 10, 11, 12, and 13. Underline also any

references to the sources of these statistics. Reviewing these, how would you explain Etzioni's repeated reliance on statistics? How might his intended readers, parents of teenagers reading the *Miami Herald* newspaper, have been influenced by the statistics? Write a few sentences about your insights.

2. A responsible writer taking a position on an issue does not define an issue and assert a position on it and then walk away. On the contrary, the writer knows that an argument for a position does not begin until **reasons** are given, and Etzioni gives several. Underline the most direct statements of Etzioni's reasons, the first sentence in paragraphs 6, 15, and 16, and the last sentence in paragraph 20. Then, for yourself, make a concise list of these reasons, reducing each one to no more than four or five words. From the point of view, first, of high school students and, then, of their parents, identify the one reason likely to be most convincing and the one likely to be least convincing. Explain briefly why you made these choices. Finally, try to think of another reason Etzioni might have offered to support his position.

Commentary: Anticipating Readers' Likely Objections

At key points throughout his essay, Etzioni acknowledges readers' likely objections and then **counterargues** them. In paragraph 3 he acknowledges that some readers will believe that McDonald's-type jobs are good because they teach teenagers to become "self-reliant, work-ethic-driven, productive youngsters." Although he suggests that he shares with his readers these standards for evaluating jobs for teenagers, Etzioni makes clear that he disagrees about the value of jobs exemplified by McDonald's.

In paragraph 8 he acknowledges that Charper and Fraser's research finding that "employees develop many skills" seems to directly contradict his own claim that fast-food jobs "impart few skills that will be useful in later life" (paragraph 3). He handles this objection by accepting as fact Charper and Fraser's finding but counterarguing that the kinds of skills learned by fast-food workers are the wrong skills: "highly routinized" skills (paragraph 6) that prepare young people to work on "yesterday's assembly lines, not tomorrow's high-tech posts" (paragraph 7).

Similarly, in paragraph 10 Etzioni acknowledges as "impressive" Harrell and Wirtz's statistic showing that students who work twenty-five hours or more per week in high school are employed four years later at a higher rate than those who do not. He then counterargues, however, by noting that "many who begin as part-time employees in fast-food chains drop out of high school and are gobbled up in the world of low-skill jobs." He concludes this refutation by implicitly comparing McDonald's-type jobs to the school tracking system that separates "(non-academic)" and "college-bound" students (paragraph 11). Instead of providing minority youngsters with an opportunity to advance, he argues, such jobs "perpetuate their disadvantaged status" because they "provide no career ladders, few marketable skills, and undermine school attendance and involvement."

Etzioni has his readers very much in mind as he writes this essay. He anticipates how they might respond to his argument. Writers have three options in anticipating readers' objections: They can simply acknowledge readers' concerns, they can accommodate them by making concessions, or they can try to refute them. Etzioni chooses this third option. When you write your essay, you will face these same choices.

Considering Topics for Your Own Essay

Etzioni focuses on a single kind of part-time work, takes a position on how worthwhile it is, and recommends against it. You could write a very similar kind of essay. For example, you could take a position for or against students' participating in other kinds of part-time work or recreation during the high school or college academic year. Possibilities include playing on an interscholastic or collegiate sports team, doing volunteer work, or taking an extra class in art or music. The argument might be different for work or recreation pursued during the summer months, when students may able to use all of their time in any way that they prefer: finding paid or volunteer work related to the career they would like to pursue; focusing on learning something important to them, such as another language, roller blading, or a musical instrument; or participating in a weight-loss or exercise program. If you yourself have taken or must take the best-paying job you can find to support yourself and continue to pay for college, you could focus on why the job either strengthens or weakens you as a person, given your life and career goals. Writing for other students, you would either recommend the job or activity to them or discourage them from pursuing it, giving reasons and support for your position. Like Etzioni, on the Internet or in the library you might find studies of the gains or losses experienced by students engaging in the activity during their high school or college years.

KAREN STABINER is a journalist specializing in health, women's, and family issues. Her reports have been published in *Vogue*, the *New Yorker, Los Angeles Times*, and *New York Times*. Stabiner is the author of six books, the most recent being *All Girls: Single-Sex Education and Why It Matters* (2002) and *My Girl: Adventures with a Teen in Training* (2005). She is the mother of a teenage daughter. This essay was first published in the *Washington Post* Sunday Outlook section in 2002.

Boys Here, Girls There: Sure, If Equality's the Goal
Karen Stabiner

Many parents may be wondering what the fuss was about this past week, when the Bush administration endorsed single-sex public schools and classes. Separating the sexes was something we did in the days of auto shop and home ec, before Betty Friedan, Gloria Steinem and Title IX.[1] How, then, did an apparent return to the Fifties come to symbolize educational reform? 1

Here's how: By creating an alternate, parallel universe where smart matters more than anything, good looks hold little currency and a strong sense of self 2

---

[1] Friedan and Steinem were pioneers in the feminist movement that began in the 1960s. Title IX of the Education Amendments of 1972 is the federal legislation that bans sexual discrimination in public schools, whether in academics or athletics.

trumps a date on Saturday night — a place where "class clown" is a label that young boys dread and "math whiz" is a term of endearment for young girls.

I have just spent three years working on a book about two all-girls schools, the private Marlborough School in Los Angeles, and The Young Women's Leadership School of East Harlem (TYWLS), a six-year-old public school in New York City. I went to class, I went home with the girls, I went to dances and basketball games and faculty meetings, and what I learned is this: Single-sex education matters, and it matters most to the students who historically have been denied access to it.

Having said that, I do not intend to proselytize. Single-sex education is not the answer to everyone's prayers. Some children want no part of it and some parents question its relevance. The rest of us should not stop wondering what to do with our coeducational public schools just because of this one new option.

But single-sex education can be a valuable tool — if we target those students who stand to benefit most. For years, in the name of upholding gender equity, we have practiced a kind of harsh economic discrimination. Sociologist Cornelius Riordan says that poor students, minorities and girls stand to profit most from a single-sex environment. Until now, though, the only students who could attend a single-sex school were the wealthy ones who could afford private tuition, the relatively few lucky students who received financial aid or those in less-expensive parochial schools. We denied access to the almost 90 percent of American students who attend public schools.

For the fortunate ones — like the girls at Marlborough — the difference is one of attitude, more than any quantifiable measure; their grades and scores may be similar to the graduates of coed prep schools, but they perceive themselves as more competent, more willing to pursue advanced work in fields such as math and science.

At TYWLS, though, the difference is more profound. Students there are predominantly Latina and African American, survivors of a hostile public system. Half of New York's high school students fail to graduate on time, and almost a third never graduate. Throughout the nation, one in six Latina and one in five African American teens become pregnant every year. But most of the members of TYWLS's two graduating classes have gone on to four-year colleges, often the first members of their families to do so, and pregnancy is the stark exception.

There are now 11 single-sex public schools in the United States, all of which serve urban students, many of them in lower-income neighborhoods. Most are side-by-side schools that offer comparable programs for boys and girls in the same facility. The stand-alone girls' schools say that they are compensating for years of gender discrimination; several attempts at similar schools for boys have failed, however, casualties of legal challenges.

Now, thanks to a bipartisan amendment to President Bush's education reform bill, sponsored by Sens. Kay Bailey Hutchison (R-Tex.) and Hillary Rodham Clinton (D-N.Y.), the administration is about to revise the way it enforces Title IX, to allow for single-sex schools and classes.

The first objections last week came from the National Organization for Women and the New York Civil Liberties Union, both of which opposed the opening of TYWLS in the fall of 1996. The two groups continue to insist — as though it were

1896 and they were arguing *Plessy v. Ferguson*[2] — that separate can never be equal. I appreciate NOW's wariness of the Bush administration's endorsement of single-sex public schools, since I am of the generation that still considers the label "feminist" to be a compliment — and many feminists still fear that any public acknowledgment of differences between the sexes will hinder their fight for equality.

But brain research has shown us that girls and boys develop and process information in different ways; they do not even use the same region of the brain to do their math homework. We cannot pretend that such information does not exist just because it conflicts with our ideology. If we hang on to old, quantifiable measurements of equality, we will fail our children. If we take what we learn and use it, we have the chance to do better.

Educators at single-sex schools already get it: Equality is the goal, not the process. There may be more than one path to the destination — but it is the arrival, not the itinerary, that counts.

Some researchers complain that we lack definitive evidence that single-sex education works. There are so many intertwined variables; the students at TYWLS might do well because of smaller class size, passionate teachers and an aggressively supportive atmosphere. Given that, the absence of boys might be beside the point.

The American Association of University Women called for more research even after publishing a 1998 report that showed some girls continued to suffer in the coed classroom. But it is probably impossible to design a study that would retire the question permanently, and, as TYWLS's first principal, Celenia Chevere, liked to say, "What am I supposed to do with these girls in the meantime?"

What is this misplaced reverence for the coed school? Do not think that it was designed with the best interests of all children at heart. As education professors David and Myra Sadker explained in their 1994 book, *Failing at Fairness: How America's Schools Cheat Girls*, our schools were originally created to educate boys. In the late 1700s, girls went to class early in the morning and late in the day — and unlike the boys, they had to pay for the privilege. When families demanded that the public schools do more for their girls, school districts grudgingly allowed the girls into existing classrooms — not because it was the best way to teach children but because no one had the money to build new schools just for girls. Coed classrooms are not necessarily better. They just are.

For those who like hard data, here is a number: 1,200 girls on the waiting list for a handful of spaces in the ninth grade at TYWLS. There is a growing desire for public school alternatives, for an answer more meaningful than a vague if optimistic call for system-wide reform. The demand for single-sex education exists — and now the Bush administration must figure out how to supply it.

Implementation will not be easy. Girls may learn better without boys, but research and experience show that some boys seem to need the socializing influence of girls: Will there be a group of educational handmaidens, girls who are

---

[2] A U.S. Supreme Court decision upholding racial segregation: "Separate" facilities for blacks and whites were constitutional as long as they were "equal." This ruling was not struck down until 1954.

consigned to coed schools to keep the boys from acting out? Who will select the chosen few who get to go to single-sex schools, and how will they make that choice? Will they take students who already show promise or those who most need help? Or perhaps the philosophy of a new pair of boys' and girls' schools in Albany, N.Y., provides the answer: Take the poorest kids first.

Whatever the approach, no one is calling for a wholesale shift to segregation by gender, and that means someone will be left out. Single-sex public schools perpetuate the kind of two-tiered system that used to be based solely on family income, even if they widen the net. But that has always been true of innovative public schools, and it is no reason to hesitate.   18

The most troubling question about single-sex public education — Why now? — has nothing to do with school. When support comes so readily from opposite ends of the political spectrum, it is reasonable to ask why everyone is so excited, particularly given the political debate about vouchers and school choice.   19

If the intention is to strengthen the public school system by responding to new information about how our children learn, then these classes can serve as a model of innovative teaching techniques, some of which can be transported back into existing coed classrooms. Single-sex public schools and classes, as odd as it may sound, are about inclusion; any school district that wants one can have one and everyone can learn from the experience.   20

But if this is about siphoning off the best and potentially brightest, and ignoring the rest, then it is a cruel joke, a warm and fuzzy set-up for measures like vouchers. If single-sex becomes a satisfying distraction from existing schools that desperately need help, then it only serves to further erode the system. The new educational reform law is called the No Child Left Behind Act, an irresistible sentiment with a chilling edge to it — did we ever actually intend to leave certain children behind? The challenge, in developing these new schools and programs, is to make them part of a dynamic, ongoing reform, and not an escape hatch from a troubled system.   21

Making Connections to Personal and Social Issues: Paradoxes

Stabiner's argument for same-sex education presents a series of paradoxes. (A paradox is a seeming contradiction, something contrary to expectation, hard to believe at first.) Perhaps the most important one is the idea that girls learn math differently from the way boys learn it. Another is the possibility that girls' greatest chance for high achievement and full equality of opportunity with boys requires that girls be segregated from boys during their schooling. The first seems like a paradox because we are used to thinking of the human brain as functioning similarly among women and men. The latter seems like a paradox perhaps because of the long-standing belief that "separate" can never truly be "equal." Stabiner argues that observation, research, and science can and should contradict or overturn such traditional thinking, thereby resolving an apparent paradox.

With two or three other students, discuss paradoxes in your lives that disclose gaps between what you once thought was true but now question or doubt. First, each of you on your own should list two or three paradoxes in your life, situations where your own observations, experiences, or learning have contradicted what you were taught when you were younger either at home, in school, or in your religious (or another kind of) community. Then, together, present your paradoxes to each other and report or speculate about what kinds of new experiences, observations, or knowledge created each of the paradoxes. Mention whether you have resolved the paradoxes and are troubled or satisfied with your conclusions.

Analyzing Writing Strategies

1. Stabiner gives three **reasons** for her position. To anchor the reasons you will examine closely, first underline the position they support: the last sentence, following the colon, at the end of paragraph 3. (Notice that Stabiner reiterates this position at the beginning of paragraph 5.) Then underline the reasons, found in the first sentence of paragraphs 5, 11, and 16. Finally, write a sentence or two explaining the connection, as you see it, between the three reasons and the position statement.

2. Stabiner provides **support** for each of her reasons. To see how she supports her first reason — that single-sex education has value — underline a phrase or sentence in each of paragraphs 5, 6, and 7 that identifies a benefit she asserts for it. Then write a sentence or two explaining how this support is relevant to the reason and evaluating how convincing it is likely to be to readers who may be resisting her argument.

Commentary: Establishing Authority by Counterarguing

Stabiner **establishes her authority** with readers primarily by carefully and unhurriedly counterarguing their likely objections and anticipating their questions. In doing so, she ensures that her readers will hear her out. After she asserts her position (in paragraph 3), she immediately (in the first sentence of paragraph 4), addresses readers' likely concern that she will attempt to "proselytize" — that is, convert them to a belief that single-sex schools are "the answer to everyone's prayers." As proof that she will not do so, she quickly lists three reasons why readers may want to resist her argument: some children would not like single-sex schools, some parents would question their relevance, and other people would prefer to focus on improving coed schools. It may seem odd or even reckless of Stabiner to give readers reasons so early in the essay to resist her argument, but actually it increases her authority. And she needs all the authority and trust she can muster, because she is asking readers to consider a radical social change, a new way of organizing schooling that locates all the girls in one place and all the boys in a different place. Moreover, she is going to ask readers to believe that this change would be as beneficial to children from low-income families as to children in high-income families.

Stabiner may seem to take an even bigger risk by acknowledging that three powerful and respected groups oppose her position: the National Organization for

Women (NOW), the New York Civil Liberties Union, and the American Association of University Women (AAUW). She attempts to refute the reasons for the AAUW's caution (paragraph 14) and takes a more subtle approach to NOW's resistance (paragraphs 10–11). She first concedes that she can sympathize with NOW's reasons for refusing to acknowledge gender differences, but she then insists that NOW is negligent in ignoring brain research showing that girls and boys learn math differently.

In these ways and others, Stabiner establishes her authority by anticipating her readers' questions and objections. Without doing so, she would not even be engaged in reasoned argument, the kind of argument we advocate in this book. Stabiner shows that she is mindful of her readers in every stage of her argument, yet this mindfulness does not weaken her argument or make her unassertive: She boldly asserts her position in the debate about same-sex schooling, and she is unequivocal about her reasons for taking the position she does. There is no mistaking what she believes and why. When you write your essay taking a position, you will want to strive for this clarity while at the same time you acknowledge, concede, or refute your readers' likely questions and objections. Some writers spend even more space counterarguing than arguing, and you should not be reluctant to do so.

Considering Topics for Your Own Essay

Every community frequently debates issues of schooling. These issues range from closing an elementary school because its enrollment has dropped to deciding whether a certain book should be required reading in all high school reading classes at a certain grade level. List further issues you are aware of. (You can be more certain it's a debatable issue if you can phrase it as a *should* question.) You can broaden your list by including issues related to any kind of training or coaching in school or the workplace.

■ Purpose and Audience

Purpose and audience are closely linked when you write an essay arguing a position. In defining your purpose, you also need to anticipate your readers' views. For example, most writers compose essays arguing for a position because they care deeply about the issue. As they develop an argument with their readers in mind, however, writers usually feel challenged to think about their own as well as their readers' feelings and thoughts about the issue.

Writers with strong convictions seek to influence their readers. Assuming that reasoned argument will prevail over prejudice, they try to change readers' minds by presenting compelling reasons and support based on shared values and principles. Nevertheless, they also recognize that in cases where disagreement is profound, it is highly unlikely that a single essay will be able to change readers' minds, no matter how well written it is. When they are addressing an audience that is completely opposed to their position, most writers are satisfied if they can simply win their readers' respect for a different point of view.

Basic Features: Arguing Positions

A Focused Presentation of the Issue

Writers use a variety of strategies to present the issue and prepare readers for their argument. For current, hotly debated issues, the title may be enough to identify the issue. Estrada's allusion to the familiar children's chant in his title "Sticks and Stones and Sports Team Names" is enough to identify the issue for many readers. Statsky gives a brief history of the debate about competitive sports for children. Many writers provide concrete examples early on to make sure that readers can understand the issue. Statsky mentions Peewee Football and Little League Baseball as examples of the kind of organized sports she opposes.

How writers present the issue depends on what they assume readers already know and what they want readers to think about the issue. Therefore, they try to define the issue in a way that promotes their position. Estrada defines the issue of naming sports teams after Native Americans in terms of how it affects individuals, especially children, rather than in terms of liberal or conservative politics. Similarly, Stabiner presents the issue of single-sex education in terms of how it can improve the lives of girls — especially disadvantaged girls — and the opportunities available to them.

A Clear Position

Very often writers declare their position in a thesis statement early in the essay. This strategy has the advantage of letting readers know right away where the writer stands. Etzioni announces his thesis in the first sentence. Statsky places her thesis in the opening paragraph, and Estrada puts his in the second paragraph. Moreover, all of the writers in this chapter restate the thesis at places in the argument where readers could lose sight of the central point. And they reiterate the thesis at the end.

In composing a thesis statement, writers try to make their position unambiguous, appropriately qualified, and clearly arguable. For example, to avoid ambiguity, Estrada uses common words like *wrong*. But because readers may differ on what they consider to be wrong, Estrada demonstrates exactly what he thinks is wrong about naming teams for ethnic groups. To show readers he shares their legitimate concerns about hypersensitivity, Estrada qualifies his thesis to apply only to genuine cases of political insensitivity. Finally, to show that his position is not based solely on personal feelings, Estrada appeals to readers' common sense of right and wrong.

Plausible Reasons and Convincing Support

To argue for a position, writers must give reasons. Even in relatively brief essays, writers sometimes give more than one reason and state their reasons explicitly. Estrada, for instance, gives two reasons for his position that naming sports teams for ethnic groups is detrimental: It treats people like team mascots, and it singles out politically weak groups. Statsky gives four reasons for her opposition to competitive sports for children: They are harmful to the children both physically and psychologically, discourage most from participating, and encourage adults to behave badly.

Writers know they cannot simply assert their reasons. They must support them with examples, statistics, authorities, or anecdotes. We have seen all of these kinds of support used in this chapter. For instance, Statsky uses all of them in her essay — giving examples of common sports injuries that children incur, citing statistics indicating the high percentage of children who drop out of competitive sports, quoting authorities on the physical and psychological hazards of competitive sports for young children, and relating an anecdote of a child vomiting to show the enormous psychological pressure competitive sports put on some children. Stabiner supports one reason that she so favors single-sex education — that it benefits poor students and minorities the most —

by pointing out the facts that Latina and African American girls at a single-sex New York City high school go on to four-year colleges at a much higher rate than their counterparts at coed schools.

Anticipating Opposing Positions and Objections

Writers also try to anticipate other widely held positions on the issue as well as objections and questions readers might raise to an argument. The writers in this chapter counterargue by either accommodating or refuting opposing positions and objections. Estrada does both, implying that he shares his readers' objection to political correctness but arguing that naming sports teams after ethnic groups is a genuine case of political insensitivity and not an in-stance of hypersensitivity. Stabiner refutes the objections of several national organizations to her position that now is the time to try single-sex schooling. Etzioni refutes parents' and students' belief in the benefits of working at McDonald's by arguing that such work does nothing more than train "robots" for "yesterday's assembly lines."

Anticipating readers' positions and objections can enhance the writer's credibility and strengthen the argument. When readers holding an opposing position recognize that the writer takes their position seriously, they are more likely to listen to what the writer has to say. It can also reassure readers that they share certain important values and attitudes with the writer, building a bridge of common concerns among people who have been separated by difference and antagonism.

Arguing a Position

Invention and Research

What is a controversial issue that you have strong feelings about — or that just interests or puzzles you? Gay marriage? A community-service requirement for college graduation? Do some thinking and writing about the issue and some online research if necessary. Then come up with a tentative argument for your position. . . . **See p. 297 for more.**

Planning and Drafting

As you look over what you have written and found out about your subject so far, how can you make a convincing case for your position? How sympathetic are your readers to your point of view? What objections and questions are they likely to raise? Make a plan for your argument, and start drafting it. . . . **See p. 305 for more.**

Critical Reading Guide

What are your draft's strengths and weaknesses? Have you stated your position clearly enough? Does it need to be qualified? Have you provided enough support for all of your reasons? Get a classmate, a friend, a writing tutor, or someone else to read and respond to your essay, especially the parts you are most unsure of. . . . **See p. 310 for more.**

Revising

As you consider your essay again in light of your reader's comments, how can you improve it? Can you assert your position more confidently? Have you ignored a strong opposing argument that you need to address? Go through your draft systematically, making changes wherever necessary. . . . **See p. 312 for more.**

Editing and Proofreading

Have you checked for errors that are especially likely in writing that argues a position? Have you left out any commas that are needed before conjunctions like *and* or *but*? Any commas or semicolons that are needed with conjunctive adverbs like *however* or *consequently*? Look for and correct these and any other errors. . . . **See p. 317 for more.**

The Writing Assignment

Write an essay on a controversial issue. Learn more about the issue, and take a position on it. Present the issue to readers, and develop an argument for the purpose of confirming, challenging, or changing your readers' views on the issue.

To learn about using the *Guide* e-book for invention and drafting, go to bedfordstmartins.com/theguide.

Invention and Research

The following activities will help you find an issue, explore what you know about it, and do any necessary research to develop an argument and counterargument. Each activity is easy to do and in most cases takes only a few minutes. Spreading the activities over several days will help you think critically about your own as well as other people's positions on the issue. Keep a written record of your invention and research to use when you draft and revise your essay.

Finding an Issue to Write About

To find the best possible issue for your essay, list as many possibilities as you can. The following activities will help you make a good choice.

Listing Issues.   *Make a list of issues you might consider writing about.* Begin your list now, and add to it over the next few days. Include issues on which you already have a position and ones you do not know much about but would like to explore further. Do not overlook the issues suggested by the Considering Topics for Your Own Essay activities following the readings in this chapter.

Put the issues you list in the form of questions, like the following examples:

- Should local school boards be allowed to ban books (like *The Adventures of Huckleberry Finn* and *Of Mice and Men*) from school libraries?

- Should teenagers be required to get their parents' permission to obtain birth-control information and contraceptives?

- Should public libraries and schools be allowed to block access to selected Internet sites?

- Should undercover police officers be permitted to pose as high school students to identify sellers and users of drugs?

- Should training in music performance or art (drawing, painting, sculpting) be required of all high school students?

- Should college admission be based solely on academic achievement in high school?

- Should colleges be required to provide child-care facilities for children of students taking classes?

- Should students attending public colleges be required to pay higher tuition fees if they have been full-time students but have not graduated within four years?
- Should elected state or national representatives vote primarily on the basis of their individual conscience, their constituents' interests, or the general welfare?
- Should scientists attempt to clone human beings as they have done with animals?
- Should more money be directed into research to cure [any disease you want to name]?

■ *Listing Issues Related to Identity and Community.*   As the following suggestions indicate, many controversial issues will enable you to explore your personal interests and needs and the expectations of various communities you belong to. List issues that interest you.

- Should student athletes be required to maintain a certain grade point average to participate in college sports?
- Should parents be held responsible legally and financially for crimes committed by their children under age eighteen?
- Should students choose a college or courses that would confirm or challenge their beliefs and values?
- Should high schools or colleges require students to perform community service as a condition for graduation?
- Should children of immigrants who do not speak English be taught in their native language while they are learning English?
- Should all materials related to voting, driving, and income-tax reporting be written only in English or in other languages read by members of the community?
- Should the racial, ethnic, or gender makeup of a police force parallel the makeup of the community it serves?

■ *Listing Issues Related to Work and Career.*   Many current controversial issues will allow you to explore work and career topics. Identify issues that you would consider writing about.

- Should businesses remain loyal to their communities, or should they move wherever labor costs, taxes, or other conditions are more favorable?
- When they choose careers, should people look primarily for jobs that are well paid or for jobs that are personally fulfilling, morally acceptable, or socially responsible?
- Should the state or federal government provide job training or temporary employment to people who are unemployed but willing to work?
- Should the primary purpose of a college education be job training?
- Should drug testing be mandatory for people in high-risk jobs such as bus drivers, heavy-equipment operators, and airplane pilots?

Choosing an Interesting Issue.   *Select an issue from your list that you think would be interesting to explore further.* You may already have an opinion on the issue, or you may have chosen it because you want to learn more about it.

Your choice may be influenced by whether you have time for research or whether your instructor requires you to do research. Issues that have been written about extensively make excellent topics for extended research projects. In contrast, you may feel confident writing about a local community or campus issue without doing much, if any, research.

Exploring the Issue

To explore the issue, you need to define it, determine whether you need to do research, and decide tentatively on your position.

Defining the Issue.   *To begin thinking about the issue, write for a few minutes explaining how you currently understand it.* If you have strong feelings about the issue, briefly explain why, but do not try to present your argument at this time. Focus on clarifying the issue by considering questions like these:

- Who has taken a position on this issue, and what positions have they taken?
- How does the issue affect different groups of people? What is at stake for them?
- What is the issue's history? How long has it been an issue? Has it changed over time? What makes it important now?
- How broad is the issue? What other issues are related to it?

Confirming Your Interest in the Issue.   *If you do not know very much about the issue or the different views people have taken on it, do some research before continuing.* This brief initial period of research should enable you to learn how the issue is being defined, orient you to the debate on it, and help you decide whether you want to learn more and write about it. Talk to other people about the issue. Go online and enter a key term or phrase about the issue into a search tool such as Google or Yahoo! Directory. Or go to the library and look for a keyword or phrase in the catalog, using the keyword search option. The library can also give you access to special online resources; check the library's Web site or ask a librarian for advice. As you are learning about the issue and confirming your interest in it, you might begin keeping a list of the most promising materials you discover. For now, however, your time is better spent quickly surveying two or three issues to confirm your interest in one than in researching any single issue in depth.

If you find that you are not interested in an issue or encounter difficulty defining it, you should switch to another issue. Return to your list of possible issues, and make another choice.

Exploring Your Opinion.   *Write for a few minutes exploring your current thinking on the issue.* What is your current position? Why do you hold this position? What other positions on the issue do you know about? As you develop your argument and learn more about the issue, you may change your mind. Your aim now is merely to record your thinking as of this moment.

Analyzing Potential Readers

Write several sentences describing the readers to whom you will be addressing your argument. Begin by briefly identifying your readers; then use the following questions to help you describe them.

- What position or positions will my readers take on this issue? How entrenched are these positions likely to be?

- What do my readers know about the issue? In what contexts are they likely to have encountered it? In what ways might the issue affect them personally or professionally?

- How far apart on the issue are my readers and I likely to be? What fundamental differences in worldview or experience might keep us from agreeing? Which of my readers' values might most influence their view of the issue?

- Why would I want to present my argument to these particular readers? What could I realistically hope to achieve — convincing them to adopt my point of view, getting them to reconsider their own position, confirming or challenging some of their underlying beliefs and values?

Testing Your Choice

Decide whether you should proceed with this particular issue. Giving up on a topic after you have worked on it is bound to be frustrating, but if the issue has not come into focus for you, starting over may be the wisest course of action. (The collaborative activity on page 301 may also help you decide whether to go on with this issue or begin looking for an alternative.)

Do You Know Enough?   Review your invention notes to see whether you understand the issue well enough to continue working with it. To make this decision, try to answer the following questions:

- Do I now know enough about the issue or can I learn what I need to know in the time I have remaining?

- Have I begun to understand the issue well enough to present it to readers — to describe it for them and explain the importance or significance of the issue? (You need not understand at this point how your entire argument will develop.)

Do You Care Enough?   Unless your instructor has chosen the issue for you, you have the opportunity to choose an issue you truly care about. Commitment to an issue can flower as you research the issue and begin writing about it. This commitment is so important, however, that you should try to decide now whether you are willing to put in the time and work needed to develop a thoughtful essay arguing for your position. To decide whether you can make this commitment, try to answer the following questions:

- Do you feel a personal need to reach a deeper understanding of the issue? If so, on what in your experience might this need be based? What is there about the issue itself that draws you to it, that perhaps makes you feel impelled to write about it? What do you think you might gain by writing about the issue? Is the issue so important to you that you are willing to arrange your schedule over the next two or three weeks to spend the time and attention needed to produce an informed, thoughtful draft of your argument?

- Does the importance of the issue inspire you to want to learn about other people's points of view on the issue and to develop an argument that addresses your readers' particular concerns and questions? What could you say at this point about the social or political significance of the issue? Does it really matter to anyone but you? If you suspect that the issue is not one of current widespread concern, do you think you might be able to argue convincingly at the beginning of your essay that it ought to be of concern?

At this point in your invention work, you will find it helpful to get together with two or three other students to discuss the issue you have tentatively chosen.

Arguers: In turn, each of you identify the issue you are planning to write about. Explain briefly why you care about it personally and why you think your intended readers might see it as important. Then tell the most important reason that you have taken the position you have on the issue.

Listeners: Tell the arguer what you know about the issue and what you think makes it worth arguing about. Then try to suggest one thing the arguer could say to make the favored reason most convincing to the intended readers.

A Collaborative Activity:
Testing Your Choice

Developing Your Argument

To construct a convincing argument, you need to list reasons for your position, choose the most plausible ones, and support them.

Listing Reasons.   *Write down every reason you can think of for why you have taken your position.* You can discover reasons for your position by trying to come up with "because" statements — for example, "I believe that my college should provide day care for the young children of full-time students **because these students are most likely to drop out if they cannot count on reliable day care.**" Given that few convincing arguments rely on only one reason, try to come up with at least two or three.

Choosing the Most Plausible Reasons.   *Write several sentences on each reason to determine which reasons seem most plausible — that is, most likely to be convincing to* *your particular readers. Then identify your most plausible reasons.* If you decide that none of your reasons seems very plausible, you might need to reconsider your position, do some more research, or choose another issue.

Anticipating Readers' Objections and Questions

To construct a convincing argument, you also need to anticipate and decide how you will counterargue readers' objections and questions.

Listing Your Most Plausible Reasons. *Review the choices you made at the end of the preceding activity, and list your two or three most plausible reasons.*

Listing Objections and Questions. *Under each reason, list one or more objections to or questions about it that readers could raise.* You may know how readers will respond to some of your reasons. For others, you may need to be inventive. Imagining yourself as the reader, look for places where your argument is vulnerable. For example, think of an assumption that you are making that others might not accept or a value others might not share. Imagine how people in different situations — different neighborhoods, occupations, age groups, living arrangements — might react to your argument.

Accommodating a Legitimate Objection or Question. *Choose one objection or question that makes sense to you, and write for a few minutes on how you could accommodate it into your argument.* You may be able simply to acknowledge an objection or answer a question and explain why you think it does not negatively affect your argument. If the criticism is more serious, try not to let it shake your confidence. Instead, consider how you can accommodate it, perhaps by conceding the point and qualifying your position or changing the way you argue for it.

If the criticism seems so damaging that you cannot accommodate it into your argument, however, you may need to rethink your position or even consider writing on a different issue. If you arrive at such an impasse, discuss the problem with your instructor; do not abandon your issue unless it is absolutely necessary.

Refuting an Illegitimate Objection or Question. *Choose one objection or question that seems to challenge or weaken your argument, and write for a few minutes on how you could refute it.* Do not choose to refute only the weakest objection while ignoring the strongest one. Consider whether you can show that an objection is based on a misunderstanding or that it does not really damage your argument.

Anticipating Opposing Positions

Now that you have planned your argument and counterargument, you need to consider how you can respond to the arguments for other positions on the issue.

Considering Other Positions. *Identify one or more widely held positions other than your own that people take on the issue.* If you can, identify the individuals or groups who support the positions you list.

To learn more about opposing positions, search for your issue online. To do so, enter a key term — a word or brief phrase — of your issue into a search tool such as Google (http://www.google.com) or Yahoo! Directory (http://dir.yahoo.com). If possible, identify at least two positions different from your own. No matter how well argued, they need not weaken your confidence in your position. Your purpose is to understand opposing positions so well that you can represent one or more of them accurately and counterargue them effectively.

Bookmark or keep a record of promising sites. Download any materials that may help you represent and counterargue opposing positions.

An Online Activity: Researching Opposing Positions

Listing Reasons for the Opposing Position.   *Choose the opposing position you think is likely to be most attractive to your particular readers, and list the reasons people give for taking this position.* Given what you now know, try to represent the argument accurately and fairly. Later, you may need to do some research to find out more about this opposing position.

Accommodating a Plausible Reason.   *Choose one reason that makes sense to you, and write for a few minutes on how you could accommodate it into your argument.* Consider whether you can accommodate the point and put it aside as not really damaging to your central argument. You may also have to consider qualifying your position or changing the way you argue for it.

Refuting an Implausible Reason.   *Choose one reason that you do not accept, and write for a few minutes on how you will plan your refutation.* Do not choose to refute a position no one really takes seriously. Also be careful not to misrepresent other people's positions or to criticize people personally. Do try to get at the heart of your disagreement.

You may want to argue that the values on which the opposing argument is based are not widely shared or are just plain wrong. Or perhaps you can point out that the reasoning is flawed (for instance, showing that an example applies only to certain people in certain situations). Or maybe you can show that the argument lacks convincing support (for instance, that the opposition's statistics can be interpreted differently or that quoted authorities do not qualify as experts). If you do not have all the information you need, make a note of what you need and where you might find it. Later, you can do more research to develop this part of your argument.

Designing Your Document

Think about whether including visual or audio elements — cartoons, photographs, tables, graphs, or snippets from films, television programs, or songs — would strengthen your argument. These are not a requirement of an effective essay arguing a position, but they could be helpful. Consider also whether your readers might benefit from design features such as headings, bulleted or numbered lists, or other elements that would make your essay easier to follow. You could construct your own graphic elements, download materials from the Internet, tape images and sounds from television or other sources, or scan into your document visuals from books and magazines. If you do use visual or audio materials you did not create yourself, be sure to acknowledge your sources in your essay (and request permission from the sources if the essay will be posted on the Web).

In thinking about possible visual aids to your argument, consider the ways in which effective speakers and writers draw upon visual information and evidence to support their claims. You might think back to compelling speeches — or even sermons — you've heard, or to interesting debates or slide shows or campaign ads you've watched. You might also review Web pages for organizations making specific claims on their Web sites.

Defining Your Purpose for Your Readers

Write a few sentences, defining your purpose in writing about your position on this issue for your particular readers. Remember that you already have analyzed your potential readers and developed your argument with these readers in mind. Given these readers, try now to define your purpose by considering the following possibilities and any others that might apply to your writing situation:

- If my readers are likely to be sympathetic to my point of view, what do I hope to achieve — give them reasons to commit to my position, arm them with ammunition to make their own arguments, or win their respect and admiration?

- If my readers are likely to be hostile to my point of view, what do I hope to accomplish — get them to concede that other points of view must be taken seriously, make them defend their reasons, show them how knowledgeable and committed I am to my position, or show them how well I can argue?

- If my readers are likely to take an opposing position but are not staunchly committed to it, what should I try to do — make them question or doubt the reasons and the kinds of support they have for their position, show them how my position serves their interests better, appeal to their values and sense of responsibility, or disabuse them of their preconceptions and prejudices against my position?

Formulating a Tentative Thesis Statement

Write a few sentences that could serve as a thesis statement. Assert your position carefully. You might also forecast your reasons, mentioning them in the order in which you will take them up in your argument. In other words, draft a thesis statement that tells your readers simply and directly what you want them to think about the issue and why.

Estrada states his thesis at the end of the second paragraph: "Still, however willing I may have been to go along with the name as a kid, as an adult I have concluded that using an ethnic group essentially as a sports mascot is wrong." Perhaps the most explicit and fully developed thesis statement in this chapter's readings is Jessica Statsky's. She asserts her thesis at the end of the first paragraph and then qualifies it and forecasts her reasons in the second paragraph:

> When overzealous parents and coaches impose adult standards on children's sports, the result can be activities that are neither satisfying nor beneficial to children.
>
> I am concerned about all organized sports activities for children between the ages of six and twelve. The damage I see results from noncontact as well as contact sports, from sports organized locally as well as those organized nationally. Highly organized competitive sports such as Peewee Football and Little League Baseball are too often played to adult standards, which are developmentally inappropriate for children and can be both physically and psychologically harmful. Furthermore, because they eliminate many children from organized sports before they are ready to compete, they are actually counterproductive for developing either future players or fans. Finally, because they emphasize competition and winning, they unfortunately provide occasions for some parents and coaches to place their own fantasies and needs ahead of children's welfare.

As you formulate your own tentative thesis statement, pay attention to the language you use. It should be clear and unambiguous, emphatic but appropriately qualified, as well as arguable and based on plausible reasons. Although you will most probably refine this thesis statement as you work on your essay, trying now to articulate it will help give your planning and drafting direction and impetus.

■ Planning and Drafting

You should now review what you have learned about the issue, do further research if necessary, and plan your first draft by setting goals and making an outline.

Seeing What You Have

Pause now to reflect on your invention and research notes. Reread everything carefully to decide whether you have enough plausible reasons and convincing support to offer readers and whether you understand the debate well enough to anticipate and respond to your readers' likely objections. It may help, as you read, to annotate your invention writings. If you have done your invention writing on the computer, you may have sentences or whole paragraphs that can be copied and pasted into your draft. Reread what you have written so far to identify the potentially useful material. Look for details that will help you clarify the issue for readers, present a strong argument for your position, and counterargue possible objections and alternative positions. Highlight key words, phrases, or sentences; make marginal notes or electronic annotations.

If your invention notes are skimpy, you may not have given enough thought to the issue or know enough at this time to write a convincing argument about it. You can do further research at this stage or begin drafting and later do research to fill in the blanks.

If you fear that you are in over your head, consult your instructor to determine whether you should make a radical change. For example, your instructor might suggest that you tackle a smaller, more doable aspect of the issue, perhaps one with which you have firsthand experience. It is also possible that your instructor will advise you to give up on this topic for the time being and to try writing on a different issue.

Doing Further Research

If you think you lack crucial information that you will need to plan and draft your essay, this is a good time to do some further research. Consider possible sources, including people you could interview as well as library materials and Internet sites. Then do your research, making sure to note down all the information you will need to cite your sources.

Setting Goals

Before you begin writing your draft, consider some specific goals for your essay. The draft will be easier to write and more focused if you have some clear goals in mind. The following questions will help you set them. You may find it useful to return to them while you are drafting, for they are designed to help you look at specific features and strategies of an essay arguing a position on a controversial issue.

Your Purpose and Readers

- Who are my readers, and what can I realistically hope to accomplish by addressing them?
- Should I write primarily to change readers' minds, to get them to consider my arguments seriously, to confirm their opinions, to urge them to do something about the issue, or to accomplish some other purpose?
- How can I present myself so that my readers will consider me informed, knowledgeable, and fair?

The Beginning

- What opening would capture readers' attention?
- Should I begin as if I were telling a story, with phrases like "When I was" (Estrada) or "Over the past three decades" (Statsky)?
- Should I make clear at the outset exactly what my concerns are and how I see the issue, as Statsky does?

Presentation of the Issue

- Should I place the issue in a historical context or in a personal context, as Estrada does?
- Should I use examples — real or hypothetical — to make the issue concrete for readers, as Estrada does?

- Should I try to demonstrate that the issue is important by citing statistics, quoting authorities, or describing its negative effects, as Statsky does?
- Should I present the issue as a paradox, something hard to believe at first, as Etzioni and Stabiner do?

Your Argument and Counterargument

- How can I present my reasons so that readers will see them as plausible, leading logically to my position, as Stabiner does?
- If I have more than one reason, how should I sequence them?
- Should I forecast my reasons or counterarguments early in the essay, as Statsky does?
- Which objections should I anticipate? Can I concede any objections without undermining my argument, as Estrada and Stabiner do?
- Should I refute any objections, as Etzioni and Stabiner do?
- Which opposing positions should I anticipate? Can I counterargue by showing that the statistics offered by others are not relevant, as Etzioni does?
- Can I support my reasoning by narrating anecdotes (Estrada), pointing out benefits (Stabiner), stressing consequences and losses (Etzioni, Statsky), or quoting research (Statsky, Stabiner, Etzioni)?

The Ending

- How can I conclude my argument effectively? Should I reiterate my thesis, as Estrada and Etzioni do?
- Should I try to unite readers with different allegiances by reminding them of values we share, as Estrada and Stabiner do?
- Could I conclude by looking to the future or by urging readers to take action or make changes, as Statsky does?
- Should I conclude with a challenge, as Etzioni and Stabiner do?

Outlining

An essay arguing a position on a controversial issue contains as many as four basic parts:

1. Presentation of the issue
2. A clear position
3. Reasons and support
4. Anticipating opposing positions and objections

These parts can be organized in various ways. If you expect some of your readers to oppose your argument, you might try to redefine the issue so that these readers can see the possibility that they may share some common values with you after all. To reinforce your connection to readers, you could go on to concede the wisdom of an aspect of their position before presenting the reasons and support for your position. You would conclude by reiterating the shared values on which you hope to build agreement. In this case, an outline might look like this:

Presentation of the issue

Accommodation of some aspect of an opposing position

Thesis statement

First reason with support

Second reason with support (etc.)

Conclusion

If you have decided to write primarily for readers who agree rather than disagree with you, then you might choose to organize your argument as a refutation of opposing arguments to strengthen your readers' convictions. Begin by presenting the issue, stating your position, and reminding readers of your most plausible reasons. Then take up each opposing argument, and try to refute it. You might conclude by calling your supporters to arms. Here is an outline showing what this kind of essay might look like:

Presentation of the issue

Thesis statement

Your most plausible reasons

First opposing argument with refutation

Second opposing argument with refutation (etc.)

Conclusion

There are, of course, many other possible ways to organize an essay arguing for a position on a controversial issue, but these outlines should help you start planning your own essay.

Consider tentative any outlining you do before you begin drafting. Never be a slave to an outline. As you draft, you will usually see ways to improve on your original plan. Be ready to revise your outline, shift parts around, or drop or add parts as you draft. If you use the outlining function of your word processing program, changing your outline will be simple, and you may be able to write the essay simply by expanding the outline.

Drafting

General Advice.   Start drafting your essay, keeping in mind the goals you set while you were planning. Remember also the needs and expectations of your readers; organize, define, and explain with them in mind. Turn off your grammar checker and spelling checker at this stage if you find them distracting. Don't be afraid to skip around in your draft; jump back and fill in a spontaneous idea, or leap ahead and write a later section first if you find that easier. If, as you draft, you find that you need more information, just make a note of what you have to find out and go on to the next point. When you are done drafting, you can search for the information you need. If you get stuck while drafting, explore the problem by using some of the writing activities in the Invention and Research section of this chapter. You may want to review the general drafting advice in Chapter 1.

As you draft, keep in mind that the basis for disagreement about controversial issues often depends on values as much as on credible support. Try to think critically about the values underlying your own as well as others' views so that your argument can take these values into account. Consider the tone of your argument and how you want to come across to readers.

A Sentence Strategy: Concession Followed by Refutation. As you draft, you will need to move back and forth smoothly between direct arguments for your position and counterarguments for your readers' likely objections, questions, and preferred positions on the issue. One useful strategy for making this move is to concede the value of a likely criticism and then to attempt to refute it immediately, either in the same sentence or in the next one.

How do you introduce a brief concession followed by refutation into your argument? The following sentences from Jessica Statsky's essay illustrate several ways to do so (the concessions are in italics, the refutations in bold):

> The primary goal of a professional athlete — winning — is not appropriate for children. Their goals should be having fun, learning, and being with friends. *Although winning does add to the fun,* **too many adults lose sight of what matters and make winning the most important goal.** (paragraph 5)

> *And it is perfectly obvious how important competitive skills are in finding a job.* **Yet the ability to cooperate is also important for success in life.** (10)

In both these examples from different stages in her argument, Statsky concedes the importance or value of some of her readers' likely objections, but then firmly refutes them. (Because these illustrations are woven into an extended argument, you may be better able to appreciate them if you look at them in context by turning to the paragraphs where they appear.) The following examples come from other readings in the chapter:

> *The authors argue that the employees develop many skills such as how to operate a food-preparation machine and a cash register.* **However, little attention is paid to how long it takes to acquire such a skill, or what its significance is.** (Amitai Etzioni, paragraph 8)

> *[M]any feminists still fear that any public acknowledgment of differences between the sexes will hinder their fight for equality.*
> ***But brain research has shown us that girls and boys develop and process information in different ways; they do not even use the same region of the brain to do their math homework.*** (Karen Stabiner, paragraphs 10, 11)

> *Another argument is that ethnic group leaders are too inclined to cry wolf in alleging racial insensitivity.* **Often, this is the case. But no one should overlook genuine cases of political insensitivity in an attempt to avoid accusations of hypersensitivity and political correctness.** (Richard Estrada, paragraph 7)

The concession-refutation move, sometimes called the "yes-but" strategy, is important in most arguments; in fact, it usually recurs, as it does in all the readings in this chapter. Following is an outline of some other kinds of language authors rely on to introduce their concession-refutation moves:

Introducing the concession	*Introducing the refutation that follows*
I understand that	What I think is
I can't prove	But I think
X claims that	As it happens
It is true that	But my point is
Another argument	But
It has been argued that	Nevertheless,
We are told that	My own belief is
Proponents argue that	This argument, however,
This argument seems plausible	But experience and evidence show
One common complaint is	In recent years, however,
I'm not saying. . . . Nor am I saying	But I am saying
Activists insist	Still, in spite of their good intentions
A reader might ask	But the real issue

For more on concession followed by refutation, go to bedfordstmartins.com/theguide and click on Sentence Strategies.

In addition to making the concession-refutation move, you can strengthen your reasoned arguments with other kinds of sentence strategies as well, and you may want to study the discussions of sentences that feature appositives to identify or establish the authority of a source (pp. 177–79), that signal the stages of an argument (pp. 498–99), and that present supporting examples in parallel grammatical form (p. 499).

Critical Reading Guide

Now is the time to get a good critical reading of your draft. Your instructor may arrange such a reading as part of your coursework; if not, you can ask a classmate, friend, or family member to read it over. If your campus has a writing center, you might ask a tutor there to read and comment on your draft using this guide to critical reading. (If you are unable to have someone else review your draft, turn ahead to the Revising section for help reading your own draft with a critical eye.)

▶ **If You Are the Writer.** To provide focused, helpful comments, your reader must know your essay's intended audience, your purpose, and a problem in the draft that you need help solving. Briefly write out this information at the top of your draft.

- *Readers:* To whom are you directing your argument? What do you assume they think about this issue? Do you expect them to be receptive, skeptical, resistant, antagonistic?

- *Purpose:* What effect do you realistically expect your argument to have on these particular readers?

- *Problem:* Ask your reader to help you solve the most important problem you see in your draft. Describe this problem briefly.

▶ **If You Are the Reader.**   Use the following guidelines to help you give constructive comments to others on their position papers.

1. *Read for a First Impression.*   Tell the writer what you think the intended readers would find most and least convincing. If you personally think the argument is seriously flawed, share your thoughts. Then try to help the writer improve the argument for the designated readers.

    Next, consider the problem the writer identified, and respond briefly to that concern now. (If you find that the problem is covered by one of the other guidelines listed below, respond to it in more detail there if necessary.)

2. *Analyze the Way the Issue Is Presented.*   Look at the way the issue is presented, and indicate whether you think that most readers would understand the issue differently. If you think that readers will need more information to grasp the issue and appreciate its importance, ask questions to help the writer fill in whatever is missing.

3. *Assess Whether the Position Is Stated Clearly.*   Write a sentence or two summarizing the writer's position as you understand it from reading the draft. Then identify the sentence or sentences in the draft where the thesis is stated explicitly. (It may be restated in several places.) If you cannot find an explicit statement of the thesis, let the writer know. Given the writer's purpose and audience, consider whether the thesis statement is too strident or too timid and whether it needs to be more qualified, more sharply focused, or more confidently asserted. If you think that the thesis, as presented, is not really arguable — for example, if it asserts a fact no one questions or a matter of personal belief — let the writer know.

4. *Evaluate the Reasons and Support.*   Identify the reasons given for the writer's position. Have any important reasons been left out or any weak ones overemphasized? Indicate any contradictions or gaps in the argument. Point to any reasons that do not seem plausible to you, and briefly explain why. Then note any places where support is lacking or unconvincing. Help the writer think of additional support or suggest sources where more or better support might be found.

Making Comments Electronically
Most word processing software offers features that allow you to insert comments directly into the text of someone else's document. Many readers prefer to make their comments in this way because it tends to be faster than writing on a hard copy and space is virtually unlimited; from the writer's point of view, it also eliminates the problem of deciphering handwritten comments. Even where such special comment features are not available, simply typing comments directly into a document in a contrasting color can provide the same advantages.

For a printable version of this critical reading guide, go to bedfordstmartins.com/theguide.

5. *Assess How Well Opposing Positions and Likely Objections Have Been Handled.* Identify places where opposing arguments or objections are mentioned, and point to any where the refutation could be strengthened or where shared assumptions or values offer the potential for accommodation. Also consider whether the writer has ignored any important opposing arguments or objections.

6. *Consider Whether the Organization Is Effective.* Get an overview of the essay's organization, perhaps by making a scratch outline. Point to any parts that might be more effective earlier or later in the essay. Point out any places where more explicit cueing — transitions, summaries, or topic sentences — would clarify the relationship between parts of the essay.

   • Reread the *beginning*. Will readers find it engaging? If not, see whether you can recommend something from later in the essay that might work better as an opening.

   • Study the *ending*. Does the essay conclude decisively and memorably? If not, suggest an alternative. Could something be moved to the end?

   • Assess the *design features and visuals*. Comment on the contribution of any headings, tables, or other design features and illustrations. Help the writer think of additional design features and illustrations that could make a contribution to the essay.

7. *Give the Writer Your Final Thoughts.* What is this draft's strongest part? What part is most in need of further work?

◼ Revising

Now you are ready to revise your essay. Your instructor or other students may have given you advice on improving your draft. Nevertheless, you may have begun to realize that your draft requires not so much revising as rethinking. For example, you may recognize that your reasons do not lead readers to accept your position, that you cannot adequately support your reasons, or that you have been unable to refute damaging objections to your argument. Consequently, instead of working to improve parts of the draft, you may need to write a new draft that presents a radically different argument. It is not unusual for students — and professional writers — to find themselves in this situation. Learning to make radical revisions is a valuable lesson for all writers.

On the other hand, you may feel quite satisfied that your draft achieves most, if not all, of your goals. In that case, you can focus on refining specific parts of your draft. Very likely you have thought of ways of improving your draft, and you may even have begun improving it. This section will help you get an overview of your draft and revise it accordingly.

Getting an Overview

Consider your draft as a whole, following these two steps:

1. *Reread.* If at all possible, put the draft aside for a day or two before rereading it. When you return to it, start by reconsidering your purpose. Then read the draft straight through, trying to see it as your intended readers will.

2. *Outline.* Make a scratch outline, indicating the basic features as they appear in the draft. Consider using the headings and outline/summary functions of your word processor.

Planning for Revision.   Resist the temptation to dive in and start changing your text until after you have a clear view of the big picture. Using your outline as a guide, move through the document, using the highlighting or commenting tools of your word processor to note comments received from others and problems you want to solve (or mark on a hard copy if you prefer).

Analyzing the Basic Features of Your Own Draft.   Using the questions presented in the Critical Reading Guide on pp. 310–12, reread your draft to identify specific problems you need to solve. Note the problems on your draft.

Studying Readers' Comments.   Review all of the comments you have received from other readers, and add to your notes any suggestions you intend to act on. For each comment, look at the draft to see what might have led the reader to make that particular point. Try to be receptive to any criticism. By letting you see how other readers respond to your draft, these comments provide valuable information about how you might improve it.

Working with Sources

How you represent the views of those who disagree with your position is especially important because it affects your credibility with readers. If you do not represent your opponents' views fairly and accurately, readers very likely will — and probably should — question your honesty. One useful strategy is to insert quoted words and phrases into your summary of the source.

But how do you decide which elements to quote and which to put in your own words? The following sentences from Jessica Statsky's essay illustrate how you might make this decision. Compare the sentence on this page from paragraph 3 of Statsky's essay to the passage on the next page from her source, the Little League Web site. The words Statsky quotes are highlighted.

> Although the official Little League Web site acknowledges that children do risk injury playing baseball, it insists that "severe injuries . . . are infrequent," the risk "far less than the risk of riding a skateboard, a bicycle, or even the school bus" ("What about My Child?").

Support your counterargument by quoting key words when summarizing opposing views

(1) We know that injuries constitute one of parents' foremost concerns, and rightly so. (2) Injuries seem to be inevitable in any rigorous activity, especially if players are new to the sport and unfamiliar with its demands. (3) But because of the safety precautions taken in Little League, severe injuries such as bone fractures are infrequent. (4) Most injuries are sprains and strains, abrasions and cuts and bruises. (5) The risk of serious injury in Little League Baseball is far less than the risk of riding a skateboard, a bicycle, or even the school bus.

Statsky summarizes the Little League's acknowledgement that playing competitive sports can be harmful by condensing the second sentence ("Injuries seem to be inevitable in any rigorous activity, especially if players are new to the sport and unfamiliar with its demands.") into one simple clause ("children do risk injury playing baseball"). Note what her summary leaves out: the Little League's explanation that injuries are "inevitable in any rigorous activity," its emphasis on the increased likelihood of injury when the sport is "new" and "unfamiliar," and the claim that the Little League takes "safety precautions" to prevent serious injury. Statsky omitted these statements because they try to explain away the basic fact she wants to emphasize — that "children do risk injury playing baseball." Demonstrating that the Little League, renowned as the first and probably the most famous provider of organized sports for children, agrees with her about this basic fact lends credibility to Statsky's argument.

But when you omit language and ideas from your summary, you must take care not to misrepresent your source. Statsky makes clear in the second part of her sentence that although the Little League agrees with her on the risk of injury, it disagrees about the seriousness of that risk. By quoting ("it insists that 'severe injuries . . . are infrequent,' 'far less than the risk of riding a skateboard, a bicycle, or even the school bus.'"), she assures readers she has not distorted the Little League's position.

Using Ellipsis Marks in Quotations to Avoid Plagiarism

In an earlier draft, Statsky omitted the quotation marks around the phrase "severe injuries . . . are infrequent," either because she did not realize that brief phrases quoted from a source require quotation marks or because she did not realize that she could have multiple separate quotations from the same source in one sentence. Below is part of her original sentence, followed by the source with the quoted words highlighted.

For more help using ellipsis marks in quotations to avoid plagiarism, go to bedfordstmartins.com/theguide and click on Avoiding Plagiarism Tutorial.

it insists that severe injuries are infrequent, the risk "far less than the risk of riding a skateboard, a bicycle, or even the school bus" ("What about My Child?").

severe injuries such as bone fractures are infrequent. Most injuries are sprains and strains, abrasions and cuts and bruises. The risk of serious injury in Little League Baseball is far less than the risk of riding a skateboard, a bicycle, or even the school bus.

Even though Statsky cites the source, this failure to use quotation marks around language that is borrowed amounts to plagiarism. A simple way to avoid plagiarizing is to use ellipsis marks (. . .) to indicate that words have been omitted:

"severe injuries . . . are infrequent." When you cite sources in a position paper, use quotation marks whenever you use phrases from your source *and* indicate your source. Doing one or the other is not enough; you must do both. For more information on quoting and using ellipses to integrate language from sources into your own sentences, see pages 739–40 in Chapter 22.

Carrying Out Revisions

Having identified problems in your draft, you now need to come up with solutions and — most important — to carry them out. Basically, you have three ways of finding solutions:

1. Review your invention and planning notes for information and ideas to add to your draft.

2. Do additional invention and research to provide material you or your readers think is needed.

3. Look back at the readings in this chapter to see how other writers have solved similar problems.

The following suggestions, which are organized according to the basic features of position papers, will help you get started solving some problems common to them.

Presentation of the Issue

- ***Do readers have difficulty summarizing the issue, or do they see it differently from the way you do?*** Try to anticipate possible misunderstandings or other ways of seeing the issue.

- ***Do readers need more information?*** Consider adding examples, quoting authorities, or simply explaining the issue further.

- ***Does the issue strike readers as unimportant?*** State explicitly why you think it is important and why you think your readers should think so, too. Try to provide an anecdote, facts, or a quote from an authority that would demonstrate its importance.

A Clear Position

- ***Do readers have difficulty summarizing your position or finding your thesis statement?*** You may need to announce your thesis statement more explicitly or rewrite it to prevent misunderstanding.

- ***Do any words seem unclear or ambiguous?*** Use other words, explain what you mean, or add an example to make your position more concrete.

- ***Do you appear to be taking a position that is not really arguable?*** Consider whether your position is arguable. If you believe in your position as a matter of faith and cannot provide reasons and support, then your position probably is not arguable. Consult your instructor about writing about a different issue.

- *Could you qualify your thesis to account for exceptions or strong objections to your argument?* Add language that specifies when, where, under what conditions, or for whom your position applies.

Plausible Reasons and Convincing Support

- *Do readers have difficulty identifying your reasons?* Announce each reason explicitly, possibly with topic sentences. Consider adding a forecast early in the essay so readers know what reasons to expect.
- *Have you left out any reasons?* Consider whether adding particular reasons would strengthen your argument. To fit in new reasons, you may have to reorganize your whole argument.
- *Do any of your reasons seem implausible or contradictory?* Either delete such reasons, or show how they relate logically to your position or to your other reasons.
- *Does your support seem unconvincing or scanty?* Where necessary, explain why you think the support should lead readers to accept your position. Review your invention notes, or do some more research to gather additional examples, statistics, anecdotes, or quotations from authorities.

Anticipation of Opposing Arguments or Objections

- *Do readers have difficulty finding your responses to opposing arguments or objections?* Add transitions that call readers' attention to each response.
- *Do you ignore any important objections or arguments?* Consider adding to your response. Determine whether you should replace a response to a relatively weak objection with a new response to a more important one.
- *Are there any concessions you could make?* Consider whether you should acknowledge the legitimacy of readers' concerns or accommodate particular objections. Show on what points you share readers' values, even though you may disagree on other points. Remember that all of the authors in this chapter concede and then attempt to refute, relying on useful sentence openers like *I understand that. . .*, *What I think is*, and *It is true that . . ., but my point is. . . .*
- *Do any of your attempts at refutation seem unconvincing?* Try to strengthen them. Avoid attacking your opponents. Instead, provide solid support — respected authorities, accepted facts, and statistics from reputable sources — to convince readers that your argument is credible.

The Organization

- *Do readers have trouble following your argument?* Consider adding a brief forecast of your main reasons at the beginning of your essay and adding explicit topic sentences and transitions to announce each reason as it is developed. As all the authors do in this chapter, consider signaling explicitly the logical relations between steps and sentences in your argument. Remember that they use

Checking Sentence Strategies Electronically
To check your draft for a sentence strategy especially useful in essays arguing a position, use your word processor's highlighting function to mark places where you are either making concessions to or trying to refute opposing arguments or objections that readers might have to your argument. Then look at each place, and think about whether you could strengthen your argument at that point by combining concession and refutation, either by moving or adding a concession just before a refutation or by moving or adding a refutation immediately following a concession. For more on the concession-refutation strategy, see p. 309.

both informal signals like *yet* and *still* and formal signals like *moreover, consequently*, and *therefore*.

- ***Does the beginning seem vague and uninteresting?*** Consider adding a striking anecdote or surprising quotation to open the essay, or find something in the essay you could move to the beginning.

- ***Does the ending seem indecisive or abrupt?*** Search your invention notes for a strong quotation, or add language that will reach out to readers. Try moving your strongest point to the ending.

For a revision checklist, go to bedfordstmartins.com/theguide.

- ***Can you add illustrations or any other design features to make the essay more interesting to read and to strengthen your argument?*** Consider incorporating a visual you came across in your research or one you can create on your own.

■ Editing and Proofreading

Now is the time to edit your revised draft for errors in grammar, punctuation, and mechanics and to consider matters of style. Our research has revealed several errors that are especially likely to occur in student essays arguing a position. The following guidelines will help you check and edit your draft for these common errors. This book's Web site also provides interactive online exercises to help you learn to identify and correct some of these errors; to access the exercises for a particular error, go to the URL listed in the margin next to that section of the guidelines.

Checking for Commas before Coordinating Conjunctions. An independent clause is a group of words that can stand alone as a complete sentence. Writers often join two or more such clauses with coordinating conjunctions (*and, but, for, or, nor, so, yet*) to link related ideas in one sentence. Look at one example from Jessica Statsky's essay:

> Winning and losing may be an inevitable part of adult life, but they should not be part of childhood. (paragraph 6)

In this sentence, Statsky links two ideas: (1) that winning and losing may be part of adult life and (2) that they should not be part of childhood. In essays that argue a position, writers often join ideas in this way as they set forth the reasons and support for their positions.

When you join independent clauses, use a comma before the coordinating conjunction so that readers can easily see where one idea stops and the next one starts:

▶ The new immigration laws will bring in more skilled people, but their presence will take jobs away from other Americans.

▶ Sexually transmitted diseases are widespread, and many students are sexually active.

A Note on Grammar and Spelling Checkers
These tools are good at catching certain types of errors, but currently there is no replacement for a good human proofreader. Grammar checkers in particular are extremely limited in what they can usually find, and often they only give you summary information that is not helpful if you do not already understand the rule in question. They are also prone to give faulty advice for fixing problems and to flag correct items as wrong. Spelling checkers cause fewer problems but cannot catch misspellings that are themselves words, such as *to* for *too*.

For practice, go to bedfordstmartins.com/theguide/exercisecentral and click on Commas before Coordinating Conjunctions.

Do not use a comma when the coordinating conjunction joins phrases that are not independent clauses:

▶ Newspaper reporters have visited pharmacies, and observed pharmacists selling steroids illegally.

▶ We need people with special talents, and diverse skills to make the United States a stronger nation.

Checking the Punctuation of Conjunctive Adverbs.   When writers take a position, the reasoning they need to employ seems to invite the use of conjunctive adverbs (*consequently, furthermore, however, moreover, therefore, thus*) to connect sentences and clauses. Conjunctive adverbs that open a sentence should be followed by a comma:

▶ Consequently, many local governments have banned smoking.

▶ Therefore, talented teachers will leave the profession because of poor working conditions and low salaries.

For practice, go to bedfordstmartins.com/theguide and click on Punctuation of Conjunctive Adverbs.

If a conjunctive adverb joins two independent clauses, it must be preceded by a semicolon and followed by a comma:

▶ The recent vote on increasing student fees produced a disappointing turnout; moreover, the presence of campaign literature on ballot tables violated voting procedures.

▶ Children watching television recognize violence but not its intention; thus, they become desensitized to violence.

Conjunctive adverbs that fall in the middle of an independent clause are set off with commas:

▶ Due to trade restrictions, however, sales of Japanese cars did not surpass sales of domestic cars.

For practice, go to bedfordstmartins.com/theguide and click on A Common ESL Problem: Subtle Differences in Meaning.

A Common ESL Problem: Subtle Differences in Meaning.   Because the distinctions in meaning among some common conjunctive adverbs are subtle, nonnative speakers often have difficulty using them accurately. For example, the difference between *however* and *nevertheless* is small; each is used to introduce a statement that contrast with what precedes it. But *nevertheless* emphasizes the contrast, whereas *however* softens it. Check usage of such terms in an English dictionary rather than a bilingual one. *The American Heritage Dictionary of the English Language* has special usage notes to help distinguish frequently confused words.

A Writer at Work

■ Anticipating Objections

In this section, we look at how Jessica Statsky tried to anticipate opposing positions and respond to them. To understand Statsky's thinking about her possible counterargument, look first at the invention writing she did while analyzing her potential readers.

> I think I will write mainly to parents who are considering letting their children get involved in competitive sports and to those whose children are already on teams and who don't know about the possible dangers. Parents who are really into competition and winning probably couldn't be swayed by my arguments anyway. I don't know how to reach coaches (but aren't they also parents?) or league organizers. I'll tell parents some horror stories and present solid evidence from psychologists that competitive sports can really harm children under the age of twelve. I think they'll be impressed with this scientific evidence.
>
> I share with parents one important value: the best interests of children. Competition really works against children's best interests. Maybe parents' magazines (don't know of any specific ones) publish essays like mine.

Notice that Statsky listed three potential groups of readers — parents, coaches, and league organizers. In her essay, she addressed concerns of coaches and organizers, but she focused primarily on parents. She divided parents into two camps: those who are new to organized sports and unaware of the adverse effects of competition and those who are really into winning. Statsky decided against trying to change the minds of parents who place great value on winning. But as you will see in the next excerpt from her invention writing, Statsky gave a lot of thought to the position these parents would likely favor.

Listing Reasons for the Opposing Position

Statsky lists the following reasons for the position that organized competitive sports teach young children valuable skills:

--Because competition teaches children how to succeed in later life

--Because competition--especially winning--is fun

--Because competition boosts children's self-esteem

--Because competition gives children an incentive to excel

This list appears to pose serious challenges to Statsky's argument, but she benefits considerably before she drafts her essay by considering the reasons her readers might give for opposing her position. By preparing this list, she gains insight into how she must develop her own argument in light of these predictable arguments, and she can begin thinking about which reasons she might accommodate and which she must refute. Her essay ultimately gains authority because she can demonstrate a good understanding of the opposing arguments that might be offered by her primary readers — parents who have not considered the dangers of competition for young children.

Accommodating a Plausible Reason

Looking over her list of reasons, Statsky decides that she can accommodate readers by conceding that competitive sports can sometimes be fun for children — at least for those who win. Here are her invention notes:

> It is true that children do sometimes enjoy getting prizes and being recognized as winners in competitions adults set up for them. I remember feeling very excited when our sixth-grade relay team won a race at our school's sports day. And I felt really good when I would occasionally win the candy bar for being the last one standing in classroom spelling contests. But when I think about these events, it's the activity itself I remember as the main fun, not the winning. I think I can concede that winning is exciting to six- to twelve-year-olds, while arguing that it's not as important as adults might think. I hope this will win me some friends among readers who are undecided about my position.

We can see this accommodation in paragraph 5 of Statsky's revised essay (p. 277), where she concedes that sports should be fun. She quotes an authority who argues even fun is jeopardized when competition becomes intense.

Refuting an Implausible Reason

Statsky recognizes that she must attempt to refute the other objections in her list. She chooses one and tries out the following refutation to the first reason in her list:

> It irritates me that adults are so eager to make first and second graders go into training for getting and keeping jobs as adults. I don't see why the pressures on adults need to be put on children. Anyway, both my parents tell me that in their jobs, cooperation and teamwork are keys to success. You can't get ahead unless you're effective in working with others. Maybe we should be training children and even high school and college students in the skills necessary for cooperation, rather than competition. Sports and physical activity are important for children, but elementary schools should emphasize achievement rather than competition--race against the clock rather than against each other. Rewards could be given for gains in speed or strength instead of for defeating somebody in a competition.

This brief invention activity leads to the argument in paragraph 10 of the revised essay (p. 278), where Statsky acknowledges the importance of competition for success in school and work, but goes on to argue that cooperation is also important. To support this part of her argument, she gives examples in paragraph 11 of sports programs that emphasize cooperation over competition.

You can see from Statsky's revised essay that her refutation of this opposing argument runs through her entire essay. These invention activities advanced her thinking about her readers and purpose; they also brought an early, productive focus to her research on competition in children's sports.

Thinking About Document Design

In her report arguing that the glass ceiling still exists for women in the corporate world (see the business course project described on p. 272), the student decides to reinforce her written argument with graphics because she believes her readers may have difficulty absorbing information from text that is densely packed with numerical data.

First, she considers downloading visuals from educational and governmental Web statistics sites (such as from the Federal Glass Ceiling Commission Report, available online) but decides that some of the older reports are outdated. She tries other Web sites that offer reports with information, but finds that she cannot access the reports she's looking for without purchasing them. Eventually, she locates an article in *Business Week* (July 26, 2004) that reports on women in executive management positions at major firms. The article includes a compelling table that she decides to reproduce in her report.

She also locates a more dated but still relevant article in another issue of *Business Week* (November 22, 1999) with several easy-to-read pie charts. She decides to include *Business Week's* three pie charts showing the percentages of female and male corporate officers, corporate officers with line jobs, and top earners. The charts are simple because each compares only two items, women and men. These *Business Week* graphics are also appealing because they indicate the actual numbers of women and men so that readers can see at a glance the relatively small numbers of women who have made it into the upper echelons.

WALL STREET'S GLASS CEILING

Few women ever make it on to the executive management committees of their firms:

FIRM	PERCENT OF WOMEN ON EMC
J.P. MORGAN	20%
MERRILL LYNCH	13
AVERAGE	12
CITIGROUP	11
GOLDMAN SACHS	8
MORGAN STANLEY	7
BEAR STEARNS	0
LEHMAN BROTHERS	0

STILL AN ALL BOYS' CLUB

HOW WOMEN AND MEN COMPARE IN THE 500 LARGEST COMPANIES, BY SALES*

■ WOMEN   ■ MEN

CORPORATE OFFICERS — 12% / 88% — 1,386 WOMEN   10,295 MEN

CORPORATE OFFICERS WITH LINE JOBS — 7% / 93% — 367 WOMEN   5,052 MEN

TOP EARNERS — 3% / 97% — 77 WOMEN   2,276 MEN

*AS OF MARCH 31, 1999   DATA: CATALYST

Thinking Critically About What You Have Learned

Now that you have read and discussed several essays that argue a position on a controversial issue and written one of your own, take some time to think critically about what you have learned. What problems did you encounter as you were writing your essay, and how did you solve them? How did reading other essays that argue a position influence your own essay? How does this type of writing reflect cultural attitudes about public debate and controversy?

Reflecting on Your Writing

Write a one-page explanation, telling your instructor about a problem you encountered in writing your essay and how you solved it. Before you begin, gather your invention and planning notes, drafts, readers' comments, revision plan, and final revision. Review these materials as you complete this writing task.

1. *Identify one writing problem you needed to solve as you worked on the essay.* Do not be concerned with grammar and punctuation; concentrate instead on problems unique to developing an essay arguing for a position. For example: Did you puzzle over how to convince your readers that the issue is important? Did you have trouble asserting your position forcefully while acknowledging other points of view? Was it difficult to refute an important objection you knew readers would raise?

2. *Determine how you came to recognize the problem.* When did you first discover it? What called it to your attention? If you did not become aware of the problem until someone pointed it out to you, can you now see hints of it in your invention writings? If so, where specifically?

3. *Reflect on how you went about solving the problem.* Did you work on the wording of a passage, cut or add reasons or refutations, conduct further research, or move paragraphs or sentences around? Did you reread one of the essays

in this chapter to see how another writer handled a similar problem, or did you look back at your invention writing? If you talked about the problem with another student, a tutor, or your instructor, did talking about it help? How useful was the advice you received?

4. *Write a brief explanation of how you identified the problem and tried to solve it.* Be as specific as possible in reconstructing your efforts. Quote from your invention notes and draft essay, other readers' comments, your revision plan, or your revised essay to show the various changes your writing — and thinking — underwent as you tried to solve the problem. If you are still uncertain about your solution, say so. Taking time to explain how you identified a particular problem, how you went about solving it, and what you learned from this experience can help you solve future writing problems more easily.

Reviewing What You Learned from Reading

Write a page or two explaining to your instructor how the readings in this chapter influenced your final essay. Your own essay has undoubtedly been influenced to some extent by one or more of the essays in this chapter as well as by classmates' essays that you may have read. These other essays may have helped you decide that you needed to do further research before you could argue responsibly for your position, that you could use a personal anecdote as part of your support, or that you should try to anticipate and effectively refute readers' objections. Before you write, take time to reflect on what you have learned from the readings and how they have influenced your own writing.

1. *Reread the final revision of your essay; then look back at the selections you read before completing it.* Do you see any specific influences? For example,

did any reading influence how you decided to present the issue, use authorities, make concessions, or refute objections? Also look for ideas you got from your reading: writing strategies you were inspired to try, specific details you were led to include, and goals you sought to achieve.

2. *Write an explanation of these influences.* Did one selection have a particularly strong influence, or were several selections influential in different ways? Quote from the readings and from your final revision to show how your essay was influenced by the selections you read. Finally, based on your review of the chapter's readings, point out any further improvements you would now make in your essay.

Considering the Social Dimensions of Position Papers

Arguing positions on important social and political issues is essential in a democracy. Doing so gives us each a voice. Instead of remaining silent and on the margins, we can enter the ongoing debate. We can try to influence others, perhaps convincing them to change their minds or at least to take seriously our point of view. Airing our differences also allows us to live together in relative peace. Instead of brawling with each other at school board meetings, in legislative halls, on street corners, or in the classroom, we argue. We may raise our voices in anger and frustration, and our differences may seem insurmountable, but at least no one is physically hurt.

Anticipating the positions taken by our readers and their likely objections to our argument benefits us in another important way. It forces us to do more than merely assert our views; we must also give reasons why we think as we do. Anticipating readers' responses to our argument encourages us not only to think of reasons but also to defend them against potential criticism. To refute objections, we need to support our reasons in ways that ground our opinions in something other than personal belief — for example, in facts that can be verified, in the authority of experts, in anecdotal experiences with which others can

identify. Ideally, then, writing position papers fosters the kind of reasonable debate that enables a diverse society like ours to hold together.

Yet even though reasoned argument about controversial social issues is a highly valued activity in our society, cautious readers and writers need to be aware that this way of presenting an argument for a position may have serious shortcomings and problems.

Suppressing Dissent.   Some critics argue that society privileges reasoned argument over other ways of arguing in order to control dissent. Instead of expressing what may be legitimate outrage and inciting public concern through passionate language, dissenters are urged to be dispassionate and reasonable. They may even be encouraged to try to build their arguments on shared values even though they are arguing with people whose views they find repugnant. While it may help prevent violent confrontation, this emphasis on calmly giving reasons and support may also prevent an honest and open exchange of differences. In the end, trying to present a well-reasoned, well-supported argument may serve to maintain the status quo by silencing the more radical voices within the community.

1. *In your own experience of writing an essay arguing a position on a controversial issue, did having to give reasons and support discourage you from choosing any particular issue or from expressing strong feelings?* Reflect on the issues you listed as possible subjects for your essay and how you made your choice. Did you reject any issues because you could not come up with reasons and support for your position? When you made your choice, did you think about whether you could be dispassionate and reasonable about it?

2. *Consider the readings in this chapter and the essays you read by other students in the class.* Do you think any of these writers felt limited by the need to give reasons and support for their position? Which of the essays you read, if any, seemed to you to express strong feelings about the issue? Which, if any, seemed dispassionate?

3. ***Consider the kind of arguing you typically witness in the media — radio, television, newspapers, magazines, the Internet.*** We have said that society privileges reasoned argument, but in the media, have giving reasons and support and anticipating readers' objections been replaced with a more contentious, in-your-face style of arguing? Think of media examples of these two different ways of arguing. In the context of these examples, what can you conclude about reasoned argument stifling dissent?

4. ***Write a page or two explaining your ideas about whether the requirement to give reasons and support suppresses dissent.*** Connect your ideas to your own essay and to the readings in this chapter.

7

Proposing
a Solution

IN COLLEGE COURSES For an education class, a student develops a proposal that would require television networks to provide educational programming specifically designed to help preschool children learn English. During a meeting with his professor, he learns about the Communications Act of 1934, which required publicly owned airwaves to serve the public interest, and the Children's Television Act of 1990, which was supposed to encourage commercial stations to provide a minimum amount of educational children's programming. He also learned that, due to lax oversight, the Federal Communications Commission once accepted a station's argument that programs like "*The Jetsons* conveyed important lessons about future technologies and *The Flintstones* taught history." He decides to center his argument on the central point that these laws need to be more rigorously enforced.

Through library and Internet research, the student discovers that the national commercial networks offer little in the way of truly educational programming for children and nothing targeted to English language learners. Given what he has learned in class about early childhood education and second language learning, he decides that two programs that currently exist could be used as models for new programming: the venerable public television program *Sesame Street* and the cable television program *Mi Casita* (*My Little House*).

He uses statistics to establish the need for his proposed solution and supports his proposal with early education and language acquisition theory. He counters possible objections by citing the two model programs as evidence that his proposal can be implemented.

IN THE COMMUNITY   A social services administrator in a large northeastern city becomes increasingly concerned about the rise in the number of adolescents in jail for both minor and major crimes. His observations and the research studies he reads convince him that a partial solution to the problem would be to intervene at the first sign of delinquent behavior in eight- to twelve-year-olds. In developing a proposal to circulate among influential people in the local police department, juvenile justice system, school system, and business and religious communities, the administrator begins by describing the long-term consequences of jailing young criminals. To emphasize the problem's significance, he focuses mainly on the costs of incarceration and the high rate of return to criminal activity by juveniles after their release from jail.

He then lists and discusses at length the major components of his early intervention program. These components include assigning mentors to young people who are beginning to fail in school, placing social workers with troubled families to help out daily before and after school, and hiring neighborhood residents to work full-time on the streets to counter the influence of gangs. The administrator acknowledges that early intervention to head off serious criminal activity will require the cooperation of many city agencies, and offers to take the lead in bringing about this cooperation. He also acknowledges the financial costs of the program but points to lowered costs for incarceration if it is successful. He further suggests sources of grant money to fund it.

IN THE WORKPLACE   A driver of a heavy diesel tractor-and-trailer truck writes a proposal for trucking company owners, who face a shortage of well-qualified drivers, suggesting that they recruit more women. As she plans her proposal, she talks to the owner of the company she drives for and to the few women drivers she knows. In trucking industry magazines, she finds statistics she can use to argue that the demand for motor carriers is increasing.

She argues that the driver shortage could be solved if more women drivers, who — according to the Bureau of Labor Statistics — comprise only a little more than 5 percent of the nation's truck drivers, were trained and hired. The training program she describes would exceed the Professional Truck Driver Institute standard, which requires a minimum of forty-four hours of actual behind-the-wheel driving time. After an initial off-road training period to assure that the recruits are ready to handle a big rig, they would be assigned to experienced drivers serving as teacher/mentors who would be paid extra for their training contributions. The students would not have to pay the $4,000-plus tuition normally required by truck driving schools, but they would be required to sign a contract agreeing to drive for the company for a minimum number of months after the training period at a slightly reduced starting pay rate.

The driver argues that everyone benefits. The company gets a skilled workforce. The experienced drivers get additional income. The new drivers get hands-on experience without the up-front cost of tuition. She gives her proposal to the company president and it is eventually published in an industry newsletter.

327

Proposals are vital to a democracy. By reading and writing proposals, citizens learn about problems affecting their well-being and explore possible actions to remedy these problems. For example, one of the scenarios opening this chapter describes a concerned citizen's effort to find a way to help at-risk children before they get into trouble. Similarly, an essay later in this chapter by a policy researcher and senator's staffer tries to help families attain flexibility in their work schedules, and another by a syndicated columnist and radio commentator addresses what he calls "the biggest issue in education." Proposals, however, do not have to be about large social problems. Many concern business-related or local community problems such as the proposal to train women as truck drivers in the previous scenario and the reading later in this chapter about making bicycle riding more attractive.

You will see that proposals are written every day in business, government, education, and the professions. Even students write proposals. Like the student who proposes more children's educational television programming, you may be asked in a course you are taking to propose a solution to a problem revealed in topics or issues of the course. Or you may decide on your own that a campus problem could be improved if certain actions were taken, as Patrick O'Malley argues in his essay proposing a solution to the problem of "high-stakes exams." O'Malley wrote his essay in a composition class but it subsequently appeared in the school newspaper. You too can write a proposal that will have an impact.

As a special form of argument, proposals have much in common with position papers, described in Chapter 6. Both analyze a subject about which there is disagreement and take a definite stand on it. Both make an argument, giving reasons and support and acknowledging readers' likely objections or questions. Proposals, however, go further: They urge readers to take specific action. They argue for a proposed solution to a problem, and they succeed or fail by the strength of that argument.

Good proposals are creative as well as convincing. Problem-solving depends on a questioning attitude — wondering about alternative approaches to bringing about change, puzzling over how a goal might be achieved, questioning why a process unfolds in a particular way, posing challenges to the status quo. Above all, problem-solving demands imagination. To solve a problem, you need to see it anew, to look at it from new angles and in new contexts.

Because a proposal tries to convince readers that its way of defining and solving the problem makes sense, proposal writers must be sensitive to readers' needs and expectations. Readers need to know details of the solution and to be convinced that it will solve the problem and can be implemented. If readers initially favor a different solution, knowing why the writer rejects it will help them decide whether to support or reject the writer's proposed solution. Readers may be wary of costs, demands on their time, and grand schemes.

As you plan and draft a proposal, you will have to determine whether your readers are aware of the problem and whether they recognize its seriousness, and you will have to consider their views on possible alternative solutions. Knowing what your readers know — their knowledge of the problem and willingness to make changes, their assumptions and biases, the kinds of arguments likely to appeal to them — is a central part of proposal writing. Mastering this skill — in other words, how to communicate effectively with your readers — can be as much fun as imagineering a solution (to borrow a word coined by Walt Disney).

A Collaborative Activity: Practice Proposing a Solution to a Problem

The preceding scenarios suggest some occasions for writing proposals to solve problems. To get a sense of the complexities and possibilities involved in proposing solutions, think through a specific problem, and try to come up with a feasible proposal. Your instructor may schedule this collaborative activity as a face-to-face in-class discussion or ask you to conduct an on-line real-time discussion in a chat room. Whatever the medium, here are some guidelines to follow:

Part 1. Form a group with two or three other students, and select one person to take notes during your discussion.

- First, identify two or three problems within your college or community, and select one that you all recognize and agree needs to be solved.
- Next, consider possible solutions to this problem, and identify one solution that you can all support. You need not all be equally enthusiastic about this solution.
- Finally, determine which individual or group has the authority to take action on your proposed solution, how you would go about convincing this audience that the problem is serious and must be solved, and how to argue that your proposed solution is feasible and should be supported. Make notes also about questions this audience might have about your proposal and what objections the audience might raise.

Part 2. As a group, discuss your efforts at proposing a solution to a problem. What surprised or pleased you most about this activity? What difficulties did you encounter in coming up with arguments that the problem must be solved and that your proposed solution would solve it? How did the objections you thought of influence your confidence in your proposed solution?

Readings

PATRICK O'MALLEY wrote the following proposal while he was a first-year college student frustrated by what he calls "high-stakes exams." O'Malley's essay may strike you as unusually authoritative. This tone of authority comes in large part from the research he did exploring the problem and its possible solutions. He interviewed two professors (his writing instructor and the writing program director), talked with several students, and read published research on the subject of testing. As you read his essay, notice particularly how he anticipates professors' likely objections to his proposed solution and evaluates their preferred solutions to the problem he identifies.

More Testing, More Learning
Patrick O'Malley

To help readers see the
stress of high-stakes
exams, O'Malley opens
with a scenario showing
students' anxiety.

It's late at night. The final's tomorrow. You got a C on the midterm, so this one will make or break you. Will it be like the midterm? Did you study enough? Did you study the right things? It's too late to drop the course. So what happens if you fail? No time to worry about that now — you've got a ton of notes to go over.   1

O'Malley defines the problem by describing negative
effects.

Although this last-minute anxiety about midterm and final exams is only too familiar to most college students, many professors may not realize how such major, infrequent, high-stakes exams work against the best interests of students both psychologically and intellectually. They cause unnecessary amounts of stress, placing too much importance on one or two days in the students' entire term, judging ability on a single or dual performance. They don't encourage frequent study, and they fail to inspire students' best performance. If professors gave additional brief exams at frequent intervals, students would be spurred to study more regularly, learn more, worry less, and perform better on midterms, finals, and other papers and projects.   2

O'Malley announces his
proposed solution in a
thesis statement that also
forecasts his reasons.

Ideally, a professor would give an in-class test or quiz after each unit, chapter, or focus of study, depending on the type of class and course material. A physics class might require a test on concepts after every chapter covered, while a history class could necessitate quizzes covering certain time periods or major events. These exams should be given weekly or at least twice monthly. Whenever possible, they should consist of two or three essay questions rather than many multiple-choice or short-answer questions. To preserve class time for lecture and discussion, exams should take no more than 15 or 20 minutes.   3

To explain how to **implement** his solution, O'Malley
uses words like *could* and
might to suggest possibilities and *should* to set goals.

The main reason professors should give frequent exams is that when they do and when they provide feedback to students on how well they are doing, students learn more in the course and perform better on major exams, projects, and papers. It makes sense that in a challenging course containing a great deal of material, students will learn more of it and put it to better use if they have to apply or "practice" it frequently on exams, which also helps them find out how much they are learning and what they need to go over again. A recent Harvard study notes students' "strong preference for frequent evaluation in a course." Harvard students feel they learn least in courses that have "only a midterm and a final exam, with no other personal evaluation." They believe they learn most in courses with "many opportunities to see how they are doing" (Light, 1990, p. 32). In a review of a number of studies of student learning, Frederiksen (1984) reports that students who take weekly quizzes achieve higher scores on final exams than students who take only a midterm exam and that testing increases retention of material tested.   4

Turning to the **argument
for his solution**, O'Malley
echoes key words from his
thesis/forecast to keep
readers oriented.

To **support** his causal
argument that frequent
exams enable students to
learn more, O'Malley cites
research studies, using
APA documentation style
keyed to a References list
at the end.

Another, closely related argument in favor of multiple exams is that they encourage students to improve their study habits. Greater frequency in test taking means greater frequency in studying for tests. Students prone to cramming will be required — or at least strongly motivated — to open their textbooks and notebooks more often, making them less likely to resort to long, kamikaze nights of studying   5

To introduce his next **reason**, O'Malley echoes the
idea of the thesis/forecast
but repeats only the word
study.

for major exams. Since there is so much to be learned in the typical course, it makes sense that frequent, careful study and review are highly beneficial. But students need motivation to study regularly, and nothing works like an exam. If students had frequent exams in all their courses, they would have to schedule study time each week and gradually would develop a habit of frequent study. It might be argued that students are adults who have to learn how to manage their own lives, but learning history or physics is more complicated than learning to drive a car or balance a checkbook. Students need coaching and practice in learning. The right way to learn new material needs to become a habit, and I believe that frequent exams are key to developing good habits of study and learning. The Harvard study concludes that "tying regular evaluation to good course organization enables students to plan their work more than a few days in advance. If quizzes and homework are scheduled on specific days, students plan their work to capitalize on them" (Light, 1990, p. 33).

6   By encouraging regular study habits, frequent exams would also decrease anxiety by reducing the procrastination that produces anxiety. Students would benefit psychologically if they were not subjected to the emotional ups and downs caused by major exams, when after being virtually worry-free for weeks they are suddenly ready to check into the psychiatric ward. Researchers at the University of Vermont found a strong relationship among procrastination, anxiety, and achievement. Students who regularly put off studying for exams had continuing high anxiety and lower grades than students who procrastinated less. The researchers found that even "low" procrastinators did not study regularly and recommended that professors give frequent assignments and exams to reduce procrastination and increase achievement (Rothblum, Solomon, & Murakami, 1986, pp. 393–394).

7   Research supports my proposed solution to the problems I have described. Common sense as well as my experience and that of many of my friends support it. Why, then, do so few professors give frequent brief exams?

8   Some believe that such exams take up too much of the limited class time available to cover the material in the course. Most courses meet 150 minutes a week — three times a week for 50 minutes each time. A 20-minute weekly exam might take 30 minutes to administer, and that is one-fifth of each week's class time. From the student's perspective, however, this time is well spent. Better learning and greater confidence about the course seem a good trade-off for another 30 minutes of lecture. Moreover, time lost to lecturing or discussion could easily be made up in students' learning on their own through careful regular study for the weekly exams. If weekly exams still seem too time-consuming to some professors, their frequency could be reduced to every other week or their length to 5 or 10 minutes. In courses where multiple-choice exams are appropriate, several questions could be designed to take only a few minutes to answer.

9   Another objection professors have to frequent exams is that they take too much time to read and grade. In a 20-minute essay exam, a well-prepared student can easily write two pages. A relatively small class of 30 students might then produce 60 pages, no small amount of material to read each week. A large class of

To introduce his last **reason**, O'Malley does not repeat the word *worry* from paragraph 2 but instead uses the synonym *anxiety*, making his writing less predictable yet still easy to follow.

Here O'Malley sums up the argument for his solution and uses a **rhetorical question** to make a smooth transition to **anticipating readers' likely objections**. Paragraphs 8 and 9 counterargue two objections.

O'Malley **refutes** the first objection by trying to get the professor to see the student's point of view. He also tries to **accommodate it** by modifying his proposed solution.

O'Malley **refutes** the second objection by suggesting several ways to cut down on professors' work while testing students frequently.

Here O'Malley shifts from anticipating objections to **evaluating alternative solutions**. Paragraphs 10–12 counter three alternative solutions.

O'Malley rejects this alternative solution by giving reasons and citing research.

In responding to the next two alternative solutions, O'Malley acknowledges their benefits but also points out their shortcomings.

O'Malley **concludes** by reiterating his reasons. He

100 or more students would produce an insurmountable pile of material. There are a number of responses to this objection. Again, professors could give exams every other week or make them very short. Instead of reading them closely they could skim them quickly to see whether students understand an idea or can apply it to an unfamiliar problem; and instead of numerical or letter grades they could give a plus, check, or minus. Exams could be collected and responded to only every third or fourth week. Professors who have readers or teaching assistants could rely on them to grade or check exams. And the Scantron machine is always available for instant grading of multiple-choice exams. Finally, frequent exams could be given *in place of* a midterm exam or out-of-class essay assignment.

Since frequent exams seem to some professors to create too many problems, however, it is reasonable to consider alternative ways to achieve the same goals. One alternative solution is to implement a program that would improve study skills. While such a program might teach students how to study for exams, it cannot prevent procrastination or reduce "large test anxiety" by a substantial amount. One research team studying anxiety and test performance found that study skills training was not effective in reducing anxiety or improving performance (Dendato & Diener, 1986, p. 134). This team, which also reviewed other research that reached the same conclusion, did find that a combination of "cognitive/relaxation therapy" and study skills training was effective. This possible solution seems complicated, however, not to mention time-consuming and expensive. It seems much easier and more effective to change the cause of the bad habit rather than treat the habit itself. That is, it would make more sense to solve the problem at its root: the method of learning and evaluation. 10

Still another solution might be to provide frequent study questions for students to answer. These would no doubt be helpful in focusing students' time studying, but students would probably not actually write out the answers unless they were required to. To get students to complete the questions in a timely way, professors would have to collect and check the answers. In that case, however, they might as well devote the time to grading an exam. Even if it asks the same questions, a scheduled exam is preferable to a set of study questions because it takes far less time to write in class, compared to the time students would devote to responding to questions at home. In-class exams also ensure that each student produces his or her own work. 11

Another possible solution would be to help students prepare for midterm and final exams by providing sets of questions from which the exam questions will be selected or announcing possible exam topics at the beginning of the course. This solution would have the advantage of reducing students' anxiety about learning every fact in the textbook, and it would clarify the course goals, but it would not motivate students to study carefully each new unit, concept, or text chapter in the course. I see this as a way of complementing frequent exams, not as substituting for them. 12

From the evidence and from my talks with professors and students, I see frequent, brief in-class exams as the only way to improve students' study habits and 13 learning, reduce their anxiety and procrastination, and increase their satisfaction with college. These exams are not a panacea, but only more parking spaces and a winning football team would do as much to improve college life. Professors can't do much about parking or football, but they can give more frequent exams. Campus administrators should get behind this effort, and professors should get together to consider giving exams more frequently. It would make a difference.

References

Dendato, K. M., & Diener, D. (1986). Effectiveness of cognitive/relaxation therapy and study skills training in reducing self-reported anxiety and improving the academic performance of test-anxious students. *Journal of Counseling Psychology, 33,* 131–135.

Frederiksen, N. (1984). The real test bias: Influences of testing on teaching and learning. *American Psychologist, 39,* 193–202.

Light, R. J. (1990). *Explorations with students and faculty about teaching, learning, and student life.* Cambridge, MA: Harvard University Graduate School of Education and Kennedy School of Government.

Rothblum, E. D., Solomon, L., & Murakami, J. (1986). Affective, cognitive, and behavioral differences between high and low procrastinators. *Journal of Counseling Psychology, 33,* 387–394.

tries for a light touch at the end in talking about other ways *to improve college life.*

APA style lists sources by author's last name, puts publication date next in parentheses, and then the title and other publication information.

KAREN KORNBLUH earned a B.A. in economics and English and an M.A. from Harvard University's Kennedy School of Government. She worked in the private sector as an economist and management consultant and in the public sector as director of the office of legislative and intergovernmental affairs at the Federal Communications Commission before becoming the deputy chief of staff at the Treasury Department in the Clinton administration. Kornbluh serves currently as the policy director for Senator Barack Obama of Illinois.

As director of the Work and Family Program of the New America Foundation, a nonprofit, nonpartisan institute that sponsors research and conferences on public policy issues, Kornbluh led an effort to change the American workplace to accommodate what she calls the new "juggler family," in which parents have to juggle their time for parenting and work. Her book *Running Harder to Stay in Place: The Growth of Family Work Hours and Incomes* was published in 2005 by the New America Foundation, and Kornbluh's articles have appeared in such distinguished venues as the *New York Times*, the *Washington Post*, and the *Atlantic Monthly*. The following proposal was published in 2005 by the Work and Family Program.

As you read, think about your own experiences as a child, a parent, or both and how they affect your response to Kornbluh's proposal. Have you or your parents had to juggle your time for parenting and work — and if so, how did you or they manage it?

Win-Win Flexibility

Karen Kornbluh

Introduction

Today fully 70 percent of families with children are headed by two working parents or by an unmarried working parent. The "traditional family" of the breadwinner and homemaker has been replaced by the "juggler family," in which no one is home full-time. Two-parent families are working 10 more hours a week than in 1979 (Bernstein and Kornbluh).

To be decent parents, caregivers, and members of their communities, workers now need greater flexibility than they once did. Yet good part-time or flex-time jobs remain rare. Whereas companies have embraced flexibility in virtually every other aspect of their businesses (inventory control, production schedules, financing), full-time workers' schedules remain largely inflexible. Employers often demand workers be available around the clock. Moreover, many employees have no right to a minimum number of sick or vacation days; almost two thirds of all workers — and an even larger percentage of low-income parents — lack the ability to take a day off to care for a family member (Lovell). The Family and Medical Leave Act (FMLA) of 1993 finally guaranteed that workers at large companies could take a leave of absence for the birth or adoption of a baby, or for the illness of a family member. Yet that guaranteed leave is unpaid.

Many businesses are finding ways to give their most valued employees flexibility but, all too often, workers who need flexibility find themselves shunted into part-time, temporary, on-call, or contract jobs with reduced wages and career opportunities — and, often, no benefits. A full quarter of American workers are in these jobs. Only 15 percent of women and 12 percent of men in such jobs receive health insurance from their employers (Wenger). A number of European countries provide workers the right to a part-time schedule and all have enacted legislation to implement a European Union directive to prohibit discrimination against part-time workers.

In America, employers are required to accommodate the needs of employees with disabilities — even if that means providing a part-time or flexible schedule. Employers may also provide religious accommodations for employees by offering a part-time or flexible schedule. At the same time, employers have no obligation to allow parents or employees caring for sick relatives to work part-time or flexible schedules, even if the cost to the employer would be inconsequential.

In the 21st Century global economy, America needs a new approach that allows businesses to gain flexibility in staffing without sacrificing their competitiveness and enables workers to gain control over their work-lives without sacrificing their economic security. This win-win flexibility arrangement will not be the same in every company, nor even for each employee working within the same organization. Each case will be different. But flexibility will not come for all employees without some education, prodding, and leadership. So, employers and employees must be required to come to the table to work out a solution that benefits everyone. American businesses must be educated on strategies for giving employees flexibility without sacrificing productivity or morale. And businesses should be recognized and rewarded when they do so.

America is a nation that continually rises to the occasion. At the dawn of a new century, we face many challenges. One of these is helping families to raise our next generation in an increasingly demanding global economy. This is a challenge America must meet with imagination and determination.

Background: The Need for Workplace Flexibility

Between 1970 and 2000, the percentage of mothers in the workforce rose from 38 to 67 percent (Smolensky and Gootman). Moreover, the number of hours worked by dual-income families has increased dramatically. Couples with children worked a full 60 hours a week in 1979. By 2000 they were working 70 hours a week (Bernstein and Kornbluh). And more parents than ever are working long hours. In 2000, nearly 1 out of every 8 couples with children was putting in 100 hours a week or more on the job, compared to only 1 out of 12 families in 1970 (Jacobs and Gerson).

In addition to working parents, there are over 44.4 million Americans who provide care to another adult, often an older relative. Fifty-nine percent of these caregivers either work or have worked while providing care ("Caregiving").

In a 2002 report by the Families and Work Institute, 45 percent of employees reported that work and family responsibilities interfered with each other "a lot" or "some" and 67 percent of employed parents report that they do not have enough time with their children (Galinksy, Bond, and Hill).

Over half of workers today have no control over scheduling alternative start and end times at work (Galinksy, Bond, and Hill). According to a recent study by the Institute for Women's Policy Research, 49 percent of workers — over 59 million Americans — lack basic paid sick days for themselves. And almost two-thirds of all workers — and an even larger percentage of low-income parents — lack the ability to take a day off to care for a family member (Lovell). Thirteen percent of non-poor workers with caregiving responsibilities lack paid vacation leave, while 28 percent of poor caregivers lack any paid vacation time (Heymann). Research has shown that flexible arrangements and benefits tend to be more accessible in larger and more profitable firms, and then to the most valued professional and managerial workers in those firms (Golden). Parents with young children and working welfare recipients — the workers who need access to paid leave the most — are the least likely to have these benefits, according to research from the Urban Institute (Ross Phillips).

In the US, only 5 percent of workers have access to a job that provides paid parental leave. The Family and Medical Leave Act grants the right to 12 weeks of unpaid leave for the birth or adoption of a child or for the serious illness of the worker or a worker's family member. But the law does not apply to employees who work in companies with fewer than 50 people, employees who have worked for less than a year at their place of employment, or employees who work fewer than 1,250 hours a year. Consequently, only 45 percent of parents working in the private sector are eligible to take even this unpaid time off (Smolensky and Gootman).

Workers often buy flexibility by sacrificing job security, benefits, and pay. Part-time workers are less likely to have employer-provided health insurance or pensions and their hourly wages are lower. One study in 2002 found that 43 percent of employed parents said that using flexibility would jeopardize their advancement (Galinksy, Bond, and Hill). 12

Children, in particular, pay a heavy price for workplace inflexibility (Waters Boots 2004). Almost 60 percent of child care arrangements are of poor or mediocre quality (Smolensky and Gootman). Children in low-income families are even less likely to be in good or excellent care settings. Full-day child care easily costs $4,000 to $10,000 per year — approaching the price of college tuition at a public university. As a result of the unaffordable and low quality nature of child care in this country, a disturbing number of today's children are left home alone: Over 3.3 million children age 6-12 are home alone after school each day (Vandivere et al). 13

Many enlightened businesses are showing the way forward to a 21st Century flexible workplace. Currently, however, businesses have little incentive to provide families with the flexibility they need. We need to level the playing field and remove the competitive disadvantages for all businesses that do provide workplace flexibility. 14

This should be a popular priority. A recent poll found that 77 percent of likely voters feel that it is difficult for families to earn enough and still have time to be with their families. Eighty-four percent of voters agree that children are being short-changed when their parents have to work long hours. . . . 15

Proposal: Win-Win Flexibility

A win-win approach in the US to flexibility . . . might function as follows. It would be "soft touch" at first — requiring a process and giving business an out if it would be costly to implement — with a high-profile public education campaign on the importance of workplace flexibility to American business, American families, and American society. A survey at the end of the second year would determine whether a stricter approach is needed. 16

Employees would have the right to make a formal request to their employers for flexibility in the number of hours worked, the times worked, and/or the ability to work from home. Examples of such flexibility would include part-time, annualized hours,[1] compressed hours,[2] flex-time,[3] job-sharing, shift working, staggered hours, and telecommuting. 17

The employee would be required to make a written application providing details on the change in work, the effect on the employer, and solutions to any problems 18

---

[1] *Annualized hours* means working different numbers of hours a week but a fixed annual total.

[2] *Compressed hours* means working more hours a day in exchange for working fewer days a week.

[3] *Flex-time* means working on an adjustable daily schedule.

caused to the employer. The employer would be required to meet with the employee and give the employee a decision on the request within two weeks, as well as provide an opportunity for an internal appeal within one month from the initial request.

The employee request would be granted unless the employer demonstrated it would require significant difficulty or expense entailing more than ordinary costs, decreased job efficiency, impairment of worker safety, infringement of other employees' rights, or conflict with another law or regulation. 19

The employer would be required to provide an employee working a flexible schedule with the same hourly pay and proportionate health, pension, vacation, holiday, and FMLA benefits that the employee received before working flexibly and would be required thereafter to advance the employee at the same rate as full-time employees. 20

Who would be covered: Parents (including parents, legal guardians, foster parents) and other caregivers at first. Eventually all workers should be eligible in our flexible, 24x7 economy. During the initial period, it will be necessary to define non-parental "caregivers." One proposal is to define them as immediate relatives or other caregivers of "certified care recipients" (defined as those whom a doctor certifies as having three or more limitations that impede daily functioning — using diagnostic criteria such as Activities of Daily Living [ADL]/Instrumental Activities of Daily Living [IADL] — for at least 180 consecutive days). . . . 21

Public Education: Critical to the success of the proposal will be public education along the lines of the education that the government and business schools conducted in the 1980s about the need for American business to adopt higher quality standards to compete against Japanese business. A Malcolm Baldridge-like award[4] should be created for companies that make flexibility win-win. A public education campaign conducted by the Department of Labor should encourage small businesses to adopt best practices of win-win flexibility. Tax credits could be used in the first year to reward early adopters. 22

Works Cited

Bernstein, Jared, and Karen Kornbluh. *Running Faster to Stay in Place: The Growth of Family Work Hours and Incomes.* Washington: New America Foundation, 2005. Print.

Galinsky, Ellen, James Bond, and Jeffrey E. Hill. *Workplace Flexibility: What Is It? Who Has It? Who Wants It? Does It Make a Difference?* New York: Families and Work Inst., 2004. Print.

Golden, Lonnie. *The Time Bandit: What U.S. Workers Surrender to Get Greater Flexibility in Work Schedules.* Washington: Economic Policy Inst., 2000. Print.

Heymann, Jody. *The Widening Gap: Why America's Working Families Are in Jeopardy — and What Can Be Done About It.* New York: Basic, 2000. Print.

Jacobs, Jerry, and Kathleen Gerson. *The Time Divide: Work, Family and Gender Inequality.* Cambridge: Harvard UP, 2004. Print.

Lovell, Vicky. *No Time to Be Sick: Why Everyone Suffers When Workers Don't Have Paid Sick Leave.* Washington: Inst. for Women's Policy Research, 2004. Print.

---

[4] The Malcolm Baldridge National Quality Award is given by the U.S. President to outstanding businesses.

National Alliance for Caregiving and AARP. *Caregiving in the U.S.* NAC, 2004. *National Alliance for Caregiving.* Web. 20 May 2008.

Ross Phillips, Katherine. *Getting Time Off: Access to Leave among Working Parents.* Washington: Urban Institute, 2004. Print. New Federalism: National Survey of America's Families B-57.

Smolensky, Eugene, and Jennifer A. Gootman, eds. *Working Families and Growing Kids: Caring for Children and Adolescents.* Natl. Research Council and Inst. of Medicine, Washington: Natl. Academies P, 2004. Print.

Vandivere, Sharon, et al. *Unsupervised Time: Family and Child Factors Associated with Self-Care.* Washington: Urban Inst., 2003. Print. Assessing the New Federalism, Occasional Paper No. 71.

Waters Boots, Shelley. *The Way We Work: How Children and Their Families Fare in a 21st Century Workplace.* Washington: New America Foundation, 2004. Print.

Wenger, Jeffrey. *Share of Workers in "Nonstandard" Jobs Declines.* Washington: Economic Policy Inst., 2003. Print.

Making Connections to Personal and Social Issues: The Problem of Child Care

Many of you have probably grown up during the period Kornbluh is describing, and your family may have been configured more as a "juggler" than as a "traditional family" (paragraph 1). Kornbluh asserts in paragraph 13 that it is the children in juggler families who "pay a heavy price." She is particularly critical of child care, which she says is very expensive and of low quality, especially for low-income families. She cites Vandivere et al. to argue that more than "3.3 million children age 6–12 are home alone after school each day" (13).

With two or three other students, discuss how well Kornbluh's argument compares with your experiences as a child. Take turns talking about the following questions: Who cared for you as a preschooler—a parent, another relative, or a babysitter, or did you attend a day-care facility of some kind? When you were of school age, did you attend any after-school programs? Would you consider yourself a "latchkey child"? In other words, were you unsupervised at home while your parents were at work?

Consider also the quality of your preschool and after-school care. Discuss how you felt at the time and how you feel now looking back on your childhood. What lasting effects, if any, do you think your childhood experiences had? Based on your experience, what kinds of child-care arrangements do you think would serve children and their parents best today?

Analyzing Writing Strategies

1. For readers to understand a proposal, they need to be told precisely what the writer is proposing. Therefore, writers **describe the proposed solution** simply and directly in a way that readers cannot miss. Kornbluh announces her solution in the title of her essay and repeats it in the third heading. Notice that she

also repeats the key word *flexibility* many times. Skim the essay, underlining every time *flexibility* (in one form or another) is used. How many times is it repeated in the first section? In the last section? What do you think is the purpose of repeating the term so many times — and why repeat it in these two sections especially?

2. To **argue for her proposed solution**, Kornbluh describes how the solution can be **implemented**. Reread paragraph 5, where she sets out some general principles, and paragraphs 16–22, where she details the elements of her solution. List the steps she recommends. Notice that the procedure includes guidelines for what employees as well as what employers should do. It also includes a timetable and criteria. How well do you think this procedure satisfies the goals Kornbluh sets out in paragraph 5: "a new approach that allows businesses to gain flexibility in staffing without sacrificing their competitiveness and enables workers to gain control over their work-lives without sacrificing their economic security"? What, if anything, do you think is missing?

Commentary: Defining the Problem and Evaluating Alternative Solutions

Every proposal begins with a problem. What writers say about the problem and how much space they devote to it depend on what they assume their readers already know and think about the problem. Some problems require more explanation than others. Obviously, if readers are already immersed in discussing the problem and possible solutions, then the writer may not have to say much to **define the problem**. Nevertheless, savvy proposal writers try to redefine even familiar problems in a way that leads logically to the writer's preferred solution. For problems that are new to readers, writers not only need to explain the problem but also convince readers that it exists and is serious enough to justify taking the actions the writer thinks are necessary to solve it. Because the problem Kornbluh is writing about has not been discussed much, she assumes readers will not be familiar with it, and therefore she spends the first part of her essay introducing the problem and the second part establishing the problem's existence and seriousness. In the second part, she also begins to make the case for her proposed solution, in part by evaluating alternative solutions that readers might think are already in place.

Kornbluh uses the first section, headed "Introduction," to acquaint readers with the new concept of what she calls the "juggler family" and to set the stage for her argument that businesses should accommodate the needs of their employees. She begins by establishing that the so-called "traditional family" is no longer the norm for many Americans and that it has been replaced by the "juggler family." To support this claim, she cites two statistics from her book demonstrating that two-parent families are working more today than they were twenty-five years ago. She also cites Lovell to substantiate the claim that employees today have little flexibility to take time off from work to care for loved ones. Thus, a plan is needed to give workers a more flexible schedule. These two claims — that the juggler family is the new norm and that employees don't have flexibility — are the cornerstones of her argument that the problem does indeed exist and requires some kind of resolution.

In paragraph 3, Kornbluh adds another important element to her argument about the problem's importance when she compares America to Europe. She demonstrates that European Union members understand the gravity of the problem better than Americans do and have already solved it. In fact, "a part-time schedule" is recognized in parts of Europe as a "right" that is protected by law. This comparison puts the United States in a negative light by suggesting that it is less advanced than other Western countries. It also implies a subtle threat to business leaders that if they do not help solve the problem, a solution may be imposed on them.

Finally, in the opening paragraphs of the second section, "Background: The Need for Workplace Flexibility," Kornbluh argues that the problem requires immediate attention. She cites statistics to establish that the problem is worsening. She shows how much work time has increased over the last thirty years (paragraph 7), how many workers provide care for children or other adults (paragraph 8), and how many people feel torn between work and family responsibilities (paragraph 9). These three paragraphs taken together demonstrate the urgency of her proposal.

In addition to introducing the problem, Kornbluh prepares for her proposed solution by **evaluating alternative solutions** that readers are likely to argue already exist. One such solution is that workers can use their sick days and vacation time to care for family members. Kornbluh apparently sees nothing wrong with using sick leave this way, but she argues that it is just not available for enough people (paragraph 10). She cites statistics revealing that many Americans, particularly the working poor, do not receive pay when they are sick or on vacation. Another solution — the Family and Medical Leave Act — also falls short, as Kornbluh reminds readers, because the law grants only "unpaid leave" and applies only to "45 percent of parents working in the private sector" (paragraph 11). At the end of paragraph 10, Kornbluh anticipates readers pointing out that some firms already provide flexible work arrangements. She does not criticize this solution because it is very much like her own; however, she refutes the implied claim that there is no need for her proposal because businesses are solving the problem on their own. She reports the findings of two research studies that show only a few firms make these arrangements and only for those at the top, not for the majority of employees. In contrast, Kornbluh's proposal is designed to help "[p]arents with young children and working welfare recipients — the workers who need access to paid leave the most" (paragraph 10).

As you plan your proposal, remember that when you introduce the problem and evaluate alternative solutions you are advancing the argument for your solution. You are also attempting to earn the confidence of your readers. Kornbluh shows readers she has done her homework, knows what she is talking about, and can be trusted. She builds credibility with readers in part by citing research and in part by making clear she understands the needs of both employees and employers. Kornbluh tries to convince readers her proposal will be of advantage to both parties equally. In other words, it is a "win-win" proposition, not a zero-sum game in which one side wins and the other loses.

Considering Topics for Your Own Essay

If you are interested in the problem Kornbluh describes, you might suggest other ways of helping parents juggle their parenting and work responsibilities. For example, consider writing a proposal for increasing opportunities for one or more parents to work at home via telecommuting. Alternatively, you might consider ways of improving preschool or after-school child-care arrangements. Would it be feasible, for instance, for high schools or community colleges to train interested students who could provide child care at supervised facilities on campus? You might interview people in your community to explore alternative ways of funding after-school programs. Perhaps you could propose that local businesses sponsor sports teams or offer after-school internships to students.

MATT MILLER has a B.A. in economics and a law degree, is a nationally syndicated columnist, hosts the public radio program *Left, Right, and Center* and is a commentator on *Morning Edition*, and has a Web site, mattmilleronline.com. His articles have appeared in the *Wall Street Journal*, the *New Yorker, Time*, the *New York Times Magazine, Fortune*, and *Slate*. Miller has written one book, *The Two Percent Solution: Fixing America's Problems in Ways Liberals and Conservatives Can Love* (2003), and edited a second with Kathleen Hall Jamieson, *Presidential Campaigns: Sins of Omission* (2001). He is a senior fellow at the Center for American Progress and was a senior adviser to the White House Office of Management and Budget in the Clinton administration.

"A New Deal for Teachers" first appeared in the *Atlantic Monthly* in 2003 and was drawn from *The Two Percent Solution*. As you read, think about your experiences with teachers in grade school and high school. What do you think motivated them to teach? How would you rate the quality of your teachers? Would you ever consider teaching as a career? Why or why not?

A New Deal for Teachers
Matt Miller

No one should need convincing that schools in the nation's poor districts are in crisis. A recent Department of Education study found that fourth-grade students in low-income areas tested three grade levels behind students in higher-income areas. "Most 4th graders who live in U.S. cities can't read and understand a simple children's book," a special report in *Education Week* concluded a few years ago, "and most 8th graders can't use arithmetic to solve a practical problem."

1

2

There are probably a hundred things these schools need, and ten things that could make a very big difference, but if we had to focus on only one thing, the most important would be improving teacher quality. Owing to rising enrollments and a coming wave of retirements, more than two million teachers must be recruited over the next decade — 700,000 of them in poor districts. That means fully two thirds of the teacher corps will be new to the job. Finding top talent and not simply warm bodies is a tall order, especially in urban districts, where half of new teachers quit within three years (and studies suggest that it's the smarter half). Research shows that much of the achievement gap facing poor and minority students comes not from poverty or family conditions but from systemic differences in teacher quality; thus recruiting better teachers for poor schools is not only the biggest issue in education but the next great frontier for social justice.

3

The obstacles to improving teacher quality are great. Good teachers in urban schools have told me with dismay of the incompetence of many of their colleagues. The state competency requirements that aspiring teachers must meet are appallingly low. The late Albert Shanker, the legendary president of the American Federation of Teachers, once said that most of the state tests are so easy to pass that they keep only "illiterates" out of teaching. Yet even these minimal standards are routinely waived so that districts can issue "emergency credentials"; in our biggest cities as many as half of new hires, and up to a quarter of city teachers overall, aren't properly trained or credentialed.

4

The situation may soon get even worse, because many of the teachers now reaching retirement age are among the best in the system. Until the 1960s and 1970s schools attracted talented women and minority members to whom most higher-paying careers weren't open. Now people who might once have taught science or social studies become doctors, lawyers, and engineers. Salaries that start, on average, at $29,000 simply can't compete with the pay in other professions. In 1970 in New York City a lawyer starting out at a prestigious firm and a teacher going into public education had a difference in their salaries of about $2,000. Today that lawyer makes $145,000 (including bonus), whereas the teacher earns roughly $40,000. Sandra Feldman, the president of the American Federation of Teachers, is quite open about the problem. "You have in the schools right now, among the teachers who are going to be retiring, *very* smart people," she told me. "We're not getting in the same kinds of people. In some places it's disastrous."

5

How should we address this crisis? Most discussion so far has revolved around improving the skills of the teachers we already have. But upgrading the skills of current teachers can get us only so far when so many new teachers will be needed. Although changing the kind of person who goes into teaching may be hopelessly beyond the power of local school budgets and policies, we need to seize this moment of generational turnover in the teaching ranks to lure top college graduates to our toughest classrooms.

6

How to do this? Let's stipulate first that pay isn't everything. Teachers are the only category of people I've ever met who routinely say, without irony, that their jobs are so fulfilling they hardly care how little they make. For many of them, too, job security, good health benefits and pensions, and free summers offset the low income.

But fulfillment and fringe benefits will never suffice to attract and retain hundreds of thousands of talented new teachers for poor districts.

There's no way to get large numbers of top people without paying up. Conservatives rightly worry that pouring more money into the system will subsidize mediocrity rather than lure new talent — especially when union rules make it next to impossible to fire bad teachers. "Dismissing a tenured teacher is not a process," one California official has said. "It's a career." The effort can take years and involve hundreds of thousands of dollars. Rather than being fired, bad teachers are shuffled from school to school. In a recent five-year period only sixty-two of the 220,000 tenured teachers in California were dismissed.

A grand bargain could be struck between unions and conservatives: make more money available for teachers' salaries in exchange for flexibility in how it is spent. For instance, the standard "lockstep" union pay scale, whereby a teacher with a degree in biochemistry has to be paid the same as one with a degree in physical education if both have the same number of years in the classroom (even though the biochemist has lucrative options outside teaching) should be scrapped. Better-performing teachers should make more than worse ones. And dismissing poor performers — who, even union leaders agree, make up perhaps 10 percent of urban teachers — should be made much easier.

If the quality of urban schools is to be improved, teaching poor children must become the career of choice for talented young Americans who want to make a difference with their lives and earn a good living too. To achieve that the federal government should raise the salary of every teacher in a poor school by at least *50 percent*. But this increase would be contingent on two fundamental reforms: teachers' unions would have to abandon the lockstep pay schedules, so that the top-performing half of the teacher corps could be paid significantly more; and the dismissal process for poor-performing teachers would have to be condensed to four to six months.

In Los Angeles teachers currently earn about $40,000 to start and top out, after thirty years and a Ph.D., at about $70,000. Under this new deal those teachers would start at $60,000, and the top-performing half of teachers would make $85,000 to $90,000 a year, on average. A number of the best teachers could earn close to $150,000 a year. The plan is designed to pay America's best teachers of poor students salaries high enough to allow them to put aside a million dollars in savings by the end of their careers.

How much would this plan cost? Roughly $30 billion a year, which would lift the federal share of K–12 spending from seven percent to 14 percent of the total nationwide — only right, given that on their own poor districts can't afford the skilled teachers they need. This federal investment looks modest beside the $80 billion a year that some representatives of corporate America say they spend training ill-prepared high school graduates to work in modern industry. The plan could be administered through a program similar to Title I, which provides supplementary federal funds to poor schools. We might call it Title I for Teachers.

To find out whether this basic plan is politically feasible, I presented it to big-city superintendents, high-ranking union leaders, and assorted education experts and teachers.

"I'd endorse something like that in a hot minute," said Day Higuchi, the president of the Los Angeles teachers' union from 1996 to 2002. "Right now L.A. Unified is the employer of last resort. People who can't get jobs elsewhere come here. If we did this, we'd become the employer of first resort. High-powered college students will be taking the job." Arne Duncan, the CEO of the Chicago Public Schools, told me that now there's "very little incentive outside of pure altruism" to get someone into teaching. This proposal "would dramatically change the face of the teacher profession," he said.

13

To gauge the conservative reaction, I spoke with Chester E. Finn Jr., a long-time school reformer on the right. Finn is the president of the Thomas B. Fordham Foundation and served as an assistant secretary of education in the Reagan Administration. He expressed several concerns. "The troubling part of this proposal," he said, "is a 50 percent boost for just showing up for work, without any reference to whether anybody you teach learns a damned thing."

14

I replied that the offer was designed to make it worthwhile for the unions to accept real reform in pay and dismissal practices. And the pay increase would subsidize mediocrity only briefly, because under the new dismissal rules bad teachers could much more easily be fired.

15

Finn had his own variation to offer. "If you wanted to make this plan really interesting," he told me, "job security and tenure would be traded for this raise. The swap here ought to be that you take a risk with your employment and you don't have to be retained if you're not good at what you do. If you are good and you get retained, you get paid a whole lot more money. If current teachers can't swallow that tradeoff, make this a parallel personnel system for new ones coming in and for the existing ones who want to do it."

16

How might that work? I asked.

17

"Any current teacher is free to join this new system on its terms," Finn said, "or to stick with the old arrangement, in which they have high security and low pay. That's just a political accommodation to an existing work force for whom this might be too abrupt a shift. Over time you'll get a very different kind of person into teaching."

18

"It sounds tempting from a union point of view," Sandra Feldman told me of Finn's parallel approach. "The more voluntary you can make a system like this, the easier it is to sell. But I worry that something like that could create resentment between the people in the different tracks." Other union and district leaders, however, told me they thought that virtually every new hire would opt for the new system, as would perhaps a quarter of the senior teachers — meaning that most of the urban teacher corps would be on the plan within five years.

19

That union leaders think it makes sense to move toward serious pay differentials for teachers is important. But educators are concerned about two related questions. In determining pay rates, who will decide which teachers are better performers? And what standards will be used to assess teachers?

20

I asked Sandra Feldman if there was a consensus in the faculty lounges at most schools about who the best teachers were. "Absolutely," she said. The question is how to evaluate performance in a way that is objective and untainted by cronyism.[1]

21

---

[1] partiality to friends.

The superintendents and conservative reformers I spoke to agreed that serious weight should be given to students' test scores. In theory, so-called "value-added analysis" — the effort to track the impact of teachers on student achievement each year — is the holy grail of accountability, and thus the ideal basis for performance pay. But in reality, many people think it has serious limits. "There's just no reliable way of doing that right now," Feldman told me. This isn't only a union view. Joseph Olchefske, the superintendent of schools in Seattle, has studied the issue; he believes it would be hard to measure the value added by individual teachers. Others, however, think individual value-added analysis may soon be practical. Day Higuchi, the former L.A. union leader, argues that in elementary school, where each child has essentially one teacher, the right testing could constructively measure that teacher's impact.

22

Finn and others suggested a blended approach to teacher assessment. "You could have value-added analysis at the school level, which is clearly going to be done," Finn said, "combined with some other kind of performance reviews." Adam Urbanski, the president of the Rochester Teachers Association, who has spearheaded union-reform efforts for two decades, said, "It would be a fatal mistake not to include student learning outcomes as the ultimate test of this. It would be equally fatal to use only test scores, because you would have a huge invitation to cheating and manipulation." He and others proposed that various indicators regarded as germane to teacher assessment by educators and the public — such as dropout rates, graduation rates, peer review, specialized training, teaching technique, and student work — be considered along with test scores.

23

The superintendents all told me that principals should be the final arbiters of teacher performance. This is a sticking point with the unions. The problem with giving principals control is that many teachers think principals don't know the first thing about good teaching. Jene Galvin, a teacher who has worked in the Cincinnati school system for twenty-seven years, told me, "We don't really believe that the principals are the experts on pedagogy or classroom teaching or classroom management. The reason is they just didn't do it very long." The solution might be to have peer evaluators — mentor and master teachers — do the evaluations along with principals.

24

Experts I spoke with, including Finn, thought that all these challenges ultimately seemed surmountable. Finn said that a key to his supporting such a plan would be "that it included the ability for managers of schools to have a whole lot of control over who is working in their school."

25

If this agenda were presented as a federal challenge, in which the President or congressional leaders said, "We're putting this pot of money on the table for those communities that can come together around a plan that meets its conditions and make it work," school districts would almost surely step forward. If unions declined to come to the table, local media and business leaders could ask why they were balking at billions of dollars. Rank-and-file teachers, who might earn an extra $20,000 to $50,000 a year, would obviously have a huge stake in the plan's adoption. They might tell union leaders they supported finding ways of speedily dismissing poor performers.

26

Some Republicans may resist. After all, teachers' unions are big Democratic donors and the chief foes of Republican efforts to introduce school vouchers. The last thing we need, these Republicans might say, is a bunch of teachers with more money to spend on making sure that Republicans never get elected. 27

But some savvy Republicans think the time for a plan like this is ripe. Rick Davis, a political adviser to Senator John McCain, believes that such a plan may be inevitable. "Anybody who has looked at teacher pay as an element of the overall problem in education realizes that money matters," Davis told me. "Other than the voucher debate, we've exhausted the Republican position on education. So sooner or later we're going to get to teacher pay, because we can't be against teachers' making money. The American public is going to figure out that their teachers make less than their garbage collectors, and they're not going to be for that." 28

Making Connections to Personal and Social Issues: Improving the Quality of Schools

At the beginning of this essay, Miller acknowledges that his focus on teacher quality is only one of many approaches to solving the problems plaguing the educational system. At the beginning of paragraph 2 he writes, "There are probably a hundred things these schools need, and ten things that could make a very big difference, but if we had to focus on only one thing, the most important would be improving teacher quality."

With two or three other students, discuss your experience as a student before going to high school. You may want to begin by recalling a problem you experienced as a student in elementary or middle school. For example, one student reported that he was afraid to go to the bathroom in middle school for fear of being beaten up, another told us she was so sleepy it was hard to pay attention, and yet another said there were not enough books for everyone. Then discuss how the kinds of problems you have identified might be solved. What changes in elementary or middle school would have improved the quality of your education?

Analyzing Writing Strategies

1. To **argue for his proposed solution**, Miller needs to give readers one or more **reasons** to believe that the solution he offers will indeed help solve the problem as he has defined it. At the beginning of the second paragraph, Miller announces his proposed solution: "improving teacher quality." Reread paragraphs 2 and 3 to see how he argues that "recruiting better teachers" would close the "achievement gap," as he calls it in paragraph 2. How does he try to convince readers? What do you find most and least convincing about this argument?

2. Proposal writers often **evaluate alternative solutions** that have been or could be suggested. Reread paragraph 5 and underline the solution that has been pro-

posed. What reason does Miller give for rejecting it? Reread paragraphs 2–4 and underline the information that sets the stage for Miller's rejection of this particular alternative solution. How effective is this part of Miller's argument?

Commentary: Anticipating Readers' Objections and Questions

Proposal writers usually try to **anticipate readers' objections and questions** and respond to them by counterarguing. Writers have three strategies for counterarguing: (1) they can simply acknowledge that they are aware of critics' concerns but do nothing else to respond; (2) they can accommodate the criticism, modifying their argument by making concessions; or (3) they can defend their proposed solutions and try to refute criticism. Those seeking to convince readers to take action to solve a problem nearly always try to respond by accommodating or refuting. How writers handle objections and questions affects their credibility. Readers expect writers to be respectful of other points of view and to take criticism seriously, but readers also understand that it is important that proposal writers assertively argue for and defend their solution.

Miller does not try to guess what others might say; he actually interviews people who have a stake in how the problem is resolved. He explains: "To find out whether this basic plan is politically feasible, I presented it to big-city superintendents, high-ranking union leaders, and assorted education experts and teachers" (paragraph 12). Notice that his field research has the goal of determining whether his solution is "politically feasible." All proposed solutions have to meet a feasibility test. That is, the solution has to be possible or realistic. Miller adds the word *politically* because his proposed solution is controversial and he needs to reassure readers that the people who would be most affected by the proposal are supportive and even enthusiastic. If Miller could not demonstrate widespread support for his proposal, then readers would conclude that it might solve the problem but it could never happen — in other words, it is simply not feasible.

Let us look at a couple of examples to see how Miller handles objections and questions. In paragraphs 6 and 7, he presents his reason for raising teachers' pay and anticipates likely objections to the proposed pay raises. He begins by stipulating "pay isn't everything," initially acknowledging that various benefits other than pay attract people to teaching. But then he argues against the idea that "fulfillment and fringe benefits" alone can accomplish the goal of hiring and keeping "hundreds of thousands of talented new teachers for poor districts" (paragraph 6). Instead, he argues that "paying up" is the only way to solve the problem. Next, he anticipates another objection: "Conservatives rightly worry that pouring more money into the system will subsidize mediocrity rather than lure new talent — especially when union rules make it next to impossible to fire bad teachers" (paragraph 7). This time, however, he does not try to refute the objection but concedes it is right and incorporates it into his proposed solution: To get substantial pay increases, teachers — and their unions — must agree to make it "much easier" to fire low-performing teachers (paragraph 8).

Miller carefully choreographs his moves in these paragraphs to present himself to readers as assertive, willing to defend his proposal against objections he thinks are wrong. But he also comes across as thoughtful and reasonable, willing to concede the legitimacy of others' objections.

Miller deals with questions differently. He uses questions to introduce important elements of the solution that still need to be worked out. In paragraph 20, he reports two questions raised by educators about the assessment of teachers to determine who gets a pay raise and who gets fired: "who will decide" and according to "what standards" of assessment? If we just track the assessment question, you will see that Miller does not try to answer the question himself, but chooses instead to report what others say. First, he presents Feldman's caveat, or warning, that any method of evaluating a teacher's performance must be "objective and untainted by cronyism" (paragraph 21). Although Miller does not put this requirement in his own words, the fact that he uses it to preface the discussion suggests that he thinks it is a useful guideline to follow. Next, he reports the conservative answer to use "students' test scores" as a way "to track the impact of teachers on student achievement each year" (paragraph 22). Miller explains that this answer is based on "value-added analysis," what he calls "the holy grail of accountability, and thus the ideal basis for performance pay." It would seem that by labeling it "ideal," Miller agrees with it; however, calling it "the holy grail" may be taken as tongue in cheek or teasing. Nevertheless, he goes on to report that not everyone agrees testing is the ideal method of assessment. He offers as an alternative a "blended approach to teacher assessment," and he lists the kinds of "indicators" that could be used in combination with tests (paragraph 23). Miller presents possible answers to the question of *who* decides in much the same way.

What is important is that Miller does not impose his own answers in dealing with these questions. He agrees with the experts he interviewed that "all these challenges ultimately seemed surmountable" (paragraph 25), but, like Kornbluh, Miller does not offer a one-size-fits-all solution. Ultimately, Miller argues that "communities" should decide how to answer these central questions for themselves, but that the government should provide an incentive by "putting this pot of money on the table" (paragraph 26). Moreover, by pointing out where union leaders agree with superintendents, and conservatives agree with supposedly liberal teachers, Miller gives readers hope that community members can work together to solve the problem.

Considering Topics for Your Own Essay

Consider making a proposal to improve the operation of an organization, business, or club to which you belong. For example, you might propose that your college keep administrative offices open in the evenings or on weekends to accommodate working students or that a child-care center be opened for students who are parents of young children. For a business, you might propose a system to handle customer complaints or a fairer way for employees to arrange their schedules. If you belong to a club that has a problem with the collection of dues, you might propose a new collection system or suggest alternative ways of raising money.

GIAN-CLAUDIA SCIARA has her M.A. and is working on her Ph.D. in city and regional planning. Before beginning graduate work, she was a writer on land-use and transportation issues and served as the bicycle program director for Transportation Alternatives, a New York City-area citizens' group working for improvements to benefit bicycling, walking, and public transit. Sciara is a member of the American Institute of Certified Planners and worked as senior transportation planner for Parsons Brinckerhoff, a worldwide engineering firm. She has delivered many papers at professional conferences and her writing has appeared in the *New York Times* as well as in scholarly journals such as the *Journal of Planning Education and Research, Journal of the American Planning Association,* and *Transportation Planning and Technology.* "Making Communities Safe for Bicycles" originally appeared in *Access,* the official journal of the University of California Transportation Center.

As you read this proposal, notice the design features — the subheadings, photographs, and graph — and think about how they contribute to your understanding of the proposal. You may also notice that Sciara uses neither APA nor MLA documentation styles, nor does she include parenthetical citations or a complete list of sources. Instead she follows the requirements of *Access* and ends her essay with "Further Reading." If you have the opportunity to publish your proposal or other essay, you too will be expected to use the journal's required format. When writing for your college courses, be sure to ask your instructor which documentation style you should follow.

Making Communities Safe for Bicycles
Gian-Claudia Sciara

To those who use a bicycle for transportation, it's a simple but important machine — cheap, flexible, reliable, and environmentally friendly. Moreover, bicycles are convenient. Someone traveling by bike can usually make a trip door to door, choose among various routes, and easily add stops along the way. 1

In addition to practicality for local trips, bicycles yield measurable health benefits. Public health professionals are beginning to see bicycles and bicycle-oriented community design as part of the remedy for Americans' inactive lifestyles, obesity, and related chronic diseases. Yet despite their obvious advantages, and despite federal statutes that promote bicycle planning, bicycles account for but a tiny percentage of trips in the US, even in "bicycle friendly" communities. Less than half of one percent of Americans bicycled to work in 2000. Estimates of personal and recreational bicycle use suggest that somewhere between 65 and 100 million Americans cycle sometimes. Even so, bicycles are scarcely used for everyday trips. 2

Bicycles do not belong to mainstream transportation culture here as they do in places like Holland. Today's planners and engineers inherit a legacy of transportation infrastructure built exclusively for motor vehicles. Design, redesign, and construction of bicycle-oriented infrastructure have only recently been acknowledged as public goals. Dispersed land use patterns put many trip origins and destinations too far apart for bicycle travel. But one of the biggest reasons bicycles are underused may be safety: fear of being struck by a motor vehicle discourages many would-be bicycle commuters. 3

Thinking Big: Facility Design and Routine Accommodation

A policy of "routine accommodation" is one sweeping change that could effectively increase bicycle use and, potentially, safety. In *Accommodating Bicycle and Pedestrian Travel: A Recommended Approach*, USDOT[1] acknowledges that "ongoing investment in the nation's transportation infrastructure is still more likely to overlook . . . than integrate bicyclists." In response, DOT encourages transportation agencies "to make accommodation of bicycling and walking a routine part of planning, design, construction, operations and maintenance activities."

4

Whether with wide curb lanes or separate bicycle facilities, corridors that accommodate bicyclists will attract potential riders. New York City's Hudson River Greenway is one example. An off-street facility, this path provides a north-south route paralleling Route 9A (locally known as the West Side Highway). Opening a key connection in spring 2001 exposed the latent demand for continuous bicycle facilities among New Yorkers. As seen in Figure 1, the number of cyclists jumped dramatically after the link between 55th and 72nd Streets made the facility continuous from 125th Street in Harlem to the Battery. Already one of the most-used bike routes in the US, the Hudson River Greenway provides a direct, scenic, and virtually auto-free route to downtown Manhattan.

5

Bicycle facilities — whether dedicated off-street paths, on-street lanes, or bicycle-friendly shoulders — can be controversial, even among bike advocates. Indeed some bicycle planners have argued for decades against separate bicycle facilities. Most notable among them, John Forester argues that "cyclists fare best when they act as and are treated as drivers of vehicles," and that they "can travel with speed and safety almost everywhere a road system goes." He rejects the

6

_____
[1]the U.S. Department of Transportation

proposition that "special, safer facilities must be made for cyclists so they can ride safely." However, his position ignores the range of ability and experience among cyclists. New bicyclists are more likely to ride where roads are designed with bicyclists in mind, and improvements designed to make potential bicyclists more

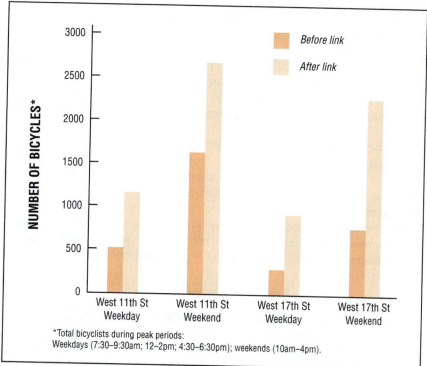

*Total bicyclists during peak periods:
Weekdays (7:30–9:30am; 12–2pm; 4:30–6:30pm); weekends (10am–4pm).

Figure 1. Route 9A Bikeway (Hudson River Greenway): Growth in bicycle use before and after Riverside South Link (2000–2001)

welcome can have dramatic results. The city of Portland, for example, attributes steadily increasing ridership from 1991 to 2001 to continued investment in its comprehensive citywide bicycle network. Portland also reports that, even with increased ridership, numbers of bicycle-motor vehicle crashes during the 1990s remained constant, which suggests a drop in the collision rate.

As policy, "routine accommodation" promises a middle ground between inflexible requirements for specific bicycle facilities and complete neglect of bicycle improvements. Bicycle design manuals (e.g., AASHTO's[2] *Guide for the Development of Bicycle Facilities*) and professional planners throughout the country have identified numerous bicycle-facility designs for a range of circumstances. But designs must be duly considered and implemented, not just cursorily reviewed and shelved. Routine accommodation implies a deliberate approach to bicycle planning and safety.

Thinking Small: Bringing Planners' Tools Up to Speed

Transportation professionals are often at a disadvantage when trying to identify bicyclists' needs, particularly with regard to safety. When asked to plan for motorized traffic, they can tap authoritative sources with detailed information about roadway volumes, network models, travel habits, collisions, etc. However, data on bicyclists, bicycle trips, and bicycle collisions are sparse. To understand how best to serve bicyclists and reduce the number and severity of bicycle collisions, it is essential to have better data than currently exist about who rides, how often, how far, how long, on what routes, etc., and especially about the causes of collisions.

Bicyclists themselves are a latent source of valuable information. Regional travel surveys and revisions to transportation demand models should routinely draw on data solicited from them. In many places bicycle advocacy groups have grown increasingly involved in local planning efforts. Planners may find cyclists to be effective partners when seeking appropriate facilities and safety measures.

Planners should be able to consult motor-vehicle collision data to identify causes — and remedies — of bicycle collisions. However, collision data are collected in a system geared toward motor vehicles. Collision report forms often do not separately identify "bicycle" as a possible party to a collision. Also, damage thresholds keep police from reporting many bicycle collisions. Although $500 may truly represent minimal damage to a motor vehicle, equivalent damage to a bicycle could render it useless. One potential remedy would require officers to report any traffic collision involving a bicycle. We might then better understand nonfatal bicycle collisions. (Fatal collisions, as a rule, are well documented.)

Education and Enforcement

Analyses of vehicle collisions have led to safety improvements through vehicle redesign, driver education, targeted enforcement, and modified vehicle codes. At the 1993 World Conference on Injury Control, Michael Brownlee pointed out that "over

_____

[2]the American Association of State Highway and Transit officials

Sensors in the pavement can make crossings safer for bicyclists

the last ten years, the accomplishments in highway safety have overshadowed all other periods in our history. About 40,000 people are alive today because of the progress made in preventing drunk driving . . . An additional 30,000 lives were saved due to increases in safety belt use." What if the safety of bicyclists were accorded comparable priority? What if bicycle and motorist education campaigns were pursued on a scale equivalent to aggressive drunk driving and seatbelt campaigns? Since 1932, the first year when estimates were recorded, over 47,000 cyclists have been killed in traffic collisions, according to the National Highway Traffic Safety Administration (NHTSA). From 1995 to 2000, cyclist fatalities trended downward; nevertheless, an average of over 750 bicyclists were killed each year. NHTSA data do not capture crashes not involving a motor vehicle or not occurring on a public roadway, but experts estimate an additional 80 bicyclists die each year, an annual total of 830 bicyclist deaths. Also, 51,000 cyclists were injured in *reported* traffic collisions in the year 2000, accounting for two percent of all reported vehicular crash injuries.

Some researchers suggest that most bicycle crashes involve only one bike and its rider, but that is not reason enough to ignore bicycle-motor vehicle conflicts. Collisions with motor vehicles can result in serious injury. And because we know many causes of bicycle-motor vehicle collisions, we also know what specific behavioral changes can reduce these conflicts. For example, at intersections and driveways, bicyclists and drivers need to make eye contact with each other. As bicyclists and motorists learn to coexist, each should be on guard for the other's bad habits. Motorists should learn to anticipate bicyclists coming from unexpected locations and directions. Also, bicyclists can actively prevent dooring (i.e., colliding

12

with a vehicle door opening into the bicyclist's path) by riding a safe distance to the left of parked vehicles. A novice bicyclist might understandably be reluctant to do this, as it means moving into ("taking") the lane; and many motorists do not recognize the danger from dooring.

Safety instruction for bicyclists is important. Bicycle-safety education efforts, where they exist, most commonly target bicyclists. Essential rules of the road for bicyclists are to obey traffic signals and stop signs, be careful entering roadways at midblock, and ride with the flow of traffic. However, motorist education is also important, though often more difficult and costly. In some states, driver education doesn't even mention bicycles. Aggressive public service campaigns are not within reach of many bicycle-planning budgets. Understandably, planners would rather use bicycle dollars to improve and build facilities than to fund costly and marginally effective advertising. Nevertheless, motorist education could save lives by emphasizing caution when pulling into the street and opening doors, consistent use of turn signals, safe speeds, and obedience to traffic signals and stop signs.   13

Making routine enforcement of traffic laws a priority would help. However, law enforcement officers who are knowledgeable about motor vehicle laws may be less informed about bicyclists' rights and responsibilities. Moreover, some officers are unfamiliar with the infractions most often associated with bicycle-motor vehicle collisions. Some bicycle advocates contend that police are quick to assume the bicyclist caused the collision, or that officers are prone to cite bicyclists illegitimately because they themselves don't know the law. One bicyclists' attorney notes that bicyclists are often cited for speeding when they are not traveling any faster than motor vehicles in the same situation. A study of Los Angeles collision data found most bicycle citations were issued for failure to ride as close as practicable to the right-hand curb, suggesting ignorance of vehicle code provi-   14

sions entitling cyclists to take the lane in circumstances where curb-hugging is unsafe or inadvisable.

Where To Go From Here

Bicycles are here to stay. Current trends suggest more commuters and recreational riders will turn to bikes for travel, particularly where the design of local transportation networks accommodates bicycles. So planners and policy makers face a choice. They can continue as they have, focusing on cars and considering bicycles only when compelled to. If so, we can expect things to remain as they are, with little support from law enforcement, marginal bicycle facilities, many bicycle injuries, and frustrated bicyclists and motorists.

Or, planners, engineers, and policy makers can acknowledge the benefits of bicycle riding and adopt a policy of routine accommodation. A 1995 survey conducted for Rodale Press queried respondents first about their current primary means of travel and second about their preferred means of travel, "all things being equal, and if good facilities [for each mode] existed." The percentage of people who chose to walk or bicycle increased from 5 to 13 percent under those hypothetical circumstances; those who chose driving alone dropped from 76 to 56 percent.

More and better facilities would enhance safety and encourage riding. More bicyclists might accustom motorists to sharing the road and in turn might encourage still more cyclists. Both factors would increase bike safety. Enhanced bike safety might encourage some motorists to try riding; more people switching to bicycles might mean fewer cars on the road, less congestion, better public health, and safer conditions for bicyclists and pedestrians — and even less competition for parking.

Further Reading

Bruce Epperson, "Demographic and Economic Characteristics of Bicyclists Involved in Bicycle-Motor Vehicle Accidents," *Transportation Research Record*, 1502: pp. 56–64, Transportation Research Board, 1995.

John Forester, "Two Views in Cycling Transportation Engineering," *Bicycle Transportation: A Handbook for Cycling Transportation Engineers*, 2nd Edition. (Cambridge, MA: The MIT Press, 1994).

James O'Day, *Synthesis of Highway Practice 192: Accident Data Quality*. National Cooperative Highway Research Program, Transportation Research Board, National Research Council. (Washington, D.C.: National Academy Press, 1993).

Parkwood Research Associates. "Pathways for People II," Rodale Press, 1995.

John Pucher, "Cycling Safety on Bikeways vs. Roads," *Transportation Quarterly*, vol. 55, no. 4, Fall 2001.

Gregory B. Rodgers et al. *Bicycle Use and Hazard Patterns in the United States*. Study No. 344. (Washington, D.C.: US Consumer Product Safety Commission, June 1994). http://www.cpsc.gov/cpscpub/pubs/344.pdf

Jane C. Stutts and William W. Hunter, "Motor Vehicle and Roadway Factors in Pedestrian and Bicyclist Injuries: An Examination Based on Emergency Department Data," *Accident Analysis and Prevention*, vol. 31, pp. 505–514, 1999.

Robert G. Thom and Alan Clayton, "Accident Requirements for Improving Cycling Safety," *Transportation Research Record*, 1405: pp. 1–6, Transportation Research Board, 1993.

Making Connections to Personal and Social Issues: Experience with Bicycles

With two or three other students, discuss Sciara's proposal to make bicycle riding more attractive. Begin by telling the others in your group whether you use a bicycle for your everyday trips and, if not, why not. Recall whether you used a bicycle for basic transportation when you were younger and how well it worked. What prevents you from using a bicycle in the same way now?

Then discuss the kinds of changes that would need to be made to make bike riding part of your own and other people's "mainstream transportation culture" (paragraph 3). Would the kinds of infrastructure changes Sciara proposes help you commute by bike to work or school? Would making it inexpensive and easy to take a bicycle on a bus, train, or even to a carpool site help?

Analyzing Writing Strategies

1. To **define the problem**, proposal writers usually need to establish both that it exists and is important. Reread paragraphs 1–3 of Sciara's proposal to identify the problem. As you read, also make notes about the kinds of information Sciara presents.

   Then, explain the problem in a sentence or two. How does the information she presents help to convince readers that the problem really exists and is important enough to be worth solving?

2. Proposal writers often try to **anticipate possible objections** to their proposed solution. Sciara does this in paragraph 6, where she discusses an objection raised by John Forester to her proposal that city planners should accommodate bicyclists by making "wide curb lanes or separate bicycle" paths. Reread the sec-

tion on "facility design and routine accommodation" in paragraphs 4–7, and underline Forester's objection. Then make notes about how Sciara counterargues his objection. Finally, evaluate how successful her counterargument seems to be for its intended readers — city planners. What seems most and least convincing in her counterargument?

Commentary: Describing and Arguing for the Proposed Solution

Like many solutions, Sciara's is multifaceted. Nevertheless, she makes every effort to describe her solution in a way that readers cannot miss. She begins by announcing simply and directly at the end of paragraph 3 that "one of the biggest reasons bicycles are underused may be safety." She then goes on to propose a tripartite approach to making bike riding safer, each part introduced by a heading:

1. "Thinking Big: Facility Design and Routine Accommodation" argues that constructing bicycle paths will ensure safety and attract riders (paragraphs 4–7);

2. "Thinking Small: Bringing Planners' Tools Up to Speed" argues that research will give planners important information to enhance safety (paragraphs 8–10);

3. "Education and Enforcement" argues that bicyclists and motorists need to be educated about safety and police need to enforce traffic laws (paragraphs 11–14).

In the first two paragraphs of the essay, Sciara presents several reasons why communities should be made safer for bicycle riders; however, she does not spell out most of her reasons. She condenses them in a few key words that she expects readers will be able to unpack for themselves: *cheap, flexible, reliable, environmentally friendly, convenient,* and *health benefits*. For example, the word *cheap* implies that bicycle riding should be promoted because it is a means of transportation accessible to most able-bodied people. *Environmentally friendly*, of course, indicates that bicycle riding could help reduce American dependence on foreign oil and also reduce pollution. The only reason for promoting bicycle riding that Sciara bothers to explain is *health benefits*, arguing that bicycling could provide a "remedy for Americans' inactive lifestyles, obesity, and related chronic diseases."

Sciara also gives reasons and support for each of the three parts of her proposed solution. For example, look at the section "Thinking Big." At the beginning of paragraph 4, she asserts the "policy of 'routine accommodation' . . . could effectively increase bicycle use and, potentially, safety." She identifies three ways to carry out this policy: "dedicated off-street paths, on-street lanes, or bicycle-friendly shoulders" (paragraph 6). To support her argument that infrastructure redesign would make bicyclists feel safer and therefore encourage bike riding, Sciara cites two examples: "New York City's Hudson River Greenway" (paragraph 5) and Portland's "comprehensive citywide bicycle network" (paragraph 6). To demonstrate that "the number of cyclists jumped dramatically" in New York with the completion of the auto-free bicycle corridor, she presents a bar graph, Figure 1, showing the statistics at a glance (paragraph 5). For the Portland example, she refers to "reports" of "steadily increasing ridership from 1991 to 2001." In addition, she suggests that because the number of accidents "remained constant" even though the number of bicyclists increased, there was actually "a drop in the collision rate" (paragraph 6).

These examples not only allow Sciara to demonstrate that infrastructure changes can attract bicyclists and enhance safety, but also show that such changes are feasible. In other words, they can be done.

Considering Topics for Your Own Essay

Sciara's essay proposes changes that would affect conventional thinking and behavior in terms of bicycle use. You might consider writing an essay proposing changes to conventional thinking and behavior of another sort. Think, for example, of the many things that happen in high school and college that reflect conventional thinking and behavior. Conventional practices that have changed very little over the years include the way exams are administered, groups are instructed, graduation ceremonies are conducted, and admission requirements for athletes are lowered. Think of additional examples of conventional practices in high school or college; then select one that you believe needs to be improved or refined in some way. What changes would you propose? What individual or group might be convinced to take action on your proposal for improvement? What questions or objections should you anticipate? How could you discover whether others have previously proposed improvements in the practice you are concerned with? Whom might you interview to learn more about the practice and the likelihood of changing it?

■ Purpose and Audience

Most proposals are calls to action. Because of this clear purpose, a writer must anticipate readers' needs and concerns more when writing a proposal than in any other kind of writing. The writer attempts not only to convince readers but also to inspire them, to persuade them to support or implement the proposed solution. What your particular readers know about the problem and what they are capable of doing to solve it determine how you address them.

Readers of proposals are often unaware of the problem. In this case, your task is clear: to present them with evidence that will convince them of its existence. This evidence may include statistics, testimony from witnesses or experts, and examples, including the personal experiences of people involved with the problem. You can also speculate about the cause of the problem and describe its ill effects.

Sometimes readers recognize the existence of a problem but fail to take it seriously. When readers are indifferent, you may need to connect the problem closely to their own concerns. For instance, you might show how much they have in common with the people directly affected by it or how it affects them indirectly. However you appeal to readers, you must do more than alert them to the problem; you must also make them care about it. You want to touch readers emotionally as well as intellectually.

At other times, readers concerned about the problem may assume that someone else is taking care of it and that they need not become personally involved. In this situation, you might want to demonstrate that the people they thought were taking care of the problem have failed. Another assumption readers might make is that a solution they supported in the past has already solved the problem. You might point out that the original solution has proved unworkable or that new solutions have become available through changed circumstances or improved technology. Your aim is to rekindle these readers' interest in the problem.

Perhaps the most satisfying proposals are addressed to parties who can take immediate action to remedy the problem. You may have the opportunity to write such a proposal if you choose a problem faced by a group to which you belong. Not only do you have a firsthand understanding of the problem, but you also have a good idea of the kinds of solutions that other members of the group will support. (You might informally survey some of them before you submit your proposal to test your definition of the problem and your proposed solution.) When you address readers who are in a position to take action, you want to assure them that it is wise to do so. You must demonstrate that the solution is feasible — that it can be implemented and that it will work.

Basic Features: Proposing Solutions

A Well-Defined Problem

A proposal is written to offer a solution to a problem. Before presenting the solution, the writer must be sure that readers know and understand what the problem is. Patrick O'Malley, for example, devotes the first three paragraphs of his essay to defining the problem of infrequent course exams. Similarly, Karen Kornbluh, Matt Miller, and Gian-Claudia Sciara describe the problem in their first few paragraphs.

Stating the problem is not enough, however; the writer also must establish the problem as serious enough to need solving. Occasionally a writer can assume that readers will recognize the problem and its seriousness, as do Miller and Sciara. Most often, writers assume readers do not understand the problem and will need to be convinced that it deserves their attention. For example, O'Malley knows other students reading the proposal will understand the seriousness of the problem, but he assumes his intended readers — professors who can remedy the problem — will need to be convinced. To help them understand the students' point of view, he begins the proposal with a scenario and a series of rhetorical questions that dramatize the plight of students studying for a high-stakes exam. Similarly, Kornbluh provides a historical context and statistics to convince readers that the "juggler family" is a new and pressing problem that must be addressed.

In defining the problem, writers usually stress its negative consequences. O'Malley, for instance, describes students' stress and poor performance on high-stakes exams. Miller examines "the achievement gap facing poor and minority students" (paragraph 2). Kornbluh shows how families are struggling to care for children and dependent parents.

A Clearly Described Solution

Once the problem is defined and its existence established, the writer must describe the solution so that readers can readily imagine what it would be like. Because O'Malley assumes that his readers know what brief exams are like, he runs little risk in not describing them. He does, however, identify their approximate lengths and possible forms — brief essay, short answer, or multiple choice. Kornbluh proposes leaving the details for a flexible work schedule up to employers to negotiate with their employees, but lists "examples" to illustrate how flexibility might be achieved: "part-time, annualized hours, compressed hours, flex-time, job-sharing, shift working, staggered hours, and telecommuting" (paragraph 17). Miller proposes what he calls a "grand bargain" that would raise the salary of successful teachers but also make it easier to fire those who perform poorly (paragraph 8).

A Convincing Argument in Support of the Proposed Solution

The main purpose of a proposal is to convince readers that the writer's solution will help solve the problem. To this end, O'Malley gives three reasons why he thinks a greater number of brief exams will solve the problem and supports each reason with published research studies as well as his own experience. Kornbluh does not have to argue that a flexible work schedule will solve the problem she is discussing because it is obvious that workers need flexibility to spend more time with children and take care of sick relatives.

Writers must also argue that the proposed solution is feasible. Kornbluh argues that her proposed solution is feasible by pointing to the fact that it has already been accomplished in Europe and that American business has already accommodated disabled workers in ways that workers with families also need. Similarly, Sciara asserts the feasibility of dedicated bicycle paths on the basis of the success of New York City's Hudson River Greenway and Portland's "citywide bicycle network" (paragraphs 5–6). Miller devotes most of his essay to demonstrating that his plan is "politically feasible" by reporting interviews with experts and stakeholders across the political spectrum (a strategy he announces in paragraph 12).

The easier a solution is to implement, the more likely it is to win readers' support. Therefore, writers sometimes set out the steps required to put the proposed solution into practice, an especially important strategy when the solution might seem difficult, time-consuming, or expensive to enact. For example, O'Malley offers professors several specific ways to give their students frequent, brief exams. Kornbluh recommends a plan and timetable to implement improvements in workplace flexibility. By not dictating a one-size-fits-all plan, she invests her proposal with the same flexibility she wants employers to make available to employees. Like Kornbluh, Miller seems flexible about the exact details of the solution, suggesting the government put a "pot of money on the table" and let "communities . . . come together around a plan" (paragraph 26).

An Anticipation of Readers' Objections and Questions

The writer arguing for a proposal must anticipate and respond to objections and questions that readers may have about the proposed solution. Both Miller and O'Malley interview people to discover what problems they might have with the proposed solution. Miller, for example, acknowledges several objections, tries to refute some, and concedes one, making it part of his proposed solution. O'Malley presents three objections — that students should be treated like adults, that there is not enough class time for so many exams, and that exams take too much time to grade — and tries to refute all of them. Sciara also raises and refutes several objections. For example, she quotes John Forester's argument against separate bicycle facilities and counterargues that Forester "ignores the range of ability and experience among cyclists" (paragraph 6).

In addition to anticipating objections, proposal writers need to respond to likely questions readers may have. Miller anticipates five predictable questions. The first three — "How should we address this crisis?"

(paragraph 5), "How to do this?" (paragraph 6), and "How much would this plan cost?" (paragraph 11) — are the kinds of questions that are likely to be asked of most any proposal: What is the proposed solution? Can it be implemented? and is it feasible? Miller's final two questions are specific to the problem he is trying to solve: "who will decide?" which teachers get a raise and which get fired, and according to "what standards?" (paragraph 20). Instead of answering these questions, Miller presents alternative points of view and concludes that the people involved have to work the answers out themselves.

An Evaluation of Alternative Solutions

Proposal writers sometimes try to convince readers that the proposed solution is preferable to other possible solutions. They may compare the proposed solution to other solutions readers may know about or ones they may think of themselves. O'Malley, for example, evaluates three alternative solutions — study-skills training, study questions, and sample exam questions as alternatives to frequent exams — and demonstrates what is wrong with each one. He rejects study-skills training because it is overly complicated, time-consuming, and expensive. He rejects study questions because, compared with exams, they would not save either students or professors any time or ensure that students each do their own individual work. He refutes the sample exam questions by arguing that they solve only part of the problem (paragraphs 10–12).

Kornbluh also evaluates three alternative solutions — sick leave or vacation time, the Family and Medical Leave Act (FMLA), and firms already providing flexible work arrangements — and shows how they are not viable because many workers do not get sick leave or vacation time, the FMLA does not guarantee paid leave, and businesses only make arrangements for highly paid executives (paragraph 2). Miller rejects the alternative solution of "upgrading the skills of current teachers" because the scale of the problem is too large (paragraph 5), but he argues that Chester E. Finn Jr.'s variation on his proposed solution should be considered seriously (paragraphs 16–19).

Proposing a Solution

Invention and Research

What is a problem that needs to be solved in a community or group you belong to? Is your dorm too noisy for you to study there? Are tips declining at your restaurant job? Do some thinking, writing, and research about possible solutions. Then decide on a tentative proposal about what action to take and who should take it. . . . **See p. 363 for more.**

Planning and Drafting

As you look over what you have written and learned about your subject so far, can you make a convincing case for your proposal? How can you engage readers' interest in the problem? What questions are they likely to have about your proposed solution? Make a plan for your proposal essay, and start drafting it. . . . **See p. 372 for more.**

Critical Reading Guide

What are your draft's strengths and weaknesses? Have you defined the problem clearly enough? Have you neglected to discuss alternative solutions that have been proposed? Get a classmate, a friend, a writing tutor, or someone else to read and respond to your essay, especially the parts you are most unsure of. . . . **See p. 378 for more.**

Revising

As you consider your essay again in light of your reader's comments, how can you improve it? Can you define the problem more clearly? Do you need to explain more fully how your solution would be implemented or how much it would cost? Go through your draft systematically, making changes wherever necessary. . . . **See p. 380 for more.**

Editing and Proofreading

Have you checked for errors that are especially likely in writing that proposes a solution? Have you used *this* or *that* ambiguously, so that readers cannot tell what noun they refer to? Do any sentences about implementing the solution not indicate clearly who should be doing so? Look for and correct these and any other errors. . . . **See p. 384 for more.**

■ The Writing Assignment

Write an essay proposing a solution to a problem. Choose a problem faced by a community or group to which you belong, and address your proposal to one or more members of the group or to outsiders who might help solve the problem.

■ Invention and Research

The following activities will help you prepare to write a proposal. You will choose a problem you can write about, analyze and define the problem, identify your prospective readers, decide on and defend your proposed solution, test your choice, offer reasons and support for adopting your proposal, and consider readers' objections and alternative solutions, among other things. These activities are easy to complete. Doing them over several days will give your ideas time to ripen and grow. Be sure to keep a written record of your invention and research to use later when you draft and revise.

Finding a Problem to Write About

You may have already thought about a problem you could write about. Or you may have been drawn to one of the problems suggested by the Considering Topics for Your Own Essay activities following one of the readings in this chapter. Even so, you will want to consider several problems that need solving before making your final choice. The following activity will help you get started.

Listing Problems. *Make a list of problems you could write about.* Make a double-column chart like the following one. Divide a piece of paper or your computer screen into two columns. In the left-hand column, list communities, groups, or organizations to which you belong. Include as many communities as possible: college, neighborhood, hometown, and cultural or ethnic groups. Also include groups you participate in: sports, musical, work, religious, political, support, hobby, and so on. In the right-hand column, list any problems that exist within each group. Here is how such a chart might begin:

Community	*Problem*
My college	Poor advising or orientation
	Shortage of practice rooms in music building
	No financial aid for part-time students
	Lack of facilities for disabled students
	Lack of enough sections of required courses
	Class scheduling that does not accommodate working students or students with children

My neighborhood   Need for traffic light at dangerous intersection
                    Unsupervised children getting into trouble
                    Megastores driving away small businesses
                    Lack of safe places for children to play

■ *Listing Problems Related to Identity and Community.*   Writing a proposal can give you special insight into issues of identity and community by helping you understand how members of a community negotiate their individual needs and concerns. You may already have made a chart of communities to which you belong and problems in those communities. The following categories may help you think of additional problems in those or other communities that you could add to your list:

- Disagreement over conforming to community standards
- Conflicting economic, cultural, or political interests within the community
- Problems with equity or fairness between men and women, rich and poor, different ethnic groups
- Lack of respect or trust among the members of the community
- Struggles for leadership of the community

■ *Listing Problems Related to Work and Career.*   Proposals are frequently written on the job and about the work people do. Based on your work experience, make a double-column chart like the following one. List the places you have worked in the left column and the problems you encountered on the job in the right column.

Workplace	*Problem*
Restaurant	Inadequate training
	Conflicts with supervisor
	Unfair shift assignments
Department store	Inadequate inventory
	Computer glitches
	Overcomplicated procedures
Office	Unfair workloads
	Changing requirements
	Inflexible work schedules
	Lack of information about procedures
	Difficulty in scheduling vacations
	Outdated technology

Choosing a Problem.   *Choose one problem from your list that seems especially important to you, that concerns others in the group or community, and that seems solvable.* (You need not know the exact solution now.) The problem should also be one that you can explore in detail and are willing to discuss in writing.

Proposing to solve a problem in a group or community to which you belong gives you an inestimably important advantage: You can write as an expert, an insider. You know about the history of the problem, have felt the urgency to solve it, and perhaps have already thought of possible solutions. Equally important, you will know precisely to whom to address the proposal, and you can interview others in the group to get their views of the problem and to understand how they might resist your solution. From such a position of knowledge and authority comes confident, convincing writing.

Should you want to propose a solution for a social problem of national scope, concentrate on one with which you have direct experience and for which you can suggest a detailed plan of action. Even better, focus on unique local aspects of the problem. For example, if you would like to propose a solution to the lack of affordable child care for children of college students or working parents, you have a great advantage if you are a parent who has experienced the frustration of finding professional, affordable child care. Moreover, even though such a problem is national in scope, it may be solvable only campus by campus, business by business, or neighborhood by neighborhood.

Analyzing and Defining the Problem

Before you can begin to consider the best possible solution, you must analyze the problem carefully and then try to define it. Keep in mind that you will have to demonstrate to readers that the problem exists, that it is serious, and that you have a more than casual understanding of its causes and consequences. If you find that you cannot do so, you will want to select some other problem to write about.

Analyzing.   *Start by writing a few sentences in response to these questions:*

- Does the problem really exist? How can I tell?
- What caused this problem? Can I identify any immediate causes? Any deeper causes? Is the problem caused by a flaw in the system, a lack of resources, individual misconduct or incompetence? How can I tell?
- What is the history of the problem?
- What are the bad effects of the problem? How does it harm members of the community or group? What goals of the group are endangered by the existence of this problem? Does it raise any moral or ethical questions?
- Who in the community or group is affected by the problem? Be as specific as possible: Who is seriously affected? Minimally affected? Unaffected? Does anyone benefit from its existence?
- What similar problems exist in this same community or group? How can I distinguish my problem from these?

Defining.   *Write a definition of the problem, being as specific as possible.* Identify who or what seems responsible for it, and give one recent, telling example.

Identifying Your Readers

In a few sentences, describe your readers, stating your reason for directing your proposal to them. Then take a few minutes to write about these readers. Whom do you need to address — everyone in the community or group, a committee, an individual, an outsider? You want to address your proposal to the person or group who can help implement it. The following questions will help you develop a profile of your readers:

- How informed are my readers likely to be about the problem? Have they shown any awareness of it?

- Why would this problem be important to my readers? Why would they care about solving it?

- Have my readers supported any other proposals to solve this problem? If so, what do those proposals have in common with mine?

- Do my readers ally themselves with any group, and would that alliance cause them to favor or reject my proposal? Do we share any values or attitudes that could bring us together to solve the problem?

- How have my readers responded to other problems? Do their past reactions suggest anything about how they might respond to my proposal?

Finding a Tentative Solution

Solving problems takes time. Apparent solutions often turn out to be impossible. After all, a solution has to be both workable and acceptable to the community or group involved. Consequently, you should strive to come up with several possible solutions whose advantages and disadvantages you can weigh. You may notice that the most imaginative solutions sometimes occur to you only after you have struggled with a number of other possibilities.

Look back at the way you defined the problem and described your readers. Then with these factors in mind, list as many possible solutions to the problem as you can think of. You might come up with only two or three possible solutions; but at this stage, the more the better. To come up with different solutions, use the following problem-solving questions:

- What solutions to this problem have already been tried?

- What solutions have been proposed for related problems? Might they solve this problem as well?

- Is a solution required that would disband or change the community or group in some way?

- What solution might eliminate some of the causes of the problem?

- What solution would eliminate any of the bad effects of the problem?

- Is the problem too big to be solved all at once? Can I divide it into several related problems? What solutions might solve one or more of these problems?

- If a series of solutions is required, which should come first? Second?

- What solution would ultimately solve the problem?

- What might be a daring solution, arousing the most resistance but perhaps holding out the most promise?

- What would be the most conservative solution, acceptable to nearly everyone in the community or group?

Give yourself enough time to let your ideas percolate as you continue to add to your list of possible solutions and to consider the advantages and disadvantages of each one in light of your prospective readers. If possible, discuss your solutions with those members of the community or group who can help you consider the advantages and disadvantages of each one.

Choosing the Most Promising Solution.   *In a sentence or two, state what you consider the best possible way of solving the problem.*

Determining Specific Steps.   *Write down the major stages or steps necessary to carry out your solution.* This list of steps will provide an early test of whether your solution can, in fact, be implemented.

Defending Your Solution

Proposals have to be feasible — that is, they must be both reasonable and practical. Imagine that one of your readers strongly opposes your proposed solution and confronts you with the following statements. *Write a few sentences refuting each one.*

- It would not really solve the problem.
- I am comfortable with things as they are.
- We cannot afford it.
- It would take too long.
- People would not do it.
- Too few people would benefit.
- I do not even see how to get started on your solution.
- We already tried that, with unsatisfactory results.
- You support this proposal merely because it would benefit you personally.

Answering these questions should help you prepare responses to possible objections. If you feel that you need a better idea of how others are likely to feel about your proposal, talk with a few people who are directly involved with or affected by the problem. The more you know about your readers' concerns, the better you will be able to anticipate their reservations and preferred alternative solutions.

Testing Your Choice

Now examine the problem and your proposed solution to see whether you can write a strong proposal. *Start by asking yourself the following questions:*

- Is this a significant problem? Do other people in the community or group really care about it, or can they be persuaded to care?

- Will my solution really solve the problem? Have you worked out how it can be implemented in an affordable way?
- Can I answer objections from enough people in the community or group to win support for my solution?

Do You Know Enough? *Review your invention notes to see whether you understand the problem well enough to argue convincingly for your solution.* To make this decision, try to answer the following questions:

- Do I now know enough about the problem or can I learn what I need to know in the time remaining?
- Do I understand the problem well enough to convince my readers that it really exists and is serious?

Do You Care Enough? In choosing a problem, you are making a commitment both to yourself and to your readers. You are obligating yourself to do the work necessary to learn what you need to know about the problem and to develop an argument supporting your solution. At the same time, you are making a commitment to your readers to make your proposal feasible. *To decide whether you can make this commitment, try to answer the following questions:*

- *Do you feel a personal interest in the problem you have chosen?* If so, on what in your experience or learning might this interest be based? Have you chosen a problem related to a special interest of yours? Have you known something about this problem for a long time, or are you just now beginning to learn about it? Is the problem so interesting to you that you are willing to arrange your time over the next two or three weeks to work on your proposal?
- *Do you think you can make a convincing argument for your proposed solution?* Are you convinced that your solution is better than the alternative solutions your readers may prefer?

As you plan and draft your proposal, you will probably want to consider these questions again. If at any point you decide that you cannot answer them with a confident yes, you may want to consider proposing a different, more feasible solution to the problem; if none exists, you may need to choose a different problem to write about.

A Collaborative Activity: Testing Your Choice

At this point, you will find it useful to get together with two or three other students and present your plans to one another. This collaborative activity will help you determine whether you can write this proposal in a way that will interest and convince others.

Presenters: Take turns briefly defining the problem you hope to solve, identifying your intended readers, and describing your proposed solution.

Listeners: Tell the presenter whether the proposed solution seems appropriate and feasible for the situation and intended readers. Suggest objections and reservations you believe readers may have.

Offering Reasons for Your Proposal

To make a convincing case for your proposed solution, you must offer your readers good reasons for adopting your proposal.

Listing Reasons.   *Write down every plausible reason you could give that might persuade readers to accept your proposal.* These reasons should answer your readers' key question: Why is this the best possible solution?

Choosing the Strongest Reasons.   *Put an asterisk next to the strongest reasons — the reasons most likely to be convincing to your intended readers.* If you do not consider at least two or three of your reasons strong, you will probably have difficulty developing a strong proposal and should reconsider your topic.

Evaluating Your Strongest Reasons.   *Now look at your strongest reasons and explain briefly why you think each one will be effective with your particular readers, the members of the group or community you are addressing.*

Considering Alternative Solutions

List alternative solutions that members of the group or community might offer when they learn about your solution, and consider the advantages and disadvantages of each one relative to your solution. Even if members are likely to consider your proposal reasonable, they will probably want to compare your proposed solution with other possible solutions. You might find it helpful to chart the information as follows:

Possible Solutions	Advantages	Disadvantages
My solution		
Alternative solution 1		
Alternative solution 2		
Etc.		

Searching the Web can be a productive way of learning about solutions other people have proposed or tried out. If possible, use your online research to identify at least two alternative solutions. Your purpose is to gain information about these solutions that will help you evaluate them fairly. Here are some specific suggestions for finding information about solutions:

- Enter keywords — words or brief phrases related to the problem or a solution — into a search tool such as Google (www.google.com) or Yahoo! (www.yahoo.com). For example, if you are concerned that many children in your neighborhood have no adult supervision after school, you could try keywords associated with the problem such as *latchkey kids* or keywords associated with possible solutions such as *after-school programs*.

- If you think solutions to your problem may have been proposed by a government agency, you could try adding the word *government* to your keywords or searching on FirstGov.gov, the U.S. government's official Web portal. For example, you might explore

An Online Activity: Researching Alternative Solutions

the problem of latchkey children by following links at the Web site of the U.S. Department of Health & Human Services (www.hhs.gov). If you want to see whether the problem has been addressed in your state or by local government, you can go to the Library of Congress Internet Resource Page on State and Local Governments (www.loc.gov/global/state/) and follow the links.

Add to your chart of the advantages and disadvantages of alternative solutions any information you find from your online research. Bookmark or keep a record of promising sites. You may want to download or copy information you could use in your essay, including visuals; if so, remember to record documentation information.

Doing Research

For guidelines on library and Internet research, see Chapter 21.

So far you have relied largely on your own knowledge and experience for ideas about solving the problem. *You may now feel that you need to do some research to learn more about the causes of the problem and to find more technical information about implementing the solution.*

If you are proposing a solution to a problem about which others have written, you will want to find out how they have defined the problem and what solutions they have proposed. You may need to acknowledge these solutions in your essay, either accommodating or refuting them. Now is a good time — before you start drafting — to get any additional information you need. If you are proposing a solution to a local problem, you will want to conduct informal interviews with several people who are aware of or affected by the problem. Find out whether they know anything about its history and current ill effects. Try out your solution on them. Discover whether they have other solutions in mind.

For more on interviewing, see Chapter 20.

Designing Your Document

Think about whether your readers might benefit from design features such as headings or numbered or bulleted lists or from visuals such as drawings, photographs, tables, or graphs. Elements like these often make the presentation of a problem easier to follow and a solution more convincing. Earlier in this chapter, for example, Karen Kornbluh's proposal about flexibility in the workplace uses headings to introduce the major sections, and Gian-Claudia Sciara's proposal about making communities safe for bicyclists uses headings, photographs, and a bar graph.

For more on document design, see Chapter 25. For guidelines on acknowledging the sources of visuals, see Chapter 22.

Consider reviewing other published proposals, either in print or online, to see how they use design elements and visuals to support and strengthen their arguments. Look back at the sample writing scenarios that open this chapter, specifically at the one about the student making a proposal to require commercial television networks to provide programming to help preschool children learn English. What design features and visuals might he use to present the statistics that establish the need for his proposed solution and the programs that he presents as models for it?

Defining Your Purpose for Your Readers

Write a few sentences defining your purpose in proposing a solution to a problem of concern to the particular readers you have in mind. Remember that you have already identified your readers in the group or community you are addressing and developed your proposal with these readers in mind. Given these readers, try now to define your purpose by considering the following questions:

- Do I seek incremental, moderate, or radical change? Am I being realistic about what my readers are prepared to do? How can I overcome their natural aversion to change of any kind?

- How can I ensure that my readers will not remain indifferent to the problem?

- Who can I count on for support, and what can I do to consolidate that support? Who will oppose my solution? Shall I write them off or seek common ground with them?

- What exactly do I want my readers to do? To take my proposed solution as a starting point for further discussion about the problem? To take action immediately to implement my solution? To commit themselves to take certain preliminary steps, like seeking funding or testing the feasibility of the solution? To take some other action?

Formulating a Tentative Thesis Statement

Write one or more sentences that could serve as your tentative thesis statement. In most essays proposing solutions to problems, the thesis statement is a concise assertion or announcement of the solution. Think about how emphatic you should make the thesis and whether you should include in it a forecast of your reasons.

Review the readings in this chapter to see how other writers construct their thesis statements. For example, recall that Patrick O'Malley states his thesis in paragraph 2: *If professors gave additional brief exams at frequent intervals, students would be spurred to study more regularly, learn more, worry less, and perform better on midterms, finals, and other papers and projects.* O'Malley's thesis announces his solution — brief, frequent exams — to the problems created for students in courses limited to anxiety-producing, high-stakes midterms and finals. The thesis lists the reasons students will benefit from the solution in the order in which the benefits appear in the essay. A forecast is not a requirement of a thesis statement, but it does enable readers to predict the stages of the argument, thereby increasing their understanding.

As you draft your own thesis statement, pay attention to the language you use. It should be clear and unambiguous, emphatic but appropriately qualified. Although you will probably refine your thesis statement as you draft and revise your essay, trying now to articulate it will help give your planning and drafting direction and impetus.

For more on thesis and forecasting statements, see Chapter 13.

For more on asserting a thesis, see Chapter 19.

■ Planning and Drafting

This section will help you review your invention writing and research notes, determine specific goals for your essay, prepare a rough outline, and get started on your first draft.

Seeing What You Have

You have now produced a lot of writing for this assignment about a problem and why it needs attention, about alternative solutions, and about the solution you want to propose and why it is preferable to the other proposed solutions. If you have done your invention writing on the computer, you may have sentences or whole paragraphs that can be copied and pasted into your draft. Reread what you have written so far to identify the potentially useful material. Look for details that will help you present a convincing argument for your solution and a strong counterargument in response to readers' likely objections to your solution and their preference for alternative solutions. Highlight key words, phrases, or sentences; make marginal notes or electronic annotations.

If at this point you doubt the significance of the problem or question the success of your proposed solution, you might want to consider a new topic. If you are unsure about these basic points, you cannot expect to produce a convincing draft.

However, if your invention material seems thin but promising, you may be able to strengthen it with additional invention writing. Ask yourself the following questions:

- Can I make a stronger case for the seriousness of the problem?
- Can I think of additional reasons for readers to support my solution?
- Are there any other ways of refuting alternative solutions to or troubling questions about my proposed solution?

Setting Goals

Before beginning to draft, think seriously about the overall goals of your proposal. Not only will the draft be easier to write once you have clear goals, but it will almost surely be more convincing as well.

Here are some questions that will help you set goals now. You may find it useful to return to them while drafting, for they are designed to help you focus on exactly what you want to accomplish with this proposal.

Your Purpose and Readers

- What do my readers already know about this problem? Should I assume, as O'Malley does, that my readers are unfamiliar with the problem? Or should I assume, as Kornbluh does, that my readers know about the problem but do not realize how serious it is?
- How can I gain readers' enthusiastic support? How can I get them to want to implement the solution? Can I convince readers that solving the problem is in everyone's interest, as Kornbluh and Sciara try to do?

- How can I present myself so that I seem both reasonable and authoritative? Can I show that I am not dictating a one-size-fits-all solution but trying to get those involved to find solutions that work for them, as O'Malley, Kornbluh, and Miller try to do?

The Beginning

- How can I immediately engage my readers' interest? Should I open, as O'Malley does, with a dramatic scenario and rhetorical questions? Or with a recitation of facts, as Sciara does, or quotations, as Miller does?

Defining the Problem

- How can I demonstrate that the problem really exists? Can I present statistics, as Kornbluh, Miller, and Sciara do?
- How can I show the seriousness and urgency of the problem? Should I stress negative consequences, as all the writers do? Can I use quotations or cite research to stress the problem's importance, as Miller and Kornbluh do?
- Will reporting or speculating about the problem's causes or history help readers understand why it needs attention? Can I use comparison and contrast, as Kornbluh does?
- How much space should I devote to defining the problem? Only a little space (like O'Malley and Sciara) or much space (like Kornbluh and Miller)?

Describing the Proposed Solution

- How can I describe my solution so that it will look like the best way to proceed? Should I give examples to show how it is feasible, as Sciara does? Or should I focus on my reasons to support it, as O'Malley does?
- Should I make the solution seem easy to implement, as O'Malley and Sciara do? Or should I acknowledge that the solution will require effort and compromise, as Kornbluh and Miller do?

Anticipating Readers' Objections or Questions

- How can I anticipate any specific objections or questions readers may have? Can I interview interested parties, as O'Malley and Miller do? Can I do library and Internet research, as all the writers do?
- How do I decide which objections to include? Can I avoid the appearance of choosing a "straw man," an objection that is too easily knocked down, by also including objections that are harder to dismiss, as Miller does?
- Has anyone already raised these objections? How can I name the source of the objection without criticizing the person? Miller, for example, refutes objections by reporting what others have said.

- Should I accommodate or concede to certain objections by modifying my proposal, as O'Malley and Miller do?
- How can I support my refutation? Should I cite statistics or research studies, as Miller does?

Evaluating Alternative Solutions

- How do I decide which alternative solutions to mention?
- How can I support my refutation of alternative solutions? Can I argue that they are too expensive and time-consuming, as O'Malley does, or that they will not really solve the problem, as Kornbluh does?
- How can I reject these other solutions without seeming to criticize their proponents? Can I provide reasons, as O'Malley does, or marshall statistics, as Kornbluh does? Can I give people with different ideas a voice in my proposal, as Miller does?

The Ending

- How should I conclude? Should I end by summarizing my solution and its advantages, as O'Malley and Sciara do? Should I end by arguing that the time is ripe for the solution to be implemented, as Miller does? Should I end with a scenario suggesting the consequences of a failure to solve the problem? Can I end with an inspiring call to action that unites everyone? Or might a shift to humor or satire to provide an effective way to end?
- Is there something special about the problem that I should remind readers of at the end, as Kornbluh does when she urges that an award be given to the companies that lead the way?

Outlining

After setting goals for your proposal, you are ready to make a working outline — a scratch outline or a more formal outline using the outlining function of your word processing program. The basic outline for a proposal is quite simple:

The problem

The solution

The reasons for accepting the solution

This simple plan is nearly always complicated by other factors, however. In outlining your material, you must take into consideration many other details, such as whether readers already recognize the problem, how much agreement exists on the need to solve the problem, how many alternative solutions are available, how much attention must be given to these other solutions, and how many objections should be expected.

Here is a possible outline for a proposal where readers may not understand the problem fully and other solutions have been proposed:

Presentation of the problem

   Its existence
   Its seriousness
   Its causes

Consequences of failing to solve the problem

Description of the proposed solution

List of steps for implementing the solution

Reasons and support for the solution

   Acknowledgment of objections
   Accommodation or refutation of objections

Consideration of alternative solutions and their disadvantages

Restatement of the proposed solution and its advantages

Your outline will of course reflect your own writing situation. As you develop it, think about what your readers know and feel about your own writing goals. Once you have a working outline, you should not hesitate to change it as necessary while drafting and revising. For instance, you might find it more effective to hold back on presenting your own solution until you have dismissed other possible solutions. Or you might find a better way to order the reasons for adopting your proposal. The purpose of an outline is to identify the basic features of your proposal and to help you organize them effectively, not to lock you into a particular structure. If you use the outlining function of your word processing program, changing your outline will be simple and you may be able to write the essay simply by expanding the outline.

Most of the information you will need to develop each feature of a proposal can be found in your invention writing and research notes. How much space you devote to each feature is determined by the topic, not the outline. Do not assume that each entry on your outline must be given one paragraph. For example, each reason for supporting the solution may require a paragraph, but you might instead present the reasons, objections, and refutations all in one paragraph.

For more on outlining, see Chapter 11.

Consider tentative any outlining you do before you begin drafting. Never be a slave to an outline. As you draft, you will usually see ways to improve on your original plan. Be ready to revise your outline, shift parts around, or drop or add parts as you draft.

Drafting

General Advice.   Start drafting your proposal, keeping in mind the goals you set while you were planning and the needs and expectations of your readers; organize, define, and argue with them in mind. Also keep in mind the two main goals of proposals: (1) to establish that a problem exists and is serious enough to require a solution and (2) to demonstrate that your proposed solution is both feasible and the best possible alternative. Use your outline to guide you as you write, but do not hesitate to stray from it whenever you find that drafting takes you in an unexpected direction.

Turn off your grammar checker and spelling checker at this stage if you find them distracting. Don't be afraid to skip around in your document. Jump back and fill in a spontaneous idea, or leap ahead and write a later section first if you find that easier. If you get stuck while drafting, explore the problem by using some of the writing activities in the Invention and Research section of this chapter (p. 363). You may want to review the general drafting advice in Chapter 1 on p. 9.

A Sentence Strategy: Rhetorical Questions.   As you draft an essay proposing a solution to a problem, you will want to connect with your readers. You will also want readers to become concerned with the seriousness of the problem and thoughtful about the challenge of solving it. Sentences that take the form of **rhetorical questions** can help you achieve these goals.

A rhetorical question is conventionally defined as a sentence posing a question to which the writer expects no answer from the reader. In proposals, however, rhetorical questions do important rhetorical work — that is, they assist a writer in realizing a particular purpose and they influence readers in certain ways. Here are three examples from Matt Miller's proposal:

- How should we address this crisis? (paragraph 5)
- How to do this? (paragraph 6)
- How much would this plan cost? (paragraph 11)

These questions, each placed at the beginning of a paragraph, function like headings. They announce the main parts of the proposal. The first question makes a transition from defining the problem to describing the solution, and the word *we* reaches out to include readers. The second question introduces the plan to implement the writer's proposed solution: the word *this* refers back to the sentence that immediately precedes the question and states the thesis of the essay. Similarly, the last question lets readers know that the focus is shifting to Miller's argument about the feasibility of his proposed solution.

Following is another pair of rhetorical questions from Miller's essay, but note that these are placed at the end of a brief paragraph instead of at the beginning:

> In determining pay rates, who will decide which teachers are better performers? And what standards will be used to assess teachers? (paragraph 20)

Positioned at the end of a paragraph, these questions serve well as a transition to readers' concerns about how Miller's proposed solution will be implemented. In fact, he frames them as questions that have been raised by "educators." Nevertheless, he treats them as rhetorical questions because he goes on to explore answers to them.

Miller uses rhetorical questions, then, to engage readers by voicing questions they are likely to have — and that others have expressed — about his proposed solution. They also help orient readers by making transitions from one topic to the next.

Other writers in this chapter also use rhetorical questions for these and similar purposes:

- Engaging readers' attention to or interest in the problem or the proposed solution:

  Will it be like the midterm? Did you study enough? Did you study the right things? It's too late to drop the course. So what happens if you fail? (Patrick O'Malley, paragraph 1)

  What if the safety of bicyclists were accorded comparable priority? What if bicycle and motorist education campaigns were pursued on a scale equivalent to aggressive drunk driving and seatbelt campaigns? (Gian-Claudia Sciara, paragraph 11)

O'Malley uses his rhetorical questions to dramatize the plight of students studying for a high-stakes exam in order to engage his primary readers — professors capable of implementing his solution — and put them in a receptive frame of mind. Sciara presents her questions after reporting the number of lives saved by drunk driving and seatbelt education campaigns. Her objective is to get readers to recognize for themselves the life-saving potential of a bicycle safety campaign.

- Orienting readers to a proposal and forecasting the plan of the argument or parts of it:

  Why, then, do so few professors give frequent brief exams? (Patrick O'Malley, paragraph 7)

O'Malley uses this rhetorical question as a transition to his anticipating objections that professors are likely to have to his proposed solution.

Writers sometimes vary their way of presenting rhetorical questions. Kornbluh uses a subheading worded like a question — "Who would be covered" — and followed by a colon to introduce the "answer" (paragraph 21). Miller presents a question indirectly:

  The question is how to evaluate performance in a way that is objective and untainted by cronyism. (paragraph 21)

He also inserts a rhetorical question into his recounting of a part of the conversation between himself and the people he interviewed:

  How might that work? I asked. (paragraph 17)

Except for Kornbluh, all of the authors in this chapter use direct rhetorical questions. Two of them — Miller and O'Malley — use five, and if we count the two indirect ones, Miller uses seven. Miller spreads his throughout the essay, while O'Malley bunches most of his questions in the opening paragraph. But even though rhetorical questions are useful, they are not a requirement for a successful proposal. They should be used for a specific purpose, and they should not be overused, because readers may begin to find them annoying.

In addition to using rhetorical questions, you can strengthen your proposal with other kinds of sentences as well; and you may want to review the discussions of sentences that introduce concession and refutation (pp. 309–10).

Critical Reading Guide

For a printable version of this critical reading guide, go to bedfordstmartins.com/theguide.

Now is the time to get a good critical reading of your draft. Writers usually find it helpful to have someone else read and comment on their drafts, and all writers know how much they learn when they read other writers' drafts. Your instructor may arrange such a reading as part of your coursework — in class or online. If not, you can ask a classmate, friend, or family member to read your draft. You could also seek comments from a tutor at your campus writing center. (If you are unable to have someone else read your draft, turn ahead to the Revising section on p. 380, where you will find guidelines for reading your own draft critically.)

▶ **If You Are the Writer.**   To provide focused, helpful comments, your reader must know your essay's intended audience, your purpose, and a problem in the draft that you need help solving. Briefly write out this information at the top of your draft.

- *Readers:* Identify the intended readers of your essay. How much do they know about the problem? How will they react to your proposed solution?

- *Purpose:* What do you want your readers to do or think as a result of reading your proposal?

- *Problem:* Ask your reader to help you solve the single most important problem you see with your draft. Describe this problem briefly.

▶ **If You Are the Reader.**   Reading a draft critically means reading it more than once — first to get a general impression and then to analyze its basic features. Use the following guidelines to help you give critical comments to others on essays that propose solutions to problems.

1. *Read for a First Impression.* Read first to get a basic understanding of the problem and the proposed solution to it. After reading the draft, briefly write out your impressions. How convincing do you think the proposal will be for its particular readers? What do you notice about the way the problem is presented and the way the solution is argued for? Next, consider the problem the writer identified, and respond briefly to that concern now. (If you find that the problem is covered by one of the other guidelines listed below, respond to it in more detail there if necessary.)

2. *Evaluate How Well the Problem Is Defined.* Decide whether the problem is stated clearly. Does the writer give enough information about its causes and consequences? What more might be done to establish its seriousness? Is there more that readers might need or wish to know about it?

3. *Consider Whether the Solution Is Described Adequately.* Does the presentation of the solution seem immediately clear and readable? How could the presentation be strengthened? Has the writer laid out steps for implementation?

Making Comments Electronically

Most word processing software offers features that allow you to insert comments directly into the text of someone else's document. Many readers prefer to make their comments in this way because it tends to be faster than writing on a hard copy and space is virtually unlimited; from the writer's point of view, it also eliminates the problem of deciphering handwritten comments. Even where such special comment features are not available, simply typing comments directly into a document in a contrasting color can provide the same advantages.

If not, might readers expect or require them? Does the solution seem practical? If not, why?

4. ***Assess Whether a Convincing Argument Is Advanced in Support of the Proposed Solution.*** Look at the reasons offered for advocating this solution. Are they sufficient? Which are likely to be most and least convincing to the intended readers? What kind of support does the writer provide for each reason? How believable do you think readers will find it? Has the writer argued forcefully for the proposal without offending readers?

5. ***Evaluate How Well the Writer Anticipates Readers' Objections and Questions.*** Which accommodations and refutations seem most convincing? Which seem least convincing? Are there other objections or reservations that the writer should acknowledge?

6. ***Assess the Writer's Evaluation of Alternative Solutions.*** Are alternative solutions discussed and either accommodated or refuted? Which are the most convincing reasons given against other solutions? Which are least convincing, and why? Has the writer sought out common ground with readers who may advocate alternative solutions? Are such solutions accommodated or rejected without a personal attack on those who propose them? Try to think of other solutions that readers may prefer.

7. ***Consider the Effectiveness of the Organization.*** Evaluate the overall plan of the proposal, perhaps by outlining it briefly. Would any parts be more effectively placed earlier or later in the essay?

   - Look at the *beginning.* Is it engaging? If not, how might it be revised to capture readers' attention? Does it adequately forecast the main ideas and the plan of the proposal? Suggest other ways the writer might begin.

   - Look closely at the way the writer *orders the argument* for the solution — the presentation of the reasons and the accommodation or refutation of objections and alternative solutions. How might the sequence be revised to strengthen the argument? Point out any gaps in the argument.

   - Look at the *ending.* Does it frame the proposal by echoing or referring to something at the beginning? If not, how might it do so? Does the ending convey a sense of urgency? Suggest a stronger way to conclude.

   - Look at any *design elements and visuals* the writer has incorporated. Assess how well they are incorporated into the essay. Point to any items that do not strengthen either the presentation of the problem or the argument in support of the solution.

8. ***Give the Writer Your Final Thoughts.*** What is the draft's strongest part? What part is most in need of further work?

■ Revising

Now you have the opportunity to revise your essay. Your instructor or other students may have given you advice on how to improve your draft. Or you may have begun to realize that your draft requires not so much revising as rethinking. For example, you may recognize that you are no longer convinced that the problem is serious, that you feel it is serious but cannot be solved now or anytime soon, that you cannot decide to whom to address the proposal, that you cannot come up with a set of convincing reasons that readers should support your solution, or that you have been unable to accommodate or refute readers' objections and questions or to evaluate alternative solutions. Consequently, instead of working to improve the various parts of your first draft, you may need to write a new draft that reshapes your argument. Many students—and professional writers—find themselves in this situation. Often a writer produces a draft or two and gets advice on them from others and only then begins to see what might be achieved.

If you feel satisfied that your draft mostly achieves what you set out to do, you can focus on refining the various parts of it. This section will help you get an overview of your draft and revise it accordingly.

Getting an Overview

Consider your draft as a whole, following these two steps:

1. *Reread.* If at all possible, put the draft aside for a day or two before rereading it. When you do go back to it, start by reconsidering your audience and purpose. Then read the draft straight through, trying to see it as your intended readers will.

2. *Outline.* Make a scratch outline, indicating the basic features as they appear in the draft. Consider using the headings and outline or summary functions of your word processor.

Planning for Revision.   Resist the temptation to dive in and start changing your text until after you have a clear view of the big picture. Using your outline as a guide, move through the document, using the change-highlighting or commenting tools of your word processor to note comments received from others and problems you want to solve (or mark a hard copy if you prefer).

Analyzing the Basic Features of Your Own Draft.   Turn to the Critical Reading Guide that begins on p. 378. Using this guide, reread the draft to identify problems you need to solve. Note the problems on your draft.

Studying Readers' Comments.   Review all of the comments you have received from other readers. For each comment, look at the draft to determine what might have led the reader to make that particular point. Try to be receptive to constructive criticism. Ideally, these comments will help you see your draft as others see it. Add to your notes any problems readers have identified.

Working with Sources

Statistics can be helpful in establishing that the problem exists and is serious. For example, Patrick O'Malley cites research to support his assertion that students prefer frequent exams to fewer high-stakes exams: "A recent Harvard study notes students' 'strong preference for frequent evaluation in a course'" (paragraph 4). But his argument would have been stronger and possibly more convincing if he had cited statistics to support the study's conclusion. Matt Miller and Gian-Claudia Sciara also cite statistics in their proposals, but Karen Kornbluh provides more statistics than either of them. Let us look at some of the ways Kornbluh uses statistics to define the problem.

Citing statistics to establish the problem's existence and seriousness

The success of Kornbluh's proposal depends on her readers accepting her argument that the problem really exists and that it is serious and widespread enough to require a solution. Therefore, she cites statistics to demonstrate that the "juggler family," as she calls it, has taken the place of the "traditional family" that had a homemaker capable of taking care of children and dependent parents:

> Today fully 70 percent of families with children are headed by two working parents or by an unmarried working parent. The "traditional family" of the breadwinner and homemaker has been replaced by the "juggler family," in which no one is home full-time. (paragraph 1)

Kornbluh begins with an impressive statistic, "fully 70 percent." But what does it mean? Seventy percent of how many? She does not answer this question with a number, but she does make clear that she is talking about nearly three-quarters of all "families with children," a number that we can infer is very large. At other points in the essay, Kornbluh does provide the raw numbers along with statistics such as percentages. Here are a couple of examples:

> In addition to working parents, there are over 44.4 million Americans who provide care to another adult, often an older relative. Fifty-nine percent of these caregivers either work or have worked while providing care ("Caregiving"). (paragraph 8)

> Over half of workers today have no control over scheduling alternative start and end times at work (Galinksy, Bond, and Hill). According to a recent study by the Institute for Women's Policy Research, 49 percent of workers — over 59 million Americans — lack basic paid sick days for themselves. (paragraph 10)

Because of the raw numbers, readers can see at a glance that the percentages Kornbluh cites are truly significant: 59 percent of 44.4 million people (who have worked while providing care to another adult) and 59 million people (who lack sick leave). Her use of statistics here is especially convincing because of the large numbers of people affected by the problem. Note that Kornbluh spells out some of the numbers she provides and uses numerals for others, depending on whether the number begins a sentence.

These statistics, like the "70 percent of families with children" in paragraph 1, focus on groups of people. But Kornbluh also compares different time periods to show that the problem has worsened over the last thirty years. Here are several examples from paragraph 7. Note that Kornbluh represents statistics in three different ways: percentages, numbers, and proportion.

> Between 1970 and 2000, the percentage of mothers in the workforce rose from 38 to 67 percent (Smolensky and Gootman). Moreover, the number of hours worked by dual-income families has increased dramatically. Couples with children worked a full 60 hours a week in 1979. By 2000 they were working 70 hours a week (Bernstein and Kornbluh). And more parents than ever are working long hours. In 2000, nearly 1 out of every 8 couples with children was putting in 100 hours a week or more on the job, compared to only 1 out of 12 families in 1970 (Jacobs and Gerson).

To establish that there is a widespread perception among working parents that the problem is serious, Kornbluh cites survey results:

> In a 2002 report by the Families and Work Institute, 45 percent of employees reported that work and family responsibilities interfered with each other "a lot" or "some" and 67 percent of employed parents report that they do not have enough time with their children (Galinksy, Bond, and Hill).

This example, from paragraph 9, shows that a large percentage, nearly half of all employees surveyed, are aware of interference between work and family responsibilities. The actual amount of interference is vague, because "some" and "a lot" may mean different things to different survey respondents. Nevertheless, the fact that such a large percentage of employees reported interference is telling. The readers Kornbluh is addressing — employers — are likely to find this statistic important because it suggests that their employees are spending time worrying about or attending to family responsibilities instead of focusing on work.

For statistics to be persuasive, they must be from sources that readers consider reliable. Readers need to know who did a study so they can determine whether its researchers can be trusted. Researchers' trustworthiness, in turn, depends on their credentials as experts in the field they are investigating and also on the degree to which they are disinterested, or free from bias.

Kornbluh provides a Works Cited list of sources that readers can follow up on to check whether the sources are indeed reliable. The fact that some of her sources are books published by major publishers (Harvard University Press and Basic Books, for example) helps establish their credibility. Other sources she cites are research institutes (such as New America Foundation, Economic Policy Institute, and Families and Work Institute) that readers can easily check on the Internet. Another factor that adds to the appearance of reliability is that Kornbluh cites statistics from a range of sources instead of relying on only one or two. Moreover, the statistics are current and clearly relevant to her argument.

Carrying Out Revisions

Having identified problems in your draft, you now need to find solutions and — most important — to carry them out. You have three ways of finding solutions:

1. Review your invention and planning notes for additional information and ideas.

2. Do further invention writing or research to provide material you or your readers think is needed.

3. Look back at the readings in this chapter to see how other writers have solved similar problems.

The following suggestions, which are organized according to the basic features of essays that propose solutions, will get you started solving some common writing problems. For now, focus on solving the problems identified in your notes. Avoid tinkering with grammar and punctuation; those tasks will come later, when you edit and proofread.

A Well-Defined Problem

- *Is the definition of the problem unclear?* Consider sketching out its history, including past attempts to deal with it, discussing its causes and consequences more fully, or comparing it to other problems that readers may be familiar with.

- *Have you failed to establish the problem's existence and seriousness?* Look for additional statistics, facts, and quotations to establish that the problem really exists. Try to dramatize its effect on people and to create a sense of urgency.

A Clearly Described Solution

- *Is the description of the solution inadequate?* Try outlining the steps or phases involved in its implementation. Help readers see how easy the first step will be, or acknowledge the difficulty of the first step. Give examples of similar solutions that have been implemented.

A Convincing Argument in Support of the Proposed Solution

- *Does the argument seem weak?* Try to think of more reasons for readers to support your proposal.

- *Is the argument hard to follow?* Try to put your reasons in a more convincing order — leading up to the strongest one rather than putting it first, perhaps.

- *Does the solution not seem feasible?* Show how your solution would really solve the problem, possibly by removing its causes. Provide additional statistical or expert support.

An Anticipation of Readers' Objections and Questions

- *Does your refutation of any objection or question seem unconvincing?* Consider accommodating it by modifying your proposal.

- *Have you left out any likely objections?* Acknowledge those objections and either accommodate or refute them.

An Evaluation of Alternative Solutions

- *Have you neglected to mention alternative solutions that some readers are likely to prefer?* Evaluate those alternatives now. Consider whether you want to accommodate or refute them. For each one, try to acknowledge its good points, but argue that it is not as effective a solution as your own. You may in fact want to strengthen your own solution by incorporating into it some of the good points from alternatives.

For a revision checklist, go to bedfordstmartins.com/theguide.

The Organization

- *Is the beginning weak?* Think of a better way to start. Would an anecdote or an example of the problem engage readers more effectively?

- *Is the ending flat?* Consider framing your proposal by mentioning something from the beginning of your essay or ending with a call for action that expresses the urgency of implementing your solution.

- *Would design elements make the problem or proposed solution easier to understand?* Consider adding headings or visuals.

◼ Editing and Proofreading

A Note on Grammar and Spelling Checkers
These tools are good at catching certain types of errors, but currently there is no replacement for a good human proofreader. Grammar checkers in particular are extremely limited in what they can usually find, and often they only give you summary information that is not helpful if you do not already understand the rule in question. They are also prone to give faulty advice for fixing problems and to flag correct items as wrong. Spelling checkers cause fewer problems but cannot catch misspellings that are themselves words, such as *to* for *too*.

Now is the time to check your revised draft for errors in grammar, punctuation, and mechanics as well as to consider matters of style. Our research has identified several errors that are especially common in essays that propose solutions. The following guidelines will help you check and edit your essay for these common errors.

Checking for Ambiguous Use of *This* and *That*. Using *this* and *that* vaguely to refer to other words or ideas can confuse readers. Because you must frequently refer to the problem and the solution in a proposal, you will often use pronouns to avoid the monotony or wordiness of repeatedly referring to them by name. Check your draft carefully for ambiguous use of *this* and *that*. Often the easiest way to edit such usage is to add a specific noun after *this* or *that*, as Patrick O'Malley does in the following example from his essay in this chapter:

> Another possible solution would be to help students prepare for midterm and final exams by providing sets of questions from which the exam questions will be selected or announcing possible exam topics at the beginning of the course. *This solution* would have the advantage of reducing students' anxiety about learning every fact in the textbook. . . . (paragraph 12)

O'Malley avoids an ambiguous *this* in the second sentence by repeating the noun *solution*. (He might just as well have used *preparation* or *action* or *approach*.)

The following sentences from proposals have been edited to avoid ambiguity:

▶ **Students would not resist a reasonable fee increase of about $40 a year.**

increase
This would pay for the needed dormitory remodeling.
　　　　　　^

▶ Compared to other large California cities, San Diego has the weakest

neglect
programs for conserving water. This and our decreasing access to Colorado River
　　　　　　　　　　　　　　　　　　^

water give us reason to worry.

one
▶ Compared to other proposed solutions to this problem, that is clearly the most
　　　　　　　　　　　　　　　　　　　　　　　　　　　^

feasible.

For practice, go to bedfordstmartins.com/theguide/exercisecentral and click on Ambiguous Use of *This* and *That*.

Checking for Sentences That Lack an Agent. A writer proposing a solution to a problem usually needs to indicate who exactly should take action to solve it. Such actors are called "agents." An agent is a person who is in a position to take action. Look at this sentence from O'Malley's proposal:

> To get students to complete the questions in a timely way, professors would have to collect and check the answers.

In this sentence, *professors* are the agents. They have the authority to assign and collect study questions, and they would need to take this action in order for this solution to be successfully implemented. Had O'Malley instead written "the answers would have to be collected and checked," the sentence would lack an agent. Naming an agent makes his argument convincing, demonstrating to readers that O'Malley has thought through one of the key parts of any proposal: who is going to take action.

The following sentences from student-written proposals illustrate how you can edit agentless sentences:

Your staff should plan a survey
▶ ~~A survey could be planned~~ to find out more about students' problems in
　^
scheduling the courses they need.

The registrar should extend
▶ ~~Extending~~ the deadline to mid-quarter◦ ~~would make sense.~~
　^

Sometimes it is appropriate to write agentless sentences, however. Study the following examples from O'Malley's essay:

> These exams should be given weekly, or at least twice monthly.

> Exams could be collected and responded to only every third or fourth week.

> Still another solution might be to provide frequent study questions for students to answer.

Even though these sentences do not name explicit agents, they are all fine because it is clear from the larger context who will perform the action. In each case, it is obvious that the action will be carried out by a professor.

For practice, go to bedfordstmartins.com/theguide/exercisecentral and click on Sentences That Lack an Agent.

A Writer at Work

■ Strengthening the Argument

This section focuses on student writer Patrick O'Malley's successful efforts to strengthen his argument for the solution he proposes in his essay, "More Testing, More Learning." Read the following three paragraphs from his draft; then compare them with paragraphs 4–6 of his final essay on pp. 330–31. As you read, take notes on the differences you observe between the draft and final versions.

The predominant reason students perform better with multiple exams is that they improve their study habits. Greater regularity in test taking means greater regularity in studying for tests. Students prone to cramming will be forced to open their textbooks more often, keeping them away from long, "kamikaze" nights of studying. Regularity prepares them for the "real world" where you rarely take on large tasks at long intervals. Several tests also improve study habits by reducing procrastination. An article about procrastination from the Journal of Counseling Psychology reports that "students view exams as difficult, important, and anxiety provoking." These symptoms of anxiety leading to procrastination could be solved if individual test importance was lessened, reducing the stress associated with the perceived burden.

With multiple exams, this anxiety decrease will free students to perform better. Several, less important tests may appear as less of an obstacle, allowing the students to worry less, leaving them free to concentrate on their work without any emotional hindrances. It is proven that "the performance of test-anxious subjects varies inversely with evaluation stress." It would also be to the psychological benefit of students if they were not subjected to the emotional ups and downs of large exams where they are virtually worry-free one moment and ready to check into the psychiatric ward the next.

Lastly, with multiple exams, students can learn how to perform better on future tests in the class. Regular testing allows them to "practice" the information they learned, thereby improving future test scores. In just two exams, they are not able to learn the instructor's personal examination style, and are not given the chance to adapt their study habits to it. The American Psychologist concludes: "It is possible to influence teaching and learning by changing the type of tests."

One difference you may have noted between O'Malley's draft and revision paragraphs is the sequencing of specific reasons that readers should accept the solution and take action on it. Whereas the draft moves in three paragraphs from improving study habits to decreasing anxiety to performing better on future tests, the revision moves from learning more and performing better on major exams to improving study habits to decreasing anxiety. O'Malley made the change after a response from a classmate and a conference with his instructor helped him see that his particular readers (professors) would probably be most convinced by the improved quality of students' learning, not by improvements in their study habits and feelings. As he continued thinking about his argument and discovering further relevant research, he shifted his emphasis from the psychological to the intellectual benefits of frequent exams.

You may also have noticed that the paragraphs of the revision are better focused than in the draft. The psychological benefits (reduced anxiety as a result of less procrastination) are now discussed mainly in a single paragraph (the third), whereas in the draft they are mixed in with the intellectual benefits in the first two paragraphs. O'Malley also uses more precise language in his revision; for example, changing "future tests" to "major exams, projects, and papers."

Another change you may have noticed is that all of the quoted research material in the draft has been replaced in the revision. Extending his library research to support his argument, O'Malley discovered the very useful Harvard report. As he found a more logical sequence, more precise terms, and fuller elaboration for his argument, he saw different ways to use the research studies he had turned up initially and quoted in the draft.

A final difference is that in the revision, O'Malley argues his reasons more effectively. Consider the draft and revised paragraphs on improved study habits. In the draft paragraph, O'Malley shifts abruptly from study habits to procrastination to anxiety. Except for study habits, none of these topics is developed, and the quotation adds nothing to what he has already said. By contrast, the revised paragraph focuses strictly on study habits. O'Malley keeps the best sentences from the draft for the beginning of the revised paragraph, but he adds several new sentences to help convince readers of the soundness of his argument that frequent exams improve students' study habits. These new sentences serve several functions: They anticipate a possible objection ("It might be argued . . ."), note a contrast between complex academic learning and familiar survival skills, and assert claims about the special requirements of regular academic study. The quotation from the Harvard report provides convincing support for O'Malley's claims and an effective way to conclude the paragraph.

Thinking About Document Design

The truck driver who wrote the proposal for recruiting and training more women (in the "In the Workplace" project described on page 327) drafted and designed her document on her computer. She was familiar with some of the features of her word processing software, such as the ability to create headings, format lists, and include photographs. More important, she recognized that these elements could serve persuasive purposes in the document she wanted to produce. She searched the Web for similar proposals that she could use as models to format her own, and eventually found several. After looking them over, she found they all contained some of the same formatting conventions: They were all single-spaced, had descriptive headings, and included some sort of visuals (tables, charts, and photographs).

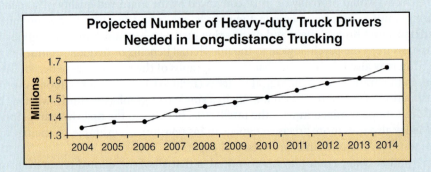

The driver decided to format her document similarly, using single-spacing and headings, and also incorporated graphs and tables gathered from several trucking industry magazines and newsletters to which she had access. To stress that carriers must increase their fleets to remain competitive within the industry, she used the line graph above showing how the skyrocketing demand for carriers over the next ten years would greatly exacerbate the current driver shortage. She used a second graph, the pie chart below, to show that current projections indicate that women will remain an underutilized group in the truck driver workforce. And to show how the trucking industry can attract women on the basis of salary, she also included a table contrasting the amount of money a woman truck driver could earn after one year, after five years, and so on, to how much women in other fields could earn over the same periods of time.

She knew that the preferred hiring solution of many companies is to recruit from truck-driving schools. However, she also knew that the region's divorced and single-parent women would likely not be able to afford such training. Therefore, she included a list comparing truck-driving school tuition rates with income statistics for women in the region to illustrate their lack of access. As an alternative solution, she proposed that companies offer after-hours training programs at various community centers in the region, which she admitted would require the companies to spend some money up front but would allow them to help the community, support the training of women, and recruit from the pool of qualified women in the region.

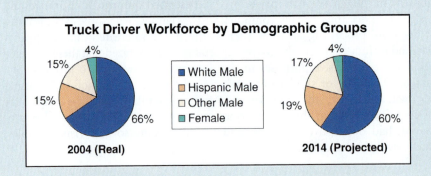

Finally, the proposal author used photographs as a framing device. She knew from her own experience that people respond to photographs and are compelled by appropriate images. Thus, toward the beginning of the proposal, she scanned in a snapshot showing herself in the double-bottom dump truck that she first learned to drive, which helped establish her authority as a trucker. Toward the end of the proposal, she included a variety of photographs like the one below, showing women truck drivers competently performing their jobs; each of these images attested to the feasibility of her proposed solution.

Thinking Critically About What You Have Learned

Now that you have worked extensively with essays that propose solutions to problems — reading them, talking about them, writing one of your own — take some time to reflect on what you have learned. What problems did you encounter while you were writing your essay, and how did you solve them? How did reading other essays proposing solutions influence your own essay? What ideas do you have about the social and cultural dimensions of this kind of writing?

Reflecting on Your Writing

Write a page or two telling your instructor about a problem you encountered in writing an essay that proposes a solution and how you solved it. Before you begin, gather all of your writing — invention and planning notes, drafts, critical comments, revision notes and plans, and final revision. Review these materials as you complete this writing task.

1. *Identify one writing problem you had to solve as you worked on your proposal essay.* Do not be concerned with grammar and punctuation; concentrate instead on problems unique to developing a proposal. For example: Did you puzzle over how to convince readers that your proposed solution would actually solve the problem you identified? Did you find it difficult to support the reasons you gave for recommending the solution? Did you have trouble coming up with alternative solutions that your readers might favor?

2. *Determine how you came to recognize the writing problem.* When did you first discover it? What called it to your attention? If someone else pointed out the problem to you, can you now see hints of it in your invention writings? If so, where specifically? When you first recognized the problem, how did you respond?

3. *Reflect on how you went about solving the problem.* Did you reword a passage, cut or add details about the problem or solution, or move paragraphs or sentences around? Did you reread one of the essays in this chapter to see how another writer handled a similar problem, or did you look back at the invention suggestions? If you discussed the writing problem with another student, a tutor, or your instructor, did talking about it help? How useful was the advice you received?

4. *Write a page or so explaining the problem and your solution.* Be as specific as possible in reconstructing your efforts. Quote from your invention notes, your draft essay, others' critical comments, your revision plan, and your revised essay to show the various changes your writing underwent as you tried to solve the problem. If you are still uncertain about your solution, say so. The point is not to prove that you have solved the problem perfectly but rather to show what you have learned about solving problems when writing proposals. Taking time to explain how you identified a particular problem, how you went about trying to solve it, and what you learned from this experience can help you solve future writing problems more easily.

Reviewing What You Learned from Reading

Write a page or two explaining to your instructor how the readings in this chapter influenced your final essay. Your own essay has probably been influenced to some extent by one or more of the proposals you have read in this chapter as well as by classmates' essays that you have read. These other proposals may have helped you decide how to show your readers the seriousness of the problem you focused on, or they may have suggested how you could convince readers that they should support your proposed solution and ignore alternative solutions. Before you write, take some time to reflect on what you have learned from these selections.

1. *Reread the final revision of your essay; then look back at the selections you read before completing it.* Do you see any specific influences? For example, if you were impressed with the way one of the readings defined the problem, built a bridge of shared concerns with readers, detailed the steps in implementing the solution, argued against an alternative solution, or demonstrated that the solution would not cost too much, look to see where you might have been striving for similar effects in your own writing. Also look for ideas you got from your reading: writing strategies you were inspired to try, specific details you were led to include, and effects you sought to achieve.

2. *Write a page or two explaining these influences.* Did one reading have a particularly strong influence on your essay, or were several readings influential in different ways? Quote from the readings and from your final revision to show how your proposal was influenced by the selections you read. Finally, based on your review of the chapter's readings, point out any further improvements you would now make in your essay.

Considering the Social Dimensions of Essays Proposing Solutions

Proposals to solve problems are essential to our society. Businesspeople, school administrators, and government officials especially depend on proposals to decide where to direct resources and energy. Proposals enable us as individuals and as a society to make things better. We probably value this kind of thinking and writing because it makes us feel effective. It convinces us that difficulties can be overcome, that we can make practical, material changes that will improve our lives and the lives of others. We tell ourselves that with a little time, hard work, and ingenuity, we can make a difference. And this attitude has produced many positive changes in our culture — improvements in civil rights, in gender equality, in business and applied sciences as diverse as bridge building and environmental protection. Even so, thorny problems persist in the very areas where the most gains have been accomplished.

Who Defines the Problem?   First, when someone proposes a solution, that proposal shapes our thinking about some aspect of our own and others' lives by labeling it a problem. Yet the individuals most directly affected by the solution may not even accept this definition and may not want to see any change. For example, not all students regard infrequent testing as a problem, but O'Malley's proposed solution would affect them nonetheless.

This question of definition becomes particularly difficult when a relatively powerless constituency in our society — the homeless, illegal immigrants, unwed teenage mothers — is designated a problem by politicians and others in the mainstream. Writers (and readers) of proposals must exercise caution in such circumstances.

1. *How specifically would the proposals you have read and written actually make things better?* Whose interests would be served by these solutions? Who would be affected without their own stated interests being served?

2. *Do any of these proposals try to improve the status of a group that is not particularly powerful?* If so, what do you think is motivating the proposal writer? Is there any evidence that the writer is a member of this group or has consulted members of the group? What gives the writer authority to speak for them?

3. *Write a page or two explaining your ideas about defining social problems in essays that propose solutions to them.* Connect your ideas to your own essay and to the readings in this chapter.

The Frustrations of Effecting Real Change. No matter how well researched and well argued, many proposals are simply never carried out. The head of a personnel department might spend weeks drawing up a persuasive and feasible proposal for establishing a company day-care center, only to have upper management decide not to commit the necessary resources. A team of educators and social scientists might spend several years researching and writing a comprehensive, book-length proposal for dealing with the nation's drastic illiteracy rate but never see their solutions carried out because of a lack of coordination among the country's various educational institutions and governing bodies. In fact, it might be argued that the most successful proposals often operate on the smallest scale. For example, a proposal suggesting ways for a single community to increase literacy rates would probably have a better chance of implementation and ultimate success than the more far-reaching national proposal. (Yet this observation does not rule out the value of the national proposal, on which the local proposal might, in fact, be based.)

Further, in choosing among competing alternative proposals, decision makers — who usually hold the power of the purse strings and necessarily represent a fairly conservative position — often go for the one that is cheapest, most expedient, and least disruptive. They may also choose small, incremental changes over more fundamental, radical solutions. While sometimes the most pragmatic choice, such immediately feasible solutions may also merely patch over a problem, failing to solve it structurally. They may even inadvertently maintain the status quo. Worse, they can cause people to give up all attempts to resolve a problem after superficial treatments fail.

1. *Consider how proposals invite writers to select problems that are solvable and how they might inadvertently attempt to solve a minor problem that is actually only a small part of a major problem.* Do any of the proposals you have read and written reveal this misdirection? If so, which ones, and what do you think is the major problem in each case? Do you think the minor problem is worth solving as a first step toward solving the major problem, or is it perhaps an unfortunate diversion?

2. *Consider how the proposals you have read and written challenge the status quo.* What existing situation do they challenge, and just how do they challenge it? What roadblocks might deter these challenges? Might the proposals be more successfully carried out on a local scale?

3. *Reflect on commentators' arguments that we should not try to solve fundamental social problems by "throwing money at them."* Do you think this objection is a legitimate criticism of most proposals to solve social problems? Or is it a manipulative justification for allowing the rich and powerful to maintain the status quo? What else, besides money, is required to solve serious social problems? Where are these other resources to come from?

4. *Write a page or two explaining your ideas about the frustrations of effecting real change.* Connect your ideas to your own essay and to the readings in this chapter.

8

Justifying an Evaluation

IN COLLEGE COURSES For a research paper in a literature in film course, a student sets out to evaluate the 1995 film *Clueless*, an adaptation of Jane Austen's novel *Emma* set in modern day Beverly Hills. Because he had already seen the film, he decides to see it again on DVD before reading the novel. Then, while he is reading the novel, he reviews key scenes in the film to see how they have been translated from the novel. He also looks closely at differences in how the main characters are portrayed in novel and film.

During this process, he takes a break and does an Internet search for reviews of *Clueless* and discovers that there is a 1996 film called *Emma* set in early nineteenth-century England like the novel. He rents the DVD and decides that his paper would be improved if he could write about the more historically accurate film as well as the looser adaptation. He goes to his professor's office hours to discuss his plan for the paper and see if there is any problem evaluating two film versions of a novel instead of one. His professor responds enthusiastically to his plan and they spend some time discussing the two films.

He then spends several days writing his essay and capturing stills from the two films to illustrate his argument that *Clueless* does a better job of presenting the novel's ironic social commentary for today's viewers than the film *Emma*. He gives two reasons: *Emma* may be aesthetically beautiful, but seems static on the screen, and viewers cannot identify with the main characters. In contrast, he argues that because the action and characters in *Clueless* are recognizable and realistic, contemporary viewers can better appreciate the social commentary.

IN THE COMMUNITY   A motorcycle enthusiast rides to York, Pennsylvania, to tour the Harley-Davidson factory there. He decides to take notes and digital photographs so that he will be able to write a review of the tour to post on his blog. Before the tour begins, he and about twenty other visitors wander through the Vaughn L. Beals Tour Center, marveling at the dozens of vintage motorcycles on display, including special police and war-era bikes. He watches a short film that relates the history of the company, which was founded in 1903, and then explores exhibits describing the plant and the manufacturing process he is about to observe firsthand.

Before entering the plant, he is given safety glasses and a headset so he can hear the tour guide on the noisy factory floor. The factory is housed in an immense building of more than 230 acres with over a thousand workers on each shift. He takes pictures and makes notes describing each part of the manufacturing and assembly process. He observes the swift, orchestrated labor in amazement, noting that workers add a new part to each bike every three minutes as it moves along a conveyor belt and is ultimately rolled off the assembly line into the crating area.

On the way home, he reflects on what he has seen and decides to title his review "Hog Heaven." At home, he spends a couple of days writing the review, enthusiastically recommending the tour and describing it as an exhilarating free ride that is great fun and educational at the same time. He illustrates his review with his photographs and then posts it for everyone to see.

IN THE WORKPLACE   For a conference panel on innovations in education, an elementary school teacher decides to give a talk on *Schoolhouse Rock!*, an animated television series developed in the 1970s and 1980s that was reissued in a DVD edition in 2002. She had enjoyed the series when she was a child, so she bought the DVD and started showing segments to her students, who seemed to enjoy them as much as she had.

To prepare her talk, she plays selected songs for the class she is currently teaching: two from the "Grammar Rock" lessons ("Conjunction Junction" and "A Noun Is a Person, Place or Thing") and two from "Multiplication Rock" ("Three Is a Magic Number" and "The Good 11"). Following each, she gives her students a quiz to see how well they have learned the lesson. Finally, she conducts an informal opinion poll to see whether the kids find this kind of learning enjoyable.

In her panel presentation, she praises the series as an entertaining and inventive way of teaching English and math fundamentals. She describes her research and gives two reasons why the series is an effective educational tool: the witty lyrics and catchy tunes make the information memorable, and the cartoon visuals make the lessons vivid and enjoyable. She supports her evaluation by screening and discussing examples of the *Schoolhouse Rock!* segments she played in class, presenting the results of the follow-up quizzes, and quoting from the opinion poll. She ends by expressing her hope that teachers and developers of multimedia educational software will learn from the example of *Schoolhouse Rock!*

Evaluation involves making judgments. Many times each day, people make judgments about subjects as diverse as the weather, food, music, computer programs, sports events, politicians, and films. In everyday conversation, you often express judgments casually ("I like it" or "I don't like it"), only occasionally giving your reasons (for example, "I hate cafeteria food because it is bland and overcooked") or supporting them with specific examples ("Take last night's spaghetti. That must have been a tomato sauce because it was red, but it didn't have the tang of tomatoes. And the noodles were so overdone that they were mushy").

When you write an evaluation, however, readers expect you to provide reasons and support for your judgment. In the scenario about the Harley-Davidson factory tour, for example, the writer gives three reasons for recommending the tour, supporting them with details and photographs. Similarly, the student evaluating two film versions of Jane Austen's novel gives two reasons for thinking *Clueless* is a more effective adaptation than *Emma*, supporting his argument with examples from both films and the novel as well as with stills from the films. The teacher who gives a presentation on *Schoolhouse Rock!* uses examples of the songs as well as her quiz grades and survey results to support her reasons for praising the old educational series.

In addition, readers need to agree that your reasons are appropriate for evaluating the subject. For example, in an evaluation of an action film like *Mission: Impossible III*, you would want to show that you are judging the film according to standards most people would use in evaluating other action films, including the first two films in the *Mission: Impossible* series. For example, in his *ReelViews* review, James Berardinelli places the film in its general category ("if you're yearning for a flashy, leave-your-brain-at-the-door summer movie"). Then he goes on to argue that even though it has all the characteristics of a summer blockbuster ("It's loud, raucous, frenetic, and blows things up real good"), he found the film disappointing because "it's testosterone without adrenaline, danger without suspense." Berardinelli shows readers that he understands they expect him to judge the film as an example of its genre, so he bases his judgment on qualities such as the film's special effects, action sequences, and most importantly, its ability to generate excitement, to be a thrilling cinematic roller-coaster ride. He even makes a point of saying that he is not criticizing the film's "plot contrivances" because "they go with the territory."

Showing readers you understand how your particular subject relates to other subjects in the same general category demonstrates that your judgment is based on reasons and standards readers recognize as appropriate for judging that kind of subject. Readers may disagree with you, but they will understand and respect your argument.

A Collaborative Activity:
Practice Evaluating a Subject

The scenarios at the beginning of this chapter suggest some occasions for evaluating a subject. You can discover how much you already know about evaluating by completing the following collaborative activity. Your instructor may schedule it for an in-class discussion or ask you to conduct an online discussion in a chat room.

Part 1. Get together with two or three other students to choose a reading from an earlier chapter that you have all already read. Review the reading, and decide whether you think the reading was helpful or unhelpful to you in learning to write well in the genre of the reading. Everyone in the group does not have to share the same judgment.

- First, take turns telling the group whether the reading was helpful in learning to write in the genre and giving two reasons for that judgment. Do not try to convince the others that your judgment is right or your reasons are sound; simply state your judgment and reasons.
- Next, after each person gives a judgment and reasons, discuss briefly as a group whether the reasons seem appropriate for judging a reading in a writing course. Again, you do not have to agree about whether the reading was helpful or unhelpful; all you have to do is discover whether you can agree on the kinds of reasons that make sense when evaluating a reading in the context of a writing course.

Part 2. As a group, spend a few minutes discussing what happened when you tried to agree on appropriate reasons for evaluating the reading:

- Begin by focusing on the reasons your group found easiest to agree on. Discuss why your group found these reasons so easy to agree on.
- Then focus on the reasons your group found hardest to agree on. Discuss why your group found these particular reasons so hard to agree on.

What can you conclude about community standards for judging readings in a writing course?

Readings

WENDY KIM immigrated to the United States from South Korea when she was eight years old. A business administration major, Kim plans to go to graduate school in business. For a composition course, she decided to research a Web site she uses regularly to decide which classes to take: RateMyProfessors.com. You may already be familiar with this site or with comparable online or campus publications evaluating professors. If not, you may want to take a look at the Web site (which has been redesigned since Kim wrote her description) to see whether you think her judgment is sound. RateMyProfessors.com, like other online professor evaluation services, is free, but you do have to register.

Grading Professors
Wendy Kim

1 "Where the Students Do the Grading" is the tagline for the Web site www.RateMyProfessors.com (RMP). Users just choose their state and find their school among the 5,962 (and counting) campuses listed, and they're ready to start grading their professors. The home page proudly displays the numbers: last I

Kim attracts readers with the title and opening quotation

She piles up statistics to show the site's popularity.

looked, there were 5,537,682 ratings, covering 753,577 professors in the United States and Canada. In fact, RMP has been so successful that it has expanded to Australia, Ireland, and the United Kingdom, and its sister-site for high school students, RateMyTeachers.com, already has a user base of 3 million students (RateMyProfessors). While not everyone agrees that these ratings provide an entirely accurate assessment, many students, like me, routinely consult RMP at the beginning of every term to decide which classes to take. Overall, the Web site is well designed, amusing, and extremely helpful.

The design of RateMyProfessors.com makes the site attractive and easy to browse. In my senior year of high school, I took a class which taught me how to make a good Web site and learned that Web site design requires care in picking colors and in organizing the layout. The layout of RMP's home page is smart, with information grouped in clearly defined rectangular boxes. Across the top is a blue banner with the name in easy to read letters. At the bottom of the banner three links ("help," "about," and "create a free account") are printed in small but easy to see white lettering. Below the banner, the page is divided into boxes, three across and two down, with plenty of white space along the left and right borders and bottom so that the page looks neatly organized and uncluttered. The top box on the left has the main menu in blue lettering against a white background with links to "Most-Rated Colleges," "Funny Ratings," "Forums," and so forth. The placement of the menu is smart because readers of English are used to reading from left to right as well as top to bottom. Below the menu a box titled "Statistics" (many of which I cited in the first paragraph) reveals how many students use the ratings.

The viewer's eye is drawn to the center box, which is three times as wide as the boxes on the sides and includes the all-important member log-in box (in white lettering against the same blue background as the top banner). The boxes on the right are ads, which pick up the same colors as the rest of the page and are not too distracting. The placement of information seems just right and the log-in box is not buried on the page but easy to see and use.

The navigation system is smooth and fast. When you log in, you get the main member page; from there, you easily link to your school's page. On the member page, you can edit your ratings, go to the message board, or manage your account. Your school's page is the destination for checking out professors whose classes you are considering, entering your own rating of a professor, or adding a professor not already listed. Finding a particular professor is quick and easy because professors' names are listed in alphabetical order. The list is easy to skim and contains lots of valuable information. To the left of each name is a face icon (which I will explain in a minute) followed by a check icon that you can click on to add your own rating. To the right of the name is the professor's department, the date he or she was last rated, the number of ratings, and the vital average ratings for overall quality and ease. Clicking on a name takes you to the professor's page, which presents even more information: a box with averages in each rating category and a list of individual users' ratings, starting with the most recent. These ratings identify the class, give the student's rating in each category, and often

Kim uses MLA style throughout to cite sources parenthetically.

Kim's thesis forecasts the reasons she will develop in subsequent paragraphs. She introduces her first reason — that the Web site is well designed — by focusing on its appearance and ease of use.

Kim takes readers on a tour of the home page, describing how the information is made visible and easily accessible. The highlighted phrases locate the various features on the page.

Kim provides more support for her first reason, showing how fast RMP's navigation system is and how easy it is to find specific professors.

2

3

4

include a comment. You can add your own rating of the professor or respond to other users' ratings. Every page displays the information clearly, without distractions. Even though there are ads, they do not flicker or get in the way. This is not the kind of Web site that takes minutes just to find what you need. Not only is it easy to browse, but it also doesn't lag because there are no large files or images to slow it down. For me, the longest it took to get to another page was two seconds using a cable modem.

5   Most important, RateMyProfessors.com is full of useful information that can help students make informed decisions when it comes to choosing teachers and preparing for a class they are about to take. A student debating whether to take a history or a sociology class, for example, can go to the Web site, first look at the overall ratings of each professor and then find user ratings for the classes being considered. Assuming the professor has been graded by other students, a great deal can be learned about the professor and possibly also about the specific class.

6   Professors are rated in several categories on a scale of 1 (worst) to 5 (best). The scores on clarity and helpfulness are averaged for the "Overall Quality rating," the overall rating that determines which icon is placed next to the professor's name: A yellow smiley face indicates "good quality," a bluish-gray sad face "poor quality," and an indifferent-looking green face "average quality." The numerical rating in each category is displayed along with the face so that students and professors can see the breakdown. In addition to evaluating the professor's clarity and helpfulness, students also rate the difficulty of the course. This rating, however, has no effect on assigning the face icon because, as the site explains, "an Easiness rating of 5 may actually mean the teacher is TOO easy." Although RMP acknowledges that easiness is "definitely the most controversial" reason for judging a class, they still present it because "many students decide what class to take based on the difficulty of the teacher." Another category that is not included in the overall rating is "Rater Interest." To explain this category the Web site quotes from a study that found student "motivation correlated with the overall evaluation," meaning that the more motivated a student was to succeed in a course, the higher the professor's overall quality score. "Instructors," however, as RMP acknowledges, "usually have little control over student motivation" (RateMyProfessors).

7   The faces and numbers are informative, but I think the comments help the most because they are so detailed. Not surprisingly, the comments on RateMyProfessors.com tend to address many of the same issues that my college's course evaluation forms do. For example, one question on my campus evaluation asks if the instructor presented the material in "an organized, understandable manner." Many of the RMP comments answer this question: from high praise ("lectures are interesting, and he's happy to answer whatever questions you could ask") to severe criticism ("lectures are BORING and POINTLESS" or "totally disorganized!! boring and reads off the power point!!"). Another question on my campus form asks if the instructor was "concerned about students learning and understanding the course material." This issue also draws many comments on

---

This topic sentence introduces the section on Kim's second reason — that RMP is extremely helpful.

Kim anticipates readers' concern about the Easiness rating. She counterargues by acknowledging the criticism and RMP's response.

Kim uses the questions in her college course evaluation form to classify comments on the Web site.

The many comments Kim quotes help readers appreciate how informative the site is.

RMP, from highly positive ("he wrote a personal whole-page response to each of my papers. So I knew exactly what he liked and how to improve on my writing") to slams ("Kinda scary and intimidating" or "He does not care if the students are learning the basic concepts. He teaches as if he were teaching a Graduate level class. This is an INTRO class, let us learn the basics 1st"). In addition to these kinds of comments, RMP also posts information that course evaluations do not include — advice on how to pass the course ("If you keep up w/ your notes and the reading, you should be fine. Pop quizzes every week." or "Has notes available on-line. Tests are extremely difficult and require a lot of reading from the book to be successful as well as attending class. Gives surprise quizzes"). The site also gives students warnings ("He's ****in' hard. Fails half his class." or "OMG, one of the worst teachers I've ever had . . . Does not know how to teach and wears the tightest pants ever . . . gross.")

Here Kim adds another category not found on course evaluations.

And as this last comment suggests, we can't forget the last rating category: Is your professor hot or not? The answer to this question makes the Web site amusing. "Hot" professors are marked with a red chili pepper beside their names. Some students also include comments in this area: "good lookin guy, nice body" and "this chick [the professor] totally blew my mind. She was sooo hot. I'm serious take this class just to check her out. SEXY!!!!" In fact, this issue may not be just a sideline to ones that supposedly are more serious. Students give professors higher overall ratings if they are hot, according to a *New York Times* article, "The Hunk Differential," which the RMP site provides as the answer to its FAQ question "Why do you have the 'hot' category?" The article, written by a professor of business, economics, and information management, reports a study that found "good-looking professors got significantly higher teaching scores" than those who did not rate as high on a beauty scale (Varian). So it may be that a professor who is considered "hot" on the site may be judged on a more lenient scale of teaching effectiveness.

Here Kim introduces her third reason — that RMP is amusing.

Kim anticipates a concern, refuting possible criticism with support from published research.

This question about the possible effect of the teacher's appearance on student response and learning leads to a more basic question about the credibility of the evaluations on RateMyProfessors.com: Are the ratings statistically valid? The simple answer, the Web site itself admits, is "Not really. They are a listing of opinions and should be judged as such" (RateMyProfessors). The results are statistically invalid, as one psychology professor explained, because the users are self-selected and not selected randomly (Harmon). And the fewer student ratings an instructor has been given, the less reliable the overall evaluation. Nevertheless, RMP claims "we often receive emails stating that the ratings are uncannily accurate, especially for schools with over 1000 ratings" (RateMyProfessors). RMP also refers readers to an article reporting a study at the University of Waterloo, Canada (UW), that found fifteen of the sixteen Distinguished Teacher Award winners at UW also had yellow smiley faces on RateMyProfessors.com (TRACE). While this correlation is reassuring, students should not approach the ratings uncritically. And evidence suggests most don't. As one college newspaper reporter put it, "students claim they do not blindly follow the comments" (Espach). A recent study of RMP published in the *Journal of Computer-Mediated Communication* found that stu-

Here, Kim anticipates a fourth, and major criticism, which she concedes. Nevertheless, she defends her positive judgment with support from researchers and students.

8

9

dents "are aware that ratings and comments on the site could reflect students exacting revenge or venting" (Kindred and Mohammed). As one student explained: "If half the ratings are bad, I will ask around about the professor. If every rating is poor I won't take the teacher" (Espach).

10   There are other Internet professor evaluation sites, but none is as widely used or as easy to use as RateMyProfessors.com. I compared RMP with three competitors: Professor Performance, Reviewum.com, and RatingsOnline. The user base of the first two sites looks too small to provide reliable information. Professor Performance has 73,040 evaluations at 1,742 colleges and universities, and Reviewum.com claims to have 20,098 records for 137 campuses. In addition, for the limited number of professors who are listed, there are only a small number of evaluations, not enough to enable students to make informed judgments.

Kim compares RMP to competing Web sites.

She compares the different sites' statistics to argue for RMP's greater reliability.

11   Although RatingsOnline does not appear to display its statistics, it claims to have ratings for "thousands of professors." However, there are only nineteen professors from my campus listed compared to 1252 on RMP. Still, RatingsOnline is better designed and includes more helpful information than the other two competitors, and it may even be better than RMP in terms of helpfulness. Students not only identify the class and term it was taken, but also are asked to list the grade they received. Of course, this information about the grade is no more reliable than any other information a user gives, but it could help students judge the user's credibility. The ratings categories on RatingsOnline also seem more specific than on RMP: prepared, enthusiastic, focused, available, material, exam prep, quality. In addition, students are prompted to indicate the percentage given to homework, quizzes, and exams in determining the final grade. This information could be useful in helping students decide which classes to take, but only if there are enough reviews posted. In its design and potential helpfulness, RatingsOnline is a very good site but not likely to be as good as RMP because its user base appears to be smaller.

Kim points out the relative strengths and weaknesses of RatingsOnline compared to RateMyProfessors.

12   When you have the option of choosing a teacher, wouldn't you really like some information? RateMyProfessors.com allows you to see what other students have to say about professors and courses you may be considering as well as to voice your opinion. As a Web site, it is not only helpful and easy to use, but it is also amusing to read.

Kim concludes by reminding readers of her reasons.

Works Cited

Espach, Alison. "RateMyProfessors.com — Blessing or Bluffing?" *The Cowl*. Providence College, 27 April 2006. Web. 15 May 2006.

Harmon, Christine. "Professors Rate Reliability of RateMyProfessors.com." *Daily Forty-Niner*. California State U., Long Beach, 15 May 2006. Web. 15 May 2006.

Kindred, Jeannette, and Shaheed N. Mohammed. "'He Will Crush You Like an Academic Ninja!': Exploring Teacher Ratings on RateMyProfessors.com." *Journal of Computer-Mediated Communication* 10.3 (2005): n. pag. Web. 15 May 2006.

Professor Performance. Professorperformance.com, n.d. Web. 19 May 2006.

RateMyProfessors. Ratemyprofessors.com, 2006. Web. 13 May 2006.

"ratemyprofessors.ca." *Teaching Matters Newsletter.* U of Waterloo Teaching Resources Office, Sept. 2001. Web. 13 May 2005.

RatingsOnline. Ratingsonline.com, n.d. Web. 19 May 2006.

Reviewum.com. Reviewum.com, n.d. Web. 19 May 2006.

Varian, Hal R. "The Hunk Differential." *New York Times.* New York Times, 28 Aug. 2003. Web. 14 May 2006.

A. O. SCOTT is a film reviewer for the *New York Times.* After graduating from college with a major in literature, he became a book reviewer for *Newsday,* a daily newspaper on Long Island, New York, and served for a time on the editorial staffs of *Lingua Franca* and *The New York Review of Books.* He still occasionally writes book reviews for the *New York Times* and contributes to other journals such as *Slate* and *The New Yorker.* He has also edited several books, including *A Bolt from the Blue and Other Essays* (2002) and the *New York Times Guide to the Best 1,000 Movies Ever Made* (2004). Scott occasionally appears on television to talk about films or books, and he sometimes lectures on college campuses.

The 2005 film *Good Night, and Good Luck* was a critical as well as a popular success (receiving six Academy Award nominations, including ones for director, screenplay, and picture). The acclaim was not only because of George Clooney, who cowrote, directed, and acted in the film, but also because of its ideas. A college journalism major whose father was a television journalist, Clooney explained in a *Columbia Journalism Review* interview that he intended the film "to reflect a great moment in journalism" when newscaster Edward R. Murrow challenged U.S. Senator Joseph R. McCarthy's scare tactic of publicly accusing people without evidence of their being Communists or traitors. Clooney said he wanted the film to stir debate about the news media's responsibility to speak truth to power.

Notice that Scott judges the film for its cinematic qualities as well as for its ideas, which he seems especially to value because of their complexity, the "shades of gray" indicated in the title of his essay. Consider, as you read, whether evaluating this kind of film for these reasons seems appropriate to you or whether you would apply different standards.

News in Black, White and Shades of Gray

A. O. Scott

Shot in a black-and-white palette of cigarette smoke, hair tonic, dark suits and pale button-down shirts, *Good Night, and Good Luck* plunges into a half-forgotten world in which television was new, the cold war was at its peak, and the Surgeon General's report on the dangers of tobacco was still a decade in the future. Though it is a meticulously detailed reconstruction of an era, the film, directed by George Clooney from a script he wrote with Grant Heslov, is concerned with more than nostalgia.

Burnishing the legend of Edward R. Murrow, the CBS newsman who in the 1940s and '50s established a standard of journalistic integrity his profession has scrambled to live up to ever since, *Good Night, and Good Luck* is a passionate, thoughtful essay on power, truth-telling and responsibility. . . . The title evokes Murrow's trademark sign-off, and I can best sum up my own response by recalling the name of his flagship program: See it now.

And be prepared to pay attention. *Good Night, and Good Luck* is not the kind of historical picture that dumbs down its material, or walks you carefully through events that may be unfamiliar. Instead, it unfolds, *cinéma-vérité* style,[1] in the fast, sometimes frantic present tense, following Murrow and his colleagues as they deal with the petty annoyances and larger anxieties of news gathering at a moment of political turmoil. The story flashes back from a famous, cautionary speech that Murrow gave at an industry convention in 1958 to one of the most notable episodes in his career — his war of words and images with Senator Joseph R. McCarthy.

While David Strathairn plays Murrow with sly eloquence and dark wit, Mr. Clooney allows the junior Senator from Wisconsin to play himself (thanks to sur-viving video clips of his hearings and public appearances), a jolt of documentary truth that highlights some of the movie's themes. Television, it suggests, can be both a potent vehicle for demagoguery[2] and a weapon in the fight against it.

Mr. Clooney, who plays Murrow's producer and partner, Fred Friendly, has clearly thought long and hard about the peculiar, ambiguous nature of the medium. It is a subject that comes naturally to him: his father, Nick, was for many years a local television newscaster in Cincinnati, and the younger Mr. Clooney's own star first rose on the small screen. Like *Good Night, and Good Luck*, his first film, *Confessions of a Dangerous Mind* (2002), used the biography of a television per-sonality (Chuck Barris of "The Gong Show") as a way of exploring the medium's ca-pacity to show the truth, and also to distort and obscure it.

Indeed, these two movies can almost be seen as companion pieces. *Confessions of a Dangerous Mind* suggests that a man with a hard time telling truth from fiction can find a natural home on the tube, while *Good Night, and Good Luck* demonstrates that a furiously honest, ruthlessly rational person may find it less com-fortable. Murrow, as conceived by the filmmakers and incarnated by Mr. Strathairn, is a man of strong ideals and few illusions. He knows that McCarthy will smear him (and offers the Senator airtime to do so), and that sponsors and government offi-cials will pressure his boss, William Paley (Frank Langella), to rein him in.

He is aware that his reports are part of a large, capitalist enterprise, and makes some necessary concessions. In addition to his investigative reports — and, in effect, to pay for them — Murrow conducts celebrity interviews, including

---

[1] *cinéma-vérité* style: In French, "films of truth." This style of filmmaking uses docu-mentary film techniques to make the drama seem life-like or realistic.

[2] demagoguery: The tactic of appealing to people's fears and prejudices instead of their reason, usually as a way to gain or retain power.

one with Liberace,[3] which Mr. Clooney has lovingly and mischievously rescued from the archives.

From that odd encounter to the kinescopes[4] of the Army-McCarthy hearings,[5] *Good Night, and Good Luck* brilliantly recreates the milieu of early television. Robert Elswit's smoky cinematography and Stephen Mirrione's suave, snappy editing are crucial to this accomplishment. It also captures, better than any recent movie I can think of, the weirdly hermetic atmosphere of a news organization at a time of crisis.

Nearly all the action takes place inside CBS headquarters (or at the bar where its employees drink after hours), which gives the world outside a detached, almost abstract quality. A telephone rings, an image flickers on a screen, a bulldog edition[6] of the newspaper arrives . . . this is what it means for information to be mediated.

But its effects are nonetheless real. While the camera never follows Friendly or Murrow home from the office, and the script never delves into psychology, we see how the climate of paranoia and uncertainty seeps into the lives of some of their co-workers. Don Hollenbeck (Ray Wise), an anchor for the New York CBS affiliate, is viciously red-baited[7] by a newspaper columnist, and Joe and Shirley Wershba (Robert Downey Jr. and Patricia Clarkson) skulk around the office like spies (though for reasons that have more to do with office politics than with national security). When Murrow, in March 1954, prepares to broadcast his exposé of McCarthy's methods, the suspense is excruciating, even if we know the outcome.

Because we do, it is possible to view *Good Night, and Good Luck* simply as a reassuring story of triumph. But the film does more than ask us, once again, to admire Edward R. Murrow and revile Joseph R. McCarthy. That layer of the story is, as it should be, in stark black-and-white, but there is a lot of gray as well, and quite a few questions that are not so easily resolved. The free press may be the oxygen of a democratic society, but it is always clouded by particles and pollutants, from the vanity or cowardice of individual journalists to the impersonal pressures of state power and the profit motive.

And while Mr. Clooney is inclined to glorify, he does not simplify. The scenes between Murrow and Paley, taking place in the latter's cryptlike office, have an almost Shakespearean gravity, and not only because Mr. Strathairn and Mr. Langella perform their roles with such easy authority. McCarthy may serve as the hissable villain, but Paley is a more complicated foil for Murrow — at once

---

[3] Liberace: A pianist who was popular in the 1950s. He never came out of the closet as a homosexual, but in the interview shown in the film he seems to be saying that, like England's Princess Margaret, he is looking for his "dream man, too."

[4] kinescopes: A method of recording television programs used in the 1950s.

[5] Army-McCarthy hearings: Nationally televised Congressional hearings in 1954 to investigate Senator McCarthy's charges that the Army was harboring Communists. In the end, McCarthy was discredited by the hearings, whose highpoint was the Army attorney Joseph Welch's exasperated comment: "Have you no sense of decency, sir, at long last? Have you left no sense of decency?"

[6] bulldog edition: The earliest morning edition of a newspaper.

[7] red-baited: To be accused and denounced as a Communist or Communist sympathizer.

patron, antagonist and protector. (Addressed by everyone else, in hushed tones, as "Mr. Paley," he is "Bill" only to Murrow.)

Most of the discussion of this movie will turn on its content — on the history it investigates and on its present-day resonance. This is a testament to Mr. Clooney's modesty (as is the fact that, on screen, he makes himself look doughy and pale), but also to his skill. Over the years he has worked with some of the smartest directors around, notably Joel Coen and Steven Soderbergh (who is an executive producer of this film). And while he has clearly learned from them, the cinematic intelligence on display in this film is entirely his own. He has found a cogent subject, an urgent set of ideas and a formally inventive, absolutely convincing way to make them live on screen.   13

Making Connections to Personal and Social Issues: A Free Press and Democracy

Scott appears to agree with Clooney that journalism plays a crucial role in maintaining democracy, saying that a "free press may be the oxygen of a democratic society" (paragraph 11). But, as Scott also points out, there are many reasons the press fails to fulfill its obligations: "from the vanity or cowardice of individual journalists to the impersonal pressures of state power and the profit motive" (paragraph 11). In today's society, there may also be problems on the receiving end. The number of newspapers in the United States has steadily declined in the last two decades, and only half of Americans today read a daily newspaper. Similarly, routine watching of television news programs has declined, from 60 percent in 1993 to 30 percent in 2000. Whereas the median age of evening news show viewers is 60 years old, young people aged 18–29 reportedly are more likely to get their news from the Internet and TV comedy shows than from other television or radio news programs, newspapers, or newsmagazines.

With two or three other students, discuss whether you try to keep informed about the news. Tell each other which of the news media — print, television, radio, or the Internet — you follow and how much time per day or week you typically spend reading or viewing news reports and opinion pieces. What are your favorite sources of information and why?

Based on your own experience and those of people you know, do you think the decline in newspaper readership and television news viewing is a problem for our country? Or do you think young people are sufficiently informed about important issues through the Internet, comedy news shows, and other sources?

Analyzing Writing Strategies

1. In evaluating a film, writers often point out details from the film as examples to **support their argument**. Reread paragraphs 8–10 and underline the details Scott presents. What are these details supposed to illustrate? How effectively do you think they support the argument?

For more information about comparing and contrasting, see Chapter 18.

2. Writers of evaluations often use comparison to **support their reasons**. One of the reasons Scott offers for his judgment of the film is that it is "a passionate, thoughtful essay on power, truth-telling and responsibility" (paragraph 2). At the beginning of paragraph 5, he observes that George Clooney "has clearly thought long and hard about the peculiar, ambiguous nature of the medium" of television, specifically its "capacity to show the truth, and also to distort and obscure it." To see how Scott uses comparison to develop and support this reason, reread paragraphs 5 and 6 where he compares *Good Night, and Good Luck* to the first film Clooney directed, *Confessions of a Dangerous Mind*. How does the comparison support Scott's argument?

Commentary: Presenting the Subject, Overall Judgment, and Reasons

Film reviews, like other evaluations, usually begin by **presenting the subject** and conveying the writer's judgment. A. O. Scott identifies the movie by name in his first sentence, and in the first four paragraphs he categorizes it as a "historical picture" in "*cinéma-vérité* style" (paragraph 3), and associates it with "documentary" films (paragraph 4). He indicates the time period in the first paragraph ("when the cold war was at its peak"), and in paragraph 10, he specifies when most of the action takes place and concisely explains what the story is about: "When Murrow, in March 1954, prepares to broadcast his exposé of McCarthy's methods." Additionally, Scott tells who the main actors are and what characters they play, and, of course, he emphasizes from the first paragraph that the film is directed and cowritten by George Clooney.

Because film reviewers need to assume their readers are trying to decide whether to see the film, they have to think carefully about how much plot detail to reveal so as not to spoil the suspense, assuming there is any. In this case, because the film depicts historical events, Scott does not try to hide the outcome but neither does he describe the climax of the story. In fact, he claims "the suspense is excruciating, even if we know the outcome" (paragraph 10).

In addition to presenting the subject, writers of evaluation usually **state their judgment** early on. In paragraph 2, Scott claims "*Good Night, and Good Luck* is a passionate, thoughtful essay on power, truth-telling and responsibility" and urges readers, "See it now." Throughout the essay, Scott makes other evaluative statements about the acting, the paranoid atmosphere the film creates, and the complexity with which the story is told. But he saves his overall judgment of the film, the thesis, until the end: "He [Clooney] has found a cogent subject, an urgent set of ideas and a formally inventive, absolutely convincing way to make them live on screen" (paragraph 13).

For more information on thesis statements, see Chapter 19.

Because it comes at the end, instead of at the beginning, this thesis summarizes the main **reasons** instead of forecasting them. The key words "subject" and "ideas" refer to what Scott writes in paragraph 2 about the film being about "power, truth-telling and responsibility." He returns in paragraphs 6 and 7 and 11 and 12 to developing and supporting this reason. First, he makes the point that broadcast news is "part of a large, capitalist enterprise" that tests and even compels compromising ideals. Then, he demonstrates that the film's idea that a "free press" is the "oxygen" needed for "a democratic society" is treated with some subtlety. Anticipating readers' possible objection to the film's apparent hero-worship of Murrow, he argues that it is not as simplistic as it might seem ("there is a lot of gray as well, and quite a few questions that are not so easily resolved" [paragraph 11]).

The second main reason for his high regard for the film relates to its being "formally inventive" (paragraph 13). In talking about the film's form, Scott is referring to its use of "*cinéma-vérité*" or "documentary" style. He shows that it is "a meticulously detailed reconstruction of an era" (paragraph 1), but as he explains in paragraph 3, it is not a traditional "historical picture that dumbs down its material, or walks you carefully through events." Instead, he shows that it is fast paced and uses flashback to frame the events. In paragraphs 9 and 10, he provides additional support by showing how Clooney's direction and screenplay combine with the cinematography and the editing to create "the weirdly hermetic atmosphere of a news organization at a time of crisis" (paragraph 8).

Because his is a rave review, Scott does not point out weaknesses of any kind. He does not qualify or limit his thesis. Most film reviews as well as other kinds of evaluations, however, combine praise and criticism. Rarely do critics find nothing to criticize. Even in highly positive evaluations, writers often acknowledge minor shortcomings to show readers that their evaluation is fair and balanced. Similarly, in negative reviews, the writer usually finds something to praise. As you read the next selection, you will see how a writer can express a positive overall judgment but still point out shortcomings.

Considering Topics for Your Own Essay

List several movies that you have seen recently, and choose one from your list that you recall especially well. Of course, if you were actually to write about this movie, you would need to see it at least twice to develop your reasons and find supporting examples. For this activity, however, you do not have to view your film again. Just be sure you have a strong overall judgment about it. Then consider how you would argue for your judgment. Specifically, what reasons do you think you would give your readers? Why do you assume that your readers would accept these reasons as appropriate for evaluating this particular film?

JONAH JACKSON has written computer game reviews for *Computer Gaming World*, Gamers.com, g4tv.com, and TechTV. This evaluation of the popular role-playing game *The Elder Scrolls III: Morrowind* was initially published on the now defunct TechTV Web site and also aired on the television show *Extended Play*. Jackson gives the game TechTV's highest rating of five stars. As you read Jackson's review, notice that he points out the game's weaknesses as well as its strengths. Consider whether balancing the good with the bad in a review like this makes the argument more convincing or less so.

The Elder Scrolls III: Morrowind

Jonah Jackson

Morrowind, the third title in Bethesda Softworks' Elder Scrolls series, has hit the shelves. In this week's episode of *Extended Play* we sink our teeth into one of the largest and most richly detailed fantasy worlds ever to wear a set of polygons.[1] There are literally hundreds of hours of gameplay. A second CD that contains a construction set promises countless more hours of gameplay as gamers all over the world work hard on [your favorite mod here].[2] It's a good time to be a gamer.

Outstanding Graphics

Morrowind would be worth the price of admission for the graphics alone. Building on past games, the island of Vvardenfell was meticulously created with dozens of climates and landscapes. Unique architectural detail differentiates cities and towns across the various regions. The sense of scope and grandeur is well maintained from the open canals of Vivec to the modest Ashlander yurt villages. Seeing the ruined ornate spires of an ancient city appear out of the mist as you walk through the countryside is something to behold.

Fog enshrouds the mountaintops, the water glistens and reflects landscape features, lightning, rain, and dust storms howl through the land, and night skies shine with stars. The Bethesda team has created a world that pulls you in with wide eyes from the moment you step off the slave boat onto the port of Seyda Neen.

Though the game is best played in the first person, there is a third-person camera position that's worth it if for nothing more than checking out the new duds you pick up in town. The few graphical quirks, such as shadows that get cast through walls and robe sleeves that obscure your ranged weapon targeting, are easy to forgive once you see your character reach up and shield his eyes while turning into the teeth of a windstorm.

Free to Explore

Morrowind begins with your arrival in Vvardenfell on an Imperial slave ship. After a short and clever character-generation

---

[1] *Polygons* are used to create virtual three-dimensional space in video games.
[2] *Mod* is a modification of a computer game's technical features.

segment disguised as a new-arrival check-in, you're off and running. Though you're given an initial task related to the game's main story, from the very beginning you're given the freedom to explore and adventure at your own pace.

Unlike many games   6
that promise you the freedom to play however you want, Morrowind goes a long way toward meeting that promise. There are hundreds of side quests and locations to explore all over the map. You'll visit many of them and have a satisfying experience by simply following the main story. Alternatively, you can head into the countryside and make your way along a story line on your own. The sheer volume of quests and plot lines ensures that independent exploration will not hamper you when you want to return to the more traditional style of RPG[3] play. Plus it's downright fun to head into the nearest ancestral tomb to pick up a few goodies while walking down a nice country road.

Still, the best way to experience Morrowind is to attach yourself to a guild   7
or two and start role-playing the quests you receive. While the ubiquitous fed-ex and find-my-lost-armor quests are well represented, many of your tasks will have more than one solution, depending on your skills, and you'll often find that the overlapping or conflicting interests of the guilds make the plot lines more interesting. The main story follows an engaging plot line as well and includes a huge back story that's interesting on its own. The island of Vvardenfell is a somewhat troubled section of the Empire. The native Dunmers or Dark Elves are at odds among themselves and with the Imperial presence. As the story unfolds you find that you play a larger and more important role in the future of Vvardenfell.

Quests and plots are revealed most often through interaction with the hun-   8
dreds of characters found throughout Vvardenfell. Conversation is based on keywords and the interface[4] keeps track of questions and responses in a separate journal. Many of the generic townspeople do begin to look and sound alike after a while and the canned responses to certain questions do get old or even nonsensical. More than once townspeople seemed completely oblivious to world-changing events that had just taken place.

---

[3] *RPG* stands for *role-playing game*.
[4] *Interface* is the part of a program that presents information and allows user input.

Customization

Every part of the game's design is implemented with an eye toward flexibility and customization to the player's desires. There are 10 races and 21 predefined classes, and you can create custom classes by choosing preferences from 27 skills among three specialization categories: Combat, Magic, and Stealth. 9

Skills are improved through training or successful use of the skill. Level advancement is based on improving a combination of any skills a total of 10 times. Level advancement brings additional Health and the opportunity to assign additional points to your base attributes. 10

Any character class can improve any skill, although advancement is easier in the skills related to your class. The game has no time limit, though, so you can work to create a mighty sorcerer who's also the most skilled swordsman and deft pickpocket in the land. 11

With a few exceptions, all skills are useful and the game is well balanced. Playing a skilled orator and acrobat with limited combat skills is just as rewarding as hacking through the hordes with a barbarian warrior. Bethesda has done an excellent job writing a story that can be played through with many different character types. 12

Control

Navigation is similar to many FPS[5] titles and will be familiar to players of the first two Elder Scrolls games. The seamless combat interface is also easy to use, although the various types of weapon swing (slash, jab, and so on) are awkwardly related to your movement direction. A group of windowed menus is available with a simple click of the right mouse button. This pauses the game and lets you ac- 13

---

[5] *FPS* refers to first-person shooter games, a multiplayer genre of computer games.

cess inventory, map, magic items, and your character's detailed status. Basics such as health, mana, and spell effects, plus a minimap, are always available on screen. Some of the interface design is less than optimal. Your inventory, which you can sort by type, can become unwieldy as you collect a lot of potions or scrolls. It's especially difficult to manage all the potion-making ingredients if your character has the Alchemy skill.

The many quests you'll receive along the way are recorded in a chronological journal that's autoindexed as you go. This journal manages to record everything of importance, but it's missing the ability to sort or group items by quest. Nor does it separate completed quests and ongoing quests. Although the sheer volume of information is a bit much in later stages, the index feature does prevent the journal from becoming unusable.   14

Sound

Bethesda gave the music and sound effects the same care it gave the visuals. The grand scope of the story is served well by the basic theme music. Given 50-plus hours of game time, it was important to produce something that was unobtrusive enough to hear a few hundred times while still providing atmosphere. The combat music is a little flat, but it does provide important auditory clues about nearby enemies. The ambiance of the game is also helped by the carefully crafted sound of footsteps, creaking doors, howling wind, moaning spirits, unsheathing swords, rippling water, and dozens of other effects that really pull the game together.   15

Summary

Morrowind is a flawed jewel, but flawed only because its scope is so grand. Beautiful graphics, compelling stories, a huge map to explore, engaging quests, and a simple interface all add up to a premier game. Its bugs and design quirks are more than compensated for by a core game that's just fantastic. It may have just missed the center of the bull's eye, but Bethesda gets five stars for hitting a target that no one else even dares aim for.   16

Making Connections to Personal and Social Issues: Freedom of Play in Computer Games

According to Jonah Jackson, an important attraction of role-playing computer games is the freedom they give players to explore and play in any way they choose. In addition, computer game enthusiasts can also join online "mod communities" to modify their favorite games.

With two or three other students, discuss your experiences with role-playing computer games. Take turns describing what kinds of games you enjoy playing and what you like about playing these particular games. For example, how much do you value the freedom to play as you choose and the opportunity to be creative? Consider also how you feel about the game's rules. Do the rules restrict your enjoyment or contribute in some way to it? Does it matter to you — and do you think it should matter to Jackson — that what he calls freedom is really scripted?

Analyzing Writing Strategies

1. Writers of evaluations give readers a lot of information about the subject in the course of the essay. But they usually **present the subject** in the opening paragraph by identifying it in certain ways. Reread paragraph 1 to see how Jackson presents the subject he is evaluating. Underline the information he gives readers, and speculate about why you think he begins with this information.

2. Jackson indicates his **overall judgment** in the opening and then reasserts it as a thesis statement in the concluding paragraph. Reread paragraph 16 to see whether the thesis statement meets the three standards for a good thesis: that it be clear and unambiguous, arguable, and appropriately qualified.

Commentary: Giving Appropriate Reasons

The argument is probably the most important part of an evaluative essay. Writers argue by giving reasons and support for their overall judgment. In addition to this direct argument, writers also usually counterargue, anticipating and responding to readers' objections and alternative judgments. Here we focus on the way writers **give reasons for their judgment**.

Reasons in evaluative arguments are often statements praising or criticizing particular qualities of the subject. Jackson uses headings to focus attention on qualities such as graphics, customization, and control. Headings make his argument easy for readers to follow. They are especially useful for text posted online, as was the case with Jackson's original review, because reading long stretches of text onscreen can be difficult. Here is a scratch outline of Jackson's essay, including the headings:

For more on the use of headings, see Chapters 13 and 25.

Introduces the subject and states the judgment (paragraph 1)

Develops and supports the first reason: "Outstanding Graphics" (2–4)

Develops and supports the second reason: "Free to Explore" (5–8)

Develops and supports the third reason: "Customization" (9–12)

Develops and supports the fourth reason: "Control" (13–14)

Develops and supports the fifth reason: "Sound" (15)

Concludes and reiterates judgment (16)

Under each heading, Jackson presents his reason in topic sentences like these:

Outstanding Graphics: Morrowind would be worth the price of admission for the graphics alone. Building on past games, the island of Vvardenfell was meticulously created with dozens of climates and landscapes. (paragraph 2)

Free to Explore: Though you're given an initial task related to the game's main story, from the very beginning you're given the freedom to explore and adventure at your own pace. (5)

Customization: Every part of the game's design is implemented with an eye toward flexibility and customization to the player's desires. (9)

Jackson does not simply assert his reasons, but supports them with particular examples. Look at the way he specifies in paragraphs 2–4 what makes the graphics good. In his topic sentence, he claims that the graphics are praiseworthy because the island was "meticulously created with dozens of climates and landscapes" (2). He supports this assertion with numerous examples. In paragraph 2, he points out how each city and town — from "the ruined ornate spires of an ancient city" to "the open canals of Vivec" and "the modest Ashlander yurt villages" — is given its own look with "[u]nique architectural detail." In paragraph 3, he specifies the different climates — fog, lightning, rain, dust storms, night skies — that the player encounters. In addition to praising the good graphics, Jackson points out the bad ones, what he calls a "few graphical quirks" (4). He gives examples of these "quirks": "shadows that get cast through walls and robe sleeves that obscure your ranged weapon targeting" (4). Supporting reasons with this kind of detail helps to convince readers that the writer is making an informed as well as a balanced evaluation. As you plan your argument, make sure that you support your reasons with specific examples.

Writers also sometimes need to argue that their **reasons are appropriate** because they are based on the kinds of standards that people knowledgeable about the subject normally use. Jackson, however, does not have to make this kind of argument because he can assume that his original TechTV audience of experienced computer game players agree that his reasons for evaluating a game are appropriate because they are based on important aesthetic and technical features of role-playing games. The order in which Jackson presents his reasons suggests that for this particular kind of game, graphics are the most important standard for judgment. Presumably, if something serious was wrong with the control interface, his review would have been much more negative, and he might have made control the first reason. Notice that he devotes eleven paragraphs to the first three reasons and only three paragraphs to the last two reasons. The Guide to Writing later in this chapter will help you decide which reasons to present, how to support them, whether you need to argue for their appropriateness, and how to organize your essay.

Considering Topics for Your Own Essay

Like Jonah Jackson, you might have a favorite computer game. Or you might do a lot of digital photography and be able to evaluate digital cameras or a software program like Photoshop. Alternatively, you might be interested in evaluating a particular Web site you use regularly, as Wendy Kim does in the annotated reading earlier in this chapter. Choose one particular game, software program, or Web site, and list its obvious strengths and weaknesses.

CHRISTINE ROMANO wrote the following essay when she was a first-year college student. In it she evaluates an argument essay written by another student, Jessica Statsky's "Children Need to Play, Not Compete," which appears in Chapter 6 of this book (pp. 276–79). Romano focuses not on the writing strategies or basic features of an essay arguing a position but rather on its logic — on whether the argument is likely to convince its intended readers. She evaluates the logic of the argument according to the standards presented in Chapter 12. You might want to review these standards on pp. 604–06 before you read Romano's evaluation. Also, if you have not already read Statsky's essay, you might want to do so now, thinking about what seems most and least convincing to you about her argument that competitive sports can be harmful to young children.

"Children Need to Play, Not Compete," by Jessica Statsky: An Evaluation

Christine Romano

Parents of young children have a lot to worry about and to hope for. In "Children Need to Play, Not Compete," Jessica Statsky appeals to their worries and hopes in order to convince them that organized competitive sports may harm their children physically and psychologically. Statsky states her thesis clearly and fully forecasts the reasons she will offer to justify her position: Besides causing physical and psychological harm, competitive sports discourage young people from becoming players and fans when they are older and inevitably put parents' needs and fantasies ahead of children's welfare. Statsky also carefully defines her key terms. By *sports*, for example, she means to include both contact and noncontact sports that emphasize competition. The sports may be organized locally at schools or summer sports camps or nationally, as in the examples of Peewee Football and Little League Baseball. She is concerned only with children six to twelve years of age.

In this essay, I will evaluate the logic of Statsky's argument, considering whether the support for her thesis is appropriate, believable, consistent, and complete. While her logic *is* appropriate, believable, and consistent, her argument also has weaknesses. I will focus on two: Her argument seems incomplete because she neglects to anticipate parents' predictable questions and objections and because she fails to support certain parts of it fully.

Statsky provides appropriate support for her thesis. Throughout her essay, she relies for support on different kinds of information (she cites eleven separate sources, including books, newspapers, and Web sites). Her quotations, examples, and statistics all support the reasons she believes competitive sports are bad for children. For example, in paragraph 3, Statsky offers the reason that "overly competitive sports" may damage children's growing bodies and that contact sports, in particular, may be especially hazardous. She supports this reason by paraphrasing Koppett's claim that muscle strain or even lifelong injury may result when a twelve-year-old throws curve balls. She then quotes Tutko on the dangers of tackle football. The opinions of both experts are obviously appropriate. They are relevant to her reason, and we can easily imagine that they would worry many parents.

Not only is Statsky's support appropriate, but it is also believable. Statsky quotes or summarizes authorities to support her argument in paragraphs 3–6, 8, 9, and 11. The question is whether readers would find these authorities credible. Since Statsky relies almost entirely on authorities to support her argument, readers must believe these authorities for her argument to succeed. I have not read Statsky's sources, but I think there are good reasons to consider them authoritative. First of all, the newspaper authors she quotes write for two of America's most respected newspapers, the *New York Times* and the *Los Angeles Times*. These newspapers are read across the country by political leaders and financial experts and by people interested in the arts and popular culture. Both have sports reporters who not only report on sports events but also take a critical look at sports issues. In addition, both newspapers have reporters who specialize in children's health and education. Second, Statsky gives background information about the authorities she quotes, which is intended to increase the person's believability in the eyes of parents of young children. In paragraph 3, she tells readers that Thomas Tutko is "a psychology professor at San Jose State University and coauthor of the book *Winning Is Everything and Other American Myths*." In paragraph 5, she announces that Martin Rablovsky is "a former sports editor for the *New York Times*," and she notes that he has watched children play organized sports for many years. Third, she quotes from two Web sites — the official Little League site and an AOL message board. Parents are likely to accept the authority of the Little League site and be interested in what other parents and coaches (most of whom are also parents) have to say.

In addition to quoting authorities, Statsky relies on examples and anecdotes to support the reasons for her position. If examples and anecdotes are to be believable, they must seem representative to readers, not bizarre or highly unusual or completely unpredictable. Readers can imagine a similar event happening elsewhere. For anecdotes to be believable, they should, in addition, be specific and true to life. All of Statsky's examples and anecdotes fulfill these requirements, and her readers would find them believable. For example, early in her argument, in paragraph 4, Statsky reasons that fear of being hurt greatly reduces children's enjoyment of contact sports. The anecdote comes from Tosches's investigative report on Peewee Football as does the quotation by the mother of an eight-year-old player who says that the children become frightened and pretend to be injured in order to stay out of the game. In the anecdote, a seven-year-old makes himself vomit to avoid playing. Because these echo the familiar "I feel bad" or "I'm sick" excuse children give when they do not want to go somewhere (especially school) or do something, most parents would find them believable. They could easily imagine their own children pretending to be hurt or ill if they were fearful or depressed. The anecdote is also specific. Tosches reports what the boy said and did and what the coach said and did.

Other examples provide support for all the major reasons Statsky gives for her position: 6

- That competitive sports pose psychological dangers — children becoming serious and unplayful when the game starts (paragraph 5)
- That adults' desire to win puts children at risk — parents fighting each other at a Peewee Football game and a coach setting fire to an opposing team's jersey (paragraph 8)
- That organized sports should emphasize cooperation and individual performance instead of winning — a coach banning scoring but finding that parents would not support him and a New York City basketball league in which all children play an equal amount of time and scoring is easier (paragraph 11)

All of these examples are appropriate to the reason they support. They are also believable. Together, they help Statsky achieve her purpose of convincing parents that organized, competitive sports may be bad for their children and that there are alternatives.

If readers are to find an argument logical and convincing, it must be consistent   7 and complete. While there are no inconsistencies or contradictions in Statsky's argument, it is seriously incomplete because it neglects to support fully one of its reasons, it fails to anticipate many predictable questions parents would have, and it pays too little attention to noncontact competitive team sports. The most obvious example of this support comes in paragraph 11, where Statsky asserts that many parents are ready for children's team sports that emphasize cooperation and individual performance. Yet the example of a Little League official who failed to win parents' approval to ban scores raises serious questions about just how many parents are ready to embrace noncompetitive sports teams. The other support, a brief description of City Sports for Kids in New York City, is very convincing but will only be logically compelling to those parents who are already inclined to agree with Statsky's position. Parents inclined to disagree with Statsky would need additional evidence. Most parents know that big cities receive special federal funding for evening, weekend, and summer recreation. Brief descriptions of six or eight noncompetitive teams in a variety of sports in cities, rural areas, suburban neighborhoods — some funded publicly, some funded privately — would be more likely to convince skeptics. Statsky is guilty here of failing to accept the burden of proof, a logical fallacy.

Statsky's argument is also incomplete in that it fails to anticipate certain objections and questions that some parents, especially those she most wants to convince, are almost sure to raise. In the first sentences of paragraphs 6, 9, and 10, Statsky does show that she is thinking about her readers' questions. She does not go nearly far enough, however, to have a chance of influencing two types of readers: those who themselves are or were fans of and participants in competitive sports and those who want their six- to twelve-year-old children involved in mainstream sports programs despite the risks, especially the national programs that have a certain prestige. Such parents might feel that competitive team sports for   8 young children create a sense of community with a shared purpose, build character through self-sacrifice and commitment to the group, teach children to face their fears early and learn how to deal with them through the support of coaches and team members, and introduce children to the principles of social cooperation and collaboration. Some parents are likely to believe and to know from personal experience that coaches who burn opposing team's jerseys on the pitching mound before the game starts are the exception, not the rule. Some young children idolize teachers and coaches, and team practice and games are the brightest moments in their lives. Statsky seems not to have considered these reasonable possibilities, and as a result her argument lacks a compelling logic it might have had. By acknowledging that she was aware of many of these objections — and perhaps even accommodating more of them in her own argument, as she does in paragraph 10, while refuting other objections — she would have strengthened her argument.

Finally, Statsky's argument is incomplete because she overlooks examples   9
of noncontact team sports. Track, swimming, and tennis are good examples that some readers would certainly think of. Some elementary schools compete in track meets. Public and private clubs and recreational programs organize competitive swimming and tennis competitions. In these sports, individual performance is the focus. No one gets trampled. Children exert themselves only as much as they are able to. Yet individual performances are scored, and a team score is derived. Because Statsky fails to mention any of these obvious possibilities, her argument is weakened.

The logic of Statsky's argument, then, has both strengths and weaknesses.   10
The support she offers is appropriate, believable, and consistent. The major weakness is incompleteness — she fails to anticipate more fully the likely objections of a wide range of readers. Her logic would prevent parents who enjoy and advocate competitive sports from taking her argument seriously. Such parents and their children have probably had positive experiences with team sports, and these experiences would lead them to believe that the gains are worth whatever risks may be involved. Many probably think that the risks Statsky points out can be avoided by careful monitoring. For those parents inclined to agree with her, Statsky's logic is likely to seem sound and complete. An argument that successfully confirms readers' beliefs is certainly valid, and Statsky succeeds admirably at this kind of argument. Because she does not offer compelling counterarguments to the legitimate objections of those inclined not to agree with her, however, her success is limited.

Making Connections to Personal and Social Issues: Competitive Team Sports and Social Cooperation

Romano reasons in paragraph 8 that some parents "feel that competitive team sports for young children create a sense of community with a shared purpose, build character through self-sacrifice and commitment to the group, teach children to face their fears early and learn how to deal with them through the support of coaches and team members, and introduce children to the principles of social co-operation and collaboration."

With two or three other students, discuss this view of the role that sports plays in developing a child's sense of social cooperation by giving children insights into how people cooperate in communities like neighborhoods, schools, workplaces, or even nations. Begin by telling one another about your own, your siblings', or your children's experiences with team sports between the ages of six and twelve. Explain how participating in sports at this young age did or did not teach social coopera-tion. If you think team sports failed to teach cooperation or had some other effect, explain the effect it did have.

Analyzing Writing Strategies

1. In paragraph 2, Romano **presents her overall judgment**. Underline the thesis statement, and evaluate it in terms of how well it meets the three standards for a good thesis: that it be clear and unambiguous, arguable, and appropriately qualified.

2. In addition to presenting her judgment in her thesis statement, Romano forecasts her reasons in paragraph 2. Reread Romano's essay, noting in the margin where she addresses each of these reasons. Then explain what you learn from the way Romano **presents her reasons**. Are they clear and easy to follow? Do you think her intended readers — her instructor and parents of young children (the same audience Statsky is trying to convince) — are likely to consider her reasons plau-sible? In other words, are these reasons appropriate for evaluating an essay that argues a position, based on standards her readers are likely to share? If you see a potential problem with any of the reasons she uses, explain the problem you see.

Commentary: Providing Convincing Support and Anticipating Readers' Possible Objections

Writers of evaluation do not merely assert the reasons for their judgment; they also provide support to back up their argument. In addition, they often try to anticipate readers' likely objections.

For more on using textual evidence as support, see Chapter 19.

Because she is writing about a text, Romano relies on textual evidence in the form of examples, summaries, and paraphrases to **support** her argument. She points to numerous examples from Statsky's essay throughout her evaluation:

The other support, *a brief description of City Sports for Kids in New York City*, is very convincing but . . . (Romano, paragraph 7)

In the first sentences of paragraphs 6, 9, and 10, Statsky does show that she is think-ing about her readers' questions. (Romano, paragraph 8)

By acknowledging that she was aware of many of these objections — and perhaps even accommodating more of them in her own argument, *as she does in paragraph 10*, while refuting other objections — she would have . . . (Romano, paragraph 8)

The first example (highlighted in italics), set off with commas in an appositive phrase, illustrates a kind of support Statsky presents in her essay. The second points to three sentences that demonstrate Statsky's use of a particular argumentative strategy. The third refers to a place where Statsky uses a different argumentative strategy. By using brief examples like these, Romano can provide many references to support her argument.

In paragraph 6, Romano presents a bulleted list of examples:

- That competitive sports pose psychological dangers — *children becoming serious and unplayful when the game starts* (paragraph 5)

- That adults' desire to win puts children at risk — *parents fighting each other at a Peewee Football game and a coach setting fire to an opposing team's jersey* (paragraph 8)

- That organized sports should emphasize cooperation and individual performance instead of winning — *a coach banning scoring but finding that parents would not support him and a New York City basketball league in which all children play an equal amount of time and scoring is easier* (paragraph 11)

Listing marshals evidence efficiently. Moreover, presenting the examples in a way that connects each example (highlighted in italics above) directly to the reason it supports helps make the examples clear and convincing.

These examples also show how Romano summarizes or paraphrases passages from Statsky's essay. A summary is a concise restatement of the original text in which only the main ideas or most important information is included. A paraphrase tends to include more details than does summary and may be as long as or even longer than the original.

Following are two side by side comparisons. The first illustrates Romano's use of summarizing and the second illustrates paraphrasing.

Romano's Summary	*Statsky's Original (paragraph 4):*
"a seven-year-old *makes himself vomit* to avoid playing" (paragraph 5).	"Coach, my tummy hurts. I can't play," he said. The coach told the player to get back onto the field. "There's nothing wrong with your stomach," he said. When the coach turned his head the seven-year-old stuck a finger down his throat and *made himself vomit*. When the coach turned back, the boy pointed to the ground and told him, "Yes there is, coach. See?" (Tosches A33)

This summary is concise, significantly shorter than the version in Statsky's original (10 instead of 69 words, a reduction of over 85 percent). Romano does use some of Statsky's words (highlighted in italics), changing Statsky's phrase *made himself vomit* from past to present tense so that the phrase fits grammatically into her own sentence. Romano uses summary here to relate the essential information. You can learn more about how Romano uses summary to support her argument in the section Working with Sources on pp. 440–42.

A good illustration of paraphrasing appears in the opening paragraph, where Romano represents Statsky's argument. Compare Romano's paraphrase to the original passage from Statsky's essay:

Romano's Paraphrase	Statsky's Original (paragraph 2)
Besides causing *physical and psychological harm, competitive sports* discourage young people from becoming *players* and *fans* when they are older and inevitably put parents' needs and fantasies ahead of children's welfare. (paragraph 1)	Highly organized *competitive sports* such as Peewee Football and Little League Baseball are too often played to adult standards, which are developmentally inappropriate for children and can be both *physically and psychologically harmful.* Furthermore, because they eliminate many children from organized sports before they are ready to compete, they are actually counterproductive for developing either future *players or fans.*

Notice that in this paraphrase, Romano tries to include many of the details from the original. Romano's paraphrase does not condense Statsky's original language very much (31 words in the paraphrase compared to 59 in the original, slightly less than 50 percent reduction). Romano does not leave very much out of her paraphrase, only the specific examples of competitive sports ("Peewee Football and Little League Baseball") and the characterization of "adult standards" as "developmentally inappropriate for children."

Writers choose summarizing over quoting when they want to emphasize the ideas rather than the language. They choose summarizing over paraphrasing when they want to stress the source's main ideas or information and skip the details. For additional information on using these strategies for presenting textual evidence see Chapter 19: Arguing, pp. 679–80 and Chapter 22: Using and Acknowledging Sources, pp. 738–46.

In addition to providing convincing support, writers of evaluation also have to **anticipate readers' objections**. The Writer at Work section on pp. 446–49 explains how Romano was made aware by her classmates that readers might raise certain objections to Statsky's argument. Romano responded by revising her essay to include these objections. In paragraph 8, for example, Romano asserts that Statsky's argument "fails to anticipate certain objections and questions that some parents, especially those she most wants to convince, are almost sure to raise." She then goes on to discuss several positive effects of competitive team sports such as creating a sense of community, building character, and teaching students to face their fears. In addition, she acknowledges that for some kids "team practice and games are the brightest moments in their lives." As you plan your own evaluation, think about your readers and how you could anticipate their possible objections. In responding to these objections, consider whether you should merely acknowledge the objection, accommodate it by making it part of your argument, or refute it — three strategies for counterarguing.

Considering Topics for Your Own Essay

List several written texts you would consider evaluating. For example, you might include in your list an essay from one of the chapters in this book. If you choose an argument from Chapters 6–10, you could evaluate its logic, its use of emotional appeals, or its credibility. You might prefer to evaluate a children's book that you read when you were young or that you now read to your own children, a magazine for people interested in a particular topic like computers or cars, a scholarly article you read for a research paper, or a short story from Chapter 10. You need not limit yourself to texts written on paper; also consider texts available online. Choose one possibility from your list, and come up with two or three reasons why it is a good or bad text.

Purpose and Audience

When you evaluate something, you seek to influence readers' judgments and possibly their actions. Your primary aim is to convince readers that your judgment is well informed and reasonable and therefore that they can feel confident in making decisions based on it. Readers do not simply accept reviewers' judgments, however, especially on important subjects. More likely they read reviews to learn more about a subject so that they can make an informed decision themselves. Consequently, most readers care less about the forcefulness with which you assert your judgment than about the reasons and support you give for it.

Effective writers develop an argument designed for their particular readers. Given what you can expect your readers to know about your subject and the standards they would apply when evaluating this kind of subject, you decide which reasons to use as well as how much and what kind of support to give.

You may want to acknowledge directly your readers' knowledge of the subject, perhaps revealing that you understand how they might judge it differently. You might even let readers know that you have anticipated their objections to your argument. In responding to objections or different judgments, you could agree to disagree on certain points but try to convince readers that on other points you do share the same or at least similar standards.

Basic Features: Evaluations

A Well-Presented Subject

The subject must be clearly identified if readers are to know what is being evaluated. Most writers name it explicitly. When the subject is a film, an essay, a video game, or a Web site, naming it is easy. When it is something more general, naming may require more imagination.

Evaluations should provide only enough information to give readers a context for the judgment. However, certain kinds of evaluations — such as reviews of films, video games, television programs, and books — usually require more information than others because reviewers have to assume that readers will be unfamiliar with the subject and are reading in part to learn more about it. For example, in reviewing *Good Night, and Good Luck*, Scott tells readers the names of the director, screenwriters, main characters and the actors who play them, as well as the place and time in which the film's story unfolds and generally what happens. For a recently released film, television program, or video game, the writer must decide how much of the plot to reveal — trying not to spoil the suspense while explaining how well or poorly the suspense is managed. In certain situations, such as when writing for your instructor and classmates, you usually do not need to worry about giving anything away.

A Clear Overall Judgment

Evaluation essays are built around an overall judgment — an assertion that the subject is good or bad or that it is better or worse than something else of the same kind. This judgment is the thesis of the essay. The thesis statement may be combined with a forecast of the reasons that will be discussed in the essay, as in Kim's essay ("Overall, the Web site is well designed, amusing, and extremely helpful."). It may also be re-

peated in the concluding paragraph, again as Kim does ("RateMyProfessors.com allows you to see what other students have to say about professors and courses you may be considering as well as to voice your opinion. As a Web site, it is not only helpful and easy to use, but it is also amusing to read."). Scott presents his judgment as advice to readers in the second paragraph: ("See it now."). He restates his overall judgment in the last paragraph and summarizes his reasons ("He has found a cogent subject, an urgent set of ideas and a formally inventive, absolutely convincing way to make them live on screen.").

Although readers expect a definitive judgment, they also appreciate a balanced one. All of the writers in this chapter, except Scott, acknowledge both good and bad qualities of the subject they are evaluating. Kim acknowledges that RatingsOnline "may even be better than [RateMyProfessors.com] in terms of helpfulness" although it is not as helpful overall because of its apparently smaller user base (paragraph 11). Similarly, Romano praises the strengths and criticizes the weaknesses of Statsky's logic. Jackson gives the computer game his show's highest five-star rating, but he also points out its shortcomings.

Appropriate Reasons and Convincing Support

Writers assert the reasons for their judgment, often explain their reasons in some detail, and provide support for their reasons. For example, one of Scott's reasons for liking the film *Good Night, and Good Luck* is that it is "formally inventive." To explain what he means by form, Scott uses the terms *"cinéma-vérité"* and "documentary," terms readers knowledgeable about film are likely to recognize as styles of filmmaking. He also specifies particular qualities of the film typical of these styles, such as "a meticulously detailed reconstruction of an era" (1). He supports his point that the film is inventive by contrasting its fast pacing to the plodding way a traditional "historical picture . . . walks you carefully through events" (3).

For an argument to be convincing, readers have to accept the reasons as appropriate for evaluating the subject. Jackson, for example, assumes that his audience of computer game players will agree that his reasons are appropriate because they are based on standards that knowledgeable gamers apply when evaluating a game.

Evaluators not only give reasons but must also support their reasons. They may use various kinds of support. Romano, for example, relies primarily on textual evidence to support her reasons, presenting it in quotations, paraphrases, and summaries. Scott, Jackson, and Kim support their argument with examples and descriptions, but Kim also cites statistics and authorities.

Many writers also use comparisons to support an evaluative argument. For example, Scott compares *Good Night, and Good Luck* to Clooney's first film, *Confessions of a Dangerous Mind*. Similarly, Jackson compares the video game he is reviewing to other role-playing games, and Kim compares RateMyProfessors.com to three competitors: Professor Performance, Reviewum.com, and RatingsOnline. Comparisons like these both support the argument and help to convince readers that the writer is an expert who knows the kinds of standards that knowledgeable people normally apply when evaluating a subject of this kind.

Anticipation of Readers' Objections and Alternative Judgments

Sometimes reviewers try to anticipate and respond to readers' possible objections and alternative judgments, but counterarguing is not as crucial for evaluation as is arguing directly for a judgment by giving reasons and support. When they do counterargue, reviewers may simply acknowledge that others perhaps disagree, may accommodate into their argument points others have made, or may try to refute objections and alternative judgments. Kim anticipates three objections readers have raised critical of RateMyProfessors.com. She uses all three ways of counterarguing: acknowledging objections to the "Easiness" rating; accommodating, or conceding that the site is not statistically valid; and refuting criticism of the "hot" rating. Romano did not anticipate objections, but her classmates helped her understand alternative judgments of competitive sports for children, leading her to modify her argument to accommodate other views. When you plan your essay, be sure to take into consideration objections and alternative judgments others have made. If you simply ignore others' views, your readers may think your evaluation is not balanced and fair.

Justifying an Evaluation

Invention and Research

What subject could you make a judgment about and then support that judgment with good reasons? A movie? A sports team? A job? Learn all you can about the subject (using online research if necessary), and do some thinking and writing about it. Then come up with a tentative overall judgment. . . . **See p. 425 for more.**

Planning and Drafting

As you look over what you have written and learned about your subject, can you make a convincing case for your evaluation? If your readers are not familiar with the subject, how can you interest them in it? Should you start off with your overall judgment or lead up to it? Make a plan for your evaluation and start drafting it. . . . **See p. 431 for more.**

Critical Reading Guide

What are your draft's strengths and weaknesses? Have you defined your standards for evaluation clearly? Does your judgment seem wishy-washy or too extreme? Get a classmate, a friend, a writing tutor, or someone else to read and respond to your essay, especially the parts you are most unsure of. . . . **See p. 437 for more.**

Revising

As you consider your essay again in light of your reader's comments, how can you improve it? Can you make the beginning more engaging? Do you need to present the subject in more detail? Are the reasons for your judgment unclear? Go through your draft systematically, making changes wherever necessary. . . . **See p. 439 for more.**

Editing and Proofreading

Have you checked for errors that are especially likely in evaluative writing? If you are comparing your subject to something else, have you left out any words necessary to make the comparison complete, logical, or clear? Look for and correct these and any other errors. . . . **See p. 444 for more.**

Guide to Writing

■ The Writing Assignment

Write an essay evaluating a particular subject. Examine your subject closely, and make a judgment about it. Give reasons for your judgment, reasons based on widely recognized standards for evaluating a subject like yours. Support your reasons with examples and other details from your subject.

To learn about using the *Guide* e-book for invention and drafting, go to bedfordstmartins.com/theguide.

■ Invention and Research

The following activities will help you choose and explore a subject, consider your judgment, and develop your argument. These activities are easy to complete. Doing them over several days will give your ideas time to ripen and grow. Keep a written record of your invention and research to use later when you draft and revise.

Finding a Subject to Write About

You may already have a subject in mind and some ideas on how you will evaluate it. Even so, it is wise to take a few minutes to consider some other possible subjects. That way you can feel confident not only about having made the best possible choice but also about having one or two alternative subjects in case your first choice does not work. The following activities will help you make a good choice.

Listing Subjects. *Make a list of subjects you might be interested in evaluating.* Make your list as complete as you can, including, for example, the subjects suggested by the Considering Topics for Your Own Essay activity following the last three readings in this chapter. The following categories may give you some ideas.

- *Culture:* Television program, magazine or newspaper, computer game, band, songwriter, recording, film, actor, performance, dance club, coffeehouse, artist, museum exhibit, individual work of art
- *Written work:* Poem, short story, novel, Web site, magazine article, newspaper column, letter to the editor, textbook, autobiography, essay from this book
- *Education:* School, program, teacher, major department, library, academic or psychological counseling service, writing center, campus publication, sports team
- *Government:* Government department or official, proposed or existing law, agency or program, candidate for public office
- *Leisure:* Amusement park, museum, restaurant, resort, sports team, sports equipment, national or state park

425

■ *Listing Subjects Related to Identity and Community.* The following are ideas for an evaluative essay on issues of identity and community.

- Evaluate how well one of the following meets the needs of residents of your town or city: a community center, public library, health clinic, college, athletic team, festival, neighborhood watch or block parent program, meals-on-wheels program, theater or symphony, school or school program, radio or TV news reports.
- Evaluate how well one of the following serves the members of your religious community: a religious school, youth or senior group, religious leader, particular sermon, bingo, revival meeting, choir, building and grounds.
- Evaluate how well one of the following aspects of local government serves the needs of the community: mayor, city council, police, courts, social services, park system, zoning commission.

■ *Listing Subjects Related to Work and Career.* Following are some suggestions for an evaluative essay on issues involving work and career.

- Evaluate a job you have had or currently have, or evaluate someone else you have observed closely, such as a coworker or supervisor.
- Evaluate a local job-training program, either one in which you have participated or one where you can observe and interview trainees.

Choosing a Subject. *Review your list, and choose the one subject that seems most promising.* Your subject should be one that you can evaluate with some authority, either one that you already know quite well or one that you can study closely over the next week or two.

Exploring Your Subject and Possible Readers

To explore the subject, you need to review what you now know about it, become more familiar with it, make a tentative judgment about it, and think seriously about who your readers may be before you proceed to study your subject in depth. You then will be in a good position to decide whether to stick with this subject for your essay or choose a different subject, making this initial brief period of invention work a very good investment of your time.

Reviewing What You Now Know about the Subject. *Write for a few minutes about what you already know about your subject right at this moment.* Focus your thinking by considering questions like these:

- Why am I interested in this subject?
- What do I like and dislike about this subject?
- What do I usually look for in evaluating a subject of this kind? What do other people look for?
- How can I arrange to become very familiar with my subject over the next week or two?

Familiarizing Yourself with the Subject.   *Take notes about what you observe and learn as you get acquainted with your subject, notes that include the kinds of details that make your subject interesting and special.* Whatever your subject, you must now take the time to experience it. If you are evaluating a one-time performance, it must be scheduled within the next few days, and you must be exceedingly attentive to the one performance and take careful notes. If you plan to evaluate a film, it would be best if you could rent the DVD or video so that you can reexamine parts you need to refer to. If you are evaluating an agency, a service, or a program, observe and talk to people and make notes about what you see and hear.

Making a Tentative Judgment.   *Review what you have written as you have been getting to know your subject; then write a few sentences stating your best current overall judgment of the subject.* Your judgment may be only tentative at this stage, or you may feel quite confident in it. Your judgment may also be mixed: You may have a high regard for certain aspects of the subject and, at the same time, a rather low assessment of other aspects. As you consider your overall judgment, keep in mind that readers of evaluative essays expect writers not only to balance their evaluation of a subject (by pointing out things they like as well as things they dislike) but also to state a definitive judgment, not a vague, wishy-washy, or undecided judgment.

Identifying and Understanding Potential Readers.   *Write several sentences about possible readers, with the following questions in mind:*

- For what particular kinds of readers do I want to write this evaluation?
- What are my readers likely to know about my subject? Will I be introducing the subject to them (as in a film or book review)? Or will they already be familiar with it, and if so, how expert on the subject are they likely to be?
- How are my readers likely to judge my subject? What about it might they like, and what might they dislike?
- What reasons might they give for their judgment?
- On what standards is their overall judgment likely to be based? Do I share these standards or at least recognize their appropriateness?

Testing Your Choice

Pause now to decide whether you have chosen a subject about which you can make a convincing evaluative argument. Reread your invention notes to see whether you know enough about your subject or can get the information you need to write a convincing evaluation for the readers you have identified. Also consider whether you feel confident in your judgment.

As you develop your argument, you should become even more confident. If, however, you begin to doubt your choice, consider beginning again with a different subject selected from your list of possibilities. Before changing your subject, however, discuss your ideas with another student or your instructor to see whether they make sense to someone else.

A Collaborative Activity:
Testing Your Choice

At this point in your invention work, you will find it helpful to get together with two or three other students to discuss your subjects and test ways of evaluating them.

Presenters: Each of you in turn briefly describe your subject without revealing your overall judgment.

Evaluators: Explain to each presenter how you would evaluate a subject of this kind. For example, would you judge a science-fiction film by the story, acting, ideas, special effects, or some other aspect of the film? Would you judge a lecture course by how interesting or entertaining the lectures are, how hard the tests are, how well the lectures are organized, or how well some other aspect of the class succeeds? In other words, tell the presenter what standards you would apply to his or her particular subject. (Presenters: Take notes about what you hear.)

Becoming an Expert on Your Subject

Now that you are confident about your choice of subject and have in mind some standards for judging it, you can confidently move ahead to become an expert on your subject. Over the next few days, you can immerse yourself in it to prepare to evaluate it confidently.

Immersing Yourself in Your Subject. *Take careful notes at every stage of gradually becoming thoroughly familiar with your subject.* If you are writing about a film, for example, you will need to view the film at least twice by attending screenings or renting a DVD or video. If you are evaluating the effectiveness of a public official, you will need to read recent public statements by the official and perhaps observe the official in action. If you decide to evaluate a local sports team, you will need to study the team, attend a game and if possible a practice, and review films of recent games. Consult with other students and your instructor about efficient strategies for becoming an expert on your subject. Your goal is to gather the details, facts, examples, or stories you will need to write an informative, convincing evaluation.

If you think you will need to do more research than time permits or you cannot view, visit, or research your subject to discover the details needed to support an evaluation of it, then you may need to consider choosing a different, more accessible subject.

Learning More about Standards for Judging Your Subject. *Make a list of prominent, widely recognized standards for judging your subject.* If you do not know the standards usually used to evaluate your subject, you could do some research. For example, if you are reviewing a film, you could read a few recent film reviews online or in the library, noting the standards that reviewers typically use and the reasons that they assert for liking or disliking a film. If you are evaluating a soccer team or one winning (or losing) game, you could read a book on coaching soccer or talk to an experienced soccer coach to learn about what makes an excellent soccer team or winning game. If you are evaluating a civic, governmental, or religious program, look for information online or in the library about what makes a good program of its type. If you are evaluating an essay in this book, you will find standards in the Purpose and Audience section and in the Basic Features section of the chapter where the essay appears. If you are evaluating an argument essay from Chapters 6–10, you will find additional standards in Evaluating the Logic of an Argument, Recognizing Emotional Manipulation, and Judging the Writer's Credibility, pp. 604–08.

Developing Your Evaluation

Now you are ready to discover how you might proceed to make a plausible, even convincing, argument to justify your judgment. Each of the following activities requires only a few minutes of your time spread out over a day or two, and they are all essential to your success in organizing and drafting your evaluation.

Listing Reasons. *Write down every reason you can think of to convince readers of your overall judgment.* Try stating your reasons like this: "My judgment is X because . . ." or "A reason I like (or dislike) X is that. . . ." Then look over your list to consider which reasons you regard as most important and likely to be most convincing to your readers. Highlight these reasons.

Finding Support. *Make notes about how to support your most promising reasons.* From your invention notes made earlier, select a few details, facts, comparisons, contrasts, or examples about your subject that might help you support each reason.

Anticipating Readers' Alternative Judgments, Questions, and Objections. *List a few questions your particular readers would likely want to ask you or objections they might have to your argument. Write for a few minutes responding to at least two of these questions or objections.* Now that you can begin to see how your argument might shape up, assume that some of your particular readers would judge your subject differently from the way you do. Remember that your responses — your counterargument — could simply acknowledge the disagreements, accommodate readers' views by conceding certain points, or refute readers' arguments as uninformed or mistaken.

One way to learn more about judgments of your subject that differ from your own judgment is to search for reviews or evaluations of your subject online. You may even decide to incorporate quotations from or references to alternative judgments as part of your counterargument, although you need not do so in order to write a successful evaluation. Enter the name of your subject — movie title, restaurant name, compact disc title, title of a proposed law, name of a candidate for public office — in a search engine such as Google (google.com) or Yahoo! Directory (http://dir.yahoo.com). (Sometimes you can narrow the search usefully by including

An Online Activity:
Researching Alternative Judgments

the keyword *review* as well.) Of course, not all subjects are conveniently searchable online, and some subjects — a local concert, a college sports event, a campus student service, a neighborhood program — will likely not have been reviewed by anyone but you.

Bookmark or keep a record of promising sites. Download any materials you might wish to cite in your evaluation, making sure you have all the information necessary to document the source.

Designing Your Document

Think about whether visual or audio elements — cartoons, photographs, tables, graphs, or snippets from films, television programs, or songs — would strengthen your argument. These are not at all a requirement of an effective evaluation essay, but they could be helpful. Consider also whether your readers might benefit by such design features as headings, bulleted or numbered lists, or other elements that would make your essay easier to follow. You could construct your own graphic elements, download materials from the Internet, tape images and sounds from television or other sources, or scan visuals into your document from books and magazines. If you do use visual or audio elements you did not create yourself, remember to document the sources in your essay (and request permission from the sources if the essay will be posted on the Web).

Think about a recent occasion where you were in a position to evaluate something, such as an essay, a television show, a magazine ad, a Web page. What information did you, or would you, present to make the most compelling analysis? In some cases, it is enough to *tell* readers, but in other cases, visuals help to *show* readers the points you are making. For instance, in evaluating the ways in which presidential candidates use body language and hand gestures to convey meaning and encourage trust, photographs from the presidential debates might support the points being made. If tone of voice is being analyzed, audio snippets from a debate embedded in, for instance, a slideshow presentation might serve to illustrate the arguments made.

Defining Your Purpose for Your Readers

Write a few sentences defining your purpose in writing this evaluation for your readers. Remember that you already have analyzed your potential readers and developed your argument with these readers in mind. Given these readers, try now to define your purpose by considering the following possibilities and any others that might apply to your writing situation:

- If my readers are likely to agree with my overall judgment, should I try to strengthen their resolve by giving them well-supported reasons, helping them refute others' judgments, or suggesting how they might respond to questions and objections?

- If my readers and I share certain standards for evaluating a subject of this kind but we disagree on our overall judgment of this particular subject, can I build a convincing argument based on these shared standards or at least get readers to acknowledge the legitimacy of my judgment?

- If my readers use different standards of judgment, what should I try to do — urge them to think critically about their own judgment, to consider seriously other standards for judging the subject, or to see certain aspects of the subject they might have overlooked?

Formulating a Tentative Thesis Statement

Write several sentences that could serve as your thesis statement. Think about how you should state your overall judgment — how emphatic you should make it, whether you should qualify it, and whether you should include in the thesis a forecast of your reasons and support. Remember that a strong thesis statement should be clear, arguable, and appropriately qualified.

Review the readings in this chapter to see how other writers construct thesis statements. For example, Romano uses the thesis statement to forecast her reasons as well as to express her overall judgment. She begins by indicating the standards she thinks are appropriate for evaluating her subject. Her thesis statement shows that she bases her reasons on these standards. In addition, it lets readers know in advance what she likes about the subject she is evaluating as well as what she does not like: "While [Statsky's] logic *is* appropriate, believable, and consistent, her argument also has weaknesses" (paragraph 2). Romano makes her thesis statement seem thoughtful and balanced. There is no ambivalence or confusion, however, about Romano's judgment. She is clear and emphatic, not vague or wishy-washy.

As you draft your own tentative thesis statement, think carefully about the language you use. It should be clear and unambiguous, emphatic but appropriately qualified. Although you will most probably refine your thesis statement as you draft and revise your essay, trying now to articulate it will help give direction and impetus to your planning and drafting.

Planning and Drafting

This section will help you review what you have learned about evaluating your subject, determine specific goals for your essay, make a tentative outline, and get started on your first draft.

Seeing What You Have

Pause now to reread your invention and research notes. Watch for language that describes the subject vividly, states your judgment clearly, presents your reasons and support convincingly, and counterargues objections to your argument or readers' alternative judgments. Highlight key words, phrases, and sentences; make marginal notes or electronic annotations. If you have done your invention writing on the computer, you may have sentences or whole paragraphs that can be copied and pasted into your draft.

If your invention notes seem skimpy, you may need to do further research at this stage, or you could begin drafting now and later do research to fill in the blanks.

If your confidence in your judgment has been shaken or if you are concerned that you will not be able to write an argument to support your judgment, consult your instructor to determine whether you should try evaluating a different subject.

Setting Goals

Before you begin drafting, set some specific goals to guide the decisions you will make as you draft and revise your essay. The draft will be easier to write and more focused if you start with clear goals in mind. The following questions will help you set goals. You may find it useful to return to them while you are drafting, for they are designed to help you focus on specific features and strategies of evaluative essays.

Your Purpose and Readers

- What do I want my readers to think about the subject after reading my evaluation? Do I want them to appreciate the subject's strengths and weaknesses, as Kim, Jackson, and Romano do? Or do I want them to see why it succeeds (as Scott does) or fails?

- Should I assume that my readers may have read other evaluations of my subject (perhaps like Scott)? Or should I assume that I am introducing readers to the subject, as Kim, Jackson, and Romano seem to do?

- How should I present myself to my readers — as someone who is an expert on the subject (perhaps like Jackson) or as someone who has examined the subject closely (like Kim and Romano)? Should I convey enthusiasm (as Kim, Scott, and Jackson do) or strike a more balanced, distanced tone (as Romano does)?

The Beginning

- How can I capture readers' attention from the start? Should I begin by naming and describing the subject, as all the writers do?

- When should I state my judgment? At the beginning of the opening paragraph like Jackson, in the middle like Romano, or at the end like Kim? Or should I wait until the second paragraph, as Scott does?

- Should I forcast the reasons for my judgment in the first couple of paragraphs, as Kim and Romano do?

The Presentation of the Subject

- How should I identify the subject? In addition to naming it, as all the writers do, should I place it in a recognizable category or genre, as Kim does when she talks about "Internet professor evaluation sites" (paragraph 10) or as Scott does when he describes the film as a "historical picture" in *cinéma-vérité* style (paragraph 2)?

- What about the subject should I describe? Can I use visuals to illustrate, as Jackson does? Should I place the subject historically, as Scott does?

- If the subject has a story, how much of it should I tell? Should I simply set the scene and identify the characters, or should I give details of the plot, as Scott and Jackson do?

The Statement of Your Judgment

- How should I state my thesis? Should I forecast my reasons early in the essay, as Romano does? Should I place my thesis at the beginning or wait until after I have provided a context?

- How can I convince readers to consider my overall judgment seriously even if they disagree with it? Should I try to present a balanced judgment by praising some things and criticizing others, as all the writers but Scott do?

Your Reasons and Support

- How can I present my reasons? Should I explain the standards on which I base my reasons, as Romano does, or can I assume that my readers will share my standards, as Jackson does?

- If I have more than one reason, how should I order them? Should I begin with the ones I think are most important for judging a subject of this kind, as Jackson does? Or should I end with the strongest reason?

- How can I support my reasons? With example, paraphrase, and summary, as all the writers do? Should I quote the text, as Kim and Romano do? Can I call on authorities and cite statistics, as Kim does?

Your Anticipation of Objections or Alternative Judgments

- What objections or alternative judgments should I anticipate? Should I acknowledge or accommodate legitimate objections and qualify my judgment, as Romano does? Are there any illegitimate objections or alternative judgments I should refute?

The Ending

- How should I conclude? Should I try to frame the essay by echoing something from the opening or from another part of the essay?

- Should I conclude by presenting or restating my overall judgment, as all the writers do?

- Should I include a rhetorical question at the end, as Kim does?

Outlining

An evaluative essay contains as many as four basic parts:

1. A presentation of the subject
2. A judgment of the subject
3. A presentation of reasons and support
4. A consideration of readers' objections and alternative judgments

These parts can be organized in various ways. If, for example, you expect readers to disagree with your judgment, you could show them what you think they have overlooked or misjudged about the subject. You could begin by presenting the subject; then you could assert your thesis, present your reasons and support, and anticipate and refute readers' likely objections.

> Presentation of the subject
>
> Thesis statement (judgment)
>
> First reason and support
>
> Anticipation and refutation of objection
>
> Second reason and support
>
> Anticipation and accommodation of objection
>
> Conclusion

If you expect some of your readers to disagree with your negative judgment even though they base their judgment on the same standard on which you base yours, you could try to show them that the subject really does not satisfy the standard. You could begin by reinforcing the standard you share and then demonstrate how the subject fails to meet it.

> Establish shared standard
>
> Acknowledge alternative judgment
>
> State thesis (judgment) that subject fails to meet shared standard
>
> First reason and support showing how subject falls short of standard
>
> Second reason and support (etc.)
>
> Conclusion

There are, of course, many other possible ways to organize an evaluative essay, but these outlines should help you start planning your own essay.

Consider tentative any outlining you do before you begin drafting. Never be a slave to an outline. As you draft, you will usually see ways to improve your original plan. Be ready to revise your outline, shift parts around, or drop or add parts as you draft. If you use the outlining function of your word processing program, changing your outline will be simple, and you may be able to write the essay simply by expanding the outline.

Drafting

General Advice.   Start drafting your essay, keeping in mind the goals you set while you were planning. Remember also the needs and expectations of your readers; organize, define, and explain with them in mind. Turn off your grammar checker and spelling checker at this stage if you find them distracting. Don't be afraid to skip around in your draft; jump back and fill in a spontaneous idea, or leap ahead and write a later section first if you find that easier. If you discover that you need more information, just make a note of what you have to find out, and go to the next point. When you are done drafting, you can search for the information you need. If you get stuck while drafting, explore the problem by using some of the writing activities in the Invention and Research section of this chapter (pp. 425–31).

You may want to review the general drafting advice on p. 9. In addition, keep in mind that in writing an evaluative argument, you must accept the burden of proof by offering reasons and support for your judgment. Remember, too, that the basis for judgment often depends on standards as much as reasons and support. Try to think critically about the standards on which you base your judgment as well as the standards that others apply to subjects of the kind you are evaluating.

Sentence Strategies: Comparing and Contrasting Your Subject with Similar Ones and Balancing Criticism and Praise.   As you draft an essay evaluating a subject, you may want to compare or contrast your subject with similar subjects to establish for readers your authority to evaluate a subject like yours. In addition, you are likely to want to balance the evaluation of your subject — by criticizing one or more aspects of the subject if you generally praise it or by praising one or more aspects of it if you generally criticize it. To do so, you will need to use sentences that clearly and efficiently express comparisons or contrasts, specifically ones that contrast criticism with praise and vice versa.

Use sentences comparing or contrasting your subject with similar subjects to help convince readers that you are knowledgeable about the kind of subject you are evaluating. These sentences often make use of key comparative terms like *more, less, most, least, as, than, like, unlike, similar,* or *dissimilar,* as readings in this chapter well illustrate.

Let us begin with three examples, all from paragraph 11 of Wendy Kim's essay "Grading Professors":

> Still, RatingsOnline is *better* designed and includes *more helpful* information than the other two competitors, and it may even be *better* than RMP in terms of helpfulness.

> The ratings categories on RatingsOnline also seem *more specific* than on RMP....

> In its design and potential helpfulness, RatingsOnline is a very good site but likely *not* to be *as good as* RMP because its user base appears to be *smaller.*

In these sentences Kim compares Internet professor evaluation sites. The first sentence compares RatingsOnline and three other sites, including RMP, the acronym for RateMyProfessors. In the second and third examples, she narrows the match-up

For more on using sentences of comparison and contrast in evaluations, go to bedfordstmartins.com/theguide and click on Sentence Strategies. For illustrations of comparisons and contrasts in different kinds of writing, see Chapter 18, pp. 664–69.

to what she considers the two best Web sites, pointing out their relative strengths and weaknesses.

> *Unlike* many games that promise you the freedom to play however you want, Morrowind goes a long way toward meeting that promise. (Jonah Jackson, paragraph 6)

In this sentence Jackson contrasts one feature of Morrowind with the corresponding feature of other computer games.

In the following examples, Scott contrasts *Good Night, and Good Luck* with other period or historical films. Notice that he leaves out the explicitly comparative term in both sentences:

> Though it is a meticulously detailed reconstruction of an era, the film . . . is concerned with *more than* nostalgia. (A. O. Scott, paragraph 1)

> *Good Night, and Good Luck* is *not the kind of historical picture* that dumbs down its material, or walks you carefully through events that may be unfamiliar. (A. O. Scott, paragraph 3)

Increase your authority with readers by using certain kinds of sentences to balance criticism and praise. The sentence strategies are similar for introducing criticism followed by praise and introducing praise followed by criticism. In general, these strategies rely on words expressing contrast, like *but, although, however, while,* and so on to set up the shift between the two responses.

Praise followed by criticism:

> This information could be useful in helping students decide which classes to take, *but* only if there are enough reviews posted. (Wendy Kim, paragraph 11)

> This journal manages to record everything of importance, *but* it's missing the ability to sort or group items by quest. (Jonah Jackson, paragraph 14)

> . . . Statsky does show that she is thinking about her readers' questions. She does not go nearly far enough, *however,* to have a chance of influencing two types of readers. . . . (Christine Romano, paragraph 8)

> The seamless combat interface is also easy to use, *although* the various types of weapon swing (slash, jab, and so on) are awkwardly related to your movement direction. (Jonah Jackson, paragraph 13)

Criticism followed by praise:

> And *while* Mr. Clooney is inclined to glorify, he does not simplify. (A. O. Scott, paragraph 12)

> The combat music is a little flat, *but* it does provide important auditory clues about nearby enemies. (Jonah Jackson, paragraph 15)

> Its bugs and design quirks are *more than compensated for* by a core game that's just fantastic. (Jonah Jackson, paragraph 16)

For more on using sentences that balance criticism and praise in evaluations, go to bedfordstmartins.com/theguide and click on Sentence Strategies.

Notice that the last example does not use an explicitly comparative term to set up the contrast.

In addition to using sentences that make comparisons or contrasts with other subjects and sentences that balance criticism and praise, you can strengthen your evaluation with other kinds of sentences as well. You may want to review the information about using appositives (pp. 177–79) and writing sentences introducing concession and refutation (pp. 309–10).

Now is the time to get a good critical reading of your draft. Writers usually find it helpful to have someone else read and comment on their drafts, and all writers know how much they learn about writing when they read other writers' drafts. Your instructor may arrange such a reading as part of your coursework — in class or online. If not, you can ask a classmate, friend, or family member to read your draft. You could also seek comments from a tutor at your campus writing center. (If you are unable to have someone else read your draft, turn ahead to the Revising section on p. 439, where you will find guidelines for reading your own draft critically.)

▶ **If You Are the Writer.** To provide focused, helpful comments, your reader must know your essay's intended audience, your purpose, and a problem in the draft that you need help solving. Briefly write out this information at the top of your draft.

- *Readers:* Identify the intended readers of your essay. What do you assume that they think about your subject? Do you expect them to be receptive, skeptical, resistant, or antagonistic?

- *Purpose:* What effect do you realistically expect your argument to have on these particular readers?

- *Problem:* Ask your reader to help you solve the most important problem you see in your draft. Describe this problem briefly.

▶ **If You Are the Reader.** Use the following guidelines to help you give constructive, critical comments to others on evaluation essays:

1. *Read for a First Impression.* Tell the writer what you think the intended readers would find most and least convincing. If you personally think the evaluation is seriously flawed, share your thoughts. Then try to help the writer improve the argument for the designated readers. Next, consider the problem the writer identified, and respond briefly to that concern now. (If you find that the problem is covered by one of the other guidelines listed below, respond to it in more detail there if necessary.)

2. *Analyze How Well the Subject Is Presented.* Locate where in the draft the subject is presented, and ask questions that will help the writer strengthen the presentation. If you are surprised by the way the writer has presented the subject, briefly explain how you usually think of this particular subject or

Critical Reading Guide

Making Comments Electronically
Most word processing software offers features that allow you to insert comments directly into the text of someone else's document. Many readers prefer to make their comments in this way because it tends to be faster than writing on a hard copy and space is virtually unlimited; from the writer's point of view, it also eliminates the problem of deciphering handwritten comments. Even where such special comment features are not available, simply typing comments directly into a document in a contrasting color can provide the same advantages.

subjects of this kind. Also indicate whether any of the information about the subject seems unnecessary. Finally, and most important, let the writer know whether any of the information about the subject seems to you possibly inaccurate or only partly true.

For a printable version of this critical reading guide, go to bedfordstmartins.com/theguide.

3. *Assess Whether the Judgment Is Stated Clearly.* Write a sentence or two summarizing the writer's judgment as you understand it from reading the draft. Then identify the sentence or sentences in the draft where the judgment is stated explicitly. (It may be restated in several places.) If you cannot find an explicit statement of the judgment, let the writer know. Given the writer's purpose and audience, consider whether the judgment is arguable, clear, and appropriately qualified. If it seems indecisive or too extreme, suggest how the writer might make it clearer or might qualify it by referring at least occasionally to the strengths of a criticized subject or the weaknesses of a praised subject.

4. *Evaluate the Reasons and Support.* Identify the reasons, and look closely at them and the support that the writer gives for them. If anything seems problematic, briefly explain what bothers you. For example, the reason may not seem appropriate for judging this kind of subject, you may not fully understand the reason or how it applies to this particular subject, the connection between a particular reason and its support may not be clear or convincing to you, the support may be too weak, or there may not be enough support to sustain the argument. Be as specific and constructive as you can, pointing out what does not work and also suggesting what the writer might do to solve the problem. For example, if the reason seems inappropriate, explain why you think so, and indicate what kinds of reasons you expect the intended readers to recognize as acceptable for judging this kind of subject. If the support is weak, suggest how it could be strengthened.

5. *Assess How Well Readers' Objections, Questions, and Alternative Judgments Have Been Handled.* Mark where the writer acknowledges, accommodates, or tries to refute readers' objections or alternative judgments, and point to any places where the counterargument seems superficial or dismissive. Suggest how it could be strengthened. Help the writer anticipate any important objections or questions that have been overlooked, providing advice on how to respond to them.

6. *Consider the Effectiveness of the Organization.* Get an overview of the essay's organization, and point out any places where more explicit cueing — transitions, summaries, or topic sentences — would clarify the relationship between parts of the essay.

   • Look at the *beginning*. Do you think readers will find it engaging? If not, propose an alternative or suggest moving something from later in the essay that might work as a better opening.

- Look at the *ending*. Does the essay conclude decisively and memorably? If not, suggest an alternative. Could something be moved to the end?
- Look at the *design features*. Comment on the contribution of figures, headings, tables, and other design features. Indicate whether any visual or audio elements that have been included fail to support the evaluation effectively, and offer suggestions for improvement. Help the writer think of additional visual or audio elements that could make a contribution to the essay.

7. ***Give the Writer Your Final Thoughts.*** What is this draft's strongest part? What part is most in need of further work?

■ Revising

Now you are ready to revise your essay. Your instructor or other students may have given you advice on improving your draft. Nevertheless, you may have begun to realize that your draft requires more rethinking than revising. For example, you may recognize that your reasons do not lead readers to accept your evaluation, that you cannot adequately support your reasons, or that you are unable to refute damaging objections to your argument. Consequently, instead of working to improve parts of the draft, you may need to write a new draft that radically reenvisions your argument. It is not unusual for students — and professional writers — to find themselves in this situation. Learning to make radical revisions is a valuable lesson for any writer.

If you feel satisfied that your draft achieves most, if not all, of your goals, you can focus on refining specific parts of it. Very likely you have thought of ways of improving your draft, and you may even have begun revising it. This section will help you get an overview of your draft and revise it accordingly.

Getting an Overview

Consider your draft as a whole, following these two steps:

1. ***Reread.*** If at all possible, put the draft aside for a day or two before rereading it. When you return to it, start by reconsidering your purpose. Then read the draft straight through, trying to see it as your intended readers will.
2. ***Outline.*** Make a scratch outline, indicating the basic features as they appear in the draft. Consider using the headings and outline/summary functions of your word processor.

Planning for Revision.   Resist the temptation to dive in and start changing your text until after you have a solid grasp of the big picture. Using your outline as a guide, move through the document, using the change-highlighting or commenting tools of your word processor to note useful comments received from others and problems you want to solve (or mark on a hard copy if you prefer).

Analyzing the Basic Features of Your Own Draft.   Using the Critical Reading Guide that begins on p. 437, identify problems that you now see in your draft.

Studying Readers' Comments.   Review all of the comments you have received from other readers, and add to your revision plan any that you intend to act on. For each comment, look at the draft to determine what might have led the reader to make that particular point. Try to be objective about any criticism. Ideally, these comments will help you see your draft as others see it, providing valuable information about how you can improve it.

Working with Sources

Using summary to support your evaluative argument

Writers of evaluation often use summary to support their argument. As the following examples show, evaluations may summarize an expert source (as Kim does in her Web site evaluation), the plot of a film or video game (as Scott and Jackson do in their film and game reviews), or an aspect of an essay or story (as Romano does in her evaluation of another essay in this book), to name just a few of the more common uses of summary.

> The results are statistically invalid, as one psychology professor explained, because the users are self-selected and not selected randomly (Harmon). (Wendy Kim, paragraph 9)

> The story flashes back from a famous, cautionary speech that Murrow gave at an industry convention in 1958 to one of the most notable episodes in his career — his war of words and images with Senator Joseph R. McCarthy. (A. O. Scott, paragraph 3)

> The island of Vvardenfell is a somewhat troubled section of the Empire. The native Dunmers or Dark Elves are at odds among themselves and with the Imperial presence. As the story unfolds you find that you play a larger and more important role in the future of Vvardenfell. (Jonah Jackson, paragraph 7)

> In the anecdote, a seven-year-old makes himself vomit to avoid playing. (Christine Romano, paragraph 5)

To get a better understanding of how summaries can support an evaluative argument, let us look closely at another example of summarizing from Christine Romano's essay. The second example, which illustrates a longer, more developed kind of summary, appears in paragraph 3. It supports Romano's argument that Statsky provides support that is "appropriate." The summary is highlighted in red:

Her quotations, examples, and statistics all support the reasons she believes competitive sports are bad for children. For example, in paragraph 3, Statsky offers the reason that "overly competitive" sports may damage children's fragile bodies and that contact sports, in particular, may be especially hazardous. She supports this reason by paraphrasing Koppett's claim that muscle strain or even lifelong injury may result when a twelve-year-old throws curve balls. She then quotes Tutko on the dangers of tackle football. The opinions of both experts are obviously appropriate. They are relevant to her reason, and we can easily imagine that they would worry many parents.

To understand how this summary works, it helps to compare it to the original:

Statsky's Original (paragraph 3)

One readily understandable danger of overly competitive sports is that they entice children into physical actions that are bad for growing bodies. Although the official Little League Web site acknowledges that children do risk injury playing baseball, they insist that severe injuries are infrequent, "far less than the risk of riding a skateboard, a bicycle, or even the school bus" ("What about My Child?"). Nevertheless, Leonard Koppett in *Sports Illusion, Sports Reality* claims that a twelve-year-old trying to throw a curve ball, for example, may put abnormal strain on developing arm and shoulder muscles, sometimes resulting in lifelong injuries (294). Contact sports like football can be even more hazardous. Thomas Tutko, a psychology professor at San Jose State University and coauthor of the book *Winning Is Everything and Other American Myths*, writes:

> I am strongly opposed to young kids playing tackle football. It is not the right stage of development for them to be taught to crash into other kids. Kids under the age of fourteen are not by nature physical. Their main concern is self-preservation. They don't want to meet head on and slam into each other. But tackle football absolutely requires that they try to hit each other as hard as they can. And it is too traumatic for young kids. (qtd. in Tosches A1)

Romano not only repeats Statsky's main ideas in a condensed form (reducing 220 words to 105), but she also describes Statsky's moves as a writer:

Statsky offers the reason. . . .

She supports this reason by paraphrasing Koppett's claim. . . .

She then quotes Tutko. . . .

Romano's description of each step in Statsky's argument shows readers exactly how Statsky uses paraphrase and quotation to support her argument about the potential for "overly competitive sports" to endanger children. Note that in summarizing, Romano here refers directly to the writer (*Statsky, She*). By naming Statsky and describing what Statsky is doing in this passage (*offers, supports, quotes*), Romano does not focus on the content of the original passage (as she does in our first example of her summarizing an anecdote in Statsky's essay). Instead, Romano focuses here on Statsky's argumentative strategy of providing support for her reasons. In the sentences (quoted above) that follow the summary, Romano explains her judgment that Statsky's use of expert opinion and examples of sports injuries is convincing. Not every summary needs to include this kind of play-by-play description of the writer's strategic moves; but when you are evaluating an argument, you can use this technique to help readers see how the original writer constructs his or her argument.

Notice also that in this summary, Romano puts quotation marks around only one of the phrases she borrows from Statsky ("overly competitive"). Perhaps the reason she uses quotation marks around this particular phrase is that Statsky uses it twice in her essay (paragraphs 3 and 11), or that Romano feels that it is a key phrase for capturing the essence of Statsky's argument that organized sports may be too competitive for children. Romano may have decided not to use quotation marks around other borrowed phrases such as *contact sports* and *tackle football* because they are common expressions and not specific to Statsky. Readers of summaries expect to see some words from the original. Because Romano makes it perfectly clear when she is re-presenting her source's language and ideas, and also includes careful citations to indicate where in the original text the material comes from, there is little concern about plagiarizing. Remember, though, that putting quotation marks around quoted words and phrases will eliminate any possible misunderstanding. If you are unsure about whether you need quotation marks, consult your instructor. (To learn more about Romano's use of summarizing together with quoting and paraphrasing, see the Commentary on page 418. For additional information, see Chapter 19: Arguing, pages 670–85, and Chapter 22: Using and Acknowledging Sources, pages 744–47.)

Carrying Out Revisions

Having identified problems in your draft, you now need to come up with solutions and — most important — to carry them out. Basically, you have three ways of finding solutions:

1. Review your invention and planning notes for information and ideas to add to your draft.

2. Do additional invention and research to provide additional material that you or your readers think is needed.

3. Look back at the readings in this chapter to see how other writers have solved similar problems.

The following suggestions, which are organized according to the basic features of evaluation essays, will help you solve some common problems in this genre.

A Well-Presented Subject

- **Is the subject unclear or hard to identify?** Try to give it a name or to identify the general category to which it belongs. If you need more information about the subject, review your invention writing to see if you have left out any details you could now add. You may also need to revisit your subject or do further invention writing to answer questions that your classmates and instructor have raised or your intended readers might have.

- *Is the subject presented in too much detail?* Cut extraneous and repetitive details. If your subject is a film or book, consider whether you are giving away too much of the plot or whether your readers will expect you to give a lot of detail.

- *Is any of the information inaccurate or only partly true?* Reconsider the accuracy and completeness of the information you present. If any of the information will be surprising to readers, consider how you might reassure them that the information is accurate.

A Clear Overall Judgment

- *Is your overall judgment hard to find?* Announce your thesis more explicitly. If your judgment is mixed — pointing out what you like and do not like about the subject — let readers know this from the beginning. Use sentences that balance praise and criticism, as most of the authors of this chapter's readings do.

- *Does your overall judgment seem indecisive or too extreme?* If your readers do not know what your overall judgment is or if they think you are either too positive or too negative, you may need to clarify your thesis statement or qualify it more carefully.

Appropriate Reasons and Convincing Support

- *Do any of the reasons seem inappropriate to readers?* Explain why you think the reason is appropriate, or show that your argument employs a standard commonly used for evaluating subjects of this kind.

- *Is any of the support thin or unconvincing?* To find additional support, review your invention writing, or reexamine the subject. Look closely again at your subject for more details that would support your reasons. As do all the authors of readings in this chapter, consider comparing or contrasting aspects of your subject with those of other subjects like yours.

- *Are any of your reasons and support unclear?* To clarify them, you may need to explain your reasoning in more detail or use examples and comparisons to make your ideas understandable. You may need to do some additional exploratory writing or research to figure out how to explain your reasoning. Consider also whether any of the reasons should be combined, separated, or cut.

Anticipation of Objections or Alternative Judgments

- *Are any important objections or questions overlooked?* Revisit your subject or invention notes to think more deeply about why and where readers might resist your argument. Try to imagine how a reader who strongly disagrees with your judgment (praising a movie or college program or restaurant for example) might respond to your evaluation.

Checking Sentence Strategies Electronically
To check your draft for a sentence strategy especially useful in evaluation essays, use your word processor's highlighting function to mark sentences where you praise or criticize various aspects of the subject. Then think about whether you could make your evaluation more authoritative and convincing to readers by making any of the sentences more balanced, either by praising something in an aspect that you have generally criticized or by criticizing something in an aspect that you have generally praised. For more on sentences that balance criticism and praise, see pp. 436–37.

The Organization

- *Does the essay seem disorganized or confusing?* You may need to add a forecasting statement, transitions, summaries, or topic sentences. You may also need to do some major restructuring, such as moving your presentation of the subject or reordering your reasons.

- *Is the beginning weak?* Review your notes to find an interesting quotation, comparison, image, or example to use in your first paragraph.

- *Is the ending weak?* See if you can restate your judgment, summarize your reasoning, or frame the essay by echoing a point made earlier.

- *Can you add any visuals or design features to make the essay more interesting to read and to strengthen your argument?* Consider taking features from your subject or creating visual or audio elements of your own.

For a revision checklist, go to bedfordstmartins.com/theguide.

■ Editing and Proofreading

Now is the time to check your revised draft for errors in grammar, punctuation, and mechanics and to consider matters of style. Our research has identified several errors that are especially likely to occur in evaluative writing. The following guidelines will help you proofread and edit your revised draft for these common errors.

Checking Comparisons.   Whenever you evaluate something, you are likely to engage in comparison. You might want to show that a new recording is inferior to an earlier one, that one film is stronger than another, that this café is better than that one. Make a point of checking to see that all comparisons in your writing are complete, logical, and clear.

Editing to Make Comparisons Complete

▶ *Jazz* is as good, if not better than, Morrison's other novels.
       as

▶ I liked the Lispector story because it's so different.
       from anything else I've ever read.

Editing to Make Comparisons Logical

▶ Will Smith's Muhammad Ali is more serious than any role he's played.
       other

▶ Ohio State's offense played much better than ~~Michigan.~~
       Michigan's did.

Check also to see that you say *different from* instead of *different than*.

▶ Carrying herself with a confident and brisk stride, Katherine Parker seems

different ~~than~~ the other women in the office.
       from

A Note on Grammar and Spelling Checkers
These tools are good at catching certain types of errors, but currently there is no replacement for a good human proofreader. Grammar checkers in particular are extremely limited in what they can usually find, and often they only give you summary information that is not helpful if you do not already understand the rule in question. They are also prone to give faulty advice for fixing problems and to flag correct items as wrong. Spelling checkers cause fewer problems but cannot catch misspellings that are themselves words, such as *to* for *too*.

For practice, go to bedfordstmartins.com/theguide/exercisecentral and click on Comparisons.

▶ Films like *Pulp Fiction* that glorify violence for its own sake are different ~~than~~ ^from^ films like *Apocalypse Now* that use violence to make a moral point.

Combining Sentences.   When you evaluate something, you generally present your subject in some detail — defining it, describing it, placing it in some context. Inexperienced writers often give such details almost one by one, in separate sentences. Combining closely related sentences can make your writing more readable, helping readers to see how ideas relate.

▶ In paragraph 5, the details provide a different impression, ~~It is~~ a comic or perhaps even pathetic impression, ~~The impression comes from~~ ^based on^ the boy's attempts to dress up like a real westerner.

From three separate sentences, this writer combines details about the "different impression" into one sentence, using two common strategies for sentence combining:

- Changing a sentence into an appositive phrase (a noun phrase that renames the noun or pronoun that immediately precedes it: "a comic or perhaps even pathetic impression")

- Changing a sentence into a verbal phrase (phrases with verbals that function as adjectives, adverbs, or nouns: "based on the boy's attempts to dress up like a real westerner")

For practice, go to bedfordstmartins.com/theguide/exercisecentral and click on Combining Sentences.

Using Appositive Phrases to Combine Sentences

▶ "Something Pacific" was created by Nam June Paik, ~~He is~~ a Korean artist who is considered a founder of video art.

▶ One of Dylan's songs ^"Talkin' John Birch Paranoid Blues"^ ridiculed the John Birch Society. ~~This song was called "Talkin' John Birch Paranoid Blues."~~

Using Verbal Phrases to Combine Sentences

▶ Spider-Man's lifesaving webbing sprung from his wristbands, ^carrying^ ~~They carried~~ Mary Jane Watson and him out of peril.

▶ The coffee bar flanks the bookshelves, ^enticing^ ~~It entices~~ readers to relax with a book.

A Writer at Work

■ Anticipating Readers' Objections and Questions

In this section, we look at how Christine Romano tried to anticipate her readers' objections and questions. The final revision of Romano's evaluation essay appears in this chapter on pp. 414–17; Statsky's argument essay (which Romano evaluates) appears in Chapter 6 (pp. 276–79).

Because Romano was applying the standards for evaluating logical arguments that are presented in Chapter 12 of this textbook, she felt confident that the standards on which she based her overall judgment of Statsky's argument would also be important to her readers. Using the Exploring Your Subject and Possible Readers activity (pp. 426–27) in this chapter's Guide to Writing, she identified two kinds of readers: her instructor, who she assumed would approve of her using the textbook standards, and parents of young children, the same audience that Statsky addresses. Romano acknowledged that parents would not know the textbook standards, but she speculated that, like her, they also would be impressed by the way Statsky supports her position. Romano noted also that she expected parents to be sympathetic to Statsky's position because they would not want their children to be hurt playing sports.

After writing for a few minutes on the Testing Your Choice activity (p. 427), Romano worked with a group of students in class on Testing Your Choice: A Collaborative Activity (p. 428). One of her group's members told her that he had been hurt playing in a Little League baseball game and had wanted to quit but that his dad had made him continue playing. He remembered crying and trying to get out of going to the next game. But looking back on the experience now, he said he was glad his father insisted because years later, when playing on the high school football team, he realized that being a serious athlete meant facing up to the fear and pain of injury. He said this was an important lesson, one that applied to everything in life, not just to playing sports. Therefore, the student told Romano, his standard for judging competitive sports for young children was based on how well the experience taught them to stick it out to conquer their pain and fear.

This student's choice of standards made Romano realize that Statsky's argument does not adequately address this compelling alternative judgment. When Romano planned and wrote her first draft, she tried to accommodate this student's point of view and others like it. In addition to praising the appropriateness, believability, and consistency of Statsky's argument, she criticized the argument for being incomplete: "[Statsky] neglects to anticipate parents' predictable questions and objections" (paragraph 2).

A few days later, Romano received some helpful advice from another student who read her draft. Using the Critical Reading Guide in this chapter (pp. 437–39), the student noted (in response to the third guideline) that she could not find a clear statement of the thesis (overall judgment) in the draft. She guessed that it might be hinted at in the final paragraph, but she was not sure what Romano's judgment was and urged Romano to state it clearly. Here is the draft version of Romano's final paragraph that the student reader commented on:

> I have been able to point out both strengths and weaknesses in the logic of Statsky's support for her argument. The strengths are appropriateness, believability, and consistency. The major weakness is incompleteness--a failure to anticipate more fully the likely objections of a wide range of readers. I have been able to show that her logic would prevent certain kinds of parents from taking her argument seriously, parents whose experience and whose children's experience of team sports lead them to believe that the gains are worth whatever risks may be involved and who believe that many of the risks Statsky points out can be avoided by careful monitoring. For parents inclined to agree with her, however, her logic is likely to seem sound and complete. An argument that successfully confirms readers' beliefs is certainly valid, and Statsky succeeds admirably at this kind of argument.

In response to item 4 in the Critical Reading Guide, the student reader noted that she thought Romano's draft essay was well supported by textual evidence and examples. She also said she found the praise of the strengths of Statsky's argument convincing but found the criticism of its weaknesses equally convincing. Therefore, she concluded by asking Romano to clarify her evaluation.

This request hit home because Romano had been trying to give Statsky's essay a mixed review but was not sure how well her own judgment was coming across. Romano was reassured by her critical reader's judgment that her argument was convincing, but she saw that she needed to clarify which standards carried the most weight for her. She revised the last paragraph, adding this final sentence to make her thesis more explicit and let readers see exactly which standards were most important in her evaluation of Statsky's argument:

> Because she does not offer compelling counterarguments to the legitimate objections of those inclined not to agree with her, however, her success is limited.

Emma is, above all, a novel about class consciousness. Marriage is here, as in all of Austen's novels, a vehicle for exploring the rigidity of social class in nineteenth-century England. However, *Emma* the film (1996) is better at capturing the feel of the period than the intricacies of social dynamics. (See Fig. 1.) Though the characters come from a range of social classes, their homes and clothing look more similar than not. When Gwyneth Paltrow plays the occasionally lovable, occasionally irritating Emma, the focus on the heroine's failure at matchmaking overshadows the fact that she is obsessed not only with manners but also with wealth. For example, she has something that even her beloved Knightley does not, an estate that she will inherit from her father as long as she does not leave him. In the novel when Knightley agrees to live in the Woodhouse home after the two marry, he goes against traditional gender roles in order to make the most of the two characters' fortunes: his wealth and her property. As it does so many times, the film misses this cue, and instead focuses on Emma's emotional inability to leave her father. In the 1996 *Emma*, social distinctions get paved over for the audience's aesthetic expectations of a romance and of a period piece.

Fig. 1. This scene from *Emma* offers a typical example of the film's attention to aesthetics.

In his comparison of the films *Emma* and *Clueless*, the student author described on p. 394 of this chapter selected movie stills to accompany his written text. He collected a number of stills from each film and chose two contrasting images that would best illustrate his argument that *Emma*, the film, looks more like Austen's England, but that *Clueless*, with its emphasis on today's social and cultural norms and its setting in contemporary suburban California, better captures the satirical spirit of the novel.

The writer used the still from *Emma* of Emma and Knightley dancing to emphasize the film's attention to aesthetics and romance. Details such as the hanging garlands, the ornate woodwork, the women's similar pale-toned dresses, the style of dancing and the musicians in the background create an image of aristocratic wealth and elegance that, the student argues, satisfies audience expectations for a romantic period piece but obscures an important part of the novel's message.

To illustrate the flavor of *Clueless*, the student chose the picture of Cher descending the stairs wearing a minidress and an outrageous hat, with shopping bags, water bottle in its holder, and cell phone. This over-the-top satiric image in *Clueless*, the student argued, was designed to emphasize the social and economic distinctions in the novel. The image captures the ridiculousness of Cher in her obvious displays of wealth and posturing. While admired and well liked by her peers, she is also naïve and too well-off for her own good.

The student builds to a concluding point that Cher's interest in reforming Tai is a result of her confidence that she could help someone to become as stylish and savvy as herself. Just as the novel makes fun of Emma for her lack of critical self-awareness, the student argued, so does *Clueless* make fun of Cher.

Clueless (1995), though it could not look less like Austen's England, better captures the spirit of the novel. Cher, who never leaves her cell phone at home and shops on Rodeo Drive, is both the consummate brat and the consummate charmer. (See Fig. 2.) Cher does more than just try to find a suitable match for the obviously not as well-off or stylish Tai; she actually works on transforming her, much as Emma does with Harriet Smith in the novel. Cher encourages Tai to cut her hair, buy new clothes, exercise, and read more nonacademic books, and she takes pride in the new person that she has tried to create. In this way, the film parallels the novel's attention not only to Emma's preoccupation with social status but also to the way she tries to use Harriet to further elevate her own reputation.

Fig. 2. *Clueless* depicts Cher as a status-conscious consumer, echoing a significant theme in Austen's novel.

Thinking Critically About What You Have Learned

Now that you have read and discussed several evaluation essays and written one of your own, take some time to think critically about what you have learned. What problems did you encounter as you were writing your essay, and how did you solve them? How did reading other evaluation essays influence your own essay? How do evaluation essays in general reflect social or cultural attitudes about making judgments?

Reflecting on Your Writing

Write a one-page explanation, telling your instructor about a problem you encountered in writing your essay and how you solved it. Before you begin, gather all of your writing — invention and planning notes, drafts, readers' comments, revision plan, and final revisions. Review these materials as you complete this writing task.

1. *Identify one writing problem you needed to solve as you worked on the essay.* Do not be concerned with grammar and punctuation problems; concentrate instead on problems unique to developing an evaluation essay. For example: Did you puzzle over how to present your subject? Did you have trouble acknowledging what you liked as well as what you disliked? Was it difficult to refute an important objection or answer a question you knew readers would raise?

2. *Determine how you came to recognize the problem.* When did you first discover it? What called it to your attention? If you did not become aware of the problem until someone else pointed it out to you, can you now see hints of it in your invention writings? If so, where specifically? When you first recognized the problem, how did you respond?

3. *Reflect on how you went about solving the problem.* Did you work on the wording of a passage, cut or add reasons or refutations, conduct further research, or move paragraphs or sen-

tences around? Did you reread one of the essays in this chapter to see how another writer handled a similar problem, or did you look back at your invention writing? If you talked about the problem with another student, a tutor, or your instructor, did talking about it help? How useful was the advice you received?

4. *Write a brief explanation of the problem and your solution.* Be as specific as possible in reconstructing your efforts. Quote from your invention notes or draft essay, others' critical comments, your revision plan, or your revised essay to show the various changes that your writing — and thinking — underwent as you tried to solve the problem. If you are still uncertain about your solution, say so. Taking time to explain how you identified a particular problem, how you went about trying to solve it, and what you learned from this experience can help you solve future writing problems more easily.

Reviewing What You Learned from Reading

Write a page or two explaining to your instructor how the readings in this chapter influenced your final draft. Your own essay may have been influenced to some extent by one or more of the essays in this chapter as well as by classmates' essays that you have read. These other essays may have helped you decide that you needed to do further research before you could argue responsibly for your overall judgment, that you could use comparisons as part of your support, or that you should try to respond to readers' likely objections and questions. Before you write, take some time to reflect on what you have learned from these selections about writing evaluations.

1. *Reread the final revision of your essay; then look back at the selections you read before completing it.* Do you see any specific influences? For

example, did any reading influence how you decided to present the subject, balance your judgment, use examples or comparisons, or respond to readers' resistance to your evaluation? Also look for ideas you got from your reading: writing strategies you were inspired to try, types of sentences you relied on, or goals you sought to achieve.

2. **Write an explanation of these influences.** Did one reading have a particularly strong influence on your essay, or were several readings influential in different ways? Quote from the readings and from your final revision to show how your essay was influenced by other essays you read. Finally, based on your review of this chapter's readings, point out any further improvements you would now make in your essay.

Considering the Social Dimensions of Evaluations

The media or arts review — someone's judgment about the quality of movies, television programs, musical performances, books, and so forth — is a special kind of evaluation. We rely on such evaluations to help us decide what movies or performances to see, what books or computer games to buy, and what exhibits to attend. They confirm or challenge our attraction to a particular television series or musical group. The best media reviewers develop impressive expertise. They come to be trusted by readers to set standards for movies, musical recordings, novels, or works of art. They educate readers, helping to shape their judgment and discrimination, building their confidence in recognizing a clumsy, a passable, or an outstanding work or performance. At their best, reviewers counterbalance advertising: Instead of enticing us to see every movie that comes to town, they help us choose among the advertised movies. A trusted media or arts reviewer for a local newspaper can come to influence a community's values — building a local consensus, for example, about what constitutes a successful musical performance and encouraging tolerance or even appreciation for new kinds of music.

Excluding and Silencing.   By deciding what to review and what to ignore, media and arts reviewers determine what receives public attention and what remains invisible, and their decisions may often be based to a large extent on economic factors: Which review is likely to sell more newspapers or bring in more advertising? (In this sense, reviewers are part of a larger publicity apparatus; indeed, in our age of giant media conglomerates, a movie or music reviewer for a national magazine may well work for the same parent company that produced or distributed the film or the recording being reviewed — a situation that may not encourage the most objective evaluations.) Community theater or musical groups without money to advertise their performances may be given only a brief listing in the local newspaper; but unless they are reviewed, they will be unlikely to attract enough ticket buyers to survive (and the less mainstream their offerings, the less likely they are to be reviewed). Similarly, a new artist is simply not likely to be reviewed as widely as an established one.

For a long time, this sort of resistance to anything new and different kept many women and minority artists from being appreciated by reviewers — both in the universities and in the media — thus making it harder for them to earn a living by their work and effectively silencing their voices. This situation has changed in some ways, especially with the advent of the Internet, where people have wider access to reviews by professionals and by people who simply want to share their judgments with others. But reviewers who work for traditional media outlets such as newspapers and television still have great power to determine what is or is not considered a successful work of art.

1. **Reflect on your own experience reading reviews on the Internet, in magazines, and in newspapers (including your college newspaper), as well as on the television or radio.** Think of one film, television program, or live performance you decided to see because of a review you read or one recording, book, or DVD you purchased after reading a review of it. Recall how the review influenced you, and explain its influence.

2. ***Consider how you usually learn about new films, music, and books.*** Do you read reviews or get your information some other way? Does your information come mainly from the mainstream media, from word of mouth, from neighborhood or alternative newspapers, or from some other source? Where do you get information about nonmainstream music, books, computer games, or films?

3. ***Reflect on any media evaluations you read in connection with this assignment (Scott's and Jackson's reviews and others) in light of the ideas presented in the introduction to this section.*** Perhaps you wrote a media review yourself.

4. ***Write a page reflecting on the role played by media reviews in excluding or silencing new, innovative, or minority performers and artists.*** If possible, connect your ideas to the readings in this chapter and to your own essay.

Hidden Assumptions of Evaluators.   Good evaluative writing provides readers with reasons and support for the writer's judgment. However, the writer's personal experiences, cultural background, and political ideology are also reflected in written evaluations. Even the most fair-minded evaluators write from the perspective of their particular ethnicity, religion, gender, age, social class, sexual orientation, academic discipline, and so on. Writers seldom make their assumptions explicit, however. Consequently, while the reasons for an evaluation may make it seem fair and objective, the writer's judgment may result from hidden assumptions that even the writer has not examined critically.

1. ***Choose one reading from this chapter, and try to identify one of the hidden assumptions of its writer.*** Think of a personal or cultural factor that may have influenced the writer's judgment of the subject. For example, how do you imagine that Romano's gender may have influenced her judgment of Statsky's essay on competitive sports for children? How do you imagine Scott's job as a journalist may have influenced his judgment of *Good Night, and Good Luck*?

2. ***Reflect on your own experience of writing an evaluation essay.*** How do you think factors such as gender, age, social class, ethnicity, religion, geographical region, or political perspective may have influenced your own evaluation? Recall the subjects that you listed as possibilities for your essay and how you chose one to evaluate. Also recall how you arrived at your overall judgment and how you decided which reasons to use and which not to use in your essay.

3. ***Write a page or two explaining your ideas about how hidden assumptions play a role in evaluation essays.*** Connect your ideas to the readings in this chapter and to your own essay.

9

Speculating about Causes

IN COLLEGE COURSES   For a college public health course, a student writes a term paper speculating about why AIDS has historically been concentrated among homosexuals in North America but among heterosexuals in sub-Saharan Africa. She chooses the topic "Compare and contrast the history of the AIDS epidemic in the United States and in some other country or region," from a list of suggested topics her professor distributes.

After she reads about AIDS in North America and in Africa from books in her college library and from online medical and public health journals available to her through the library Web site, she meets with her professor to discuss her focus and plans, as he requires. She tells him that she chose the topic because one of her cousins has AIDS, and, as she has learned during the course, public health experts typically cannot stop a dangerous epidemic until they understand what causes it. She explains her plans to speculate that differences in three areas — sexual practices, attitudes towards courtship and marriage, and the impact of AIDS-prevention programs — explain the different patterns of the disease between the United States and Canada and countries in southern Africa.

Following her professor's suggestions to look at reports by hospice workers, doctors, and sociologists, she discovers several visuals and other evidence that convincingly support her causal speculations. Based on her professor's advice for further revisions to the finished paper and his encouragement, she submits the paper to the annual campus competition for the dozen best research papers by undergraduates.

IN THE COMMUNITY   For a big-city newspaper, a science reporter with a 12-year-old son and a 10-year-old daughter writes an article speculating about the reasons for increasing intolerance in the United States of what she calls "boyish behavior." After reviewing recent research in medical journals, she describes various disorders that boys are being diagnosed with at a higher rate than girls and muses that a modern Tom Sawyer or Huckleberry Finn would be diagnosed with attention-deficit hyperactivity disorder and put on medication. Reflecting on her prior knowledge of the research on biological differences between boys and girls, she contends that these differences cannot account for the increasing concern with boyish behavior. Instead, she argues that economic changes and altered cultural expectations best explain it.

For example, she speculates that adults attempt to stamp out any early signs of aggression in boys, such as shouting, playing rambunctiously, teasing girls, or interacting with adults in unmannerly and abrupt ways because our society has become extremely fearful of crime. In addition, because school classrooms are increasingly group-oriented, boyish expressions of individualism and humor are perceived by teachers as disruptive. Finally, the writer speculates that boys' fidgeting at their desks is seen as a threat to career success in an economy that increasingly values sitting still and concentrating for seven or more hours a day.

Within a week after her report is published, she receives twenty-six e-mail responses from teachers accusing her of having no understanding of what it is like to try to teach in a rowdy classroom and only nine responses from teachers or parents praising her speculations as insightful.

IN THE WORKPLACE   Writing for a monthly journal read by other school administrators, a high-school principal speculates about conditions that might make violence likely at a school site. She reviews a few recently published reports of violence in high schools, focusing on conditions in those schools that allowed students to attack teachers and other students with guns, knives, or explosives. She argues that a major cause of school violence is that bathrooms, cafeterias, hallways, and recreational spaces that used to be monitored by teachers, counselors, and administrators are now monitored by people from the community who are not taken seriously by students. Other causes, she argues, include reluctance to inspect everything that students carry into a school, and lockers, which permit students to store weapons, ammunition, or explosives.

Recognizing that her analysis of the problem implies unpopular solutions — assigning teachers to monitor all school spaces, removing lockers, and installing backpack-screening equipment — she anticipates the reservations that other principals will have to her reasoning. For support, she quotes from research studies and reports that agree or imply agreement with her speculations. Then she concludes by describing briefly how she went about implementing her recommendations at her own school, assuming that unless she did so she would not be taken seriously by her readers. Soon after her journal article is published, she receives a dozen phone calls from other principals around the country inviting her to come speak to their teachers and school-district administrators.

We all quite naturally try to explain causes. Because we assume that everything has a cause, we predictably ask "Why?" when we notice something new or unusual or puzzling.

Many things can be fully and satisfactorily explained. When children ask, "Why is the sky blue in the day and black at night?" parents can — perhaps after doing a little research — provide an answer. But we can answer other questions only tentatively: Why since the 1980s has the cost of a college education increased faster than the cost of living? Why are more women than men attending college and completing degrees? Questions such as these often have only plausible, not definitive, explanations, because we cannot design a scientific experiment to identify the cause conclusively. The decline in men's college attendance, for example, has been attributed to men's excessive television viewing and the time they spend playing video games rather than reading. Although these causes are plausible, we cannot know for certain that television and video games are indeed responsible. Because the phenomenon remains problematic, however, informed speculation, based on the best available evidence and experience, is called for. *To speculate* means primarily "to examine or ponder something," but it also means "to question," "to be curious," and even "to take risks." Without some understanding of the possible causes of a personal or social problem, solutions to it cannot confidently be proposed: To propose a solution to a problem, you have to reduce at least some of the uncertainty over how it came about. Consequently, this kind of thinking and writing is necessary to everyday life.

Writing that speculates about the causes of things that may never be answered definitively plays an important role in academic and professional life. Government specialists seek to understand the causes of unemployment or homelessness. Business executives study the reasons for declines in sales or increases in worker productivity. Officials at a four-year college may speculate about why so many students transfer to other colleges to complete their degrees.

This chapter presents several essays that speculate about the causes of a phenomenon or trend. A **phenomenon** is something notable about the human condition or social order — fear of failure, for example, or the high rate of intermarriage among ethnic and racial groups in the United States. A **trend** is a significant change that occurs over some period of time, generally months or years. It can be identified by an increase or a decrease — for example, a rise in the political influence of evangelical Christians or a decline in the percentage of people who attend college right after graduating from high school.

When you speculate about causes, you describe your subject, propose some causes for it, and argue that one cause (or more) is the best available explanation. You do not have to prove that your explanation is right, but you must attempt to convince readers that it is plausible by supporting your explanation with examples, facts, statistics, or anecdotes. To make your argument convincing, you will need to anticipate readers' questions about or objections to it.

Speculating about why things are the way they are or why things change will call for your most astute judgment as you evaluate possible causes and choose plausible ones. It will exercise your reasoning as you argue to support your speculations. You will learn to write an important genre that will be useful to you in many aspects of your life.

Your instructor may schedule this collaborative activity as an in-class discussion or ask you to conduct an online discussion in a chat room. Whatever the medium, here are some guidelines to follow.

To get a sense of this special kind of argument, choose a current trend, and speculate about its causes.

Part 1. Get together with two or three other students, and select one person to take notes.

1. Make a list of five or six trends — such as the decline in voter turnout in the United States, the increasing cost of a college education, or the increasing rate of smoking among young people. Choose one trend that interests all of you.

2. Together, list as many likely causes for this trend as you can in different areas, including economic, cultural, and psychological causes.

3. Select two or three causes that seem most likely to provide a partial explanation for the trend. Discuss how you might support each of these causes — that is, how you would convince others that these causes are plausible or likely explanations for the trend.

Part 2. When you have finished speculating, take a few more minutes to reflect on the process you have been engaged in.

- Where did your ideas about causes come from — reading, television, your own experience?
- How did you differentiate among the causes, rejecting some and accepting others as most likely?
- What kinds of support did you come up with? Where do you think you might find further support?

A Collaborative Activity:
Practice Speculating about Causes

Readings

SHEILA McCLAIN wrote this causal-speculation essay for her first-year college composition course. In it, she speculates about the causes of the U.S. public's growing interest in health and fitness. She carefully documents the trend and then offers four possible causes to explain it. As you read, reflect on your own efforts to achieve physical fitness — your interest or disinterest in it and efforts you have made, if any — and evaluate how plausibly McClain explains its appeal.

Fitness Culture: A Growing Trend in America
Sheila McClain

1   Twenty years ago the exercise and fitness industry catered to a small, select group of hard-core athletes and bodybuilders. Now the interest in physical fitness has an increasingly broad appeal to people of all ages, and the evidence can be seen

McClain cites her sources using MLA style.

She names the trend and establishes its existence by documenting a threefold increase in fitness industry profits and memberships.

The first of four causes of the trend is introduced: people have become more aware of the relation between physical fitness and health. The link between exercise, diet, and health is both a background and a perpetuating cause: It launches and sustains the trend. McClain argues to support this cause with reports of research and of programs launched by government, employers, insurers, and schools.

Here McClain speculates about a second cause, the attraction of fitness classes and health clubs. This is a key step in her argument because public awareness of the importance of fitness would not necessarily have turned people toward group, rather than solitary, exercise.

everywhere (Merritt). These days a person cannot turn on the television without seeing an infomercial featuring the latest exercise machine. Yoga, Tai Chi, and other popular forms of exercise are depicted in movies and on television and are advertised across the country. Products such as herbs and muscle-building supplements, fitness wear, exercise mats, workout videos, and new age music for meditation line the shelves of department stores. As one source points out, sales of fitness equipment for use at home have been booming since the early 1990s, and wholesalers in this market saw an increase in profits from just under $1 billion in 1990 to nearly $3 billion in 2001. Furthermore, health club memberships among people 55 and older jumped 273 percent between 1987 and 2001 ("Wellness"). Several causes have contributed to the growth of this "fitness culture" in America.

One of the most obvious causes is the increase in public awareness about the benefits of health and fitness. As noted in a 1992 report (Leepson), numerous clinical studies and scientific reports confirm that exercise together with a proper diet helps prevent heart disease as well as many other serious health problems. In fact, a healthy lifestyle may even reverse the effects of certain ailments. Because "clinical studies in 1989 done by the United States Preventive Services Task Force, a government appointed panel of experts, found 'a strong association between physical activity and decreased risk of several medical conditions, as well as overall mortality'" (Leepson), the federal government has attempted to increase awareness about the benefits of exercise. It, along with some state governments, has also implemented programs designed to increase the health and fitness of the public. With doctors, health experts, and even the government supporting the health and fitness trend, employers and health insurance providers are encouraging the "wellness culture" as well. There are now well-recognized economic benefits for companies that sponsor fitness programs, because healthy people are more productive and make fewer insurance claims (Goldberg). Increasingly, companies even pay for employee fitness club memberships, and some insurance companies give price breaks to businesses who encourage their employees to make healthy lifestyle changes. Increased public awareness about health and fitness is also seen in our nation's schools, where health and physical education are today required subjects. As a nation, we are now much more aware of the ways that physical fitness contributes to health, longevity, and productivity.

We all know the benefits of being healthy, but why the popularity of fitness clubs and group activities? The answer may be in part that these fulfill the basic human desire for a sense of community and belonging. Social institutions small and large, from local book clubs to national campaigns to protect endangered forests or wild animal species, were once widespread in the United States. Instead of joining others in such activities, people these days may be more likely to stay at home to watch television, play video games, search for entertainment online, or use up generous calling-time allowances on their cell phones. In families, both parents may be working full time, with little time left for volunteer activities. As a result, Americans have become more solitary and family oriented. At the same time, they are growing more aware that they must stay fit to be healthy and realize that fitness classes and health clubs can have the added advantage of bringing them

2

3

into contact with others. Glenn Colarossi, co-owner of the Stamford (Connecticut) Athletic Club, says this about why people join clubs and attend classes: "People like to belong to something. They like the support and added incentive of working out with others" (qtd. in Glenn). Catherine Larner, a writer on health and lifestyle issues, considers "increasing one's circle of friends" among the benefits of going to the gym (1). Group exercise creates positive peer pressure that keeps many going where they might give up were they exercising alone. A sense of community and belonging to a group also creates a sense of responsibility toward that community, enabling the members to encourage one another and drawing them closer together, fulfilling the need for companionship as well as the need to keep fit.

4   Another, somewhat surprising cause of the increase in popularity of fitness activities may be the fear and anxiety people feel from threats of terrorism along with the stress of modern life. The fact that exercise provides a release of built-up negative emotions and that exercising regularly can reduce stress has long been recognized. As Mary Sisson notes in an article in *Crain's New York Business*, health club chains saw an increase in revenues immediately after 9/11 and even expanded, one of them opening four new clubs, despite an economic downturn for most other industries. This article gives several plausible reasons why fear and stress cause people to exercise more and to do so together: (1) under stressful conditions people want the sense of community provided by gyms and classes, (2) working out gives people a sense of empowerment which counteracts feelings of helplessness, (3) traveling less provided many people with more leisure time to fill after 9/11, and (4) people make personal reassessments after a major catastrophe. For example, one woman descended forty flights of stairs evacuating the World Trade Center. Thereafter, realizing how out-of-shape she was, she took up regular exercise (Sisson). Nurturing class instructors and the meditation techniques used in many popular fitness classes also contribute to their stress-relieving properties.

A third cause: public anxiety in a changed world after 9/11 and the need people feel for communal reassurance. This is an immediate cause.

5   I have a friend who is very cynical about the fitness trend because she suspects it is fueled mainly by women who want bodies like celebrity movie and HBO actresses. It is not fitness and good health these women desire but rather eye-catching, man-enticing bodies, she insists. I tried this skeptical idea out on my exercise physiology professor, and she agreed that some people purchase celebrity-endorsed health products and are motivated to begin exercise programs by the desire to reshape their bodies, not to become more fit and healthy. She doubted that people with these motives could explain the huge increase in attendance at fitness gyms and clubs, however, because research in her field has shown that people with these motives are more likely to become discouraged easily and drop out of fitness classes (Harton).

McClain considers an objection to her argument and refutes it with the help of one of her professors, gaining authority with readers by bringing the objection directly into her essay. Notice how, in the next paragraph, she confidently reasserts her speculation about what has sustained the trend.

6   Therefore, only increased awareness of the health benefits of physical fitness, not a desire for a more beautiful body, could be sustaining the long-term trend of participation in fitness programs. In addition, attitudes towards exercise are changing. It used to be seen as hard work involving lots of pain and little gain. Moreover, people often exercised so sporadically that the only noticeable change was increased muscle soreness. These days the forms of exercise available are more engaging, more interesting, and gentler than in the past, and they vary greatly to

She introduces a fourth cause: people's changing attitude toward exercise. This cause seems necessary for the trend to be sustained. To argue for it, she tries humor.

appeal to a wide range of people. Consider classes in belly dancing (you know what that is), strip tease aerobics (look it up!), and spinning (indoor group stationary cycling, led by an instructor) — these are just a few examples. People's attitudes change when they stick with exercise long enough to experience the body's release of endorphins, hormones known to induce "runner's high." David Glenn, writing a business journal, points to the impacts of these life-changing attitudes: "People look to personal fitness as a lifestyle and a way to enjoy life, not as a way to look like Arnold Schwarzenegger." Gabriela Lukas, a New Yorker who has been exercising regularly since 2001, finds it emotionally satisfying and says it makes her "feel alive" (qtd. in Sisson). More and more people are changing their attitudes about physical fitness as they recognize that they feel better, have more energy, and are actually improving the quality of their lives by exercising regularly.

The "fitness culture" in America continues to grow and shows no signs of slowing down anytime soon. As we become increasingly aware of the costs of ill health and a lack of physical fitness — and daily newspapers and popular magazines still seem determined to make us aware — and as we experience more stress and anxiety, we are bound to have ever more need of friendship, community, and the endorphins provided by our bodies when we exercise. As more and more people continue to experience the benefits of exercise, the good news about regular exercise spreads wider. As people talk up the pleasures of belonging to a club or fitness center where familiar people welcome them, more will join. Together, these causes snowball, ensuring the continued growth of the fitness industry.

7

McClain concludes by summarizing her argument and predicting that the trend will continue.

Works Cited

Glenn, David J. "Exercise Activities Mellowing Out." *Fairfield County Business Journal* 2 June 2003: 22. *Regional Business News*. Web. 19 May 2006.

Goldberg, Carol. "Fitness Industry: Shaping Up for a Good Run." *Long Island Business News* 16 Dec. 1996: 21-22. *Regional Business News*. Web. 19 May 2006.

Harton, Dorothy. Personal interview. 9 May 2006.

Larner, Catherine. "Will Gym Fix It for You?" *Challenge Newsline* 31.1 (2003): 1-2. *Academic Search Premier*. Web. 2 May 2006.

Leepson, Marc. "Physical Fitness." *CQ Researcher* 2.41 (1992): 955-74. *Academic Search Premier*. Web. 2 May 2006.

Merritt, Greg. "The 20 Biggest Changes of the Past 20 Years." *FLEX* Nov. 2003: 286-92. *Health Source*. Web. 5 May 2006.

Sisson, Mary. "Gyms Dandy." *Crain's New York Business* 26 Aug. 2002: 1-2. *Regional Business News*. Web. 6 May 2006.

"Wellness: Finally a Well-Rooted Concept." *American Fitness* 21.1 (2003): n. pag. *Academic Search Premier*. Web. 2 May 2006.

McClain cites eight sources using the MLA system of documentation.

STEPHEN KING is America's best-known writer of horror fiction. In 2003, he won a Lifetime Achievement Award from the Horror Writers Association, and he has also won many other awards, including the 2003 National Book Foundation Medal for Distinguished Contribution to American Letters. He is a prolific novelist and short-story writer, his most recent novels being *The Colorado Kid* (2005), *Cell* (2006), and *Lisey's Story* (2006). Many movies and TV movies have been based on King's work, including *Dreamcatcher* (2003), *Riding the Bullet* (2004), *Desperation* (2005), and *Nightmares and Dreamscapes* (2006). He has published a book about writing, *On Writing* (2000), where he asserts that if you want to become a better writer, "you have to read a lot and write a lot. There's no way around these two things . . . no shortcut. . . . I take a book with me everywhere I go . . . to read in small sips as well as in long swallows. . . . You can even read while you're driving, thanks to the audiobook revolution."

In this essay excerpted from *Playboy* magazine, King speculates about the popular appeal of horror movies. Before you begin reading, think about your own attitude toward horror films. Do you enjoy them? "Crave" them? Dislike them? Or are you indifferent? As you read, notice how King tries to explain why some people are attracted to horror movies.

For more about Stephen King, check his official Web site: http://stephenking.com.

Why We Crave Horror Movies
Stephen King

1   I think that we're all mentally ill; those of us outside the asylums only hide it a little better — and maybe not all that much better, after all. We've all known people who talk to themselves, people who sometimes squinch their faces into horrible grimaces when they believe no one is watching, people who have some hysterical fear — of snakes, the dark, the tight place, the long drop . . . and, of course, those final worms and grubs that are waiting so patiently underground.

2   When we pay our four or five bucks and seat ourselves at tenth-row center in a theater showing a horror movie, we are daring the nightmare.

3   Why? Some of the reasons are simple and obvious. To show that we can, that we are not afraid, that we can ride this roller coaster. Which is not to say that a really good horror movie may not surprise a scream out of us at some point, the way we may scream when the roller coaster twists through a complete 360 or plows through a lake at the bottom of the drop. And horror movies, like roller coasters, have always been the special province of the young; by the time one turns 40 or 50, one's appetite for double twists or 360-degree loops may be considerably depleted.

4   We also go to re-establish our feelings of essential normality; the horror movie is innately conservative, even reactionary. Freda Jackson as the horrible melting woman in *Die, Monster, Die!* confirms for us that no matter how far we may be removed from the beauty of a Robert Redford or a Diana Ross, we are still light-years from true ugliness.

5   And we go to have fun.

Ah, but this is where the ground starts to slope away, isn't it? Because this is a very peculiar sort of fun, indeed. The fun comes from seeing others menaced — sometimes killed. One critic has suggested that if pro football has become the voyeur's version of combat, then the horror film has become the modern version of the public lynching.

It is true that the mythic, "fairy tale" horror film intends to take away the shades of gray. . . . It urges us to put away our more civilized and adult penchant for analysis and to become children again, seeing things in pure blacks and whites. It may be that horror movies provide psychic relief on this level because this invitation to lapse into simplicity, irrationality, and even outright madness is extended so rarely. We are told we may allow our emotions a free rein . . . or no rein at all.

If we are all insane, then sanity becomes a matter of degree. If your insanity leads you to carve up women like Jack the Ripper or the Cleveland Torso Murderer, we clap you away in the funny farm (but neither of those two amateur-night surgeons was ever caught, heh-heh-heh); if, on the other hand, your insanity leads you only to talk to yourself when you're under stress or to pick your nose on your morning bus, then you are left alone to go about your business . . . though it is doubtful that you will ever be invited to the best parties.

The potential lyncher is in almost all of us (excluding saints, past and present; but then, most saints have been crazy in their own ways), and every now and then, he has to be let loose to scream and roll around in the grass. Our emotions and our fears form their own body, and we recognize that it demands its own exercise to maintain proper muscle tone. Certain of these emotional muscles are accepted — even exalted — in civilized society; they are, of course, the emotions that tend to maintain the status quo of civilization itself. Love, friendship, loyalty, kindness — these are all the emotions that we applaud, emotions that have been immortalized in the couplets of Hallmark cards and in the verses (I don't dare call it poetry) of Leonard Nimoy.

When we exhibit these emotions, society showers us with positive reinforcement; we learn this even before we get out of diapers. When, as children, we hug our rotten little puke of a sister and give her a kiss, all the aunts and uncles smile and twit and cry, "Isn't he the sweetest little thing?" Such coveted treats as chocolate-covered graham crackers often follow. But if we deliberately slam the rotten little puke of a sister's fingers in the door, sanctions follow — angry remonstrance from parents, aunts, and uncles; instead of a chocolate-covered graham cracker, a spanking.

But anticivilization emotions don't go away, and they demand periodic exercise. We have such "sick" jokes as "What's the difference between a truckload of bowling balls and a truckload of dead babies?" (You can't unload a truckload of bowling balls with a pitchfork . . . a joke, by the way, that I heard originally from a ten-year-old.) Such a joke may surprise a laugh or a grin out of us even as we recoil, a possibility that confirms the thesis: If we share a brotherhood of man, then we also share an insanity of man. None of which is intended as a defense of either the sick joke or insanity but merely as an explanation of why the best horror films, like the best fairy tales, manage to be reactionary, anarchistic, and revolutionary all at the same time.

The mythic horror movie, like the sick joke, has a dirty job to do. It deliberately appeals to all that is worst in us. It is morbidity unchained, our most base instincts let free, our nastiest fantasies realized . . . and it all happens, fittingly enough, in the dark. For those reasons, good liberals often shy away from horror films. For myself, I like to see the most aggressive of them — *Dawn of the Dead*, for instance — as lifting a trap door in the civilized forebrain and throwing a basket of raw meat to the hungry alligators swimming around in that subterranean river beneath.   12

Why bother? Because it keeps them from getting out, man. It keeps them down there and me up here. It was Lennon and McCartney who said that all you need is love, and I would agree with that.   13

As long as you keep the gators fed.   14

Making Connections to Personal and Social Issues: Media Violence

"The potential lyncher is in almost all of us," says Stephen King, ". . . and every now and then, he has to be let loose to scream and roll around in the grass" (paragraph 9). King seems to say that horror films perform a social function by allowing us to exercise (or possibly exorcise) our least civilized emotions. Some religious groups and politicians believe that film violence — of any kind in any type of film — inspires people, especially the impressionable young, to commit violence, a belief quite different from King's.

With two or three other students, discuss these different positions about violence in movies. Begin by describing, in turn, a specific incident of violence in a movie you saw recently at a theater, on television, or on a DVD. Then together explore the question of whether film violence exorcises or inspires violence. If you find that the members of your group disagree on this issue, what reasons can you give for your positions? How do you think film violence has influenced you personally?

Finally, if you believe that media violence inspires real violence, do you support censorship of movies, television programs, books, or magazines that portray violence? For children or adults or both? If you oppose censorship, do you support movie rating systems or the television V-chip, which gives parents some control over what their children watch?

Analyzing Writing Strategies

1. King's subject is not simply horror movies but more: what they contribute to keeping people balanced mentally or psychologically, as he understands this needed balance. Reread paragraphs 1 and 2 to study how he **presents the subject** of his essay. Underline two or three key words that identify the mental states of interest to him. Also underline the first clause beginning "I think that" and the last clause, beginning "we are daring." Then evaluate how well this introduction orients readers to the subject and prepares them for what

follows. Finally, compare paragraphs 1 and 2 to paragraphs 13 and 14. Together, these paragraphs **frame** the essay; the end refers to the beginning. How would you describe this reference and explain its likely usefulness to readers?

2. King offers several kinds of **support** for the causes he proposes. Underline these examples: analogy in the last phrase of the last sentence of paragraph 12, example in the last sentence of paragraph 4, and comparison in the last sentence of paragraph 6. Then consider what general statement King is trying to support in each case and describe how the analogy, example, or comparison supports the general statement. Finally, evaluate whether the support is likely to be convincing for King's readers.

Commentary: Plausible Causes and Logical Sequence of Causes

King proposes three **causes** of our craving for horror movies:

- We go to horror movies to prove that we can sit through them. (paragraphs 2–3)
- We go to reassure ourselves that we are normal. (4)
- We go because we enjoy seeing others in danger. (5–14)

King begins with a cause that seems obvious but is still worth mentioning: We go to horror films because we want to prove something to ourselves, just as we ride roller coasters to show ourselves and others that we have the courage to do so (paragraph 3). We can surmise that King mentions this cause right away because he assumes that readers will be thinking of it. By connecting to a common experience of his readers and setting an obvious cause aside, he can move on to the not-so-obvious causes that are the heart of his argument.

King next entertains a very different cause: We go to horror movies "to re-establish our feelings of essential normality" (paragraph 4). This cause is much less predictable than the first and is based on a popular theory that says we engage all of the arts, even horror movies, to make ourselves feel better. Although this cause is also plausible, it moves us from *obvious causes* toward the one *hidden* (unexpected, unlikely, risky) *cause* that King argues at length — that we "crave" horror movies (not just attend them casually) in order to manage our uncivilized emotions of fear, violence, and aggression.

In your own causal analysis essay, your first goal will be to speculate creatively about your subject so that you can come up with at least one not-so-obvious cause. Like King, you may want to place this cause last, after discussing other more obvious causes, and to argue for it at length and with ingenuity.

Considering Topics for Your Own Essay

Consider speculating about a popular cultural phenomenon that interests you. For instance, have you ever wondered why romance novels, newspaper comics, a dance craze, a type of music, a television series, or a style of dress is so popular? Police shows or soap operas or MTV? Coffee houses or drive-through fast-food restaurants? Video games, roller derby, or professional football? A board game, toy, or doll? Science fiction novels about alien invaders or the genomics revolution? Christian pop? Think about how you might present the phenomenon to your readers. What obvious and not-so-obvious causes might you propose to explain the popularity of the phenomenon?

ERICA GOODE is an award-winning newspaper writer. After earning a master's degree in social psychology in 1979, she was awarded a mass-media fellowship sponsored by the American Association for the Advancement of Science. She then spent six years at the *San Francisco Chronicle* as a general assignment reporter and a science writer specializing in psychology and mental health; a year on an invited fellowship at the Center for Advanced Study in the Behavioral Sciences; and several years as senior writer and assistant managing editor at *U.S. News & World Report.* She moved in 1998 to the *New York Times,* where she writes about human behavior. She has won awards for her writing from the National Mental Health Association and the American Psychiatric Association.

In this essay, Goode argues that Americans eat too much — 22 percent of us are obese — not entirely because of our lack of self-control but also because of the ways food is priced, advertised, made available, and consumed away from home. As you read, notice how she relies on recent research studies in nutrition and public health to support her speculations. Notice also how the visuals she or her editors chose complement her text. After you finish reading, take a moment to evaluate whether your own experience eating out inclines you to take her speculations seriously or to resist or even want to challenge them.

The Gorge-Yourself Environment
Erica Goode

From giant sodas to supersize burgers to all-you-can-eat buffets, America's approach to food can be summed up by one word: Big. Plates are piled high, and few crumbs are left behind. Today's blueberry muffin could, in an earlier era, have fed a family of four.   1

But social norms change. Free love has given way to safe sex. Smokers have become pariahs. The gin fizz and the vodka gimlet have yielded to the mojito and the cosmopolitan. Now many health experts are hoping that, in the service of combating an epidemic of obesity, the nation might be coaxed into a similar cultural shift in its eating habits.   2

Traditionally, the prescription for shedding extra pounds has been a sensible diet and increased exercise. Losing weight has been viewed as a matter of personal responsibility, a private battle between dieters and their bathroom scales.   3

More Food, More Choices, More Eating
In an affluent society, decisions about what and how much to eat are dictated by many factors besides hunger. Bigger, cheaper and more varied meals, heavily advertised and widely available, may induce people to eat more than they need to.

But a growing number of studies suggests that while willpower obviously plays a role, people do not gorge themselves solely because they lack self-control.

Rather, social scientists are finding, a host of environmental factors — among them, portion size, price, advertising, the availability of food and the number of food choices presented — can influence the amount the average person consumes. "Researchers have underestimated the powerful importance of the local environment on eating," said Dr. Paul Rozin, a professor of psychology at the University of Pennsylvania, who studies food preferences. Give moviegoers an extra-large tub of popcorn instead of a container one size smaller and they will eat 45 to 50 percent more, as Dr. Brian Wansink, a professor of nutritional science and

4

marketing at the University of Illinois, showed in one experiment. Even if the pop-corn is stale, they will still eat 40 to 45 percent more. Keep a tabletop in the office stocked with cookies and candy, and people will nibble their way through the work-day, even if they are not hungry. Reduce prices or offer four-course meals instead of single tasty entrees, and diners will increase their consumption.

In a culture where serving sizes are mammoth, attractive foods are ubiqui-tous, bargains are abundant and variety is not just the spice but the staple of life, many researchers say, it is no surprise that waistlines are expanding. Dr. Kelly D. Brownell, a professor of psychology at Yale and an expert on eating disorders, has gone so far as to label American society a "toxic environment" when it comes to food.   5

Health experts and consumer advocates point to the studies of portion size and other environmental influences in arguing that fast-food chains and food man-ufacturers must bear some of the blame for the country's weight problem. "The food industry has used portion sizes and value marketing as very effective tools to try to increase their sales and profits," said Margo Wootan, the director of nutrition policy at the Center for Science in the Public Interest, an advocacy group financed by private foundations.   6

Trial lawyers met in Boston last month to discuss legal approaches to obesity, including lawsuits against fast-food chains and food manufacturers on grounds like false advertising, failure to provide labeling about caloric content or even fostering food addiction. At least seven such lawsuits have been filed, with varying success, said John F. Banzhaf III, a professor of public interest law at George Washington University. Professor Banzhaf, who led the way in litigation against tobacco com-panies, is now channeling similar energy into reforming fast food.   7

The food industry, however, dismisses such suits as a device to deposit more money in lawyers' bank accounts. The onus for eating healthfully, industry spokesmen say, rests entirely with the consumer. "If you don't want a large ham-burger in a restaurant, usually there is a smaller hamburger," said Steven Anderson, the president and chief executive of the National Restaurant Association. "You can get a grilled chicken sandwich in almost any restaurant I've ever been in. There are the options there and it's for the individual to decide." Still, at least one company, Kraft Foods, the maker of Oreos and Lunchables, recently announced its intention to "help encourage healthy lifestyles" by reducing portion sizes for some products.   8

Some scientists have mixed feelings about taking the obesity issue into court. "Whenever trial lawyers get hold of an issue, I worry," said Dr. Adam Drewnowski, the director for the Center for Public Health Nutrition at the University of Washington. But none dispute that an increasing number of studies show that how food is served, presented and sold plays at least some role in what and how much people eat.   9

Price is a powerful influence. In a series of studies, researchers at the University of Minnesota have demonstrated that the relative cost of different products has an even more potent effect on food choice than nutritional labeling. Dr. Simone French, an associate professor of epidemiology, and her colleagues   10

Portion Size

Many foods and beverages have gotten steadily bigger since they were introduced. Consider Burger King hamburgers.

1954 HAMBURGER SANDWICH

3.9 OZ.

2002 SANDWICHES OFFERED

HAMBURGER 4.4 OZ.

WHOPPER JR. 6.0

DOUBLE HAMBURGER 6.1

WHOPPER 9.9

DOUBLE WHOPPER 12.6

Source: Dr. Lisa R. Young, New York University

Availability

Reflecting greater choice, nearly half of Americans' food dollar is spent away from home.

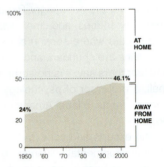

Source: U.S. Department of Agriculture

Advertising

Food industry ad spending is weighted in ways that have little to do with an ideal diet.

BREAKFAST CEREALS $792

CANDY, GUM 765

BEER 728

CARBONATED SOFT DRINKS 549

SNACKS, NUTS 330

COFFEE, TEA, COCOA 322

1997 ad spending, in millions.

FRUITS, VEGETABLES 105

Source: U.S. Department of Agriculture

Price

A study found that labeling vending-machine snacks as low in fat did little to increase sales.

ADDING A LABEL 1% INCREASE IN SALES

ADDING LABEL AND A SIGN 7%

But lowering the price of those same snacks vs. higher-fat ones had a big effect on sales of the low-fat items.

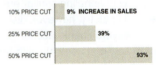

10% PRICE CUT 9% INCREASE IN SALES

25% PRICE CUT 39%

50% PRICE CUT 93%

Source: Dr. Simone French, University of Minnesota

Variety

More choices lead to more eating. When study subjects were served a four-course meal of four different foods, they ate much more than when given four servings of just one food.

CALORIES EATEN

FOUR FOODS: 1,094 CAL.

ONE FOOD: 684 CAL.

POUNDS OF FOOD EATEN

FOUR FOODS: 1.28 LBS.

ONE FOOD: 0.89 LBS.

Source: Dr. Barbara Rolls, Pennsylvania State University

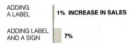

manipulated the prices of high-fat and low-fat snacks in vending machines at 12 high schools and 12 workplaces. In some cases, the snacks were labeled to indicate their fat content. "The most interesting finding was that the price changes were whopping in effect," compared with the labels, Dr. French said. Dropping the price of the low-fat snacks by even a nickel spurred more sales. In contrast, orange stickers signaling low-fat content or cartoons promoting the low-fat alternatives had little influence over which snacks were more popular.

Packaging can change the amount people consume. Dr. Wansink and his colleagues have showed that, fooled by a visual illusion, people drink more from short, wide glasses than thinner, taller ones, but they think they are drinking less.   11

Having more choices also appears to make people eat more. In one study, Dr. Barbara Rolls, whose laboratory at Pennsylvania State University has studied the effects of the environment on eating, found that research subjects ate more when offered sandwiches with four different fillings than they did when they were given sandwiches with their single favorite filling. In another study, participants served a four-course meal with meat, fruit, bread and a pudding — foods with very different tastes, flavors and textures — ate 60 percent more food than those served an equivalent meal of only their favorite course.   12

To anyone who has survived Christmas season at the office, it will come as no surprise that the availability of food has an effect as well. Dr. Wansink and his colleagues varied the placement of chocolate candy in work settings over three weeks. When the candy was in plain sight on workers' desks, they ate an average of nine pieces each. Storing the sweets in a desk drawer reduced consumption to six pieces. And chocolates lurking out of sight, a couple of yards from the desk, cut the number to three pieces per person.   13

Researchers have long suspected that large portions encourage people to eat more, but studies have begun to confirm this suspicion only in the last several years. There is little question that the serving size of many foods has increased since McDonald's introduced its groundbreaking Big Mac in 1968. For her doctoral dissertation, Dr. Lisa Young, now an adjunct assistant professor in the department of nutrition, food studies and public health at New York University, tracked portion sizes in national restaurant chains, in foods like cakes, bread products, steaks and sodas and in cookbook recipes from the 1970's to the late 1990's. The amount of food allotted for one person increased in virtually every category Dr. Young examined. French fries, hamburgers and soda expanded to portions that were two to five times as great as they had been at the beginning of the period Dr. Young studied. Steaks, chocolate bars and bread products grew markedly. Cookbooks specified fewer servings (and correspondingly larger portions) for the same recipe appearing in earlier editions. "Restaurants are using larger dinner plates, bakers are selling larger muffin tins, pizzerias are using larger pans and fast-food companies are using larger drink and French fry containers," Dr. Young wrote in a paper published last year in *The American Journal of Public Health*. Even the cup holders in automobiles have grown larger to make room for giant drinks, Dr. Young noted.   14

She and other experts think it is no coincidence that obesity began rising sharply in the United States at the same time that portion sizes started increasing.   15

Big portions at low prices lead to big waistlines, researchers say.

But cause and effect cannot be proved. And the food industry rejects the idea of a connection. Mr. Anderson of the restaurant association, for example, says that lack of exercise, poor eating habits and genetic influences are largely responsible for Americans' struggle with extra fat. Still, in cultures where people are thinner, portion sizes appear to be smaller. Take France, where the citizenry is leaner in body mass and where only 7.4 percent of the population is obese, a contrast to America, where 22.3 percent qualify. Examining similar restaurant meals and supermarket foods in Paris and Philadelphia, Dr. Rozin and colleagues at Penn found that the Parisian portions were significantly less hefty. Cookbook portions were also smaller. Even some items sold at McDonald's — the chicken sandwich, for example — are smaller than their American counterparts.

"There is a disconnect between people's understanding of portions and the idea that a larger portion has more calories," said Dr. Marion Nestle, chairwoman of the N.Y.U. nutrition and food policy department and the author of "Food Politics: How the Food Industry Influences Nutrition and Health." The Double Gulp, a 64-ounce soft drink sold by 7-Eleven, Dr. Nestle noted, has close to 800 calories, more than a third of many people's daily requirement, but she said people were often shocked to learn this.   16

And, as studies by Dr. Rolls, Dr. Wansink and others suggest, faced with larger portions, people are likely to consume more, an effect, Dr. Rolls noted, that is not limited to people who are overweight. "Men or women, obese or lean, dieters, nondieters, plate-cleaners, non-plate-cleaners — it's pretty much across the board," she said. In one demonstration of this, Dr. Rolls and her colleagues varied the portions of ziti served at an Italian restaurant, keeping the price for the dish the same but on some days increasing the serving by 50 percent. On the days of the increase, Dr. Rolls said, customers ate 45 percent more, and while diners rated the bigger portion size as a better value, they deemed both servings appropriate. The researchers have also shown that after downing large plates of food, people do not usually compensate by eating less at their next meal.   17

Very young children, studies suggest, are relatively immune to the pressures that huge food seems to impose on adults. Three-year-olds served three different portion sizes of macaroni and cheese for lunch on three different days, Dr. Rolls and her colleagues discovered, ate the same amount each time. Five-year-olds, however, already showed signs of succumbing to adult overindulgence, eating more when more was put in front of them.   18

Researchers have yet to cement the link between larger portions and a fatter public. But add up the studies, Dr. Rolls and other experts say, and it is clear Americans might have more success slimming down if plates were not quite so large and a tempting snack did not await on every corner. Obviously, people have responsibility for deciding what to eat and how much, Dr. Rolls said. "The problem is," she said, "they're not very good at it."   19

Making Connections to Personal and Social Issues: Controlling Public Environments for Eating

Goode assumes, for sound scientific reasons, that weight control is basically a matter of calorie control — that is, the more calories you eat, the more you weigh. She also assumes, again for good reasons, that if people weigh too much in relation to their height, their health will suffer.

With two or three other students, in turn tell each other briefly about one or two recent incidents when you were aware that the environment — by which Goode means specific places and occasions for eating, mainly away from home — led you to eat more than you ordinarily would, or encouraged you to do so even if you resisted successfully. Where were you? What did you eat? What was there about the environment that permitted or encouraged or even pressured you to eat more?

Then discuss whether the food industry bears any responsibility for such overindulgence, as Goode implies. Do you think this industry needs to be challenged and sued for damages in court or that laws need to be passed controlling various aspects of the environments in which we eat, as laws have been passed to curtail smoking? Do you think that federal and state health agencies should launch advertising campaigns against overeating, as they have launched campaigns warning about the dangers of smoking? If states can pass laws to require motorcycle riders to wear helmets, can they — should they — also pass laws to redefine environments in which food is purchased and consumed? Recall that the helmet laws were passed because motorcycle riders could not be trusted to wear helmets, thereby reducing public expense to get them back on their feet following serious accidents. By analogy, if obesity is a public health crisis, as some claim, should we not also have laws to control the ways food is purchased and consumed outside the home?

Analyzing Writing Strategies

1. To increase her authority with readers, Goode must acknowledge any certain or likely questions about or objections to her speculations; that is, she must bring the question or objection directly into her argument and then **counterargue** it. Goode does so in paragraphs 14–19. Underline the first sentence in paragraphs 14 and 15 and label each "large portions" in the margin. Then put a bracket around the next three sentences in paragraph 15 and label them "objection" in the margin. In the remainder of the essay, Goode counterargues this objection, attempting to **refute** it through research findings. Read to the end and reflect on how convincing Goode's refutation is likely to be for her readers. Write a few sentences explaining your insights.

2. Goode advances five **causes** to explain the U.S. obesity epidemic. To mark them, underline the first sentence in paragraphs 10, 11, 12, 13, and 14. Notice how visible each cause is to readers. Notice also that Goode's argument to support her speculations about each cause varies considerably in length. With her whole argument in mind, reflect on how plausible each cause seems to be and why she might have sequenced the causes in this order. Write a sentence or two offering a possible justification for her ordering.

Commentary: Presentation of the Subject

Goode devotes almost a third of her essay to **presenting the subject** she speculates about. Contrast this attention to presenting the subject to King's presentation, where he announces his subject in two sentences, perhaps assuming that all of his readers will have seen a horror movie and will recognize immediately and fully the subject of his speculations. Goode, however, must assume that her readers will initially be thinking about the usual ways to curtail their food intake: diet, exercise, self-control. She wants readers to think about quite a different possibility, that environmental factors associated with occasions for buying and consuming food can at least partially explain why more and more Americans are obese. She defines her subject most concisely in paragraph 4 by listing the environmental (as opposed to personal) factors of most concern to her and several researchers: "portion size, price, advertising, the availability of food and the number of food choices." Then, aware that some readers may doubt that such influences on food consumption are important or decisive, she **supports** her perspective on the subject by writing about research findings and court challenges (through paragraph 9). The article's graphics support these causes and contribute greatly to her argument. When you present the subject of your causal speculations, you will need to define and describe it for your readers as fully as may be needed, based on your assessment of how much they know about it. (Following the convention of newspapers and newsmagazines, Goode does not formally cite her sources but does identify them informally within her essay. Your instructor may want you to cite your sources more formally, using one of the two citation styles detailed in Chapter 22.)

Considering Topics for Your Own Essay

Like Goode, consider writing about the causes of a current social problem. Your guiding question is either *what causes something to occur* or *why is it increasing or decreasing over time*. For example: What causes juvenile suicides? or Why have juvenile suicides been increasing or decreasing over time? Consider these current social problems: domestic violence, child abuse, access to health insurance, decay of a particular neighborhood in your city, crime rates, rates of incarceration, unequal funding of public schools, hunger, identity theft, income inequality, cost of a college education, the higher divorce rate in the South, gambling addiction, teen pregnancy. These suggestions will help you think of other social problems.

BILL SAPORITO is editor-at-large of *Time*, an influential U.S. weekly newsmagazine. He directs the magazine's coverage of business, the economy, personal finance, and sports while occasionally doing his own writing and reporting. He has worked at *Time* for almost twenty years. Previously, he was senior editor at *Fortune* magazine and a member of the board of editors there. He began his career as a reporter at the *New York Daily News*. This essay was published in 2004 in *Time*.

In this essay, Saporito speculates about a recent change in the behavior of players and fans in both professional sports and college sports. It has become commonplace for players to trash-talk each other on the court or field and for fans to trash the players from the sidelines. Fights have erupted and new rules and penalties have been enacted to control this behavior. As you read, notice the wide range of causes Saporito comes up with in an effort to better understand this new sports phenomenon. Notice particularly causes that surprise you, that you could not have predicted.

Why Fans and Players Are Playing So Rough
Bill Saporito

As brawls go, it was hardly the worst that sport has to offer. Europeans accustomed to soccer's bloodbaths must have been chuckling: You call that a riot? In five minutes of mayhem that was repeated thousands of times on TV, Indiana Pacers forward Ron Artest was seen leading a fast break into the stands at the Palace in Auburn Hills, Mich. Artest was charging down a local lout, John Green, who hit him with a full beverage cup after Artest got into an on-court scuffle with the Detroit Pistons' Ben Wallace. Several teammates joined Artest, punching anyone they could reach. The referees ended the game with 45.9 sec. left, and the Pacers were forced to exit through a shower of popcorn, beer and venom from Detroit fans. Nine fans were hurt, none seriously. But the rumble in Detroit quickly turned into another spectacularly American experience — bad sports behavior morphing into trash television. *Booyah!* Artest, apologetic but clueless, was soon appearing on the *Today* show promoting the rap album he had just produced, looking as though he had scheduled everything on his Palm Pilot: Friday? beat the pom-poms out of a fan; Monday, work on that p.r. campaign! Green, who has had three DUI arrests, may not be able to dribble in a straight line, but he found himself on *Larry King Live* arguing the cause of those who feel that buying an overpriced ticket for a sporting event is a license to spew nastiness at people guilty of possessing far more athletic talent than they do. 1

The riot in Detroit also set off a second battle across the country, as everyone from sports-radio yakkers to families gathered for Thanksgiving dinner tried to assign blame for the rise of incivility in sports — the athletes or the fans? Call it a jump ball. It's easy to view Artest and Wallace as typical modern athletes: too wealthy and too self-involved. Traveling in chartered jets, surrounded by hangers-on, coddled by agents, they have more in common with CEOs than ordinary Joes. But the distance between athletes and the people who pay to see them may be increasing out of necessity. Some fans who were once happy to cheer for the home team have now turned every contest into a hate-test. Opposing players must be verbally eviscerated, their personal problems made fodder for derision. Home-team players who don't measure up aren't spared either. And the fans are hardly discouraged by arena managers happy to sell them overpriced booze and pump up the atmosphere with lasers and loud music. So does the fault lie in our stars or in ourselves? 2

NBA commissioner David Stern was outraged by his players. He suspended Artest for the rest of the season, costing him some $5.5 million in lost wages. Indiana's Stephen Jackson, who accompanied him into the stands, was docked 30 games, and Jermaine O'Neal, who clocked one fan from a running start, got 25. (Anthony Johnson, another Pacer, got a five-game rest; Detroit's Wallace, whose shove of Artest set off the chain of events, was iced for six.) The NBA Players Association has appealed Artest's suspension as unreasonable. Oakland County, Mich., authorities are reviewing game and security tapes to determine what 3 charges may be filed against Pacers and fans, although it's not likely that anything beyond a misdemeanor will result. Lawyers for injured fans like Mike Ryan, a 5-ft. 9-in. pilot who was clocked by Artest, are already putting on the full-court press.

But Stern wants the fight to set off a national debate about what he calls the "social contract" between fans and players, which seems to have been voided. "Over the years, at all sporting events, there's developed a combination of things," says Stern. "First, the professional heckler, who feels empowered to spend the entire game directing his attention to disturbing the other team at any decibel level, at any vocabulary. Then, an ongoing permissiveness that runs the gamut from college kids who don't wear shirts and paint their faces and think that liberates them to say anything, to NBA fans who use language that is not suitable to family occasions."

How did fan behavior become so vile? Practice. In cities like Boston, New York and Philadelphia, fans are notorious for their raucous behavior. Emotions in Yankees-Red Sox games get so high that during the closing innings of the sixth game of this year's play-offs, when police had to ring the field, veteran fans scarcely batted an eye. In Philadelphia, fans frustrated by the team's awful play once famously booed Santa Claus during half time. Behavior at Eagles games got so bad that officials seven years ago set up an on-site court in Veterans Stadium — with a jail — to handle the worst offenders. Eagles president Joe Banner says the jail only "moderately improved" behavior at the Vet; it took a move to a new stadium, with a high-tech security system equipped with 100 cameras to spot trouble, to quiet things down, at least for now.

Baseball was birthed by brutes, on the field and off. Games in the late 19th century and early 20th century were filled with violence, from Ty Cobb barreling into second base with spikes flying to crowds storming the field. Still, fans pretty much calmed down until fairly recent times. In a 2002 game between the Chicago White Sox and the Kansas City Royals, a father-son combo leaped out of the Comiskey Park stands and for no apparent reason attacked Kansas City first-base coach Tom Gamboa. This year, another fan at Comiskey tried to tackle umpire Laz Diaz. "There is no question — you can ask any coach on any team, they would concur — that the anger in the voice of this small percentage of fans has escalated," says Gamboa. "I have no idea when this started, but there are some people now, when they pay for a sports event, instead of watching it, they feel like they're entitled to partake in it."

Wharton School[1] professor Ken Shropshire, who has written several sports books, including *In Black and White: Race and Sports in America*, thinks change in the way fans relate to their teams is fueled by everything from close-up TV coverage to video games. "With the realistic, violent sports video games and the pervasiveness of sports on television, there's closeness, and fans feel they're actually part of this thing now," he says. "From a marketing aspect, all the major sports convey that fans are right in the middle. So they feel they should be part of the game."

---

[1] The prestigious business school of the University of Pennsylvania.

THEN AND NOW
At Madison Square Garden in 1948, jackets for men and hats for ladies signaled a more decorous time. In 2004, Duke fans taunted a Tennessee-Martin player during the Blue Devils' season opener in Durham, N.C.

Many commentators have delicately cited race as a factor in the brawl (all the players involved were black, most of the fans white), but Shropshire argues that race is less a factor than it was during the 1970s, when the predominance of black players in the NBA gained widespread attention — not to mention in an earlier era when black players in any sport were a novelty. "Look at what Jackie Robinson had to endure," Shropshire says. "For three years, he never went into the stands, and the abuse hurled at that time was more severe. A small percentage of fans have forever done the wrong thing. It's up to the individual athletes to decide to do the right thing."   8

A bigger factor, says Shropshire, may be the class differences between fans and players, particularly as star salaries soar ever higher. "The working-class   9 guy who has pulled together the money to go to that game is spending a significant portion of his income," he says. "And the most visible thing he sees is that his money is going to the salaries of these players." Stern calls that ridiculous, arguing that fans still consider athletes their heroes. (Just look at this year's Boston Red Sox.) "Nobody is saying Shaq [O'Neal] and Kevin Garnett don't deserve the salaries they get," he says. "Because they are MVP candidates, and they never let up."

For their part, most NBA players insist that they either ignore the abuse or use it as motivation. "The hostile arenas make the game fun," says New York Knicks guard Allan Houston. "They make you want to hit a big shot so you can silence them." Houston, one of the league's gentlemen, admits, "As a player, it's hard not to go after some people, but you have to be a bigger person than that. If you hold back, it makes them look bad. It puts the stain on them." 10

In some respects, the fans are just taking a cue from the players. Beating the opposition isn't good enough; in-your-face humiliation is preferable. Profane language among players on the court got so pervasive that the NBA had to make it a violation. In football, the NFL has started calling penalties against players for taunting and excessively celebrating after touchdowns. Still, it's players like Philadelphia receiver Terrell Owens — who trampled the Dallas Cowboys logo after a touchdown this fall — who get most of the attention, since their antics are replayed and reinforced on ESPN and sports talk shows. 11

Mix those strutting pros and hardened fans in today's hoop arenas, and the chemistry is ripe for agitation. Games aren't mere athletic contests; they are in-your-face productions. Laser-light-show introductions, clatter-making Thunder Stix and scoreboard exhortations for more noise contribute to an atmosphere of confrontation. Players shooting free throws used to be accorded an almost respectful silence. Now fans attempt to distract them by jeering and waving towels. It doesn't work, but that doesn't stop the fans' behavior. 12

Alcohol, of course, plays a part too. In the NFL, serious tailgaters fuel up before they even enter the stadium. Many teams are sponsored in part by a brewer, and beer sales make up a significant percentage of a stadium's concession revenues — a spigot that teams are not eager to cut off. Still, to head off trouble, most basketball and football venues stop selling beer by the end of the third quarter (as does the Palace in Auburn Hills). 13

The obnoxiousness isn't limited to pro sports either. Many college venues take great pride in their lack of hospitality for visiting teams. At Duke University the denizens of the Cameron Indoor Stadium, known as the Cameron Crazies, specialize in personal taunts that often cross the line. They once showered condoms on a Maryland player who had been accused of sexual assault. Last season they dangled chicken nuggets on a fishing pole near chunky Tar Heels center Sean May. The Crazies are "an integral part of our success," says Duke assistant athletic director of communication Jon Jackson. "The Crazies have had fun without being abusive." Some fun. 14

Many commentators see the general decline in sports behavior as consistent with falling standards in society as a whole. What do we expect of sports fans in a 15

TUMULT IN THE STANDS

The Pacers aren't the only team to mix it up with fans. In recent years, confrontations between players or officials and crowds have been getting increasingly nasty.

FOOTBALL
Incoming! Enraged that a last-minute call went against the hometown Cleveland Browns, fans pitched beer bottles and other debris at the refs as the team suffered a 15-10 loss to the Jacksonville Jaguars in December 2001.

HOCKEY
In Philadelphia, a notoriously tough town for visiting teams, a Flyers fan climbed over the glass three seasons ago to get at Toronto Maple Leafs bad boy Tie Domi. The man got his way. Domi pulled him into the penalty box and began wrestling him.

BASEBALL
In Oakland this fall, Texas pitcher Frank Francisco answered a couple who heckled his team by tossing a chair that broke the woman's nose. Last year in Boston, two Yankees scuffled with a Red Sox grounds-crew member in New York's bullpen.

nation where episodes of humiliation, greed and win-at-all-costs behavior (from *Survivor* to *My Big Fat Obnoxious Boss*) pass for family entertainment? "Incivility, boorishness and crassness are everywhere in the idiot culture that we live in," says veteran NBC sportscaster Bob Costas. "And yet we celebrate all this as edginess. This behavior is encouraged."

Meanwhile, back on the court, the Pacers, even with three of their best players suspended, went on to win three of their next four games, while Detroit, the defending NBA champion, is struggling to regain its championship form. The two teams will meet again this season — in Indianapolis on Christmas Day. They are not likely to be exchanging gifts.

16

Making Connections to Personal and Social Issues: Sports Fans' Behavior

Both Saporito and National Basketball Association Commissioner David Stern respond very moralistically to player and fan misbehavior. Stern not only imposes huge fines on some players, but also expresses outrage and complains about "permissiveness." One pro football team sets up a jail and court within its stadium. Saporito asks how fan behavior has come to be "vile" (paragraph 5). Yet cheering and booing have always been a part of sports events, large and small, professional and amateur. Crowds in the Roman Colosseum roared in support of their favorite gladiator of a pair who were fighting to kill each other. Alcohol consumed before or during a game or both has been a part of college and professional sports for decades. It seems, then, that Stern and Saporito are worried about something new: personal attacks by fans on individual players by insulting or taunting them, throwing things at them, ridiculing them, attempting to humiliate them.

With two or three other students discuss this new kind of fan behavior. Begin by telling each other about one example of it that you observed, either at a live game or on TV. Describe what happened and what you thought about it. (Maybe you participated in it!) Then together discuss the morality of this kind of fan behavior. Maybe you agree with Saporito and Stern, or maybe you do not see a problem so long as fans are not throwing anything at players. Maybe you think it adds to the liveliness of sports events. What do you wish fans would start doing or stop doing for you to have a more enjoyable time at sports events?

Analyzing Writing Strategies

1. To learn more about how Saporito uses sources to **support** his argument, focus on paragraphs 7–9, where he relies on commentary by a college professor, Ken Shropshire. Saporito first must establish the authority of Shropshire. To see how he does so, underline three facts about Shropshire in the first sentence of paragraph 7. In paragraph 8 underline two or three words or phrases that reveal Shropshire's historical perspective on professional basketball. Then in paragraphs 7–9, reread the five quotations Saporito selects from Shropshire and decide whether their language and content give you any reason to doubt Shropshire's authority. (At the end of paragraph 9, Saporito reveals enough confidence in Shropshire's expertise to allow the commissioner of the National Basketball Association, David Stern, to challenge it.) Finally, write a few sentences summarizing what you have learned about the ways Saporito uses Shropshire's commentary to support his argument.

2. In paragraphs 1–4 Saporito **presents his subject**, confrontations between players and fans at professional and college sports events. Reread each of these paragraphs and write a phrase or two after each one that identifies what it contributes to your understanding of the subject. Then, reflecting on this introduction from your perspective of having read the whole essay, write a few sentences evaluating how well it presents the subject. Think about

whether it makes the subject seem worth speculating about and engaging to both fans and non-fans, whether it makes understanding its causes seem urgent, and whether it establishes Saporito's authority to speculate about it.

Commentary: Plausible Causes

Saporito speculates about seven causes that he believes explain the relatively new phenomenon of incivility by fans at sports events: fan practice at behaving badly, close-up TV coverage of games along with video-game addiction, racial prejudice against black players, fan envy of players' high salaries, profane language and taunting by players as a model for fan behavior, excessive drinking of alcohol before and during games, and a general decline in standards of behavior. Perhaps he advances so many causes because he does not want readers to notice that he has left out some possible cause. The seven causes certainly do make his speculations seem comprehensive: a serious, thoughtful effort.

Saporito attempts to support — to argue — every cause. He relies on a wide range of sources: print, media, personal contacts. He has written about sports for many years and seems to care about his subject. Consequently, his argument seems plausible. Though he never inserts his personal views, perhaps because he has been a reporter for so long, readers probably infer that he wishes sports events were more civil, for both the players and the fans. Even readers who have little interest in big-time college or professional sports events are likely to find his speculations informative, more or less convincing, and highly readable.

Considering Topics for Your Own Essay

For your own essay, you could speculate about the causes of some other sports phenomenon: doping, overtraining, team cohesion, sports celebrity, sports as a religion, successful coaching, improvement in athletic performance, dedication of parents to Little League baseball, March Madness, becoming a sports fan, indifference to sports, inferior facilities and/or less money allocated to college women's teams; the motivation to win, the training effectiveness of a particular regimen, the Superbowl craze, the appeal of watching team sports (live or on television); the success of a particular team or why a successful team chokes. Or you could speculate about the causes of a recent rise in the popularity of a sport.

■ Purpose and Audience

The fundamental purpose of writing a causal argument is to engage readers in making sense of the world. The possible causes of puzzling phenomena or trends are worth thinking about and irresistibly interesting. Indeed, humans are probably unable *not* to speculate about causes, since so much of what we want to understand can never be known definitively.

If we assume that we can engage readers in our subject and our speculations about it, then our purpose becomes to help them understand their world better, to show them a new way to think about a subject. For example, like McClain and King, you might hope to lead readers to think about popular culture in new ways. Or like Goode or Saporito, you might want readers to appreciate the significance of a major behavioral phenomenon or social change.

The chief purpose of an essay speculating about causes is to convince readers that the proposed causes are plausible. Therefore, you must construct a coherent, logical, authoritative argument that readers will take seriously. Sometimes, like McClain and King, you may want readers to look at a phenomenon in a new way or to go beyond obvious or familiar explanations. At other times, like Goode and Saporito, you may hope to get readers to reexamine their own behaviors or to spark change in the conditions that contribute to some behaviors.

Your audience will also affect your purpose. If you think that your readers are only mildly curious about the subject and know little about it, you might write partly to stimulate their interest in the subject itself. You could then concentrate on convincing them of the plausibility of your proposed causes. If you expect that readers will know a lot about the subject and oppose or be skeptical of your speculations, you could devote a lot of attention to conceding and refuting what you assume to be their preferred causes. If you believe that the distance between you and them is unbridgeable, you could even accentuate your differences, forcefully refuting their likely objections to your causes and refuting their preferred causes.

Basic Features:
Speculating about Causes

A Presentation of the Subject

First, it is necessary to describe the subject. Depending on what readers know or need to know, writers sometimes devote a large portion of the essay to presenting the subject — describing it with specific details and examples and establishing that it actually exists (or existed) by citing statistics and statements by authorities.

In writing about a phenomenon he knows will be familiar to his readers, Stephen King simply asserts in his title that horror movies are widely popular. In contrast, Erica Goode's less immediately obvious subject — the contribution of environmental factors, as opposed to simple lack of willpower, to increasing obesity among Americans — requires considerable detail. Goode devotes almost a third of her essay to presenting research findings and expert testimony supporting the idea that matters such as portion size, the availability of food, value pricing, and advertising play "at least some role in what and how much people eat" (paragraph 9).

In an essay about a trend, a writer must always demonstrate that the trend exists. Sheila McClain, for example, demonstrates that the trend exists by citing statistics documenting a dramatic eleven-year increase in fitness industry profits. In some cases, a writer may have to show that the subject is an established, significant trend as opposed to a fad, a fluctuation, or a superficial change. For example, a new form of exercise might become a fad if many people try it out for a few months. This brief popularity would not make it a trend, but it might be part of a trend — a general increase in health con-sciousness, perhaps, such as the one that McClain writes about.

Plausible Causes

No matter how well presented the subject may be, a causal argument goes nowhere unless it offers plausible causes as a possible explanation. In many causal arguments, readers first encounter the writer's causes in a **forecast** — a list of causes in the order in which they will be taken up in the argument. Erica Goode provides a forecast of sorts in paragraph 4, although the order in which she takes up each cause varies slightly in the actual outline of the essay.

Speculating about the reasons for Americans' increasing interest in physical fitness, Sheila McClain comes up with four plausible causes based on her own observations and what she has learned through research. The first cause is increased awareness of the benefits of fitness, resulting from governmental and other educational programs. The second cause is a personal need for community and support that leads people to join fitness clubs. The third cause is the intense anxiety many Americans experienced after 9/11, a feeling of stress and fearfulness that working out at a gym could alleviate. Finally, the fourth cause is the greater variety in the forms of exercise available today, which means that exercise can now appeal to a wider range of people than in the past. At first glance, even without McClain's arguments to support them, these causes seem likely and worth taking seriously. They do not immediately provoke readers' resistance or skepticism. They are, in short, plausible.

A Logical Sequence of Causes

Causes must be presented in a logical sequence. The reader needs to be aware of a meaningful step-by-step sequence of causes: The second cause follows from the first in some meaningful way, the third from the second, and so forth. Maybe an obvious cause prepares for a hidden cause, as in Stephen King's essay, or one cause creates a necessary condition for the next cause, as in Sheila McClain's essay, or every cause is a consequence of the preceding cause and predates the following cause, a logical sequence sometimes referred to as a **line of reasoning**. Alternatively, causes may be presented in what the writer sees as an ascending or descending order of importance. For example, Erica Goode orders causes in such a way that she ends with what she clearly sees as the most important environmental cause for overeating, portion size. Bill Saporito orders causes from ones that are relatively narrowly defined to those that are broader and farther reaching.

Convincing Support

The support for every cause is the heart of causal speculation. A list of causes is not an argument. Writers of essays speculating about causes know that argument — or support — is required because a definitive, unarguable explanation for the subject is not available. Causal speculation is quintessentially argumentative; every cause must be argued for — or supported — if readers are going to be convinced that the explanation, though tentative, throws some light on the subject.

To provide convincing support for a cause requires both knowledge and creativity. Stephen King supports his causes with his understanding of psychology and his many years of writing horror novels and movies. Sheila McClain, Erica Goode, and Bill Saporito use examples, statistics, and authorities to support their arguments. Because she is writing for a college course, McClain cites and documents her sources.

A Consideration of Readers' Objections and Alternative Causes

Writers of causal speculation choose plausible causes and convincing support and sequence them logically in the essay. However, in nearly every writing situation requiring causal argument, writers must also imaginatively anticipate readers' objections and possible alternative causes and then acknowledge, accommodate, or refute these points in the counterargument. It is not enough simply to be aware that readers may have objections or alternative causes that they prefer over the writer's. These objections must be addressed within and become part of the argument, making it complete.

Stephen King anticipates that some readers will be skeptical that horror movies are popular because they appeal to and help us control the dark, dangerous side within us. He devotes roughly half of his essay to trying to convince readers that this cause is plausible. Erica Goode devotes four paragraphs to refuting the objection that no causal connection can be established between increased portion size and increased obesity among Americans.

Speculating About Causes

Invention and Research

What is something that has made you wonder "why?" Why is voter turnout so low? Why have pedicures become so popular? Do some thinking and writing about how you might answer this question, and some research about how others have answered it. Then come up with a tentative speculation of your own about the cause(s). . . . **See p. 485 for more.**

Planning and Drafting

As you look over what you have written and learned about your subject so far, can you make a convincing case for what causes it? Do you need to prove that it has one main cause, multiple causes, one cause that started it and a different cause that sustained it? Make a plan for your argument and start drafting it. . . . **See p. 495 for more.**

Critical Reading Guide

What are your draft's strengths and weaknesses? Is there enough evidence that a trend actually exists? Instead of A causing B, might B actually cause A? Get a classmate, a friend, a writing tutor, or someone else to read and respond to your essay, especially the parts you are most unsure of. . . . **See p. 500 for more.**

Revising

As you consider your essay again in light of your reader's comments, how can you improve it? Can you provide more evidence for a trend's existence? More support for your claim about the main cause of a phenomenon? Go through your draft systematically, making changes wherever necessary. . . . **See p. 502 for more.**

Editing and Proofreading

Have you checked for errors that are especially likely in essays speculating about causes? Have you violated any rules for using words or figures in dates, percentages, fractions, and other numbers? Have you used any "reason is because" constructions? Look for and correct these and any other errors. . . . **See p. 506 for more.**

Guide to Writing

■ The Writing Assignment

Write an essay about an important or intriguing phenomenon or trend, and speculate about why it might have occurred. Describe your subject, demonstrate its existence, if necessary, and propose possible causes for it. Discover a way to sequence the causes logically. Then support or argue for the causes so that your readers will find them plausible.

To learn about using the *Guide* e-book for invention and drafting, go to bedfordstmartins.com/theguide.

■ Invention and Research

The following activities will help you find a subject, explore what you know about it, do any necessary research, and develop the parts of your causal argument. These activities are easy to complete. Doing them over several days will give your ideas time to ripen and grow. Be sure to keep a written record of your invention and research to use later when you draft and revise.

Finding a Subject to Write About

You may already have a subject in mind and some ideas about what might have caused it to occur. Even so, you should take some time to consider other possible subjects to ensure the best possible choice. Remember to consider both phenomena and trends as possible subjects for this writing assignment:

- A *phenomenon* is something notable about the human condition or the social order — fear of speaking to a group, for example, or opposition to gun-control legislation.

- A *trend* is a significant change extending over many months or years. It can be identified by an increase or a decrease — a rise in the birthrate, a decline in test scores.

Some subjects can be approached as either phenomena or trends. For example, you could speculate about the causes of the changing suicide rate among young people (a trend), or you could ignore the change and simply speculate about the causes of such suicides (a phenomenon).

The following activities will help you choose a subject for your essay. Make your lists of possible phenomena and trends as complete as possible, including, for example, the subjects suggested by the Considering Topics for Your Own Essay activity following each reading in this chapter.

Listing Phenomena.   *Make a list of current phenomena that you could write about.* Here are some possibilities to consider. Start with a few of them, and see whether they bring to mind other topics of interest to you.

- *College:* A noisy library, insufficient parking, an instructor's skill or popularity, cheating on exams, a successful or an unsuccessful class or course, women as the majority of college students

- *Personal life:* Competitiveness, idealism, creativity, popularity, jealousy, laziness, workaholism, high achievement, contentiousness, rage, stuttering, depression, low self-esteem, anxiety disorder, alcoholism, single homelessness, personal bankruptcy, child abuse

- *Politics and government:* Hostility toward politicians, low voter turnout, satisfactions of jury duty, stability of our system of government, negative campaigning, high percentage of minority inmates in U.S. prisons, the rise and fall in value of the dollar in relation to currency values in other countries, world overpopulation, lack of social mobility (moving to a higher income group), lack of educational opportunity, rural poverty, prosperity, collapse of an earlier civilization

- *Environment:* Pollution, nuclear waste disposal, limited popularity of recycling programs, unsafe or borderline-safe food production, global warming

- *Life stages:* The "terrible twos," teenage alienation or rebellion, postponement of motherhood, midlife crisis, abrupt career changes

- *The arts:* Popularity of rap or jazz, decline of musical theater, impulse to censor the arts, child prodigies, maintaining competence playing an instrument

- *Culture:* Continuing influence or popularity of a book, movie, actor, novelist, social activist, athlete, politician, religious leader, or television program; popularity of online and print catalog buying; limited appeal of movies with subtitles

Listing Trends.   *Make a list of several trends, from the past as well as the present, that you would like to understand better.* Consider both trends you have studied and can research and ones you know about firsthand. Be sure that the possibilities you list are trends, not fads or short-term fluctuations. To start, consider the following possibilities:

- *Shifting patterns in education:* Increasing interest in teaching as a career, increase in home schooling, increase in community college enrollments, declining numbers of math and science majors, increase in the number of white students attending historically black colleges, declining percentage of men attending college, increasing cost of textbooks

- *Changes in patterns of leisure or entertainment:* Increasing consumption of fast food, declining interest in a particular style of music, increase in competitive cycling, increase or decrease in a magazine's circulation

- *Shifts in religious practices:* Declining church attendance, increasing incidence of women ministers or rabbis, increasing interest in Asian religions, increased membership in fundamentalist churches, growth of "megachurches"

- *New patterns of political behavior:* Increase in conservatism or liberalism, decline in support for legalized abortion, developing power of minorities and women, increase in support for same-sex marriage

- *Societal changes:* Increases in the number of working women with children, single-parent households, telecommuters, ethnic intermarriages, grandparents raising their grandchildren, vegetarians

- *Changes in political or world affairs:* Spreading influence of capitalism, increasing resistance to globalization, increasing numbers of women elected to political office, growing ethnic or religious conflicts, increasing numbers of women becoming suicide bombers

- *Changes in economic conditions:* Increasing cost of medical care, decline in real median wage for families and individuals since 1973, increasing gap between wealthiest and poorest Americans, decreasing family savings rate, increasing cost of college

- *Historical emergence of noteworthy movements and other trends:* Rise of community colleges, comprehensive high schools, cities; emergence of Impressionism, pop art, arts and crafts movement; achievement of female suffrage; development of industrialization, unionization of labor, public health systems, a national highway system; settlement of the West

■ *Listing Subjects Related to Identity and Community.*   These suggestions may bring to mind topics related to identity and community.

Phenomena

- A particular conflict in a community to which you belong
- The popularity of athletes or other groups of students in high school
- The lack of understanding and sympathy between the young and the old
- The obsession of many young women and men with their weight and body image
- The continued high numbers of pregnant teenagers despite widely available birth control
- The deterioration of children's attachment to one or both parents during adolescence
- The watching of more hours of TV than people say they would like
- The experience of high school as generally unpleasant by some students

Trends

- Increasing prejudice against new immigrants
- Increasing incidence of people abandoning or abusing aged relatives
- Increasing incidence of domestic violence against spouses or children
- Increasing popularity of twelve-step, self-help programs
- Increasing popularity of sororities and fraternities on college campuses
- Increasing sexual activity before age fifteen
- Increasing incidence of depression among young adolescents (ages thirteen to fifteen)

- Increasing obesity among children
- Increasing numbers of college athletes graduating from college
- Increasing use of plastic surgery to enhance self-image
- Increasing numbers of young people choosing to remain virgins until they marry
- Increasing rate of cigarette smoking among young people

■ *Listing Subjects Related to Work and Career.* The following suggestions will help you to think of subjects related to work and career.

Phenomena

- Students' expectations of less financial success than their parents
- A preference for self-employment even though people who own their own businesses work harder for more hours each day than do other workers
- College students who hold part-time jobs
- Business majors
- The importance or difficulty of arranging working internships while in college
- Older students who attend college

Trends

- Rising employment among young people
- Increasing numbers of full-time and part-time temporary or contingent workers
- Increasing types of service-related careers

Choosing a Subject. *Look over your list of possibilities, and choose one subject to write about.* Describe the subject in two or three sentences. You may or may not already have some ideas about why this phenomenon or trend occurred. As you analyze it in detail, you will have the opportunity to consider possible causes and to decide which ones are the most plausible.

Of the two types of subjects — a phenomenon or a trend — a trend may be more challenging to examine because you must nearly always do research to demonstrate that the phenomenon actually exists or that it has been increasing or decreasing over an extended period of time. (Usually one or two references will be adequate.) Since a trend begins at a specific point, you must take care that the causes you propose as the sources of the trend actually precede its onset. You may also need to differentiate between causes that launched the trend and those that perpetuate it.

It may help you in choosing a subject if you tentatively identify your ultimate readers. They could be either a general adult readership or adult readers who already have some special interest or stake in your subject. They could be instructors, administrators, coworkers, or employers. They could be members of a particular community or region.

Exploring What You Know about Your Subject

Write for several minutes about the subject you have chosen. Note everything you now know about it. (When you start writing, you may be surprised at how much you do know.) Try to describe why you are interested in this trend or phenomenon, and speculate about where you might find more information about it.

Considering Causes

Think now about what might have caused your selected phenomenon or trend to occur. List possible causes, and then analyze the most promising ones.

Listing Possible Causes.   *Write down all the things you can think of that might have caused the phenomenon or trend.* Consider each of the following:

- Immediate causes (those responsible for making the phenomenon or trend begin when it did)
- Remote, background causes (those from before the phenomenon or trend began)
- Perpetuating causes (those that may have contributed to sustaining or continuing the phenomenon or trend)
- Obvious causes
- Hidden causes

Selecting the Most Promising Causes.   *Review your list, and select five or six causes that seem to you to provide a plausible explanation of your subject.* Since you will next need to analyze these causes, it might be helpful to list them in table form. If you are writing on paper, skip five or six lines between each cause in your list.

Analyzing Promising Causes.   *Below each cause in your list, explain why you think it is real and important.* Consider the following questions as you analyze each cause:

- Is it a necessary cause? Without it, could the phenomenon or trend have occurred anyway?
- Is it a sufficient cause? Could it alone have caused this phenomenon or trend?
- Would this cause affect everybody the same way?
- Would this cause always lead to phenomena or trends like this one?
- What particular anecdotes or examples might demonstrate the importance of the cause?
- Do you know of any authorities who have suggested that it is an important cause?
- Is it a remote or background cause or an immediate cause?
- Is it a perpetuating cause, sustaining the phenomenon or trend?
- Is it an obvious cause or a hidden cause?
- Could it actually be a *result* of the phenomenon or trend rather than a *cause*?

Researching Your Subject

In exploring your subject, you may have found that you already know enough to describe or define it adequately for your readers. If not, you will need to consult library and Internet sources or interview a faculty or community expert to learn more about the subject.

If you are speculating about the causes of a trend, you will also need to do some research to confirm that it actually is a trend and not just a fluctuation or a fad. To do so, you will need to find examples and probably statistics that show an increase or a decrease in the trend over time and that indicate the date when this change began. (For example, recall that Sheila McClain cites dates and statistics to demonstrate that participation in fitness activities has actually increased.) If you are unable to find evidence to confirm that a trend exists, then it is probably just a fad or short-term fluctuation. In this case, you will have to choose a different subject for your essay.

An Online Activity: Researching the Phenomenon or Trend

Searching the Web may help you establish the existence of the phenomenon or trend and provide information you can use in presenting it to your readers. Enter a key term describing your subject in a search engine such as Google (google.com) or Yahoo! Directory (dir.yahoo.com). Adding the word *trend* to your key term may help — for example, *religion trends or dieting trends*.

If you are interested in trends in education, you might find information at the National Center for Education Statistics Web site (http://nces.ed.gov/ssbr/pages/trends.asp). For other national trends, look for the relevant statistics link on the U.S. government Web site (http://firstgov.gov/).

Bookmark or keep a record of promising sites. Download any materials you might wish to cite in your evaluation, remembering to record the source information required to document them.

Considering Your Readers

Write a careful analysis of your readers. Because you will be trying to make a convincing case for some particular readers, you should know as much as possible about them. Only after you have analyzed your readers can you confidently decide how to present these causes in your essay — which causes you will emphasize, which causes will require the most convincing evidence, which causes will be obvious or not so obvious. Take a few minutes to answer the following questions:

- Who are my readers? (Describe them briefly.)

- What do my readers know about my subject? Will I have to prove its existence to them? How extensively will I have to define or describe it for them?

- What attitudes do my readers have about my subject? Do they care about it? Are they indifferent to it? Might they understand it differently from the way I understand it?

- What causes would they be most likely to think of?

Testing Your Choice

Now that you have explored your subject, considered its possible causes, and confirmed its existence, take some time to review your material and decide whether your subject is workable. Despite the work you have done so far, if you find you have serious doubts about how well you can write about your subject, then you are probably better off choosing a new one. The questions and the collaborative activity that follow will help you test your choice.

Do You Know Enough?   Review your invention notes to see whether you understand the phenomenon or trend and its possible causes well enough to continue working with it. To make this decision, try to answer the following questions:

- Do I now know enough or do I have time to find out what I need to know to describe and define my subject in a way that will interest readers and convince them that the phenomenon or trend actually exists?

- Have I been able to come up with several possible causes? Can I convince readers that these causes are plausible?

- Am I certain that the causes I propose are not simply obvious ones that will not be informative or challenging to most readers?

Do You Care Enough?   It is important that you pick a phenomenon or trend that you are truly interested in because you will be devoting a lot of time and energy to researching and writing about it. In choosing a subject, you are obligating yourself to do the work necessary to understand the phenomenon or trend and its causes as fully as possible. At the same time, you are making a commitment to your readers to develop an argument speculating about the causes of the phenomenon or trend that is informative, convincing, and interesting to read. To decide whether you can make this commitment, try to answer the following questions.

- *Do you feel a personal interest in the phenomenon or trend you have chosen?* Is it something that affects you directly or that you feel strongly about? Is it something that intrigues you and sparks your curiosity so that you want to explore its possible causes and convince readers of their plausibility? Are you willing to devote the time necessary to writing a full and convincing argument about this subject?

- *Do you think this is a subject you can present to readers in an interesting and engaging way?* If so, what can you bring to your exploration of the phenomenon or trend and its causes that readers will not have thought of or realized before? Will your approach to the subject challenge readers' expectations? If this is not possible given the subject, will your approach be informative to readers so that they will learn something important from your essay? Can you use statistics or other information in a way that will surprise readers? Can you counterargue their possible objections?

A Collaborative Activity:
Testing Your Choice

At this point, you will find it helpful to get together with two or three other students to discuss and get feedback on your subject and list of causes. This collaborative activity will help you determine whether you are ready to start developing your causal argument.

Presenters: Briefly identify your subject, and ask the listeners what causes immediately come to their minds as plausible explanations for your subject. Make a list of these causes as the listeners talk. Finally, tell the listeners the causes you propose to argue for, and ask them whether they accept these as likely or plausible. Take notes about their objections and questions. (When you plan and draft your essay, these lists and notes may suggest further causes you will want to argue for, and they will help you anticipate your readers' likely questions and objections to your proposed causes.)

Listeners: Respond imaginatively to the presenter's request for causes that you think initially explain the subject. When the presenter tells you the causes he or she proposes to argue for, praise those that seem plausible, but also ask all the questions and raise all the objections you can think of. In this way, you will help the presenter anticipate readers' likely questions and objections.

Researching Causes

Some causal arguments can be made fully and convincingly on the basis of your own knowledge and intuition. In fact, you may have to rely on your own ideas to explain very recent phenomena or emerging trends. Most subjects, however, will have already been noticed by others, and you will want to learn what they have said about the causes. Doing research can be helpful in several ways:

- To confirm or challenge your own ideas
- To identify further causes to add to your own explanation
- To provide support for causes that you want to argue for
- To identify causes that your readers may prefer more than the ones you find plausible
- To reveal some of the reservations that readers may have about the causes you suggest

As you discover causes others have proposed, add the most interesting or most plausible ones to your list. Analyze these as you did your own proposed causes. In your essay, you may want to accommodate them by integrating them in full or in part into your own argument.

As you gather evidence about causes, remember to record the information you will need to acknowledge your sources.

Developing Your Argument

Try out an argument in writing to support a key cause. Once you have figured out what to expect of your readers, review your list of causes and analyses, and make a new, shorter list of all the causes that you believe provide a plausible explanation of your subject. Then write a one-page argument for one cause that you think readers may find most plausible or interesting or unexpected. Begin by identifying the cause. Then use some of the support you have found to make the cause seem plausible or likely to your readers. As part of your argument to support this cause, you may want to respond to readers' likely questions or objections.

Anticipating Objections

Try responding to the most likely objections to your causes. You should expect that readers will evaluate your essay critically by considering each cause and your support for it carefully before they decide that you have devised a plausible explanation. It would be wise, therefore, to account for any possible objections your readers could raise.

Consider the two most likely objections, and think about how you would acknowledge, concede, or refute them. Write several sentences, trying out your response.

Anticipating Alternative Causes

Try responding to alternative causes that your readers may prefer to your own proposed causes. As they read your essay, your readers may think of other causes that seem more plausible to them than your causes. Try to think of two or three such causes now, and write several sentences about each one, explaining why you do not consider it important, why you specifically reject it, or why you think it is less plausible than your causes.

Designing Your Document

Think about whether your readers might benefit from design features such as headings, numbered lists, or other elements that would make the development of your causal argument easier to follow. Consider also whether visuals — drawings, photographs, tables, or graphs — would strengthen your argument. These are not at all a requirement for an essay speculating about causes, but they can be helpful, as you can see in Erica Goode's essay. You may come across promising visuals in your research and either download them from the Internet or make photocopies from library materials. Or you may find statistics that you can use to construct your own visuals, such as tables or graphs. If you do use visuals or statistics, be sure to document their sources and ask permission from the source if you want to post a visual on the Web.

For more information about including visuals in your work, see Chapter 25.

Defining Your Purpose for Your Readers

Write a few sentences defining why you are writing this argument speculating about causes. Recall that in an earlier invention activity you identified your readers and considered what they know about your subject. Given these readers, try now to define your purpose by considering the following questions:

- How can I interest readers in my subject, establishing its significance for them personally, so that they will care about my speculations about its possible causes?

- Do I attempt to give my readers a fresh, new way of thinking about a phenomenon or trend that they may not have strong feelings about, or must I dissuade them from their present way of thinking about a phenomenon or trend that is already of significant concern to them?

- How much resistance should I expect from my readers to each of the causes I want to propose? Will the readers be largely receptive? Skeptical but convincible? Resistant and perhaps even antagonistic?

- How can I best respond to my readers' likely questions and objections and to the alternative causes they may prefer to my own? Shall I concede where I can or refute at every opportunity, and how can I refute without seeming dismissive of my readers' ideas?

Formulating a Tentative Thesis Statement

Write a sentence or two that could serve as your thesis statement. In an essay speculating about causes, the thesis statement focuses on the subject and announces the causes that are argued for in the piece. You will already have described the trend or phenomenon that is your subject. As readers approach your causal speculations, they need to know what causes you consider plausible and want them to take seriously. Though forecasting is optional, readers will often benefit from knowing how you have sequenced the causes.

Readings in this chapter illustrate effective thesis statements. For instance, Erica Goode presents her thesis this way: "But a growing number of studies suggests that while willpower obviously plays a role, people do not gorge themselves solely because they lack self-control. Rather, social scientists are finding a host of environmental factors — among them, portion size, price, advertising, the availability of food and the number of food choices presented — can influence the amount the average person consumes" (paragraphs 3–4). Goode refers back to her subject — "an epidemic of obesity" (paragraph 2) — and then lists the contributing environmental causes she will go on to argue for in the essay.

After describing his subjects — bad behavior among sports players and fans — Bill Saporito asserts his viewpoint on the topic and poses the question his essay will set out to answer: "But the distance between athletes and the people who pay to see them may be increasing out of necessity. Some fans who were once happy to cheer for the home team have now turned every contest into a hate-test. Opposing players must be verbally eviscerated, their personal problems made fodder for derision. Home-team players who don't measure up aren't spared either. And the fans are hardly discouraged by arena managers happy to sell them overpriced booze and pump up the atmosphere with lasers and loud music. So does the fault lie in our stars or in ourselves?" (paragraph 2).

■ Planning and Drafting

This section will help you review your invention writing, determine specific goals for your essay, make a tentative outline, and get started on your first draft.

Seeing What You Have

Pause now to reflect on your invention and research notes. Reread what you have written so far to see what you have. Watch for language that establishes the trend or phenomenon, argues convincingly for the causes you think are most plausible, and counterargues readers' likely objections to your causes as well as their alternative causes. Highlight key words, phrases, and sentences; make marginal notes or electronic annotations about any material you think could be useful. If you have done your invention writing on the computer, you may have sentences or whole paragraphs that can be copied and pasted into your draft.

Ask yourself the following questions:

- Could I research my subject more fully to make it seem more significant and worth speculating about?

- If I am speculating about the causes of a trend, do I have enough information to establish convincingly that the trend is (or was) increasing or decreasing over time?

- Will I be able to sequence my causes logically and argue for them convincingly?

- Have I been able to anticipate a wide range of readers' likely questions and objections?

- Have I been able to identify a few alternative causes readers may prefer over my causes?

Setting Goals

Before you begin drafting, set some specific goals to guide the decisions you will make as you draft and revise your essay. The draft will be easier to write and more convincing if you start with clear goals in mind. The following questions will help you set goals. You may find it useful to return to them while you are drafting, for they are designed to help you focus on specific elements of causal speculation essays.

Your Purpose and Readers

- What are my readers likely to know about my subject?

- How can I interest them in understanding its causes?

- How can I present myself so that my readers will consider me informed and authoritative?

The Beginning

- What opening would make readers take this subject seriously and really want to think about its causes? Should I provide a specific, significant example, as Bill Saporito does? Assert the subject's seriousness and importance, as Erica Goode does? Provide a historical perspective, as Sheila McClain does?

- Should I personalize my subject by connecting it to my firsthand experience? Should I begin with an anecdote? Should I cite surprising statistics, as McClain does?

The Presentation of the Subject

- Do I need to demonstrate that my subject really exists, as Goode, Saporito, and McClain do?

- If I am analyzing a trend, do I need to demonstrate that it is not just a fluctuation or a fad, as McClain does?

- How much and what kind of support do I need for these points?

The Causal Argument

- How many causes should I propose?

- How can I present my proposed causes in the most effective sequence? Should I arrange them from least to most important or vice versa, as Goode does? From most obvious to least obvious, as Stephen King does, or vice versa? From immediate to remote or vice versa?

- Do I need to make other distinctions among causes, such as differentiating a cause that starts a trend from one that keeps it going?

- How much and what kind of support do I need to offer to make each cause plausible to my readers? Are any causes so obvious that support is unnecessary? Do I need to demonstrate to readers that all of my causes existed before the phenomenon or trend began?

- How can I anticipate readers' objections to my proposed causes? Should I just acknowledge the existence of some objections without responding to them? Concede other objections, as King does? Refute other objections, as Goode does?

- How can I anticipate alternative causes readers might propose? Should I acknowledge one or more of these causes? Concede the plausibility of other causes? Refute other causes as not worth taking seriously, as McClain and Saporito do?

The Ending

- How should I end my essay? Should I try to frame the essay by echoing something from the beginning, as Saporito does?

- Should I summarize my causes, as McClain does, or, as King does, refocus on the key cause?
- Should I conclude with a conjecture about larger implications?

Outlining

A causal analysis may contain as many as four basic parts:

1. A presentation of the subject
2. Plausible causes, logically sequenced
3. Convincing support for each cause
4. A consideration of readers' questions, objections, and alternative causes

These parts can be organized in various ways. If your readers are not likely to think of any causes other than the ones you are proposing, you may want to begin by describing the subject and indicating its importance or interest. Then state your first proposed cause, supporting it convincingly and accommodating, conceding, or refuting readers' likely questions and objections. Follow the same pattern for any other causes you propose. Your conclusion could then mention — and elucidate — the lack of other explanations for your subject.

> Presentation of the subject
>
> First proposed cause with support and consideration of objections, if any
>
> Second proposed cause with support and consideration of objections, if any (etc.)
>
> Conclusion

If you need to account for alternative causes that are likely to occur to readers, you could discuss them first and give your reasons for conceding or rejecting them before offering your own proposed causes. Many writers save their own causes for last, hoping that readers will remember them best.

> Presentation of the subject
>
> Alternative causes and consideration of them
>
> Proposed causes with support and consideration of objections, if any
>
> Conclusion

Another option is to put your own causes first, followed by alternatives. This pattern helps you show the relative likelihood of your causes over the others. You might then end with a restatement of your causes.

> Presentation of the subject
>
> Proposed causes with support and consideration of objections, if any
>
> Alternative causes compared with your causes
>
> Concluding restatement of your proposed causes

There are, of course, many other possible ways to organize a causal analysis, but these outlines should help you start planning your own essay.

Consider any outlining you do before you begin drafting to be tentative. Never be a slave to an outline. As you draft, you will usually see ways to improve on your original plan. Be ready to revise your outline, shift parts around, or drop or add parts as you draft. If you use the outlining function of your word processing program, changing your outline will be simple, and you may be able to write the essay simply by expanding the outline.

Drafting

General Advice.   Start drafting your essay, keeping in mind the goals you set while you were planning. Remember also the needs and expectations of your readers; organize, define, explain, and argue with them in mind. Turn off your grammar checker and spelling checker at this stage if you find them distracting. Don't be afraid to skip around in your draft; jump back and fill in a spontaneous idea, or leap ahead and write a later section first if you find that easier. If, as you draft, you discover that you need more information, make a note of what you need to find out, and go on to the next point. Later you can interview an expert, survey a group, or do further library or Internet research to get the information you need. If you get stuck while drafting, explore the problem by using some of the writing activities in the Invention and Research section of this chapter.

You may want to review the general drafting advice on p. 9. These tips may also help you draft your essay:

- Remember that in writing about causes, you are dealing with probabilities rather than certainties. Therefore, resist the urge to claim that you have the final, conclusive answer; instead, simply assert that your explanation is plausible. Qualify your statements, and acknowledge readers' objections and alternative causes.

- Try to enliven your writing and to appeal to your readers' interests and concerns. Causal analysis is potentially rather dry.

Sentence Strategies: Topic Sentences to Signal Stages of the Argument and Examples in Parallel Form.   As you draft an essay speculating about the causes of a phenomenon or trend, you will want to ensure that your readers can readily recognize the stages of your argument and that they can easily understand the support you offer for each of your proposed causes. Two sentence strategies that can help you achieve these goals are using clear topic sentences, especially ones that are grammatically parallel, and using grammatically parallel sentences to present examples.

Signal the stages of your causal argument with easy-to-recognize topic sentences. Topic sentences are usually placed first or very early in a paragraph. They can announce a new cause, introduce counterargument (the writer's response to readers' likely questions or alternative causes), or identify different parts of the support for a cause or counterargument. They may include key terms that the writer has introduced in a thesis statement at the beginning of the essay, and they may take identical or similar sentence forms so that readers can recognize them more easily. Here are examples from Stephen King's essay. They identify what King believes to be the three main causes for many moviegoers' attraction to horror movies:

> Why? Some of the reasons are simple and obvious. To show that we can, that we are not afraid, that we can ride this roller coaster. (paragraph 3)

> We also go to re-establish our feelings of essential normality. (4)

> And we go to have fun. . . . The fun comes from seeing others menaced — sometimes killed. (5–6)

King assists readers in identifying each new stage of his argument by introducing the grammatical subject *we* in the first topic sentence and then repeating it to signal the next two stages: *we can, we also go, And we go.* You will find similarly prominent topic sentences in the essays by Sheila McClain, Erica Goode, and Bill Saporito.

Do not hesitate to make your sequences of causes very visible and accessible to your readers. Readers like to follow a logical, step-by-step argument. You can avoid frustrating their expectations by taking care to satisfy them — chiefly through the content of your argument, but also with visible signals.

Consider presenting examples supporting a cause in parallel grammatical form to help readers understand that the examples are related. Here is a sequence of three related examples from one paragraph in Erica Goode's causal argument:

> Give moviegoers an extra-large tub of popcorn instead of a container one size smaller and they will eat 45 to 50 percent more. . . . (paragraph 4)

> Keep a tabletop in the office stocked with cookies and candy, and people will nibble their way through the workday. . . . (4)

> Reduce prices or offer four-course meals instead of single tasty entrees, and diners will increase their consumption. (4)

Note how Goode relates these examples by beginning each sentence with a verb in the imperative mood ("Give," "Keep," "Reduce") and in the second clause predicting what will happen if the imperative is carried out using a future tense verb ("will eat," "will nibble," "will increase"). The three sentences are almost exactly parallel grammatically. In the following examples from another paragraph, Goode again links two related examples by opening her sentences with grammatically similar constructions:

> In one study, Dr. Barbara Rolls . . . found that research subjects ate more. . . . (paragraph 12)

> In another study, participants served a four-course meal. . . . (12)

The repetition of grammatical form (as well as the content of the sentences) tells readers that the examples are related, making the ideas easier to follow and contributing to the effectiveness of the argument.

For more on using topic sentences to signal the main stages of a causal argument, go to bedfordstmartins.com/theguide and click on Sentence Strategies.

For more on relating examples to one another by repeating grammatical forms, go to bedfordstmartins.com/theguide and click on Sentence Strategies.

In addition to using topic sentences that help readers follow the stages of your argument and using parallel grammatical form to present related examples, you can strengthen your causal argument with other kinds of sentences as well. You may want to review the information about sentences with appositives (pp. 177–79) and sentences that introduce concession and refutation (pp. 309–10).

Critical Reading Guide

Now is the time to get a good critical reading of your draft. Writers usually find it helpful to have someone else read and comment on their drafts, and all writers know how much they learn about writing when they read other writers' drafts. Your instructor may arrange such a reading as part of your coursework — online or in class. If not, you can ask a classmate, friend, or family member to read your draft. You could also seek comments from a tutor at your campus writing center. (If you are unable to have someone else read your draft, turn ahead to the Revising section on pp. 502–06, where you will find guidelines for reading your own draft critically.)

▶ **If You Are the Writer.**   To provide focused, helpful comments, your reader must know your essay's intended audience, your purpose, and a problem in the draft that you need help solving. Briefly write out this information at the top of your draft.

- *Readers:* Identify the intended readers of your essay. What do you assume they already know and think about your subject and its causes? Do you expect them to be receptive, skeptical, resistant, or antagonistic?

- *Purpose:* What do you hope to accomplish with your readers?

- *Problem:* Ask your reader to help you solve the most important problem you see in your draft. Describe this problem briefly.

▶ **If You Are the Reader.**   Reading a draft critically means reading it more than once — first to get a general impression and then to analyze its basic features. Use the following guidelines to assist you in giving critical comments to others on essays that speculate about the causes of phenomena or trends:

1. *Read for a First Impression.*   Read the essay straight through. As you read, try to notice any words or passages that contribute to your first impression, and identify those that make weak contributions as well as strong ones.

    After you have finished reading the draft, write a few sentences describing your overall impression. Does the essay hold your interest? What in it most surprises you? What do you like best? Do you find the causal argument convincing? Next, consider the problem the writer identified, and

Making Comments Electronically

Most word processing software offers features that allow you to insert comments directly into the text of someone else's document. Many readers prefer to make their comments in this way because it tends to be faster than writing on a hard copy and space is virtually unlimited; from the writer's point of view, it also eliminates the problem of deciphering handwritten comments. Even where such special comment features are not available, simply typing comments directly into a document in a contrasting color can provide the same advantages.

respond briefly to that concern now. (If you find that the problem is covered by one of the other guidelines listed below, respond to it in more detail there if necessary.)

2. *Evaluate How Well the Subject Is Presented.* How well does the draft present the phenomenon or trend? Does it give enough information to make readers understand and care about the subject? Does it establish that the subject actually exists? If the subject is a trend, does the writer demonstrate a significant increase or decrease over time? Where might additional details, examples, or statistics be helpful?

3. *Consider Whether the Causes and Support Are Convincing.* Look first at the proposed causes, and list them. Do there seem to be too many? Too few? Do any seem either too obvious (not worth mentioning) or too obscure (remote in time or overly complicated)?

    Next, examine the support for each cause — anecdotes, examples, statistics, reference to authorities, and so on. Which support is most convincing? Which seems unconvincing? Where would more support or a different kind of support strengthen the argument?

    Check for errors in reasoning. Does the argument mistakenly take something for a cause just because it occurred before or at the start of the phenomenon or trend? Are any of the proposed causes of the subject actually *effects* of the subject?

4. *Assess Whether Readers' Likely Objections and Questions Are Anticipated Adequately.* Look for places where the writer acknowledges readers' possible objections to or questions about the proposed causes. How well are objections handled? Should any of them be taken more seriously? Help the writer see other ways of either accommodating or refuting objections. Do any of the refutations attack or ridicule the persons raising the objections? Try to think of other likely questions or objections the writer has overlooked.

5. *Assess Whether Alternative Causes Are Adequately Anticipated.* If alternative causes are acknowledged by the writer, are they presented fairly? Is it clear why they have been accommodated or rejected? Do the refutations seem convincing? Do any of the refutations attack or ridicule the persons proposing the alternative causes? Try to think of other plausible causes readers might prefer.

6. *Consider Whether the Organization Is Effective.* Given the expected readers, are the causes presented in an effective sequence? If not, suggest a more logical sequence.

    - *Look at the beginning.* Is it engaging? Imagine at least one other way to open the essay. Look for something later in the essay that could be moved to the beginning — an intriguing anecdote, for instance, or a surprising statistic.

For a printable version of this critical reading guide, go to bedfordstmartins.com/theguide.

- *Look at the ending.* Is the ending decisive and memorable? Think of an alternative ending. Could something from earlier in the essay be moved to or restated at the end?

- *Look again at any visuals the writer has incorporated.* Assess how well the visuals are integrated into the essay. Point to any items that do not provide support for the writer's argument.

7. ***Give the Writer Your Final Thoughts.*** What is this draft's strongest part? What about it is most memorable? What part is most in need of further work?

▪ Revising

Now you have the opportunity to revise your essay. Your instructor or other students may have given you advice on how to improve your draft. Or you may have begun to realize that your draft requires not so much revising as rethinking. For example, you may recognize that your causes are too obvious, that your causes lack a logical relationship to each other that would allow you to sequence them in a chain of reasoning, or that you have not anticipated readers' objections or alternative causes. Consequently, instead of working to improve the various parts of your first draft, you may need to write a new draft that radically reshapes your argument. Many students—and professional writers—find themselves in this situation. Often a writer produces a draft or two, gets advice on them from others, and only then begins to see what might be achieved.

If you feel satisfied that your draft mostly achieves what you set out to do, you can focus on refining the various parts of it. Very likely you have thought of ways to improve your draft, and you may even have begun improving it. This section will help you get an overview of your draft and revise it accordingly.

Getting an Overview

Consider your draft as a whole, following these two steps:

1. *Reread.* If at all possible, put the draft aside for a day or two before rereading it. When you go back to it, start by reconsidering your audience and your purpose. Then read the draft straight through, trying to see it as your intended readers will.

2. *Outline.* Make a scratch outline, indicating the basic features as they appear in the draft. Consider using the headings and outline/summary functions of your word processor.

Planning for Revision. Resist the temptation to dive in and start changing your text until after you have a solid grasp of the big picture. Using your outline as a guide, move through the document, using the highlighting or commenting tools of your word processor to note comments received from others and problems you want to solve (or mark on a hard copy if you prefer).

Analyzing the Basic Features of Your Own Draft.   Turn now to the Critical Reading Guide that begins on p. 500, and use it to identify problems in your draft. Note the problems on your draft.

Studying Readers' Comments.   Review all of the comments you have received from other readers. For each comment, look at the draft to determine what might have led the reader to make that particular point. Try to be objective about any criticism. Ideally, these comments will help you see your draft as others see it. Add to your notes any problems that you intend to act on.

Working with Sources

Writers of essays speculating about the causes of a phenomenon or trend must establish that the causes they offer are plausible. To do so, they often rely on evidence from experts or others who have researched and thought about the topic. But using too few sources or sources that are too narrow in scope can undercut the effectiveness of the argument because readers may feel they are being provided with only a limited vision of it. Consequently, it can be important to offer information from a number of sources and from sources that reflect a variety of areas of expertise.

Look, for example, at the sources that Erica Goode refers to in speculating about the extent to which environmental factors can affect how much people eat in her essay "The Gorge-Yourself Environment," which appears on page 465. She cites a professor of psychology with an interest in food preferences and a professor of nutritional science and marketing in paragraph 4, a professor of psychology with an interest in eating disorders in paragraph 5, the director of nutrition policy at an advocacy group in paragraph 6, and the chair of a university's nutrition and food policy department in paragraph 16. She also cites the specific findings of at least six academic research projects (paragraphs 10, 11, 12, 14, 17, and 18). All together, the number of expert research projects she cites is impressive and the variety of her sources adds to her credibility.

In her essay "Fitness Culture: A Growing Trend in America" (p. 457), Sheila McClain cites two articles from fitness magazines (one by Greg Merritt from *FLEX* and one titled "Wellness: Finally a Well-Rooted Concept" from *American Fitness*). But a look at her Works Cited list reveals that she doesn't rely solely — or even primarily — on such sources, which because of their editorial mission might be biased toward the position she is taking. Rather, much of the expert testimony she cites comes from business publications (*Fairfield County Business Journal, Long*

Citing a variety of sources to support your causal speculations

For help working with sources, go to bedfordstmartins.com/ theguide.

Island Business News, Crain's New York Business), an online general interest publication with a focus on religious issues (*Challenge Newsline*), and a government publication (*The CQ Researcher Online*). She also cites an interview with her exercise physiology professor — whom she identifies in the text of her essay — to help refute a counterargument. Again, the number of sources and their variety in terms of approach to the subject lend credibility to the writer's speculations.

As you determine how many and what kinds of sources to cite in your essay, keep in mind that readers of essays speculating about causes are more likely to be persuaded if the sources you rely on are neither too few nor too narrowly focused. If, when you begin to draft, you find that your research seems skimpy, you may need to return to your sources, and to new sources, as well, to cast a wider net.

Carrying Out Revisions

Having identified problems in your draft, you now need to find solutions and — most important — ways to implement them. Basically, you have three ways of finding solutions:

1. Review your invention and planning notes for other information and ideas.
2. Do additional invention writing or research to provide material that you or your readers think is needed.
3. Look back at the readings in this chapter to see how other writers have solved similar problems.

The following suggestions, which are organized according to the basic features of essays that speculate about causes, will get you started solving some problems that are common to them.

A Presentation of the Subject

- ***Is your subject unclear, or is its existence not clearly established?*** Discuss it in greater detail. Consider adding anecdotes, statistics, citations from authorities, or other details. If your subject is a trend, be sure you show evidence of a significant increase or decrease over an extended period.

Plausible Causes

- ***Do you propose too many causes?*** Clarify the role each one plays: Is it obvious? Hidden? Immediate, remote, or perpetuating? (You need not use these labels.) In addition, you may need to emphasize one or two causes or delete some that seem too obvious, too obscure, or relatively minor.
- ***Do you propose too few causes for a complex subject?*** Try to think of other possible causes, especially hidden or remote ones. Conduct further research if necessary.

Convincing Support

- *Is your support skimpy or weak?* Look for more or stronger types of support.

- *Do you make errors in reasoning?* Correct them. For example, if you cannot provide convincing support that a proposed cause occurred before the phenomenon or trend began and also contributed to it, you will have to delete that cause or at least present it more tentatively. If you have confused a cause with an effect, clarify their relationship.

A Logical Sequence of Causes

- *Do your readers find the argument disorganized or hard to follow?* Consider grouping related causes together, rearranging the causes in order of increasing or decreasing importance, or moving your refutations of alternative causes to precede your argument on behalf of the causes that you favor. Try to forge a logical chain of reasoning from cause to cause. Your plan may be more understandable if you forecast it at the beginning. Provide summaries, transitions, and other cues for readers. Remember that all the authors in this chapter signal clearly and visibly the stages of their arguments, especially where they introduce each separate cause for the phenomenon or trend.

A Consideration of Readers' Objections and Questions

- *Are any of your refutations of possible objections to your proposed causes unconvincing?* Try to provide stronger evidence. If you cannot do so, you may want to accommodate the objections.

- *Do any refutations attack or ridicule people?* Revise them to focus on the objections, not on the people who are making them.

- *Do your readers raise questions about your argument that you have not considered or have not answered clearly?* You may need to provide more information about your subject or more support for proposed causes.

- *Do your readers make any objections that you have not considered or not taken seriously enough?* Consider whether you can explain why they are wrong or should acknowledge their validity and incorporate them into your own argument.

Responses to Alternative Causes

- *Do any of your refutations of alternative causes seem unconvincing?* Try to provide a stronger counterargument, or consider accommodating the alternative causes.

- *Do any refutations attack or ridicule people?* Revise to focus on specific alternative causes that you believe to be implausible rather than on the people who are proposing these causes.

- *Do your readers suggest any causes that you have not considered?* Decide whether the causes are plausible and should be integrated into your argument. If they seem implausible, decide whether to mention and refute them.

Checking Sentence Strategies Electronically
To check your draft for a sentence strategy especially useful in essays speculating about causes, use your word processor's highlighting function to mark the sentences where you introduce each cause of the phenomenon or trend. Then look at whether each sentence indicates clearly to readers that you are moving on to a new stage in your causal argument. If any do not, think about how you could make the structure of the argument clearer, such as by repeating key terms from your thesis statement in these sentences or putting them into parallel grammatical form. For more on using topic sentences to signal the stages of a causal argument, see pp. 498–99.

The Beginning and Ending

- *Is the beginning dull?* Try opening with a surprising fact or an engaging anecdote or by emphasizing your subject's puzzling nature.
- *Is the ending weak?* Try to make it more emphatic or more interesting, perhaps by restating your main cause or causes, framing (referring to something mentioned at the beginning), or inviting readers to speculate further.

For a revision checklist, go to bedfordstmartins.com/theguide.

■ Editing and Proofreading

Now is the time to check your revised draft for errors in grammar, punctuation, and mechanics and to consider matters of style. Our research has identified several errors that are especially likely to occur in essays speculating about causes. The following guidelines are designed to help you check and edit your essay for these common errors.

A Note on Grammar and Spelling Checkers

These tools are good at catching certain types of errors, but currently there is no replacement for a good human proofreader. Grammar checkers in particular are extremely limited in what they can usually find, and often they only give you summary information that is not helpful if you do not already understand the rule in question. They are also prone to give faulty advice for fixing problems and to flag correct items as wrong. Spelling checkers cause fewer problems but cannot catch misspellings that are themselves words, such as *to* for *too*.

Checking Your Use of Numbers.   Whether they are indicating the scope of a phenomenon or citing the increase or decrease of a trend, writers who are speculating about causes often cite dates, percentages, fractions, and other numbers. Look, for example, at these sentences from an essay about increasing reports of sexual harassment in the workplace:

> According to a 1994 survey conducted by the Society for Human Resource Management, the percentage of human resource professionals who have reported that their departments handled at least one sexual harassment complaint rose from 35 percent in 1991 to 65 percent in 1994.

> The jury awarded Weeks $7.1 million in punitive damages, twice what she sought in her lawsuit.

The writer follows the convention of spelling out numbers ("one") that can be written as one or two words and using a combination of numerals and words for a large number ("$7.1 million"). She could have used numerals for the large number: $7,100,000. She uses numerals for dates and percentages.

Conventions for presenting numbers in writing are easy to follow. The following sentences, taken from student essays that speculate about causes, have each been edited to demonstrate conventional ways of using numbers in academic writing.

Spelling Out Numbers and Fractions of One or Two Words

▶ According to the World Health Organization, as many as ~~1~~ *one* person in every ~~50~~ *fifty* may be infected with HIV.

▶ Maybe ~~2/3~~ *two-thirds* of the smoke from a cigarette is released into the air.

Using Figures for Numbers and Fractions of More than Two Words

▶ That year the Japanese automobile industry produced only ~~four thousand eight hundred thirty-seven~~ *4,837* vehicles, mostly trucks and motorbikes.

▶ This study shows that Americans spend an average of ~~five and one-third~~ *5 1/3* hours a day watching television.

Writing Percentages and Dates with Figures

▶ Comparing 1980 to 1960, we can see that time spent viewing television increased ~~twenty-eight~~ *28* percent.

Spelling Out Numbers That Begin a Sentence

▶ *Thirty* ~~30~~ percent of commercial real estate in Washington, D.C., is owned by foreigners.

For practice, go to bedfordstmartins.com/theguide/exercisecentral and click on Numbers.

Checking for *Reason Is Because* Constructions. When you speculate about causes, you need to offer reasons and support for your speculations. Consequently, essays that speculate about causes often contain sentences constructed around a *reason is because* pattern. Since *because* means "for the reason that," such sentences say essentially that "the reason is the reason."

REDUNDANT The *reason* we lost the war *is because* troop morale was down.

If you find this pattern in your writing, here are two ways to edit out the redundancy:

CLEAR The reason we lost the war is that troop morale was down.

CLEAR We lost the war because troop morale was down.

▶ Her research suggests that one reason women attend women's colleges is ~~because~~ *that* they want to avoid certain social pressures.

▶ ~~A reason older~~ *Older* Americans watch so much television ~~is~~ because they tend to be sedentary.

A Writer at Work

■ Analyzing Causes

When a writer is planning an essay that speculates about causes, identifying and analyzing possible causes are the most important parts of invention and research. Here we look at an invention table of causes and analyses that Sheila McClain developed for "Fitness Culture: A Growing Trend in America," which appears in this chapter on pp. 457–60.

McClain worked on this invention in stages, and her table of causes shows how her ideas about her subject evolved. She began the activity with the idea that her subject would be an increase in the number of Americans joining health clubs. Later, as she did research and considered her subject in more detail, she decided it was too narrow and modified it to focus on an increase in interest in fitness and exercise more broadly, with the increase in health-club memberships being one element of this trend for which she could also speculate about causes. As you read through her invention table, notice how the causes and analyses reflect McClain's developing ideas about her subject. With her initial subject in mind, she entered the first three causes in the table and a partial analysis. Then, after she researched her subject and decided to focus on fitness and exercise, she added the other three causes and completed the analysis.

Table of Possible Causes and Analyses

Causes	Analyses
1. Sense of community in going to the gym	Obvious cause. Positive peer pressure keeps people going — they are more likely to exercise on a regular basis and have a greater sense of commitment than if exercising alone. Also, going to a gym substitutes for social activities many people don't have time for today. My mom joined a gym because she said it was motivation for her to do something outside of the home and her office. This could be considered a perpetuating cause.
2. Variety of equipment and activities offered by gyms	Traditional exercises are boring and can be seen as hard work. At a gym, people have the opportunity to work out as strenuously or as gently as they care to, depending on the kind of equipment and classes they choose. Many types of exercise offered by gyms, such as aerobics, are actually considered fun. This could be seen as a sufficient cause for the popularity of gyms.

3. Desire to look better	An increasing emphasis on body image in the media means that people want to look like models and film stars. Going to a gym can help them do so. Again, a perpetuating cause. But would this really be a reason to go to a gym? People with this motivation could run or work out at home.
4. Greater awareness of the benefits of fitness and exercise	Government studies on the benefits of physical activity in the late 80s led both the federal and state governments to make the public more aware of these benefits. This remote cause led to a perpetuating cause. Employers and insurance companies have jumped on the bandwagon — encouraged by insurers, many more companies now pay for employee health-club memberships, leading many more people to participate in exercise. Health and phys ed required in more schools also.
5. Reaction to 9/11	Definitely a hidden and surprising cause. Research has shown an increase in the number of health clubs since the terrorist attacks on the World Trade Center for several reasons — stress leads people to want to be part of a group, working out can empower people feeling helpless, and the tragedy led people to reassess their lifestyle choices and seek out ways of improving themselves.
6. Changing attitudes toward exercise	Combine with #2 above. Inside and outside of gyms, more people are beginning to recognize the emotional benefits of exercise, the endorphin release known as runner's high. As one writer says, exercise is now seen as "a way to enjoy life." Exercise is also a way to improve the quality of one's life.

Once McClain had analyzed these possible causes, she could decide how to use them to make her explanation of her subject convincing. She decided to focus first on cause 4 because it seemed the most fundamental to the trend of increased interest in exercise and fitness, then to write about cause 1 and cause 5, and finally to combine her analyses of causes 2 and 6 because they were closely related. She thought her readers would find these clauses plausible, and she knew she had enough statistics and examples to support them. After discussing her ideas with a friend, she reevaluated cause 3 and found it an objection to her new subject, an increasing interest in "fitness culture." Citing the response of her exercise physiology professor to this objection, she tried with at least some success to refute it.

For more on different types of visuals, see Chapter 25.

The report that the biology student wrote about the possible causes of the difference between the AIDS epidemic in sub-Saharan Africa and North America (described on p. 454) was accompanied by several visuals, including a color map, downloaded from the Internet, that depicted rates of HIV infection across the continent of Africa and a series of pie charts that showed the relationship between gender and AIDS in North America and in two regions of Africa. The student also incorporated several tables that presented statistics and other information that would have otherwise taken up unnecessary space and been difficult to grasp (such as, a bar graph that represents HIV infections at 5-year intervals, showing the spike in infections over the last 20 years).

As seen in these examples, maps, tables, graphs, charts, and diagrams can be used to convey information in a way that is easy to read and comprehend. Readers can glean information from these visuals much more quickly and efficiently than they can from statistics that are contained only in written text.

Color can be an important element in selecting or designing visuals. Considering colors for your visuals can be much like selecting the most effective words to convey your written ideas. In both cases, you want your choices to enhance readers' understanding of and interest in the argument you are making. In the map of Africa, for instance, the seven colors used are clearly distinguishable. The brightest, most vibrant color represents the areas of highest infection rates, while gray appropriately represents areas for which information is not available.

Although visuals can help convey information and make an argument, they cannot do all the work for writers. Visuals can represent information but cannot interpret it. The writer must comment on the in-

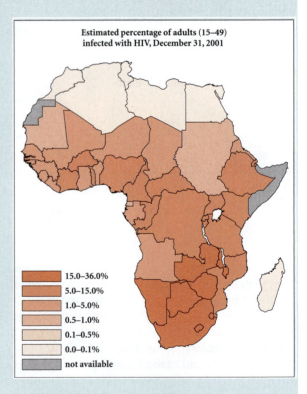

Estimated percentage of adults (15–49) infected with HIV, December 31, 2001

- 15.0–36.0%
- 5.0–15.0%
- 1.0–5.0%
- 0.5–1.0%
- 0.1–0.5%
- 0.0–0.1%
- not available

Spread of AIDS in Sub-Saharan Africa

formation illustrated in visuals — for example, by referring directly to a visual in text, explaining why the information is important, and suggesting what the implications of such information might be.

For an example of an instructional process narrative containing diagrams, see Figure 14.3, p. 637.

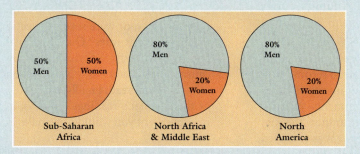

Proportion of Reported AIDS Cases by Gender

Thinking Critically About What You Have Learned

Now that you have worked extensively with essays that speculate about causes — reading them, talking about them, writing one of your own — take some time to reflect on what you have learned about causal speculation. What problems did you encounter while you were writing your essay, and how did you solve them? How did reading other causal speculation essays influence your own essay? What ideas do you have about the social or cultural dimensions of this kind of writing?

Reflecting on Your Writing

Write an explanation of a page or two, telling your instructor about a problem you encountered in writing your essay and how you solved it. Before you begin, gather your invention and planning notes, drafts, readers' comments, revision notes and plans, and final revision. Review these materials as you complete this writing task.

1. ***Identify one writing problem you needed to solve as you worked on your essay.*** Do not be concerned with grammar and punctuation; concentrate instead on problems unique to developing an essay that speculates about causes. For example: Did you have trouble demonstrating that a trend exists? Was it difficult to decide on a logical sequence for presenting causes? Did you worry about the need to identify and address alternative causes?

2. ***Determine how you came to recognize the problem.*** When did you first discover it? What called it to your attention? If someone else pointed out the problem to you, can you now see hints of it in your invention writing? If so, where specifically? When you first recognized the problem, how did you respond?

3. ***Reflect on how you went about solving the problem.*** Did you change the wording of a passage, cut or add causes or refutations, conduct

further research, or move paragraphs or sentences around? Did you reread one of the essays in this chapter to see how another writer handled a similar problem, or did you look back at the invention suggestions? If you talked about the problem with another student, a tutor, or your instructor, did talking about it help? How useful was the advice you received?

4. ***Write an explanation of the problem and your solution.*** Be as specific as possible in reconstructing your efforts. Quote from your invention notes or draft essay, other readers' comments, your revision plan, or your revised essay to show the various changes your writing underwent as you tried to solve the problem. Taking time to explain how you identified a particular problem, how you went about trying to solve it, and what you learned from this experience can help you solve future writing problems more easily.

Reviewing What You Learned from Reading

Write a page or two explaining to your instructor how the readings in this chapter influenced your final essay. Your own essay has undoubtedly been influenced to some extent by one or more of the essays in this chapter as well as by classmates' essays that you have read. These other essays may have helped you decide on an appropriate subject, suggested the need to consider both immediate and background causes, or shown you how to accommodate or refute an important alternative cause. Before you write, take some time to reflect on what you have learned about writing causal speculation from these selections.

1. ***Reread the final revision of your essay; then look back at the selections you read before completing it.*** Do you see any specific influences? For example, if you were impressed with the way one of the readings established the existence of a trend, presented causes in a logical order, used authorities or personal experience and observation to support a cause, or argued convincingly against an alternative cause, look to see where you might have been striving for similar effects in your own

writing. Also look for ideas you got from your reading: writing strategies you were inspired to try, specific details you were led to include, effects you sought to achieve.

2. ***Write an explanation of these influences.*** Did one selection have a particularly strong influence on your essay, or were several selections influential in different ways? Quote from the readings and from your final revision to show how your causal speculation essay was influenced by the selections you read. Finally, based on your review of this chapter's readings, point out any further improvement you would now make in your essay.

Considering the Social Dimensions of Causal Speculation

Persuasive writing, as we define it in this text, deals with probabilities and possibilities, not with certainties. Causal speculation is persuasive writing par excellence because it confronts aspects of social life that we do not yet understand and may never fully understand. Without this great social resource, we would feel helpless in the face of threatening social problems. They would seem like random acts of a chaotic universe. Instead, when confronted with the alarming evidence that the teenage suicide rate is high, we can start speculating about why many teenagers are ending their own lives. We can evaluate competing causes and decide which are the most plausible. Finally, we can take action toward changing the trend, feeling reassured that our knowledge is sound, even though it is speculative and likely to change over time. Nevertheless, cautious readers and writers need to be aware of several problems posed by causal speculation.

The Power of Authority and Ideology.   First, we need to keep in mind that what seems to be the best current explanation for the causes of a trend or phenomenon is not necessarily the only explanation. Speculating about causes tends to give greater voice to certain interests and to minimize or silence others. Some analyses — particularly those of experts such as economists, psychologists, and popular authors — are often granted more authority than analyses favored by parents, teachers, community and religious leaders, and other persons most directly affected.

In addition, we need to remember that causal reasoning is always shaped by the analyst's ideology — the beliefs, values, and attitudes that determine a person's worldview. For example, Stephen King — a horror writer — has a real interest in establishing the horror movie as a legitimate literary and cinematic form; not surprisingly, then, he emphasizes the psychological benefits of horror movies. Erica Goode, whose educational background is in social psychology, is clearly sympathetic to the work of the various psychologists and social scientists she quotes to support her claim that subtle environmental factors contribute to how much people eat. For reasons of their own, spokespersons for the fast-food industry blame very different factors — such as lack of exercise and genetic makeup — for increasing obesity among Americans.

Even the way we define a phenomenon or a trend can affect our explanation of its causes. For example, when four white Los Angeles police officers were videotaped beating a black motorist but acquitted of assault charges in the spring of 1992, many people took to the streets, starting fires, looting, and killing 55 people and injuring 2,383. While some observers called the disturbance a "riot," others used a more sympathetic term — "uprising." These two terms reflect two ways of understanding what happened in the city that spring, pointing to entirely different sets of possible causes. A great deal is at stake when society must decide whether the causes of violent crimes were linked to frustration with racism and unequal justice, on the one hand, or to lack of an adequate police "presence" and respect for the law, on the other hand.

1. *Consider how the readings and your own essay are exercises in exerting authority.* We have said that because causal speculation deals with possibilities instead of certainties, writers must be somewhat tentative about their speculations. However, if causal argument is to be convincing, it cannot be too timid. Writers who have studied a subject carefully may feel that they are justified in exerting their authority. Compare the Erica Goode and Bill Saporito essays. Which seems more assertive? What accounts for your response?

What seems to you assertive or unassertive about your own essay? Was it your knowledge or your ideology — your way of looking at the world — or both that gave you the confidence to be authoritative?

2. *Consider how easy it is to accept a causal explanation.* We have also said that if readers are not alert, they may begin to think that the explanation offered is the only possible one. Is either Goode's or Saporito's argument so seductive that you find yourself accepting it without question? Explain briefly.

3. *Write a page or two explaining your ideas about authority and ideology in essays speculating about causes.* Connect your ideas to your own essay and to the readings in this chapter.

Causes and Blame. Causal speculations sometimes become exercises in assigning blame. For example, not long ago, a woman's "provocative" attire could be cited in court as a cause (and possible justification) for her being raped. Similarly, more recently, homosexuals with AIDS have been blamed for their "lifestyle choices" and immigrants have been blamed for taking jobs and businesses from nonimmigrant Americans. In cases like these, causal speculation can become a way for people to avoid confronting social responsibilities and put off working toward solving serious social problems.

1. *Draw some conclusions about individual and social influences on behavior.* Americans are often divided about whether individuals are primarily responsible for their circumstances or whether social, economic, and political conditions best explain people's difficulties and suffering. Where does Goode position herself on this issue? Explore your own position as well. If you were to write about the causes of obesity among Americans, which kinds of causes — individual or social — would you emphasize? Why?

2. *Write a page or two explaining your ideas on how essays speculating about causes can become exercises in assigning blame.* Connect your ideas to your own essay and to the readings in this chapter.

10 Interpreting Stories

Stories have a special place in most cultures. Elders relate family and cultural history through stories; lessons are taught through moral fables and parables. The bonds of family and community are often strengthened by sharing stories.

Stories have the power to stimulate our feelings and imagination, allowing us to escape our everyday routine and become aware of the wider world around us. They can lead us to look at others with sensitivity and, for a brief time, to see the world through another person's eyes. They can also lead us to see ourselves differently, to gain insight into our innermost feelings and thoughts.

The stories you will read in this chapter may remind you of the essays about remembered events you read and wrote in Chapter 2. Like an autobiographical essay, a story succeeds largely on how well it conveys to readers the significance of an event. As you may remember, essays about remembered events convey significance primarily through vivid descriptive detail showing people in particular places engaged in some kind of dramatic action. Fictional stories work the same way, only the people are called the *characters*, places are called the *setting*, the dramatic action is called the *plot*, and the significance is called the *theme* or *meaning*.

In this chapter, you will be reading and writing essays interpreting a story. The essay interpreting a story is a special kind of academic writing — like the lab report in biology, the ethnography in anthropology, and the brief in law. College students can expect to write interpretive or analytical essays, as they are sometimes called, in English and film studies courses. Although the genre of essays interpreting stories is specialized, you do not have to be an English major to write a successful interpretive essay. Once you have learned the conventions of presenting an interpretive argument, you will be able to use your experience of listening to, viewing, reading, and telling stories to write insightfully about the fictional stories you read.

A Collaborative Activity:
Practice Interpreting a Story

This activity invites you to practice arguing for your interpretation of a story. Get together with two or three other students to discuss your interpretations of a story you have all read. Your instructor may assign a story or may invite you to choose one from this chapter, and he or she may schedule this activity as a face-to-face in-class discussion or ask you to conduct an online real-time discussion. Whatever the medium, here are some guidelines to follow:

Part 1. Begin by picking a question for interpretation for your story from the list below. Members of your group may choose the same question or different ones.

Next take a few minutes to make notes of what you will say. Take turns telling the other group members your interpretation and your reasons for it. The others will react, indicating where they agree and disagree with your interpretation.

Questions for Interpretation

For "The Story of an Hour" (p. 516), how do you interpret the following?

1. The meaning of the final paragraph

2. What Mrs. Mallard feels "was approaching to possess her" and why she tries "to beat it back" in paragraph 10

3. Mrs. Mallard's thoughts in paragraph 14

For "Sunday in the Park" (p. 518), how do you interpret the following?

1. The portrayal of the other boy's father

2. Morton's threat to discipline Larry at the end of the story

3. The relationship between the wife and Morton

For "The Use of Force" (p. 521), how do you interpret the following?

1. The doctor's ambivalence in paragraph 32 about his own actions

2. The doctor's attitude in paragraph 22 toward the girl and her parents

3. The girl's behavior

For "Videotape" (p. 524), how do you interpret the following?

1. The narrator's — and perhaps our society's — fascination with public spectacle and so-called "reality TV"

2. The idea in paragraph 34 that there is a causal connection between serial or other crime and technologies that enable "taping and playing"

3. The behaviors of the "Video Kid" and of the narrator, especially toward his wife

For "Araby" (p. 527), how do you interpret the following?

1. How the boy sees himself at the end of the story

2. Mangan's sister compared to the boy's representation of her

3. The changes the boy undergoes in the story

Part 2. After you have all presented your interpretations and gotten feedback from the group, use the following questions to explore what you learned about interpreting stories:

- What was most challenging for you: choosing a question, responding to it, or giving reasons for your interpretation?

- What one thing said by other members of your group, either in response to your interpretation or in presenting their own interpretations, might lead you to change your interpretation or how you argue for it?

An Anthology of Short Stories

Following are five short stories: "The Story of an Hour," by Kate Chopin; "Sunday in the Park," by Bel Kaufman; "The Use of Force," by William Carlos Williams; "Videotape," by Don DeLillo; and "Araby," by James Joyce. Your instructor may invite the whole class or small groups to discuss one or more of these stories. You may also be asked to choose one of these stories for your interpretive essay.

KATE CHOPIN (1851–1904) was born in St. Louis and lived in Louisiana until her husband died in 1882, leaving her with six children. Encouraged by friends, Chopin wrote her first novel, *At Fault* (1890), when she was nearly forty years old. She wrote many short stories for popular magazines such as *Century*, *Harper's*, and *Vogue*, in which "The Story of an Hour" first appeared in 1894. She published two collections of stories and a second novel, her best-known work, *The Awakening* (1899).

The Story of an Hour
Kate Chopin

Knowing that Mrs. Mallard was afflicted with a heart trouble, great care was taken to break to her as gently as possible the news of her husband's death. [1]

It was her sister Josephine who told her, in broken sentences; veiled hints that revealed in half concealing. Her husband's friend Richards was there, too, near her. It was he who had been in the newspaper office when intelligence of the railroad disaster was received, with Brently Mallard's name leading the list of "killed." He had only taken the time to assure himself of its truth by a second telegram, and had hastened to forestall any less careful, less tender friend in bearing the sad message. [2]

She did not hear the story as many women have heard the same, with a paralyzed inability to accept its significance. She wept at once, with sudden, wild abandonment, in her sister's arms. When the storm of grief had spent itself she went away to her room alone. She would have no one follow her. [3]

There stood, facing the open window, a comfortable, roomy armchair. Into this she sank, pressed down by a physical exhaustion that haunted her body and seemed to reach into her soul. [4]

She could see in the open square before her house the tops of trees that were all aquiver with the new spring life. The delicious breath of rain was in the air. In the street below a peddler was crying his wares. The notes of a distant song which some one was singing reached her faintly, and countless sparrows were twittering in the eaves. [5]

There were patches of blue sky showing here and there through the clouds that had met and piled one above the other in the west facing her window. [6]

She sat with her head thrown back upon the cushion of the chair, quite motionless, except when a sob came up into her throat and shook her, as a child who has cried itself to sleep continues to sob in its dreams.

She was young, with a fair, calm face, whose lines bespoke repression and even a certain strength. But now there was a dull stare in her eyes, whose gaze was fixed away off yonder on one of those patches of blue sky. It was not a glance of reflection, but rather indicated a suspension of intelligent thought.

There was something coming to her and she was waiting for it, fearfully. What was it? She did not know; it was too subtle and elusive to name. But she felt it, creeping out of the sky, reaching toward her through the sounds, the scents, the color that filled the air.

Now her bosom rose and fell tumultuously. She was beginning to recognize this thing that was approaching to possess her, and she was striving to beat it back with her will — as powerless as her two white slender hands would have been.

When she abandoned herself a little whispered word escaped her slightly parted lips. She said it over and over under her breath: "free, free, free!" The vacant stare and the look of terror that had followed it went from her eyes. They stayed keen and bright. Her pulses beat fast, and the coursing blood warmed and relaxed every inch of her body.

She did not stop to ask if it were or were not a monstrous joy that held her. A clear and exalted perception enabled her to dismiss the suggestion as trivial.

She knew that she would weep again when she saw the kind, tender hands folded in death; the face that had never looked save with love upon her, fixed and gray and dead. But she saw beyond that bitter moment a long procession of years to come that would belong to her absolutely. And she opened and spread her arms out to them in welcome.

There would be no one to live for her during those coming years; she would live for herself. There would be no powerful will bending hers in that blind persistence with which men and women believe they have a right to impose a private will upon a fellow-creature. A kind intention or a cruel intention made the act seem no less a crime as she looked upon it in that brief moment of illumination.

And yet she had loved him — sometimes. Often she had not. What did it matter! What could love, the unsolved mystery, count for in face of this possession of self-assertion which she suddenly recognized as the strongest impulse of her being!

"Free! Body and soul free!" she kept whispering.

Josephine was kneeling before the closed door with her lips to the keyhole, imploring for admission. "Louise, open the door! I beg; open the door — you will make yourself ill. What are you doing, Louise? For heaven's sake open the door."

"Go away. I am not making myself ill." No; she was drinking in a very elixir of life through that open window.

Her fancy was running riot along those days ahead of her. Spring days, and summer days, and all sorts of days that would be her own. She breathed a quick prayer that life might be long. It was only yesterday she had thought with a shudder that life might be long.

She arose at length and opened the door to her sister's importunities. There [20] was a feverish triumph in her eyes, and she carried herself unwittingly like a goddess of Victory. She clasped her sister's waist, and together they descended the stairs. Richards stood waiting for them at the bottom.

Some one was opening the front door with a latchkey. It was Brently Mallard [21] who entered, a little travel-stained, composedly carrying his gripsack and umbrella. He had been far from the scene of accident, and did not even know there had been one. He stood amazed at Josephine's piercing cry; at Richards' quick motion to screen him from the view of his wife.

But Richards was too late. [22]

When the doctors came they said she had died of heart disease — of joy that kills. [23]

BEL KAUFMAN (b. 1911) wrote *Up the Down Staircase* (1965), called by *Time* magazine "easily the most popular novel about U.S. public schools in history" and made into both a film and a play. Her story "Sunday in the Park" won the National Education Association/PEN Short Story Contest in 1983. The granddaughter of the great short-story writer Sholom Aleichem, Kaufman grew up in Russia and learned English after she came to the United States at age twelve.

Sunday in the Park

Bel Kaufman

It was still warm in the late-afternoon sun, and the city noises came muffled [1] through the trees in the park. She put her book down on the bench, removed her sunglasses, and sighed contentedly. Morton was reading the *Times Magazine* section, one arm flung around her shoulder; their three-year-old son, Larry, was playing in the sandbox: a faint breeze fanned her hair softly against her cheek. It was five-thirty of a Sunday afternoon, and the small playground, tucked away in a corner of the park, was all but deserted. The swings and seesaws stood motionless and abandoned, the slides were empty, and only in the sandbox two little boys squatted diligently side by side. *How good this is*, she thought, and almost smiled at her sense of well-being. They must go out in the sun more often; Morton was so city-pale, cooped up all week inside the gray factory-like university. She squeezed his arm affectionately and glanced at Larry, delighting in the pointed little face frowning in concentration over the tunnel he was digging. The other boy suddenly stood up and with a quick, deliberate swing of his chubby arm threw a spadeful of sand at Larry. It just missed his head. Larry continued digging; the boy remained standing, shovel raised, stolid and impassive.

"No, no, little boy." She shook her finger at him, her eyes searching for the [2] child's mother or nurse. "We mustn't throw sand. It may get in someone's eyes and hurt. We must play nicely in the nice sandbox." The boy looked at her in unblinking expectancy. He was about Larry's age but perhaps ten pounds heavier, a husky little boy with none of Larry's quickness and sensitivity in his face. Where was his mother? The only other people left in the playground were two women and a little girl on roller skates leaving now through the gate, and a man on a bench a few feet away. He was a big man, and he seemed to be taking up the whole bench as he held the Sunday comics close to his face. She supposed he was the child's father. He did not look up from his comics, but spat once deftly out of the corner of his mouth. She turned her eyes away.

At that moment, as swiftly as before, the fat little boy threw another spadeful of sand at Larry. This time some of it landed on his hair and forehead. Larry looked up at his mother, his mouth tentative; her expression would tell him whether to cry or not.   3

Her first instinct was to rush to her son, brush the sand out of his hair, and punish the other child, but she controlled it. She always said that she wanted Larry to learn to fight his own battles.   4

"Don't *do* that, little boy," she said sharply, leaning forward on the bench. "You mustn't throw sand!"   5

The man on the bench moved his mouth as if to spit again, but instead he spoke. He did not look at her, but at the boy only.   6

"You go right ahead, Joe," he said loudly. "Throw all you want. This here is a *public* sandbox."   7

She felt a sudden weakness in her knees as she glanced at Morton. He had become aware of what was happening. He put his *Times* down carefully on his lap and turned his fine, lean face toward the man, smiling the shy, apologetic smile he might have offered a student in pointing out an error in his thinking. When he spoke to the man, it was with his usual reasonableness.   8

"You're quite right," he said pleasantly, "but just because this is a public place. . . ."   9

The man lowered his funnies and looked at Morton. He looked at him from head to foot, slowly and deliberately. "Yeah?" His insolent voice was edged with menace. "My kid's got just as good right here as yours, and if he feels like throwing sand, he'll throw it, and if you don't like it, you can take your kid the hell out of here."   10

The children were listening, their eyes and mouths wide open, their spades forgotten in small fists. She noticed the muscle in Morton's jaw tighten. He was rarely angry; he seldom lost his temper. She was suffused with a tenderness for her husband and an impotent rage against the man for involving him in a situation so alien and so distasteful to him.   11

"Now, just a minute," Morton said courteously, "you must realize. . . ."   12

"Aw, shut up," said the man.   13

Her heart began to pound. Morton half rose; the *Times* slid to the ground. Slowly the other man stood up. He took a couple of steps toward Morton, then stopped. He flexed his great arms, waiting. She pressed her trembling knees together. Would there be violence, fighting? How dreadful, how incredible. . . . She   14 must do something, stop them, call for help. She wanted to put her hand on her husband's sleeve, to pull him down, but for some reason she didn't.

Morton adjusted his glasses. He was very pale. "This is ridiculous," he said unevenly. "I must ask you. . . ." 15

"Oh, yeah?" said the man. He stood with his legs spread apart, rocking a little, looking at Morton with utter scorn. "You and who else?" 16

For a moment the two men looked at each other nakedly. Then Morton turned his back on the man and said quietly, "Come on, let's get out of here." He walked awkwardly, almost limping with self-consciousness, to the sandbox. He stooped and lifted Larry and his shovel out. 17

At once Larry came to life; his face lost its rapt expression and he began to kick and cry. "I don't *want* to go home, I want to play better, I don't *want* any supper, I don't *like* supper. . . ." It became a chant as they walked, pulling their child between them, his feet dragging on the ground. In order to get to the exit gate they had to pass the bench where the man sat sprawling again. She was careful not to look at him. With all the dignity she could summon, she pulled Larry's sandy, perspiring little hand, while Morton pulled the other. Slowly and with head high she walked with her husband and child out of the playground. 18

Her first feeling was one of relief that a fight had been avoided, that no one was hurt. Yet beneath it there was a layer of something else, something heavy and inescapable. She sensed that it was more than just an unpleasant incident, more than defeat of reason by force. She felt dimly it had something to do with her and Morton, something acutely personal, familiar, and important. 19

Suddenly Morton spoke. "It wouldn't have proved anything." 20

"What?" she asked. 21

"A fight. It wouldn't have proved anything beyond the fact that he's bigger than I am." 22

"Of course," she said. 23

"The only possible outcome," he continued reasonably, "would have been — what? My glasses broken, perhaps a tooth or two replaced, a couple of days' work missed — and for what? For justice? For truth?" 24

"Of course," she repeated. She quickened her step. She wanted only to get home and to busy herself with her familiar tasks; perhaps then the feeling, glued like heavy plaster on her heart, would be gone. *Of all the stupid, despicable bullies,* she thought, pulling harder on Larry's hand. The child was still crying. Always before she had felt a tender pity for his defenseless little body, the frail arms, the narrow shoulders with sharp, winglike shoulder blades, the thin and unsure legs, but now her mouth tightened in resentment. 25

"Stop crying," she said sharply. "I'm ashamed of you!" She felt as if all three of them were tracking mud along the street. The child cried louder. 26

If there had been an issue involved, she thought, *if there had been something to fight for. . . . But what else could he possibly have done? Allow himself to be beaten? Attempt to educate the man? Call a policeman? "Officer, there's a man in the park who won't stop his child from throwing sand on mine. . . ."* The whole thing was as silly as that, and not worth thinking about. 27

"Can't you keep him quiet, for Pete's sake?" Morton asked irritably.   28

"What do you suppose I've been trying to do?" she asked.   29

Larry pulled back, dragging his feet.   30

"If you can't discipline this child, I will," Morton snapped, making a move toward the boy.   31

But her voice stopped him. She was shocked to hear it, thin and cold and penetrating with contempt. "Indeed?" she heard herself say. "You and who else?"   32

WILLIAM CARLOS WILLIAMS (1883–1963) is one of the most important poets of the twentieth century, best known for his long poem *Paterson* (1946–1958). He also wrote essays, plays, novels, and short stories. "The Use of Force" was published initially in *The Doctor Stories* (1933), a collection loosely based on Williams's experiences as a pediatrician.

The Use of Force
William Carlos Williams

They were new patients to me, all I had was the name, Olson. Please come down as soon as you can, my daughter is very sick.   1

When I arrived I was met by the mother, a big startled-looking woman, very clean and apologetic, who merely said, Is this the doctor? and let me in. In the back, she added. You must excuse us, doctor, we have her in the kitchen where it is warm. It is very damp here sometimes.   2

The child was fully dressed and sitting on her father's lap near the kitchen table. He tried to get up, but I motioned for him not to bother, took off my overcoat and started to look things over. I could see that they were all very nervous, eyeing me up and down distrustfully. As often, in such cases, they weren't telling me more than they had to, it was up to me to tell them; that's why they were spending three dollars on me.   3

The child was fairly eating me up with her cold, steady eyes, and no expression to her face whatever. She did not move and seemed, inwardly, quiet; an unusually attractive little thing, and as strong as a heifer in appearance. But her face was flushed, she was breathing rapidly, and I realized that she had a high fever. She had magnificent blonde hair, in profusion. One of those picture children often reproduced in advertising leaflets and the photogravure sections of the Sunday papers.   4

She's had a fever for three days, began the father, and we don't know what it comes from. My wife has given her things, you know, like people do, but it don't do no good. And there's been a lot of sickness around. So we tho't you better look her over and tell us what is the matter.   5

As doctors often do I took a trial shot at it as a point of departure. Has she had a sore throat?   6

Both parents answered me together, No . . . No, she says her throat don't hurt her.   7

Does your throat hurt you? added the mother to the child. But the little girl's expression didn't change nor did she move her eyes from my face.   8

Have you looked?   9

I tried, said the mother, but I couldn't see.   10

As it happens we had been having a number of cases of diphtheria in the school to which this child went during that month and we were all, quite apparently, thinking of that, though no one had as yet spoken of the thing.   11

Well, I said, suppose we take a look at the throat first. I smiled in my best professional manner and asking for the child's first name I said, come on, Mathilda, open your mouth and let's take a look at your throat.   12

Nothing doing.   13

Aw, come on, I coaxed, just open your mouth wide and let me take a look. Look, I said opening both hands wide, I haven't anything in my hands. Just open up and let me see.   14

Such a nice man, put in the mother. Look how kind he is to you. Come on, do what he tells you to. He won't hurt you.   15

At that I ground my teeth in disgust. If only they wouldn't use the word "hurt" I might be able to get somewhere. But I did not allow myself to be hurried or disturbed but speaking quietly and slowly I approached the child again.   16

As I moved my chair a little nearer suddenly with one catlike movement both her hands clawed instinctively for my eyes and she almost reached them too. In fact she knocked my glasses flying and they fell, though unbroken, several feet away from me on the kitchen floor.   17

Both the mother and father almost turned themselves inside out in embarrassment and apology. You bad girl, said the mother, taking her and shaking her by one arm. Look what you've done. The nice man . . .   18

For heaven's sake, I broke in. Don't call me a nice man to her. I'm here to look at her throat on the chance that she might have diphtheria and possibly die of it. But that's nothing to her. Look here, I said to the child, we're going to look at your throat. You're old enough to understand what I'm saying. Will you open it now by yourself or shall we have to open it for you?   19

Not a move. Even her expression hadn't changed. Her breaths however were coming faster and faster. Then the battle began. I had to do it. I had to have a throat culture for her own protection. But first I told the parents that it was entirely up to them. I explained the danger but said that I would not insist on a throat examination so long as they would take the responsibility.   20

If you don't do what the doctor says you'll have to go to the hospital, the mother admonished her severely.   21

Oh yeah? I had to smile to myself. After all, I had already fallen in love with the savage brat, the parents were contemptible to me. In the ensuing struggle they grew more and more abject, crushed, exhausted while she surely rose to magnificent heights of insane fury of effort bred of her terror of me.   22

The father tried his best, and he was a big man, but the fact that she was his daughter, his shame at her behavior and his dread of hurting her made him release her just at the critical times when I had almost achieved success, till I wanted to kill him. But his dread also that she might have diphtheria made him tell me to go on, go on though he himself was almost fainting, while the mother moved back and forth behind us raising and lowering her hands in an agony of apprehension. 23

Put her in front of you on your lap, I ordered, and hold both her wrists. 24

But as soon as he did the child let out a scream. Don't, you're hurting me. Let go of my hands. Let them go I tell you. Then she shrieked terrifyingly, hysterically. Stop it! Stop it! You're killing me! 25

Do you think she can stand it, doctor! said the mother. 26

You get out, said the husband to his wife. Do you want her to die of diphtheria? 27

Come on now, hold her, I said. 28

Then I grasped the child's head with my left hand and tried to get the wooden tongue depressor between her teeth. She fought, with clenched teeth, desperately! But now I also had grown furious — at a child. I tried to hold myself down but I couldn't. I know how to expose a throat for inspection. And I did my best. When finally I got the wooden spatula behind the last teeth and just the point of it into the mouth cavity, she opened up for an instant but before I could see anything she came down again and gripping the wooden blade between her molars she reduced it to splinters before I could get it out again. 29

Aren't you ashamed, the mother yelled at her. Aren't you ashamed to act like that in front of the doctor? 30

Get me a smooth-handled spoon of some sort, I told the mother. We're going through with this. The child's mouth was already bleeding. Her tongue was cut and she was screaming in wild hysterical shrieks. Perhaps I should have desisted and come back in an hour or more. No doubt it would have been better. But I have seen at least two children lying dead in bed of neglect in such cases, and feeling that I must get a diagnosis now or never I went at it again. But the worst of it was that I too had got beyond reason. I could have torn the child apart in my own fury and enjoyed it. It was a pleasure to attack her. My face was burning with it. 31

The damned little brat must be protected against her own idiocy, one says to oneself at such times. Others must be protected against her. It is a social necessity. And all these things are true. But a blind fury, a feeling of adult shame, bred of a longing for muscular release are the operatives. One goes on to the end. 32

In a final unreasoning assault I overpowered the child's neck and jaws. I forced the heavy silver spoon back of her teeth and down her throat till she gagged. And there it was — both tonsils covered with membrane. She had fought valiantly to keep me from knowing her secret. She had been hiding that sore throat for three days at least and lying to her parents in order to escape just such an outcome as this. 33

Now truly she was furious. She had been on the defensive before but now she attacked. Tried to get off her father's lap and fly at me while tears of defeat blinded her eyes. 34

DON DeLILLO (b. 1936) writes stories, essays, plays, and screenplays but is best known for his novels, including *White Noise* (1985), winner of the National Book Award, and *Underworld* (1997), winner of the William Dean Howells Award. "Videotape" was originally published in 1994 in *Antaeus*, a literary magazine, but later it became a section of *Underworld*.

Videotape

Don DeLillo

It shows a man driving a car. It is the simplest sort of family video. You see a man at the wheel of a medium Dodge. 1

It is just a kid aiming her camera through the rear window of the family car at the windshield of the car behind her. 2

You know about families and their video cameras. You know how kids get involved; how the camera shows them that every subject is potentially charged, a million things they never see with the unaided eye. They investigate the meaning of inert objects and dumb pets and they poke at family privacy. They learn to see things twice. 3

It is the kid's own privacy that is being protected here. She is twelve years old and her name is being withheld even though she is neither the victim nor the perpetrator of the crime but only the means of recording it. 4

It shows a man in a sport shirt at the wheel of his car. There is nothing else to see. The car approaches briefly, then falls back. 5

You know how children with cameras learn to work the exposed moments that define the family cluster. They break every trust, spy out the undefended space, catching mom coming out of the bathroom in her cumbrous robe and turbaned towel, looking bloodless and plucked. It is not a joke. They will shoot you sitting on the pot if they can manage a suitable vantage. 6

The tape has the jostled sort of noneventness that marks the family product. Of course the man in this case is not a member of the family but a stranger in a car, a random figure, someone who has happened along in the slow lane. 7

It shows a man in his forties wearing a pale shirt open at the throat, the image washed by reflections and sunglint, with many jostled moments. 8

It is not just another video homicide. It is a homicide recorded by a child who thought she was doing something simple and maybe halfway clever, shooting some tape of a man in a car. 9

He sees the girl and waves briefly, wagging a hand without taking it off the wheel — an underplayed reaction that makes you like him. 10

It is unrelenting footage that rolls on and on. It has an aimless determination, a persistence that lives outside the subject matter. You are looking into the mind of home video. It is innocent, it is aimless, it is determined, it is real. 11

He is bald up the middle of his head, a nice guy in his forties whose whole life seems open to the hand-held camera. 12

But there is also an element of suspense. You keep on looking not because you know something is going to happen — of course you do know something is going to happen and you do look for that reason but you might also keep on looking if you came across this footage for the first time without knowing the outcome. There is a crude power operating here. You keep on looking because things combine to hold you fast — a sense of the random, the amateurish, the accidental, the impending. You don't think of the tape as boring or interesting. It is crude, it is blunt, it is relentless. It is the jostled part of your mind, the film that runs through your hotel brain under all the thoughts you know you're thinking.

The world is lurking in the camera, already framed, waiting for the boy or girl who will come along and take up the device, learn the instrument, shooting old Granddad at breakfast, all stroked out so his nostrils gape, the cereal spoon baby-gripped in his pale fist.

It shows a man alone in a medium Dodge. It seems to go on forever.

There's something about the nature of the tape, the grain of the image, the sputtering black-and-white tones, the starkness — you think this is more real, truer-to-life than anything around you. The things around you have a rehearsed and layered and cosmetic look. The tape is superreal, or maybe underreal is the way you want to put it. It is what lies at the scraped bottom of all the layers you have added. And this is another reason why you keep on looking. The tape has a searing realness.

It shows him giving an abbreviated wave, stiff-palmed, like a signal flag at a siding.

You know how families make up games. This is just another game in which the child invents the rules as she goes along. She likes the idea of videotaping a man in his car. She has probably never done it before and she sees no reason to vary the format or terminate early or pan to another car. This is her game and she is learning it and playing it at the same time. She feels halfway clever and inventive and maybe slightly intrusive as well, a little bit of brazenness that spices any game.

And you keep on looking. You look because this is the nature of the footage, to make a channeled path through time, to give things a shape and a destiny.

Of course if she had panned to another car, the right car at the precise time, she would have caught the gunman as he fired.

The chance quality of the encounter. The victim, the killer, and the child with a camera. Random energies that approach a common point. There's something here that speaks to you directly, saying terrible things about forces beyond your control, lines of intersection that cut through history and logic and every reasonable layer of human expectation.

She wandered into it. The girl got lost and wandered clear-eyed into horror. This is a children's story about straying too far from home. But it isn't the family car that serves as the instrument of the child's curiosity, her inclination to explore. It is the camera that puts her in the tale.

You know about holidays and family celebrations and how somebody shows up with a camcorder and the relatives stand around and barely react because they're numbingly accustomed to the process of being taped and decked and shown on the VCR with the coffee and cake.

He is hit soon after. If you've seen the tape many times you know from the hand wave exactly when he will be hit. It is something, naturally, that you wait for. You say to your wife, if you're at home and she is there, Now here is where he gets it. You say: Janet, hurry up, this is where it happens.

24

Now here is where he gets it. You see him jolted, sort of wire-shocked — then he seizes up and falls toward the door or maybe leans or slides into the door is the proper way to put it. It is awful and unremarkable at the same time. The car stays in the slow lane. It approaches briefly, then falls back.

25

You don't usually call your wife over to the TV set. She has her programs, you have yours. But there's a certain urgency here. You want her to see how it looks. The tape has been running forever and now the thing is finally going to happen and you want her to be here when he's shot.

26

Here it comes, all right. He is shot, head-shot, and the camera reacts, the child reacts — there is a jolting movement but she keeps on taping, there is a sympathetic response, a nerve response, her heart is beating faster but she keeps the camera trained on the subject as he slides into the door and even as you see him die you're thinking of the girl. At some level the girl has to be present here, watching what you're watching, unprepared — the girl is seeing this cold and you have to marvel at the fact that she keeps the tape rolling.

27

It shows something awful and unaccompanied. You want your wife to see it because it is real this time, not fancy movie violence — the realess beneath the layers of cosmetic perception. Hurry up, Janet, here it comes. He dies so fast. There is no accompaniment of any kind. It is very stripped. You want to tell her it is realer than real but then she will ask what that means.

28

The way the camera reacts to the gunshot — a startle reaction that brings pity and terror into the frame, the girl's own shock, the girl's identification with the victim.

29

You don't see the blood, which is probably trickling behind his ear and down the back of his neck. The way his head is twisted away from the door, the twist of the head gives you only a partial profile and it's the wrong side, it's not the side where he was hit.

30

And maybe you're being a little aggressive here, practically forcing your wife to watch. Why? What are you telling her? Are you making a little statement? Like I'm going to ruin your day out of ordinary spite. Or a big statement? Like this is the risk of existing. Either way you're rubbing her face in this tape and you don't know why.

31

It shows the car drifting toward the guardrail and then there's a jostling sense of two other lanes and part of another car, a split-second blur, and the tape ends here, either because the girl stopped shooting or because some central authority, the police or the district attorney or the TV station, decided there was nothing else you had to see.

32

This is either the tenth or eleventh homicide committed by the Texas Highway Killer. The number is uncertain because the police believe that one of the shootings may have been a copycat crime.

33

And there is something about videotape, isn't there, and this particular kind of serial crime? This is a crime designed for random taping and immediate playing. You sit there and wonder if this kind of crime became more possible when the means of taping and playing an event — playing it immediately after the taping — became part of the culture. The principal doesn't necessarily commit the sequence

34

of crimes in order to see them taped and played. He commits the crimes as if they were a form of taped and played event. The crimes are inseparable from the idea of taping and playing. You sit there thinking that the serial murderer has found its medium, or vice versa — an act of shadow technology, of compressed time and repeated images, stark and glary and unremarkable.

It shows very little in the end. It is a famous murder because it is on tape and because the murderer has done it many times and because the crime was recorded by a child. So the child is involved, the Video Kid as she is sometimes called because they have to call her something. The tape is famous and so is she. She is famous in the modern manner of people whose names are strategically withheld. They are famous without names or faces, spirits living apart from their bodies, the victims and witnesses, the underage criminals, out there somewhere at the edges of perception.   35

Seeing someone at the moment he dies, dying unexpectedly. This is reason alone to stay fixed to the screen. It is instructional, watching a man shot dead as he drives along on a sunny day. It demonstrates an elemental truth, that every breath you take has two possible endings. And that's another thing. There's a joke locked away here, a note of cruel slapstick that you are willing to appreciate even if it makes you feel a little guilty. Maybe the victim's a chump, a dope, classically unlucky. He had it coming, in a way, like an innocent fool in a silent movie.   36

You don't want Janet to give you any crap about it's on all the time, they show it a thousand times a day. They show it because it exists, because they have to show it, because this is why they're out there. The horror freezes your soul but this doesn't mean that you want them to stop.   37

JAMES JOYCE (1882–1941), a native of Dublin, Ireland, is considered one of the most influential writers of the early twentieth century. "Araby," one of his most often anthologized stories, first appeared in the collection *Dubliners* in 1914. Like his novel *Portrait of the Artist as a Young Man*, published two years later, it relies on scenes from Joyce's own boyhood.

Araby

James Joyce

North Richmond Street, being blind,[1] was a quiet street except at the hour when the Christian Brothers' School set the boys free. An uninhabited house of two storeys stood at the blind end, detached from its neighbours in a square ground. The other houses of the street, conscious of decent lives within them, gazed at one another with brown imperturbable faces.   1

---

[1] A dead end. The young Joyce in fact lived for a time on North Richmond Street in Dublin.

The former tenant of our house, a priest, had died in the back drawing-room. Air, musty from having been long enclosed, hung in all the rooms, and the waste room behind the kitchen was littered with old useless papers. Among these I found a few paper-covered books, the pages of which were curled and damp: *The Abbot*, by Walter Scott, *The Devout Communicant* and *The Memoirs of Vidocq*.[2] I liked the last best because its leaves were yellow. The wild garden behind the house contained a central apple-tree and a few straggling bushes under one of which I found the late tenant's rusty bicycle-pump. He had been a very charitable priest; in his will he had left all his money to institutions and the furniture of his house to his sister.

When the short days of winter came dusk fell before we had well eaten our dinners. When we met in the street the houses had grown sombre. The space of sky above us was the colour of ever-changing violet and towards it the lamps of the street lifted their feeble lanterns. The cold air stung us and we played till our bodies glowed. Our shouts echoed in the silent street. The career of our play brought us through the dark muddy lanes behind the houses where we ran the gauntlet of the rough tribes from the cottages, to the back doors of the dark dripping gardens where odours arose from the ashpits, to the dark odorous stables where a coachman smoothed and combed the horse or shook music from the buckled harness. When we returned to the street light from the kitchen windows had filled the areas. If my uncle was seen turning the corner we hid in the shadow until we had seen him safely housed. Or if Mangan's sister came out on the doorstep to call her brother in to his tea we watched her from our shadow peer up and down the street. We waited to see whether she would remain or go in and, if she remained, we left our shadow and walked up to Mangan's steps resignedly. She was waiting for us, her figure defined by the light from the half-opened door. Her brother always teased her before he obeyed and I stood by the railings looking at her. Her dress swung as she moved her body and the soft rope of her hair tossed from side to side.

Every morning I lay on the floor in the front parlour watching her door. The blind was pulled down to within an inch of the sash so that I could not be seen. When she came out on the doorstep my heart leaped. I ran to the hall, seized my books and followed her. I kept her brown figure always in my eye and, when we came near the point at which our ways diverged, I quickened my pace and passed her. This happened morning after morning. I had never spoken to her, except for a few casual words, and yet her name was like a summons to all my foolish blood.

Her image accompanied me even in places the most hostile to romance. On Saturday evenings when my aunt went marketing I had to go to carry some of the parcels. We walked through the flaring streets, jostled by drunken men and bargaining women, amid the curses of labourers, the shrill litanies of shop-boys who stood on guard by the barrels of pigs' cheeks, the nasal chanting of street-

---

[2] *The Devout Communicant* is a collection of religious meditations. *The Abbot* is a historical romance set in the court of Mary, Queen of Scots, a Catholic, who was beheaded for plotting to assassinate her Protestant cousin, Queen Elizabeth I. *The Memoirs of Vidocq* is a collection of sexually suggestive stories about a French criminal turned detective.

singers, who sang a *come-all-you* about O'Donovan Rossa,³ or a ballad about the troubles in our native land. These noises converged in a single sensation of life for me: I imagined that I bore my chalice safely through a throng of foes. Her name sprang to my lips at moments in strange prayers and praises which I myself did not understand. My eyes were often full of tears (I could not tell why) and at times a flood from my heart seemed to pour itself out into my bosom. I thought little of the future. I did not know whether I would ever speak to her or not or, if I spoke to her, how I could tell her of my confused adoration. But my body was like a harp and her words and gestures were like fingers running upon the wires.

One evening I went into the back drawing-room in which the priest had died. It was a dark rainy evening and there was no sound in the house. Through one of the broken panes I heard the rain impinge upon the earth, the fine incessant needles of water playing in the sodden beds. Some distant lamp or lighted window gleamed below me. I was thankful that I could see so little. All my senses seemed to desire to veil themselves and, feeling that I was about to slip from them, I pressed the palms of my hands together until they trembled, murmuring: *"O love! O love!"* many times.

At last she spoke to me. When she addressed the first words to me I was so confused that I did not know what to answer. She asked me was I going to Araby. I forgot whether I answered yes or no. It would be a splendid bazaar, she said she would love to go.⁴

"And why can't you?" I asked.

While she spoke she turned a silver bracelet round and round her wrist. She could not go, she said, because there would be a retreat that week in her convent. Her brother and two other boys were fighting for their caps and I was alone at the railings. She held one of the spikes, bowing her head towards me. The light from the lamp opposite our door caught the white curve of her neck, lit up her hair that rested there and, falling, lit up the hand upon the railing. It fell over one side of her dress and caught the white border of a petticoat, just visible as she stood at ease.

"It's well for you," she said.

"If I go," I said, "I will bring you something."

What innumerable follies laid waste my waking and sleeping thoughts after that evening! I wished to annihilate the tedious intervening days. I chafed against the work of school. At night in my bedroom and by day in the classroom her image came between me and the page I strove to read. The syllables of the word *Araby* were called to me through the silence in which my soul luxuriated and cast an Eastern enchantment over me. I asked for leave to go to the bazaar on Saturday night. My aunt was surprised and hoped it was not some Freemason affair.⁵ I answered few questions in class. I watched my master's face pass from amiability

---

³ A contemporary leader of an underground organization opposed to British rule of Ireland.

⁴ Traveling bazaars featured cafés, shopping stalls, and entertainment. Araby was the name of an English bazaar that visited Dublin when Joyce was a boy.

⁵ The Freemasons is a secretive fraternal order that has a long history and that has traditionally been opposed by the Catholic Church.

to sternness; he hoped I was not beginning to idle. I could not call my wandering thoughts together. I had hardly any patience with the serious work of life which, now that it stood between me and my desire, seemed to me child's play, ugly monotonous child's play.

On Saturday morning I reminded my uncle that I wished to go to the bazaar in the evening. He was fussing at the hallstand, looking for the hatbrush, and answered me curtly: 13

"Yes, boy, I know."   14

As he was in the hall I could not go into the front parlour and lie at the window. I left the house in bad humour and walked slowly towards the school. The air was pitilessly raw and already my heart misgave me.   15

When I came home to dinner my uncle had not yet been home. Still it was early. I sat staring at the clock for some time and, when its ticking began to irritate me, I left the room. I mounted the staircase and gained the upper part of the house. The high cold empty gloomy rooms liberated me and I went from room to room singing. From the front window I saw my companions playing below in the street. Their cries reached me weakened and indistinct and, leaning my forehead against the cool glass, I looked over at the dark house where she lived. I may have stood there for an hour, seeing nothing but the brown-clad figure cast by my imagination, touched discreetly by the lamplight at the curved neck, at the hand upon the railings and at the border below the dress.   16

When I came downstairs again I found Mrs. Mercer sitting at the fire. She was an old garrulous woman, a pawnbroker's widow, who collected used stamps for some pious purpose. I had to endure the gossip of the tea-table. The meal was prolonged beyond an hour and still my uncle did not come. Mrs. Mercer stood up to go: she was sorry she couldn't wait any longer, but it was after eight o'clock and she did not like to be out late, as the night air was bad for her. When she had gone I began to walk up and down the room, clenching my fists. My aunt said: 17

"I'm afraid you may put off your bazaar for this night of Our Lord."   18

At nine o'clock I heard my uncle's latchkey in the halldoor. I heard him talking to himself and heard the hallstand rocking when it had received the weight of his overcoat. I could interpret these signs. When he was midway through his dinner I asked him to give me the money to go to the bazaar. He had forgotten.   19

"The people are in bed and after their first sleep now," he said.   20

I did not smile. My aunt said to him energetically: 21

"Can't you give him the money and let him go? You've kept him late enough as it is."   22

My uncle said he was very sorry he had forgotten. He said he believed in the old saying: "All work and no play makes Jack a dull boy." He asked me where I was going and, when I had told him a second time he asked me did I know *The Arab's Farewell to His Steed*. When I left the kitchen he was about to recite the opening lines of the piece to my aunt.   23

I held a florin tightly in my hand as I strode down Buckingham Street towards the station. The sight of the streets thronged with buyers and glaring with gas recalled to me the purpose of my journey. I took my seat in a third-class carriage   24 of a deserted train. After an intolerable delay the train moved out of the station slowly. It crept onward among ruinous houses and over the twinkling river. At Westland Row Station a crowd of people pressed to the carriage doors; but the porters moved them back, saying that it was a special train for the bazaar. I remained alone in the bare carriage. In a few minutes the train drew up beside an improvised wooden platform. I passed out on to the road and saw by the lighted dial of a clock that it was ten minutes to ten. In front of me was a large building which displayed the magical name.

I could not find any sixpenny entrance and, fearing that the bazaar would be closed, I passed in quickly through a turnstile, handing a shilling to a weary-looking man. I found myself in a big hall girdled at half its height by a gallery. Nearly all the stalls were closed and the greater part of the hall was in darkness. I recognised a silence like that which pervades a church after a service. I walked into the centre of the bazaar timidly. A few people were gathered about the stalls which were still open. Before a curtain, over which the words *Café Chantant*[6] were written in coloured lamps, two men were counting money on a salver. I listened to the fall of the coins.

Remembering with difficulty why I had come I went over to one of the stalls and examined porcelain vases and flowered tea-sets. At the door of the stall a young lady was talking and laughing with two young gentlemen. I remarked their English accents and listened vaguely to their conversation.

"O, I never said such a thing!"

"O, but you did!"

"O, but I didn't!"

"Didn't she say that?"

"Yes. I heard her."

"O, there's a . . . fib!"

Observing me the young lady came over and asked me did I wish to buy anything. The tone of her voice was not encouraging; she seemed to have spoken to me out of a sense of duty. I looked humbly at the great jars that stood like eastern guards at either side of the dark entrance to the stall and murmured:

"No, thank you."

The young lady changed the position of one of the vases and went back to the two young men. They began to talk of the same subject. Once or twice the young lady glanced at me over her shoulder.

I lingered before her stall, though I knew my stay was useless, to make my interest in her wares seem the more real. Then I turned away slowly and walked down the middle of the bazaar. I allowed the two pennies to fall against the sixpence in my pocket. I heard a voice call from one end of the gallery that the light was out. The upper part of the hall was now completely dark.

Gazing up into the darkness I saw myself as a creature driven and derided by vanity; and my eyes burned with anguish and anger.

---

[6] Literally, *singing café* (French), a music hall.

Readings

The following two readings are essays written by students. Sally Crane and David Ratinov argue for different ways of understanding the ending of "Araby," the preceding short story by James Joyce. The Analyzing Writing Strategies section and the Commentary following each reading touch on a few features best illustrated by that essay, capturing its special qualities and strengths.

SALLY CRANE wrote this interpretive essay about James Joyce's "Araby" (p. 527) for her composition course. As her title suggests, Crane focuses on what the final scene tells about the boy's character. During class discussion, most of the other students said they thought the boy changes at the end of the story. In her essay, Crane argues that he is just as much in the dark at the end of the story as he was at the beginning. (*Note:* In citing paragraphs, Crane followed her instructor's special directions rather than MLA style.)

Gazing into the Darkness
Sally Crane

Crane takes a position in the debate on the final scene's meaning.

Here she forecasts her reasons.

Paragraphs 3–6 develop and support Crane's first reason: the imagery of blindness.

Readers of "Araby" often focus on the final scene as the key to the story. They assume the boy experiences some profound insight about himself when he gazes "up into the darkness" (para. 37). I believe, however, that the boy sees nothing and learns nothing — about either himself or others. He's not self-reflective; he's merely self-absorbed. [1]

The evidence supporting this interpretation is the imagery of blindness and the ironic point of view of the narrator. There can seem to be a profound insight at the end of the story only if we empathize with the boy and adopt his point of view. In other words, we must assume that the young boy is narrating his own story. But if the real narrator is the grown man looking back at his early adolescence, then it becomes possible to read the narrative as ironic and to see the boy as confused and blind. [2]

The story opens and closes with images of blindness. The street is "blind" with an "uninhabited house . . . at the blind end" (para. 1). As he spies on Mangan's sister, from his own house, the boy intentionally limits what he is able to see by lowering the "blind" until it is only an inch from the window sash (para. 4). At the bazaar in the closing scene, "the light was out," and the upper part of the hall was "completely dark" (para. 36). The boy is left "gazing up into the darkness," seeing nothing but an inner torment that burns his eyes (para. 37). [3]

This pattern of imagery includes images of reading, and reading stands for the boy's inability to understand what is before his eyes. When he tries to read [4]

532

at night, for example, the girl's "image [comes] between [him] and the page," in effect blinding him (para. 12). In fact, he seems blind to everything except this "image" of the "brown-clad figure cast by [his] imagination" (para. 16). The girl's "brown-clad figure" is also associated with the houses on "blind" North Richmond Street, with their "brown imperturbable faces" (para. 1). The houses stare back at the boy, unaffected by his presence and gaze.

The most important face he tries and fails to read belongs to Mangan's sister. His description of her and interpretation of the few words she says to him can be seen as further evidence of his blindness. He sees only what he wants to see, the "image" he has in his mind's eye (para. 5). This image comes more from what he's read than from anything he's observed. He casts her simultaneously in the traditional female roles of angel and whore:

> While she spoke she turned a silver bracelet round and round her wrist. She could not go, she said, because there would be a retreat that week in her convent. . . . She held one of the spikes, bowing her head towards me. The light from the lamp opposite our door caught the white curve of her neck, lit up her hair that rested there and, falling, lit up the hand upon the railing. It fell over one side of her dress and caught the white border of a petticoat, just visible as she stood at ease. (para. 9)

Her angelic qualities are shown in her plans to attend a convent retreat and in her bowed head. Her whorish qualities come through in the way she flirtatiously plays with the bracelet, as if she were inviting him to buy her an expensive piece of jewelry at the bazaar. The "white curve of her neck" and the "white border of a petticoat" combine the symbolic color of purity, associated with the Madonna, with sexual suggestiveness (para. 9). The point is that there is no suggestion here or anywhere else in the story that the boy is capable of seeing Mangan's sister as a real person. She only exists as the object of his adoring gaze. In fact, no one seems to have any reality for him other than himself.

He is totally self-absorbed. But at the same time, he is also blind to himself. He says repeatedly that he doesn't understand his feelings: "Her name sprang to my lips at moments in strange prayers and praises which I myself did not understand. My eyes were often full of tears (I could not tell why)" (para. 5). His adoration of her is both "confused" and confusing to him. He has no self-understanding (para. 5).

The best insight we have into the boy comes from the language he uses. Much of his language seems to mimic the old priest's romantic books: "Her name was like a summons to all my foolish blood" (para. 4); "I imagined that I bore my chalice safely through a throng of foes" (para. 5); "my body was like a harp and her words and gestures were like fingers running upon the wires" (para. 5). Language like this sounds as though it comes out of a popular romance novel, something written by Danielle Steele perhaps. The mixing of romance with soft porn is unmistakable. Perhaps the boy has spent too much time reading the priest's sexually seductive stories from *The Memoirs of Vidocq* (para. 2).

5   In paragraphs 5 and 6, to support her argument about the boy's inability to "read" Mangan's sister, Crane quotes and analyzes a passage from the story.

6   Here Crane develops more support for her first reason, pointing out the boy's lack of *self*-awareness.

7   To introduce her second reason, about the narrator's ironic viewpoint, she quotes a series of phrases from the story.

Here Crane explains why she thinks the story is ironic, making fun of the boy's romantic "quest."

I think this language is meant to be ironic, to point to the fact that the narrator is not the young boy himself but the young boy now grown and looking back at how "foolish" he was (para. 4). This interpretation becomes likely when you think of "Araby" as a fictionalized autobiography. In autobiographical stories, remembered feelings and thoughts are combined with the autobiographer's present perspective. The remembered feelings and thoughts in this story could be seen as expressing the boy's point of view, but we read them ironically through the adult narrator's present perspective. The romantic, gushy language the boy uses is laughable. It reveals the boy's blindness toward everyone, including himself. He sees himself as Sir Galahad, the chivalric hero on his own grail quest to Araby. The greatest irony comes at the end when his quest is exposed as merely a shopping trip and Araby as merely a suburban mall.

Crane concludes by summarizing the main points of her argument.

Most people interpret the ending as a moment of profound insight, and the language certainly seems to support this interpretation: "Gazing up into the darkness I saw myself as a creature driven and derided by vanity; and my eyes burned with anguish and anger" (para. 37). But here again we see the narrator using inflated language that suggests an ironic stance. So even in the moment of apparent insight, the boy is still playing a heroic role. He hasn't discovered his true self. He's just as self-absorbed and blind in the end as he was at the beginning.

Analyzing Writing Strategies

For more on reasons and support, see Chapter 19, pp. 674–80.

1. To see how interpretive essays develop and **support** their reasons, reread paragraph 5, where Crane argues that the boy cannot see the reality of Mangan's sister, only the two competing images of women he has learned from his religious training and romantic reading. To support this reason, Crane quotes a long passage from the story. Describe what she does in the rest of the paragraph following the indented quote.

2. One of the **reasons** Crane gives for her interpretation, first stated in paragraph 1, that the boy does not experience "some profound insight about himself" at the end of "Araby" is developed in paragraphs 6–8. Reread these paragraphs and summarize the argument.

Commentary: An Interesting and Clearly Stated Interpretation

For more on thesis statements, see Chapter 19, pp. 670–74.

Like position papers, evaluations, proposals, and causal speculations, essays interpreting stories make arguments. They state a thesis — asserting an idea about the story's meaning or significance — and try to convince readers that this interpretation is plausible. Like those of other arguments, the **thesis statement** of an interpretive essay must meet three basic standards: It must be arguable, clear, and appropriately qualified. In addition, the interpretation must be perceived by readers as interesting.

Sally Crane's thesis statement identifies itself as arguable by setting up a contrast between her interpretation of the story's ending and that of other readers:

> Readers of "Araby" often . . . assume the boy experiences some profound insight about himself when he gazes "up into the darkness." I believe, however, that the boy sees nothing and learns nothing — about either himself or others. He's not self-reflective; he's merely self-absorbed.
>
> The evidence supporting this interpretation is the imagery of blindness and the ironic point of view of the narrator. (paragraphs 1–2)

Crane summarizes the debate simply: Either the boy "experiences some profound insight" at the end, or as Crane herself argues, he "sees nothing and learns nothing."

As we pointed out in the headnote, Crane knew about this debate over the ending from class discussion. Because her essay continues the conversation, she can be confident that the readers of her essay — her instructor and classmates — will find her interpretation interesting, even if they disagree with it. To make her interpretation even more interesting, she uses critical approaches she has learned in English classes. Readers who are not conversant with concepts like *imagery, irony,* and *point of view* may not even understand what Crane is talking about, let alone find it interesting. Your instructor and the Suggestions for Interpreting (pp. 545–48) will help you develop an interpretation that is interesting as well as arguable.

In addition to being arguable and interesting, Crane's thesis statement is clear and appropriately qualified. Readers familiar with the concepts Crane uses are likely to understand her thesis statement, but some readers will probably think it is not appropriately qualified because she makes the broad generalization: "the boy sees nothing and learns nothing." To qualify a thesis statement, writers typically add limiting words like "usually" and "most" in place of absolutes like "nothing" and "all." However, writers who can offer readers convincing support for their generalizations do not hedge. They generalize confidently, letting readers decide for themselves whether the thesis statement is appropriate or needs to be qualified.

Not only does a good thesis statement assert the interpretation, but it also uses key terms to **forecast** the reasons and support that will be offered and to indicate the order in which they will come up in the essay. Crane's first key term, *sees nothing,* introduces the first reason she thinks the boy ultimately "learns nothing" — because throughout the story he cannot understand with any accuracy his own feelings and motivations or anyone else's. In the first sentence of paragraph 2, Crane forecasts that she will support this reason by showing how the story uses "imagery of blindness."

Writers with little experience reading and writing essays interpreting stories may think that stating the thesis at the beginning and forecasting the argument gives too much away. Although stories seldom state their meanings explicitly, essays interpreting stories are expected to do so. Interpretive arguments are most effective when readers have a clear sense of what they are arguing and why.

DAVID RATINOV wrote the following essay about "Araby" (p. 527) for freshman composition. Like Sally Crane (p. 532), Ratinov is curious about what the boy's final statement might mean. But unlike Crane, Ratinov concludes that the boy does gain insight from seeing the hypocrisy of other characters as well as his own. As you read, notice how Ratinov's interpretation differs from Crane's. (*Note:* Like Crane, Ratinov cites paragraphs, following his instructor's directions rather than MLA style.)

From Innocence to Insight: "Araby" as an Initiation Story
David Ratinov

"Araby" tells the story of an adolescent boy's initiation into adulthood. The story is narrated by a mature man reflecting on his adolescence and the events that forced him to face the disillusioning realities of adulthood. The minor characters play a pivotal role in this initiation process. The boy observes the hypocrisy of adults in the priest and Mrs. Mercer; and his vain, self-centered uncle introduces him to another disillusioning aspect of adulthood. The boy's infatuation with the girl ultimately ends in disillusionment, and Joyce uses the specific example of the boy's disillusionment with love as a metaphor for disillusionment with life itself. From the beginning, the boy deludes himself about his relationship with Mangan's sister. At Araby, he realizes the parallel between his own self-delusion and the hypocrisy and vanity of the adult world.

From the beginning, the boy's infatuation with Mangan's sister draws him away from childhood toward adulthood. He breaks his ties with his childhood friends and luxuriates in his isolation. He can think of nothing but his love for her: "From the front window I saw my companions playing below in the street. Their cries reached me weakened and indistinct and, leaning my forehead against the cool glass, I looked over at the dark house where she lived" (para. 16). The friends' cries are weak and indistinct because they are distant emotionally as well as spatially. Like an adult on a quest, he imagines he carries his love as if it were a sacred object, a chalice: "Her image accompanied me even in places the most hostile to romance. . . . I imagined that I bore my chalice safely through a throng of foes" (para. 5). Even in the active, distracting marketplace, he is able to retain this image of his pure love. But his love is not pure.

Although he worships Mangan's sister as a religious object, his lust for her is undeniable. He idolizes her as if she were the Virgin Mary: "her figure defined by the light from the half-opened door. . . . The light from the lamp opposite our door caught the white curve of her neck, lit up her hair that rested there and, falling, lit up the hand upon the railing" (paras. 3, 9). Yet even this image is sensual with the halo of light accentuating "the white curve of her neck." The language makes obvious that his attraction is physical rather than spiritual: "Her dress swung as she moved her body and the soft rope of her hair tossed from side to side" (para. 3). His desire for her is strong and undeniable: "her name was like a summons to all my foolish blood" (para. 4); "my body was like a harp and her words and gestures were like fingers running upon the wires" (para. 5). But in order to justify his love, to make it socially acceptable, he deludes himself into thinking that his love is pure. He is being hypocritical, although at this point he does not know it.

Hypocrisy is characteristic of the adults in this story. The priest is by far the most obvious offender. What is a man of the cloth doing with books like *The Abbot* (a romantic novel) and *The Memoirs of Vidocq* (a collection of sexually suggestive tales)? These books imply that he led a double life. Moreover, the fact that he had money to give away when he died suggests that he was far from saintly. Similarly, at first glance Mrs. Mercer appears to be religious, but a closer look reveals that she too is materialistic. Her church work — collecting used stamps for some "pious purpose" (presumably to sell for the church) — associates her with money and profit (para. 17). Even her name, Mercer, identifies her as a dealer in merchandise. In addition, her husband is a pawnbroker, a profession that the church frowns on. Despite being linked to money, she pretends to be pious and respectable. Therefore, like the priest, Mrs. Mercer is hypocritical.

The uncle, as the boy's only living male relative, is a failure as a role model and the epitome of vanity. He is a self-centered old man who cannot handle responsibility: When the boy reminds him on Saturday morning about the bazaar, the uncle brushes him off, devoting all his attention to his own appearance. After being out all afternoon the uncle returns home at 9:00, talking to himself. He rocks the hallstand when hanging up his overcoat. These details suggest that he is drunk. "I could interpret these signs" indicates that this behavior is typical of his uncle (para. 19). The uncle is the only character in the story the boy relies on, but the uncle fails him. Only after the aunt persuades him does the uncle give the boy the money he promised. From the priest, Mrs. Mercer, and his uncle, the boy learns some fundamental truths about adulthood, but it is only after his visit to Araby that he is able to recognize what he has learned.

Araby to the adolescent represents excitement, a chance to prove the purity of his love and, more abstractly, his hope; however, Araby fulfills none of these expectations. Instead, the boy finds himself in utter disillusionment and despair. Araby is anything but exciting. The trip there is dreary and uneventful, lonely and intolerably slow — not the magical journey he had expected. When he arrives, Araby itself is nearly completely dark and in the process of closing. With his excitement stunted, he can barely remember why he came there (to prove the purity of his love by buying a gift for Mangan's sister).

The young lady selling porcelain and her gentleman friends act as catalysts, causing the boy to recognize the truth of his love for Mangan's sister. Their conversation is flirtatious — a silly lovers' game that the boy recognizes as resembling his own conversation with Mangan's sister. He concludes that his love for her is no different than the two gentlemen's love for this "lady" (para. 26). Neither love is pure. He too had only been playing a game, flirting with a girl and pretending that it was something else and that he was someone else.

His disillusionment with love is then extended to life in general. Seeing the last rays of hope fading from the top floors of Araby, the boy cries: "I saw myself as a creature driven and derided by vanity; and my eyes burned with anguish and anger" (para. 37). At last he makes the connection — by deluding himself, he has been hypocritical and vain like the adults in his life. Before these realizations he believed that he was driven by something of value (such as purity of love), but now he realizes that his quest has been in vain because honesty, truth, and purity are only childish illusions and he can never return to the innocence of childhood.

Analyzing Writing Strategies

For more on thesis state-
ments, see Chapter 19,
pp. 670–74.

1. Find the thesis statement in Ratinov's essay, and underline its key terms. Then find and circle where Ratinov uses these key terms in the rest of his essay. Are all of the key terms in the essay easy to find, or do any drop out of sight? Also determine whether Ratinov's key terms enable him to satisfy the standards of a well-written interpretive thesis statement: Is it interesting, arguable, clear, and appropriately qualified?

For more on topic sentence
strategies, see Chapter 13,
pp. 613–16.

2. Look closely at each opening sentence in paragraphs 2–8 to see if it functions as an effective **topic sentence**. Does it connect the preceding paragraph to the one it introduces? What other functions do these opening sentences have?

To learn more about com-
menting on quotations, turn
to Sentence Strategies,
pp. 553–54.

3. In paragraph 2, underline the two quotations. Then analyze what Ratinov does before and after each quotation to provide a context for it and a comment on it. How does he prepare you to read each quote? How does he attempt to show you the relevance and point of each quote?

Commentary: Plausible Reasons and Convincing Support

Ratinov presents three interrelated reasons for his interpretation of the story's ending. His first reason is that the boy deludes himself by imagining his love for Mangan's sister to be noble. Second, he argues that the boy sees the adult characters in the story as hypocritical and self-centered. Finally, he argues that at the bazaar, the boy suddenly connects the adults' hypocrisy to his own. His self-delusion ends, thus completing his initiation into adulthood.

For more on textual evi-
dence, see Chapter 19,
pp. 679–80.

This chain of reasoning seems plausible. Whether readers accept it as such depends on how well Ratinov supports the argument. He supports it with **textual evidence**, primarily quotations of significant passages from the story. He may quote individual words (paragraph 7), short phrases (paragraph 4), a single sentence (paragraph 8), or strings of sentences (paragraph 2). Unlike Crane, who uses a block quotation (paragraph 5), Ratinov does not use any quotes long enough to require indentation — more than four lines, according to MLA style. Like Crane, Ratinov uses ellipsis marks (. . .) to indicate where he has omitted words from his quotation (paragraph 2). Both writers also parenthetically cite the paragraph numbers to indicate where the quotations can be found in the story. By citing paragraphs instead of the author and page number as MLA style dictates, these students are following their instructors' directions. Be sure to follow your instructor's preferred format for citing sources.

For more on MLA quotation
style, see Chapter 22,
pp. 750–63, and
pp. 562–63 in this chapter.

Notice that, like Crane, Ratinov does more than merely quote words from the story. He tells readers what the words mean in the context of the argument he is making. In paragraph 2, for example, Ratinov makes an assertion, which he then supports by quoting two sentences. To make certain that readers understand how the quotation supports his assertion, Ratinov discusses two word choices and their implications.

Purpose and Audience

When you write an essay interpreting a story, you cannot simply tell readers, who may have different interpretations, what you think and expect them to accept your interpretation or even to understand it fully. You need to show how you read the story. Ideally, your readers will see something new in the story after reading your essay. But even if they continue to read the story differently from the way you read it, they may still acknowledge that your interpretation reflects an imaginative, thoughtful reading of the story.

Interpreting a story, then, is not a competition for the "correct" interpretation. Your aim is to develop an interpretation that is insightful and interesting to readers who are already engaged in conversation with other readers about their different ways of reading the story. Readers do not require you to come up with a startling new idea, though they would be pleased if you did. Your readers will be disappointed, however, if your essay is unfocused, if the key terms in your thesis statement are unclear, if you do not give reasons for your interpretation or you do not support them with quotations from the story, or if your essay fails to provide the necessary cues to keep readers on track. Readers will be especially disappointed if they think you are retelling the story rather than developing your own interpretation of the story's meaning or significance.

Basic Features: Interpreting Stories

An Appropriately Presented Subject

The essays interpreting stories in this chapter both focus on a specific subject — one particular story. When an interpretive essay responds to a class discussion or writing assignment, all the writer needs to do is identify the story by name. The readers — the instructor and other students in the class — already know who the author is and when the story was written. Both student writers in this chapter simply refer to "Araby" in the first few words of their opening sentence: "'Araby' tells the story . . ." (David Ratinov) and "Readers of 'Araby' . . ." (Sally Crane).

Sometimes, students are asked to choose from a list of stories or to find a story on their own. On such occasions, you may need to give readers a little more information about the story — such as the name of the author and the date the story was originally published. To acquaint readers with the story, you also can briefly describe the situation. But avoid retelling the story in detail.

An Interesting and Clearly Stated Interpretation

An interpretation is an idea asserted about the meaning of the story. A good interpretation illuminates the story for readers by adding something interesting to the ongoing conversation in which readers are engaged. The main idea or thesis is usually presented explicitly in a thesis statement near the beginning of the essay and may be summarized again at the conclusion. In addition to being interesting, the thesis statement must be arguable, not a simple statement of fact that anyone who reads the story will know (such as stating that the boy in "Araby" lives in Dublin with his aunt and uncle). Nor should the thesis be obvious, a conclusion that most readers would make (the boy has a crush on Mangan's sister). A good thesis statement should also be clear, not vague or ambiguous, and appropriately qualified, not overgeneralized or exaggerated. Crane states her thesis in the second sentence of the opening paragraph: "I believe, however, that the boy sees nothing and learns nothing — about either himself or others." (The word *however* refers to the preceding sentence, which summarizes an opposing interpretation expressed by other students in her class.)

A good thesis statement forecasts the reasons the writer will use in the essay to develop and support the thesis. Inexperienced writers sometimes are afraid they are ruining the surprise by announcing their thesis and forecasting their argument at the beginning. But readers familiar with this kind of writing have come to expect writers to preview the argument in the opening paragraphs. Explicit forecasting is a convention of literary interpretation similar in purpose to the abstract that precedes many articles in scientific journals. Explicitness does not mean that you have to sacrifice subtlety or complexity in your interpretation. All it means is that you are striving to make your ideas as comprehensible as possible to readers.

Ratinov's opening paragraph provides a good example of explicit forecasting. He explains his main idea, beginning with his thesis, in the first sentence: "'Araby' tells the story of an adolescent boy's initiation into adulthood." Then, in the five sentences that follow, he previews his argument. Finally, in the last sentence of the opening paragraph, Ratinov provides a succinct summary of his reasons: "At Araby, he realizes the parallel between his own self-delusion and the hypocrisy and vanity of the adult world." Together with *initiation*, the key term in the opening sentence, the last sentence sets out three additional key terms: *self-delusion, hypocrisy*, and *vanity*. These additional key terms signal for readers the steps in Ratinov's argument, specifying what he means when he asserts that the boy's experience can be understood as an initiation story. For key terms to be useful to readers, they must be clear and consistent. Moreover, the reasons that the key terms stand for should be directly connected to the thesis and be well supported.

A Plausible Chain of Reasons with Convincing Support

Writers must argue for their interpretation. They can usually assume that their readers will be familiar with the story, but they can never assume that readers will understand or accept their interpretation.

Writers argue for their interpretation not so much to convince readers to adopt it but rather to convince them that it is plausible. An essential strategy writers typically follow is to show readers how they read the story. They do this by supporting their interpretation with textual evidence and explaining

what they think these quotations mean in light of the thesis.

The primary source of support for your argument, then, is the story itself, particularly examples gleaned from it. Writers quote, summarize, and paraphrase passages from the story. They do more than just refer readers to a specific passage, however: They also explain the meaning of the passage and its relevance to their thesis. We can see an example of the way writers explain their textual support in the following passage from Ratinov's essay, where he describes what happens when the boy's uncle finally comes home from work, having forgotten that the boy was waiting for him:

> When the boy reminds him on Saturday morning about the bazaar, the uncle brushes him off, devoting all his attention to his own appearance. After being out all afternoon the uncle returns home at 9:00, talking to himself. He rocks the hallstand when hanging up his overcoat. These details suggest that he is drunk. "I could interpret these signs" indicates that this behavior is typical of his uncle. The uncle is the only character in the story the boy relies on, but the uncle fails him. (paragraph 5)

Notice that Ratinov summarizes the most important details, paraphrasing some of the language, and that he quotes sparingly — only one especially telling phrase. Everything else in this paragraph is Ratinov's commentary. Like Ratinov and Crane, you will want to combine explanatory commentary with quotation, summary, and paraphrase to support and develop your argument.

Interpreting Stories

Invention and Research

If you are not assigned a story, try going online to find one that interests you. Would you like to focus on interpreting character development, theme, or some other aspect of the story? Analyze and annotate the story with this focus in mind, and do some writing to explore your annotations, list ideas, and develop connections among them. Then come up with a tentative main idea for your essay. . . . **See p. 543 for more.**

Planning and Drafting

As you look over what you have written and learned about your subject, can you make a convincing case for your interpretation? If your readers are not familiar with the story, how much do you need to tell them about it? How much textual support for your argument should you include? Make a plan for your essay and start drafting it. . . . **See p. 551 for more.**

Critical Reading Guide

What are your draft's strengths and weaknesses? Have you provided a clear statement of and textual support for your interpretation? Are the connections between ideas hard to follow? Get a classmate, a friend, a writing tutor, or someone else to read and respond to your essay, especially the parts you are most unsure of. . . . **See p. 555 for more.**

Revising

As you consider your essay again in light of your reader's comments, how can you improve it? Is the thesis too obvious and thus uninteresting? Do you need to present more details of the story or more explanations of material you quote? Go through your draft systematically, making changes wherever necessary. . . . **See p. 556 for more.**

Editing and Proofreading

Have you checked for errors that are especially likely in essays interpreting stories? Are items in a series all in parallel grammatical form? Have you used ellipsis marks correctly to indicate material deleted from quotations? Look for and correct these and any other errors. . . . **See p. 561 for more.**

The Writing Assignment

Write an essay interpreting some aspect of a short story. Aim to convince readers that your view of the story is interesting and adds to the ongoing conversation among those who read stories and write about them. Back up your interpretation with reasons and support from the story.

To learn about using the *Guide* e-book for invention and drafting, go to bedfordstmartins.com/theguide.

Invention and Research

The following activities will help you choose a short story, analyze it, write to explore your annotations, formulate a tentative thesis statement, test your choice, revise your thesis statement, and find additional support in the story for your thesis. To make these activities as useful as possible, spread them out over several days, and keep a written record of your invention work.

Choosing a Story to Write About

Choose a story that fascinates, surprises, or puzzles you, one that will be worth spending time on because it excites your imagination. You may have chosen a story already, or your instructor may have assigned you one. If so, go on to the next section, Analyzing the Story.

If you need to choose a story on your own, read several stories before deciding on one to write about. Do not choose a story that seems obvious to you. Your instructor can help you decide whether you have made a good choice.

■ *Considering Stories Related to Identity and Community.* If you are studying the topic of identity and community, you will see immediately how the stories in this chapter relate to these concerns. Almost any story you choose to write about would allow you to think more about how people develop their individuality and their connections to others. Here are a few widely anthologized stories you might consider writing about:

"The Monkey Garden," by Sandra Cisneros

"The Open Boat," by Stephen Crane

"Fleur," by Louise Erdrich

"A Rose for Emily," by William Faulkner

"My Kinsman, Major Molineux," by Nathaniel Hawthorne

"A Clean, Well-Lighted Place," by Ernest Hemingway

"The Lottery," by Shirley Jackson

"The Metamorphosis," by Franz Kafka

"The Ones Who Walk Away from Omelas," by Ursula Le Guin

"A Pair of Tickets," by Amy Tan

"My Father's Chinese Wives," by Sandra Tsing Loh

"Everyday Use," by Alice Walker

■ ***Considering Stories Related to Work and Career.*** "The Use of Force" (in this chapter) would be useful in writing about the topic of work and career. Here are some additional stories you might consider for exploring this topic:

"Sonny's Blues," by James Baldwin

"The Yellow Wallpaper," by Charlotte Perkins Gilman

"The Birthmark," by Nathaniel Hawthorne

"Reena," by Paule Marshall

"Shiloh," by Bobbie Ann Mason

"Bartleby the Scrivener," by Herman Melville

"Picasso," by Gertrude Stein

"The Catbird Seat," by James Thurber

"A&P," by John Updike

"Why I Live at the P.O.," by Eudora Welty

An Online Activity:
Finding a Story

If your instructor has not assigned a story for you to write about, you may be able to find one that interests you by searching online. Simply entering the keyword *short stories* into a search engine such as Google (http://www.google.com) or Yahoo! Directory (http://dir.yahoo.com) will lead to Web sites with stories you could consider writing about. Many of these sites feature stories that have not been published in print, but others, such as the following, are collections of classic stories:

Twenty Great American Short Stories <http://www.americanliterature.com/SS/SSINDX.HTML>

Classic Short Stories <http://www.bnl.com/shorts/>

Classic Reader <http://www.classicreader.com/toc.php/sid.6/>

Bibliomania: Short Stories <http://www.bibliomania.com/0/5/frameset.html>

If your instructor needs to approve your choice, be sure to include information about the Web site along with the printout of the story you have chosen.

Analyzing the Story

To help you analyze the story, this section offers suggestions for interpreting that may help you annotate for potentially meaningful details. As you annotate the story, your goal will be to decide on a thesis, an idea about the story's meaning, for which you can develop a reasoned, well-supported argument.

Choosing a Suggestion for Interpreting.   *Select one or more suggestions for interpreting that will help you focus on some aspects of the story that seem significant or about which you have questions.* For example:

- If on first reading the story you wondered why a character acts in a particular way, look at the suggestions for interpreting *character*.

- If you were struck by the language used to describe the scene, look at the suggestions for interpreting *setting*.

- If you noticed any kind of pattern in the events in the story, look at the suggestions for interpreting *plot structure*.

- If you had questions about the way the story is narrated, look at the suggestions for interpreting *point of view*.

- If you recognized a familiar motif (for example, a coming-of-age story) or theme (alienation), look at the suggestions for interpreting *literary motif* or *theme*.

You may want to read and annotate the story several times, keeping in mind the different suggestions for interpreting, before you decide on an idea you can use as a working thesis for your draft. Notice also that rereading the story with different suggestions in mind can help you to discover how different aspects of the story work together and can lead you to construct a more fully developed thesis.

Character

To interpret the character psychologically:

- Identify the character's motivations, inner conflicts, and doubts.

- Consider whether the character changes or learns anything in the course of the story.

- Focus on how the character relates to other characters, noting how the character deals with intimacy, commitment, and responsibility.

- Note whether the character seems depressed, manic, abusive, fearful, egotistical, or paranoid. Look for another character who may represent the character's alter ego — the "flip side" of the character's personality.

To interpret the character ethically or morally:

- Decide what you consider to be the character's virtues and/or vices.

- Consider what influences your judgment of the character — something in the story (such as what the narrator or another character says), something you bring to the story (your views of right and wrong, based on your family upbringing or religious teachings), or something else.

- See whether any of the other characters have different moral values that could be compared and contrasted to the character's values.

To interpret the character from a social perspective:

- Consider how the character fits into and is defined by society — in terms of race, ethnicity, socioeconomic class, sexual orientation, age, or gender.
- Notice who in the story exercises power over whom, what causes the difference in power, what its effects are, and whether the balance of power changes during the story.

Setting

To interpret the setting in relation to the action, mood, or characters:

- Consider how the setting signals what is happening and whether it comments (possibly ironically) on the action.
- Notice how the setting affects the mood — for example, how it heightens suspense or foreboding.
- Look for cause-and-effect connections between the setting and what characters are thinking, doing, or feeling.

To interpret the setting historically or culturally:

- Think of how the historical period or cultural context in which the story is set might affect what happens and does not happen and why.
- Imagine how the meaning might be different if the historical time or cultural situation were different.

To interpret the setting metaphorically or symbolically:

- Assume that the setting is a projection of the thoughts and feelings of the narrator, and then consider what the setting tells you about the narrator's state of mind.
- Assume that the setting symbolizes the social relations among characters in the story, and then consider what the setting tells you about these relationships.
- Assume that the setting stands for something outside the characters' control (such as nature, God, or some aspect of society), and then consider what the setting tells you about the pressures and rules under which the characters function.

Plot Structure

To interpret the plot as realistic (as resembling real-life experience):

- Think of the story as a sequence of stages or steps leading somewhere, mark where each new stage begins, and consider how the sequence could be understood.

- Think of the story as having not only a main plot but also subplots that mirror, undercut, or comment in some way on the main plot.

To interpret the plot as surrealistic (as having symbolic rather than literal meaning):

- Think of the story as a series of images, more like a collage or a dream rather than a realistic portrayal of actual events, and look for ways of understanding the arrangement of these images.

Point of View

To interpret the point of view in terms of what the narrator can see:

- Consider whether the narrator is a character in the story or an all-knowing, disembodied voice who knows what every character thinks, feels, and does.
- Identify any important insights or ideas the narrator has.
- Consider how factors such as the narrator's gender, age, and ethnicity may influence what he or she notices as important.
- Consider what the narrator is not able to see or what the narrator distorts — for example, certain truths about himself or herself, about other characters, or about what happens in the story.

To interpret the point of view in terms of how the narrator represents what he or she sees:

- Characterize the narrator's tone at various points in the story — for example, as satirical, celebratory, angry, bitter, or optimistic.
- Infer what there is about the narrator (or about the situation) that could account for each tone you identify.
- Consider what special agenda or motive may have led the narrator to this particular way of describing characters and scenes or telling the story.
- Imagine how your interpretation might differ if the story were narrated from another character's point of view or by an all-knowing voice.

Literary Motif or Theme

To interpret the story in terms of a traditional story motif (or an ironic reversal of the tradition), consider whether it could be seen as:

- An initiation (or coming-of-age or rite-of-passage) story
- A heroic quest (for love, truth, fame, fortune, salvation of oneself or the community)
- A story about a character's disillusionment or fall from innocence
- A story about family or surrogate families
- A story about storytelling (or some other art) or about becoming a writer or an artist

To interpret the story in terms of a common literary theme, consider whether the following themes are found in the story:

- the American dream
- dynamics of power
- social construction of femininity or masculinity
- popular culture
- race relations
- alienation
- imagination

For examples of Ratinov's annotations and invention writings, see the Writer at Work section on pp. 563–66.

Annotating with the Suggestions for Interpreting in Mind. *Annotate details in the story that relate to the focus you have chosen for your interpretation.* To annotate, simply underline, bracket, or highlight words and phrases that seem significant. Circle words to be defined, and write their definitions in the margins. Draw lines to connect related words and images. Make marginal notes indicating what you are learning about the story by annotating with the suggestions for interpreting in mind. Write down any further questions you have as you annotate.

Writing to Explore Your Annotations

Write at least a page exploring what you have discovered about the story from analyzing it with the suggestions for interpreting in mind. If you have reread the story several times with different suggestions for interpreting, you may be able to write several pages.

It may help to begin by reviewing the suggestions for interpreting you used and writing your thoughts about each suggestion. For example, if you focused on the suggestions to interpret the character psychologically, you could begin by explaining what you now think are the character's motivations, inner conflicts, and doubts. Then you could go on to discuss how the character changes — what precipitated the change, how it proceeded, how you can tell the character has changed, and why the change is significant.

You may also find it productive to write about patterns of words, figures of speech, characters, or events you found as you were annotating. For instance, when David Ratinov reflected on the annotations he had made using the suggestions for interpreting character, he discovered that several minor characters, in addition to the main character, were hypocritical.

Formulating a Tentative Thesis Statement

Using the suggestions for interpreting, you have annotated the story and explored your annotations. Your aim now is to list ideas you can support with details from the story, explore the connections among these ideas, and draft a tentative thesis statement.

Listing Ideas.   *Write several sentences stating the ideas you have discovered using one or more of the suggestions for interpreting to annotate the story and to explore your annotations.* The only requirement is that you feel confident that you could find specific details and quotations in the story to support each idea. Do not worry about how these ideas relate to one another or even about whether they are contradictory. Simply write down every idea you can think of.

The suggestions for interpreting you used to annotate the story and explore your annotations should lead you, as they led Ratinov, to assert your ideas about the story. For example, writing about several of the characters in "Araby" convinced Ratinov that he could confidently assert the idea that "all the adult characters are hypocrites."

Writing to Develop Connections among Your Ideas.   *Write for ten minutes contemplating how the ideas you listed can make a chain of reasons leading to a general conclusion or main idea about the story that would be your thesis.* As you write, you may decide to drop some of the ideas, reformulate others, or add new ideas. Focus your writing on these questions:

- What are the key terms in each idea? (For example, the key term in Ratinov's idea that "all the adult characters are hypocrites" is *hypocrite.*)
- Could any of these ideas be links in a chain of reasons leading to some new, main idea about the story I can make now? (For example, Ratinov links the idea that the boy in "Araby" is *self-deluded* and the idea that adults are *hypocrites* to the boy's discovery that he is a hypocrite too [key terms italicized].)

Drafting the Thesis Statement.   *Now that you have asserted some ideas, thought about what their key terms enable you to say about the story, and considered how the terms could work together, write a few sentences stating your main idea or thesis and your reasons or supporting ideas.* Try completing the following sentence for each reason:

For more on thesis statements, see Chapter 13, pp. 610–12, and Chapter 19, pp. 670–74.

I think [main idea] about the story because [reason 1, 2, etc.].

Formulating a thesis statement (even one you know you will revise later) can be a challenge. It may help to review the thesis statements David Ratinov and Sally Crane wrote and to think about how they worded their key terms (italicized):

> "Araby" tells the story of an adolescent boy's *initiation* into adulthood . . . [by which] he realizes the parallel between his own *self-delusion* and the *hypocrisy* and *vanity* of the adult world. (Ratinov)

> I believe, however, that the boy *sees nothing* and *learns nothing* — about either himself or others. He's not self-reflective; he's merely *self-absorbed.* (Crane)

As you draft your own tentative thesis statement, pay attention to the language you use. It should be clear and unambiguous, emphatic but appropriately qualified. Although you will most probably refine your thesis statement as you draft and revise your essay, trying now to articulate it will help give your planning and drafting direction and impetus.

Testing Your Choice

Now that you have developed a tentative thesis statement, you need to be sure that it says what you want it to say, that your readers will find your interpretation interesting, and that you will be able to find support for it in the story. Review the key terms in your thesis to make sure you can find evidence for each point. Also consider whether your ideas still work together to form a logical chain of reasons. If your ideas still seem workable, you have probably made a good choice. However, if your ideas seem unworkable — that is, if you now think you cannot find examples in the story to support your ideas, or if your ideas seem too obvious or factual — you may need to return to Formulating a Tentative Thesis Statement or even to Analyzing the Story to develop your ideas or find new ones. You even may need to choose a different story and start over. If you are thinking of starting over, discuss the possibility with your instructor before doing so.

A Collaborative Activity:
Testing Your Choice

At this point, you will find it helpful to get together with two or three other students who have read your story and to get responses to one another's thesis statements. Your partners' feedback will help you determine whether your thesis or main idea is workable and whether you can construct a well-reasoned argument to support it.

Writers: Take turns reading your tentative thesis statement aloud. Then take notes as your partners tell you what your thesis statement leads them to expect from your essay.

Listeners: As the writer speaks, note down what you think are the key terms in the thesis statement. Remember that each of these key terms stands for an idea or a link in the chain of reasons arguing for the overall thesis. So tell the writer what the ideas are that you expect will be developed in the essay. Also indicate if you think the writer will have difficulty supporting any of these ideas, if you do not see how the ideas work together, or if you think any of the ideas are obvious or uninteresting. For example, if you were a member of David Ratinov's group, you might have said that his thesis statement led you to expect his essay to demonstrate three things: (1) the boy is *self-deluded*, (2) the adults are *hypocritical*, and (3) the boy ultimately realizes he has been self-deluded because of his *vanity*, and that this discovery completes his *initiation* into adulthood (key terms are italicized).

Revising the Thesis Statement

Try to improve your thesis statement. Consider whether you want to change your argument to alter the thesis statement or the reasons for it. Clear up any ambiguity or vagueness in your key terms, and qualify them more appropriately if necessary. Make explicit why you think your thesis is interesting and arguable by indicating how other readers disagree.

Finding Additional Support

If you do not have enough support for your reasons, reread the story, making additional annotations in passages where you find details you might be able to use. With your key terms in mind, evaluate the support you already have to determine whether it is sufficient to explain and illustrate each reason. Wherever support is lacking, fill it in by doing further annotating. If you cannot find any support for one of your reasons, you need to reconsider whether you should use that reason.

If you find details in the story that contradict any of your reasons, do not ignore the contradiction. Instead, analyze the details to see how you should modify your argument.

■ Planning and Drafting

This section will help you review your invention notes, determine specific goals for your essay, make an outline, and get started on your first draft.

Seeing What You Have

Review your invention writing and annotated text. If some time has elapsed since you last read the story, you may want to reread it now. As you review what you have discovered about the story, consider whether your thesis is arguable and whether you have stated it clearly and directly. Also decide whether you have sufficient support and whether you might have overlooked anything important that could contradict or weaken your argument.

If you cannot find support for all of your reasons, you may not be ready to write a complete draft. You may, however, be ready to begin drafting the parts for which you do have support. Then you can return to the story to search for support for your other reasons. But if your ideas still seem obvious or not likely to be interesting to your readers, you may need to reconsider the direction in which you are going and possibly begin again.

Setting Goals

Before you start drafting, set some goals to guide the decisions you will make as you draft. Consider what you want to say about the story you are interpreting. Here are some questions that will help you set your goals and enable you to get across to your readers exactly what you want to tell them about the story:

Your Purpose and Readers

- Are my readers likely to know this story? If not, how much do I need to tell them about the story so that they can follow my argument? If so, how can I lead them to see my interpretation as interesting, whether or not they agree with it?

- Should I acknowledge readers' possible questions or differing interpretations, as Crane does?

The Interpretation

- How can I explicitly state my thesis and forecast my plan, as Crane and Ratinov do, without sounding stilted or mechanical?
- Which key terms will accurately forecast my reasons?

Reasons and Support

- How can I organize my reasons so that my readers will see how they interrelate or form a chain of reasoning, as Crane and Ratinov do?
- How can I integrate quotations smoothly into my writing?
- How can I connect quotations to my reasons so that readers will know why I have chosen these passages to quote?
- How can I make my argument sound authoritative and thoughtful?
- How much textual support must I include for my argument to be convincing?

The Ending

- Should I repeat my key terms, as Crane and Ratinov do?
- Should I reiterate my thesis statement?
- Should I end with a provocative question or with larger implications suggested by my interpretation?

Outlining

For more on outlining, see Chapter 12, pp. 593–95.

After setting goals for your essay, you are ready to make a working outline — a scratch outline or a formal outline using the outlining function of your word processing program. Remember that an outline is a tentative plan; you may change your plan as you make further discoveries while drafting.

Drafting

General Advice.   Start drafting your essay, keeping in mind your purpose for writing and the goals you set while you were planning: You want to convince readers that your thesis is plausible. Explain your reasons fully and directly. Do not expect readers to guess at how a supporting quotation illustrates a reason; spell out the connections you want readers to see. Remember that your readers may have different ways of interpreting the passages to which you refer. Indicate exactly why you are citing specific details from the story and how you interpret the writer's choice of words.

If you get stuck while drafting, explore the problem by using some of the writing activities in the Invention and Research section of this chapter (pp. 543–51).

Turn off your grammar checker and spelling checker at this stage if you find them distracting. Don't be afraid to skip around in your document. Jump back and fill in a spontaneous idea, or leap ahead and write a later section first if you find that easier. You may want to review the general drafting advice in Chapter 1 on p. 9.

Sentence Strategies: Frequent Short Quotations and Commenting on Quotations or Paraphrases.   As you draft an essay interpreting a short story, you will need to support your interpretation with quotations and paraphrases (restatements of quotations using mostly your own words) and with comments on them. Frequently quoting single words and brief phrases rather than whole sentences or passages and using language that refers directly to your quotations and paraphrases will help you achieve these goals.

Use short quotations frequently to support your interpretation of the story. Here are examples of short quotations from this chapter's two student essays:

> At the bazaar in the closing scene, "the light was out," and the upper part of the hall was "completely dark." (Sally Crane, paragraph 3)

> Her church work — collecting used stamps for some "pious purpose" (presumably to sell for the church) — associates her with money and profit. (David Ratinov, paragraph 4)

Crane and Ratinov do occasionally quote complete sentences — together they do so seven times — and one time Crane quotes several sentences in a row, set off as a block quotation (paragraph 5). The majority of their quotations, however, are brief phrases and single words from the stories they are interpreting. These additional examples illustrate the wide range of possibilities:

> The "white curve of her neck" and the "white border of a petticoat" combine the symbolic color of purity, associated with the Madonna, with sexual suggestiveness. (Sally Crane, paragraph 5)

> Yet even this image is sensual with the halo of light accentuating "the white curve of her neck." (David Ratinov, paragraph 3)

> He concludes that his love for her is no different than the two gentlemen's love for this "lady." (David Ratinov, paragraph 7)

Short word and phrase quotations like these will usually be part of the grammar of your own sentences — that is, they become the subjects, verbs, direct objects, and so on of your sentences. When you quote a complete sentence from a story, however, you will nearly always do so in a way that separates it from the grammar of your own sentence that introduces it, as in this example:

> Most people interpret the ending as a moment of profound insight, and the language certainly seems to support this interpretation: "Gazing up into the darkness I saw myself as a creature driven and derided by vanity; and my eyes burned with anguish and anger." (Sally Crane, paragraph 9)

Brief quotations are not in themselves superior to sentence and block quotations, but they allow you to sample more of the exact language of the story,

For more on using frequent short quotations to support your interpretation of a story, go to bedfordstmartins.com/theguide and click on Sentence Strategies.

making your argument more lively and interesting. They also enable you to bring together efficiently evidence from different parts of a story to support one part of your argument.

Comment directly on your quotations or paraphrases so that readers will understand their relevance to your interpretation of a story. The relevance, importance, or point of each of your quotations and paraphrases will rarely be obvious to your readers unless you provide a context for it, a comment in which you directly connect the quotation or paraphrase to the idea you are trying to support. Two prominent strategies that writers rely on in their comments are referring to quotations or paraphrases with *this* and *these* and repeating key nouns in them.

Referring to Quotations or Paraphrases with **This** *and* **These**

After mentioning images of looking, seeing, and blindness, Sally Crane comments, "*This pattern of imagery* includes images of reading, and reading stands for the boy's inability to understand what is before his eyes" (paragraph 4).

After quoting three of the boy's romantic thoughts about the girl, Sally Crane comments, "*Language like this* sounds as though it comes out of a popular romance novel, something written by Danielle Steele perhaps" (paragraph 7).

After paraphrasing the uncle's activities, David Ratinov comments, "*These details* suggest that he is drunk" (paragraph 5).

Referring to Quotations or Paraphrases by Repeating Key Nouns

After quoting the image of North Richmond Street houses with their "brown imperturbable faces," Sally Crane comments, "*The houses* stare back at the boy, unaffected by his presence and gaze" (paragraph 4).

After quoting three sentences that describe the boy's observations of his friends as they play in the street below his house, a quotation that mentions the friends' "cries," or shouts, David Ratinov comments, "*The friends' cries* are weak and indistinct because they are distant emotionally as well as spatially" (paragraph 2).

After paraphrasing information in the story about the priest, Mrs. Mercer, and the boy's uncle, David Ratinov comments, "From *the priest, Mrs. Mercer, and his uncle*, the boy learns some fundamental truths about adulthood, but it is only after his visit to Araby that he is able to recognize what he has learned" (paragraph 5).

There are many other ways to introduce comments on quotations and paraphrases, but using *this* and *these* and repeating key nouns are reliable and effective.

In addition to using frequent short quotations and commenting directly on your quotations and paraphrases, you can strengthen your interpretive writing with other kinds of sentences as well, and you may want to review the discussions of absolute phrases (p. 116) and comparison and contrast (pp. 435–37).

For more on commenting on quotations and paraphrases, go to bedfordstmartins.com/theguide and click on Sentence Strategies.

Now is the time to get a good critical reading of your draft. Most writers find it helpful to have someone else read and comment on their drafts, and all writers know how much they learn about writing when they read other writers' drafts. Your instructor may arrange such a reading as part of your coursework. If not, you can ask a classmate, friend, or family member to read your draft. You could also seek comments from a tutor at your campus writing center. The guidelines in this section can be used by *anyone* reviewing an essay interpreting a story. (If you are unable to have someone else read your draft, turn ahead to the Revising section, where you will find advice for reading your own draft critically.)

▶ **If You Are the Writer.**   To provide focused, helpful comments, your reader must know your essay's intended audience, your purpose, and a problem in the draft that you need help solving. The reader must also have read the story you are writing about. Attach a copy of the story to your draft if you think your reader may not already have one, and write out brief answers to the following questions at the top of your draft:

- *Readers:* How do you think your interpretation builds on or contradicts the interpretations your readers are likely to have of the story?

- *Purpose:* What specifically do you want your readers to learn about the story from reading your essay?

- *Problem:* What is the most important problem you see in your draft?

▶ **If You Are the Reader.**   Use the following guidelines to help you give critical comments to others on essays interpreting stories:

1. *Read for a First Impression.*   Read first to grasp the writer's interpretation of the story. As you read, identify any passages that are particularly convincing as well as any that seem unclear or unsupported. Remember that even if you interpret the story differently, your goal now is to help the writer present his or her interpretation as effectively as possible.

   Write a one-sentence summary of the essay's thesis. Also indicate generally whether you think the writer's interpretation makes sense. Next, consider the problem the writer identified, and respond briefly to that concern now. (If you find that the problem is covered by one of the other guidelines listed below, respond to it in more detail there if necessary.)

2. *Evaluate the Thesis Statement and How Well It Forecasts the Argument.* Find the thesis statement, and highlight or underline its key terms. If you cannot find the thesis statement or cannot identify the key terms, let the writer know. Evaluate the thesis statement on the basis of whether it makes an interesting and arguable assertion (rather than a statement of fact or an obvious point), is clear and precise (neither ambiguous nor vague), and is appropriately qualified (neither overgeneralized nor exaggerated).

Critical Reading Guide

Making Comments Electronically
Most word processing software offers features that allow you to insert comments directly into the text of someone else's document. Many readers prefer to make their comments in this way because it tends to be faster than writing on a hard copy and space is virtually unlimited; from the writer's point of view, it also eliminates the problem of deciphering handwritten comments. Even where such special comment features are not available, simply typing comments directly into a document in a contrasting color can provide the same advantages.

For a printable version of this critical reading guide, go to bedfordstmartins.com/theguide.

Then skim the rest of the essay, highlighting or underlining each key term as it is brought up. If you cannot find a key term later in the essay but you do see where the reason it stands for is developed and supported, let the writer know where the key term should be added. If a reason introduced by a key term in the thesis statement is left out of the essay altogether, tell the writer. Also note any important reasons that are developed in the essay but are not announced in the thesis statement.

3. *Indicate Whether Each Reason Is Well Supported.*   Look closely at the sections where the reasons are developed. Note whether each reason is supported adequately with textual evidence such as quotations, paraphrases, or summaries. Indicate where support is lacking, and let the writer know if you do not understand how a particular quotation relates to the reason it is supposed to support. Point out any passages in the story that the writer could use to bolster this part of the argument or that undermine it.

4. *Evaluate the Argument as a Chain of Reasons.*   Summarize briefly for the writer your understanding of how the reasons work together to argue for the thesis. If you do not see how a particular reason fits in, say so. Also note where logical connections linking the chain of reasons could be added, strengthened, or made more explicit.

5. *Suggest How the Organization Could Be Improved.*   Consider the overall plan, perhaps by making a scratch outline. Note any places where the argument is hard to follow or where transitions are missing or do not work well.

   • Look again at the *beginning* to see if it adequately forecasts the rest of the essay.

   • Look at the *ending* to see if it is too abrupt, repetitive, or goes off in a new and surprising direction.

6. *Give the Writer Your Final Thoughts.*   What is the draft's strongest part? What part is most in need of further work?

▪ Revising

This section will help you get an overview of your draft and revise it accordingly.

Getting an Overview

Consider your draft as a whole, following these two steps:

1. *Reread.* If at all possible, put the draft aside for a day or two. When you do reread, start by reconsidering your purpose. Then read the draft straight through, trying to see it as your intended readers will.

For more on scratch outlining, see Chapter 12, pp. 593–95.

2. *Outline.* Make a scratch outline, indicating the basic features as they appear in the draft. Consider using the headings and outline/summary functions of your word processor.

Planning for Revision.   Resist the temptation to dive in and start changing your text until after you have a clear view of the big picture. Using your outline as a guide, move through the document, using the change-highlighting or commenting tools of your word processor to note comments received from others and problems you want to solve (or mark on a hard copy if you prefer).

Analyzing the Basic Features of Your Own Draft.   Turn now to the Critical Reading Guide that begins on p. 555. Using this guide, identify problems you now see in your draft. Note the problems on your draft.

Studying Readers' Comments.   Review all of the comments you have received from other readers. For each comment, look at the draft to determine what might have led the reader to make that particular point. Try to be objective about any criticism. Ideally, these comments will help you see your draft as others see it. Add to your notes any problems readers have identified that you intend to act on.

Working with Sources

The primary source writers interpreting stories use is the story itself. They may also use secondary sources providing information about the author or the period in which the story was written or set in addition to sources offering alternative interpretations of the story. Neither Sally Crane nor David Ratinov used secondary sources; instead, their instructors required them to focus solely on the story itself. Their essays illustrate the many different ways writers use quotations from the text they are analyzing to support their interpretive argument.

Crane and Ratinov both quote the same passage in "Araby" but they use it to support different arguments. By looking closely at how Crane and Ratinov use quotations differently, we can see why writers cannot simply drop quotations into their essays and expect them to speak for themselves. Like all writers interpreting stories, Crane and Ratinov need to show how they understand the language they quote and why they think the quotations demonstrate their argument about the story's meaning.

Here is the original passage from "Araby" followed by a side-by-side comparison showing how Crane and Ratinov quote from the same passage (blue highlighting):

"Araby" (paragraphs 7–11)

At last she spoke to me. When she addressed the first words to me I was so confused   7
that I did not know what to answer. She asked me was I going to Araby. I forgot whether
I answered yes or no. It would be a splendid bazaar, she said she would love to go.

"And why can't you?" I asked.   8

While she spoke she turned a silver bracelet round and round her wrist. She could   9
not go, she said, because there would be a retreat that week in her convent. Her brother
and two other boys were fighting for their caps and I was alone at the railings. She held
one of the spikes, bowing her head towards me. The light from the lamp opposite our
door caught the white curve of her neck, lit up her hair that rested there and, falling,

Quoting from the story to support your interpretation

For help working with sources, go to bedfordstmartins.com/theguide.

lit up the hand upon the railing. It fell over one side of her dress and caught the white border of a petticoat, just visible as she stood at ease.

10   "It's well for you," she said.

11   "If I go," I said, "I will bring you something."

Crane's Essay (paragraph 5)

The most important face he tries and fails to read belongs to Mangan's sister. His description of her and interpretation of the few words she says to him can be seen as further evidence of his blindness. He sees only what he wants to see, the "image" he has in his mind's eye. This image comes more from what he's read than from anything he's observed. He casts her simultaneously in the traditional female roles of angel and whore:

> While she spoke she turned a silver bracelet round and round her wrist. She could not go, she said, because there would be a retreat that week in her convent. . . . She held one of the spikes, bowing her head towards me. The light from the lamp opposite our door caught the white curve of her neck, lit up her hair that rested there and, falling, lit up the hand upon the railing. It fell over one side of her dress and caught the white border of a petticoat, just visible as she stood at ease. (para. 9)

Her angelic qualities are shown in her plans to attend a convent retreat and in her bowed head. Her whorish qualities come through in the way she flirtatiously plays with the bracelet, as if she were inviting him to buy her an expensive piece of jewelry at the bazaar. The "white curve of her neck" and the "white border of a petticoat" combine the symbolic color of purity, associated with the Madonna, with sexual suggestiveness (para. 9). The point is that there is no suggestion here or anywhere else in the story that the boy is capable of seeing Mangan's sister as a real person. She only exists as the object of his adoring gaze. In fact, no one seems to have any reality for him other than himself.

Ratinov's Essay (paragraph 3):

Although he worships Mangan's sister as a religious object, his lust for her is undeniable. He idolizes her as if she were the Virgin Mary: "her figure defined by the light from the half-opened door. . . . The light from the lamp opposite our door caught the white curve of her neck, lit up her hair that rested there and, falling, lit up the hand upon the railing" (paras. 3, 9). Yet even this image is sensual with the halo of light accentuating "the white curve of her neck." The language makes obvious that his attraction is physical rather than spiritual: "Her dress swung as she moved her body and the soft rope of her hair tossed from side to side" (para. 3). His desire for her is strong and undeniable: "her name was like a summons to all my foolish blood" (para. 4); "my body was like a harp and her words and gestures were like fingers running upon the wires" (para. 5). But in order to justify his love, to make it socially acceptable, he deludes himself into thinking that his love is pure. He is being hypocritical, although at this point he does not know it.

Notice that whereas Crane quotes nearly all of paragraph 9 from "Araby," Ratinov quotes only one sentence from that paragraph. Because she is quoting five or more lines, Crane uses a block quotation. She also uses ellipsis marks to indicate where she has omitted a sentence from her quotation (a description of what the other boys are doing that is not relevant to the point she is making about the boy's "blindness" in regard to Mangan's sister). Ratinov also uses ellipsis marks, but cuts several paragraphs to connect two descriptions of Mangan's sister on the steps of her house. Here is the description from paragraph 3 of "Araby" with the language Ratinov quotes italicized:

> She was waiting for us, *her figure defined by the light from the half-opened door.* Her brother always teased her before he obeyed and I stood by the railings looking at her. *Her dress swung as she moved her body and the soft rope of her hair tossed from side to side.*

Ratinov chose to connect this first passage from paragraph 3 in "Araby" to the passage from paragraph 9 because they both display the boy's adoring gaze and the romantic backlit image of the girl he sees.

Both Crane and Ratinov precede and follow quotations with their own words (yellow highlighting) explaining how the quotations substantiate their arguments. Crane uses the block quote from "Araby" to argue that the boy's "blindness" makes him misread Mangan's sister. Following the block quotation, Crane focuses on certain words and phrases from "Araby" — paraphrasing (purple highlighting) and quoting (teal highlighting) — to explain why she thinks the story's language demonstrates that the boy sees the girl in contrasting "angelic" and "whorish" stereotypes. This argument supports the reason Crane is developing to support her overall thesis about the boy's lack of insight.

Ratinov uses the same passage, interpreting it similarly as revealing a combination of religious idolization with sexual desire. But instead of arguing that this combination of images reveals the boy's blindness to his own feelings, Ratinov argues that they reveal his hypocrisy. Like Crane, Ratinov introduces and follows the quotation from paragraph 9 of "Araby" (together with quotations from other parts of the story) with his own words (yellow highlighting). Also like Crane, he repeats language that he wants to focus readers' attention on: describing the light from the doorway as a "halo of light" and repeating the quotation "the white curve of her neck" to emphasize that the boy's view of the girl confuses spirituality and sensuality. At the end of the paragraph, Ratinov explicitly states the reason he is developing and repeats keywords from his essay's thesis: The boy "deludes himself" and is "hypocritical."

When you quote from the story to support your interpretation, be sure to frame the quotation with your own language explaining your ideas about the quotation and how your reasoning relates to your overall thesis.

Carrying Out Revisions

Having identified problems in your draft, you now need to figure out solutions and — most important — carry them out. Basically, you have three ways of finding solutions:

1. Review your invention and planning notes for additional support and ideas.
2. Do further invention writing to answer questions your readers raised or to provide material you or your readers think is needed.
3. Look back at the student essays by Sally Crane and David Ratinov to see how other writers have solved similar problems.

The following suggestions, which are organized according to the basic features of essays interpreting stories, will get you started solving some writing problems common in such essays.

Your Purpose and Readers

- Will readers recognize which story is the subject of this interpretation? State the title early on in the essay. Consider whether readers need to know the author or date of publication.

- Do readers need to be reminded about what happens in the story? If readers may not remember much about the story, briefly describe it for them, but avoid giving too much plot summary.

The Interpretation

- *Is your thesis statement hard for readers to find?* State explicitly at the beginning what your essay will demonstrate, announcing your thesis and forecasting the reasons you will use to argue for it.

- *Is your thesis statement perceived as unarguable or uninteresting?* Revise the thesis to make it clear that you are not stating a simple fact about the story or making an obvious point. Relate your interpretation to class discussion, as Crane does.

- *Are your key terms unclear or not appropriately qualified?* Revise your key terms to avoid ambiguity and vagueness. If you need to limit or qualify your thesis or reasons, add words like *some* or *usually*.

- *Are the key terms in the thesis statement not repeated later in the essay?* Delete any key term from the thesis statement that you do not discuss later in the essay or add language that develops and supports the reason for which this key term stands. If necessary, rewrite the paragraph's topic sentence using the key term.

Reasons and Support

- *Does the thesis or do any of the reasons used to argue for it seem superficial or thin?* Try developing your reasons more fully by comparing or contrasting related reasons; classifying your reasons or dividing them into their subparts; or discussing the social, political, and cultural implications of your way of interpreting the story. Consider elaborating on your reasons by rereading the story with another related suggestion for interpreting in mind.

Checking Sentence Strategies Electronically
To check your draft for sentence strategies especially useful in essays interpreting stories, use your word processor's highlighting function to mark quotations from the story. Then look at how many of the quotations are short (words and phrases) and how many are more extended (sentences and passages). If you have used mostly extended rather than short quotations, think about whether using more short ones (perhaps by using only words or phrases from some of the longer ones) would make your argument more lively and interesting. Also look to make sure that you have commented on each quotation, explaining its relevance to your interpretation of the story. For more on using quotations in literary interpretation, see pp. 553–54.

- *Does support seem lacking?* Add textual evidence by quoting, paraphrasing, or summarizing key passages. Focus your discussion more closely on the writer's choice of words, explaining what particular word choices mean in relation to your reasons. Consider using other kinds of support, such as information about the story's historical or cultural context.

- *Does the connection between a reason and its support seem vague?* Clarify your point by explaining why you think the support you have given illustrates the reason. Do not simply quote from the story. Explain how you interpret each quotation, which words seem significant, and how they demonstrate the point you are making. Remember that both Crane and Ratinov comment on the relevance or point of each quotation immediately after they introduce it.

- *Are there contradictions or gaps in your argument?* You may need to rewrite sections of your essay to eliminate contradictions or fill in gaps. Before cutting anything, consider whether the contradiction is real or apparent. If it is only apparent, explain more fully and clearly how your reasons relate logically to one another as well as to your thesis. To fill in gaps, you may have to lay out your train of thought more explicitly so that readers can more easily follow your logic.

The Organization

- *Is the essay hard to follow?* Provide more explicit cues: better forecasting, clear topic sentences, logical transitions, brief summaries.

- *Does the opening fail to prepare readers for your argument?* You may need to revise it to forecast your reasons more directly or to give readers a clearer context to help them understand your point.

- *Does the ending seem abrupt?* You may need to tie all the strands of the essay together, reiterate your thesis, or discuss its implications.

For a revision checklist, go to bedfordstmartins.com/theguide.

■ Editing and Proofreading

Now is the time to check your revised draft for problems in grammar, punctuation, and mechanics and to consider matters of style. It may help you to recognize problems if you study your draft in separate passes — first for paragraphs, then for sentences, and finally for words. Our research has identified two problems that occur often in essays interpreting stories: lack of parallel structure (a matter of style) and the misuse of ellipsis marks (a matter of punctuation). The following guidelines will help you check your draft for these common problems. This book's Web site also provides interactive online exercises to help you learn to identify and correct one of these errors; to access these exercises, go to the URL listed in the margin next to that section of the guidelines.

A Note on Grammar and Spelling Checkers
These tools are good at catching certain types of errors, but currently there's no replacement for a good human proofreader. Grammar checkers in particular are extremely limited in what they can usually find, and often they only give you summary information that is not helpful if you don't already understand the rule in question. They are also prone to give faulty advice for fixing problems and to flag correct items as wrong. Spelling checkers cause fewer problems but can't catch misspellings that are themselves words, such as *to* for *too*.

Checking for Parallelism in Your Writing.   When you present similar items together, you must present them in the same grammatical form. All items in a series should be parallel in form — all nouns, all prepositional phrases, all adverb clauses, and so on. Notice, for example, how Sally Crane edited her first-draft sentences to introduce parallel structure:

▶ I believe, however, that the boy sees nothing and ~~is incapable of learning~~ *learns nothing —*

either about himself or others~~₀ because he is so~~ *He's not self-reflective; he's merely* self-absorbed.

▶ This image comes more from ~~his reading~~ *what he's read* than from anything he's observed.

▶ The greatest irony comes at the end when his quest is exposed as merely a shopping trip, *and Araby as merely a suburban mall.*

The parallelism makes Crane's sentences easier to read and helps her emphasize some of her points. The parallelism of "sees nothing" and "learns nothing" emphasizes the relationship between these two conditions in a way that the first-draft wording did not; the same is true of "what he's read" and "anything he's observed." In the final sentence, Crane added a parallel phrase as an ironic comment.

Following are several more examples from other student essays, each edited to show ways of making writing parallel.

For practice, go to bedfordstmartins.com/theguide/exercisecentral and click on Parallelism.

▶ To Kafka, loneliness, ~~being isolated~~ *isolation*, and regrets are the price of freedom.

▶ Sarah really cares about her brother and ~~to maintain~~ *values* their relationship. She lets us know that she was injured by her mother's abuse but avoids saying what she felt after the incident, how others reacted to the incident, and ~~the~~ *what* physical pain she endured.

Checking Your Use of Ellipsis Marks.   Ellipsis marks are three spaced periods. They are used to indicate that something has been omitted from quoted text. You will often quote other sources when you interpret a story, and you must be careful to use ellipsis marks to indicate places where you delete material from a quotation. Look, for example, at the way Sally Crane uses ellipsis marks in quoting from "Araby."

ORIGINAL TEXT	North Richmond Street, being blind, was a quiet street except at the hour when the Christian Brothers' School set the boys free. An uninhabited house of two storeys stood at the blind end, detached from its neighbours in a square ground.
QUOTED WITH ELLIPSIS MARKS	The street is "blind," with an "uninhabited house . . . at the blind end."

If you are using MLA style, follow these few simple rules about using ellipsis marks:

- When you delete words from the *middle of a quoted sentence*, add ellipsis marks, and leave a single space before and after each ellipsis point.
- When you delete words from the *end of a quoted sentence* and a grammatically complete sentence remains, add a period after the last word and then three ellipsis marks.
- Leave a single space after the period and the first two ellipsis marks. Do not leave a space between the last mark and the closing quotation mark.
- When you delete material from the middle of a passage of *two or more sentences*, use ellipsis marks where the text is omitted and a period after the preceding text if it is grammatically a complete sentence.
- When you delete words from the *beginning of a quoted sentence*, use ellipsis marks only if the remainder of the sentence begins with a capitalized word and is grammatically a complete sentence.
- Single words and brief phrases can be quoted without ellipsis marks.

The following sentences from other student essays interpreting "Araby" have been edited to correct problems with the use of ellipsis marks:

For more on ellipsis marks, see Chapter 22, pp. 739–40.

For practice, go to bedfordstmartins.com/theguide/exercisecentral and click on Ellipsis Marks.

▶ We learn that a former tenant of the boy's house, "... a priest, had died in

the back drawing-room ... He had been a very charitable priest; in his will he

had left all his money to institutions and the furniture of his house to his sister."

▶ The boys lived on "a quiet street ..."

▶ The light shone on "... the white border of a petticoat ..."

A Writer at Work

Using the Suggestions for Interpreting To Analyze a Story

In this Writer at Work section, you will see some of the invention work that David Ratinov did for his essay interpreting "Araby," which appears earlier in this chapter (pp. 536–38). Using the Guide to Writing in this book, Ratinov chose the suggestions for interpreting character to guide his analysis of the story. As you will see, he annotated a portion of the story focusing on two characters (Mrs. Mercer and the boy's uncle), wrote to explore his annotations on the passages, and listed ideas for formulating his tentative thesis statement. You will be able to infer from his invention work how his ideas came to form the thesis he developed for his final essay.

Annotating

Ratinov annotated paragraphs 13–24 of "Araby" as he reread them with the suggestions for interpreting character in mind. The annotated passages are reproduced here. Notice the diversity of his annotations. In the text itself, he underlined key words, circled words to be defined, and connected related words and ideas. In the margin, Ratinov defined words, made comments, and posed questions. He also expressed his tentative insights, reactions, and judgments.

2nd mention of uncle fussing — vain? irritable? rude

On Saturday morning I reminded my uncle that I wished to go to the bazaar in the [13] evening. He was fussing at the hallstand, looking for the hatbrush, and answered me curtly:

"Yes, boy, I know." [14]

always unkind to the boy? uncle's effect on the boy

As he was in the hall I could not go into the front parlour and lie at the window. I left [15] the house in bad humour and walked slowly towards the school. The air was pitilessly raw and already my heart misgave me.

uncle will be late sudden change in mood; big contrast

When I came home to dinner my uncle had not yet been home. Still it was early. I sat [16] staring at the clock for some time and, when its ticking began to irritate me, I left the room. I mounted the staircase and gained the upper part of the house. The high cold

liberated from uncle?

empty gloomy rooms liberated me and I went from room to room singing. From the front window I saw my companions playing below in the street. Their cries reached me weakened

isolated from friends

and indistinct and, leaning my forehead against the cool glass, I looked over at the dark house where she lived. I may have stood there for an hour, seeing nothing but the brown-

romantic, even sensual

clad figure cast by my imagination, touched discreetly by the lamplight at the curved neck , at the hand upon the railings and at the border below the dress.

merchandise

When I came downstairs again I found Mrs. Mercer sitting at the fire. She was an [17]

talkative hypocritically religious

old garrulous woman, a pawnbroker's widow, who collected used stamps for some pious purpose. I had to endure the gossip of the tea-table. The meal was prolonged beyond an

boy doesn't seem to like or trust the adults

hour and still my uncle did not come. Mrs. Mercer stood up to go: she was sorry she couldn't wait any longer, but it was after eight o'clock and she did not like to be out late,

uncle and Mercer both try to give a false impression

as the night air was bad for her. When she had gone I began to walk up and down the room, clenching my fists. My aunt said:

"I'm afraid you may put off your bazaar for this night of Our Lord."

At nine o'clock I heard my uncle's latchkey in the halldoor. I heard him talking to himself and heard the hallstand rocking when it had received the weight of his overcoat. I could interpret these signs. When he was midway through his dinner I asked him to give me the money to go to the bazaar. He had forgotten.

"The people are in bed and after their first sleep now," he said.

I did not smile. My aunt said to him energetically:

"Can't you give him the money and let him go? You've kept him late enough as it is."

My uncle said he was very sorry he had forgotten. He said he believed in the old saying: "All work and no play makes Jack a dull boy." He asked me where I was going and, when I had told him a second time he asked me did I know *The Arab's Farewell to His Steed*. When I left the kitchen he was about to recite the opening lines of the piece to my aunt.

I held a florin tightly in my hand as I strode down Buckingham Street towards the station. The sight of the streets thronged with buyers and glaring with gas recalled to me the purpose of my journey. I took my seat in a third-class carriage of a deserted train. After an intolerable delay the train moved out of the station slowly. It crept onward among ruinous houses and over the twinkling river. At Westland Row Station a crowd of people pressed to the carriage doors; but the porters moved them back, saying that it was a special train for the bazaar. I remained alone in the bare carriage. In a few minutes the train drew up beside an improvised wooden platform. I passed out on to the road and saw by the lighted dial of a clock that it was ten minutes to ten. In front of me was a large building which displayed the magical name.

Margin annotations:
- 18 — 19   aunt religious, but hypocritical?
- boy knows uncle is drunk
- 20   boy's fears are justified excuses
- 21
- 22   aunt to the rescue
- 23   hypocritical what a bore!
- boy determined to go to bazaar to buy girl a gift
- 24   boy focused on his task
- language shows boy's impatience
- boy still isolated

As you can see, annotating this section of the story with the suggestions for interpreting character in mind led Ratinov to notice how negatively Mrs. Mercer and the uncle are portrayed by Joyce.

Exploratory Writing

Following the instructions in Writing to Explore Your Annotations in this chapter (p. 548), Ratinov discovered that the two characters are criticized primarily because of their hypocrisy. Here is what he wrote to explore this portion of his annotations:

Mrs. Mercer may be a good neighbor to the boy's aunt, but the boy dislikes her. Joyce plants many clues that she is a hypocrite. She thinks of herself as a good religious Christian, but she is pious (an exaggerated Christian, not a believable one), she collects stamps to sell for charity instead of doing good works firsthand (my guess), and she gossips. Her husband got his money in an un-Christian way. Does the boy know all this or only the narrator much later? I'm sure the boy senses it. He says he has to endure Mrs. Mercer and her gossiping with his aunt. Now that I've looked over the evidence for the uncle's hypocrisy, it seems that his unguardianlike actions toward the boy--his irresponsibility toward him--are just as big a flaw as is his hypocrisy. He seems to be trying to hide something by drinking and being obsessive about his appearance--a failure to advance at work? He tries to impress people with a bigger house than he can afford. Says he believes in things that don't apply to his own actions. I think I can show that he's a hypocrite like Mrs. Mercer. Because the boy distrusts him, he must sense this hypocrisy.

As Ratinov wrote about the hypocrisy of Mrs. Mercer and the uncle, he became increasingly confident that he had not only an interesting idea, but one he could also find support for in the story.

Listing Ideas for the Thesis

Following the advice given in Formulating a Tentative Thesis Statement in this chapter (p. 548), Ratinov listed ideas he felt confident he could support. In all, he listed five ideas, but notice that the first one came from the exploratory writing he did about Mrs. Mercer and the uncle (shown above):

-- All the adult characters are hypocrites.

-- If this is just a story about romance, then all the adult characters wouldn't have to be so weak and flawed.

-- Mangan's sister is different from the adults, but through her the boy has to face up to what the adult world is all about.

-- The adults are initiating the boy into adulthood, but he doesn't see it until the end of the story.

-- Growing up means being able to see the world for what it actually is, not what you want it to be.

From these ideas about hypocrisy, romance, initiation into the adult world, and the connection between growing up and learning to see reality, Ratinov was able to devise the thesis statement he eventually used in his final essay.

Thinking Critically About What You Have Learned

Now that you have read and discussed several essays interpreting a story and have written such an essay yourself, take some time to think critically about what you have learned. What problems did you encounter while you were writing your essay, and how did you solve them? How did reading other essays that interpret a story influence your own essay? What ideas do you have about the social and cultural dimensions of literary interpretation?

Reflecting on Your Writing

Write a one-page explanation, telling your instructor about a problem you encountered in writing your essay and how you solved it. Before you begin, gather your invention and planning notes, drafts and readers' comments, revision plan, and final revision. Review these materials as you complete this writing task.

1. ***Identify* one *significant writing problem you encountered while writing the essay.*** Do not be concerned with grammar and punctuation; focus instead on a problem specific to writing an interpretation. For example, were you uncertain about which suggestions for interpreting to use for analyzing the story? Did you puzzle over how best to state your thesis and forecast your argument? Did you have trouble deciding which passages from the story to use as support or whether to quote, summarize, or paraphrase them?

2. ***Determine how you came to recognize the problem.*** When did you first discover it — when you were trying to analyze the story, to find supporting evidence, or to sequence your reasons? If someone else pointed out the problem to you, can you now see signs of it in your invention work? If so, where specifically? When you first recognized the problem, how did you respond?

3. ***Reflect on how you went about solving the problem.*** Did you consider using a different suggestion for interpreting? Did you reread one of the essays in this chapter to see how another writer handled a similar problem, or did you do additional invention work such as rereading the story to fill in gaps in your original annotations? Did you reword, reorganize, or simply cut something that was problematic? If you talked about the problem with another student, a tutor, or your instructor, how did talking about it help?

4. ***Write a brief explanation of the problem and your solution.*** Be as specific as possible in reconstructing your efforts. Quote from your invention notes or draft essay, other readers' comments, your revision plan, and your final revision to show the various changes your writing and thinking underwent as you tried to solve the problem. If you are still uncertain about your solution, say so. Taking time to explain how you identified a particular problem, how you went about trying to solve it, and what you learned from this experience can help you solve future writing problems more easily.

Reviewing What You Learned from Reading

Write a page or so explaining to your instructor how the readings in this chapter influenced your final draft. Your own essay interpreting a story may have been influenced to some extent by the essays in this chapter — the two selections on "Araby" — and by classmates' essays that you have read. Before you write, take some time to reflect on what you have learned from these readings.

1. *Reread the final revision of your essay; then look back at the essays you read before completing it.* Do you see any specific influences? For example, did one of the essays influence the suggestions for interpreting you used or the organization you followed? If you were impressed by the way another writer stated a thesis clearly and emphatically, forecasted reasons, or used quotations as support, look to see where you might have been striving for similar effects in your own essay. Look for ideas you got from your reading: writing strategies you were inspired to try, details you were led to include, effects you sought to achieve.

2. *Write an explanation of these influences.* Did one selection have a particularly strong influence on your essay, or were parts of several selections influential in similar or different ways? Give examples from the readings and from your final revision to show how you built on what you have learned from other writers. Finally, based on your review of the chapter's readings, point out any further improvements you would now make in your essay.

Considering the Social Dimensions of Essays Interpreting Stories

Some genres, like position papers, have a broad general audience, composed of people whose knowledge of current controversial issues varies widely. Other genres, like essays interpreting stories, are highly specialized, read and written by a comparatively small group of people who share certain kinds of knowledge and interests. Students in English courses, whether they major in English or some other field, learn certain ways of reading and writing about stories. For example, they learn that interpretive essays are arguments, requiring arguable assertions, reasons, and supporting evidence.

But to write effectively in this genre, students also must learn what kinds of interpretations are likely to interest their particular readers — people engaged in an ongoing conversation about stories and other works of literature. They need to know some of the specialized vocabulary English majors use as well as

the critical approaches to interpreting stories they find useful. English instructors determine which approaches their students need to become conversant with and they introduce these subjects in lecture and class discussion. They choose stories to read and assign essays to write that will give students opportunities to use these approaches.

The essays written by Sally Crane and David Ratinov reflect the kinds of approaches students in English classes are likely to encounter. Both student writers are concerned with the character or character development of the boy in "Araby." They focus on what the boy says to himself at the end, the meaning of which is not obvious but requires interpretation. Their interpretations of the ending differ, but the kinds of interpretations they make fit comfortably within the usual conversation among English majors. Crane writes about the way the story is narrated, arguing that the boy is an unreliable narrator, unable to read others or himself accurately; therefore what he says is ironic, meaning the opposite of what it seems to say. Ratinov writes about a theme common to many stories, the theme of initiation. Crane and Ratinov also discuss images of women, although they emphasize different aspects of the boy's cultural background. Crane emphasizes the chivalric tradition about which the boy reads and Ratinov stresses his religious education. These subjects — irony, initiation, and images of women — are included in the suggestions for interpreting in the Guide to Writing because they represent some of the ways in which English majors understand stories.

1. List some of the subjects you and your classmates discussed in class and wrote about. Where did these subjects come from — class discussion, the suggestions for interpreting in the Guide to Writing, your instructor's questions or lecture, other English classes?

2. Consider whether any subjects were deemed by your instructor or other students as uninteresting or not appropriate for interpreting stories. Why were these subjects rejected?

3. Write a page or two about your experience making interpretations in this and other English classes.

Part Two
Critical Thinking Strategies

11

A Catalog of Invention Strategies

Writers are like scientists: They ask questions, systematically inquiring about how things work, what they are, where they occur, and how more information can be learned about them. Writers are also like artists in that they use what they know and learn to create something new and imaginative.

The invention and inquiry strategies — also known as **heuristics** — described in this chapter are not mysterious or magical. They are available to all writers, and one or more of them may appeal to your common sense and experience. These techniques represent ways creative writers, engineers, scientists, composers — in fact, all of us — solve problems.

Once you have mastered these strategies, you can use them to tackle many of the writing situations you will encounter in college, on the job, and in the community. The best way to learn them is to use them as you write an actual essay. Chapters 2–10 show you when these strategies can be most helpful and how to make the most efficient use of them. The Guides to Writing in those chapters offer easy-to-use adaptations of these general strategies, adaptations designed to satisfy the special requirements of each kind of writing. You will learn how and when to use these strategies and see how to combine them to achieve your goals.

The strategies for invention and inquiry in this chapter are grouped into two categories:

Mapping: A brief visual representation of your thinking or planning

Writing: The composition of phrases or sentences to discover information and ideas and to make connections among them

These invention and inquiry strategies can be powerful tools for thinking about your topic and planning your writing. They will help you explore and research a topic fully before you begin drafting and then help you creatively solve problems as you draft and revise your draft. In this chapter, strategies are arranged alphabetically within each of the two categories.

■ Mapping

Mapping strategies involve making a visual record of invention and inquiry. Many writers find that mapping helps them think about a topic. In making maps, they usually use key words and phrases to record material they want to remember, questions they need to answer, and new sources of information they want to check. The maps show the ideas, details, and facts they are examining. They also show possible ways to connect and focus materials. Maps might be informal graphic displays with words and phrases circled and connected by lines to show relationships, or they might be formal sentence outlines. Mapping can be especially useful for working in collaborative writing situations, for preparing oral presentations, and for creating visual aids for written or oral reports. Mapping strategies include clustering, listing, and outlining.

Clustering

Clustering is a strategy for revealing possible relationships among facts and ideas. Unlike listing (the next mapping strategy), clustering requires a brief period of initial preparation when you divide your topic into parts or main ideas. Clustering works as follows:

1. In a word or phrase, write your topic in the center of a piece of paper. Circle it.
2. Also in words or phrases, write down the main parts or ideas of your topic. Circle these, and connect them with lines to the topic in the center.
3. Next, think of facts, details, examples, or ideas related in any way to these main parts. Cluster these around the main parts.

Clustering can be useful for any kind of writing. You can use it in the early stages of planning an essay to find subtopics and organize information. You may try out and discard several clusters before finding one that is promising. Many writers use clustering to plan brief sections of an essay as they are drafting or revising. (A model of clustering is shown in Figure 11.1 on the next page.)

Listing

Listing is a familiar activity. We make shopping lists and lists of errands to do or people to call. Listing can also be a great help in planning an essay. It enables you to recall what you already know about a topic and suggests what else you may need to find out. It is an easy way to get started with your invention writing, instead of just worrying about what you will write. A list rides along on its own momentum, the first item leading naturally to the next.

A basic activity for all writers, listing is especially useful to those who have little time for planning — for example, reporters facing deadlines and college students taking essay exams. Listing lets you order your ideas quickly. It can also serve as a first step in discovering possible writing topics.

Software-based Diagramming Tools

Software vendors have created a variety of electronic tools to help people working in business and technical fields better visualize complex projects. The features of these software packages allow you to enter, store, and rearrange information in a variety of visual formats such as flowcharts, webs, and outlines. For some types of complex writing assignments, these graphical depictions can make it easier for you (or your instructor) to see how to proceed on the project, where more information is needed, or other pitfalls that might not otherwise be apparent. If you are comfortable with any of these packages or if you are primarily a visual thinker, you may find the use of a diagramming tool helpful during the invention stage as well as in later stages of your project.

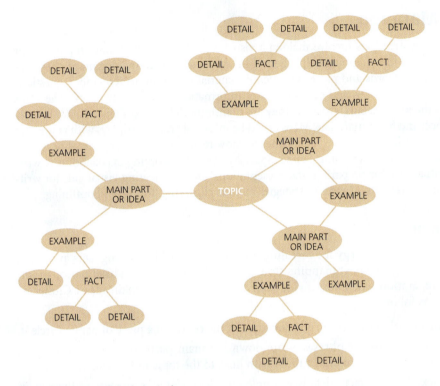

Figure 11.1 A model of clustering

Listing is a solitary form of brainstorming, a popular technique of problem solving in groups. When you work with a group to generate ideas for a collaborative writing project, you are engaged in true brainstorming. Here is how listing works best for invention work:

1. Give your list a title that indicates your main idea or topic.
2. Write as fast as you can, relying on short phrases.
3. Include anything that seems at all useful. Try not to be judgmental at this point.
4. After you have finished or even as you write, reflect on the list, and organize it in the following way. This step is very important, for it may lead you to further discoveries about your topic.

Put an asterisk next to the most promising items.

Number key items in order of importance.

Put items in related groups.

Cross out items that do not seem promising.

Add new items.

Outlining

Like listing and clustering, **outlining** is both a means of inventing what you want to say in an essay and a way of organizing your ideas and information. As you outline, you nearly always see new possibilities in your subject, discovering new ways of dividing or grouping information and seeing where you need additional information to develop your ideas. Because outlining lets you see at a glance where your essay's strengths and weaknesses lie, outlining can also help you read and revise your essay with a critical eye.

There are two main forms of outlining: informal outlining and formal topic or sentence outlining. Among the several types of informal outlining, scratch outlines are perhaps the most adaptable to a variety of situations. Chunking is another useful method. (Clustering also may be considered a type of informal outlining.)

A *scratch outline* is little more than a list of the essay's main points. You have no doubt made scratch outlines many times—to plan essays or essay exams, to revise your own writing, and to analyze a difficult reading passage. Here are sample scratch outlines for two different kinds of essays. The first is an outline for Rick Bragg's essay in Chapter 2, and the second shows one way to organize a position paper (Chapter 6):

The Planning and Drafting sections of the Guides to Writing in Chapters 2–10 illustrate many different scratch outlines. See also p. 595.

Scratch Outline: Essay about a Remembered Event

1. Gives background on his quest since boyhood for "a car built for speed"
2. Recalls the 1969 muscle car he bought the summer before his senior year of high school, how he paid for it, and his uncle's warning
3. Recalls how the car conveyed status to him among his peers
4. Recalls winning his first parking-lot race in the car and his subsequent thrill over speeding the car down country roads
5. Turns to specific incident two weeks after he got the car when, during a high-speed race through the country, he braked suddenly because he saw a police cruiser and flipped the car into a ditch
6. Describes how, miraculously, he was relatively unhurt, hanging upside down and pinned in by the low adjustment of the steering wheel
7. Reflects on the inappropriateness of his initial mental response: to turn down the radio
8. Describes being pulled from the car by a state trooper and the trooper's comment that he should have been killed in the accident ("The Lord was riding with you, son")
9. Describes his mother's stunned reaction
10. Tells about the authorities' decision not to charge him
11. Remembers the sight of the crushed car once it had been flipped back over
12. Recalls the wrecker operator's echo of the trooper's comment
13. Ends with a reflection about an imagined newspaper headline that humorously summarizes his experience

Turn to pp. 33–36 to compare this outline to Bragg's essay.

Scratch Outline: Essay Arguing a Position

Presentation of the issue

Concession of some aspect of an opposing position

Thesis statement

First reason with support

Second reason with support (etc.)

Conclusion

Remember that the items in a scratch outline do not necessarily coincide with paragraphs. Sometimes two or more items may be developed in the same paragraph or one item may be covered in two or more paragraphs.

Chunking, a type of scratch outline commonly used by professional writers in business and industry and especially well suited to writing in the electronic age, consists of a set of headings describing the major points to be covered in the final document. What makes chunking distinctive is that the blocks of text — or "chunks" — under each heading are intended to be roughly the same length and scope. These headings can be discussed and passed around among several writers and editors before writing begins, and different chunks may be written by different authors, simply by typing notes or text on a word processor into the space under each heading. The list of headings is subject to change during the writing, and new headings may be added or old ones subdivided or discarded as part of the drafting and editing process.

The advantage of chunking in your own writing is that it breaks the large task of drafting into smaller tasks in a simple, evenly balanced way; once the headings are determined, the writing becomes just a matter of filling in the specifics that go in each chunk. Organization tends to improve as you get a sense of the weight of different parts of the document while filling in the blanks. Places where the essay needs more information or there is a problem with pacing tend to stand out because of the chunking structure, and the headings can either be taken out of the finished essay or left in as devices to help guide readers. If they are left in, they should be edited into parallel grammatical form like the items in a formal topic or sentence outline, as discussed below.

Topic and *sentence outlines* are considered more formal than scratch outlines because they follow a conventional format of numbered and lettered headings and subheadings:

I. (Main topic)

  A. (Subtopic of I)

  B.

    1. (Subtopic of I.B)

    2.

      a. (Subtopic of I.B.2)

      b.

        (1) (Subtopic of I.B.2.b)

        (2)

C.

    1. (Subtopic of I.C)

    2.

The difference between a topic and sentence outline is obvious: Topic outlines simply name the topics and subtopics, whereas sentence outlines use complete or abbreviated sentences. To illustrate, here are two partial formal outlines of an essay arguing a position, Jessica Statsky's "Children Need to Play, Not Compete," from Chapter 6.

Turn to pp. 276–79 to compare these outlines to Statsky's essay.

Formal Topic Outline

I. Organized sports harmful to children

  A. Harmful physically

    1. Curve ball (Koppett)

    2. Tackle football (Tutko)

  B. Harmful psychologically

    1. Fear of being hurt

      a. Little League Online

      b. Mother

      c. Reporter

    2. Competition

      a. Rablovsky

      b. Studies

Formal Sentence Outline

I. Highly organized competitive sports such as Peewee Football and Little League Baseball can be physically and psychologically harmful to children, as well as counterproductive for developing future players.

  A. Physically harmful because sports entice children into physical actions that are bad for growing bodies.

    1. Koppett claims throwing a curve ball may put abnormal strain on developing arm and shoulder muscles.

    2. Tutko argues that tackle football is too traumatic for young kids.

  B. Psychologically harmful to children for a number of reasons.

    1. Fear of being hurt detracts from their enjoyment of the sport.

      a. Little League Online ranks fear of injury seventh among the seven top reasons children quit.

      b. One mother says, "kids get so scared. . . . They'll sit on the bench and pretend their leg hurts."

      c. A reporter tells about a child who made himself vomit to get out of playing Peewee Football.

  2. Too much competition poses psychological dangers for children.
      a. Rablovsky reports: "The spirit of play suddenly disappears, and sport becomes joblike."
      b. Studies show that children prefer playing on a losing team to "warming the bench on a winning team."

In contrast to an informal outline in which anything goes, a formal outline must follow many conventions. The roman numerals and capital letters are followed by periods. In topic and sentence outlines, the first word of each item is capitalized, but items in topic outlines do not end with a period as items in sentence outlines do. Every level of a formal outline except the top level (identified by the roman numeral *I*) must include at least two items. Items at the same level of indentation in a topic outline should be grammatically parallel — all beginning with the same part of speech. For example, *I.A.* and *I.B.* are parallel when they both begin with an adverb (*Physically harmful* and *Psychologically harmful*) or with a noun (*Harmful physically* and *Harmful psychologically*); they would not be parallel if one began with an adverb (*Physically harmful*) and the other with a noun (*Harmful psychologically*).

▪ Writing

Writing is itself a powerful tool for thinking. As you write, you can recall details, remember facts, develop your ideas, find connections in new information you have collected, examine assumptions, and critically question what you know.

Unlike most mapping strategies, **writing strategies** of invention invite you to produce complete sentences. Sentences provide considerable generative power. Because they are complete statements, they take you further than listing or clustering. They enable you to explore ideas and define relationships, bring ideas together or show how they differ, and identify causes and effects. Sentences can also help you develop a logical chain of thought.

Some of these invention and inquiry strategies are systematic, while others are more flexible. Even though they call for complete sentences that are related to one another, they do not require preparation or revision. You can use them to develop oral as well as written presentations.

These writing strategies include cubing, dialoguing, dramatizing, keeping a journal, looping, questioning, and quick drafting.

Cubing

Cubing is useful for quickly exploring a writing topic, probing it from six different perspectives. It is known as *cubing* because a cube has six sides. These are the six perspectives in cubing:

  Describing: What does your subject look like? What size is it? What is its color? Its shape? Its texture? Name its parts.

  Comparing: What is your subject similar to? Different from?

Associating: What does your subject make you think of? What connections does it have to anything else in your experience?

Analyzing: What are the origins of your subject? What are its parts or features? How are its parts related?

Applying: What can you do with your subject? What uses does it have?

Arguing: What arguments can you make for your subject? Against it?

Here are some guidelines to help you use cubing productively.

1. Select a topic, subject, or part of a subject. This can be a person, a scene, an event, an object, a problem, an idea, or an issue. Hold it in focus.

2. Limit your writing to three to five minutes for each perspective. The whole activity should take no more than half an hour.

3. Keep going until you have written about your subject from all six perspectives. Remember that cubing offers the special advantage of enabling you to generate multiple perspectives quickly.

4. As you write from each perspective, begin with what you know about your subject. However, do not limit yourself to your present knowledge. Indicate what else you would like to know about your subject, and suggest where you might find that information.

5. Reread what you have written. Look for bright spots, surprises. Recall the part that was easiest for you to write. Recall the part where you felt a special momentum and pleasure in the writing. Look for an angle or an unexpected insight. These special parts may suggest a focus or topic within a larger subject, or they may provide specific details to include in a draft.

Dialoguing

A dialogue is a conversation between two or more people. You can use **dialoguing** to search for topics, find a focus, explore ideas, or consider opposing viewpoints. When you write a dialogue as an invention strategy, you need to make up all parts of the conversation (unless, of course, you are writing collaboratively — on a network, for example). To construct a dialogue by yourself, imagine two particular people talking, hold a conversation yourself with some imagined person, or simply talk out loud to yourself. To construct a dialogue independently or collaboratively, follow these steps:

See pp. 61–62 for an example of dialogue used for invention.

1. Write a conversation between two speakers. Label the participants *Speaker A* and *Speaker B*, or make up names for them.

2. If you get stuck, you might have one of the speakers ask the other a question.

3. Write brief responses to keep the conversation moving fast. Do not spend much time planning or rehearsing responses. Write what first occurs to you, just as in a real conversation, where people take quick turns to prevent any awkward silences.

Dialogues can be especially useful with personal experience and persuasive essays because they help you remember conversations and anticipate objections.

Dramatizing

Dramatizing is an invention activity developed by the philosopher Kenneth Burke as a way of thinking about how people interact and as a way of analyzing stories and films.

Thinking about human behavior in dramatic terms can be very productive for writers. Drama has action, actors, setting, motives, and methods. Since stars and acting go together, you can use a five-pointed star to remember these five points of dramatizing: Each point on the star provides a different perspective on human behavior (see Figure 11.2). We can think of each point independently and in combination. Let us begin by looking at each point to see how it helps us to analyze people and their interactions.

Action.   An action is anything that happens, has happened, will happen, or could happen. Action includes events that are physical (running a marathon), mental (thinking about a book you have read), and emotional (falling in love). This category also refers to the results of activity (an essay).

Actor.   The actor is involved in the action — either responsible for it or simply affected by it. (The actor does not have to be a person. It can be a force, something that causes an action. For example, if the action is a rise in the price of gasoline, the actor could be increased demand or short supply.) Dramatizing may also include a number of coactors working together or at odds.

Setting.   The setting is the situation or background of the action. We usually think of setting as the place and time of an event, but it may also be the historical background of an event or the childhood of a person.

Motive.   The motive is the purpose or reason for an action — the actor's intention. Actions may have multiple, even conflicting, motives.

Figure 11.2 Dramatizing

Method.   The method explains how an action occurs, including the techniques an actor uses. It refers to whatever makes things happen.

Each of these points suggests a simple invention question:

Action: What?

Actor: Who?

Setting: When and where?

Motive: Why?

Method: How?

This list looks like the questions reporters typically ask. But dramatizing goes further: It enables us to ask a much fuller set of invention questions that we generate by considering relations between and among these five elements. We can think about actors' motives, the effect of the setting on the actors, the relations between actors, and so on.

You can use this invention strategy to learn more about yourself or about other significant people in your life. You can use it, as well, to explore, analyze, or evaluate characters in stories or movies. Moreover, dramatizing is especially useful in analyzing the readers you want to inform or convince.

To use dramatizing, imagine the person you want to understand better in a particular situation. Holding this image in mind, write answers to any questions in the following list that apply. You may draw a blank on some questions, have little to say to some, and find a lot to say to others. Be exploratory and playful with the questions. Write responses quickly, relying on words and phrases, even drawings.

- What is the actor doing?
- How did the actor come to be involved in this situation?
- Why does the actor do what he or she does?
- What else might the actor do?
- What is the actor trying to accomplish?
- How do other actors influence — help or hinder — the main actor?
- What do the actor's actions reveal about him or her?
- What does the actor's language reveal about him or her?
- How does the event's setting influence the actor's actions?
- How does the time of the event influence what the actor does?
- Where does this actor come from?
- How is this actor different now from what he or she used to be?
- What might this actor become?
- How is this actor like or unlike the other actors?

Keeping a Journal

Professional writers often use **journals** to keep notes, and so might you. Starting a writer's journal is easy. Buy a special notebook, or open a new file on your computer, and start writing. Here are some possibilities:

- Keep a list of new words and concepts you learn in your courses. You could also write about the progress and direction of your learning in particular courses — the experience of being in the course, your feelings about what is happening, and what you are learning.

- Respond to your reading, both assigned and personal. As you read, write about your personal associations, reflections, reactions, and evaluations. Summarize or copy memorable or especially important passages, and comment on them. (Copying and commenting have been practiced by students and writers for centuries in special journals called *commonplace books.*)

- Write to prepare for particular class meetings. Write about the main ideas you have learned from assigned readings and about the relationship of these new ideas to other ideas in the course. After class, write to summarize what you have learned. List questions you have about the ideas or information discussed in class. Journal writing of this kind involves reflecting, evaluating, interpreting, synthesizing, summarizing, and questioning.

- Record observations and overheard conversations.

- Write for ten or fifteen minutes every day about whatever is on your mind. Focus these meditations on your new experiences as you try to understand, interpret, and reflect on them.

- Write sketches of people who catch your attention.

- Organize your time. Write about your goals and priorities, or list specific things to accomplish and what you plan to do.

- Keep a log over several days or weeks about a particular event unfolding in the news — a sensational trial, an environmental disaster, a political campaign, a campus controversy, the fortunes of a sports team.

You can use a journal in many ways. All of the writing in your journal has value for learning. You may also be able to use parts of your journal for writing in your other courses.

Looping

Looping is especially useful for the first stages of exploring a topic. As its name suggests, **looping** involves writing quickly to explore some aspect of a topic and then looping back to your original starting point or to a new starting point to explore another aspect. Beginning with almost any starting point, looping enables you to find a center of interest and eventually a thesis for your essay. The steps are simple:

1. Write down your area of interest. You may know only that you have to write about another person or a movie or a cultural trend that has caught your

attention. Or you may want to search for a topic in a broad historical period or for one related to a major political event. Although you may wander from this topic as you write, you will want to keep coming back to it. Your purpose is to find a focus for writing.

2. Write nonstop for ten minutes. Start with the first thing that comes to mind. Write rapidly, without looking back to reread or to correct anything. *Do not stop writing. Keep your pencil moving or keystrokes clacking.* Continuous writing is the key to looping. If you get stuck for a moment, rewrite the last sentence. Trust the act of writing to lead you to new insights. Follow diversions and digressions, but keep returning to your topic.

3. After ten minutes, pause to reread what you have written. Decide what is most important — a single insight, a pattern of ideas, an emerging theme, a visual detail, anything at all that stands out. Some writers call this a "center of gravity" or a "hot spot." To complete the first loop, restate this center in a single sentence.

4. Beginning with this sentence, write nonstop for another ten minutes.

5. Summarize in one sentence again to complete the second loop.

6. Keep looping until one of your summary sentences produces a focus or thesis. You may need only two or three loops; you may need more.

Questioning

Asking **questions** about a subject is a way to learn about it and decide what to write. When you first encounter a subject, however, your questions may be scattered. Also, you are not likely to think right away of all the important questions you ought to ask. The advantage of having a basic list of questions for invention, like the ones for cubing and for dramatizing discussed earlier in this chapter, is that it provides a systematic approach to exploring a subject.

The questions that follow come from classical rhetoric (what the Greek philosopher Aristotle called *topics*) and a modern approach to invention called *tagmemics.* Based on the work of linguist Kenneth Pike, tagmemics provides questions about different ways we make sense of the world, the ways we sort and classify experience in order to understand it.

Here are the steps in using questions for invention:

1. In a sentence or two, identify your subject. A subject could be any event, person, problem, project, idea, or issue — in other words, anything you might write about.

2. Start by writing a response to the first question in the following list, and move right through the list. Try to answer each question at least briefly with a word or a phrase. Some questions may invite several sentences or even a page or more of writing. You may draw a blank on a few questions. Skip them. Later, when you have more experience with questions for invention, you can start anywhere in the list.

3. Write your responses quickly, without much planning. Follow digressions or associations. Do not screen anything out. Be playful.

What Is Your Subject?

- What is your subject's name? What other names does it have? What names did it have in the past?
- What aspects of the subject do these different names emphasize?
- Imagine a still photograph or a moving picture of your subject. What would it look like?
- What would you put into a time capsule to stand for your subject?
- What are its causes and results?
- How would it look from different vantage points or perspectives?
- What particular experiences have you had with the subject? What have you learned?

What Parts or Features Does Your Subject Have, and How Are They Related?

- Name the parts or features of your subject.
- Describe each one, using the questions in the preceding subject list.
- How is each part or feature related to the others?

How Is Your Subject Similar to and Different from Other Subjects?

- What is your subject similar to? In what ways are these subjects alike?
- What is your subject different from? In what ways are the subjects different?
- What seems to you most unlike your subject? In what ways are the two things unlike each other? Now, just for fun, note how they are alike.

How Much Can Your Subject Change and Still Remain the Same?

- How has your subject changed from what it once was?
- How is it changing now — moment to moment, day to day, year to year?
- How does each change alter your way of thinking about your subject?
- What are some different forms your subject takes?
- What does it become when it is no longer itself?

Where Does Your Subject Fit in the World?

- When and where did your subject originate?
- What would happen if at some future time your subject ceased to exist?
- When and where do you usually experience the subject?
- What is this subject a part of, and what are the other parts?
- What do other people think of your subject?

Quick Drafting

Sometimes you know what you want to say or have little time for invention. In these situations, **quick drafting** may be a good strategy. There are no special rules for quick drafting, but you should rely on it only if you know your subject well, have had experience with the kind of writing you are doing, and will have a chance to revise your draft. Quick drafting can help you discover what you already know about the subject and what you need to find out. It can also help you develop and organize your thoughts.

12

A Catalog of Reading Strategies

This chapter presents strategies to help you become a thoughtful reader. A thoughtful reader is above all a patient *re*reader, concerned not only with comprehending and remembering but also with interpreting and evaluating. Reading this way, you alternate between understanding and questioning — on the one hand, striving to understand the text on its own terms; on the other hand, taking care to question its ideas and authority.

The strategies here complement and supplement reading strategies presented in Part One, Chapters 2–10. Thoughtful reading is central to your success with the writing assignments in those chapters. The Making Connections to Personal and Social Issues activity following each reading in Part One helps you think about the selection in light of your own experience and awareness of social issues, while the Analyzing Writing Strategies questions help you understand how the text works and evaluate how well it achieves its purpose with its readers. A Critical Reading Guide in each Part One chapter helps you read other students' drafts as well as your own to find out what is working and what needs improvement.

Reading is, after all, inextricably linked to writing, and the reading strategies in this chapter can help you enrich your thinking as a reader and participate in conversations as a writer. These strategies include the following:

- *Annotating:* Recording your reactions to, interpretations of, and questions about a text as you read it
- *Taking inventory:* Listing and grouping your annotations and other notes to find meaningful patterns
- *Outlining:* Listing the text's main ideas to reveal how it is organized
- *Paraphrasing:* Restating what you have read to clarify or refer to it
- *Summarizing:* Distilling the main ideas or gist of a text
- *Synthesizing:* Integrating into your own writing ideas and information gleaned from different sources
- *Contextualizing:* Placing a text in its historical and cultural contexts
- *Exploring the significance of figurative language:* Examining how metaphors, similes, and symbols are used in a text to convey meaning and evoke feelings

- *Looking for patterns of opposition:* Analyzing the values and assumptions embodied in the language of a text
- *Reflecting on challenges to your beliefs and values:* Examining the bases of your personal responses to a text
- *Evaluating the logic of an argument:* Determining whether a thesis is well reasoned and adequately supported
- *Recognizing emotional manipulation:* Identifying texts that unfairly and inappropriately use emotional appeals based on false or exaggerated claims
- *Judging the writer's credibility:* Considering whether writers represent different points of view fairly and know what they are writing about

These reading strategies can help you connect information from different sources and relate it to what you already know; distinguish fact from opinion; uncover and question assumptions; and subject other people's ideas as well as your own to reasoned argument. You can readily learn these strategies and apply them not only to the reading selections in Part One but also to your other college reading. Although mastering the strategies will not make critical reading easy, it can make your reading much more satisfying and productive and thus help you handle even difficult material with confidence. These reading strategies will, in addition, often be useful in your reading outside of school — for instance, these strategies can help you understand, evaluate, and comment on what political figures, advertisers, and other writers are saying.

■ Annotating

Annotations are the marks — underlines, highlights, and comments — you make directly on the page as you read. **Annotating** can be used to record immediate reactions and questions, outline and summarize main points, and evaluate and relate the reading to other ideas and points of view. Especially useful for studying and preparing to write, annotating is also an essential element of many other critical reading strategies. Your annotations can take many forms, such as the following:

Writing comments, questions, or definitions in the margins

Underlining or circling words, phrases, or sentences

Connecting ideas with lines or arrows

Numbering related points

Bracketing sections of the text

Noting anything that strikes you as interesting, important, or questionable

Most readers annotate in layers, adding further annotations on second and third readings. Annotations can be light or heavy, depending on the reader's purpose and the difficulty of the material. Your purpose for reading also determines how you use your annotations.

Annotating Onscreen
Although this discussion of annotating assumes you are reading printed pages, you can also annotate many kinds of text on the computer screen by using your word processor's highlighting and commenting functions. Even if these functions are not available, you may be able to type annotations into the text using a different color or font. If electronic annotation is impossible, print out the text, and annotate by hand.

The following selection, excerpted from Martin Luther King Jr.'s "Letter from Birmingham Jail," is annotated to illustrate some of the ways you can annotate as you read. Add your own annotations, if you like.

MARTIN LUTHER KING JR. (1929–1968) first came to national notice in 1955, when he led a successful boycott against the policy of restricting African American passengers to rear seats on city buses in Montgomery, Alabama, where he was minister of a Baptist church. He subsequently formed a national organization, the Southern Christian Leadership Conference, that brought people of all races from all over the country to the South to fight nonviolently for racial integration. In 1963, King led demonstrations in Birmingham, Alabama, that were met with violence; a bomb was detonated in a black church, killing four young girls. King was arrested for his role in organizing the protests, and while in prison, he wrote the famous "Letter from Birmingham Jail" to answer the criticism of local clergy and to justify to the nation his strategy of civil disobedience, which he called "nonviolent direct action."

King begins his letter by discussing his disappointment with the lack of support he has received from white moderates, such as the group of clergy who published criticism in the local newspaper. As you read the following excerpt, try to infer from King's written response what the clergy's specific criticisms might have been. Also, notice the tone King uses to answer his critics. Would you characterize the writing as apologetic, conciliatory, accusatory, or in some other way?

An Annotated Sample from "Letter from Birmingham Jail"
Martin Luther King Jr.

¶1. White moderates block progress.

I must confess that over the past few years I have been gravely 1 disappointed with the white moderate. I have almost reached the regrettable conclusion that the Negro's [great stumbling block in his stride toward freedom] is not the White Citizen's Counciler or the Ku Klux Klanner, but the white moderate, who is more de-

negative vs. positive

voted to "order" than to justice; who prefers a negative peace which is the absence of tension to a positive peace which is the presence of justice; who constantly says: "I agree with you in the goal you seek, but I cannot agree with your methods of direct

order vs. justice

ends vs. means

treating others like children

action"; who paternalistically believes he can set the timetable for another man's freedom; who lives by a mythical concept of time and who constantly advises the Negro to wait for a "more convenient season." Shallow understanding from people of good will is more frustrating than absolute misunderstanding from people of ill will. Lukewarm acceptance is much more bewildering than outright rejection.

¶2. Tension necessary for progress.

I had hoped that the white moderate would understand that law and order exist for the purpose of establishing justice and that when they fail in this purpose they become the [dangerously structured dams that block the flow of social progress.] I had hoped that the white moderate would understand that the present tension in the South is a necessary phase of the transition from an [obnoxious negative peace,] in which the Negro passively accepted his unjust plight, to a [substantive and positive peace,] in which all men will respect the dignity and worth of human personality. Actually, we who engage in nonviolent direct action are

Tension already exists anyway.

not the creators of tension. We merely bring to the surface the hidden tension that is already alive. We bring it out in the open, where it can be seen and dealt with. [Like a boil that can never

True?

be cured so long as it is covered up but must be opened with all its ugliness to the natural medicines of air and light, injustice must be exposed, with all the tension its exposure creates, to the light of human conscience and the air of national opinion before it can be cured.]

simile: hidden tension is "like a boil"

¶3. Questions clergymen's logic: condemning his actions = condemning victims, Socrates, Jesus.

In your statement you assert that our actions, even though peaceful, must be condemned because they precipitate violence. But is this a logical assertion? Isn't this like condemning a robbed man because his possession of money precipitated the evil act of robbery? Isn't this like condemning Socrates because his unswerving commitment to truth and his philosophical inquiries precipitated the act by the misguided populace in which they made him drink hemlock? Isn't this like condemning Jesus

2

3

because his unique God-consciousness and never-ceasing devotion to God's will precipitated the evil act of crucifixion? We must come to see that, as the federal courts have consistently affirmed, it is wrong to urge an individual to cease his efforts to gain his basic constitutional rights because the question may precipitate

Yes!

violence. [Society must protect the robbed and punish the robber.]

I had also hoped that the white moderate would reject the 4 myth concerning time in relation to the struggle for freedom. I have just received a letter from a white brother in Texas. He

example of a white moderate

writes: "All Christians know that the colored people will receive equal rights eventually, but it is possible that you are in too great a religious hurry. It has taken Christianity almost two thousand years to accomplish what it has. The teachings of Christ take time to come to earth." Such an attitude stems from a tragic misconception of time, from the strangely irrational notion that there is something in the very flow of time that will inevitably cure all ills. Actually, time itself is neutral; it can be used either destructively or constructively. More and more I feel that the people of ill will have used time much more effectively than have the people of good will. We will have to repent in this generation not

Silence is as bad as hateful words and actions.

merely for the [hateful words and actions of the bad people] but for the [appalling silence of the good people.] Human progress never rolls in on [wheels of inevitability;] it comes through the tireless efforts of men willing to be co-workers with God, and without this hard work, time itself becomes an ally of the forces of social

metaphor

¶4. Time must be used to do right.

stagnation. [We must use time creatively, in the knowledge that

not moving

the time is always ripe to do right.] Now is the time to make real the promise of democracy and transform our pending [national elegy] into a creative [psalm of brotherhood.] Now is the time to

metaphors

lift our national policy from the [quicksand of racial injustice] to the [solid rock of human dignity.]

You speak of our activity in Birmingham as <u>extreme</u>. At first 5 I was rather disappointed that fellow clergymen would see my nonviolent efforts as those of an extremist. I began thinking about the <u>fact</u> that <u>I stand in the middle of two opposing forces in the Negro community</u>. One is a [force of complacency,] made up in part of Negroes who, as a result of long years of oppression, are so drained of self-respect and a sense of "somebodiness" that they have adjusted to segregation; and in part of a few middle-class Negroes, who because of a degree of academic and economic security and because in some ways they profit by segregation, have become insensitive to the problems of the masses. The other [force is one of bitterness and hatred,] and it comes perilously close to advocating violence. It is expressed in the various <u>black nationalist</u> [groups that are springing up] across the nation, the largest and best-known being <u>Elijah Muhammad's Muslim movement</u>. Nourished by the Negro's frustration over the continued existence of racial discrimination, this movement is made up of people who have lost faith in America, who have absolutely repudiated Christianity, and who have concluded that the white man is an incorrigible "devil."

<u>I have tried to stand between these two forces</u>, saying that 6 we need emulate neither the "do-nothingism" of the complacent nor the hatred and despair of the black nationalist. For there is <u>the more excellent way of love and nonviolent protest</u>. I am grateful to God that, through the influence of the Negro church, the way of nonviolence became an integral part of our struggle.

If this philosophy had not emerged, by now many streets of 7 the South would, I am convinced, be flowing with blood. And I am further convinced that if our white brothers dismiss as "rabble-rousers" and "outside agitators" those of us who employ nonviolent direct action, and if they refuse to support our nonviolent

---

King accused of being an extremist.

¶5. King in middle of two extremes: complacent & angry.

Malcolm X?

¶6. King offers better choice.

How did nonviolence become part of King's movement?

¶7. King's movement prevented racial violence. Threat?

Gandhi?

The church?

If . . . then . . .

efforts, millions of Negroes will, out of frustration and despair, seek (solace) and security in black-nationalist ideologies — a development that would inevitably lead to a frightening racial nightmare.

comfort

(Oppressed people cannot remain oppressed forever.) The yearning for freedom eventually manifests itself, and that is what has happened to the American Negro. Something within has reminded him of his birthright of freedom, and something without has reminded him that it can be gained. Consciously or uncon-

8

worldwide uprising against injustice

sciously, he has been caught up by the (Zeitgeist,) and with his black brothers of Africa and his brown and yellow brothers of Asia, South America and the Caribbean, the United States Negro is moving with a sense of great urgency toward the [promised land of racial justice.] If one recognizes this [vital urge that has engulfed the Negro community,] one should readily understand why public demonstrations are taking place. The Negro has many [pent-up resentments] and latent frustrations, and he must release them. So let him march; let him make prayer pilgrimages to the city hall; let him go on freedom rides — and try to understand why he must do so. If his repressed emotions are not released in nonviolent ways, they will seek expression through violence; this is not a threat but a fact of history. So I have not said to my people: "Get rid of your discontent." Rather, I have tried to say that this normal and healthy discontent can be [channeled into the creative outlet of nonviolent direct action.] And now this approach is being termed extremist.

spirit of the times

Not a threat?

¶8. Discontent is normal and healthy but must be channeled.

But though I was initially disappointed at being categorized as an extremist, as I continued to think about the matter I gradually gained a measure of satisfaction from the label. Was not Jesus an extremist for love: "Love your enemies, bless them

9

that curse you, do good to them that hate you, and pray for them which despitefully use you, and persecute you." Was not (Amos) an extremist for justice: "Let justice roll down like waters and righteousness like an ever-flowing stream." Was not (Paul) an extremist for the Christian gospel: "I bear in my body the marks of the Lord Jesus." Was not Martin Luther an extremist: "Here I stand; I cannot do otherwise, so help me God." And (John Bunyan:) "I will stay in jail to the end of my days before I make a butchery of my conscience." And (Abraham Lincoln:) "This nation cannot survive half slave and half free." And (Thomas Jefferson:) "We hold these truths to be self-evident, that all men are created equal. . . ."

So the question is not whether we will be extremists, but what kind of extremists we will be. Will we be extremists for hate or for love? Will we be extremists for the preservation of injustice or for the extension of justice? In that dramatic scene on Calvary's hill three men were crucified. We must never forget that all three were crucified for the same crime — the crime of extremism. Two were extremists for immorality, and thus fell below their environment. The other, (Jesus Christ,) was an extremist for love, truth and goodness, and thereby rose above his environment. Perhaps the South, the nation and the world are in dire need of creative extremists.

I had hoped that the white moderate would see this need. 10 Perhaps I was too optimistic; perhaps I expected too much. I suppose I should have realized that few members of the oppressor race can understand the deep groans and passionate yearnings of the oppressed race, and still fewer have the vision to see that [injustice must be rooted out] by strong, persistent and determined action. I am thankful, however, that some of our white brothers in the South have grasped the meaning of this

Hebrew prophet

Christian apostle

English preacher

Founded Protestantism

No choice but to be extremists: But what kind?

¶9. Creative extremists are needed.

Disappointed in the white moderate

¶10. Some whites have supported King.

social revolution and committed themselves to it. They are still all

too few in quantity, but they are big in quality. Some — such

as Ralph McGill, Lillian Smith, Harry Golden, James McBride   *Who are they?*

Dabbs, Ann Braden and Sarah Patton Boyle — have written

what they did   about our struggle in eloquent and prophetic terms. Others have

marched with us down nameless streets of the South. They have

languished in filthy, roach-infested jails, suffering the abuse and   *been left unaided*

brutality of policemen who view them as "dirty nigger-lovers."

Unlike so many of their moderate brothers and sisters, they have

recognized the urgency of the moment and sensed the need for

[powerful "action" antidotes] to combat the [disease of segregation.]

CHECKLIST: ANNOTATING

1. Mark the text using notations like these:
   - Circle words to be defined in the margin.
   - Underline key words and phrases.
   - Bracket important sentences and passages.
   - Use lines or arrows to connect ideas or words.
2. Write marginal comments like these:
   - Number and summarize each paragraph.
   - Define unfamiliar words.
   - Note responses and questions.
   - Identify interesting writing strategies.
   - Point out patterns.
3. Layer additional markings on the text and comments in the margins as you reread for different purposes.

■ Taking Inventory

An inventory is simply a list or grouping of items. **Taking inventory** helps you analyze your annotations for different purposes. When you take inventory, you make various kinds of lists to explore patterns of meaning you find in the text. For instance, in reading the annotated passage by Martin Luther King Jr., you might have noticed that certain similes and metaphors are used or that many famous people are named. By listing the names (Socrates, Jesus, Luther, Lincoln, and so on) and then grouping them into categories (people who died for their beliefs, leaders, teachers, and religious figures) you could better understand why the writer refers to these particular people. Taking inventory of your annotations can be helpful in writing about a text you are reading.

Outlining

Outlining is an especially helpful reading strategy for understanding the content and structure of a reading. **Outlining**, which identifies the text's main ideas, may be part of the annotating process, or it may be done separately. Writing an outline in the margins of the text as you read and annotate makes it easier to find information later. Writing an outline on a separate piece of paper gives you more space to work with, and therefore such an outline usually includes more detail.

The key to outlining is distinguishing between the main ideas and the supporting material such as examples, quotations, comparisons, and reasons. The main ideas form the backbone, which holds the various parts and pieces of the text together. Outlining the main ideas helps you uncover this structure.

Making an outline, however, is not simple. The reader must exercise judgment in deciding which are the most important ideas. Because importance is relative, different readers can make different — and equally reasonable — decisions based on what interests them in the reading. Readers also must decide whether to use the writer's words, their own words, or a combination of the two. The words used in an outline reflect the reader's interpretation and emphasis. Reading is never a passive or neutral act; the process of outlining shows how constructive reading can be.

You may make either a formal, multileveled outline with roman (I, II) and arabic (1, 2) numerals together with capital and lowercase letters or an informal scratch outline that lists the main idea of each paragraph. A *formal outline* is harder to make and much more time-consuming than a scratch outline. You might choose to make a formal outline of a reading about which you are writing an in-depth analysis or evaluation. For example, here is a formal outline a student wrote for a paper evaluating the logic of the King excerpt. Notice that the student uses roman numerals for the main ideas or claims, capital letters for the reasons, and arabic numerals for supporting evidence and explanation.

For more on the conventions of formal outlines, see pp. 573–76.

Formal Outline

I. "[T]he Negro's great stumbling block in his stride toward freedom is . . . the white moderate. . . ."

   A. Because the white moderate is more devoted to "order" than to justice (paragraph 2)

      1. Law and order should exist to establish justice.

      2. Law and order compare to "dangerously structured dams that block the flow of social progress."

   B. Because the white moderate prefers a "negative peace" (absence of tension) to a "positive peace" (justice) (paragraph 2)

      1. The tension already exists.

      2. It is not created by nonviolent direct action.

      3. Society that does not eliminate injustice compares to a boil that hides its infections. Both can be cured only by exposure (boil simile).

   C. Because even though the white moderate agrees with the goals, he does not support the means to achieve them (paragraph 3)

      1. The argument that the means--nonviolent direct action--are wrong because they precipitate violence is flawed.

      2. An analogy compares black people to the robbed man who is condemned because he had money.

      3. Analogies compare black people with Socrates and Jesus.

   D. Because the white moderate paternalistically believes he can set a timetable for another man's freedom (paragraph 4)

      1. King rebuts the white moderate's argument that Christianity will cure man's ills and man must wait patiently for that to happen.

      2. He argues that "time itself is neutral" and that people "must use time creatively" for constructive rather than destructive ends.

II. Creative extremism is preferable to moderation.

   A. Classifies himself as a moderate (paragraphs 5–8)

      1. "I . . . stand between . . . two forces": the white moderate's complacency and the Black Muslim's rage.

      2. If nonviolent direct action were stopped, more violence, not less, would result.

      3. "[M]illions of Negroes will, out of frustration and despair, seek solace and security in black-nationalist ideologies . . ." (paragraph 7).

      4. Repressed emotions will be expressed--if not in nonviolent ways, then through violence (paragraph 8).

   B. Redefines himself as a "creative extremist" (paragraph 9)

      1. Extremism for love, truth, and goodness is creative extremism.

      2. He identifies himself with other extremists--Jesus, Amos, Paul, Martin Luther, John Bunyan, Abraham Lincoln, and Thomas Jefferson.

C. Not all white people are moderates; some are committed to "this social revolution" (paragraph 10).

   1. He lists the names of white writers.

   2. He refers to other white activists.

Making a scratch outline takes less time than making a formal outline but still requires careful reading. A *scratch outline* will not record as much information as a formal outline, but it is sufficient for most critical reading purposes. To make a scratch outline, you first need to locate the topic of each paragraph in the reading. The topic is usually stated in a word or phrase, and it may be repeated or referred to throughout the paragraph. For example, the opening paragraph of the King excerpt (p. 586) makes clear that its topic is the white moderate.

After you have found the topic of the paragraph, figure out what is being said about it. To return to our example: King immediately establishes the white moderate as the topic of the opening paragraph and at the beginning of the second sentence announces the conclusion he has come to — namely, that the white moderate is "the Negro's great stumbling block in his stride toward freedom." The rest of the paragraph specifies the ways the white moderate blocks progress.

For each paragraph in the King excerpt, the annotations include a summary of the paragraph's topic. Here is an outline that lists those paragraph topics:

Paragraph Scratch Outline

¶1. white moderates block progress in the struggle for racial justice

¶2. tension necessary for progress

¶3. clergymen's criticism not logical

¶4. time must be used to do right

¶5. King is in the middle of two extremes: complacent and angry

¶6. King offers better choice

¶7. King's movement has prevented racial violence

¶8. discontent normal and healthy but must be channeled

¶9. creative extremists needed

¶10. some whites have supported King

CHECKLIST: OUTLINING

1. Reread each paragraph, identifying the topic and the comments made about the topic. Do not include examples, specific details, quotations, or other explanatory and supporting material.

2. List the author's main ideas in the margin of the text or on a separate piece of paper.

Paraphrasing

Paraphrasing is restating something you have read by using mostly your own words. It can help you clarify the meaning of an obscure or ambiguous passage. It is one of the three ways of integrating other people's ideas and information into your own writing, along with *quoting* (reproducing exactly the language of the source text) and *summarizing* (distilling the main ideas or gist of the source text) (p. 597). You might choose to paraphrase rather than quote when the source's language is not especially arresting or memorable. You might paraphrase short passages but summarize longer ones.

Following are two passages. The first is from paragraph 2 of the excerpt from King's "Letter." The second passage is a paraphrase of the first:

Original

I had hoped that the white moderate would understand that law and order exist for the purpose of establishing justice and that when they fail in this purpose they become the dangerously structured dams that block the flow of social progress. I had hoped that the white moderate would understand that the present tension in the South is a necessary phase of the transition from an obnoxious negative peace, in which the Negro passively accepted his unjust plight, to a substantive and positive peace, in which all men will respect the dignity and worth of human personality.

Paraphrase

King writes that he had hoped for more understanding from white moderates--specifically that they would recognize that law and order are not ends in themselves but means to the greater end of establishing justice. When law and order do not serve this greater end, they stand in the way of progress. King expected the white moderate to recognize that the current tense situation in the South is part of a transition process that is necessary for progress. The current situation is bad because although there is peace, it is an "obnoxious" and "negative" kind of peace based on blacks passively accepting the injustice of the status quo. A better kind of peace--one that is "substantive," real and not imaginary, as well as "positive"--requires that all people, regardless of race, be valued.

When you compare the paraphrase to the original, you can see that the paraphrase contains all the important information and ideas of the original. Notice also that the paraphrase is somewhat longer than the original, refers to the writer by name, and encloses King's original words in quotation marks. Although the paraphrase tries to be *neutral*, to avoid inserting the reader's opinions or distorting the original writer's ideas, it does inevitably express the reader's interpretation of the original text's meaning. Another reader might paraphrase the same passage differently.

CHECKLIST: PARAPHRASING

1. Reread the passage to be paraphrased, looking up unfamiliar words in a college dictionary.

2. Translate the passage into your own words, putting quotation marks around any words or phrases you quote from the original.

3. Revise to ensure coherence.

Summarizing

Summarizing is one of the most widely used reading strategies for critical reading because it helps the reader understand and remember what is most important in the reading. Another advantage of summarizing is that it creates a condensed version of the reading's ideas and information, which can be referred to later or inserted into the reader's own writing. Along with quoting and paraphrasing, summarizing enables you to refer to and integrate other writers' ideas into your own writing.

A summary is a relatively brief restatement, primarily in the reader's own words, of the reading's main ideas. Summaries vary in length, depending on the reader's purpose. Some summaries are very brief — a sentence or even a subordinate clause. For example, if you were referring to the excerpt from "Letter from Birmingham Jail" and simply needed to indicate how it relates to your other sources, your summary might focus on only one aspect of the reading. It might look something like this: "There have always been advocates of extremism in politics. Martin Luther King Jr., in 'Letter from Birmingham Jail,' for instance, defends nonviolent civil disobedience as an extreme but necessary means of bringing about racial justice." If, however, you were surveying the important texts of the civil rights movement, you might write a longer, more detailed summary that not only identifies the reading's main ideas but also shows how the ideas relate to one another.

Many writers find it useful to outline the reading as a preliminary to writing a summary. A paragraph-by-paragraph scratch outline (like the one on p. 595) lists the reading's main ideas in the sequence in which they appear in the original. But summarizing requires more than merely stringing together the entries in an outline. It fills in the logical connections between the author's ideas. Notice also in the following example that the reader repeats selected words and phrases and refers to the author by name, indicating, with verbs like *expresses*, *acknowledges*, and *explains*, the writer's purpose and strategy at each point in the argument.

Summary

King expresses his disappointment with white moderates who, by opposing his program of nonviolent direct action, have become a barrier to progress toward racial justice. He acknowledges that his program has raised tension in the South, but he explains that tension is necessary to bring about change. Furthermore, he argues that tension already exists. But because it has been unexpressed, it is unhealthy and potentially dangerous.

He defends his actions against the clergy's criticisms, particularly their argument that he is in too much of a hurry. Responding to charges of extremism, King claims that he has actually prevented racial violence by channeling the natural frustrations of oppressed blacks into nonviolent protest. He asserts that extremism is precisely what is needed now--but it must be creative, rather than destructive, extremism. He concludes by again expressing disappointment with white moderates for not joining his effort as some other whites have.

A summary presents only ideas. While it may use certain key terms from the source, it does not otherwise attempt to reflect the source's language, imagery, or tone; and it avoids even a hint of agreement or disagreement with the ideas it summarizes. Of course, however, a writer might summarize ideas in a source like "Letter from Birmingham Jail" to show readers that he or she has read it carefully and then proceed to use the summary to praise, question, or challenge King's argument. In doing so, the writer might quote specific language that reveals word choice, imagery, or tone.

CHECKLIST: SUMMARIZING

1. Make a scratch outline of the reading.
2. Write a paragraph or more that presents the author's main ideas largely in your own words. Use the outline as a guide, but reread parts of the original text as necessary.
3. To make the summary coherent, fill in connections between ideas.

◾ Synthesizing

Synthesizing involves presenting ideas and information gleaned from different sources. It can help you see how different sources relate to one another — for example, offering supporting details or opposing arguments.

When you synthesize material from different sources, you construct a conversation among your sources, a conversation in which you also participate. Synthesizing contributes most when writers use sources not only to support their ideas, but to challenge and extend them as well.

In the following example, the reader uses a variety of sources related to the King passage (pp. 586–92). The synthesis brings the sources together around a central idea. Notice how quotation, paraphrase, and summary are all used to present King's and the other sources' ideas.

Synthesis

When King defends his campaign of nonviolent direct action against the clergymen's criticism that "our actions, even though peaceful, must be condemned because they precipitate violence" (King excerpt, paragraph 3), he is using what Vinit Haksar calls Mohandas Gandhi's "safety-valve argument" ("Civil Disobedience and Non-Cooperation" 117). According to Haksar, Gandhi gave a "non-threatening warning of worse things to come" if his demands were not met. King similarly makes clear that advocates of actions more extreme than those he advocates are waiting in the wings: "The other force is one of bitterness and hatred, and it comes perilously close to advocating violence" (King excerpt, paragraph 5). King identifies this force with Elijah Muhammad, and although he does not name him, King's contemporary readers would have known that he was referring also to Malcolm X who, according to Herbert J. Storing, "urged that Negroes take seriously the idea of revolution" ("The Case against Civil Disobedience" 90). In fact, Malcolm X accused King of being a modern-day Uncle Tom, trying "to keep us under control, to keep us passive and peaceful and nonviolent" (Malcolm X Speaks 12).

CHECKLIST: SYNTHESIZING

1. Find and read a variety of sources on your topic, annotating the passages that give you ideas about the topic.

2. Look for patterns among your sources, possibly supporting or refuting your ideas or those of other sources.

3. Write a paragraph or more synthesizing your sources, using quotation, paraphrase, and summary to present what they say on the topic.

Contextualizing

All texts were written sometime in the past and therefore may embody historical and cultural assumptions, values, and attitudes different from your own. To read thoughtfully, you need to become aware of these differences. **Contextualizing** is a critical reading strategy that enables you to make inferences about a reading's historical and cultural context and to examine the differences between its context and your own.

The excerpt from King's "Letter from Birmingham Jail" is a good example of a text that benefits from being read contextually. If you knew little about the history of slavery and segregation in the United States, Martin Luther King Jr., or the civil rights movement, it would be difficult to understand the passion for justice and impatience with delay expressed in this passage from King's writings. To understand the historical and cultural context in which King organized his demonstrations and wrote his "Letter from Birmingham Jail," you could do some library or Internet research. A little research would enable you to appreciate the intense emotions that swept the nation at the time. You would see that the threat of violence was all too real. Comparing the situation at the time King wrote the "Letter" in 1963 to situations with which you are familiar would help you understand some of your own attitudes toward King and the civil rights movement.

Here is what one reader wrote to contextualize King's writing:

Notes from a Contextualized Reading

1. I am not old enough to know what it was like in the early 1960s when Dr. King was leading marches and sit-ins, but I have seen television documentaries showing

demonstrators being attacked by dogs, doused by fire hoses, beaten and dragged by helmeted police. Such images give me a sense of the violence, fear, and hatred that King was responding to.

The tension King writes about comes across in his writing. He uses his anger and frustration creatively to inspire his critics. He also threatens them, although he denies it. I saw a film on Malcolm X, so I could see that King was giving white people a choice between his own nonviolent way and Malcolm's more confrontational way.

2. Things have certainly changed since the sixties. Legal segregation has ended, but there are still racists like the detective in the O. J. Simpson trial. African Americans like Colin Powell and Condoleezza Rice are highly respected and powerful. The civil rights movement is over. So when I'm reading King today, I feel like I'm reading history. But then again, every once in a while there are reports of police brutality because of race (think of Amadou Diallo) and of what we now call hate crimes.

CHECKLIST: CONTEXTUALIZING

1. Describe the historical and cultural situation as it is represented in the reading and in other sources with which you are familiar. Your knowledge may come from other reading, television or film, school, or elsewhere. (If you know nothing about the historical and cultural context, you could do some library or Internet research.)

2. Compare the historical and cultural situation in which the text was written to your own historical and cultural situation. Consider how your understanding and judgment of the reading is affected by your own context.

■ Exploring the Significance of Figurative Language

Figurative language — metaphor, simile, and symbolism — enhances literal meaning by embodying abstract ideas in vivid images and by evoking feelings and associations.

Metaphor implicitly compares two different things by identifying them with each other. For instance, when King calls the white moderate "the Negro's great stumbling block in his stride toward freedom" (paragraph 1), he does not mean that the white moderate literally trips the Negro who is attempting to walk toward freedom. The sentence makes sense only if understood figuratively: The white moderate trips up the Negro by frustrating every effort to achieve justice.

Simile, a more explicit form of comparison, uses the word *like* or *as* to signal the relationship of two seemingly unrelated things. King uses simile when he says that injustice is "like a boil that can never be cured so long as it is covered up" (paragraph 2). This simile makes several points of comparison between injustice and a boil. It suggests that injustice is a disease of society as a boil is a disease of the body and that injustice, like a boil, must be exposed or it will fester and infect the entire body.

Symbolism compares two things by making one stand for the other. King uses the white moderate as a symbol for supposed liberals and would-be supporters of civil rights who are actually frustrating the cause.

How these figures of speech are used in a text reveals something of the writer's feelings about the subject. Exploring possible meanings in a text's figurative language involves (1) annotating and then listing the metaphors, similes, and symbols you find in a reading; (2) grouping and labeling the figures of speech that appear to express related feelings or attitudes; and (3) writing to explore the meaning of the patterns you have found.

The following example shows the process of exploring figures of speech in the King excerpt.

Listing Figures of Speech

"stumbling block in his stride toward freedom" (paragraph 1)

"law and order . . . become the dangerously structured dams" (2)

"the flow of social progress" (2)

"Like a boil that can never be cured" (2)

"the light of human conscience and the air of national opinion" (2)

"the quicksand of racial injustice" (4)

Grouping and Labeling Figures of Speech

Sickness: "like a boil" (2); "the disease of segregation" (10)

Underground: "hidden tension" (2); "injustice must be exposed" (2); "injustice must be rooted out" (10)

Blockage: "dams," "block the flow" (2); "Human progress never rolls in on wheels of inevitability" (4); "pent-up resentments" (8); "repressed emotions" (8)

Writing to Explore Meaning

The patterns labeled underground and blockage suggest a feeling of frustration. Inertia is a problem; movement forward toward progress or upward toward the promised land is stalled. The strong need to break through the resistance may represent King's feelings both about his attempt to lead purposeful, effective demonstrations and his effort to write a convincing argument.

The simile of injustice being "like a boil" links the two patterns of underground and sickness, suggesting something bad, a disease, is inside the people or the society. The cure is to expose or to root out the blocked hatred and injustice as well as to release the tension or emotion that has long been repressed. This implies that repression itself is the evil, not simply what is repressed. Therefore, writing and speaking out through political action may have curative power for individuals and society alike.

CHECKLIST: EXPLORING THE SIGNIFICANCE OF FIGURATIVE LANGUAGE

1. Annotate all the figures of speech you find in the reading — metaphors, similes, and symbols — and then list them.

2. Group the figures of speech that appear to express related feelings and attitudes, and label each group.

3. Write one or two paragraphs exploring the meaning of these patterns. What do they tell you about the text?

■ Looking for Patterns of Opposition

All texts carry within themselves voices of opposition. These **patterns of opposition** may echo the views and values of critical readers the writer anticipates or predecessors to whom the writer is responding in some way; they may even reflect the writer's own conflicting values. Careful readers look closely for such a dialogue of opposing voices within the text.

When we think of oppositions, we ordinarily think of polarities: *yes* and *no, up* and *down, black* and *white, new* and *old*. Some oppositions, however, may be more subtle. The excerpt from King's "Letter from Birmingham Jail" is rich in such oppositions: *moderate* versus *extremist, order* versus *justice, direct action* versus *passive acceptance, expression* versus *repression*. These oppositions are not accidental; they form a significant pattern that gives a reader important information about the essay.

A careful reading will show that King always values one of the two terms in an opposition over the other. In the passage, for example, *extremist* is valued over *moderate* (paragraph 9). This preference for extremism is surprising. The reader should ask why, when white extremists like members of the Ku Klux Klan have committed so many outrages against African Americans, King would prefer extremism. If King is trying to convince his readers to accept his point of view, why would he represent himself as an extremist? Moreover, why would a clergyman advocate extremism instead of moderation?

Studying the patterns of opposition enables you to answer these questions. You will see that King sets up this opposition to force his readers to examine their own values and realize that they are in fact misplaced. Instead of working toward justice, he says, those who support law and order maintain the unjust status quo. By getting his readers to think of white moderates as blocking rather than facilitating peaceful change, King brings them to align themselves with him and perhaps even embrace his strategy of nonviolent resistance.

Looking for patterns of opposition involves annotating words or phrases in the reading that indicate oppositions, listing the opposing terms in pairs, deciding which term in each pair is preferred by the writer, and reflecting on the meaning of the patterns. Here is a partial list of oppositions from the King excerpt, with the preferred terms marked by an asterisk:

Listing Patterns of Opposition

moderate	*extremist
order	*justice
negative peace	*positive peace
absence of justice	*presence of justice
goals	*methods
*direct action	passive acceptance
*exposed tension	hidden tension

CHECKLIST: LOOKING FOR PATTERNS OF OPPOSITION

1. Annotate the selection for words or phrases indicating oppositions.

2. List the pairs of oppositions. (You may have to paraphrase or even supply the opposite word or phrase if it is not stated directly in the text.)

3. For each pair of oppositions, put an asterisk next to the term that the writer seems to value or prefer over the other.

4. Study the patterns of opposition. How do they contribute to your understanding of the essay? What do they tell you about what the author wants you to believe?

◼ Reflecting on Challenges to Your Beliefs and Values

To read thoughtfully, you need to scrutinize your own assumptions and attitudes as well as those expressed in the text you are reading. If you are like most readers, however, you will find that your assumptions and attitudes are so ingrained that you are not fully aware of them. A good strategy for getting at these underlying beliefs and values is to identify and reflect on the ways the text challenges you, how it makes you feel — disturbed, threatened, ashamed, combative, or some other way.

For example, here is what one student wrote about the King passage:

Reflections

In paragraph 1, Dr. King criticizes people who are "more devoted to 'order' than to justice." This criticism upsets me because today I think I would choose order over justice. When I analyze my feelings and try to figure out where they come from, I realize that what I feel most is fear. I am terrified by the violence in society today. I'm afraid of sociopaths who don't respect the rule of law, much less the value of human life.

I know Dr. King was writing in a time when the law itself was unjust, when order was apparently used to keep people from protesting and changing the law. But things are different now. Today, justice seems to serve criminals more than it serves law-abiding citizens. That's why I'm for order over justice.

CHECKLIST: REFLECTING ON CHALLENGES TO YOUR BELIEFS AND VALUES

1. Identify challenges by marking the text where you feel your beliefs and values are being opposed, criticized, or unfairly characterized.

2. Write a few paragraphs reflecting on why you feel challenged. Do not defend your feelings; instead, analyze them to see where they come from.

▪ Evaluating the Logic of an Argument

An argument includes a thesis backed by reasons and support. The *thesis* asserts an idea, a position on a controversial issue, or a solution to a problem that the writer wants readers to accept. The *reasons* tell readers why they should accept the thesis, and the *support* (such as examples, statistics, authorities, and textual evidence) gives readers grounds for accepting it. For an argument to be considered logically acceptable, it must meet the three conditions of what we call the ABC test:

For more on argument, see Chapter 19. For an example of the ABC test, see Christine Romano's essay in Chapter 8, pp. 414–17.

The ABC Test

A. The reasons and support must be appropriate to the thesis.

B. The reasons and support must be *believable*.

C. The reasons and support must be *consistent* with one another as well as *complete*.

Testing for Appropriateness

To evaluate the logic of an argument, you first decide whether the argument's reasons and support are appropriate and clearly related to the thesis. To test for appropriateness, ask these questions: How does each reason or piece of support relate to the thesis? Is the connection between reasons and support and the thesis clear and compelling? Or is the argument irrelevant or only vaguely related to the thesis?

For more on analogy, see Chapter 18, pp. 668–69. For invoking authorities, see Chapter 19, pp. 677–78.

Readers most often question the appropriateness of reasons and support when the writer argues by analogy or by invoking authority. For example, in paragraph 2, King argues that when law and order fail to establish justice, "they become the dangerously structured dams that block the flow of social progress." The analogy asserts the following logical relationship: Law and order are to progress toward justice what a dam is to water. If you do not accept this analogy, the argument fails the test of appropriateness.

King uses both analogy and authority in the following passage: "Isn't this like condemning Socrates because his unswerving commitment to truth and his philosophical inquiries precipitated the act by the misguided populace in which they made him drink hemlock?" (paragraph 3). Not only must you judge the appropriateness of the analogy comparing the Greek populace's condemnation of Socrates to the white moderates' condemnation of King, but you must also judge whether it is appropriate to accept Socrates as an authority on this subject. Since Socrates is generally respected for his teaching on justice, his words and actions are likely to be considered appropriate to King's situation in Birmingham.

Testing for Believability

Believability is a measure of your willingness to accept as true the reasons and support the writer gives in defense of a thesis.

To test for believability, ask: On what basis am I being asked to believe this reason or support is true? If it cannot be proved true or false, how much weight does it carry?

In judging facts, examples, statistics, and authorities, consider the following points.

Facts are statements that can be proved objectively to be true. The believability of facts depends on their *accuracy* (they should not distort or misrepresent reality), their *completeness* (they should not omit important details), and the *trustworthiness* of their sources (sources should be qualified and unbiased). King, for instance, asserts as fact that the African American will not wait much longer for racial justice (paragraph 8). His critics might question the factuality of this assertion by asking, is it true of all African Americans? How much longer will they wait? How does King know what African Americans will and will not do?

Examples and *anecdotes* are particular instances that may or may not make you believe a general statement. The believability of examples depends on their *representativeness* (whether they are truly typical and thus generalizable) and their *specificity* (whether particular details make them seem true to life). Even if a vivid example or gripping anecdote does not convince readers, it usually strengthens argumentative writing by clarifying the meaning and dramatizing the point. In paragraph 5 of the King excerpt, for example, King supports his generalization that some African American nationalist extremists are motivated by bitterness and hatred by citing the specific example of Elijah Muhammad's Black Muslim movement. Conversely, in paragraph 9, he refers to Jesus, Paul, Luther, and others as examples of extremists motivated by love and Christianity. These examples support his assertion that extremism is not in itself wrong and that any judgment of extremism must be based on its motivation and cause.

Statistics are numerical data, including correlations. The believability of statistics depends on the *comparability* of the data (the price of apples in 1985 cannot be compared to the price of apples in 2006 unless the figures are adjusted to account for inflation), the *precision* of the methods employed to gather and analyze data (representative samples should be used and variables accounted for), and the *trustworthiness* of the sources (sources should be qualified, unbiased, and — except in historical contexts — as recent as possible).

Authorities are people to whom the writer attributes expertise on a given subject. Not only must such authorities be appropriate, as mentioned earlier, but they must be believable as well. The believability of authorities depends on their *credibility*, on whether the reader accepts them as experts on the topic at hand. King cites authorities repeatedly throughout his essay. He refers to religious leaders (Jesus and Luther) as well as to American political leaders (Lincoln and Jefferson). These figures are likely to have a high degree of credibility among King's readers.

Testing for Consistency and Completeness

In looking for consistency, you should be concerned that all the parts of the argument work together and that none of the reasons or support contradict any of the other reasons or support. In addition, the reasons and support, taken together, should be sufficient to convince readers to accept the thesis or at least take it seriously. To test for consistency and completeness, ask: Are any of the reasons and support contradictory? Do they provide sufficient grounds for accepting the thesis? Does the writer fail to counterargue (to acknowledge, accommodate, or refute any opposing arguments or important objections)?

For more on counterarguing, see Chapter 19, pp. 681–84.

A thoughtful reader might regard as contradictory King's characterizing himself first as a moderate between the forces of complacency and violence and later as an extremist opposed to the forces of violence. King attempts to reconcile this apparent contradiction by explicitly redefining extremism in paragraph 9. Similarly, the fact that King fails to examine and refute every legal recourse available to his cause might allow a critical reader to question the sufficiency of his argument.

> ### CHECKLIST: EVALUATING THE LOGIC OF AN ARGUMENT
>
> Use the ABC test:
>
> A. *Test for appropriateness* by checking that the reasons and support are clearly and directly related to the thesis.
>
> B. *Test for believability* by deciding whether you can accept the reasons and support as true.
>
> C. *Test for consistency and completeness* by ascertaining whether the argument has any contradictions and whether any important objections or opposing arguments have been ignored.

■ Recognizing Emotional Manipulation

Many different kinds of essays appeal to readers' emotions. Tobias Wolff's remembered-event essay (in Chapter 2) may be terrifying to some readers; John Edge's attempts to eat a pickled pig lip (in Chapter 3) may disgust some readers, especially vegetarians; and Richard Estrada's position paper (in Chapter 6) may be annoying to some readers because of his accommodating tone.

Writers often try to arouse emotions in readers to excite their interest, make them care, or move them to take action. There is nothing wrong with appealing to readers' emotions. What is wrong is manipulating readers with false or exaggerated appeals. Therefore, you should be suspicious of writing that is overly or falsely sentimental, that cites alarming statistics and frightening anecdotes, that demonizes others and identifies itself with revered authorities, or that uses symbols (flag waving) or emotionally loaded words (such as *racist*).

King, for example, uses the emotionally loaded word *paternalistically* to refer to the white moderate's belief that "he can set the timetable for another man's freedom" (paragraph 1). In the same paragraph, King uses symbolism to get an emotional reaction from readers when he compares the white moderate to the "Ku Klux Klanner." To get readers to accept his ideas, he also relies on authorities whose names evoke the greatest respect, such as Jesus and Lincoln. But some readers might object that comparing King's crusade to that of Jesus and other leaders of religious and political groups is pretentious and manipulative. A critical reader might also consider King's discussion of African American extremists in paragraph 7 to be a veiled threat designed to frighten readers into agreement.

> ### CHECKLIST: RECOGNIZING EMOTIONAL MANIPULATION
>
> 1. Annotate places in the text where you sense emotional appeals are being used.
> 2. Assess whether any of the emotional appeals are unfairly manipulative.

■ Judging the Writer's Credibility

Writers often try to persuade readers to respect and believe them. Because readers may not know them personally or even by reputation, writers must present an image of themselves in their writing that will gain their readers' confidence. This image cannot be made directly but must be made indirectly, through the arguments, language, and system of values and beliefs expressed or implied in the writing. Writers establish credibility in their writing in three ways:

By showing their knowledge of the subject

By building common ground with readers

By responding fairly to objections and opposing arguments

Testing for Knowledge

Writers demonstrate their knowledge through the facts and statistics they marshal, the sources they rely on for information, and the scope and depth of their understanding. You may not be sufficiently expert on the subject yourself to know whether the facts are accurate, the sources are reliable, and the understanding is sufficient. You may need to do some research to see what others say about the subject. You can also check credentials — the writer's educational and professional qualifications, the respectability of the publication in which the selection first appeared, and reviews of the writer's work — to determine whether the writer is a respected authority in the field. For example, King brings with him the authority that comes from being a member of the clergy and a respected leader of the Southern Christian Leadership Conference.

Testing for Common Ground

One way writers can establish common ground with their readers is by basing their reasoning on shared values, beliefs, and attitudes. They use language that includes their readers (*we*) rather than excludes them (*they*). They qualify their assertions to keep them from being too extreme. Above all, they acknowledge differences of opinion and try to make room in their argument to accommodate reasonable differences. You want to notice such appeals.

King creates common ground with readers by using the inclusive pronoun *we*, suggesting shared concerns between himself and his audience. Notice, however, his use of masculine pronouns and other references ("the Negro . . . he," "our brothers"). Although King addressed his letter to male clergy, he intended it to be published in the local newspaper, where it would be read by an audience of both men and women. By using language that excludes women, a common practice at the time the selection was written, King misses the opportunity to build common ground with half of his readers.

Testing for Fairness

Writers reveal their character by how they handle opposing arguments and objections to their argument. As a critical reader, pay particular attention to how writers treat possible differences of opinion. Be suspicious of those who ignore differences and pretend that everyone agrees with their viewpoints. When objections or opposing views are represented, consider whether they have been distorted in any way; if they are refuted, be sure they are challenged fairly — with sound reasoning and solid support.

One way to gauge the author's credibility is to identify the tone of the argument, for it conveys the writer's attitude toward the subject and toward the reader. Examine the text carefully for indications of tone: Is the text angry? Sarcastic? Evenhanded? Shrill? Condescending? Bullying? Do you feel as if the writer is treating the subject — and you, as a reader — with fairness? King's tone might be characterized in different passages as patient (he doesn't lose his temper), respectful (he refers to white moderates as "people of good will"), or pompous (comparing himself to Jesus and Socrates).

CHECKLIST: JUDGING THE WRITER'S CREDIBILITY

1. Annotate for the writer's knowledge of the subject, how well common ground is established, and whether the writer deals fairly with objections and opposing arguments.

2. Decide what in the essay you find credible and what you question.

Part Three

Writing Strategies

13

Cueing the Reader

Readers need guidance. To guide readers through a piece of writing, a writer can provide five basic kinds of **cues** or signals:

1. Thesis and forecasting statements, to orient readers to ideas and organization
2. Paragraphing, to group related ideas and details
3. Cohesive devices, to connect ideas to one another and bring about coherence and clarity
4. Connectives, to signal relationships or shifts in meaning
5. Headings and subheadings, to group related paragraphs and help readers locate specific information quickly

This chapter illustrates how each of these cueing strategies works.

▧ Orienting Statements

To help readers find their way, especially in difficult and lengthy texts, you can provide two kinds of **orienting statements**: a thesis statement, which declares the main point, and a forecasting statement, which previews subordinate points, showing the order in which they will be discussed in the essay.

Thesis Statements

To help readers understand what is being said about a subject, writers often provide a thesis statement early in the essay. The **thesis statement** operates as a cue by letting readers know which is the most important general idea among the writer's many ideas and observations. Here are three thesis statements from essays in Part One:

Toufexis expresses her thesis statement in one sentence.

> O.K., let's cut out all this nonsense about romantic love. Let's bring some scientific precision to the party. Let's put love under a microscope.
>
> When rigorous people with Ph.D.s after their names do that, what they see is not some silly, senseless thing. No, their probe reveals that love rests firmly on the foundations of evolution, biology and chemistry.
>
> — Anastasia Toufexis, Chapter 4

It seems to me that what Native Americans are saying is that what would be intolerable for Jews, blacks, Latinos and others is no less offensive to them. Theirs is a request not only for dignified treatment, but for fair treatment as well. For America to ignore the complaints of a numerically small segment of the population because it is small is neither dignified nor fair.

— RICHARD ESTRADA, Chapter 6

Estrada expresses his thesis statement in three sentences.

. . . I could not shake the idea that sooner or later I would get the rifle out again. All my images of myself as I wished to be were images of myself armed. Because I did not know who I was, any image of myself, no matter how grotesque, had power over me. This much I understand now. But the man can give no help to the boy, not in this matter nor in those that follow. The boy moves always out of reach.

— TOBIAS WOLFF, Chapter 2

Wolff's thesis statement is explicit, but in many auto-biographical essays, the thesis statement is implied.

Readers naturally look for something that will tell them the point of an essay, a focus for the many diverse details and ideas they encounter as they read. The lack of an explicit thesis statement can make this task more difficult. Therefore, careful writers keep readers' needs and expectations in mind when deciding how to state the thesis as clearly and directly as possible.

Another important decision is where to place the thesis statement. Most readers expect to find some information early on that will give them a context for reading the essay, particularly if they are reading about a new and difficult subject. Therefore, a thesis statement, like that of Toufexis, placed at the beginning of an essay enables readers to anticipate the content of the essay and helps them understand the relationships among its various ideas and details.

Occasionally, however, particularly in fairly short, informal essays and in some autobiographical and argumentative essays, a writer may save a direct statement of the thesis until the conclusion, which is where Estrada and Wolff put theirs. Ending with the thesis brings together the various strands of information or supporting details introduced over the course of the essay and makes clear the essay's main idea.

EXERCISE 13.1

In the essay by Jessica Statsky in Chapter 6, underline the thesis statement, the last sentence in paragraph 1. Notice the key terms in this thesis, the words that seem to be essential to presenting Statsky's ideas: "overzealous parents and coaches," "impose adult standards," "children's sports," "activities . . . neither satisfying nor beneficial." Then skim the essay, stopping to read the sentence at the beginning of each paragraph. Also read the last paragraph.

Consider whether the idea in every paragraph's first sentence is anticipated by the thesis' key terms. Consider also the connection between the ideas in the last paragraph and the thesis' key terms. What can you conclude about how a thesis might assert the point of an essay, anticipate the ideas that follow, and help readers relate the ideas to each other?

Forecasting Statements

Some thesis statements include a **forecast**, which overviews the way a thesis will be developed, as in the following example.

> In the three years from 1348 through 1350 the pandemic of plague known as the Black Death, or, as the Germans called it, the Great Dying, killed at least a fourth of the population of Europe. It was undoubtedly the worst disaster that has ever befallen mankind. Today we can have no real conception of the terror under which people lived in the shadow of the plague. For more than two centuries plague has not been a serious threat to mankind in the large, although it is still a grisly presence in parts of the Far East and Africa. Scholars continue to study the Great Dying, however, as a historical example of human behavior under the stress of universal catastrophe. In these days when the threat of plague has been replaced by the threat of mass human extermination by even more rapid means, there has been a sharp renewal of interest in the history of the fourteenth-century calamity. With new perspective, students are investigating its manifold effects: demographic, economic, psychological, moral and religious.
>
> — WILLIAM LANGER, "The Black Death"

Langer's thesis statement forecasts the five main categories of effects of the Black Death his essay will examine.

This introductory paragraph informs us that Langer's article is about the effects of the Black Death. His thesis (highlighted) states that there is renewed interest in studying the social effects of the bubonic plague and that these new studies focus on five particular categories of effects. As a reader would expect, Langer then goes on to divide his essay into explanations of the research into these five effects, addressing them in the order in which they appear in the forecasting statement.

EXERCISE 13.2

Turn to Erica Goode's essay in Chapter 9, and underline the forecasting statement in paragraph 4. Then skim the essay, pausing to read the first sentence in each paragraph. Notice whether Goode takes up every point she mentions in the forecasting statement and whether she sticks to the order she promises readers. How well does her forecasting statement help you follow her essay? Would you offer any suggestions for improvement?

◼ Paragraphing

For additional visual cues for readers, see Headings and Subheadings on pp. 623–24.

Paragraph cues as obvious as indentation keep readers on track. You can also arrange material in a paragraph to help readers see what is important or significant. For example, you can begin with a topic sentence, help readers see the relationship between the previous paragraph and the present one with an explicit transition, and place the most important information toward the end.

Paragraph Cues

One **paragraph cue** — the indentation that signals the beginning of a new paragraph — is a relatively modern printing convention. Old manuscripts show that paragraph divisions were not always marked. To make reading easier, scribes and printers began to use the symbol ¶ to mark paragraph breaks, and later, indenting became common practice. Even that relatively modern custom, however, has been abandoned by most business writers, who now distinguish one paragraph from another by leaving a line of space above and below each paragraph. Writing on the Internet is also usually paragraphed in this way.

Paragraphing helps readers by signaling when a sequence of related ideas begins and ends. Paragraphing also helps readers judge what is most important in what they are reading. Writers typically emphasize important information by placing it at the two points where readers are most attentive — the beginning and the end of a paragraph. Many writers put information to orient readers at the beginning of a paragraph and save the most important information for last.

You can give special emphasis to information by placing it in its own paragraph.

EXERCISE 13.3

Turn to Patrick O'Malley's essay in Chapter 7, and read paragraphs 4–6 with the following questions in mind: Does all the material in each paragraph seem to be related? Do you feel a sense of closure at the end of each paragraph? Does the last sentence offer the most important or significant or weighty information in the paragraph?

Topic Sentence Strategies

A **topic sentence** lets readers know the focus of a paragraph in simple and direct terms. It is a cueing strategy for the paragraph, much as a thesis or forecasting statement is for the whole essay. Because paragraphing usually signals a shift in focus, readers expect some kind of reorientation in the opening sentence. They need to know whether the new paragraph will introduce another aspect of the topic or develop one already introduced.

Announcing the Topic.   Some topic sentences simply announce the topic. Here are some examples taken from Barry Lopez's book *Arctic Dreams*:

A polar bear walks in a way all its own.

What is so consistently striking about the way Eskimos used parts of an animal is the breadth of their understanding about what would work.

The Mediterranean view of the Arctic, down to the time of the Elizabethan mariners, was shaped by two somewhat contradictory thoughts.

Lopez's topic sentences identify topics and also indicate how they will be developed in subsequent sentences.

The following paragraph shows how one of Lopez's topic sentences (highlighted) is developed:

What is so consistently striking about the way Eskimos used parts of an animal is the breadth of their understanding about what would work. Knowing that muskox horn is more flexible than caribou antler, they preferred it for making the side prongs of a fish spear. For a waterproof bag in which to carry sinews for clothing repair, they chose salmon skin. They selected the strong, translucent intestine of a bearded seal to make a window for a snowhouse — it would fold up for easy traveling and it would not frost over in cold weather. To make small snares for sea ducks, they needed a springy material that would not rot in salt water — baleen fibers. The down feather of a common eider, tethered at the end of a stick in the snow at an angle, would reveal the exhalation of a quietly surfacing seal. Polar bear bone was used anywhere a stout, sharp point was required, because it is the hardest bone.

— Barry Lopez, Arctic Dreams

EXERCISE 13.4

Turn to David Ratinov's essay in Chapter 10. Underline the topic sentence (the first sentence) in paragraphs 3–5. Consider how these sentences help you anticipate the paragraph's topic and method of development.

Making a Transition.   Not all topic sentences simply point to what will follow. Some also refer to earlier sentences. Such sentences work both as topic sentences, stating the main point of the paragraph, and as transitions, linking that paragraph to the previous one. Here are a few topic sentences from "Quilts and Women's Culture," by Elaine Hedges:

> Within its broad traditionalism and anonymity, however, variations and distinctions developed.

> Regionally, too, distinctions were introduced into quilt making through the interesting process of renaming.

> With equal inventiveness women renamed traditional patterns to accommodate to the local landscape.

> Finally, out of such regional and other variations come individual, signed achievements.

> Quilts, then, were an outlet for creative energy, a source and emblem of sisterhood and solidarity, and a graphic response to historical and political change.

Hedges uses specific transitions to tie each topic sentence to a previous statement.

Sometimes the first sentence of a paragraph serves as a transition, and a subsequent sentence states the topic, as in the following example:

> . . . What a convenience, what a relief it will be, they say, never to worry about how to dress for a job interview, a romantic tryst, or a funeral!
>
> Convenient, perhaps, but not exactly a relief. Such a utopia would give most of us the same kind of chill we feel when a stadium full of Communist-bloc athletes in identical sports outfits, shouting slogans in unison, appears on TV. Most people do not want to be told what to wear any more than they want to be told what to say. In Belfast recently four hundred Irish Republican prisoners "refused to wear any clothes at all, draping themselves day and night in blankets," rather than put on

The highlighted sentences serve as transitions.

prison uniforms. Even the offer of civilian-style dress did not satisfy them; they insisted on wearing their own clothes brought from home, or nothing. Fashion is free speech, and one of the privileges, if not always one of the pleasures, of a free world.

— ALISON LURIE, *The Language of Clothes*

Occasionally, whole paragraphs serve as transitions, linking one sequence of paragraphs with those that follow, as below:

Yet it was not all contrast, after all. Different as they were — in background, in personality, in underlying aspiration — these two great soldiers had much in common. Under everything else, they were marvelous fighters. Furthermore, their fighting qualities were really very much alike.

— BRUCE CATTON, "Grant and Lee: A Study in Contrasts"

This transition paragraph summarizes the contrasts between Grant and Lee and sets up an analysis of the similarities of the two men.

EXERCISE 13.5

Turn to the Stephen King essay in Chapter 9, and read paragraphs 8–12. As you read, underline the part of the first sentence in paragraphs 9–12 that refers to the previous paragraph, creating a transition from one to the next. Notice the different ways King creates these transitions. Consider whether they are all equally effective.

Positioning the Topic Sentence. Although topic sentences may occur anywhere in a paragraph, stating the topic in the first sentence has the advantage of giving readers a sense of how the paragraph is likely to be developed. The beginning of the paragraph is therefore the most common position for a topic sentence.

A topic sentence that does not open a paragraph is most likely to appear at the end. When a topic sentence concludes a paragraph, it usually summarizes or generalizes preceding information:

Even black Americans sometimes need to be reminded about the deceptiveness of television. Blacks retain their fascination with black characters on TV: Many of us buy *Jet* magazine primarily to read its weekly television feature, which lists every black character (major or minor) to be seen on the screen that week. Yet our fixation with the presence of black characters on TV has blinded us to an important fact that *Cosby*, which began in 1984, and its offshoots over the years demonstrate convincingly: There is very little connection between the social status of black Americans and the fabricated images of black people that Americans consume each day. The representation of blacks on TV is a very poor index to our social advancement or political progress.

— HENRY LOUIS GATES JR., "TV's Black World Turns — but Stays Unreal"

Gates does not explicitly state his topic until the last sentence.

When a topic sentence is used in a narrative, it often appears as the last sentence as a way to evaluate or reflect on events:

A cold sun was sliding down a gray fall sky. Some older boys had been playing tackle football in the field we took charge of every weekend. In a few years, they'd be called to Southeast Asia, some of them. Their locations would be tracked with pushpins in red, white, and blue on maps on nearly every kitchen wall. But that afternoon, they were quick as young deer. They leapt and dodged, dove from each other and collided in midair. Bulletlike passes flew to connect them. Or the ball spiraled in a high arc across the frosty sky one to another. In short, they were mindlessly agile in a way that captured as audience every little kid within running distance of the yellow goalposts.

— MARY KARR, Cherry

Karr's topic sentence reflects on narrated events described earlier in the paragraph.

It is possible for a single topic sentence to introduce two or more paragraphs. Subsequent paragraphs in such a sequence have no separate topic sentences of their own:

Anthropologists Daniel Maltz and Ruth Borker point out that boys and girls socialize differently. Little girls tend to play in small groups or, even more common, in pairs. Their social life usually centers around a best friend, and friendships are made, maintained, and broken by talk — especially "secrets." If a little girl tells her friend's secret to another little girl, she may find herself with a new best friend. The secrets themselves may or may not be important, but the fact of telling them is all-important. It's hard for newcomers to get into these tight groups, but anyone who is admitted is treated as an equal. Girls like to play cooperatively; if they can't cooperate, the group breaks up.

Tannen's topic sentence states the topic of two paragraphs: the one in which it appears and the one that follows it.

Little boys tend to play in larger groups, often outdoors, and they spend more time doing things than talking. It's easy for boys to get into the group, but not everyone is accepted as an equal. Once in the group, boys must jockey for their status in it. One of the most important ways they do this is through talk: verbal display such as telling stories and jokes, challenging and sidetracking the verbal displays of other boys, and withstanding other boys' challenges in order to maintain their own story — and status. Their talk is often competitive talk about who is best at what.

— DEBORAH TANNEN, That's Not What I Meant!

EXERCISE 13.6

Consider the variety and effectiveness of the topic sentences in your most recent essay. Begin by underlining the topic sentence in each paragraph after the first one. The topic sentence may not be the first sentence in a paragraph, though often it will be.

Then double-underline the part of the topic sentence that provides an explicit transition from one paragraph to the next. You may find a transition that is separate from the topic sentence. You may not always find a topic sentence.

Reflect on your topic sentences, and evaluate how well they serve to orient your readers to the sequence of topics or ideas in your essay.

◾ Cohesive Devices

Cohesive devices guide readers, helping them follow your train of thought by connecting key words and phrases throughout a passage. Among such devices are pronoun reference, word repetition, synonyms, repetition of sentence structure, and collocation.

Pronoun Reference

One common cohesive device is **pronoun reference**. As noun substitutes, pronouns refer to nouns that either precede or follow them and thus serve to connect phrases or sentences. The nouns that come before the pronouns are called *antecedents*.

> In New York from dawn to dusk to dawn, day after day, you can hear the steady rumble of tires against the concrete span of the George Washington Bridge. The bridge is never completely still. It trembles with traffic. It moves in the wind. Its great veins of steel swell when hot and contract when cold; its span often is ten feet closer to the Hudson River in summer than in winter.
>
> — GAY TALESE, "New York"

The pronouns form a chain of connection with their antecedent.

This example has only one pronoun-antecedent chain, and the antecedent comes first, so all the pronouns refer back to it. When there are multiple pronoun-antecedent chains with references forward as well as back, writers have to make sure that readers will not mistake one pronoun's antecedent for another's.

Word Repetition

To avoid confusion, writers often use **word repetition**. The device of repeating words and phrases is especially helpful if a pronoun might confuse readers:

> Some odd optical property of our highly polarized and unequal society makes the poor almost invisible to their economic superiors. The poor can see the affluent easily enough — on television, for example, or on the covers of magazines. But the affluent rarely see the poor or, if they do catch sight of them in some public space, rarely know what they're seeing, since — thanks to consignment stores and, yes, Wal-Mart — the poor are usually able to disguise themselves as members of the more comfortable classes.
>
> — BARBARA EHRENREICH, *Nickel and Dimed*

Ehrenreich repeats words instead of using pronouns.

In the next example, several overlapping chains of word repetition prevent confusion and help the reader follow the ideas:

> Natural selection is the central concept of Darwinian theory — the fittest survive and spread their favored traits through populations. Natural selection is defined by Spencer's phrase "survival of the fittest," but what does this famous bit of jargon really mean? Who are the fittest? And how is "fitness" defined? We often read that fitness involves no more than "differential reproductive success" — the production of more surviving offspring than other competing members of the population. Whoa! cries Bethell, as many others have before him. This formulation defines fitness in terms of survival only. The crucial phrase of natural selection means no more than "the survival of those who survive" — a vacuous tautology. (A tautology is a phrase — like "my father is a man" — containing no information in the predicate ["a man"] not inherent in the subject ["my father"]. Tautologies are fine as definitions, but not as testable scientific statements — there can be nothing to test in a statement true by definition.)
>
> — STEPHEN JAY GOULD, *Ever Since Darwin*

Gould uses repetition, with some variation of form, to keep readers focused on key concepts.

Synonyms

In addition to word repetition, you can use **synonyms**, words with identical or very similar meanings, to connect important ideas. In the following example, the author develops a careful chain of synonyms and word repetitions:

> Over time, small bits of knowledge about a region accumulate among local residents in the form of stories. These are remembered in the community; even what is unusual does not become lost and therefore irrelevant. These narratives comprise for a native an intricate, long-term view of a particular landscape. . . . Outside the region this complex but easily shared "reality" is hard to get across without reducing it to generalities, to misleading or imprecise abstraction.
>
> — BARRY LOPEZ, *Arctic Dreams*

Note the variety of synonym sequences:

"particular landscape," "region"

"local residents," "community," "native"

"stories," "narratives"

"accumulate," "remembered," "does not become lost," "comprise"

"intricate, long-term view," "complex . . . reality," "without reducing it to generalities"

The result is a coherent paragraph that constantly reinforces the author's point.

Sentence Structure Repetition

Writers occasionally use **sentence structure repetition** to emphasize the connections among their ideas, as in this example:

> But the life forms are as much part of the structure of the Earth as any inanimate portion is. It is all an inseparable part of a whole. If any animal is isolated totally from other forms of life, then death by starvation will surely follow. If isolated from water, death by dehydration will follow even faster. If isolated from air, whether free or dissolved in water, death by asphyxiation will follow still faster. If isolated from the Sun, animals will survive for a time, but plants would die, and if all plants died, all animals would starve.
>
> — ISAAC ASIMOV, "The Case against Man"

Collocation

Collocation — the positioning of words together in expected ways around a particular topic — occurs quite naturally to writers and usually forms recognizable networks of meaning for readers. For example, in a paragraph on a high school graduation, a reader might expect to encounter such words as *valedictorian, diploma, commencement, honors, cap and gown,* and *senior class.* The paragraph that follows uses five collocation chains:

housewife, cooking, neighbor, home

clocks, calculated cooking times, progression, precise

obstinacy, vagaries, problem

sun, clear days, cloudy ones, sundial, cast its light, angle, seasons, sun, weather

cooking, fire, matches, hot coals, smoldering, ashes, go out, bed-warming pan

The seventeenth-century housewife not only had to make do without thermometers, she also had to make do without clocks, which were scarce and dear throughout the sixteen hundreds. She calculated cooking times by the progression of the sun; her cooking must have been more precise on clear days than on cloudy ones. Marks were sometimes painted on the floor, providing her with a rough sundial, but she still had to make allowance for the obstinacy of the sun in refusing to cast its light at the same angle as the seasons changed; but she was used to allowing for the vagaries of sun and weather. She also had a problem starting her fire in the morning; there were no matches. If she had allowed the hot coals smoldering under the ashes to go out, she had to borrow some from a neighbor, carrying them home with care, perhaps in a bed-warming pan.

— WAVERLY ROOT AND RICHARD DE ROUCHEMENT, *Eating in America*

EXERCISE 13.7

Now that you know more about pronoun reference, word repetition, synonyms, sentence structure repetition, and collocation, turn to Amanda Coyne's essay in Chapter 3 and identify the cohesive devices you find in paragraphs 1–4. Underline each cohesive device you can find; there will be many. You might also want to connect with lines the various pronoun, related-word, and synonym chains you find. You could also try listing the separate collocation chains. Consider how these cohesive devices help you read and make sense of the passage.

EXERCISE 13.8

Choose one of your recent essays, and select any three contiguous paragraphs. Underline every cohesive device you can find; there will be many devices. Try to connect with lines the various pronoun, related-word, and synonym chains you find. Also try listing the separate collocation chains.

You will be surprised and pleased at how extensively you rely on cohesive ties. Indeed, you could not produce readable text without cohesive ties. Consider these questions relevant to your development as a writer: Are all of your pronoun references clear? Are you straining for synonyms when repeated words would do? Do you ever repeat sentence structures to emphasize connections? Do you trust yourself to put collocation to work?

■ Connectives

A **connective** serves as a bridge to connect one paragraph, sentence, clause, or word with another. It also identifies the kind of connection by indicating to readers how the item preceding the connective relates to the one that follows it. Connectives help readers anticipate how the next paragraph or sentence will affect the meaning of what they have just read. There are three basic groups of connectives, based on the relationships they indicate: logical, temporal, and spatial.

Logical Relationships

Connectives help readers follow the **logical relationships** within an argument. How such connectives work is illustrated in this tightly and passionately reasoned paragraph by James Baldwin:

> Baldwin uses connectives to reinforce the logic of his argument.

> The black man insists, by whatever means he finds at his disposal, that the white man cease to regard him as an exotic rarity and recognize him as a human being. This is a very charged and difficult moment, for there is a great deal of will power involved in the white man's naïveté. Most people are not naturally malicious, and the white man prefers to keep the black man at a certain human remove because it is easier for him thus to preserve his simplicity and to avoid being called to account for crimes committed by his forefathers, or his neighbors. He is inescapably aware, nevertheless, that he is in a better position in the world than black men are, nor can he quite put to death the suspicion that he is hated by black men therefore. He does not wish to be hated, neither does he wish to change places, and at this point in his uneasiness he can scarcely avoid having recourse to those legends which white men have created about black men, the most unusual effect of which is that the white man finds himself enmeshed, so to speak, in his own language which describes hell, as well as the attributes which lead one to hell, as being black as night.
>
> — JAMES BALDWIN, "Stranger in the Village"

Connectives Showing Logical Relationships

- *To introduce another item in a series:* first, second; in the second place; for one thing . . . , for another; next; then; furthermore; moreover; in addition; finally; last; also; similarly; besides; and; as well as

- *To introduce an illustration or other specification:* in particular; specifically; for instance; for example; that is; namely

- *To introduce a result or a cause:* consequently; as a result; hence; accordingly; thus; so; therefore; then; because; since; for

- *To introduce a restatement:* that is; in other words; in simpler terms; to put it differently

- *To introduce a conclusion or summary:* in conclusion; finally; all in all; evidently; clearly; actually; to sum up; altogether; of course

- **To introduce an opposing point:** but; however; yet; nevertheless; on the contrary; on the other hand; in contrast; still; neither; nor

- **To introduce a concession to an opposing view:** certainly; naturally; of course; it is true; to be sure; granted

- **To resume the original line of reasoning after a concession:** nonetheless; all the same; even though; still; nevertheless

Temporal Relationships

In addition to showing logical connections, connectives may indicate **temporal relationships** — a sequence or progression in time — as this example illustrates:

> That night, we drank tea and then vodka with lemon peel steeped in it. The four of us talked in Russian and English about mutual friends and American railroads and the Rolling Stones. Seryozha loves the Stones, and his face grew wistful as we spoke about their recent album, *Some Girls*. He played a tape of "Let It Bleed" over and over, until we could translate some difficult phrases for him; after that, he came out with the phrases at intervals during the evening, in a pretty decent imitation of Jagger's Cockney snarl. He was an adroit and oddly formal host, inconspicuously filling our teacups and politely urging us to eat bread and cheese and chocolate. While he talked to us, he teased Anya, calling her "Piglet," and she shook back her bangs and glowered at him. It was clear that theirs was a fiery relationship. After a while, we talked about ourselves. Anya told us about painting and printmaking and about how hard it was to buy supplies in Moscow. There had been something angry in her dark face since the beginning of the evening; I thought at first that it meant she didn't like Americans; but now I realized that it was a constant, barely suppressed rage at her own situation.
>
> — ANDREA LEE, *Russian Journal*

Lee uses connectives to show the relationship of events transpiring over one evening.

Connectives Showing Temporal Relationships

- **To indicate frequency:** frequently; hourly; often; occasionally; now and then; day after day; every so often; again and again

- **To indicate duration:** during; briefly; for a long time; minute by minute; while

- **To indicate a particular time:** now; then; at that time; in those days; last Sunday; next Christmas; in 2003; at the beginning of August; at six o'clock; first thing in the morning; two months ago; when

- **To indicate the beginning:** at first; in the beginning; since; before then

- **To indicate the middle:** in the meantime; meanwhile; as it was happening; at that moment; at the same time; simultaneously; next; then

- **To indicate the end and beyond:** eventually; finally; at last; in the end; subsequently; later; afterward

Spatial Relationships

Connectives showing **spatial relationships** orient readers to the objects in a scene, as illustrated in these paragraphs:

Least Heat Moon uses connectives to show where the direction of his narrative occurs.

On Georgia 155, I crossed Troublesome Creek, then went through groves of pecan trees aligned one with the next like fenceposts. The pastures grew a green almost blue, and syrupy water the color of a dusty sunset filled the ponds. Around the farmhouses, from wires strung high above the ground, swayed gourds hollowed out for purple martins.

The land rose again on the other side of the Chattahoochee River, and Highway 34 went to the ridgetops where long views over the hills opened in all directions. Here was the tail of the Appalachian backbone, its gradual descent to the Gulf. Near the Alabama stateline stood a couple of LAST CHANCE! bars. . . .

— WILLIAM LEAST HEAT MOON, *Blue Highways*

Connectives Showing Spatial Relationships

- ***To indicate closeness:*** close to; near; next to; alongside; adjacent to; facing

- ***To indicate distance:*** in the distance; far; beyond; away; there

- ***To indicate direction:*** up/down; sideways; along; across; to the right/left; in front of/behind; above/below; inside/outside; toward/away from

EXERCISE 13.9

Turn to Rick Bragg's essay in Chapter 2. Relying on the lists of connectives just given, underline the *logical* and *temporal* connectives in paragraphs 1–6. Consider how the connectives relate the ideas and events from sentence to sentence. Suggest any further connectives that could be added to make the relationships even clearer.

EXERCISE 13.10

Select a recent essay of your own. Choose at least three paragraphs, and, relying on the lists of connectives given in the text, underline the logical, temporal, and spatial connectives. Depending on the kind of writing you were doing, you may find few, if any, connectives in one category or another. For example, an essay speculating about causes may not include any spatial connectives; writing about a remembered event might not contain connectives showing logical relationships.

Consider how your connectives relate the ideas from sentence to sentence. Comparing your connectives to those in the lists, do you find that you are making full use of the repertoire of connectives? Do you find gaps between any of your sentences that a well-chosen connective would close?

◼ Headings and Subheadings

Headings and subheadings — brief phrases set off from the text in various ways — can provide visible cues to readers about the content and organization of a text. Headings can be distinguished from text in numerous ways, including the selective use of capital letters, bold or italic type, or different sizes of type. To be most helpful to readers, headings should be phrased similarly and follow a predictable system.

Heading Systems and Levels

In this chapter, the headings in the section Paragraphing, beginning on p. 612, provide a good example of a system of headings that can readily be outlined:

◼ Paragraphing

Paragraph Cues

Topic Sentence Strategies

Announcing the Topic.

Making a Transition.

Positioning the Topic Sentence.

Notice that in this example the heading system has three levels. The first-level heading sits on its own line and is preceded by a square bullet; this heading stands out most visibly among the others. The second-level heading also sits on its own line, but appears in a smaller font and without the square bullet. The first of these second-level headings has no subheadings beneath it, while the second has three. These third-level headings run into the paragraph they introduce, as you can see if you pause now to turn to pp. 613–15.

All of these headings are set apart from the surrounding text by the special use of font size or spacing or both. At each level, they follow a parallel grammatical structure: nouns at the first level, which you can confirm by skimming the chapter in order to look at the other four first-level heads; nouns at the second level ("cues" and "strategies"); and "-ing" nouns at the third level.

To learn more about distinguishing headings from surrounding text and about setting up systems of headings, see Headings and Body Text, p. 811 in Chapter 25, Designing Documents.

Headings and Genres

Headings may not be necessary in the short essays you will be writing for this composition course. Short essays offer readers thesis statements, forecasting statements, well-positioned topic sentences, and transition sentences so that they have all the cues they may need. Headings are rare in some genres, like essays about remembered events (Chapter 2) and essays profiling people and places (Chapter 3). Headings appear more frequently in genres such as concept explanations, explanations of opposing positions in debates, position papers, public policy proposals, evaluations, and speculations about social problems (Chapters 4–9).

Frequency and Placement of Headings

Before dividing their essays into sections with headings and subheadings, writers need to make sure their discussion is detailed enough to support at least one heading at each level. The frequency and placement of headings depend entirely on the content and how it is divided and organized. Keep in mind that headings do not reduce the need for other cues to keep readers on track.

EXERCISE 13.11

Turn to Gian-Claudia Sciara's essay in Chapter 7, and survey that essay's system of headings. If you have not read the essay, read or skim it now. Also read Basic Features: Proposing Solutions at the end of the Chapter 7 Readings section (pp. 360–61) to familiarize yourself with the genre — proposing a solution. Consider how Sciara's headings help readers anticipate what is coming and how the argument is organized. Decide whether the headings substitute for or complement a strong system of other cues for keeping readers on track. Consider whether the headings grammatically are parallel.

EXERCISE 13.12

Select one of your essays that might benefit from headings. Develop a system of headings, and insert them where appropriate. Be prepared to justify your headings in light of the discussion about headings in this section.

Narrating 14

Narrating is a basic writing strategy for representing action and events. As the term's Latin root, *gnarus* ("knowing"), implies, narrating also helps people make sense of events they are involved in, as well as events they observe or read about. From earliest childhood, we use narrating to help us reflect on what has happened, to explain what is happening, and to imagine what could happen.

Narrating is one of the most versatile writing strategies and serves many different purposes. It can be used to report on events, present information, illustrate abstract ideas, support arguments, explain procedures, and entertain with stories. This chapter begins by describing and illustrating five basic narrating strategies and concludes by looking at two types of process narrative — explanatory and instructional.

▪ Narrating Strategies

Whether the purpose is to make clear exactly what happened or to dramatize events so that readers can imagine what the experience was like, writers use an array of narrating strategies. Strategies such as calendar and clock time, temporal transitions, verb tense, specific narrative action, and dialogue give narrative its dynamic quality, the sense of events unfolding in time. They also help readers track the order in which the events occurred and understand how they relate to one another.

Calendar and Clock Time

Presenting a clear sequence of action is essential to narrative. One of the simplest ways of constructing a clear time sequence is to place events on a timeline with years or precise dates and times clearly marked. Look, for example, at the chronology in Figure 14.1, which presents a series of events in the history of genetics. Chronologies like this one often appear in books and magazines as sidebars accompanying written narratives. A chronology is not itself a narrative, but it shares with narrative two basic elements: Events are presented in chronological order, and each event is marked (in this case, by year) so that readers can understand clearly when events occurred in relation to one another.

1866 Austrian botanist and monk Gregor Mendel proposes basic laws of heredity based on cross-breeding experiments with pea plants. His findings, published in a local natural-history journal, are largely ignored for more than 30 years.

1882 While examining salamander larvae under a microscope, German embryologist Walther Fleming spots tiny threads within the cells' nuclei that appear to be dividing. The threads will later turn out to be chromosomes.

1883 Francis Galton, a cousin of Charles Darwin's and an advocate of improving the human race by means of selective breeding, coins the word eugenics.

1910 U.S. biologist Thomas Hunt Morgan's experiments with fruit flies reveal that some genetically determined traits are sex linked. His work also confirms that the genes determining these traits reside on chromosomes.

1926 U.S. biologist Hermann Muller discovers that X rays can cause genetic mutations in fruit flies.

1932 Publication of Aldous Huxley's novel *Brave New World,* which presents a dystopian view of genetic engineering.

Figure 14.1 Chronology of events in the history of genetics
From *Time*, January 11, 1999, pp. 46–47.

Look now at a brief but fully developed narrative reconstructing the discovery of the bacterial cause of stomach ulcers. This narrative was written by Martin J. Blaser for *Scientific American*, a journal read primarily by nonspecialists interested in science. As you read, notice the same narrating strategies you saw in the chronology in Figure 14.1: sequencing events in chronological order and marking the passage of time by specifying when each event occurred (each time marker is highlighted):

> Blaser cites specific years, months, days, and a holiday to convey the passage of time and indicate when each event occurred.

In 1979 J. Robin Warren, a pathologist at the Royal Perth Hospital in Australia, made a puzzling observation. As he examined tissue specimens from patients who had undergone stomach biopsies, he noticed that several samples had large numbers of curved and spiral-shaped bacteria. Ordinarily, stomach acid would destroy such organisms before they could settle in the stomach. But those Warren saw lay underneath the organ's thick mucus layer — a lining that coats the stomach's tissues and protects them from acid. Warren also noted that the bacteria were present only in tissue samples that were inflamed. Wondering whether the microbes might somehow be related to the irritation, he looked to the literature for clues and learned that German pathologists had witnessed similar organisms a century earlier. Because they could not grow the bacteria in culture, though, their findings had been ignored and then forgotten.

Warren, aided by an enthusiastic young trainee named Barry J. Marshall, also had difficulty growing the unknown bacteria in culture. He began his efforts in 1981. By April 1982 the two men had attempted to culture samples from 30-odd patients — all without success. Then the Easter holidays arrived. The hospital laboratory staff accidentally held some of the culture plates for five days instead of the usual two. On the fifth day, colonies emerged. The workers christened them *Campylobacter pyloridis* because they resembled pathogenic bacteria of the *Campylobacter* genus found in the intestinal tract. Early in 1983 Warren

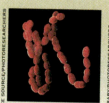

1944 Working with pneumococcus bacteria, Oswald Avery, Colin MacLeod and Maclyn McCarty prove that DNA, not protein, is the hereditary material in most living organisms.

1950 British physician Douglas Bevis describes how amniocentesis can be used to test fetuses for Rh-factor incompatibility. The prenatal test will later be used to screen for a battery of genetic disorders.

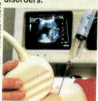

1953 American biochemist James Watson and British biophysicist Francis Crick announce their discovery of the double-helix structure of DNA, the molecule that carries the genetic code.

1964 Stanford geneticist Charles Yanofsky and colleagues prove that the sequence of nucleotides in DNA corresponds exactly to the sequence of amino acids in proteins.

1969 A Harvard Medical School team isolates the first gene: a snippet of bacterial DNA that plays a role in the metabolism of sugar.

1970 University of Wisconsin researchers synthesize a gene from scratch.

1973 American biochemists Stanley Cohen and Herbert Boyer insert a gene from an African clawed toad into bacterial DNA, where it begins to work. Their experiment marks the beginning of genetic engineering.

and Marshall published their first report, and within months scientists around the world had isolated the bacteria.

> — MARTIN J. BLASER, "The Bacteria behind Ulcers"

In addition to calendar time (years, months, days), writers sometimes also refer to clock time (hours, minutes, seconds). Here is a brief narrative from an essay profiling the emergency room at Bellevue Hospital in New York City:

9:05 P.M. An ambulance backs into the receiving bay, its red and yellow lights flashing in and out of the lobby. A split second later, the glass doors burst open as a nurse and an attendant roll a mobile stretcher into the lobby. When the nurse screams, "Emergency!" the lobby explodes with activity as the way is cleared to the trauma room. Doctors appear from nowhere and transfer the bloodied body of a black man to the treatment table. Within seconds his clothes are stripped away.

> — GEORGE SIMPSON, "The War Room at Bellevue"

The references to clock time establish the sequence and contribute to dramatic intensity.

EXERCISE 14.1

Turn to the remembered-event essay "100 Miles per Hour, Upside Down and Sideways," by Rick Bragg, in Chapter 2, and underline the references to calendar time in paragraphs 2, 6, and 8. How do you think these calendar time markers function in the narrative? What do they tell you about the impression Bragg wants to create about his younger self?

EXERCISE 14.2

Read through "The New York Pickpocket Academy" by John McPhee, in Chapter 3, and underline any references to clock time that you find. What does McPhee's use of clock time contribute to his essay?

Temporal Transitions

For a more extensive list of connectives showing temporal relationships, see Chapter 13.

Whereas calendar and clock time tend to be used sparingly, writers regularly use **temporal transitions** such as *when, at that moment, before,* and *while.* Temporal transitions establish a clear sequence of actions in time. They are used to narrate both onetime and recurring events.

Onetime Events.   Writers and readers rely on temporal transitions to show readers how events relate to one another, indicating which event came first, which event followed, and which events happened at the same time. To see how temporal transitions work, let us look at the concluding paragraphs of a remembered-event essay in which Russell Baker recounts what happened after his final flight test, his last chance to become a pilot. The "he" Baker refers to is the flight check pilot, T. L. (nicknamed "Total Loss") Smith.

Baker uses temporal transitions to show what he and Smith were doing after the flight test.

> Back at the flight line, when I'd cut the ignition, he climbed out and tramped back toward the ready room while I waited to sign the plane in. When I got there he was standing at a distance talking to my regular instructor. His talk was being illustrated with hand movements, as pilots' conversations always were, hands executing little loops and rolls in the air. After he did the falling-leaf motion with his hands, he pointed a finger at my instructor's chest, said something I couldn't hear, and trudged off. My instructor, who had flown only with the pre-hangover Baker, was slack-jawed when he approached me.
>
> "Smith just said you gave him the best check flight he's ever had in his life," he said. "What the hell did you do to him up there?"
>
> "I guess I just suddenly learned to fly," I said.
>
> — Russell Baker, "Smooth and Easy"

Look closely at the two transitions in the first sentence. The word *when* presents actions in chronological order (first Baker stopped the plane, and then Smith got out). *While* performs a different function, showing that the next two actions occurred at the same time (Baker signed in as the instructor returned to the ready room). There is nothing complicated or unusual about this set of actions, but it would be hard to represent them in writing without temporal transitions.

Recurring Events.   Temporal transitions also enable writers to show what recurring events typically happened over a longer period of time. In the following narrative by Monica Sone about her daily life in an internment camp for Japanese Americans during World War II, we can see how transitions (highlighted) help the writer represent actions she routinely performed.

With the time marker *first,* Sone starts describing her typical work routine. In the third sentence, she tells of her surreptitious actions *in the first few months and every morning.*

> First I typed on pink, green, blue and white work sheets the hours put in by the 10,000 evacuees, then sorted and alphabetized these sheets, and stacked them away in shoe boxes. My job was excruciatingly dull, but under no circumstances did I want to leave it. The Administration Building was the only place which had modern plumbing and running hot and cold water; in the first few months and every morning, after I had typed for a decent hour, I slipped into the rest room and took a complete sponge bath with scalding hot water. During the remainder of the day,

I slipped back into the rest room at inconspicuous intervals, took off my head scarf and wrestled with my scorched hair. I stood upside down over the basin of hot water, soaking my hair, combing, stretching and pulling at it.

— MONICA SONE, "Camp Harmony"

EXERCISE 14.3

Turn to the remembered-event essay "On Being a Real Westerner," by Tobias Wolff, in Chapter 2. Underline the temporal transitions in paragraph 9, where Wolff relates a onetime event, and paragraph 5, where he presents recurring events. Notice the number of transitions he uses and how each one functions. What can you conclude about Wolff's use of temporal transitions from your analysis of these two paragraphs? How well do these transitions create a sense of time passing? How effectively do they help you follow the sequence of actions?

EXERCISE 14.4

Turn to "Love: The Right Chemistry," by Anastasia Toufexis, in Chapter 4. Read paragraph 3, underlining the temporal transitions Toufexis uses to present the sequence of evolutionary changes that may have contributed to the development of romantic love. How important are these transitions in helping you follow her narrative?

Verb Tense

In addition to time markers like calendar time and temporal transitions, writers use **verb tense** to represent action in writing and to help readers understand when each action occurred in relation to the other actions. Let us look at some of the ways writers use verb tense to narrate onetime and recurring events.

Onetime Events.   Writers typically use the past tense to represent onetime events that began and ended at some time in the past. Here is a brief passage from a remembered-person essay by Amy Wu. In addition to the temporal transitions *once* and *when* in the opening sentence, which let readers know that this particular event occurred many years earlier, the writer also uses simple past-tense verbs (highlighted):

Once, when I was 5 or 6, I interrupted my mother during a dinner with her friends and told her that I disliked the meal. My mother's eyes transformed from serene pools of blackness into stormy balls of fire. "Quiet!" she hissed, "do you not know that silent waters run deep?"

— AMY WU, "A Different Kind of Mother"

> Wu uses the simple past tense to indicate that actions occurred in a linear sequence.

In the next example, by Chang-Rae Lee, we see how verb tense can be used to show more complicated relationships between past actions:

When Uncle Chul amassed the war chest he needed to open the wholesale business he had hoped for, he moved away from New York.

— CHANG-RAE LEE, "Uncle Chul Gets Rich"

> Lee employs both the simple past (*amassed, needed, moved*) and the past perfect tense (*had hoped*).

You do not have to know the names of these verb tenses to know that the hopes came before the money was amassed. In fact, most readers of English can understand complicated combinations of tenses without knowing their names.

Let us look at another verb tense combination used frequently in narrative: the simple past and the past progressive.

Malcolm X uses the simple past tense (*overheard*, *was*) and past progressive tense (*was leaving*, *was appearing*).

> When Dinah Washington was leaving with some friends, I overheard someone say she was on her way to the Savoy Ballroom where Lionel Hampton was appearing that night — she was then Hamp's vocalist.
>
> — MALCOLM X, *The Autobiography of Malcolm X*

This combination of tenses plus the temporal transition *when* shows that the two actions occurred at the same time in the past. The first action ("Dinah Washington was leaving") continued during the period that the second action ("I overheard") occurred.

Occasionally, writers use the present instead of the past tense to narrate one-time events. Process narratives and profiles typically use the present tense to give the story a sense of "you are there" immediacy.

Edge uses present-tense verbs to give readers a sense that they are in the room with him.

> Slowly, the dank barroom fills with grease-smeared mechanics from the truck stop up the road and farmers straight from the fields, the soles of their brogans thick with dirt clods. A few weary souls make their way over from the nearby sawmill. I sit alone at the bar, one empty bottle of Bud in front of me, a second in my hand. I drain the beer, order a third, and stare down at the pink juice spreading outward from a crumpled foil pouch and onto the bar.
> *I'm not leaving until I eat this thing*, I tell myself.
>
> — JOHN T. EDGE, "I'm Not Leaving Until I Eat This Thing"

Recurring Events.   Verb tense, usually combined with temporal transitions, can also help writers narrate events that occurred routinely.

Morris uses the helping verb *would* along with temporal transitions to show recurring actions.

> Many times, walking home from work, I would see some unknowing soul venture across that intersection against the light and then freeze in horror when he saw the cars ripping out of the tunnel toward him. . . . Suddenly, the human reflex would take over, and the pedestrian would jackknife first one way, then another, arms flaying the empty air, and often the car would literally skim the man, brushing by him so close it would touch his coat or his tie. . . . On one occasion, feeling sorry for the person who had brushed against the speeding car, I hurried across the intersection after him to cheer him up a little. Catching up with him down by 32nd I said, "That was good legwork, sir. Excellent moves for a big man!" but the man looked at me with an empty expression in his eyes, and then moved away mechanically and trancelike, heading for the nearest bar.
>
> — WILLIE MORRIS, *North toward Home*

Notice also that Morris shifts to the simple past tense when he moves from recurring actions to an action that occurred only once. He signals this shift with the temporal transition *on one occasion*.

EXERCISE 14.5

Turn to the remembered-event essay "Calling Home," by Jean Brandt, in Chapter 2. Read paragraph 3, and underline the verbs, beginning with *got, took, knew,* and *didn't want* in the first sentence. Brandt uses verb tense to reconstruct her actions and reflect on their effectiveness. Notice also how verb tense helps you follow the sequence of actions Brandt took.

Specific Narrative Action

The narrating strategy we call **specific narrative action** uses active verbs and modifying phrases and clauses to present action vividly. Specific narrative action is especially suited to representing the intense, fast-moving, physical actions of sports events. The following example by George Plimpton shows how well specific narrative actions (highlighted) work to show what happened during a practice scrimmage. Plimpton participated in the Detroit Lions football training camp while writing a book profiling professional football. This is what he experienced:

> Since in the two preceding plays the concentration of the play had been elsewhere, I had felt alone with the flanker. Now, the whole heave of the play was toward me, flooding the zone not only with confused motion but noise — the quick stomp of feet, the creak of football gear, the strained grunts of effort, the faint *ah-ah-ah* of piston-stroke regularity, and the stiff calls of instruction, like exhalations. "Inside, inside! Take him inside!" someone shouted, tearing by me, his cleats thumping in the grass. A call — a parrot squawk — may have erupted from me. My feet splayed in hopeless confusion as Barr came directly toward me, feinting in one direction, and then stopping suddenly, drawing me toward him for the possibility of a button-hook pass, and as I leaned almost off balance toward him, he turned and came on again, downfield, moving past me at high speed, leaving me poised on one leg, reaching for him, trying to grab at him despite the illegality, anything to keep him from getting by. But he was gone, and by the time I had turned to set out after him, he had ten yards on me, drawing away fast with his sprinter's run, his legs pinwheeling, the row of cleats flicking up a faint wake of dust behind.
>
> — GEORGE PLIMPTON, *Paper Lion*

Though Plimpton uses active verbs, he describes most of the action through modifying phrases and clauses.

The two most common kinds of modifiers that writers employ to present specific narrative action are:

Participial phrases: tearing by me, stopping suddenly, moving past me at high speed

Absolute phrases: his cleats thumping in the grass, his legs pinwheeling, the row of cleats flicking up a faint wake of dust behind

As with verb tense, most English speakers know how to construct these phrases and clauses without knowing their grammatical names. By piling up specific narrative actions, Plimpton reconstructs for readers the texture and excitement of his experience on the football field. Combined with vivid sensory description (*the creak of football gear, the strained grunts of effort, the faint* ah-ah-ah *of piston-stroke regularity*), these specific narrative actions re-create the sights and sounds of people in motion.

EXERCISE 14.6

Turn to paragraph 2 of the profile essay "The Long Good-Bye: Mother's Day in Federal Prison" by Amanda Coyne, in Chapter 3. Underline any specific narrative actions you find in this brief paragraph. Then reflect on how they help the reader envision the scene in the prison's visiting room.

EXERCISE 14.7

Make a videotape of several brief — two- or three-minute — televised segments of a fast-moving sports competition such as a football or basketball game. Then review the tape, and choose one segment to narrate using specific narrative actions to describe in detail what you see.

If you cannot videotape a televised game, narrate a live-action event (for example, people playing touch football, a dog catching a Frisbee, or a skateboarder or inline skater practicing a trick). As you watch the action, take detailed notes of what you see. Then, based on your notes, write a few sentences using specific narrative actions to describe the action you witnessed firsthand.

Dialogue

Dialogue reconstructs choice bits of conversation and does not try to present an accurate and complete record. It is most often used in narratives that dramatize events. In addition to showing people interacting, dialogue can give readers insight into character and relationships. Dialogue may be quoted to make it resemble the give-and-take of actual conversation, or it may be summarized to give readers the gist of what was said.

The following example from Gary Soto's *Living up the Street* shows how a narrative can combine quoted and summarized dialogue. In this passage, Soto recalls his first experience as a migrant worker in California's San Joaquin Valley.

So it went. Two pans equaled one tray — or six cents. By lunchtime I had a trail of thirty-seven trays behind me while Mother had sixty or more. We met about halfway from our last trays, and I sat down with a grunt, knees wet from kneeling on dropped grapes. I washed my hands with the water from the jug, drying them on the inside of my shirt sleeve before I opened the paper bag for the first sandwich, which I gave to Mother. I dipped my hand in again to unwrap a sandwich without looking at it. I took a first bite and chewed it slowly for the tang of mustard. Eating in silence I looked straight ahead at the vines, and only when we were finished with cookies did we talk.

"Are you tired?" she asked.

"No, but I got a sliver from the frame," I told her. I showed her the web of skin between my thumb and index finger. She wrinkled her forehead but said it was nothing.

"How many trays did you do?"

I looked straight ahead, not answering at first. I recounted in my mind the whole morning of bend, cut, pour again and again, before answering a feeble "thirty-seven." No elaboration, no detail. Without looking at me she told me how she had done field work in Texas and Michigan as a child. But I had a difficult time listening to her stories. I played with my grape knife, stabbing it into the ground, but stopped when Mother reminded me that I had better not lose it. I left the knife sticking up like a small, leafless plant. She then talked about school, the junior high I would be going to that fall, and then about Rick and Debra, how sorry they would be that they hadn't come out to pick grapes because they'd have no new clothes for the school year. She stopped talking when she peeked at her watch, a bandless one she kept in her pocket. She got up with an "Ay, Dios," and told me that we'd work until three, leaving me cutting figures in the sand with my knife and dreading the return to work.

— GARY SOTO, "One Last Time"

> Soto uses signal phrases with the first two quotations but not with the third, where it is clear who is speaking. The fourth quotation, *thirty-seven*, is preceded by a narrative that tells what Soto did and thought before speaking.

Quoted dialogue is easy to recognize, of course, because of the quotation marks. Summarized dialogue can be harder to identify. In this case, however, Soto embeds signal phrases (*she told me* and *she then talked*) in his narrative. He summarizes what his mother talked about without going into detail or quoting words she might have used. Summarizing leaves out information the writer decides readers do not need. In this passage about a remembered event, Soto has apparently chosen to focus on his own feelings and thoughts rather than his mother's.

For more on deciding when to quote, see Chapter 22.

EXERCISE 14.8

Read the essay "100 Miles per Hour, Upside Down and Sideways" in Chapter 2, and consider Rick Bragg's use of both direct quotation and summaries for reporting speech. When does Bragg choose to quote directly, and why might he have made this decision?

EXERCISE 14.9

If you wrote a remembered-event essay in Chapter 2 or wrote a bit of narrative in some other essay, reread your essay, looking for one example of each of the following narrating strategies: calendar or clock time, temporal transitions, past-tense verbs in onetime events, specific narrative action, and dialogue. Do not worry if you cannot find examples of all of the strategies. Pick one strategy you did use, and comment on what it contributes to your narrative.

■ Narrating a Process

Process narratives explain how something was done or instruct readers on how it could or should be done. Whether the purpose is explanatory or instructional,

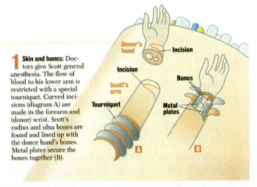

A Second Hand, A Second Chance

It took a 17-member surgical team about 15 hours to complete Matthew Scott's hand transplant, the first in the United States. The operation is extremely complex. Unlike a solid organ transplant—a kidney, for example—a hand reattachment involves multiple tissues: skin, muscle, tendon, bone, nerves and blood vessels. At right, the procedure:

50   NEWSWEEK   FEBRUARY 8, 1999

1 **Skin and bones:** Doctors give Scott general anesthesia. The flow of blood to his lower arm is restricted with a special tourniquet. Curved incisions (diagram A) are made in the forearm and (donor) wrist. Scott's radius and ulna bones are found and lined up with the donor hand's bones. Metal plates secure the bones together (B).

Figure 14.2 Presentation of an explanatory process
The two-page layout reproduced here shows how "A Second Hand, A Second Chance" was designed as a sidebar accompanying a longer article, "To Have and to Hold." From *Newsweek*, February 8, 1999, pp. 50–51.

process narratives must convey clearly each necessary action and the exact order in which the actions occur.

Explanatory Process Narratives

Explanatory process narratives often relate particular experiences or elucidate processes followed by machines or organizations. Let us begin with an excerpt from a remembered-event essay by Mary Mebane. She uses process narrative to let readers know what happened the first time she worked on an assembly line putting tobacco leaves on the conveyor belt.

> The job seemed easy enough as I picked up bundle after bundle of tobacco and put it on the belt, careful to turn the knot end toward me so that it would be placed right to go under the cutting machine. Gradually, as we worked up our tobacco, I had to bend more, for as we emptied the hogshead we had to stoop over to pick up the tobacco, then straighten up and put it on the belt just right. Then I discovered the hard part of the job: the belt kept moving at the same speed all the time and if

Temporal transitions and simple past-tense verbs place the actions in time.

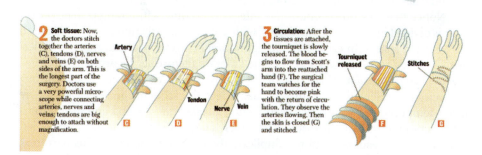

2 **Soft tissue:** Now, the doctors stitch together the arteries (C), tendons (D), nerves and veins (E) on both sides of the arm. This is the longest part of the surgery. Doctors use a very powerful microscope while connecting arteries, nerves and veins; tendons are big enough to attach without magnification.

Artery
Tendon   Nerve   Vein
G   D   E

3 **Circulation:** After the tissues are attached, the tourniquet is slowly released. The blood begins to flow from Scott's arm into the reattached hand (F). The surgical team watches for the hand to become pink with the return of circulation. They observe the arteries flowing. Then the skin is closed (G) and stitched.

Tourniquet released   Stitches
F   G

the leaves were not placed on the belt at the same tempo there would be a big gap where your bundle should have been. So that meant that when you got down lower, you had to bend down, get the tobacco, straighten up fast, make sure it was placed knot end toward you, place it on the belt, and bend down again. Soon you were bending down, up; down, up; down, up. All along the line, heads were bobbing — down, up; down, up — until you finished the barrel. Then you could rest until the men brought you another one.

— MARY MEBANE, "Summer Job"

Here, specific narrative actions (*bend down, get the tobacco, straighten up fast*) become a series of staccato movements (*down, up; down, up; down, up*) that emphasize the speed and machinelike actions Mebane had to take to keep up with the conveyor belt.

The next example shows how a laser printer functions.

To create a page, the computer sends signals to the printer, which shines a laser at a mirror system that scans across a charged drum. Whenever the beam strikes the drum, it removes the charge. The drum then rotates through a toner chamber filled with thermoplastic particles. The toner particles stick to the negatively charged areas of the drum in the pattern of characters, lines, or other elements the computer has transmitted and the laser beam mapped.

Once the drum is coated with toner in the appropriate locations, a piece of paper is pulled across a so-called transfer corona wire, which imparts a positive electrical charge. The paper then passes across the toner-coated drum. The positive charge on the paper attracts the toner in the same position it occupied on the drum. The final phase of the process involves fusing the toner to the paper with a set of high-temperature rollers.

— RICHARD GOLUB AND ERIC BRUS, *Almanac of Science and Technology*

Like Mebane's process narrative, this one sequences the actions chronologically from beginning ("the computer sends signals to the printer") to end ("fusing the toner to the paper"). Temporal transitions (*then, once, then, final*), present-tense verbs, and specific narrative actions (*sends, shines, scans, strikes*) convey the passage of time and place the actions clearly in this chronological sequence.

Our last explanatory process narrative is a graphic sidebar of the type commonly used in magazines and books. This one comes from a *Newsweek* magazine feature on

> Because the inanimate objects performing the action change from sentence to sentence, the writers must construct a clearly marked chain, introducing the object's name in one sentence and repeating the name or using a synonym in the next.

Matthew Scott, only the third person to receive a hand transplant. "A Second Hand, A Second Chance," shown in Figure 14.2, illustrates the process narrative.

Notice that this process narrative integrates writing with graphics. The procedure is divided into three distinct steps, with each step clearly numbered and labeled (*1. Skin and bones*). In each step, the figure captions refer to the graphics with letters — *Curved incisions* (*diagram A*). The graphics themselves incorporate labels — *Donor's hand, Incision, Tourniquet released*. The writer uses some basic narrating strategies to present the actions and make clear the sequence in which they were taken: temporal transitions (*now, while, after*), present-tense verbs, and specific narrative actions, mostly in the form of active verbs (*secure, stitch, watches*). Much is left out, of course. Readers could not duplicate the procedure based on this narrative, but it does give *Newsweek* readers a clear sense of what was done during the fifteen hours of surgery.

EXERCISE 14.10

In Chapter 3, read paragraph 6 of Brian Cable's profile of a local mortuary, "The Last Stop." Here Cable narrates the process that the company follows once it has been notified of a client's death. As you read, look for and mark the narrating strategies discussed in this chapter that Cable uses. Then reflect on how well you think the narrative presents the actions and their sequence.

Instructional Process Narratives

For guidelines on designing your own documents, see Chapter 25.

Unlike explanatory process narratives, **instructional process narratives** must include all of the information a reader needs to perform the procedure presented. Depending on the reader's experience, the writer might need to define technical terms, list tools that should be used, give background information, and account for alternatives or possible problems.

Figure 14.3 presents a detailed instructional process narrative from the Sunset *Home Repair Handbook* that gives readers directions for replacing a broken plug.

The instructions begin with general advice on when to replace a plug, followed by a classification of three common types of plugs that also are illustrated in the accompanying graphic. Notice that even though the graphic is not referred to explicitly in the text, readers are unlikely to be confused because the graphic is right next to the relevant paragraph and is clearly titled "Types of plugs."

Paragraphs 4 and 5 briefly explain the procedure for replacing two- and three-prong plugs. These procedures are spelled out in greater detail in the accompanying graphics titled "Replacing a plug with terminal screws" and "Replacing three special types of plugs." The first of these graphics includes four steps that are clearly numbered, illustrated, and narrated. Each step presents several actions to be taken, and its graphic shows what the plug should look like when these actions have been com-

■ Replacing Plugs ■

Any plug with a cracked shell or loose, damaged, or badly bent contacts should be replaced. Also replace plugs that transmit power erratically or get warm when used. If a plug arcs when it's pushed into or pulled out of a receptacle, examine the wires; if they're not firmly attached to the terminal screws, tighten the connections.

The two kinds of common plugs are terminal-screw and self-connecting. In plugs with terminal screws, the wires are attached to screws inside the plug body. Self-connecting plugs clamp onto wires, making an automatic connection. These plugs, as well as two-prong plugs with terminal screws, are commonly used for lamps and small appliances. Three-prong grounding plugs are used for larger appliances and power tools. Detachable cords for small appliances have female plugs with terminal screws.

NOTE: Many old-style plugs with terminal screws have a removable insulating disc covering the terminals and wires. The NEC now requires "dead-front" plugs; such plugs have a rigid insulating barrier.

To replace a plug, cut off the old one plus at least an inch of the cord. For plugs that have terminal screws, split the cord insulation to separate the wires; then strip the insulation from the ends *(page 159)*.

When replacing a two-prong plug, connect the identified conductor to the silver-colored screw. For a three-prong grounding plug, attach the wires to the terminal screws as follows: white neutral wire to silver screw, black hot wire to brass screw, and green grounding wire to green terminal screw.

Types of plugs

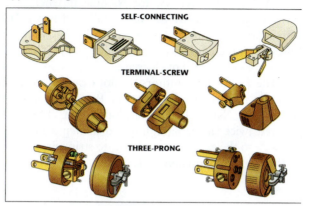

Replacing a plug with terminal screws

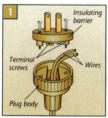
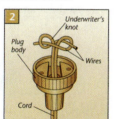
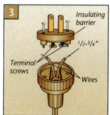
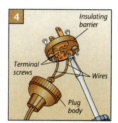

1 Unscrew and remove the new plug's insulating barrier. Using a utility knife, split the end of the cord to separate the wires; push the cord through the plug body.

2 Make two loops with the wires, pass the loose ends of the wires through the loops, and pull to form an Underwriter's knot (to prevent strain on connections).

3 Strip ¹/₂ to ³/₄ inch of insulation off the wire ends, being careful not to nick the wires *(page 159)*. Unscrew the terminal screws to allow space for the wires.

4 Form loops on wires and wrap them clockwise three-quarters of the way around screws. Tighten the screws, trim excess wire, and reattach the barrier to the body.

Replacing three special types of plugs

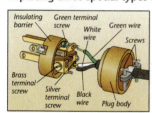
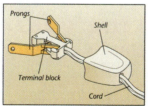
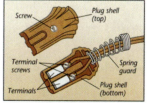

Three-prong grounding plug. Unscrew the insulating barrier; push stripped wires through the plug body into the correct terminal slots. Tighten the terminal screws and reassemble the plug.

Self-connecting plug. Push the cord (don't strip it) through the shell and into the terminal block; squeeze the prongs together to grip the cord and slide into the shell.

Female appliance plug. Unscrew the plug shell; feed the cord through the spring guard. Strip the wire ends *(page 159)*, wrap them clockwise around the terminal screws, and tighten; reassemble the plug.

Figure 14.3 Replacing plugs
From *Home Repair Handbook* (Menlo Park, Calif.: Sunset, 1999), pp. 156–57.

pleted. We can identify the actions by looking at the verbs. Step 1 in "Replacing a plug with terminal screws," for example, instructs readers to take four separate actions, each signaled by the verb (italicized here): "*Unscrew* and *remove* the new plug's insulating barrier. Using a utility knife, *split* the end of the cord to *separate* the wires; *push* the cord through the plug body." These are active verbs, and the sentences are in the form of clear and efficient commands.

The anonymous authors do not assume that readers know very much, especially on important safety matters. Paragraph 3, for example, presents a note explaining the National Electrical Code ("NEC") for old-style plugs. Also, readers are referred twice (in paragraph 4 and in step 3 of "Replacing a plug with terminal screws") to the explanation of how to strip wires safely, which appears on page 159 of the *Home Repair Handbook.*

EXERCISE 14.11

Write a one- to two-page instructional process narrative that tells readers how to make a peanut butter and jelly sandwich or perform some other equally simple procedure such as logging on to the Internet, shortening a pair of pants, separating egg whites from yolks, potting a plant, or filling a fountain pen. Address your narrative to readers who have never done the procedure before or to those who may know something about the procedure but would be interested in how you go about doing it.

Describing

Describing comes from the Latin *describere*, meaning "to sketch" or "to copy in writing." Written descriptions help readers imagine what is being described. Vivid description creates an intense, distinctive image, one that seems to bring the words on the page to life. Good description can also be evocative, calling up memories or suggesting feelings associated with the subject being described. Writers can use description for many purposes: to give readers an impression of a person or place, to illustrate abstract ideas, to make information memorable, or to support an argument. This chapter presents the three basic descriptive techniques of naming, detailing, and comparing; surveys the words writers typically use to evoke vivid sense impressions; and examines how writers use description to create a dominant impression.

Naming

Naming calls readers' attention to observable features of the subject being described. To describe a room, for example, you might name objects you see as you look around, such as a bed, pillows, blankets, dresser, clothes, books, a CD player, and CDs. These objects suggest what kind of room it is and begin to give readers an impression of what it is like to be in this particular room.

Look closely at the following passage describing a weasel that the writer, Annie Dillard, encountered in the woods:

> He was ten inches long, thin as a curve, a muscled ribbon, brown as fruitwood, soft-furred, alert. His face was fierce, small and pointed as a lizard's; he would have made a good arrowhead. There was just a dot of chin, maybe two brown hairs' worth, and then the pure white fur began that spread down his underside. He had two black eyes I didn't see, any more than you see a window.
>
> — ANNIE DILLARD, *Teaching a Stone to Talk*

Dillard names the weasel's many distinctive features.

With these names, readers can begin to put together a mental image of the animal Dillard is describing. She uses simple, everyday nouns, like *chin*, to identify the weasel's features, not technical words like *maxilla* or *mandible*. Words like *chin* are also concrete nouns that refer to specific, observable parts of a weasel's face. The piling up of simple, concrete nouns helps readers imagine what the weasel looked like to Dillard.

Although writers most commonly name what they see, sight is not the only sense contributing to vivid descriptions, as in the following passage:

Kazin names smells, sounds, tastes, and tactile qualities.

> When the sun fell across the great white pile of the new Telephone Company building, you could smell the stucco burning as you passed; then some liquid sweetness that came to me from deep in the rings of the freshly cut lumber stacked in the yards, and the fresh plaster and paint on the brand-new storefronts. Rawness, sunshiny rawness down the end streets of the city, as I thought of them then — the hot ash-laden stink of the refuse dumps in my nostrils and the only sound at noon the resonant metal plunk of a tin can I kicked ahead of me as I went my way.
>
> — Alfred Kazin, *A Walker in the City*

EXERCISE 15.1

Go to a place where you can sit for a while, and observe the scene. It might be a landscape or a cityscape, indoors or outdoors, crowded or solitary. It could be a familiar or a new place. For five minutes, list everything in the scene that you can name using nouns. (A simple way to test if a word is a noun is to see if you can put the word *the, a,* or *an* in front of the word.) Remember, you can name objects you see (*dog, hydrant*) as well as impressions such as smells or sounds you experience at the place (*stench, hiss*).

Then write a page or so that describes the scene for someone who is not there with you. You could choose to write for readers who have been to the place but have not seen what you are seeing there now, or you could write for readers who have never been to this particular place to let them know what to expect when they get there.

EXERCISE 15.2

Turn to "An American Childhood," by Annie Dillard, in Chapter 2. Read paragraphs 12 and 13 and underline the names that Dillard uses to describe the circuitous route she runs while the stranger is chasing her. Begin underlining with the words *house, path, tree,* and *bank* in the opening sentence. How do you think the amount of naming Dillard does contributes to the description's vividness — measured by your ability to imagine the chase scene?

■ Detailing

Naming identifies the notable features of the subject being described; **detailing** makes the features more specific or particularized. Naming answers the questions "What is it?" and "What are its parts or features?" Detailing answers questions like these:

What size is it?

How many are there?

What is it made of?

Where is it located?

What is its condition?

How is it used?

Where does it come from?

What is its effect?

What is its value?

To add details to names, add modifiers — adjectives and adverbs, phrases and clauses. *Modifiers* make nouns more specific by supplying additional information. Notice how many modifying details Dillard provides in her description of the weasel.

> He was ten inches long, thin as a curve, a muscled ribbon, brown as fruitwood, soft-furred, alert. His face was fierce, small and pointed as a lizard's; he would have made a good arrowhead. There was just a dot of chin, maybe two brown hairs' worth, and then the pure white fur began that spread down his underside. He had two black eyes I didn't see, any more than you see a window.
>
> — ANNIE DILLARD, *Teaching a Stone to Talk*

Dillard provides details about size, shape, color, texture.

Dillard's details provide information that particularizes the weasel, showing readers what a specific weasel looked like. Her weasel has certain qualities that make it an individual, such as its length and color. Just as objective physical details like these help readers picture the weasel, other details convey subjective information about Dillard's thoughts and feelings during the encounter. For example, when Dillard writes that the weasel's "face was fierce," she is making a judgment. She uses details like this to make readers see the weasel as a wild animal, not a soft and cuddly pet.

In describing people, writers often combine physical details with details characterizing aspects of the individual's personality. These characterizations or evaluations let readers know something about the writer's thoughts about the person, as the following examples illustrate:

> My father, a fat, funny man with beautiful eyes and a subversive wit . . .
>
> — ALICE WALKER, "Beauty: When the Other Dancer Is the Self"

> I was afraid of her higharched bony nose, her eyebrows lifted in half-circles above her hooded, brilliant eyes, and of the Kentucky R's in her speech, and the long steps she took in her hightop shoes. I did nothing but fear her bearing-down authority. . . .
>
> — EUDORA WELTY, "Miss Duling"

Walker uses both physical description (*fat*) and evaluative details (*funny, beautiful*) to express her feelings about her father. Welty combines physical detail (*higharched bony nose*) with subjective judgment (*bearing-down authority*) to help readers understand her fear.

Sometimes physical details alone can be enough to symbolize a person's character or the writer's feelings toward that person, as in the following passage:

> Rick was not a friendly looking man. He wore only swim trunks, and his short, powerful legs rose up to meet a bulging torso. His big belly was solid. His shoulders, as if to offset his front-heaviness, were thrown back, creating a deep crease of

The physical details suggest a powerful and threatening character.

excess muscle from his sides around the small of his back, a crease like a huge frown. His arms were crossed, two medieval maces placed carefully on their racks, ready to be swung at any moment. His round cheeks and chin were darkened by traces of black whiskers. His hair was sparse. Huge, black, mirrored sunglasses replaced his eyes. Below his prominent nose was a thin, sinister mustache. I couldn't believe this menacing-looking man was the legendary jovial Rick.

— BRAD BENIOFF, "Rick"

EXERCISE 15.3

Return to the description you wrote in Exercise 15.1. Put brackets around the details you used to help describe the scene. Add any other details you think of now — details that indicate size, quantity, makeup, location, condition, use, source, effect, value, or any other quality that would make the description more specific and particularized for readers. Then reread your description. What do you think the detailing contributes to the description you wrote?

EXERCISE 15.4

Look again at paragraphs 12 and 13 of Annie Dillard's essay in Chapter 2. In Exercise 15.2, you underlined the names Dillard used. Now put brackets around the details. You might begin, for example, with the modifiers *yellow* and *backyard*. How do you think detailing contributes to Dillard's description? How do these details help you imagine Dillard's experience of the chase?

EXERCISE 15.5

Turn to paragraphs 10 and 13 of Amanda Coyne's essay in Chapter 3. Read and put brackets around the words that detail the description of Stephanie and her son Ellie. If you have not read the entire essay, read it now, and consider how Coyne uses these contrasting descriptions of the inmate and her son to emphasize her main point in the essay.

■ Comparing

In addition to naming and detailing, writers sometimes use **comparing** to make their description more vivid for readers. Look again at Annie Dillard's description of a weasel, paying attention this time to the comparisons:

Dillard uses similes and metaphors to describe the weasel.

He was ten inches long, thin as a curve, a muscled ribbon, brown as fruitwood, soft-furred, alert. His face was fierce, small and pointed as a lizard's; he would have made a good arrowhead. There was just a dot of chin, maybe two brown hairs' worth, and then the pure white fur began that spread down his underside. He had two black eyes I didn't see, any more than you see a window.

— ANNIE DILLARD, *Teaching a Stone to Talk*

Dillard uses two kinds of comparison in this description: simile and metaphor, both of which point out similarities in things that are essentially dissimilar. A *simile* expresses the similarity directly by using the words *like* or *as* to announce the comparison. A *metaphor,* by contrast, is an implicit comparison in which one thing is described as though it were the other.

Similes and metaphors can enhance the vividness of a description by giving readers additional information to help them picture the subject. For example, Dillard uses the word *thin* to detail the weasel's body shape. But *thin* is a relative term, leading readers to wonder, how thin? Dillard gives readers two images for comparison, a curve and a ribbon, to help them construct a fuller mental image of the weasel.

Comparing can also convey to readers what the writer feels about the subject. The following comparison from Brad Benioff's description of Coach Rick suggests the writer's feelings: "His arms were crossed, two medieval maces placed carefully on their racks, ready to be swung at any moment." Sometimes the similes or metaphors writers use are suggestive but hard to pin down. What do you think Dillard means, for example, by comparing the weasel's eyes to a window: "He had two black eyes I didn't see, any more than you see a window"?

EXERCISE 15.6

Return to the description you wrote in Exercise 15.1 and may have added to in Exercise 15.3. Reread it, and mark any comparing you did. Try to add one or two similes or metaphors to your description. How do you think your use of comparing may help readers imagine the subject or get a sense of what you feel about it?

■ Using Sensory Description

When writers use **sensory description** to describe animals, people, or scenes, they usually rely on the sense of sight more than the other senses. Our vocabulary for reporting what we see is larger and more varied than our vocabulary for reporting other sense impressions. Quite a few nouns and verbs designate sounds; a smaller number of nouns, but few verbs, describe smells; and very few nouns or verbs convey touch and taste. It also seems easier to use naming to describe what we see. Nonvisual sense perceptions seem to be less readily divided into distinguishing features. For example, we have many names to describe the visible features of a car but few to describe the sounds a car makes. Nevertheless, writers can detail the qualities and attributes of nonvisual sensations — the loudness or tinniness or rumble of an engine, for instance. They can also use comparing to help readers imagine what something sounds, feels, smells, or tastes like.

The Sense of Sight

When people describe what they see, they identify the objects in their field of vision. Here are two brief examples of visual description.

On Christmas Eve I saw that my mother had outdone herself in creating a strange menu. She was pulling black veins out of the backs of fleshy prawns. The kitchen was littered with appalling mounds of raw food: A slimy rock cod with bulging eyes that pleaded not to be thrown into a pan of hot oil. Tofu, which looked like stacked wedges of rubbery white sponges. A bowl soaking dried fungus back to life. A plate of squid, their backs crisscrossed with knife markings so they resembled bicycle tires.

— AMY TAN, "Fish Cheeks"

She was thirty-four. She wore a white skirt and yellow sweater and a thin gold necklace, which she held in her fingers, as if holding her own reins, while waiting for children to answer. Her hair was black with a hint of Irish red. It was cut short to the tops of her ears, and swept back like a pair of folded wings. She had a delicate cleft chin, and she was short — the children's chairs would have fit her. . . . Her hands kept very busy. They sliced the air and made karate chops to mark off boundaries. They extended straight out like a traffic cop's, halting illegal maneuvers yet to be perpetrated. When they rested momentarily on her hips, her hands looked as if they were in holsters.

— TRACY KIDDER, *Among Schoolchildren*

EXERCISE 15.7

Write a few sentences describing a teacher, friend, or family member. Do not rely on memory for this exercise; describe someone who is before you as you write so that you can describe in detail what you see. Later, when you are alone, reread what you have written, and make any changes you think will help make this visual description more vivid for your readers.

The Sense of Hearing

In reporting auditory impressions, writers seldom name the objects from which the sounds come without also naming the sounds themselves: the murmur of a voice, the rustle of the wind, the squeak of a hinge, the sputter of an engine. *Onomatopoeia* is the term for names of sounds that echo the sounds themselves: *squeak, murmur, hiss, boom, plink, tinkle, twang, jangle, rasp, chirr.* Sometimes writers make up words like *sweesh* and *cara-wong* to imitate sounds they wish to describe. Qualitative words like *powerful* and *rich* as well as relative terms like *loud* and *low* often specify sounds further. For detailing sounds, writers sometimes use the technique called *synesthesia*, applying words commonly used to describe one sense to another, such as describing sounds as *sharp* and *soft*; they sometimes also use simile or metaphor to compare one sound to another.

To write about the sounds along Manhattan's Canal Street, Ian Frazier uses many of these describing and naming techniques.

The traffic on Canal Street never stops. It is a high-energy current jumping constantly between the poles of Brooklyn and New Jersey. It hates to have its flow pinched in the density of Manhattan, hates to stop at intersections. Along Canal Street, it moans and screams. Worn brake shoes of semitrucks go "Ooohhhh nooohhhh" at stoplights, and the sound echoes in the canyons of warehouses and Chinatown tenements. People lean on their horns from one end of Canal Street to the other. They'll honk nonstop for ten minutes at a time, until the horns get tired and out of breath. They'll try different combinations: shave-and-a-hair-cut, long-long-long, short-short-short-long. Some people have musical car horns; a person purchasing a musical car horn seems to be limited to a choice of four tunes — "La Cucaracha," "Theme from *The Godfather*," "Dixie," and "Hava Nagila."

— IAN FRAZIER, "Canal Street"

EXERCISE 15.8

Turn to paragraph 6 of Tobias Wolff's essay, "On Being a Real Westerner," in Chapter 2, and find the place where Wolff uses onomatopoeia to describe sound. Then look at paragraph 9, where Wolff describes the sound created by firing the rifle. What do you think these descriptions of sound contribute to this particular essay, which takes place mostly in the silence of Wolff's home?

EXERCISE 15.9

Find a noisy spot — a restaurant, a football game, a nursery school, a laundry room — where you can perch for about half an hour. Listen attentively to the sounds of the place, and make notes about what you hear. Then write a page or so describing the place through its sounds.

The Sense of Smell

The English language has a meager stock of words to express the olfactory sense. In addition to the word *smell*, fewer than a dozen commonly used nouns name this sensation: *odor, scent, vapor, fume, aroma, fragrance, perfume, bouquet, stench, stink*. Although there are other, rarer words like *fetor* and *effluvium*, few writers use them, probably for fear that their readers will not know them. Few verbs describe receiving or sending odors — *smell, sniff, waft* — but a fair number of detailing adjectives are available: *redolent, pungent, aromatic, perfumed, stinking, musty, rancid, putrid, rank, fetid, malodorous, foul, acrid, sweet*, and *cloying*.

Here is an example of how Amanda Coyne, in her essay in chapter 3, uses smell in a description:

Occasionally, a mother will pick up her present and bring it to her nose when one of the bearers of the single flower — her child — asks if she likes it. . . . But most of what is being smelled today is the children themselves. While the other adults are plunking coins into the vending machines, the mothers take deep whiffs from the backs of their children's necks, or kiss and smell the backs of their knees, or take off their shoes and tickle their feet and then pull them close to their noses. They hold them tight and take in their own second scent — the scent assuring them that these are still their children and that they still belong to them.

— AMANDA COYNE, "The Long Good-Bye: Mother's Day in Federal Prison"

Coyne uses smell to describe "convict moms" and their children in a prison visiting room.

In addition to using *smell* as a verb, Coyne describes the repeated action of bringing the object being smelled to the nose, an act that not only signifies the process of smelling but also underscores its intimacy. To further emphasize intimacy, Coyne connects smelling with other intimate acts of kissing, tickling, pulling close, and holding tight.

Because she is not describing her own experience of smell, Coyne does not try to find words to evoke the effect the odor has. In the next passage, however, Frank Conroy uses comparing in addition to naming and detailing to describe how the smell of flowers affected him:

> The perfume of the flowers rushed into my brain. A lush aroma, thick with sweetness, thick as blood, and spiced with the clear acid of tropical greenery.
> — FRANK CONROY, *Stop-Time*

Naming the objects from which smells come can also be very suggestive.

> The odor of these houses was different, full of fragrances, sweet and nauseating. On 105th Street the smells were of fried lard, of beans and car fumes, of factory smoke and home-made brew out of backyard stills. There were chicken smells and goat smells in grassless yards filled with engine parts and wire and wood planks, cracked and sprinkled with rusty nails. These were the familiar aromas: the funky earth, animal and mechanical smells which were absent from the homes my mother cleaned.
> — LUIS J. RODRIGUEZ, *Always Running: Gang Days in L.A.*

EXERCISE 15.10

Turn to "I'm Not Leaving Until I Eat This Thing," by John T. Edge, in Chapter 3, and read paragraph 16. Underline the words describing the sense of smell. How do you think this bit of sensory description helps readers imagine the scene?

EXERCISE 15.11

Choose a place with noticeable, distinctive smells where you can stay for ten or fifteen minutes. You may choose an eating place (a cafeteria, a doughnut shop), a place where something is being manufactured (a sawmill, a bakery), or some other place that has strong, identifiable odors (a fishing dock, a garden, a locker room). While you are there, take notes on what you smell, and then write a page or so describing the place primarily through its smells.

The Sense of Touch

Few nouns and verbs name tactile sensations besides words like *touch, feel, tickle, brush, scratch, sting, itch,* and *tingle*. Probably as a consequence, writers describing the sense of touch tend not to name the sensation directly or even to report the act of feeling. Nevertheless, a large stock of words describes temperature (*hot, warm, mild, tepid, cold, arctic*), moisture content (*wet, dry, sticky, oily, greasy, moist, crisp*), texture (*gritty, silky, smooth, crinkled, coarse, soft, leathery*), and weight (*heavy, light, ponderous, buoyant, feathery*). Read the following passages with an eye for descriptions of touch.

> A small slab of roughly finished concrete offered a place to stand opposite a square of tar from which a splintered tee protruded.
>
> — WILLIAM RINTOUL, "Breaking One Hundred"

> The earth was moldy, a dense clay. No sun had fallen here for over two centuries. I climbed over the brick retaining wall and crawled toward the sound of the kitten. As I neared, as it sensed my presence was too large to be its mother, it went silent and scrabbled away from the reach of my hand. I brushed fur, though, and that slight warmth filled me with what must have been a mad calm because when the creature squeezed into a bearing wall of piled stones, I inched forward on my stomach.
>
> — LOUISE ERDRICH, "Beneath the House"

Here is an example of a writer recalling a childish fantasy of aggression toward her younger sister. Notice the tactile description she uses.

> She was baby-soft. I thought that I could put my thumb on her nose and push it bonelessly in, indent her face. I could poke dimples into her cheeks. I could work her face around like dough.
>
> — MAXINE HONG KINGSTON, "The Quiet Girl"

EXERCISE 15.12

Do something with your hands, and then write a sentence or two describing the experience of touch. For example, you might pet a dog, dig a hole and put a plant into the earth, make a pizza, sculpt with clay, bathe a baby, scrub a floor, or massage a friend's back. As you write, notice the words you consider using to describe temperature, moisture content, texture, weight, or any other tactile quality.

EXERCISE 15.13

Turn to "The Last Stop," by Brian Cable, in Chapter 3, and read paragraph 28. Underline the language that describes the sense of touch. What does this detail add to your understanding of the scene, and why might Cable have chosen to save it for the last paragraph of his profile?

The Sense of Taste

Other than *taste, savor,* and *flavor,* few words name gustatory sensations directly. Certain words do distinguish among types of tastes — *sweet (saccharine, sugary, cloying); sour (acidic, tart); bitter (acrid, biting); salty (briny, brackish)* — and several other words describe specific tastes (*piquant, spicy, pungent, peppery, savory, toothsome*).

In the following passage, M. F. K. Fisher describes the surprisingly "delicious" taste of tar:

> Tar with some dust in it was perhaps even more delicious than dirty chips from the iceman's wagon, largely because if we worked up enough body heat and had the right amount of spit we could keep it melted so that it acted almost like chewing gum, which was forbidden to us as vulgar and bad for the teeth and in general to be shunned. Tar was better than anything ever put out by Wrigley and Beechnut, anyway. It had a high, bright taste. It tasted the way it smelled, but better.
>
> — M. F. K. FISHER, "Prejudice, Hate, and the First World War"

Fisher tries to evoke the sense of taste by comparing tar that acted like chewing gum to actual Wrigley and Beechnut chewing gum. More surprisingly, she compares the taste of tar to its smell.

Ernest Hemingway, in a more conventional passage, tries to describe taste primarily by naming the foods he consumed and giving details that indicate the intensity and quality of the tastes:

> As I ate the oysters with their strong taste of the sea and their faint metallic taste that the cold wine washed away, leaving only the sea taste and the succulent texture, and as I drank their cold liquid from each shell and washed it down with the crispy taste of the wine, I lost the empty feeling and began to be happy and to make plans.
>
> — ERNEST HEMINGWAY, *A Moveable Feast*

Writers often use words like *juicy, chewy*, and *chunky* to evoke both the taste and the feel of food in the mouth.

Fisher uses suggestive words not typically associated with taste.

Hemingway combines taste and touch (the feel of the food in his mouth).

EXERCISE 15.14

In the manner of Hemingway, take notes as you eat a particular food or an entire meal. Then write a few sentences describing the tastes you experienced.

EXERCISE 15.15

Turn to John T. Edge's "I'm Not Leaving Until I Eat This Thing" in Chapter 3, an essay about pickled pig's lips. Read paragraphs 7 and 18, underlining any language that describes or suggests the sense of taste. How well does this sensory description help you participate in the writer's experience?

■ Creating a Dominant Impression

The most effective description creates a **dominant impression**, a mood or an atmosphere that reinforces the writer's purpose. Writers often attempt to create a dominant impression — for example, when they describe a place to set a scene and make readers aware of its atmosphere. Naming, detailing, comparing, and sensory language — all the choices about what to include and what to call things — come together to create this effect, as the following passage by Mary McCarthy illustrates. Notice that McCarthy directly states the idea she is trying to convey in the last sentence of the paragraph.

> Whenever we children came to stay at my grandmother's house, we were put to sleep in the sewing room, a bleak, shabby, utilitarian rectangle, more office than bedroom, more attic than office, that played to the hierarchy of chambers the role of a poor relation. It was a room seldom entered by the other members of the family, seldom swept by the maid, a room without pride; the old sewing machine, some cast-off chairs, a shadeless lamp, rolls of wrapping paper, piles of pins, and remnants of material united with the iron folding cots put out for our use and the bare floor boards to give an impression of intense and ruthless temporality. Thin, white spreads, of the kind used in hospitals and charity institutions, and naked blinds at the windows reminded us of our orphaned condition and of the ephemeral character of our visit; there was nothing here to encourage us to consider this our home.
>
> — MARY MCCARTHY, *Memories of a Catholic Girlhood*

McCarthy names objects and provides details that support the overall impression she seeks to convey.

Everything in the room made McCarthy and her brothers feel unwanted, discarded, orphaned. The room itself is described in terms applicable to the children: Like them, it "played to the hierarchy of chambers the role of a poor relation."

Sometimes writers comment directly in a description, as McCarthy does. Often, however, writers want description to speak for itself, as in the following example.

> Hanging from the ceiling there was a heavy glass chandelier on which the dust was so thick that it was like fur. And covering most of one wall there was a huge hideous piece of junk, something between a sideboard and a hall-stand, with lots of carving and little drawers and strips of looking-glass, and there was a once-gaudy carpet ringed by the slop-pails of years, and two gilt chairs with burst seats, and one of those old-fashioned armchairs which you slide off when you try to sit on them. The room had been turned into a bedroom by thrusting four squalid beds in among the wreckage.
>
> — GEORGE ORWELL, *The Road to Wigan Pier*

Orwell uses language that *shows* objects and details that convey an impression.

EXERCISE 15.16

Turn to Rick Bragg's essay in Chapter 2 and read paragraph 2 describing Bragg's car. What seems to you to be the dominant impression of this description? What do you think contributes most to this impression?

16

Defining

Defining is an essential strategy for all writing. Autobiographers, for example, must occasionally define objects, conditions, events, and activities for readers likely to be unfamiliar with particular terms, as in the following example.

Gray defines *psoriasis* in this example of autobiographical writing.

> My father's hands are grotesque. He suffers from psoriasis, a chronic skin disease that covers his massive, thick hands with scaly, reddish patches that periodically flake off, sending tiny pieces of dead skin sailing to the ground.
>
> — Jan Gray, "Father"

When writers share information or explain how to do something, they must often define important terms for readers who are unfamiliar with the subject, as in this example.

Olson defines *shifting baselines* in this example of explanatory writing.

> Shifting baselines are the chronic, slow, hard-to-notice changes in things, from the disappearance of birds and frogs in the countryside to the increased drive time from L.A. to San Diego.
>
> — Randy Olson, "Shifting Baselines: Slow-Motion Disaster below the Waves"

To convince readers of a position or an evaluation or to move them to act on a proposal, a writer must often define concepts important to an argument.

Ehrenreich defines *extreme poverty* in this example of argument.

> You would come across news of a study showing that the percentage of Wisconsin food-stamp families in "extreme poverty" — defined as less than 50 percent of the federal poverty line — has tripled in the last decade to more than 30 percent.
>
> — Barbara Ehrenreich, *Nickel and Dimed*

As these examples illustrate, there are many kinds of definitions and many forms that they can take. Some published essays and reports are concerned primarily with the definition of a little-understood or problematic concept or thing. Usually, however, definition is only a part of an essay. A long piece of writing, like a term paper, textbook, or research report, may include many kinds of brief and extended definitions, all of them integrated with other writing strategies.

This chapter illustrates various types of sentence definitions, the most common in writing. When writers use sentence definitions, they rely on various sentence patterns to provide concise definitions. The chapter also provides illustrations of multisentence extended definitions, including definition by word history, or etymology, and by stipulation.

■ Sentence Definitions

Every field of study, every institution, and every activity has its own unique concepts and terms. Coming to a new area for the first time, a participant or a reader is often baffled by the many unfamiliar names for objects and activities. In college, introductory courses in all the academic disciplines often seem like courses in definitions of new terms. In the same way, newcomers to a sport like sailing or rock climbing often need to learn a great deal of specialized terminology. In such cases, writers of textbooks and manuals rely on brief **sentence definitions**, involving a variety of sentence strategies.

The following examples, from introductory college textbooks, illustrate various sentence strategies an author may use to name and define terms for readers.

The most obvious sentence strategies simply announce a definition.

A *karyotype* is a graphic representation of a set of chromosomes.

Then, within the first week, the cells begin to *differentiate* — to specialize in structure and function.

B lymphocytes form in the bone marrow and release antibodies that fight bacterial infections.

Geologists refer to the processes of mountain building as *orogenesis* (from the Greek *oro*, "mountain," and *genesis*, "birth").

Posthypnotic suggestions (suggestions to be carried out after the hypnosis session has ended) have helped alleviate headaches, asthma, warts, and stress-related skin disorders.

These sentences present their definitions directly.

All of these sentence strategies declare in a straightforward way that the writer is defining a term. Other strategies, signaled by subordinate clauses, are less direct but still quite apparent.

During the *oral stage*, which lasts throughout the first 18 months, the infant's sensual pleasures focus on sucking, biting, and chewing.

Hemophilia is called the bleeder's disease because the affected person's blood does not clot.

The definitions in the subordinate clauses add details, express time and cause, or indicate conditions or tentativeness.

Another common defining strategy is the appositive phrase. Here one word or phrase defines another word or phrase in a brief inserted phrase called an *appositive*.

Taxonomy, the science of classifying groups (taxa) of organisms in formal groups, is hierarchical.

The actual exchange of gases takes place in small air sacs, the *alveoli*, which are clustered in branches like grapes around the ends of the smallest bronchioles.

These sentences use appositives to present either the definition or the word to be defined.

EXERCISE 16.1

Look up any three of the following words or phrases in a dictionary. Define each one in a sentence. Try to use a different sentence pattern, like the ones just illustrated, for each of your definitions.

bull market	ecumenism	samba
carcinogen	edema	seasonal affective disorder
caricature	harangue	sonnet
clinometer	hyperhidrosis	testosterone
ectomorph	mnemonic	zero-based budgeting

EXERCISE 16.2

Turn to the essay in Chapter 4 titled "Cannibalism: It Still Exists" by student writer Linh Kieu Ngo, and analyze the sentence definitions in paragraphs 5, 6, 7, 8, and 11. Notice the different kinds of sentence patterns Ngo relies on. (You need not be able to analyze the sentences grammatically to examine their patterns.) Keeping in mind that Ngo's purpose is to introduce readers to the concept of cannibalism and its varieties, how helpful do you find these sentence definitions? How do they work with Ngo's use of examples?

■ Extended Definitions

At times a writer may need to go further than a brief sentence definition and provide readers with a fuller, **extended definition** extending over several sentences, as in the following example.

Castro provides an extended definition of the term *contingent worker*.

> Every day, 1.5 million temps are dispatched from agencies like Kelly Services and Manpower — nearly three times as many as 10 years ago. But they are only the most visible part of America's enormous new temporary work force. An additional 34 million people start their day as other types of "contingent" workers. Some are part-timers with some benefits. Others work by the hour, the day or the duration of a project, receiving only a paycheck without benefits of any kind. The rules of their employment vary widely and so do the attempts to label them. They are called short-timers, per-diem workers, leased employees, extra workers, supplementals, contractors — or in IBM's ironic computer-generated parlance, "the peripherals." They are what you might expect: secretaries, security guards, salesclerks, assembly-line workers, analysts and CAD/CAM designers. But these days they are also what you'd never expect: doctors, high school principals, lawyers, bank officers, X-ray technicians, biochemists, engineers, managers — even chief executives.
> — Janice Castro, "Contingent Workers"

Castro begins by comparing contingent workers to the more familiar temporary workers ("temps") managed by temporary employment agencies. Then she gives examples of contingent workers' working arrangements and lists many names by which these workers are known. Finally, she identifies the various categories of contingent workers. These strategies — comparisons, examples, synonyms, and classification — are often found in extended definitions and in fact in all kinds of explanatory writing. Castro never concisely defines the word *contingent* in the phrase "contingent worker" because she assumes that readers can infer that it means roughly the opposite of permanent, continuing worker.

In this next example, Marie Winn offers an extended definition of television addiction. Like Janice Castro, Winn begins with a comparison. These two experienced writers know that comparison or contrast is often the most effective way to present an unfamiliar term or concept to readers. The key is to know your readers well enough to find a term nearly all of them will know to compare to the unfamiliar term.

> People often refer to being "hooked on TV." Does this, too, fall into the light-hearted category of cookie eating and other pleasures that people pursue with unusual intensity, or is there a kind of televison viewing that falls into the more serious category of destructive addiction? . . .
>
> Let us consider television viewing in the light of the conditions that define serious addictions.
>
> Not unlike drugs or alcohol, the television experience allows the participant to blot out the real world and enter into a pleasurable and passive mental state. The worries and anxieties of reality are as effectively deferred by becoming absorbed in a television program as by going on a "trip" induced by drugs or alcohol. And just as alcoholics are only inchoately aware of their addiction, feeling that they control their drinking more than they really do ("I can cut it out any time I want — I just like to have three or four drinks before dinner"), people similarly overestimate their control over television watching. Even as they put off other activities to spend hour after hour watching television, they feel they could easily resume living in a different, less passive style. But somehow or other while the television set is present in their homes, the click doesn't sound. With television pleasures available, those other experiences seem less attractive, more difficult somehow. . . .
>
> The self-confessed television addict often feels he "ought" to do other things — but the fact that he doesn't read and doesn't plant his garden or sew or crochet or play games or have conversations means that those activities are no longer as desirable as television viewing. In a way a heavy viewer's life is as imbalanced by his television "habit" as a drug addict's or an alcoholic's. He is living in a holding pattern, as it were, passing up the activities that lead to growth or development or a sense of accomplishment. This is one reason people talk about their television viewing so ruefully, so apologetically. They are aware that it is an unproductive experience, that almost any other endeavor is more worthwhile by any human measure.
>
> Finally, it is the adverse effect of television viewing on the lives of so many people that defines it as a serious addiction. The television habit distorts the sense of time. It renders other experiences vague and curiously unreal while taking on a greater reality for itself. It weakens relationships by reducing and sometimes eliminating normal opportunities for talking, for communicating.
>
> And yet television does not satisfy, else why would the viewer continue to watch hour after hour, day after day? "The measure of health," writes Lawrence Kubie, "is flexibility . . . and especially the freedom to cease when sated." But the television viewer can never be sated with his television experiences — they do not provide the true nourishment that satiation requires — and thus he finds that he cannot stop watching.
>
> — MARIE WINN, "TV Addiction"

In Winn's extended definition of *TV addiction*, she compares her subject to drug and alcohol addiction, describes its effects on addicts, and speculates on why breaking the addiction is so difficult.

Extended definitions may also include *negative definitions* — explanations of what the thing being defined is *not*:

Bakker uses a negative definition, explaining that *dinosaurs* are not lizards.

It's important to be clear about the reverse definition, as well: what dinosaurs are not. Dinosaurs are not lizards, and vice versa. Lizards are scaly reptiles of an ancient bloodline. The oldest lizards antedate the earliest dinosaurs by a full thirty million years. A few large lizards, such as the man-eating Komodo dragon, have been called "relics of the dinosaur age," but this phrase is historically incorrect. No lizard ever evolved the birdlike characteristics peculiar to each and every dinosaur. A big lizard never resembled a small dinosaur except for a few inconsequential details of the teeth. Lizards never walked with the erect, long-striding gait that distinguishes the dinosaur like ground birds today or the birdlike dinosaurs of the Mesozoic.

— ROBERT T. BAKKER, *The Dinosaur Heresies*

EXERCISE 16.3

Choose one term that names some concept or feature of central importance in an activity or a subject you know well. For example, if you sail, you know terms like *tacking* and *coming about*. If you are studying biology, you have probably encountered terms like *morphogenesis* and *ecosystem*. Choose a word with a well-established definition. Write an extended definition of several sentences for this important term. Write for readers your own age who will be encountering the term for the first time when they read your definition.

EXERCISE 16.4

In his essay in Chapter 4, Richard A. Friedman presents an extended definition. After reading his essay, how would you define *hyperthymia*? Reread the first five paragraphs of the essay to see which strategies he uses to define the term.

■ Historical Definitions

Occasionally, a writer will trace the history of a word, from its first use to its adoption into other languages to its shifting meanings over the centuries. Such a strategy can be a rich addition to an essay, bringing surprising depth and resonance to the definition of a concept. A **historical definition** may begin with the roots of a word but extends well beyond the word's origins to trace its history over a long period of time. Such a history should always serve a writer's larger purpose, as the example here shows.

In this example, from a special issue of *Time* magazine on the future uses of cyberspace and its potential impact on the economy, Philip Elmer-DeWitt provides a historical definition of the term *cyberspace*.

It started, as the big ideas in technology often do, with a science-fiction writer. William Gibson, a young expatriate American living in Canada, was wandering past the video arcades on Vancouver's Granville Street in the early 1980s when something about the way the players were hunched over their glowing screens struck him as odd. "I could see in the physical intensity of their postures how *rapt* the kids were," he says. "It was like a feedback loop, with photons coming off the screens into the kids' eyes, neurons moving through their bodies and electrons moving through the video game. These kids clearly *believed* in the space the games projected."

That image haunted Gibson. He didn't know much about video games or computers — he wrote his breakthrough novel *Neuromancer* (1984) on an ancient manual typewriter — but he knew people who did. And as near as he could tell, everybody who worked much with the machines eventually came to accept, almost as an article of faith, the reality of that imaginary realm. "They develop a belief that there's some kind of *actual space* behind the screen," he says. "Some place that you can't see but you know is there."

Gibson called that place "cyberspace," and used it as the setting for his early novels and short stories. In his fiction, cyberspace is a computer-generated landscape that characters enter by "jacking in" — sometimes by plugging electrodes directly into sockets implanted in the brain. What they see when they get there is a three-dimensional representation of all the information stored in "every computer in the human system" — great warehouses and skyscrapers of data. He describes it in a key passage in *Neuromancer* as a place of "unthinkable complexity," with "lines of light ranged in the nonspace of the mind, clusters and constellations of data. Like city lights, receding. . . ."

In the years since, there have been other names given to that shadowy space where our computer data reside: the Net, the Web, the Cloud, the Matrix, the Metaverse, the Datasphere, the Electronic Frontier, the information superhighway. But Gibson's coinage may prove the most enduring. By 1989 it had been borrowed by the online community to describe not some science-fiction fantasy but today's increasingly interconnected computer systems — especially the millions of computers jacked into the Internet.

— PHILIP ELMER-DeWITT, "Welcome to Cyberspace"

Elmer-DeWitt begins with a story about how William Gibson created the name *cyberspace* for a strange phenomenon he observed — young people's intense concentration while playing video games. *Cybernetics* was already a familiar term used to describe computer-controlled processes like robots in factories. Gibson borrowed the *cyber* portion and combined it with *space* to reflect his imagined realm, the "place that you can't see but you know is there." Elmer-DeWitt also offers details about how Gibson imagined humans would gain access to cyberspace and how it was constructed. Finally, bringing the historical definition into the present, Elmer-DeWitt lists competing terms that have failed to supplant *cyberspace* as the term most people now use to identify the realm of computer data and electronic communication.

EXERCISE 16.5

Any good dictionary tells the origins of words. Historical, or etymological, dictionaries, however, give much more information, enough to trace changes in the use of a word over long periods of time. The preeminent historical dictionary of our language is the

Oxford English Dictionary. Less imposing is *A Dictionary of American English*, and more accessible still is *A Dictionary of Americanisms*. Look up the historical definition of any one of the following words in *A Dictionary of Americanisms*, and write several sentences on its roots and development.

basketball	bushwhack	gerrymander	rubberneck
bazooka	canyon	jazz	sashay
bedrock	carpetbag	lobbying	Scot-free
blizzard	dugout	pep	two-bit
bogus	eye-opener	picayune	
bonanza	filibuster	podunk	

Stipulative Definitions

To stipulate means to seek or assert agreement on something. In a **stipulative definition**, the writer declares a certain meaning, generally not one found in the dictionary.

In her autobiography, Annie Dillard defines *football* as she understood it as a nine-year-old.

> Dillard provides a stipulative definition of *football* as she understood it when she was nine years old.

Some boys taught me to play football. This was fine sport. You thought up a new strategy for every play and whispered it to the others. You went out for a pass, fooling everyone. Best, you got to throw yourself mightily at someone's running legs. Either you brought him down or you hit the ground flat out on your chin, with your arms empty before you. It was all or nothing. If you hesitated in fear, you would miss and get hurt: you would take a hard fall while the kid got away, or you would get kicked in the face while the kid got away. But if you flung yourself wholeheartedly at the back of his knees — if you gathered and joined body and soul and pointed them diving fearlessly — then you likely wouldn't get hurt, and you'd stop the ball. Your fate, and your team's score, depended on your concentration and courage. Nothing girls did could compare with it.

— ANNIE DILLARD, *An American Childhood*

For Dillard's complete essay, see Chapter 2.

There are recognizable elements of grown-up football in Dillard's definition. Her focus is less on rules and strategy, however, than on the "concentration and courage" required to make a successful tackle and, of course, on the sheer thrill of doing it. She stipulates this definition because it suits her purposes in telling a remembered incident about how she and her fellow football players were chased by a man whose car they had bombed with snowballs.

This next example illustrates how a newspaper columnist might create a stipulative definition of a term to support an argument.

Ozone depletion and the greenhouse effect are human disasters. They happen to occur in the environment. But they are urgent because they directly threaten man. A sane environmentalism, the only kind of environmentalism that will win universal public support, begins by unashamedly declaring that nature is here to serve man. A sane environmentalism is entirely anthropocentric: it enjoins man to pre-serve nature, but on the grounds of self-preservation.

A sane environmentalism does not sentimentalize the earth. It does not ask people to sacrifice in the name of other creatures. After all, it is hard enough to ask people to sacrifice in the name of other humans. (Think of the chronic public resistance to foreign aid and welfare.) Ask hardworking voters to sacrifice in the name of the snail darter, and, if they are feeling polite, they will give you a shrug.

— CHARLES KRAUTHAMMER, "Saving Nature, but Only for Man"

> Krauthammer uses his stipu-lative definition of *environ-mentalism* to argue for a more realistic approach to protecting the environment.

EXERCISE 16.6

Look at Karen Kornbluh's essay "Win-Win Flexibility" in Chapter 7. Kornbluh begins the argument with contrasting stipulative definitions of the "traditional" family and the "juggler" family. What is her stipulative definition of each type of family? How does she use these definitions to support her overall argument?

EXERCISE 16.7

Write several sentences of a stipulative definition for one of the following.

1. Define in your own way game shows, soap operas, police dramas, horror movies, or some other form of entertainment. Try for a stipulative definition of what your subject is generally like. In effect, you will be saying to your readers — other students in your class who are familiar with these entertainments — "Let's for now define it this way."

2. Define in your own way some hard-to-define concept, such as "loyalty," "love," "bravery," "shyness," or "masculinity."

3. Think of a new development or phenomenon in contemporary romance, music, television, leisure, fashion, or eating habits, or in your line of work. Invent a name for it, and write a stipulative definition for it.

17

Classifying

Classifying is an essential writing strategy for thinking about and organizing ideas, information, and experience. The process of **classifying** involves either grouping or dividing. Writers group related items (such as *apples, oranges, bananas, strawberries, cantaloupes,* and *cherries*) and label the general class of items they grouped together (*fruit*). Or they begin classifying with a general class (such as *fruit*) and then divide it into subclasses of particular types (*apples, oranges,* etc.).

This chapter shows how you can organize and illustrate a classification you have read about or constructed yourself.

■ Organizing Classification

Classifying in writing serves primarily as a means of **organization**, of creating a framework for the presentation of information, whether in a few paragraphs of an essay or in an entire book. This section surveys several examples of classifying, ranging from a simple two-level classification to a complex multilevel system.

The simplest classification divides a general topic into two subtopics. Here is an example by Edward J. Loughram from a proposal to keep at-risk teenagers out of jail and help them lead productive lives. Before he can present his proposed solution, Loughram has to get readers to see that all juvenile offenders are not the same. He does this by explaining that although statistics show that the number of juvenile offenders is rising, they do not take into account the fact that there are two distinct groups of young people getting into trouble. He classifies juvenile offenders into these two categories to argue that the problem of delinquency can be solved, at least in part, by interrupting the criminal paths of the second group.

> Two primary factors explain the growing numbers of juvenile offenders. First, there is indeed a rise in serious crime among young people, fueled by the steady stream of drugs and weapons into their hands. These dangerous offenders are committed — legitimately — to juvenile-correction agencies for long-term custody or treatment.
>
> But a second, larger group is also contributing to the increase. It consists of 11-, 12-, and 13-year-old first-time offenders who have failed at home, failed in school, and fallen through the cracks of state and community social-service

Loughram's two categories show that the basis for his classification is the seriousness of the crimes.

agencies. These are not serious offenders, or even typical delinquents. But they are coming into the correctional system because we have ignored the warning signs among them.

— EDWARD J. LOUGHRAM, "Prevention of Delinquency"

From Loughram's essay, we see how a writer can use a simple two-category classification to advance an argument. The next example, excerpted from a concept explanation essay by Janice Castro, presents a somewhat more complicated classification system:

Every day, 1.5 million temps are dispatched from agencies like Kelly Services and Manpower — nearly three times as many as 10 years ago. But they are only the most visible part of America's enormous new temporary work force. An additional 34 million people start their day as other types of "contingent" workers. Some are part-timers with some benefits. Others work by the hour, the day or the duration of a project, receiving only a paycheck without benefits of any kind. The rules of their employment vary widely and so do the attempts to label them. They are called short-timers, per-diem workers, leased employees, extra workers, supplementals, contractors — or in IBM's ironic computer-generated parlance, "the peripherals." They are what you might expect: secretaries, security guards, salesclerks, assembly-line workers, analysts and CAD/CAM designers. But these days they are also what you'd never expect: doctors, high school principals, lawyers, bank officers, X-ray technicians, biochemists, engineers, managers — even chief executives. . . .

Already the temping phenomenon is producing two vastly different classes of untethered workers: the mercenary work force at the top of the skills ladder, who thrive; and the rest, many of whom, unable to attract fat contract fees, must struggle to survive.

— JANICE CASTRO, "Contingent Workers"

Castro explains that "contingent" is only one of many labels used to identify this general class of part-time and temporary workers. Although she only indirectly labels these two types of contingent workers, we can see that her basis for differentiating between these two groups is the amount of money they are paid. We can label these groups *well-paid* and *low-paid*. Readers sometimes have to supply labels to clarify for themselves the categories in a classification.

So far, Castro's is a simple two-part classification system like Loughram's. It has two levels: the general class of contingent workers and two subclasses of well-paid and low-paid contingent workers. Castro, however, adds a third level to her classification by listing several types of jobs that fall under her two subclasses. Here is a tree diagram that graphically displays Castro's three-level classification:

> Castro classifies contingent workers into two categories: the well-paid and the low-paid.

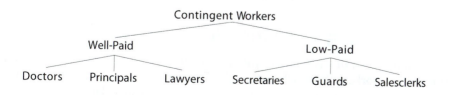

Later in the essay, Castro identifies another class of workers who are not contingent workers but are "a permanent cadre of 'core workers.'" To add this class of core workers to the tree diagram, we should also add a new general class at the top that includes all of the subclasses below it. We could label this most general class "corporate workers." Here is what the expanded tree diagram would look like:

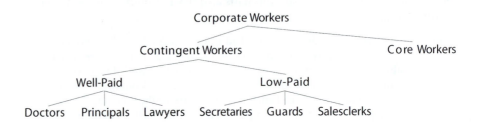

What the tree diagrams show at a glance is that in a classification system, some categories are on the same level, or *coordinate*. Some are on a higher level, *superordinate*. And some are on a lower level, *subordinate*. The highest level represents the most general category, and each lower level identifies increasingly specific types. If Castro took her classification to the most specific level, she would name individuals as examples of workers in each type of job. Whether you construct your own classification system or use someone else's, you want to make sure that each item is placed in an appropriate category on the proper level.

EXERCISE 17.1

Turn to the concept explanation in Chapter 4, "Cannibalism: It Still Exists," and make a tree diagram of the classification in paragraphs 5–12. What do you think is Linh Kieu Ngo's basis for classification? Does each item seem to be placed in an appropriate category and on the proper level?

EXERCISE 17.2

Review the essays you have written so far for this class or for another class, looking for an essay in which you used classifying. What was the purpose of your essay and your basis for classifying? Construct a tree diagram of your classification to see whether each item can be placed in an appropriate category and on the proper level.

■ Illustrating Classification

We used tree diagrams as an **illustration** of the categories and levels of Castro's classification of workers. Writers, however, sometimes integrate graphics into their own writing to make their classification easy for readers to see at a glance.

Here is an example from *Newsweek* magazine in which Sharon Begley and Martha Brant explain the problem of drug abuse by Olympic athletes.

If doping is, as [the head of IOC's Medical Commission Prince Alexandre] de Merode noticed, suddenly "an important problem," it is partly because the newest doping agents pose the risk of serious health problems, and even death. But the larger reason is that it is ridiculously easy to dope and not get caught. Doping and detection are like an arms race. First, trainers discover a performance-enhancing drug. Then, sports officials develop a test for it. Trainers retaliate by inventing a way to elude the detectors. So far, doping has stayed a lap ahead. "Undetectable drugs are 90 percent of estimated doping cases," says Hein Verbruggen, head of international cycling.

Czech tennis pro Petr Korda tested positive for the steroid nandrolone after the Wimbledon quarterfinals last May, for instance. (Protesting that he did not know how the chemicals got into his system, he avoided the one-year suspension the International Tennis Association is supposed to impose.) But American pro Jim Courier charged that steroids are far from the worst abuse in tennis. "EPO is the problem," Courier told *Newsweek*. "I have pretty strong suspicions that guys are using it on the tour. I see guys who are out there week in and week out without taking rests. EPO can help you when it's the fifth set and you've been playing for four-and-a-half hours." Although the endurance-building effects of EPO last for about two weeks, its use can't be detected in urine at all or in blood for more than a day or so after the athlete stops taking it.

EPO is only one weapon in a pharmaceutical arsenal of performance-enhancing substances flowing through sports. Stimulants like amphetamines, ephedrine and caffeine were the first substances to land on the IOC's list of banned agents, and they're still popular. They provide a quick pop of energy, and so are a favorite of sprinters, cyclists and swimmers. They are an ingredient of many asthma medications. Exercise-induced asthma has inexplicably stricken many Olympians, including 60 percent of the U.S. team in 1994, and medical use of stimulant inhalants is allowed. Are stimulants detectable? Sure, if your trainer's IQ matches his hat size. They clear the urine in hours, so all an athlete has to do is not take them too close to her event. If you've been using too soon before your race, there are always "masking agents." Probenecid, for one, inhibits substances from reaching the urine. And urine tests are all the IOC requires: blood tests, which can detect more substances, are deemed too invasive.

Anabolic steroids, almost all of them derivatives of the hormone testosterone, are the mothers of all doping agents. They build muscles. By most estimates, an athlete can improve strength at least 5 percent by taking steroids either orally or through injection during high-intensity training. Drug-detection machines, such as the high-resolution mass spectrometer used at the Atlanta Games in 1996, can be tuned to detect any synthetic steroid; the Atlanta lab tested for 100 different types. But the Dr. Feelgoods of sport can tinker with the molecular structure of common steroids, so they slip through. "There are 72 banned steroids," says one American coach who says he developed drug regimes for athletes in Atlanta, "but the testosterone molecule is changeable in millions of ways. All you have to do is make a steroid not on the list." Or, simply by going cold turkey a few weeks before competition, an athlete can get the muscle-bulking effects without getting caught. If that seems too chancy, athletes can use a diuretic. These drugs, which are also banned, dilute the urine. That makes illicit substances virtually undetectable.

More and more athletes are turning to the source of all steroids: testosterone itself. Natural levels vary, so sports federations and the IOC try to detect doping in-

Begley and Brant classify performance-enhancing drugs into five categories and explain what each type of drug does, how detectable it is, and what its health risks are.

Drug	What Does It Do?	Masking/Detection	Risks
Human growth hormone (hGH)	Stimulates the intra-cellular breakdown of body fat, allowing more to be used for energy.	This is a natural hormone, so added amounts don't show up in blood or urine tests.	Muscle and bone disfigure-ment — jutting forehead, elongated jaw. Also: heart and metabolic problems.
Erythropoietin (EPO)	Increases the number of red blood cells without having to "dope" using one's own blood.	It's extremely difficult to detect because the extra blood cells are the athlete's own.	Extra cells can make blood the consistency of yogurt. This can lead to a clot, heart attack or stroke.
Testosterone	Used to build muscles. It lets the body recover quickly from strenuous exercise.	Rules allow up to five times the natural body level, giving athletes latitude.	Unnatural levels can cause heart disease, liver cancer and impotence.
Steroids/ androstenedione	Anabolic steroids are in-carnations of testosterone; androstenedione is a pre-cursor molecule.	Water-based steroids (most common) are undetectable in urine after several weeks.	Synthetic testosterone car-ries the same risks as nat-urally occurring testosterone.
Stimulants	The first category that the IOC tested for. They delay the symptoms of fatigue.	Stimulants such as amphetamines can be detected; diuretics can dilute them in urine.	Fatigue is the body saying "stop" — overriding that message can be dangerous.

The essay's organizational plan is illustrated in the chart; the chart sometimes repeats information in the text but more often comple-ments or adds to the text.

directly. They measure the relative amounts of testosterone and another natural steroid called epitestosterone. In most people, testosterone levels are no more than twice epi levels. But to allow for individual variation, the IOC set the prohibited level at anything over 6 to 1. That means an athlete can dope himself up to, say, five times his normal testosterone levels, and get away with it. How much of an edge would that provide? A male athlete with a typical testosterone/epitestosterone ratio of 1.3 to 1 could boost that to 6 to 1, stay within the IOC limit and improve his per-formance at least 10 percent. Women, with a natural ratio of 2.5 to 1, could do even better, since they have less testosterone to begin with and so are more sensitive to added amounts. Testosterone can give women beards, deep voices and tough skin. It can make men's breasts swell and testicles shrivel.

The doping agents of choice today are substances that cannot be detected in urine: EPO and human growth hormone. Even though the performance-enhancing effects of hGH are unproved, many athletes believe it boosts energy. (Athletes dubbed the Atlanta Olympics "The Growth Hormone Games.") hGH can also cause grotesque skeletal deformations by stimulating abnormal bone growth. EPO, by increasing the production of red blood cells up to tenfold, can turn blood the consistency of yogurt, making it too thick to flow freely. The misuse of EPO has apparently killed at least 18 Dutch and Belgian cyclists since 1987.

— SHARON BEGLEY AND MARTHA BRANT, "The Real Scandal"

Although most readers would expect the chart to present the drugs in the order they appear in the essay, that is not the case here. In the essay, the drugs are discussed in this order: EPO, stimulants, steroids, testosterone, and human growth hormone (hGH). But in the chart, the order is hGH, EPO, testosterone, steroids, and stimulants. Except for EPO, the order in the chart reverses the order in the text. If you include a chart with your classification, be sure that your chart corresponds to the written text.

For more information on designing documents with graphics, see Chapter 25.

Maintaining Clarity and Coherence

The next example illustrates how writers can help readers follow a classification system by maintaining **clarity and coherence** — even when the subject is new and difficult. The passage comes from a book on physics by Gary Zukav. He uses classifying to explain the concept of mass. Simply defined, mass in physics is a measure of the matter in an object.

> There are two kinds of mass, which means that there are two ways of talking about it. The first is gravitational mass. The gravitational mass of an object, roughly speaking, is the weight of the object as measured on a balance scale. Something that weighs three times more than another object has three times more mass. Gravitational mass is the measure of how much force the gravity of the earth exerts on an object. Newton's laws describe the effects of this force, which vary with the distance of the mass from the earth. . . .
>
> The second type of mass is inertial mass. Inertial mass is the measure of the resistance of an object to acceleration (or deceleration, which is negative acceleration). For example, it takes three times more force to move three railroad cars from a standstill to twenty miles per hour (positive acceleration) than it takes to move one railroad car from a standstill to twenty miles per hour. . . . Similarly, once they are moving, it takes three times more force to stop three cars than it takes to stop the single car. This is because the inertial mass of the three railroad cars is three times more than the inertial mass of the single railroad car.
>
> — GARY ZUKAV, *The Dancing Wu Li Masters: An Overview of the New Physics*

Zukav explains the concept of mass by classifying it into two types, gravitational and inertial, and provides cues to help readers understand the classification.

From this passage, we can see some of the cues writers use to make a classification clear and coherent. Zukav begins by forecasting the classification he will develop (*There are two kinds of mass*). He then introduces each category in its own paragraph, announced with the transition (*first* and *second*) and presented in the same sentence pattern (*The first is . . .* and *The second type of mass is . . .*). Careful cueing like this can help make a classification clear to readers.

EXERCISE 17.3

Look back at the paragraphs from Linh Kieu Ngo's essay on cannibalism that you used to make a tree diagram in Exercise 17.1 or at the example by Begley and Brant earlier in this chapter to examine the strategies these authors use to make their classifications clear and coherent. Notice how each category is introduced and the transitions are used to help readers keep track of the categories. What conclusions can you draw about how writers maintain clarity and coherence from your analysis?

EXERCISE 17.4

Look back at the classification you examined in Exercise 17.2 to see how well you were able to maintain clarity and coherence in your classification. What changes would you make, if any, to improve clarity and coherence?

General strategies for coherence are discussed in Chapter 13.

18 Comparing and Contrasting

Comparing and contrasting make writing more memorable when you analyze and evaluate two or more things. You might compare two people you know well, two motorcycles you are considering buying for a cross-country tour, three Stephen King novels, four tomato plants being grown under different laboratory conditions, or two theories about the relationship between inflation and wages. But as soon as you begin to compare two things, you usually begin to contrast them as well, for rarely are two things alike in all respects. The contrasts, or differences, between the two motorcycles are likely to be more enlightening than the similarities, many of which may be so obvious as to need no analysis. Comparison, then, brings similar things together for examination, to see how they are alike. Contrast is a form of comparison that emphasizes differences.

The use of comparison and contrast is more than a writing strategy, of course. It is a way of thinking and learning. According to research on learning, we acquire new concepts most readily if we can see how they are similar to or different from concepts we already know.

Professional writers say that comparison and contrast is a basic strategy they would not want to be without. In some writing situations (like the ones we mentioned), it has no substitute. Indeed, some writing is essentially extended comparison. But for all kinds of writing situations, writers regularly alternate comparison and contrast with other writing strategies when they present information.

Chances are that you will confront many test questions and essay assignments asking you to compare and contrast — two poems, three presidents, four procedures. This strategy is popular in all academic disciplines, for it is one of the best ways to challenge students intellectually.

Two Ways of Comparing and Contrasting

There are two ways to organize comparison and contrast in writing: in chunks and in sequence. In **chunking**, each object of the comparison is presented separately; in sequencing, the items are compared point by point. For example, a chunked comparison of two motorcycles would first detail all pertinent features of the Pirsig Z-1700 XL and then consider all features of the Kawazuki 1750XL, whereas a

sequenced comparison would analyze the Pirsig and the Kawazuki feature by feature. In a chunked comparison, the discussion is organized around each separate item being compared. In a sequenced comparison, it is organized around characteristics of the items being compared.

In the following example of chunked comparison, Jane Tompkins contrasts popular nineteenth-century "sentimental" novels with the "Western" novels that provided a reaction against them:

> The female, domestic, "sentimental" religion of the best-selling women writers — Harriet Beecher Stowe, Susan Warner, Maria Cummins, and dozens of others — whose novels spoke to the deepest beliefs and highest ideals of middle-class America, is the real antagonist of the Western.
>
> You can see this simply by comparing the main features of the Western with the sentimental novel. In these books . . . a woman is always the main character, usually a young orphan girl, with several other main characters being women too. Most of the action takes place in private spaces, at home, indoors, in kitchens, parlors, and upstairs chambers. And most of it concerns the interior struggles of the heroine to live up to an ideal of Christian virtue — usually involving uncomplaining submission to difficult and painful circumstances, learning to quell rebellious instincts, and dedicating her life to the service of God through serving others. In these struggles, women give one another a great deal of emotional and material support, and they have close relationships verging on what today we would identify as homosocial and homoerotic. There's a great deal of Bible reading, praying, hymn singing, and drinking of tea. Emotions other than anger are expressed very freely and openly. Often there are long, drawn-out death scenes in which a saintly woman dies a natural death at home. . . .
>
> The elements of the typical Western plot arrange themselves in stark opposition to this pattern, not just vaguely and generally but point for point. First of all, in Westerns (which are generally written by men), the main character is always a full-grown adult male, and almost all of the other characters are men. The action takes place either outdoors — on the prairie, on the main street — or in public places — the saloon, the sheriff's office, the barber shop, the livery stable. The action concerns physical struggles between the hero and a rival or rivals, and culminates in a fight to the death with guns. In the course of these struggles the hero frequently forms a bond with another man — sometimes his rival, more often a comrade — a bond that is more important than any relation he has with a woman and is frequently tinged with homoeroticism. There is very little free expression of the emotions. The hero is a man of few words who expresses himself through physical action — usually fighting. And when death occurs it is never at home in bed but always sudden death, usually murder.
>
> — JANE TOMPKINS, *West of Everything: The Inner Life of Westerns*

Tompkins discusses sentimental novels and Westerns separately, presenting each point of contrast for the two subjects in the same order (chunking).

Tompkins signals the shift from one subject to the other with a transition sentence at the start of the third paragraph.

Schematically, a chunked comparison looks simple enough. As the preceding example shows, it is easy to block off such a discussion in a text and then provide a clean transition between the various parts. And yet it can in fact be more complicated for a writer to plan than a sequenced comparison. Sequenced comparison may be closer to the way people perceive and think about similarities or differences in things. For example, you may have realized all at once that two navy blazers are different, but you would identify the specific differences — buttons, tailoring, fabric — one at a time. A sequenced comparison would point to the differences in just this way, one at a time, whereas a chunked comparison would present all the features of one blazer and then do the same for the second. A writer using the chunked strategy, then, must organize all the points of comparison before starting to write and then be sure that the points of comparison are presented in the same order in the discussion of each item being compared. With sequencing, however, the writer can take up each point of comparison as it comes to mind.

EXERCISE 18.1

Identify the specific items contrasted in the example comparing sentimental novels and Westerns. Number in sequence each contrast, and underline both parts of the contrast. To get started, in the paragraph about sentimental novels, underline "a woman is always the main character, usually a young orphan girl," and number it "1" in the margin. In the paragraph about Westerns, underline "the main character is always a full-grown adult male," and number this "1" also to complete your identification of both parts of the comparison. Then look for contrast 2 and underline and number the contrasted items, and so on.

Look over your work and consider the pattern of these contrasts. Were they easy to identify? If so, what made them easy to identify? Was any contrast left incomplete? In general, how successsful and informative do you find this set of contrasts?

In the next example, from a natural history of the earth, David Attenborough uses sequencing to contrast bird wings and airplane wings:

Bird wings have a much more complex job to do than the wings of an aeroplane, for in addition to supporting the bird they must act as its engine, rowing it through the air. Even so the wing outline of a bird conforms to the same aerodynamic principles as those eventually discovered by man when designing his aeroplanes, and if you know how different kinds of aircraft perform, you can predict the flight capabilities of similarly shaped birds.

Short stubby wings enable a tanager and other forest-living birds to swerve and dodge at speed through the undergrowth just as they helped the fighter planes of the Second World War to make tight turns and aerobatic manoeuvres in a dog-fight. More modern fighters achieve greater speeds by sweeping back their wings while in flight, just as peregrines do when they go into a 130 kph dive, stooping to a kill. Championship gliders have long thin wings so that, having gained height in a thermal up-current, they can soar gently down for hours and an albatross, the largest of flying birds, with a similar wing shape and a span of 3 metres, can patrol the ocean for hours in the same way without a single wing beat. Vultures and hawks circle at very slow speeds supported by a thermal and they have the broad rectangular wings that very slow flying aircraft have. Man has not been able to adapt wings to provide hovering flight. He has only achieved that with the whirling horizontal blades of a helicopter or the downward-pointing engines of a vertical landing jet. Hummingbirds have paralleled even this. They tilt their bodies so that they are almost upright and then beat their wings as fast as 80 times a second producing a similar down-draught of air. So the hummingbird can hover and even fly backwards.

— DAVID ATTENBOROUGH, *Life on Earth*

> Attenborough uses a limited, focused basis for the comparison of bird wings and airplane wings: their shape.

Although birds and planes both fly, they have almost nothing else in common. But Attenborough finds a valid — and fascinating — basis for comparison and develops it in a way that both informs and entertains his readers. A successful comparison always has these qualities: a valid basis for comparison, a limited focus, and information that will catch a reader's attention.

EXERCISE 18.2

Identify the specific items compared in the preceding selection comparing bird wings and aircraft wings. Underline both items, and number the pair in the margin. To get started, underline *tanager* and *fighter planes* in the first sentence of the second paragraph. In the margin, number this pair "1." Then identify pair 2 and so on.

Consider the pattern and ordering of the comparisons you have identified. Were the pairs of items easy to identify? If so, what made them easy to identify? Some comparisons begin by naming a bird, some by identifying a category of aircraft. Did this lack of predictability present problems for you? Do you see any possible justification for the writer's having given up the predictability of always beginning each comparison with either a bird or an aircraft? In general, how successful and informative did you find this comparison of birds' wings and aircrafts' wings?

EXERCISE 18.3

Write a page or so comparing or contrasting any one of the following subjects. Be careful to limit the basis for your comparison, and underline the sentence that states that basis. Use chunking or sequencing to organize the comparison.

Two ways of achieving the same goal (for example, travel by bus or subway or using flattery or persuasion to get what you want)

A good and bad job interview

Your relationship with two friends or relatives

Two or more forms of music, dance, film, or computer software

Two religions or congregations

Two methods of doing some task at home or on the job

EXERCISE 18.4

Read closely the specified comparisons in the following essays from Part One. How is each comparison organized? (It may or may not be neatly chunked or sequenced.) Why do you think the writer organizes the comparison in that way? What is the role of the comparison in the whole essay? How effective is it?

"Love: The Right Chemistry," paragraph 14 (Chapter 4)

"Born to Be Happy," paragraphs 5–6 (Chapter 4)

"The Gorge-Yourself Environment," paragraph 14 (Chapter 9)

■ Analogy

An **analogy** is a special form of comparison in which one part of the comparison is used simply to explain the other, as in the following example.

McPhee uses two analogies — the 12-month calendar and the distance along two widespread arms — to explain the duration of geologic time.

> In like manner, geologists will sometimes use the calendar year as a unit to represent the time scale, and in such terms the Precambrian runs from New Year's Day until well after Halloween. Dinosaurs appear in the middle of December and are gone the day after Christmas. The last ice sheet melts on December 31st at one minute before midnight, and the Roman Empire lasts five seconds. With your arms spread wide . . . to represent all time on earth, look at one hand with its line of life. The Cambrian begins in the wrist, and the Permian Extinction is at the outer end of the palm. All of the Cenozoic is in a fingerprint, and in a single stroke with a medium-grained nail file you could eradicate human history. Geologists live with the geologic scale. Individually, they may or may not be alarmed by the rate of exploitation of the things they discover, but, like the environmentalists, they use these repetitive analogies to place the human record in perspective — to see the Age of Reflection, the last few thousand years, as a small bright sparkle at the end of time.
>
> — JOHN McPHEE, *Basin and Range*

Analogies are not limited to abstract, scientific concepts. Writers often use analogies to make nontechnical descriptions and explanations more vivid or to make an imaginative point of comparison that serves a larger argument. Consider the following example.

Ehrenreich suggests, by analogy, that the working poor in the United States are among society's "major philanthropists."

> But now that government has largely withdrawn its "handouts" [to the welfare poor], now that the overwhelming majority of the poor are out there toiling in Wal-Mart or Wendy's — well, what are we to think of them? Disapproval and condescension no longer apply, so what outlook makes sense?
>
> Guilt, you may be thinking warily. Isn't that what we're supposed to feel? But guilt doesn't go anywhere near far enough; the appropriate emotion is shame — shame at our own dependency, in this case, on the underpaid labor of others. When someone works for less pay than she can live on — when, for example, she goes hungry so that you can eat more cheaply and conveniently — then she has made a great sacrifice for you, she has made you a gift of some part of her abilities, her health, and her life. The "working poor," as they are approvingly termed, are in fact the major philanthropists of our society. They neglect their own children so that the children of others will be cared for; they live in substandard housing so that other homes will be shiny and perfect; they endure privation so that inflation will be low and stock prices high. To be a member of the working poor is to be an anonymous donor, a nameless benefactor, to everyone else. As Gail, one of my restaurant coworkers put it, "you give and you give."
>
> — BARBARA EHRENREICH, *Nickel and Dimed*

Analogies are tricky. They can be useful, but analogies rarely are consistently accurate at all major points of comparison. For example, in the preceding analogy, the working poor can be seen as philanthropists in the sense that they have "made a great sacrifice" but not in the sense that they are selflessly sharing their wealth. Analogies can powerfully bring home a point, but skilled writers exercise caution with them.

Nevertheless, you will run across analogies regularly; indeed, it would be hard to find a book without at least one. For abstract information and in certain writing situations, analogy is often the writing strategy of choice.

EXERCISE 18.5

Write a one-paragraph analogy that explains a principle or process to a reader who is unfamiliar with it. Choose a principle or process that you know well. You might select a basic principle from the natural or social sciences, like morphogenesis, Federalism, or ethnocentrism; or you could consider a bodily movement, like running; a physiological process, like digestion; or a process from your job, like assembling a product. Look for something very familiar to compare it with that will help the reader understand the principle or process without a technical explanation.

19

Arguing

Arguing involves reasoning as well as making assertions. When you write an essay in which you assert a point of view, you are obliged to come up with reasons for your point of view and to find ways to support your reasons. In addition to arguing for your point of view, you must think carefully about what your readers know and believe to argue against — to **counterargue** — opposing points of view. If you ignore what your readers may be thinking, you will be unlikely to convince them to take your argument seriously.

This chapter presents the basic strategies for making assertions and reasoning about a writing situation. We focus on asserting a thesis, backing it up with reasons and support, and anticipating readers' questions and objections (counterarguing).

■ Asserting a Thesis

Central to any argument is the **thesis** — the point of view the writer wants readers to consider. The thesis statement may appear at the beginning of the essay or at the end, but wherever it is placed, its job is simple: to announce as clearly and straightforwardly as possible the main point the writer is trying to make in the essay.

There are five kinds of argumentative essays in Part One of this book. Each of these essays requires a special kind of assertion and reasoning. Here we first define each type of assertion and suggest a question it is designed to answer. Then we illustrate each assertion and question with a thesis from a reading in Chapters 6–10:

Chapters 6–10 contain essays that argue for each of these kinds of assertions, along with guidelines for constructing an argument to support such an assertion.

- *Assertion of opinion:* What is your position on a controversial issue? (Chapter 6, "Arguing a Position")

  When overzealous parents and coaches impose adult standards on children's sports, the result can be activities that are neither satisfying nor beneficial to children.
  — Jessica Statsky, "Children Need to Play, Not Compete"

- *Assertion of policy:* What is your understanding of a problem, and what do you think should be done to solve it? (Chapter 7, "Proposing a Solution")

  Although this last-minute anxiety about midterm and final exams is only too familiar to most college students, many professors may not realize how such major, infrequent, high-stakes exams work against the best interests of students both psychologically and intellectually. . . . If professors gave additional brief exams at frequent intervals, students would be spurred to study more regularly, learn more, worry less, and perform better.

— Patrick O'Malley, "More Testing, More Learning"

- *Assertion of evaluation:* What is your judgment of a subject? (Chapter 8, "Justifying an Evaluation")

Morrowind is a flawed jewel, but flawed only because its scope is so grand. Beautiful graphics, compelling stories, a huge map to explore, engaging quests, and a simple interface all add up to a premier game.

— Jonah Jackson, "The Elder Scrolls III: Morrowind"

- *Assertion of cause:* What do you think made a subject the way it is? (Chapter 9, "Speculating about Causes")

The mythic horror movie, like the sick joke, has a dirty job to do. It deliberately appeals to all that is worst in us. It is morbidity unchained, our most base instincts let free, our nastiest fantasies realized . . . and it all happens, fittingly enough, in the dark.

— Stephen King, "Why We Crave Horror Movies"

- *Assertion of interpretation:* What does a story mean, or what is significant about it? (Chapter 10, "Interpreting Stories")

"Araby" tells the story of an adolescent boy's initiation into adulthood. . . . From the beginning, the boy deludes himself about his relationship with Mangan's sister. At Araby, he realizes the parallel between his own self-delusion and the hypocrisy and vanity of the adult world.

— David Ratinov, "From Innocence to Insight: 'Araby' as an Initiation Story"

As these different thesis statements indicate, the kind of thesis you assert depends on the occasion for which you are writing and the question you are trying to answer for your readers. Whatever the writing situation, to be effective, every thesis must satisfy the same three standards: It must be *arguable, clear,* and *appropriately qualified.*

Arguable Assertions

Reasoned argument seems called for when informed people disagree over an issue or remain divided over how best to solve a problem, as is so often the case in social and political life. Hence the thesis statements in reasoned arguments make **arguable assertions** — possibilities or probabilities, not certainties. Argument becomes useful in situations in which there are uncertainties, situations in which established knowledge and facts cannot provide the answers.

Therefore, a statement of fact could not be an arguable thesis statement because facts are easy to verify — whether by checking an authoritative reference book, asking an authority, or observing the fact with your own eyes. For example, these statements assert facts:

> Jem has a Ph.D. in history.
>
> I am less than five feet tall.
>
> Eucalyptus trees were originally imported into California from Australia.

Each of these assertions can be easily verified. To find out Jem's academic degree, you can ask him, among other things. To determine a person's height, you can use a tape measure. To discover where California got its eucalyptus trees, you can refer to a source in the library. There is no point in arguing over such statements (though you might question the authority of a particular source or the accuracy of some- one's measurement). If a writer asserts something as fact and attempts to support the assertion with authorities or statistics, the essay is considered not an argument but a report of information.

Like facts, expressions of personal feelings are not arguable assertions. Whereas facts are unarguable because they can be definitively proved true or false, feelings are unarguable because they are purely subjective. Personal feelings can be explained, but it would be unreasonable to attempt to convince others to change their views or take action solely on the basis of your personal feelings.

You can declare, for example, that you love Ben & Jerry's Chunky Monkey ice cream or that you detest eight o'clock classes, but you cannot offer an argument to support such assertions. All you can do is explain why you feel as you do. Even though many people agree with you about eight o'clock classes, it would be point- less to try to convince others to share your feelings. If, however, you were to restate the assertion as "Eight o'clock classes are counterproductive," you could then con- struct an argument that does not depend solely on your subjective feelings, memo- ries, or preferences. Your argument could be based on reasons and support that apply to others as well as to yourself. For example, you might argue that students' ability to learn is at an especially low ebb immediately after breakfast and provide scientific support, in addition, perhaps, to personal experience and interviews with your friends.

Clear and Precise Wording

The way a thesis is worded is as important as its arguability. The wording of a thesis, especially its key terms, must be clear and precise.

Consider the following assertion: "Democracy is a way of life." The meaning of this claim is uncertain, partly because the word *democracy* is abstract and partly be- cause the phrase *way of life* is inexact. Abstract ideas like democracy, freedom, and pa- triotism are by their very nature hard to grasp, and they become even less clear with overuse. Too often, such words take on connotations that may obscure the meaning you want to emphasize. *Way of life* is fuzzy: What does it mean? Moreover, can a form of government be a way of life? It depends on what is meant by *way of life*. Does it refer to daily life, to a general philosophy or attitude toward life, or to something else?

Thus a thesis is vague if its meaning is unclear; it is ambiguous if it has more than one possible meaning. For example, the statement "My English instructor is mad" can be understood in two ways: The teacher is either angry or insane. Obviously, these are two very different assertions. You would not want readers to think you mean one when you actually mean the other.

Whenever you write argument, you should pay special attention to the way you phrase your thesis and take care to avoid vague and ambiguous language.

Appropriate Qualification

In addition to being arguable and clear, an argument thesis must make **appropriate qualifications** that suit your writing situation. If you are confident that your case is so strong that readers will accept your argument without question, state your thesis emphatically and unconditionally. If, however, you expect readers to challenge your assumptions or conclusions, you must qualify your statement. Qualifying a thesis makes it more likely that readers will take it seriously. Expressions like *probably, very likely, apparently,* and *it seems* all serve to qualify a thesis.

EXERCISE 19.1

Write an assertion of opinion that states your position on one of the following controversial issues:

Should English be the official language of the United States and the only language used in local, state, and federal government agencies in oral and written communications?

Should teenagers be required to get their parents' permission to obtain birth control information and contraceptives?

Should high schools or colleges require students to perform community service as a condition for graduation?

Should girls and boys be treated differently by their families or schools?

Should businesses remain loyal to their communities, or should they move wherever labor costs, taxes, or other conditions are more favorable?

These issues are complicated and have been debated for a long time. Constructing a persuasive argument would obviously require careful deliberation and research. For this exercise, however, all you need to do is construct a thesis on the issue you have chosen, a thesis that is arguable, clear, and appropriately qualified.

EXERCISE 19.2

Find the thesis in one of the argument essays in Chapters 6–10. Then decide whether the thesis meets the three requirements: that it be arguable, clear, and appropriately qualified.

EXERCISE 19.3

If you have written or are currently working on one of the argument assignments in Chapters 6–10, consider whether your essay thesis meets the three requirements: that it be arguable, clear, and appropriately qualified. If you believe it does not meet the requirements, revise it appropriately.

Giving Reasons and Support

Whether you are arguing a position, proposing a solution, justifying an evaluation, speculating about causes, or interpreting a story, you need to give **reasons and support** for your thesis.

Reasons can be thought of as the main points arguing for a thesis. Often they answer the question "Why do you think so?" For example, if you assert among friends that you value a certain movie highly, one of your friends might ask, "Why do you like it so much?" And you might answer, "*Because* it has challenging ideas, unusual camera work, and memorable acting." Similarly, you might oppose restrictions on students' use of offensive language at your college *because* they would make students reluctant to enter into frank debates on important issues, offensive speech is hard to define, and restrictions violate the free-speech clause of the First Amendment. These *because* phrases are your reasons. You may have one or many reasons, depending on your subject and your writing situation.

For your argument to succeed with your readers, you must not only give reasons but also provide support. The main kinds of support writers use are examples, statistics, authorities, anecdotes, and textual evidence. Following is a discussion and illustration of each kind, along with standards for judging the reliability of that particular type of support.

Examples

Examples may be used as support in all types of arguments. They are an effective way to demonstrate that your reasons should be taken seriously. For examples to be believable and convincing, they must be representative (typical of all the relevant examples you might have chosen), consistent with the experience of your readers (familiar and not extreme), and adequate in number (numerous enough to be convincing and yet selective and not likely to overwhelm readers).

The following illustration comes from a book on illiteracy in America by Jonathan Kozol, a prominent educator and writer.

Illiterates cannot read the menu in a restaurant.

They cannot read the cost of items on the menu in the *window* of the restaurant before they enter.

Illiterates cannot read the letters that their children bring home from their teachers. They cannot study school department circulars that tell them of the

Kozol presents several examples to support his argument that the human costs of illiteracy are high.

courses that their children must be taking if they hope to pass the SAT exams. They cannot help with homework. They cannot write a letter to the teacher. They are afraid to visit in the classroom. They do not want to humiliate their child or themselves.

Illiterates cannot read instructions on a bottle of prescription medicine. They cannot find out when a medicine is past the year of safe consumption; nor can they read of allergenic risks, warnings to diabetics, or the potential sedative effect of certain kinds of nonprescription pills. They cannot observe preventive health care admonitions. They cannot read about "the seven warning signs of cancer" or the indications of blood-sugar fluctuations or the risks of eating certain foods that aggravate the likelihood of cardiac arrest.

— Jonathan Kozol, *Illiterate America*

These examples probably seem to most readers to be representative of all the examples Kozol collected in his many interviews with people who could neither read nor write. Though all of his readers are literate and have never experienced the frustrations of adult illiterates, Kozol assumes they can recognize that the experiences are a familiar part of illiterates' lives. Most readers will believe the experiences to be neither atypical nor extreme.

EXERCISE 19.4

Identify the examples in paragraphs 9 and 11 in Jessica Statsky's essay "Children Need to Play, Not Compete" in Chapter 6 and paragraphs 16–18 in Amitai Etzioni's essay "Working at McDonald's" in Chapter 6. If you have not read the essays, pause to skim them so that you can evaluate these examples within the context of the entire essay. How well do the examples individually and as a set meet the standards of representativeness, consistency with experience of readers, and adequacy in number? You will not have all the information you need to evaluate the examples — you rarely do unless you are an expert on the subject — but make a judgment based on the information available to you in the headnotes and the essays.

Statistics

In many kinds of arguments about economic, educational, or social issues, **statistics** may be essential. When you use statistics in your own arguments, you will want to ensure that they are up-to-date (they should be current, the best presently available facts on the subject), relevant (they should be appropriate for your argument), and accurate (they should not distort or misrepresent the subject). In addition, take care to select statistics from reliable sources and to use statistics from the sources in which they originally appeared if at all possible. For example, you would want to get medical statistics from a reputable and authoritative professional periodical like the *New England Journal of Medicine* rather than from a supermarket tabloid or an unaffiliated Web site. If you are uncertain about the most authoritative sources, ask a reference librarian or a professor who knows about your topic.

The following selection, written by a Harvard University professor, comes from an argument speculating about the decline of civic life in the United States. Civic life includes all of the clubs, organizations, and activities people choose to participate in.

> The culprit is television.
>
> First, the timing fits. The long civic generation was the last cohort of Americans to grow up without television, for television flashed into American society like lightning in the 1950s. In 1950 barely 10 percent of American homes had television sets, but by 1959, 90 percent did, probably the fastest diffusion of a major technological innovation ever recorded. The reverberations from this lightning bolt continued for decades, as viewing hours grew by 17–20 percent during the 1960s and by an additional 7–8 percent during the 1970s. In the early years, TV watching was concentrated among the less educated sectors of the population, but during the 1970s the viewing time of the more educated sectors of the population began to converge upward. Television viewing increases with age, particularly upon retirement, but each generation since the introduction of television has begun its life cycle at a higher starting point. By 1995 viewing per TV household was more than 50 percent higher than it had been in the 1950s.
>
> Most studies estimate that the average American now watches roughly four hours per day (excluding periods in which television is merely playing in the background). Even a more conservative estimate of three hours means that television absorbs 40 percent of the average American's free time, an increase of about one-third since 1965. Moreover, multiple sets have proliferated: By the late 1980s three-quarters of all U.S. homes had more than one set, and these numbers too are rising steadily, allowing ever more private viewing. . . . This massive change in the way Americans spend their days and nights occurred precisely during the years of generational civic disengagement.
>
> — ROBERT D. PUTNAM, "The Strange Disappearance of Civic America"

Putnam uses statistics to support his opinion that, since the early 1960s, Americans have devoted less and less time to civic life because they are watching more and more television.

These statistics come primarily from the U.S. Bureau of the Census, a nation-wide count of the number of Americans and a survey, in part, of their buying habits, levels of education, and leisure activities. The Census reports are widely considered to be accurate and trustworthy. They qualify as original sources of statistics.

Chapter 21 provides help finding statistical data in the library.

EXERCISE 19.5

In Chapter 6, underline the statistics in paragraphs 5 and 6 of Jessica Statsky's essay. If you have not read the essay, pause to skim it so that you can evaluate the writer's use of statistics within the context of the whole essay. How well do the statistics meet the standard of up-to-dateness, relevance, accuracy, and reliance on the original source? (If you find that you do not have all the information you need, base your judgments on whatever information is available to you.) Does the writer indicate where the statistics come from? What do the statistics contribute to the argument?

Authorities

To support an argument, writers often cite experts on the subject who agree with their point of view. Quoting, paraphrasing, or even just referring to a respected **authority** can add to a writer's credibility. Authorities must be selected as carefully as facts and statistics. One qualification for authorities to support arguments is suggested by the way we refer to them: They must be authoritative — that is, trustworthy and reputable. They must also be specially qualified to contribute to the subject you are writing about. For example, a well-known expert on the American presidency might be a poor choice to support an argument on whether adolescents who commit serious crimes should be tried in the courts as adults. Finally, qualified authorities must have training at respected institutions or have unique real-world experiences, and they must have a record of research and publications recognized by other authorities.

The following example comes from a *New York Times* article about some parents' and experts' heightened concern over boys' behavior. The author believes that the concern is exaggerated and potentially dangerous to boys, and she wants to understand why it is increasing. In the full argument, she is particularly concerned about the number of boys who are being given Ritalin, a popular drug for treating attention-deficit hyperactivity disorder.

> Today, the world is no longer safe for boys. A boy being a shade too boyish risks finding himself under the scrutiny of parents, teachers, guidance counselors, child therapists — all of them on watch for the early glimmerings of a medical syndrome, a bona fide behavioral disorder. Does the boy disregard authority, make snide comments in class, push other kids around and play hooky? Maybe he has a conduct disorder. Is he fidgety, impulsive, disruptive, easily bored? Perhaps he is suffering from attention-deficit hyperactivity disorder, or ADHD, the disease of the hour and the most frequently diagnosed behavioral disorder of childhood. Does he prefer computer games and goofing off to homework? He might have dyslexia or another learning disorder.
>
> "There is now an attempt to pathologize what was once considered the normal range of behavior of boys," said Melvin Konner of the departments of anthropology and psychiatry at Emory University in Atlanta. "Today, Tom Sawyer and Huckleberry Finn surely would have been diagnosed with both conduct disorder and ADHD." And both, perhaps, would have been put on Ritalin, the drug of choice for treating attention-deficit disorder.
>
> — NATALIE ANGIER, "Intolerance of Boyish Behavior"

Angier establishes Melvin Konner's professional qualifications by naming the university where he teaches and his areas of study.

In this example, the writer relies on *informal* citation within her essay to introduce the authority she quotes. In newspapers, magazines, and some books, writers rely on informal citation, mentioning the title or author in the essay itself. In other books and in research reports, writers rely on a *formal* style of citation that allows them to refer briefly in an essay to a detailed list of works cited appearing at the end of the essay. This list provides the author, title, date, and publisher of every source of information referred to in the essay. To evaluate the qualifications of an authority in an argument relying on a list of works cited, you may have to rely solely on the information provided in the list.

For examples of two formal citation styles often used in college essays, see Chapter 22.

EXERCISE 19.6

Analyze how authorities are used in paragraphs 4 and 5 of Patrick O'Malley's essay "More Testing, More Learning" in Chapter 7 and in paragraphs 4–7 of Erica Goode's essay "The Gorge-Yourself Environment" in Chapter 9. Begin by underlining the authorities' contributions to these paragraphs, whether through quotation, summary, or paraphrase. On the basis of the evidence you have available, decide to what extent each source is authoritative on the subject: qualified to contribute to the subject, trained appropriately, and recognized widely. How does the writer establish each authority's credentials? Then decide what each authority contributes to the argument as a whole. (If you have not read the essays, take time to read or skim them.)

Anecdotes

Anecdotes are brief stories about events or experiences, recounted in an engaging way. If they are relevant to the argument, well told, and true to life, they can provide convincing support. To be relevant, an anecdote must strike readers as more than an entertaining diversion; it must seem to make an irreplaceable contribution to an argument. If it is well told, the narrative or story is easy to follow, and the people and scenes are described memorably, even vividly. There are many concrete details that help readers imagine what happened. A true-to-life anecdote is one that seems to represent a possible life experience of a real person. It has to be believable, even if the experience is foreign to readers' experiences.

See Chapter 14, Narrating, and Chapter 2, Remembering Events, for more information about narrating anecdotes.

The following anecdote appeared in an argument taking a position on a familiar issue: gun ownership and control. The writer, an essayist, poet, and environmental writer who is also a rancher in South Dakota, always carries a pistol and believes that other people may have an urgent personal need to carry one and should have the right to do so.

To support her argument, Hasselstrom tells an engaging anecdote and, in the last paragraph, explains its relevance.

I was driving the half-mile to the highway mailbox one day when I saw a vehicle parked about midway down the road. Several men were standing in the ditch, relieving themselves. I have no objection to emergency urination, but I noticed they'd dumped several dozen beer cans in the road. Besides being ugly, cans can slash a cow's feet or stomach.

The men noticed me before they finished and made quite a performance out of zipping their trousers while walking toward me. All four of them gathered around my small foreign car, and one of them demanded what the hell I wanted.

"This is private land. I'd appreciate it if you'd pick up the beer cans."

"What beer cans?" said the belligerent one, putting both hands on the car door and leaning in my window. His face was inches from mine, and the beer fumes were strong. The others laughed. One tried the passenger door, locked; another put his foot on the hood and rocked the car. They circled, lightly thumping the roof, discussing my good fortune in meeting them and the benefits they were likely to bestow upon me. I felt very small and very trapped and they knew it.

"The ones you just threw out," I said politely.

"I don't see no beer cans. Why don't you get out here and show them to me, honey?" said the belligerent one, reaching for the handle inside my door.

"Right over there," I said, still being polite, " — there, and over there." I pointed with the pistol, which I'd slipped under my thigh. Within one minute the cans and the men were back in the car and headed down the road.

I believe this incident illustrates several important principles. The men were trespassing and knew it; their judgment may have been impaired by alcohol. Their response to the polite request of a woman alone was to use their size, numbers, and sex to inspire fear. The pistol was a response in the same language. Politeness didn't work; I couldn't match them in size or number. Out of the car, I'd have been more vulnerable. The pistol just changed the balance of power.

— LINDA M. HASSELSTROM, "Why One Peaceful Woman Carries a Pistol"

Most readers would readily agree that this anecdote is well told. It has many concrete, memorable details. As in any good story, something happens: There is action, suspense, climax, resolution. There is even dialogue. It is about a believable, possible experience.

EXERCISE 19.7

Analyze the way an anecdote is used in paragraphs 1–3 of Richard A. Friedman's essay "Born to Be Happy" in Chapter 4. Consider whether the story is well told and true to life. Decide whether it seems to be relevant to the whole argument. Does the writer make the relevance clear? Do you find the anecdote convincing?

Textual Evidence

When you argue claims of value (Chapter 8) and interpretation (Chapter 10), **textual evidence** will be very important. In your other college courses, if you are asked to evaluate a controversial book, you must quote, paraphrase, or summarize passages so that readers can understand why you think the author's argument is or is not credible. If you are interpreting a novel for one of your classes, you must include numerous excerpts to show just how you arrived at your conclusion. In both situations, you are integrating bits of the text you are evaluating or interpreting into your own text and building your argument on these bits.

For textual evidence to be considered effective support for an argument of evaluation or interpretation, it must be carefully selected to be relevant to the thesis and reasons. You must help readers see the connection between each piece of evidence and the reason it supports. Textual evidence must also be highly selective — that is, chosen from among all the available evidence to provide the support needed without overwhelming the reader with too much evidence or weakening the argument with marginally relevant evidence. Textual evidence usually has more impact if it is balanced between quotation and paraphrase from the text. For these selective, balanced choices of evidence to be comprehensible and convincing to readers, the evidence must be smoothly integrated into the sentences of the argument. Finally, the relevance of textual evidence is rarely obvious: The writer must ordinarily explain the link between the evidence and the writer's intended point.

The following example comes from a student essay in Chapter 10 in which the writer argues that the main character (referred to as "the boy") in the short story "Araby" by James Joyce is so self-absorbed that he learns nothing about himself or other people.

You can read "Araby" in Chapter 10, pp. 527–31.

Crane cites textual evidence from "Araby" to convince readers to take her argument seriously.

> The story opens and closes with images of blindness. The street is "blind" with an "uninhabited house . . . at the blind end." As he spies on Mangan's sister, from his own house, the boy intentionally limits what he is able to see by lowering the "blind" until it is only an inch from the window sash. At the bazaar in the closing scene, the "light was out," and the upper part of the hall was "completely dark." The boy is left "gazing up into the darkness," seeing nothing but an inner torment that burns his eyes.
>
> This pattern of imagery includes images of reading, and reading stands for the boy's inability to understand what is before his eyes. When he tries to read at night, for example, the girl's "image [comes] between [him] and the page," in effect blinding him. In fact, he seems blind to everything except this "image" of the "brown-clad figure cast by [his] imagination." The girl's "brown-clad figure" is also associated with the houses on "blind" North Richmond Street, with their "brown imperturbable faces." The houses stare back at the boy, unaffected by his presence and gaze.
>
> — SALLY CRANE, "Gazing into the Darkness"

Notice first how the writer quotes selected words and phrases about blindness to support her reasoning that the boy learns nothing because he is blinded. There are twelve quotations in these two paragraphs, all of them relevant and perhaps not so many as to overwhelm the reader. The writer relies not only on quotes but also on paraphrases of information in the story. The second and third sentences in paragraph 1 are largely paraphrases. The quotations in particular are integrated smoothly into the sentences so that readers' momentum is not blocked. Most important, the writer does not assume that the evidence speaks for itself; she comments and interprets throughout. For example, in the first paragraph, all the sentences except the fourth one offer some comment or explanation.

For more information on paraphrasing, see pp. 595–97 in Chapter 12.

EXERCISE 19.8

Analyze the use of evidence in paragraphs 2 and 3 of David Ratinov's essay "From Innocence to Insight: 'Araby' as an Initiation Story" in Chapter 10. If you have not read this essay, pause to skim or read it so that you can evaluate the effectiveness of the evidence in these paragraphs in the context of Ratinov's full argument. The quotes are easy to identify. The paraphrases you could identify with confidence only by reading the story, but you can probably identify some of them without doing so. Then try to identify the phrases or sentences that comment on or explain the evidence. Finally, consider whether Ratinov's evidence in these two paragraphs seems relevant to his thesis and reasons, appropriately selective, well balanced between quotes and paraphrases, integrated smoothly into the sentences he creates, and explained helpfully.

■ Counterarguing

Asserting a thesis and backing it with reasons and support are essential to a successful argument. Thoughtful writers go further, however, by **counterarguing**—anticipating and responding to their readers' objections, challenges, and questions. To anticipate readers' concerns, try to imagine other people's points of view, what they might know about the subject, and how they might feel about it. Try also to imagine how readers would respond to your argument as it unfolds step by step. What will they be thinking and feeling? What objections would they raise? What questions would they ask?

To counterargue, writers rely on three basic strategies: acknowledging, accommodating or conceding, and refuting. Writers show they are aware of readers' objections and questions (acknowledge), modify their position to accept readers' concerns they think are legitimate (accommodate), or explicitly show why readers' objections are invalid or why their concerns are irrelevant (refute). Writers may use one or more of these three strategies in the same essay. According to research by rhetoricians and communications specialists, readers find arguments more convincing when writers have anticipated their concerns in these ways. Acknowledging readers' concerns and either accommodating or refuting them wins readers' respect, attention, and sometimes even agreement.

Acknowledging Readers' Concerns

When you **acknowledge** readers' questions or objections, you show that you are aware of their point of view and you take it seriously even if you do not agree with it, as in the following example.

> The homeless, it seems, can be roughly divided into two groups: those who have had marginality and homelessness forced upon them and want nothing more than to escape them, and a smaller number who have at least in part chosen marginality, and now accept, or, in a few cases, embrace it.
>
> I understand how dangerous it can be to introduce the idea of choice into a discussion of homelessness. It can all too easily be used for all the wrong reasons by all the wrong people to justify indifference or brutality toward the homeless, or to argue that they are getting only what they deserve.
>
> And I understand, too, how complicated the notion can become: Many of the veterans on the street, or battered women, or abused and runaway children, have chosen this life only as the lesser of evils, and because, in this society, there is often no place else to go.
>
> And finally, I understand how much that happens on the street can combine to create an apparent acceptance of homelessness that is nothing more than the absolute absence of hope.
>
> Nonetheless we must learn to accept that there may indeed be people on the street who have seen so much of our world, or have seen it so clearly, that to live in it becomes impossible.
>
> — Peter Marin, "Go Ask Alice"

Marin acknowledges three doubts his readers may have regarding his argument that some of America's homeless have chosen that way of life.

You might think that acknowledging readers' objections in this way — addressing readers directly, listing their possible objections, and discussing each one — would weaken an argument. It might even seem reckless to suggest objections that not all readers would think of. On the contrary, however, readers who expect writers to explore an issue thoroughly respond positively to this strategy because it makes the writer seem thoughtful and reasonable, more concerned with seeking the truth than winning an argument. By researching your subject and your readers, you will be able to use this strategy confidently in your own argumentative essays. And you will learn to look for it in arguments you read and use it to make judgments about the writer's credibility.

EXERCISE 19.9

Richard Estrada acknowledges readers' concerns in paragraphs 6 and 7 of his essay in Chapter 6. How, specifically, does Estrada attempt to acknowledge his readers' concerns? What do you find most and least successful in his acknowledgment? How does the acknowledgment affect your judgment of the writer's credibility?

Accommodating Readers' Concerns

To argue effectively, you must often take special care to **accommodate readers' concerns** by acknowledging their objections, questions, and alternative positions, causes, or solutions. Occasionally, however, you may have to go even further. Instead of merely acknowledging your readers' concerns, you may decide to accept some of them and incorporate them into your own argument. This strategy can be very disarming to readers. It is sometimes referred to as **concession**, for it seems to concede that opposing views have merit. The following example comes from an essay enthusiastically endorsing e-mail.

After supporting his own reasons for embracing e-mail, Kinsley accommodates readers' likely reservations by conceding that e-mail poses certain problems.

To be sure, egalitarianism has its limits. The ease and economy of sending email, especially to multiple recipients, makes us all vulnerable to any bore, loony, or commercial or political salesman who can get our email address. It's still a lot less intrusive than the telephone, since you can read and answer or ignore email at your own convenience. But as normal people's email starts mounting into the hundreds daily, which is bound to happen, filtering mechanisms and conventions of etiquette that are still in their primitive stage will be desperately needed.

Another supposed disadvantage of email is that it discourages face-to-face communication. At Microsoft, where people routinely send email back and forth all day to the person in the next office, this is certainly true. Some people believe this tendency has more to do with the underdeveloped social skills of computer geeks than with Microsoft's role in developing the technology email relies on. I wouldn't presume to comment on that. Whether you think email replacing live conversation is a good or bad thing depends, I guess, on how much of a misanthrope you are. I like it.

— MICHAEL KINSLEY, "Email Culture"

Notice that Kinsley's accommodation or concession is not grudging. He readily concedes that e-mail brings users a lot of unwanted messages and may discourage conversation in the workplace.

EXERCISE 19.10

How does Patrick O'Malley attempt to accommodate readers in paragraphs 7 and 8 of his Chapter 7 essay arguing for more frequent exams? What seems successful or unsuccessful in his argument? What do his efforts at accommodation contribute to the essay?

Refuting Readers' Objections

Your readers' possible objections and views cannot always be accommodated. Sometimes they must be refuted. When you **refute readers' objections**, you assert that they are wrong and argue against them. Refutation does not have to be delivered arrogantly or dismissively, however. Writers can refute their readers' objections in a spirit of shared inquiry in solving problems, establishing probable causes, deciding the value of something, or understanding different points of view in a controversy. Differences are inevitable. Reasoned argument provides a peaceful and constructive way for informed, well-intentioned people who disagree strongly to air their differences.

In the following example, a social sciences professor refutes one argument for giving college students the opportunity to purchase lecture notes prepared by someone else.

> Now, it may well be argued that universities are already shortchanging their students by stuffing them into huge lecture halls where, unlike at rock concerts or basketball games, the lecturer can't even be seen on a giant screen in real time. If they're already shortchanged with impersonal instruction, what's the harm in offering canned lecture notes?
>
> The amphitheater lecture is indeed, for all but the most engaging professors, a lesser form of instruction, and scarcely to be idealized. Still, Education by Download misses one of the keys to learning. Education is a meeting of minds, a process through which the student educes, draws from within, a response to what the teacher teaches.
>
> The very act of taking notes — not reading someone else's notes, no matter how stellar — is a way of engaging the material, wrestling with it, struggling to comprehend or take issue, but in any case entering into the work. The point is to decide, while you are listening, what matters in the presentation. And while I don't believe that most of life consists of showing up, education does begin with that — with immersing yourself in the activity at hand, listening, thinking, judging, offering active responses. A download is a poor substitute.
>
> — TODD GITLIN, "Disappearing Ink"

Gitlin first concedes a possible objection, and then even partially agrees with this view. In the second paragraph, however, he begins to refute the objection.

As this selection illustrates, writers cannot simply dismiss readers' possible concerns with a wave of their hand. Gitlin states a potential objection fully and fairly but then goes on to refute it by claiming that students need to take their own lecture notes to engage and comprehend the material that is being presented to them.

Effective refutation requires a restrained tone and careful argument. Although you may not accept this particular refutation, you can agree that it is well reasoned and supported. You do not feel attacked personally because the writer disagrees with you.

EXERCISE 19.11

Analyze and evaluate the use of refutation in Karen Stabiner's essay "Boys Here, Girls There: Sure, If Equality's the Goal" (paragraphs 10–15) in Chapter 6. How does Stabiner signal or announce the refutation? How does she support the refutation? What is the tone of the refutation, and how effective do you think the tone would be in convincing readers to take the writer's argument seriously?

■ Logical Fallacies

Fallacies are errors or flaws in reasoning. Although essentially unsound, fallacious arguments seem superficially plausible and often have great persuasive power. Fallacies are not necessarily deliberate efforts to deceive readers. Writers may introduce a fallacy accidentally by not examining their own reasons or underlying assumptions critically, by failing to establish solid support, or by using unclear or ambiguous words. Here is a summary of the most common logical fallacies (listed alphabetically):

- *Begging the question:* Arguing that a claim is true by repeating the claim in different words (sometimes called *circular reasoning*)
- *Confusing chronology with causality:* Assuming that because one thing preceded another, the former caused the latter (also called *post hoc, ergo propter hoc* — Latin for "after this, therefore because of this")
- *Either-or reasoning:* Assuming that there are only two sides to a question and representing yours as the only correct one
- *Equivocating:* Misleading or hedging with ambiguous word choices
- *Failing to accept the burden of proof:* Asserting a claim without presenting a reasoned argument to support it
- *False analogy:* Assuming that because one thing resembles another, conclusions drawn from one also apply to the other
- *Hasty generalization:* Offering only weak or limited evidence to support a conclusion

- *Overreliance on authority:* Assuming that something is true simply because an expert says so and ignoring evidence to the contrary
- *Oversimplifying:* Giving easy answers to complicated questions, often by appealing to emotions rather than logic
- *Personal attack:* Demeaning the proponents of a claim instead of refuting their argument (also called *ad hominem* — Latin for "against the man" — *attack*)
- *Red herring:* Attempting to misdirect the discussion by raising an essentially unrelated point
- *Slanting:* Selecting or emphasizing the evidence that supports your claim and suppressing or playing down other evidence
- *Slippery slope:* Pretending that one thing inevitably leads to another
- *Sob story:* Manipulating readers' emotions to lead them to draw unjustified conclusions
- *Straw man:* Directing the argument against a claim that nobody actually makes or that everyone agrees is very weak

Part Four

Research
Strategies

20

Field Research

In universities, government agencies, and the business world, field research can be as important as library research or experimental research. If you major in education, communication, or one of the social sciences, you will probably be asked to do writing based on your own observations, interviews, and questionnaire results. You will also read large amounts of information based on these methods of learning about individuals, groups, and institutions. You also might use observations or interviews to help you select or gain background for a service-learning project.

For more on service learning, see Chapter 28.

Observations and interviews are essential for writing profiles (Chapter 3). Interviewing could be helpful, as well, in documenting a trend or phenomenon and exploring its causes (Chapter 9): You might interview an expert or conduct a survey to establish the presence of a trend, for example. In proposing a solution to a problem (Chapter 7), you might want to interview people involved; or if many people are affected, you might find it useful to prepare a questionnaire. In writing to explain an academic concept (Chapter 4), you might want to interview a faculty member who is a specialist on the subject. As you consider how you might use such research most appropriately, ask your instructor whether your institution requires you to obtain approval for your field research.

■ Observations

This section offers guidelines for planning an observational visit, taking notes on your observations, writing them up, and preparing for follow-up visits. Some kinds of writing are based on observations from single visits — travel writing, social workers' case reports, insurance investigators' accident reports — but most observational writing is based on several visits. An anthropologist or a sociologist studying an unfamiliar group or activity might observe it for months, filling several notebooks with notes. If you are profiling a place (Chapter 3), you almost certainly will want to make more than one observational visit, some of them perhaps combined with interviews.

Second and third visits to observe further are important because as you learn about a place from initial observations, interviews, or reading, you will discover new ways to look at it. Gradually, you will have more and more questions that can be answered only by follow-up visits.

Planning the Visit

To ensure that your observational visits are productive, you must plan them carefully.

Getting Access.   If the place you propose to visit is public, you will probably have easy access to it. If everything you need to see is within view of anyone passing by or using the place, you can make your observations without any special arrangements. Indeed, you may not even be noticed. However, most observational visits require special access. Hence, you will need to arrange your visit, calling ahead or stopping by to introduce yourself, state your purpose, and get acquainted. Find out the times you may visit, and be certain you can gain access easily.

Announcing Your Intentions.   State your intentions directly and fully. Say who you are, where you are from, and what you hope to do. You may be surprised at how receptive people can be to a college student on assignment for a class or a service-learning project. Not every place you wish to visit will welcome you, however. In addition, private businesses as well as public institutions place a variety of constraints on outside visitors. But generally, if people know your intentions, they may be able to tell you about aspects of a place or an activity you would not have thought to observe.

Taking Your Tools.   Take a notebook with a firm back so that you will have a steady writing surface. Remember also to take a pen. Some observers dictate their observations into a tape recorder and transcribe their notes later. You might want to experiment with this method. We recommend, though, that you record your first observations in writing. Your instructor or other students in your class may want to see your notes, and transcribing a recording can take a lot of time.

Observing and Taking Notes

Here are some basic guidelines for observing and taking notes.

Observing.   Some activities invite the observer to watch from multiple vantage points, whereas others may limit the observer to a single perspective. Take advantage of every perspective available to you. Come in close, take a middle position, and stand back. Study the scene from a stationary position, and then try to move around it. The more varied your perspectives, the more details you are likely to observe.

Your purposes in observing are twofold: to describe the activity or place and to analyze it. Therefore, you will want to look closely at the activity or place itself, and you will also want to discover the perspective you want to take on it and develop insights into it.

Try initially to be an innocent observer: Pretend that you have never seen anything like this activity or place before. Then consider your own and your readers' likely preconceptions. Ask yourself what details are surprising and what reinforces expectations.

Taking Notes.   You will undoubtedly find your own style of notetaking, but here are a few pointers.

- Write on only one side of the paper. Later, when you organize your notes, you may want to cut up the pages and file notes under different headings.
- Take notes in words, phrases, or sentences. Draw diagrams or sketches if they will help you see and understand the place or activity or recall details of it later on.
- Use abbreviations as much as you like, but use them consistently and clearly.
- Note any ideas or questions that occur to you.
- If you are expecting to see a certain behavior, try not to let this expectation influence what you actually do see.
- Use quotation marks around any overheard remarks or conversations you record.

Perhaps the most important advice about notetaking during an observational visit is to record as many details as possible about the place or activity and to write down your insights (ideas, interpretations, judgments) as they come to mind. Do not focus on taking notes in a systematic way. Be flexible. Later you will have the chance to reorganize your notes and fill in gaps. At the same time, however, you want to be sure to include details about the setting, the people, and your reactions.

■ *The Setting.*   Describe the setting: Name or list objects you see there, and then record details of some of them — their color, shape, size, texture, function, relation to similar or dissimilar objects. Although your notes will probably contain mainly visual details, you might also want to record details about sounds and smells. Be sure to include some notes about the shape, dimensions, and layout of the place as a whole. How big is it? How is it organized?

■ *The People.*   Note the number of people you observe, their activities, their movements and behavior. Describe their appearance or dress. Record parts of overheard conversations. Indicate whether you see more men than women, more members of one nationality or ethnic group than of another, more older than younger people. Most important, note anything surprising, interesting, or unusual about the people and how they interact with each other.

■ *Your Personal Reactions.*   Write down your impressions, questions, ideas, or insights as they occur to you.

Reflecting on Your Observations

Immediately after your observational visit (within a few minutes, if possible), find a quiet place to reflect on what you saw, review your notes, and fill in any gaps with additional details or ideas. Give yourself at least a half-hour to add to your notes and to write a few sentences about your perspective on the place or activity. Ask yourself the following questions:

- What did I learn from my observational visit?
- How did what I observed fit my own or my readers' likely preconceptions of the place or activity?
- What perspective on the place do my notes seem to convey?
- What, if anything, seemed contradictory or out of place?

Writing Up Your Notes

Your instructor may ask you to write up your notes on the observational visit, as Brian Cable did after visiting the Goodbody mortuary for his profile essay. If so, review your notes, looking for a meaningful pattern in the details you have noted down. You might find clustering or taking inventory useful for discovering patterns in your notes.

Clustering is described in Chapter 11, pp. 571–72. Inventory-taking is described in Chapter 12, pp. 592–93.

Assume that your readers have never been to the place, and decide on the perspective of the place you want to convey to them. Choose details that will convey this. Then draft a brief description of the place. Your purpose is to select details from your notes that will help readers imagine the place and understand it.

See Chapter 15 for a full discussion of describing strategies.

EXERCISE 20.1

Arrange to meet with a small group (three or four students) for an observational visit somewhere on campus, such as the student center, campus gym, cafeteria or restaurant, or any other place where some activity is going on. Take notes by assigning each person in your group a specific task; one person can take notes on the appearance of the people, for example; another can take notes on their activities; another on their conversations; and another on what the place looks and smells like. Take about twenty to thirty minutes, and then report to each other on your observations. This will give you some good practice on what you will need to do when you observe on your own, and you will get to see some of the difficulties associated with observing people and places.

Preparing for Follow-Up Visits

Rather than repeat yourself in follow-up visits, try to build on what you have already discovered. You should probably do some interviewing and reading before another observational visit so that you will have a greater understanding of the subject when you observe it again. You might want to present your notes from your first visit to your instructor or to a small group from your class so that you could use their responses as well, especially if you are working on a specific assignment such as a profile. It is also important to develop a plan for your follow-up visits: questions to be answered, insights to be tested, types of information you would like to discover.

▪ Interviews

Like making observations, interviewing tends to involve four basic steps: (1) planning and setting up the interview, (2) taking notes during the interview, (3) reflecting on the interview, and (4) writing up your notes.

Planning and Setting Up the Interview

The initial steps in interviewing involve choosing an interview subject and then arranging and planning for the interview.

Choosing an Interview Subject.   First, choose someone to interview. If you are writing about some activity in which several people are involved, choose subjects representing a variety of perspectives — a range of roles, for example. For a profile of a single person, most or all of your interviews would be with that person. But for a service-learning project, for instance, you might interview several members of an organization to gain a more complete picture of its mission or activities. You should be flexible because you may be unable to speak with the person you initially targeted and may wind up interviewing someone else — the person's assistant, perhaps. Do not assume that this interview subject will be of little use to you. With the right questions, you might even learn more from the assistant than you would from the person you had originally expected to see.

Arranging an Interview.   You may be nervous about calling up a busy person and asking for some of his or her time. Indeed, you may get turned down. But if so, it is possible that you will be referred to someone who will see you, someone whose job it is to talk to the public.

Do not feel that just because you are a student, you do not have the right to ask for people's time. You will be surprised at how delighted people are to be asked about themselves, particularly if you reach them when they are not feeling harried. Most people love to talk — about anything! And since you are a student on assignment, some people may feel that they are performing a public service by talking with you.

When introducing yourself to arrange the interview, give a short and simple description of your project. If you talk too much, you could prejudice or limit the interviewee's response. At the same time, it is a good idea to exhibit some sincere enthusiasm for your project. If you lack enthusiasm, the person may see little reason to talk with you.

Keep in mind that the person you want to interview will be donating valuable time to you. Be certain that you call ahead to arrange a specific time for the interview. Arrive on time. Dress appropriately. Bring all the materials you need. Express your thanks when the interview is over. Finally, try to represent your institution well, whether your interview is for a single course assignment or part of a larger service-learning project.

Planning for the Interview.   The best interview is generally the well-planned interview. Making an observational visit and doing some background reading beforehand can be helpful. In preparation for the interview, you should consider your
objectives and prepare some questions.

Think about your main objectives:

- Do you want an orientation to the place or your topic (the "big picture") from
  this interview?
- Do you want this interview to lead you to interviews with other key people?
- Do you want mainly facts or opinions?
- Do you need to clarify something you have heard in another interview,
  observed, or read?
- Do you want to learn more about the person, the place, or the activity through
  the interview — or all of these?

The key to good interviewing is flexibility. You may be looking for facts, but
your interview subject may not have any to offer. In that case, you should be able to
shift gears and go after whatever your subject is in a position to discuss. Be aware
that the person you are interviewing represents only one point of view. You may
need to speak with several people to get a more complete picture. Talking with more
than one person may also help you discover contradictions or problems that could
contribute to the significance you decide to emphasize.

Composing Questions.   Take care in composing the questions you prepare in
advance; they can be the key to a successful interview. Any question that places unfair limits on respondents is a bad question. Avoid forced-choice questions and
leading questions.

Forced-choice questions impose your terms on respondents. If you are interviewing a counselor at a campus rape crisis center and want to know what he or she
thinks is the motivation for rape, you could ask this question: "Do you think rape is
an expression of passion or of power and anger?" But the counselor might not think
that either passion or power and anger satisfactorily explain the motivation for
rape. A better way to phrase the question would be as follows: "People often fall into
two camps on the issue of rape. Some think it is an expression of passion, while others argue it is an expression of anger and insecurity. Do you think it is either of
these? If not, what is your opinion?" Phrasing the question in this way allows the interviewee to react to what others have said but also gives the interviewee freedom to
set the terms for his or her response.

Leading questions assume too much. An example of this kind of question is
this: "Do you think the number of rapes has increased because women are perceived
as competitors in a highly competitive economy?" This question assumes that there
is an increase in the occurrence of rape, that women are perceived (apparently by
rapists) as economic competitors, and that the state of the economy is somehow
related to acts of rape. A better way of asking the question might be to make the
assumptions more explicit by dividing the question into its parts: "Do you think the

number of rapes has increased? What could have caused this increase? I've heard some people argue that the economy has something to do with it. Do you think so? Do you think rapists perceive women as competitors for jobs? Could the current economic situation have made this competition more severe?"

Good questions come in many different forms. One way of considering them is to divide them into two basic types: open and closed. **Open questions** give the respondent range and flexibility. They also generate anecdotes, personal revelations, and expressions of attitudes. **Closed questions** usually request specific information.

Suppose you are interviewing a small-business owner, for example. You might begin with a specific (closed) question about when the business was established and then follow up with an open-ended question such as, "Could you take a few minutes to tell me something about your early days in the business? I'd be interested to hear how it got started, what your hopes were, and what problems you had to face." Consider asking directly for an anecdote ("What happened when your employees threatened to strike?"), encouraging reflection ("What do you think has helped you most? What has hampered you?"), or soliciting advice ("What advice would you give to someone trying to start a new business today?"). Here are some examples of open and closed questions:

Open Questions

- What do you think about (*name a person or an event*)?
- Describe your reaction when (*name an event*) happened.
- Tell me about a time you were (*name an emotion*).

Closed Questions

- How do you (*name a process*)?
- What does (*name a word or phrase*) mean?
- What does (*name a person, object, or place*) look like?
- How was it made?

The best questions encourage the subject to talk freely but to the point. If an answer strays too far from the point, you may need to ask a follow-up question to refocus the talk. Another tack you might want to try is to rephrase the subject's answer, to say something like "Let me see if I have this right" or "Am I correct in saying that you feel . . . ?" Often, a person will take the opportunity to amplify the original response by adding just the anecdote or quotable comment you have been looking for.

Bringing Your Tools.   As for an observational visit, when you interview someone, you will need a notebook with a firm back so you can write in it easily without the benefit of a table or desk. You might find it useful to divide several pages into two columns by drawing a line about one-third of the width of the page from the left margin. Use the left-hand column to note details about the scene, the person, the mood of the interview, and other impressions. Head this column *Details and Impressions*. At the top of the right-hand column, write several questions. You may not use them, but they will jog your memory. This column should be titled *Information*. In it, you will record what you learn from answers to your questions.

For an example of notes of this sort, see Chapter 3, pp. 125–27.

Taking Notes during the Interview

Because you are not taking a verbatim transcript of the interview (if you want a literal account, use a tape recorder or shorthand), your goals are to gather information and to record a few quotable bits of information, comments, and anecdotes. In addition, because the people you interview may be unused to giving interviews and so will need to know you are paying attention, it is probably a good idea to do more listening than notetaking. You may not have much confidence in your memory, but if you pay close attention, you are likely to recall a good deal of the conversation afterward. Take some notes during the interview: a few quotations; key words and phrases; details of the scene, the person, and the mood of the interview. Remember that how something is said is as important as what is said. Look for material that will give texture to your writing — gesture, verbal inflection, facial expression, body language, physical appearance, dress, hair, or anything that makes the person an individual.

Reflecting on the Interview

As soon as you finish the interview, find a quiet place to reflect on it and review your notes. This reflection is essential because so much happens in an interview that you cannot record at the time. Spend at least a half-hour adding to your notes and thinking about what you learned.

At the end of this time, write a few sentences about your main impressions from the interview. Ask yourself these questions:

- What did I learn?
- What seemed contradictory or surprising about the interview?
- How did what was said fit my own or my readers' likely expectations about the person, activity, or place?
- How can I summarize my impressions?

Writing Up Your Notes

Your instructor may ask you to write up your interview notes. If so, review them for useful details and ideas. Decide what perspective you want to take on this person. Choose details that will contribute to this perspective. Select quotations and paraphrases of information you learned from the person.

You might also review notes from any related observations or other interviews, especially if you plan to combine these materials in a profile, ethnographic study, or other project.

■ Questionnaires

Questionnaires let you survey the opinions and knowledge of large numbers of people. You could carry out many face-to-face or phone interviews to get the same information, but questionnaires have the advantages of economy, efficiency, and anonymity. Some questionnaires, such as the ones you filled out when entering college, just collect demographic information: your name, age, sex, hometown, religious preference, intended major. Others, such as the Gallup and Harris polls, collect opinions on a wide range of issues. Before elections, we are bombarded with the results of such polls. Still other kinds of questionnaires, such as those used in academic research, are designed to help answer important questions about personal and societal problems.

This section briefly outlines procedures you can follow to carry out an informal questionnaire survey of people's opinions or knowledge and then write up the results. There are many good texts on designing questionnaires. A sample questionnaire appears in this section (Figure 20.1).

Focusing Your Study

A questionnaire survey usually has a limited focus. You might need to interview a few people to find this focus. Or you may already have a limited focus in mind. If you are developing a questionnaire as part of a service-learning project, discuss your focus with your supervisor or other staff members.

As an example, let us assume that you go to your campus student health clinic and have to wait over an hour to see a doctor. Sitting in the waiting room with many other students, you decide that this long wait is a problem that would be an ideal topic for a writing assignment you have been asked to do for your writing class, an essay proposing a solution to a problem (Chapter 7).

You do not have to explore the entire operation of the clinic to study this problem. You are not interested in how nurses and doctors are hired or in how efficient the clinic's system of ordering supplies is, for example. Your primary interests are how long students usually wait for appointments, what times are most convenient for students to schedule appointments, how the clinic accommodates students when demand is high, and whether the long wait discourages many students from getting the treatment they need. With this limited focus, you can collect valuable information using a fairly brief questionnaire. To be certain about your focus, however, you should talk informally with several students to find out whether they also think there is a problem with appointment scheduling at the clinic. You might want to talk with staff members, too, explaining your plans and asking for their views on the problem.

Whatever your interest, be sure to limit the scope of your survey. Try to focus on one or two important questions. With a limited focus, your questionnaire can be brief, and people will be more willing to fill it out. In addition, a survey based on a limited amount of information will be easier to organize and report on.

Writing Questions

The same two basic types of questions used for interviews, closed and open, are also useful in questionnaires. Figure 20.1 illustrates how these types of questions may be employed in the context of a questionnaire about the student health clinic problem. Notice that the questionnaire uses several forms of *closed questions* (in items 1–6): two-way questions, multiple-choice questions, ranking scales, and checklists. You will probably use more than one form of closed question in a questionnaire to collect different kinds of information. The sample questionnaire also uses several *open questions* (items 7–10) that ask for brief written answers. You may want to combine closed and open questions in your questionnaire because both offer advantages: Closed questions will give you definite answers, while open questions can elicit information you may not have anticipated as well as provide lively quotations for your essay explaining what you have learned.

Whatever types of questions you develop, try to phrase them in a fair and unbiased manner so that your results will be reliable and credible. As soon as you have a collection of possible questions, try them out on a few typical respondents. You need to know which questions are unclear, which seem to duplicate others, and which provide the most interesting responses. These tryouts will enable you to assess which questions will give you the information you need. Readers can also help you come up with additional questions.

Designing the Questionnaire

Begin your questionnaire with a brief, clear introduction stating the purpose of your survey and explaining how you intend to use the results. Give advice on answering the questions, and estimate the amount of time needed to complete the questionnaire (see Figure 20.1 for an example). You may opt to give this information orally if you plan to hand the questionnaire to groups of people and have them fill it out immediately. However, even in this case, your respondents will appreciate a written introduction that clarifies what you expect and helps keep them on track.

Select your most promising questions, and decide how to order them. Any logical order is appropriate. You might want to arrange the questions from least to most complicated or from general to specific. You may find it appropriate to group the questions by subject matter or format. Certain questions may lead to others. You might want to place open questions at the end (see Figure 20.1 for an example).

Design your questionnaire so that it looks attractive and readable. Make it look easy to complete. Do not crowd questions together to save paper. Provide plenty of space for readers to answer questions, especially open questions, and encourage them to use the back of the page if they need more space.

Two-way question

Multiple-choice questions

Ranking scale

Checklist

Ranking scale

Open questions

This is a survey about the scheduling of appointments at the campus Student Health Clinic. Your participation will help determine how long students have to wait to use clinic services and how these services might be more conveniently scheduled. The survey should take only 3 to 4 minutes to complete. All responses are confidential. Thank you for your participation.

1. Have you ever made an appointment at the clinic?   (Circle one.)

    Yes   No

2. How frequently have you had to wait more than 10 minutes at the clinic for a scheduled appointment?   (Circle one.)

    Always   Usually   Occasionally   Never

3. Have you ever had to wait more than 30 minutes at the clinic for a scheduled appointment?   (Circle one.)

    Yes   No   Uncertain

4. From your experience so far with the clinic, how would you rank its system for scheduling appointments?   (Circle one.)

0	1	2	3	4	5
no experience	inadequate	poor	adequate	good	outstanding

5. Given your present work and class schedule, when are you able to visit the clinic?   (Check all applicable responses.)

    _____ 8–10 AM   _____ 1–3 PM
    _____ 10 AM–Noon   _____ 3–5 PM
    _____ 12–1 PM

6. Given your present work and class schedule, which times during the day (Monday through Friday) would be the most and least convenient for you to schedule appointments at the clinic?   (Rank the four choices from 1 for most convenient time to 4 for least convenient time.)

    _____ Morning (7 AM – Noon)   _____ Dinnertime (5–7 PM)
    _____ Afternoon (12–5 PM)   _____ Evening (7–10 PM)

7. How would you evaluate your most recent appointment at the clinic?

8. Based on your experiences with scheduling at the clinic, what advice would you give to other students about making appointments?

9. What do you believe would most improve the scheduling of appointments at the clinic?

10. If you have additional comments about scheduling at the clinic, please write them on the back of this page.

Figure 20.1 Sample questionnaire: Scheduling at the Student Health Clinic

Testing the Questionnaire

Make a few copies of your first-draft questionnaire, and ask at least three readers to complete it. Time them as they respond, or ask them to keep track of how long they take to complete it. Discuss with them any confusion or problems they experience. Review their responses with them to be certain that each question is eliciting the information you want it to elicit. From what you learn, reconsider your questionnaire, and make any necessary revisions to your questions and design or format.

Administering the Questionnaire

Decide who you want to fill out your questionnaire and how you can arrange for them to do so. The more respondents you have, the better, but constraints of time and expense will almost certainly limit the number. You can mail or e-mail questionnaires, distribute them to dormitories, or send them to campus or workplace mailboxes, but the return will be low. Half the people receiving questionnaires in the mail usually fail to return them. If you do mail the questionnaire, be sure to mention the deadline for returning it. Give directions for its return, and include a stamped, self-addressed envelope, if necessary. Instead of mailing the questionnaire, you might want to arrange to distribute it yourself to groups of people in class or around campus, at dormitory meetings, or at work. Some colleges and universities have restrictions about the use of questionnaires, so you should check your institution's policy before sending one out.

Note that if you want to do a formal questionnaire study, you will need a scientifically representative group of readers (a random or stratified random sample). Even for an informal study, you should try to get a reasonably representative group. For example, to study satisfaction with appointment scheduling at the clinic, you would want to include students who have been to the clinic as well as those who have avoided it. You might even want to include a concentration of seniors rather than first-year students because, after four years, seniors would have made more visits to the clinic. If many students commute, you would want to be sure to have commuters among your respondents. Your essay will be more convincing if you demonstrate that your respondents represent the group whose opinions or knowledge you claim to be studying. As few as twenty-five respondents could be adequate for an informal study.

Writing Up the Results

Once you have the completed questionnaires, how do you write up the results?

Summarizing the Results. Begin by tallying the results from the closed questions. Take an unused questionnaire, and tally the responses next to each choice. Suppose that you had administered the student health clinic questionnaire to twenty-five students. Here is how the tally might look for the checklist in question 5 of Figure 20.1.

5. Given your present work and class schedule, when are you able to visit the clinic? (Check all applicable responses.)

_____ 8–10 AM 𝍫𝍫𝍫 III (18)   _____ 1–3 PM III (3)

_____ 10 AM–Noon 𝍫 II (7)   _____ 3–5 PM 𝍫 IIII (9)

_____ 12–1 PM 𝍫𝍫 III (13)

Each tally mark represents one response to that item. The totals add up to more than twenty-five because respondents were asked to check all the times when they could make appointments.

Next, consider the open questions. Read all respondents' answers to each question separately to see the kinds and variety of responses they gave. Then decide whether you want to code any of the open questions so that you can summarize results from them quantitatively, as you would with closed questions. For example, you might want to classify the types of advice given as responses to question 8 in the clinic questionnaire: "Based on your experiences with scheduling at the clinic, what advice would you give to other students about making appointments?" You could then report the numbers of respondents (of your twenty-five) who gave each type of advice. For an opinion question (for example, "How would you evaluate your most recent appointment at the clinic?"), you might simply code the answers as positive, neutral, or negative and then tally the results accordingly for each kind of response. However, you'll probably want to use the responses to most open questions as a source of quotations for your report or essay.

You can give the results from the closed questions as percentages, either within the text itself or in one or more tables. You can find table formats in texts you may be using or even in magazines or newspapers. Conventional table formats for the social sciences are illustrated in the *Publication Manual of the American Psychological Association*, 5th edition (Washington, DC: American Psychological Association, 2001).

For strategies for integrating quoted material, see Chapter 22, pp. 741–42.

Because readers' interests can be engaged more easily with quotations than with percentages, plan to use open responses in your essay. You can quote responses to the open questions within your text, perhaps weaving them into your discussion like quoted material from published sources. Or you can organize several responses into lists and then comment on them.

You can use computer spreadsheet programs to tabulate the results from closed questions and even print out tables or graphs that you can insert into your essay. For a small, informal survey, however, such programs will probably not save you much time.

Organizing the Write-up.   In organizing your results, you might want to consider a plan that is commonly followed in the social sciences.

Reporting Your Survey

Statement of the problem

    Context for your study
    Question or questions you wanted to answer

Need for your survey
Brief preview of your survey and plan for your report

Review of other related surveys (if you know of any)

Procedures

Questionnaire design
Selection of participants
Administration of the questionnaire
Summary of the results

Results: Presentation of what you learned, with limited commentary or interpretation

Summary and discussion

Brief summary of your results
Brief discussion of their significance (commenting, interpreting, exploring implications, and possibly comparing to other related surveys)

21

Library and Internet Research

Research requires patience, careful planning, good advice, and even luck. The rewards are many, however. Each new research project leads you to unexplored regions of the library or of cyberspace. You may find yourself in a rare-book room reading a manuscript written hundreds of years ago or involved in a lively discussion on the Internet with people hundreds of miles away. One moment you may be keyboarding commands, and the next you may be threading a microfilm reader, viewing a videodisk, or squinting at the fine print in an index. You may breeze through an encyclopedia entry introducing you to a new subject or struggle with a just-published report of a highly technical research study on the same subject.

This chapter is designed to help you learn how to use the resources available in your college library and on the Internet. It gives advice on how to learn about the library and the Internet, develop efficient search strategies, keep track of your research, locate appropriate sources, and read them with a critical eye. Chapter 22 provides guidelines for using and acknowledging these sources in an essay. It also presents a sample research paper on home schooling that was written for an assignment to write an essay speculating about the causes of a trend.

■ Integrating Library and Internet Research

Although this chapter includes separate sections on the library and the Internet, these two ways to find research information are closely intertwined. You can often use the Internet to access many of the library's resources — the catalog of books and other items, indexes to periodical articles, and other kinds of electronic databases — from your own computer in your home or dorm room. On the other hand, you will need or want to go through the library's computers rather than your own to access many Web-based resources, including those that charge fees for subscriptions or for downloading and printing out documents.

For most research topics, you will need to find source materials both in the library and on the Internet because each offers material not available from the other. The vast majority of books and articles published in print are not available online, and so you will almost certainly need to consult some of these print sources to avoid getting a skewed perspective on your topic, especially if it deals with events that occurred more than a few years ago. As discussed later in this chapter, print sources also tend to offer more reliable information than online ones. Likewise, though, very little online material ever appears in print, and especially for current topics, you will almost certainly want to check the Web for the latest developments or research findings. Compared with print sources, online sources usually take less time and effort both to find and to integrate into your own writing. So in some ways, they can help you do a more thorough job of research within the time available to you. Still, be careful not to rely too heavily on the Web just because it is easy to use.

■ Orienting Yourself to the Library

To conduct research in most college libraries, you will need to become familiar with a wide variety of resources. Public-access catalogs, almost all of them now electronic, provide information on books. Periodical indexes and abstracts, used to locate magazine and journal articles, are available both in print volumes and in various electronic forms: on CD-ROMs, through the library catalog, or through the World Wide Web. The materials you find may be in print, in reduced-size photographic formats like microfilm and microfiche that require special machines to read, or in electronic text files accessible through an electronic periodical index or library Web site.

Taking a Tour

Make a point of getting acquainted with your campus library. Your instructor may arrange a library orientation tour for your composition class. If not, you can join one of the regular orientation tours scheduled by the librarians or design your own tour (for suggestions, see Table 21.1). Because nearly all college libraries are more complex and offer more services than typical high school or public libraries, you will need to learn how your campus library's catalog and reference room are organized, how you can access computer catalogs and databases, whom to ask for help if you are confused, and where you can find books, periodicals, and other materials.

Nearly every college library offers a Web site and handouts describing its resources and services. Pick up copies of any available pamphlets and guidelines. Also look for a floor map of materials and facilities. See whether your library offers any research guidelines, special workshops, or presentations on strategies for locating resources. Many library Web sites offer tutorials for using the library's electronic resources.

Consulting a Librarian

Think of college librarians as instructors whose job is to help you understand the library and get your hands on sources you need to complete your research projects. Librarians at the information or reference desk are there to provide reference services, and most have years of experience answering the very questions you are likely

Table 21.1 Designing Your Self-Guided Library Tour

Here is a list of important locations or departments to look for in your college library.

Library Location	What You Can Do at These Locations
Loan desk	Obtain library cards, check out materials, place holds and recalls, pay fees or fines.
Reference desk	Obtain help from reference librarians to locate and use library resources.
Information desk	Ask general and directional questions.
Reserves desk	Gain access to books and journal articles that are on reserve for specific classes.
Interlibrary loan department	Request materials not available on site; you can do this electronically through the catalog at many libraries.
Public-access computers	Gain access to the library catalog, electronic periodical indexes and abstracts, the campus network, and the Internet.
Current periodicals	Locate unbound current issues of newspapers, journals, and magazines.
Directories of books and journals	Use directories to find the location of books and journals shelved by call numbers.
Reference collection	Find reference materials such as encyclopedias, dictionaries, handbooks, atlases, bibliographies, statistics, and periodical indexes and abstracts.
Government publications department	Locate publications from federal, state, and local government agencies.
Multimedia resources	Locate nonprint materials such as videos, CD-ROMs, and audiotapes.
Microforms	Locate materials on microfilm (reels) and microfiche (cards).
Special collections	Find rare and valuable materials not readily available in most library collections; in larger libraries only.
Archives	Find archival materials, collections of papers from important individuals and organizations that provide source material for original research (in larger libraries only).
Maps and atlases	Locate maps and atlases in a special location because of their size and format.
Copy service	Use self-service and special-function copiers.
Reading rooms	Read in quiet, comfortable areas.
Study rooms	Study in rooms reserved for individuals or small groups.
Computer labs	Use networked computers for word processing, research, and other functions.

to ask. You should not hesitate to approach them with any questions you have about locating sources. Remember, however, that they can be most helpful when you can explain your research assignment clearly and ask questions that are as specific as possible. You need not do so face-to-face: Many library Web sites now offer "virtual reference" chat rooms that connect library users to a reference librarian who can offer advice, send electronic documents, and demonstrate electronic searches.

Knowing Your Research Task

Before you go to the library to start an assigned research project, learn as much as you can about the assignment. Ask your instructor to clarify any confusing terms and to define the purpose and scope of the project. Find out how you can narrow or focus the project once you begin the research. Asking a question or two in advance can prevent hours — or even days — of misdirected work. Should you need to ask a librarian for advice, have the assignment in writing. You should try to get to the library as soon as you understand the assignment. If many of your class-mates will be working on similar projects, you may be competing with them for a limited number of books and other resources.

A Library Search Strategy

For your library research to be manageable and productive, you will want to work carefully and systematically. Although specific search strategies may vary to fit the needs of individual research tasks, the general process presented in Figure 21.1 should help you get started, keep track of all your research, use library materials to get an overview of your subject, locate the sources you need, and read those sources with a critical eye. Remember that research is a recursive, repetitive process, not a linear one. You will be constantly refining and revising your research strategy as you find out more about your topic.

■ Keeping Track of Your Research

As you research your topic, you will want to keep a careful record of all the sources you locate by setting up a working bibliography. You will also want to take notes on your sources in some systematic way.

Keeping a Working Bibliography

A **working bibliography** is a preliminary, ongoing record of books, articles, Web sites — all the sources of information you discover as you research your subject. In addition, you can use your working bibliography to keep track of any encyclopedias, bibliographies, and indexes you consult, even though these general sources are not identified in an essay.

Each entry in a working bibliography is called a **bibliographic citation**. The information you record in each bibliographic citation will help you to locate the source in the library and then, if you end up using it in your paper, to *cite* or *docu-ment* it in the final **bibliography** — the list of references or works cited you provide at the end of an essay. Recording this information for each possible source as you

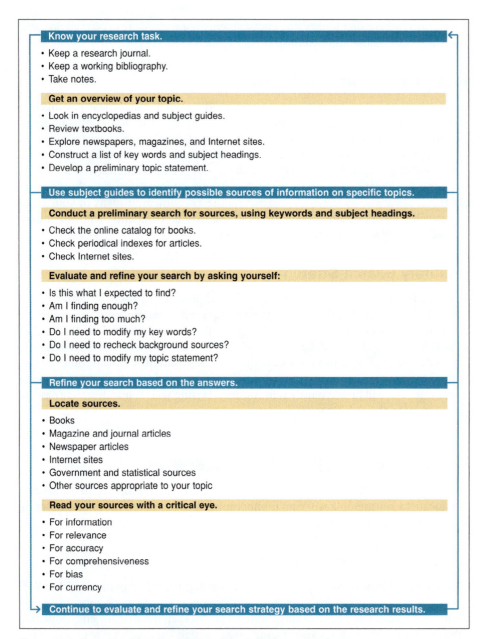

Figure 21.1 Overview of an information search strategy

identify it, rather than reconstructing it later, will save you hours of work. In addition to the bibliographic information, note the library location where the source is kept and any index or other reference work where you learned about it, just in case you have to track it down again. (See Figures 21.2 and 21.3 for guidelines on how to record bibliographic and other information for a book or a print periodical article. For guidelines for Internet sources, see Figure 21.6 on page 732.)

As you locate books in the library, record this information in your working bibliography for each book you look up.

Author: _____

Title: _____

Place of publication: _____

Publisher: _____

Date of publication: _____

Library where book is located: _____

Call number: _____

Special location (such as in reference or government publications dept.): _____

Is the book available or checked out?: _____

Figure 21.2 Information for working bibliography — books

As you locate articles in the library, record this information in your working bibliography for each article you look up.

Author of article: _____

Title of article: _____

Title of journal: _____

Volume number: _____ Issue number: _____

Date of issue: _____ Inclusive page numbers: _____

Library and special location: _____

Index where you found the article: _____

Figure 21.3 Information for working bibliography — periodical articles

Confirm with your instructor which documentation style is required for your assignment so that you can follow that style for all the sources you put into your working bibliography. Chapter 22 presents two common documentation styles — one adopted by the Modern Language Association (MLA) and widely used in the humanities and the other advocated by the American Psychological Association (APA) and used in the social sciences. Individual disciplines often have their own preferred styles of documentation.

Practiced researchers keep their working bibliography on index cards, in a notebook, or in a computer file. Many researchers find index cards convenient because the cards are easy to arrange in the alphabetical order required for the list of works cited or references. Others find cards too easy to lose and prefer instead to keep everything — working bibliography, notes, and drafts — in one notebook. Researchers who use computers for their working bibliography can either record the information in a file in their word processing program or use one of the software programs that format the information according to a preset documentation style (such as MLA or APA) or a customized style created by the user. These programs can also create and insert the citations that are required — within the essay text or in footnotes or endnotes — and can format the final list of works cited. Some programs can even download source information from electronic indexes and other databases into a bibliographic file and then automatically format the information.

Whether you use index cards, a notebook, or a computer file for your working bibliography, your entries need to be accurate and complete. If the call number you record for a book is incomplete or inaccurate, for example, you may not be able to easily find the book in the stacks. If the author's name is misspelled, you may have trouble finding the book in the catalog. If the volume number for a periodical is incorrect, you may not be able to locate the article. If you initially get some bibliographic information from a catalog or index, check it again for accuracy when you examine the source directly.

Taking Notes

Outlining, paraphrasing, and summarizing are discussed in Chapter 12, and quoting is discussed in Chapter 22.

After you have identified some possible sources and found them in print or online, you will want to begin taking notes. If you can make a photocopy of the relevant items or download them onto your computer, you may want to annotate on the page or on the screen. Otherwise, you should paraphrase, summarize, and outline useful information as separate notes. In addition, you will want to record quotations you might want to use in your essay.

You may already have a method of notetaking you prefer. Some researchers like to use index cards for notes as well as for their working bibliography. They use 3- by 5-inch cards for their bibliography and larger ones (4- by 6-inch or 5- by 7-inch) for notes, and some also use cards of different colors to organize their notes. Other people prefer to keep their notes in a notebook, and still others enter their notes into a computer file. Whatever method you use, be sure to keep accurate notes.

For tips on avoiding plagiarism, see Chapter 22, p. 748.

Careful notetaking is the most important way to minimize the risks of misquoting and of copying facts incorrectly. Another common error in notetaking is copying an author's words without enclosing them in quotation marks. This error leads easily to **plagiarism**, the unacknowledged and therefore improper use of another's words or ideas. Double-check all your notes, and be as accurate as you can. Be sure to include the page numbers where you find information, so that you can go back and reread if necessary; you will also need to give page numbers when you document sources.

You might consider photocopying materials from print sources that look especially promising. All libraries house photocopy machines or offer a copying service. Photocopying can facilitate your work, allowing you to reread and analyze important sources as well as to highlight material you may wish to quote, summarize, or paraphrase. However, because photocopying can be costly, you will want to be selective. Be sure to photocopy title pages or other publication information for each source you copy, or write this information on the photocopied text, especially if you are copying excerpts from several sources. Bring paper clips or a stapler with you to the library to help keep your photocopies organized.

For electronic sources you find in the library, download the material to a disk, and print it out if at all possible, especially if the source is on the Web. Downloading gives you the same options for rereading, highlighting, and annotating as photocopying does, and the printout serves as a "hard copy" in case the source changes or disappears. Be sure the printout includes all the information required by the documentation system you are using.

■ Getting Started

"But where do I start?" That common question is easily answered. You first need an overview of your topic. If you are researching a concept or an issue in a course you are taking, a bibliography in your textbook or your course materials provides the obvious starting point. Your instructor can advise you about other sources that provide overviews of your topic. If your topic is currently in the news, you will want to consult newspapers, magazines, or Internet sites. For all other topics — and for background information — encyclopedias and disciplinary (subject) guides are often the place to start. They introduce you to diverse aspects of a subject that might lead you to find a focus for your research.

Consulting Encyclopedias

General encyclopedias, such as the *Encyclopaedia Britannica* and the *Encyclopedia Americana*, give basic information about many topics; however, general encyclopedias alone are not adequate resources for college research. Specialized encyclopedias cover topics in the depth appropriate for college writing. In addition to providing an overview of a topic, a specialized encyclopedia often includes an explanation of issues related to the topic, definitions of specialized terminology, and selective bibliographies of additional sources.

As starting points, specialized encyclopedias have two distinct advantages: (1) They provide a comprehensive introduction to key terms related to your topic, terms that are especially useful in identifying the subject headings used to locate material in catalogs and indexes, and (2) they provide a comprehensive presentation of a subject, enabling you to see many possibilities for focusing your research on one aspect of it.

The following list identifies some specialized encyclopedias in the major academic disciplines:

ART	*Dictionary of Art.* 34 vols. 1996.
BIOLOGY	*Concise Encyclopedia Biology.* 1995.
CHEMISTRY	*Concise Encyclopedia Chemistry.* 1993.
COMPUTERS	*Encyclopedia of Computer Science and Technology.* 45 vols. 1975–.
ECONOMICS	*Fortune Encyclopedia of Economics.* 1993.
EDUCATION	*Encyclopedia of Educational Research.* 1992.
ENVIRONMENT	*Encyclopedia of the Environment.* 1994.
FOREIGN RELATIONS	*Encyclopedia of U.S. Foreign Relations.* 1997. *Encyclopedia of the Third World.* 1992.
HISTORY	*Encyclopedia USA.* 29 vols. 1983–. *New Cambridge Modern History.* 14 vols. 1957–1980, 1990–.
LAW	*Corpus Juris Secundum.* 1936. *American Jurisprudence,* 2d series. 1962.
LITERATURE	*Encyclopedia of World Literature in the Twentieth Century.* 5 vols. 1981–1993. *Encyclopedia of Literature and Criticism.* 1990.
MEDICINE	*American Medical Association's Complete Medical Encyclopedia.* 2003.
MUSIC	*New Grove Dictionary of Music and Musicians,* 2nd ed. 29 vols. 2001.
NURSING	*Miller-Keane Encyclopedia and Dictionary of Medicine, Nursing, and Allied Health.* 1997
PHILOSOPHY	*Routledge Encyclopedia of Philosophy.* 10 vols. 1998.
PSYCHOLOGY	*Encyclopedia of Psychology.* 8 vols. 2000.
RELIGION	*Encyclopedia of Religion.* 15 vols. 2005.
SCIENCE	*McGraw-Hill Encyclopedia of Science and Technology.* 20 vols. 2002.
SOCIAL SCIENCES	*International Encyclopedia of the Social Sciences.* 19 vols. 1968–.
SOCIOLOGY	*Encyclopedia of Sociology.* 5 vols. 2000.
WOMEN'S STUDIES	*Women's Studies Encyclopedia,* Rev. ed. 3 vols. 1999.

You can locate any of these in the library by doing a title search in the online catalog and looking for the encyclopedia's call number. Find other specialized encyclopedias by looking in the catalog under the subject heading for the discipline, such as "psychology," and adding the subheading "encyclopedia" or "dictionary."

Three particular reference sources can help you identify other specialized encyclopedias covering your topic:

ARBA Guide to Subject Encyclopedias and Dictionaries, 2nd ed. (1997): Lists specialized encyclopedias by broad subject categories, with descriptions of coverage, focus, and any special features. Also available online.

Subject Encyclopedias: User Guide, Review Citations, and Keyword Index (1999): Lists specialized encyclopedias by broad subject categories and provides information about articles within them. By looking under the key terms that describe a topic, you can search for related articles in any of over four hundred specialized encyclopedias.

Kister's Best Encyclopedias: A Comparative Guide to General and Specialized Encyclopedias, 2nd ed. (1994): Surveys and evaluates more than a thousand encyclopedias, both print and electronic. Includes a title index and a topic index that you can use to find references to encyclopedias on special topics.

Consulting Disciplinary Guides

Once you have a general overview of your topic, you can consult one of the research guides within the discipline. The following guides can help you identify the major handbooks, encyclopedias, bibliographies, journals, periodical indexes, and computer databases in the various disciplines. You need not read any of these extensive works straight through, but you will find them to be valuable references. The *Guide to Reference Books,* 11th ed. (1996), edited by Robert Balay, will help you find disciplinary guides for subjects not listed here.

ANTHROPOLOGY	*Introduction to Library Research in Anthropology,* 2nd ed. 1998. By John M. Weeks.
ART	*Fine Arts: A Bibliographic Guide to Basic Reference Works, Histories, and Handbooks,* 3rd ed. 1990. By Donald L. Ehresmann.
	Visual Arts Research: A Handbook. 1986. By Elizabeth B. Pollard.
BUSINESS	*Encyclopedia of Business Information Sources,* 1970–(annual). Also available online.
	Strauss's Handbook of Business Information: A Guide for Librarians, Students, and Researchers, 2nd ed. 2004. By Rita W. Moss.
EDUCATION	*Education: A Guide to Reference and Information Sources,* 2nd ed. 2000. By Lois Buttlar and Nancy O'Brien.
FILM	*On the Screen: A Film, Television, and Video Research Guide.* 1986. By Kim N. Fisher.
GENERAL HISTORY	*Guide to Reference Books,* 11th ed. 1996. Edited by Robert Balay.
	A Student's Guide to History, 9th ed. 2004. By Jules R. Benjamin.
HUMANITIES	*The Humanities: A Selective Guide to Information Sources,* 5th ed. 2000. By Ron Blazek and Elizabeth S. Aversa. Also available online.

LITERATURE	*Reference Works in British and American Literature,* 2nd ed. 1998. By James K. Bracken. Also available online. *Literary Research Guide: An Annotated Listing of Reference Sources in English Literary Studies,* 4th ed. 2002. By James L. Harner.
MUSIC	*Music: A Guide to the Reference Literature.* 1987. By William S. Brockman.
PHILOSOPHY	*Philosophy: A Guide to the Reference Literature,* 2nd ed. 1997. By Hans E. Bynagle. Also available online.
POLITICAL SCIENCE	*Political Science: A Guide to Reference and Information Sources.* 1990. By Henry York.
PSYCHOLOGY	*Library Use: A Handbook for Psychology,* 3rd ed. 2003.
SCIENCE AND TECHNOLOGY	*Information Sources in Science and Technology.* 1998. By Charlie Hurt.
SOCIAL SCIENCES	*The Social Sciences: A Cross-Disciplinary Guide to Selected Sources,* 3rd ed. 2002. By Nancy L. Herron. Also available online.
SOCIOLOGY	*Sociology: A Guide to Reference and Information Sources,* 3rd ed. 2005. By Stephen H. Aby.
WOMEN'S STUDIES	*Women's Studies: A Guide to Information Sources.* 1990. By Sarah Carter and Maureen Ritchie.

Consulting Bibliographies

Like encyclopedias and disciplinary guides, bibliographies give an overview of what has been published on the subject. A **bibliography** is simply a list of publications on a given subject. Its scope may be broad or narrow. Some bibliographers try to be exhaustive, including every title they can find, but most are selective. To discover how selections were made, check the bibliography's preface or introduction. Occasionally, bibliographies are annotated with brief summaries and evaluations of the entries. Bibliographies may be found in a variety of places: in encyclopedias, in the library catalog, and in research guides. All specialized encyclopedias and disciplinary guides have bibliographies. Research articles include bibliographies to document their sources of information.

Even if you attend a large research university, your library is unlikely to hold every book or journal article that a bibliography might direct you to. The library catalog and serial record (a list of periodicals the library holds) will tell you whether the book or journal is available on site or through interlibrary loan.

■ Identifying Subject Headings and Keywords

To extend your research beyond encyclopedias, you need to find appropriate subject headings and keywords. **Subject headings** are specific words and phrases used in library catalogs, periodical indexes, and other databases to categorize the contents of books and articles so that people can look for materials about a particular topic. One way to begin your search for subject headings is to consult the *Library of Congress Subject Headings* (LCSH), which your library probably makes available both in print and online. This work lists the standard subject headings used in library catalogs. Here is an example from the LCSH:

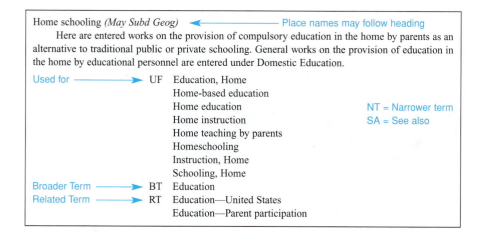

Home schooling *(May Subd Geog)* ← ——————— Place names may follow heading
Here are entered works on the provision of compulsory education in the home by parents as an alternative to traditional public or private schooling. General works on the provision of education in the home by educational personnel are entered under Domestic Education.

Used for ——→ UF   Education, Home
Home-based education
Home education   NT = Narrower term
Home instruction   SA = See also
Home teaching by parents
Homeschooling
Instruction, Home
Schooling, Home
Broader Term ——→ BT   Education
Related Term ——→ RT   Education—United States
Education—Parent participation

This sample entry proved particularly useful because when one student researching this topic found nothing listed in the library catalog under "Home schooling," she tried the other headings until "Education — Parent participation" and "Education — United States" yielded information on three books. Note, too, that this entry explains the types of books that would be found under these headings and those that would be found elsewhere.

Instead of looking for likely headings in the LCSH, however, you can usually locate useful subject headings faster by searching the catalog or other database using **keywords**, words or phrases that you think describe your topic. As you read about your subject in an encyclopedia or other reference book, you should keep a list of keywords that may be useful. (Make sure you spell your keywords correctly. Databases are often unforgiving of spelling errors.) As you review the results of a keyword search, look for the titles that seem to match most closely the topics that you are looking for. When you call up the detailed information for these titles, look for the section labeled "Subject" or "Subject Heading," which will show the headings under which the book or article is classified. (In the example that follows, this section is abbreviated as "Subj-lcsh.") In many computerized catalogs and databases, these subject headings are links that you can click on to get a list of other materials on the same subject. Keep a list in your working bibliography of all the subject headings you find that relate to your topic, so that you can refer to them each time you

For an example of an online catalog reference to a periodical, see p. 727.

start looking for information. Here is an example of an online catalog listing for a book on home schooling:

| Title: | Kingdom of children: culture and controversy in the homeschooling movement / Mitchell L. Stevens |
| Imprint: | Princeton, NJ: Princeton University Press, c2001. |

LOCATION	CALL NO	STATUS
Coe	LC40.S74 2001	NOT CHCKD OUT

Description:	xiii, 228 p.; 24 cm
Series:	Princeton studies in cultural sociology
Subj-lcsh	**Home Schooling — United States**
	Educational sociology — United States
Note(s):	Includes bibliographical references (p. 199 – 224) and index

Subject headings

Determining the Most Promising Sources

As you follow a subject heading into the library catalog and periodical indexes, you will discover many seemingly relevant books and articles. How do you decide which ones to track down and examine? You may have little to go on but author, title, date, and publisher or periodical name, but these details actually provide useful clues. Look again, for example, at the online catalog reference to a book on home schooling (see above). The title, *Kingdom of Children: Culture and Controversy in the Homeschooling Movement,* is the first clue to the subject coverage of the book. Note that the publication date, 2001, is fairly recent. From the subject headings, you can see that the geographic focus of the book is the United States. Finally, from the notes, you can see that the book includes an extensive bibliography that could lead you to other sources.

Now look at Figure 21.4, search results from *ERIC,* an electronic periodical database, searched through EBSCOhost.

For a discussion of periodical indexes, see p. 721.

This screen lists articles that address different aspects of home schooling, briefly describing some of the articles. You can see that the first article deals with the issue from a British point of view, which might provide an interesting cross-cultural perspective for your essay. The second and third articles, both from a journal devoted to the topic of college admissions, might give you a sense of how well home schooling prepares students for college. Be careful, though, to stay focused on your specific research topic or thesis, especially if you are pressed for time and cannot afford to become distracted exploring sources that sound interesting but are unlikely to be useful.

In addition, each entry contains the information that you will need to locate it in a library, and some databases provide links to the full text of articles from selected periodicals. Going back to the second article, here is what each piece of information means.

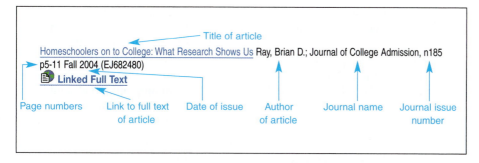

When you look in catalogs and indexes, consider the following points when deciding whether you should track down a particular source:

- **Relevance to your topic:** Do the title, subtitle, description, subject headings, and abstract help you determine how directly the particular source addresses your topic?

- **Publication date:** How recent is the source? For current controversies, emerging trends, and scientific or technological developments, you must consult recent material. For historical or biographical topics, you will want to start with

Figure 21.4 EBSCOhost: "Homeschooling," results of ERIC search

present-day perspectives but eventually explore older sources that offer authoritative perspectives. You may also want or need to consult sources written at the time of the events or during the life of the person you are researching.

- *Description:* Does the length indicate a brief treatment of the topic or an extended treatment? Does the work include illustrations that may elaborate on concepts discussed in the text? Does it include a bibliography that could lead you to other works or an index that could give you an overview of what is discussed in the text? Does the abstract indicate the focus of the work?

From among the sources that look promising, select publications that seem by their titles to address different aspects of your topic or to approach it from different perspectives. Try to avoid selecting sources that are mostly by the same author, from the same publisher, or in the same journal. Common sense will lead you to an appropriate decision about diversity in source materials.

◼ Searching Online Library Catalogs and Databases

Computerized library catalogs and other databases consist of thousands or millions of records, each representing an individual item such as a book, an article, or a government publication. The record is made up of different fields describing the item and allowing users to search for it and retrieve it from the database.

Using Different Search Techniques

Basic search strategies include author, title, and subject searches. When you request an **author search**, the computer looks for a match between the name you type and the names listed in the author field of all the records in the online catalog or other database. When you request a **title search** or a **subject search**, the computer looks for a match in the title field or the subject field, respectively. Computers are very literal. They try to match only the exact terms you enter, and most do not recognize variant or incorrect spellings. That is an incentive to become a good speller and a good typist. However, because most library catalogs and databases also offer the option of searching for titles and subjects by keywords, you need not enter the full exact title or subject heading. In addition, you can be flexible where the computer cannot. For instance, if you were researching the topic of home schooling, you could do a subject search not only for "home schooling" but also for "homeschooling" and "home-schooling." Table 21.2 on p. 717 describes some search capabilities commonly offered by library catalogs and databases.

Doing Advanced Searches and Using Boolean Operators

The real power of using an online catalog or other database is demonstrated when you need to look up books or articles using more than one keyword. For example, suppose you want information about home schooling in California. Rather than

Table 21.2 Common Search Capabilities Offered by Library Catalogs and Databases

Type of Search	How the Computer Conducts the Search	Things to Know
Author search (**exact**) • Individual *(Guterson, David)* • Organization *(U.S. Department of Education)*	Looks in the author field for the words entered	• Author searches generally are exact-match searches, so authors' names are entered *last name, first name* (for example, "Shakespeare, William"). • Organizations can be considered authors. Enter the name of the organization in natural word order. • An exact-match author search is useful for finding books and articles by a particular author.
Title search (**exact**) • Book title • Magazine or journal title • Article title	Looks in the title field for words in the exact order you enter them	An exact-match title search is useful for identifying the location of known items, such as when you are looking for a particular journal or book.
Subject search (**exact**)	Looks in the subject heading or descriptor field for words in the exact order you enter them	An exact-match subject search is useful when you are sure about the subject heading.
Keyword search	Looks in the title, note, subject, abstract, and text fields for the words entered	A keyword search is the broadest kind you can use. It is useful during early exploration of a subject.
Title word search • Book title • Magazine or journal title • Article title	Looks in the title field of the record for the words entered and ignores word order	Since this is not an exact-match search, entering "home and schooling" will retrieve the same records as entering "schooling and home."
Subject word search	Looks in the subject heading or descriptor field of the record for the words entered and ignores word order	Since this is not an exact-match search, entering "education privatization" will retrieve the same records as "privatization education."

looking through an index listing all the articles on home schooling and picking out those that mention California, you can ask the computer to do the work for you by linking your two keywords. Many online catalogs and databases now offer the option of an **advanced search**, sometimes on a separate page from the main search page, that allows you to search for more than one keyword at a time, search for certain keywords while excluding others, or search for an exact phrase. Or you may be able to create this kind of advanced search yourself by using the **Boolean operators** AND, OR, and NOT along with quotation marks and parentheses.

To understand the operation of **Boolean logic** (developed by and named after George Boole, a nineteenth-century mathematician), picture one set of articles about home schooling and another set of articles about California. A third set is formed by articles that are about both home schooling and California. The figures below provide an illustration of how each Boolean operator works.

Using Truncation

Another useful search strategy employs **truncation**. With this technique, you drop the ending of a word or term and replace it with a symbol, which indicates you want to retrieve records containing any term that begins the same way as your term. For example, by entering the term "home school#" you would retrieve all the records that have terms such as "home school," "home schooling," "home schools," "home schooled," or "home schoolers." Truncation is useful when you want to retrieve both the plural and singular forms of a word or any word for which you are not sure of the ending. Truncation symbols vary with the catalog or database. The question mark (?), asterisk (*), and pound sign (#) are frequently used.

AND

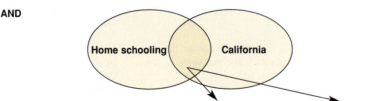

Returns references that contain both the term **home schooling** AND the term **California**

- Narrows the search
- Combines unrelated terms
- Is the default used by most online catalogs and databases

OR

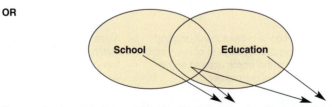

Returns all references that contain either the term **school** OR the term **education** OR both terms
- Broadens the search (**"OR is more"**)
- Is useful with synonyms and variant spellings: ("home schooling" and "homeschooling")

NOT

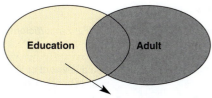

Returns references that include the term **education** but NOT the term **adult**
- Narrows the search

Caution: By narrowing your search, you may eliminate relevant material.

Table 21.3 on p. 720 offers some suggestions for expanding or narrowing your electronic search.

■ Locating Sources

The following are guidelines for finding books, various kinds of periodical articles, government documents and statistical information, and other types of sources.

Finding Books

The primary source for books is the library's computerized catalog. Besides allowing you to flexibly search keywords and subject headings, the catalog may tell you whether a book is currently available or checked out. It also allows you to print out source information rather than having to copy the material by hand. However, the catalog will require correct spelling for searches and may contain only materials received and cataloged after a certain date. Look again at the sample catalog listing for a book on home schooling:

Finding Books
1. Determine keywords or subject headings.
2. Enter terms in the online catalog.
3. Evaluate results.
4. Refine results if necessary.
5. Locate the books.

| Title: | Kingdom of children: culture and controversy in the homeschooling movement / Mitchell L. Stevens |
| Imprint: | Princeton, NJ: Princeton University Press, c2001. |

LOCATION	CALL NO	STATUS
Coe	LC40.S74 2001	NOT CHCKD OUT

Description:	xiii, 228 p.; 24 cm
Series:	Princeton studies in cultural sociology
Subj-lcsh	**Home Schooling — United States**
	Educational sociology — United States
Note(s):	Includes bibliographical references (p. 199 – 224) and index

The "imprint" line provides publication information.

The "description" is sometimes called the "physical description."

Table 21.3 Electronic Search Tips

If You Find Too Many Sources on Your Topic:	If You Find Insufficient Information on Your Topic:
• Use a subject heading search instead of a keyword search. • Add a concept word to your search. • Use a more precise vocabulary to describe your topic. • Use the "limits" link on your library catalog's search page to restrict your findings by date, format, language, or other options.	• Use a keyword or title search instead of a subject heading search. • Eliminate unimportant words or secondary concepts from your search terms. • Try truncated forms of your keyword. • Use different words to describe your topic. • Check the spelling of each term you type.

Whether you search a library catalog by author, title, subject, or keyword, each record you find will provide the following standard information. You will need this information to enter the book in your working bibliography and to locate it in the library.

1. *Call number:* This number, which usually appears on a separate line in the computerized catalog record, is your key to finding the book in the library. Most college libraries use the Library of Congress call-number system, and most public libraries and some small college libraries use the Dewey system. The Library of Congress system uses both letters and numbers in the call number, and both are needed to locate a book. Call numbers serve two purposes: They provide an exact location for every book in the library, and because they are assigned according to subject classifications, they group together books on the same topic. When you go to the stacks to locate the book, therefore, always browse for other useful material on the shelves around it. Call numbers also give information about special collections of books kept in other library locations such as the reference room or government publications department. If the online catalog covers more than one library, the name of the library that has the book will also be included.

Examples of records in online catalogs are shown on p. 714.

2. *Author:* The author's name usually appears last name first, followed by birth and death dates. For books with multiple authors, the record includes an author entry under each author's name.

3. *Title:* The title appears exactly as it does on the title page of the book, except that only the first word and proper nouns and adjectives are capitalized.

4. *Publication information:* The place of publication (usually just the city), the publisher, and the year of publication are listed. If the book was published simultaneously in the United States and abroad, both places of publication and both publishers are indicated.

5. *Physical description:* This section provides information about the book's page length and size. A roman numeral indicates the number of pages devoted to front matter (such as a preface, table of contents, and acknowledgments).

6. *Notes:* Any special features such as a bibliography or an index are listed here.

7. *Subject headings:* Assigned by the Library of Congress, these headings indicate how the book is listed in the subject catalog. They also provide useful links for finding other books on the same subject.

For more on the Library of Congress Subject Headings (LCSH), see pp. 712–14.

Finding Periodical Articles

The most up-to-date information on a subject is usually found not in books but in articles published in periodicals. A **periodical** is a publication such as a magazine, newspaper, or scholarly journal that is published on an ongoing basis, at regular intervals (for instance, daily, weekly, monthly, or annually), and with different content in each issue. Many print periodicals now publish online versions as well, although the contents may be somewhat different. In addition, some magazines and journals are published exclusively on the Web. Examples of periodicals include *Sports Illustrated* (magazine), the *New York Times* (newspaper), *Tulsa Studies in Women's Literature* (scholarly journal), *Kairos* (online journal), and *Slate* (online magazine).

Articles in periodicals are usually not listed in the library catalog; to find them, you must use library reference works called **periodical indexes**. Some periodical indexes include **abstracts** or short summaries of articles. In the library, indexes may be available in print, in microform, on CD-ROM, through the computerized catalog, or as online databases. Many are available in both print and electronic formats, and some electronic indexes give you access to the full text of articles. Regardless of format, periodical indexes all serve the same basic function of leading the user to articles on a specific topic. If you understand how to use one, you will be able to use others.

> **Finding Periodical Articles**
>
> 1. Select an appropriate periodical index or database.
> 2. Select a search option.
> 3. Display and evaluate the results of the search.
> 4. Refine your search strategy if necessary.
> 5. Interpret results to locate the articles.
> 6. Print, e-mail, or download results for later use.

Distinguishing Scholarly Journals and Popular Magazines

Although they are both called periodicals, journals and magazines have important differences. **Journals** publish articles written by experts in a particular field of study, frequently professors or researchers in academic institutions. Journals are usually specialized in their subject focus, research oriented, and extensively reviewed by specialists prior to publication. They are intended to be read by experts and students conducting research. **Magazines**, in contrast, usually publish general-interest articles written by journalists. The articles are written to entertain and educate the general public, and they tend to appeal to a much broader audience than journal articles.

Journals contain a great deal of what is called **primary literature**, reporting the results of original research. For example, a scientist might publish an article in a medical journal about the results of a new treatment protocol for breast cancer. **Secondary literature**, published in magazines, is intended to inform the general public about new and interesting developments in scientific and other areas of research. If a reporter from *Newsweek* writes an article about this scientist's cancer research, this article is classified as secondary literature. Table 21.4 summarizes some of the important differences between scholarly journals and popular magazines.

Table 21.4 How to Distinguish a Scholarly Journal from a Popular Magazine

Scholarly Journal	*Popular Magazine*
• The front or back cover lists the contents of the issue. • The title of the publication contains the word *Journal*. • You see the journal only at the library.	• The cover features a color picture. • The title may be catchy as well as descriptive. • You see the magazine for sale at the grocery store, in an airport, or at a bookstore.
• It either does not include advertisements or advertises products such as textbooks, professional books, and scholarly conferences. • The authors of articles have *Ph.D.* or academic affiliations after their names. • Many articles have more than one author.	• It has lots of colorful advertisements in it. • The authors of articles are journalists or reporters. • Most articles have a single author but may quote experts.
• A short summary (abstract) of an article may appear on the first page. • Most articles are fairly long, 5 to 20 pages.	• A headline or engaging description may precede the article. • Most of the articles are fairly short, 1 to 5 pages.
• The articles may include charts, tables, figures, and quotations from other scholarly sources. • The articles have a bibliography (list of references to other books and articles) at the end. • You probably would not read it at the beach.	• The articles have color pictures and side-bar boxes • The articles do not include a bibliography. • You might bring it to the beach to read.

Selecting an Appropriate Periodical Index or Abstract

Periodical indexes and abstracts are of two types: general and specialized. Both provide you with information that will help you locate articles on a topic. In addition to the lists on pp. 723–26, a reference librarian can help you identify other indexes and abstracts that may be useful for your topic.

General Indexes.   These indexes are a good place to start your research because they cover a broad range of subjects. Most have separate author and subject listings as well as a list of book reviews. General indexes usually list only articles from popular magazines and newspapers, although some of them include listings from basic scholarly journals. Here is a list of the most common general indexes:

The Readers' Guide to Periodical Literature (1900–; online, 1983–; updated quarterly): Covers about two hundred popular periodicals and may help you launch your search for sources on general and current topics. Even for general topics, however, you should not rely on it exclusively. Nearly all college libraries house far more than two hundred periodicals, and university research libraries house twenty thousand or more. The *Readers' Guide* does not even attempt to cover the research journals that play such an important role in college writing. Here is an example of an entry for home education:

> **HOME SCHOOLING**
> Geography in the genes. il *National Geographic*
> v204 no5 p insert32 N 2003
> Keeping it in the family. S. Hunt. por *Black Issues Book Review* v5
> no5 p20–1 S/O 2003
> My home is my classroom. S. Payne. por *New York Times*
> *Upfront* v136 no2 p30 S 22 2003

Magazine Index (on microfilm, 1988–; online as part of InfoTrac, 1973–; see below): Indexes over four hundred magazines.

InfoTrac (online): Time coverage varies by subscription. Includes three indexes: (1) the *General Periodicals Index*, which covers over twelve hundred general-interest publications, incorporating the *Magazine Index* and including the *New York Times* and the *Wall Street Journal*; (2) the *Academic Index*, which covers four hundred scholarly and general-interest publications, including the *New York Times*; and (3) the *National Newspaper Index*, which covers the *Christian Science Monitor*, *Los Angeles Times*, *New York Times*, *Wall Street Journal*, and *Washington Post*. Some entries include abstracts or the full text of articles.

Alternative Press Index (1970–; online through Biblioline): Indexes alternative and radical publications.

Humanities Index (1974–; online, 1984–): Covers more than five hundred periodicals in archaeology, history, classics, literature, performing arts, philosophy, and religion.

Social Sciences Index (1974–; online, 1983–): Covers more than five hundred periodicals in economics, geography, law, political science, psychology, public administration, and sociology.

Public Affairs Information Service Bulletin (1915–; online, 1972–): Covers articles and other publications by public and private agencies on economic and social conditions, international relations, and public administration. Subject listings only.

Specialized Indexes and Abstracts.   These publications list or summarize articles devoted to technical or scholarly research. As you learn more about your topic, you will turn to specialized indexes and abstracts to find references to scholarly articles. The example in Figure 21.5 from ERIC, which indexes and summarizes

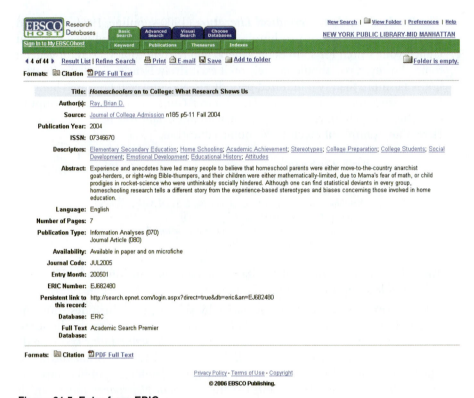

Figure 21.5 Entry from ERIC

articles from a wide range of periodicals that publish educational research, is typical of entries found in specialized indexes.

Here is a list of specialized periodical indexes that cover various disciplines:

Accounting and Tax Index (1964–; online)

America: History and Life (1954–; online, 1964–)

American Statistics Index (1973–)

Applied Science and Technology Index (1958–; online, 1983–)

Art Index (1929–; online as *Art Abstracts*, 1984–)

Biological and Agricultural Index (1964–; online as *Bio Abstracts*, 1985–)

Education Index (1929–; online as *Education Abstracts*, 1983–)

Engineering Index (1920–; online)

Historical Abstracts (1955–; online, 1982–)

Index Medicus (1961–; online as MEDLINE)

MLA International Bibliography of Books and Articles in the Modern Languages and Literature (1921–; online)

Music Index (1949–; online, 1981–)

Philosopher's Index (1957–; online)

Physics Abstracts (1898; online as INSPEC)

Psychological Abstracts (1927; online as PsycINFO)

Science Abstracts (1898)

Sociological Abstracts (1952; online as Sociofile)

Most periodical indexes and abstracts use their own system of subject headings. The print version of *Sociological Abstracts*, for example, has a separate volume for subject headings. Check the opening pages or, for an electronic index or abstract, the opening screen or home page to see how subjects are classified. Then look for periodicals or articles under your most useful subject heading from the LCSH or the heading that seems most similar to it. If you are using an electronic index, the items in the subject heading field for particular articles may function as links to lists of related materials.

Indexes to Periodicals Representing Particular Viewpoints.   Some specialized periodical indexes tend to represent particular viewpoints and may help you identify different positions on an issue.

Chicano Index (1967–): Indexes general and scholarly articles about Mexican Americans. Articles are arranged by subject with author and title indexes. (Before 1989, the title was *Chicano Periodical Index*.)

G. K. Hall Index to Black Periodicals (1999–); previously published as *Index to Black Periodicals* (1984–1998): Provides an author and subject index to general and scholarly articles about African Americans.

Left Index (1982–; online only, 2000–): Indexes by author and subject over eighty periodicals with a Marxist, radical, or left perspective. Listings cover primarily topics in the social sciences and humanities.

Another useful source for identifying positions is *Editorials on File*, described on p. 728.

Full-Text Electronic Services.   In addition to the electronic indexes and abstracts listed earlier, many libraries subscribe to other electronic database services that provide the full text of periodical articles, often in particular subject areas. The text is available either in the database itself (so you can see it onscreen and download it or print it out) or by mail or fax for a fee. Subscriptions to these services tend to be expensive, so they may not be available in small college libraries, and the articles available may be limited to those in recent issues. Nevertheless, be sure to check with a librarian about what is available at your library. Some of these services include the following:

ERIC (Educational Resources Information Center) (online, 1966–): Indexes, abstracts, and provides some full texts of articles from 750 education journals.

Business Periodicals Ondisc (1988–) and *ABI/INFORM* (1988–): Provide full-text articles from business periodicals that can be printed on your library's printer.

PsycBooks (online, 2004–): Indexes books and book chapters in psychology.

Ingenta (1998–; http://www.ingenta.com): An online document delivery service, Ingenta lists articles from more than 5,400 online journals and 26,000 other publications. For a fee, you can receive the full text of the article, online or by fax.

LEXIS-NEXIS Academic Universe (time coverage varies by source; http://www.lexis-nexis.com/lncc/academic): Provides the full text of articles from academic journals and other sources containing legal, news, and government information and statistics.

JSTOR (http://www.jstor.org): Provides the full text of articles from older issues of more than three hundred journals in the humanities and social sciences.

Project Muse (1996–; http://muse.jhu.edu): Provides the full text of articles from more than three hundred journals in the humanities, social sciences, and mathematics from Johns Hopkins University Press and selected not-for-profit publishers.

Hein Online (2000–; http://www.11.georgetown.edu/lib/gulconly/hein/hein.html): Provides a collection of legal periodical titles with full-text access.

Science Direct (1997–; http://www.sciencedirect.com): Provides the full text of articles from more than a thousand journals in science, technology, medicine, and the social sciences from Elsevier Press.

Interlibrary networks: Known by different names in different regions, these networks allow you to search in the catalogs of colleges and universities in your area and across the country. In many cases, you can request a book by interlibrary loan, although it may take several weeks to be delivered to your library. You can also request a copy of an article from a journal to which your own library does not subscribe. Most libraries do not lend their journals but will copy and forward articles for a fee.

Searching Electronic Periodical Databases

Although you can search an electronic periodical database by author or title, you will probably more often want to do searches using keywords. As with searches for books in the library catalog, make your keywords as precise as possible so that your search results in a manageable list of sources relevant to your topic. Most databases include a thesaurus of keywords and an advanced-search mechanism or set of guidelines for using Boolean operators or other keyword-combining procedures. In addition, many databases include a browse function. When you enter a keyword, this function automatically lists the terms that are close to the keyword alphabetically. If you enter a very general keyword, the function provides a list of subtopics that you can use to narrow your search before you ask the system to retrieve records.

Once you have typed your keywords, the computer searches the database and lists every reference to them that it finds. You can usually print the results or download the records to your own disk. Because online databases contain so much information, you may want to consult with a librarian to develop an efficient search strategy. Also keep in mind that some electronic indexes cover only the last fifteen to twenty years; you may need to consult older printed versions of indexes as well.

Locating Periodicals in the Library

When you identify a promising magazine or journal article in a periodical index, you must go to the library's online catalog or periodicals database to learn whether the library subscribes to the periodical, whether the article is available in print or electronic form or both, and where you can find the magazine or journal issue you need. No library can subscribe to every periodical, so as you go through indexes and abstracts, be sure to identify more articles than you actually need. This will save you from having to repeat your catalog or database search later when you find out that your library does not subscribe to some of the magazines or journals that contain your possible sources.

Although every library arranges its print periodicals differently, recent issues are usually arranged alphabetically by title on open shelves. Older issues may be bound like books (shelved by call numbers or alphabetically by title) or filmed and available in microform. Ask a librarian at the reference desk how the periodicals in your library are arranged.

Suppose you want to look up an article on home schooling from *Journal of College Admission* that you found indexed in *ERIC*. Here is a typical record for the journal from a library's online catalog or periodicals database. Notice that the title search refers to the title of the journal, not the title of the article.

You searched TITLE **Journal of College Admission**

Title of the journal

Where the journal is published

Title:	Journal of college admission
Imprint:	Skokie, Ill., National Association of College Admission Counselors [etc.]

Library where the journal is located and location of current (unbound) issues

LOCATION:	MAIN-Latest in Curr Per LB 2301.A77x	Call number
LIB. HAS:	B100-183(1984-2004)	Bound volumes and years the library owns
Latest Received:	Fall 2005 No. 189	Most recent issue received

In this instance, you would learn that the library does subscribe to *Journal of College Admission* and that you could locate the 2004 article in the library's current periodicals collection.

Finding Newspaper Articles and Other News Sources

Newspapers provide useful information for many research topics in such areas as foreign affairs, economics, public opinion, and social trends. Libraries usually photograph newspapers and store them in miniature form on microfilm (reels) or microfiche (cards) that must be placed in viewing machines to be read. Newspaper indexes such as the *Los Angeles Times Index, New York Times Index,* and *London Times Index,* which are available online as well as in print, can help you locate specific articles on your topic. College libraries usually have indexes to local newspapers as well.

Your library may also subscribe to newspaper article and digest services, such as the following:

National Newspaper Index (microfilm, 1989–; online as part of InfoTrac, 1979–) (see p. 723): Indexes the *Christian Science Monitor, Los Angeles Times, New York Times, Wall Street Journal,* and *Washington Post.*

NewsBank (microfiche and CD-ROM, 1970–; online): Provides full-text articles from five hundred U.S. newspapers; a good source of information on local and regional issues and trends.

Newspaper Abstracts (1988–; online, 1989–): Indexes and gives brief abstracts of articles from nineteen major regional, national, and international newspapers; available through Proquest.

Facts on File (weekly; CD-ROM, 1980): Provides a digest of U.S. and international news events arranged by subject, such as foreign affairs, arts, education, religion, and sports.

Editorials on File (twice monthly): Provides a digest of editorials from 150 U.S. and Canadian newspapers with brief descriptions of editorial subjects followed by fifteen to twenty editorials on the subject, reprinted from different newspapers.

CQ Researcher (online, 1991–; previously published since 1924 as Editorial Research Reports): Reports on current and controversial topics, including brief histories, statistics, editorials, journal articles, endnotes, and supplementary reading lists.

Foreign Broadcast Information Service (FBIS) (1980–; online, 1990–): Provides a digest of foreign broadcast scripts, newspaper articles, and government statements from Asia, Europe, Latin America, Africa, Russia, and the Middle East.

Keesing's Record of World Events (1931–; also online): Provides a monthly digest of events in all countries, compiled from British and other reporting services; includes speeches and statistics and chronological, geographic, and topical indexes.

Finding Government and Statistical Information

Federal, state, and local governments now make many of their publications and reference services available through the World Wide Web, though college libraries still maintain print collections of government publications. Ask a reference librarian for assistance in locating governmental sources in the library or on the Web. In particular, consider consulting the following sources for information on political subjects and national trends. Although these publications are not always listed in library catalogs or databases, they can usually be found in the reference area or the government documents department of college libraries. If these works are not listed in your library's catalog, ask for assistance in locating them.

Sources for Researching Political Subjects.   Two publications that report developments in the federal government can be rich sources of information on political issues. Types of material they cover include congressional hearings and debates, presidential proclamations and speeches, U.S. Supreme Court decisions and dissenting opinions, and compilations of statistics.

> *Congressional Quarterly Almanac* (annual): A summary of legislation; provides an overview of government policies and trends, including analysis as well as election results, records of roll-call votes, and the text of significant speeches and debates.

> *CQ Weekly* (online, 1998–; formerly published as *Congressional Quarterly Weekly Report*): A news service; includes up-to-date summaries of congressional committee actions, congressional votes, and executive branch activities as well as overviews of current policy discussions and other activities of the federal government.

Sources for Researching Trends.   Research can help you identify trends to write about and, most important, provide the statistical evidence you need to demonstrate the existence of a trend. The following resources can be especially helpful:

For guidance on developing an argument that speculates about the causes of a trend, see Chapter 9.

> *Statistical Abstract of the United States* (annual; some content online, http:// www.census.gov/statab/www): A publication of the Bureau of the Census; provides a variety of social, economic, and political statistics, often covering several years, including tables, graphs, charts, and references to additional sources of information.

> *American Statistics Index* (1974–; annual with monthly supplements): Attempts to cover all federal government publications containing statistical information of research significance and includes brief descriptions of references.

> *Statistical Reference Index* (1980–): Provides a selective guide to American statistical publications from sources other than the U.S. government, including economic, social, and political statistical sources.

> *World Almanac and Book of Facts* (annual): Presents information on a variety of subjects drawn from many sources, including a chronology of the year, climatological data, and lists of inventions and awards.

> *The Gallup Poll: Public Opinion* (1935–): Provides a chronological listing of the results of public opinion polls, including information on social, economic, and political trends.

In addition to researching the trend itself, you may want to research others' speculations about its causes. If so, the reports of federal government activities described in the preceding section may be helpful.

Finding Other Library Sources

Libraries hold vast amounts of useful materials other than books, periodicals, and government documents. Some of the following library sources and services may be appropriate for your research.

- *Vertical files:* Pamphlets and brochures from government and private agencies
- *Special collections:* Manuscripts, rare books, and materials of local interest
- *Audio collections:* Records, audiotapes, music CDs, readings, and speeches
- *Video collections:* Slides, filmstrips, videotapes, and DVDs
- *Art collections:* Drawings, paintings, and engravings
- *Interlibrary loans:* As noted above, many libraries can arrange to borrow books from other libraries or have copies of journal articles sent from other libraries as part of an interlibrary network program. Ask your librarian how long it will take to get the material you need (usually several weeks) and how to use the loan service (some libraries allow you to send an electronic request to the local interlibrary loan office).
- *Computer resources:* Interactive computer programs that combine text, video, and audio resources in history, literature, business, and other disciplines

Using the Internet for Research

By now, most of you are familiar with searching the Internet. This section introduces you to some tools and strategies that will help you use the Net more efficiently to find information on a topic.

As you use the Internet for conducting research, keep the following concerns and guidelines in mind:

- *The Internet has no central system of organization.* On the Internet, a huge amount of information is stored on many different networks and servers and in many different formats, each with its own system of organization. The Internet has no central catalog, reference librarian, or standard classification system for the vast resources available there.
- *Many significant electronic sources are not part of the Internet or require a paid subscription or other fees.* Computerized library catalogs, electronic periodical indexes, full-text article databases, and other electronic resources are often stored on CD-ROMs or on campus computer networks rather than on the Internet and so are available to students only through the library or other campus computers. Furthermore, some databases on the Web charge for a sub-

scription or for downloading or printing out content. For these reasons (as well as the one discussed below), you should plan to use the library or campus computer system for much of your electronic research, since it will give you access to more material at a lower cost. You will not need to pay for subscriptions, and you may be able to download or print out material for free as well.

- ***Internet sources that you find on your own are generally less reliable than print sources or than electronic sources to which your library or campus subscribes.*** Because it is relatively easy for anyone to publish on the Internet, judging the reliability of online information is a special concern. Depending on your topic, purpose, and audience, the sources you find on the Internet may not be as credible or authoritative as print sources or subscription electronic sources, which have usually been screened by publishers, editors, librarians, and authorities on the topic. For some topics, most of what you find on the Internet may be written by highly biased or amateur authors, so you will need to balance or supplement these sources with information from your library or campus and print sources. When in doubt about the reliability of an online source for a particular assignment, check with your instructor. (See Reading Sources with a Critical Eye on pp. 734–37 for more specific suggestions.)

- ***Internet sources are not as stable as print sources or the electronic sources to which your library or campus subscribes.*** A Web site that existed last week may no longer be available today, or its content may have changed.

- ***Internet sources must be documented, and so you need to include them in your working bibliography.*** A working bibliography is an ongoing record of all the possible sources you discover as you research your subject. The working bibliography becomes the draft for the list of references or works cited at the end of your essay, even if you do not include all these sources in your final list. You will need to follow appropriate conventions for quoting, paraphrasing, summarizing, and documenting the online sources you use, just as you do for print sources. Because an Internet source can change or disappear quickly, be sure to record the information for the working-bibliography entry when you first find the source. Whenever possible, download and print out the source to preserve it. Make sure your download or printout includes all the items of information required for the entry or at least all those you can find. Citation forms for Internet sources typically require more information than those for print sources, but the items are often harder (or impossible) to identify because Internet sources do not appear in the kinds of standard formats that print sources do. (See Figure 21.6 for an example of how to organize bibliographic information for an Internet source.)

Citing Internet sources using MLA style is discussed in Chapter 22, pp. 750–63; APA style is discussed on pp. 763–70.

▪ Finding the Best Information Online

Because the World Wide Web does not have a central directory that will point you to specific resources, **search tools** like Google and Yahoo! are important resources for searching the Web for information on your topic. To use these tools effectively, you should understand their features, strengths, and limitations.

As you locate potentially useful Internet sources, record this information (as much as applies) for each site:

Author(s) of work: _____

Title of work: _____

Title of site: _____

Editor(s) of site: _____

Sponsor of site: _____

Publication information for print version of work: _____

Range or total number of pages, paragraphs, screens, or other sections of the work, if numbering

    appears on screen: _____

Name of database and online service: _____

Date of electronic publication or latest update: _____

Date you accessed the source: _____

Electronic addrress (URL): _____

Keyword(s) or sequence of links you used to access the source: _____

_____

Figure 21.6 Information for working bibliography — Internet sources

Most search tools now allow you to look for sources using both search engines and subject directories. **Search engines** are based on keywords. They are simply computer programs that scan the Web — or that part of the Web that is in the particular search engine's database — looking for the keyword(s) you have entered. **Subject directories** are based on categories, like the subject headings in a library catalog or periodical index. Beginning with a menu of general subjects, you click on increasingly narrow subjects (for example, going from Science to Biology to Genetics to DNA Mapping), until you reach either a list of specific Web sites or a point where you have to do a keyword search within the narrowest subject you have chosen. Search engines are useful whenever you have a good idea of the appropriate keywords for your topic or if you are not sure under what category the topic falls. But subject directories can help quickly narrow your search to those parts of the Web that are likely to be most productive and thus avoid keyword searches that produce hundreds or thousands of results.

Always click on the link called Help, Hints, or Tips on a search tool's home page to find out more about the recognized commands and advanced-search techniques for that specific search tool. Most search engines either allow searches using the Boolean operators discussed on pp. 716–19 or incorporate Boolean logic into an advanced-search page. Many also let you limit a search to specific dates, languages, or other criteria.

As with searches of library catalogs and databases, the success of a Web search depends to a great extent on the keywords you choose. Remember that many different words often describe the same topic. If your topic is ecology, for example, you may find information under the keywords *ecosystem, environment, pollution,* and *endangered species,* as well as a number of other related keywords, depending on the focus of your research. When you find a source that seems promising, be sure to create a bookmark for the Web page so that you can return to it easily later on. No matter how precise your keywords are, search engines can be unreliable, and you may not find the best available resources. You might instead begin your search at the Web site of a relevant and respected organization. If you want photos of constellations, go to the NASA Web page. If you want public laws, go to a government Web page like GPO Access. In addition, be sure to supplement your Internet research with other sources from your library, including books, reference works, and articles from appropriate periodicals.

Two other, more recent sources of online information are **blogs** and **RSS**. A blog, or Web log, is a Web site, often based on a particular topic, that is maintained by an individual or organization and updated on a regular basis, often many times a day. Blogs may contain postings written by the sponsor(s) of the site; information such as news articles, press releases, and commentary from other sites; and comments posted by readers. Blogs are usually organized chronologically, with the newest post at the top. Because they are not subjected to the same editorial scrutiny as published books or periodical articles and may reflect just one person's opinions and biases, it's a good idea to find several blogs from multiple perspectives about your subject. Some Web sites, such as Blogwise (www.blogwise.com) and Blogger (www.blogger.com), provide directories and search functions to help you find blogs on a particular topic.

If you are researching a very current topic and need to follow constantly updated news sites and blogs, you can use a program called an **aggregator**, which obtains news automatically from many sources and assembles it through a process called RSS (really simple syndication). Using an aggregator, you can scan the information from a variety of sources by referring to just one Web page and then click on links to the news stories to read further. Many aggregators, such as NetNewsWire, NewsGator, and SharpReader, are available as software that you can download to your computer; others are Web sites you can customize to your own preferences, such as Bloglines (www.bloglines.com) and NewsIsFree (www.newsisfree.com).

■ Using E-mail and Online Communities for Research

You may find it possible to use your computer to do research in ways other than those already discussed in this chapter. In particular, if you can find out the e-mail address of an expert on your topic, you may want to contact the person and ask whether he or she would agree to a brief online (or telephone) interview. In addition, several kinds of electronic communities available on the Internet may possibly be helpful. Many Web sites consist of or incorporate tools known as **bulletin boards** or **message boards**, in which anyone who registers may post messages to and receive them from other members. Older Internet servers known as news servers also provide access to bulletin boards or variants called **newsgroups**. Another kind of community, **mailing lists**, are groups of people who subscribe to receive e-mail messages shared among all the members simultaneously. Finally, **chat rooms** allow users to meet together at the same time in a shared message space, using either a Web-based or generally available chat software application.

These different kinds of online communities often focus on a specific field of shared interest, and the people who frequent them are sometimes working professionals or academics with expertise in topics that are obscure or difficult to research otherwise. Such experts are often willing to answer both basic and advanced questions and will sometimes consent to an e-mail or telephone interview. Even if they are not authorities in the field, online community members may stimulate your thinking about the topic in new directions or save you a large amount of research time by pointing you to a range of other available resources that might otherwise have taken you quite a while to uncover. Many communities provide some kind of indexing or search mechanism so that you can look for "threads" of postings related to your topic, and some also provide daily "digests" of postings.

As with other sources, however, evaluate the credibility and reliability of online communities with a critical eye. Also be aware that while some communities and some members of them welcome guests and newcomers, others may perceive your questions as intrusive or unwanted. What may seem new and exciting to you may be old news for veterans. Finally, remember that some online communities are more active than others; survey the dates of posts and frequency of activity to determine whether a given group is still lively or has gone defunct.

You can probably access a variety of newsgroups related to your topic through your college library; go to www.groups.google.com to find a list. For mailing lists, you have to register for a subscription to the list. Remember that unless a digest option is available, each subscription means you will be receiving a large amount of e-mail, so think about the implications before you sign up.

■ Reading Sources with a Critical Eye

From the beginning of your library and Internet search, you should evaluate potential sources to determine which ones you should take the time to examine more closely and then which of these you should use in your essay. Obviously, you must decide which sources provide information relevant to the topic. But you must also read sources with a critical eye to decide how credible or trustworthy they are. Just because a book or an essay appears in print or online does not necessarily mean that an author's information or opinions are reliable.

Selecting Relevant Sources

Begin your evaluation of sources by narrowing your working bibliography to the most relevant works. Consider them in terms of scope, date of publication, and viewpoint.

Scope and Approach.   To decide how relevant a particular source is to your topic, you need to examine the source in depth. Do not depend on title alone, for it may be misleading. If the source is a book, check its table of contents and index to see how many pages are devoted to the precise subject you are exploring. In most cases, you will want an in-depth, not a superficial, treatment of the subject. Read the preface or introduction to a book or the abstract or opening paragraphs of an article and any biographical information given about the author to determine the author's basic approach to the subject or special way of looking at it. As you attend to these elements, consider the following questions:

- Does the source provide a general or specialized view? General sources are helpful early in your research, but then you need the authority or up-to-date coverage of specialized sources. Extremely specialized works, however, may be too technical.

- Is the source long enough to provide adequate detail?

- Is the source written for general readers? Specialists? Advocates? Critics?

- Is the author an expert on the topic? Does the author's way of looking at the topic support or challenge your own views? (The fact that an author's viewpoint challenges your own does not mean that you should reject the author as a source, as you will see from the discussion on viewpoints.)

- Is the information in the source substantiated elsewhere? Does its approach seem to be comparable to, or a significant challenge to, the approaches of other credible sources?

Date of Publication.   Although you should always consult the most up-to-date sources available on your subject, older sources often establish the principles, theories, and data on which later work is based and may provide a useful perspective for evaluating it. If older works are considered authoritative, you may want to become familiar with them. To determine which sources are authoritative, note the ones that are cited most often in encyclopedia articles, bibliographies, and recent works on the subject. If your source is on the Web, consider whether it has been regularly updated.

Viewpoint.   Your sources should represent multiple viewpoints on the subject. Just as you would not depend on a single author for all of your information, so you do not want to use only authors who belong to the same school of thought. (For suggestions on determining authors' viewpoints, see the following Identifying Bias section.)

Using sources that represent a variety of different viewpoints is especially important when developing an argument for one of the essay assignments in Chapters 6–10. During the invention work in those chapters, you may want to research what others have said about your subject to see what positions have been staked out and what arguments have been made. You will then be able to define the issue more carefully, collect arguments supporting your position, and anticipate arguments opposing it.

Identifying Bias

One of the most important aspects of evaluating a source is identifying any bias in its treatment of the subject. Although the word *bias* may sound accusatory, most writing is not neutral or objective and does not try or claim to be. Authors come to their subjects with particular viewpoints. In using sources, you must consider carefully how these viewpoints are reflected in the writing and how they affect the way authors present their arguments.

Although the text of the source will give you the most precise indication of the author's viewpoint, you can often get a good idea of it by looking at the preface or introduction or at the sources the author cites. When you examine a reference, you can often determine the general point of view it represents by considering the following elements.

Title.   Does the title or subtitle indicate the text's bias? Watch for loaded words or confrontational phrasing.

Author.   What is the author's professional title or affiliation? What is the author's perspective? Is the author in favor of something or at odds with it? What has persuaded the author to take this stance? How might the author's professional affiliation affect his or her perspective? What is the author's tone? Information on the author may be available in the book, article, or Web site itself or in biographical sources available in the library. You could also try entering the author's name into a search engine and see what you learn from the sites it finds.

For more detail on these argumentative strategies, see Chapter 19.

Presentation of Argument.   Almost every written work asserts a point of view or makes an argument for something the author considers important. To determine this position and the reason behind it, look for the main point. What evidence does the author provide as support for this point? Is the evidence from authoritative sources? Is the evidence persuasive? Does the author make concessions to or refute opposing arguments?

Publication Information.   Is the book published by a commercial publisher, a corporation, a government agency, or an interest group? Is the Web site sponsored by a business, a professional group, a private organization, an educational institution, a government agency, or an individual? What is the publisher's or sponsor's position on the topic? Is the author funded by or affiliated with the publisher or sponsor?

Editorial Slant.   What kind of periodical published the article — popular, academic, alternative? If you found the article on a Web site, is the site maintained by a commercial or academic sponsor? Does the article provide links to other Web resources? For periodicals, knowing some background about the publisher can help to determine bias because all periodicals have their own editorial slants. Where the periodical's name does not indicate its bias, reference sources may help you determine this information. Two of the most common are the following:

Gale Directory of Publications and Broadcast Media (1990–, updated yearly): A useful source providing descriptive information on newspapers and magazines. Entries often include an indication of intended audience and political or other bias.

Magazines for Libraries (1997): A listing of over 6,500 periodicals arranged by academic discipline. For each discipline, this book lists basic indexes, abstracts, and periodicals. Each individual listing for a periodical includes its publisher, the date it was founded, the places it is indexed, its intended audience, and an evaluation of its content and editorial focus. Here is an example of one such listing:

> 2605. *Growing Without Schooling.* [ISSN: 0745-5305]
> 1977. bi-m. $25. Susannah Sheffer. Holt Assocs., 2269 Massachusetts Ave., Cambridge, MA 02140. Illus., index, adv. Sample. Circ: 5,000.
> *Bk. rev:* 0–4, 400–600 words, signed. *Aud:* Ga, Sa.
> GWS is a journal by and for home schoolers. Parents and students share their views as to why they chose home schooling and what they like about it. While lesson plans or activities are not included, home schoolers could get ideas for interesting activities from articles chronicling their experiences ("Helping Flood Victims," "Legislative Intern"). "News and Reports" offers home schoolers information on legal issues while the "Declassified Ads" suggest resources geared toward home schoolers. This is an important title for public libraries and should be available to students and faculty in teacher preparation programs.

22

Using and Acknowledging Sources

In addition to your own firsthand observation and analysis, your writing in college will be expected to use and acknowledge secondary sources — readings, interviews, Web sites, computer bulletin boards, lectures, and other print and nonprint materials.

When you cite material from another source, you need to acknowledge the source, usually by citing the author and page or date (depending on the documentation system) in your text and including a list of works cited or references at the end of your paper. It is necessary to acknowledge sources correctly and accurately to avoid *plagiarism*, the undesirable act of using the words and ideas of others as if they were your own. By citing sources correctly, you give credit to the originator of the words and ideas you are using, give your readers the information they need to consult those sources directly, and build your own credibility.

This chapter provides guidelines for using sources effectively and acknowledging them accurately. It includes model citations for both the Modern Language Association (MLA) and American Psychological Association (APA) documentation styles and presents a sample research paper that follows the MLA format.

■ Using Sources

Writers commonly use sources by quoting directly, by paraphrasing, and by summarizing. This section provides guidelines for deciding when to use each of these three methods and how to do so effectively.

Deciding Whether to Quote, Paraphrase, or Summarize

As a general rule, quote only in these situations: (1) when the wording of the source is particularly memorable or vivid or expresses a point so well that you cannot improve it without destroying the meaning, (2) when the words of reliable and respected authorities would lend support to your position, (3) when you wish to highlight the author's opinions, (4) when you wish to cite an author whose opinions challenge or vary greatly from those of other experts, or (5) when you are going to discuss the source's choice of words. Paraphrase passages whose details you wish to note completely but whose language is not particularly striking. Summarize any long passages whose main points you wish to record selectively as background or general support for a point you are making.

Quoting

Quotations should duplicate the source exactly. If the source has an error, copy it and add the notation *sic* (Latin for "thus") in brackets immediately after the error to indicate that it is not your error but your source's:

> According to a recent newspaper article, "Plagirism [sic] is a problem among journalists and scholars as well as students" (Berensen 62).

However, you can change quotations (1) to emphasize particular words by italicizing them, (2) to omit irrelevant information or to make the quotation conform grammatically to your sentence by using ellipsis marks, and (3) to make the quotation conform grammatically or to insert information by using brackets.

Using Italics for Emphasis. You may italicize any words in the quotation that you want to emphasize; add a semicolon and the words *emphasis added* (in regular type, not italicized) to the parenthetical citation.

> In her 2001 exposé of the struggles of the working class, Ehrenreich writes, "The wages Winn-Dixie is offering--*$6 and a couple of dimes to start with*--are not enough, I decide, to compensate for this indignity" (14; emphasis added).

Using Ellipsis Marks for Omissions. A writer may decide to leave certain words out of a quotation because they are not relevant to the point being made or because they add information readers will not need in the context in which the quotation is being used. When you omit words from within a quotation, you must use ellipsis marks — three spaced periods (. . .) — in place of the missing words. When the omission occurs within a sentence, include a space before the first ellipsis mark and after the closing mark. There should also be spaces between the three marks.

> Hermione Roddice is described in Lawrence's *Women in Love* as a "woman of the new school, full of intellectuality and . . . nerve-worn with consciousness" (17).

When the omission falls at the end of a sentence, place a sentence period *directly after* the final word of the sentence, followed by a space and three spaced ellipsis marks.

> But Grimaldi's commentary contends that for Aristotle rhetoric, like dialectic, had "no limited and unique subject matter upon which it must be exercised. . . .

Instead, rhetoric as an art transcends all specific disciplines and may be brought into play in them" (6).

A period plus ellipsis marks can indicate the omission of the rest of the sentence as well as whole sentences, paragraphs, or even pages.

When a parenthetical reference follows the ellipsis marks at the end of a sentence, place the three spaced periods after the quotation, and place the sentence period after the final parenthesis:

> But Grimaldi's commentary contends that for Aristotle rhetoric, like dialectic, had "no limited and unique subject matter upon which it must be exercised. . . . Instead, rhetoric as an art transcends all specific disciplines . . ." (6).

When you quote only single words or phrases, you do not need to use ellipsis marks because it will be obvious that you have left out some of the original.

> More specifically, Wharton's imagery of suffusing brightness transforms Undine before her glass into "some fabled creature whose home was in a beam of light" (21).

For the same reason, you need not use ellipsis marks if you omit the beginning of a quoted sentence unless the rest of the sentence begins with a capitalized word and still appears to be a complete sentence.

Using Brackets for Insertions or Changes.   Use brackets around an insertion or a change needed to make a quotation conform grammatically to your sentence, such as a change in the form of a verb or pronoun or in the capitalization of the first word of the quotation. In this example from an essay on James Joyce's "Araby," reprinted in Chapter 10, the writer adapts Joyce's phrases "we played till our bodies glowed" and "shook music from the buckled harness" to fit the grammar of her sentences:

> In the dark, cold streets during the "short days of winter," the boys must generate their own heat by "play[ing] till [their] bodies glowed." Music is "[shaken] from the buckled harness" as if it were unnatural, and the singers in the market chant nasally of "the troubles in our native land" (30).

You may also use brackets to add or substitute explanatory material in a quotation:

> Guterson notes that among Native Americans in Florida, "education was in the home; learning by doing was reinforced by the myths and legends which repeated the basic value system of their [the Seminoles'] way of life" (159).

Some changes that make a quotation conform grammatically to another sentence may be made without any signal to readers: (1) A period at the end of a quotation may be changed to a comma if you are using the quotation within your own sentence, and (2) double quotation marks enclosing a quotation may be changed to single quotation marks when the quotation is enclosed within a longer quotation.

Integrating Quotations

Depending on its length, a quotation may be incorporated into your text by being enclosed in quotation marks or set off from your text in a block without quotation marks. In either case, be sure to blend the quotation into your essay rather than drop it in without appropriate integration.

In-Text Quotations.   Incorporate brief quotations (no more than four typed lines of prose or three lines of poetry) into your text. You may place the quotation virtually anywhere in your sentence:

At the Beginning

"To live a life is not to cross a field," Sutherland, quoting Pasternak, writes at the beginning of her narrative (11).

In the Middle

Woolf begins and ends by speaking of the need of the woman writer to have "money and a room of her own" (4)--an idea that certainly spoke to Plath's condition.

At the End

In *The Second Sex*, Simone de Beauvoir describes such an experience as one in which the girl "becomes an object, and she sees herself as object" (378).

Divided by Your Own Words

"Science usually prefers the literal to the nonliteral term," Kinneavy writes, "--that is, figures of speech are often out of place in science" (177).

When you quote poetry within your text, use a slash (/) with spaces before and after to signal the end of each line of verse:

Alluding to St. Augustine's distinction between the City of God and the Earthly City, Lowell writes that "much against my will / I left the City of God where it belongs" (4-5).

Block Quotations.   In the MLA style, use the block form for prose quotations of five or more typed lines and poetry quotations of four or more lines. Indent the quotation an inch (ten character spaces) from the left margin, as shown in the following example. In the APA style, use block form for quotations of forty words or more. Indent the block quotation one-half inch (five to seven spaces), keeping your indents consistent throughout your paper.

In a block quotation, double-space between lines just as you do in your text. *Do not* enclose the passage within quotation marks. Use a colon to introduce a block quotation, unless the context calls for another punctuation mark or none at all.

When quoting a single paragraph or part of one in the MLA style, do not indent the first line of the quotation more than the rest. In quoting two or more paragraphs, indent the first line of each paragraph an extra quarter inch (three spaces). If you are using the APA style, the first line of subsequent paragraphs in the block quotation indents an additional half inch or five to seven spaces from the block quotation indent.

> In "A Literary Legacy from Dunbar to Baraka," Margaret Walker says of Paul Lawrence Dunbar's dialect poems:
>
> > He realized that the white world in the United States tolerated his literary genius only because of his "jingles in a broken tongue," and they found the old "darky" tales and speech amusing and within the vein of folklore into which they wished to classify all Negro life. This troubled Dunbar because he realized that white America was denigrating him as a writer and as a man. (70)

Introducing Quotations

Statements that introduce in-text quotations take a range of punctuation marks and lead-in words. Here are some examples of ways writers typically introduce quotations.

Introducing a Quotation Using a Colon

A colon usually follows an independent clause placed before the quotation.

> As George Williams notes, protection of white privilege is critical to patterns of discrimination: "Whenever a number of persons within a society have enjoyed for a considerable period of time certain opportunities for getting wealth, for exercising power and authority, and for successfully claiming prestige and social deference, there is a strong tendency for these people to feel that these benefits are theirs 'by right'" (727).

Introducing a Quotation Using a Comma

A comma usually follows an introduction that incorporates the quotation in its sentence structure.

> Similarly, Duncan Turner asserts, "As matters now stand, it is unwise to talk about communication without some understanding of Burke" (259).

Introducing a Quotation Using that

No punctuation is generally needed with *that*, and no capital letter is used to begin the quotation.

> Noting this failure, Alice Miller asserts that "the reason for her despair was not her suffering but the impossibility of communicating her suffering to another person" (255).

Punctuating within Quotations

Although punctuation within a quotation should reproduce the original, some adaptations may be necessary. Use single quotation marks for quotations within the quotation:

Original from Guterson (16–17)

E. D. Hirsch also recognizes the connection between family and learning, suggesting in his discussion of family background and academic achievement "that the significant part of our children's education has been going on outside rather than inside the schools."

Quoted Version

Guterson claims that E. D. Hirsch "also recognizes the connection between family and learning, suggesting in his discussion of family background and academic achievement 'that the significant part of our children's education has been going on outside rather than inside the schools'" (16-17).

If the quotation ends with a question mark or an exclamation point, retain the original punctuation:

"Did you think I loved you?" Edith later asks Dombey (566).

If a quotation ending with a question mark or an exclamation point concludes your sentence, retain the question mark or exclamation point, and put the parenthetical reference and sentence period outside the quotation marks:

Edith later asks Dombey, "Did you think I loved you?" (566).

Avoiding Grammatical Tangles

When you incorporate quotations into your writing, and especially when you omit words from quotations, you run the risk of creating ungrammatical sentences. Three common errors you should try to avoid are verb incompatibility, ungrammatical omissions, and sentence fragments.

Verb Incompatibility.   When this error occurs, the verb form in the introductory statement is grammatically incompatible with the verb form in the quotation. When your quotation has a verb form that does not fit in with your text, it is usually possible to use just part of the quotation, thus avoiding verb incompatibility.

► The narrator suggests his bitter disappointment when *he describes seeing himself* "~~I saw myself~~

"as a creature driven and derided by vanity" (35).

As this sentence illustrates, use the present tense when you refer to events in a literary work.

Ungrammatical Omission.   Sometimes omitting text from a quotation leaves you with an ungrammatical sentence. Two ways of correcting the grammar are (1) adapting the quotation (with brackets) so that its parts fit together grammatically and (2) using only one part of the quotation.

▶ **From the moment of the boy's arrival in Araby, the bazaar is presented as a**

  commercial enterprise: "I could not find any sixpenny entrance and . . .
  hand[ed]
  ~~handing~~ **a shilling to a weary-looking man" (34).**
  ^

▶ **From the moment of the boy's arrival in Araby, the bazaar is presented as a**

  commercial enterprise: "I *He* **could not find any sixpenny entrance" and . . .**
  ^
  so had to pay a shilling to get in (34).
  ~~handing a shilling to a weary-looking man" (34).~~
  ^

Sentence Fragment.   Sometimes when a quotation is a complete sentence, writers neglect the sentence that introduces the quote — for example, by forgetting to include a verb. Make sure that the quotation is introduced by a complete sentence.

  leads
▶ **The girl's interest in the bazaar ~~leading~~ the narrator to make what amounts**
  ^
  to a sacred oath: "If I go . . . I will bring you something" (32).

Paraphrasing and Summarizing

In addition to quoting sources, writers have the option of paraphrasing or summarizing what others have written.

Paraphrasing.   In a **paraphrase**, the writer restates primarily in his or her own words all the relevant information from a passage, without any additional comments or any suggestion of agreement or disagreement with the source's ideas. A paraphrase is useful for recording details of the passage when the order of the details is important but the source's wording is not. Because all the details of the passage are included, a paraphrase is often about the same length as the original passage. Paraphrasing allows you to avoid quoting too much. Anyway, it is better to paraphrase than to quote ordinary material, where the author's way of expressing things is not worth special attention.

Here is a passage from a book on home schooling and an example of an acceptable paraphrase of it:

Original Source

Bruner and the discovery theorists have also illuminated conditions that apparently pave the way for learning. It is significant that these conditions are unique to each learner, so unique, in fact, that in many cases classrooms can't provide them. Bruner also contends that the more one discovers information in a great variety of circumstances, the more likely one is to develop the inner categories required to organize that information. Yet life at school, which is for the most part generic and predictable, daily keeps many children from the great variety of circumstances they need to learn well.

— David Guterson, *Family Matters: Why Homeschooling Makes Sense*, p. 172

Acceptable Paraphrase

According to Guterson, the "discovery theorists," particularly Bruner, have found that there seem to be certain conditions that help learning to take place. Because each individual requires different conditions, many children are not able to learn in the classroom. According to Bruner, when people can explore information in many different situations, they learn to classify and order what they discover. The general routine of the school day, however, does not provide children with the diverse activities and situations that would allow them to learn these skills (172).

Readers assume that some words in a paraphrase are taken from the source. Indeed, it would be nearly impossible for paraphrasers to avoid using any key terms from the source, and it would be counterproductive to try to do so because the original and paraphrase necessarily share the same information and concepts. Notice, though, that of the total of 86 words in the paraphrase, the paraphraser uses only a name (*Bruner*) and a few other key nouns and verbs (*discovery theorists, conditions, children, learn[ing], information, situations*) for which it would be awkward to substitute other words or phrases. If the paraphraser had wanted to use other kinds of language from the source — for example, the description of life at school as "generic and predictable" — these adjectives should have been enclosed in quotation marks.

In fact, the paraphraser puts quotation marks around only one of the terms from the source: "discovery theorists," a technical term likely to be unfamiliar to readers. The source of all the material in the paraphrase is identified by the author's name (*Guterson*) in the first sentence and by the page number (*172*) in the last sentence, which indicates where the paraphrased material appears in David Guterson's book. This source citation follows the style of the Modern Language Association (MLA). Notice that placing the citation information in this way indicates clearly to readers where the paraphrase begins and ends, so that they understand clearly where the text is expressing ideas taken from a source and where it is expressing the writer's own ideas (or ideas from a different source). Should readers want to check the accuracy or completeness of the paraphrase, they could turn to the alphabetically arranged list of works cited at the end of the essay in which the paraphrase appeared, look for Guterson's name, and find there all the information they would need to locate the book and check the source.

Although it is acceptable and often necessary to reuse a few key words or quote striking or technical language, paraphrasers must avoid borrowing too many words from a source and repeating the sentence structures of a source. Here is a paraphrase of the first sentence in the Guterson passage that repeats too many of the words and phrases in the source, making the paraphrase unacceptable.

Unacceptable Paraphrase: Too Many Borrowed Words and Phrases

Apparently, some conditions, which have been illuminated by Bruner and other discovery theorists, pave the way for people to learn.

If you compare the source's first sentence and the paraphrase of it, you will see that the paraphrase borrows almost all of its key language from the source sentence, including the entire phrase *pave the way for*. Even if you cite the source, this heavy borrowing would be considered plagiarism, using the ideas and words of others as though they were your own.

Here is another paraphrase of the same sentence that too closely resembles the structure of the source sentence, again making the paraphrase unacceptable.

Unacceptable Paraphrase: Sentence Structure Repeated Too Closely

Bruner and other researchers have also identified circumstances that seem to ease the path to learning.

If you compare the source's first sentence and this paraphrase of it, you will see that the paraphraser has borrowed the phrases and clauses of the source and arranged them in an identical sequence, simply substituting synonyms for most of the key terms: *researchers* for *theorists, identified* for *illuminated, circumstances* for *conditions, seem to* for *apparently,* and *ease the path to* for *pave the way for.* This paraphrase would also be considered plagiarism, even though most of the key terms have been changed and even if you cite the source.

Summarizing. Like a paraphrase, a **summary** may rely on key words from the source but is made up mainly of words supplied by the writer. It presents only the main ideas of a source, leaving out examples and details. Consequently, summaries allow you to bring concisely into your writing large amounts of information from source material.

Here is an example of a summary of five pages from the David Guterson book. You can see at a glance how drastically some summaries condense information, in this case from five pages to five sentences. Depending on the summarizer's purpose, the five pages could be summarized in one sentence, the five sentences here, or two or three dozen sentences.

> In looking at different theories of learning that discuss individual-based programs (such as home schooling) versus the public school system, Guterson describes the disagreements among "cognitivist" theorists. One group, the "discovery theorists," believes that individual children learn by creating their own ways of sorting the information they take in from their experiences. Schools should help students develop better ways of organizing new material, not just present them with material that is already categorized, as traditional schools do. "Assimilationist theorists," by contrast, believe that children learn by linking what they don't know to information they already know. These theorists claim that traditional schools help students learn when they present information in ways that allow children to fit the new material into categories they have already developed (171-75).

In this summary, the source of the summarized material is identified by the author's name in the first sentence and the page numbers of the material in the last sentence, following the citation style of the Modern Language Association. As in paraphrases, putting the citation information at the beginning and the end of the summary in this way makes clear to the reader the boundaries between the ideas in the source and the writer's own ideas (or the ideas in a different source).

Though this summarizer puts quotation marks around three technical terms from the original source, summaries usually do not include quotations: Their purpose is not to display the source's language but to present its main ideas. Longer summaries like this one are more than a dry list of main ideas from a source. They are instead a coherent, readable new text composed of the source's main ideas. Summaries provide balanced coverage of a source, following the same sequence of ideas and avoiding any hint of agreement or disagreement with them.

Acknowledging Sources

Notice in the preceding examples of paraphrasing and summarizing that the source is acknowledged by name. Even when you use your own words to present someone else's information, you must acknowledge that you borrowed the information. The only types of information that do not require acknowledgment are common knowledge (John F. Kennedy was assassinated in Dallas), facts widely available in many sources (U.S. presidents used to be inaugurated on March 4 rather than January 20), well-known quotations ("To be or not to be. That is the question"), or material you created or gathered yourself, such as photographs that you took or data from surveys that you conducted. Remember that you need to acknowledge the source of any visual (photograph, table, chart, graph, diagram, drawing, map, screen shot) that you did not create yourself or of any information that you used to create your own visual. (You should also request permission from the source of a visual you want to borrow if your essay is going to be posted on the Web.) When in doubt about whether you need to acknowledge a source for something, it is safer to do so.

The documentation guidelines later in this section present various styles for citing sources. Whichever style you use, the most important thing is that your readers be able to tell where words or ideas that are not your own begin and end. You can accomplish this most readily by taking and transcribing notes carefully, by placing parenthetical source citations correctly, and by separating your words from those of the source with **signal phrases** such as "According to Smith," "Peters claims," and "As Olmos asserts." (When you cite a source for the first time in a signal phrase, you may use the author's full name; after that, use just the last name.)

Avoiding Plagiarism

Writers — students and professionals alike — occasionally fail to acknowledge sources properly. The word **plagiarism**, which derives from the Latin word for "kidnapping," refers to the unacknowledged use of another's words, ideas, or information. Students sometimes get into trouble because they mistakenly assume that plagiarizing occurs only when another writer's exact words are used without acknowledgment. In fact, plagiarism applies to such diverse forms of expression as musical compositions and visual images as well as ideas and statistics. So keep in mind that, with the exceptions listed above, you must indicate the source of any borrowed information or ideas you use in your essay, whether you have paraphrased, summarized, or quoted directly from the source or have reproduced it or referred to it in some other way.

Remember especially the need to document electronic sources fully and accurately. Perhaps because it is so easy to access and distribute text and visuals online and to copy material from one electronic document and paste it into another, many students do not realize or forget that information, ideas, and images from electronic sources require acknowledgment in even more detail than those from print sources do (and are often easier to detect if they are not acknowledged).

Some people plagiarize simply because they do not know the conventions for using and acknowledging sources. This chapter makes clear how to incorporate sources into your writing and how to acknowledge your use of those sources. Others plagiarize because they keep sloppy notes and thus fail to distinguish between their own and their sources' ideas. Either they neglect to enclose their sources' words in quotation marks, or they fail to indicate when they are paraphrasing or summarizing a source's ideas and information. If you keep a working bibliography and careful notes, you will not make this serious mistake.

For more on keeping a working bibliography, see Chapter 21, pp. 705–08.

Another reason some people plagiarize is that they doubt their ability to write the essay by themselves. They feel intimidated by the writing task or the deadline or their own and others' expectations. If you experience this same anxiety about your work, speak to your instructor. Do not run the risk of failing a course or being expelled because of plagiarism. If you are confused about what is and what is not plagiarism, be sure to ask your instructor.

Understanding Documentation Styles

Although there is no universally accepted system for acknowledging sources, most documentation styles use parenthetical in-text citations keyed to a separate list of works cited or references. The information required in the in-text citations and the order and content of the works cited entries vary across academic disciplines. This section presents the basic features of two styles: the author-page system that is advocated by the Modern Language Association (MLA) and widely used in the humanities and the author-year system that is advocated by the American Psychological Association (APA) and widely used in the natural and social sciences.

In Part One of this book, you can find examples of student essays that follow the MLA style (Linh Kieu Ngo, Chapter 4; Jessica Statsky, Chapter 6) and the APA style (Patrick O'Malley, Chapter 7). For more information about these documentation styles, consult the *MLA Handbook for Writers of Research Papers*, Seventh Edition (2009), or the *Publication Manual of the American Psychological Association*, Sixth Edition (2010).

Check with your instructor about which of these styles you should use or whether you should use some other style. A list of common documentation style manuals is provided in Table 22.1.

Table 22.1 Some Commonly Used Documentation Style Manuals

Subject	Style Manual	Online Source
General	*The Chicago Manual of Style*. 15th ed. 2003.	http://www.chicagomanualofstyle.org
	A Manual for Writers of Research Papers, Theses, and Dissertations. 7th ed. 2007.	http://www.turabian.org
Online Sources	*Columbia Guide to Online Style*. 2nd. ed. 2006.	http://cup.columbia.edu/book/978-0-231-13210-7/the-columbia-guide-to-online-style
Biological Sciences	*Scientific Style and Format: The CSE Manual for Authors, Editors, and Publishers*. 7th ed. 2006.	http://www.councilscienceeditors.org/publications/style.cfm
Chemistry	*The ACS Style Guide*. 3rd ed. 2006.	http://www.pubs.acs.org/page/books/styleguide/index.html
Government Documents	*The Complete Guide to Citing Government Documents*. Rev. ed. 1993.	http://exlibris.memphis.edu/resource/unclesam/citeweb.html
Humanities	*MLA Handbook for Writers of Research Papers*. 7th ed. 2009.	http://www.mla.org
	MLA Style Manual and Guide to Scholarly Publishing. 3rd ed. 2008.	
Psychology/Social Sciences	*Publication Manual of the American Psychological Association*. 6th ed. 2010.	http://www.apastyle.apa.org

The MLA System of Documentation

Citations in Text

The MLA author-page system generally requires that in-text citations include the author's last name and the page number of the passage being cited. There is no punctuation between author and page. The parenthetical citation should follow the quoted, paraphrased, or summarized material as closely as possible without disrupting the flow of the sentence.

> Dr. James is described as a "not-too-skeletal Ichabod Crane" (Simon 68).

Note that the parenthetical citation comes before the final period. With block quotations, however, the citation comes after the final period, preceded by a space (see p. 742 for an example).

If you mention the author's name in your text, supply just the page reference in parentheses.

> Simon describes Dr. James as a "not-too-skeletal Ichabod Crane" (68).

A WORK WITH MORE THAN ONE AUTHOR

To cite a source by two or three authors, include all the authors' last names; for works with more than three authors, use all the authors' names or just the first author's name followed by *et al.*, meaning "and others," in regular type (not italicized or underlined).

> Dyal, Corning, and Willows identify several types of students, including the "Authority-Rebel" (4).

> The Authority-Rebel "tends to see himself as superior to other students in the class" (Dyal, Corning, and Willows 4).

> The drug AZT has been shown to reduce the risk of transmission from HIV-positive mothers to their infants by as much as two-thirds (Van de Perre et al. 4-5).

TWO OR MORE WORKS BY THE SAME AUTHOR

Include the author's last name, a comma, a shortened version of the title, and the page number(s).

> When old paint becomes transparent, it sometimes shows the artist's original plans: "a tree will show through a woman's dress" (Hellman, *Pentimento* 1).

A WORK WITH AN UNKNOWN AUTHOR

Use a shortened version of the title, beginning with the word by which the title is alphabetized in the works-cited list. ("Awash in Garbage" was the title in the following example.)

An international pollution treaty still to be ratified would prohibit all plastic garbage from being dumped at sea ("Awash" 26).

TWO OR MORE AUTHORS WITH THE SAME LAST NAME CITED IN YOUR ESSAY

In addition to the last name, include each author's first initial in the citation. If the first initials are also the same, spell out the authors' first names.

Chaplin's *Modern Times* provides a good example of montage used to make an editorial statement (E. Roberts 246).

A CORPORATE OR GOVERNMENT AUTHOR

In a parenthetical citation, give the full name of the author if it is brief or a shortened version if it is long. If you name the author in your text, give the full name even if it is long.

A tuition increase has been proposed for community and technical colleges to offset budget deficits from Initiative 601 (Washington State Board 4).

According to the Washington State Board for Community and Technical Colleges, a tuition increase . . . from Initiative 601 (4).

A MULTIVOLUME WORK

When you use two or more volumes of a multivolume work in your paper, include the volume number and the page number(s), separated by a colon and one space, in each citation.

According to Forster, modernist writers valued experimentation and gradually sought to blur the line between poetry and prose (3: 150).

If you cite only one volume, give the volume number in the works cited (see p. 755) and include only the page number(s) in the parenthetical citation.

A LITERARY WORK

For a novel or other prose work available in various editions, provide the page numbers from the edition used as well as other information that will help readers locate the quotation in a different edition, such as the part or chapter number.

In *Hard Times*, Tom reveals his utter narcissism by blaming Louisa for his own failure: "'You have regularly given me up. You never cared for me'"(Dickens 262; bk. 3, ch. 9).

For a play in verse, such as a Shakespearean play, indicate the act, scene, and line numbers instead of the page numbers.

At the beginning, Regan's fawning rhetoric hides her true attitude toward Lear: "I profess / myself an enemy to all other joys . . . / And find that I am alone felicitate / In your dear highness' love" (*King Lear* 1.1.74-75, 77-78).

For a poem, indicate the line numbers and stanzas or sections (if they are numbered), instead of the page numbers. If the source gives only line numbers, use the term *lines* in the first citation and give only the numbers in subsequent citations.

> In "Song of Myself," Whitman finds poetic details in busy urban settings, as when he describes "the blab of the pave, tires of carts . . . the driver with his interrogating thumb" (8.153-54).

A RELIGIOUS WORK

For the Bible, indicate the book, chapter, and verse instead of the page numbers. Abbreviate books with names of five or more letters in your parenthetical citation, but spell out full names of books in your text.

> She ignored the admonition "Pride goes before destruction, and a haughty spirit before a fall" (*New Oxford Annotated Bible*, Prov. 16.18).

A WORK IN AN ANTHOLOGY

Use the name of the author of the work, not the editor of the anthology, but use the page number(s) from the anthology.

> In "Six Days: Some Rememberings," Grace Paley recalls that when she was in jail for protesting the Vietnam War, her pen and paper were taken away and she felt "a terrible pain in the area of my heart--a nausea" (191).

A QUOTATION FROM A SECONDARY SOURCE

Include the secondary source in your list of works cited. In your parenthetical citation, use the abbreviation *qtd. in* (in regular type, not italicized) to acknowledge that the original was quoted in a secondary source.

> E. M. Forster says "the collapse of all civilization, so realistic for us, sounded in Matthew Arnold's ears like a distant and harmonious cataract" (qtd. in Trilling 11).

AN ENTIRE WORK

Include the reference in the text without any page numbers or parentheses.

> In *The Structure of Scientific Revolutions*, Thomas Kuhn discusses how scientists change their thinking.

A WORK WITHOUT PAGE NUMBERS

If a work has no page numbers or is only one page long, you may omit the page number. If a work uses paragraph numbers instead, use the abbreviation *par.* (or *pars.*, plural) and use a comma after the author's name.

The average speed on Montana's interstate highways, for example, has risen by only 2 miles per hour since the repeal of the federal speed limit, with most drivers topping out at 75 (Schmid).

Whitman considered African American speech "a source of a native grand opera" (Ellison, par. 13).

TWO OR MORE WORKS CITED IN THE SAME PARENTHESES

When two or more different sources are used in the same passage of your essay, it may be necessary to cite them in the same parentheses. Separate the citations with a semicolon. Include any specific pages, or omit pages to refer to the whole work.

A few studies have considered differences between oral and written discourse production (Scardamalia, Bereiter, and Goelman; Gould).

MATERIAL FROM THE INTERNET

Give enough information in the citation to enable readers to locate the Internet source in the list of works cited. If the author is not named, give the document title. Include page, section, paragraph, or screen numbers, if available.

In handling livestock, "many people attempt to restrain animals with sheer force instead of using behavioral principles" (Grandin).

List of Works Cited

Providing full information for the citations in the text, the list of works cited identifies all the sources the writer uses. Entries are alphabetized according to the first author's last name or by the title if the author is unknown. Every source cited in the text must refer to an entry in the list of works cited. Conversely, every entry in the list of works cited must correspond to at least one in-text citation.

In the MLA style, multiple works by the same author (or same group of authors) are alphabetized by title. The author's name is given for the first entry only; in subsequent entries, three hyphens and a period are used.

Kingsolver, Barbara. *High Tide in Tucson: Essays from Now or Never*. New York: HarperCollins, 1995. Print.

---. *Small Wonder*. New York: HarperCollins, 2002. Print.

The information presented in a works-cited entry for a book follows this order: author, title, publication source, year of publication, and medium of publication. The MLA style requires a "hanging indent," which means that the first line of a works-cited entry is not indented but subsequent lines of the entry are. The MLA specifies an indent of half an inch or five character spaces.

Note that, in the list of works cited, publishers' names are given in shortened form. Compound or hyphenated names are usually limited to the first name only (with *Bedford*, for example, used for *Bedford/St. Martin's*) The words *University* and *Press* are shortened to *U* and *P*, respectively.

Books

Here is an example of a basic MLA-style entry for a book:

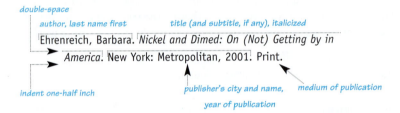

A BOOK BY A SINGLE AUTHOR

Lamb, Sharon. *The Secret Lives of Girls*. New York: Free, 2002. Print.

A BOOK BY AN AGENCY OR A CORPORATION

American Medical Association. *Family Medical Guide*. 4th ed. Hoboken: Wiley, 2004. Print.

A BOOK BY MORE THAN ONE AUTHOR

Saba, Laura, and Julie Gattis. *The McGraw-Hill Homeschooling Companion*. New York: McGraw, 2002. Print.

Wilmut, Ian, Keith Campbell, and Colin Tudge. *The Second Creation: Dolly and the Age of Biological Control*. New York: Farrar, 2000. Print.

A WORK BY MORE THAN THREE AUTHORS

The MLA lists all the authors' names *or* the name of the first author followed by *et al.* (in regular type, not italicized).

Hunt, Lynn, et al. *The Making of the West: Peoples and Cultures*. Boston: Bedford, 2001. Print.

A BOOK BY AN UNKNOWN AUTHOR

Use the title in place of the author.

Rand McNally Commercial Atlas and Marketing Guide. Skokie: Rand, 2003. Print.

A BOOK WITH AN AUTHOR AND AN EDITOR

If you refer to the author's text, begin the entry with the author's name.

Arnold, Matthew. *Culture and Anarchy*. Ed. Samuel Lipman. New Haven: Yale UP, 1994. Print.

If you cite the editor in your paper, begin the entry with the editor's name.

Lipman, Samuel, ed. *Culture and Anarchy*. By Matthew Arnold. 1869. New Haven: Yale UP, 1994. Print.

AN EDITED COLLECTION

Waldman, Diane, and Janet Walker, eds. *Feminism and Documentary*. Minneapolis: U of Minnesota P, 1999. Print.

A WORK IN AN ANTHOLOGY OR A COLLECTION

Lahiri, Jhumpa. "Nobody's Business." *The Best American Short Stories 2002*. Ed. Sue Miller. Boston: Houghton, 2002. 136-72. Print.

TWO OR MORE WORKS FROM THE SAME ANTHOLOGY

To avoid repetition, you may create an entry for the collection and cite the collection's editor to cross-reference individual works to the entry.

Boyd, Herb, ed. *The Harlem Reader*. New York: Three Rivers, 2003. Print.

Wallace, Michelle. "Memories of a Sixties Girlhood: The Harlem I Love." Boyd 243-50.

ONE VOLUME OF A MULTIVOLUME WORK

If only one volume from a multivolume set is used, indicate the volume number after the title.

Freud, Sigmund. *The Standard Edition of the Complete Psychological Works of Sigmund Freud*. Vol. 8. Trans. and ed. James Strachey. New York: Norton, 2000. Print.

TWO OR MORE VOLUMES OF A MULTIVOLUME WORK

Sandburg, Carl. *Abraham Lincoln*. 6 vols. New York: Scribner's, 1939. Print.

A BOOK THAT IS PART OF A SERIES

After the medium of publication, include the series title in regular type (not italicized or in quotation marks), followed by the series number and a period. If the word *Series* is part of the name, include *Ser.* before the number. Common abbreviations may be used for selected words in the series title.

Zigova, Tanya, et al. *Neural Stem Cells: Methods and Protocols*. Totowa: Humana, 2002. Print. Methods in Molecular Biology 198.

A REPUBLISHED BOOK

Provide the original year of publication after the title of the book, followed by publication information for the edition you are using.

Alcott, Louisa May. *An Old-Fashioned Girl*. 1870. New York: Puffin, 1995. Print.

A LATER EDITION OF A BOOK

Rottenberg, Annette T., and Donna Haisty Winchell. *The Structure of Argument*. 6th ed. Boston: Bedford, 2009. Print.

A BOOK WITH A TITLE IN ITS TITLE

Do not italicize a title normally italicized when it appears within the title of a book.

Hertenstein, Mike. *The Double Vision of* Star Trek: *Half-Humans, Evil Twins, and Science Fiction*. Chicago: Cornerstone, 1998. Print.

O'Neill, Terry, ed. *Readings on* To Kill a Mockingbird. San Diego: Greenhaven, 2000. Print.

Use quotation marks around a work normally enclosed in quotation marks when it appears within the title of a book.

Miller, Edwin Haviland. *Walt Whitman's "Song of Myself": A Mosaic of Interpretation*. Iowa City: U of Iowa P, 1989. Print.

A TRANSLATION

If you refer to the work itself, begin the entry with the author's name.

Tolstoy, Leo. *War and Peace*. Trans. Constance Garnett. New York: Modern, 2002. Print.

If you cite the translator in your text, begin the entry with the translator's name.

Garnett, Constance, trans. *War and Peace*. By Leo Tolstoy. 1869. New York: Modern, 2002. Print.

A DICTIONARY ENTRY OR AN ARTICLE IN A REFERENCE BOOK

"Homeopathy." *Webster's New World College Dictionary*. 4th ed. 1999. Print.

Rowland, Lewis P. "Myasthenia Gravis." *The Encyclopedia Americana*. 2001 ed. Print.

AN INTRODUCTION, PREFACE, FOREWORD, OR AFTERWORD

Graff, Gerald, and James Phelan. Preface. *Adventures of Huckleberry Finn*. By Mark Twain. 2nd ed. New York: Bedford, 2004. iii-vii. Print.

Articles

Here is an example of a basic MLA-style entry for an article in a periodical:

author, last name first   article title, in quotation marks

Simon, Robin W. "Revisiting the Relationship among Gender, Marital Status, and Mental
    ►   Health." *American Journal of Sociology*   107.4   (2002):   1065-96.   Print.

double-space;   periodical title, italicized   volume   date, in   page numbers   medium
indent second and   and   parentheses,
subsequent lines   issue   followed by
one-half inch   number   colon

Scholarly journals are typically identified using their volume and issue numbers, separated by a period. If a journal does not use volume numbers, provide the issue number only, following the title of the journal.

Fee, Margery. "Predators and Gardens." *Canadian Literature* 197 (2008): 6-9. Print.

If the article is not on a continuous sequence of pages, give the first page number followed by a plus sign, as in the following example.

AN ARTICLE FROM A DAILY NEWSPAPER

Stoll, John D., et al. "U.S. Squeezes Auto Creditors." *Wall Street Journal* 10 Apr. 2009: A1+.
     Print.

Note that magazines and newspapers are identified not by volume and issue number but by date, with the names of most months abbreviated.

AN ARTICLE FROM A WEEKLY OR BIWEEKLY MAGAZINE

Doig, Will. "America's Real First Family." *Advocate* 17 July 2007: 46-50. Print.

AN ARTICLE FROM A MONTHLY OR BIMONTHLY MAGAZINE

Shelby, Ashley. "Good Going: Alaska's Glacier Crossroads." *Sierra* Sept.-Oct. 2005: 23. Print.

AN EDITORIAL

"Addiction Behind Bars." Editorial. *New York Times* 12 Apr. 2009: A20. Print.

A LETTER TO THE EDITOR

Orent, Wendy, and Alan Zelicoff. Letter. *New Republic* 18 Nov. 2002: 4-5. Print.

A REVIEW

Cassidy, John. "Master of Disaster." Rev. of *Globalization and Its Discontents*, by Joseph
     Stiglitz. *New Yorker* 12 July 2002: 82-86. Print.

If the review does not include an author's name, start the entry with the title of the review and alphabetize by that title. If the review is untitled, begin with the words *Rev. of* and alphabetize under the title of the work being reviewed.

AN UNSIGNED ARTICLE

Begin with the article title, alphabetizing the entry according to the first word after any initial *A, An,* or *The.*

> "A Shot of Reality." *U.S. News & World Report* 1 July 2003: 13. Print.

Electronic Sources

Electronic sources present special problems in documentation for several reasons. Their content frequently changes or disappears without notice; and because it is not organized in the kinds of standard ways that print books and periodicals are, finding the information needed for documentation is often difficult. If you cannot find some of this information, just include what you do find. You may also be able to get answers to some of your questions by going to www.mla.org.

Much of the information required in citations of electronic sources takes the same form as in corresponding kinds of print sources. For example, if you are citing an article from an online periodical, put the article title in quotation marks and italicize the name of the periodical. If the source has been previously or simultaneously published in print, include the print publication information if it is available. You also should include information specific to electronic sources, where it is appropriate and available, including the following:

- The version or edition used
- The publisher or sponsor of the site; if not available, use *N.p.*
- Date of publication; if not available, use *n.d.*
- Medium of publication (*Web*)
- The date you accessed the source

Here is an example of a basic MLA-style entry for the most commonly cited kind of electronic source, a specific document from a Web site:

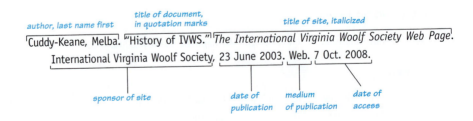

AN ENTIRE WEB SITE

Gardner, James Alan. *A Seminar on Writing Prose*. N.p., 2001. Web. 4 June 2008.

If the author's name is not known, begin the citation with the title.

The International Virginia Woolf Society Web Page. International Virginia Woolf Society,
31 Aug. 2002. Web. 21 Feb. 2008.

For an untitled personal site, put a description such as *Home page* (in regular type,
not italicized), followed by a period, in the position a title would normally be cited.

Chesson, Frederick W. Home page. N.p., 1 Apr. 2003. Web. 26 Apr. 2006.

AN ONLINE SCHOLARLY PROJECT

For a complete project, provide the title, italicized, and the name of the editor, if
given. Then give the electronic publication information — the version number (if
any), the name of the sponsoring organization, and the date of electronic publication or latest update—followed by the medium and date of access.

The Darwin Correspondence Project. Ed. Duncan Porter. Cambridge U Library, 2 June 2003.
Web. 28 Nov. 2008.

A BOOK OR SHORT WORK WITHIN A SCHOLARLY PROJECT

Begin with the author's name and the title (italicized for a book or in quotation
marks for an article, essay, poem, or other short work). Follow with the print publication information, if any, and the information about the project.

Corelli, Marie. *The Treasure of Heaven*. London: Constable, 1906. *Victorian Women Writer's
Project*. Indiana U, 10 July 1999. Web. 10 Sept. 2008.

Heims, Marjorie. "The Strange Case of Sarah Jones." *The Free Expression Policy Project*. FEPP,
24 Jan. 2003. Web. 13 Mar. 2008.

MATERIAL FROM AN ONLINE DATABASE

If you accessed material through an online database, then after the print publication
information, give the name of the database (in italics), the medium, and the date of
access.

Braus, Patricia. "Sex and the Single Spender." American Demographics 15.11 (1993):
28-34. *Academic Search Premier*. Web. 13 Aug. 2008.

A NONPERIODIC PUBLICATION ON A CD-ROM

Picasso: The Man, His Works, the Legend. Danbury: Grolier Interactive, 1996. CD-ROM.

AN ARTICLE FROM AN ONLINE SCHOLARLY JOURNAL

Include the volume number and issue number, if given, after the title of the journal. Also include the number of pages, paragraphs, or other sections, if given, after the date of publication; if none are given, use *n. pag.*

Cesarini, Paul. "Computers, Technology, and Literacies." *The Journal of Literacy and Technology* 4.1 (2004/2005): n. pag. Web. 12 Oct. 2008.

A POSTING TO A DISCUSSION GROUP OR NEWSGROUP

Include the author's name (if you know it), the group name, the sponsor, the title or subject line of the posting (in quotation marks), the posting date, the medium, and the access date.

Willie, Otis. "In the Heat of the Battle." *Soc.history.war.us-revolution*. Google, 27 Sept. 2005. Web. 7 Oct. 2008.

Martin, Francesca Alys. "Wait--Did Somebody Say 'Buffy'?" *Cultstud-l*. U of SFL, 8 Mar. 2000. Web. 8 Mar. 2008.

AN EMAIL MESSAGE

The subject line of the message is enclosed in quotation marks. Identify the persons who sent and received it and the date it was sent. End with the medium (*E-mail*).

Olson, Kate. "Update on State Legislative Grants." Message to the author. 5 Nov. 2008. E-mail.

Note that MLA style hyphenates *E-mail*.

COMPUTER SOFTWARE

How Computers Work. Indianapolis: Que, 1998. CD-ROM.

Other Sources

A LECTURE OR PUBLIC ADDRESS

Birnbaum, Jack. "The Domestication of Computers." Conf. of the Usability Professionals Association. Hyatt Grand Cypress Resort, Orlando. 10 July 2002. Lecture.

A GOVERNMENT DOCUMENT

If the author is known, the author's name may either come first or be placed after the title, introduced with the word *By*.

> United States. Dept. of Health and Human Services. *Trends in Underage Drinking in the United States, 1999-2007*. By Gabriella Newes-Adeyi, et al. Washington: GPO, 2009. Print.

A PAMPHLET

> BoatU.S. Foundation for Boating Safety and Clean Water. *Hypothermia and Cold Water Survival*. Alexandria, VA: BoatU.S. Foundation, 2001. Print.

PUBLISHED PROCEEDINGS OF A CONFERENCE

If the name of the conference is part of the title of the publication, it need not be repeated. Use the format for a work in an anthology (see p. 755) to cite an individual presentation.

> Duffett, John, ed. *Against the Crime of Silence*: Proceedings of the International War Crimes Tribunal. Nov. 1967, Stockholm. New York: Clarion-Simon, 1970. Print.

A PUBLISHED DOCTORAL DISSERTATION

Cite as you would a book, but add pertinent dissertation information before publication data.

> Botts, Roderic C. *Influences in the Teaching of English, 1917-1935: An Illusion of Progress*. Diss. Northeastern U, 1970. Ann Arbor: UMI, 1971. Print.

> Jones, Anna Maria. *Problem Novels/Perverse Readers: Late-Victorian Fiction and the Perilous Pleasures of Identification*. Diss. U of Notre Dame, 2001. Ann Arbor: UMI, 2001. Print.

AN UNPUBLISHED DOCTORAL DISSERTATION

Enclose the title of an unpublished dissertation in quotation marks.

> Bullock, Barbara. "Basic Needs Fulfillment among Less Developed Countries: Social Progress over Two Decades of Growth." Diss. Vanderbilt U, 1986. Print.

A LETTER

Use *MS* ("manuscript") if written by hand, and *TS* ("typescript") if produced using technology.

> Duhamel, Grace. Letter to the author. 22 Mar. 2008. TS.

A MAP OR CHART

Map of Afghanistan and Surrounding Territory. Map. Burlington: GiziMap, 2001. Print.

A CARTOON OR COMIC STRIP

Provide the title (if given) in quotation marks directly following the artist's name.

Cheney, Tom. Cartoon. *New Yorker*. 10 October 2005: 55. Print.

AN ADVERTISEMENT

Hospital for Special Surgery. Advertisement. *New York Times* 13 Apr. 2009: A7. Print.

A WORK OF ART OR MUSICAL COMPOSITION

De Goya, Francisco. *The Sleep of Reason Produces Monsters*. 1799. Etching with watercolor. Norton Simon Museum, Pasadena.

Beethoven, Ludwig van. *Violin Concerto in D Major, Op. 61*. 1809. New York: Edwin F. Kalmus, n.d. Print.

Gershwin, George. *Porgy and Bess*. 1935. New York: Alfred, 1999. Print.

If a photograph is not part of a collection, identify the subject, the name of the person who photographed it, and when it was photographed.

Washington Square Park, New York. Personal photograph by author. 24 June 2006.

A PERFORMANCE

Proof . By David Auburn. Dir. Daniel Sullivan. Perf. Mary-Louise Parker. Walter Kerr Theatre, New York. 9 Sept. 2001. Performance.

A TELEVISION PROGRAM

"Murder of the Century." *American Experience*. Narr. David Ogden Stiers. Writ. and prod. Carl Charlson. PBS. WEDU, Tampa, 14 July 2003. Television.

A FILM OR VIDEO RECORDING

Space Station. Prod. and dir. Toni Myers. Narr. Tom Cruise. IMAX, 2002. Film.

Casablanca. Dir. Michael Curtiz. Perf. Humphrey Bogart, Ingrid Bergman, and Paul Henreid. 1942. Warner Home Video, 2003. DVD.

A MUSIC RECORDING

Begin the entry with the name of the musician, composer, or group. Follow with the title of the recording (in italics unless your citation is for an instrumental piece designated only by form, key, or number); and the performers or conductor (if applicable). End with publication information and medium (such as *LP*, *CD*, or *Audiocassette*).

Beethoven, Ludwig van. Violin Concerto in D Major, Op. 61. U.S.S.R. State Orch. Cond. Alexander Gauk. Perf. David Oistrikh, Allegro, 1980. Audiocassette.

Springsteen, Bruce. "Dancing in the Dark." *Born in the USA*. Columbia, 1984. CD.

AN INTERVIEW

Ashrawi, Hanan. "Tanks vs. Olive Branches." Interview with Rose Marie Berger. *Sojourners Magazine* Feb. 2005: 22-26. Print.

Ellis, Trey. Personal interview. 3 Sept. 2008.

The APA System of Documentation

Citations in Text

AUTHOR INDICATED IN PARENTHESES

The APA author-year system calls for the last name of the author and the year of publication of the original work in the citation. If the cited material is a quotation, you also need to include the page number(s) of the original. If the cited material is not a quotation, the page reference is optional. Use commas to separate author, year, and page in a parenthetical citation. The page number is preceded by *p.* for a single page or *pp.* for a range. Use an ampersand (&) to join the names of multiple authors.

The conditions in the stockyards were so dangerous that workers "fell into the vats; and when they were fished out, there was never enough of them left to be worth exhibiting" (Sinclair, 2005, p. 134).

Racial bias does not necessarily diminish through exposure (Johnson & Tyree, 2001).

If you are citing an electronic source without page numbers, give the paragraph number if it is provided, preceded by the abbreviation *para*. If no paragraph number is given, give the heading of the section and the number of the paragraph within it where the material appears, if possible.

The subjects were tested for their responses to various stimuli, both positive and negative (Simpson, 2002, para. 4).

AUTHOR INDICATED IN SIGNAL PHRASE

If the author's name is mentioned in your text, cite the year in parentheses directly following the author's name, and place the page reference in parentheses before the final sentence period. Use *and* to join the names of multiple authors.

> Sinclair (2005) wrote that workers sometimes "fell into the vats; and when they were fished out, there was never enough of them left to be worth exhibiting" (p. 134).

> As Jamison and Tyree (2001) have found, racial bias does not diminish merely through exposure to individuals of other races (Conclusion section, para. 2).

SOURCE WITH MORE THAN TWO AUTHORS

To cite works with three to five authors, use all the authors' last names the first time the reference occurs and the last name of the first author followed by *et al.* (in regular type, not italicized or underlined) subsequently. If a source has six or more authors, use only the last name of the first author and *et al.* at first and subsequent references.

First Citation in Text

> Rosenzweig, Breedlove, and Watson (2005) wrote that biological psychology is an interdisciplinary field that includes scientists from "quite different backgrounds" (p. 3).

Subsequent Citations

> Biological psychology is "the field that relates behavior to bloody processes, especially the workings of the brain" (Rosenzweig et al., 2005, p. 3).

TWO OR MORE WORKS BY THE SAME AUTHOR

To cite one of two or more works by the same author or group of authors, use the author's last name plus the year (and the page, if you are citing a quotation). When more than one work being cited was published by an author in the same year, the works are alphabetized by title and then assigned lowercase letters after the date (2005a, 2005b).

> Middle-class unemployed workers are better off than their lower-class counterparts, because "the white collar unemployed are likely to have some assets to invest in their job search" (Ehrenreich, 2005b, p. 16).

UNKNOWN AUTHOR

To cite a work listed only by its title, the APA uses a shortened version of the title.

> An international pollution treaty still to be ratified would prohibit all plastic garbage from being dumped at sea ("Awash," 1987).

SECONDARY SOURCE

To quote material taken not from the original source but from a secondary source that quotes the original, give the secondary source in the reference list, and in your essay acknowledge that the original was quoted in a secondary source.

> E. M. Forster said "the collapse of all civilization, so realistic for us, sounded in Matthew Arnold's ears like a distant and harmonious cataract" (as cited in Trilling, 1955, p. 11).

List of References

The APA follows this order in the presentation of information for each source listed: author, publication year, title, and publication source; for an article, the page range is given as well. Titles of books, periodicals, and the like should be italicized, if possible.

When the list of references includes several works by the same author, the APA provides the following rules for arranging these entries in the list:

- Same-name single-author entries precede multiple-author entries:

Zettelmeyer, F. (2000).

Zettelmeyer, F., Morton, F. S., & Silva-Risso, J. (2006).

- Entries with the same first author and a different second author are alphabetized under the first author according to the second author's last name:

Dhar, R., & Nowlis, S. M. (2004).

Dhar, R., & Simonson, I. (2003).

- Entries by the same authors are arranged by year of publication, in chronological order:

Golder, P. N., & Tellis, G. J. (2003).

Golder, P. N., & Tellis, G. J. (2004).

- Entries by the same authors with the same publication year should be arranged alphabetically by title (according to the first word after *A, An,* or *The*), and lowercase letters (*a, b, c,* and so on) are appended to the year in parentheses:

Aaron, P. (1990a). *Basic* . . .

Aaron, P. (1990b). *Elements* . . .

The APA recommends that the first line of each entry be indented one-half inch (or five spaces) in papers intended for publication but notes that student writers may use a hanging indent of five spaces. Ask your instructor which format is preferred. The following examples demonstrate a hanging indent of one-half inch.

Books

A BOOK BY A SINGLE AUTHOR

Ehrenreich, B. (2001). *Nickel and dimed: On (not) getting by in America*. New York, NY:
    Metropolitan.

A BOOK BY AN AGENCY OR A CORPORATION

American Medical Association. (2004). *Family medical guide*. Hoboken, NJ: Wiley.

A BOOK BY MORE THAN ONE AUTHOR

Saba, L., & Gattis, J. (2002). *The McGraw-Hill homeschooling companion*. New York, NY:
    McGraw-Hill.

Hunt, L., Po-Chia Hsia, R., Martin, T. R., Rosenwein, B. H., Rosenwein, H., & Smith, B. G.
    (2001). *The making of the West: Peoples and cultures*. Boston, MA: Bedford/St. Martin's.

If there are more than seven authors, list only the first six, then insert three periods, and
add the last author's name.

A BOOK BY AN UNKNOWN AUTHOR

Use the title in place of the author.

Rand McNally commercial atlas and marketing guide. (2003). Skokie, IL: Rand McNally.

When an author is designated as "Anonymous," identify the work as "Anonymous"
in the text, and alphabetize it as "Anonymous" in the reference list.

A BOOK WITH AN AUTHOR AND AN EDITOR

Arnold, M. (1994). *Culture and anarchy* (S. Lipman, Ed.). New Haven, CT: Yale University
    Press. (Original work published 1869)

AN EDITED COLLECTION

Waldman, D., & Walker, J. (Eds.). (1999). *Feminism and documentary*. Minneapolis, MN:
    University of Minnesota Press.

A WORK IN AN ANTHOLOGY OR A COLLECTION

Fairbairn-Dunlop, P. (1993). Women and agriculture in western Samoa. In J. H. Momsen
    & V. Kinnaird (Eds.), *Different places, different voices* (pp. 211-226). London,
    England: Routledge.

A TRANSLATION

Tolstoy, L. (2002). *War and peace* (C. Garnett, Trans.). New York, NY: Modern Library.
    (Original work published 1869)

AN ARTICLE IN A REFERENCE BOOK

Rowland, R. P. (2001). Myasthenia gravis. In *Encyclopedia Americana* (Vol. 19, p. 683). Danbury, CT: Grolier.

AN INTRODUCTION, PREFACE, FOREWORD, OR AFTERWORD

Graff, G., & Phelan, J. Preface (2004). In M. Twain, *Adventures of Huckleberry Finn* (pp. iii-vii). New York, NY: Bedford/St. Martin's.

Articles

AN ARTICLE FROM A DAILY NEWSPAPER

Peterson, A. (2003, May 20). Finding a cure for old age. *The Wall Street Journal*, pp. D1, D5.

AN ARTICLE FROM A WEEKLY OR BIWEEKLY MAGAZINE

Gross, M. J. (2003, April 29). Family life during war time. *The Advocate*, 42-48.

AN ARTICLE FROM A MONTHLY OR BIMONTHLY MAGAZINE

Shelby, A. (2005, September/October). Good going: Alaska's glacier crossroads. *Sierra, 90*, 23.

AN ARTICLE IN A SCHOLARLY JOURNAL WITH CONTINUOUS ANNUAL PAGINATION

The volume number follows the title of the journal.

Shan, J. Z., Morris, A. G., & Sun, F. (2001). Financial development and economic growth: A chicken and egg problem? *Review of Economics, 9*, 443-454.

AN ARTICLE IN A SCHOLARLY JOURNAL THAT PAGINATES EACH ISSUE SEPARATELY

The issue number appears in parentheses after the volume number.

Tran, D. (2002). Personal income by state, second quarter 2002. *Current Business, 82*(11), 55-73.

AN ANONYMOUS ARTICLE

Communities blowing whistle on street basketball. (2003). *USA Today*, p. 20A.

A REVIEW

Cassidy, J. (2002, July 12). Master of disaster [Review of the book *Globalization and its discontents*]. *The New Yorker*, 82-86.

If the review is untitled, use the bracketed information as the title, retaining the brackets.

Electronic Sources

For more information on using the Internet for research, see Chapter 21, pp. 730–31.

For answers to frequently asked questions on citing Internet sources in the APA style, go to http://www.apastyle.apa.org/elecref/html.

The following guidelines are derived from the *Publication Manual of the American Psychological Association*, Sixth Edition (2010).

For most sources accessed on the Internet, you should provide the following information:

- Name of author (if available)
- Date of publication or most recent update (in parentheses; if unavailable, use the abbreviation *n.d.*)
- Title of document
- Publication information, including volume and issue numbers for periodicals
- Retrieval information necessary to locate the document

A WEB SITE

When you cite an entire Web site, the APA does not require an entry in the list of references. You may instead give the name of the site in your text and its Web address in parentheses. To cite a document that you have accessed through a Web site, follow these formats:

> American Cancer Society. (2003). How to fight teen smoking. Retrieved from http://www.cancer.org/docroot/ped/content/ped_10_14_how_to_fight_teen_smoking.asp

> Heins, M. (2003, January 24). The strange case of Sarah Jones. *The Free Expression Policy Project*. Retrieved from http://www.fepproject.org/commentaries/sarahjones.html

ARTICLE FROM A DATABASE

Follow the guidelines for a comparable print source, but conclude the retrieval statement with the article's DOI (Digital Object Identifier), if any. If there is no DOI, conclude with the URL of the journal home page.

> Houston, R. G., & Toma, F. (2003). Home schooling: An alternative school choice. *Southern Economic Journal, 69*(4), 920-936. Retrieved from http://www.southerneconomic.org

> Tharp, R. G. (1989). Psychocultural variables and constants: Effects on teaching and learning in schools. *American Psychologist, 44*(2), 349-359. doi: 10.1037/0003-006X.44.2.349

AN ARTICLE FROM AN ONLINE PERIODICAL

Include the same information you would for a print document. If the article has a DOI, include it; if not, include the URL for the article or the periodical's home page.

Jauhar, S. (2003, July 15). A malady that mimics depression. *The New York Times*. Retrieved from http://www.nytimes.com

Retrieval information is always required for periodicals that are published only online.

Cesarini, P. (2004/2005). Computers, technology, and literacies. *The Journal of Literacy and Technology, 4*(1). Retrieved from http://www.literacyandtechnology.org/v4 /cesarini.htm

ONLINE POSTINGS

Include online postings in your list of references only if you can provide data that would allow retrieval of the source. Provide the author's name, the date of the posting, the subject line, and any other identifying information. Include the words *Retrieved from* followed by the URL where the message can be found. Include the name of the list, newsgroup, or blog, if this information is not part of the URL.

Paikeday, T. (2005, October 10). "Esquivalience" is out [Electronic mailing list message]. Retrieved from http://listserv.linguistlist.org/cgi-bin/wa?A1=ind0510b&L=ads-1#1

Ditmire, S. (2005, February 10). NJ tea party [Newsgroup message]. Retrieved from http:// groups.google.com/group/TeaParty

AN E-MAIL MESSAGE

In the APA style, it is not necessary to list personal correspondence, including e-mail, in your reference list. Simply cite the person's name in your text, and in parentheses give the notation *personal communication* (in regular type, not underlined or italicized) and the date.

COMPUTER SOFTWARE

If an individual has proprietary rights to the software, cite that person's name as you would for a print text. Otherwise, cite as you would an anonymous print text.

How Computers Work [Software]. (1998). Available from Que: http://www.how computerswork.net

Other Sources

A GOVERNMENT DOCUMENT

U.S. Department of Health and Human Services. (2009). *Trends in underage drinking in the United States, 1991-2007*. Washington, DC: GPO.

AN UNPUBLISHED DOCTORAL DISSERATION

Bullock, B. (1986). *Basic needs fulfillment among less developed countries: Social progress over two decades of growth* (Unpublished doctoral dissertation). Vanderbilt University, Nashville, TN.

A TELEVISION PROGRAM

Charlsen, C. (Writer and producer). (2003, July 14). Murder of the century [Television series episode]. In M. Samels (Executive producer), *American Experience*. Boston, MA: WGBH.

A FILM OR VIDEO RECORDING

Myers, T. (Writer and producer). (2002). *Space station* [Film]. New York, NY: IMAX.

A MUSIC RECORDING

If the recording date differs from the copyright date, the APA requires that it should appear in parentheses after the name of the label. If it is necessary to include a number for the recording, use parentheses for the medium; otherwise, use brackets.

Beethoven, L. van. (1806). Violin concerto in D major, op. 61 [Recorded by USSR State Orchestra]. (Cassette Recording No. ACS 8044). New York, NY: Allegro. (1980)

Springsteen, B. (1984). Dancing in the dark. On *Born in the U.S.A.* [CD]. New York, NY: Columbia.

AN INTERVIEW

When using the APA style, do not list personal interviews in your references list. Simply cite the person's name (last name and initials) in your text, and in parentheses give the notation *personal communication* (in regular type, not italicized or underlined) followed by a comma and the date of the interview. For published interviews, use the appropriate format for an article.

■ Some Sample Research Papers

As a writer, you will want or need to use sources on many occasions. You may be assigned to write a research paper, complete with formal documentation of outside sources. Several of the writing assignments in this book present opportunities to do library or field research — in other words, to turn to outside sources. Among the readings in Part One, the essays listed here cite and document sources. (The documentation style each follows is given in parentheses.)

An Annotated Research Paper

On the following pages is a student research paper speculating about the causes of a trend—the increase in homeschooling. The author cites statistics, quotes authorities, and paraphrases and summarizes background information and support for her argument. She uses the MLA documentation style.

1/2"
Dinh 1

1"

Double-spaced

Cristina Dinh

Professor Cooper

1"   English 100

15 May. 2009

Double-spaced
Title centered; no
underlining, quotes,
or italics

Educating Kids at Home

Every morning, Mary Jane, who is nine, doesn't have to worry about   1"
gulping down her cereal so she can be on time for school. School for
Mary Jane is literally right at her doorstep.

Paragraphs indented
one-half inch

In this era of serious concern about the quality of public education,
increasing numbers of parents across the United States are choosing to educate their children at home. These parents believe they can do a better job
teaching their children than their local schools can. *Homeschooling*, as this
practice is known, has become a national trend over the past thirty years,

Author named in text;
no parenthetical page
reference because source
not paginated

and, according to education specialist Brian D. Ray, the homeschooled population is growing at a rate between 5 and 12 percent per year. A 2008 report by the U.S. Department of Education's Institute of Education Sciences

Abbreviated title used in
parenthetical citation
because works cited lists
two sources by government
author (named in text); no
punctuation between title
and page number

estimated that, nationwide, the number of homeschooled children rose from
850,000 in 1999 to approximately 1.5 million in 2007 (*1.5 Million* 1).
Some home-schooling advocates believe that even these numbers may be
low because not all states require formal notification when parents decide
to teach their children at home.

Author named in text;
parenthical page
reference falls at end
of sentence

What is home schooling, and who are the parents choosing to be
homeschoolers? David Guterson, a pioneer in the homeschooling movement,
defines home schooling as "the attempt to gain an education outside of institutions" (5). Homeschooled children spend the majority of the conventional school day learning in or near their homes rather than in traditional
schools; parents or guardians are the prime educators. Former teacher and
homeschooler Rebecca Rupp notes that homeschooling parents vary considerably in what they teach and how they teach, ranging from those who follow a highly traditional curriculum within a structure that parallels the
typical classroom to those who essentially allow their children to pursue

1"

Dinh 2

whatever interests them at their own pace (3). Homeschoolers commonly combine formal instruction with life skills instruction, learning
fractions, for example, in terms of monetary units or cooking measurements (Saba and Gattis 89). According to the U.S. Department of
Education's 2008 report, while homeschoolers are also a diverse group
politically and philosophically--libertarians, conservatives, Christian fun-
damentalists--most say they homeschool for one of three reasons:
they are concerned about the quality of academic instruction, the
general school environment, or the lack of religious or moral instruction
(*1.5 Million* 2).

    The first group generally believes that children need individual atten-
tion and the opportunity to learn at their own pace to learn well. This
group says that one teacher in a classroom of twenty to thirty children
(the size of typical public-school classes) cannot give this kind of attention.
These parents believe they can give their children greater enrichment and
more specialized instruction than public schools can provide. At home, parents can work one-on-one with each child and be flexible about time, allowing their children to pursue their interests at earlier ages. Many of these
parents, like homeschooler Peter Bergson, believe that

> home schooling provides more of an opportunity to continue
> the natural learning process that's in evidence in all children.
> [In school,] you change the learning process from self-directed
> to other-directed, from the child asking questions to the
> teacher asking questions. You shut down areas of potential
> interest. (qtd. in Kohn 22)

    This trend can be traced back to the 1960s, when many people
began criticizing traditional schools. Various types of "alternative
schools" were created, and some parents began teaching their children at
home (Friedlander 20). Parents like this mention several reasons for their
disappointment with public schools and for their decision to home
school. A lack of funding, for example, leaves children without new textbooks. In a 2002 survey, 31 percent of teachers said that their students
are using textbooks that are more than ten years old, and 29 percent said

Work by two authors cited

*Quotation of more than
four lines typed as a block
and indented ten spaces*
*Brackets indicate addition
to quotation*

*Parenthetical citation of
secondary source falls after
period*

Dinh 3

Corporate author's name ————— that they do not have enough textbooks for all of their students (National Education Association). Many schools also cannot afford to buy laboratory equipment and other teaching materials. At my own high school, the chemistry teacher told me that most of the lab equipment we used came from a research firm he worked for. In a 2006 Gallup poll, lack of proper financial support ranked first on the list of the problems in public schools (Rose and Gallup).

Parents also cite overcrowding as a reason for taking their kids out of school. The more students in a classroom, the less learning that goes on, as Cafi Cohen discovered before choosing to homeschool; after spending several days observing what went on in her child's classroom, she found that administrative duties, including disciplining, took up to 80 percent of a teacher's time with only 20 percent of the day devoted to learning (6). Moreover, faced with a large group of children, a teacher ends up gearing lessons to the students in the middle level, so children at both ends miss out. Gifted children and those with learning disabilities particularly suffer in this situation. At home, parents of these children say they can tailor the material and the pace for each child. Studies show that homeschooling methods seem to work well in preparing children academically. Lawrence Rudner, director of the ERIC Clearinghouse on Assessment and Evaluation at the University of Maryland and a researcher on homeschooling, found that testing of homeschooled students showed them to be between one and three years ahead of public school students their age (xi). Homeschooled children have also made particularly strong showings in academic competitions; since the late 1990s, 10 percent of National Spelling Bee participants have been homeschooled, as have two National Spelling Bee and two National Geographic Bee winners (Lyman). More and more selective colleges are admitting, and even recruiting, homeschooled applicants (Basham, Merrifield, and Hepburn 15).

Parents in the second group--those concerned with the general school environment--claim that their children are more well-rounded than those in school. Because they don't have to sit in classrooms all day, homeschooled

Dinh 4

kids can pursue their own projects, often combining crafts or technical skills with academic subjects. Homeschoolers participate in outside activities such as 4-H competitions, field trips with peers in homeschool support groups, science fairs, musical and dramatic productions, church activities, and Boy Scouts or Girl Scouts (Saba and Gattis 59-62). In fact, they may even be able to participate to some extent in actual school activities. A 1999 survey conducted by the U.S. Department of Education's Institute of Education Sciences found that 28 percent of public schools allowed homeschooled students to participate in extracurricular activities alongside enrolled students, and 20 percent allowed homeschooled students to attend some classes (Blumenfeld 12).

Many homeschooling parents believe that these activities provide the social opportunities kids need without exposing their children to the peer pressure they would have to deal with as regular school students. For example, many kids think that drinking and using drugs are cool. When I was in high school, my friends would tell me a few drinks wouldn't hurt or affect driving. If I had listened to them, I wouldn't be alive today. Four of my friends were killed under the influence of alcohol. Between 1992 and 2008, the number of high school seniors surveyed who had used any illicit drug in the last year climbed from 27.1 percent to 36.6 percent (Johnston, et al. 59).

Work by more than three authors cited

Another reason many parents decide to homeschool their kids is that they are concerned for their children's safety. Samuel L. Blumenfeld notes that "physical risk" is an important reason many parents remove their children from public schools as "[m]ore and more children are assaulted, robbed, and murdered in school" and a "culture of violence, abetted by rap music, drug trafficking, . . . and racial tension, has engulfed teenagers" (4). Beginning in the mid-1990s, a string of school shootings--including the 1999 massacres in Littleton, Colorado, and Conyers, Georgia, and the 2001 massacre in Santee, California--has led to increasing fears that young people are simply not safe at school.

Dinh 5

While all of the reasons mentioned so far are important, perhaps the single most significant cause of the growing homeschooling trend is Christian fundamentalist dissatisfaction with "godless" public schools.

Sociologist Mitchell L. Stevens, author of one of the first comprehensive studies of homeschooling, cites a mailing sent out by Basic Christian Education, a company that markets homeschooling materials, titled "What Really Happens in Public Schools." This publication sums up the fears of fundamentalist homeschoolers about public schools: that they encourage high levels of teenage sexual activity and pregnancies "out of wedlock"; expose children to "violence, crime, lack of discipline, and, of course, drugs of every kind"; present positive portrayals of communism and socialism and negative portrayals of capitalism; and undermine children's Christian beliefs by promoting "New Age philosophies, yoga, Transcendental Meditation, witchcraft demonstrations, and Eastern religions" (51).

As early as 1988, Luanne Shackelford and Susan White, two Christian homeschooling mothers, were claiming that because schools expose children to "[p]eer pressure, perverts, secular textbooks, values clarification, TV, pornography, rock music, bad movies . . . [h]ome schooling seems to be the best plan to achieve our goal [to raise good Christians]" (160).

As another mother more recently put it:

> I don't like the way schools are going. . . . What's wrong with Christianity all of a sudden? You know? This country was founded on Christian, on religious principles. [People] came over here for religious freedom, and now all of a sudden all religious references seem to be stricken out of the public school, and I don't like that at all. (qtd. in Stevens 67)

Although many nonfundamentalist homeschoolers make some of these same criticisms, those who cite the lack of "Christian values" in public schools have particular concerns of their own. For example, homeschooling leader Raymond Moore talks of parents who are "'sick and tired of the teaching of evolution in the schools as a cut-and-dried fact,' along with other evidence of so-called secular humanism" (Kohn 21), such as

---

Brackets used to indicate changes in capitalization and addition to quotation for clarification

Ellipsis marks used to indicate words left out of quotations

Quotation cited in a secondary source

Single quotation marks indicate a quotation within a quotation

Citation placed close to quotation, before comma but after quotation marks

Dinh 6

textbooks that contain material contradicting Christian beliefs. Moreover, parents worry that schools undermine their children's moral values. In particular, some Christian fundamentalist parents object to sex education in schools, saying that it encourages children to become sexually active early, challenging values taught at home. They see the family as the core and believe that the best place to instill family values is within the family. These Christian homeschooling parents want to provide their children not only with academic knowledge but also with a moral grounding consistent with their religious beliefs.

Still other homeschooling parents object to a perceived government-mandated value system that they believe attempts to override the values, not necessarily religious in nature, of individual families. For these parents, homeschooling is a way of resisting what they see as unwarranted intrusion by the federal government into personal concerns (*Alliance*).

Armed with their convictions, parents such as those who belong to the Christian Home School Legal Defense Association have fought in court and lobbied for legislation that allows them the option of homeschooling. In the 1970s, most states had compulsory attendance laws that made it difficult, if not illegal, to keep school-age children home from school. Today, homeschooling is permitted in every state, with strict regulation required by only a few (Home School). As a result, Mary Jane is one of hundreds of thousands of American children who can start her school day without leaving the house.

Internet source cited by shortened form of title; author's name and page numbers unavailable

Shortened form of corporate author's name cited

Works cited begin on a new page, one inch from top margin

*Title centered
Double-spaced*

Entries in alphabetical order by authors' last names

Entry begins flush with left margin; subsequent lines indent one-half inch

Period after author, title, publication, medium and date of access

1"   Dinh 7

Works Cited

Alliance for the Separation of School and State. Home page. Alliance for the
    Separation of School and State, 26 Feb. 2009. Web. 10 Apr. 2009.

Basham, Patrick, John Merrifield, and Claudia R. Hepburn. *Home Schooling: From
    the Extreme to the Mainstream.* 2nd ed. Vancouver: The Fraser Institute,
    2007. Studies in Education Policy. *Fraser Institute.* Web. 13 Apr. 2009.

Blumenfeld, Samuel L. *Homeschooling: A Parent's Guide to Teaching
    Children.* Bridgewater: Replica, 1999. Print.

Cohen, Cafi. *And What about College?: How Homeschooling Leads to Admissions to
    the Best Colleges and Universities.* Cambridge: Holt, 1997. Print.

Friedlander, Tom. "A Decade of Home Schooling." *The Homeschool Reader.* Ed.
    Mark Hegener and Helen Hegener. Tonasket: Home Education, 1988. Print.

Guterson, David. *Family Matters: Why Homeschooling Makes Sense.* San Diego:
    Harcourt, 1992. Print.

Home School Legal Defense Association. "State Action Map." *HSLDA: Advocates
    for Homeschooling.* HSLDA, 2009. Web. 5 Apr. 2009.

Johnston, Lloyd D., et al. *Monitoring the Future: National Results on Adolescent
    Drug Use, Overview of Key Findings, 2008.* Bethesda: National Institute on
    Drug Abuse, 2009. Web. 20 Apr. 2009.

Kohn, Alfie. "Home Schooling." *Atlantic Monthly* Apr. 1988: 20-25. Print.

Lyman, Isabel. "Generation Two." *American Enterprise* Oct./Nov. 2002:
    48-49. *InfoTrac OneFile.* Web. 10 May 2009.

National Education Association. *2002 Instructional Materials Survey.* Sept.
    2002. Association of American Publishers. 2002. Web. 21 Apr. 2009.

Ray, Brian D. "Research Facts on Homeschooling." *National Home Education
    Research Institute.* NHERI, 2008. Web. 10 Apr. 2009.

Rose, Lowell C., and Alec M. Gallup. "The 38th Annual PDK/Gallup Poll of the
    Public's Attitudes Toward the Public Schools." *Phi Delta Kappan* 88.1
    (2006): n. pag. *Phi Delta Kappa International.* Web. 1 May 2009.

Rudner, Lawrence. Foreword. *The McGraw-Hill Homeschooling Companion.* By
    Laura Saba and Julie Gattis. New York: McGraw, 2002. Print.

Dinh 8

Rupp, Rebecca. *The Complete Home Learning Source Book*. New York: Three Rivers, 1998. Print.

Saba, Laura, and Julie Gattis. *The McGraw-Hill Homeschooling Companion*. New York: McGraw, 2002. Print.

Shackelford, Luanne, and Susan White. *A Survivor's Guide to Home Schooling*. Westchester: Crossway, 1988. Print.

Stevens, Mitchell L. *Kingdom of Children: Culture and Controversy in the Homeschooling Movement*. Princeton: Princeton UP, 2001. Print.

United States. Dept. of Education. Institute of Education Sciences. *Homeschooling in the United States: 1999*. Washington: GPO, 2001. *National Center for Education Statistics*. Web. 23 Apr. 2009.

---. ---. ---. *1.5 Million Homeschooled Students in the United States in 2007*. Washington: GPO, 2008. *National Center for Education Statistics*. Web. 23 Apr. 2009.

Part Five

Writing for Assessment

23

Essay Examinations

Essay exams are inescapable. Even though the machine-scorable multiple-choice test has sharply reduced the number of essay exams administered in schools and colleges, essay exams will continue to play a significant role in the education of liberal arts students. Many instructors — especially in the humanities and social sciences — still believe that an exam that requires you to write is the best way to find out what you have learned and, more important, help you consolidate and reinforce your learning. Instructors who give essay exams want to be sure you can sort through the large body of information covered in a course, identify what is important or significant, and explain your decision. They want to see whether you understand the concepts that provide the basis for a course and whether you can use those concepts to interpret specific materials, to make connections on your own, to see relationships, to draw comparisons and find contrasts, and to synthesize diverse information in support of an original assertion. They may even be interested in your ability to justify your own evaluations based on appropriate standards of judgment and to argue your own opinions with convincing reasons and supporting evidence. Remember that your instructors want to encourage you to think more critically and analytically about a subject; they feel, therefore, that a written exam provides the best demonstration that you are doing so.

As a college student, then, you will face a variety of essay exams, from short-answer identifications that require only a few sentences to take-home exams that may involve hours of planning and writing. You will find that the writing activities and strategies discussed in Parts One and Three of this book — particularly narrating, describing, defining, comparing and contrasting, classifying, and arguing — as well as the critical thinking strategies in Part Two will help you to do well on these exams. This chapter provides some more specific guidelines for you to follow in preparing for and writing essay exams and analyzes a group of typical exam questions to help determine which strategies will be most useful.

But you can also learn a great deal from your experiences with essay exams in the past — the embarrassment and frustration of doing poorly on one and the great pleasure and pride of doing well. Do you recall the best exam you ever wrote? Do you remember how you wrote it and why you were able to do so well? How can you be certain to approach such writing tasks confidently and to complete them successfully? Keep these questions in mind as you consider the following guidelines.

■ Preparing for an Exam

First of all, essay exams require a comprehensive understanding of large amounts of information. Because exam questions can reach widely into the course materials — and in such unpredictable ways — the best way to ensure that you will do well on them is to keep up with readings and assignments from the very start of the course. Do the reading, go to lectures, take careful notes, participate in discussion sessions, and organize small study groups with classmates to explore and review course materials throughout the semester. Trying to cram weeks of information into a single night of study will never allow you to do your best.

Then, as an exam approaches, find out what you can about the form it will take. No question is more irritating to instructors than the pestering inquiry "Do we need to know this for the exam?" but it is generally legitimate to ask whether the questions will require short or long answers, how many questions there will be, whether you may choose which questions to answer, and what kinds of thinking and writing will be required of you. Some instructors may hand out study guides for exams or even lists of potential questions. However, you will often be on your own in determining how best to go about studying.

Try to avoid simply memorizing information aimlessly. As you study, you should be clarifying the important issues of the course and using these issues to focus your understanding of specific facts and particular readings. If the course is a historical survey, distinguish the primary periods, and try to see relations among the periods and the works or events that define them. If the course is thematically unified, determine how the particular materials you have been reading relate to those themes. If the course is a broad introduction to a general topic, concentrate on the central concerns of each study unit, and see what connections you can discover among the various units. Try to place all you have learned into perspective, into a meaningful context. How do the pieces fit together? What fundamental ideas have the readings, the lectures, and the discussions seemed to emphasize? How can those ideas help you digest the information the course has covered?

One good way to prepare yourself for an exam is by making up questions you think the instructor might ask and then planning answers to them with classmates. Returning to your notes and to assigned readings with specific questions in mind can help enormously in your process of understanding. The important thing to remember is that an essay exam tests more than your memory of specific information; it requires you to use specific information to demonstrate a comprehensive grasp of the topics covered in the course.

■ Reading the Exam Carefully

Before you answer a single question, read the entire exam so that you can apportion your time realistically. Pay particular attention to how many points you may earn in different parts of the exam; notice any directions that suggest how long an answer should be or how much space it should take up. As you are doing so, you may wish to make tentative choices of the questions you will answer and decide on the order in which you will answer them. If you have immediate ideas about how you would organize any of your answers, you might also jot down partial scratch outlines. But before you start to complete any answers, write down the actual clock time you expect to be working on each question or set of questions. Careful time management is crucial to your success on essay exams; giving some time to each question is always better than using up your time on only a few and never getting to others.

You will next need to analyze each question carefully before beginning to write your answer. Decide what you are being asked to do. Following your immediate impulse to cast about for ideas indiscriminately at this point might cause you to become flustered, to lose concentration, or even to go blank. But if you first look closely at what the question is directing you to do and try to understand the sort of writing that will be required, you can begin to recognize the structure your answer will need to take. This tentative structure will help you focus your attention on the particular information that will be pertinent to your answer. Consider this question from a sociology final:

> Drawing from lectures and discussions on the contradictory aspects of American values, the "bureaucratic personality," and the behaviors associated with social mobility, discuss the problems of attaining economic success in a relatively "open," complex, post-industrial society such as the United States.

Such a question can cause momentary panic, but you can nearly always define the writing task you face. Look first at the words that give you directions: *draw from* and *discuss*. The term *discuss* probably invites you to list and explain the problems of attaining economic success. The categories of these problems are already identified in the opening phrases: "contradictory . . . values," "bureaucratic personality," and "behaviors." Therefore, you would plan to begin with an assertion (or thesis) that included the key words in the final clause ("attaining economic success in a relatively open, complex, post-industrial society") and then take up each category of problem — and perhaps other problems you can think of — in separate paragraphs.

This question essentially calls for organization, recall, and clear presentation of facts from lectures and readings. Though the question looks confusing at first, once you sort it out, you will find that it contains the key terms for the answer's thesis, as well as the main points of development. The next section presents some further examples of the kinds of questions often found on essay exams. Pay particular attention to how the directions and the key words in each case can help you define the writing task involved.

■ Some Typical Essay Exam Questions

Following are nine categories of exam questions, divided according to the sort of writing task involved and illustrated by examples. Although the wording of the examples in a category may differ, the essential directions are similar.

All of the examples are unedited and were written by instructors in six different departments in the humanities and social sciences at two different universities. Drawn from short quizzes, midterms, and final exams for a variety of first- and second-year courses, these questions demonstrate the range of writing you may be expected to do on exams.

Define or Identify

Some questions require you to write a few sentences defining or identifying material from readings or lectures. Such questions almost always allow you only a few minutes to complete your answer.

See Chapter 16 for more on defining.

You may be asked for a brief overview of a large topic, as in Question 23.1. This question, from a twenty-minute quiz in a literature course, was worth as much as 15 of the 100 points possible on the quiz.

Question 23.1

Name and describe the three stages of African literature.

Answering this question would simply involve following the specific directions. A student would probably *name* the periods in historical order and then *describe* each period in a separate sentence or two.

Other questions, like Question 23.2, supply a list of specific items to identify. This example comes from a final exam in a communication course, and the answer to each part was worth as much as 4 points on a 120-point exam.

Question 23.2

Define and state some important facts concerning each of the following:

A. demographics

B. instrumental model

C. RCA

D. telephone booth of the air

E. penny press

With no more than three or four minutes for each part, students taking this exam would offer a concise definition (probably in a sentence) and briefly expand the definition with facts relevant to the main topics in the course.

Sometimes the list of items to be identified can be complicated, including quotations, concepts, and specialized terms; it may also be worth a significant number of points. The next example contains the first five items in a list of fifteen that opened a literature final. Each item was worth 3 points, for a total of 45 out of a possible 130 points.

Question 23.3

Identify each of the following items:

1. projection
2. "In this vast landscape he had loved so much, he was alone."
3. Balducci
4. *pied noir*
5. the Massif Central

Although the directions do not say so specifically, a crucial aspect of this question is not just to identify each item but also to explain its significance in terms of the overall subject. In composing a definition or an identification, always ask yourself a simple question: Why is this item important enough to be on the exam?

Recall Details of a Specific Source

For more on paraphrasing and summarizing, see Chapter 12, pp. 595–98.

Sometimes instructors will ask for a straightforward summary or paraphrase of a specific source — for example, a report on a book or a film. To answer such questions, the student must recount details directly from the source and is not encouraged to interpret or evaluate. In the following example from a sociology exam, students were allowed about ten minutes and required to complete the answer on one lined page provided with the exam.

Question 23.4

In his article "Is There a Culture of Poverty?" Oscar Lewis addresses a popular question in the social sciences: What is the "culture of poverty"? How is it able to come into being, according to Lewis? That is, under what conditions does it exist? When does he say a person is no longer a part of the culture of poverty? What does Lewis say is the future of the culture of poverty?

The phrasing here invites a fairly clear-cut structure. Each of the five specific questions can be turned into an assertion and supported with illustrations from Lewis's article. For example, the first two questions could become assertions like these: "Lewis defines the culture of poverty as _____," and "According to Lewis, the culture of poverty comes into being through _____." The important thing in this case is to summarize accurately what the writer said and not waste time evaluating or criticizing his ideas.

Explain the Importance or Significance

Another kind of essay exam question asks students to explain the importance of something covered in the course. Such questions require specific examples as the basis for a more general discussion of what has been studied. This type of question often involves interpreting a literary or cinematic work by concentrating on a particular aspect of it, as in Question 23.5. This question was worth 10 out of 100 points and was to be answered in seventy-five to one hundred words.

Question 23.5

In the last scene of *The Paths of Glory*, the owner of a café brings a young German woman onto a small stage in his café to sing for the French troops, while Colonel Dax looks on from outside the café. Briefly explain the significance of this scene in relation to the movie as a whole.

In answering this question, a student's first task would be to reconsider the whole movie, looking for ways in which this one brief scene illuminates or explains larger issues or themes. Then, in a paragraph or two, the student would summarize these themes and point out how each element of the specific scene fits into the overall context.

You may also be asked to interpret specific information to show that you understand the fundamental concepts of a course. The following example from a communication midterm was worth a possible 10 of 100 points and was allotted twenty minutes of exam time.

Question 23.6

Chukovsky gives many examples of cute expressions and statements uttered by small children. Give an example or two of the kinds of statements that he finds interesting. Then state their implications for understanding the nature of language in particular and communication more generally.

Here the student must start by choosing examples of children's utterances from Chukovsky's book. These examples would then provide the basis for demonstrating the student's grasp of the larger subject.

Questions like these are usually more challenging than definition and summary questions because you must decide for yourself the significance, importance, or implications of the information. You must also consider how best to organize your answer so that the general ideas you need to communicate are clearly developed.

Apply Concepts

Very often, courses in the humanities and the social sciences emphasize significant themes, ideologies, or concepts. A type of common essay exam question asks students to apply the concepts to works studied in the course. Rather than providing specific information to be interpreted more generally, such questions present you with a general idea and require you to illustrate it with specific examples from your reading.

See Chapter 4 for more on explaining a concept.

On a literature final, an instructor posed this writing task. It was worth 50 points out of 100, and students had about an hour to complete it.

Question 23.7

Many American writers have portrayed their characters or their poetic speaker as being engaged in a quest. The quest may be explicit or implicit, it may be external or psychological, and it may end in failure or success. Analyze the quest motif in the work of four of the following writers: Edwards, Franklin, Hawthorne, Thoreau, Douglass, Whitman, Dickinson, James, Twain.

On another literature final, the following question was worth 45 of 130 points. Students had about forty-five minutes to answer it.

Question 23.8

Several works studied in this course depict scapegoat figures. Select two written works and two films, and discuss how their authors or directors present and analyze the social conflicts that lead to the creation of scapegoats.

Question 23.7 instructs students to *analyze*, and Question 23.8 instructs them to *discuss*; yet the answers for both questions would be structured similarly. An introductory paragraph would define the concept — the *quest* or a *scapegoat* — and refer to the works to be discussed. Then a paragraph or two would be devoted to the works, developing specific support to illustrate the concept. A concluding paragraph would probably attempt to bring the concept into clearer focus, which is, after all, the point of answering these questions.

Comment on a Quotation

On essay exams, an instructor will often ask students to comment on a quotation they are seeing for the first time. Usually, such quotations will express some surprising or controversial opinion that complements or challenges basic principles or ideas in the course. Sometimes the writer being quoted is identified, sometimes not. In fact, it is not unusual for instructors to write the quotation themselves.

A student choosing to answer the following question from a literature final would have risked half the exam — in points and time — on the outcome.

Question 23.9

Argue for or against this thesis: "In *A Clockwork Orange*, both the heightened, poetic language and the almost academic concern with moral and political theories deprive the story of most of its relevance to real life."

The directions here clearly ask for an argument. A student would need to set up a thesis indicating that the novel either is or is not relevant to real life and then point out how its language and its theoretical concerns can be viewed in light of this thesis.

The next example comes from a midterm exam in a history course. Students had forty minutes to write their answers, which could earn as much as 70 points on a 100-point exam.

Question 23.10

"Some historians believe that economic hardship and oppression breed social revolt; but the experience of the United States and Mexico between 1900 and 1920 suggests that people may rebel also during times of prosperity."

Comment on this statement. Why did large numbers of Americans and Mexicans wish to change conditions in their countries during the years from 1900 to 1920? How successful were their efforts? Who benefited from the changes that took place?

Although here students are instructed to "comment," the three questions make clear that a successful answer will require an argument: a clear *thesis* stating a position on the views expressed in the quotation, specific *reasons* for that thesis, and *support* for the thesis from readings and lectures. In general, such questions do not require a "right" answer: Whether you agree or disagree with the quotation is not as important as whether you can argue your case reasonably and convincingly, demonstrating a firm grasp of the subject matter.

See Chapter 19 for more on these components of an argument.

Compare and Contrast

Instructors are particularly fond of essay exam questions that require a comparison and contrast of two or three principles, ideas, works, activities, or phenomena. To answer this kind of question, you need to explore fully the relations between things of importance in the course, analyze each thing separately, and then search out specific points of likeness or difference. Students must thus show a thorough knowledge of the things being compared, as well as a clear understanding of the basic issues on which comparisons and contrasts can be made.

Often, as in Question 23.11, the basis of comparison will be limited to a particular focus; here, for example, students are asked to compare two works in terms of their views of colonialism.

Question 23.11

Compare and analyze the views of colonialism presented in Memmi's *Colonizer and the Colonized* and Pontecorvo's *Battle of Algiers*. What are the significant differences between these two views?

Sometimes instructors will simply identify what is to be compared, leaving students the task of choosing the basis of the comparison, as in the next three examples from communication, history, and literature exams, respectively.

Question 23.12

In what way is the stage of electronic media fundamentally different from all the major stages that preceded it?

Question 23.13

What was the role of the United States in Cuban affairs from 1898 until 1959? How did its role there compare with its role in the rest of Spanish America during the same period?

Question 23.14

Write an essay on one of the following topics:

1. Squire Western and Mr. Knightley
2. Dr. Primrose and Mr. Elton

See Chapter 18 for more on comparing and contrasting.

Whether the point of comparison is stated in the question or left for you to define for yourself, your answer needs to be limited to the aspects of similarity or difference that are most relevant to the general concepts or themes covered in the course.

Synthesize Information from Various Sources

For more on synthesizing, see Chapter 12, pp. 598–99.

In a course with several assigned readings, an instructor may give students an essay exam question that requires them to pull together (synthesize) information from several or even all the readings.

The following example was one of four required questions on a final exam in a course in Latin American studies. Students had about thirty minutes to complete their answer.

Question 23.15

On the basis of the articles read on El Salvador, Nicaragua, Peru, Chile, Argentina, and Mexico, what would you say are the major problems confronting Latin America today? Discuss the major types of problems with references to particular countries as examples.

For more on forecasting statements, see Chapter 13, p. 612.

This question asks students to do a lot in thirty minutes. They must first decide which major problems to discuss, which countries to include in each discussion, and how to use material from many readings to develop their answers. To compose a coherent essay, a student will need a carefully developed forecasting statement.

Analyze Causes

See Chapter 9 for more on analyzing causes.

In humanities and social science courses, much of what students study concerns the causes of trends, actions, and events. Hence, it is not surprising to find questions about causes on essay exams. In such cases, the instructor expects students to analyze causes of various phenomena discussed in readings and lectures. These examples come from midterm and final exams in literature, sociology, cultural studies, and communication courses, respectively.

Question 23.16

Why do Maurice and Jean not succumb to the intolerable conditions of the prison camp (the Camp of Hell) as most of the others do?

Question 23.17

Given that we occupy several positions in the course of our lives and given that each position has a specific role attached to it, what kinds of problems or dilemmas arise from those multiple roles, and how are they handled?

Question 23.18

Explain briefly the relationship between the institution of slavery and the emergence of the blues as a new African American musical expression.

Question 23.19

Analyze the way in which an uncritical promotion of the new information technology (computers, satellites, etc.) may support, unintentionally, the maintenance of the status quo.

Although these questions are presented in several ways ("what kinds of problems," "explain the relationship," "analyze the way"), they all require a list of causes in the answer. The causes would be organized under a thesis statement, and each cause would be argued and supported by referring to lectures or readings.

Criticize or Evaluate

Occasionally, instructors will include essay exam questions that invite students to evaluate a concept or a work. Nearly always, they want more than opinion: They expect a reasoned, documented judgment based on appropriate standards of judgment. Such questions test students' ability to recall and synthesize pertinent information and to understand and apply criteria taught in the course.

See Chapter 8 for more on evaluation.

On a final exam in a literature course, a student might have chosen one of the following questions about novels read in the course. Each would have been worth half the total points, with about an hour to answer it.

Question 23.20

Evaluate *A Passage to India* from a postcolonial critical standpoint.

Question 23.21

A Clockwork Orange and *The Comfort of Strangers* both attempt to examine the nature of modern decadence. Which does so more successfully?

See Chapter 18 for more on comparing and contrasting.

To answer either of these questions, a student would have to be very familiar with the novels under discussion and would have to establish standards for evaluating works of literature. The student would initially have to make a judgment favoring one novel over the other (though not necessarily casting one novel as "terrible" and the other as "perfect"). The student would then give reasons for this judgment, with supporting quotations from the novels, and probably use the writing strategies of comparison and contrast to develop the argument.

This next question was worth 10 of 85 points on a communication course midterm. Students were asked to answer "in two paragraphs."

Question 23.22

Eisenstein and Mukerji both argue that movable print was important to the rise of Protestantism. Cole extends this argument to say that print set off a chain of events that was important to the history of the United States. Summarize this argument, and criticize any part of it if you choose.

Here students are asked to criticize or evaluate an argument in several course readings. The instructor wants to know what students think of this argument and even though this is not stated, why they judge it as they do. Answering this unwritten "why" part of the question is the challenge: Students must come up with reasons and support appropriate to evaluating the argument.

■ Planning Your Answer

The amount of planning you do for a question will depend on how much time it is allotted and how many points it is worth. For short-answer definitions and identifications, a few seconds of thought will probably be sufficient. (Be careful not to puzzle too long over individual items like these. Skip over any you cannot recognize fairly quickly; often, answering other questions will help jog your memory.) For answers that require a paragraph or two, you may want to jot down several ideas and examples to focus your thoughts and give you a basis for organizing your information.

For longer answers, though, you will need to develop a much more definite strategy of organization. You have time for only one draft, so allow a reasonable period—as much as a quarter of the time allotted the question—for making notes, determining a thesis, and developing an outline. Jotting down pertinent ideas is a good way to begin; then you can plan your organization with a scratch outline (just a listing of points or facts) or a cluster.

For questions with several parts (different requests or directions, a sequence of questions), make a list of the parts so that you do not miss or minimize one part. For questions presented as questions (rather than directives), you might want to rephrase each question as a writing topic. These topics will often suggest how you should outline the answer.

You may have to try two or three outlines or clusters before you hit on a workable plan. But be realistic as you outline: You want a plan you can develop within the limited time allotted for your answer. Hence, your outline will have to be selective. It will contain not everything you know on the topic but rather what you know that you can develop clearly within the time available.

For information on clustering and outlining, see Chapter 11, pp. 571–76.

Writing Your Answer

As with planning, your strategy for writing depends on the length of your answer. For short identifications and definitions, it is usually best to start with a general identifying statement and then move on to describe specific applications or explanations. Two sentences will almost always suffice, but make sure you write complete sentences.

For longer answers, begin by stating your forecasting statement or thesis clearly and explicitly. An essay exam is not an occasion for indirectness: You want to strive for focus, simplicity, and clarity. In stating your point and developing your answer, use key terms from the question; it may look as though you are avoiding the question unless you use key terms (the same key terms) throughout your essay. If the question does not supply any key terms, you will find that you have provided your own by stating your main point. Use these key terms throughout the answer.

If you have devised a promising outline for your answer, you will be able to forecast your overall plan and its subpoints in your opening sentences. Forecasting shows readers how your essay is organized and has the practical advantage of making your answer easier to read. You might also want to use briefer paragraphs than you ordinarily do and signal clear relations between paragraphs with transition phrases or sentences.

See Chapter 13 for more on forecasting and transitions.

As you begin writing your answer, freely strike out words or even sentences you want to change by drawing through them neatly with a single line. Do not stop to erase, and try not to be messy. Instructors do not expect flawless writing, but they are put off by unnecessary messiness.

As you continue to write, you will certainly think of new subpoints and new ideas or facts to include later in the essay answer. Stop briefly to make a note of these on your original outline. If you find that you want to add a sentence or two to sections you have already completed, write them in the margin or at the top of the page, with a neat arrow pointing to where they fit in your answer.

Do not pad your answer with irrelevancies and repetitions just to fill up space. You may have had an instructor who did not seem to pay much attention to what you wrote, but most instructors read exams carefully and are not impressed by the length of an answer alone. Within the time available, write a comprehensive, specific answer without padding.

Watch the clock carefully so that you do not spend too much time on one answer. You must be realistic about the time constraints of an essay exam, especially if you know the material well and are prepared to write a lot. If you write one dazzling answer on an exam with three required questions, you earn only 33 points, not enough to pass at most colleges. Being required to answer more than one question may seem unfair, but keep in mind that instructors plan exams to be reasonably comprehensive. They want you to write about the course materials in two or three or more ways, not just one way.

If you run out of time when you are writing an answer, jot down the remaining main ideas from your outline, just to show that you know the material and with more time could have continued your exposition.

Write legibly and proofread what you write. Remember that your instructor will likely be reading a large pile of exams. Careless scrawls, misspellings, omitted words, and missing punctuation (especially missing periods needed to mark the ends of sentences) will only make that reading difficult, even exasperating. A few minutes of careful proofreading can improve your grade.

■ Model Answers to Some Typical Essay Exam Questions

Here we analyze several successful answers and give you an opportunity to analyze one for yourself. These analyses, along with the information we have provided elsewhere in this chapter, should greatly improve your chances of writing successful exam answers.

Short Answers

A literature midterm opened with ten items to identify, each worth 3 points. Students had about two minutes for each item. Here are three of Brenda Gossett's answers, each one earning her the full 3 points.

> Rauffenstein: He was the German general who was in charge of the castle where Boeldieu, Marical, and Rosenthal were finally sent in The Grand Illusion. He, along with Boeldieu, represented the aristocracy, which was slowly fading out at that time.

> Iges Peninsula: This peninsula is created by the Meuse River in France. It is there that the Camp of Hell was created in The Debacle. The Camp of Hell is where the French army was interned after the Germans defeated them in the Franco-Prussian War.

> Pache: He was the "religious peasant" in the novel The Debacle. It was he who inevitably became a scapegoat when he was murdered by Loubet, La Poulle, and Chouteau because he wouldn't share his bread with them.

The instructor said only "identify the following" but clearly wanted students both to identify the item and to indicate its significance to the work in which it appeared. Gossett does both and gets full credit. She mentions particular works, characters, and events. Although she is rushed, she answers in complete sentences. She does not misspell any words or leave out any commas or periods. Her answers are complete and correct.

Paragraph-Length Answers

One question on a weekly literature quiz was worth 20 points of the total of 100. With only a few minutes to answer the question, students were instructed to "answer in a few sentences." Here is the question and Camille Prestera's answer:

> In *Things Fall Apart*, how did Okonkwo's relationship with his father affect his attitude toward his son?

> Okonkwo despised his father, who was lazy, cowardly, and in debt. Okonkwo tried to be everything his father wasn't. He was hardworking, wealthy, and a great warrior and wrestler. Okonkwo treated his son harshly because he was afraid he saw the same weakness in Nwoye that he despised in his father. The result of this harsh treatment was that Nwoye left home.

Prestera begins by describing Okonkwo and his father, contrasting the two sharply. Then she explains Okonkwo's relationship with his son Nwoye. Her answer is coherent and straightforward.

Long Answers

Many final exams include at least one question requiring an essay-length answer. John Pixley had an hour to plan and write this essay for a final exam in a literature course in response to Question 23.7:

> Many American writers have portrayed their characters or their poetic speaker as being engaged in a quest. The quest may be explicit or implicit, it may be external or psychological, and it may end in failure or success. Analyze the quest motif in the work of four of the following writers: Edwards, Franklin, Hawthorne, Thoreau, Douglass, Whitman, Dickinson, James, Twain.

John Pixley's Answer

1   Americans pride themselves on being ambitious and on being able to strive for goals and to tap their potential. Some say that this is what the "American Dream" is all about. It is important for one to do and be all that one is capable of. This entails a quest or search for identity, experience, and happiness. Hence, the idea of the quest is a vital one in the United States, and it can be seen as a theme throughout American literature.

Key term, quest, is mentioned in introduction and thesis.

2   In eighteenth-century colonial America, Jonathan Edwards dealt with this theme in his autobiographical and personal writings. Unlike his fiery and hard-nosed sermons, these autobiographical writings present a sensitive, vulnerable man trying

First writer is identified immediately.

to find himself and his proper, satisfying place in the world. He is concerned with his spiritual growth, in being free to find and explore religious experience and happiness. For example, in <u>Personal Narrative</u>, he very carefully traces the stages of religious beliefs. He tells about periods of abandoned ecstasy, doubts, and rational revelations. He also notes that his best insights and growth came at times when he was alone in the wilderness, in nature. Edwards's efforts to find himself in relation to the world can also be seen in his "Observations of the Natural World," in which he relates various meticulously observed and described natural phenomena to religious precepts and occurrences. Here, he is trying to give the world and life, of which he is a part, some sense of meaning and purpose.

Edwards's work and the details of his quest are presented.

Although he was a contemporary of Edwards, Benjamin Franklin, who was very involved in the founding of the United States as a nation, had a different conception of the quest. He sees the quest as being one for practical accomplishment, success, and wealth. In his <u>Autobiography</u>, he stresses that happiness involves working hard to accomplish things, getting along with others, and establishing a good reputation. Unlike Edwards's, his quest is external and bound up with society. He is concerned with his morals and behavior, but, as seen in part 2 of the <u>Autobiography</u>, he deals with them in an objective, pragmatic, even statistical way, rather than in sensitive pondering. It is also evident in this work that Franklin, unlike Edwards, believes so much in himself and his quest that he is able to laugh at himself. His concern with society can be seen in <u>Poor Richard's Almanac</u>, in which he gives practical advice on how to find success and happiness in the world, how to "be healthy, wealthy, and wise."   3

Transition sentence identifies second writer. Key term (quest) is repeated.

Contrast with Edwards adds coherence to essay.

Another key term from the question, external, is used.

Franklin's particular kind of quest is described.

Still another version of the quest can be seen in the mid-nineteenth-century poetry of Walt Whitman. The quest that he portrays blends elements of those of Edwards and Franklin. In "Song of Myself," which is clearly autobiographical, the speaker emphasizes the importance of finding, knowing, and enjoying oneself as part of nature and the human community. He says that one should come to realize that one is lovable, just as are all other people and all of nature and life. This is a quest for sensitivity and awareness, as Edwards advocates, and for great self-confidence, as Franklin advocates. Along with Edwards, Whitman sees that peaceful isolation in nature is important; but he also sees the importance of interacting with people, as Franklin does. Being optimistic and feeling good — both in the literal and figurative sense — are the objects of this quest. Unfortunately, personal disappointment and national crisis (i.e., the Civil War) shattered Whitman's sense of confidence, and he lost the impetus of this quest in his own life.   4

Transition sentence identifies third writer. Key term is repeated.

Comparison of Whitman to Edwards and Franklin sustains coherence of essay.

Whitman's quest is defined.

This theme of the quest can be seen in prose fiction as well as in poetry and autobiography. One interesting example is "The Beast in the Jungle," a short story written by Henry James around 1903. It is interesting in that not only does the principal character, John Marcher, fail in his lifelong quest, but his failure comes about in a most subtle and frustrating way. Marcher believes that something momentous is going to happen in his future. He talks about his belief to only one person, a   5

Transition: Key term is repeated, and fourth writer is identified.

woman named May. May decides to befriend him for life and watch with him for the momentous occurrence to come about, for "the beast in the jungle" to "pounce." As time passes, May seems to know what this occurrence is and eventually even says that it has happened; but John is still in the dark. It is only long after May's death that the beast pounces on him in his recognition that the "beast" was his failure to truly love May, the one woman of his life, even though she gave him all the encouragement that she possibly, decently could. Marcher never defined the terms of his quest until it was too late. By just waiting and watching, he failed to find feeling and passion. This tragic realization, as someone like Whitman would view it, brings about John Marcher's ruin.

Quest of James character is described.

6   As seen in these few examples, the theme of the quest is a significant one in American literature. Also obvious is the fact that there are a variety of approaches to, methods used in, and outcomes of the quest. This is an appropriate theme for American literature seeing how much Americans cherish the right of "the pursuit of happiness."

Conclusion repeats key term.

Pixley's answer is strong for two reasons: He has the information he needs, and he has organized it carefully and presented it coherently.

EXERCISE 23.1

The following essay was written by Dan Hepler. He answered the same essay exam question as his classmate John Pixley. Analyze Hepler's essay to discover whether it meets the criteria of a good essay exam answer. Review the criteria mentioned earlier in this chapter in Writing Your Answer and in the annotated commentary of John Pixley's answer. Try to identify the features of Hepler's essay that contribute to or work against its success.

Dan Hepler's Answer

1   The quest motif is certainly important in American literature. By considering Franklin, Thoreau, Douglass, and Twain, we can see that the quest may be explicit or implicit, external or psychological, a failure or a success. Tracing the quest motif through these four authors seems to show a developing concern in American literature with transcending materialism to address deeper issues. It also reveals a drift toward ambiguity and pessimism.

2   Benjamin Franklin's quest, as revealed by his Autobiography, is for material comfort and outward success. His quest may be considered an explicit one because he announces clearly what he is trying to do: perfect a systematic approach for living long and happily. The whole Autobiography is a road map intended for other people to use as a guide; Franklin apparently meant rather literally for people to imitate his methods. He wrote with the assumption that his success was reproducible. He is possibly the most optimistic author in American literature because he enjoys

life, knows exactly <u>why</u> he enjoys life, and believes that anyone else willing to follow his formula may enjoy life as well.

By Franklin's standards, his quest is clearly a success. But his <u>Autobiography</u> portrays only an external, not a psychological, success. This is not to suggest that Franklin was a psychological failure. Indeed, we have every reason to believe the contrary. But the fact remains that Franklin <u>wrote</u> only about external success; he never indicated how he really felt emotionally. Possibly it was part of Franklin's overriding optimism to assume that material comfort leads naturally to emotional fulfillment.   3

Henry David Thoreau presents a more multifaceted quest. His <u>Walden</u> is, on the simplest level, the chronicle of Thoreau's physical journey out of town and into the woods. But the moving itself is not the focus of <u>Walden</u>. It is really more of a metaphor for some kind of spiritual quest going on within Thoreau's mind. Most of the action in <u>Walden</u> is mental, as Thoreau contemplates and philosophizes, always using the lake, the woods, and his own daily actions as symbols of higher, more eternal truths. This spiritual quest is a success in that Thoreau is able to appreciate the beauty of nature and to see through much of the sham and false assumptions of town life and blind materialism.   4

Thoreau does not leave us with nearly as explicit a "blueprint" for success as Franklin does. Even Franklin's plan is limited to people of high intelligence, personal discipline, and sound character; Franklin sometimes seems to forget that many human beings are in fact weak and evil and so would stand little chance of success similar to his own. But at least Franklin's quest could be duplicated by another Franklin. Thoreau's quest is more problematic, for even as great a mystic and naturalist as Thoreau himself could not remain in the woods indefinitely. This points toward the idea that the real quest is all internal and psychological; Thoreau seems to have gone to the woods to develop a spiritual strength that he could keep and take elsewhere on subsequent dealings with the "real world."   5

The quest of Frederick Douglass was explicit in that he needed physically to get north and escape slavery, but it was also implicit because he sought to discover and redefine himself through his quest, as Thoreau did. Douglass's motives were more sharply focused than either Franklin's or Thoreau's; his very humanness was at stake, as well as his physical well-being and possibly even his life. But Douglass also makes it clear that the most horrible part of slavery was the mental anguish of having no hope of freedom. His learning to read, and his maintenance of this skill, seems to have been as important as the maintenance of his material comforts, of which he had very few. In a sense, Douglass's quest is the most psychological and abstract so far because it is for the very essence of freedom and humanity, both of which were mostly taken for granted by Franklin and Thoreau. Also, Douglass's quest is the most pessimistic of the three; Douglass concludes that physical violence is the only way out, as he finds with the Covey incident.   6

7   Finally, Mark Twain's <u>Huckleberry Finn</u> is an example of the full range of mean- ing that the quest motif may assume. Geographically, Huck's quest is very large. But again, there is a quest defined implicitly as well as one defined explicitly, as Huck (without consciously realizing it) searches for morality, truth, and freedom. Twain's use of the quest is ambiguous, even more so than the previous writers', because while he suggests success superficially (i.e., the "happily ever after" scene in the last chapter), he really hints at some sort of ultimate hopelessness inherent in soci- ety. Not even Douglass questions the good or evil of American society as deeply as Twain does; for Douglass, everything will be fine when slavery is abolished; but for Twain, the only solution is to "light out for the territories" altogether — and when Twain wrote, he knew that the territories were no more.

8   Twain's implicit sense of spiritual failure stands in marked contrast to Franklin's buoyant confidence in material success. The guiding image of the quest, however, is central to American values and, consequently, a theme that these writers and others have adapted to suit their own vision.

EXERCISE 23.2

Analyze the following essay exam questions to decide what kind of writing task they present. What is being asked of the student as a participant in the course and as a writer? Given the time constraints of the exam, what plan would you propose for writing the answer? Following each question is the number of points it is worth and the amount of time allotted to answer it.

1. Cortazar is a producer of fantastic literature. Discuss first what fantastic literature is. Then choose any four stories by Cortazar as examples, and discuss the fantastic elements in these stories. Refer to the structure, techniques, and narrative styles that he uses in these four stories. If you like, you may refer to more than four, of course. (Points: 30 of 100. Time: 40 of 150 minutes.)

2. During the course of the twentieth century, the United States experienced three significant periods of social reform — the progressive era, the age of the Great Depression, and the decade of the 1960s. What were the sources of reform in each period? What were the most significant reform achievements of each period as well as the largest failings? (Points: 35 of 100. Time: 75 of 180 minutes.)

3. Since literature is both an artistic and ideological product, writers comment on their material context through their writing.

   a. What is Rulfo's perspective of his Mexican reality, and how is it portrayed through his stories?

   b. What particular themes does he deal with, especially in these stories: "The Burning Plain," "Luvina," "They Gave Us the Land," "Paso del Norte," and "Tell Them Not to Kill Me"?

   c. What literary techniques and structures does he use to convey his perspective? Refer to a specific story as an example.

   (Points: 30 of 100. Time: 20 of 50 minutes.)

4. Why is there a special reason to be concerned about the influence of television watching on kids? In your answer, include a statement of the following:

   a. Your own understanding of the *general communication principles* involved for any television watcher.

   b. What is special about television and kids.

   c. How advertisers and producers use this information. (You should draw from the relevant readings as well as lectures.)

   (Points: 20 of 90. Time: 25 of 90 minutes.)

5. Analyze the autobiographical tradition in American literature, focusing on differences and similarities among authors and, if appropriate, changes over time. Discuss four authors in all. In addition to the conscious autobiographers — Edwards, Franklin, Thoreau, Douglass — you may choose one or two figures from among the following fictional or poetic quasi-autobiographers: Hawthorne, Whitman, Dickinson, Twain. (Points: 50 of 120. Time: 60 of 180 minutes.)

6. How does the system of (media) sponsorship work, and what, if any, ideological control do sponsors exert? Be specific and illustrative. (Points: 33 of 100. Time: 60 of 180 minutes.)

7. Several of the works studied in this course analyze the tension between myth and reality. Select two written works and two films, and analyze how their authors or directors present the conflict between myth and reality and how they resolve it, if they resolve it. (Points: 45 of 130. Time: 60 of 180 minutes.)

8. *Man's Hope* is a novel about the Spanish Civil War written while the war was still going on. *La Guerre Est Finie* is a film about Spanish revolutionaries depicting their activities nearly thirty years after the civil war. Discuss how the temporal relationship of each of these works to the civil war is reflected in the character of the works themselves and in the differences between them. (Points: 58 of 100. Time: 30 of 50 minutes.)

9. Write an essay on one of these topics: The role of the narrator in *Tom Jones* and *Pride and Prejudice* or the characters of Uncle Toby and Miss Bates. (Points: 33 of 100. Time: 60 of 180 minutes.)

Writing Portfolios

24

A writing portfolio displays your work. Portfolios for college composition courses usually include a selection of your writing for the course and an essay reflecting on your learning in the course. The contents of a portfolio will, of course, vary from writer to writer and from instructor to instructor. This chapter provides some advice for assembling a writing portfolio using the resources in *The St. Martin's Guide to Writing*.

The Purposes of a Writing Portfolio

Portfolios are widely used for many purposes, most generally to display an individual's accomplishments. Artists present portfolios of their work to gallery owners and patrons. Designers and architects present portfolios of their most successful and imaginative work to show potential clients what they can do. Some colleges request applicants to submit portfolios of high school writing; outstanding portfolios sometimes qualify students for college credit or placement in advanced courses. Graduating seniors may be asked to submit a portfolio of their best work for evaluation, sometimes leading to special recognition or rewards. Instructors applying for new positions or advancement may compile a portfolio to demonstrate excellence or innovation in their teaching. No matter what the specific purpose or occasion, a portfolio can present a rich opportunity to show what you can do.

Creating a portfolio for a composition course enables you to present your best, most representative, or most extensively revised writing and, to some extent, collaborate with your instructor in assessing your work. Your instructor will assign the final grade, but how you select the materials included in your portfolio and describe them in your introductory essay may have some influence on your instructor's judgment. Most important, selecting your work and composing a reflective essay gives you an opportunity to think critically about your learning in the course. Thinking critically, as we explain in Chapter 1, is a kind of metacognition that helps learners consolidate, reinforce, and therefore better remember and apply what they have learned. Putting together your portfolio, you reflect on what you have learned about the basic features of different genres, the writing strategies that help your writing achieve its purpose for your particular readers, the composing strategies that enable you to manage complex and challenging writing assignments, and the reading and researching strategies that contribute to your success in college. In addition,

For more on the process of thinking critically, see pp. 12–14.

reviewing your work can increase your satisfaction with your courses as you become more aware of the specific ways in which your knowledge is growing. Finally, it can give you insights into your own intellectual development, help you recognize your strengths and weaknesses, and discover your interests.

Whether or not you are asked to turn in a writing portfolio, you might want to consider keeping one as a valuable personal record of an important period in your intellectual development. You might even wish to update the portfolio each term, adding interesting work from all your courses or perhaps from all the courses in your major.

Assembling a Portfolio for Your Composition Course

Some instructors give students free rein in deciding what to include in their portfolio, but most instructors specify what the portfolio should include. They usually ask students to select a certain number of the essays assigned in the course. They may specify that certain types of essays be included, such as one based on personal experience or observation and another based on library and Internet research, along with other materials like in-class writing or responses to readings. Many instructors also ask students to include materials that reflect their writing process for at least one of the essays (such as invention work, drafts, and critical responses). In addition to a selection of course materials, instructors usually require a reflective essay or letter that introduces the portfolio and evaluates the writer's own work.

Instructors who require portfolios often do not assign grades to individual drafts or revisions but wait until the end of the term to grade the entire portfolio. In such cases, instructors may ask students to submit a midterm portfolio for an in-progress course evaluation. A midterm portfolio usually includes plans for revising further one or more of the assigned essays.

There are many possible ways of assembling portfolios, and you will need to determine exactly what your instructor expects your portfolio to include. Here are some of the variables:

- Of the essays assigned in the course, how many should be included in the portfolio?
- How many of the essays assigned throughout the course may be revised further for the portfolio?
- What process work should be included?
- What other material written or collected for the course should be included (such as exercises, notes from collaborative activities, analyses of readings, downloaded Web pages)?

For more on service learning, see Chapter 28.

- What material from other courses, workplace projects, or service-learning projects may be included?
- Should the portfolio be introduced by a reflective essay or letter? If so, how long should it be? Are there any special requirements for this essay?

- How should the portfolio be organized? Should there be a table of contents? How should each entry be labeled and each page be numbered?
- Will the essays be graded when they are turned in, at midterm, or only at the end of the term when the final portfolio is submitted?

The following sections review specific resources in *The St. Martin's Guide to Writing* that can help you select work to include in your portfolio, reflect on what you have learned, and organize your portfolio.

Selecting Work

Your instructor will very likely specify a list of what to include in your portfolio. Whatever materials you include, you have some important decisions to make, and these decisions reveal a lot about you as a writer. Here are some suggestions to help you make selections:

- If you are asked to select only your best essays, you might begin by rereading your essays to see how well each one develops the basic features of its genre. Also review any critical responses you received from your instructor, classmates, writing center tutors, or other critical readers.
- If you are asked to make further revisions to one or more of your essays, you might begin by rereading the latest revision of each essay, using the Critical Reading Guide for that genre; or getting a critical response to each essay from your instructor, a classmate, or a writing center tutor. It may also help to review any critical responses you received on earlier drafts and the revision chart you made earlier to see what else you could do to improve the essay. Be sure to edit and proofread your essays carefully.
- If you are asked to select essays based on personal experience, you might choose from the remembering events essay you wrote for Chapter 2. If you are asked for essays based on firsthand observation and analysis, look at what you wrote for the profile (Chapter 3), the story interpretation (Chapter 10), or the concept explanation (Chapter 4). If you are asked to include argument essays, review the writing you did for Chapters 6–9.
- If you are asked to select essays incorporating library or Internet research, look at the essays you wrote for Chapters 4–9.
- If you are asked to select essays with a range of different purposes and audiences, you might begin by reviewing the Purpose and Audience sections of the Part One chapters you used. Then reread your invention notes defining the particular purpose and audience for each essay you wrote.
- If you are asked to include examples of your writing process work, look in your process materials for your most imaginative invention work, for a first draft and one or more revisions showing significant rethinking or reorganization, for your critical reading response to another student's draft showing perceptive criticism and helpful suggestions, or for sentences you edited and the chart of your common errors.

- If you are asked to include a complete process for one essay, you might choose process materials that show the quality as well as quantity of work you have done. To reflect the quality of your work, look for examples of thoughtful invention and substantive revision you can point out in your reflective essay.

- If you are asked to select essays that show the progress you have made in the course, you may want to choose essays that underwent radical change through the term.

Reflecting on Your Work and Your Learning

Many instructors require a written statement in the form of an essay or letter introducing the portfolio. Some ask for a simple description of the work presented in your portfolio; others prefer an evaluation of your work; still others may want you to connect your learning in this course to other courses and to work you hope to do in the future. Keeping the following considerations in mind will help you write a thoughtful, well-organized statement to your instructor about what you have learned:

- *Introduce and describe your work.* Because you will need to refer to several works or parts of a work, name each item in your portfolio in a consistent way. In describing an essay, give its title, genre (using the title of the chapter in *The St. Martin's Guide*), purpose, audience, and topic.

- *Justify your choices.* When you justify what you see as your "best" work, you think critically about the standards you are using to evaluate good writing in each genre. *The St. Martin's Guide* sets forth clear criteria for each kind of writing in the Basic Features and Critical Reading sections in Chapters 2–10. Review these sections as you judge the success of your essay, and refer to them as you explain your choice.

If you need help writing an evaluation, review Chapter 8.

- *Illustrate your growth as a writer with specific examples.* You may have selected work to show how you have grown as a writer, but you should not assume your readers will read the portfolio as you do without some guidance. You need to show them where they can find evidence that supports your statements by citing relevant examples from the work included in your portfolio. Summarize or quote your examples and be sure to tell readers what you think the examples illustrate. Also refer to them in a way that will help readers locate them with ease — perhaps by page and paragraph number (see the next section for some suggestions for organizing your portfolio).

- *Use* **The St. Martin's Guide** *to help you reflect on your learning.* Your instructor may ask you to consider what you learned in writing and revising a particular essay as well as what you learned about the process of writing that essay. In either case, it will help you to anchor your reflections in the specific work you have done using this book. Consider what you have learned analyzing and discussing the readings, inventing and researching, participating in group inquiry, planning and drafting, getting and giving critical comments, and revising and editing. Look again at the Thinking Critically About What You Have Learned sections in Chapters 2–10. There you will find questions that will help you reflect on how you solved problems when revising an essay, how reading influenced your writing, and how your writing can be situated and understood in a larger social context. You may well be able to use material you have already written for these sections in your portfolio reflective essay.

Organizing the Portfolio

Some instructors prescribe the portfolio's design and organization, while others allow students to be creative. Portfolios may be presented in an inexpensive manila folder, a looseleaf, or on a Web site. Follow your instructor's specific guidelines. Here are some possibilities for organizing your portfolio:

- *Include a cover or front page.* The design of the front page may be left up to you. But be sure to indicate the class section number, the instructor's name, your own name, and the date.

- *Include a table of contents.* Portfolios, like books, need a table of contents so that readers can see at a glance what is included and where it is located. The table of contents should appear at the beginning of the portfolio, identify all of the parts of the portfolio, and specify the page on which each part begins. You may decide to renumber all of the pages in the portfolio consecutively even though some of the material already has page numbers. If you add new page numbers, consider using a different color, putting the new page numbers in a new place, or using a letter- or word-number sequence (such as *Event-1, Position-1,* etc.). Whatever you decide, be consistent.

- *Include a reflective essay or letter.* Most instructors want the reflective essay to be the first item in the portfolio following the table of contents. In this position, the reflective essay introduces the material in the portfolio. Your instructor may use your reflective essay as a guide, reading the sections of the portfolio you specifically refer to in your essay before skimming the rest of the material.

- *Label each item.* If your instructor does not specify how you should label your work, you need to develop a clear system on your own. You may need to explain your system briefly in a note on the table of contents or in your reflective essay where you refer to particular items in your portfolio. For example, you could use *The St. Martin's Guide* chapter number to identify each essay assignment. To indicate process materials, consider using the chapter number and title and the relevant heading from that chapter's Guide to Writing section (such as Chapter 2, Exploring Your Present Perspective). To identify different drafts, you could write on the top left margin of every page the chapter number, essay title, and draft number. For drafts that received a critical reading, you might want to add the notation "Read by S." You should also date all of your work.

- *Sequence the material.* If your instructor does not indicate how you should order the work included in your portfolio, you will have to decide yourself. The sequence of materials should be consistent with the way you introduce your work in the reflective essay. If your instructor asks you to present two or more examples of your best work, you may want to begin with the essay you consider your very best. If your instructor asks you to show the progress you have made in the course, you could begin with your weakest essay and either show how you improved it or how later essays were stronger. If your instructor asks you to demonstrate growth, you might organize your work by the particular areas that improved. For example, you could show that you learned to revise substantively by presenting earlier and later revisions of an essay from early in the course and following them with a pair of revisions from a subsequent and more extensively reworked essay. Or to show that you learned to edit or altogether avoid certain sentence errors, you could give examples of a particular error being corrected in a revision and the same error being avoided in a later first draft.

Part Six

Writing and Speaking to Wider Audiences

25

Designing Documents

This chapter introduces basic components of document design, discusses some common formats for paper and electronic documents you may be asked to create in your college courses or in the workplace, and offers guidelines for designing effective documents.

For more MLA or APA style, see Chapter 22.

When you are required to use a particular document format, such as the MLA or APA style, for an academic writing assignment, you will not have many design choices. Your instructor will expect you to follow the MLA or APA rules for spacing, margins, heading formats, and so on. For writing assignments that do not require you to follow a particular academic format, you will often have more flexibility. Furthermore, the design possibilities for a Web page or slideshow presentation extend beyond those for the print page (including, for example, transitions, movement, and audio and video clips) and require careful consideration.

Paper and electronic documents differ in important ways, but both employ basic principles of design and use type, visuals, and white space to enhance readability. These principles have been developed over the centuries as increasing numbers of people have gained access to reading material, and designers today benefit not only from this accumulated knowledge but also from studies that have examined how the eye moves over the page, what expectations readers bring to documents, and how reading takes place within different contexts.

The arrangement of text, visuals, and white space on a page — called **page layout** — has a major impact on the readability of a document and may influence the reader's attitude toward it. A well-designed page is inviting to read and easy to scan.

Considering Context

When considering page layout and other aspects of document design, you will want to analyze the context in which your document will be read. For instance, if you are writing an essay for a college course, your instructor will read it carefully. Your design decisions should make sustained reading as easy as possible; therefore, you will want to present a neat, clearly printed paper. Fonts that are too small to read easily or print that is too light to see clearly will make the reader's job unnecessarily difficult. Use double-spaced text and one-inch margins to leave your instructor room to write comments on the page.

When you write for other audiences, however, you cannot expect all readers to read your writing closely. Some readers may skim through your blog entries looking for interesting points; readers might scan a report or memo for information important specifically to them. For these readers, headings, bullets, and chunking are important design elements that help them "see" the main points of your writing as well as find the information of most interest to them.

Frequently, too, your other page-layout and document design decisions will be predetermined by the kind of document you are preparing. Business letters and memos, for example, traditionally follow specific formats. Because your readers will bring certain long-held expectations to these kinds of documents, altering an established format can cause confusion.

To analyze the context in which a document is read or used, ask yourself the following questions:

- *Where will my document be read?* Will the document be read on paper in a well-lighted, spacious, quiet room? Or will it be read on a laptop computer screen on a noisy, lurching city bus?
- *Do my readers have specific expectations for this kind of document?* Am I writing a memo, letter, or report that my readers expect will follow certain design conventions?
- *How will the information be used?* Are my readers reading to learn, to be entertained, or to complete an assigned task? Are they most likely to skim the document or to read it carefully?

Elements of Document Design

Readable fonts, informative headings, bulleted or numbered lists, and appropriate use of color, white space, and visuals like photographs, charts, and diagrams all help readers find their place on the page with ease.

Font Style and Size

Typography is a design term for the letters and symbols that make up the print on a page or a screen. You are already using important aspects of typography when you use capital letters, italics, boldface, or different sizes of type to signal a new sentence, identify the title of a book, or distinguish a heading from body text.

Word processing programs enable you to use dozens of different fonts, or typefaces; bold and italic versions of these fonts; and a range of font sizes. Fortunately, you can rely on some simple design principles to make good typographic choices for your documents.

Perhaps the most important advice for working with typography is to choose fonts that are easy to read. Some fonts are meant for decorative, or otherwise very minimal use, and are hard to read in extended chunks. Font style, font size, and combinations of style and size are features that can add to or distract from readability.

Considering Font Style.   For most academic and business writing, you will probably want to choose a traditional font that is easy to read, such as **Arial** or Times New Roman. This book is set in Minion. Sentences and paragraphs printed in fonts that imitate *calligraphy* (typically called script fonts) or those that mimic *handwriting* are not only difficult to read but also too informal in appearance for most academic and business purposes.

Some Fonts Appropriate for Academic and Business Writing

Arial

Georgia

Tahoma

Times New Roman

Verdana

Considering Font Size.   To ensure that your documents can be read easily, you also need to choose an appropriate font size (traditionally measured in units called **points**). For most types of academic writing, a 12-point font is standard for the main (body) text. However, for Web pages, you should consider using a slightly larger font to compensate for the difficulty of reading from a computer monitor. For overhead transparencies and computer-projected displays, you should use an even larger font size (such as 32-point, and typically no smaller than 18-point) to ensure that the text can be read from a distance.

Combining Font Styles and Sizes.   Although computers now make hundreds of font styles and sizes available to writers, you should avoid confusing readers with too many different ones in one document. Limit the fonts in a document to one or two that complement each other well. A common practice, for instance, is to choose one font for all titles and headings (such as Arial, 14-pt, boldface) and another for the body text (such as Times New Roman, 12-pt), as shown in the example here.

This is an Example Heading

This is body text. This is body text.
This is body text. This is body text.
This is body text. This is body text.

This is an Example Heading

This is body text. This is body text.
This is body text. This is body text.
This is body text. This is body text.

Headings and Body Text

Titles and headings are often distinguished from body text by boldface, italics, or font size. These elements of typography are helpful in calling attention to certain parts or sections of a piece of writing, showing the hierarchy of its headings and subheadings as well as offering readers visual cues to its overall organization. However, you should always check with your instructor about the conventions for using (or not using) these elements in the particular discipline you are studying.

Distinguishing between Headings and Subheadings.   Typically, headings for major sections (level-one headings) must have more visual impact than those subdividing these sections (level-two headings), which should be more prominent than headings within the subdivisions (level-three headings). The typography should reflect this hierarchy of headings. Here is one possible system for distinguishing among three levels of headings:

LEVEL-ONE HEADING
Level-Two Heading
Level-Three Heading

Notice that the level-one and level-two headings are given the greatest prominence by the use of boldface and that they are distinguished from one another by the use of all capital letters for the major heading versus capital and lowercase letters for the subheading. The third-level heading, italicized but not boldfaced, is less prominent than the other two headings but can still be readily distinguished from body text. Whatever system you use to distinguish headings and subheadings, be sure to apply it consistently throughout your document.

For more on selecting appropriate headings and subheadings, see Chapter 13, pp. 623–24.

Positioning Headings Consistently.   In addition to keeping track of the font size and style of headings, you need to position headings in the same way throughout a piece of writing. You will want to consider the spacing above and below headings and determine whether the headings should be aligned with the left margin, indented a fixed amount of space, or centered. In this book, headings like the one that begins this paragraph — **Positioning Headings Consistently** — are aligned with the left margin and followed by a period and a fixed amount of space.

Using Type Size to Differentiate Headings from Text.   In documents that do not need to observe the MLA or APA style, you may wish to use font size to help make headings visually distinct from the body of the text. If you do so, avoid making the headings too large. To accompany 12-point body text, for instance, a 14-point heading will suffice. The default settings for heading and body text styles on most word processing and desktop publishing programs are effective, and you may want to use them to autoformat your heading and text styles.

Numbered and Bulleted Lists

Lists are often an effective way to present information in a logical and visually coherent way. Use a **numbered list** (1, 2, 3) to present the steps in a process or to list items that readers will need to refer back to easily (for instance, see the sample e-mail message on p. 827). Use a **bulleted list** (marking each new item with a "bullet" — a dash, circle, or box) to highlight key points when the order of the items is not significant (for instance, see the sample memo on p. 824). Written instructions, such as recipes, are typically formatted using numbered lists, whereas a list of supplies, for example, is more often presented in the form of a bulleted list.

Colors

Although you should avoid using color in most academic writing, in other writing situations color can help readers follow the organization of the document. For an example, notice the use of color to differentiate headings in one of the Guides to Writing in Chapters 2–10 of this book.

Color printers, photocopiers, and online technology facilitate the use of color, but color does not necessarily make text easier to read. In most academic writing, the only color you should use is black. If you think using an additional color will increase your readers' understanding of what you have to say, experiment with a color that contrasts well with the black type and white background to see whether the mix of colors provides you with the flexibility you need. Consider, however, whether your readers might be color-blind or whether they will have access to a full-color version of the document.

Although the slideshow design in Figure 25.1 is visually interesting and the heading is readable, the bulleted text is very hard to read because there is too little contrast between the text color and the background color.

In Figure 25.2, it is clear that the person who created the pie chart carefully chose the colors to represent the different data. What the person did not consider, however, is how the colors would look when printed out on a black-and-white printer. It is impossible to associate the labels with the slices of the pie, and thus to read the chart.

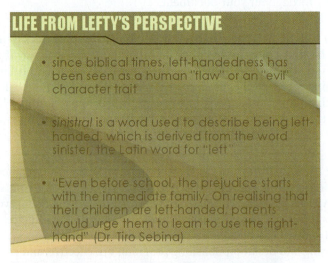

Figure 25.1 A document with too little color contrast

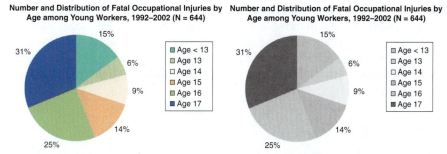

Figure 25.2 A pie chart that requires a color printer to be understandable
Source: National Institute for Occupational Safety and Health, "Data on Young Worker Injuries and Illnesses in Worker Health" (2004).

Also consider the meanings associated with different colors. For example, in the United States, blue is often associated with consistency, trustworthiness, and dependability. Bright yellow and rich red are used in most fast-food signs, as studies have shown that this color combination is appetite-inducing. Note also that a color may have different emotional resonance for people of other cultures. In the United States and other Western cultures, white typically is associated with goodness and purity; in China, however, white represents grief and mourning. Although your use of color in an essay, a Web page, or a slideshow presentation might not carry such deep meaning, bear in mind that most people have emotional or psychological responses to colors and color combinations.

White Space

Another basic element of document design, white space, is the open or blank space surrounding the text on a printed page or computer screen. White space is usually used between a heading, for instance, and the paragraph that follows the heading. You also use white space when you set the margins on the page, and even when you double-space between lines of text. In all of these cases, the space makes your document easier to read. When used generously, white space facilitates reading by keeping the pages of a document uncluttered and by helping the eye find and follow the text.

Chunking.   **Chunking**, the breaking up of text into smaller units, also facilitates reading. Paragraphing is a form of chunking that divides text up into units of closely related information. In most academic essays and reports, text is double-spaced, and paragraphs are distinguished by indenting the first line one-half inch.

In single-spaced text, you may want to facilitate easier reading by adding extra space between paragraphs, rather than indenting the first lines of paragraphs. This format is referred to as **block style** and is often used in memos, letters, and electronic documents. When creating electronic documents, especially Web pages, you might consider chunking your material into separate "pages" or screens, with links connecting the chunks.

Margins.   Adequate margins are an important component of white space and general readability. If the margins are too small, your page will seem cluttered. Generally, for academic essays, use one-inch margins on all sides unless your instructor (or the style manual you are following) advises differently. Some instructors ask students to leave large margins to accommodate marginal comments.

◼ Visuals

Tables, graphs, charts, diagrams, photographs, maps, and screen shots add visual interest and are often more effective in conveying information than prose alone. Be certain, however, that each visual has a valid role to play in your work; if the visual is merely a decoration, leave it out or replace it with a visual that is more appropriate.

You can create visuals on a computer, using the drawing tools of a word processing program, the charting tools of a spreadsheet program, or software specifically designed for creating visuals. You can also download visuals from the World Wide Web or photocopy or scan visuals from print materials. If your essay is going to be posted on the Web on a site that is not password-protected and a visual you want to use is from a source that is copyrighted, you should request written permission from the copyright holder (such as the photographer, publisher, or site sponsor). For any visual that you borrow from or create based on data from a source, be sure to cite the source in the caption, your bibliography, or both, according to the guidelines of the documentation system you are using.

Choose Appropriate Visuals and Design the Visuals with Their Final Use in Mind

One important thing to think about when considering visuals is to select the types that will best suit your purpose. The following list identifies various types of visuals, explains what they are best used for, and provides examples. If you plan to incorporate a visual into an overhead transparency or a computer-projected display, try to envision the original version as it would appear enlarged on a screen. Similarly, if you intend the visual for use on a Web page, consider how it will appear when displayed on a computer screen.

- *Tables.* A table is used to display numerical or textual data that is organized into columns and rows to make it easy to understand. A table usually includes several items as well as variables for each item. For example, the first column of Table 25.1 includes cities and states; the next two columns show the city population in 1990 and in 2000; and the final two columns show the change in population from 1990 to 2000 in number and percentage.

- *Bar graphs.* A bar graph typically compares numerical differences, often over time, for one or more items. For example, Figure 25.3 shows the rise in Internet access across five years (1997–2001) for U.S. households of varying incomes.

Table 25.1 Population Change for the Ten Largest U.S. Cities, 1990 to 2000

City and State	Population		Change, 1990 to 2000	
	April 1, 2000	April 1, 1990	Number	Percentage
New York, NY	8,008,278	7,322,564	685,714	9.4
Los Angeles, CA	3,694,820	3,485,398	209,422	6.0
Chicago, IL	2,896,016	2,783,726	112,290	4.0
Houston, TX	1,953,631	1,630,553	323,078	19.8
Philadelphia, PA	1,517,550	1,585,577	−68,027	−4.3
Phoenix, AZ	1,321,045	983,403	337,642	34.3
San Diego, CA	1,223,400	1,110,549	112,851	10.2
Dallas, TX	1,188,580	1,006,877	181,703	18.0
San Antonio, TX	1,144,646	935,933	208,713	22.3
Detroit, MI	951,270	1,027,974	−76,704	−7.5

Source: U.S. Census Bureau, Census 2000; 1990 Census, Population and Housing Unit Counts, United States (1990 CPH-2-1).

- **Line graphs.** A line graph charts change over time, typically, with only one variable represented (unlike in Figure 25.3, where the bar chart data is organized into six variables). For example, Figure 25.4 shows the amount of government spending for low-income children between 1966 and 2002.
- **Pie charts.** A pie chart shows the sizes of parts making up a whole. For instance, the whole (100 percent) in the chart shown in Figure 25.5 is the average annual

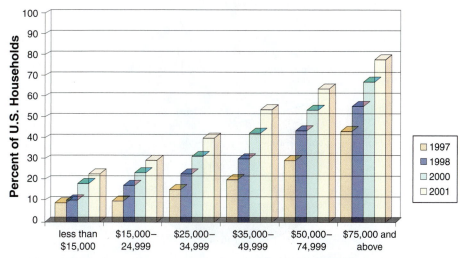

Figure 25.3 **Percent of U.S. households with Internet access by income**
Source: http://www.bc-net.org/Broadband/FixedWirelessBroadbandProject.nsf/
c39905004594509b85256c020048da39/fd5c34c8ce893c7185256c06004b05b5/
$FILE/bringing_a_nation.pdf

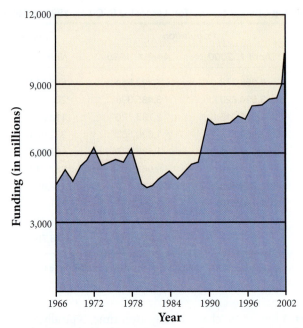

Figure 25.4 Title I spending for low-income children (in constant dollars)
Source: U.S. Department of Education.

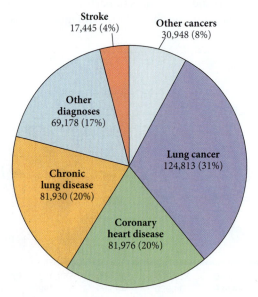

Figure 25.5 Average annual U.S. deaths attributable to cigarette smoking, 1995–1999
Source: Data from U.S. Centers for Disease Control.
Note: Total annual average is 406,290 deaths.

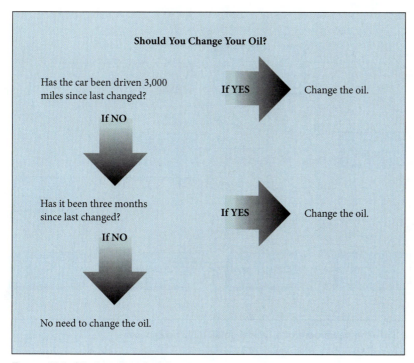

Should You Change Your Oil?

Has the car been driven 3,000 miles since last changed?

If YES → Change the oil.

If NO ↓

Has it been three months since last changed?

If YES → Change the oil.

If NO ↓

No need to change the oil.

Figure 25.6 Oil-changing decision process

number of deaths in the United States attributable to cigarette smoking; the parts are the specific causes of death, such as lung cancer (31 percent) and coronary heart disease (20 percent).

- **Flowcharts.** A flowchart shows a process broken down into parts or stages. Flowcharts are particularly helpful for explaining a process or facilitating a decision based on a set of circumstances, as shown, for instance, in Figure 25.6.

- **Organization charts.** An organization chart does what its name suggests — it creates a map of lines of authority within an organization, such as a company. Typically, the most important person — the person to whom most employees report — appears at the top of the chart, as seen in Figure 25.7, where the managing editor, who oversees the entire daily newspaper, appears at the top.

- **Diagrams.** A diagram depicts an item or its properties, often using symbols. It is typically used to show relationships or how things function. (See Figure 25.8.)

- **Drawings and cartoons.** A drawing shows a simplified version or an artist's interpretation of an object or situation. Cartoons, like the one in Figure 25.9, are drawings typically used to make an argumentative point, usually in a humorous way.

- **Photographs.** Photographs are used when an author wants to represent a real and specific object, place, or person, often for its emotional impact. For instance,

For another example of a diagram, see Chapter 14, p. 637.

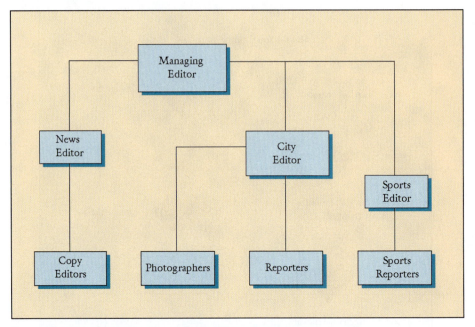

Figure 25.7 The newsroom of a typical small daily newspaper

a student selected Figure 25.10, a photo of a burrowing owl, to be included in a report about the ways in which local development was affecting endangered species. Although photographic images are generally assumed to duplicate what the eye sees, a photograph may, in fact, be manipulated in a variety of ways for special effects. Photographs that have been altered should be so identified.

- *Maps.* Maps are used to show geographical areas, lay out the spatial relationships of objects, or make a historical or political point. Figure 25.11 identifies Western Relocation Authority Centers and states that had a high Japanese-American population. The map reveals the fact that people were often relocated a great distance from their homes. (See Figure 25.11).

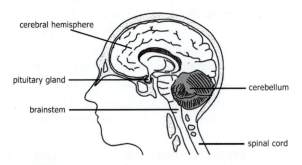

Figure 25.8 A cross-section of the human brain

Figure 25.9 A cartoon that makes an argument about
using Native American names for sports teams

- *Screen shots.* A screen shot duplicates the appearance of a specific computer
  screen or of a window or other section within it. Screen shots can be used to
  capture a Web page to include in a print document or to describe steps or instructions for using a piece of software (see Figure 25.12).

Number and Title Your Visuals

Number your visuals in sequential order and give each one a title. Refer to tables as
Table 1, Table 2, and so on, and to other types of visuals as *Figure 1, Figure 2*, and so

Figure 25.10 The burrowing owl

Figure 25.11 Western relocation authority centers
During World War II, ethnic prejudice was strong, and although they posed no threat to national security, Japanese Americans were forced to go to "Western Relocation Authority" camps. As the map indicates, people were often taken a great distance from their homes.

on. (In a long work with chapters or sections, you may also need to include the chapter or section number [*Figure 25.1*], as is done in this chapter of this book).

Make sure each visual has a title that reflects the subject of the visual (for example, income levels) and its purpose (to compare and illustrate changes in those in-

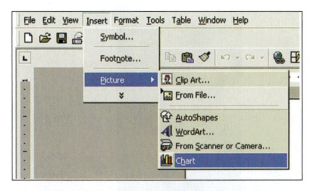

Figure 25.12 Screen capture to accompany written instructions, "How to Insert a Chart into a Word Processing Document"

come levels): *Figure 1. Percentage of U.S. Households in Three Income Ranges, 1990–2000.* Notice that MLA style requires that the title for a table be placed above the table and the title for a figure be placed below the figure.

Label the Parts of Your Visuals and Include Descriptive Captions

To help readers understand a visual, clearly label all of its parts. In a table, for instance, give each column a heading; likewise, label each section of a pie chart with the percentage and the item it represents. You may place the label on the chart itself if it is readable and clear; if that is not practical, place a legend next to the chart.

Some visuals may require a caption that provides a fuller description than the title alone does. Your caption might also include an explanation helpful to understand the visual, as in Figure 25.11.

Cite Your Visual Sources

Finally, if you borrow a visual from another source or create a visual from borrowed information, you must cite the source, following the guidelines for the documentation style you are using (see Figure 25.2 and Table 25.1 for examples). In addition, be sure to document the source in your list of works cited or references.

Integrate the Visual into the Text

Visuals should facilitate, not disrupt, the reading of the body text. To achieve this goal, you need to first introduce and discuss the visual in your text and then insert the visual in an appropriate location.

Introducing the Visual. Ideally, you should introduce each visual by referring to it in your text immediately *before* the visual appears. An effective textual reference answers the following questions:

- What is the number of the visual?
- Where is it located?
- What kind of information does it contain?
- What important point does it make or support?

Here is an example of an effective introduction for the line graph shown earlier (Figure 25.4):

> Note the sharp increase between 1990 and 2002 in federal spending for disadvantaged children (see Figure 25.4), which rose steadily over this period despite fluctuations in partisan control of Congress and the White House.

Placing the Visual in an Appropriate Location. MLA style requires and APA style recommends that you place a visual in the body of your text as soon after the discussion as possible, particularly when the reader will need to consult the visual. In

Stanford University anchors the reputation and identity of their law school via their Web site (see Figure 1). The page includes rich colors: vibrant, deep blue; rich, robust red; and an eye-friendly cream. The page includes rotating graphics that change each time the page is reloaded: photos of classrooms, palm trees, a bicycle stand, people walking through campus, and floating key words (such as "international law," "law and business," "conflict resolution," and "Silicon Valley"). These rotating graphics are meant to represent the various facets of Stanford Law School.

Figure 1: Home Page of Stanford Law School (image captured on July 28, 2006 from http://www.law.stanford.edu).

Along with the photographs, the "News" section of the home page is most prominent. Although it is a bit difficult to read, the "News" section clearly works to catch the reader's eye, as it is the only part of the site in more-traditional black

Figure 25.13 Excerpt from sample student paper with figure

APA style, visuals can also be grouped at the end of an essay if they contain supplemental information that may not be of interest to the reader or if the visuals take up multiple pages. (See Figure 25.13 for a page from a sample student paper with a figure included. Note that the figure is mentioned in the text and placed directly after this introduction, and that it includes a descriptive title with source information.)

Use Common Sense When Creating Visuals on a Computer

If you use a computer program to create visuals, keep this advice in mind:

- *Make the decisions that your computer cannot make for you.* A computer can automatically turn spreadsheet data into a pie chart or bar graph, but only you can decide which visual — or what use of color, if any — is most appropriate for your purpose.

- *Avoid "chart junk."* Many computer programs provide an array of special effects that can be used to alter visuals, including three-dimensional renderings, textured backgrounds, and shadowed text. Such special effects often detract from the intended message of the visual by calling attention to themselves instead. Use them sparingly, and only when they complement or emphasize key information.

- *Use clip art sparingly.* Clip art consists of icons, symbols, and other simple, typically abstract, copyright-free drawings. Because clip art simplifies ideas, it is of limited use in conveying the complex information contained in most academic writing.

▮ Sample Documents

Earlier in this chapter you saw examples of various types of visuals; in this section you will take a look at various types of documents that you may be asked to prepare. Each sample document is accompanied by a discussion of appropriate design conventions.

As you examine the documents, try also to analyze the way that typography, color, white space, and visuals are used to guide the reader's eye across the page. What design features make the documents easy to read? What features make finding specific information within the documents easy? What features make the document easy to use?

In addition to examining the sample documents with these questions in mind, look at the sample research paper in Chapter 22, pp. 772–79.

Memos

Memos, such as the one shown in Figure 25.14 on p. 824, are documents sent between employees of the same organization (in contrast to business letters, which are sent to people outside the organization). The following conventions for writing a memo are well-established and, in most cases, should not be altered. In addition, some organizations have specific guidelines for memos (such as the use of preprinted letterhead or memo forms).

- *Heading.* A memo should carry the major heading *Memorandum* or *Memo*. If you are using letterhead stationery, position the heading just below the letterhead. The heading may be centered on the page or positioned at the left margin (depending on your organization's guidelines). In either case, the heading should be distinguished in some way from the rest of the body text, such as by a large font size, boldface type, or capital letters.

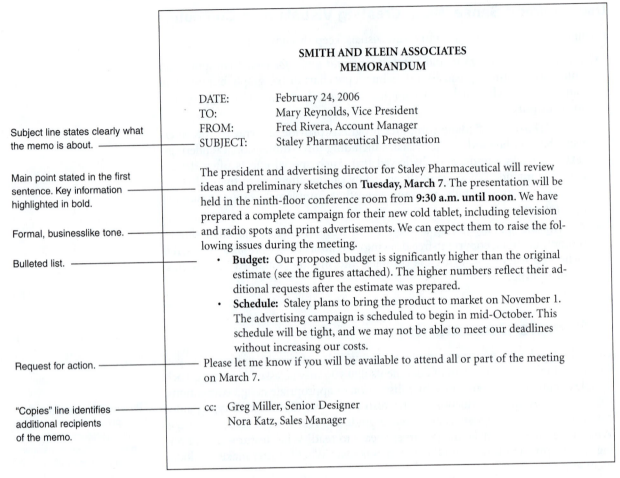

Subject line states clearly what the memo is about.

Main point stated in the first sentence. Key information highlighted in bold.

Formal, businesslike tone.

Bulleted list.

Request for action.

"Copies" line identifies additional recipients of the memo.

SMITH AND KLEIN ASSOCIATES
MEMORANDUM

DATE: February 24, 2006
TO: Mary Reynolds, Vice President
FROM: Fred Rivera, Account Manager
SUBJECT: Staley Pharmaceutical Presentation

The president and advertising director for Staley Pharmaceutical will review ideas and preliminary sketches on **Tuesday, March 7.** The presentation will be held in the ninth-floor conference room from **9:30 a.m. until noon.** We have prepared a complete campaign for their new cold tablet, including television and radio spots and print advertisements. We can expect them to raise the following issues during the meeting.

- **Budget:** Our proposed budget is significantly higher than the original estimate (see the figures attached). The higher numbers reflect their additional requests after the estimate was prepared.
- **Schedule:** Staley plans to bring the product to market on November 1. The advertising campaign is scheduled to begin in mid-October. This schedule will be tight, and we may not be able to meet our deadlines without increasing our costs.

Please let me know if you will be available to attend all or part of the meeting on March 7.

cc: Greg Miller, Senior Designer
      Nora Katz, Sales Manager

Figure 25.14 A sample memo

- ***Content headings.*** Just below the heading and separated by at least one line of space are the content headings: *Date, To, From,* and *Subject.* Place the content headings at the left margin and in the same size font as the body text.
- ***Body text.*** The main text of a memo is usually presented in block style: single-spaced with an extra line of space between paragraphs. (Do not indent the first line of paragraphs in block style.) If you need to call attention to specific information, consider presenting it in a numbered or bulleted list, or highlight the information visually by using boldface or extra white space above and below it. In a memo announcing a meeting, for example, you might boldface the date, time, and place of the meeting so the reader can quickly find the information, or you might set off the date, time, and place on separate lines.

Letters

The **business letter** (such as the one shown in Figure 25.15) is the document most often used for correspondence between representatives of one organization and representatives of another, though e-mail messages are increasingly being used in place of business letters. Business letters are written to obtain information about a company's products, to register a complaint, to respond to a complaint, or to introduce other documents (such as a proposal) that accompany the letter. As with memos, the design conventions for letters are long-established, although letters have more variations. Check to see whether there are specific business letter guidelines for your organization.

The heading of a business letter consists of the contact information for both the sender and the recipient of the letter. Block style is the most commonly used format for business letters.

Be sure to state the purpose of your letter in the first few lines and to provide supporting information in the paragraphs that follow. Always maintain a courteous and professional tone throughout a business letter. Include enough information to identify clearly any documents you refer to in the letter.

E-mail

Increasingly, students and instructors rely on electronic mail to exchange information about assignments and schedules as well as to follow up on class discussions (see Figure 25.16 on p. 827). **E-mail** messages are usually concise, direct, relatively informal, and limited to a single subject. Effective e-mails include a clear subject line.

In many organizations, e-mail messages are replacing handwritten or typed memos. When you send a memo electronically, make sure the headings automatically provided by the e-mail program convey the same essential information as the content headings in a traditional memo. If you are part of a large or complex organization, you may want to repeat your name and add such information as your job title, division, and telephone extension in a "signature" at the end of the document.

E-mail is a broader medium of communication than the business memo. Nevertheless, in anything other than quick e-mails to friends, you should maintain a professional tone. Avoid sarcasm and humor, which may not come across as you intend, and be sure to proofread and spell-check your message before sending it. Also, because e-mail messages are accessible to many people other than the person to whom you are writing, always be careful about what you write in an e-mail message.

While e-mail messages are among the simplest forms of electronic documents, new software programs allow you to attach files, insert hypertext links, and even insert pictures and graphics into your e-mail documents. As a matter of courtesy, check to be sure that the recipient of your e-mail message has the software to read these electronic files before you include them with the message.

For information on Web pages, which are another common type of electronic document, see pp. 831–34.

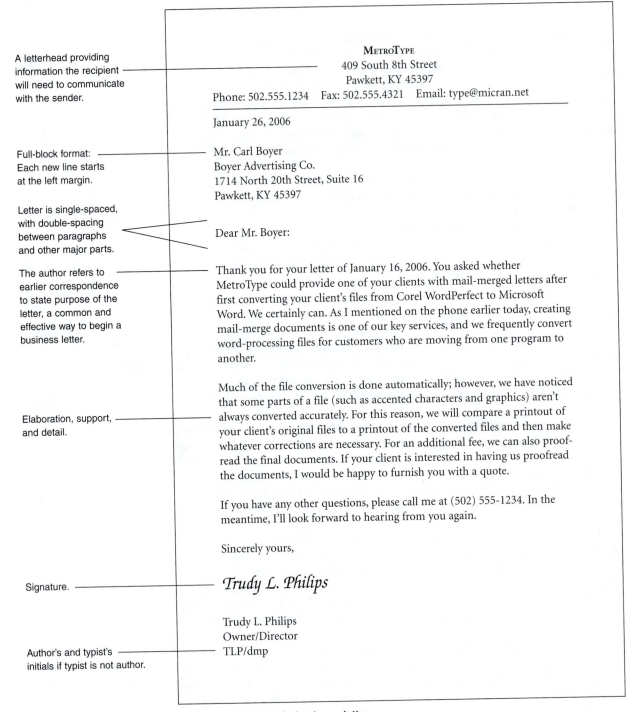

A letterhead providing information the recipient will need to communicate with the sender.

Full-block format: Each new line starts at the left margin.

Letter is single-spaced, with double-spacing between paragraphs and other major parts.

The author refers to earlier correspondence to state purpose of the letter, a common and effective way to begin a business letter.

Elaboration, support, and detail.

Signature.

Author's and typist's initials if typist is not author.

MᴇᴛʀᴏTʏᴘᴇ
409 South 8th Street
Pawkett, KY 45397
Phone: 502.555.1234   Fax: 502.555.4321   Email: type@micran.net

January 26, 2006

Mr. Carl Boyer
Boyer Advertising Co.
1714 North 20th Street, Suite 16
Pawkett, KY 45397

Dear Mr. Boyer:

Thank you for your letter of January 16, 2006. You asked whether MetroType could provide one of your clients with mail-merged letters after first converting your client's files from Corel WordPerfect to Microsoft Word. We certainly can. As I mentioned on the phone earlier today, creating mail-merge documents is one of our key services, and we frequently convert word-processing files for customers who are moving from one program to another.

Much of the file conversion is done automatically; however, we have noticed that some parts of a file (such as accented characters and graphics) aren't always converted accurately. For this reason, we will compare a printout of your client's original files to a printout of the converted files and then make whatever corrections are necessary. For an additional fee, we can also proofread the final documents. If your client is interested in having us proofread the documents, I would be happy to furnish you with a quote.

If you have any other questions, please call me at (502) 555-1234. In the meantime, I'll look forward to hearing from you again.

Sincerely yours,

Trudy L. Philips

Trudy L. Philips
Owner/Director
TLP/dmp

Figure 25.15 A sample business letter

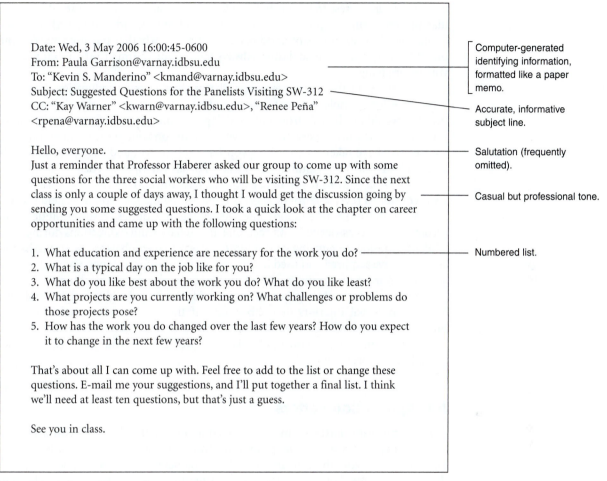

Date: Wed, 3 May 2006 16:00:45-0600
From: Paula Garrison@varnay.idbsu.edu
To: "Kevin S. Manderino" <kmand@varnay.idbsu.edu>
Subject: Suggested Questions for the Panelists Visiting SW-312
CC: "Kay Warner" <kwarn@varnay.idbsu.edu>, "Renee Peña"
<rpena@varnay.idbsu.edu>

Hello, everyone.
Just a reminder that Professor Haberer asked our group to come up with some
questions for the three social workers who will be visiting SW-312. Since the next
class is only a couple of days away, I thought I would get the discussion going by
sending you some suggested questions. I took a quick look at the chapter on career
opportunities and came up with the following questions:

1. What education and experience are necessary for the work you do?
2. What is a typical day on the job like for you?
3. What do you like best about the work you do? What do you like least?
4. What projects are you currently working on? What challenges or problems do
   those projects pose?
5. How has the work you do changed over the last few years? How do you expect
   it to change in the next few years?

That's about all I can come up with. Feel free to add to the list or change these
questions. E-mail me your suggestions, and I'll put together a final list. I think
we'll need at least ten questions, but that's just a guess.

See you in class.

Callouts (right margin):
Computer-generated identifying information, formatted like a paper memo.
Accurate, informative subject line.
Salutation (frequently omitted).
Casual but professional tone.
Numbered list.

Figure 25.16 A sample e-mail message

Résumés

A **résumé** is used to acquaint a prospective employer with your work experience,
education, and accomplishments. All résumés contain such basic information as
your name, address, phone number, and e-mail address.

The résumé is a good example of why the context in which a document is read
is so important. An employer may receive dozens of résumés for one position. Your
résumé may not be read closely in a first screening. Consequently, your résumé
should highlight your important qualifications visually so that the reader can
quickly find the pertinent information by scanning the page.

The format of résumés varies among disciplines and professions. Some professions require traditional formatting, while others allow for some flexibility in

design. Be sure to research your field and the potential employers to see if a particular résumé format is preferred; consider consulting recently published reference books that show examples of good résumés. Also see whether putting your résumé on a Web page might be advisable. Always tailor your résumé to the job for which you are applying.

Résumés may also vary in terms of what is emphasized — educational or work experience, for example. A recent college graduate and a professional with years of experience would not benefit from emphasizing the same aspects of their background. If you have little work experience, focus your résumé on your grade point average, the courses you have taken, the projects you have completed, and the applicable skills and abilities you have acquired in college. (For an example of such a résumé, see Figure 25.17 on p. 829.) If you have extensive, relevant, and continuous work experience, consider a reverse-chronological résumé, listing the jobs you have held (beginning with the most recent job) and describing the duties, responsibilities, and accomplishments associated with each one. If you have shifted directions during your adult life, consider organizing your résumé in a way that emphasizes the strengths and skills you have acquired and used in different settings — for instance, your experience speaking in front of groups, handling money, or working with machinery.

Do not include such personal information as your height, weight, and age. Mention personal interests or hobbies only if they are relevant to the position. Finally, proofread your résumé carefully; it must be error-free. Your résumé is the first impression you make on a potential employer. Do everything you can to make a good first impression.

Job-Application Letters

A **job-application letter** (sometimes called a **cover letter**) is sent with a résumé when you apply for a job. The primary purpose of the job-application letter is to persuade your reader that you are a qualified candidate for employment and to introduce your résumé. For college students and recent graduates, most job-application letters (such as the one shown in Figure 25.18) consist of four paragraphs:

1. The *first paragraph* identifies the position you are applying for and how you became aware of its availability. If you are not applying for a particular position, the first paragraph expresses your desire to work for the particular organization.

2. The *second paragraph* briefly describes your education, focusing on specific achievements, projects, and relevant course work.

3. The *third paragraph* briefly describes your work experience, focusing on relevant responsibilities and accomplishments.

   Note that the second and third paragraphs should not merely restate what is in your résumé; rather, they should help persuade your reader that you are qualified for the job.

4. The *fourth paragraph* expresses your willingness to provide additional information and to be interviewed at the employer's convenience.

Ample margins.

Kim Hua

Current Address: MS 1789, Union College, Union, PA 55342 —— Contact information.
Permanent Address: 702 Good Street, Borah, ID 83702
Phone: (412) 555-1234 Email: khua@mailer.union.edu

EDUCATION

| Union College | Bachelor of Arts, | Anticipated May 2007 |
| Union, PA | Child Development | GPA: 3.7 |

Relevant Courses: Lifespan Human Development, Infancy and Early Childhood, Parent-Child Relations, Fundamentals of Nutrition, Education of the Preschool Child

Relevant Projects: Coordinator, collaborative research project analyzing educational goals for local Head Start program. Lead writer, report on parent-child relations, delivered to the Borah, Idaho, School Board.

CHILD DEVELOPMENT WORK EXPERIENCE

- *Summer 2005, Union College Child-Care Center, Union College, Union, PA* —— Work experience begins with most current employment.

  Child Care Provider: Provided educational experiences and daily care for three 2-year-olds and four 3-year-olds. Prepared daily activity agendas.

- *Summer 2004, St. Alphonsus Day Care Center, St. Alphonsus Hospital, Union, PA*

  Child Care Provider: Provided educational experiences and daily care for a group of nine children ages six through ten.

- *Fall 2003, Governor's Commission for the Prevention of Child Abuse, Union, PA*

  Intern: Located online resources relevant to the prevention of child abuse. —— Relevant volunteer work.
  Recommended which resources to include in the Web site of the Governor's Commission.

OTHER WORK EXPERIENCE

2003 to present, Union Falls Bed & Breakfast, Union, PA

Payroll Manager: Maintain daily payroll records for all employees, compile daily —— Other experience showing dependability and responsibility.
and weekly reports of payroll costs for the manager, and ensure compliance with all applicable state and federal laws governing payroll matters.

PROFESSIONAL AFFILIATIONS

Past President, Union College Child and Family Studies Club; Student Member, American Society of Child Care Professionals; Member, National Child Care Providers

Figure 25.17 A sample résumé

Modified block format: Your address, the date, and the signature block begin at the center of the page.

308 Fairmont Street
Warren, CA 07812
June 9, 2006

Ms. Ronda Green
Software Engineer
Santa Clara Technology
P.O. Box 679
Santa Clara, CA 09145

Dear Ms. Green:

Purpose of the letter.

I am responding to your February 10 posting on Monster.com (reference #91921) that Santa Clara Technology is accepting résumés for an entry-level engineer position in the Quality Assurance Department. I think that my experience as an intern in quality assurance and my educational background qualify me for this position.

Education paragraph.

As my résumé states, I graduated this past May from the University of Southern California (USC) with a Bachelor of Science degree in Interdisciplinary Studies. The Interdisciplinary Studies program at USC allows students to develop a degree plan spanning at least two disciplines. My degree plan included courses in computer science, marketing, and technical communication. In addition to university courses, I have completed courses in team dynamics, project management, and C and C++ programming offered by the training department at PrintCom, a manufacturer of high-end laser printers.

Work-experience paragraph.

Throughout last summer, I worked as an intern in the quality-assurance department of PrintCom. I assisted quality-assurance engineers in testing printer drivers, installers, and utilities. In addition, I maintained a database containing the results of these tests and summarized the results in weekly reports. This experience gave me valuable knowledge of the principles of quality assurance and of the techniques used in testing software.

Concluding paragraph.

I would appreciate the opportunity to discuss further the education, skills, and abilities I could bring to Santa Clara Technology. You can reach me any workday after 3 p.m. (PDT) at (907) 555-1234 or by e-mail at sstur17@axl.com.

Sincerely yours,

Shelley Sturman

Shelley Sturman

Enclosure: résumé

Figure 25.18 A sample job-application letter

Lab Reports

A **lab report** is written to summarize the results of an experiment or test, and generally consists of the following five sections:

1. The *Introduction* provides background information: the hypothesis of the experiment, the question to be answered, how the question arose.

2. The *Methods* section describes how the research was conducted or how the experiment was performed.

3. The *Results* section describes what happened as a result of your research or experiment.

4. The *Discussion* section consists of your explanation of and reasoning about your results.

5. The *References* section cites the sources used in conducting the research, performing the experiment, or writing the report.

The content and format of a lab report may vary from discipline to discipline or from course to course. Before writing a lab report, be certain that you understand your instructor's requirements. The sample in Figure 25.19 shows excerpts from a lab report written by two students in a soils science course. It uses the documentation format advocated by the Council of Science Editors (CSE).

Electronic Documents: Web Pages

Electronic documents range from simple e-mail messages to complex, interactive World Wide Web pages. While electronic documents often offer the potential for expanded use of color and visuals (including animation and video), the general principles of design used for paper documents can be applied to electronic ones with some modification. Again, you will want to analyze the context in which the document will be read. Will your reader be reading from a computer screen or printing the document on paper for reading? If the reading takes place on a computer screen, how big is the screen and how good is its resolution? Reading from a computer screen is more difficult than reading on paper, so you will want to avoid small fonts and confusing backgrounds that distract from the core content.

For a discussion of e-mail and a sample document, see pp. 825–27.

A significant issue that makes electronic texts different from print texts is the technological ability to create links to additional text or graphics, to other Web pages, or to short clips of video, animation, or sound. As an author, it's important to consider that, because of the linking capacities of electronic texts, readers may navigate your text in a nonlinear fashion, starting almost anywhere they like and branching off whenever a link piques their curiosity. To help readers to find their way around, Web authors often provide a navigation scheme across the pages that make up a Web site. Site maps and "index" pages are also good cues to provide to readers.

Software programs called **HTML editors** provide those not familiar with HTML programming with an easy way to create Web pages, and most new word processing programs allow a document to be converted into HTML (which stands for hypertext markup language) and saved as a Web page.

Bulk Density and Total Pore Space

Joe Aquino and Sheila Norris
Soils 101
Lab Section 1
February 20, 2006

Introduction

Background information that the reader will need to understand the experiment.

Soil is an arrangement of solids and voids. The voids, called pore spaces, are important for root growth, water movement, water storage, and gas exchange between the soil and atmosphere. A medium-textured soil good for plant growth will have a pore-space content of about 0.50 (half solids, half pore space). The total pore space is the space between sand, silt, and clay particles (micropore space) plus the space between soil aggregates (macropore space).[1]

[The Introduction continues with a discussion of the formulas used to calculate bulk density, particle density, and porosity.]

Methods

Detailed explanation of the methods used.

To determine the bulk density[2] and total pore space of two soil samples, we hammered cans into the wall of a soil pit (Hagerstown silt loam). We collected samples from the Ap horizon and a Bt horizon. We then placed a block of wood over the cans so that the hammer did not smash them. After hammering the cans into the soil, we dug the cans, now full of soil, out of the horizons; we trimmed off any excess soil. The samples were dried in an oven at 105°C for two days and weighed. We then determined the volume of the cans by measuring the height and radius, as follows:

volume = 1/4 r^2h

We used the formulas noted in the Introduction to determine bulk density and porosity of the samples. Particle density was assumed to be 2.65 g/cm^3. The textural class of each horizon was determined by feel; that is, we squeezed and kneaded each sample and assigned it to a particular textural class.

Figure 25.19 A sample lab report

Results

We found both soils to have relatively light bulk densities and large porosities, but the Bt horizon had greater porosity than the Ap. Furthermore, we determined that the Ap horizon was a silt loam, whereas the Bt was a clay (see Table 1).

Table 1 Textural class, bulk density, and porosity of two Hagerstown soil horizons

Textural Class	Ap Silt Loam	Bt Clay
Bulk density (g/cm³)	1.20	1.08
Porosity	0.55	0.59

[The Results section continues with sample calculations.]

Discussion

Both soils had bulk densities and porosities in the range we would have expected from the discussions in the lab manual and textbook. The Ap horizon is a medium-textured soil and is considered a good topsoil for plant growth, so a porosity around 0.5 is consistent with those facts. The Bt horizon is a fine-textured horizon (containing a large amount of clay), and the bulk density is in the predicted range.

[The Discussion section continues with further discussion of the results.]

[The References section begins on a new page.]

References

1. Brady NC, Weil RR. The nature and properties of soils. 11th ed. New York: Prentice-Hall; 1996. 291 p.
2. Blake GR, Hartge KH. Bulk density. In: Klute A, editor. Methods of soil analysis. Part 1. 2nd ed. Agronomy 1986;9:363-376.

Presents the results of the experiment, with a table showing quantitative data.

Explains what was significant about the results of the research.

The references are in the format recommended by the Council of Science Editors (CSE).

As you design a Web page, beware of letting fancy or gratuitous graphics and multimedia elements distract from your message. Yes, you *can* add a textured background to the screen that will make it look like marble or cloth, but will that background make reading the text easier? Will a sound file improve communication of your main points, or are you adding sound simply because you can? Consider the following guidelines when designing a Web page:

- *Make sure your text is easy to read.* Many Web pages are difficult to read because of textured and brightly colored backgrounds. Keep the background of a Web page light in tone so that your text can be read with ease. Color type can also be difficult to read; avoid vibrant colors for long blocks of text. Bear in mind that most readers are used to reading dark (typically black) text on a light (typically white) background.

- *Chunk information carefully and keep your Web pages short.* Because many people have difficulty reading long documents on a computer screen, be sure to chunk your information into concise paragraphs. Also, readers often find it difficult to read a Web page that requires extensive scrolling down the screen. Break up long text blocks into separate Web pages that require no more than one or two screens of scrolling. Use hypertext links to connect the text blocks and to help readers navigate across the pages.

- *Limit the file size of your Web pages.* A Web page that is filled with visuals and sound files can be slow and clunky to load, especially for users with old computers or dial-up connections to the Internet. Limiting your use of visuals and sound files so that your pages load quickly will help ensure that your documents are read.

- *Use hypertext links effectively.* Make sure that all of your links work correctly and that all the pages of your Web site include a link back to your home page so readers can access it easily. You can make your text easier to read by judiciously limiting the number of links you embed in text. In addition to embedded text links, consider including a list of important links on a separate page for readers' convenience.

- *Use the elements of document design.* Remember what you have learned in this chapter about typography, white space, color, and visuals when you create Web pages. Most principles of good paper document design apply to Web page design as well.

Oral Presentations 26

At some point in your academic career, you will probably be asked to give an oral presentation. In fact, you may give many oral presentations before you graduate, and you almost certainly will give oral presentations on the job. This chapter contains practical suggestions for preparing and giving effective oral presentations.

Be Ready

Many people are terrified at the thought of public speaking, particularly people who have little experience with it. Even experienced public speakers can become jittery before giving an oral presentation. The key to defeating nervousness and anxiety is to research and prepare. If you have researched your subject thoroughly and have planned your presentation in detail, then you should be able to relax. If you find that you are still anxious, take a few slow, deep breaths before starting your presentation. It is also helpful not to think of your presentation as a performance. Remember that you are communicating a message. Think of your presentation as simply talking to an audience.

Understand the Kind of Oral Presentation You Have Been Asked to Give

The list that follows identifies the four basic types of oral presentations.

- *Impromptu presentation.* An impromptu oral presentation is given without preparation. In a history class, for example, your instructor may call on you to explain briefly a concept you are studying, such as "manifest destiny." As best you can, you would recall what you have read and summarize the information. While impromptu presentations are given without preparation, they do require knowledge of the subject matter.

- *Extemporaneous presentation.* In an extemporaneous presentation, you prepare beforehand and speak from notes or an outline. For example, in a management class, you might prepare a report on a business that you recently visited. In most academic and business situations, extemporaneous talks are preferred because they are informal yet well organized. Extemporaneous presentation often includes outlining your major points on a board or as a transparency for an overhead projector.

- *Scripted presentation.* Reading from a script is one way to ensure that you say exactly what you want to say — and that you take no more than the time you have been allotted. Because you read to your audience, a scripted presentation can be stiff and boring unless it is carefully planned and rehearsed. Scripted presentations also need to be written so that the audience can easily follow the presentation by just hearing it. Sentences often need to be shorter than in a document that is read. You will also need to provide more transitions and cues than in documents that are read. (See Use Cues to Orient Listeners on the next page.) A simple guideline to remember is that if your writing is difficult for you to read aloud, it will be difficult to hear as well.

- *Memorized presentation.* This type of oral presentation is written and committed to memory beforehand. For instance, at a sales meeting, you might evaluate a new product in relation to its competition. However, most people prefer scripted talks because of the difficulty of memorizing a lengthy oral presentation.

Assess Your Audience and Purpose

To give effective oral presentations you need to assess your audience and your purpose. Even for an impromptu presentation, you should take a few moments to think about whom you are speaking to and why. To assess your audience, ask the same questions you would ask about readers: Why are the members of my audience here? What do they already know about my subject? How do they feel about my topic? What objections might they have to my argument?

Define your purpose by completing the following statement: "In this oral presentation, I want to. . . ." For instance, you may want to speculate on the causes of the recent trend of companies' hiring numerous part-time and temporary contingent workers or argue your position on the ethics of this new hiring policy.

Determine How Much Information You Can Present in the Allotted Time

Your presentation should be exactly as long as the time allotted. Using substantially less time will make your presentation seem incomplete or superficial; using substantially more time may alienate your audience. Plan your presentation to allocate sufficient time for an introduction, concluding remarks, and follow-up questions (if a question-and-answer session is to be part of the presentation). If you are giving a scripted presentation, each double-spaced page of text will probably take two minutes to deliver. Time yourself to be sure.

Use Cues to Orient Listeners

Listening is one of the most difficult ways to comprehend information, in part because listeners cannot look back at previous information or scan forward, as readers can. To help your audience follow your oral presentation, use the same cues you would use to orient readers — but use them more frequently and overtly. Here are four basic cues that are especially helpful for listeners.

- *Thesis and forecasting statements.* Begin your presentation with thesis and forecasting statements that announce to audience members what you intend to communicate (your thesis) and the order in which you will present your material (your forecast). For instance, if you will present an argument about deregulation in the telecommunications industry, you can begin by asserting your position and preview the reasons you will offer to support your position.
- *Transitions.* Provide transitions when you move from one point to the next to help your audience follow the twists and turns of your presentation. For example, when you have finished discussing your first reason, state explicitly that you are now turning to your second reason.
- *Summaries.* End your oral presentation with a summary of the main points you have made. Also look for opportunities to use summaries throughout the presentation, particularly when you have spent a long time discussing something complicated. A brief summary that indicates the point you are making and its relation to your overall thesis can help listeners understand how the parts of your argument fit together to support your thesis.
- *Visuals.* Visual presentation of these cues will reinforce them. Your thesis, forecasting statements, transitions, and summaries can all be presented visually.

For further discussion and illustration of orienting cues, see Chapter 13.

Prepare Effective and Appropriate Visuals

For presentations that you plan ahead of time, you can use a variety of visuals — from simple lists and graphs to sophisticated computer demonstrations — to help both you and your audience. For instance, an overhead transparency or other projected image listing the major points of your presentation will help you make a forecasting statement that your listeners will pay attention to and remember. You can even leave the visual on display as you talk, referring to it to make a transition or adding to it as you answer questions.

Various technologies are available for displaying visuals. Writing on a board or flip chart has several advantages: low cost, high visibility, and simplicity for composing or altering on the spot. To present a long passage or detailed graphic, photocopied handouts are preferable, although they can be distracting.

Overhead transparencies are a popular way to display visuals during a presentation. An overhead transparency consists of text, graphics, or both printed on a sheet of 8 1/2-by-11-inch film (see Figure 26.1 for an example). When illuminated by an overhead projector, the material is enlarged and projected on a screen. Overhead transparencies can help your audience follow and remember your presentation.

Simple design

Bulleted list to define
main points

Large, easy-to-read font

Ample space around
text and graphics

Illustration that
clarifies text and adds
visual interest

Figure 26.1 Sample overhead transparency

If you use them, think of them as integral to your presentation, not just decorative. They should be concise, easy to read, and uncluttered. You may use an overhead transparency to list the main points of your presentation, to signal transitions from one topic to another, and to summarize information you have presented.

Easy-to-use computer presentation software such as Microsoft PowerPoint is becoming increasingly widespread and extends the capabilities of the overhead transparency to include animation.

As you prepare visuals, keep in mind that they must be legible to everyone in your audience, including people seated in the back of the room. Use a large, easy-to-read font and generous amounts of space around text.

For more on designing documents, see Chapter 25.

Verify That You Will Have the Correct Equipment and Supplies

Well before your presentation is scheduled to begin, verify that the presentation room contains all of the equipment and supplies you will need. For example, if you plan to use an overhead projector, make sure it is in the room, placed correctly, and working well. Anticipating your needs (bring a marker) as well as potential problems (bring a spare bulb) will make your presentation go smoothly and help reduce your anxiety.

Rehearse Your Presentation

Rehearsing will help you become more familiar with your material, fit the material into the allotted time, and feel more confident about speaking in public. If possible, rehearse in the same room in which you will give the presentation, using the same equipment. Also try to rehearse before an audience of colleagues or friends who can give you constructive criticism. Rehearsing a script or memorized presentation will enable you to plan your delivery. For a scripted talk, mark cues very selectively on your printed text to remind yourself when to pause or emphasize a word or phrase.

Deliver the Oral Presentation Professionally

Before your presentation, try to relax: Take a few deep breaths, drink some water, or step outside for some fresh air. If someone is to introduce you, give that person information about yourself and your presentation. Otherwise, begin by introducing yourself and your title or topic.

These guidelines will help you make a professional impression:

- As you speak, try to make eye contact with the people in the room.
- Use your hands to gesture as you would in a conversation; your hands should be neither clamped rigidly at your sides nor doing something distracting such as playing with your jewelry.
- If you are behind a lectern, avoid slouching, leaning on it, or gripping it tightly throughout the presentation.
- If you are using visuals, be careful not to block the audience's view of them. After introducing a new visual, resume making eye contact with audience members; talk to the audience, not the visual.
- Try to avoid distracting vocal mannerisms, such as repeatedly saying "uh," "like," or "you know."
- Speak loudly enough so that all members of the audience can hear you, and speak clearly and distinctly. Nervousness may cause you to speak too rapidly, so watch your pace.
- Do not speak in a monotone. Instead, let the pitch of your voice rise and fall naturally, especially when giving a scripted presentation.
- Dress appropriately for your audience and the formality of the situation in which you are speaking. The focus should be on your message, not on how you are dressed.

End Your Presentation Graciously

If no question-and-answer session is scheduled to follow your presentation, end the presentation by thanking your audience for giving you the opportunity to speak. If appropriate, offer to answer any questions in a private conversation or in a follow-up correspondence.

If a question-and-answer session follows your presentation, politely invite questions by saying something like, "If you have any questions, I would be happy to try to answer them now."

27 Working with Others

Although writing usually requires a solitary, individual effort, writers often seek advice and feedback from friends, colleagues, or mentors on their own *individual writing projects*. For instance, they may ask the advice of a librarian about researching their subject in the library or on the Internet, try out their argument on a coworker or fellow student, seek help to improve a draft, or get someone to check for grammar errors. On some occasions, writers also work together in small groups or teams to research, plan, and compose written reports — what we call *joint writing projects*.

Working with others is often referred to as *collaboration*, a term that we use throughout this chapter to mean working cooperatively with others to make writing better. Because collaborating with others on individual projects and especially on joint writing projects can be challenging and sometimes difficult, the following advice will help you anticipate the difficulties so that you can realize the full potential of collaboration.

■ Working with Others on Your Individual Writing Projects

From the very beginning of your work on an assignment in this book, you are collaborating with others to write the best essay you possibly can. Your instructor is a collaborator, as are other students in your class. For instance, their comments about the readings will help you understand more about the genres you will be writing, and their responses to your invention work and to drafts of your essays will give you many ideas. Of course, you yourself collaborate with other students when you give them your insights on the readings and on their writing.

In every assignment chapter, four special activities enable you to collaborate with other students in a purposeful way. Chapter 6, Arguing a Position, for example, has these activities:

A Collaborative Activity: Practice Arguing a Position. In this activity toward the beginning of the chapter, you work with two or three other students to try out a brief argument and discover how much you already know about this genre.

Making Connections to Personal and Social Issues. This activity, following each of the readings, invites you to examine with other students some of the important ideas and underlying assumptions of the reading. In small-group discussion, you can explore your responses and develop your understanding.

Testing Your Choice: A Collaborative Activity. Partway through the invention work, at a point where you need to assess realistically whether you have made a wise topic choice, this activity guides you in presenting your topic to a few other students and getting their response and advice. From discovering what you have to say about your topic in this first public tryout and from reflecting on what other students have to say, you can decide whether you have chosen a topic you can write about convincingly.

Critical Reading Guide. Once you have a draft of your essay, anyone using the Critical Reading Guide can give you a comprehensive evaluation of your draft, and you can do likewise for others with their drafts. Because in Chapter 6 the Critical Reading Guide reflects the particular requirements of a successful essay arguing a position on a controversial issue, anyone using it to evaluate your draft will be able to give you focused, relevant advice. When you use the guide to evaluate another student's draft, you will be learning how to evaluate position essays, including your own.

In these four formal activities, you collaborate with others to develop your individual writing projects by discovering what you may know about a project before you get very far into it, assessing your progress after a period of initial work, and evaluating your first attempts to draft a complete essay. There are many other occasions for fruitful collaboration in the assignment chapters. You may use the activities informally with another student, or your instructor may ask you to do them in class or on your own time. For instance, in Chapter 6 you might work with other students to complete the Analyzing Writing Strategies tasks that follow every reading. You and another student might exchange revisions of your essays to help each other with final editing and proofreading. Or you might meet or exchange e-mail messages with two or three other students to work on the challenging task, Considering the Social Dimensions of Position Papers, that concludes the chapter. These activities may seem easier or more enjoyable if you work on them with other students. But collaborative activities will also very likely be more productive, increasing your understanding of writing that takes positions on issues through the exchange of many more ideas than you might have come up with on your own.

Collaboration on your individual projects need not always be so purposeful and organized. It continues usefully in the most casual, brief encounter with a classmate on or off campus. You might lament the upcoming deadline for a first draft of the essay, telling each other what you still have to accomplish in the little time remaining. You might talk about what happened when you tried one of the book's collaborative activities. You might continue a discussion of a reading that began in class. You might describe the most formidable problem you must solve before you can complete your draft. If you are both doing library research on the same or a similar issue, you might tell each other about useful sources you have discovered.

Following are guidelines for successful collaboration on individual writing projects. These guidelines apply to formal, planned meetings to improve writing itself — from invention work through planning and revising:

- Whenever you read someone else's writing, have the writer inform you about his or her purpose and readers. Collaboration is always more effective when writers focus on helping other writers achieve their purposes for their particular readers. If a writer is explaining a concept to readers who know nothing about it, as might be the case in Chapter 4, Explaining a Concept, your comments are likely to be unhelpful if you assume the essay is addressed to someone who shares your understanding of the concept.

- Know the genre the writer is working in. If a writer is proposing a solution to a problem and you are evaluating the writing as though it were an essay arguing a position, your advice is likely to be off the mark.

- When you evaluate another writer's work, be sure you know the stage of its development. Is it a set of tentative notes for a first draft? A partial draft? A complete draft? A revision? If it is a draft, you want to focus on helping the writer develop and organize ideas; if it is a revision, you might focus exclusively on cueing and coherence or editing and proofreading.

- When you evaluate someone's writing, be helpful and supportive but also frank and specific. You do a writing partner no favor if you shrink from criticizing and giving advice. If your criticism seems grounded in the purpose, audience, and genre, it will probably not seem arbitrary or personal to your partner.

- Bring as much writing as possible to a scheduled meeting with other writers. The further along your writing is, the more you can learn from the collaboration, and your partners will feel that their time has been well spent.

- Try to be receptive to criticism. Later, you can decide whether to change your essay, and how.

Working with Others on Joint Writing Projects

In addition to collaborating with others on your individual writing projects, you may be given the opportunity to write an essay with other students — a joint project in which you collaborate to produce a single essay. For instance, in Chapter 6, Arguing a Position, you could collaborate to construct a persuasive argument for a position you share with two or three other students on a controversial issue. In Chapter 4, Explaining a Concept, you could work with a few other students to research and explain a concept, perhaps using graphics or hands-on activities to help others grasp the concept and its implications. In Chapter 7, Proposing a Solution, you have an opportunity to practice researching and writing proposals, by far the most common type of joint writing project in college, business, and the community.

Consider the following workplace writing example. A pharmaceuticals company decided to invest time and money in finding a solution to a problem the company saw as damaging to its business as well as to the community. The company assigned a team of seven division managers and a technical writer, gave them a budget to pay for outside consultants, and asked them to present a written proposal to the state legislature and local school board in six months' time.

The pharmaceuticals team divided the project into a series of research and writing tasks like those outlined in the Guide to Writing in Chapter 7. The team members scheduled due dates for each task and progress reports to identify problems as they arose. They assigned responsibility for each task to either individuals or small groups and identified which tasks might need consultation with outside experts.

When people collaborate on large writing projects like that of the pharmaceutical company, they usually divide up the work. For example, they might divide responsibilities according to the expertise of different group members. Someone who knows the problem firsthand might work on developing ways to explain the problem to those who have not experienced it directly. People who have experience making forecasts and planning budgets or hiring and managing people might be assigned to research and draft those aspects of the proposal. Everyone in the group might read and suggest revisions in the draft, and individuals may be assigned parts to strengthen and clarify. When a final draft seems near, one person might be assigned the job of improving cueing and coherence, another might be in charge of editing and proofreading, and a third might work on document design.

Writing collaboratively on a joint project certainly has benefits. Collaboration not only draws on the expertise and energy of different people but can also be synergistic, creating an outcome that is greater than the sum of its parts. One difficulty of collaborative writing projects, however, is that learning how to work effectively with others takes time and effort. Writers working on a joint project need to spend a lot of time communicating with one another. They must learn to anticipate conflicts and resolve them constructively. They should be realistic in scheduling and do their assigned tasks responsibly. They have to be flexible in their writing processes and open to different points of view.

Your instructor may decide how large your group should be and may even assign students to particular groups. If you are unhappy being in a particular group, discuss the situation with your instructor as soon as possible. To help group members work together constructively on joint writing projects, here are some ground rules you will want to discuss and implement:

- Begin by establishing clear and easy means of communicating with one another. Exchange e-mail addresses or establish a listserv, but also exchange phone numbers in case servers go down.

- Expect to spend a lot of time planning the project together and discussing who will do what and when. Discuss how the group should divide responsibilities. To decide how best to collaborate, you will need to plan the project so that you know what needs to be accomplished and in what order. Remember, however, to remain flexible and keep lines of communication open to deal with problems as they arise.

- Set a schedule of regular meetings. The meetings can take place in person, over the Internet, or by telephone. Agree on how to run the meetings. For example, should someone lead each discussion and should the role of discussion leader rotate? Should notes or minutes be taken at each meeting and then reviewed subsequently to make sure that nothing important has been left out or misunderstood? Should each meeting have an agenda and, if so, how and when should it be developed for each subsequent meeting? Should votes be taken or should everything be decided by consensus?

- Try to treat each other with respect and consideration, but do not be surprised by disagreements and personality conflicts. Arguing can stimulate thinking — inspiring creativity as well as encouraging each person to explain ideas clearly and systematically. But arguing can also encourage aggressiveness in some people and withdrawal in others. Recognize that people interact differently in groups and have different ways of contributing. If there is a problem in the way the group interacts, address it immediately, perhaps by calling a special meeting to work out a solution. Try to avoid placing blame. Consider, for example, whether taking turns would ensure that everyone contributes to the discussion and no one dominates. Urge everyone to refrain from characterizing other people and instead to speak only about what they themselves think and feel by making "I" rather than "you" statements.

- Keep track of everyone's progress. Consider creating a chart so that all members can see at a glance what they need to do and when. Schedule regular progress reports so that any problems can be identified immediately. If someone is having difficulty completing a particular task, other group members should volunteer to help so that the project is not stalled.

For more on oral presentations, see Chapter 26.

- If the group will make an oral presentation of the written proposal, plan it carefully, giving each person a role. Rehearse the presentation as a group to make sure it satisfies the time limit and other requirements of the assignment.

After setting its ground rules, the pharmaceuticals team divided its work in much the same way as that suggested in the Guide to Writing a proposal in Chapter 7. Here are some highlights of the team's researching and writing process:

- To answer the kinds of questions listed on p. 365 of the Guide to Writing, under Analyzing and Defining the Problem (such as what caused the problem? what is its history? what are its bad effects?), the team assigned a small group to conduct library and Internet research. From this initial research, a specialist in the field of vocational training was interviewed and subsequently hired as a consultant by the team.

- As their attempts to analyze the problem continued, the team members turned to the next task in the Guide to Writing, Identifying Your Readers (p. 365). They assigned several small groups to do field research: to observe and conduct interviews at local high schools, to interview school board members and others in the community, and to interview state legislators who would be involved eventually in judging the proposal.

- They turned next to finding a solution. In researching the problem, they had collected many ideas on how the problem might be solved as well as criticisms of each possible solution. The whole team reviewed this material and after lengthy discussion agreed on the principles a good solution to this problem would need to have: (1) Students would have to begin vocational training as early as the tenth grade, (2) equipping area high schools and hiring specialized teachers would be too expensive, and (3) on-site training would not only make modern equipment and specialized teachers readily available to students but also motivate students and help them learn efficiency and accountability.

- Before figuring out how to implement these principles, the team members tested their ideas by consulting with a variety of people, many of whom they had interviewed earlier. This research helped them anticipate objections to their proposed solution and consider the specific steps necessary to implement their solution. Half of the team focused on drafting arguments to defend the solution, while the other half focused on drafting the implementation section. Leaders of the two groups kept in close communication.

- When they had a coherent argument for their solution and a plan for implementation worked out, the team members met to review the entire draft. They identified some problems and asked the drafting groups to do some revision.

- They showed the revised draft to a wide array of people, including business leaders, school board members, parent groups, representatives of teachers' unions, and interested students. They then categorized the problems and suggestions for revision offered by these critical readers and sent the draft back to the original drafting groups for another revision.

- The final revised draft was reviewed for clarity, coherence, and mechanics before being submitted to the company's board of directors and, after minor revisions, distributed to the state legislature and the local school board. It was also published in local newspapers and business magazines and on the company's Web site.

If you collaborate with other students to develop a proposal, you will not have as many outside resources as the pharmaceuticals company team in this model. The decisions this team made, however, mirror the kinds of decisions you and your fellow students will have to make.

28 Writing in Your Community

Service learning combines classroom education with life experience. Through partnerships with community organizations, colleges and universities can offer students ways to see how the knowledge that they are gaining in school can be put to work beyond the campus. Research and experience show that such programs provide valuable service to those who need it and also help students learn and retain course content. Students also often discover that their skills and knowledge can help others. If your composition class has a service-learning component, you will have an opportunity to learn more about your community, to become an active participant in that community, and to apply your writing skills to your community experience.

In service-learning programs, students are most often placed in off-campus positions with government bureaus such as local parks and recreation departments or nonprofit organizations that offer community support services such as care for the homeless. In these positions students apply what they are studying in class. Here are a few examples:

- Nursing students teach expectant mothers about prenatal and infant care.
- Chemistry students tour local elementary schools demonstrating the fun of science.
- Botany students teach fourth graders about plants native to their region.
- Zoology students help gather samples for a study of local amphibian populations.
- Political science students work with the local government to increase voter turnout.
- English-speaking students tutor grade school children who are having trouble learning to read and write English.

Whatever form your service-learning experience takes, it can serve as a valuable resource for your writing. While you will probably find much to write about in your service experience, you may also find writing is a part of your service. When writing is part of your service, you move beyond having classmates and instructors as your primary audience and enter the realm of public discourse.

▪ Using Your Service Experience as Source Material

Finding a Topic

One of the many advantages of service learning is that it can make finding an engaging topic for your writing much easier and more rewarding. The service experience should present numerous topics that might be fruitfully explored through your writing. Simply paying attention to the issues that come to bear on your service experience should help you generate a substantial list of ideas. You might ask yourself some simple questions:

- Who is most affected by the situation, and how are these people affected?
- How long has this situation existed?
- What are the results of this situation?
- What forces shape the situation? Can anything be done to alter these forces?
- How have other organizations successfully handled this issue? How else might the situation be improved?
- What common perceptions do people hold about this situation? What are my own perceptions?
- Are these perceptions inaccurate? How might they be changed?

For example, if your service experience includes working at a clinic that serves low-income families without health insurance, you might write a report explaining the known long-term effects of insufficient medical care on children. You might also write a proposal to address the problem faced by people who have little or no medical coverage. Or perhaps you are interested in arguing a position that advocates universal health care coverage. There are dozens of possible essay topics in any service experience.

Gathering Sources

In traditional college writing settings, research is often limited, by time and availability, to what one can find in the library or on the Internet. A service-learning environment can provide field research sources that would otherwise be difficult to tap. The most significant of these potential sources is the people who run the organization in which you are doing your service. If you have focused your writing on the kinds of issues that are relevant to your service, these people can serve as experts. Many of the people you work with will have years of experience and specialized training and probably will have researched the subject themselves. Take advantage of your opportunity to tap their knowledge. When approached courteously, people are often more than willing to discuss their thoughts on something important to them.

Depending on the situation, your service site might also be a good place to circulate a questionnaire or conduct a survey to help you gather information about your subject. Of course, your own observations and experiences as you perform

For suggestions on making observations, conducting interviews, and creating questionnaires, see Chapter 20.

your service will prove to be valuable as well. You might consider keeping a daily journal in which you record your experiences and observations as you perform your service. When you are ready to begin writing, you will already have done some early invention work.

The service organization itself might also be a good source of information. Such organizations often collect and produce literature that is relevant to their mission. Your organization might even maintain its own small library of resource materials that you could borrow or use. Frequently such organizations are also part of a network of similar groups that share their expertise through newsletters, trade journals, Web sites, or online discussion groups. Explore these unique resources.

Keep in mind the ethical considerations that are involved. Many service-learning environments, such as those that involve counseling, tutoring, or teaching, can give you access to information that should be kept confidential, especially if you are working with minors. Be sure that you are open about your information-gathering and that everyone whom you might use as a source knows your intentions. Any questionnaires should include a disclosure stating what you intend to do with the information gathered. Any information gained from interviews should be properly attributed, but you should consider carefully maintaining the anonymity of anyone whom you use for examples in your writing, unless you have your subjects' explicit permission to use their names. Err on the side of caution and consideration, and ask your instructor for guidance if you have any questions about how to treat sensitive material.

Writing *about* Your Service Experience

Writing in a service-learning program is really no different from other writing situations. You still must identify for yourself the kind of writing you are doing, generate ideas through invention, and refine those ideas through a process of drafting and revision. Service learning, however, may put you in a position to write for a nonacademic audience. For example, you might write an editorial for your campus or local newspaper in which you argue for increased support for your service organization or project. You might craft a letter to local government officials or even representatives to the state or national legislature suggesting a solution to a specific problem. Remember that writing is action, and as such it can be a powerful tool.

The service-learning experience can provide you with subject matter for many of the academic writing activities discussed in Part One of this textbook. While you can no doubt generate your own list of ideas, here are some to consider:

Chapter 2: Remembering Events

- Write about your first day of service. What happened? How did you feel? What did you learn? How did it differ from what you expected to learn?
- Write about a particularly difficult day. Why was it difficult? How did you handle the situation? What would you do differently? What did you learn from the experience?

Chapter 3: Writing Profiles

- Write about the place where you are doing your service. What does it look like? How does it make you feel? How does the location reflect or affect what goes on there? What does go on there?

- Write about one of the people you have met doing your service. What is he or she like? How is he or she typical (or atypical) of other people in the same position? What makes this person special or different?

Chapter 4: Explaining a Concept

- Write about a concept with which you were unfamiliar before you did your service. What does the concept mean? How is it important in the context of your service experience? How does what you learned about this concept make you think differently now?

- Write about a concept that you knew but now understand differently because of your service. How has your understanding of the concept changed? What caused that change? How might you explain that change to someone who does not share your experience?

Chapter 5: Explaining a Debate

- Write about a debate that is relevant to the type of service you are doing and briefly describe each position in the debate. (Note that there may be more than two.) Who are the major proponents of each side of the debate? What are the main reasons and evidence given to support each position?

Chapter 6: Arguing a Position

- Write an argument in support of the service organization you are working with. Why should people support it? How can they support it? Why is it a worthwhile endeavor?

- Write an argument about the value of service learning. What have you gained from this experience? Who should participate? What are the advantages of service learning to individuals and the community?

Chapter 7: Proposing a Solution

- Write about a process or procedure within or affecting the organization you are working with that you think needs to be improved. Why does it need to be improved? How might it be improved? What would the effect of the improvements be?

- Write about a policy, law, or practice that you think should be eliminated or revised because it negatively affects the organization you are working with. What would be the benefit of eliminating or revising it? Why was it created or instituted in the first place? What steps would need to be taken in order to change the policy, law, or practice?

Chapter 8: Justifying an Evaluation

- Write about how effectively the organization you are working with satisfies its objectives. How do you measure its effectiveness? In what ways does it succeed? In what ways does it fail?

- Write about your school's service-learning program. In what ways is it most successful? In what ways could it be improved?

Chapter 9: Speculating about Causes

- Write about the causes for a problem or situation that you have encountered through your service-learning experience. What brought the problem about? What circumstances perpetuate it?

- Write about why service-learning programs have become common. What function do they serve that traditional education models do not? What demand do they meet? Why are so many colleges and universities involved in such partnerships?

Writing *for* Your Service Organization

Some service-learning situations will put you in a position not just to write *about* your service experience but also to write *as part of* your service experience. You might be asked to create flyers, brochures, press releases, or Web pages for a community organization. You might help craft presentations or reports. While these may not be academic writing activities, they are still writing activities, and the strategies presented in this text still apply. You might be asked, for example, to help write a brochure that explains the purpose and function of the organization. In effect, you would be writing an explanation, and you would need to keep in mind the basic features of this genre outlined in Chapter 4.

Such writing situations give you an opportunity to practice recognizing the kinds of writing you are asked to do. While in class you might be asked to select a topic and write an essay in which you argue a position (Chapter 6) or propose a solution (Chapter 7), in your service experience you might simply be asked to create a flyer that explains the importance of a no-kill animal shelter or a brochure that urges people to carpool as a way of cutting down traffic congestion. By identifying what kind of writing activity you are being asked to do, you can identify what basic features your readers will expect to find.

Writing in organizations is frequently a collaborative process. Everyone involved in the process is expected to do his or her part. When your written document will be used to represent your organization in any way, respect the expertise of the staff, especially when their assessment of the audience differs from your own. In some situations, your service writing may be heavily edited — or not used at all. Make sure your instructor and service-learning program administrators are aware of any instances in which you and members of the organization are having difficulty reaching a consensus.

For suggestions on how to make such collaboration run smoothly and successfully, see Chapter 27.

Finally, remember that nonacademic writing often requires greater attention to presentation than most kinds of academic writing. One-inch margins and double-spaced text simply are not enough when you are trying to create eye-catching documents such as brochures and press releases. Document design can not only make a piece of writing more visually attractive and thereby stimulate readers' interest but can also help readers with different needs identify which parts of the document they will find most relevant. Therefore, carefully consider the layout and configuration of your document, and take advantage of the flexibility that even a simple word processing program can give you.

For more on document design, see Chapter 25.

Handbook

■ Introduction

Use this Handbook to help you correct errors in grammar and punctuation. Use it as well when you need advice about how to write clearer, more effective sentences. Finally, when you need to know whether to capitalize a word or whether to underline a title or put quotation marks around it, this Handbook is the first place to check. Because the Handbook is based on extensive research and is designed to be used efficiently, you can rely on it to enhance your command of standard edited English.

You may use the Handbook on your own when you edit your essays, or your instructor may guide you in using the Handbook to correct certain errors in your writing. If you are using the Handbook on your own, check the Handbook Contents on the next page, or look in the index for the category of error you are concerned about — for example, "pronoun reference," "commas," "quotation marks," or "parallelism." If you cannot identify the relevant category of error or locate the information you need, ask your instructor or another student for advice.

Your instructor may use the Handbook's letter-and-number system to lead you directly to the page where you can learn how to correct the error. For example, the code "P1-b" indicates that a comma is needed after an introductory word, phrase, or clause. Referring to the Detailed Handbook Contents inside the back cover, you would discover that P1-b is on or near p. H-57 in the Handbook. As an alternative, you can find P1-b by flipping through the text and looking at the orange tabs at the tops of the pages. Each tab indicates the section code for that page. The orange tabs on each page also include an abbreviation or a symbol for the topic covered on that page. If your instructor indicates errors in your sentences with conventional correction symbols such as *cap*, *frag*, or *ww*, you can find the section where the error is covered by checking the chart of correction symbols near the back of this book.

When you locate the Handbook section that will help you correct an error or make a sentence more concise or more graceful, you will find a brief explanation and a sentence or two illustrating correct usage. The section also provides several hand-corrected sentences so that you can see immediately how to edit your own sentence. Most of these sample sentences come from student essays written for assignments in this book. Grammatical terms are defined in the margin. In addition, below the heading of each numbered Handbook section is a URL that you can use to access interactive online exercises for practice in the topics covered in that section.

HANDBOOK CONTENTS

To design a handbook that would provide an efficient quick reference for students, we carried out extensive research. Ten college writing instructors and four professional editors worked together to identify errors* in more than five hundred student essays from colleges across the country. All of the essays were written in first-year composition courses by students using *The St. Martin's Guide to Writing*. We used this research to determine the error categories listed in the Handbook Contents. The errors are listed below in order of descending frequency and can guide you in editing your own writing. The numbers in bold following each error indicate where in this Handbook you can find help with understanding and correcting each error.

_____

* Spelling errors were not included.

1. Wordiness **W1-a–W1-c**
2. Misused word **W2-a, W2-e**
3. Incorrect or ambiguous pronoun reference **G1**
4. Verb tense errors **G5-a, G5-b**
5. Missing comma between independent clauses **P1-a**
6. Problems with hyphens between compound adjectives **M1-a**
7. Missing comma after introductory elements **P1-b**
8. Capitalization of proper or common nouns **M2-a**
9. Unnecessary comma between compound elements **P2-a**
10. Incorrect spacing **M3**
11. Missing words **E1-a–E1-d**
12. Missing comma with nonrestrictive word groups **P1-c**
13. Comma splice or fused sentence **S1, S2**
14. Problems in using quotation marks with other punctuation **P6-b**
15. Missing or unnecessary hyphens in compound nouns **M1-b**
16. Missing comma with transitional and parenthetical expressions, absolute phrases, and contrasted elements **P1-d**
17. Problems of pronoun-antecedent agreement **G2**
18. Incorrect preposition **W2-b, L3**
19. Misuse of *who, which,* or *that* **G3**
20. Unnecessarily complex sentence structure **W1-b**
21. Spelling out or using figures for numbers incorrectly **M4**
22. Problems with apostrophes in possessive nouns **P7-a**
23. Sentence fragment **S3**
24. Missing comma in items in a series **P1-e**
25. Unnecessary comma with restrictive word groups **P2-b**

This list of the top twenty-five errors can be categorized into the following five major patterns of errors. You may find it useful to keep these patterns in mind as you edit your work.

1. Missing or unnecessary commas (**P1-a–P1-d, P2-a–P2-g**)
2. Errors in word choice (**W1-a–W1-d, W2-a–W2-d**)
3. Errors in pronoun reference, agreement, or use (**G1, G2, G3**)
4. Verb tense errors (**G5-a, G5-b**)
5. Errors in recognizing and punctuating sentences — comma splices, fused sentences, fragments (**S1, S2, S3**)

■ Keeping a Record of Your Own Errors

In addition to checking your work for the errors college students usually make, you will find it useful to keep a record of the errors that *you* usually make. Recording errors in your writing can help you discover your own most frequent errors and error patterns. You can then work toward avoiding them.

To use the Record of Errors form below, note the name and section number of each error you make in the left-hand column. (See the Handbook Contents on p. H-2 or the list of correction symbols at the back of the book for the names of errors.) For example, if in your first essay your instructor or another student marks a vague use of the pronoun *this* at the beginning of two of your sentences, locate the section that provides help in correcting this error (G1), and enter the error name in the left column along with the section number: Vague use of *this*, *that*, and *which*, G1. Then under *Essay 1* and next to the name of the error, enter the number *2* to indicate how many times you made this error. As you edit subsequent essays, you can easily review this section in the Handbook to make sure you have avoided this pronoun problem.

By your second or third essay, you should begin to see patterns in the errors you make and to understand how to recognize and correct them.

RECORD OF ERRORS

Name of Error and Section Number in the Handbook	FREQUENCY						
	Essay 1	Essay 2	Essay 3	Essay 4	Essay 5	Essay 6	Essay 7

S   Sentence Boundaries

S1   Comma Splices

For practice, go to bedfordstmartins.com/theguide/csplice

In a comma splice, two **independent clauses** are improperly joined by a comma.

```
     ┌── INDEPENDENT ──┐  ┌── INDEPENDENT CLAUSE ──┐
                CLAUSE
```
COMMA SPLICE   I know what to do, I just don't know how to do it.

> **independent (main) clause** A word group with a subject and a predicate that can stand alone as a separate sentence. (A predicate is the part of a clause that includes a complete verb and says something about the subject.)

Because a comma splice can be edited in many ways, first consider how the ideas in the two independent clauses relate. For example, are they equally important, or does one depend on or explain the other? Then select the strategy below that will best clarify this relationship for a reader. To edit the example just given, for example, the writer might change the comma to a period.

> ► I know what to do⸴ I just don't know how to do it.

Add a subordinating conjunction to one of the clauses, rewording as necessary.

> ► *After*
> ~~The~~ New York City police began to crack down on minor offenders, a significant decrease in major crime resulted as well.

> ► *Though*
> *Midnight Cowboy* ~~was~~ rated X in the early 1970s, ~~it~~ contained one scene that was considered "sexually explicit," ~~yet~~ the movie was tastefully done and could not be considered pornographic by today's standards.

> **subordinating conjunction** A word or phrase (such as *although, because, since*, or *as soon as*) that introduces a dependent clause and relates it to an independent clause.

By beginning a clause with a subordinating conjunction, you indicate that the clause is subordinate to — and dependent on — the main clause. Usually, the **dependent clause** explains or qualifies the **independent clause**. Select the subordinating conjunction carefully so that it tells the reader how the ideas in the dependent clause relate to the ideas in the independent clause.

Separate the independent clauses with a comma and a coordinating conjunction.

> ► On the album *Other People's Songs*, Erasure has produced an eclectic collection
> *and*
> of cover treatments, the result highlights the group's strengths and
> weaknesses throughout its thirty-year recording career.

> **dependent (subordinate) clause** A word group that has a subject, a predicate, and a subordinating word (such as *because*) at the beginning; it cannot stand by itself as a sentence but must be connected to an independent (main) clause.

> **coordinating conjunction** A word that joins comparable and equally important sentence elements: *for, and, or, but, nor, yet*, or *so*.

> ▶ By 1988, the average American car had achieved a high of 26 mpg, *but* by 2003 that figure had fallen to less than 21 mpg.

The coordinating conjunction tells the reader that the ideas in the two clauses are closely related and equally important.

Separate the independent clauses with a semicolon.

> ▶ The tattoo needle appeared to be like an extension of his arm ; the needle was his brush, and the human body, his canvas.

> ▶ Nate was very lucky ; he lived to see his hundredth birthday.

The semicolon tells the reader that the ideas in the two clauses are closely connected, but it implies the connection rather than stating it. Occasionally, a colon may be used to introduce a second independent clause (see P4-a).

Separate the independent clauses with a semicolon or a period, and add a conjunctive adverb or a transitional phrase such as *for example* or *in other words*.

conjunctive adverb A word or phrase (such as *finally, however,* or *therefore*) that tells how the ideas in two sentences or independent clauses are connected.

> ▶ He doesn't need the map right now ; *instead,* he just follows the direction Kiem pointed out to him before and checks it with the compass.

> ▶ He doesn't need the map right now . *Instead,* he just follows the direction Kiem pointed out to him before and checks it with the compass.

The semicolon tells the reader that the ideas in the two clauses are closely connected, and the conjunctive adverb describes the connection. The period shows a stronger break. Conjunctive adverbs are used more frequently in formal than in informal writing.

subordinating conjunction A word or phrase (such as *although, because, since,* or *as soon as*) that introduces a dependent clause and relates it to an independent clause.

Note: A **subordinating conjunction** always begins a clause, but a conjunctive adverb can appear in other positions within a clause. If the conjunctive adverb appears in the middle of one clause rather than between two clauses, the semicolon is still placed between the clauses, not before the adverb.

> ▶ The importance of English as a link between those who have little else in common is clear ; the true controversy , *in fact,* lies in other issues.

Turn the independent clauses into separate sentences.

▶ At high noon we were off, paddling down the Potomac River, we were two
to a canoe, leaving space in the middle for our gear. *[We]*

▶ Unfortunately, not many people realize how much scientific research with
animals means to the medical world, ~~only~~ the scientists themselves and the
diseased patients who suffer and hope for new cures can fully understand the
importance of animal testing. *[Only]*

The period at the end of the first independent clause tells the reader that one
complete sentence is ending and another is beginning.

Turn one independent clause into a phrase that modifies the other.

▶ At high noon we were off, paddling down the Potomac River, ~~we were~~ two to a
canoe with space in the middle for our gear.

Eliminating the subject and verb in the second clause turns this clause into
a **modifying phrase,** reducing the number of words and closely connecting the
ideas.

modifying phrase A word
group that serves as an
adjective or adverb.

S2   Fused Sentences

For practice, go to bedfordstmartins.com/theguide/fused

A fused or run-on sentence consists of two **independent clauses** run together with
no punctuation.

	┌INDEPENDENT CLAUSE┐──────── INDEPENDENT CLAUSE────────
FUSED	Her mood was good I took the opportunity to ask if she had a
SENTENCE	few minutes to answer some questions.

**independent (main)
clause** A word group with
a subject and a predicate
that can stand alone as a
separate sentence. (A
predicate is the part of a
clause that includes a complete verb and says some-
thing about the subject.)

Because a fused sentence can be edited in many ways, first consider how the
ideas in the two independent clauses are related, and then select the most appropriate strategy below. In the example just given, the writer might emphasize the causal
relationship between the clauses.

▶ ~~Her~~ mood was good, I took the opportunity to ask if she had a few minutes
to answer some questions. *[Because her]*

Make one of the clauses subordinate to the other by adding a subordinating conjunction and rewording as necessary.

> *that*
> ► Kids can be so cruel to each other it is a wonder we all make it through childhood.

> *Although kids can be extremely   amazingly⌃*
> ► ~~Kids can be so~~ cruel to each other, ~~it is a wonder~~ we all make it through childhood.

By beginning a clause with a subordinating conjunction, you indicate that the clause is subordinate to — and dependent on — the main clause. Usually, the **dependent clause** explains or qualifies the independent clause. Choose the subordinating conjunction carefully so that it tells the reader how the dependent clause relates to the independent clause.

Add a comma and a coordinating conjunction to separate the independent clauses.

> ⌃ *and*
> ► The beast was upon me I could feel his paws pressing down on my chest.

The coordinating conjunction tells the reader that the ideas in the two clauses are equally important.

Separate the independent clauses with a semicolon.

> ► I looked around at the different monitors, most were large color monitors, many of which were connected to the supercomputer.

The semicolon tells the reader that the ideas in the two clauses are closely connected, but it implies the connection rather than stating it. Occasionally, a colon may be used to introduce a second independent clause (see P4-a).

Separate the independent clauses with a semicolon or a period, and add a conjunctive adverb or a transitional phrase such as *for example* or *in other words*.

> ⌃ *instead*⌃
> ► Most students do not do their homework during the day they do it in the evening.

> ⊙ *Instead*⌃
> ► Most students do not do their homework during the day they do it in the evening.

The semicolon indicates that the ideas in the two clauses are closely connected, and the conjunctive adverb explains the connection. The period indicates a stronger break. Conjunctive adverbs appear more frequently in formal than in informal writing.

---

subordinating conjunction A word or phrase (such as *although, because, since,* or *as soon as*) that introduces a dependent clause and relates it to an independent clause.

dependent (subordinate) clause A word group that has a subject, a predicate, and a subordinating word (such as *because*) at the beginning; it cannot stand by itself as a sentence but must be connected to an independent (main) clause.

coordinating conjunction A word that joins comparable and equally important sentence elements: *for, and, or, but, nor, yet,* or *so.*

conjunctive adverb A word or phrase (such as *finally, however,* or *therefore*) that tells how the ideas in two sentences or independent clauses are connected.

Note: A **subordinating conjunction** always *introduces* a clause, but a conjunctive adverb can occupy different positions within a clause. If the conjunctive adverb appears in the middle of one clause rather than between two clauses, the semicolon is still placed between the clauses, not before the adverb.

> ; ↑instead↑
> ▶ Most students do not do their homework during the day they do it in the evening.

Turn the independent clauses into separate sentences.

> His
> ▶ He was only eight. his life hadn't even started.

> ▶ I couldn't believe it. I had fallen into a puddle of mud.

The period at the end of the first independent clause tells the reader that one complete sentence is ending and another is beginning.

Turn one independent clause into a phrase that modifies the other.

> ▶ The beast was upon me, I could feel his paws pressing down on my chest.

Eliminating the subject and verb in the second clause turns this clause into a **modifying phrase**, reducing the number of words and closely linking the ideas.

S3   Sentence Fragments

For practice, go to bedfordstmartins.com/theguide/frag

A fragment is either an incomplete sentence, lacking a complete **subject** or **predicate**, or a **dependent clause** punctuated as a sentence. Even though a fragment begins with a capital letter and ends with a period, it cannot stand alone as a sentence.

FRAGMENT   Tonight it's my turn. *A ride-along with Sergeant Rob Nether of the Green Valley Police Department.*

Because a fragment can often be edited in several ways, begin by considering what the fragment lacks and how its ideas relate to those in the sentences before and after it. Then use one of the following strategies to change the fragment into a complete sentence. To edit the fragment in the example, the writer might connect it to the preceding sentence.

> for a
> ▶ Tonight it's my turn, A ride-along with Sergeant Rob Nether of the Green Valley Police Department.

modifying phrase A word group that serves as an adjective or adverb.

subject The part of a clause that identifies who or what is being discussed: At the checkpoint, *we* unloaded the canoes.

predicate The part of a clause that includes a complete verb and says something about the subject: At the checkpoint, we *unloaded the canoes.*

dependent (subordinate) clause A word group that has a subject, a predicate, and a subordinating word (such as *because*) at the beginning; it cannot stand by itself as a sentence but must be connected to an independent (main) clause: *Although it was raining*, we loaded our gear onto the buses.

Connect the fragment to a complete sentence.

▶ Frank turned the tarot cards one at a time. ~~Each~~ *each* time telling me something about my future.

▶ A unique design has the distinct advantage of becoming associated with its role. ~~For~~ *for* example, the highly successful Coke bottle shape, which is now associated with soft drinks.

Eliminate the subordinating word or words that make a clause dependent.

▶ The world that I was born into demanded continuous work. ~~Where nobody~~ *Nobody* got ahead, and everyone came home tired.

Add or complete the verb or the subject to change a fragment into a complete sentence.

▶ The crowd in the lounge is basically young. The teenage and early twenties generation *gathers there*.

▶ Children are brought up in different ways. Some *grow up* around violence.

Note: Sometimes writers use fragments intentionally for emphasis or special effect.

The bare utility of the clock echoes the simplicity of the office. No sign of a large hardwood desk or a pillowy leather chair or even a wall with shelves filled with imposing law books.

Use intentional fragments cautiously. Especially in academic writing, many readers may perceive them as errors, regardless of your intentions. In the example above, for instance, the same impact might also be achieved by using a colon or dash.

G Grammatical Sentences

G1 Pronoun Reference

For practice, go to bedfordstmartins.com/theguide/pref

Make sure that each **pronoun** clearly refers to one specific **antecedent**.

> ***The elderly and children*** are victims when no one bothers to check on ***them***.

In this example, the pronoun *them* refers to a specific antecedent, *the elderly and children*.

Rewrite to eliminate vague uses of *they, it,* or *you*.

▶ Lani explained that everything is completely supported by individual
The organization receives
contributions. ~~They receive~~ no tax support.

▶ Often, a guest such as Caroline Kennedy or Kevin Costner may appear
having the same guest return
more than once. Although ~~it~~ seems repetitious, it actually is not because the

guest discusses different topics each time.

▶ Parents argue that beginning the program in the sixth grade is too early.
They say that   *encourages*
~~By~~ exposing teens to sex education early, ~~you encourage~~ them to go out and

have sex.

Add a noun, change the pronoun to a noun, or revise the sentence to eliminate vague uses of *this, that,* or *which*.

▶ Researchers have noticed that men interrupt women more than women
finding
interrupt men. This may explain why women sometimes find it difficult to start

and sustain conversations with men.

good grades
▶ I was an *A* student, and I thought ~~that~~ should have been enough for any teacher.

pronoun A word that replaces a specific noun (such as *she, it, his, they, them, yours, ours, myself, whose,* or *which*), points out a specific noun (such as *this, these,* or *that*), or refers to an unspecified person or object (such as *everybody* or *each*).

antecedent The word or words that a pronoun replaces and to which it refers.

▶ The brevity of the first story prevents the reader from dwelling on the plot

Because these

and caring about the outcome. ~~These~~ faults are not present in "The Soft

is

Voice of the Serpent," ~~which makes~~ it much more fulfilling to read.

Add a missing antecedent, or eliminate a pronoun with no clear antecedent.

▶ In addition to the cars your tenants actually drive, five or six vehicles are

your tenants

always on and around the property. As a result, not only do ~~they~~ park ~~some of~~

~~them~~ in front of their neighbors' homes, but their questionable visitors park up

and down the street as well.

Adding an antecedent (specifying *your tenants* instead of *they*) and eliminating a pronoun (reducing *park some of them* to *park*) simplify and clarify the sentence.

Identify a specific antecedent if a pronoun refers vaguely to a clause or a whole sentence.

▶ After the long ride, we reached the place for our expedition at Pine Heaven

the trip

Forest in western Virginia. At my age, ~~it~~ seemed to take forever.

Rewrite to eliminate an ambiguous reference to two possible antecedents.

if

▶ Students may now sue their schools ~~if they~~ are underperforming.

underperforming

▶ Students may now sue their schools. ~~if they are underperforming.~~

Rewrite to eliminate an implied reference.

In this   the singer

▶ ~~This~~ song tells about being carefree and going through life without any worries.

Years later, though, he starts to remember his past, and things do not seem so

problem-free anymore.

In this example, adding *the singer* specifies an antecedent for *he*.

Note: Sometimes the implied noun may be present in another form, such as a possessive (*Mary's* for *Mary*) or as part of another word (*child* in *childhood*).

▶ Radaker's ~~arguments~~ irritated everyone at the lecture because he failed to

his arguments
support ~~them~~ with examples or evidence.
^

G2 Pronoun Agreement

For practice, go to bedfordstmartins.com/theguide/pagree

Make sure that a **pronoun** and its **antecedent** agree in **number,** in **person,** and in **gender.** In the following examples, the arrows connect the pronouns and their antecedents.

The *scientists* did not know what *they* were creating.

I thought about Punita's offer while watching the movie. *My* curiosity won.

After we went back to the lab, *Punita* started concentrating on *her* work.

The form of the antecedent and the form of the pronoun must correspond — agree — so that a reader is not troubled by inconsistencies or confused about how many, who, or which gender you mean.

G2-a Use either singular or plural forms consistently for both a pronoun and its antecedent.

If the antecedent of a pronoun is singular, the pronoun must be singular so that both agree in number. Likewise, if the antecedent is plural, the pronoun must be plural.

The *shelter* gets most of *its* cats and dogs from *owners* who cannot keep *their* pets.

When the pronoun and its antecedent do not agree, change one or the other so that both are singular or both are plural, or rewrite the sentence to eliminate the inconsistency. See also E2-b.

Change either the pronoun or its antecedent so that both are singular or plural.

he or she is
▶ The patient is fully aware of the decision that ~~they are~~ making.
^

Patients are
▶ ~~The patient is~~ fully aware of the decision that they are making.
^

Note: As an alternative, you may be able to eliminate the pronoun.

each
▶ The patient is fully aware of ~~the~~ decision, ~~that they are making.~~
^

---

pronoun A word that replaces a specific noun (such as *she, it, his, they, them, yours, ours, myself, whose,* or *which*), points out a specific noun (such as *this, these,* or *that*), or refers to an unspecified person or object (such as *everybody* or *each*).

antecedent The word or words that a pronoun replaces and to which it refers.

number The form of a word that shows whether it refers to one thing (singular) or more than one (plural): *parent, parents; child, children.*

person The form of a word that shows whether it refers to *I* or *we* (first person), to *you* (second person), or to *he, she, it,* or *they* (third person).

gender The form of a word that shows whether it refers to a male (*he*) or a female (*she*).

Revise the sentence to eliminate the inconsistency.

▶ Roommates get agitated at always being told to clean, and the roommate

complaining.
doing the yelling gets tired of ~~hearing their own voice complain.~~
       ^

Use a singular pronoun to refer to a singular indefinite pronoun, or reword the sentence.

▶ Whether student, teacher, faculty member, graduate, or parent, each wants

his or her
~~their~~ school to be the one that remains open.
   ^
All students, teachers, faculty members, graduates, and parents want
▶ ~~Whether student, teacher, faculty member, graduate, or parent, each wants~~
their school to be the one that remains open.
   ^
                                       students
▶ This event would be a good chance for ~~everyone~~ to come out, socialize, and
                                             ^
enjoy themselves.

▶ This event would be a good chance for everyone to come out, socialize, and

a relaxing afternoon.
enjoy ~~themselves.~~
   ^

Consider the level of formality of your writing as you choose among your options. Participants in a casual conversation may not mind if an indefinite pronoun and its antecedent do not agree, but such errors are not acceptable in most formal writing.

Use a singular pronoun in most cases if the antecedent is a collective noun.

                                                                its
▶ The Santa Barbara School District has a serious problem on ~~their~~ agenda.
                                                                  ^

A collective noun may sometimes be considered plural if it refers to the group members as individuals: The *couple* decided it was time to consolidate *their* bank accounts.

See also G6-b.

G2-b **Use masculine, feminine, or gender-free forms to match a pronoun with its antecedent.**

Match a masculine pronoun with a masculine antecedent and a feminine pronoun with a feminine antecedent so that the pronoun and its antecedent agree in **gender**.

I first met *Mark* the day *he* was hired.

If an antecedent might be either masculine or feminine, avoid using a pronoun that stereotypes by gender. See also W3-c.

Match a plural antecedent with a plural pronoun to include both sexes.

▶ Many people believe that ~~a boy or girl is~~ *children are* better off with a family that is able to provide for all of their needs than with a poverty-stricken parent.

Use a phrase that includes both masculine and feminine singular pronouns (such as *his or her*) to refer to both sexes.

▶ Many people believe that a child is better off with a family that is able to provide for all of ~~their~~ *his or her* needs than with a poverty-stricken parent.

Note: If repeating a phrase such as *his* or *her* seems cumbersome or repetitious, try using plural forms or eliminating the pronouns altogether, as the following strategy suggests.

Rewrite to eliminate unneeded or awkward pairs of masculine and feminine pronouns when you are referring to both men and women.

▶ This solution, of course, assumes that the bus ~~driver~~ *drivers* will be where ~~he/she is~~ *they are* supposed to be; boredom sometimes inspires ~~a driver~~ *drivers* to make up new and exciting variations on ~~his or her~~ *the* designated routes.

Note: Avoid using *he/she* in all but the most informal writing situations.

G3   Relative Pronouns

For practice, go to bedfordstmartins.com/theguide/relp

Use personal **relative pronouns** to refer to people: *who, whom, whoever, whomever,* and *whose.*

> This reaction is unlike the response of the boys, *who* had trouble focusing on a subject.

Use nonpersonal relative pronouns to refer to things: *which, whichever, whatever,* and *whose* (*whose* can be used as a nonpersonal relative pronoun as well as a personal one).

relative pronoun A pronoun (such as *who, whom, whose, which,* or *that*) that introduces an adjective clause (a clause that modifies a noun or pronoun).

These interruptions, 75 percent of *which* come solely from males, disrupt conversations.

Use *that* for general references to things and groups.

Sensory modalities are governed by the side of the brain *that* is not damaged.

See also G6-e.

G3-a   Select *who* for references to people, *which* for nonrestrictive references to things, and *that* for restrictive references to groups and things.

My attention focused on a little dark-haired boy *who* was crying.

The tournament, *which* we had worked for all year, was the most prestigious event of the season.

Save Our Sharks tried to promote a bill *that* would forbid the killing of certain sharks.

Change *that* to *who* to refer to a person.

▶ Illness phobics have countless examinations despite the reassurance of each

physician <s>that</s> *who* examines them.

▶ It was his parents <s>that</s> *who* made him run for student council, play the piano, and go out for sports.

Note: Rewriting a sentence to simplify its structure sometimes eliminates a problem with pronouns.

▶ <s>It was his</s> *His* parents <s>that</s> made him run for student council, play the piano, and go out for sports.

See also G3-b for information on *who* and *whom*.

Change *that* to *which* when a nonrestrictive clause supplies extra, nondefining information.

▶ Caroline had the prettiest jet-black hair, <s>that</s> *which* went down to the middle of her back.

(See P1-c on using commas with nonrestrictive word groups.)

Change *which* to *that* when a restrictive clause supplies essential information defining a thing or a group.

> ▶ From the moment we are born, we come into a society ~~which~~ *that* assimilates us into its culture.

> ▶ In addition to the equipment and technology ~~which~~ *that* fill the trauma room, a team of experts assembles before the patient arrives.

(See P2-b on unnecessary commas with restrictive word groups.)

Note: Which is usually used only in nonrestrictive clauses, but sometimes writers use it in restrictive clauses as well.

restrictive clause A clause, not set off by commas, that provides information essential to defining or identifying the noun or pronoun it modifies.

G3-b   Use *who* as a subject and *whom* as an object.

Two strategies can help you to figure out which word to use.

1. Mark the phrase or clause, and then arrange its words in subject-verb-object order or **preposition**-object order. In this standard order, a subject (*who*) is followed by a verb, but an object (*whom*) follows a subject and verb or follows a preposition.

2. Look for the subject of the clause. If the verb in the clause has another subject, use *whom;* if the verb in the clause has no other subject, use *who.*

SUBJECT	We remember [*who* tips well] and [*who* doesn't].
OBJECT OF VERB	*I will always admire whom.* Mr. Scott is someone [*whom* I will always admire].
OBJECT OF PREPOSITION	The university employs a large number of foreign teaching assistants [for *whom* English is a second language].

object The part of a clause that receives the action of the verb (At the checkpoint, we unloaded *the canoes*) or the part of a phrase that follows a preposition (We dragged them to *the river*).

preposition A word (such as *between, in,* or *of*) that always appears as part of a phrase and indicates the relation between a word in a sentence and the object of the preposition: The water splashed *into* the canoe.

Change *who* to *whom* when the pronoun is an object within another clause that has a subject and a verb.

> ▶ He has the ability to attract guests ~~who~~ *whom* people want to hear.

Change *who* to *whom* when the pronoun is the object of a preposition.

> ▶ He also met his wife, ~~who~~ *whom* he was married to for fifty-two years.

> ▶ He also met his wife, ~~who~~ *to whom* he was married ~~to~~ for fifty-two years.

Change *whom* to *who* when the pronoun is the subject of a clause, followed by a verb.

▶ The libraries are staffed by professionals ~~whom~~ *who* have instituted methods to keep students informed of new materials.

G4   Pronoun Case

For practice, go to bedfordstmartins.com/theguide/pcase

A pronoun can take different forms or cases, depending on its role in a sentence.

subject complement A word or word group that follows a linking verb (such as *seems*, *appears*, or *is* and other forms of *be*) and describes or restates the subject: The tents looked *old and dirty*.

- Subject or **subject complement:** *I, we, you, he, she, it, they* (subjective form)

  "*You*'d better be careful," *she* said.

  It is *we* you owe the money to.

- Object of a verb or a **preposition:** *me, us, you, him, her, it, them* (objective form)

  This realization spurred *me* to hasten the search.

  Her dog, Peter the Great, went with *her* on the excavation in southern Siberia.

- Possession or ownership: *mine, ours, yours, his, hers, theirs, my, our, your, his, her, its, their* (possessive form)

  I trusted *his* driving.

  I finished putting *my* gear on and rolled over backward into the ocean.

  See R2-a for more on pronouns.

reflexive pronoun A pronoun such as *myself* or *ourselves* that refers to a noun or a personal pronoun in the same clause.

Replace a reflexive pronoun that does not refer to another noun or pronoun in the clause.

▶ Kyle and ~~myself~~ *I* went upstairs to see how she was doing.

A reflexive pronoun does not belong in this sentence because *myself* does not refer to a preceding *I*.

compound subject Two or more words acting as a subject and linked by *and*.

Change a pronoun to the subjective form if it is part of a compound subject.

▶ Even though Annie and ~~me~~ *I* went through the motions, we didn't understand the customs of our host.

Change a pronoun to the objective form if it is an object (or part of a compound object) of a preposition or a verb.

>   There was an invisible wall between ~~she~~ *her* and ~~I~~ *me*.

(marginal note) **compound object** Two or more words acting as an object and linked by *and*.

Change a pronoun to the possessive form when it modifies a gerund.

>   One of the main reasons for ~~me~~ *my* wanting to stay home with my children until they enter grade school is that I would miss so much.

(marginal note) **gerund** A verb form that is used as a noun and ends in *-ing*: *arguing, throwing.*

Change the form of a pronoun to fit the implied or understood wording of a comparison using *than* or *as*.

>   I was still faster than ~~her~~ *she*.

Test whether a pronoun form fits by filling in the implied wording.

| INCORRECT PRONOUN | I was still faster than *her* [was fast]. |
| CORRECT PRONOUN | I was still faster than *she* [was fast]. |

Use *we* to precede a subject or *us* to precede an object.

We is the subjective form, and *us* is the objective form. Select the form that matches the role of the noun in the sentence.

>   Whenever ~~us~~ *we* neighborhood kids would go out and play, I would always be goalie.

Test your choice of pronoun by reading the sentence with the noun left out.

| INCORRECT PRONOUN | Whenever *us* would go out and play, I would always be goalie. |
| CORRECT PRONOUN | Whenever *we* would go out and play, I would always be goalie. |

G5   Verbs

For practice, go to bedfordstmartins.com/theguide/verbs

Use standard verb forms in the appropriate **tense**, **mood**, and **voice**.

(marginal note) **tense** The form of a verb that shows the time of the action or state of being.

G5-a **Select the appropriate verb tense to place events in past, present, and future time.**

Most of the time you will probably choose the correct verb tense without thinking about it. (See R2-a for a review of the basic verb tenses.) In a few situations, however,

(marginal note) **mood** The form of a verb that shows the writer's attitude toward a statement.

(marginal note) **voice** The form of a verb that indicates (active) or deemphasizes (passive) the performer of the action.

you will need to pay special attention to conventional usage or to the relationships among different verbs within the context of your essay.

> ## For ESL Writers
>
> See L2 for advice on how to use the correct tense in conditional clauses, two-word verbs, and helping (auxiliary) verbs and whether to use a gerund or infinitive form after a verb.

Change verbs from the past tense to the present when discussing events in a literary work or film, general truths, ongoing principles, and facts.

> ▶ In the "Monkey Garden," the girl ~~knew~~ *knows* it ~~was~~ *is* time to grow up but still
>
> ~~wanted~~ *wants* to play with the other kids in her make-believe world.

> ▶ In the film, Virginia Woolf (Nicole Kidman) ~~was~~ *is* an intensely neurotic woman
>
> whose diet ~~seemed~~ *seems* to consist entirely of cigarettes.

Academic readers expect this use of the present tense in a literary analysis, as if the action in a work is always present and ongoing. Readers also expect general truths, facts, and ongoing principles to be stated in the present tense. See also E2-a.

GENERAL TRUTH The family *is* the foundation for a child's education.

ONGOING
PRINCIPLE Attaining self-sufficiency *is* one of the most important priorities of our energy policy.

FACT The earth *is tilted* at an angle of 23 degrees.

Note: Some style guides make different recommendations about verb tense, depending on the field and its conventions. The style guide of the American Psychological Association (APA), for example, recommends using the past tense for past studies and past research procedures but using the present tense for research implications and conclusions.

APA STYLE Davidson *stated* that father absence *is* more than twice as common now as in our parents' generation.

Change the verb from the past tense to the past perfect (using *had*) to show that one past action already had taken place before another past action occurred.

> ▶ The victim's roommate also claimed that she *had* called the dorm office two days prior to the suicide attempt.

The past action identified by the verb *had called* occurred before the past action identified by the verb *claimed*.

> **For ESL Writers**
>
> Certain verbs — ones that indicate existence, states of mind, and the senses of sight, smell, touch, and so on — are rarely used in the **progressive tense**. Such verbs include *appear, be, belong, contain, feel, forget, have, hear, know, mean, prefer, remember, see, smell, taste, think, understand,* and *want.*
>
>   *belong*
> ▶ I ~~am belonging~~ to the campus group for foreign students.

progressive tense A tense that shows ongoing action, consisting of a form of *be* plus the *-ing* form of the main verb: I *am waiting*.

G5-b **Use the correct verb endings and verb forms.**

The five basic forms of regular verbs (such as *talk*) follow the same pattern, adding *-s, -ed,* and *-ing* as shown here. The forms of irregular verbs (such as *speak*) do not consistently follow this pattern in forming the past and the past participle. (See R2-a.)

- Infinitive or base: *talk* or *speak*

  Every day I *talk* on the phone and *speak* to my friends.

- Third-person singular present (*-s* form): *talks* or *speaks*

  He *talks* softly, and she *speaks* slowly.

- Past: *talked* or *spoke*

  I *talked* to my parents last week, and I *spoke* to Jed on Tuesday.

- Present participle (*-ing* form): *talking* or *speaking*

  She is *talking* on the phone now, and he is *speaking* to a friend.

- Past participle (*-ed* form): *talked* or *spoken*

  I have *talked* to her many times, but she has not *spoken* to him yet.

Add an *-s* or *-es* ending to a verb when the subject is in the third-person singular (*he, she, it,* or a singular noun).

    treats
▶ The national drug control policy ~~treat~~ drug abuse as a law enforcement problem.

    accounts
▶ This group ~~account~~ for more than 10 percent of the total U.S. population.

For ESL Writers

Choosing the correct verb form is sometimes complicated by English expressions. For example, *used to* followed by the base form of the verb does not mean the same as *get used to* followed by a gerund.

In the United States, most people *used to live* in rural areas. [This situation existed in the past but has changed.]

My daughter *is getting used to going* to school every day. [She is getting in the habit of attending school.]

(For more on choosing correct word forms, see W2.)

Delete an *-s* or *-es* ending from a verb when the subject is in the first person (*I, we*), second person (*you*), or third-person plural (*they*).

▶ Because I didn't tell you about the movie, I really ~~suggests~~ *suggest* that you go see it.

Add a *-d* or an *-ed* ending to a regular verb to form the past tense or the past participle.

▶ This movie was filmed in New Orleans because it resembles the city where the story is ~~suppose~~ *supposed* to take place.

▶ As we walked through the library, she ~~explain~~ *explained* the meaning of the yellow signs.

Check to be sure you have used the correct form of an irregular verb.

If you are uncertain about a verb form, refer to the list of irregular verbs in R2-a or check your dictionary.

▶ The hostess greeted us and ~~lead~~ *led* us to our seats.

▶ We could tell our food had just ~~came~~ *come* off the grill because it still sizzled.

Note: Some verbs with different meanings are confusing because they have similar forms. For example, the verb *lie* (*lie, lay, lain, lying*) means "recline," but the verb *lay* (*lay, laid, laid, laying*) means "put or place." Check such verbs in the Glossary of Frequently Misused Words at the end of this Handbook or in a dictionary to make sure that you are using the correct forms of the word you intend.

▶ I thought everyone was going to see my car ~~laying~~ *lying* on its side.

G5-c Choose the correct form of a verb to show the indicative, imperative, or subjunctive mood.

INDICATIVE	There *was* Ward, the perfect father, who *served* as sole provider for the family.
	Where *are* the Cleavers today?
IMPERATIVE	*Take* me to the mall.
SUBJUNCTIVE	If it *were* to rain on the day of the picnic, we would simply bring everything indoors.

The subjunctive is often used in clauses with *if* or *that*. Always use the **base form** of the verb for the present subjunctive (see G5-b). For the past tense of the verb *be*, the subjunctive form is *were*, not *was*.

▶ Even if this claim ~~was~~ *were* true, it would raise a very controversial issue.

▶ It was as if he ~~was~~ *were* stretching his neck to pick leaves or fruit out of a high tree.

G5-d Use verbs primarily in the active voice.

The **active voice** calls attention to the actor performing an action. By contrast, the **passive voice** emphasizes the recipient of the action or the action itself while omitting or deemphasizing the actor.

ACTIVE	The monkey *lived* in the garden.
PASSIVE	The story *is told* by a girl as she reflects on her own childhood.

Change passive verbs to active in most writing situations.

Straightforward and direct, the active voice creates graceful, clear writing that emphasizes actors.

▶ The ~~story is told by the girl~~ *girl tells the story* as she reflects on her own childhood.

▶ ~~Physicians are attracted by the~~ *The* monetary rewards of high-tech research *attract physicians*.

Rewrite to eliminate awkward, unnecessary passive verbs.

▶ The guests cluster like grapes *seeking others with similar interests* ~~as similar interests are sought~~.

---

indicative mood The verb form that is ordinarily used for statements and questions.

imperative mood The verb form used for commands or directions.

subjunctive mood The verb form that is used for wishes, suggestions, and conditions that are hypothetical, impossible, or unlikely.

base form The uninflected form of a verb: I *eat;* to *play.*

active voice The verb form that shows the subject in action: The cat *caught* the mouse.

passive voice The verb form that shows something happening to the subject: The mouse *was caught* by the cat.

Note: The passive is sometimes useful if you want to shift information to the end of a sentence. It is also frequently used in impersonal writing that focuses on an action rather than an actor, as in a scientific research report.

> When the generator *is turned on,* water *is forced* down the tunnel, and the animals swim against the current. Their metabolism *is measured.* They have participated in this experiment before, and the results from that run and this new one *will be compared.*

G6   Subject-Verb Agreement

For practice, go to bedfordstmartins.com/theguide/svagree

Use **subjects** and **verbs** that agree in **person** and **number.** Agreement problems often occur when a sentence has a complicated subject or verb, especially when the subject and verb are separated by other words.

>   *are*
> ▶ The large amounts of money that are associated with sports ~~is~~ not the problem.

The plural subject, *amounts,* requires a plural verb, *are.* See also R2-a to check the correct forms of *be* and other irregular verbs.

G6-a   **Make sure the subject and verb agree even if they are separated by other words.**

> The *relationship* between artists and politicians *has become* a controversial issue.

First identify the subject and the verb; then change one to agree with the other.

>   *is*
> ▶ The pattern of echoes from these sound waves ~~are~~ converted by computer into a visual image.
>
> ▶ The ~~pattern of~~ echoes from these sound waves are converted by computer into a visual image.

G6-b   **Use a singular verb with a subject that is a collective noun.**

> The *association distributes* information on showing bison, selling bison, and marketing bison meat.

Change the verb to a singular form if the subject is a collective noun.

> *fights*
> ► If a military team ~~fight~~ without spirit and will, it will probably lose.
> ^

Note: A collective noun is generally considered singular because it treats a group as a single unit. If it refers to the members of the group as individuals, however, it may be considered plural.

SINGULAR (GROUP AS A UNIT)	The *staff is* amiable.
PLURAL (INDIVIDUAL MEMBERS)	The *staff exchange* greetings and small talk as *they begin* putting on *their* surgical garb.

G6-c   Use a verb that agrees with a subject placed after it.

In most sentences, the subject precedes the verb, but some sentences are inverted. For example, sentences beginning with *there is* and *there are* reverse the standard order, putting the subject after the verb.

VERB┌────SUBJECT────────┐
There *are no busy lines and brushstrokes* in the paintings.

VERB┌SUBJECT┐
There *is interaction* between central and peripheral visual fields.

In inverted sentences, change the verb so that it agrees with the subject that follows it, or rewrite the sentence.

> *were*
> ► The next morning, there ~~was~~ Mike and Cindy, acting as if nothing had happened.
> ^

> *were*
> ► The next morning, ~~there was~~ Mike and Cindy, acting as if nothing had happened.
> ^

G6-d   Use a plural verb with a compound subject.

┌────SUBJECT────────┐VERB
She and her husband have a partnership with her in-laws.

Two subjects joined by *and* require a plural verb.

> *accumulate,*
> ► Dust and dirt ~~accumulates,~~ bathrooms get mildewy, and kitchens get greasy.
> ^

Note: If two subjects are joined by *or* or *nor*, the verb should agree with the subject that is closer to it.

Most nights, my daughter or my sons *start* dinner.

compound subject Two or more words acting as a subject and linked by *and*.

antecedent The word or words that a pronoun replaces and to which it refers.

G6-e Use a verb that agrees with the **antecedent** of the pronoun *who, which,* or *that.*

Its staff consists of nineteen *people* who *drive* to work in any kind of weather to make sure the station comes through for its listeners.

To check agreement, identify the antecedent of the pronoun.

▶ Within the ordered chaos of the trauma room are diagnostic tools, surgical

devices, and X-ray equipment, which ~~is~~ *are* required for Sharp to be designated a

trauma center.

▶ The males choose topics that enable them to establish dominance over others

in the group, while the females tell personally moving stories that ~~encourages~~ *encourage*

others to show their feelings.

Note: With the phrase *one of the* followed by a plural noun, use a verb that agrees with the noun.

One of the *features* that *make* the monitor different is that it doubles as a television.

G6-f Use a singular verb with an **indefinite pronoun.**

Everything on the playground *is* child friendly.

During informal conversation, people sometimes treat indefinite pronouns as plural forms. In formal writing, however, an indefinite pronoun usually refers to a single person or object and agrees with a singular verb.

indefinite pronoun A pronoun that does not refer to a particular person or object, such as *anybody, each, one, everyone, everything, somebody, something, neither, none,* or *nobody* (which take the singular); *few, many,* and *several* (which take the plural); and *all, most,* and *some* (which can take either the singular or plural).

▶ There are two alternatives to this solution, and neither ~~seem~~ *seems* feasible.

Note: If an indefinite pronoun such as *all, none,* or *some* refers to a plural noun, use a plural form of the verb. If it refers to a singular noun, use a singular form.

Some manage to find jobs that fit their schedule, the surf schedule.

Most are respectable people.

All of the money *is* missing.

G6-g Use a verb that agrees with the subject rather than a subject complement.

The shark's favorite *diet is* elephant seals and sea lions.

When either the subject or the subject complement names a group or category, the choice between a singular or plural verb becomes confusing. Make sure that the verb agrees with the actual subject. If necessary, rewrite the sentence.

▶ Big blocks of color in a simple flat shape ~~is~~ *are* his artistic trademark.

▶ *He favors big* ~~Big~~ blocks of color in a simple flat shape. ~~is his artistic trademark.~~

subject complement A word or word group that follows a linking verb (such as *seems, appears,* or *is* and other forms of *be*) and describes or restates the subject: The tents looked *old and dirty.*

G7 Adjectives and Adverbs

For practice, go to bedfordstmartins.com/theguide/adjadv

Distinguish **adjectives** from **adverbs** so that you select the correct forms of these **modifiers**. See also R2-a.

ADJECTIVES	Because *angry* drivers are *dangerous* drivers, it is *imperative* that the county implement *a* solution.
ADVERB	Installing traffic lights would *quickly* alleviate three important aspects of the problem.

adjective A word that modifies a noun or a pronoun, adding information about it.

adverb A word that modifies a verb, an adjective, or another adverb, often telling when, where, why, how, or how often.

G7-a Select an adverb, not an adjective, to modify an adjective, another adverb, or a verb.

Often ending in *-ly*, adverbs tell how, when, where, why, and how often.

Despite a *very* busy work schedule, Caesar finds time in the afternoon to come *directly* to the high school and work as a volunteer track coach.

Change an adjective that modifies another adjective, an adverb, or a verb to an adverb form.

▶ This man yelled at me so ~~loud~~ *loudly* that I began to cry.

Note: Adjective forms that are common in informal conversation should be changed to adverb forms in more formal writing.

modifier A word, phrase, or clause functioning as an adjective or adverb that adds information and detail about a noun, a verb, or another word.

SPOKEN	The day was going *slow,* and I repeatedly caught my lure on the riverbed or a tree limb.

WRITTEN   The day was going *slowly*, and I repeatedly caught my lure on the riverbed or a tree limb.

G7-b Select an adjective, not an adverb, to modify a noun or a pronoun.

I am enamored of the *cool* motor, the *massive* boulder in the middle of the lake, and the sound of the wake *splashing* against the side of the two-seater.

Change an adverb that modifies a noun or a pronoun to an adjective.

> Working within a ~~traditionally~~ *traditional* chronological plot, Joyce develops the protagonist's emotional conflict.

An adjective generally appears immediately before or after the word it modifies. When an adjective acts as a **subject complement**, however, it is separated from the word it modifies by a **linking verb**.

My grandfather is *amazing*.

Note: Some verbs act as linking verbs only in certain contexts. When one of these verbs connects a subject and its complement, use an adjective form: She looked *ill*. When the verb is modified by the word that follows it, however, use an adverb: She looked *quickly*.

subject complement A word or word group that follows a linking verb (such as *seems, appears,* or *is* and other forms of *be*) and describes or restates the subject: The tents looked *old and dirty*.

linking verb *Be, seem, appear, become, taste,* or another verb that connects a subject with a subject complement that describes or modifies it: The chips *taste* salty.

For ESL Writers

ESL writers sometimes have trouble choosing between past and present participles (*looked, looking*) used as adjectives. See L6 for help in selecting the correct form.

G7-c Select the correct forms of adjectives and adverbs to show comparisons.

Add *-er* or *-est* to short words (usually of one or two syllables), and use *more, most, less,* and *least* with longer words and all *-ly* adverbs.

The southern peninsula's *smallest* kingdom was invaded continually by its two *more powerful* neighbors.

Use *-er, more,* or *less* (the comparative form) to compare two things.

I had always been a little bit *faster* than she was.

Use *-est, most,* or *least* (the superlative form) to compare three or more.

An elite warrior corps grew that soon gained the respect of even its *most bitter* foes.

Change the forms of adjectives and adverbs to show comparison precisely.

▶ She has clearly been the ~~least~~ *less* favored child in the sense that she is not as beautiful or as intelligent as her sister.

E   Effective Sentences

E1   Missing Words

For practice, go to bedfordstmartins.com/theguide/mword

To write effective prose, you need to supply all words necessary for clarity, completeness, and logic.

> **For ESL Writers**
>
> If English is not your native language, you may have special trouble with omitted words. See also L4.

E1-a   Supply small words such as prepositions, conjunctions, infinitive parts, articles, and verb parts needed for clarity and completeness.

When you forget to include these small words, the reader may be puzzled or have to pause momentarily to figure out what you mean. Proofread your essays carefully, even out loud, to catch these omitted words.

Insert missing prepositions.

> ▶ The car began to skid *in* the other direction.

> ▶ He graduated *from* high school at the top of his class.

> ▶ A child his age shouldn't be playing outside *at* that time of night.

> **For ESL Writers**
>
> If you are not a native speaker of American English, prepositions may be especially difficult for you because they are highly idiomatic. In other words, native speakers of English use prepositions in ways that do not translate directly into other languages. The best way to understand when prepositions are needed in English sentences is to read widely and study the work of other writers. See also L3.

Insert missing conjunctions.

> ▶ Most families and patients will accept the pain, inconvenience, financial *and* emotional strain as long as the patient can achieve a life "worth living."

---

preposition A word (such as *between, in*, or *of*) that always appears as part of a phrase and indicates the relation between a word in a sentence and the object of the preposition: The water splashed *into* the canoe.

conjunction A word that relates sentence parts by coordinating, subordinating, or pairing elements, such as *and, because*, or *either . . . or*.

▶ The heads of these golf clubs can be made of metal, wood, *or* graphite and often
have special inserts in the part of the club that hits the ball.

A conjunction is generally needed to connect the final item in a series, such as
financial and emotional strain in the first example and *graphite* in the second.

Restore the *to* omitted from an infinitive if it is needed for clarity.

▶ They decided *to* start the following Monday morning.

▶ I noticed how he used his uncanny talent for acting *to* make a dreary subject come
alive.

> **infinitive** A verb form
> consisting of the word *to*
> plus the base form of the
> verb: *to run, to do.*

Insert missing articles.

▶ This incident ruined the party, but it was only *the* beginning of the worst.

▶ But such *a* condition could be resolved by other means.

> **article** An adjective that
> precedes a noun and iden-
> tifies a definite reference to
> something specific (*the*) or
> an indefinite reference to
> something less specific (*a*
> or *an*).

For ESL Writers

Nonnative speakers of English sometimes have trouble understanding when and
when not to use the articles *a, an,* and *the.* For more advice on the use of articles,
see L1.

Insert other missing words that help clarify or complete a sentence.

▶ Malaria was once a widespread disease *it may* and become so again.

▶ In these scenes, women are often *shown* with long, luxurious hair.

▶ Finally, and I'm embarrassed to admit, *it* I pushed Cindy against the wall.

E1-b   Insert the word *that* if it is needed to prevent confusion or misreading.

CONFUSING   I would like to point out golf is not just a game for rich old men
in ugly pants.

CLEARER   I would like to point out *that* golf is not just a game for rich old men
in ugly pants.

Without *that*, the reader may think at first that the writer is pointing out golf and have to double back to understand the sentence. In the revised sentence, *that* tells the reader exactly where the **dependent clause** begins.

> Dryer says, *that* as people grow older, they may find themselves waking up early, usually at dawn.

> Another problem parents will notice is *that* the child leaves out certain words.

Note: If the meaning of a sentence is clear without *that*, it may be left out.

dependent (subordinate) clause A word group that has a subject, a predicate, and a subordinating word at the beginning; it cannot stand by itself as a sentence but must be connected to an independent (main) clause.

E1-c   Add enough words to a comparison to show that the items are of the same kind and to make the comparison logical, clear, and complete.

Because a comparison, by definition, connects two or more things for the reader, you should name both things and state the comparison fully. In addition, the items you are comparing should be of the same kind. For example, compare a person with another person, not with an activity or a situation.

> The old student center has a *general store* that carries *as many books or supplies as* the *Saver Center.*

This sentence compares two stores, which are entities of the same kind. See also E7-c.

Reword a comparison to specify comparable items of the same kind.

> Five-foot-five-inch Maria finds climbing to be more challenging ~~than~~ *for her than it is for* her six-foot-five-inch companions, who can reach the handholds more easily.

The original version of this sentence says that climbing is more challenging than companions (illogically comparing an activity to people). The edited sentence says that climbing is more challenging for Maria than it is for her companions (logically comparing one person to other people).

Reword a comparison to identify clearly and completely all items being compared.

> Danziger's article is interesting and lightly laced with facts, definitely more entertaining, *than Solomon's article.*

Note: In some types of comparative sentences, standard English requires the coordinated use of *as.*

> Millie is *as* graceful *as*, if not more graceful than, Margot.

> ► Students opting for field experience credits would learn as much, or more ,than students who take only classes.

(inserted above: as ⌒; carets below "much" and "than")

E1-d Supply all words needed to clarify the parts of a compound structure.

Although words may be left out of compound structures to avoid unnecessary repetition, these omitted words must fit in each part of the compound.

> Women tend to express feelings *in the form of* requests, whereas men tend to express them *in* [*the form of*] commands.

When the same words do not fit in each part, you need to supply the missing words even if they are simply different forms of the same word.

> ► Water buffalo meat has been gaining popularity in America and being sold to the public.

(inserted above: is)

> ► Observable behaviors that relate to classroom assault can be dealt with prior, during, and after an attack.

(inserted above: to ⌒)

> **compound structure** A sentence element, such as a subject or a verb, that consists of two or more items linked by *and* or another conjunction.

E2 Shifts

For practice, go to bedfordstmartins.com/theguide/shifts

Follow the same pattern throughout a sentence or passage to avoid a shift in tense, person, number, mood, voice, or type of discourse.

E2-a Use one verb tense consistently in a sentence or passage unless a tense change is needed to show a time change.

> ► The nurse tried to comfort me by telling jokes and explaining that the needle wouldn't hurt. With a slight push, the long, sharp needle ~~pierces~~ through my skin and ~~finds~~ its way to the vein.

(inserted above: pierced; inserted above: found)

> **tense** The form of a verb that shows the time of the action or state of being.

If you tend to mix verb tenses as you draft, perform a special edit of your entire essay, concentrating on this one issue.

Change the tense of any verbs that do not follow the established tense in a passage unless they show logical time changes.

▶ I noticed much activity around the base. Sailors and chiefs ~~are~~ *were* walking all over

the place. At 8:00 a.m., all traffic, foot and vehicle, halted. Toward the piers,

the flag ~~is rising~~ *rose* up its pole. After the national anthem ~~ends,~~ *ended,* salutes ~~are~~ *were*

completed, and people ~~go~~ *went* on with what they ~~are~~ *had been* doing.

Change verbs to the present tense to discuss events in literature, general truths, facts, and other ongoing principles.

▶ In 2003, the Supreme Court ruled that antisodomy laws are unconstitutional

because such laws ~~went~~ *go* against "our tradition [that] the state is not

omnipresent in our homes."

▶ In the story, when the boy ~~died,~~ *dies,* Kathy ~~realized~~ *realizes* that it ~~was~~ *is* also time for her

childhood to die, and so she ~~returned~~ *returns* to her South African home as an adult.

Note: The conventional use of the present tense for events in literary works and for enduring facts and principles may require tense shifts in a sentence or text. See also G5-a.

PRESENT TENSE   When Dr. Full *is introduced* in the story, he *is* very poor and dependent on alcohol.

PRESENT TENSE WITH LOGICAL SHIFT TO FUTURE   Each cell *has* forty-six chromosomes that *carry* the genetic traits the individual *will have* when he or she *is* born.

person The form of a word that shows whether it refers to *I* or *we* (first person), to *you* (second person), or to *he, she, it,* or *they* (third person).

number The form of a word that shows whether it refers to one thing (singular) or more than one (plural): *parent, parents; child, children.*

E2-b **Change the nouns and pronouns in a passage to a consistent person and number.**

▶ Lynn informs all the members of helpful programs for ~~you and your pet.~~ *them and their pets.*

▶ Lynn informs ~~all the members~~ *you* of helpful programs for you and your pet.

In casual conversation, people often shift between singular and plural nouns and pronouns or between the third person and the second (or even the first). In writing, however, such shifts may be confusing or may make the essay poorly focused.

Note: Besides making sure that the nouns and pronouns are consistent in person and number within a sentence or series of sentences, consider how your choice of person suits the tone or approach of your essay. The first or second person, for example, will usually strike a reader as less formal than the third person.

E2-c   Establish a consistent mood and voice in a passage.

> *knew*
> ► Each time I entered his house, I ~~could~~ always ~~know~~ when he was home.

The original sentence shifts from the indicative mood (*I entered*), used for statements and questions, to the subjunctive mood (*I could know*), used to indicate hypothetical, impossible, or unlikely conditions.

> *to take the test.*
> ► I stepped out of the car with my training permit, a necessary document ~~for the test to be taken.~~

Although mood and voice may need to change to fit the context of a sentence, unneeded shifts may seem inconsistent. See also G5-c on mood, G5-d on voice, and L2-a on conditional clauses.

Change the verbs in a conditional clause or passage to a consistent mood.

> *would*
> ► If the mother should change her mind and keep the child, the couple ~~will~~ be reimbursed for their expenses.

> *changes*   *keeps*
> ► If the mother ~~should change~~ her mind and ~~keep~~ the child, the couple will be reimbursed for their expenses.

Change the verbs in a passage to a consistent voice, preferably the active voice.

> ► I will judge the song according to the following criteria: the depth with which the lyrics treat each issue and the clarity with which
> *the music presents each issue.*
> ~~each issue is presented in the music.~~

See also G5-d and W1-b.

E2-d   Use either direct or indirect quotation without mixing the two.

Writers use direct quotation to present statements or questions in a speaker's or another writer's own words; they use indirect quotation to present the person's words without quoting directly.

---

mood The form of a verb that shows the writer's attitude toward a statement.

voice The form of a verb that indicates (active) or deemphasizes (passive) the performer of the action.

> *you want to me.*
> ▶ "~~Do whatever they wanted to her,~~ she cried, "but don't harm Reza."

> *They could do*   *they shouldn't*
> ▶ ~~Do~~ whatever they wanted to her, she cried, but ~~don't~~ harm Reza.

To avoid shifts between direct and indirect quotation, make sure that your pronouns are consistent in **person** (see G2) and your verbs are consistent in **mood** (see G5-c).

E3   Noun Agreement

For practice, go to bedfordstmartins.com/theguide/nagree

In most instances, use nouns that agree in **number** when they refer to the same topic, person, or object.

> The treatment consists of *injections* of minimal *doses* of the *allergens* given at regular *intervals*.

Sometimes, however, the context calls for both singular and plural nouns.

> **Students** who want to make the most of *their* college years should pursue *a major course of study* while choosing *electives* or *a few minor courses of study* from the liberal arts.

Note: When you use a noun with a plural possessive such as *their,* the thing possessed can be expressed as a singular noun if each individual could possess only one item.

> By the time the *calves* reach two months of age, *their coat* has turned dark brown.

E3-a   Select corresponding singular or plural forms for related references to a noun.

When several nouns are used to develop a topic, they may describe and expand the characteristics of a key noun, act as synonyms for one another, or develop related points in the discussion. A sentence or passage that includes such nouns will generally be clearer and more effective if the nouns agree in number.

> ▶ Many people tend to "take their jobs to bed" with them and stay awake
>
> *promotions,*
> thinking about what needs to be done the next day. They also worry about ~~a~~
>
> *layoffs, or shifts*
> ~~promotion, a layoff, or a shift~~ in responsibilities.

E3-b   Decide whether a noun should be singular or plural on the basis of its relationship to other words in the sentence and the meaning of the sentence as a whole.

A noun may need to agree with another word in the sentence or may need to be singular or plural to fit the context or idiomatic usage.

---

person The form of a word that shows whether it refers to *I* or *we* (first person), to *you* (second person), or to *he, she, it,* or *they* (third person).

mood The form of a verb that shows the writer's attitude toward a statement.

number The form of a word that shows whether it refers to one thing (singular) or more than one (plural): *parent, parents; child, children.*

Minnows are basically inedible because *they* have very little meat on *their bodies.*

In this sentence the writer consistently uses plural forms (*they, their*, and *bodies*) to refer to the minnows but also uses *meat*, which conventionally takes a singular form in a context like this one.

Note: Nouns such as *kind, type*, or *sort* are singular, although they have plural forms (*kinds, types*). Use *this* and *that* instead of *these* and *those* to modify the singular forms of these and similar words. Expressions with *kind of* or *sort of* are usually singular.

▶ To comprehend ~~these~~ *this* type of ~~articles,~~ *article,* it helps to have a strong background in statistics.

▶ RAs are allowed to choose what kind of ~~programs~~ *program* they want to have.

Change a noun to singular or to plural to agree with a preceding indefinite adjective.

▶ Under some ~~circumstance,~~ *circumstances,* parents aren't there to supervise their kids.

indefinite adjective A word that modifies a noun or another adjective and indicates an unspecific quantity, such as *few, many,* or *some.*

Consider changing a noun to singular or to plural to reflect its context in the sentence.

Sometimes it is customary to treat an abstract quality (such as *justice* or *power*) as a singular noun. In other cases, a noun should be singular or plural to fit with the grammar or logic of the rest of the sentence.

▶ As soon as immigrants get to the United States, they realize that to get ~~a better job~~ *better jobs* and better living conditions, they need to learn English.

Note: Some common idiomatic expressions mix singular and plural forms.

IDIOMATIC WORDING   The penalties set for offenders might be enough to help them see *the error of their ways* and eventually help them reform their social habits.

E4   Modifiers

For practice, go to bedfordstmartins.com/theguide/mod

Put a **modifier** next to or very close to the particular word that it modifies so that the connection between the two is clear.

Fourteen teenage idealists *with nervous stomachs* waited *for their moment in front of the onlookers.*

We had raised all the money *that we needed for the five-day trip.*

modifier A word, phrase, or clause functioning as an adjective or adverb that adds information and detail about a noun, a verb, or another word.

A modifier's position in a sentence generally tells the reader what word the modifier qualifies.

E4-a   **Place a word, phrase, or clause next to or close to the word that it modifies.**

My *frozen* smile faltered as my chin quivered.

The flurry *of fins, masks, weights, and wet suits* continued.

Beyond the chairs loomed the object *that I feared most* —

a beautiful, black Steinway grand piano *that gleamed under the bright stage lights.*

If a modifier is too far away from the word it modifies, a reader may assume that it modifies another word closer to it. As a result, a *misplaced modifier* can create confusion, ambiguity, or even unintended humor.

Move a modifier closer to the word it modifies.

▶ The ~~attempted~~ number of *attempted* suicides this semester was four.

▶ The women have to do all the hard work, *needed to maintain the family,* especially in subsistence culture, ~~needed to maintain the family.~~

▶ He and the other people start to look for any sign of a boat, an island, or an oil platform, *as hard as they can* ~~as hard as they can.~~

Rewrite to clarify the sentence.

▶ *In organizing meetings open to all neighbors,* community ~~Community~~ leaders should *select* ~~organize meetings open to all neighbors at~~ convenient times and locations.

▶ We were friends until I *turned eighteen and* became too popular and obnoxious for anyone to stand, ~~when I turned eighteen.~~

E4-b   **Place a modifier so that it qualifies the meaning of a particular word in the sentence instead of dangling.**

A phrase that does not modify a specific word is called a *dangling modifier.* A dangling modifier usually occurs at the beginning of a sentence and is likely to be a **participial phrase** or a **prepositional phrase.**

participial phrase A group of words that begins with a present participle (*dancing, freezing*) or a past participle (*danced, frozen*) and modifies a noun or a pronoun: We boarded the bus, *expecting to leave immediately.*

prepositional phrase A group of words that begins with a preposition and indicates the relation between a word in a sentence and the object following the preposition: Her sunglasses slid *under the seat.*

▶ By far the best song on the album, ~~the~~ vocal performance and musical

"Don't Know Why," has a

arrangement ~~of "Don't Know Why"~~ create a perfect harmony.

that

Rewrite the sentence, placing a word that could logically be modified immediately after the modifying phrase.

▶ Rather than receiving several painful shots in the mouth before a cavity is

a patient may find that

filled, hypnosis can work just as effectively.

▶ After surveying the floor on which I live, the residents of my dorm don't care

I concluded that

much for floor programs.

Rewrite the sentence by changing the modifying phrase into a dependent clause.

Unlike a phrase, a clause includes both a **subject** and a **predicate**. By changing a phrase to a clause, you can correct a dangling modifier by supplying the information or connection that is missing. Be sure to add words and rewrite so that both the subject and the predicate are clearly stated and the clause fits the rest of the sentence.

If the school board decides to close

▶ ~~By closing~~ Dos Pueblos, the remaining high schools ~~would~~ have larger student

will

bodies and increased budgets.

I concluded

▶ After ~~concluding~~ my monologue on the hazards of partying, she smiled broadly

and said, "OK, Mom, I'll be more careful next time."

E4-c   **Place a limiting modifier just before the word it modifies to avoid ambiguity.**

A limiting modifier creates confusion or ambiguity when it is misplaced because it often could modify several words in the same sentence.

▶ Landfills in Illinois are going to be filled to capacity by 2015, and some

even

experts ~~even~~ say sooner.

When *even* precedes *say* in the example above, the sentence suggests that the experts are "even saying," not that the date will be even sooner.

dependent (subordinate) clause A word group that has a subject, a predicate, and a subordinating word (such as *because*) at the beginning; it cannot stand by itself as a sentence but must be connected to an independent (main) clause.

subject The part of a clause that identifies who or what is being discussed: At the checkpoint, *we* unloaded the canoes.

predicate The part of a clause that includes a complete verb and says something about the subject: At the checkpoint, we *unloaded the canoes.*

limiting modifier A modifier such as *almost, just,* or *only* that should directly precede the word or word group it limits.

infinitive A verb form consisting of the word *to* plus the base form of the verb: *to run, to do*.

E4-d   **Keep the two parts of an infinitive together.**

When other words follow the *to*, they "split" the infinitive, separating *to* from the base form of the verb. These other words can usually be moved elsewhere in the sentence. Be especially alert to **limiting modifiers** that split infinitives. See also E4-c.

> *always*
> ▶ His stomach seemed to ~~always~~ hang over his pants.

Note: Occasionally, moving intervening words creates a sentence more awkward than the version with the split infinitive. In such cases, leaving the split infinitive may be the better choice.

E5   Mixed Constructions

For practice, go to bedfordstmartins.com/theguide/mix

The beginning and ending of a sentence must match, and its parts should fit together. If a sentence changes course in the middle or its parts are mixed up, a reader will have to guess at the pattern or connection you intend.

E5-a   **Begin and end a sentence with the same structural pattern to avoid a mixed construction.**

A sentence is mixed if it combines several grammatical patterns. You usually need to rewrite a mixed construction so that its parts fit together.

> *If we save*   *we will have*
> ▶ ~~The~~ more oil ~~that we save~~ now, ~~means~~ much more in the future.

Choose one of the grammatical patterns in a mixed sentence, and rewrite to use it consistently throughout the sentence.

> *place where*
> ▶ School is another ~~resource for~~ children who don't have anyone to talk to can get educated about the problem of teen pregnancy.

> ▶ School is another resource for children who don't have anyone to talk to can
> *provide information*
> ~~get educated~~ about the problem of teen pregnancy.

Rewrite a mixed sentence if neither part supplies a workable pattern for the whole.

> *The*
> ▶ ~~This is something the~~ shelter prides itself on ~~and is~~ always looking for new volunteers and ideas ~~for the shelter.~~

▶ The ~~next part of the~~ *next detailed* essay ~~was where~~ the results of the study ~~were detailed~~

and ~~finally included~~ *concluded with* a commentary section~~.~~ ~~concluding the article.~~

E5-b Match the subject and the predicate in a sentence so that they are compatible.

subject The part of a clause that identifies who or what is being discussed.

predicate The part of a clause that includes a complete verb and says something about the subject.

You can solve the problem of a logically mismatched subject and predicate — called *faulty predication* — by rewriting either the subject or the predicate so that the two fit together.

▶ *Students attending schools*
~~Schools~~ that prohibited paddling behaved as well as *those at* schools that permitted corporal punishment.

To test a sentence for faulty predication, ask yourself whether the subject can do what the predicate says: For example, do schools behave? If not, revise the sentence.

Revise the subject so that it can perform the action described in the predicate.

▶ Bean's service is top notch, *the staff* and is striving continually to meet student needs.

Revise the predicate so that it fits logically with the subject.

▶ Ironically, the main character's memory of Mangan's sister on the porch step

always includes
~~cannot recall the image without~~ the lamplight.

E5-c Order words logically so that the meaning of the sentence will be clear.

▶ *Entering traffic*
~~Traffic entering~~ will be dispersed into a perimeter pattern of flow.

E5-d Eliminate the phrase *is where*, *is when*, or *the reason is because*, and then rewrite the sentence so that it is clear and logical.

Often you can replace an *is where* or *is when* phrase with a noun specifying a category or type.

▶ This *part makes* ~~is where~~ the irony *seem* ~~seems to be~~ most evident.

▶ An absolutist position is *a stance taken by someone who* ~~when someone~~ strongly opposes any restrictions on speech.

To eliminate *the reason is because*, rewrite the sentence, or use *the reason is that* or *because* instead.

> ▶ ~~Another reason~~ *In addition,* radio stations should not play songs with sexually explicit lyrics ^is because children like to sing along.

> ▶ Another reason radio stations should not play songs with sexually explicit lyrics is ~~because~~ *that* children like to sing along.

E6   Integrated Quotations, Questions, and Thoughts

For practice, go to bedfordstmartins.com/theguide/int

When you use sources or write dialogue, merge your quotations, questions, and thoughts smoothly into your text so that the reader can tell who is speaking, thinking, or providing information.

> The expense of being a teenager has caused many youths to join the workforce just because "they were offered a job" (Natriello 60).

> "Hello," I replied, using one of the few words I knew.

> I told myself, Don't move.

Use introductory phrases to link ideas and provide necessary background and context. Refer to the source or the speaker in the sentence, varying your words to avoid repeating *says* or *states*. See also P6 and P10.

E6-a   Introduce, connect, and cite source material with grammatically correct and logical wording when you integrate a direct quotation into a sentence.

direct quotation A speaker's or writer's exact words, which are enclosed in quotation marks.

Writers often introduce quotations by mentioning the name of the person being quoted. Although *says* and *states* are acceptable, consider using more precise verbs and phrases that establish exact logical connections and provide variety. Examples include *agrees, asserts, charges, claims, confirms, discusses, emphasizes,* and *suggests.*

> In the words of American Motors President M. Paul Tippitt, "The cardinal rule of the new ballgame is change" (Sobel 259).

Readers expect quotations and text to fit gracefully so that the writer's ideas and the material from supporting sources are unified and coherent. See also E2-d.

Rewrite to cite a source smoothly, without jumping from sentences of text to quotation.

Identifying the author of your source in the main part of your sentence often supplies the context a reader needs.

▶ Most people are not even aware of the extent to which television plays a role

As Mitroff and Bennis point out,

in their lives. "Television defines our problems and shapes our actions; in

(xi)

short, how we define our world" ~~(Mitroff and Bennis xi).~~

Mitroff and Bennis assert that most

▶ ~~Most~~ people are not even aware of the extent to which ~~television plays a role~~

"television   *" (xi)*

~~in their lives. "Television~~ defines our problems and shapes our actions; ~~in short,~~

~~how we define our world" (Mitroff and Bennis xi).~~

If you were writing for a magazine or newspaper, you would usually include a publication name and date in your sentence. In academic writing, however, you should cite the author's name and the date of the publication in your text and provide full publication information in a list of works cited (see Chapter 22).

FOR A MAGAZINE   Andrew DePalma's 2003 *New York Times* article, "Preparing to 'Tell Us about Yourself,'" explains this point clearly.

FOR AN ACADEMIC ESSAY OR A SCHOLARLY PUBLICATION   Andrew DePalma (2003) explains this point clearly.

Rewrite the text that introduces or integrates the quotation, and reselect the words you are quoting if necessary.

▶ The average American child ~~who~~ is "exposed to violence from every medium"

and

~~. . . in addition listens to~~ "music that advocates drug use" (Hollis 624).

E6-b Integrate a question so that its source is clear.

Enclose a **direct quotation** in quotation marks, identifying the speaker and using his or her exact words. Do not use quotation marks for an **indirect quotation** or a question that you address to the reader.

DIRECT QUOTATION   "Can you get my fins?" he asked.

direct quotation A speaker's or writer's exact words, which are enclosed in quotation marks.

indirect quotation A reworded statement or question that presents a speaker's or writer's ideas without quoting directly or using quotation marks.

INDIRECT QUOTATION	Without much hesitation, I explained my mission to her and asked whether she would help me out.
QUESTION ADDRESSED TO READER	Should sex education be a required class in public schools?

As in any dialogue, begin a new paragraph to show each change of speaker.

▶ "The refrigeration system is frozen solid. Come back later," Once again *he said, once* turning his back to me. I asked

I asked, "When would it be best for me to come back?"

E6-c Integrate thoughts so that they are clearly identified and consistently punctuated.

If you supply the exact words that you or someone else thinks, follow the guidelines for direct quotations. Quotation marks are optional, but be consistent throughout an essay.

Go eighty feet for thirty minutes, she reminded herself.

▶ Wife and kids? I thought.

▶ "Wife and kids?" I thought.

E7   Parallelism

For practice, go to bedfordstmartins.com/theguide/para

Use parallel grammatical form to present items as a pair or in a series.

Imagine that you and your daughter are *walking* in the mall or *eating* in a popular restaurant.

By implementing this proposal, administrators could enhance the reputation of the university with quality *publications, plays, concerts,* and *sports teams.*

An interruption has the potential *to disrupt turns at talk, to disorganize the topic of conversation,* and *to violate the current speaker's right to talk.*

The grammatical similarity of the items in the pair or series strongly signals the reader that they are equally important, similar in meaning, and related in the same way to the rest of the sentence.

E7-a Rewrite any item in a series that does not follow the same grammatical pattern as the other items.

Items in a series are usually linked by *and* or *or*. Each item should be parallel to the others, presented as a **noun,** an **infinitive,** a **gerund,** or another grammatical form.

> ► The children must deal with an overprotective parent, sibling rivalry, and ~~living~~ *life* in a single-parent home.

> ► Drivers destined for Coronado can choose to turn left, right, or ~~proceeding~~ *proceed* straight into the city.
> *turn*   *proceed*

noun A word that names a specific or general thing, person, place, concept, characteristic, or other idea.

infinitive A verb form consisting of the word *to* plus the base form of the verb: *to run, to do.*

gerund A verb form that is used as a noun and ends in *-ing*: *arguing, throwing.*

E7-b Rewrite one item in a pair so that both follow the same grammatical pattern.

Items in a pair are usually linked by *and* or *or*.

> ► While Simba is growing up, he is told of things he should do and things not ~~to~~ do.
> *he should*

E7-c Rewrite one item in a comparison using *than* or *as* so that it matches the other in grammatical form.

> ► They feel that using force is more comprehensible to the children than abstract consequences.
> *threatening*

E7-d Use parallel form for items joined by correlative conjunctions.

> ► At that time, the person is surprised not only about where he is but also
> *about*
> ~~unable to account for~~ what has happened.

Besides presenting the word pairs in parallel form, position the conjunctions so that each introduces a comparable point.

correlative conjunctions Word pairs that link sentence elements; the first word anticipates the second: *both . . . and, either . . . or, neither . . . nor, not only . . . but also.*

E8   Coordination and Subordination

For practice, go to bedfordstmartins.com/theguide/cosu

Use coordination and subordination to indicate the relationships among sentence elements.

E8-a   Use coordination to join sentence elements that are equally important.

The sheriff's department lacks both the *officers* and the *equipment* to patrol every road in the county.

Most of us would agree with the evil queen's magic mirror that this Disney girl, with her *skin as white as snow, lips as red as blood,* and *hair as black as ebony,* is indeed, "the fairest one of all."

Writers use coordination to bring together in one sentence two or more elements of equal importance to the meaning. These elements can be words, phrases, or clauses, including **independent clauses** within the same sentence.

The sport of windsurfing dates back only to 1969, but *it already has achieved full status as an Olympic event.*

Children like to sing along with songs they hear on the radio; consequently, *radio stations should not play songs with language that demeans women.*

E8-b   Use subordination to indicate that one sentence element is more important than other elements.

After Dave finished his mutinous speech, the corners of Dan's mouth slowly formed a nearly expressionless grin.

Political liberals, *who trace their American roots to the Declaration of Independence,* insist that the federal government should attempt to reduce inequalities of income and wealth.

Writers frequently subordinate information within a single sentence. The most important information appears in an independent clause, and the less important or subordinate information appears in words, **phrases,** or **dependent clauses** attached to the independent clause or integrated into it. (Often, the most important information in a sentence will be information that is new to a reader.)

---

independent (main) clause A word group with a subject and a predicate that can stand alone as a separate sentence. (A predicate is the part of a clause that includes a complete verb and says something about the subject: At the checkpoint, we *unloaded the canoes.*)

phrase A group of words that does *not* contain both a subject and a verb and is always part of an independent clause. Common types of phrases include *prepositional* (After a flash of lightning, I saw a tree split in half) and *verbal* (Blinded by the flash, I ran into the house).

dependent (subordinate) clause A word group that has a subject, a predicate, and a subordinating word (such as *because*) at the beginning; it cannot stand by itself as a sentence but must be connected to an independent (main) clause: *Although it was raining,* we loaded our gear onto the buses.

W Word Choice

Effective language is concise, exact, and appropriate for the context.

> **Tears stream down James's face as he sits scrunched up in the corner of the shabby living room, wishing that he had anyone else's life.**
>
> **We need traffic signals for this dangerous intersection.**

Well-chosen words engage the reader, conveying impressions or claims clearly and convincingly.

W1 Concise Sentences

For practice, go to bedfordstmartins.com/theguide/csent

Sentences with redundant phrasing, repetitive wording, wordy expressions, and unnecessary intensifiers are tiresome to read and may be difficult to understand. Concentrate on choosing words well, simplifying sentence stucture, and avoiding words that are unnecessary or evasive.

> ▶ ~~In many cases, this~~ situation may ~~be due to the fact that~~ these women ~~were~~ ~~not given the~~ opportunity to work.
>
> *This* *occur because* *have had no*

Note: Even though you may need to add detail or examples to clarify your ideas, cutting out useless words will make your writing more focused and precise.

W1-a Eliminate redundancies and repetition.

Redundant phrasing adds unnecessary words to a sentence. Repetitive wording says the same thing twice.

Eliminate or rewrite redundant expressions that repeat the same point in different words.

The phrase *blue in color* is redundant because it repeats obvious information, adding a category name to a description. The following phrases do the same: *large-sized, a reluctant manner, to an extreme degree, a helpless state, a crisis-type situation, the area of population control,* and *passive kind of behavior.* In addition, expressions such as *past memories, advance planning,* and *mix together* include modifiers that repeat information already provided in the word modified. After all, all memories are of the past, planning is always done in advance, and *mix* means "put together."

Other expressions such as *the fact is true, bisect in half,* and *in my opinion, I be-lieve* are redundant because they contain obvious implications: *Truth* is implied by *fact, bisect* means "to divide in half," and *in my opinion* says the same thing as *I be-lieve.* Pare down these and any similar expressions.

▶ Many machines in the drilling area need to be [modernized] ~~updated to better and more modern equipment.~~

▶ All these recommendations are interconnected. ~~to one another.~~

▶ ~~The~~ [California] colleges ~~in the state of California~~ rely too much on the annual income of a student's parents and not enough on the parents' true financial situation.

Delete extra words from a redundant or repetitive sentence.

▶ In addition, there is a customer service center. [convenient] ~~for the convenience of the customers.~~

▶ Student volunteers will no longer be [exhausted] ~~overworked, overburdened, and overexhausted~~ from working ~~continuously at the jobs~~ without ~~any~~ breaks because of the shortage. [labor] ~~of labor.~~

W1-b   Eliminate words that do not add to the meaning of a sentence.

Rewrite a wordy sentence to reduce the number of clauses and phrases.

Concentrate on turning clauses into phrases or replacing phrases, especially strings of **prepositional phrases,** with individual words. Sometimes you can even consolidate a series of sentences into one.

▶ [Michael Jordan is an excellent recent example] ~~One of the best examples in recent times~~ of an athlete. [overexposed] ~~being completely overexposed is that of Michael Jordan.~~

▶ ~~It is this~~ [This] exaggeration ~~that serves to provide the~~ [provides the characters'] comic appeal. ~~of the characters.~~

▶ ~~There are many other possible alternative solutions to teen pregnancy. One~~ [No single alternative will solve the problem of teen pregnancy, and all the possible] ~~solution is not going to work alone to solve the problem. But there are~~ [solutions have disadvantages.] ~~disadvantages that come along with them.~~

prepositional phrase A group of words that begins with a preposition and indicates the relation between a word in a sentence and the object following the preposition: Her sunglasses slid *under the seat.*

Eliminate wordy expressions, or replace them with fewer words.

Extra, empty words can creep into a sentence in many ways.

▶ Demanding Eldridge's resignation ~~at this point in time~~ will not solve the problem.
                                                    now

▶ However, in most neighborhoods, the same ~~group of~~ people who write the

    newsletters ~~are the ones who~~ organize and participate in the activities.
                also

Here are examples of a few common wordy phrases and clearer, more concise alternatives.

Wordy Phrases	*More Concise Alternatives*
due to the fact that in view of the fact that the reason for for the reason that this is why in light of the fact that on the grounds that	for, because, why, since
despite the fact that regardless of the fact that	although, though
as regards in reference to concerning the matter of where . . . is concerned	concerning, about, regarding
it is necessary that there is a need for it is important that	should, must
has the ability to is able to is in a position to	can
in order to for the purpose of	to
at this point in time	now
on the subject of	on, about
as a matter of fact	actually
be aware of the fact that	know [that]
to the effect that	that
the way in which	how
in the event that	if, when

Rewrite a wordy sentence to simplify its structure.

Watch particularly for *there is* or *there are* at the beginning of a sentence or for a verb in the passive voice. These indirect structures have their uses. Often, however, you can express your ideas more directly and forcefully by editing to eliminate *there is* or *there are* or by changing from the passive to the active voice.

▶ ~~There are always five~~ *Five ... are always* or six spots open at the ends of the rows.

▶ ~~The topic is initiated by a~~ *A ... initiates* member who has nothing to gain by the discussion ~~of~~ the topic.

Note: Often, as in these examples, the verb *be* is far less precise than another verb might be. Whenever possible, replace *am, are, is, was,* and other forms of *be* with a stronger verb that clearly defines an action.

W1-c   **Rewrite a sentence to eliminate unnecessary intensifiers or hedges.**

▶ Your choice could ~~very possibly~~ make the difference between a saved or lost life.

Delete unnecessary intensifiers such as *very, really, clearly, quite*, and *of course*.

Although intensifiers can strengthen statements, eliminating them or substituting more forceful words is often more effective.

▶ The plot of this movie is ~~really great.~~ *thrilling.*

Some intensifiers are unnecessary because the words they modify are already as strong as possible, such as *very unique.* (Something either is or is not unique; it cannot be *very* or *slightly* unique.)

▶ The arrangement of the plain blocks ~~is so unique that it~~ *unique* makes the sculpture seem textured.

Eliminate unnecessary hedges.

Writers use hedges such as *apparently, seem, perhaps, possibly, to a certain extent, tend,* and *somewhat* to avoid making claims that they cannot substantiate. Hedges add subtlety to prose, appear careful and thoughtful, and acknowledge the possibility of important exceptions. Too many hedges, however, make writing tentative and uncertain.

▶ ~~In most cases, realistic~~ *Realistic* characteristics ~~tend to~~ *often* undermine comedy's primary function of making us laugh at exaggerated character traits.

W1-d Eliminate unnecessary prepositions.

▶ I went to the hospital so the clerk could admit me ~~in.~~

If the word following a preposition is the object of a verb, the preposition may be unnecessary.

▶ Nothing happened, and my doctor ordered ~~for~~ them to stop inducing labor.

▶ Consequently, student volunteers will not be inclined to leave and seek ~~for~~ smaller hospitals with less intense shifts.

Note: Another alternative is to change the verb.

▶ Consequently, student volunteers will not be inclined to leave and ~~seek~~ *look* for smaller hospitals with less intense shifts.

preposition A word (such as *between*, *in* or *of*) that always appears as part of a phrase and indicates the relation between a word in a sentence and the object of the preposition: The water splashed *into* the canoe.

For ESL Writers

Prepositions also combine with verbs to form two- or three-word (or phrasal) verbs whose meaning cannot be understood literally (*handed in, longed for*). When a preposition is part of a two- or three-word verb, it is called a *particle*. See L2-b.

W2 Exact Words

For practice, go to bedfordstmartins.com/theguide/eword

Effective writers choose words carefully, paying attention to meaning, form, idiomatic phrasing, and freshness.

The central library stands like a giant concrete mushroom, towering above the surrounding eucalyptus groves. The strong, angular lines are softened by a few well-placed, sweeping curves on the stabilizing pylons and the shrouds around the low windows.

W2-a Replace incorrect words with the exact words you intend, or omit incorrect words if they are unnecessary.

Check a dictionary when you are uncertain of the meaning of a word. Watch for incorrect words and for words similar in meaning or sound. See also the Glossary of Frequently Misused Words.

▶ Louis kicked him into a river ~~invested~~ *infested* with crocodiles.

▶ How do we stop offshore oil drilling and yet offer an alternative to ~~appease~~ *alleviate* the energy crisis?

▶ Some universities have chosen to go ~~literally~~ *literally* underground to avoid public scrutiny.

preposition A word (such as *between, in* or *of*) that always appears as part of a phrase and indicates the relation between a word in a sentence and the object of the preposition: The water splashed *into* the canoe.

W2-b Use correct prepositions.

Short as they generally are, prepositions define crucial relationships for the reader.

The levels increase *in* width *from* the scrawny third floor *up to* the immense sixth story (*over* two hundred feet across).

A building's beauty must be determined *by* the harmony *of* its design.

If prepositions are a problem in your writing, note how other writers use them.

▶ Unlike many of the other pieces of art ~~about~~ *on* campus, the statues seemed to fit well.

For ESL Writers

If you find prepositions difficult, pay special attention to them as you read. For a review of the meanings of some common prepositions, see L3.

idiom An expression whose meaning cannot be determined from its parts but must be learned (*call off* for "cancel"; *look after* for "take care of").

W2-c Use standard idioms, the conventional expressions generally used in American English.

Read and listen carefully to get a sense of standard idioms, especially the ones that consist of small words, such as **prepositions,** and verb forms.

▶ The most serious problems of many developing countries stem ~~to~~ *from* lack of educational and economic opportunity.

For ESL Writers

Idiomatic two- and three-word verbs (*put down, set up*) and combinations of verbs or adjectives and prepositions (*look for, afraid of*) can be especially troublesome for writers whose first language is not English. See L2-b for more help with these expressions.

W2-d Eliminate or rewrite clichés or overused expressions.

Readers prefer lively, original expressions to familiar, overused phrases.

> During ~~the thick of~~ the night, he must walk alone with only a flashlight for company.

> *erupts in gasps and nervous giggles*
> The audience ~~is on pins and needles,~~ wondering whose plan will falter first.

cliché An overused expression that has lost its original freshness, such as *hard as a rock*.

W2-e Select the correct form of the word that fits the context of your essay and conveys the meaning you intend.

If you are learning to use an unfamiliar word or are struggling to find a word whose meaning fits, you may use the wrong form of the word you intend. If so, change the word to the correct form when you discover your mistake or a reader notes it for you. Proofread your essays carefully for words written incorrectly. A good dictionary can help you determine which form of a word fits your context.

> *introduces*
> The phrase "you know" ~~is an introductory to~~ someone's opinion.

> *manicurist*
> I found out that becoming a ~~manicure~~ is increasingly popular because it takes only a few months of training.

W2-f Use appropriate figures of speech.

Figures of speech, such as **similes** and **metaphors,** are vivid and original means of expressing comparisons. They help a reader perceive a similarity, often creating a striking image or a surprising but engaging idea.

> Our dog Tiger rolls around in the warm mud and sinks his head into the soft ground like a hippo basking in the African sun.

> If you think of the *Journal of the American Medical Association* article as a two-hour documentary on PBS, the *American Health* essay is a thirty-second sound bite.

A figure of speech can make a complex idea easier to understand or bring a scene or character to life for your readers. Make sure that any figure of speech that you use is clear, appropriate, and consistent.

INACCURATE METAPHOR The children would jump from car to car *as if they were mushrooms.* [Mushrooms cannot jump.]

figures of speech Images such as similes and metaphors that suggest a comparison (or analogy) between objects that are generally unlike each other.

simile A direct comparison that uses *like* or *as: like a tree bending in the strong wind.*

metaphor An indirect comparison that refers to or describes one thing as if it were the other: *The mob sharpened its claws.*

mixed metaphor An in-consistent metaphor, one that mixes several images rather than completing one.

Also avoid **mixed metaphors,** as in the following example, in which the soul is compared to both a criminal defendant and a plant.

**MIXED
METAPHOR**
> Karma is an inorganic process of development in which the soul not only *pays the price* for its misdeeds but also *bears the fruit* of the *seeds sown* in former lives.

W3   Appropriate Words

For practice, go to bedfordstmartins.com/theguide/aword

When you choose words carefully, your writing will have the appropriate level of formality, without slang, biased wording, or stuffy, pretentious language. Taken from a profile of a large city's trauma system, the following sentences illustrate how appropriate words can convey a sense of the environment.

> At 6:50 p.m., the hospital's paging system comes alive.

> Lying on the table, the unidentified victim can only groan and move his left leg.

> All the components are in place: a countrywide trauma system, physicians and staff who care and are willing to sacrifice, and private hospitals serving the community.

Readers appreciate appropriate language choices that produce smooth, integrated writing, without sudden jumps from formal to informal language.

W3-a   Use the level of formality expected in your writing situation.

Many problems with appropriate language occur when writers use language accepted in informal conversation in a more formal writing situation. For example, a phone conversation or e-mail exchange with your friend will be more informal than a memo to your employer or a report for your political science class.

LESS FORMAL
> One cool morning in May, I stood on the edge of Mount Everest, or at least that's what it seemed like to me.

MORE FORMAL
> Mistreatment of the elderly is an unusually sensitive problem because it involves such value-laden ideas as *home* and *family*.

Taking into account the kind of essay you are writing, reword as necessary to avoid shifts in the level of formality.

> ▶ What makes an excellent church, auditorium, or theater makes a ~~lousy~~ *poor* library.

>   *is*
> ▶ The average cost to join a gymnasium ~~can run you~~ around $40 a month, ~~and~~
>
>   *Even if*
> ~~that's only~~ when you sign a membership contract. ~~I bet~~ you thought you
>
> *could not*
> ~~couldn't~~ afford a membership. ~~Well,~~ you can.

W3-b   Limit the use of slang in formal writing situations.

Although slang may be appropriate to define a character or a situation in a narrative or description, it is likely to be out of place in more formal academic writing.

APPROPRIATE SLANG	"This weather is *awesome* for peeling out. You *oughta* try it sometime." [appropriate for the dialogue in an essay about a remembered event]
INAPPROPRIATE SLANG	Parties are an excellent way to *blow off steam* and take a break from the pressures of college. [too informal in a proposal addressed to college administrators]

Replace inappropriate slang expressions with more formal words.

>   *criticize*
> ▶ We shouldn't ~~dis~~ these girls.
>
>   *impressive.*
> ▶ The cast of the movie was ~~awesome.~~

Replace slang with precise, more descriptive words.

>   *vividly embodied the historical characters.*
> ▶ The cast of the movie ~~was awesome.~~

W3-c   Use nonsexist language that includes rather than excludes.

Avoid using masculine pronouns (such as *he* or *his*) to refer to people who might be either men or women. Also avoid using words referring to men to represent people in general. See also G2-b.

Revise a sentence that uses masculine pronouns to represent people in general.

Use plural forms, eliminate the pronouns, or use both masculine and feminine pronouns.

---

slang Informal language that tends to change rapidly.

nonsexist language Language that describes people without using words that make assumptions about gender or imply acceptance of gender-based stereotypes.

▶ *A student's* **Students'** eligibility for alternative loans is based on whether or not ~~his~~ **their**

school decides ~~he is~~ **they are** entitled to financial aid.

▶ Abstract expressionism is art that is based on the artist's spontaneous feelings

at the moment when he is creating ~~his~~ **or she   a** work.

Replace masculine nouns used to represent people in general with more inclusive words.

▶ Oligarchies have existed throughout ~~the history of man.~~ **human history.**

▶ Every individual has his **or her** rightful place in the social hierarchy.

▶ Every individual has ~~his~~ **a** rightful place in the social hierarchy.

Rewrite language that implies or reinforces stereotypes or discrimination.

▶ Oligarchies were left to ~~barbaric tribesmen~~ **the tribes** and herders ~~who were beyond the reach of civilization.~~ **outside the empire.**

▶ A doctor who did not keep up with his colleagues would be forced to update ~~his~~ **or her** procedures.

W3-d   Replace pretentious language with simpler, more direct wording.

pretentious language
Fancy or wordy language used primarily to impress.

Using impressive words is sometimes part of the pleasure of writing, but such words may be too elaborate for the situation or may seem to be included for their own sake rather than the reader's understanding. Use words that best express your idea, and balance or replace distractingly unusual words with simpler, more familiar choices.

▶ Perhaps ~~apprehension toward instigating~~ **fear of** these changes stems from financial concern.

▶ Expanded oil exploration may seem relatively innocuous, but this proposal is a deplorable suggestion to all but the most ~~pernicious, specious entities.~~ **deceptive, destructive groups.**

P Punctuation

P1 Commas

For practice, go to bedfordstmartins.com/theguide/comma

Use a comma to set off and separate sentence elements.

P1-a Add a comma between independent clauses joined by a coordinating conjunction.

|——INDEPENDENT CLAUSE——| |——INDEPENDENT CLAUSE——|
Perhaps my father had the same dream, and perhaps my grandfather did as well.

When independent clauses are joined by a coordinating conjunction, a comma is required to tell the reader that another independent clause follows the first one.

▶ In 2002, women's ice hockey became a full Olympic medal sport, and the
   Canadian team brought home the gold.

▶ Researchers have studied many aspects of autism, but they readily acknowledge
   that they have much more to learn.

Note: If the independent clauses are brief and unambiguous, a comma is not required, though it is never wrong to include it.

   The attempt fails and Spider-Man must let go.

Note: When a coordinating conjunction joins two elements other than independent clauses, no comma is needed (see P2-a).

P1-b Place a comma after an introductory word, phrase, or clause.

Sentences often begin with words, phrases, or clauses that precede the **independent clause** and modify an element within it.

   Naturally, this result didn't help him any.

   With a jerk, I lofted the lure in a desperate attempt to catch a fish and please my dad.

   When we entered the honeymoon suite, the room smelled of burnt plastic and was
   the color of Pepto Bismol.

The comma following each introductory element lets the reader know where the modifying word or phrase ends and the main clause begins.

independent (main) clause A word group with a subject and a predicate that can stand alone as a separate sentence.

coordinating conjunction A word that joins comparable and equally important sentence elements: *for, and, or, but, nor, yet,* or *so.*

▶ In a poor family with no father, a boy can find the gangs more appealing than the tough life of poverty.

▶ When I picked up the receiver, I heard an unfamiliar voice.

▶ Forgetting my mission for a moment, I took time to look around.

Note: If an introductory phrase or clause is brief — four words or fewer — the comma may be omitted unless it is needed to prevent misreading.

Without hesitation I dived into the lake.

P1-c   Use commas to set off a nonrestrictive word group.

To test whether a word group is *nonrestrictive* (supplemental, nondefining, and thus nonessential) or *restrictive* (defining and thus essential), read the sentence with and without the word group. If the sentence is less informative but essentially unchanged in meaning without it, the word group is nonrestrictive. Use commas to set it off. Conversely, if omitting the word group changes the meaning of the sentence by removing a definition or limitation, it is restrictive. In this case, do not use commas.

NONRESTRICTIVE   The oldest fishermen, *grizzly sea salts wrapped in an aura of experience,* led the way.

RESTRICTIVE   Blood and violence can give video games a sense of realism *that was not previously available.*

In the first sentence, the commas tell the reader that the word group presents extra information. The sentence would be essentially unchanged without the word group: *The oldest fishermen led the way.* In the second sentence, the word group is not set off with commas because it provides essential information about the realism of video games. The sentence would not have the same meaning without it.

Insert a comma to set off a nonrestrictive (nonessential) word group at the end of a sentence.

▶ We all stood, anxious and prepared for what he was about to say.

▶ The next period is the preoperational stage, which begins at age two and lasts until age seven.

▶ He was learning useful outdoor skills, such as how to tie knots and give first aid.

Insert a pair of commas to set off a nonrestrictive (nonessential) word group in the middle of a sentence.

▶ The most common moods are happiness‸when the music is in a major key‸ or sadness, when the music is in a minor key.

▶ Laura‸ our neighbor and best friend‸ appeared at the kitchen window.

▶ My dog‸ Shogun‸ was lying on the floor doing what he does best, sleeping.

The last example illustrates the importance of context for deciding what is essential in a sentence. Here, the writer has only one dog, so the dog's name is nonrestrictive (nonessential) information and is placed between commas. If the writer had more than one dog, however, the name would be essential to identify which dog and would not be set off by commas.

See also P2-b.

P1-d **Use commas to set off a transitional, parenthetical, or contrasting expression or an absolute phrase.**

Often used to begin sentences, *transitional expressions* help the reader follow a writer's movement from point to point, showing how one sentence is related to the next. *Parenthetical comments* interrupt a sentence with a brief aside. *Contrasting expressions* generally come at the end of a sentence, introduced by *not, no,* or *nothing*. *Absolute phrases*, which can appear anywhere within a sentence, modify the whole clause and often include a past or present **participle** as well as modifiers.

TRANSITIONAL	*Besides,* it is summer.
PARENTHETICAL	These are all indications, *I think,* of Jan's drive for power and control.
CONTRASTING	Nick is the perfect example of a young, hungry manager trying to climb to the top, *not bothered by the feelings of others.*
ABSOLUTE	"Did I ever tell you about the time I worked with Danny Kaye at Radio City Music Hall?" she asked, *her eyes focusing dreamily into the distance.*

> **participle** A verb form showing present tense (*dancing, freezing*) or past tense (*danced, frozen*) that can also act as an adjective. In a participial phrase, a group of words begins with a present or past participle and modifies a noun or pronoun: We boarded the bus, *expecting to leave immediately.*

By using commas to set off such expressions, you signal that they are additions, supplementing or commenting on the information in the rest of the sentence.

Insert a comma to set off a transitional, parenthetical, or contrasting expression or an absolute phrase that begins or ends a sentence.

▶ For example‸ in our society a wedding gown is worn by the bride only once, on her wedding day.

▶ We had an advantage, thanks to P.T.'s knowledge.

▶ My uncle talked to me as if I were a person, not a child.

▶ "Well, well," he'd grin, his crooked mouth revealing his perfect white teeth.

Insert a pair of commas to set off a transitional, parenthetical, or contrasting expression or an absolute phrase that falls in the middle of a sentence.

▶ Students, therefore, often complain about their TA's inability to speak English.

▶ At every response, I defended those innocent people and emphasized that no one, absolutely no one, can decide whether or not a person is worthy of living.

▶ He uttered his famous phrase, "If you don't have time to do something right, you definitely don't have time to do it over," for the first, but not the last, time.

▶ I followed her, both of us barefoot and breathing white mist, out the door into the blood-reddened snow.

Note: If a transitional element, such as a **conjunctive adverb**, links two **independent clauses** within one sentence, add a semicolon between the clauses to avoid a **comma splice**. (See P3-d and S1.)

▶ One can see how delicate he is, yet this fragility does not detract from his masculinity; instead, it greatly enhances it.

conjunctive adverb A word or phrase (such as *finally, however*, or *therefore*) that tells how the ideas in two sentences or independent clauses are connected.

independent (main) clause A word group with a subject and a predicate that can stand alone as a separate sentence.

comma splice The improper joining of two independent clauses with only a comma.

P1-e **Use a comma to separate three or more items in a series, placing the final comma before the conjunction.**

He was wearing a camouflage hat, a yellow sweatshirt, and a pair of blue shorts.

The commas in a series separate the items for the reader.

▶ He always tells me about the loyalty, honor, and pride he feels as a Marine.

▶ Our communities would get relief from the fear and despair that come from having unremitting violence, addiction, and open-air drug markets in their midst.

Note: You will notice that newspapers, magazines, and British publications will often omit the comma before the conjunction. In your academic writing, however, you should always include it for clarity.

Occasionally, a writer will separate the last two items in a series with a comma but omit *and*. Or a writer may join all the items in a series with *and* or *or* and thus need no commas at all. Use such alternatives sparingly.

▶ In her, I found a woman with character, integrity, intelligence.

P1-f   Use a comma before a trailing nonrestrictive participial phrase.

Participial phrases are generally **nonrestrictive word groups.** When they follow the **independent (main) clause** in a sentence, they should be set off with commas. (See P1-c.)

PARTICIPIAL
PHRASE
The plane lifted off as he opened the package, *expecting to find cookies and a mushy love letter.*

The comma before the phrase signals the end of the main clause and sets off the important modifying phrase.

▶ Every so often, a pelican agilely arcs high over the water, twisting downward gracefully to catch an unsuspecting mackerel.

▶ I sat down, confused and distraught.

Note: If the participial phrase is restrictive, providing essential information, do not use a comma. (See P1-c and P2-b.)

Now at our disposal were the essential elements of life: the snow, Julie, me, and an entire pantry *stocked with food.*

I noticed his tiny form amid the crowd of vacationers *emerging from the terminal gate.*

Both participial phrases define or limit the nouns they modify, telling readers what kind of pantry and what kind of crowd. Consequently, they are not set off by commas.

P1-g   Place a comma between a complete direct quotation and the text identifying the speaker.

I answered, "Okay, let me grab the ladder."

"Discipline is effective if you get the students to adopt your values," explained Fathman.

---

participial phrase A group of words that begins with a present participle (*dancing, freezing*) or a past participle (*danced, frozen*) and modifies a noun or a pronoun.

nonrestrictive word group A group of words, set off by commas, that provides extra or nonessential information and could be eliminated without changing the meaning of the noun or pronoun it modifies.

independent (main) clause A word group with a subject and a predicate that can stand alone as a separate sentence.

direct quotation A speaker's or writer's exact words, which are enclosed in quotation marks.

The comma, along with the quotation marks, helps the reader determine where the quotation begins and ends. See also P6.

▶ So I asked her, "Momma, who you talkin' to?"

▶ "It will be okay," Coach reassured me, as he motioned for the emergency medical technicians to bring a board.

▶ Dr. Carolyn Bailey says, "I view spanking as an aggressive act."

P1-h Add a comma (or pair of commas in the middle of a sentence) to set off expressions commonly included in dialogue.

direct address Words that are spoken directly to someone else who is named.

Use commas to set off the name of a person **directly addressed** by a speaker, words such as *yes* and *no*, and mild **interjections**. Also use a comma to set off a question added to the end of a sentence.

"Chadan, you're just too compassionate."

"Yes, sir," replied Danny.

Boy, did we underestimate her.

That's not very efficient, is it?

interjection An exclamatory word that indicates strong feeling or attempts to command attention: *Shhh! Oh! Ouch!*

A comma marks the division between the main part of the sentence and a comment that precedes or follows it:

▶ "Well, son, what are you doing?"

▶ "No, sir."

▶ So, this is to be a battle of wills, is it? Fine, I'll play.

▶ "Besides, it'll be good for me."

P1-i Use a comma between **coordinate adjectives**.

coordinate adjectives Two or more adjectives that modify a noun equally and independently: the *large, red* hat.

If you can change the order of a series of adjectives or add *and* between them without changing the meaning, they are coordinate and should be separated with a comma.

There are reasons for her *erratic, irrational* behavior.

The comma signals that the adjectives are equal, related in the same way to the word modified.

If the adjectives closest to the noun cannot logically be rearranged or linked by *and*, they are noncoordinate adjectives (also called *cumulative adjectives*) and should not be separated by commas.

> **I pictured myself as a *professional race car* driver.**

noncoordinate adjectives
Two or more adjectives that do not modify a noun equally. Instead, one or two of the adjectives closest to the noun form a noun phrase that the remaining adjectives modify: *colorful hot-air* balloons.

Once you have determined that adjectives are coordinate, add a comma between them.

▶ **I can still remember the smell of his cigar and his old, oily clothing.**

▶ **Professionals who use this five-step, systematic approach are less likely to injure or be injured during an assault.**

Note: The same rule applies to coordinate adjectives that follow the noun they modify or are otherwise separated from it in the sentence.

> **Skippy was a good-looking guy, *tall, blond,* and *lean*.**

P1-j Add commas where needed to set off dates, numbers, and addresses.

When you include a full date (month, day, and year), use a pair of commas to set off the year.

▶ **In the July 8, 2002, issue of the *New Yorker*, Elizabeth Kolbert described Sidney Hook as "one of the most prominent public intellectuals of his generation" (23).**

If you present a date in reverse order (day, month, and year), do not add commas.

▶ **In the ~~July 8,~~ 8 July 2002 issue of the *New Yorker*, Elizabeth Kolbert described Sidney Hook as "one of the most prominent public intellectuals of his generation" (23).**

If a date is partial (month and year only), do not add commas.

> **This intriguing article appeared in the April 2003 issue of *Personnel Journal*.**

In large numbers, separate groups of three digits (thousands, millions, and so forth) with commas.

▶ **As of 2000, there were about 900,000 speakers of Korean in the United States.**

When you write out an address, add commas between the parts, setting off the street address, the city, and the state with the zip code. When an address or place name is embedded in a complete sentence, add a comma after the last element.

▶ Mrs. Wilson relocated to Bowie⌄ Maryland⌄ after moving from Delaware.

P1-k Add a comma if needed for clarity when a word is omitted, is repeated twice, or might be grouped incorrectly with the next words.

Such instances are rare. Check the guidelines in P1 and P2 so that you do not add unnecessary or incorrect commas.

▶ The statistics reveal that in 1997⌄ 648,000 Hispanic students (48 percent of all Hispanic students) were enrolled in Hispanic-Serving Institutions (HSIs).

P2   Unnecessary Commas

For practice, go to bedfordstmartins.com/theguide/uncom

Because commas are warranted in so many instances, it is easy to use them unnecessarily or incorrectly, particularly with compound sentence elements, with restrictive elements, and between verbs and subjects or verbs and objects.

P2-a Omit the comma when items in a pair joined by *and* or another
coordinating conjunction are not independent clauses.

Many word pairs can be joined by *and* or another coordinating conjunction, including **compound predicates, compound objects,** and **compound subjects.** None of these pairs should be interrupted by a comma.

coordinating conjunction A word that joins comparable and equally important sentence elements: *for, and, or, but, nor, yet,* or *so.*

independent (main) clause A word group with a subject and a predicate that can stand alone as a separate sentence.

compound predicate Two or more verbs or verb phrases linked by *and.*

compound object Two or more words acting as an object and linked by *and.*

compound subject Two or more words acting as a subject and linked by *and.*

COMPOUND PREDICATE   *I grabbed my lunchbox* and *headed out to the tree.*

COMPOUND OBJECT   As for me, I wore *a pink short set with ruffles* and *a pair of sneakers.*

COMPOUND SUBJECT   My *father* and *brother* wore big hiking boots.

Two independent clauses joined by a coordinating conjunction require a comma (see P1-a). The comma shows the reader where one independent clause ends and the other begins. Using a comma in other situations thus sends the wrong signal.

▶ According to Ward, many Custer fans believe that Custer was a "hero⌿" and "represents certain endangered manly virtues."

▶ The school district could implement more programs at both the junior high and the high school⌿and thus could offer the students more opportunities.

▶ I was running out of time⌿and patience.

▶ Culture is not what we do, but how we do things, and why we do them in a
particular way.

P2-b Omit any comma that sets off a restrictive word group.

Use commas to set off a nonrestrictive word group but not a restrictive word group.
A *restrictive word group* distinguishes the noun it modifies from similar nouns or
precisely defines its distinguishing characteristics. A *nonrestrictive word group* provides extra or nonessential information.

RESTRICTIVE   She demonstrates this shortcoming in her story *"Is There Nowhere
Else We Can Meet?"*

NONRESTRICTIVE   The supercomputer center, *which I had seen hundreds of times*, still
held many mysteries for me.

The context helps to determine which information is necessary and which is
extra. In the first example, *"Is There Nowhere Else We Can Meet?"* identifies a specific story, distinguishing it from other stories by the same writer. In the second,
which I had seen hundreds of times adds supplementary information, but the reference to the mysteries of the supercomputer center would be the same without
this addition.

A comma signals that a word group is not essential to the meaning of the
sentence. If a comma incorrectly sets off a restrictive word group, it undermines
the meaning, suggesting to the reader that essential information is not important. See also P1-c.

▶ The ten people from the community would consist of three retired people, over
the age of sixty, three middle-aged people, between the ages of twenty-five and
sixty, and four teenagers.

▶ Although divorce is obviously a cause of the psychological problems, a child
will face, the parents need to support their child through the anxiety and
turmoil.

P2-c Omit any commas that unnecessarily separate the main elements of the sentence — subject and verb or verb and object.

Even in a complicated sentence, a reader expects the core elements — **subject, verb,**
and **object** — to lead directly from one to the other. A comma that separates two of
these elements confuses matters by suggesting that some other material has been
added, such as an introductory or trailing element or a transitional or parenthetical
expression.

subject The part of a
clause that identifies who
or what is being discussed.

verb A word or phrase that
expresses action or being
and, along with a subject,
is a basic component of a
sentence.

object The part of a clause
that receives the action of
the verb: At the checkpoint,
we unloaded *the canoes.*

Delete a comma that unnecessarily separates a subject and its verb.

▶ *Bilateral*/means that both the left and the right sides of the brain are involved in processing a stimulus.

▶ This movie's only fault/is that it does not set a good example for younger children.

Delete a comma that unnecessarily separates a verb and its object.

▶ Now the voters must decide/the issue of term limits.

▶ Unlike Kaoma, many other groups or solo singers try without success to incorporate in their works/music from different cultures.

P2-d **Omit a comma that separates the main part of the sentence from a trailing adverbial clause.**

adverbial clause A clause that nearly always modifies a verb, indicating time, place, condition, reason, cause, purpose, result, or another logical relationship.

When an adverbial clause appears at the beginning of a sentence, it is usually set off by a comma because it is an introductory element. When the clause appears at the end of a sentence, however, a comma is ordinarily not needed.

When Pirates of the Caribbean *finally reaches its climax,* the ending is a doozy.

Depp shows his charm *when Sparrow seduces the governor's daughter.*

Omitting this unnecessary comma makes the sentence flow more smoothly.

▶ I found the tables turned/when he interviewed me about the reasons for my tattoo.

P2-e **Leave out any comma that separates noncoordinate adjectives.**

noncoordinate adjectives Two or more adjectives that do not modify a noun equally. Instead, one or two of the adjectives closest to the noun form a noun phrase that the remaining adjectives modify: *colorful hot-air* balloons.

If you cannot rearrange the adjectives before a noun or add *and* between them, they are probably noncoordinate adjectives (sometimes called *cumulative adjectives*). Such adjectives are not equal elements; do not separate them with a comma. In contrast, **coordinate adjectives** should be separated by commas (see P1-i).

┌**COORDINATE ADJECTIVES**┐
Wearing a pair of jeans, *cutoff, bleached,* and *torn,* with an embroidered blouse

coordinate adjectives Two or more adjectives that modify a noun equally and independently: the *large, red* hat.

NONCOORDINATE ADJECTIVES
and *soft leather* sandals, she looked older and more foreign than Julie.

Leather modifies *sandals,* and *soft* modifies *leather sandals* as a unit. Thus the meaning is cumulative, and a comma would interrupt the connection between the adjectives and the noun.

▶ Huge⁄neighborhood parties could bring the people in our community together.

P2-f   Omit any comma that appears before or after a series of items.

Although commas should be used to separate the items in a list, they should not be used before the first item or after the final one.

▶ Race, sex, religion, financial situation, or any other circumstance beyond the
control of the applicant⁄should not be considered.

See also P1-e.

P2-g   Omit or correct any other unnecessary or incorrect commas.

Check your essays carefully for the following typical comma problems.

Omit a comma that follows a coordinating conjunction.

A comma is needed *before* a coordinating conjunction if it links two independent clauses but not if it links a pair of other sentence elements. A comma is never needed *after* a coordinating conjunction, however. Be especially alert to this unnecessary comma when *but* or *yet* appears at the beginning of a sentence.

> **coordinating conjunction**
> A word that joins comparable and equally important sentence elements: *for, and, or, but, nor, yet,* or *so.*

▶ But⁄since sharks are not yet classified as endangered species, the members of
Congress were not very sympathetic, and the bill was not passed.

Note: A conjunction may or may not be needed for transition or dramatic effect, depending on the context of the sentence in your essay.

Since
▶ ~~But, since~~ sharks are not yet classified as endangered species, the members of
Congress were not very sympathetic, and the bill was not passed.

Omit a comma following a coordinating conjunction joining two independent clauses, even if the conjunction is followed by a transitional or introductory expression.

▶ The ominous vision of the piano wavered before my eyes, and⁄before I knew it,
I was at the base of the steps to the stage, steps that led to potential public
humiliation.

▶ I had finally felt the music deep in my soul, and, when I sang, I had a great feeling of relief knowing that everything was going to be all right.

Omit a comma after the word that introduces a dependent clause.

dependent (subordinate) clause A word group that has a subject, a predicate, and a subordinating word at the beginning; it cannot stand by itself as a sentence but must be connected to an independent (main) clause.

Watch for words such as *who, which, that, whom, whose, where, when, although, because, since, though,* and other **subordinating conjunctions**.

▶ This trend was evident as I entered a college where, the first-year enrollment had been rising.

▶ The drinking age should be raised because, drunk driving has become the leading cause of death among young people between the ages of fifteen and twenty-five.

subordinating conjunction A word or phrase that introduces a dependent clause and relates it to an independent clause.

Omit a comma preceding *that* when it introduces an indirect quotation.

indirect quotation A reworded statement or question that presents a speaker's or writer's ideas without quoting directly or using quotation marks.

Unlike a direct quotation, an indirect quotation is not set off by a comma or quotation marks.

▶ After looking at my tests, the doctor said, that I had calcification.

Omit a comma immediately following a preposition.

preposition A word (such as *between, in,* or *of*) that always appears as part of a phrase and indicates the relation between a word in a sentence and the object of the preposition: The water splashed *into* the canoe.

A comma may follow a complete **prepositional phrase** at the beginning of a sentence, but a comma should not follow the preposition or interrupt the phrase.

▶ Despite, multiple recruitment and retention problems, the number of public school teachers increased by 27 percent between 1986 and 1999.

Omit unnecessary commas that set off a prepositional phrase in the middle of a sentence.

prepositional phrase A group of words that begins with a preposition and indicates the relation between a word in a sentence and the object following the preposition: Her sunglasses slid *under the seat.*

When a prepositional phrase appears in the middle of a sentence or at the end, it is usually not set off by commas. When it acts as an introductory element, however, it is generally followed by a comma.

▶ "I've seen the devil b'fore," he grumbled, in a serious tone, with his blue eyes peering into mine.

▶ The children's trauma team gathers in the Resuscitation Room, at the same time that John Doe is being treated.

Rewrite a sentence that is full of phrases and commas to simplify both the sentence structure and the punctuation.

▶ ~~The researchers could monitor, by~~ *By* looking through a porthole window, how *the researchers could monitor*
much time ~~was spent, by Noah,~~ *Noah spent* in the dome.

P3   Semicolons

For practice, go to bedfordstmartins.com/theguide/semi

Use semicolons to join closely related independent clauses and to make long sentences with commas easier to read.

P3-a   Use a semicolon to join independent clauses if the second clause restates or sets up a contrast to the first.

> **In fact, she always had been special; we just never noticed.**

independent (main) clause A word group with a subject and a predicate that can stand alone as a separate sentence.

Although two independent clauses could be separated by a period, the semicolon tells the reader that they are closely related, emphasizing the restatement or sharpening the contrast.

▶ **Davie was not an angel; he was always getting into trouble with the teachers.**

Note: When the independent clauses are linked by *and, but,* or another coordinating conjunction, use a comma rather than a semicolon (see P1-a) unless the independent clauses include internal punctuation (see P3-c).

P3-b   Use semicolons to separate items in a series when they include internal commas.

> **Studies of gender differences in conversational interaction include an Elizabeth Aries article titled "Interaction Patterns and Themes of Male, Female, and Mixed Groups," a study conducted in a research laboratory setting; a Pamela Fishman article titled "Interaction: The Work Women Do," a study researched by naturalistic observation; and an article by Candace West and Don Zimmerman titled "Small Insults: A Study of Interruptions in Cross-Sex Conversation between Unacquainted Persons," a study conducted in a research laboratory setting.**

Because the reader expects items in a series to be separated with commas, other commas within items can be confusing. The solution is to leave the internal commas as they are but to use a stronger mark, the semicolon, to signal the divisions between items.

▶ Appliances that use freon include air conditioners, small models as well as central systems, refrigerators, and freezers, both home and industrial types.

P3-c   Use a semicolon to join a series of independent clauses when they include other punctuation.

independent (main)
clause A word group with
a subject and a predicate
that can stand alone as a
separate sentence.

Sometimes independent clauses include elements set off by internal punctuation. In such cases, use semicolons between the independent clauses if the other punctuation is likely to confuse a reader or make the sentence parts difficult to identify.

▶ He was the guide, and he was driving us in this old Ford sedan, just the two of us and him, and I had noticed early on that the car didn't have a gas cap.

Independent clauses like these could also be separated by periods, but semicolons let the reader know that the information in each clause is part of a continuing event.

P3-d   Use a semicolon to join two independent clauses when the second clause contains a conjunctive adverb or a transitional expression.

conjunctive adverb A
word or phrase (such as *finally, however,* or *therefore*)
that tells how the ideas in
two sentences or independent clauses are connected.

transitional expression A
word or group of words
that expresses the relationship between one sentence
and the next.

Because a semicolon shows a strong relationship between independent clauses, writers often use it to reinforce the connection expressed by the adverb or transition. Always place the semicolon between the two clauses, no matter where the conjunctive adverb or transitional expression appears. Place the semicolon *before* the conjunctive adverb or transition if it begins the second independent clause. See also P1-d.

▶ Ninety-five percent of Americans recognize the components of a healthy diet, however, they fail to apply their nutritional IQ when selecting foods.

P3-e   Omit or correct a semicolon used incorrectly to replace a comma or other punctuation mark.

Use semicolons to join two independent clauses or to separate the items in a series when they include other punctuation, but do not use semicolons in place of other punctuation.

appositive A word or word
group that identifies or
gives more information
about a noun or pronoun
that precedes it.

Replace a semicolon with a comma to link an independent clause to a phrase or to set off an appositive.

▶ The threat of a potentially devastating malpractice suit promotes the practice of defensive medicine, doctors ordering excessive and expensive tests to confirm a diagnosis.

Replace a semicolon with a comma to join two independent clauses linked by a coordinating conjunction.

coordinating conjunction
A word that joins comparable and equally important
sentence elements: *for,
and, or, but, nor, yet,* or *so.*

▶ The ashtrays would need to be relocated to that area; and it could then become an outdoor smoking lounge.

See also P1-a.

Replace a semicolon with a colon to introduce a list.

▶ Our county ditches fill up with old items that are hard to get rid of: old refrigerators, mattresses, couches, and chairs, just to name a few.

Note: For introducing an in-text list as in this example, a dash (see P5-b) is a less formal and more dramatic alternative to the colon (see P4-a).

P4 Colons

For practice, go to bedfordstmartins.com/theguide/colon

Besides introducing specific sentence elements, colons conventionally appear in works cited or bibliography entries, introduce subtitles, express ratios and times, and follow the salutations in formal letters.

P4-a Use a colon to introduce a list, an appositive, a quotation, a question, or a statement.

appositive A word or word group that identifies or gives more information about a noun or pronoun that precedes it.

Usually, a colon follows an **independent clause** that makes a general statement; after the colon, the rest of the sentence often supplies specifics — a definition, a quotation or question, or a list (generally in grammatically parallel form; see E7).

independent (main) clause A word group with a subject and a predicate that can stand alone as a separate sentence.

Society's hatred, violence, and bigotry take root here: the elementary school playground.

Use the colon selectively to alert readers to closely connected ideas, a significant point, a crucial definition, or a dramatic revelation.

Note: Because a colon follows but does not interrupt an independent clause, it is not used after words such as *is, are, consists of, including, such as, for instance,* and *for example* (see P4-b).

Consider using a colon to introduce a list.

You can use a colon to introduce a list if the list is preceded by an independent clause. Be careful not to interrupt the clause in the middle (see P4-b).

▶ Most young law school graduates become trial lawyers in one of three ways/: by going to work for a government prosecutor's office, by working for a private law firm, or by opening private offices of their own.

Consider using a colon to emphasize an appositive.

Although you can always use commas to set off an appositive, try using a colon occasionally when you need special emphasis.

▶ The oldest fishermen are followed by the younger generation of middle-aged fathers, excited by the chance to show their sons what their fathers once taught them. Last to arrive are the novices/: the thrill seekers.

Consider using a colon to introduce a formal quotation, a question, a statement, or another independent clause.

▶ We learn that the narrator is a troublemaker in paragraph twelve/: "I got thrown out of the center for playing pool when I should've been sewing."

▶ I ran around the office in constant fear of his questions/: What do you have planned for the day? How many demonstrations are scheduled for this week? How many contacts have you made?

▶ Both authors are clearly of the same opinion/: recycling scrap tires is no longer an option.

▶ I guess the saying is true/: Absence does make the heart grow fonder.

Do not capitalize the first word following a colon that introduces an incomplete sentence. However, when the first word following a colon introduces a complete sentence, you can either capitalize the word or not, depending on your preference (see M2-b). Whichever choice you prefer, be consistent. When you introduce a quotation with a colon, always capitalize the word that begins the quotation. See also P6-b.

P4-b   **Delete or correct an unnecessary or incorrect colon.**

As you proofread your writing, watch out for the following incorrect uses of the colon.

Omit a colon that interrupts an independent clause, especially after words such as *is, are, include, composed of, consists of, including, such as, for instance,* and for *example.*

**independent (main)
clause** A word group with
a subject and a predicate
that can stand alone as a
separate sentence.

▶ The tenets include; courtesy, integrity, perseverance, self-control, indomitable spirit, and modesty.

Replace an inappropriate colon with the correct punctuation mark.

▶ As I was touring the different areas of the shop, I ran into Christy, one of the owners; "Hi, Kim," she said with a smile on her face.

P5   Dashes

For practice, go to bedfordstmartins.com/theguide/dashes

A dash breaks the rhythm or interrupts the meaning of a sentence, setting off information with greater emphasis than another punctuation mark could supply. Writers often use dashes to substitute for other punctuation in quick notes and letters to friends. In many kinds of published writing, dashes are an option used sparingly — but often to good effect.

P5-a   Type, space, and position a dash correctly.

Type a dash (—) as two hyphens (--) in a row with no spaces before or after. Use one dash before a word or words set off at the end of the sentence. Use two dashes — one at the beginning and one at the end — if the word or words are in the middle of the sentence.

The rigid structure and asymmetrical arrangements of the sculpture blend well with three different surroundings--the trees, the library building, and the parking lots.

Retype a dash using two hyphens and no spaces.

▶ Of all public stations in Maryland, WBJC reaches the largest audience--almost 200,000 listeners per week.

▶ And of course, the trees in the sculpture were more than just imitation--they spoke!

Note: Most word processing programs will allow you to insert a solid dash (—) instead of two hyphens (--).

Use a pair of dashes, not just one, to mark the beginning and end of a word group that needs emphasis.

▶ I could tell that the people in the room work in uncomfortable conditions —

they all wear white lab coats, caps, and gloves ⁄ but they joke or laugh while

building the guns.

If the word group includes commas or other internal punctuation, the dashes tell the reader exactly where the expression that is being set off begins and ends.

P5-b   Consider using a dash to set off material from the rest of the sentence.

That smell completely cut off the outside world — the smell of the ocean, the soft

breeze, the jubilation of young people under the sun.

Because the dash marks a strong break, it alerts the reader to the importance of the material that follows it.

Consider inserting a dash or pair of dashes to emphasize a definition, a dramatic statement, a personal comment, or an explanation.

▶ Binge eating ⁄ larger than normal consumption of high-calorie foods ⁄ starts with
   emotional distress and depression.

▶ But unlike the boys, the girls often turn to something other than violence ⁄
   motherhood.

▶ In many cases it may be more humane and I personally believe it is much

more humane to practice euthanasia than to cause the patient prolonged

suffering and pain.

Consider inserting a dash or pair of dashes to emphasize a list.

If the list appears in the middle of the sentence, use one dash at the beginning and another at the end to signal exactly where the list begins and ends.

▶ Another problem is that certain toy figures The Hulk, Spider-Man, and the

X-Men, to name just a few ⁄ are characters from movies that portray violence.

P5-c Rewrite a sentence that uses the dash inappropriately or excessively.

Use dashes purposefully; avoid relying on them instead of using other punctuation marks or developing clear sentences and transitions.

▶ Finally the TV people were finished with their interviewing—now they wanted *and*

to do a shot of the entrance to the restaurant.

If you are not sure whether you have used a dash or pair of dashes appropriately, try removing the material that is set off. If the sentence does not make logical and grammatical sense, one or both of the dashes are misused or misplaced.

▶ That's a tall order — and a reason to start / amassing some serious capital soon.

P6 Quotation Marks

For practice, go to bedfordstmartins.com/theguide/quote

Use double quotation marks, always in pairs, to indicate direct quotations, to set off special uses of words, and to mark some types of titles. Proofread carefully to be sure that you have added quotation marks at both the beginning and the end of each quotation.

P6-a Set off direct quotations with quotation marks.

A direct quotation is set off by a pair of quotation marks and by an initial capital letter. **Indirect quotations,** however, do not use quotation marks or capital letters.

"Mary," I finally said, "I can't keep coming in every weekend."

Field Marshall Viscount Montgomery stated, "A good beating with a cane can have a remarkable sense of awakening on the mind and conscience of a boy" (James, 1963, p. 13).

Ms. Goldman is saying that it's time to face the real issues.

When a phrase such as *she said* interrupts the quotation, do not capitalize the first word after the phrase unless the word actually begins a new quoted sentence.

▶ The commissioners came to the conclusion that alcohol prohibition was, in

the words of Walter Lippman, a helpless failure."

direct quotation A speaker's or writer's exact words, which are enclosed in quotation marks.

indirect quotation A reworded statement or question that presents a speaker's or writer's ideas without quoting directly or using quotation marks.

MLA style Conventions set forth in the guidelines of the Modern Language Association for preparing research papers and documenting sources. See Chapter 22.

APA style Conventions set forth in the guidelines of the American Psychological Association for preparing research papers and documenting sources. See Chapter 22.

Note: In a research paper, indent a long quotation as a block, double spaced, and omit quotation marks. If you are following **MLA style**, indent a long quotation (five typed lines or more) ten spaces, or an inch from the left margin. If you are following **APA style,** indent a long quotation (forty words or more) five spaces.

> The mother points out the social changes over Dee's and her lifetime, contrasting the two time periods.
>
> > Who can even imagine me looking a strange white man in the eye? It seems to me I have talked to them always with one foot raised in flight, with my head turned in whichever way is farthest from them. Dee, though. She would always look anyone in the eye. (Walker 49)

P6-b Follow convention in using punctuation at the end of a quotation, after a phrase such as *he said* or *she said*, and with other punctuation in the same sentence.

Using other punctuation with quotation marks can be tricky at times.

Place a comma or a period inside the closing quotation mark.

▶ Fishman also discusses utterances such as "umm," "oh," and "yeah."

▶ Grandpa then said, "I guess you haven't heard what happened."

▶ "At that point I definitely began to have my doubts, but I tried to go on with my 'normal life.'"

In a research paper following either MLA style or APA style, the closing quotation mark should follow the last quoted word, but the period at the end of the sentence should follow the parentheses enclosing the citation.

▶ Senator Gabriel Ambrosio added that "an override would send a terrible message, particularly to the young people (Schwaneberg 60)."

Note: Place a colon or semicolon outside the closing quotation mark.

> The doctor who tells the story says that the girl is "furious"; she shrieks "terrifyingly, hysterically" as he approaches her.

Follow an introductory phrase such as *he said* with either a comma or the word *that*.

▶ I looked down and said, "I was trying on your dress blues."

▶ Eberts and Schwirian bluntly point out that, "control attempts aimed at constraining or rehabilitating individual criminals or at strengthening local police forces are treating the symptoms or results of social conditions" (98).

When you introduce a formal quotation with an independent clause, you can instead follow the introduction with a colon. (See P4-a.)

Place a question mark or an exclamation point inside the closing quotation mark if it is part of the quotation, or outside if it is part of your own sentence.

▶ My father replied, "What have I ever done to you?"

▶ How is it possible that he could have kept repeating to our class, "You are too dumb to learn anything?"?

Note: You do not need to add a period if a question mark or an exclamation point concludes a quotation at the end of the sentence.

▶ Miriam produces a highlighter from her bookbag with an enthusiastic "Voilà!"

Supply a closing quotation mark at the end of a paragraph to show that a new quotation begins in the next paragraph.

In a dialogue, enclose each speaker's words in quotation marks, and begin a new paragraph every time the speaker changes.

▶ "Come on, James," Toby said. "Let's climb over the fence." "I don't think it's a good idea!" I replied.

Omit the closing quotation mark if a quotation continues in the next paragraph.

If a quotation from a speaker or writer continues from one paragraph to the next, omit the closing quotation mark at the end of the first paragraph, but begin the next paragraph with a quotation mark to show that the quote continues.

▶ ". . . I enjoy waiting on these people because they also ask about my life, instead of treating me like a servant.

"However, some customers can be rude and very impatient. . . ."

P6-c   Consider using double quotation marks to set off words being defined.

Set off words sparingly (see P6-f), using quotation marks only for those you define or use with a special meaning. You may also use underlining or italics rather than quotation marks to set off words. (See M5-b.)

> ▶ The two most popular words in the state statutes are "reasonable" and "appropriate," used to describe the manner of administration.

Note: Occasionally, quotation marks identify words used ironically. In general, keep such use to a minimum. (See P6-f.)

P6-d Enclose titles of short works (such as articles, chapters, essays, short stories, short poems, episodes in a television program, and songs) in quotation marks.

Note: Titles of longer works are underlined or italicized. (See M5-a.)

> ▶ The short story The Use of Force, by William Carlos Williams, is an account of a doctor's unpleasant experience with his patient.

> ▶ Charlene Marner Solomon, author of Careers under Glass, writes an excellent, in-depth article on obstacles working women encounter when trying to move up the corporate ladder.

Place the quotation marks around the exact title of the work mentioned.

> ▶ The "Use of Force," by William Carlos Williams, is at first just another story of a doctor's visit.

Note: When you supply your own title at the beginning of your own essay, do not enclose it in quotation marks.

P6-e Use single quotation marks inside double quotation marks to show a quotation within a quotation.

Single quotation marks indicate that the quoted words come from another source or that the source added quotation marks for emphasis.

> ▶ Flanagan and McMenamin say, "Housing values across the United States have acted more like a fluctuating stock market than the 'sure' investment they once were."

P6-f Omit or correct quotation marks used excessively or incorrectly.

Avoid using quotation marks unnecessarily when you wish to set off words or include direct or indirect quotations.

Omit unneeded quotation marks used for emphasis, irony, or distance.

Avoid using quotation marks just to emphasize certain words, to show irony, or to distance yourself from **slang, clichés,** or trite expressions. Reserve quotation marks for words that you define or use with a special meaning. (See P6-c.)

> ▶ Environmental groups can wage war in the hallways of Washington and Sacramento and drive oil companies away from our ~~"~~sacred shores.~~"~~

slang Informal language that tends to change rapidly.

cliché An overused expression that has lost its original freshness, such as *hard as a rock.*

Add quotation marks to show direct quotations, and omit them from indirect quotations, rewording as necessary to present material accurately.

> ▶ To start things off, he said, "*While* farming in Liberty, Texas, at the age of eighteen, the spirit of God ^*inspired his move to Houston.*~~came to him to go to Houston.~~"

added: that ᵛwhile ... ᵛ inspired his move to Houston.

Whenever you quote a written source or a person you have interviewed, check your notes to make sure that you are using quotation marks to enclose only the speaker's or writer's exact words.

direct quotation A speaker's or writer's exact words, which are enclosed in quotation marks.

indirect quotation A reworded statement or question that presents a speaker's or writer's ideas without quoting directly or using quotation marks.

P7   Apostrophes

For practice, go to bedfordstmartins.com/theguide/apo

Use an apostrophe to mark the **possessive form** of nouns and some pronouns, the omission of letters or figures, and the plural of letters or figures.

possessive form The form that shows that a thing belongs to someone or to something.

P7-a   Use an apostrophe to show the possessive form of a noun.

The form of a possessive noun depends on whether it is singular (one item) or plural (two or more items).

Add -'s to a singular noun to show possession.

| a student's parents | the rabbit's eye | Ward's essay |

Be sure to include the apostrophe and to place it before the *-s* so that the reader does not mistakenly think that the noun is plural.

> ▶ The ~~apartments~~ *apartment's* design lacks softening curves to tame the bare walls.
> ▶ Mrs. Johnson says that 90 percent of the ~~libraries~~ *library's* material is on the first floor.

Indicate shared or joint possession by adding -'s to the final noun in a list; indicate individual possession by adding -'s to each noun.

father and mother's room (joint or shared possession)

father's and mother's patterns of conversation (individual possession)

Indicate possession by adding -'s to the last word in a compound.

mother-in-law's

Note: Even if a singular noun ends in *s*, add an apostrophe and -*s*. If the second *s* makes the word hard to pronounce, it is acceptable to add only an apostrophe.

Louis's life   Williams's narrator   Cisneros's story   Sophocles' plays

To show possession, add only an apostrophe to a plural noun that ends in *s* but -'s if the plural noun does not end in *s*.

their neighbors' homes   other characters' expressions

the children's faces   the women's team

▶ Males tend to interrupt ~~females~~ conversations. *(females')*

Note: Form the plural of a family name by adding -*s* without an apostrophe (the Harrisons); add the apostrophe only to show possession (the Harrisons' house).

P7-b   Add an apostrophe to show where letters or figures are omitted from a contraction.

▶ "~~Lets~~ go back inside and see if you can do it my way now." *(Let's)*

▶ Many people had cosmetic surgery in the ~~80s.~~ *('80s)*

Note: The possessive forms of **personal pronouns** do not have apostrophes (*yours, its, hers, his, ours, theirs*) but are sometimes confused with contractions (such as *it's* for *it is*).

▶ A huge 10- by 4-foot painting of the perfect wave in all ~~it's~~ glorious detail *(its)* hangs high up on the wall of the surfing club.

personal pronoun A pronoun that refers to a specific person or object and changes form depending on its function in a sentence, such as *I, me, my, we, us,* and *our.*

P7-c   Add -'s to form the plural of a number, a letter, or an abbreviation.

perfect 10's   mostly *A*'s and *B*'s   training the R.A.'s

▶ The participants were shown a series of ~~3s~~ that configured into a large 5. *(3's)*

To show that a date refers to a decade, add -*s* without an apostrophe.

Women have come a long way in the business world since the 1950s.

Note: Some style guides, such as the MLA guide, prefer no apostrophes with plural abbreviations: *ATMs.*

P7-d **Add -'s to form the possessive of an indefinite pronoun.**

▶ Everyone knows that good service can make or break ~~ones~~ *one's* dining experience.

Note: The possessive forms of **personal pronouns,** however, do not have apostrophes: *my, mine, your, yours, hers, his, its, our, ours, their, theirs.*

P7-e **Omit unnecessary or incorrect apostrophes.**

Watch for an apostrophe incorrectly added to a plural noun ending in *s* when the noun is not a possessive.

▶ Autistic ~~patient's~~ *patients* can be high, middle, or low functioning.

Also remove an apostrophe added to a possessive **personal pronoun** (*yours, its, hers, his, ours, theirs*), watching especially for any forms confused with contractions (such as *it's* for *it is*). See also P7-b.

▶ That company does not use animals to develop ~~it's~~ *its* products.

P8   Parentheses

For practice, go to bedfordstmartins.com/theguide/paren

Parentheses are useful for enclosing material — a word, a phrase, or even a complete sentence — that interrupts a sentence. Place words in parentheses anywhere after the first word of the sentence as long as the placement is appropriate and relevant and the sentence remains easy to read.

P8-a **Add parentheses to enclose additions to a sentence.**

Parentheses are useful for enclosing citations of research sources (following the format required by your style guide); for enclosing an **acronym** or abbreviation at first mention; for adding dates, definitions, illustrations, or other elaborations; and for numbering or lettering a list (always using a pair of marks).

▶ Americans are not utilizing their knowledge, and as a result, their children are (not benefiting *American Dietetic Association*, 1990, p. 582).

▶ *People for the Ethical Treatment of Animals* (PETA) is a radical animal liberation group.

indefinite pronoun A pronoun that does not refer to a particular person or object, such as *all, anybody, anywhere, each, enough, every, everyone, everything, one, somebody, something, either, more, most, neither, none,* or *nobody.*

personal pronoun A pronoun that refers to a specific person or object and changes form depending on its function in a sentence, such as *I, me, my, we, us,* and *our.*

acronym A word formed from the first letters of the phrase that it abbreviates, such as *BART* for *Bay Area Rapid Transit.*

▶ The bill ~~called~~ (S-2232) was introduced to protect people who smoke off the job against employment discrimination.

▶ Signals would 1) prevent life-threatening collisions, 2) provide more efficient and speedy movement of traffic, and 3) decrease frustration and loss of driver judgment.

Note: Use commas to separate the items in a numbered list. If the items include internal commas, use semicolons. (See P3-b.)

P8-b   Correct the punctuation used with parentheses, and omit unnecessary parentheses.

When you add information in parentheses, the basic pattern of the sentence should remain logical and complete, and the punctuation should be the same as it would be if the parenthetical addition were removed. Delete any comma *before* a parenthesis mark.

▶ As I stood at the salad bar, a young lady asked if the kitchen had any cream cheese, (normally served only at breakfast).

Parentheses are unnecessary if they enclose information that could simply be integrated into the sentence.

▶ He didn't exhibit the uncontrollable temper and the high-velocity swearing (typical of many high school coaches).

P9   Brackets

For practice, go to bedfordstmartins.com/theguide/brack

Use brackets to insert editorial notes into a quotation and to enclose parenthetical material within text that is already in parentheses. In a quotation, the brackets tell the reader that the added material is yours, not the original author's. See also P10.

▶ " 'The gang is your family,' he [Hagan] explains."

If the original quotation includes a mistake, add [sic], the Latin word for "so," in brackets to tell the reader that the error occurs in the source. Often you can reword your sentence to omit the error.

Replace inappropriate brackets with parentheses.

▶ The American Medical Society has linked "virtual" violence [violence in the

various media] to real-life acts of violence (Hollis 623).

P10   Ellipsis Marks

For practice, go to bedfordstmartins.com/theguide/ellip

Use ellipsis marks to indicate a deliberate omission within a quotation or to mark a dramatic pause in a sentence. Type ellipsis marks as three spaced periods (. . .), with a space before the first period and following the last period.

> Aries also noticed this reaction in her research: "The mixed group setting seems to benefit men more than women . . . allowing men more variation in the ways they participate in discussions" (32).

If you omit the end of a quoted sentence or if you omit a sentence or more from the middle of a quoted passage, add a sentence period and a space before the first ellipsis mark. (If a quotation that ends with ellipsis marks is followed by a parenthetical citation, put the sentence period at the very end — after the closing quotation mark and the citation.)

Do not use opening or closing ellipsis marks if the quotation is clearly only part of a sentence.

▶ According to the environmental group Earthgreen, U.S. oil reserves ". . . will be
economically depleted by 2018 at the current consumption rate . . ."
(Miller 476).

See pp. 562–63 and pp. 739–40 for more on ellipsis marks.

P11   Slashes

For practice, go to bedfordstmartins.com/theguide/slash

Use a slash to separate quoted lines of poetry and to separate word pairs that present options or opposites.

> In "A Poison Tree," William Blake gives the same advice: "I was angry with my friend: / I told my wrath, my wrath did end."

Note: When you use a slash to show the lines in poetry, leave a space before and after the mark. If you quote four lines or more, omit the quotation marks and slashes and present the poetry line for line as a block quotation, double spaced. Following **MLA style,** indent each line of a block quotation ten spaces or an inch from the left margin. See also P6-a.

P12   Periods

For practice, go to bedfordstmartins.com/theguide/period

Use a period to mark the end of a **declarative sentence,** an **indirect question,** or an abbreviation.

▶ Another significant use for clinical hypnosis would be to replace anesthesia.

▶ She asked her professor why he was not as tough on her as he was on the male students?.

▶ Mrs. Drabin was probably one of the smartest people I knew.

Note: Some abbreviations do not include periods (see M6); always check your dictionary to be sure. In addition, many specialized professional and academic fields have their own systems for handling abbreviations.

P13   Question Marks

For practice, go to bedfordstmartins.com/theguide/quest

Add a question mark after a direct question.

▶ Did they even read my information sheet/?

Avoid using question marks to express irony or sarcasm. Use them sparingly to question the accuracy of a preceding word or figure.

P14   Exclamation Points

For practice, go to bedfordstmartins.com/theguide/excl

Use an exclamation point to show strong emotion or emphasis.

He fell on one knee and exclaimed, "Marry me, my beautiful princess!"

Use exclamation points sparingly. Replace inappropriate or excessive exclamation points with periods.

▶ If parents know which disciplinary methods to use, they can effectively protect their children!.

MLA style Conventions set forth in the guidelines of the Modern Language Association for preparing research papers and documenting sources. See Chapter 22.

declarative sentence A sentence that makes a statement rather than asking a question or exclaiming.

indirect question A statement that tells what a question asked without directly asking the question.

M   Mechanics

M1   Hyphens

Hyphens are used to form **compound words** and to break words at the end of a line. Depending on the word and its position in a sentence, a compound may be written as separate words with no hyphen between them, as one word with no space or hyphen between the parts, or as a hyphenated word.

moonshine	postmaster	shipboard
vice versa	place kick	highly regarded
like-minded	once-over	all-around
father-in-law	take-it-or-leave-it	mid-December

> **compound word** A word formed from two or more words that function together as a unit.

M1-a   **Use a hyphen to join the parts of a compound adjective when it precedes a noun but not when it follows a noun.**

Before Noun	*After Noun*
after-school activities	activities after school
well-known athlete	athlete who is well known
fast-growing business	business that is fast growing

> **compound adjective** An adjective formed from two or more words that function as a unit.

When a compound adjective precedes a noun, the hyphen clarifies that the compound functions as a unit.

▶ People usually think of locusts as hideous looking creatures that everyone dislikes and wants to squash.

▶ I was a nineteen year old second semester sophomore.

▶ People are becoming increasingly health conscious.

When two different prefixes or initial words are meant to go with the same second word, use a hyphen and a space at the end of the first prefix or word.

Over twenty people crowd the small trauma room, an army of green- and blue-hooded medical personnel.

Note: Some compound adjectives are nearly always hyphenated, before or after a noun, including those beginning with *all-* or *self-*.

all-inclusive fee   self-sufficient economy
fee that is all-inclusive   economy that is self-sufficient

▶ The use of ethanol will be a self perpetuating trend.

A compound with an -*ly* **adverb** preceding an **adjective** or a **participle** is always left as two words.

brilliantly clever scheme	rapidly growing business	highly regarded professor

M1-b   **Present a compound noun as one word, as separate words, or as a hyphenated compound.**

If you are not certain about a particular compound noun, look it up in your dictionary. If you cannot find it, spell it as separate words.

Close up the parts of a compound noun spelled as one word.

▶ Another road in our county now looks like an appliance grave yard.

Omit hyphens in a compound noun spelled as separate words.

▶ First, make the community aware of the problem by writing a letter-to-the-editor.

Add any hyphens needed in a hyphenated compound noun.

Hyphenate fractions, compound numbers (up to ninety-nine), and other nouns that are hyphenated in your dictionary.

▶ Almost two thirds of women who marry before age eighteen end up divorced,

twice the number of women who marry at twenty one or older.

Note: Some compound words have more than one acceptable spelling (*workforce* and *work force*, for example); if you use such a compound, choose one spelling and use it consistently. If you are unsure about whether to use a hyphen, check your dictionary, or follow the common usage of professional publications in that field.

M1-c   **Spell words formed with most prefixes (including *anti-*, *co-*, *mini-*, *multi-*, *non-*, *post-*, *pre-*, *re-*, *sub-*, and *un-*) as one word with no hyphen.**

antismoking	coauthor	multicultural	nonviolent
postwar	repossess	submarine	unskilled

---

adverb A word that modifies a verb, an adjective, or another adverb, often telling when, where, why, how, or how often.

adjective A word that modifies a noun or a pronoun, adding information about it.

participle A verb form showing present tense (*dancing, freezing*) or past tense (*danced, frozen*) that can also act as an adjective.

compound noun A noun formed from two or more words that function as a unit.

▶ This possibility is so rare as to be non-existent.

Note: Insert a hyphen in a compound noun beginning with *ex-*, *great-*, or *self-* (unless it is followed by a suffix, as in *selfhood*) or ending in *-elect* or *-in-law*. Check your dictionary in case of a question.

    ex-husband   self-esteem   secretary-elect

▶ Self-sufficiency is not the only motivation.

Note: Use a hyphen in a word that includes a prefix and a **proper name**.

    un-American   anti-American   pro-American

> **proper name** The capitalized name of a specific person, group, place, or thing.

M1-d Use a hyphen when necessary to avoid ambiguity.

Sometimes a hyphen is necessary to prevent a reader from confusing a word with a prefix (*re-cover* or *re-creation*) with another word (*recover* or *recreation*) or from stumbling over a word in which two or three of the same letters fall together (*anti-inflammatory, troll-like*).

The police officers asked for the *recreation* facility's logbook to help them
re-create the circumstances surrounding the crime.

M1-e Insert a hyphen between syllables to divide a word at the end of a line.

If you must divide a word, look for a logical division, such as between syllables, between parts of a compound word, or between the root and a prefix or suffix. If you are uncertain about where to divide a word, check your dictionary.

go-ing	height-en	mus-cu-la-ture	back-stage
dis-satis-fied	com-mit-ment	honor-able	philos-ophy

Although many word processors will automatically divide words, writing is easier to read without numerous broken words. Check with your instructor or consult the style manual used in a specific field for advice about whether to use the hyphenation function.

M2 Capitalization

Capitalize proper names, the first word in a sentence or a quotation that is a sentence, and the main words in a title.

M2-a Capitalize proper names but not common nouns.

Capitalize specific names of people, groups, places, streets, events, historical periods, monuments, holidays, days, months, and directions that refer to specific geographic areas.

> **common noun** The general name of a person, place, or thing.

World War II	the Great Depression	Lincoln Memorial
Independence Day	Passover	Ramadan
Monday	January	Colorado College
the Northeast	Native Americans	Magnolia Avenue

▶ It is difficult for americans to comprehend the true meaning of freedom.

When a reference is general, use a common noun (uncapitalized) rather than a proper one (capitalized). Do not capitalize general names of institutions, seasons, compass directions, or words that you want to emphasize.

summer vacation	last winter	university requirements
church service	southern exposure	western life

▶ The Federal institutions never even review the student's real financial situation.

▶ I work in a Law Office that specializes in settling accident cases.

Note: Adjectives derived from proper nouns should be capitalized: *Mexican, Napoleonic.* Common nouns such as *street* and *river* are capitalized only when they are part of a proper name: *Main Street, the Mississippi River.*

M2-b Capitalize the word that begins a sentence.

▶ the garden was their world.

If a sentence appears within parentheses and is not part of a larger sentence, capitalize the first word.

Note: When you use a colon to introduce an **independent clause** — usually a dramatic or emphatic statement, a question, or a quotation — you may either capitalize the first word of the clause or not capitalize it, but be consistent within an essay. When you use a colon to introduce any other type of clause, phrase, or word, as in a list, do not capitalize the first word. (See P4-a.)

> **independent (main) clause** A word group with a subject and a predicate that can stand alone as a separate sentence.

M2-c Capitalize the first word in a quotation unless it is integrated into your own wording or continues an interrupted quotation.

Lucy Danziger says, "Forget about the glass ceiling" (81).

Marilyn describes the adult bison as having an "ugly, shaggy, brown coat."

Writers often incorporate short quotations and quotations introduced by *that* into their sentences; neither needs an initial capital letter. When a phrase such as *she said* interrupts a quotation, capitalize the first word in the quotation but not the first word after the phrase unless it begins a new sentence. See also P6.

▶ **Toby said, "trust me — we won't get caught."**

▶ **"renting," she insists, "deprives you of big tax breaks."**

Note: If you quote from a poem, capitalize words exactly as the poet does.

M2-d Capitalize the first and last words in a title and subtitle plus all other words except for articles, coordinating conjunctions, and prepositions.

War and Peace *Stranger in a Strange Land* *The Grand Canyon Suite*

Tragedy: Vision and Form "On First Looking into Chapman's Homer"

Titles of short works are placed in quotation marks (see P6-d), and titles of long works are underlined or italicized (see M5-a).

▶ **In her article "The Gun In The Closet," Straight tells of booming Riverside, California, a city east of Los Angeles.**

article An adjective that precedes a noun and identifies a definite reference to something specific (*the*) or an indefinite reference to something less specific (*a* or *an*).

coordinating conjunction A word that joins comparable and equally important sentence elements: *for, and, or, but, nor, yet,* or *so.*

preposition A word (such as *between, in,* or *of*) that always appears as part of a phrase and that indicates the relation between a word in a sentence and the object of the preposition: The water splashed *into* the canoe.

M2-e Capitalize a title that precedes a person's name but not one that follows a name or appears without a name.

Professor John Ganim	Aunt Alice
John Ganim, my professor	Alice Jordan, my favorite aunt

▶ **At the state level, Reverend Green is President of the State Congress of Christian Education and Moderator of the Old Landmark Association.**

Note: References to the President (of the United States) and other major public figures are sometimes capitalized in all contexts.

M2-f Avoid overusing capitalization for emphasis.

Although in some writing situations a word that appears entirely in capital letters can create a desired effect, you should limit this use of capital letters to rare occasions.

The powerful SMACK of the ball on the rival's thigh brings an abrupt, anticlimactic end to the rising tension.

In most cases, follow the conventions for capitalizing described in this section.

▶ The principles are called the ~~TENETS OF TAE KWON DO.~~ *tenets of Tae Kwon Do.*

M3   Spacing

Allow standard spacing between words and punctuation marks. Writers have traditionally left two spaces after a period at the end of a sentence and one after a comma. Style guides such as **APA** now recommend leaving one space after a sentence period. **MLA** and APA also supply specific directions about spacing source citations.

M3-a   Supply any missing space before or after a punctuation mark.

Although spell-checkers can help identify some misspelled words, they do not indicate spacing errors unless the error links two words or splits a word. Even if you write on a word processor, proofread carefully for spacing errors around punctuation marks.

▶ My curiosity got the best of me, so I flipped through the pages to see what would happen.

▶ "I found to my horror, "Nadine later wept, "that I was too late!"

▶ "I would die without bread!" Roberto declared. "In my village, they made fresh bread every morning."

▶ Pet adoption fees include the cost of spaying or neutering all dogs and cats four months old or older (if needed).

M3-b   Close up any unnecessary space between words and punctuation marks.

▶ Karl did not know why this war was considered justifiable by the U.S. government .

▶ The larger florist shops require previous experience , but the smaller , portable wagons require only a general knowledge of flowers.

▶ Do you remember the song " The Wayward Wind" ?

M4   Numbers

Conventions for the treatment of numbers vary widely. In the humanities, writers tend to spell out numbers as recommended here, but in the sciences and social sciences, writers are far more likely to use numerals.

one out of ten   1 out of 10

APA style Conventions set forth in the guidelines of the American Psychological Association for preparing research papers and documenting sources. See Chapter 22.

MLA style Conventions set forth in the guidelines of the Modern Language Association for preparing research papers and documenting sources. See Chapter 22.

M4-a Spell out whole numbers *one* through *ninety-nine*, numbers that begin sentences, and very large round numbers in most nonscientific college writing.

Five or six vehicles, in various states of disrepair, are on the property.

Forty-eight percent of students enrolling in bachelor's programs at public colleges fail to graduate.

There are more than eleven thousand regular parking spaces and almost a thousand metered spaces.

Spell out whole numbers *one* through *ninety-nine* in most nonscientific college writing.

▶ A hefty $7,000 is paid to Wells Fargo Security for ~~4~~ *four* guards who patrol the grounds ~~24~~ *twenty-four* hours a day.

▶ Only ~~15~~ *fifteen* years ago, it was difficult to find any public figures who were openly gay.

Note: Depending on the type of writing that you do and the conventions of your field, you may decide to spell out only numerals up to ten. Either rule is acceptable. Just be sure to follow it consistently.

Be consistent also in expressing related numbers. The following sentence expresses a range as "5 to 17." Ordinarily, *five* and *seventeen* would be spelled out, but because they appear in context with larger numbers expressed as numerals, they too are presented as numerals.

The dentists examined the mouths of 42,500 children, aged 5 to 17, at 970 schools across the nation.

Note: If two numbers occur in succession, use a combination of spelled-out words and numerals for clarity.

eight 39-cent stamps   ten 3-year-olds

Spell out a number that begins a sentence, or rewrite so that the number is no longer the first word.

▶ ~~41,000~~ *Forty-one thousand* women die from breast cancer each year.

▶ *Each year,* 41,000 women die from breast cancer.

Spell out very large round numbers, or use a combination of numerals and words.

3.5 million dollars *or* $3.5 million   nearly 14 million
five thousand   a billion

M4-b Use numerals for numbers over a hundred, in fractions and percentages, with abbreviations and symbols, in addresses and dates, and for page numbers and sections of books.

99%   73 percent   3 cm   185 lbs.   5 a.m.   10:30 p.m. $200
175 Fifth Avenue   May 6, 1970   the 1980s   18.5   1/2
page 44   chapter 22   volume 8   289 envelopes

▶ A woman with the same skills as her coworkers may earn an additional ~~eight~~ *8* to ~~twenty~~ *20* percent just by being well groomed.

Note: Either the word *percent* or the % symbol is acceptable as long as it is used consistently throughout a paper.

▶ The movie *Midnight Cowboy* was rated X in the late ~~nineteen sixties~~ *1960s*.

M5 Underlining (Italics)

When they are printed, underlined words appear in the slanted type called *italics*. Most word processors now include an italics option, but your instructor may prefer that you continue to underline.

M5-a Underline or italicize titles of long or self-contained works.

Titles of books, newspapers, magazines, scholarly journals, pamphlets, long poems, movies, videotapes, CDs and DVDs, television and radio programs, long musical compositions, plays, comic strips, and works of art are underlined or italicized.

Hemingway's novel *The Sun Also Rises*   *Beowulf*   *Citizen Kane*
the *Washington Post*   *60 Minutes*   *Pride and Prejudice*

I found that the article in the *Journal of the American Medical Association* had more information and stronger scientific proof than the article in *American Health*.

Note: The Bible and its divisions are not underlined.

Titles of short works or works contained in other works, such as chapters, essays, articles, stories, short poems, and individual episodes of a television program, are not underlined but are placed in quotation marks. See also P6-d.

▶ The hit Reese Witherspoon film "Legally Blonde" was based on a novel by
Amanda Brown, whose most recent book is "Family Trust."

▶ The original "Star Trek" episode "The Trouble with Tribbles" was hugely
popular.

M5-b Underline or italicize words used as words and letters and numbers
used as themselves.

the word *committed*   three *7*'s   a *q* or a *g*

▶ Rank order is a term that Aries uses to explain the way that some individuals
take the role as the leader and the others fall in behind.

M5-c Underline or italicize names of vehicles (airplanes, ships, and trains),
foreign words that are not commonly used in English, and occasional words that need special emphasis.

Lindbergh's *Spirit of St. Louis*   Amtrak's *Silver Star*

Resist the temptation to emphasize words by putting them in bold type. In most
writing situations, underlining provides enough emphasis.

▶ Upon every table is a vase adorned with a red carnation symbolizing amore (the
Italian word for "love").

(no bold)

▶ This situation could exist because it is just that, **reverse** socialization.

M5-d Underline or italicize when appropriate, but not in place of or in addition to other conventional uses of punctuation and mechanics.

Eliminate any unusual uses of underlining or italics.

UNUSUAL   The commissioner of the NFL, Paul Tagliabue, said, *"I do not
believe playing [football] in Arizona is in the best interests of the NFL."*

APPROPRIATE   The commissioner of the NFL, Paul Tagliabue, said, "I do not
believe playing [football] in Arizona is in the best interests of the NFL."

M6   Abbreviations

Although abbreviations are more common in technical and business writing than
in academic writing, you may sometimes want to use them to avoid repetition. Use

the full word in your first reference, followed by the abbreviation in parentheses. Then use the abbreviation in subsequent references.

San Diego Humane Society (SDHS)   prisoners of war (POWs)

Abbreviations composed of all capital letters are generally written without periods or spaces between letters. When capital letters are separated by periods, do not include a space after the period, except for the initials of a person's name, which should be spaced.

USA   CNN   UPI   B.A.   Ph.D.   T. S. Eliot

M6-a   Use abbreviations that your readers will recognize for names of agencies, organizations, countries, and common technical terms.

FBI   IRS   CBS   NATO   NOW   DNA   GNP   CPM

The SDHS is an independently run nonprofit organization.

Note: Do not abbreviate geographic names in formal writing unless the areas are commonly known by their abbreviations (*Washington, D.C.*).

M6-b   Use a.m., p.m., *No.,* $, BC, and AD only with specific numerals or dates.

7:15 a.m.	10:30 p.m.
$172.18 *or* $38	No. 18 *or* no. 18 [item or issue number of a source]
72 BC [before Christ]	72 BCE [before the Common Era]
AD 378 [*anno Domini*]	378 CE [Common Era]

Note: AD, for *anno Domini* ("in the year of our Lord"), is placed before the date, not after it.

M6-c   Use commonly accepted abbreviations for titles, degrees, and Latin terms.

Change a title or a degree to an accepted abbreviation. Avoid duplication by using a title before a person's name or a degree after the name but not both.

Rev. Jesse Jackson	Mr. Roger Smith	Ms. Martina Navratilova
Diana Lee, M.D.	Dr. Diana Lee	James Boyer, D.V.M.
Ann Hajek, Ph.D.	Ring Lardner Jr.	Dr. Albert Einstein

According to Dr. Ira Chasnoff of Northwestern Memorial, cocaine produces a dramatic fluctuation in blood pressure.

Reserve Latin terms primarily for source citations or comments in parentheses rather than using them in the text of your essay.

c. (*or* ca.)	"circa" or about (used with dates)
cf.	compare
e.g.	for example
et al.	and others (used with people)
etc.	and so forth
i.e.	that is
vs. (*or* v.)	versus (used with titles of legal cases)

Some adult rights (e.g., the right to vote) clearly should not be extended to children.

Roe v. Wade **is still the law of the land.**

M6-d Use abbreviations when appropriate, but do not use them to replace words in most writing.

In formal writing, avoid abbreviating units of measurement or technical terms (unless your essay is technical), names of time periods (months, days, or holidays), course titles or department names, names of states or countries (unless the abbreviation is the more common form), names of companies, and parts of books.

▶ **The Pets for People program gives older people the companionship they need,**
  especially
  esp. if they live alone.
  ^

▶ **I called the closest site on Hancock St̶. to ask for a tour.**
  Street
  ^

▶ **The walkout followed an incident on Sept̶. 27.**
  September
  ^

M7 Titles and Headings

Use an appropriate title and headings that follow the format required for an essay or research paper. Consult your instructor or a style guide in your field to determine whether you are expected to supply a title page, running heads, text headings, or other design features.

M7-a Place your heading and title on the first page of a research paper, following MLA style.

If you are following MLA style, do not include a title page. Instead, begin your first page with a double-spaced heading one inch from the top of the page and aligned

MLA style Conventions set forth in the guidelines of the Modern Language Association for preparing research papers and documenting sources. See Chapter 22.

with the left margin. In the heading, list your name, your instructor's name, the class name and number, and the date on separate, double-spaced lines. Double-space again and center your title, following the rules for capitalizing titles (see M2) but omitting the quotation marks.

Then begin the first paragraph of your text, indenting it and all other paragraphs five spaces or one-half inch and double-spacing every part of the text (including references to sources and quotations). Throughout your paper, leave one-inch margins on all four sides of the text, except for the **running head** with the page number (see M7-b). If your computer program has a feature that aligns the right margin (called "right justification"), turn this function off because it may produce odd spaces in your text and make it hard to read. Also turn off the "auto-hyphenation" feature. You may want to refer to the format of the sample paper in Chapter 22 (pp. 772–79). See M7-b and M8-a for other MLA requirements.

If you are following **APA style**, supply a title page (see M7-c), a brief abstract, and text headings (see M7-d).

M7-b   Use an appropriate running head to number the pages of a research paper.

If you are following **MLA style**, provide a running head on each page, starting on page 1, that includes your last name and the page number. Position this heading one-half inch below the top of the page, aligned with the right margin. (Most word processing programs have a feature that will allow you to print a running head automatically on each page.) See the sample paper in Chapter 22 (p. 772). Other style guides recommend different running heads — such as the shortened title with the page number required by **APA** — so follow any directions carefully.

M7-c   Prepare a title page for your essay or research paper if required.

Supply a separate title page if it is customary in a particular field or expected by your instructor. (If you are following MLA style, a separate title page is not required; see M7-a.) If you have not been given guidelines by your instructor, center your title about halfway down the page. Beginning about three inches up from the bottom of the page, list your name, your teacher's name, the class name and number, and the date, each on a separate line, centered and double-spaced.

M7-d   Use text headings if required to identify the sections of a research paper.

In many fields, a research paper or report is expected to follow a particular structure and to include section headings so that a reader can easily identify the parts of the discussion. The APA, for example, recommends preparing an abstract or a closing summary, an introduction, and separate sections on the method, results, and implications of the study's findings (see pp. 700–701). References and appendixes conclude the paper. Follow whatever guidelines your instructor or department provides.

running head (header) A heading at the top of a page that usually includes the page number and other information.

APA style Conventions set forth in the guidelines of the American Psychological Association for preparing research papers and documenting sources. See Chapter 22.

Even if specific headings are not required, a long essay may be easier for a reader to follow if headings are supplied for each section. Such headings, however, cannot replace adequate transitions within your text, and they need to reflect your audience and purpose. A heading may be centered or aligned with the left margin of the paper. It may be spaced so that it is set off from the text or be followed directly by text on the same line. Follow your instructor's advice, and be consistent so that comparable headings are set up the same way — same type size and style, same capitalization, and same position on the page. Such consistency lets the reader know that sections are of similar weight or that one section is subsidiary to another.

M8 Special Design Features

Because computers make it easy to use different typefaces, type sizes, margin widths, and indents in your documents, you may be tempted to impose an elaborate design on a simple essay and fill it with variations and special features. Resist this temptation unless your instructor specifically encourages such experimentation. Use conventional design features and layouts to make your essay easy to follow, easy to read, and easy to understand.

M8-a Prepare your essay following any required conventions.

If you are required to follow a standard style, such as **MLA** or **APA**, check with your instructor about its requirements for margins, type size, and so forth. If you have not been given specific requirements, follow a fairly conservative style, like the MLA, to avoid excessive formatting that may not appeal to academic readers.

However you prepare your essay, most college instructors will hold you responsible if it should be lost. Always print a second copy, save the file on a backup disk, duplicate a typed or handwritten copy, or keep drafts so that you can replace a lost essay. Some instructors, especially in composition, require that you hand in planning materials and drafts or submit a complete portfolio at the end of the term. Keep any materials that may be needed later in the term.

For an MLA-style essay or research paper, use only one side of plain, white, nonerasable paper (8½-by-11-inch sheets). If your final version looks messy from corrections or smudges, hand in a clean duplicate made on a good copier. Make sure your printer is in good condition so that your final drafts are neat with dark, readable type. If your instructor will accept a handwritten essay or research paper, prepare it neatly, writing clearly in black or blue ink on only one side of each page. See M7-a for directions about MLA margin widths and other spacing.

> **MLA style** Conventions set forth in the guidelines of the Modern Language Association for preparing research papers and documenting sources. See Chapter 22.

> **APA style** Conventions set forth in the guidelines of the American Psychological Association for preparing research papers and documenting sources. See Chapter 22.

M8-b Use bold, italic, or unusual type styles or sizes sparingly.

A typical word-processor setting for text is double-spaced 12-point type. If you want to use bold or italic type, unusual fonts, or special sizes of type, check first with your instructor. Most college instructors prefer simplicity, although some might allow you to use slightly larger (14-point) type for the title, bold section headings in a long essay, additional spacing between sections, or slightly smaller (10-point) type in a crowded chart. Even so, use only features that will make your text easy to read and easy to follow. Be clear and consistent. Dramatic type variations are more suitable for a newsletter or brochure than an academic essay or report.

In **MLA style**, as in the style guides for other academic fields, the use of different type styles is essentially limited to underlining certain titles and words (see M5).

UNUSUAL	She finally let out a laughing smile and said, *"I am so happy, Shellah."*
APPROPRIATE	She finally let out a laughing smile and said, "I am so happy, Shellah."
UNUSUAL	The effect is the same: **Any violent behavior will not be tolerated.**
APPROPRIATE	The effect is the same: Any violent behavior will not be tolerated.

MLA style Conventions set forth in the guidelines of the Modern Language Association for preparing research papers and documenting sources. See Chapter 22.

M8-c   Use extra capital letters, icons, symbols, or other atypical features sparingly.

Although you may occasionally capitalize all of the letters in a word for emphasis, most college instructors will expect you to follow the standard conventions for capitalization (see M2). If you are preparing special tables, charts, boxes, or other visual materials, ask your instructor's advice about variations in capitalization, type size and style, special symbols, and so forth.

▶ When all of these components are pulled together, the lyrics become powerful,

as proven by De Garmo *and* & Key.

M9   Spelling

Try several (or all) of the following suggestions for catching and correcting your spelling errors.

- Proofread your writing carefully to catch transposed letters (*becuase* for *because*), omitted letters (*becaus*), and other careless errors (*then* for *than*). When you proofread for spelling, read the text backward, beginning with the last word. (This strategy keeps you from reading for content and lets you focus on each word.)

- Check a good dictionary for any words you are uncertain about. When you are writing and doubt the spelling of a word, put a question mark by the word but wait to check it until you have finished drafting. (Check a misspeller's dictionary if you are unsure of the first letters of the word.)

- Keep a list of words you often misspell so that you can try to pinpoint your personal patterns. Although misspellings nearly always follow a pattern, you are not likely to misspell every word of a particular type, or you may spell the same word two different ways in the same essay.

M9-a Study the spelling rules for adding **prefixes and suffixes** to words.

Although English has a large number of words with unusual spellings, many follow the patterns that spelling rules describe.

Add a prefix to a root without doubling or dropping letters.

distrust	misbehave	unable
dissatisfy	misspell	unnatural

Add a suffix beginning with a vowel (such as *-ing*) in accord with the form of the root word.

Double the final consonant if the word has a single syllable that ends in a single consonant preceded by a single vowel.

begging	hidden	fitting

Do the same if the word has a final stressed syllable that ends in a single consonant preceded by a single vowel.

beginning	occurrence

The final consonant does not double if the word ends in a double consonant or has a double vowel.

acting	parted	seeming	stooped

In some cases, the stress shifts to the first syllable when a suffix is added. When it does, do not double the final consonant.

prefér:	preférring,	preférred
	préference,	préferable

Add a suffix that begins with *y* or a vowel by dropping a final silent *e*.

achieving	icy	location
grievance	lovable	continual

Note: Keep the final silent *e* to retain a soft *c* or *g* sound, to prevent mispronunciation, or to prevent confusion with other words.

changeable	courageous	noticeable
eyeing	mileage	canoeist
dyeing	singeing	

prefix A word part, such as *pre-*, *anti-*, or *bi-*, that is attached to the beginning of a word to form another word: *preconceived, unbelievable.*

suffix A word part, such as *-ly*, *-ment*, or *-ed*, that is added to the end of a word to change the word's form (*bright, brightly*) or tense (*call, called*) or to form another word (*govern, government*).

Add a suffix that begins with a consonant by keeping a final silent *e*.

achievement   discouragement   sincerely

Exceptions: acknowledgment, argument, awful, judgment, truly, wholly.

Form the plural of a singular noun in accord with its form.

If a singular noun ends in a consonant followed by *y*, change *y* to *i* and add *-es*.

baby, babies   cry, cries

Note: Simply add *-s* to proper names: her cousin *Mary*, both *Marys*.

If a singular noun ends in a vowel followed by *y*, add *-s*.

trolley, trolleys   day, days

If a singular noun ends in a consonant and *o*, add *-es*.

potato, potatoes   echo, echoes   veto, vetoes

Exceptions: autos, dynamos, pianos, sopranos.

If a singular noun ends in a vowel and *o*, add *-s*.

video, videos   rodeo, rodeos   radio, radios

If a singular noun ends in *s, ss, sh, ch, x,* or *z*, add *-es*.

Jones, Joneses   hiss, hisses   bush, bushes

match, matches   suffix, suffixes   buzz, buzzes

Note: The plural of *fish* is *fish;* the plural of *thesis* is *theses.*

Check the dictionary for the plural of a word that originates in another language.

criterion, criteria   datum, data

medium, mediums *or* media

hors d'oeuvre, hors d'oeuvres *or* hors d'oeuvre

M9-b **Study the spelling rules (and the exceptions) that apply to words you routinely misspell.**

Add *i* before *e* except after *c*.

Most people remember this rule because of the jingle "Write *i* before *e* / Except after *c* / Or when sounded like *ay* / As in *neighbor* and *weigh*." *Exceptions:* either, foreign, forfeit, height, leisure, neither, seize, weird.

Spell most words ending in the sound "seed" as -cede.

precede   recede   secede   intercede

Exceptions: proceed, succeed, supersede.

For ESL Writers

If you have learned Canadian or British English, you may have noticed some differences in the way that words are spelled in U.S. English.

U.S. English	*Canadian or British English*
color	colour
realize	realise (*or* realize in Canadian English)
center	centre
defense	defence

M9-c **Watch for words that are often spelled incorrectly because they sound like other words.**

In English, many words are not spelled as they sound. The endings of some words may be dropped in speech but need to be included in writing. For example, speakers often pronounce *and* as *an'* or drop the *-ed* ending on verbs. Other common words sound the same but have entirely different meanings. Watch carefully for words such as the following.

already ("by now": He is *already* in class.)

all ready ("fully prepared": I'm *all ready* for the test.)

an (article: Everyone read *an* essay last night.)

and (conjunction: The class discussed the problem *and* the solution.)

its (possessive pronoun: The car lost *its* shine.)

it's ("it is": *It's* too cold to go for a walk.)

maybe ("perhaps": *Maybe* we should have tacos for dinner.)

may be (verb showing possibility: They *may be* arriving tonight.)

than (conjunction showing comparison: The house was taller *than* the tree.)

then (adverb showing time sequence: First she knocked and *then* she opened the door.)

their (possessive pronoun: They decided to sell *their* old car.)

there (adverb showing location: The car dealer is located *there* on the corner.)

they're ("they are": *They're* going to pick up the new car tonight.)

your (possessive pronoun: I can see *your* apartment.)

you're ("you are": Call me when *you're* home.)

For distinctions between other words such as *affect/effect, principal/principle,* and *to/too,* see the Glossary of Frequently Misused Words.

Watch for and correct misspelled words that sound the same as other words.

▶ I started packing my gear, still ~~vary~~ *very* excited about the trip.

▶ The campfire had ~~burn~~ *burned* down to a sizzle.

▶ I just ~~new~~ *knew* it was a bear, and I was going to be its dinner.

▶ As students pay ~~there~~ *their* fees, part of this money goes toward purchasing new books and materials.

▶ Pushing off from Anchovy Island, the boat sets its ~~coarse~~ *course*.

M9-d   Watch for words that are often misspelled.

Check your essays for the following words, which are often spelled incorrectly. Look up any other questionable words in a dictionary, and keep a personal list of words that you tend to misspell.

absence	apparently	cannot	dependent
accidentally	appearance	categories	desperate
accommodate	appropriate	changeable	develops
accomplish	argument	choose	disappear
achievement	arrangement	chose	eighth
acknowledge	attendance	coming	eligible
acquaintance	basically	commitment	embarrass
acquire	before	committed	emphasize
against	beginning	competitive	environment
aggravate	believe	conscience	especially
all right	benefited	conscious	every day
a lot	business	convenient	exaggerated
although	businesses	criticize	exercise
analyze	calendar	definitely	exercising

experience

explanation

finally

foreign

forty

fourth

friend

government

harass

height

heroes

immediately

incredible

indefinitely

interesting

irrelevant

knowledge

loose

lose

maintenance

maneuver

mischievous

necessary

noticeable

occasion

occur

occurred

occurrences

particularly

performance

phenomena

phenomenon

physically

playwright

practically

precede

preference

preferred

prejudice

preparation

privilege

probably

proceed

professor

quiet

quite

receive

recommend

reference

referred

roommate

schedule

separate

similar

studying

succeed

success

successful

therefore

thorough

truly

unnecessarily

until

usually

whether

without

woman

women

L   ESL Troublespots

This section provides advice about problems of grammar and standard usage that are particularly troublesome for speakers of English as a second language (ESL).

L1   Articles

For practice, go to bedfordstmartins.com/theguide/art

The rules for using articles (*a, an,* and *the*) are complicated. Your choice depends on whether the article appears before a **count, noncount,** or **proper noun.** An *article* is used before a common noun to indicate whether the noun refers to something specific (*the* moon) or whether it refers to something that is one among many or has not yet been specified (*a* planet, *an* asteroid). In addition, for some nouns, the absence of an article indicates that the reference is not specific.

count noun A noun that names people and things that can be counted: one *teacher*, two *teachers*; one *movie*, several *movies*.

noncount noun A noun that names things or ideas that are not or cannot be counted: *thunder, money, happiness*.

proper noun The capitalized name of a specific person, group, place, or thing.

L1-a   Select the correct article to use with a count noun.

- Use *a* or *an* with nonspecific singular count nouns.
- Use no article with nonspecific plural count nouns.
- Use *the* with specific singular and plural count nouns.

Note: The article *a* is used before a consonant and *an* before a vowel; exceptions include words beginning with a long *u,* such as *unit.*

Use *a* or *an* before a singular count noun when it refers to one thing among many or something that has not been specifically identified.

▶ We, as *a* society, have to educate our youth about avoiding teen pregnancy.

▶ ~~Darkroom~~ *A darkroom* is a room with no light where photographs are developed.

Use *the* before a singular or plural count noun when it refers to one or more specific things.

After you have used *a* or *an* with a count noun, subsequent references to the noun become specific and are marked by *the.*

When I walked into the office, *a* woman in her mid-forties was waiting to be called.

As I sat down, I looked at *the* woman.

Exceptions include a second reference to one among many.

I was guided to *a* classroom. It was *a* bright room, filled with warm rays of
Hawaiian sunlight.

Note: In most situations, use *the* with a count noun modified by a superlative
adjective.

the most frightening moment   the smallest person

But: He gave *a* most unusual response.

Nouns such as *sun* generally refer to unique things; for instance, the only sun visible in the sky. Nouns such as *house* and *yard* often refer to things that people own.
A writer may talk about *the yard* meaning his or her own yard. In most situations,
both types of nouns can be preceded by the definite article *the*.

Don't look directly at *the sun*. [Only one sun could be meant.]

I spent Saturday cleaning *the house*. [The reader will infer that the writer is refer

ring to his or her own house.]

Note: You can also introduce count nouns referring to specific entities with possessive nouns or pronouns (*Maya's* friends) or demonstrative pronouns (*these* friends).
Indefinite count and noncount nouns can also be introduced by words that indicate
amount (*few* friends, *some* sand).

COUNT NOUN   She stayed with *her* eight children.

NONCOUNT NOUN   Her family wanted *some* happiness.

**Delete any article before a plural count noun when it does not refer to
something specific.**

▶ ~~The people~~ People like Dee cannot forget their heritage.

L1-b **Select the correct article to use with a noncount noun.**

The many kinds of noncount nouns include the following.

Natural phenomena: *thunder, steam, electricity*
Natural elements: *gold, air, sunlight*
Manufacturing materials: *steel, wood, cement*
Fibers: *wool, cotton, rayon*
General categories made up of a variety of specific items: *money, music, furniture*
Abstract ideas: *happiness, loyalty, adolescence, wealth*
Liquids: *milk, gasoline, water*

noncount noun A noun
that names things or ideas
that are not or cannot be
counted: *thunder, money,
happiness*.

Some nouns naming foodstuffs are always noncount (*pork, rice, broccoli*); others are noncount when they refer to food as it is eaten (*We ate barbecued chicken and fruit*) but count when they refer to individual items or varieties (*We bought a plump chicken and various fruits*).

Delete any article before a noncount noun when it refers to something general.

▶ What is needed is ~~a~~ reasonable and measured legislation.

▶ The destruction caused by the war drew artists away from ~~the~~ reality, which is painful and cruel, and toward ~~the~~ abstract art that avoids a sense of despair.

Use *the* before a noncount noun when it refers to something specific or when it is specified by a prepositional phrase or an adjective clause.

The coffee is probably cold by now.

The water on the boat has to be rationed.

The water that we have left has to be rationed.

Note: You can also introduce noncount nouns referring to specific things with possessive nouns or pronouns (*her* money) or demonstrative pronouns (*that* money). Indefinite noncount nouns can also be introduced by words that indicate amount (*some* money).

prepositional phrase A group of words that begins with a preposition and indicates the relation between a word in a sentence and the object following the preposition: Her sunglasses slid *under the seat.*

adjective clause A clause that modifies a noun or pronoun and is generally introduced by a relative pronoun (such as *that* or *which*).

proper noun The capitalized name of a specific person, group, place, or thing.

L1-c   **Select the correct article to use with a proper noun.**

Most plural proper nouns require *the*: *the* United States, *the* Philippines, *the* Black Hills, *the* Clintons, *the* Los Angeles Dodgers. Exceptions include business names (Hillshire Farms, Miller Auto Sales).

Delete any article before most singular proper nouns.

In general, singular proper nouns are not preceded by an article: Dr. Livingston, New York City, Hawaii, Disneyland, Mount St. Helens, Union Station, Wrigley Field.

▶ ~~The~~ Campus Security is a powerful deterrent against parties because if you are written up twice, you can lose your housing contract.

Note: The is used before proper noun phrases that include *of* (*the* Rock of Gibraltar, *the* Gang of Four). *The* is also required before proper nouns that name the following things:

1. Bodies of water, except when the generic part of the name precedes the specific name: *the* Atlantic Ocean, *the* Red River, but Lake Erie
2. Geographic regions: *the* West Coast, *the* Sahara, *the* Grand Canyon
3. Vehicles for transportation: *the* Concorde
4. Named buildings and bridges: *the* World Trade Center, *the* Golden Gate Bridge
5. National or international churches: *the* Russian Orthodox Church
6. Governing bodies preceded by a proper adjective: *the* British Parliament
7. Titles of religious and political leaders: *the* Dalai Lama, *the* president
8. Religious and historical documents: *the* Bible, *the* Magna Carta
9. Historical periods and events: *the* Gilded Age, *the* Civil War

L2 Verbs

For practice, go to bedfordstmartins.com/theguide/everb

Section R2-a reviews the basic English verb forms and includes a list of common irregular verbs. As you edit your writing, pay particular attention to conditional clauses, two-word verbs, helping (auxiliary) verbs, and gerund or infinitive forms after verbs.

L2-a Select verb tenses carefully in main clauses and conditional clauses.

Conditional clauses beginning with *if* or *unless* generally indicate that one thing causes another (a factual relationship); predict future outcomes or possibilities; or speculate about the past, present, future, or impossible events or circumstances.

┌────CONDITIONAL CLAUSE────┐ ┌──────────MAIN CLAUSE──────────┐
If we *use* television correctly, it *can give* us information and entertainment.

┌────CONDITIONAL CLAUSE────┐ ┌──────────MAIN CLAUSE──────────┐
If we *use* television incorrectly, it *will control* our families and our community.

Change both verbs to the same tense (generally present or past) to express general or specific truths or actions that happen together habitually.

▶ When we moved to America, my family ~~has~~ *had* good communication.

Change the verb in the main clause to the future and the verb in the conditional clause to the present to express future possibilities or predictions.

▶ If you ask in any of her restaurants, the manager ~~would~~ *will* tell you about working with her all these years.

independent (main) clause A word group with a subject and a predicate that can stand alone as a separate sentence.

base form The uninflected form of a verb: I *eat;* to *play.*

Change the verb in the main clause to *would*, *could*, or *might* plus the base form and change the verb in the *if* conditional clause to the past tense to speculate about events or conditions that are unreal, improbable, or contrary to fact.

Use *were* rather than *was* in an *if* clause.

▶ Some people believe that if the Health Department ~~gives~~ *were to give* out clean needles, the number of people using drugs would increase.

participle A verb form showing present tense (*dancing, freezing*) or past tense (*danced, frozen*) that can also act as an adjective.

Change the verb in the main clause to *would have*, *might have*, *could have*, or *should have* plus the past participle, and change the verb in the *if* clause to the past perfect to speculate about actions in the past that did not in fact occur.

▶ If the computer lab *had* added more hours during finals week, students would not have had to wait to use a computer.

Note: Do not add *would have* to the *if* clause.

L2-b   Learn the meanings of the idiomatic two- and three-word verbs used in English.

Idiomatic two- or three-word (or phrasal) verbs usually combine a verb with a word that appears to be a preposition or an adverb (called a *particle*). The combined meaning cannot be understood literally, and similar expressions often have very different meanings.

hand in means "submit"
hand out means "distribute"
look into means "investigate"
look out for means "watch carefully"
run away means "leave without warning"
run into means "meet by chance"
walk out on means "abandon"
want out means "desire to be free of responsibility"

Native speakers of English will notice misuses of these idiomatic verbs even though they use the verbs without thinking about their literal meanings. When you are unsure of the meaning or usage of such verbs, consult a dictionary designed for nonnative speakers of English, or ask a native speaker.

L2-c   Use the correct verb forms after helping verbs.

base form The uninflected form of a verb: I *eat;* to *play.*

After the helping (auxiliary) verbs *do, does,* and *did,* always use the **base form** of the main verb. After the helping verbs *have, has,* and *had,* always use the past **participle** form of the main verb. (See R2-a and G5.)

cooperate
▶ They do not ~~cooperated~~ with the police.

done
▶ They have ~~doing~~ these things for a long time.

been
▶ They have doing these things for a long time.

Note: A modal such as *will* sometimes precedes *have, has,* or *had.*

By Friday I *will have finished* this project.

Following the helping verbs *be, am, is, are, was, were,* and *been* (forms of *be*), use the present participle to show ongoing action (progressive tense).

giving
▶ **The president is ~~given~~ a speech on all major networks.**

Note: Use one of the modal verbs with *be.* Use *have, has,* or *had* with *been.*

Terence *could be making* some calls while I go out.

I *have been* working hard.

After the helping verbs *am, is, are, was,* and *were* (forms of *be*), use the past participle to form the **passive voice**.

canceled
▶ **Regular programming is ~~cancel~~ for tonight.**

To form the passive, *be, being,* and *been* need another helping verb in addition to the past participle.

Tonya *will be challenged* in graduate school this fall.

After a **modal**, use the **base form**.

The Senate *might* vote on this bill next week.

L2-d Follow verbs with **gerunds** or **infinitives**, depending on the verb and your meaning.

1. Verbs that can be followed by either a gerund or an infinitive with no change in meaning

begin	continue	like	prefer
can't stand	hate	love	start

The roof *began leaking.*

The roof *began to leak.*

passive voice The verb form that shows something happening to the subject: The mouse *was caught* by the cat.

modals The helping verbs *can, could, may, might, must, shall, should, will,* and *would,* which must be used in conjunction with another (main) verb: I *may go* to the bank.

base form The uninflected form of a verb: I *eat;* to *play.*

gerund A verb form that is used as a noun and ends with *-ing: arguing, throwing.*

infinitive A verb form consisting of the word *to* plus the base form of the verb: *to run, to do.*

2. Verbs that change their meaning, depending on whether a gerund or an infinitive follows

| forget | remember | stop | try |

Salam *remembered going* to the park on Saturday. [Salam recalled a weekend visit to a park.]

Salam *remembered to go* to the park on Saturday. [Salam remembered that he had to go to the park on Saturday.]

3. Verbs that can be followed by a gerund but not an infinitive

admit	deny	keep	recall
appreciate	discuss	miss	resist
avoid	dislike	postpone	risk
can't help	enjoy	practice	suggest
consider	finish	put off	tolerate
delay	imagine	quit	

> ► I recall ~~to see~~ Michel there.
> *seeing*

Note: Not or *never* can separate the verb and the gerund.

We discussed *not* having a party this year.

4. Verbs that can be followed by an infinitive but not a gerund

agree	expect	need	refuse
ask	fail	offer	venture
beg	have	plan	wait
choose	hope	pretend	want
claim	manage	promise	wish
decide	mean		

> ► Children often only pretend ~~eating~~ food they dislike.
> *to eat*

Note: In a sentence with a verb followed by an infinitive, the meaning changes depending on the placement of a negative word such as *not* or *never*.

I *never* promised to eat liver. [I did not make the promise.]

I promised *never* to eat candy. [I promised not to do it.]

5. Verbs that must be followed by a noun or pronoun and an infinitive

advise	encourage	order	teach
allow	force	persuade	tell
cause	instruct	remind	urge
command	invite	require	warn
convince	need		

Magda taught *her parrot to say* a few words.

Note: Use an infinitive, not *that*, following a verb such as *want* or *need*.

▶ José wants ~~that~~ his new car ^*to stay* ~~stays~~ in good condition.

6. The verbs *let, make* ("force"), and *have* ("cause") must be followed by a noun or pronoun and the **base form** of the verb (not the infinitive)

He *let me borrow* the car.

The drill sergeant *makes the recruits stand* at attention.

I *had the children draw* in their notebooks.

base form The uninflected form of a verb: I *eat*; to *play*.

L3   Prepositions

For practice, go to bedfordstmartins.com/theguide/prep

Use the prepositions *in, on,* and *at* to indicate location and time.

preposition A word (such as *between, in,* or *of*) that always appears as part of a phrase and indicates the relation between a word in a sentence and the object of the preposition: The water splashed *into* the canoe.

Location

- *In* usually means *within a geographic place or enclosed area* (*in* Mexico, *in* a small town, *in* the park, *in* my bedroom, *in* a car).
- *On* means *on top of* (*on* the shelf, *on* a hill, *on* a bicycle); it is also used with modes of mass transportation (*on* a train, *on* the subway), streets (*on* Broadway), pages (*on* page 5), floors of buildings (*on* the tenth floor), and tracts of private land (*on* a farm, *on* the lawn).
- *At* refers to specific addresses and named locations (*at* 1153 Grand Street, *at* Nana's house, *at* Macy's), to general locations (*at* work, *at* home, *at* the beach), and to locations that involve a specific activity (*at* the mall, *at* the gym, *at* a party, *at* a restaurant).

Time

- *In* is used with months (*in* May), years (*in* 1999), and seasons (*in* the fall), as well as with *morning, afternoon,* and *evening* (*in* the morning).

- *On* is used with days of the week (*on* Wednesday) and dates (*on* June 2, 2006).
- *At* is used with specific times (*at* 7:30, *at* noon, *at* midnight) and with *night* (*at* night).

Change any incorrect prepositions so that *in, on,* and *at* convey time and location correctly.

▶ People are driving at 55 or 60 miles per hour ~~in~~ *on* the highway.

Change any incorrect prepositions to idiomatic usage.

▶ Is life worse in the refugee camps or in Vietnam? You would find answers ~~from~~ *in* his article.

▶ Williams gives readers insight ~~to~~ *into* the doctor's insecurity.

L4   Omitted or Repeated Words

For practice, go to bedfordstmartins.com/theguide/oword

> **subject** The part of a clause that identifies who or what is being discussed.

In English, every sentence, with rare exceptions, should have both a **subject** and a **verb.** If your native language allows you to omit either subject or verb, check your drafts carefully to be sure that you include both in your writing.

┌SUBJECT┐ ┌VERB┐
My brother has been very successful in his job.

> **verb** A word or phrase that expresses action or being and, along with a subject, is a basic component of a sentence.

Supply both a subject and a verb in each sentence, but do not repeat the subject or other words that duplicate grammatical functions.

Add a missing subject.

▶ On the contrary, *the compliments* increase his irritability.

Add a missing verb.

▶ Mr. Yang *is* a man who owns a butcher shop.

Supply a missing expletive (*there* or *it*) if the subject follows the verb.

▶ ~~Are~~ *There are* many ways to help poor people get jobs.

Delete a repeated subject.

▶ The elderly woman ~~she~~ must have an eye infection.

Delete other words that repeat grammatical functions.

▶ People say that the cost of insurance ~~has~~ never goes down anymore.

▶ Only a few people ~~that~~ are rich.

L5   Adjective Order

For practice, go to bedfordstmartins.com/theguide/order

Adjectives generally appear in the following order in English sentences.

1. Article, pronoun, or other determiner: *a, an, the, that, his, their, Janine's*
2. Evaluation or judgment: *beautiful, ugly, elegant, magnificent, impressive*
3. Size or dimension: *short, tall, long, large, small, big, little*
4. Shape: *round, rectangular, square, baggy, circular, octagonal*
5. Age: *new, young, old, aged, antique*
6. Color: *pink, turquoise, gray, orange*
7. History or origin (country and religion): *Asian, Norwegian, Thai, American, Protestant, Mongolian, Buddhist, Muslim, Catholic, Jewish*
8. Material: *copper, cotton, plastic, oak, linen*
9. Noun used as a descriptive adjective: *kitchen* (sink), *bedroom* (lamp)

When you use several adjectives to modify a noun, arrange them in the order expected in English.

| 1 | 2 | 4 | 6 | | | 1 | 3 | 5 |
a beautiful, round, turquoise stone   *her skinny, young* cousin

L6   Participles

For practice, go to bedfordstmartins.com/theguide/part

Use the present form of the participle (*-ing*) if it describes someone or something *causing* or *producing* a mental state. Use the past form (*-ed*) if it describes someone or something *experiencing* the mental state. Problem participles include the following pairs.

annoying/annoyed	exhausting/exhausted
boring/bored	pleasing/pleased
confusing/confused	surprising/surprised
disappointing/disappointed	terrifying/terrified
exciting/excited	tiring/tired

participle A verb form showing present tense (*dancing, freezing*) or past tense (*danced, frozen*) that can also act as an adjective.

The class was *confused* by the *confusing* directions.

The teacher was *surprised* by the *surprising* number of questions.

Change a participle to its present form (-*ing*) if it describes someone or something causing or producing a situation.

> ▶ Parents must not accept the ~~frightened~~ *frightening* behavior that their children learn in gangs.

Change a participle to its past form (-*ed*) if it describes someone or something experiencing a situation.

> ▶ I was not ~~pleasing~~ *pleased* with the information about religion in this article.

R   Review of Sentence Structure

As you write, your primary concern will be with rhetoric, not parts of speech or sentence structure. You will focus on learning how to develop ideas, illustrate general statements, organize an argument, and integrate information. Yet sentence structure is important. Writing clear and correct sentences is part of being a competent writer. This and the other sections in the Handbook will help you achieve that goal.*

R1   Basic Sentence Structure

This review of basic sentence structure will look first at the elements that make up simple sentences and then at how simple sentences produce compound and complex sentences.

R1-a   Words, Phrases, and Clauses

The basic building blocks of sentences are, of course, words, which can be combined into discrete groupings or *phrases*.

Words and phrases are further combined to create clauses. A *clause* is a group of at least two words that both names a topic and makes some point about that topic; every clause can be divided into a subject and a predicate. The *subject* identifies the topic or theme of the sentence — what is being discussed — while the *predicate* says something about the subject and is the focus of information in the clause. A clause can be either *independent* (that is, a complete idea in itself) or *dependent* (combined with an independent clause to create a complete idea). Dependent (or subordinate) clauses are discussed in R2-b.

R1-b   Sentence Units

To introduce the principles of sentence structure, it is useful to consider *simple sentences*, those with only a single independent clause made up of a subject and a predicate.

---

* English sentence structure has been described with scientific precision by linguists. This brief review is based on an extraordinary sentence grammar, *A Grammar of Contemporary English* (New York: Harcourt, 1972), which is available in a revised and expanded edition titled *A Comprehensive Grammar of the English Language* (New York: Addison Wesley, 1985). Two of its authors, Sidney Greenbaum and Sir Randolph Quirk, have written a shorter version, *A Student's Grammar of the English Language* (New York: Addison Wesley, 1990), which you might wish to consult for elaboration on any of the points discussed here.

Subject	Predicate
Native Americans	introduced baked beans to the New England settlers.
The Native Americans	cooked their beans in maple sugar and bear fat.

Subject	Predicate
The settlers	used molasses and salt pork instead.
Both baked-bean dishes	were essentially the same.

The subject and the predicate may each be a single word or a group of words. In addition to its verb, the predicate may include **objects, complements,** and **adverbial modifiers.** Simple sentences, then, are composed of some combination of these basic units: subject, verb, direct object, indirect object, subject complement, object complement, and adverbial modifier.

Of these seven units, two — subject and verb — are required in every sentence. Note that the subject determines whether the verb in the predicate is singular or plural: In the last of the preceding examples, the plural subject *dishes* requires the plural verb *were.*

The basic sentence units can be defined as follows.

Subjects. The simplest subject can be a single noun or pronoun, but a subject may also commonly consist of a noun phrase (including adjectives and other sentence elements) or even a noun clause. Subjects may also be *compound* when two or more nouns or pronouns are linked by a conjunction. (See R2 for definitions and examples of these various elements.)

Verbs. These can be classified as *transitive,* when they occur with an object, or *intransitive,* when they occur without an object. Intransitive verbs that occur with complements are often called *linking verbs.* Like subjects, verbs may be compound.

Objects. These include *direct* and *indirect* objects, which, like subjects, can be nouns, noun phrases, noun clauses, or pronouns. Objects usually follow the subject and verb.

Complements. These are either subject complements or object complements: *Subject complements* refer to the subject, *object complements* to an object. Like subjects and objects, complements can be nouns or pronouns, noun phrases or noun clauses (sometimes referred to as *predicate nominatives*). Complements can also be adjectives or adjective phrases (sometimes called *predicate adjectives*). Like objects, complements usually follow the subject and verb. They also follow any objects.

Adverbials. These are modifiers that refer to the verb in the sentence. They can be adverbs, adverb phrases, or adverb clauses.

---

object The part of a clause that receives the action of the verb (At the checkpoint, we unloaded *the canoes*) or the part of a phrase that follows a preposition (We dragged them to *the river*).

complement A word or word group that describes or restates a subject or an object.

adverbial modifier A word or word group that modifies a verb, an adjective, or another adverb.

R1-c   Types of Simple Sentences

The basic sentence elements listed in R1-b can be put together in various ways to produce seven general types of simple sentences. The basic units are subject (S), verb (V), direct object (DO), indirect object (IO), subject complement (SC), object complement (OC), and adverbial modifier (A).

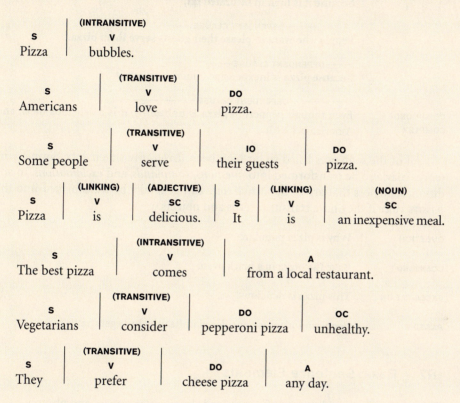

	(INTRANSITIVE)		
S	V		
Pizza	bubbles.		

	(TRANSITIVE)	
S	V	DO
Americans	love	pizza.

	(TRANSITIVE)		
S	V	IO	DO
Some people	serve	their guests	pizza.

	(LINKING)	(ADJECTIVE)		(LINKING)	(NOUN)
S	V	SC	S	V	SC
Pizza	is	delicious.	It	is	an inexpensive meal.

	(INTRANSITIVE)	
S	V	A
The best pizza	comes	from a local restaurant.

	(TRANSITIVE)		
S	V	DO	OC
Vegetarians	consider	pepperoni pizza	unhealthy.

	(TRANSITIVE)		
S	V	DO	A
They	prefer	cheese pizza	any day.

R1-d   Combinations and Transformations

The simple sentence patterns shown in R1-c can be combined and transformed to produce all of the sentences writers of English need. Two or more clauses may be combined with a coordinating conjunction (such as *and* or *but*) or a pair of correlative conjunctions (such as *either . . . or*) to create a *compound sentence*. Writers create *complex sentences* by combining independent clauses with a subordinating conjunction (such as *although* or *because*) or by linking two clauses with a relative pronoun (such as *which* or *who*); clauses that contain subordinating conjunctions or relative pronouns are *dependent clauses* and can no longer stand on their own as simple sentences. Clauses can also be combined to produce *compound-complex sentences* (compound sentences that contain dependent clauses). Conjunctions and dependent clauses are discussed in more detail in R2.

COMPOUND   Pizza is delicious, and it is an inexpensive meal. Either Americans love pizza, or they consider it junk food.

COMPLEX   Vegetarians consider pepperoni pizza unhealthy

┌────── **DEPENDENT CLAUSE** ──────┐
because it is high in saturated fat.

┌────── **DEPENDENT CLAUSE** ──────┐
People who want to please their guests serve them pizza.

┌────── **DEPENDENT CLAUSE** ──────┐
Because pizza is inexpensive, Americans love it.

┌────── **DEPENDENT CLAUSE** ──────┐
COMPOUND-   Even though pepperoni pizza is unhealthy, it is a delicious meal, and
COMPLEX   Americans love it.

All of the sentences listed so far have been *declarative* statements. Simple sentences may also be transformed into *questions*, *commands*, and *exclamations*. In addition, sentences that are in the *active voice* can generally be transformed into the *passive voice* if they have transitive verbs and objects.

QUESTION   Why is pizza popular?

COMMAND   Bake the pizza in a brick oven.

EXCLAMATION   This pizza is delicious!

PASSIVE   Pepperoni pizza is considered unhealthy by vegetarians.

R2 Basic Sentence Elements

This section reviews the parts of speech and the types of clauses and phrases.

R2-a Parts of Speech

There are ten parts of speech: nouns, pronouns, adjectives, adverbs, verbs, prepositions, conjunctions, articles, demonstratives, and interjections.

Nouns. Nouns function in sentences or clauses as **subjects**, **objects**, and **subject complements**. They also serve as objects of various kinds of **phrases** and as **appositives**. They can be proper (*Burger King, Bartlett pear, Julia Child, General Foods*) or common (*tomato, food, lunch, café, waffle, gluttony*). Common nouns can be abstract (*hunger, satiation, indulgence, appetite*) or concrete (*spareribs, soup, radish, champagne, gravy*). Nouns can be singular (*biscuit*) or plural (*biscuits*); they may also be collective (*food*). They can be marked to show possession (*gourmet's*

---

subject The part of a clause that identifies who or what is being discussed: At the checkpoint, *we* unloaded the canoes.

object The part of a clause that receives the action of the verb (At the checkpoint, we unloaded *the canoes*) or the part of a phrase that follows a preposition (We dragged them to *the river*).

subject complement A word or word group that follows a linking verb (such as *seems, appears*, or *is* and other forms of *be*) and describes or restates the subject: The tents looked *old and dirty*.

phrase A group of words that does *not* contain both a subject and a verb and is always part of an independent clause.

appositive A word or word group that identifies or gives more information about a noun or pronoun that precedes it.

choice, lambs' kidneys). Nouns take determiners (*that lobster, those clams*), quantifiers (*many hotcakes, several sausages*), and articles (*a milkshake, the eggnog*). They can be modified by adjectives (*fried chicken*), adjective phrases (*chicken in a basket*), and adjective clauses (*chicken that is finger-licking good*). See also E3.

Pronouns. Pronouns come in many different forms and have a variety of functions in clauses and phrases.

Personal pronouns function as replacements for nouns and come in three case forms:

1. Subjective, for use as subjects or subject complements: *I, we, you, he, she, it, they*.

2. Objective, for use as objects of verbs and prepositions: *me, us, you, him, her, it, them*.

3. Possessive: *mine, ours, yours, his, hers, theirs*. Possessive pronouns also have a determiner form for use before nouns: *my, our, your, his, her, its, their*.

> **Calvin Trillin says the best restaurants in the world are in Kansas City, but *he* was born there.**

> **If *you* ever have the spareribs and french-fried potatoes at Arthur Bryant's, *you* will never forget *them*.**

> ***Your* memory of that lunch at Bryant's is clearer than *mine*.**

Personal pronouns come in three persons (first person: *I, me, we, us*; second person: *you*; third person: *he, him, she, her, it, they, them*), three genders (masculine: *he, him*; feminine: *she, her*; neuter: *it*), and two numbers (singular: *I, me, you, he, him, she, her, it*; plural: *we, us, you, they, them*).

Reflexive pronouns, like personal pronouns, function as replacements for nouns, nearly always replacing nouns or personal pronouns in the same clause. Reflexive pronouns include *myself, ourselves, yourself, yourselves, himself, herself, oneself, itself, themselves*.

> **Aunt Odessa prided *herself* on her chocolate sponge cake.**

Reflexive pronouns may also be used for emphasis.

> **Barry baked the fudge cake *himself*.**

Indefinite pronouns do not refer to a specific person or object: *each, all, everyone, everybody, everything, everywhere, both, some, someone, somebody, something, somewhere, any, anyone, anybody, anything, anywhere, either, neither, none, nobody, many, few, much, most, several, enough*.

> **Not *everybody* was enthusiastic about William Laird's 1698 improvement on apple cider — Jersey lightning applejack.**

In the Colonies, *most* preferred rum.

Taverns usually served *both*.

Relative pronouns introduce **adjective (or relative) clauses**. They come in three forms: personal, to refer to people (*who, whom, whose, whoever, whomever*), non-personal (*which, whose, whichever, whatever*), and general (*that*).

In 1846, Nancy Johnson invented a small hand-operated machine, *which* was the forerunner of today's portable ice-cream freezer.

It was Jacob Fussell of Baltimore *who* established the first wholesale ice-cream business in 1851.

The fact *that* we had to wait until 1896 for someone to invent the ice-cream cone is surprising.

Interrogative pronouns have the same forms as relative pronouns but have different functions. They serve to introduce questions.

Who invented the ice-cream sundae?

Of chocolate and vanilla ice cream, *which* do you prefer?

The waiter asked, "*Whose* chocolate walnut sundae is this?"

Demonstrative pronouns are pronouns used to point out particular persons or things: *this, that, these, those*.

This dish is what Mandy likes best for brunch: pecan waffles with blueberry syrup.

Of everything on the menu, *these* must be most fattening.

See also G1–G4.

Adjectives. Adjectives modify nouns and pronouns. Adjectives often occur immediately before or after nouns they modify. As **subject complements** (sometimes called predicate adjectives), they may be separated by the verb from nouns or pronouns they modify.

Creole cooking can be found in *many* diners along the Gulf of Mexico.

Gumbo is a *spicy* soup.

Jambalaya tastes *delicious*, and it is *cheap*.

---

adjective clause A clause that modifies a noun or pronoun and is generally introduced by a relative pronoun (such as *that* or *which*).

subject complement A word or word group that follows a linking verb (such as *seems, appears,* or *is* and other forms of *be*) and describes or restates the subject: The tents looked *old* and *dirty*.

Some adjectives change form in comparisons.

Gumbo is *spicier* than crawfish pie.

Gumbo is the *spiciest* Creole soup.

Some words can be used as both pronouns and adjectives; nouns are also sometimes used as adjectives.

ADJ.   ADJ.   PRON.
Many people love *crawfish* pie, and *many* prefer gumbo.

See also G7-b.

Adverbs. Adverbs modify verbs (*eat well*), adjectives (*very big appetite*), and other adverbs (*extremely well done*). They often tell when, how, where, why, and how often.
A number of adverbs are formed by adding *-ly* to an adjective (*hearty* appetite, eat *heartily*).

Walter Jetton started the charcoal fires *early*. [when]

He basted the sizzling ribs *liberally* with marinade. [how]

Pots of beans simmered *nearby*. [where]

Like adjectives, adverbs can change form for comparison.

He ate the buttermilk biscuits *fast*. [*faster* than Bucky ate his biscuits, *fastest* of all the hungry diners]

With adverbs that end in *-ly*, the words *more* and *most* are used when making comparisons.

Junior drank the first cold lemonade *quickly*. [*more quickly* than Billy Joe, *most quickly* of all those at the table]

The *conjunctive adverb* (or simply the *connective*) is a special kind of adverb used to connect the ideas in two sentences or independent clauses. Familiar connectives include *consequently, however, therefore, similarly, besides*, and *nevertheless*.

The inspiration for Tex-Mex food came from Mexico. *Nevertheless,* it is considered a native American cuisine.

Finally, adverbs may evaluate or qualify the information in a sentence.

Barbecue comes from *barbacoa*, a word the Spaniards *probably* picked up from the Arawak Indians.

See also G7-a.

Verbs. Verbs tell what is happening in a sentence by expressing action (*cook, stir*) or a state of being (*be, stay*). Depending on the structure of the sentence, a verb can be **transitive** (*Jerry bakes cookies*) or **intransitive** (*Jerry bakes for a living*); an intransitive verb that is followed by a **subject complement** (*Jerry is a fine baker, and his cookies always taste heavenly*) is often called a **linking verb**.

Nearly all verbs have several forms (or principal parts), many of which may be irregular rather than follow a standard pattern. In addition, verbs have various forms to indicate *tense* (time of action or state of being), *voice* (performer of action), and *mood* (statement, command, or possibility). Studies have shown that because verbs can take so many forms, the most common errors in writing involve verbs. See also G5.

Verb Phrases. Verbs divide into two primary groups: (1) *main* (*lexical*) *verbs* and (2) *auxiliary* (*helping*) *verbs* that combine with main verbs to create verb phrases. The three primary auxiliary verbs are *do, be,* and *have,* in all their forms.

>*do:* does, did, doing, done
>
>*be:* am, is, are, was, were, being, been
>
>*have:* has, had, having

These primary auxiliary verbs can also act as main verbs in sentences. Other common auxiliary verbs (*can, could, may, might, shall, should, will, would, must, ought to, used to*), however, cannot be the main verb in a sentence but are used in combination with main verbs in verb phrases. The auxiliary verb works with the main verb to indicate tense, mood, and voice.

A favorite cheese in the United States *has* always been cheddar.

When the cheese curd forms, it *must* be separated from the whey.

After cheddar cheese is shaped into a block, it *should* be aged for at least several months.

By the year 2011, Americans *will have been* eating cheese for four hundred years.

Principal Parts of Verbs. All main verbs (as well as the primary auxiliary verbs *do, be,* and *have*) have five forms. The forms of a large number of verbs are regular, but many verbs have irregular forms.

---

transitive verb A verb that needs an object — something that receives the action of the verb — to make its meaning complete.

intransitive verb A verb that does not need an object to make its meaning complete.

subject complement A word or word group that follows a linking verb (such as *seems, appears,* or *is* and other forms of *be*) and describes or restates the subject: The tents looked *old* and *dirty.*

linking verb *Be, seem, appear, become, taste,* or another verb that connects a subject with a subject complement that describes or modifies it: The chips *taste* salty.

Form	Regular	Irregular
Infinitive or base	sip	drink
Third-person singular present (-s form)	sips	drinks
Past	sipped	drank
Present participle (-ing form)	sipping	drinking
Past participle (-ed form)	sipped	drunk

The past and past participle for most verbs in English are formed by simply adding -d or -ed (posed, walked, pretended, unveiled). However, a number of verbs have irregular forms, most of which are different for the past and the past participle.

For regular verbs, the past and past participle forms are the same: sipped. Even though regular verbs have predictable forms, they pose certain spelling problems, having to do mainly with dropping or doubling the last letter of the base form before adding -ing, -d, or -ed. (See M9-a.) All new verbs coming into English have regular forms: format, formats, formatted, formatting.

Irregular verbs have unpredictable forms. (Dictionaries list the forms of irregular verbs under the base form.) Their -s and -ing forms are generally predictable, just like those of regular verbs, but their past and past participle forms are not. In particular, be careful to use the correct past participle form of irregular verbs.

Listed here are the principal parts of fifty-three commonly troublesome irregular verbs. Check your dictionary for a more complete listing.

Base	Past Tense	Past Participle
be: am, is, are	was, were	been
beat	beat	beaten
begin	began	begun
bite	bit	bitten
blow	blew	blown
break	broke	broken
bring	brought	brought
burst	burst	burst
choose	chose	chosen
come	came	come
cut	cut	cut
deal	dealt	dealt
do	did	done
draw	drew	drawn
drink	drank	drunk
drive	drove	driven
eat	ate	eaten

Base	Past Tense	Past Participle
fall	fell	fallen
fly	flew	flown
freeze	froze	frozen
get	got	got (gotten)
give	gave	given
go	went	gone
grow	grew	grown
have	had	had
know	knew	known
lay	laid	laid
lead	led	led
lie	lay	lain
lose	lost	lost
ride	rode	ridden
ring	rang	rung
rise	rose	risen
run	ran	run
say	said	said
see	saw	seen
set	set	set
shake	shook	shaken
sink	sank	sunk
sit	sat	sat
speak	spoke	spoken
spring	sprang (sprung)	sprung
steal	stole	stolen
stink	stank	stunk
swear	swore	sworn
swim	swam	swum
take	took	taken
teach	taught	taught
tear	tore	torn
throw	threw	thrown
wear	wore	worn
win	won	won
write	wrote	written

Tense. Native speakers of English know the **tense** system and use it confidently. They comprehend time as listeners and readers. As talkers, they use the system in combination with adverbs of time to identify the times of actions. As writers, however, even native speakers may find it difficult to put together sentences that express time clearly through verbs: Time has to be expressed consistently from sentence to sentence, and shifts in time perspective must be managed smoothly. In addition, certain conventions permit time to be expressed in unusual ways: History can be written in present time to dramatize events, or characters in novels may be presented as though their actions are in present time. The following examples of verb tense provide only a partial demonstration of the complex system indicating time in English.

tense The form of a verb that shows the time of the action or state of being.

Present. There are three basic types of present time: timeless, limited, and instantaneous. Timeless present-tense verbs express habitual action.

> Some Americans *grow* their own fruits and vegetables.

Limited present-tense verbs express an action in process and of limited duration.

> The neighbors *are preparing* watermelon rind preserves this week.

Instantaneous present-tense verbs express action being completed at the moment.

> Laura *is eating* the last ripe strawberry.

Present-tense verbs can also be emphatic.

> I certainly *do enjoy* homemade strawberry preserves in the middle of winter.

Past. There are several kinds of past time. Some actions must be identified as having taken place at a particular time in the past.

> While he *was waiting*, Jake *ordered* a ham sandwich on whole wheat bread.

In the *present perfect tense*, actions may be expressed as having taken place at no definite time in the past or as occurring in the past and continuing into the present.

> Jake *has eaten* more ham sandwiches than he can count.

> The Downtown Deli *has sold* delicious ham sandwiches on homemade bread for as long as he can remember.

Action can even be expressed as having been completed in the past prior to some other past action or event (the *past perfect tense*).

> Before he *had taken* a bite, Jake dropped his sandwich on the floor.

Future. The English verb system offers writers several different ways of expressing future time. Future action can be indicated with the modal auxiliary *will.*

> **Fast-food restaurants *will grow* in popularity.**

A completed future action can even be viewed from some time farther in the future (*future perfect tense*).

> **Within a decade or two, Americans *will have given up* cooking their own meals.**

Continuing future actions can be expressed with *will be* and the *-ing* form of the verb.

> **Americans *will* soon *be eating* every second meal away from home.**

The right combination of verbs with *about* can express an action in the near future.

> **Jeremiah *is about to eat* his third hamburger.**

Future arrangements, commands, or possibilities can be expressed.

> **Junior and Mary Jo *are to be married* at McDonald's.**

> **You *have to be* there by noon to get a good table.**

> **If Junior *is to lose* weight, he must give up french fries.**

Voice. A verb is in the *active* voice when it expresses an action taken by the subject. A verb is said to be in the *passive* voice when it expresses something that happens to the subject.

In sentences with active verbs, it is apparent who is performing the action expressed in the verb.

> **The chef *disguised* the tasteless broccoli with a rich cheese sauce.**

In sentences with passive verbs, it may not be clear who is performing the action.

> **The tasteless broccoli *was disguised* with a rich cheese sauce.**

The writer could reveal the performer by adding a phrase (*by the chef*), but the revision would also create a clumsy sentence. Graceful, clear writing relies on active, rather than passive, verbs. Passive forms do fulfill certain purposes, however, such as expressing the state of something.

> **The broccoli *is disguised.***

> **The restaurant *was closed.***

Passives can give prominence to certain information by shifting it to the end of the sentence.

> ***Who* closed this restaurant? It was closed by *the Board of Health.***

Writers also use passives to make sentences more readable by shifting long **noun clauses** to the end.

> ACTIVE *That the chef disguised the tasteless broccoli* with a cheese sauce disgusted Elvira.

> PASSIVE Elvira was disgusted *that the chef disguised the tasteless broccoli* with a cheese sauce.

Mood. Mood refers to the writer's attitude toward a statement. There are three moods: indicative, imperative, and subjunctive. Most statements or questions are in the *indicative mood.*

> The chuck wagon *fed* cowboys on the trail.

> *Did* cowboys ever *tire* of steak and beans?

Commands or directions are given in the *imperative mood.*

> *Eat* those beans!

The *subjunctive mood* is used mainly to indicate hypothetical, impossible, or unlikely conditions.

> If I *were* you, I'd compliment the cook.

> *Had* they *been* here yesterday, they would have had hot camp bread.

Prepositions. Prepositions occur in **phrases**, followed by **objects**. (The uses of prepositional phrases are explained in R2-c.) Most prepositions are single words (*at, on, by, with, of, for, in, under, over, by*), but some consist of two or three words (*away from, on account of, in front of, because of, in comparison with, by means of*). They are used to indicate relations — usually of place, time, cause, purpose, or means — between their objects and some other word in the sentence.

> I'll meet you *at* El Ranchero *for* lunch.

> The enchiladas are stuffed *with* cheese.

> You can split an order *with* [Georgette and me].

Objects of prepositions can be single or compound nouns or pronouns in the **objective case** (as in the preceding examples) or phrases or clauses acting as nouns.

> Herman began making nachos *by* [grating the cheese].

> His guests were happy *with* [what he served].

noun clauses Word groups that can function like nouns, acting as subjects, objects, or complements in independent clauses.

phrase A group of words that does *not* contain both a subject and a verb and is always part of an independent clause. Common types of phrases include *prepositional* (*After a flash of lightning*, I saw a tree split in half) and *verbal* (*Blinded by the flash*, I ran into the house).

object The part of a clause that receives the action of the verb (At the checkpoint, we unloaded *the canoes*) or the part of a phrase that follows a preposition (We dragged them to *the river*).

objective case The form a pronoun takes when it is an object (receiving the action of the verb): We helped *him*.

Conjunctions. Like prepositions, conjunctions show relations between sentence elements. There are coordinating, subordinating, and correlative conjunctions.

Coordinating conjunctions (*and, but, for, nor, or, so,* or *yet*) join logically comparable sentence elements.

> Guacamole is made with avocados, tomatoes, onions, *and* chiles.
>
> You may add a little lemon or lime juice, *but* be careful not to add too much.

Subordinating conjunctions (*although, because, since, though, as though, as soon as, rather than*) introduce **dependent clauses**.

> *As soon as* the waitress came, Susanna ordered an iced tea.
>
> She dived into the salsa and chips *because* she was too hungry to wait for her combination plate.

Correlative conjunctions come in pairs, with the first element anticipating the second (*both . . . and, either . . . or, neither . . . nor, not only . . . but also*).

> Charley wanted to order *both* the chile relleno *and* the enchiladas verdes.

Articles. There are only three articles in English: *the, a,* and *an. The* is used for definite reference to something specific; *a* and *an* are used for indefinite reference to something less specific. *The Mexican restaurant in Westbury* is different from *a Mexican restaurant in Westbury.* (See L1.)

Demonstratives. *This, that, these,* and *those* are demonstratives. Sometimes called demonstrative adjectives, they are used to point to something specific.

> Put one of *these* maraschino cherries at each end of the banana split.
>
> The accident left pineapple milkshake all over the front seat of *that* pickup truck.

Interjections. Interjections indicate strong feeling or an attempt to command attention: *phew, shhh, damn, oh, yea, yikes, ouch, boo.*

R2-b   Dependent Clauses

Like independent clauses, all dependent clauses have a **subject** and a **predicate** (which may also have objects, complements, and adverbial modifiers). Unlike independent clauses, however, dependent clauses cannot stand by themselves as complete sentences; they always occur with independent clauses as part of either the subject or the predicate.

INDEPENDENT   Ribbon-shaped pasta is popular in northern Italy.

---

dependent (subordinate) clause A word group that has a subject, a predicate, and a subordinating word (such as *because*) at the beginning; it cannot stand by itself as a sentence but must be connected to an independent (main) clause.

subject The part of a clause that identifies who or what is being discussed: At the checkpoint, *we* unloaded the canoes.

predicate The part of a clause that includes a complete verb and says something about the subject: At the checkpoint, we *unloaded the canoes.*

DEPENDENT   ..., while tubular-shaped pasta is popular in southern Italy.

..., which is generally made by hand, ...

Although it originally comes from China, ...

There are three types of dependent clauses: adjective, adverb, and noun.

Adjective Clauses. Also known as *relative clauses*, adjective clauses modify nouns and pronouns in independent clauses. They are introduced by relative pronouns (*who, whom, which, that, whose*) or adverbs (*where, when*), and most often they immediately follow the noun or pronoun they modify. Adjective clauses can be either *restrictive* (essential to defining the noun or pronoun they modify) or *nonrestrictive* (not essential to understanding the noun or pronoun); nonrestrictive clauses are set off by commas, and restrictive clauses are not (see P1-c and P2-b).

Vincent bought a package of agnolotti, *which is a pasta used in soup.*

We went back to the restaurant *where they serve that delicious veal.*

Everyone *who likes Italian cooking* **knows Romano cheese well.**

Adverb Clauses. Introduced by subordinating conjunctions (such as *although, because,* and *since*), adverb clauses nearly always modify verbs in independent clauses, although they may occasionally modify other elements (except nouns). Adverb clauses are used to indicate a great variety of logical relations with their independent clauses: time, place, condition, concession, reason, cause, circumstance, purpose, result, and so on. They are generally set off by commas.

Although the finest olive oil in Italy comes from Lucca, **good-quality olive oil is produced in other regions of the country.** [concession]

When the tomato sauce comes to a boil, **reduce the heat and simmer.** [time]

If you know mushrooms, **you probably prefer them fresh.** [condition]

Ken carefully watches the spaghetti *because he does not like it to be overcooked.* [reason]

Noun Clauses. Like nouns, noun clauses can function as **subjects, objects,** or **complements** (or predicate nominatives) in independent clauses. They are thus essential to the structure of the **independent clause** in which they occur and so, like restrictive adjective clauses, are not set off by commas. A noun clause usually begins with a **relative pronoun,** but the introductory word may sometimes be omitted.

┌─────── SUBJECT ───────┐
That we preferred the sausage surprised us.

┌────────── OBJECT ──────────┐
Harold did not know for sure *whether baloney came from Bologna.*

---

subject The part of a clause that identifies who or what is being discussed: At the checkpoint, *we* unloaded the canoes.

object The part of a clause that receives the action of the verb (At the checkpoint, we unloaded *the canoes*) or the part of a phrase that follows a preposition (We dragged them to *the river*).

subject complement A word or word group that follows a linking verb (such as *seems, appears,* or *is* and other forms of *be*) and describes or restates the subject: The tents looked *old and dirty.*

independent (main) clause A word group with a subject and a predicate that can stand alone as a separate sentence. (A predicate is the part of a clause that includes a complete verb and says something about the subject: At the checkpoint, *we unloaded the canoes.*)

relative pronoun A pronoun (such as *who, whom, whose, which,* or *that*) that introduces an adjective clause (a clause that modifies a noun or pronoun).

SUBJECT COMPLEMENT
He assumed *that it did.*

┌────DIRECT OBJECT────┐
Hillary claims *no one eats pizza in Italy.* [relative pronoun *that* dropped]

PREP. ┌────OBJECT OF PREPOSITION────┐
Gnocchi may be flavored with *whatever fresh herbs are available.*

R2-c Phrases

Like **dependent clauses**, phrases can function as nouns, adjectives, or adverbs in sentences. However, unlike clauses, phrases do not contain both a subject and a verb. (A phrase, of course, cannot stand on its own but occurs as part of an **independent clause**.) The six most common types of grammatical phrases are *prepositional, appositive, participial, gerund, infinitive,* and *absolute.*

Prepositional Phrases. Prepositional phrases always begin with a **preposition** and function as either an adjective or adverb.

Food *in Hunan* is noticeably different from that *in Sichuan.*
ADJECTIVE PHRASE   ADJECTIVE PHRASE

The perfect egg roll is crisp *on the outside* and crunchy *on the inside.*
ADVERB PHRASE   ADVERB PHRASE

Appositive Phrases. Appositive phrases identify or give more information about a noun or pronoun just preceding. They take several forms. A single noun may also serve as an appositive.

The baguette, *the most popular bread in France,* is a loaf about two feet long.

The king of the breakfast rolls, *the croissant,* is shaped like a crescent.

The baker *Marguerite* makes superb croissants.

Participial Phrases. Participles are verb forms used to indicate certain tenses (present: *sipping;* past: *sipped*). They can also be used as verbals — words derived from verbs — and function as adjectives.

At breakfast, we were first served *steaming* coffee and a simple *buttered* roll.

A participial phrase is an adjective phrase made up of a participle and any complements or modifiers it might have. Like participles, participial phrases modify nouns and pronouns in sentences.

Two-thirds of the breakfasts *consumed in the diner* included sausage and eggs.

Prepared in the chef's personal style, the vegetable omelets are served with a cheese sauce *flavored with garlic and herbs.*

---

dependent (subordinate) clause A word group that has a subject, a predicate, and a subordinating word (such as *because*) at the beginning; it cannot stand by itself as a sentence but must be connected to an independent (main) clause: *Although it was raining,* we loaded our gear onto the buses.

preposition A word (such as *between, in,* or *of*) that always appears as part of a phrase and indicates the relation between a word in a sentence and the object of the preposition: The water splashed *into the canoe.*

Mopping up the cheese sauce with the last of his roll, Mickey thought to himself, I could get used to this.

Gerund Phrases. Like a participle, a gerund is a verbal. Ending in *-ing*, it even looks like a present participle, but it functions as a noun, filling any noun slot in a clause. Gerund phrases include **complements** and any modifiers of the gerund.

┌SUBJECT┐
Roasting is the quickest way to cook a turkey.

┌──────SUBJECT──────┐
Preparing a stuffed turkey takes several hours.

You begin by *mixing the dressing.*
OBJECT OF PREPOSITION

complement A word or word group that describes or restates a subject or an object.

Infinitive Phrases. Like participles and gerunds, infinitives are verbals. The infinitive is the base form of the verb, preceded by *to: to simmer, to broil, to fry.* Infinitives and infinitive phrases function as nouns, adjectives, or adverbs.

Tamales can be complicated *to prepare.*
ADVERB

To assemble the tamales, begin by cutting the kernels off the corncobs.
ADVERB

┌──────NOUN──────┐
Remembering *to save the corn husks* is important.
OBJECT OF GERUND PHRASE

Anyone's first tamale dinner is a meal *to remember for a long time.*
ADJECTIVE

Absolute Phrases. The absolute phrase does not modify or replace any particular part of a clause; it modifies the whole clause. An absolute phrase includes a noun or pronoun and often includes a past or present participle as well as modifiers. Nearly all modern prose writers rely on absolute phrases. Some style historians consider them a hallmark of modern prose.

Her eyes glistening, Lucy checked out the cases of doughnuts at Krispy Kreme Doughnuts.

She stood patiently in line, *her arms folded to control her hunger, her book pack hanging off one shoulder.*

She walked slowly to a table, *each hand bearing a treasure.*

GL Glossary of Frequently Misused Words

Sometimes writers choose a word that is incorrect, imprecise in meaning, pronounced the same as the correct word (a homophone), or used widely but unacceptable in formal writing situations. In addition, problems can arise with idiomatic phrases, common everyday expressions that may or may not fit, or words whose denotations or connotations do not precisely suit the context of a particular sentence. In general, you should avoid imprecise popular usages in formal writing.

accept/except *Accept* is a verb ("receive with favor"). *Except* may be a verb ("leave out") but is more commonly used as a preposition ("excluding"). Other forms: *acceptance, acceptable; exception.*

> **None of the composition instructors will *accept* late papers, *except* Mr. Siu.**

> **Her *acceptance* of the bribe *excepts* her from consideration for the position.**

adapt/adopt *Adapt* means "adjust to make more suitable." *Adopt* means "take as one's own." Other forms: *adaptable, adaptation; adoption.*

> **To *adopt* an older child, parents must be willing to *adapt* themselves to the child's needs.**

advice/advise *Advice* is a noun; *advise* is a verb. Other forms: *advisable, adviser.*

> **Everyone *advised* him to heed the expert's *advice*.**

affect/effect *Affect* is commonly used as a verb, most often meaning "influence"; in psychology, the noun *affect* is a technical term for an emotional state. *Effect* is generally a noun ("result or consequences"); it is only occasionally used as a verb ("bring about"), although the adjective form (*effective*) is common.

> **Researchers are studying the *effect* of stress.**

> **How does stress *affect* the human body?**

all right *All right* is the preferred spelling, rather than *alright*, which many people regard as unacceptable.

a lot A common expression meaning "a large number," *a lot* is always written as two words. Because it is vague and informal, avoid it in college writing.

among/between Use *among* when you are referring to more than two objects; limit *between* to references to only two objects.

It is hard to choose one winner *among* so many highly qualified candidates for the scholarship.

Between the two extreme positions lies a vast middle ground.

amount/number   *Amount* refers to the quantity of a unit ("amount of water," "amount of discussion"), whereas *number* refers to the quantity of individual items ("number of papers," "number of times"). In general, use *amount* only with a singular noun.

anxious/eager   *Anxious* means "nervous" or "worried"; *eager* means "looking forward [impatiently]." Avoid using *anxious* to mean *eager*.

The students were *eager* to learn their grades.

They were *anxious* they wouldn't pass.

between/among   See **among/between**.

capital/capitol   *Capital* is the more common word and has a variety of meanings, among them the principal city in a state or country; *capitol* refers only to a government building.

cite/sight/site   *Cite* as a verb means "refer to as proof" or "summon to appear in court." *Site* is a noun meaning "place or location." *Sight* may be a verb or a noun and always refers to seeing or what is seen ("a sight for sore eyes").

Can you *cite* your sources for these figures?

A new dormitory will be built at this *site*.

When she *sighted* the speeding car, the officer *cited* the driver for recklessness.

complement/compliment   *Complement* refers to completion, the making of a satisfactory whole, whereas *compliment* indicates admiration or praise; both can be used as either nouns or verbs. *Complementary* means "serving to complete" or "contrasting in color"; *complimentary* means "given free."

The dean *complimented* the school's recruiters on the full *complement* of students registered for the fall.

The designer received many *compliments* on the way the elements of the room *complemented* one another.

Buy a new refrigerator and receive a *complimentary* ice maker in a *complementary* color.

could of/should of/would of In standard speech, "could have," "should have," and "would have" sound very much like "could of," "should of," and "would of"; however, substituting *of* for *have* in this construction is too casual for written work. The same holds true for "might of," "must of," and "will of."

council/counsel *Council* is a noun ("an assembly of people who deliberate or govern"). *Counsel* is a verb meaning "advise" or a noun meaning "advice." Other forms: *councilor* ("member of a council"); *counselor* ("one who gives advice").

The *council* on drug abuse has issued guidelines for *counseling* troubled students.

Before voting on the important fiscal issue, City *Councilor* Lopez sought the *counsel* of her constituents.

desert/dessert As a noun or an adjective, *desert* (dez´ ert) means "a dry, uncultivated region"; as a verb, *desert* (di zurt´) means "abandon." A *dessert* is a sweet dish served at the end of a meal.

The hunters were alone in the arid *desert, deserted* by their guides.

After a heavy meal, sherbet is the perfect *dessert.*

eager/anxious See **anxious/eager.**

effect/affect See **affect/effect.**

emigrant/immigrant An *emigrant* moves out of a country; an *immigrant* moves into a country. Other forms: *emigrate, emigration, émigré; immigrate, immigration.*

Congress passed a bill to deal with illegal *immigrants* living in the United States.

Members of her family *emigrated* from Cuba to Miami and Madrid.

etc. An abbreviation of the Latin words *et cetera* ("and other things"), *etc.* should never be preceded by *and* in English. Also be careful to spell the abbreviation correctly (*not* "ect."). In general, use *etc.* sparingly, if at all, in college writing.

except See **accept/except.**

count noun A noun that names people and things that can be counted: one *teacher*, two *teachers*; one *movie*, several *movies*.

fewer/less Use *fewer* when referring to **count nouns**; reserve *less* for amounts you cannot count.

The new cookies have *fewer* calories than the other brand because they contain *less* sugar.

fortuitous/fortunate Often used incorrectly, the adjective *fortuitous* means "by chance" or "unplanned" and should not be confused with *fortunate* ("lucky").

Because the two candidates wished to avoid each other, their *fortuitous* meeting in the parking lot was not a *fortunate* event for either party.

hisself/theirselves In nonstandard speech, "hisself" is sometimes used for *himself* and "theirselves" for *themselves*, but such usage is not acceptable in written work.

hopefully In conversation, *hopefully* is often used as a convenient shorthand to suggest that some outcome is generally to be hoped for ("Hopefully, our nominee will win the election"); this usage, however, is not acceptable in most written work. Better substitutes include *I hope, let's hope, everyone hopes,* and *it is to be hoped,* depending on your meaning. The adverb *hopefully* ("full of hope") should always modify a specific verb or adverb.

I *hope* my brother will win the election.

We should all *hope* his brother will win the election.

Her sister is *hopeful* that she will win the election.

The candidate inquired *hopefully* about the results.

immigrant See **emigrant/immigrant**.

its/it's *Its* is a possessive pronoun; *it's* is the contraction of *it is.*

This job has *its* advantages.

When *it's* well grilled, there's nothing like a steak.

lay/lie The verb *lay,* meaning "put, place," is **transitive** (forms of *lay* are *lay, laid, laid*). The verb *lie,* meaning "recline," is **intransitive** (forms of *lie* are *lie, lay, lain*). Writers may incorrectly use *laid* as the past tense of *lie,* or *lay* as the present tense of *lie.* Other forms: *laying, lying.*

The lion *lies* in wait for the approach of its prey.

Joseph *laid* down his shovel, took a shower, and *lay* down for a nap.

> **transitive verb** A verb that needs an object — something that receives the action of the verb — to make its meaning complete.

> **intransitive verb** A verb that does not need an object to make its meaning complete.

less/fewer See **fewer/less**.

literally *Literally* means "exactly as stated, actually" and is often used to suggest that a cliché has in fact come true. However, to say, "The movie made my hair literally stand on end" is to misuse the word (although a person who suffered a fatal heart attack brought on by a fearful shock might correctly be said to have *literally* died of fright).

loose/lose *Lose* is a verb ("mislay, fail to maintain"); *loose* is most often used as an adjective ("not fastened tightly").

A *loose* board may make someone *lose* his or her balance.

number/amount See **amount/number**.

persecute/prosecute *Persecute* means "mistreat or oppress"; *prosecute* most often means "bring a legal suit or action against."

> A biased majority can easily *persecute* minority groups.

> The law may *prosecute* only those who are indicted.

prejudice/prejudiced *Prejudice* is a noun or a verb. When used adjectivally, it should take the form of the past tense of the verb: *prejudiced*.

> We should fight *prejudice* wherever we find it.

> He was *prejudiced* against the candidate because she spoke with an accent.

principal/principle *Principal* implies "first in rank, chief," whether it is used as an adjective ("the principal cities of the Midwest") or a noun ("the principal of a midwestern high school"). *Principle* is generally a noun meaning "a basic law or truth."

> In *principle*, you are correct.

> The *principle* of free speech will be the *principal* topic of discussion.

prosecute/persecute See **persecute/prosecute**.

sensual/sensuous Both *sensual* and *sensuous* suggest the enjoyment of physical pleasure through the senses. However, *sensual* generally implies self-indulgence, particularly in terms of sexual activity; *sensuous* has a more positive meaning and suggests the ability to appreciate intellectually what is received through the senses. Other forms: *sensuality; sensuousness*.

> When drunk, the emperor gave himself up to brutal *sensuality*.

> Anyone can enjoy a *sensuous* spring night.

set/sit The difference between the verbs *sit* and *set* is similar to that between *lie* and *lay*: *Sit* is generally intransitive ("rest on one's buttocks"), and *set* is transitive ("put [something] in a certain place"). *Set* also has a number of uses as a noun. The past tense and past **participle** forms of *sit* are both *sat*; these forms for *set* are both *set*.

participle A verb form showing present tense (*dancing, freezing*) or past tense (*danced, frozen*) that can also act as an adjective.

> He would rather *sit* than stand and would rather lie than *sit*.

> He *set* his suitcase on the ground and then *sat* on it.

should of See **could of/should of/would of.**

sight/site See **cite/sight/site**.

stationary/stationery *Stationary* is an adjective meaning "fixed, remaining in one place" ("Concrete will make the pole stationary"). *Stationery* refers to writing paper. One way to keep the distinction in mind is to associate the *er* in *paper* with that in *stationery*.

that/which When used as a **subordinating conjunction**, *that* always introduces a **restrictive word group**; *which* is generally used for **nonrestrictive word groups.** Although it is acceptable to use *which* before a restrictive word group, *that* is generally preferred to make it clear that the clause is restrictive. (See the discussion of restrictive and nonrestrictive word groups in P1-c and P2-b, and the review of sentence structure and sentence elements on p. H-115.)

> Her first bid for the Senate was the only election *that* she ever lost.

> Her first bid for the Senate, *which* was unsuccessful, brought her to prominence.

> The Senate election *that* resulted in her defeat took place in 1968.

their/there/they're *Their* is a possessive pronoun; *there* specifies a place or functions as an expletive; and *they're* is a contraction of *they are.*

> The coauthors say *there* are no copies of *their* script in their office, but *they're* not telling the truth.

theirselves See **hisself/theirselves.**

to/too/two *To* is a preposition, *too* is an adverb, and *two* is generally an adjective. The most common error here is the substitution of *to* for *too.*

> It is *too* early *to* predict either of the *two* scores.

unique To be precise, *unique* means "one of a kind, like no other." Careful writers do not use it loosely to mean simply "unusual or rare." Nor can it correctly take a comparative form ("most unique"), although advertisers sometimes use it this way.

> Her generosity is not *unique*, although today it is increasingly rare.

> This example of Mayan sculpture is apparently *unique*; none other like it has so far been discovered.

used to In colloquial speech, *used to* often sounds like "use to." However, *used to* is the correct form for written work.

---

subordinating conjunction A word or phrase (such as *although*, *because*, *since*, or *as soon as*) that introduces a dependent clause and relates it to an independent clause.

restrictive word group A group of words, not set off by commas, that provides information essential to defining or identifying the noun or pronoun it modifies.

nonrestrictive word group A group of words, set off by commas, that provides extra or nonessential information and could be eliminated without changing the meaning of the noun or pronoun it modifies.

My grandfather *used to* be a Dodgers fan until the team moved to Los Angeles.

weather/whether *Weather* is a noun ("atmospheric conditions"); *whether* is a conjunction.

The *weather* forecast indicates *whether* there will be sun or rain.

which See **that/which**.

who's/whose *Who's* is the contraction of *who is* or *who has; whose* is a possessive pronoun.

Who's up next?

She's the only student *who's* done her work correctly.

Whose work is this?

The man *whose* job I took has retired.

would of See **could of/should of/would of**.

Acknowledgments

Text Credits

Mirko Bagaric. "A Case for Torture." From *The Age* 17, May 2005. Copyright © 2005 by Mirko Bagaric. Reprinted with permission of the author and *The Age.*

Rick Bragg. "100 Miles per Hour, Upside Down and Sideways." From *All Over But the Shoutin'* by Rick Bragg. Copyright © 1997 by Rick Bragg. Used by permission of Pantheon Books, a division of Random House, Inc.

Amanda Coyne. "The Long Good-bye: Mother's Day in Federal Prison." Copyright © 1997 by Harper's Magazine. All rights reserved. Reproduced from the May issue by special permission.

Don DeLillo. "Videotape." From *Underworld* by Don DeLillo. Copyright © 1997 by Don DeLillo. Reprinted with permission of Scribner, an imprint of Simon & Schuster Adult Publishing Group. All rights reserved.

Annie Dillard. Excerpt from *An American Childhood* by Annie Dillard. Copyright © 1987 by Annie Dillard. Reprinted by permission of HarperCollins Publishers.

John T. Edge. "I'm Not Leaving Until I Eat This Thing." From *The Oxford American* (September/October 1999). Copyright © John T. Edge. Photograph by Shannon Brinkman. Reproduced with permission.

Richard Estrada. "Sticks and Stones and Sports Team Names." From *The Los Angeles Times*, October 29, 1995. Copyright © 1995 The Washington Post Syndicate. Reprinted with permission of The Washington Post Writers Group.

Amos Esty. "Investigating a Mega-Mystery." From *American Scientist*, August 2005. Copyright © 2005 by American Scientist. Reprinted with permission.

Amitai Etzioni. "Working at McDonald's" Copyright © 1986 by Amitai Etzioni. Author of *The Spirit of Community*. Director, George Washington University Center for Communication Policy Studies. Reproduced with the permission of the author.

Noah Feldman. "America's Church-State Problem." Excerpted from *Divided by God: America's Church-State Problem — and What We Should Do About It* by Noah Feldman. Reprinted with the permission of Farrar, Straus & Giroux, LLC.

Richard A. Friedman. "Born to Be Happy, Through a Twist of Human Hard Wire." From *The New York Times*, December 31, 2002. Copyright © 2002 by The New York Times Company. Reprinted with permission.

Erica Goode. "The Gorge-Yourself Environment." From *The New York Times*, July 22, 2003. Copyright © 2003 by The New York Times Company. Reprinted with permission.

Bob Holmes. "In the Blink of an Eye." From *New Scientist*, July 2005. Copyright © 2005 by New Scientist. Reprinted with the permission of New Scientist.

Jonah Jackson. "The Elder Scrolls III: Morrowind." Courtesy G4Media, Inc. Images from *The Elder Scrolls III: Morrowind 7*. © 2002 Bethesda Softworks LLC, a ZeniMax Media Company. The Elder Scrolls, Morrowind, Bethesda Softworks and ZeniMax are registered trademarks of ZeniMax Media Inc. All rights reserved.

Kermit D. Johnson. "Inhuman Behavior: A Chaplain's View of Torture." From *The Christian Century*, April 18, 2006. Copyright © 2006 by Christian Century. www.christiancentury.org. Subscriptions $49/year from P.O. Box 378, Mt. Morris, Illinois 61054. 1-800-208-4097. Reprinted with permission.

Bel Kaufman. "Sunday in the Park." From *The Available Press/PEN Short Story Collection*, Ballantine Books, 1985. Reproduced by permission of the author.

Martin Luther King Jr. "Letter from Birmingham Jail." Copyright © 1963 Martin Luther King Jr., Copyright renewed 1991 Coretta Scott King. Reprinted by arrangement with the Estate of Martin Luther King Jr., c/o Writers House as agent for the proprietor, New York, NY.

Stephen King. "Why We Crave Horror Movies." Originally appeared in *Playboy*, 1982. © Stephen King. All rights reserved. Reprinted with permission.

Karen Kornbluh. "Win-Win Flexibility." From New American Foundation, June 29, 2005. Copyright © 2005. Reprinted with the permission of the author.

John McPhee. "The New York Pickpocket Academy." From *Giving Good Weight* by John McPhee. Copyright © 1979 by John McPhee. Reprinted with the permission of Farrar, Straus & Giroux, LLC.

Matthew Miller. "A New Deal for Teachers." From *Two Percent Solution* by Matthew Miller. Copyright © 2003 by Matthew Miller. Reprinted by permission of Public Affairs, a member of Perseus Books, LLC. Originally published in *The Atlantic Monthly*, July/August 2003. Letter to the editor by Walt Gardner, Philip Fried, and Matthew Miller's response are reprinted with the permission of *The Atlantic Monthly*.

Rod Paige. "Testing Has Raised Students' Expectations, and Progress in Learning Is Evident Nationwide." From *Insight on the News*, May 11, 2004. Copyright © 2004 by News World Communications. Reprinted with permission.

Bill Saporito. "Why Fans and Players are Playing So Rough." From *Time*, December 6, 2004. © 2004 Time Inc. Reprinted by permission.

Gian-Claudia Sciara. "Making Communities Safe for Bicycles." Originally published in *Access* 22 (Spring 2003): 28–33. Reprinted with permission of the author and Access magazine.

A. O. Scott. "News in Black, White and Shades of Gray." From *The New York Times*, September 23, 2005. Copyright © 2005 by The New York Times Company. Reprinted by permission.

Jane S. Shaw. "Nature in the Suburbs." From *Backgrounder* #1724, February 18, 2004. Reprinted with the permission of The Heritage Foundation.

Karen Stabiner. "Boys Here, Girls There: Sure, If Equality's the Goal." Originally published in *The Washington Post*, May 12, 2002. Copyright © 2002 by Karen Stabiner. Reprinted with permission of the author.

Jutka Terris. "Unwelcome Human Neighbors: The Impact of Sprawl on Wildlife." Originally published by the Natural Resources Defense Council (NRDC), 1999. Reprinted with permission.

Anastasia Toufexis. "Love: The Right Chemistry." From *Time*, February 15, 1993. © 1993 Time Inc. Reprinted by permission.

Reg Weaver. "NCLB's Excessive Reliance on Testing Is Unrealistic, Arbitrary, and Frequently Unfair." From *Insight on the News*, May 11, 2004. Copyright © 2004 by News World Communications. Reprinted with permission.

William Carlos Williams. "The Use of Force." From *The Collected Stories of William Carlos Williams*. Copyright © 1938 by William Carlos Williams. Reprinted by permission of New Directions Publishing Corp.

Tobias Wolff. "On Being a Real Westerner." Excerpt from *This Boy's Life* by Tobias Wolff. Copyright © 1989 by Tobias Wolff. Reprinted with permission of Grove/Atlantic, Inc.

Picture Credits

16 © Zave Smith/zefa/Corbis; 17 (left) David Epperson/Getty Images; (right) image100/Alamy; 72 Bill Aron/PhotoEdit, Inc.; 73 (left) David Young-Wolff/PhotoEdit, Inc.; (right) © Jon Feingersh/CORBIS; 134 David Young-Wolff/ PhotoEdit, Inc.; 135 (left) DigitalGlobe/Getty Images; (right) Comstock Images/Alamy; 142 Diagram by Nigel Holmes for TIME Magazine; 154 Michael Patrick O'Neill/NHPA; 156 (top) Andrew Hendry; (bottom) Rod Planck/Photo Researchers, Inc.; 158 Francois Gohier/ardea; 159 From "In the Blink of an Eye," by Bob Holmes, *New Scientist*, July 9, 2005; 160 Francois Gohier/ardea; 188 Maria Burwell; 192 © James Cavalini/BSIP/Phototake; 193 (left) © Najilah Feanny/CORBIS SABA; (right) Scott Camazine/Photo Researchers, Inc.; 272 David De Lossy/Getty Images; 273 (left) Michael Newman/PhotoEdit; (right) © Roger Ressmeyer/CORBIS; 321 (top) "Wall Street's Glass Ceiling" from *Business Week*, July 26, 2004. © 2004 Business Week, Inc. Reprinted with permission; (bottom) "Still an All Boys' Club" from *Business Week*, November 22, 1999, ©1999 Business Week, Inc. Reprinted with permission; 326 Getty Images; 327 (left) David Young-Wolff/PhotoEdit, Inc.; (right) Blend Images/Alamy; 350 Mitche Manitou; 351 (top and bottom) Mitche Manitou; 353 Mitche Manitou; 354 Mitche Manitou; 355 Mitche Manitou; 389 Gabe Palmer; 394 Photofest; 395 (left) © Nancy Richmond/The Image Works; (right) © Norbert Schaefer/CORBIS; 408 © 2003 Bethesda Softworks LLC, a ZeniMax Media Company. All Rights Reserved; 409 © 2003 Bethesda Softworks LLC, a ZeniMax Media Company. All Rights Reserved; 410 © 2003 Bethesda Softworks LLC, a ZeniMax Media Company. All Rights Reserved; 448 Photofest; 449 Photofest; 454 © Joel Stettenheim/CORBIS; 455 (left) © Randy Faris/Corbis; (right) AP Images/David Duprey; 466 (left) Ozier Muhammad/The New York Times/Redux; (right) COPYRIGHT NORMAN Y. LONO/Contract Photographer; 468 © The New York Times Graphics; 470 Ozier Muhammad/The New York Times/Redux; 476 (top) Gjon Mili/Time Life Pictures/Getty Images; (bottom) AP Images/Grant Halverson; 478 (top left) Bob Self/The Florida Times-Union; (top right) AP Images/Miles Kennedy; (bottom) D. Ross Cameron/Oakland Tribune/Polaris; 626–627 © 1999 Time Inc. Reprinted by permission; 626 (left) © Bettmann/CORBIS; (center) The Granger Collection, New York; (right) Book Cover (HarperPerennial edition) from BRAVE NEW WORLD by ALDOUS HUXLEY. Copyright 1932, 1960 by Aldous Huxley. Reprinted by permission of HarperCollins Publisher; 627 (far left) Hank Morgan/ Science Source/Photo Researchers; (center left) Saturn Stills-Science Photo Library/Photo Researchers; (center right) © Bettmann/CORBIS; (far right) Kenneth Highfill/Photo Researchers, Inc.; 634–635 Diagram by Christoph Blumrich. © 1999 Newsweek, Inc. All Rights Reserved. Reprinted by permission; 634 Jeanne Friebert/Sipa; 637 From *Home Repair Handbook* (Menlo Park, Calif.: Sunset, 1999), pp. 156–157; 715 © 2006 EBSCO Publishing, Inc. All rights reserved.

Author and Title Index

Subject Index

ABC test, 604
ABI/INFORM, 726
absolute phrases, 83, 116, 631
abstracts, 721, 723–25
accommodating readers' concerns, 682–83
accuracy, 605
acknowledging readers' concerns, 681–82
active voice, H-35
ad hominem attacks, 685
adjective clauses, punctuation of, 185–86
adjectives, H-27–29
  as complements, H-116
  compound, hyphens for, H-85–86
  coordinate, commas between, H-62–63
  noncoordinate, commas not needed to
    separate, H-66–67
  order of (ESL problem), 124–25
  order of (ESL troublespot), H-113
adverb clauses, H-129
adverbial clauses, trailing, commas and,
  H-66
adverbial modifiers, H-116
adverbials, H-116
adverbs, H-27–29, H-121–22
  conjunctive. *See* conjunctive adverbs
advice/advise, H-132
affect/effect, H-132
agent, sentences that lack an, 385
aggregator, 733
all right, H-132
Alternative Press Index, 723
alternative solutions, evaluating, proposals
  for solutions and, 339–41, 346,
  361–62, 369–70, 374, 379, 384
ambiguity, hyphens to avoid, H-87
American Statistics Index, 729
among/between, H-132–33
amount/number, H-133

analogies, false, 684
analogy, 668–69
anecdotes, 151–52
  as support for an argument, 678–79
  testing for believability and, 605
annotated research paper, sample, 771–79
annotating (annotations)
  interpretations of stories, 548, 564–65
  as reading strategy, 585–92
antecedents, 617
  pronoun agreement and, H-15
  pronoun reference and, H-12
anticipating opposing positions, objec-
    tions, alternatives, and questions
  evaluations, 418–20, 423, 429, 433, 443,
    446
  proposals for solutions, 347–48, 356,
    361, 373, 379, 383
  reasoned arguments, 287, 293, 295, 302,
    316, 319–20, 323
  speculations about causes, 483, 493, 501,
    505
anxious/eager, H-133
APA style
  block quotations, H-76
  design features and conventions,
    H-97–98
  in-text citations, 763–65
    author indicated in parentheses, 763
    author indicated in signal phrase, 764
    first citation in text, 764
    secondary source, 765
    source with more than two authors,
      764
    subsequent citations, 764
    two or more works by the same au-
      thor, 764
    unknown author, 764

  list of references. *See* list of references
    (APA style)
  section headings, H-96–97
apostrophes, H-79–81
appeal to readers' interests, 164, 184
appositive phrases, 445, H-130
appositives, 177–78
  colons to emphasize, H-72
appropriateness, testing for, 604–5
appropriate qualifications, 673–74
*ARBA Guide to Subject Encyclopedias and
  Dictionaries*, 711
arguable assertions, 671–72
arguing (arguments), 670–85. *See also*
    counterarguing; position papers;
    reasoned arguments; thesis
  appropriate qualifications in, 673–74
  arguable assertions, 671–72
  asserting a thesis, 670–74
  clear and precise wording in, 672–73
  evaluating the logic of, 604–6
  logical fallacies and, 684–85
  service-learning experience and, 849
  speculations about causes, 492–93
art collections, 730
articles (*a, an,* and *the*), H-128
  ESL troublespots, H-104–7
  missing, H-31
articles in periodicals. *See* periodicals
as, 643
  pronoun case and, H-19
audience (readers). *See also* anticipating
    opposing positions, objections, al-
    ternatives, and questions; critical
    comments from other readers
  accommodating readers' concerns,
    682–83
  acknowledging readers' concerns, 681–82

Index for ESL Writers

Submitting Your Essays for Publication

We hope that we'll be able to include many new essays by students in the next editions of *The St. Martin's Guide to Writing* and its companion collections. Please let us see the best essays you've written using *The Guide*. Send them with this submission form and copies of the agreement form on the back of this page (one for each essay you submit) to English Editor — Student Essays, Bedford/St. Martin's, 33 Irving Place, 10th Floor, New York, NY 10003.

PAPER SUBMISSION FORM

Student's Name _____

Instructor's Name _____

School _____

Department _____

Writing Assignment (circle one)

Remembering an Event   Proposing a Solution

Writing Profiles   Justifying an Evaluation

Explaining a Concept   Speculating about Causes

Explaining Opposing Positions   Interpreting Stories

Arguing a Position

Agreement Form

I hereby assign to Bedford/St. Martin's ("Bedford") all of my right, title and interest throughout the world, including without limitation, all copyrights, in and to my essay, _____, and any notes and drafts pertaining to it (the sample essay and such materials being referred to as the "Essay").

I understand that Bedford in its discretion has the right but not the obligation to publish the Essay in any form(s) or format(s) that it may desire; that Bedford may edit, revise, condense, or otherwise alter the Essay as it deems appropriate in order to prepare the same for publication. I understand that Bedford has the right to use and to authorize the use of my name as author of the Essay in connection with any work that contains the Essay (or a portion of it).

I represent that the Essay is wholly original and was completely written by me, that publication of it will not infringe upon the rights of any third party, and that I have not granted any rights in it to any third party.

In the event Bedford determines to publish any part of the Essay in one of its print books, I will receive one free copy of the work in which it appears.

Student's signature _____

Name _____ Date _____

Permanent address _____

_____

Phone number(s) _____

Email address(es) _____

A Note to the Student:

When a writer creates something — a story, an essay, a poem — he or she automatically possesses all of the rights to that piece of writing, no trip to the U.S. Copyright Office needed. When a writer — an historian, a novelist, a sportswriter — publishes his or her work, he or she normally transfers some or all of those rights to the publisher, by formal agreement. The form above is one such formal agreement. By entering into this agreement, you are engaging in a modern publishing ritual — the transfer of rights from writer to publisher. If this is your first experience submitting something for publication, you should know that you are in good company: every student who has published an essay in one of our books entered into this agreement, and just about every published writer has entered into a similar one.

Thank you for submitting your essay.

CORRECTION SYMBOLS

Letters and numbers in bold type refer to sections of the Handbook.

ab	faulty abbreviation	**M6**
ad	misuse of adverb or adjective	**G7**
agr n	error in noun agreement	**E3**
agr p/a	error in pronoun-antecedent agreement	**G2**
agr s/v	error in subject-verb agreement	**G6**
appr	inappropriate word	**W3**
art	error in the use of an article	**L1**
cap	use a capital letter	**M2**
case	error in pronoun case	**G4**
cs	comma splice	**S1**
dm	dangling modifier	**E4-b**
ESL	English as a second language	**L**
exact	inexact word	**W2**
frag	sentence fragment	**S3**
fs	fused sentence	**S2**
hyph	error in use of hyphen	**M1**
inc	incomplete construction	**E1**
integ	question, quotation, or thought has not been integrated smoothly **E6**	
mixed	mixed construction	**E5**
mm	misplaced modifier	**E4-a**
mood	error in mood	**G5-c**
ms	manuscript form	**M7, M8**
no ab	do not abbreviate	**M6-d**
no cap	do not capitalize	**M2-f**
no und	do not underline (italicize) **M5-d**	
num	error in use of numbers	**M4**
p	error in punctuation	**P**
⌄	comma	**P1**
no ⌄	no comma	**P2**
;	semicolon	**P3-a, b, c, d**

no ;	no semicolon	**P3-e**
:	colon	**P4-a**
no :	no colon	**P4-b**
—	dash	**P5**
no —	no dash	**P5-c**
❝ ❞	quotation marks	**P6**
no ❝ ❞	no quotation marks	**P6-f**
⸂	apostrophe	**P7**
no ⸂	no apostrophe	**P7-e**
( )	parentheses	**P8**
[ ]	brackets	**P9**
. . .	ellipsis marks	**P10**
/	slash	**P11**
.	period	**P12**
?	question mark	**P13**
!	exclamation point	**P14**
pron	error in pronoun use	**G3**
ref	error in pronoun reference	**G1**
shift	passage contains a shift in tense, person, number, mood, voice, or from direct to indirect discourse **E2**	
sp	spelling	**M9**
t	error in verb tense	**G5-a**
und	underline (italics)	**M5**
vb	error in verb form	**G5-b, L2**
voice	ineffective use of passive voice **G5-d**	
w	wordy	**W1**
wc	ineffective word choice	**W**
ww	wrong word	**GL**
//	faulty parallelism	**E7**
#	add a space	**M3-a**
⌒	close up space	**M3-b**
∧	insert	
℘	delete	
X	obvious error	

DIRECTORY OF DOCUMENTATION MODELS

MLA Style

APA Style

Citations in Text

Reference Entries

Books

Articles

Electronic Sources

Other Sources

HANDBOOK CONTENTS